717394.

PEOPLES, J. AND MAZUR

MEN AN~~IT~~

~~TI~~ONS.

~~19~~00.

Metropolitan Borough of Wandsworth.

D1437236

Men & Nations

A WORLD HISTORY

Anatole G. Mazour & John M. Peoples

RUPERT HART-DAVIS   *Soho Square London*   *1963*

10031 6061

900 MAZO

717394

m 34415

Copyright © 1961, 1959 by Harcourt, Brace & World, Inc.

All rights reserved

Printed in the United States of America

Designed by Peter Oldenburg

Picture editor, Frances L. Orkin

Maps and charts by Visual Services, Inc.

Drawings by Walter B. Humphrey and Monroe Eisenberg

Acknowledgments for other illustrations
  follow the Index

Men and Nations

A WORLD HISTORY

Contents

TIME CHARTS

GRAPHS AND DIAGRAMS

Men and Nations

A WORLD HISTORY

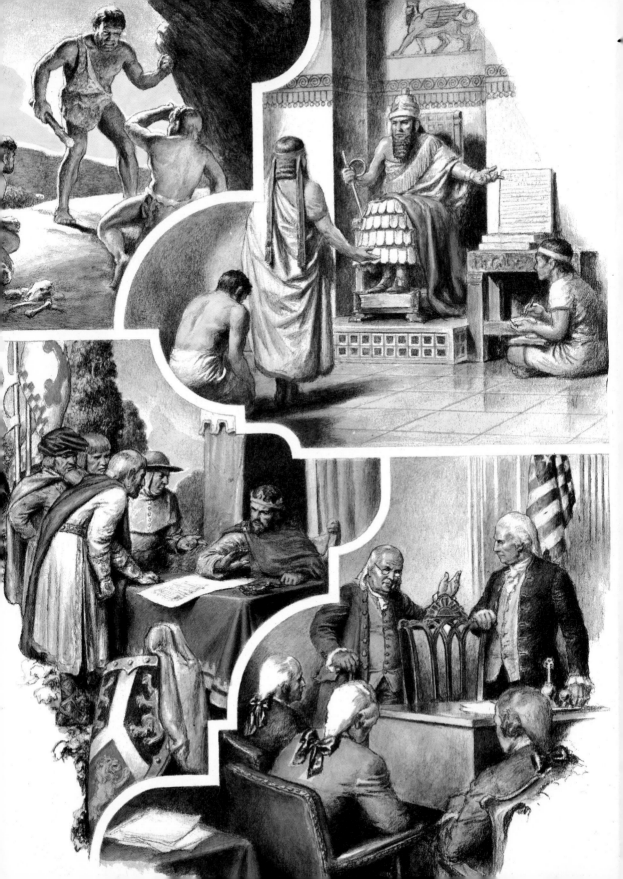

History and You

THE NATIONS OF THE WORLD today face a host of problems. None of these problems is completely new. Each has roots in the past—often centuries deep in the past. When we study history we can trace the record of how men have dealt with their problems from the Stone Age to modern times. We can find great themes, major topics in the story of mankind, running through history. We can watch ways of life start and grow and change for the worse or for the better.

The pictures opposite illustrate one major theme, the development of ideas about government and law. For many thousands of years men lived without government as we know it. They had neither congresses nor presidents nor governors nor mayors nor police. There were no laws to obey or to break. Families and tribes might be loosely organized under fathers and clan leaders. Often the only rule that governed life was that the fastest man with a club or rock could take what he wanted—until some still faster man came along. The top, left picture shows a scene that was probably common in the Stone Age.

The second picture shows a degree of progress. Here is a king of Mesopotamia about four thousand years ago, literally laying down the law to his subjects. As the centuries went by people learned to live together in groups larger than tribes. Strong leaders ruled these groups. Cities and nations came into being under the leadership of kings and emperors. Some laws were set up as rules for living.

One great ruler had his laws written down so that his subjects could know what rules they were supposed to obey. This was a long stride forward, but these rulers were still autocratic —we would call them dictatorial. No subject of the king could vote. Only a few privileged men, the princes and nobles, could take part in government. If there was any code of law, the law could be changed according to the king's will.

Moving down and to the left in the picture, we now see one of the great events in man's progress toward democratic government. Here is shown a group of English noblemen presenting the Magna Carta to King John in the year 1215. Though reluctant, the king approved this Great Charter, which guaranteed certain rights of his subjects. (One was the right of an accused person to be tried by a jury.) Fundamentally, the acceptance of the Magna Carta meant that there were laws that even the king had to obey. People were beginning to stand up for the idea that they should have something to say about government. Here was a major step toward the establishment of the principle that government should be based on law rather than on one man's will.

The last picture brings us closer to our own times. The date is 1787 (not long ago in terms of world history). The scene is the convention that drew up the Constitution of the United States. Benjamin Franklin and George Washington stand before the convention. The members of this convention drew up a set of laws which stated what sort of government the new nation should have. The citizens agreed upon laws establishing their government; the laws govern all citizens and protect the rights of all citizens. No man can take what he wants by force. The laws can be changed only by lawful processes. Thus, a look at world history shows that we have made great progress in law, in government, in freedom of the individual citizen.

The democratic government set up in America under the Constitution has lasted and grown stronger in spite of great wars and other crises. In recent years this democratic ideal of government has been challenged by dictatorships of various kinds. Since World War II the challenge has come from the Communist form of despotic government. The clash between the democracies of the world and the Communist states could prove to be a life and death matter for all people. The more we can understand these two ways of life, the better we can maintain our own way. Knowing how different ideas of government grew up in the past will help us face this great challenge to our pattern of life and government.

We cannot hope to solve the problems of the modern world unless we understand them. We cannot understand them unless we know how they developed. We must know history. The world can advance only through the efforts of thoughtful, informed men and women. Knowing history, having learned lessons from the long story of men and nations, the men and women of today and tomorrow can reach wise solutions to their great problems.

In a democracy, where every citizen has a voice in his own government, decisions depend on the voting citizens. This is where *you* come into history. You may never be president, secretary of state, or a member of Congress and have to make our national policies yourself. But you will have to decide which policies seem wisest, which men are to have your support and your vote. This task needs the best you can give it.

Great themes in history

As you read history, watch for great themes. One has already been mentioned. This and others are summarized here:

▶ What sort of *government* have people believed in? Has power been held by a despot of one kind or another, or have people tried to govern themselves by a democratic system? Have the *rights and liberties of the individual* been valued and guarded? What kind of *laws* have been made? How well have the laws and the various branches of the government worked in practice?

▶ What has caused *the decline and fall of great civilizations of the past?* Many nations were unable to establish strong, efficient governments. Many nations proved unable to solve such problems as poverty, ignorance, and disease. They failed to give freedom and opportunity to most people. These failures weakened the nations. Then they were attacked, conquered, and destroyed, usually by powerful but less civilized powers. Will this process of history continue?

▶ What has been done with the great issues of *war and peace?* What has caused wars? What has been done to preserve peace? When efforts to keep the peace have failed, why did they fail? What can be done to reduce rivalries and tensions among the great powers?

▶ How have *science and invention* contributed to civilization? What effect have scientific discoveries had on the history of the world? Are there links between the science of earlier times and the discoveries of our atomic age?

▶ How have people lived and worked? What was the importance at various periods of *farming, trade, manufacturing,* and other ways of earning a living? What forms of *transportation* and *communication* have been used? How much or how little did people enjoy in the way of *food, clothing, and shelter?* Did they have necessities, and even luxuries, or was poverty a problem?

►What contributions did different ages make in the *fine arts,* such as literature, painting, sculpture, architecture, music? Why have some peoples produced great art, others almost none?

►What form of *religion* did men believe in? Was it a noble one, in which all could share? How did the great religions grow in importance?

►What was the role given to *education* in different civilizations?

►How has *geography* influenced history? How, for example, do mountains, rivers, and seaports affect the way people live and work?

If you try to find answers to these questions as you study history, you will be learning about the many forces that have worked together to make the world what it is. For example, you will learn of the power of ideas. One powerful idea is the democratic belief that every human being has worth and dignity that must be respected. As you read history you can watch ideas such as these appear, develop gradually, become strong, and finally be accepted by enough people to be put into effect.

The same forces that shaped the past are working now in your world, shaping the future. You are about to read the history of the past. You are living in the history of the present. You are watching the world change day by day. The one certain thing in history is that conditions change. You must ask whether these changes represent progress—movement toward a goal, a better world.

Features of this book

As you read, make full use of all the features of this book that have been planned to help the reader.

►The *table of contents* gives a preview of the book. Note that the text is divided into ten parts and fifty-six chapters. The *index* is a classified directory for the book. Use it to find names and topics. The index includes a *guide to pronunciation* for new or difficult words.

►Each of the ten parts of the book opens with an *introductory picture and a page of text.* These pages point up great themes to watch for in the coming chapters. These introductions will help you to read thoughtfully, watching for the main ideas.

►Following the introduction to each part you will find a *time chart* for that section of history. These charts will help you to see the relationship of major events to one another. A look down the columns of a chart shows the order of events in different areas of the world.

►At the end of each chapter you will find a *review* section. If you are familiar with the "People, places, and things" listed, and if you can answer the questions under "Events in review," you have covered the main points of the chapter. The "Problems and projects" sections contain suggestions for discussion, debate, or extra study.

►Each of the ten parts ends with a brief *review of that part.* These questions are to help you keep track of major themes within each part and trace themes from one period of history to another.

►Each part has its *suggested reading* list. You may want to learn more about a person or an event than one book can tell you. Any book listed can add something valuable to your knowledge of history. A list of basic reference books is found at the end of this introduction.

▶ Accompanying the text are 82 specially prepared *maps*. Each map was drawn to help you visualize some fact of history, such as the geographic location of Italy or the campaigns of World War II. Use these maps regularly as you read.

▶ In the back of the book there is a *16-page map supplement* in full color. These maps show highlights of world history and geography. They are a handy place to find cities, seas, nations, and other world features.

▶ The book has hundreds of *illustrations*. These range from a drawing of a stone axe to a diagram of a medieval manor to a photograph of an earth satellite. They have been selected to help make clear what the text is saying, or to tell you a little more about a topic. The *captions* point out features in the illustrations and relate them to the text.

▶ To add further information and interest, the book has *four special sections in full color* (see the table of contents). These show samples of the world's civilization at different periods. Such things as Egyptian wall paintings, Greek temples, medieval stained glass windows, and eighteenth-century costumes are shown in full color.

All these parts of the book are planned to work together to enable you to acquire an understanding of the past that will help you to live wisely in the present.

A basic library for the study of World History

Encyclopedias and almanacs

Britannica Junior (Encyclopaedia Britannica, Inc., 1958).
Compton's Pictured Encyclopedia (F. E. Compton & Co., 1957).
Encyclopaedia Britannica (Encyclopaedia Britannica, Inc., 1958).
Information Please Almanac (Published annually by Macmillan).
World Almanac (Published annually by the *New York World-Telegram and Sun*).
World Book Encyclopedia (Field Enterprises Educational Corporation, 1958).

Atlases

Goode's World Atlas (Rand McNally, 1953).

*Books marked with a star (*) are easy reading.

Hammond's Library World Atlas (Hammond, 1957).
Hammond's Historical Atlas (Hammond, 1957).
Rand McNally Cosmopolitan World Atlas, Centennial ed. (Rand McNally, 1955).
Shepherd, W. R. *Historical Atlas* (Barnes and Noble, 1957).

Dictionaries

Thorndike-Barnhart Comprehensive Desk Dictionary (Doubleday, 1956).
Thorndike-Barnhart High School Dictionary (Scott, Foresman, 1957).
Webster's Biographical Dictionary (Merriam, 1956).
Webster's Geographical Dictionary, rev. ed. (Merriam, 1955).

Webster's New International Dictionary, 2nd ed. (Merriam, 1957).

Webster's Students Dictionary (American Book, 1956).

Art, literature, music, and science

*Bakeless, Katherine. *Story-Lives of Great Composers,* rev. ed. (Lippincott, 1953). Short biographies of the greatest men of music.

*Bauer, Marion, and Peyser, Ethel. *How Music Grew; from Prehistoric Times to the Present Day* (Putnam, 1939). The development of music through the ages, clearly described.

Benét, William R. (Ed.) *Reader's Encyclopedia; an Encyclopedia of World History and the Arts* (Crowell, 1955).

*Bolton, Sarah K. *Famous Men of Science* (Crowell, 1946). Brief biographies of leading scientists.

*Chandler, Anna C. *Story-Lives of Master Artists* (Stokes, 1933).

*Craven, Thomas. *Rainbow Book of Art* (World Publishing Company, 1956). A short survey of the world's art. Many reproductions of famous pictures.

De Kruif, Paul. *Microbe Hunters* (Harcourt, Brace, 1939). Lively accounts of the lives and work of great bacteriologists.

*Guerber, Helene A. *Book of the Epic; the World's Great Epics Told in Story* (Lippincott, 1913). Epics from Europe, Asia, and America told in simple and interesting story form.

*Hillyer, Virgil M., and Edward G. Huey. *Child's History of Art* (Appleton-Century, 1933).

Jaffe, Bernard. *Crucibles; the Story of Chemistry,* rev. ed. (Simon & Schuster, 1948).

*Lamprey, Louise. *All the Ways of Building* (Macmillan, 1933). Architecture and building forms throughout history.

Reinach, Salomon. *Apollo; an Illustrated Manual of the History of Art Throughout the Ages* (Scribner, 1935). Perhaps the best general history of art.

General works

*Augur, Helen. *Book of Fairs* (Harcourt, Brace, 1939). The fascinating stories of fairs from prehistoric to recent times.

*Bart, Barry. *Book of Battles* (Garden City, 1942). Sixteen decisive battles in world history. The illustrations show the weapons and armor used at different periods.

Eaton, Jeanette. *Leaders in Other Lands* (Heath, 1950).

Evans, Mary. *Costume Throughout the Ages,* rev. ed. (Lippincott, 1950). A condensed and well-illustrated account of clothing since ancient times.

Fish, Helen D. *Pegs of History* (Stokes, 1943). The key dates of world history with a brief account of the meaning of each.

Gibson, Charles Edmund. *Story of the Ship from the Earliest Days to the Present* (Abelard-Schuman, 1958).

Hagedorn, Hermann. *Book of Courage* (Winston, 1942). Socrates and twenty-five other men and women who influenced the times in which they lived.

*Hartman, Gertrude. *The World We Live In and How It Came To Be* (Macmillan, 1935). A well-illustrated, simply written history of the highlights of world civilization.

Leeming, Joseph. *Costume Book* (Stokes, 1938). Historic costumes from early days through the mid-19th century.

The editors of *Life*. *Life's Picture History of Western Man*. An excellent summary of the history of the Western World, with splendid illustrations.

*Stuart, Dorothy M. *Boy Through the Ages* (Doran, 1926).

*———. *Girl Through the Ages* (Lippincott, 1933). Boy and girl customs, costumes, and lore from early times. The greatest emphasis is on Egypt and Europe.

*Van Loon, Hendrik W. *Story of Mankind* (Liveright, 1951). A very readable general world history which stresses general trends.

———. *Van Loon's Lives* (Simon & Schuster, 1942). Imaginary dinner parties with famous guests from many centuries.

Part One THE BEGINNINGS

Part One covers a tremendous span of time. This part starts with the days before there was any recorded history or anything we would call civilization and tells how, over many thousands of years, men built up great cultures in such lands as Egypt. The picture on the facing page shows one important part of the growth of civilization. No great king or warrior is involved, but rather some unknown priests and workmen who had learned a basic and highly useful fact of geometry. Any triangle that is three feet (or yards, or any other unit) long on one side, four on another, and five on the third side, is a right triangle. The Egyptians learned to knot a cord so as to mark off three units on one side, four on the second, five on the third. When this cord was pegged down at the corners, it formed a right triangle. Architects and builders used the right angle in laying out temples, palaces, and other structures.

The Egyptians had none of the textbooks and few or none of the tools for measuring that we take for granted; hence the discovery of a way to lay out a 90 degree angle was an important step toward civilization. Part One will tell about many other contributions ancient Egypt made to the world.

Before taking up Egypt, the book must go back to the beginning of man's story. Chapter 1 tells a small part of the story of the earliest men. They are called prehistoric because they were unable to keep any written records. Over many thousands of years they made slow, stumbling progress toward civilization. Among these people were many unknown benefactors of the human race. There was the man who first learned how to kindle a fire, the man who learned to plant seeds, and many others.

Chapters 2, 3, 4, and 5 tell the story of the beginnings of civilization in two of the four great regions of early civilization: the valley of the Nile River in Egypt, and the region of Mesopotamia in Asia Minor. You will learn why the earliest civilizations were found in such river valleys, how they began, how they developed, and what they were like.

Look at the time chart on pages 10–11. The area covered by a block of color contains major events from Chapters 2 through 5. One column records dates from Egyptian history. The next column shows the order of events in the Fertile Crescent (the name given to an area running from Palestine over to Mesopotamia). This chart starts at 4000 years before the birth of Christ (4000 B.C.) or about the beginning of recorded history. This chart could not be made large enough to cover the millions of years of prehistory. (For approximate dates in early times, see page 13.)

The three columns to the right on the time chart show key dates in other lands. A look at the chart will show what history was being made in the rest of the world at the time of the events described in Part One.

Part One THE BEGINNINGS

	EGYPT	FERTILE CRESCENT

4000 B.C.

c. 4000   Copper used

4000-2900   Age of Sumerian city-states

c. 3500   Alphabet developed

c. 3400   Menes unites two kingdoms

c. 3400   Sumerians keep written records

3400-2500   Old Kingdom

3000 B.C.

c. 3000   Copper used

2776   Solar calendar

c. 2500   Cheops builds Great Pyramid

c. 2100-1800   Middle Kingdom

2000 B.C.

c. 2000   Canal dug, Nile River to Red Sea
Bronze used

c. 2000   Indo-Europeans in Iran

Hammurabi

c. 1800   Hyksos invade Egypt

1580   Empire Age begins

c. 1550   Hatshepsut rules

c. 1500   Iron used

c. 1375   Ikhnaton, Monotheism

1292-1225   Rameses II, the Great

1000 B.C.

c. 1000   Zoroaster

1000-700   Phoenician commercial supremacy; colonies

933-722   Kingdom of Israel

525   Persians conquer Egypt

612   Destruction of Nineveh

550   Cyrus of Persia

332   Alexander conquers Egypt

530-330   Persian Empire at height

331   Alexander conquers Persia

31   Rome conquers Egypt

A.D.

EUROPE	INDIA	CHINA
	c. 4000-2000 Earliest known civilization	
	  c. 2500 Highly developed civilization in Indus River Valley	
c. 2000 Indo-Europeans move into Greece 1600-1100 Aegean civilization 1500-1200 Mycenaean Age of Greece	c. 2000 Indo-Europeans enter India 	c. 1700 Shang dynasty: unified government c. 1500 Written records begin 1122-255 Chou dynasty: foundations of Chinese culture
c. 1000 Phoenician alphabet reaches Greece c. 850 Homer 776 First recorded Olympic games 509 Roman republic founded 480 Greeks defeat Persians 338 Alexander conquers Greece Hellenistic Age begins 264-146 Punic Wars	 c. 563 Birth of Buddha 326 Alexander to Indus River 273-232 Asoka: spread of Buddhism	604 Lao-tse 551-478 Confucius 228-210 Great Wall built 202 Han dynasty begins

Chapter 1

Prehistoric Man Moves along the Road to Civilization

HISTORIANS divide the history of the human race into two main periods: before and since men learned to write. The period since the discovery, or invention, of writing is called *historic time*. Written records tell us most of what we know of people in the past. The period before this development is called *prehistoric time*. Historic time makes up only a small part of the lifetime of the human race. Records go back only about six thousand years.

The small time chart on the facing page shows important periods in prehistoric and early historic time. Notice that, through the Old Stone Age, the dates have question marks after them and that all dates are in round numbers. Down to the Copper Age men kept no written records. Hence all dates for prehistory are estimates. Even in early historic times, dates are approximate. The importance of this chart is to show the great span of early times and the order and approximate length of various periods such as the Old Stone Age and New Stone Age. (All these dates, of course, are marked B.C., meaning before Christ.)

Scientists are able to make educated guesses about dates in prehistoric time. Also they are able to tell us many things about early man. They do this by studying three kinds of remains: (1) the bones of early man, which show his size and appearance; (2) the bones of animals found near him; (3) the weapons, tools, and other utensils found with him. Scientists call these tools and weapons *artifacts* (things made by human skill and work).

Earliest men: Peking, Java, and Heidelberg

What the scientists have found shows that men probably appeared on the earth sometime around 1,000,000 B.C. Remains have been found at two widely separated places: in a cave near Peking, China, and on the great island of Java off the coast of southeast Asia.

Little can be learned about these earliest men. Complete skeletons have never been found. Scientific guesses about their appearance have been made on the basis of the remains that have been found. Early men were not handsome by our standards. They were short, squatty, and powerfully built. They had powerful jaws with sharply receding chins. Their foreheads were low, with heavy eyebrow ridges. In fact, scientists call Java man *Pithecanthropus erectus,* which means something like "the man who looks like an ape and walks on his hind legs." Crude stone fist hatchets were found with Peking man, but no artifacts were found with Java man.

We have no sign of men for hundreds of thousands of years after the time of Peking and Java men. A great glacier covered much of the northern half of the earth.

The next evidence of man's existence was found near Heidelberg, Germany. In an ancient river bed scientists uncovered the jaw and lower teeth of a man who lived after the glacier had retreated, probably around 500,000 B.C. No tools or weapons were found with Heidelberg man. We know only that he existed and disappeared.

The Old Stone Age

● *Neanderthal man*

We move far into the Old Stone Age (or *Paleolithic Age*) before finding further traces of man. Nearly half a million years passed between the times of the Peking and Heidelberg men. Almost as many years passed before the next man about whom we have evidence. Again remains were found in Germany, in caves in the valley of the Neander River. The German word for valley is *thal,* so he is called Neanderthal man. He lived, probably, from about 50,000 B.C. until sometime after 25,000 B.C. He was short and powerfully built, with bowed legs, heavy jaw, thick eyebrows and large nose.

Neanderthal man made more progress than the men who preceded him. He made better tools. He lived in caves and wore clothes of animal skins. He learned how to make a fire when he wanted one. This was indeed a great step forward!

Neanderthal man differed from earlier men in another way: he buried his dead. What is more, he buried with them tools, weapons, and even food. He must have expected these offerings to be of use later. In other words, he believed in some form of life after death. We do not know what his belief was, but he surely had some kind of religion.

Like the earlier men, Neanderthal man disappeared. We do not know why. Glaciers

EARLY TIMES

8000 B. C.
New Stone Age
(Neolithic Age)

4000 B. C.
Copper Age

1,000,000? B. C.
First Glacial Age:
Java man—Peking man

500,000? B. C.
Second Glacial Age:
Heidelberg man

2000 B. C.
Bronze Age

25,000–10,000 B. C.
Fourth Glacial Age:
Cro-Magnon man

2,000,000,000? B. C.
Origin of the earth

400,000? B. C.
Old Stone Age

5,000,000? B. C.
Age of Reptiles

1,000,000,000? B. C.
Early forms of life

50,000 B. C.
Neanderthal man

300,000 B. C.
Third Glacial Age

1500 B. C.
Early Iron Age

had again advanced far south; he may have died out from the cold. Some scientists believe he moved on to Siberia and Arctic America. He may have been overcome by stronger and more advanced men.

Reconstructions of the heads of prehistoric men. Notice the development from Java man (left) to Neanderthal man (center) and to Cro-Magnon man (right).

● Cro-Magnon man appears

A new kind of man appeared in Europe about 25,000 B.C. Scientists call him Cro-Magnon, from the region in France where his remains have been found. Europe was very cold then, for the polar icecap extended far south of its present limits. This is known because, with Cro-Magnon's remains, there were found the remains of plants and animals that live only in a very cold climate.

Cro-Magnon man appeared in Europe at about the time Neanderthal man disappeared. He may have moved in from Asia or Africa. He took over Neanderthal man's caves, possibly by driving him out or killing him. Cro-Magnon man was equipped to overcome Neanderthal man. He had made more progress, and had better tools and weapons.

Much more is known about Cro-Magnon man than about any of the others. More remains have been found. Then, too, Cro-Magnon man has told us more. He could not

write, but he could draw and paint. In the caves in southern France and in Spain where Cro-Magnon man lived, the walls are covered with his paintings of himself and of the animals he hunted. Among the animals he painted were the wooly mammoth and the reindeer, which live only in very cold climates. They are excellent paintings, full of life and movement. He also made small clay or limestone statues of animals, men, and women. Cro-Magnon man was the earliest artist.

Neanderthal man and Cro-Magnon man lived toward the end of the Old Stone Age. To sum up, here is what is known or can be guessed about man's life during that long period: He lived as a wandering hunter, following game and good climate. In unfavorable weather he found shelter in caves. He learned to use fire and to make clothing of animal skins. His food consisted of animals, fish, shellfish, and any berries, roots, and vegetables he found. He had only a few possessions, and these were mostly tools or weapons of flint or bone. He probably lived in groups: families, clans, or tribes. He had some primitive form of religion. And he disappeared.

The New Stone Age: Neolithic man

The scientific name for the New Stone Age is *Neolithic,* from Greek words which mean *new* and *stone.* Neolithic man made many advances toward civilization.

The Neolithic Age got its name from the method of making tools. Some clever men learned that stone tools can be polished to a fine edge and point on a flat piece of sandstone. They learned to use stones other than flint. Tools and weapons were grooved and tied to handles. Many special tools were made: awls, wedges, saws, drills, chisels, needles, and barbed harpoons. Stone, wood, bone, and horn were all used.

More people appeared in Europe as the icecap retreated. Increased population created a housing shortage: there were not enough caves to go around. The Neolithic people began to build homes. They built furniture of wood, developed a crude kind of pottery, wove cloth, and made nets for fishing. They built boats. They began to live in organized village communities. Undoubtedly they had governments of some sort.

Earlier people had been wanderers; Neolithic people settled down in villages. They could do so because of their two greatest discoveries: agriculture and the taming (domestication) of animals.

A model of one type of house built by Neolithic men. Scientists have reconstructed these New Stone Age houses from remains found in lakes in Switzerland. These lake dwellers built huts on platforms that were perched on pilings sunk into the lake bottom.

It is not quite clear how people learned that seeds could be planted and made to grow year after year. The discovery may have been accidental, or the work of some unknown genius. It revolutionized life on earth. Wheat, barley, rice, and millet were planted in ground worked with stone hoes. Crops were harvested with wooden-handled flint sickles. Grain was ground into flour on stone hand mills. Bread appeared on the table.

Domestication of animals also provided a surer food supply. Dogs, cattle, horses, goats, sheep, and pigs were tamed and made the servants of man. Some of them supplied power when it was needed. Almost all of them were food stored on the hoof. Cows, goats, and sheep were living producers of milk and cheese. When they were slaughtered, they were stores of meat as well as hides and wool for clothing. People could now be sure enough of a food supply to settle down permanently.

This settling down is probably the reason for the great inventiveness of Neolithic men. Food did not need to be hunted constantly; it could be produced and stored. There was more time to work on better tools, more time

A painting of a bison, photographed from a cave in Altamira, Spain. This picture was painted perhaps 200 centuries ago by an artist of the Cro-Magnon period.

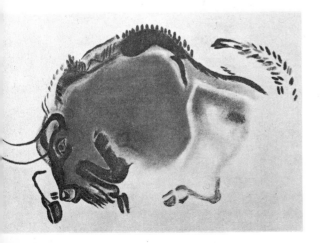

for art and other things. More people could live together in communities. They accumulated more property. They developed rules to regulate their living, because it was necessary to do so.

Neolithic people used spoons of horn or wood; perhaps table manners appeared for the first time. Girls will be interested to know that bone hairpins have been found.

●*Four centers of Neolithic life*

The two sources of food supply—plants and animals—produced two different economies (ways of getting food and other essentials) and cultures (ways of living). The farmer who settled down in an agricultural village needed a very special kind of environment. The soil had to be fertile and clear of trees, for the farmer lacked the tools to clear forest land. There had to be enough water, either rain at the right time of year or streams from which he could irrigate. The climate also had to be right. There were many small districts on earth that met these conditions naturally, but in Neolithic times four great regions were ideal: (1) the Nile River Valley in Egypt; (2) the valley of the Tigris and Euphrates rivers in southwestern Asia, called Mesopotamia—the "land between the rivers"; (3) the Indus River Valley in northwestern India; and (4) the valley of the Yellow River in northern China.

The herdsman also needed a special environment for his economy, or way of making a living. His greatest requirement was grass pasture land, with enough water for the animals. He did not like heavily forested regions. Open grasslands were his choice, for here he could move his flocks and herds easily from one feeding-place to another.

Four great grass zones were ideal: (1) the Sahara region of North Africa (in Neolithic times not so dry as now) with enough grass to support considerable flocks of animals; (2) the peninsula of Arabia, between Africa and Asia; (3) the plains of Mongolia, in east

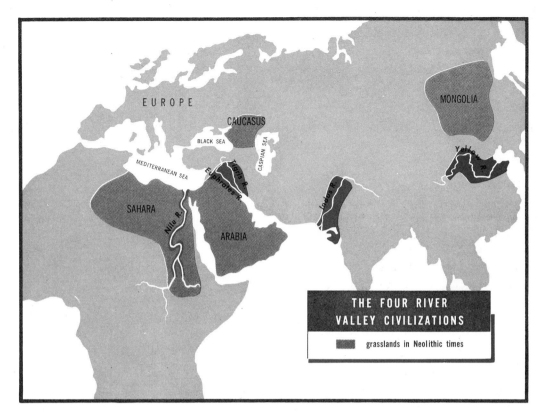

THE FOUR RIVER
VALLEY CIVILIZATIONS

grasslands in Neolithic times

central Asia; (4) the great grassland plain that stretches north of the Black and Caspian seas.

The economy of the herdsman made possible a life more secure than that of the hunter. However, it did not develop great civilizations. Herdsmen wandered about in small groups or tribes, with no permanent homes. The development of high civilization seems to require that men live together in groups, in permanent, settled conditions. Therefore, the great early civilizations of the earth grew up in the four valleys of the Nile, the Tigris-Euphrates, the Indus, and the Yellow rivers.

Civilization begins: The Age of Metals

Agricultural life in the river valleys required better tools than the polished stone of Neolithic times. The first metal used was copper. Its discovery was probably accidental, rather than an attempt to meet a need. Perhaps someone built a fire on some copper ore and noticed the bright, shining lumps of the metal in the ashes.

Sometime around 4000 B.C., men in the Nile Valley and Mesopotamia were producing copper by smelting (extracting metal from ore by heat). Copper could be hammered into weapons, tools, utensils, and jewelry. It could also be poured into sand molds.

Copper was used for tools and weapons for several thousand years. It was not entirely satisfactory. It was too soft to hold an edge, or for heavy work. After a long time a better metal came into use. This was bronze, a mixture of copper and tin. This mixture is much harder than copper. Since some copper ore contains tin, the discovery of bronze may also have been accidental. Bronze was used in Egypt and Mesopotamia by 3000 B.C. At first it was used only for jewelry and weapons. Since tin ore was much scarcer than copper, bronze was expensive. By 2000 B.C., however, bronze was available for many uses, and the Bronze Age began.

At some point in his development, early man learned to irrigate land and thereby raise better crops. The upper picture shows a means of irrigation used in ancient Egypt. This wall painting of a garden dates from about 1250 B.C. The lower picture (taken in Egypt about 1950 A.D.) shows the same sort of well-sweep arrangement still in use to water the land. Note the shape of the buckets in both pictures and the cut-off tree trunks used to support the long poles.

Iron is a much better material than either copper or bronze. Iron ore is found in more places and in larger amounts than either copper or tin. Yet its use came much later than the others, for the process of getting the metal out of the ore is much more difficult.

Learning how to make iron could hardly have been accidental. In the process, charcoal is added to the ore in a fire so hot that it can be produced only by bellows. The resulting hot metal must be hammered to get out the impurities. If the impurities are left in, they weaken the metal beyond use.

There is no record of when, where, or by whom the process of making iron was discovered. Recent evidence seems to show that Negro smiths in central Africa had learned to smelt iron when the rest of the world was still in the Stone Ages. The knowledge spread very slowly. Iron was used a little in Egypt about 1500 B.C.

The first people to use iron extensively were the Hittites, around 1400 B.C. They lived in Asia Minor, in part of present-day Turkey. They had copper and silver mines; they traded these metals with other people for goods they wanted. The Hittites did not trade their iron, nor the knowledge of how they made it. They kept the process secret. With superior iron weapons they defended themselves against stronger and more numerous people, and conquered much land. Finally, though, they were conquered. After that happened, traders spread the secret to Egypt, Europe, Mesopotamia, and India.

● *Civilization spreads as trade develops*

The river valley civilizations produced their food by agriculture. In time, methods of farming improved, and it took only a part of the people to produce enough food for all. Gone were the days when all of the people had to spend most of their time getting food. Several things resulted from this:

1. People were divided into classes. Some did not work at all, but lived from the labor

of others. These were the kings, nobles, and priests. They got control of the land in various ways. Then they compelled others to do the work and pay them part of the crops as rent.

2. Division of labor took place. Some men were able to specialize in other kinds of work besides farming. Experts at tool and weapon making could devote all their time to this work. They traded their products for food and other things they needed. Thus a class of skilled workers, or *artisans,* appeared. Merchants, or traders, also appeared. They made their living by buying or trading from the farmer or artisan, and selling or trading to anyone who needed the goods. The traders carried ideas as well as goods. Merchants carried not only Hittite iron but also the knowledge of how to make it.

Trade became increasingly important as the river valley civilization developed. Egypt and Mesopotamia lacked good supplies of copper, tin, and iron. They traded for them, exchanging surplus food and other things.

● *The invention of writing brings prehistoric times to an end*

Settled community life required rules to make living together possible, and to protect property. Forms of government appeared, and with them came taxation to pay the costs of government. Life in the farming river valleys needed much teamwork. The yearly floods had to be controlled. Irrigation systems had to be built. Men could not accomplish these things working as individuals. Coöperation was necessary. There had to be agreements as to who should do what work, and how, and when. As trade developed, records of transactions, or "deals," were required. All of these things called for a means of keeping permanent records.

What was needed was the development of written language. It took an amount of skill greater than that required for any other great advance toward civilization. With the development of writing, prehistoric times ended, and historic times began.

Review of Chapter 1

People, places, and things

Identify: Heidelberg man, Cro-Magnon man, artifacts, Neanderthal man, Hittites.

Locate: The Nile Valley, the valley of the Tigris and Euphrates Rivers, the Indus River, the valley of the Yellow River in China, the plains of Mongolia, the grassland between the Black and Caspian seas, the peninsula of Arabia, the Sahara region in Africa.

Events in review

1. How much of the lifetime of the human race comes within the period of *historic* time? How have we obtained information about prehistoric ages?
2. Contrast the Old Stone Age with the New Stone Age with respect to the following: tools, food, housing.

3. Name the two greatest discoveries made by Neolithic men.
4. Why did the great early civilizations grow up in four geographic regions?
5. Where, and approximately when, did copper, bronze, and iron come into use?
6. Why was a written language needed after men began to live in communities?

Problems and projects

1. Prove by using prehistoric times as an example that history is a slow and always continuing process.
2. Write an imaginary account of a camping trip in which you have at your disposal only the knowledge and equipment possessed by primitive man.
3. Make sketches of ancient reptiles or make clay models of these vanished animals.

Chapter 2 Civilization Develops in Two Regions

THE map on page 22 shows the lands you are about to study. The region around the eastern end of the Mediterranean Sea is often called the Near East. Three continents—Europe, Asia, and Africa—come together here. Notice the land bridge that unites the three continents. This land bridge has been a roadway linking Africa and Europe and Asia since earliest times. Civilization developed early in two regions of the world: the Nile Valley in Africa and the Fertile Crescent in Asia Minor. In both regions, geography helped civilization get started and grow.

Geographic advantages in Egypt and Mesopotamia

On the map, Egypt looks like a fairly large country. If you were to fly over it in a plane, you would see that it is almost all a sandy desert, dotted here and there with little oases of palm trees where there is water. You would see the bright green of growing crops and vegetation only in one long, narrow strip. This is the valley of the Nile River, which flows northward out of the mountains of Africa to the Mediterranean Sea.

● *Egypt and the Nile*

The Nile is 2,000 miles long. In its 2,000 miles there are six cataracts; these are rapids where the river is forced into a narrow channel to cut through hard rocks. The valley averages about ten miles in width. Through-

out the whole length of the river desert plateaus rise to heights of 200 feet above the valley. Where the river flows into the Mediterranean, it divides into several branches and spreads out over a wider territory, like our Mississippi River. Here it drops much of the sediment it carries, forming a region partly plain, partly marsh. This region is called the Nile Delta, because it is shaped like the Greek letter Delta, or Δ.

Herodotus, the Greek historian, said: "All Egypt is the gift of the Nile." He spoke truly. Each year, from May to October, spring rains and melting snow (far back where the Nile begins) cause the river to rise twenty to forty feet above its normal level. It overflows its banks and spreads out over the flatlands of the valley. There it deposits its silt, a layer of very fertile soil. Each year, then, the soil of the valley is renewed. This is important. The land has been farmed continuously for more than 6,000 years, and is still fertile. Except during the spring there is very little rain along the Nile. Water for irrigation must be taken from the river during the dry months.

The first people to move into the valley found a few other natural resources besides fertile soil and good climate. There were deposits of clay, granite, sandstone, and limestone for building. They needed these materials because there were few forests to furnish lumber. There was some copper, some gold, and there were a few precious stones. There was no iron or coal. You can understand, then, why Egypt developed an agricultural economy and has remained a farming country to the present day.

There was one other thing that could be called a natural resource: this was the valley's location. The valley is surrounded on all sides by deserts and seas. These furnished a natural protection against invaders. Egyptians had little to fear from their neighbors, because they had few neighbors. The natural barriers were broken in only one place: the Isthmus of Suez, which joins Egypt and Asia Minor. Throughout history it has been the route for both traders and invading armies.

● *The Fertile Crescent*

You may wonder at the term *Fertile Crescent*. Look again at the map. See the shaded strip of land that begins at the Isthmus of Suez. It runs up along the eastern end of the Mediterranean Sea and swings over in a half-circle south of the highlands of Armenia and Anatolia. Then it goes down the valley of the Tigris-Euphrates River to the Persian Gulf. Its shape is something like the new moon, so it is called a crescent.

There are two parts to the Fertile Crescent. One is a narrow strip of land along the eastern end of the Mediterranean Sea. The region is about 350 miles long, and 35 miles across at its widest. The southern part, Palestine, lies along the valley of the Jordan River.

Across the desert eastward is the eastern part of the Fertile Crescent—Mesopotamia, which means "land between the rivers." Here was the location of the other great early civilization of the Near East. The map shows you that the Tigris and Euphrates rivers rise in the great mountain plateaus of Armenia and Anatolia in northern Asia Minor. They flow southeast, one straight and one in a great loop, to the Persian Gulf. They now join some distance from the gulf. In ancient days they were separate (see map).

As in the Nile Valley, the soil of the Tigris-Euphrates region was made fertile by silt from floods. Excavations show that at one time a layer of silt eight feet deep was deposited over the whole of Mesopotamia, the result of a huge flood. Every people who lived in the valley had a legend of a great flood, like the one described in the Bible. The land was hot and dry except in flood time. Irrigation was necessary.

The southern end of the valley was called the Plain of Sumer. It was formed by the soil that the rivers poured into the Persian Gulf, century after century. This part of the valley was especially fertile. Historians think that it was the location of the Garden of Eden which the Bible describes. Here Neolithic men, called Sumerians, settled and grew crops.

Like Egypt, Mesopotamia was surrounded by deserts and mountains. There was one great difference in geography that made the history of the two countries very different. The deserts and highlands around Mesopotamia were not so barren as those around Egypt. There was enough grass and other plant life to support tribes of herdsmen.

These desert wanderers were wild, fierce, and toughened by their way of life. They envied the richer, easier life of the valley people. At various times, the valley people grew weak, either from easier living or because of failure to build a strong, united government. Then the desert men moved in, conquered, and settled down. The history of Mesopotamia is the story of a succession of peoples. Each held and ruled the valley for a time. Each in turn was conquered and enslaved by another people who were stronger, more warlike, and usually less civilized.

Common developments bring the two regions into historic times

● *The use of metal*

As you know, metal was first used in the two valleys. In both places copper was used for needles, chisels, and jewelry about 5000

B.C. Bronze, the stronger alloy of copper and tin, was developed in Egypt after 3000 B.C. Its use came later in Mesopotamia. The Bronze Age lasted until about 1000 B.C. in both valleys.

● The calendar

Very early each region developed a workable calendar. This was a great accomplishment. Ancient men did not know that a day is the length of time it takes the earth to spin around on its axis and that a year is the length of time it takes the earth to move around the sun. From what they could see, they believed they lived on a flat earth. The sky was like a huge bowl over a plate. Sun, moon, and stars moved around overhead in the area under the bowl.

The people were farmers, and the changes of the seasons were very important to them. They had to know when the spring floods would start and stop. The most natural way was to divide the time from flood to flood by the moon, the time from new moon to the next new moon. Twelve moons equal one year. The trouble is that a lunar (moon) month is only 29½ days long. Twelve "moons" equal only 354 days, not 365.

The lunar calendar was very unsatisfactory. Months came earlier each year; so it was not much help in farming. In Egypt someone noticed that just before the floods came, a very bright star began to appear in the sky. This was Sirius, the Dog Star. The interval from one rising of Sirius to the next was 365 days; this was a year. The Egyptians divided the year into twelve months of thirty days each. This left them with five extra days. Like the wise people they were, they used them for holidays and feasting.

Numbering the years was no great problem. In the beginning, years were known by an outstanding event: the year of the great flood or the year the locusts were bad. Later, the people used the reigns of kings: the first, second, or twentieth year of the reign of a

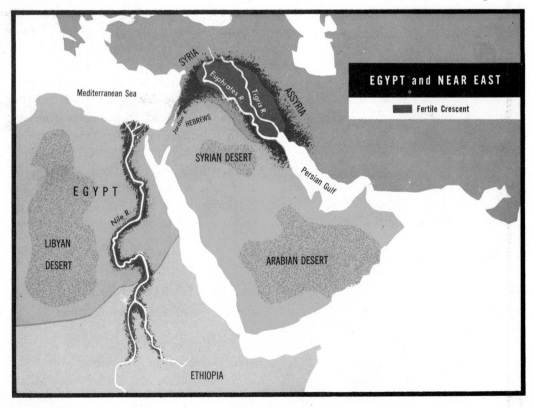

EGYPT and NEAR EAST

■ Fertile Crescent

Mediterranean Sea

SYRIA

Euphrates R.

Tigris R.

ASSYRIA

Jordan R.

HEBREWS

SYRIAN DESERT

Persian Gulf

EGYPT

Nile R.

LIBYAN DESERT

ARABIAN DESERT

ETHIOPIA

certain king. By this method we can trace back the record in Egypt to 4241 B.C. Some historians believe that this is the first recorded date in history. The Egyptians perfected the solar (sun and stars) calendar in 2776 B.C.

The Sumerians developed a moon calendar but did not improve it. Their years had twelve lunar months. When the passage of years threw their calendar out of joint, they added a thirteenth month to bring the calendar back into line with the seasons.

You have noticed that the letters B.C. and A.D. are used with dates to show divisions of time: B.C. means "*Before the birth of Christ*"; A.D. stands for the Latin phrase *Anno Domini,* meaning "in the year of our Lord," or since the birth of Christ. Of course, no ancient man ever dated anything B.C. A moment's thought will tell you why. This method of reckoning time is used only in those parts of the world and by those people who follow the Christian religion. Mohammedans, Chinese, Hebrews, and Hindus have other ways of counting the years. For example, our year A.D. 1960 corresponds with the Chinese year 4658.

● *Irrigation, flood control, and government*

Farming in both great valleys depended on irrigation and flood control; therefore, the people had to learn to work together in groups. It took teamwork to build dikes to control floods, and ditches and canals for irrigation. The people set up governments to plan, direct, and make the rules for this work.

The first valley dwellers had moved into both valleys in small groups or tribes. Each group settled in a village along a river. They lived together in the village for greater protection, and went out to work the surrounding land. The kind of government that grew up is called a *city-state:* a town or city and the surrounding land it controls.

Strong forces tended to bring city-states together. Two or more villages often had to work together for flood control or irrigation.

However, quarrels over land, water rights, and commerce often caused trouble and kept the city-states divided.

● *The development of writing*

The development of written language marks the difference between prehistoric and historic times. Only three peoples have created original written languages: the Egyptians, the Sumerians, and the Chinese.

There are four steps in the development of a true and simple form of writing:

1. A picture represents a word or an idea. Many peoples have gone this far, among them some American Indians. Picture writing has several drawbacks. Pictures must be very simple and always drawn alike. A great many pictures are needed. *Ideas* are very difficult to show in pictures. A thing, such as man, tree, or horse, is easily shown. But how would you show an idea, such as truth, or God, or life after death?

2. A picture is used to represent two words that sound alike, such as *I* and *eye, be* and *bee.* This is the first step toward having a sign represent a sound rather than a word or idea. It requires fewer pictures.

3. An agreed sign stands for a special speech sound, a syllable like *ab* or *ed.* Syllable signs are combined to form words; pictures are no longer used. This is called *phonetic* (or sound) writing.

4. An alphabet is developed, in which each sign (letter) represents a speech sound. Letters are combined to form words. Fewer letters are needed than signs for syllable sounds.

● *Egyptian writing and writing material*

In the beginning the Egyptians used pictures only. There were more than 600 of them, many representing more than one word or idea. This is called *hieroglyphic,* or picture writing. Later they developed phonetic (sound) signs, and produced an alphabet. Using twenty-four letters, they could write a

Hieroglyphic writing reproduced from a papyrus scroll.

running hand instead of forming each letter separately.

At first Egyptians wrote or carved on rock, a long and difficult process, not suited to ordinary use. Searching for a better writing material, they used what they found near them. Large reeds, called papyrus, grew in the marshes near the river. The Egyptians cut the stems in long, thin slices, wove them into a mat, joined the surface with a kind of glue, and pressed and dried the mat. They called the product *papyrus,* from which we get the word *paper.*

They wrote on the papyrus with ink made from vegetable gum and soot. For a pen they made a pointed reed. Papyrus was made in long, narrow strips and left that way. Instead of cutting it into pages they rolled it; an ancient Egyptian book is a roll of paper.

● *Sumerian writing and writing material*

Sumerian writing was very different. They also began with pictures and then developed phonetic signs for syllables. They never developed an alphabet, however. Their written language contained about 600 syllable signs. Most of them were like triangles or wedges. The Latin word for wedge is *cuneus;* so we call Sumerian writing *cuneiform.*

The Sumerians also used what they had at hand for writing material. They did not have the papyrus reed; so they did not learn papermaking. They did have plenty of clay. They rolled out a lump of soft clay and made their wedge-shaped marks on it with a pointed stick called a stylus. Then they allowed the clay tablet to bake until it was hard, after which it would last indefinitely. It might shatter, but, as with pottery, the pieces could always be fitted together.

● *The Rosetta Stone and Behistun Rock*

Modern men learned to read the two ancient languages as a result of clever detective work on two famous rocks: the Rosetta Stone and the Behistun Rock.

In 1798 A.D. a French army under Napoleon Bonaparte invaded Egypt. The following year an engineer officer found, on the Rosetta branch of the Nile, in the delta, a stone slab. It was carved with writing in three languages:

A clay tablet from Babylonia, showing cuneiform writing.

rian solved the mystery. He proved that all three inscriptions gave the law of an Egyptian ruler. From the Greek, which he knew, he was able to work out twelve of the twenty-four consonant signs. Other scholars using other clues worked out a complete key.

The puzzle of cuneiform writing was solved in much the same way. Darius the Great, ruler of Persia, had put down a rebellion led by nine chiefs, whom he punished. To discourage other rebellions he ordered the story to be carved on a limestone cliff at Behistun, both in pictures and writing.

The Behistun cliff, or rock, is huge. The carving shows Darius I giving judgment on nine rebel chiefs, who are standing with their hands bound behind them. The writing is in three languages: Persian, which was partly known; Susian, a native language of the region; Babylonian, the same as Sumerian cuneiform. A brilliant Englishman was able to work out from the Behistun Rock the syllable signs of cuneiform writing.

Greek, hieroglyphics, and the running hand of the later Egyptians.

Scholar-detectives guessed, but could not be sure, that the three all told the same story. After twenty years a brilliant French histo-

Review of Chapter 2

People, places, and things

Identify: the Garden of Eden, hieroglyphic writing, phonetic writing, papyrus, Darius, cuneiform, B.C., A.D.

Locate: Egypt, Mesopotamia, the Near East, the Nile Valley, the Fertile Crescent, the Tigris-Euphrates Valley, the Persian Gulf.

Events in review

1. What historian said that Egypt was the "gift of the Nile"? Why did he say this?
2. What was the importance of (a) the Rosetta Stone and (b) the Behistun Rock in increasing our knowledge of ancient civilizations?
3. Why did early peoples find the lunar calendar unsatisfactory?

4. Did Egypt and Mesopotamia have the same natural resources? Name two advantages of each region.
5. Why did Egypt throughout history remain a farming country?

Problems and projects

1. Discuss the importance of geography in determining history. Use examples from both ancient and modern times. (For instance, river valleys were centers for early civilizations. Have rivers been important in American history?)
2. One of the great contributions of the ancient nations to modern times has been the calendar. Do you agree or disagree with this statement? Give reasons.

Chapter 3

The Egyptians Build a High Civilization

ONE of the greatest civilizations of all time grew up in ancient Egypt. We will study first the *political* development of Egypt—how the country was organized and governed.

Political developments

●*Egypt becomes a united kingdom*

Over the centuries the early city-states (page 23) were united to form the two kingdoms of Upper and Lower Egypt. Menes was the first ruler to unite all Egypt into one kingdom. He wanted some sign or symbol to show his new power. So he wore a double crown which combined the white crown of Upper Egypt with the red crown of Lower Egypt. Menes and his successors put down rebellions, gained more territory, regulated irrigation, and promoted trade and prosperity.

Much of their power came from the fact that they were religious as well as political leaders. They claimed to be descended from the gods—to be half-god and half-man. They took the title *Pharaoh*, which means "Great House." He was such a wonderful and fearful person, this half-god and half-king, that it was not proper for his subjects to call him directly by his name. They called him by the title of the palace in which he lived.

In the 3,000 years from the time of Menes to the birth of Christ there were thirty dynasties (families) of pharaohs. The events of the times divide these years into several ages.

●*The Old Kingdom: The Pyramid Age, 3000–2300 B.C.*

The Pyramid Age was probably the greatest period of all Egyptian history. Almost all the important discoveries in science and the arts took place then. It was the age of the building of the great pyramids which have become symbols of Egyptian civilization (see the picture on page 31).

The pharaoh was an autocrat; that is, he alone had power to make, enforce, and interpret laws. He was in part a god, not just the agent of a god like the Sumerian priests. Although he had absolute power, it was his duty to protect and care for his people.

The pharaoh appointed all government officials and priests. He claimed all the land. Farmers paid him one fifth of the crop as rent; if they failed to do so, they would be cut off from irrigation water. They also owed him services, like army duty or work on the irrigation system. They helped build the great pyramids.

Toward the end of the Old Kingdom the pharaohs became weaker. For 300 years the country was torn by civil wars as rival leaders claimed the throne. Finally a strong line of rulers reunited the country.

●*The Middle Kingdom: The Feudal Age, 2000–1800 B.C.*

The strong pharaohs of the Middle Kingdom restored order and prosperity in Egypt, but these good times lasted only for a while.

The problems of making all the decisions and seeing that they were carried out were too great for all but the strongest and ablest rulers. There was just too much power in the hands of one man. Gradually the pharaohs lost some of their powers to others. The chief minister (vizier) gained the power of supervising the minor officials, like tax collectors. Governors of provinces became powerful and, in time, made their positions hereditary (passing from father to son). Priests were important not only as conductors of religious ceremonies, but also as healers of disease. They performed many government duties and became very wealthy. The position of priest also became hereditary.

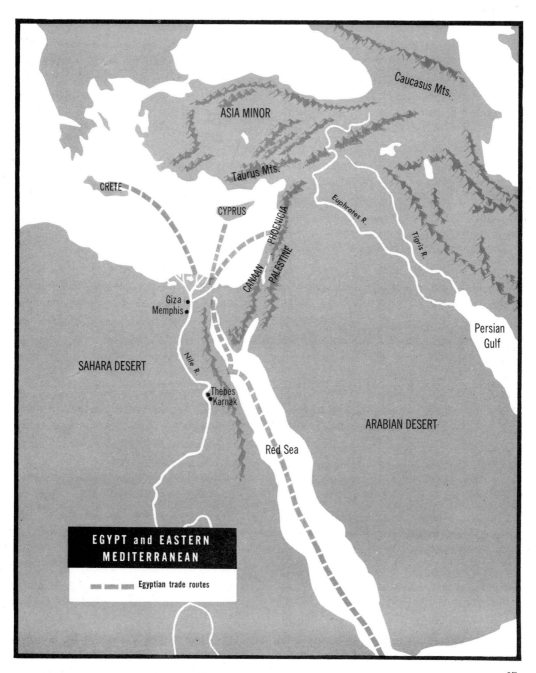

EGYPT and EASTERN
MEDITERRANEAN

▬ ▬ ▬ ▬ Egyptian trade routes

Thus the power of the pharaoh was weakened by the rise of a hereditary class of officials, nobles, and priests. These often rivaled each other as well as the pharaoh for wealth and power. This condition gives the period its name of Feudal Age or Age of Nobles. In a feudal system all the land is owned by a few rich people, and the workers on the land are almost the slaves of the owners.

The Middle Kingdom also ended in disorder. The country was weakened by rivalries, conflicts, and the division of power. In 1750 B.C. Egypt was invaded for the first time in many centuries. An Asiatic people called the Hyksos, under rulers known as the Shepherd Kings, crossed the isthmus and conquered the delta region. They had a well-organized army, better equipped than the Egyptians because they had horses and chariots. They ruled parts of Egypt for 200 years, but added nothing to Egyptian culture.

● *The Empire Age, 1600–1200 B.C.*

The nobles of Upper Egypt, the region up the Nile from the delta, rebelled against the Hyksos and drove them from the country. Then Egypt was united under a succession of strong pharaohs who ruled from Thebes. This new line of pharaohs regained much of the power of the older group of pharaohs. They kept strict control of the government and all the officials, and created a strong army and navy. They adopted the horse-drawn chariots of the Hyksos, and began to use weapons of iron.

But, like so many rulers in history, even today, the pharaohs were not satisfied to rule Egypt only. They wanted more and more territory; they wanted to rule over an empire—and they did so: they conquered Ethiopia, and Syria, the western end of the Fertile Crescent. At one time the Egyptians controlled almost all of Mesopotamia.

However, like many others, the Egyptians found it easier to conquer territory than to hold and rule it. Usually they allowed the native prince of a conquered region to act as governor. To be sure of his loyalty and obedience, they took his son back to Egypt to be trained at the palace at Thebes. But only the ablest pharaohs could hold the empire together. Whenever the government of Egypt became weak, some part of the empire revolted and tried to break away. All through your study of history you will see that people would rather have their own government, even a poor one, than be ruled by outsiders.

Some of the pharaohs of the Empire Age have become very famous. One of these might be called the first famous woman in history. Her name was Hatshepsut. It was not unusual for a queen to rule as pharaoh, but Hatshepsut was unusually able. She was more interested in the welfare of her country than in war and conquest. She tried to make Egypt prosperous by increasing trade and by governing wisely and efficiently. She ordered the construction of temples to the gods and many other public buildings.

Hatshepsut was succeeded by Thutmose III, her husband and also her half-brother. This illustrates a strange custom of Egyptian rulers. Since the pharaoh was half-god, it was not proper for him to marry an ordinary human being. He usually married his sister or half-sister. Thutmose was much younger than Hatshepsut. While she lived, he was not really king, but just the queen's husband. After she died, he showed his jealousy by having her name struck off all the public buildings erected at her order.

When he became the real pharaoh, Thutmose III proved to be an able ruler and general. He extended the boundaries of the empire to its greatest limits. From the Tigris River to the island of Crete, from Asia Minor to Nubia far up the Nile River, Thutmose ruled as emperor. His system of government was so good and his armies so powerful that Egypt was secure for years after his death.

The third pharaoh, Amenhotep IV, was not a famous conqueror, nor even a very good ruler. He is famous because he brought about a social and religious revolution in Egypt. When he came to the throne, he found that the priests of the sun-god Amon had become so powerful that they interfered in all affairs. He wanted to break their power, and he was also interested in a new idea of religion.

Amenhotep IV believed that the sun-god was the *only* god, not just the first among many gods. What was more, Amon was a kindly god who loved and cared for his people. This belief in one god only is known as *monotheism.* Amenhotep IV changed the name of his god to Aton, to show his new nature. In his honor he changed his own name to Ikhnaton. To help break the power of the priests of Amon he moved his capital from Thebes, where the great temple of Amon was located, to a new city which he ordered built. He forbade the worship of any god but Aton.

You may be sure that the priests of Amon and of the other gods were displeased. Their rich and easy living was being destroyed by the order of the pharaoh. So they began to cause trouble. Because they had a great hold over the people, they were able to stir them against the king. Soon Ikhnaton learned that he could not change people's religious beliefs just by passing a law. The bitter struggle between king and priests caused much disorder in Egypt. When Ikhnaton died, the priests of Amon re-established their power. They forced his successor, Tutankhamen, to move the capital back to Thebes. "King Tut's" tomb was discovered in 1922 A.D.

● *The decline*

After the death of Ikhnaton there were few strong rulers in Egypt. For four or five hundred years the government grew steadily weaker. The empire was lost, and foreign invaders came into Egypt itself. The country was conquered and ruled, in turn, by the Ethiopians, the Assyrians, and the Persians. Alexander the Great of Macedon conquered it in 332 B.C. The Romans took and held it

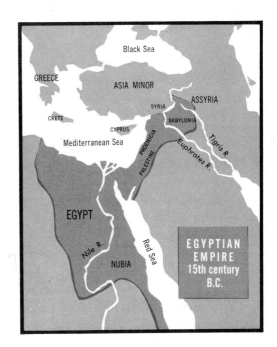

for three centuries. In the seventh century A.D. it was conquered by the Mohammedan Arabs. For several hundred years it was part of the Turkish Empire. During the late 1800's it became a protectorate of England. Only in the twentieth century did Egypt become an independent country again.

Cultural development in Egypt

● *Agriculture, industry, and commerce*

Most of the Egyptian farm land was owned by the pharaoh, the nobles, and the priests, in very large estates. Farming was done by peasants and slaves, with very crude tools. The light soil was broken with hoes or wooden plows drawn either by oxen or by the peasants themselves. These primitive methods did not improve much with the passage of time. However, they produced very good crops, often three a year, because of the rich soil and warm climate. The men who did the work kept only part of the crop. The rest went for rent and taxes.

The Nile floods determined the year's work. In November, when the flood had subsided, the land was cultivated and planted.

29

The growing season lasted until May, when the floods began again. Wheat and barley were the main grain crops. Flax was grown for the weaving of linen. Cotton was also grown, just as it is today in Egypt, and woven into cloth. There were crops of vegetables, and some vineyards and fruit orchards.

In spite of crude farming methods and the unfair division of land and crops, Egypt produced more food than her people needed. The surplus food was traded with other people for the things Egypt needed. Inside the country, the Nile was the great highway of trade. Even in Neolithic times Egyptians built wooden boats. Later they were among the first to build seagoing ships. These they sailed into the eastern Mediterranean and Aegean seas, the Red Sea, and even the Indian Ocean. Using first donkeys and later camels, their caravans went overland into Asia Minor and deep into Africa.

The Egyptians also had the products of their artisans to trade. There were products of metal, pottery, glass, and wood, as well as woven cloth, jewelry, paper, carved stone, and ships. These craftsmen did very fine work, and their products were greatly prized.

The people: social classes

The first person in Egyptian society was, of course, the pharaoh. His position as half-god placed him far above common mortals. He was head of government, judge, high priest, and general of the armies combined.

Below the pharaoh came the wealthy class of nobles and priests, who had been able to make their positions hereditary. They owned great estates of rich land, and grew wealthy from the work of peasants and slaves. Their sons attended the schools in the temples and the great university. These rich people gave great feasts, had fine clothing, jewelry, and household furnishings. Their homes were large and spacious, built with wood frames covered with bricks. Beautiful woven hang-ings often served for partitions. Walls, floors, and ceilings were decorated with paintings. Surrounding the houses were lovely gardens. Around the whole place were high walls.

Next in order came a small middle class of merchants, businessmen, owners of workshops, and members of the professions. Below them came the artisans, skilled workmen in many crafts. At the bottom of the pyramid were the vast majority of the people—the peasants and slaves.

The life of the poor was wretched indeed. Their houses were mud huts with thatched roofs and scanty, poorly built furniture. Rows of houses were separated by narrow alleys. The people lived in filth and ignorance. In the farming villages they had a little more room, but not much else.

A very attractive feature of Egyptian culture was the favorable position held by women. A woman owned property in her own right and could pass it on by inheritance to her daughter. Women were the equals of their husbands in their social and business affairs. A man, even of the wealthy class, usually had only one wife, which was not true among other ancient peoples. It was common for a queen to rule the country or to share the throne with her husband. A queen could pass on the right of kingship to her children. In many ways the Egyptian woman was better off than her sisters in any other civilization until very recent times.

Architecture and engineering

When you think of Egypt, it is likely that the first things that come to your mind are the pyramids. These huge structures can still be seen along the lower Nile, although they were built four or five thousand years ago. Pyramids were built as tombs for the pharaohs. Old Kingdom Egyptians believed that only the pharaoh, a god, was sure to have a life after death; he might grant immortality to a chosen few of his favorites. Even after death he would continue to look after the welfare of his people. It was therefore important that his burial place should fit his splendid position. The Egyptian people were forced to help build such a burial place.

There was great rivalry among the Old Kingdom pharaohs to see which could have the most magnificent pyramid. The winner was Khufu, whom the Greeks called Cheops. His final resting place is the Great Pyramid. It is a truly magnificent structure. Each side, at the ground, is 755 feet long, about the length of two city blocks. It is more than half a mile around at the base. The pyramid is nearly 480 feet high, more than one third the height of the tallest building in the United States.

The Great Pyramid is built of huge stone blocks, each weighing two and a half tons. There are two and a half million blocks in all. They were so carefully cut and joined that the sides do not vary one tenth of a foot. The joints between the blocks are one thousandth of an inch wide. This is less than

the clearance of the moving parts of a modern automobile, yet the stone blocks of the pyramids were cut with copper saws.

The stone was quarried many miles from the site, and roads were built to drag them to place. It is said that it took 10,000 men ten years to build the road, and that it took twenty years to erect the pyramid. However, it is probable that they did not work continuously. Taking care of the crops and other duties caused interruptions in the work. The huge blocks of stone were moved by being placed on rollers. They were then dragged and pushed by hundreds of slaves. The blocks were put in place in the pyramid by rolling them up ramps (inclined planes) built up with earth.

Egyptian engineers and scientists were among the ablest in the ancient world. The

The Great Pyramid, built around 2500 B.C. as the tomb of the Pharaoh Khufu, or Cheops.

engineers built huge pyramids and temples. These engineers also built dams. One of them, built during the Middle Kingdom, was large enough to irrigate 27,000 acres, about forty-two square miles. They built a canal to join the Nile River and the Red Sea. Egyptian engineers developed the ramp, the long slope to move things up more easily, and the principle of the lever. When you see a man move a log or other heavy object by placing one end of a crowbar under it, a stone or block under the bar, and then pushing or pulling down on the other end of the bar, he is using this principle.

● Other sciences

Early in their history the Egyptians recognized the need for exact measurements and a science of numbers. They developed a number system based on ten. They made great developments in mathematics. In arithmetic they used fractions as well as whole numbers. They used geometry to fix the boundaries of fields after the floods subsided, and to lay out canals and ditches. They had formulas for measuring the area of a circle and the contents of a silo shaped like a round column. They learned and perfected many principles of algebra.

The Egyptians also made discoveries in medicine. They knew a great deal about the anatomy of the human body—the way it is put together—and used the knowledge in treating illness and in preparing mummies. *The Book of Healing Diseases,* written during the Middle Kingdom, catalogued and classified diseases according to symptoms. It named the herbs and drugs for treating each

Pillars in the temple at Karnak, showing hieroglyphic writing. The pictures of men are approximately life size. The style of architecture shown here is typical of Egyptian buildings: columns supporting heavy beams. This is known as post and lintel construction.

illness. Some of the treatments were magic spells, but many were more scientific. Egyptian physicians made a special study of the blood. They knew that it circulated through the body, and that the heart was the center of the circulatory system. After Egyptian times this knowledge was lost and not rediscovered until the seventeenth century A.D.

Egyptian medical schools were located in the temples. Each doctor specialized in the treatment of a particular disease. The skill of Egyptian doctors was recognized throughout the ancient world. They performed good bone surgery. They knew how to treat wounds, disinfecting them with a salt solution. Egyptian dentists made inlays of gold foil to fill cavities in teeth. Many physicians were oculists, because diseases of the eye were very common in that land of glaring sun and dust.

The arts

Egyptian art was as good as their architecture and science. Sculpture ranged in size from huge stone figures like the Sphinx, weighing hundreds of tons, to small, lifelike figures of kings and sacred animals, beautifully shaped from copper, bronze, stone, wood, or ivory. Egyptian painting, seen in wall and ceiling decorations, was very accurate. However, the painters did not make much use of lights and shadows, nor had they learned the trick

Part of an Egyptian wall painting showing farmers at work, hoeing, using mallets to break up clods, plowing, and scattering seed. Notice that the second row of figures is drawn above the first row. Egyptian artists did not know how to get perspective in their pictures. They drew distant figures above rather than behind the figures in foreground.

of perspective, which gives depth and distance to a painting.

Education

It would have been impossible for the Egyptians to gather and pass on so much knowledge over so many years without a system of education. Their schools were usually in temples, because education was partly religious. Education was mostly for children of noble and priestly families, although children of the middle class and of artisans often attended schools.

Children remained in the care of the mother until the age of four, after which boys went to school. The boy learned to read, and to write by copying passages from the great books of Egypt. He learned arithmetic and the sacred songs of his religion. Discipline was very severe. A boy who neglected his work was beaten harshly. Girls did not have any formal schooling. This is one way in which women were not treated equally.

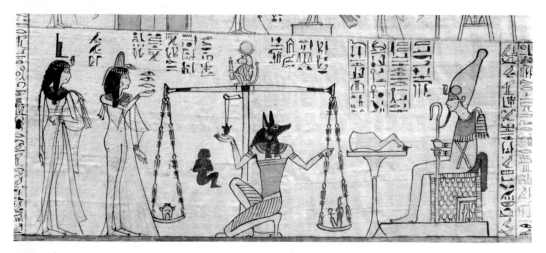

When this elementary education was finished, the educational paths separated. Sons of artisans went with their fathers to learn trades. Sons of the wealthy, the nobles or priests, went on to higher schools. They studied astronomy and religion for the priesthood, or science, engineering, or medicine. The greatest university of ancient Egypt was at Heliopolis. It was famous throughout the ancient world. Many famous Greeks studied there. It is thought that Moses, who led the Hebrews out of Egypt back to their homeland in Asia Minor, was educated at Heliopolis.

The great masses of the poor and the slaves were uneducated. In fact, the ability to read and write was the basis of a respected and profitable Egyptian profession, that of *scribe*. For a fee, the scribe would read or write for those who could not. He might also be employed by a wealthy man to keep accounts. He might even rise high in government service, and in time become a noble.

Religion

Already in this book you have read of the importance of religion in Egyptian life and culture. The Egyptians worshipped natural forces such as the sun, moon, and stars. In early days each village and district had its local god or gods. In time some of these were accepted and worshipped throughout

Part of the Book of the Dead *of a princess, showing some of the Egyptian beliefs about life after death. She stands next to the scales in the judgment hall of the god Osiris. The god Anubis weighs her heart against truth. At the right is Osiris on his throne. The figure behind the princess is the goddess Isis.*

the country. Each god had an animal as his symbol. Among the sacred animals were the cat, the bull, the crocodile, and the scarab (a beetle). Some of the important gods were:

1. Ra, or Amon-Ra, the sun-god, was first in importance and reverence. He was the source of life and goodness, lord of all other gods, the giver of victories. His temples were filled with gifts of thanks, and his priests became wealthy and powerful.
2. Isis, the moon-goddess, was mother of the universe, queen of the world and the heavens. She was the wife of Osiris.
3. Horus, god of the rising sun, was the son of Osiris.
4. Set was the god of evil.
5. Osiris, god of the Nile River and of fertility, was loved the most. He was lord of the realm of the dead—the judge who could give eternal life to all.

Thus the Egyptians came to believe in life after death for the spirits of both people and animals. They believed that the spirit would be happier if the body were preserved; so they worked out a way of preserving the body by mummification. Even today we do not know how to preserve a body as well as did these people thousands of years ago.

The mummy was placed in the tomb and provided with clothing, food, jewelry, toilet articles, tools, weapons, and even servants (small sculptured figures). These were necessary for the long journey to the Realm of the Dead. On this journey the soul was beset by serpents, dragons, and demons. To guard against them there was put in the tomb a copy of the *Book of the Dead,* a collection of hymns, prayers, and magic chants.

When the soul reached the Realm of the Dead it entered the Hall of Truth, where Osiris sat in judgment. Here it must testify to the kind of life it had lived on earth. It must take oath that it had not lied, or murdered, or been too proud and haughty. Perhaps the finest part of the oath required it to say: "I have made no man weep; I have not inflicted pain." This is a noble idea of character in any age.

When the soul had testified and taken oath, it was weighed on the great scale against a feather, the symbol of truth. If it had sworn falsely, it was thrown to a horrible monster called the Eater of the Dead. But if it had spoken truly, it could enter into the presence of the sun god and eternal happiness, in the "fields of content."

Thus you can see that good character and a good life were very important to Egyptians because they would be rewarded hereafter. At first they thought that this reward could come only to the pharaoh and a chosen few. Later they believed that everyone could enter the hereafter.

Review of Chapter 3

People, places, and things

Identify: pharaoh, Menes, Hyksos, Amenhotep IV, Aton, scribe, monotheism, mummification, *The Book of Healing Diseases.*

Locate: Egypt, Ethiopia, Syria, the Fertile Crescent, Memphis. Trace the sea routes of the ancient Egyptians.

Events in review

1. To what extent was Egyptian agriculture dependent upon the Nile?
2. Describe the Egyptian economy, showing that it was based on both agriculture and trade.
3. What products were produced by (a) Egyptian farmers, (b) Egyptian artisans.
4. Why were the pyramids built?
5. Why is the construction of the pyramids considered a great engineering accomplishment?
6. Did all Egyptian children receive the same education? Explain.
7. What were two of the notable discoveries made by Egyptian doctors?
8. Describe briefly the Egyptian idea of life after death.

Problems and projects

1. Describe briefly three characteristics of life in ancient Egypt that were similar to the way of life in America today.
2. List a number of political and economic problems of Egypt at the present time. Did any of these problems exist in ancient times?
3. Discuss the importance of Egypt in the world of today. How does the geographical location of Egypt affect Egypt's role in world affairs?
4. Contrast the schools of ancient Egypt with modern schools. How could the Egyptian schools have been improved?
5. Draw or trace a map of Egypt and the surrounding lands. Show in color the Egyptian empire at its greatest extent.
6. Suppose you were preparing a tour for visitors to Egypt. What sights would you advise them to see in order to get a picture of the great civilization of ancient Egypt?

Chapter 4 Mesopotamia Is Ruled by a Series of Peoples

WHILE one great civilization was growing in the Nile Valley, other civilizations were rising and declining in Mesopotamia. A series of peoples ruled this area: the Sumerians and Babylonians, the Hittites, the Assyrians, the Chaldeans, and the Persians.

Sumerians and Babylonians

The Sumerians, as you know, moved into the Plain of Sumer in lower Mesopotamia toward the end of the New Stone Age, possibly before 6000 B.C. By the time 2000 years had passed, about 4000 B.C., they were using metal and had developed a form of writing.

●*The Sumerian city-states*

The city-state form of government was used very early. Each city-state had its own god or gods. The high priest was the head of the government. He gained his power by claiming to be the god's representative or agent, able to speak for him and give his commands. The position of high priest became hereditary. The priests were supported by a class of nobles and a well-organized army. Both nobles and priests owned much land, and the priests controlled irrigation.

The Sumerian city-states were never united into one government for the entire region. There was much rivalry among them, and among the peoples who held other parts of the great valley. Failure to unite weakened them, and the Sumerians, able and civilized in so many ways, were finally conquered by a less civilized but more warlike people.

●*The Babylonians*

Sometime after 2300 B.C. a new people invaded Mesopotamia. They built a new city as their capital and called it Babylon; from it they have been called Babylonians. They conquered all of Sumeria, and eventually much of the rest of Mesopotamia. The Babylonians moved into Mesopotamia in groups, and, group by group, took over the city-states with their form of government. About 2000 B.C. a very strong and able ruler managed to conquer all the city-states and unite the whole country. He was Hammurabi.

Hammurabi was more than a great military leader. He turned out to be an able organizer and a wise and just statesman as well. He is best known because he drew up and had published a *code,* or collection, of written laws. In it he speaks of himself as the father of his people, their "pastor, savior, and good protecting shadow."

●*Hammurabi's code of laws*

Hammurabi's code of 282 articles controlled all parts of Babylonian life. Agriculture, commerce, and industry were carefully regulated. Men who failed to cultivate their

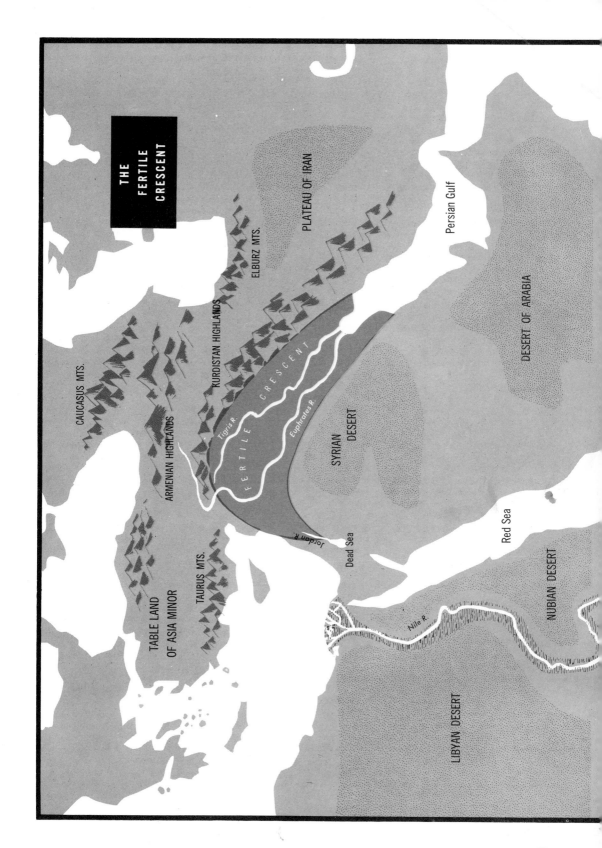

THE FERTILE CRESCENT

PLATEAU OF IRAN

ELBURZ MTS.

KURDISTAN HIGHLANDS

CAUCASUS MTS.

ARMENIAN HIGHLANDS

Tigris R.

FERTILE CRESCENT

Euphrates R.

Persian Gulf

DESERT OF ARABIA

SYRIAN DESERT

TABLE LAND OF ASIA MINOR

TAURUS MTS.

Jordan R.

Dead Sea

Red Sea

Nile R.

NUBIAN DESERT

LIBYAN DESERT

37

fields or to keep up the irrigating canals and ditches were punished. Wages, hours, and conditions of work were regulated. There were sections dealing with property rights and bankruptcy. Others dealt with marriage contracts, breach of promise suits, and divorce. The laws were enforced by judges, under supervision by the king's advisers and officials. There were very severe penalties for trying to bribe a judge or a witness.

The laws of Hammurabi gave some degree of justice to everyone. Thus government under Hammurabi was better than the political and social customs of the rest of the ancient world. According to our ideas today, Hammurabi's laws had several weaknesses. One was his idea of punishment—the old idea of "an eye for an eye; a tooth for a tooth." If a man caused another to lose an eye, then his eye was put out. If a son struck his father, his hand was cut off. A second weakness was that justice was not equal for all people. If a wealthy man destroyed the eye of a poor man, he did not lose his eye; he only paid a fine. A thief who could not repay what he had stolen was put to death; if he had money, he had only to repay more than he had stolen. Today it is believed that the law should be the same for rich and poor alike. However, Hammurabi's laws were more just than others of their time and even of later times.

After the death of Hammurabi the Babylonian government grew weaker. The Babylonians were very superstitious, and the priests gained great power over them through their claims to be able to ward off evil spirits and to foretell the future. Finally, the Babylonians in their turn were conquered by other invaders of the fertile valley.

Before we go on to these new conquerors, let us see how far the Babylonians traveled on the long road of civilization.

The ideas, customs, institutions, and things that made up Sumerian culture were fully as rich and as highly developed as those of the Egyptians. Historians used to believe that the Egyptians were first in almost everything. Recent evidence seems to show that civilization may have developed first in Sumeria.

Agriculture, commerce, and industry

Most of the Sumerian people were farmers; they raised large crops of grain, vegetables, and dates. They had domestic animals: cows, sheep, and goats, oxen for plowing, and donkeys to pull their carts and chariots. They developed a dairy industry

A corner of a room in the ruins of a Sumerian house. The archway clearly shows the sun-dried bricks the Sumerians used as building materials.

very early. They wove fine woolen goods. They raised flax and made linen cloth.

Most of the land was owned by priests and soldiers. The work was done by tenants, by laborers who worked for wages, or by slaves.

Tenants paid their rent with part of the crop, sometimes as much as two thirds.

As in Egypt, food production was enough to allow many people to work in trade and industry. Sumerians traded with other parts of the Near East before 3000 B.C. Merchants had agents in far places, and salesmen who traveled from city to city. The Babylonians carried on trade with other parts of Asia Minor, with Egypt, and even with India and China.

Social classes

Both Sumerians and Babylonians had distinct social classes. At the top were land-owning aristocrats, the priests, and the government officials. Next came the owners of small farms, the artisans, and the merchants. At the bottom were the slaves. Both peoples treated slaves fairly well compared to other ancient peoples. Babylonians often set slaves free, and the child of a male slave and a free woman was considered free.

As in Egypt, there were great differences in living conditions. The poor lived in mud huts with thatched roofs and only the poorest furnishings. The homes of the wealthy were large and comfortable. They were usually two stories high, built around an inner court. The furniture was handsome: chairs, tables, and beds were beautifully built of wood. There were many utensils of wood, stone, and copper.

Women were respected and well treated, as in Egypt. Other ancient peoples considered women as property to be owned, to be treated as slaves. Sumerian, Babylonian, and Egyptian women were treated as equals in most ways. True, in Mesopotamia a husband could sell his wife and children to pay his debts; but in other ways women fared better.

Babylonian women could enter the trades and professions, and even become priestesses. There is some evidence that they were paid as well as men doing the same work. In this respect we do not do as well even today.

Architecture, engineering, science, and the arts

For building materials the Sumerians used sun-dried clay bricks. Their structures did not last as long as those of the Egyptians, but their architecture was good. The Sumerians seem to have invented several important architectural devices. One was the arch, one of the strongest forms in building. (Note the picture on page 38.) They made vaults and domes on their buildings. They knew and used the ramp, or inclined walkway. They even built sewers beneath their buildings, covered with arches of brick.

The most striking Sumerian buildings were the temples, built on artificial mountains to rise high above the flat valley. They were in the form of large blocks or terraces, one on top of another. Ramps led from one story to the next. Each was a little smaller than the one below; thus they looked a little like our step-back skyscrapers. Each story was painted a different color, and each was dedicated to a different star or planet. Usually there were seven stories. The top one was the shrine of the god.

Sumerians excelled in metal work and jewelry. They knew how to make alloys (combinations of two or more metals), and they made fine metal castings. They used copper, bronze, silver, and gold in their metal work, and carved jewelry from ivory, fine wood, and precious stones. Their sculpture was magnificent.

Sumerian engineers and scientists made many important discoveries. It is thought that the principle and use of the wheel were first found in Sumeria in Neolithic times. Someone has said that almost every machine is a development, in some way, of the wheel. Later Sumerians developed many mathematical principles of arithmetic, algebra, and geometry. They used a number system based on sixty. They divided a circle into 360 degrees, each degree with sixty minutes, each minute with sixty seconds. When you look at the face of a compass or a watch, you are seeing a principle discovered by the Sumerians thousands of years ago.

Sumerian scientists were greatly interested in astronomy. They made careful observations of the positions of the stars and planets at various times. They noticed and recorded unusual events such as eclipses of the sun and moon. Many of the constellations that we talk about were first noticed and named by the Sumerian astronomers.

The Babylonians copied the Sumerian art, architecture, way of writing, and science, but they seldom did as well as the Sumerians had done. Many times in history you will read of conquerors who adopted the culture of the people they conquered. In a way it is hard to say who were the conquerors and who the conquered.

● Education

Both Sumerians and Babylonians considered education very important, although it was only for children of the wealthy. Schools were usually in the temples, conducted by priests. Both boys and girls were educated. In this way the girls of Mesopotamia were better off than their Egyptian sisters.

Writing and spelling were very important subjects. As the child entered the classroom, he was given a ball of soft clay and a stylus; these were his tablet and pencil. He flattened the clay with his hands and made the wedge-shaped marks with the stylus (note the drawing on page 36). Writing was learned by copying religious books and songs.

The child also learned reading, history, foreign languages, and map-making. Boys learned to shoot with bows and arrows, and took part in other outdoor activities. In the higher schools they studied mathematics, astronomy, law, medicine, and surgery. Much time was spent learning *divination,* that is, foretelling the future from various signs and omens.

● Religion

The Sumerians believed in many gods. These gods were the forces of nature, like the sun, moon, and stars. They thought of their gods as supermen, with the same habits and passions as men but much more powerful.

A reconstruction of a model of a Sumerian chariot. The original copper model, dating from about 2800 B.C., was found by archeologists in what is now Iraq. Notice the construction of the wheel.

Tammuz, the sun god, was the most powerful. Ishtar was the goddess of love, motherhood, and fertility.

The priests were powerful and important. They claimed to be able to intercede in the next world for good people, and also to foretell the future. In addition to leading the religion, they directed the government and conducted much of the business. The temples were shrines for ceremonies and festivals, but they also contained schools, offices, storehouses, and workshops.

Sumerian belief about the future life was vague. They did not believe in reward or punishment (heaven or hell), but thought there was some sort of life after death. They feared ghosts: they thought that if they did not bury personal objects, like jewelry, the spirit would be displeased, and would return to haunt the house and family.

The Babylonians took over many Sumerian religious ideas. Marduk, god of the city of Babylon, became the principal god, but Ishtar remained the chief goddess. Babylonians were even more superstitious than Sumerians. They thought they were constantly surrounded by evil spirits. Unless these evil spirits were warded off by charms and spells, they could cause accidents, illness, insanity, or death. The Babylonians made many sacrifices to their gods—not in the hope of a better future life but for such things as good harvests and business gains. They believed that life after death was gloomy and hopeless. It was spent in a place called The Land of No Return.

Babylonian priests were as powerful as the Sumerian, gaining much power from giving charms and spells against evil spirits. They claimed the power of divination by studying the liver of a sacrificed sheep. They also practiced astrology, the prediction of the future from the stars. They believed that comets, eclipses, and changes in the position of stars and planets were caused by the gods, and that these phenomena in the sky influenced the lives of people.

Now in the long procession of conquerors and conquered, we come to another invading people. Three or four hundred years had passed since the days of the great Hammurabi, and the Babylonians were soon to move off the stage in favor of other peoples.

Rise and fall of the Hittites

The Hittites were one of the most powerful people of the ancient world. They are also one of the most mysterious because there are so many things about them we do not know. Originally they were herdsmen of the grasslands north of the Black and Caspian seas. About 2000 B.C. they migrated south to the high plateau of Anatolia in Asia Minor.

The Hittites were the first people to learn to smelt iron and use it for weapons. They used this advantage to conquer and expand over all of Asia Minor. When the Babylonians grew weaker, the Hittites invaded Mesopotamia, conquering and looting Babylon itself. At that time Syria, at the western end of the Fertile Crescent, was ruled by Egypt. When Ikhnaton was making his social and religious reforms in Egypt, he did not pay much attention to his empire. The Hittites were quick to take advantage. As Egyptian power declined, they gained control of most of the Near East. Then, for some unknown reasons, they fell.

Possibly their downfall was a result of their failure to keep their great secret—the process of smelting iron. Among those who learned to make and use iron weapons were the Assyrians, the fiercest, cruelest, most aggressive and warlike of all ancient peoples. Now it was their turn to play the role of the conqueror.

The Assyrians

The Assyrians were another of the desert tribes who moved into the Fertile Crescent

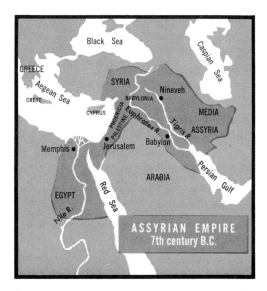

ASSYRIAN EMPIRE
7th century B.C.

An Assyrian cavalryman. This carving comes from the palace of King Sennacherib at Nineveh. The sculptor showed the weapons of this warrior—spear, bow and quiver of arrows, and short sword —and the trappings of the horse.

deported to other places and replaced by Assyrian colonists. Thus conquered lands were more easily held, and Assyria had many slaves. The Bible tells how the Assyrians captured Samaria and the northern kingdom of the Hebrews, carrying the people into captivity and slavery. When they captured Babylon, the Assyrians looted the city and then destroyed it completely, turning the waters of the river over the site. Small wonder that the people of the ancient world hated and feared the Assyrians!

● *Assyrian government*

Assyrian government was strictly a one-man business. The king had absolute power. Every priest and government official took orders from and was responsible to the king. He himself was responsible only to the god Assur, whose representative he claimed to be.

The government of the Assyrian empire was cruel and harsh but very efficient. Roads were built so that troops could move about quickly. Conquered lands were ruled by governors who collected heavy taxes. To check on them the kings established a postal service. Governors had to make regular and frequent reports. There was always an army of occupation, usually of paid soldiers recruited from among other conquered peoples. It was paid for, you may be certain, by the conquered peoples.

Aside from this new form of imperial government, the Assyrians contributed little to civilization. Their religion contained no new ideas. In literature, art, and sculpture they were imitators, not creators. They used cuneiform writing, and did improve it a little. They were very proud of their power and grandeur, and showed their pride by building huge palaces and temples.

● *Greatness and decline*

After the Assyrians became powerful, they built a new capital city called Nineveh. Here they gathered all their splendor—the wealth

just as soon as they saw a chance to do so. They settled along the Tigris River, in the northeast, and built a city-state called Assur, from which both the people and the region took their name. When the Egyptians, Babylonians, and Hittites grew weak, the Assyrians were ready. They conquered the entire Fertile Crescent, and even ruled Egypt for a time.

Assyrians were specialists in warfare. They used cavalry instead of chariots. Both horsemen and foot soldiers were armed with lances, swords, bows and arrows, and protected by breast-plates, helmets, and shields, all of iron. They developed tactics of fighting both on foot and on horseback which other peoples of their time could not resist. They also developed methods of besieging cities and tearing down their brick walls with huge battering rams and other machines.

And how cruel they were! Enemies captured in battle were put to death, often by dreadful methods. Conquered peoples were

42

from the spoils and taxes of conquered countries and from the labor of slaves. Nineveh was the symbol of the pride and cruelty of this barbarous people. They tried to make it the strongest fortified city in the world. A huge double wall fifty feet thick and one hundred feet high stretched for seven miles around the city. There were fifteen gates, each beautifully decorated and strongly defended. Eighteen mountain streams flowed through the city to assure a supply of water.

But powerful Nineveh was not powerful enough. In their turn the Assyrians grew weaker, possibly because of the great number of miserable slaves and their use of mercenaries, or paid soldiers from the conquered peoples. As so often happens with a bully, the others "ganged up" on the Assyrians. There were plenty of enemies. Finally the Chaldeans, the Medes, the Persians, and the Egyptians joined forces. They captured and destroyed Nineveh, and later conquered the entire empire. The whole Near East could breathe a sigh of relief. Three hundred years later the Macedonian Alexander the Great from over in Europe led his army to the site of Nineveh. There was almost nothing left of the once great city.

The Chaldeans

The people who organized and led the combination of armies against Assyrians were the Chaldeans. They took the largest share of the Assyrian empire and rebuilt the old city of Babylon as their capital. Under a very able ruler named Nebuchadnezzar they conquered all of Mesopotamia and took Syria from Egypt. They captured Jerusalem and took all of Palestine, carrying many Hebrews into slavery in Babylon. The strength of the Chaldeans seemed to lie in the ability of Nebuchadnezzar. Within thirty years after his death Babylon was captured by the Persians, and the Chaldean Empire ended.

The rebuilt city of Babylon was a thing of wonder. Its thick outer wall stretched for thirteen miles around an area larger than the city of Philadelphia. The whole was enclosed by a deep ditch filled with water. Part of the enclosed land was used for farming so that the city had a food supply for a siege.

The Chaldeans liked very large buildings. The most striking and beautiful of all was the Palace of Nebuchadnezzar. The building itself was of glazed or enameled brick. It had an enormous courtyard and huge rooms. Its crowning glory was the Hanging Gardens. There is a legend that Nebuchadnezzar's wife had lived in the mountains and was homesick on the flat plains of Mesopotamia. To please her he had built, on the roof of the palace, terraced gardens covered with plants and tropical flowers. The Greeks called the Hanging Gardens one of the seven wonders of the ancient world.

Like the Assyrians, the Chaldeans gave little to civilization. They were deeply interested in astrology. It is thought that the "Wise Men of the East," who followed the star to Bethlehem, were Chaldean astrologers. These beliefs in astrology were passed on to later civilizations. They had great influence on Roman thinking.

The Hanging Gardens of Babylon.

The Persians

The greatest of all the peoples who ruled Mesopotamia were the Persians. You have read of tribes of herdsmen in the great grasslands of the Caucasus Mountains, north of the Black and Caspian seas. The Sumerians may have come from this region; the Hittites surely did. Many different tribes migrated from the Caucasus. Some went west

● Cyrus, Darius, and Xerxes

About 550 B.C. Cyrus, one of the ablest men in all history, became governor of Persia, the southern part of Iran. He led a revolt against the Medes, defeated their king, and became ruler of the two tribes. The Persians were fierce fighters who made great use of horsemen and archers. Herodotus, the Greek historian, wrote that Persian education empha-

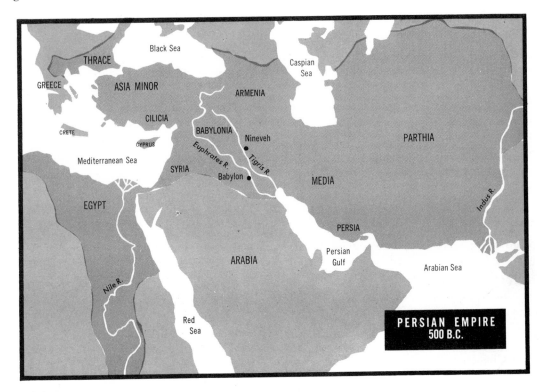

sized three things above all others: to ride, to draw the bow, and to speak the truth.

and south to Greece and Italy, some south to Asia Minor and Mesopotamia, some east and south to India. About 2000 B.C. two such tribes, the Medes and the Persians, moved south to the high plateau of Iran, east of Mesopotamia. Stronger peoples then held the valley, so the Medes and Persians stayed in Iran, living in their tribal groups and herding their sheep. In time they became united under the Medes, and they joined in the alliance that overthrew the cruel Assyrian Empire. After the victory over Assyria the Medes and Persians held all of Iran and northern Mesopotamia.

After defeating the Median king, Cyrus began a career of conquest. He and his successors conquered a vast empire. Cyrus defeated the Chaldeans, captured Babylon, and gained all Mesopotamia. He then took the rest of Asia Minor, including the western end of the Fertile Crescent—the part along the Mediterranean. Cyrus' son conquered Egypt. A later ruler, Darius, added the regions south and east of Iran all the way to the Indus River in India. Darius and his son Xerxes invaded Greece, but were unable to conquer it. At its peak the Persian Empire stretched from the Indus in India to the Nile in Africa, and north to the Black and Caspian seas—the greatest empire the world had ever seen.

The early Persian kings were not only great generals; they were also wise rulers. They were all-powerful, but they showed great concern for justice and fair dealings. Tax collection and the administration of justice were very fair. Cyrus was especially concerned that the laws should be applied equally, without favor to anyone. He was a kind man. He allowed the Hebrews who had been carried into slavery by the Assyrians and Chaldeans to return to Palestine and rebuild their temple in Jerusalem.

Persian government

In governing their huge empire the rulers chose the ablest officials they could find—often men from the conquered people. They paid great attention to the customs of the local peoples. When a conquered people paid taxes and tribute to the Persians, they were allowed to keep their own laws, customs, and religion. This tolerant practice won the favor of the priests and the loyalty of the people.

Three sets of officials were used in governing the empire. First, a governor and his officials. Second, a general and his troops. The Persians believed, as is believed today, that civil and military governments should be kept separate. The third set of officials were the inspectors, called "the King's Eyes and Ears." They checked on the governors and generals to see that they used their power wisely.

The Persians built roads and bridges throughout the empire, and set up a royal postal service so that governors could make regular reports. The roads were built primarily for the army, of course, but they were used by merchants, too. There was a great interchange of customs, ideas, and cultures among all the different peoples of the empire.

Persian religion: Zoroaster

The Persians' greatest cultural contribution was in the field of religion. They produced one of the great original religious thinkers. At first, like other early peoples, they worshipped many gods. About 600 B.C. a great prophet and religious reformer completely changed their religious ideas. His name was Zoroaster.

Zoroaster taught that the god Ahura Mazda had created the world as a place where human beings were trained for a future life. Between the forces of good and evil there was a great struggle. The forces of good, symbolized by light, were led by Ahura Mazda, god of light and order, truth and purity, creator and upholder of the universe. He was assisted by Mithra, the savior. The forces of evil or darkness were led by the god Ahriman. Human beings could choose sides and help in this struggle. Those who chose the good would be rewarded with eternal life. Those who chose evil would have darkness and misery after death. In the far, far distant future the forces of good would finally triumph. Then the earth would disappear, for it would have served its purpose as the stage on which the great conflict took place.

Zoroaster's ideas greatly influenced the lives of the Persians. The thinking of the Hebrews and, later, the Christians seems to have been affected by his idea of a struggle here on earth between good and evil, and a final judgment in which reward or punishment depended on man's choice. According to Zoroaster, nothing is so shameful as lying. Persian children were taught that they must always tell the truth. Getting into debt was considered a form of lying; therefore, debt was shameful.

The early Persian rulers were influenced by Zoroaster's teachings. Darius had these words carved on the Behistun Rock (see page 25): "On this account Ahura Mazda brought me health. . . . Because I was not wicked, nor was I a liar, nor was I a tyrant; neither I nor any of my line. We have ruled according to righteousness."

The Persian kings who followed Xerxes were neither so strong nor so wise. As time went on, both the government and the army grew weak. The army was made up of men from all the subject nations, commanded by Mede and Persian officers. In 331 B.C. Alexander the Great of Macedon defeated the Persian king and ruled the Persian Empire. After Alexander's death the empire fell apart.

Review of Chapter 4

People, places, and things

Identify: Hammurabi, "The Land of No Return," Marduk, Nineveh, the Hanging Gardens, Nebuchadnezzar, Cyrus, Darius, Zoroaster, Ahura Mazda, Mithra, Ahriman, Xerxes.

Locate: Mesopotamia, Iran (Persia), the Black Sea, the Caspian Sea, the Caucasus, Palestine, Jerusalem, Assyria, Chaldea.

Events in review

1. Why were the Sumerians conquered by the Babylonians?
2. What was the Code of Hammurabi? Why is the Code important?
3. Explain the importance of Sumerian civilization in the ancient world. Include in your answer (a) the sources of information about this civilization, (b) cultivation of crops, (c) domestication of animals, (d) trade, (e) influence of Sumerian civilization on that of other countries.
4. Name an outstanding cultural contribution to the world made by each of the following people: Sumerians, Babylonians, Chaldeans, Persians. Did Assyrian civilization make any real contribution to the world?
5. List some of the important discoveries made by Sumerian scientists and engineers.
6. What is meant by "divination"?
7. State briefly some of the main ideas of the Zoroastrian faith.

Problems and projects

1. Compare the social life of ancient Mesopotamia with that of the United States today. Include (a) social classes, (b) position of women, (c) family life.
2. Discuss the educational system of the Sumerians and Babylonians. In what way did their system differ from ours?
3. Compare the Hittites with the Assyrians as conquerors. Which would you consider the more successful? Why?
4. Make a model or draw a picture of an ancient Sumerian temple.
5. In an encyclopedia or other source book look up Hammurabi's Code. Make a list of five of the most interesting laws. Explain their interest to you. How do the laws of Babylon compare with our laws today?
6. Form a committee to prepare a travel folder which has as its purpose the attraction of tourists to Nebuchadnezzar's Babylonia.

Chapter 5

Phoenicians and Hebrews: Weak Peoples Make Great Contributions

THE WESTERN END of the Fertile Crescent is a narrow strip of land along the eastern end of the Mediterranean Sea. Here in ancient times were two regions inhabited by people who have had great influence on the modern world. The entire region is about three hundred fifty miles long. At its widest point, it is about thirty-five miles across. The southern part is Palestine. Today the northern part is part of Lebanon, but in ancient times it was called Phoenicia.

The Phoenicians

Phoenicia was less than 200 miles long and averaged about twelve miles in width. Unlike other regions you have studied, it was not a river valley. It was hilly, even mountainous, and no large-scale farming was possible. The mountains hemmed it in against the sea.

● *Trade*

From the very earliest times its people turned to the sea and to commerce for their living. The Phoenicians became the greatest traders of the ancient world. They were not

MEDITERRANEAN SEA

PHOENICIA

SYRIA

Lebanon Mts.

● Sidon

Mt. Hermon ● Damascus

● Tyre

ARAMEANS

SEA OF GALILEE

Mt. Carmel

KINGDOM

● Samaria

OF ISRAEL

Mt. Gilead

AMMON

Jordan R.

PHILISTINES

CANAAN

Jerusalem ●
Bethlehem ●

KINGDOM

DEAD SEA

MOAB

OF JUDAH

PALESTINE AND PHOENICIA ABOUT EIGHTH CENTURY BC

47

fighters; they preferred to make things and to buy and sell them. Seldom in their history were they really independent. In turn they were conquered by, or paid tribute to, the Babylonians, Egyptians, Hittites, Assyrians, Chaldeans, Persians, and Greeks. But always the Phoenician people worked and always they traded.

Phoenicia was a loose union of city-states, each with its king. The largest, Tyre and Sidon, were seaports which became world famous. The Phoenicians built seagoing ships very early. To us they look pitifully small and frail, but the Phoenicians were skillful and fearless sailors. With their one or two sails and their one or two tiers of oarsmen they traveled all over the Mediterranean Sea. They even went out through the Straits of Gibraltar to the west coast of Africa and to England in search of tin, copper, iron, gold, silver, and ivory. In those days, without instruments for navigation, it took great courage to sail a ship out of sight of land, toward the meeting place of sky and sea. People be-

lieved that in those vast, lonely spaces lived monsters that devoured ships.

Phoenicia lacked natural resources of fertile land or minerals. Its only natural resource was lumber, the beautiful, straight-grained cedar trees of the Lebanon Mountains that so many ancient peoples used in their building. The Phoenicians became skilled artisans. They took the metals of other lands and turned them into beautiful objects of gold, silver, copper, and bronze. They wove the finest woolen cloth of the ancient world. From the Egyptians they learned how to blow glass. They surpassed their teachers and made exquisite glassware. Along their seacoast they found a shellfish called murex, from which they learned to make purple dye. Phoenician woolen cloth, dyed purple, was a prized possession of the ancient world. It was so expensive that only the wealthy could afford it. That is the reason why purple became the color worn by kings —the royal purple. Always they built ships, for themselves or for sale. They traded over-

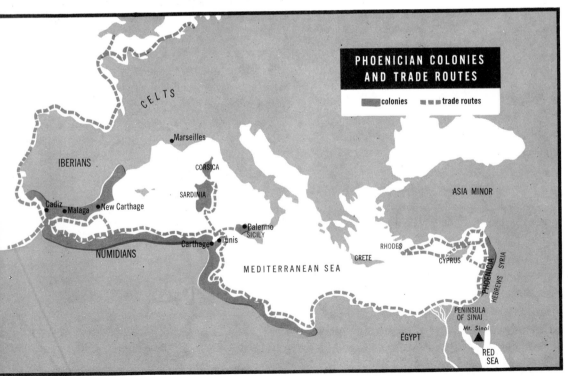

PHOENICIAN COLONIES AND TRADE ROUTES

colonies ▪▪▪ trade routes

CELTS

Marseilles

IBERIANS

CORSICA

SARDINIA

Cadiz Malaga New Carthage

Palermo
SICILY

Carthage Tunis

NUMIDIANS

MEDITERRANEAN SEA

ASIA MINOR

RHODES

CRETE

CYPRUS

PHOENICIA

HEBREWS SYRIA

PENINSULA OF SINAI

Mt. Sinai

EGYPT

RED SEA

land, too; Phoenician caravans even made the long journey to China to bring back beautiful silk for themselves and their customers.

● *Phoenician colonies*

For a short time, from about 1000 to 700 B.C., Near Eastern conditions favored the Phoenicians. Both the Egyptian and Babylonian empires were declining. The Hittites were growing weaker, and the Assyrians had not yet started their empire-building. The Phoenician city-states were united under Tyre, and they built an overseas empire. They established colonies on distant shores to trade with the natives. Marseilles, in southern France, and Cadiz, in Spain, were originally Phoenician colonies. Greatest of all was Carthage in North Africa, near the site of the present city of Tunis. Founded by the Phoenicians about 850 B.C., it grew and prospered until it became a greater trading center than either Tyre or Sidon. For a time Carthage claimed control of the entire Mediterranean.

● *Phoenician culture*

Culturally the Phoenicians were imitators and improvers rather than creators. They were businessmen rather than philosophers. They copied their government and most of their culture from the Egyptians and Babylonians. They added nothing to the world's knowledge of mathematics, science, or medicine.

The religion of the Phoenicians was not attractive. They worshiped many gods, of whom the principal one was Baal. He was a difficult and angry god. To soothe him they made sacrifices of the things they valued most. Sometimes they even sacrificed their own children to win Baal's favor. They had no belief in an afterlife; they called it "the time of nonexistence."

Although the Phoenicians created little that was original, one of their improvements

A Phoenician ship.

has had far-reaching effects. They have been given most credit for improving the alphabet, which they learned to use from the Hebrews and Egyptians. The Egyptians developed an alphabet of consonants, but continued to use their picture symbols, or hieroglyphics, with it. The Hebrews and Phoenicians took over the consonant letter symbols, but not the pictures.

To the practical Phoenicians writing was useful in their business for making records of contracts, bills of lading (goods in a ship or caravan), and bills of sale. Phoenician commerce spread the knowledge of alphabetical writing through the Mediterranean world. It is told that the Greeks, when they first saw the Phoenician paper with its mysterious signs, feared it as magic. They overcame their fear and improved the alphabet greatly. The Greeks added symbols for the vowel sounds. The Romans copied from the Greeks, with some changes, and it is the Roman alphabet that is in use today in the Western World. Thus the letter symbols you are now reading trace back through the Romans and Greeks to the improvements of Hebrews and Phoenicians on the creation of the Egyptians.

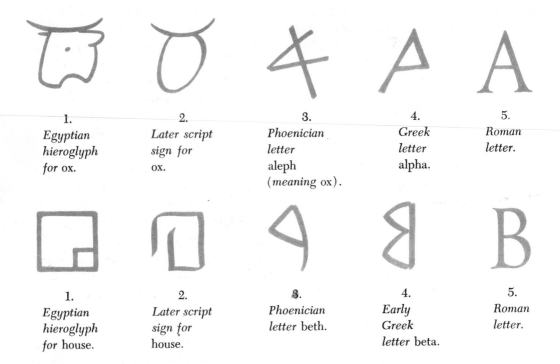

1. Egyptian hieroglyph for ox.	2. Later script sign for ox.	3. Phoenician letter aleph (*meaning* ox).	4. Greek letter alpha.	5. Roman letter.
1. Egyptian hieroglyph for house.	2. Later script sign for house.	3. Phoenician letter beth.	4. Early Greek letter beta.	5. Roman letter.

These pictures show five stages in the development of writing. Over many thousands of years, picture symbols were modified until they ceased to be pictures and became letter symbols—letters. The early Egyptian sign for ox (around 3000 B.C.) was a simple sketch of an ox's head. This picture was simplified as the centuries went by. The Phoenicians further simplified the sign, so that it looked more like the later Greek letter alpha. The Romans changed alpha to the letter A we now use.

Similar developments can be traced for the second letter of our alphabet. The Egyptians started with a drawing of a house for their hieroglyphic writing. The original sketch was changed at various times. The Hebrew-Phoenician word for house was beth. The Phoenician sign for beth is shown above. The Greeks transformed this into the letter beta. In later Greek writing beta was turned around to face the right. In that form it closely resembled the Roman letter B.

Even the word *alphabet* can be so traced. The Hebrew-Phoenician first letter was *aleph,* the second *beth.* The Greeks changed them to *alpha* and *beta.* These first two letters are combined in the word *alphabet.*

The Hebrews

Palestine is a small land, not more than 150 miles long, seldom as much as thirty miles wide. It is really two regions. The northern part, at the lower end of the Fertile Crescent, is watered by the Jordan River. There the soil is fertile enough to grow grain, olives, figs, and grapes. The southern region, around and south of the Dead Sea, is mostly desert. The soil is poor and rocky; there is not enough rainfall for farming. In ancient times it supported only an economy of herdsmen with sheep and goats.

Ancient Palestine had few natural resources. There were not many minerals, not much good soil, no forests. It did have the advantage of location. It lay along the great land bridge between Asia and Africa. Through it ran the route from Egypt to Asia

Minor and Mesopotamia. The merchants who carried the goods, and also the ideas, of these two great civilized regions traveled this route. The location was not always an advantage, for armies also passed along the road. The peoples of Palestine had to fight for freedom against Egyptians, Hittites, Assyrians, Chaldeans, and Persians. They were conquered often, for they were not powerful.

Like Mesopotamia, Palestine was inhabited by a series of peoples. The people who had the greatest influence on their own times and on all history since were the Hebrews, or Jews. They did not always live in Palestine. Abraham, the legendary founder of the Jewish people, once lived in Sumeria. He left there and led his people across the Syrian Desert to the borders of Canaan, northern Palestine. Some Jews stayed there in the bordering deserts. Others crossed the Isthmus of Suez into Egypt. They settled in the Land of Goshen, in the delta region. It was swampy country, not very desirable. The Jews settled down, improved the land, and began to prosper.

The Hebrews in Egypt

These Hebrews lived peacefully in Egypt for several centuries at least. You may have read the Bible story of Joseph, who was sold by his brothers into slavery in Egypt. By his great ability he rose to become a favorite of the Pharaoh and was made governor of all Egypt. In time, though, the Hebrews fell from favor. Perhaps they had made their part of the country too prosperous, so that the Egyptians were envious. They were forced to work on the roads and to help build the great buildings. This lasted for many years.

Then there came a great leader among the Hebrews. Moses had been raised and educated as an Egyptian in the palace of a princess. He may have attended the great university at Heliopolis. In spite of his upbringing and high position he had great sympathy for the sufferings of his people, the Jews. In time he came to believe that Jehovah had called him to lead his people out of slavery. You may remember the Bible story of how Moses tried to persuade the Pharaoh to set the Hebrews free. When the Pharaoh refused, ten great plagues came to punish the Egyptians. In the tenth plague the angel of death came to every Egyptian household and took the oldest child, but he passed over the houses of the Hebrews. This is the origin of the great Jewish festival of the Passover. The Pharaoh at last consented to free the Hebrews. Moses led them across the branch of the Red Sea to the Sinai Peninsula. When the Pharaoh changed his mind and sent an army to bring them back to slavery, the Bible tells that the waters of the sea closed on the Egyptians and drowned them.

The Jews move to Palestine

Many of the Hebrews were unhappy in the Sinai Desert. They and their ancestors had lived in Egypt for centuries. They had accepted Egyptian customs and worshipped Egyptian gods. Life in Egypt, even in slavery, was better than living in the harsh desert, or so they thought. It was then that Moses went up Mount Sinai and came back to them with the Ten Commandments and the renewed idea of Jehovah as their own God. Moses also worked out the code of laws by which they were to live, and began to tell them of Palestine as the Promised Land. Thus, with a God of their own, with Commandments as a standard for living, and with a code of laws to govern them, they went on, not back.

Ikhnaton was pharaoh in Egypt when the Jews began to try to enter Palestine. Those Jews who had come from Egypt joined their efforts with those who had lived for so long on the borders of Canaan. By this time they were all desert tribes again, hardened by the harsh life of desert herdsmen. But winning a homeland in Palestine was not easy going. The good land was held by the Canaanites and Philistines, who fought hard to hold it.

The struggle went on for more than a century. The Canaanites were first to be conquered, so that some of the Hebrews were able to settle down in the Jordan Valley. The Philistines were fiercer. The Hebrews drove them back to the seacoast, but never conquered them completely.

As desert wanderers the Hebrews were divided into twelve tribes. Each was led by judges, who were religious leaders. The long years of fighting for Palestine united them under a king—first Saul, then David, then Solomon.

After conquering Palestine the Hebrews did not remain united very long. Those of northern Canaan settled down in towns, making their living by farming. They adopted the customs of the conquered Canaanites: They lived in houses, wore woolen clothing instead of sheepskins, and many worshipped the Canaanite gods instead of Jehovah. Southern Palestine remained a rural, herdsman's region. People clung to their old ideas, ways of living, and religion. They criticized the northerners for giving up these old tribal ways and beliefs.

The reign of Solomon brought the final split. He was famous for wisdom, but also for love of luxury and good living. To beautify Jerusalem he built a great temple and a palace for himself. He brought in architects, artisans, and building materials from Egypt and Phoenicia. The cost was great for a poor country. Taxes were heavy, and many men were forced to work on the great buildings without pay. At the end of Solomon's reign there was a revolution, and the kingdom split in two. The northern kingdom, Israel, had its capital at Samaria. The southern kingdom was Judah, with Jerusalem as the capital.

● *Conquests of Palestine*

You already know some of the rest of the story. The Assyrians captured Samaria, conquered Israel, and carried many Jews into captivity and slavery. Later, the Chaldeans captured Jerusalem. They destroyed Solomon's temple and took the southern Hebrews into captivity.

Thereafter the history of the Jews is a long story of conquest by one people after another, and of wandering over the earth. Cyrus the Persian allowed the Jews of Babylon to return to Jerusalem, rebuild the temple, and fortify the city. This independence did not last long. Alexander of Macedon made Palestine part of his empire. The Romans took it in 63 B.C. and held it for four hundred years. It was under Roman rule when Jesus was born. After the Romans the Mohammedan Arabs held the country until they, in turn, were conquered by the Turks. The Turks held Palestine until the end of the First World War, in 1918, when it was given to the British. In 1948 it was divided between the Arabs and the newly formed Republic of Israel, to which Jews from all over the world have returned. Since then there has been much trouble between Arabs and Jews.

Jewish contributions to civilization

You can see that there is nothing in the political history of the Jews to make them great, or to set them apart from their neighbors of the ancient world. It may seem strange, then, that they have had as large a part in forming Western civilization as any of their more powerful neighbors, and a much larger share than some. The Jews were great as thinkers and writers. They made a supreme gift to the world in three magnificent works: a code of laws, a great work of literature, and a truly noble religion.

● *The laws of Moses*

The Jewish laws are the laws of Moses. When you compare them with the other great collection of laws of the ancient world—the Code of Hammurabi—the superiority of the Jewish laws is plain. Mosaic laws demand "an eye for eye," but they set a much higher

value on human life than Hammurabi's. The laws of Moses accepted slavery, for it was the custom of the ancient world. However, Jewish law demanded kindness for slaves; Hammurabi's code punished a slave more severely than a freeman for the same act. Jewish laws required, as Babylonian laws did not, kindness to the poor and to strangers. Mosaic law was most severe against witchcraft (astrology) and sacrifices to idols. These were crimes carrying the death penalty. In Hebrew thinking, man need only trust in Jehovah and the religious leaders, and he would learn all he needed to know. There was no need for astrologers or soothsayers.

● The Old Testament

The great Hebrew work of literature is, of course, the Old Testament of the Bible. What a rich and varied piece of writing it is! The first five books contain the story of creation, the early history of man, and the laws of Moses. Next come the sermons and poetry of

Ruins of a synagogue in Palestine, built many centuries ago by the Hebrews as a place of worship. In the distance is Mount Hermon, in Lebanon.

the great Jewish prophets. Among the Jews, a prophet was a great religious thinker and teacher, not necessarily a man who could foretell the future. Then there are other writings: hymns, poems, proverbs, stories, and prophecies. Together with the later, Christian, writings of the New Testament, no other book has so much influenced the thinking and living of the people of the Western World.

● The Hebrew religion

The religion of the Hebrews was great because it developed rather than stood still. The early Hebrews worshipped Jehovah as a God who belonged to them alone. He was what might be called a tribal war god. In some ways He was not very attractive. It is interesting to think of the description of Him in the

53

Ten Commandments. He is to be the only God, and He is described as a jealous God. If a man sins against Him, not only will the man be punished, but his children, and their children, and their children. This was a God to fear, not to love.

The growth of the Hebrews' idea of Jehovah came partly from the many trials and sorrows they suffered, and partly from the teachings and writings of their great prophets. Amos taught that Jehovah wanted justice for all men. Hosea wrote that Jehovah loved and forgave men. When Jews of the northern region adopted the Canaanite practice of worshipping idols and making sacrifices to them, Micah rebuked them sternly. Jehovah (Micah told the people) was not interested in sacrifices:

"And I will cut off witchcrafts out of thine hand; and thou shalt have no more soothsayers.

"Thy graven images also will I cut off, and thy standing images out of the midst of thee; and thou shalt no more worship the work of thine hands." (Micah, Chapter 5, verses 12 and 13.)

Next Micah described one of the noblest standards of conduct man has ever known—one that anyone may learn and try to follow:

"He has showed thee, oh man, what is good. And what doth the lord require of thee, but to do justly, and to love mercy, and to walk humbly with thy God?" (Micah, Chapter 6, verse 8.)

The Jews came to think of Jehovah as a loving father, a universal power who lived in the hearts of his worshippers. Other ancient people thought of their gods as human beings, but more powerful. To the Jews, Jehovah was not like a human being. He was a spiritual force. The kings of other ancient peoples had to claim to be gods, or gods' representatives, to gain power. Jewish kings were mortal beings; only Jehovah was divine.

The belief in one God, who is just, kind, merciful, loving, and forgiving, who is a spirit, not like a human being, who is universal, belonging to everyone, is called *monotheism*. It is the supreme gift of the Hebrews to civilization. It is not an invention or a discovery to make life easier. It is a great and noble idea; and ideas, as you know, are powerful. No other single idea has so influenced western civilization.

Review of Chapter 5

People, places, and things

Identify: Baal, Moses, Solomon, Passover, Ten Commandments, Promised Land, Philistines, Canaanites, monotheism.

Locate: Palestine, Phoenicia, Tunis, Cadiz, Carthage, Tyre, Sidon, Marseilles, the Sinai Desert, the Sinai Peninsula, the Red Sea, the Jordan Valley, Canaan.

Events in review

1. How did geography and location affect the occupations of the Phoenicians?
2. State the origin of the expression "the royal purple."
3. What world conditions favored Phoenician expansion into an empire?

4. Which of the Phoenician colonies can be considered the greatest? Why?
5. Why was the improvement of the alphabet by the Phoenicians of such far-reaching effect?
6. What different lands did the Hebrews live in, from the time of Abraham to the time of Solomon?
7. What is the great Hebrew work of literature? What different kinds of writings are found in this work?
8. What is the greatest gift of the Hebrews to world civilization?

Problems and projects

1. Compare the Laws of Moses with the Code of Hammurabi.

Review continues after color supplement

ANCIENT TIMES

This and the seven following pages show samples of the art and architecture of the ancient world, particularly Egypt and Greece. Paintings, statues, and buildings tell us many things about the people who created them: what skills they possessed, what they thought was striking or beautiful, what subjects interested them, what their activities were.

There were fine artists in prehistoric times (see page 16). The paintings above, found in a cave in Lascaux, France, are believed to be more than 20,000 years old. The Stone Age artists painted animals that were important in their lives—stags, a wild horse, a bull. (Photo by Braun, Paris.)

Samples of Egyptian art. Facing
page 54C: Sculptured relief of a
pharaoh.

This page 54B: Four Egyptian wall
paintings, perhaps 3,500 years old.
Contrast the figures here with the
animals in the cave painting on
page 54A. (All five pictures from
UNESCO.)

Above: Figures of a man and an ibis.
Note the hieroglyphic writing
above the figures (see page 24).

Left: The jackal-headed god
Anubis and a mummy.

Right: An Egyptian noble hunting
waterfowl among the reeds at the
Nile's edge. The great man is
drawn many times larger than his
subjects.

Left: Figures of gods and humans
shown on a typical Egyptian boat.

Egyptian architecture and sculpture were on a grand scale. Above, left: The Sphinx and the Great Pyramid (see page 31). Above, right: The temple of Queen Hatshepsut in the Valley of the Queens.

Left: A statue of Rameses II at Luxor. The man in the foreground shows the scale of this piece of sculpture. Rameses ruled Egypt for 67 years during the thirteenth century B.C.

Facing page: A mummy case. As noted on pages 34 and 35, the Egyptians carefully preserved the bodies of dead persons. The mummies of wealthy persons were placed in elaborate carved and painted cases.

A highly-developed civilization existed on the island of Crete from about 2000 B.C. to 1400 B.C. Above is a view of the remains of a great palace at Cnossus (see pages 64-65). Notice that Cretan architects, like the Egyptians, used columns. Brightly colored paintings decorate the walls.

Some of the world's greatest examples of art and architecture were created in Greece. At right are ruins of the Parthenon, the marble temple built on the Acropolis in Athens about 447 B.C. (see page 77).

Above: A model of the Parthenon as it is
believed to have looked when built.
(Metropolitan Museum of Art, New York.)
Compare this model with the photograph on
page 54F. Notice that the Greeks used color
to ornament the building.

Below: A Greek statue of a Sphinx made around
540 B.C. (Metropolitan Museum of Art.)

Above: The painting on this Greek vase shows
a scene in a shoemaker's shop. (Museum of
Fine Arts, Boston.)

Above: A painted carving on stone dating from about 530 B.C. This shows a Greek warrior mounting his chariot. The helmet, shield, and long spear were typical equipment for Greek soldiers. (Metropolitan Museum of Art, New York.)

Left: A Greek vase. The picture shows a wrestling match. Wrestling was one of the events in the Olympic Games (see page 66). (Metropolitan Museum of Art, New York.)

2. Discuss a problem of the Hebrews in ancient times and compare it with a problem that the people of Israel face today.

3. Make a model of a Phoenician ship.
4. For discussion: Why have the Phoenicians been called "the carriers of civilization"?

Review of the Beginnings

1. Early man had to "start from scratch" to build his life. List five of the discoveries and inventions he had to make in order to progress toward civilization.
2. Geography had an important influence on the development of early civilizations. Name three civilizations that grew up in river valleys. Why were the rivers important?
3. Name at least one people that became powerful though they did *not* live in a river valley. How did geography influence this civilization?
4. Make a three-column chart. List the contributions to civilization made by the Egyptians, the Mesopotamians, the Hebrews.
5. Which of the peoples studied in Part One made the greatest contributions in the following fields: architecture, art, education, engineering, development of the alphabet, trading and colonizing, law, religion? Give details to support your answer.
6. How did trade help to spread civilization from one country to another?
7. Imagine yourself a boy or girl of ancient times. In which of the civilizations studied in Part One would you prefer to live? Give reasons for your choice. (Consider family life, schools, housing, food, safety from aggressive enemies, art, religion, and other features of life.)
8. Part One tells of the rise to power, and the decline, of Egyptians, Sumerians, Babylonians, Persians, and others. Can you think of any nations of modern times that have risen to great strength and then have declined or been overthrown?

Books about prehistoric man, Egypt, and the Fertile Crescent

Barclay, Isabel. *Worlds Without End* (Doubleday, 1956). A history of world exploration from the Egyptian Hannu's expedition to the Land of Punt 4,000 years ago—to the polar discoveries of Amundsen and Byrd.

The Bible. Selections from the Old Testament (see above, pages 53–54).

*Breasted, James H. *Ancient Times* (Ginn, 1935). A simply-written textbook. Chapter 1 has an illustrated account of people, tools, and animals of Stone Age times.

*Books in these lists marked with a star (*) are easy reading.

Breasted, James H. *Conquest of Civilization* (Harper, 1938). A storehouse of information about ancient peoples. Highly recommended.

——. *A History of Egypt from the Earliest Times to the Persian Conquest* (Scribner, 1912). One of the most comprehensive surveys of Egyptian history. Five illustrations.

*Browne, Lewis. *This Believing World* (Macmillan, 1944). A popular account of the world's great religions.

Burrows, Millar. *Founders of the Great Religions* (Scribner, 1931). A brief biography of Moses, among others.

Chiera, Edward. *They Wrote on Clay; Babylonian Tablets Speak Today* (University of Chicago, 1938). The clay tablets tell of the everyday life and great events of ancient Mesopotamia.

Colbert, Edwin H. *Origin of the Dog* (American Museum of Natural History, 1945). The museum publishes a series of pamphlets, all worth reading. Some others are *Age of Man, Rise of Mammals, Triumph of Mammals.*

Contenau, Georges. *Everyday Life in Babylon and Assyria* (St. Martin's, 1954). Survey of the period between 700 and 530 B.C.

Easton, S. C. *Heritage of the Past, from the Earliest Times to the Close of the Middle Ages* (Rinehart, 1955). This is the first volume of a two-volume history of world civilization from the dawn of man to the emergence of our modern national states.

Edwards, I. E. S. *The Pyramids of Egypt* (Penguin, 1947). A fine source for any student who wants to learn more about the history and construction of the pyramids.

*Evans, Eva. *All About Us* (Capitol, 1947). Interesting accounts of how early man wandered over the earth and how different environments produced differences in skin color, customs, and language.

*Gatti, Ellen, and Gatti, Attilio. *Here is Africa* (Scribner, 1943). A very attractive story of Egypt, ancient and modern, with many excellent illustrations.

Goldman, Irving. *First Men; the Story of Human Beginnings* (Abelard-Schuman, 1955). Discusses man's beginnings and traces his development to the present day with special emphasis on primitive cultures of today.

Hartman, Gertrude. *Builders of the Old World* (Heath, 1955). A history of man which traces the influence of each country's geography, climate, and natural resources.

*——. *World We Live In and How It Came To Be* (Macmillan, 1935). Very readable chapters on Egypt and the Near East. Good illustrations.

Hayes, William C. "Daily Life in Ancient Egypt," with 32 paintings by H. M. Herger. In *National Geographic Magazine,* October 1941, pp. 419–515.

Heaton, Eric William. *Everyday Life in Old Testament Times* (Scribner, 1956). The ordinary circumstances, problems, attitudes, and ways of thinking and doing things of the Hebrews from 1250 to 586 B.C.

*Hoffman, Gail. *Land and People of Israel* (Lippincott, 1955). The story of Palestine from Old Testament days to the present.

Jessup, Ronald Frederick. *Wonderful World of Archeology* (Garden City Books, 1956). Enthusiastic accounts of some of the puzzles solved by archeology.

*Lamprey, Louise. *All the Ways of Building* (Macmillan, 1933). Egyptian and Near-Eastern architecture.

Life, various issues, 1955–56. "The Story of Man."

*Linton, Ralph and Adelin. *Man's Way from Cave to Skyscraper* (Harper, 1947). The ways of living of men everywhere.

Marek, Kurt W. (C. W. Ceram, pseud.) *Gods, Graves, and Scholars* (Knopf, 1951). Translated from the German by E. B. Garside. This account of the adventures of the great archeologists brings to life the mysterious past of mankind.

——. (C. W. Ceram, pseud.) *Secret of the Hittites* (Knopf, 1955). Translated from the German by Richard and Clara Winston. Fascinating reconstruction of the role of the Hittites in 2000 B.C.

*Meadowcroft, Enid L. *Gift of the River; a History of Ancient Egypt* (Crowell, 1937). A simply-written history which will interest people of any age-group. It stresses the influence of the Nile on Egypt.

*Mills, Dorothy. *Book of the Ancient World for Younger Readers* (Putnam, 1923). One of the best accounts of ancient times, covering all the peoples studied in Part One.

Ogg, Oscar. *Twenty-six Letters* (Crowell, 1948). The development of written language.

Orlinsky, Harry M. *Ancient Israel* (Cornell, 1954). A scholarly history of the Jewish people in Old Testament times. Tells of their religion along with the rest of their history.

*Quennell, C. H. B., and Quennell, Marjorie. *Everyday Life in the Old Stone Age* (Putnam, 1956).

*———, and Quennell, Marjorie. *Everyday Life in the New Stone, Bronze, and Early Iron Ages* (Putnam, 1955). These valuable and well-illustrated books compare the lives of primitive peoples today with the way we think Stone Age men lived. Highly recommended.

Robinson, Charles Alexander. *Ancient History* (Macmillan, 1951). An interpretation of ancient history from prehistoric times to the death of Justinian—in terms of art, literature, law, and economic development.

Steindorff, Georg and Seele, K. C. *When Egypt Ruled the East* (Univ. of Chicago Press, 1957). The early periods are traced, the Empire Age more thoroughly covered. The chapters on religion and art are especially good. Interesting, easily read, and beautifully illustrated.

*Van Loon, Hendrik W. *Story of Mankind* (Liveright, 1951). Good reading for this as for other units.

Wells, Herbert George. *Outline of History* (Garden City Books, 1956). A fascinating history of life and mankind, revised and brought up to the end of World War II by Raymond Postgate.

White, Anne T. *Lost Worlds: Adventures in Archeology* (Random House, 1941). The discoveries of the remains of ancient civilizations in Egypt and the Near East, told like a fast-moving adventure story. Highly recommended.

———. *First Men in the World* (Random House, 1953). Tells the story of archeology's gradual and often controversial discovery of our ancestors.

Good stories about early times

*Davis, William S. *Belshazzar* (Macmillan, 1925). Story of the fall of Babylon. The historical background is correct, the plot is interesting, and the style is readable.

*Gere, Frances K. *Boy of Babylon* (Longmans, Green, 1941). Simply written, well-illustrated, highly readable stories of life in ancient Babylon.

*Kummer, Frederic. *First Days of History* (Doran, 1925). These stories, written in an easy style, give numerous details of everyday life in five of the centers of civilization in the ancient world: China, India, Babylon, Egypt, and Persia.

*———. *Great Road* (Winston, 1938). The road from Egypt to Babylon, and the colorful traffic over it.

*Lamprey, Louise. *Long Ago in Egypt* (Little, Brown, 1926). A story of Egypt under Queen Hatshepsut.

*Reason, Joyce. *Bran the Bronze-Smith* (Dutton, 1932). A story of ancient times in Ireland, England, and France.

Rolt-Wheeler, Francis W. *The Finder of Fire* (Appleton-Century, 1927).

*Waterloo, Stanley. *Story of Ab* (Doubleday, 1937). A convincing group of stories about a cave man.

Williamson, Thames R. *Cave Mystery* (Harcourt, Brace, 1935). A mystery story involving Cro-Magnon relics. Much information about prehistoric life.

———. *Messenger to the Pharaoh* (Longmans, Green, 1937). A young Egyptian solves a mystery during the building of the Great Pyramid. Good details on life in ancient Egypt.

Part Two GREECE : THE FOUNDATION OF WESTERN CIVILIZATION

Part One ranged over half a dozen great civilizations in the large area known as the Near East. Part Two will concentrate on a single great civilization in one small corner of Europe—Greece. This small country needs intensive study because it can rightly be called the foundation of our Western civilization. There are many important links between ancient Greece and our world today.

The picture on the facing page shows one of these links. When the citizens of a democratic nation go to the polls to vote, they are carrying on an ideal that began with the Greeks. The citizens of city-states like Athens had a direct voice in their own government. One of their rights was to vote to *ostracize* (banish from the city) any man whom they considered a threat to the government or the city. They voted by writing names on pieces of pottery (like the one sketched above) and placing the pieces in a jar.

In Egypt and Mesopotamia governments never progressed beyond the despotism of the king-gods. Individual men had no share in government and few rights of any kind. In Greece the individual citizen was a free man whose liberty was protected. He was a voter and had an active share in his government. The ideas of modern democracy originated in Greece. Here you can trace one of the great themes of world history.

The Greeks made great contributions in other fields besides government. The picture opposite suggests a little of the richness of Greek architecture and sculpture, which have never been surpassed. Greek scientists laid the foundations of a number of the sciences. Greek philosophers rank among the world's great thinkers. Greek historians set the standards for the writing of history. Greek dramatists left works which are still performed in the theater and read with pleasure. The Greek individual set a standard of critical thinking and had a fierce love of liberty and a zest for living which have rarely been equalled.

Chapter 6 tells how Greek civilization began and how it grew. By the start of the fifth century B.C. (see the time chart on the next two pages) the Greeks were strong enough to repel two invasions by the massive armies of the Persian Empire. Chapter 7 describes the Golden Age of Greece—one of the most glorious eras in the record of man's culture. The art, literature, and philosophy of this period rank among the greatest achievements of our world. Chapter 8 describes how this high civilization was disrupted by civil war. Ancient Greece never became a united nation but remained a collection of rival city-states. Weakened by their own disputes, the city-states were conquered by the Macedonians and became part of the empire of Alexander the Great. Greek culture did not disappear, however. Its influence spread widely in the Mediterranean world.

Part Two GREECE

AMERICA	AEGEAN AREA

1500 B.C.

Stone Age civilization

Cretan Kings rule Aegean area

c. 1194-1184 Trojan War

1000 B.C.

c. 1000 Mayan civilization
in Central America

1000-500 Migrations into Greece

c. 850 Homer

776 First recorded Olympic Games

594 Solon

500 B.C.

Persian Wars: **490** Marathon; **480** Salamis

c. 484 Birth of Herodotus

479-404 Athenian Empire

c. 469 Birth of Socrates

461-429 Age of Pericles

459-404 Peloponnesian Wars

c. 427 Birth of Plato

384 Birth of Aristotle

360 Praxiteles. the sculptor

338 Battle of Chaeronea: Macedonia conquers Greece

338 Hellenistic Age begins

c. 300 Euclid's *Elements of Geometry*

c. 287 Birth of Archimedes

A.D.

NEAR EAST	EUROPE	INDIA AND CHINA
Empire Age in Egypt		c. 1500 Written records begin in China
		1122 Chou dynasty begins: foundation of Chinese culture
c. 973-937 Reign of Solomon in Palestine	c. 1000-c. 700 Phoenician traders in Mediterranean	
	c. 800 Carthage founded	
	c. 753 Rome founded	
612 Nineveh destroyed End of Assyrian Empire	c. 600 Greek colonies in Sicily and Italy	
530 Persian Empire reaches height	c. 509 Roman Republic founded	c. 563 Buddha
		c. 551 Confucius
332 Macedonia conquers Egypt. Alexander founds city of Alexandria, soon a center of Hellenistic culture		326 Alexander reaches Indus River
331 Macedonia conquers Persian Empire	264-146 Romans at war with Carthage, Punic Wars	202 Han dynasty in China

Chapter 6 Greece Dominates the Mediterranean World

TO BEGIN the study of Greek civilization, take a look at the map on the facing page. Geography is important in the history of Greece because the location of the various cities and areas influenced the way they grew and what happened to them.

The European side of the Mediterranean Sea consists of three peninsulas jutting southward: the Iberian, the Italian, and the Balkan. Each peninsula is cut off from the rest of Europe by a range of mountains: the Pyrenees, the Alps, and the Balkans. (The map on page 120 shows these features.)

The word "mediterranean" means "in the midst of land." The Mediterranean is the world's largest inland sea. It borders the shores of three continents and has many good harbors. Islands are numerous and close together, especially in the eastern end. The climate is between temperate and tropical. Very early in history the Mediterranean Sea became a pathway of trade and ideas, and the Mediterranean area was the center of Western civilization for many centuries.

The Aegean Sea is a branch of the Mediterranean. It is at the northeastern end, bordered by the Balkan Peninsula and Asia Minor. Look at its many islands, and see how close they are to one another. Early men could go between them, even in small boats. From Egypt and the Fertile Crescent people took their ideas and knowledge to the islands and the peninsula of Greece. There they developed cultures of their own, based on these ideas, and began the great European civilization that we have inherited.

It seems surprising that Greece was the scene of such great development. Geography was unkind in many ways. To be sure, there were many good harbors, and the long irregular coastline brought every part of the peninsula close to the sea. But notice how the land is cut up and divided by short mountain ranges. Compared to the Alps they are not high, but they are rugged and hard to cross. Geography made it difficult for the people of the peninsula to get together.

Greece was not a river valley civilization, for it has no rivers worth mentioning. But there was enough good soil, and the mild climate brought enough rain, to grow grain, grapes, and olives in the small valleys. Also, the foothills of the mountains gave pasture for sheep and goats. However, there was never enough food for the population; so the Greeks had to be traders to live. Their long coastline and many good harbors turned them to the sea; they became fishermen, sailors, pirates, traders, and colonizers.

Look again at the islands of the Aegean, which lie like stepping stones between Greece and Asia Minor and the long island of Crete to the south. It was here that the earliest civilizations of the region began.

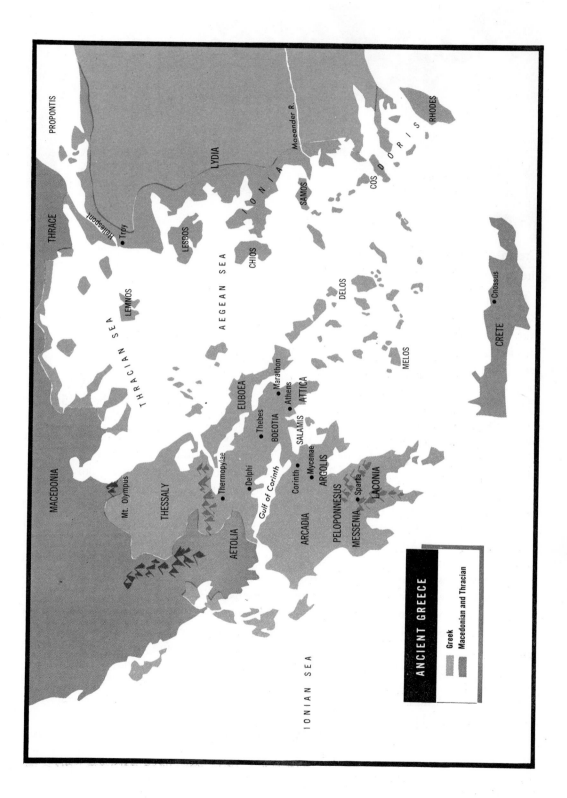

ANCIENT GREECE

Greek

Macedonian and Thracian

PROPONTIS

THRACE

Hellespont

Troy

LYDIA

Moeander R.

IONIA

SAMOS

DORIS

COS

RHODES

LESBOS

CHIOS

AEGEAN SEA

THRACIAN SEA

LEMNOS

DELOS

CRETE

Cnossus

MELOS

MACEDONIA

Mt. Olympus

THESSALY

Thermopylae

Delphi

Gulf of Corinth

EUBOEA

Marathon

Athens

ATTICA

Thebes

BOEOTIA

SALAMIS

Corinth

Mycenae

ARGOLIS

AETOLIA

ARCADIA

PELOPONNESUS

Sparta

LACONIA

MESSENIA

IONIAN SEA

Cretan and Aegean civilizations: the forerunners

Human beings had lived on Crete and the Aegean Islands even during the New Stone Age. They learned to use copper and bronze, and to make beautiful pottery. The Cretans were influenced by the great civilizations of nearby Egypt and the Fertile Crescent, but they added ideas of their own. They controlled the Aegean Islands, and planted colonies on the mainlands of Greece and Asia Minor. Mycenae in Greece and Troy in Asia Minor became centers of Cretan, or Aegean, culture.

Crete remained the center of the empire, which it controlled with its navy. The capital was Cnossus. The sea kings of Crete were so confident in their navy that they did not fortify Cnossus, as they did Troy and Mycenae. Their trust was justified for a long time, but finally they were conquered by people from the Greek peninsula, and Cnossus was destroyed.

The Aegean civilization which was then destroyed was a fine one. Its people made beautiful carved figures of ivory, stone, gold, silver, and bronze. They developed two kinds of writing, a hieroglyphic and a cuneiform style. In the palace and the homes of the nobles there was running water, and there were bathrooms with pipes and drains.

This painting from the palace at Cnossus shows a famous Cretan sport—vaulting over the back of a charging bull.

The beginnings of Greek civilization, 1000–500 B.C.

● *Migrations into Greece*

The people who destroyed the Aegean civilization were the same ones who had invaded the Greek peninsula. Between 2000 and 1000 B.C. three groups of people entered Greece from the north. Like the Hittites, Medes, and Persians they were herdsmen from the grasslands of the Caucasus region.

The newcomers were at a much lower level of civilization than the Aegean peoples. After the coming of the third group the art of writing disappeared, and it was several centuries later before it was brought back by the Phoenicians. These wild tribes from the north had iron weapons, which helped them to conquer the bronze-armed Aegeans. They were organized into clans and tribes. Several related families formed a clan, with a chief. A number of clans made up a tribe, with a head chief. The clan chiefs formed a council to help in governing.

Because of both the geography of Greece and their own tribal organization, the newcomers settled down in city-states. Tribal chiefs became kings and head-priests; clan chiefs became nobles. Land was owned in common by the tribe. There were few skilled workmen, and there was little commerce. Warfare was constant, and piracy was an honorable profession.

● *The nobles and the tyrants*

In time the nobles took power from the kings. Tribal ownership of land was replaced by private ownership. Some small farms were owned by peasants, but nobles took most of the land. These wealthy nobles also built ships and encouraged trading; so a commercial class (businessmen) appeared in the cities. These men had money, but no political power or social position.

Warfare was still frequent. Nobles formed groups which struggled for political power. Often the new merchant class fought for political or social advantages. The common people, especially the small farmers, were very badly off and discontented. Population was increasing, but the amount of good land stayed the same. Land was inherited only by the eldest son; others had to find their ways of making a living. Men who could not pay their debts were sold into slavery. The increasing number of slaves made it difficult for free laborers to earn a living.

Considering all these circumstances, it is not surprising that Greeks began to leave the peninsula and go out to establish colonies. Colonization was often very well planned. Colonizing groups were formed with a leader chosen in advance. The groups usually agreed on a form of government and laws before they left. Greek colonies were planted all over the Mediterranean world.

For about two centuries the nobles controlled the Greek city-states. During this time many changes took place to weaken their power. Foot soldiers became more important in war, so the chariot-driving noble was not needed. The nobles were weakened by fighting among themselves. The merchant class had money to hire armies of their own and

to fight for power. Great numbers of people were discontented with noble rule. Many had lost their land and were ready to follow any leader who promised better things.

The men who appeared with the promises were called *tyrants*. To the Greeks this meant a man who seized and held power by force, without legal right. Tyrants usually came from the commercial class. They always promised to bring peace and prosperity and to defend the poor against the nobles and officials. Many of the tyrants were excellent rulers. Their interest in commerce made them want peace. Hence they stopped the political fighting of the nobles, encouraged trade, and passed good laws. As time went on, some of them became harsh, unjust, and dictatorial, giving the word tyrant its present bad meaning—a ruler who is not restrained by laws or a national constitution; a man who exercises absolute power in a brutal manner, an oppressor. The Greeks had no love for tyrants, good or bad. To kill a tyrant was always considered a noble deed.

● *Greek culture 1000–500* B.C.

Most of the Greek people remained farmers or shepherds. Commerce and industry developed chiefly in the cities, and increased with the establishment of colonies. Greece exported metal work, woven cloth, and pottery, and imported grain, fish, and metal ores. Manufacturing production increased with the growing number of slaves (debtors and war prisoners). Free laborers and peasants found earning a living harder.

The most important works of Greek literature were the epics of Homer. The *Iliad* is the story of the war of the Greeks against Troy, or Ilium, over in Asia Minor. The *Odyssey* tells of the wanderings of the hero Odysseus on his way home from the wars. These books tell us so much about the life of the Greeks in the Age of Kings (1000–800 B.C.) that this time is sometimes called the Homeric Period. They also tell so much about the gods and

The modern Olympic Games open with rituals copied from ancient times. The picture above shows the Olympic flame being lit at Olympia in 1956. A chain of 350 Greek runners carried the torch, by relays, to Athens. Next it was flown to Australia for ceremonies opening the Olympics at Melbourne.

their ways that the Greeks considered them great religious books as well as great works of literature.

● *Religion*

Greek religion developed during this period. The Greeks believed in a great number of gods and goddesses, each of whom ruled over some part of earth or heaven, or had some power over people.

Zeus was the supreme god; he made storms and hurled bolts of lightning when he was angry. *Hera* was his sister and wife, the protectress of women and marriage. She was a nagging wife, and he often slipped away on adventures of his own. *Poseidon,* brother of Zeus, was god of the sea. *Pluto,* another brother, was lord of Hades, the underworld. *Persephone,* daughter of Zeus, was Pluto's wife. She spent six months of the year with

him in Hades. During the other six months she returned to earth to make sure that plants grew and that both animals and people had offspring. This was the Greek explanation for the apparent disappearance of life from earth during winter and its return in spring. *Athena,* daughter of Zeus, was the virgin goddess of wisdom and womanly virtue, the special protectress of Athens, which was named for her. *Aphrodite,* another daughter, was goddess of love and beauty. *Apollo* was god of light, music, poetry, and symbol of manly beauty. *Hermes* with his winged feet was the swift messenger of the gods. *Eros,* son of Aphrodite, shot the arrows which brought love to those they struck.

The Greeks believed that the gods, if kept friendly by ceremonies and sacrifices, would give aid and guidance. Men could learn their wishes by studying the behavior of sacred animals, or the condition of their entrails (internal organs) after they had been sacrificed. The Greeks consulted omens before beginning any important venture.

The Greek idea of a future life was not very attractive. All souls went to Hades, the gray and gloomy place ruled over by Pluto and Persephone. A favored few heroes went to the Elysian Fields of the Blessed. A few especially wicked people, who had defied the will of the gods, suffered eternal torment in Tartarus, a region below Hades.

● *The Olympic Games*

The gods were thought to be pleased by displays of manly strength and courage, and the Greeks held athletic contests in their honor. Most famous were the games at Olympia, held every fourth year in honor of Zeus. The first games took place in 776 B.C. From this date the later Greeks reckoned their time in four-year periods called Olympiads. At first the Greek games consisted only of a foot-race, but later jumping, javelin and discus throwing, boxing, wrestling, and chariot racing were added. Winners received only wreaths of wild olive branches at the games, but when they returned home they were shown many honors and received rich gifts.

After an interval of fifteen centuries the Olympic Games were revived in 1896 for athletes from all over the world.

● The city-state organization

During the latter part of this early period there were many influences that might have led the Greeks to unite. They spoke a common language and had a common religion. Great religious festivals like the Olympic Games brought them together. They joined in common management of great temples like that of Apollo at Delphi. However, two things stronger than all the forces of unity kept the people apart. One was geography: rugged mountains separated the small valleys from each other. The second dividing force was the development of the city-state organization which became typical of Greek civilization and culture. It was a basic reason for both the greatness and weakness of Greece.

The Greek word for city-state was *polis.* Originally it meant a fort on a high place, a refuge during danger, the location of the temple. As a village or city grew up around the fort, *polis* came to mean the fort, the city, and the surrounding region. It also meant the government. The Greek word *polis* gives us our words politics, policy, and metropolis.

Greek city-states differed in many ways, but they were alike in a number of important ways. They had certain physical things in common: (1) Small size. Athens at its greatest was smaller than Rhode Island. Sparta, the largest, was three-fourths the size of Connecticut. (2) Small population. The Greeks considered the ideal city-state population to be 5,000 to 10,000 citizens plus slaves and strangers. Most of them had less. Athens at its peak had about 40,000 citizens. Only three others had half as many. (3) The polis. There was an acropolis, or top city, on a hill or mountain, fortified for defense.

● Representative government

Representative government was an even greater point of likeness. It is the most original and important thing the Greeks gave to the world. They deserve special honor for it. Governments of city-states were not all alike. Some were aristocracies, ruled by a king and nobles. Others were democracies, in which all citizens took part in the government. But all of them had some kind of representative government and certain other institutions and ideas that were alike: (1) A council. In the aristocracies a council of nobles checked the power of the king. In democracies the council was a small elected body which carried on the business of government between meetings of the assembly of all citizens. (2) A public meeting place where all citizens

The baton changes hands in the 400 meter relay at the Melbourne Olympic Games. The United States team set a world record.

could gather. Sometimes it was the city market place. (3) Division of citizens into groups or clans. The division was usually based on wealth, the amount of land owned. (4) A passion for independence. Each city-state had its own laws, religion, calendar, coinage, weights and measures. (5) Great patriotism. Citizens loved their city and were willing to spend their lives in its service.

So much for the things that were alike about city-states. To learn how different they could be, let us look at the two that were largest, most important, and most widely different of all: Sparta and Athens. Although both were parts of Greece, these two city-states provide a striking contrast of cultures.

Sparta

The last and least civilized of the invaders that came into Greece moved south to the Peloponnesus. The Peloponnesus is the large peninsula at the southern tip of Greece. The newcomers conquered and settled a region called Laconia and made the city of Sparta their capital. The native inhabitants of the region numbered twenty times as many as the Spartans, but the Spartans controlled them by force.

Spartan government

Spartan government was for citizens only. An Assembly of all citizens over thirty years of age elected all officials and voted on major policies. A Council of Elders, men over sixty years of age, proposed the laws and policies which the Assembly voted on, and acted as administrators. The real rulers of Sparta were five *ephors* (overseers), elected by the Assembly. They had unlimited power to act as guardians of the state and its citizens. Finally, there were two kings, elected by the Assembly from two royal families. They served as high priests, judges, army commanders, and members of the Council of Elders. They were less powerful than the ephors.

The military machine

The population of Sparta was divided into three classes. Most important were the citizens, or *Spartiates*. Although they controlled the government, their lives from birth to death were strictly regulated. All the regulations were aimed to make every adult male

Warriors of ancient Greece, as shown on old coins. The fighting men of Athens and Sparta wore crested helmets and carried large, round shields of the type shown here. A spear, a favorite Greek weapon, can be seen on the coin at the left. Silver money of this type came into use in the seventh century B.C.

citizen part of an efficient military machine. This army was needed to control the conquered people and to extend Spartan power.

The citizen began his military service at the age of twenty. At thirty he was compelled to marry, but remained in the army. He remained in the army until he was sixty. There was very little home or family life. The citizen spent most of his time in military training. He ate his meals and spent his leisure time in a military club which he had to join. He was not allowed to engage in any trade or business, because business activities and love of money were considered bad for military discipline. To support the citizen and his family the government divided equally among citizens all the land which it owned. With each piece of land went a certain number of slaves to work it.

Sparta's rulers were greatly afraid that their people would come to love money and luxuries, which would weaken them. So they prohibited the use of gold and silver and made a money of iron bars. The bars were too heavy to carry around, and would not buy much. They also feared that contact with outside peoples and ideas would weaken discipline and obedience. Therefore, citizens were not allowed to travel except on military or government business. Foreign visitors were not welcome. They were closely watched by the secret police, and often made to leave the country.

The Spartans called the second class of people by a word that meant "neighbors." They were free, but not citizens. They lived in the towns and cities, and most of them engaged in commerce and industry.

The lowest class were the slaves, called *helots*. They were assigned to citizens to cultivate the land and act as servants. The citizen was required to see that his land produced enough food for himself and his family. If it did not, it was taken back by the government. Therefore, he supervised his slaves very carefully. The Spartans lived in constant fear of

a slave revolt; so they tried to prevent the slaves from developing any leaders. At regular intervals all helots who were outstanding either mentally or physically were killed. The system worked. There never was a successful helot rebellion.

● *Training Spartan citizens*

The Spartan citizen may seem to be an unnatural kind of person, but Spartan rulers had given much thought to developing just such a person. They wanted men skilled in warfare, obedient to orders, and willing to die for Sparta. They got them by training and education. In a way, the education of a Spartan began at birth. Newly born children were examined by a group of officials. Any child

Spartan boys in training. Since strength and endurance were among the "Spartan virtues," boys got hard workouts in such ways as wrestling, throwing heavy weights, and pulling against one another on ropes.

who seemed weak, unhealthy, or deformed in any way was taken up the mountainside and exposed (left to die). Only strong and healthy people could be Spartans! At the age of seven the surviving boys were taken to live in barracks, in military groups. They were trained in the use of weapons and in the "Spartan virtues": courage, strength, endurance, cunning, and devotion to Sparta. They were taught to read and write, but the greater part of their education was military.

It was indeed a harsh education. To teach endurance, boys wore only a single garment, summer and winter. They never wore shoes. Often they were beaten publicly so that they would bear pain without crying out. To teach them to forage for themselves in wartime, their food was so coarse and scanty that they had to steal food to keep from starving. If caught they were beaten, not for stealing but for being so clumsy as to be caught. They were taught to walk in silence, their eyes downcast, and to use the fewest possible words in speaking. Today such short, abrupt speech is called *laconic,* from Laconia, the location of Sparta. Always they were taught the glories of Sparta, and how noble it was to die in battle for the fatherland.

The girls were the future mothers of soldiers; so they too had to be healthy. They were given strict physical training for strength and endurance. They were also trained in patriotic devotion to the fatherland. Many stories have come down to us, but one will be enough to show the attitude of Spartan women. A Spartan mother was told that her five sons had been killed in battle. Her reply was, "That is not what I want to know, but did Sparta win?" When told that Sparta had won, she exclaimed, "Then let us give thanks."

Today there is a name for the Spartan kind of civilization. A system in which the individual exists only for the benefit of the government, and which glorifies war, is called *totalitarian.* The Spartan culture was certainly that kind. It did produce an efficient government and an almost unconquerable army. But it produced nothing else: no art, no literature, no philosophy, no science or inventions, no poetry or drama.

Athens

Another tribe of invaders settled on the peninsula of Attica, on the east-central coast of Greece. Much of the soil of Attica was rocky and unproductive, good only for raising grapes and olives and providing pasture for sheep and goats. The Athenians were compelled to look to the sea for much of their living. Nevertheless they built Athens some six miles inland for protection against pirates. There was, and is, a special port city, Piraeus.

Athens was a typical polis. The city was built around a rocky, fortified hill, the acropolis, or upper city. The entire city was surrounded by a strong wall. It was a place of defense for the whole peninsula in time of war.

● *Social classes and government*

As in Sparta, the population was divided into three classes. First were the citizens, subdivided by clans into four groups according to the amount of land they owned. Next came the aliens, who were called *metics.* They were merchants and skilled workmen, who paid special taxes and were allowed special privileges. Lowest were the slaves, fewer in Athens than in most city-states. Even so, at the time of its greatest glory more than half of the population consisted of metics and slaves.

The original invaders set up an aristocratic form of government with a number of classes of citizens. Only the three highest classes of citizens could vote. They met in an Assembly and elected nine *archons,* members of the two highest classes. These were the real rulers. There was a king, but he was only one of the archons; so he was no more powerful than any other. The archons appointed all officials and made all the laws, but these laws, in spite of Hammurabi's example, were not written. The judges, who were always nobles, said what the law was and applied it in each case. Needless to say the laws always seemed to work for the benefit of the noble class.

Athens depended on trade and industry. It had to export manufactured goods to pay for the food and raw materials it imported. So there appeared a class of businessmen who did not like the rule of the nobles. The

not make much change in the existing laws; therefore, his code was harsh and severe. Almost every offense was punished by death. It was easy for a borrower to lose his land. A man who could not pay his debts became a slave. Today we call a harsh law *Draconian*.

Conditions in Athens remained bad. Nobles and metics grew wealthy from trade, but farmers got poorer. If a crop was bad, a farmer had to borrow, mortgaging his land and sometimes himself and his family. He had little chance to repay; more and more citizens

lower classes of citizens were also discontented. Either they had no voice in the government, or they found it always run for the benefit of the upper classes. In time, tyrants gained control of the government. Three of these rulers carried out programs of reform. As a result of the work of Draco, Solon, and Cleisthenes, Athens was changed into the greatest democracy of the ancient world.

● *Draco*

The first of these tyrants was Draco. Draco's change was to have the laws written so that everyone could know them. He did

Buildings of the style typical of public structures in Greece. This is a model of Olympia, site of the original Olympic Games. The long building in the center was a temple to Zeus. Other buildings included temples and clubhouses for the men from different Greek cities. Beyond lay the Stadium and the Hippodrome.

were being sold into slavery for debt. The poor demanded that their debts be canceled and that the land be divided equally. The nobles opposed both of these demands. War between the classes seemed certain. In this emergency power was given to a widely-trusted businessman. He was a politician, a general, a traveler, and a poet. His name was Solon.

Greek chariots, pictured on coins.

● Solon

Solon showed wisdom and moderation by not giving either class all that it wanted. He canceled the debts of the poor, and his laws provided that there should be no more enslavement for debt. He freed those who had been enslaved for nonpayment. He did not divide the land equally, but he set a limit to the amount of land a man could own. Every man was required to teach his sons a trade.

Solon allowed the fourth class of citizens to vote, and the third class to hold office. To check the power of the archons he set up a Council of Four Hundred, with members chosen by lot from the three upper classes. The Council proposed the laws which the Assembly voted on. To check the power of the judges he set up a court composed of large numbers of citizens. Any man who thought a judge's decision unfair could appeal it to this popular court. Solon's reforms started Athens on the way to democracy. Today a wise lawmaker is called a *solon*.

Athens still had much unrest. The upper three officeholding classes formed political parties and struggled for control of the government. Nobles plotted to seize the government and take away the political rights of the lower classes. Then a third great tyrant gained power by promising to protect and restore the political rights of the people.

● Cleisthenes

Cleisthenes was a member of a famous Athenian family, a man of wealth and of social position. He was deeply interested in the welfare of the common people. He opposed the class division based on differences in wealth, and made a new division in which all citizens were politically equal. All male citizens over twenty years of age were made members of the Assembly. The Council was increased to 500 members, drawn by lot from all citizens over thirty. The Council took over most of the powers and duties formerly held by the archons.

To safeguard the democracy of Athens Cleisthenes began a practice that was long followed. Once a year each citizen was given a ballot—a piece of pottery called an *ostrakon*. On it he could write the name of any man he thought was opposed to the government, or who threatened its safety. A man whose name received enough such votes was compelled to leave the country and go into exile for ten years. This custom was called *ostracism*. Sometimes today a person does something so unpopular that his neighbors will not speak to him or have anything to do with him. It is said then that he is ostracized.

Cleisthenes' reforms made Athens almost a complete democracy. The Assembly of all citizens had full and final power. It chose archons and generals, and could judge and punish them. The Council of Five Hundred proposed the laws to the Assembly. The court was completely democratic. There were no judges and no lawyers; each man could plead his own case. The jury of citizens was the entire court. Juries were very large; 501 was a common number. Each juror voted by secret ballot. Jurors, officeholders, and Council members were chosen by lot, to show the Athenian belief in the equality and fitness of all citizens for government service.

For the citizens it was true democracy—probably the most complete of any government in history. You must remember, though, that half or more of the residents were not citizens. Many an Athenian was able to give so much of his time and services to his government because he was supported by slaves.

Athenians loved their city, and felt for it a loyalty and devotion as great as Spartans felt for Sparta. It was their city and their government; therefore, they gave as much attention to public affairs as to their private business. The wealthy felt a sense of duty to give much to the state for its protection and beauty. The poor man felt that at least in government he was anyone's equal.

Expansion and conflict:
Greeks vs. Persians

As you have learned, the Greek city-states established many colonies around the shores of the Aegean, Black, and Mediterranean Seas. It is surprising that these colonies, and Greece itself, were allowed to develop for so long without interference from the powerful empires of the Near East. This freedom did not last forever.

In 546 B.C. Cyrus, the great Persian ruler, conquered Asia Minor and with it the Greek colonies along the shores. He gave these city-states the same tolerant rule that the rest of his empire enjoyed. They paid tribute, but were allowed to keep their own local government, laws, and religion. However, Greeks in Asia Minor loved independence as much as their brothers on the peninsula. Some of their leaders denounced the "tyranny" of the Persians and stirred up revolts. The Persians easily put down the uprisings and did not punish the cities very severely.

● *The First Persian War:*
  Marathon, 490 B.C.

When Darius came to the Persian throne, he faced another problem. A fierce tribe from the Danube River region was invading Asia Minor. Darius decided to keep them out by setting up a "buffer" (frontier) state in Thrace, a region between the Aegean and Black seas. He planned to control the Aegean Sea with his fleet.

All the Greek city-states in Greece, Asia Minor, and on the Black Sea were alarmed at this prospect. Athens especially feared to lose control of the Aegean Sea, on which her commercial life depended. She encouraged the city-states in Asia Minor to revolt again and sent them help. The Persians once more put down the revolt easily. Again the penalty was not as severe as might have been expected. However, the incident made Darius determined to control the city-states of the Greek peninsula as well as the Greek colonies. In an effort to get what he wanted peacefully, Darius sent ambassadors to Greece to ask the city-states to accept him as their king. If they did so, and paid tribute, he would allow them to keep their government, laws, and religion. They were told to send him earth and water as a sign that they acknowledged him ruler of land and sea.

Darius had not counted on the Greeks' fierce love of independence. Both Athens and Sparta refused his terms. He then gathered two great armies and fleets, one to conquer Thrace, the other to strike at Athens.

It was in the year 490 B.C. that the Persians landed on the coast of Attica and advanced to the plain of Marathon, not far from Athens. At Marathon they were met by the Athenian army. Herodotus, the Greek historian, tells that the Athenians had 10,000 troops, and that the Persians outnumbered them ten to one. It is likely that he exaggerated the odds to make the story better. The smaller Athenian army attacked bravely, routing the Persians. One report tells that the Persians lost 6,000 men, the Athenians 192. That was the end of the first invasion.

● *The Second Persian War:*
  Thermopylae and Salamis, 480 B.C.

After the defeat at Marathon, the Persians went home, threatening to come back with a larger army and conquer all Greece. Soon afterward Darius died, but his son Xerxes began to gather another large army and fleet for a second invasion of Greece.

In 480 B.C. the dreaded news came. Xerxes had raised a great army. He moved his army, partly by land and partly by sea, north to the Hellespont, the narrow strait separating Asia Minor from Thrace. There he built a bridge of ships which his army crossed. They marched through Thrace, Macedonia, and Thessaly with little opposition.

To come from Thessaly into central Greece the Persians had to march through the narrow mountain pass of Thermopylae. There they were met by King Leonidas of Sparta and a force of less than five hundred men. Leonidas appealed for reinforcement, but none of the states was ready to send more troops. Now the Spartan training proved its worth. Leonidas and his men scorned to retreat; to surrender would be a disgrace. For three days they held the narrow pass against the entire Persian army. Finally a Greek traitor offered, for pay, to show the Persians a secret pass through the mountains. The Spartans were surrounded. Still refusing to surrender, they fought on until every man was killed. To this day the name Thermopylae stands for a brave fight against great odds.

With the pass cleared the Persians were able to move out onto the central plains. Every city-state was in danger, and there was no army in the field. Athens was in a turmoil: should they try to defend the city, or abandon it in their fleet? The omens gave confusing advice. The able Greek general Themistocles persuaded the Athenians to abandon their city and let the ships take them to the island of Salamis. The Persians captured Athens, and Xerxes made good the vow of his father by destroying the walls and most of the city.

Now the Greek leader Themistocles used strategy. Pretending to be a traitor, he sent word to advise Xerxes to attack with his fleet in the narrow waters between Salamis island and the coast. Xerxes ordered the attack and set up his throne on a high coastal point to watch the defeat of the Athenian fleet. To his horror he saw the small Greek ships outmaneuver the larger Persian ships, ramming and sinking many of them. Xerxes ordered his fleet to withdraw. Just then he received news of revolts in the Persian Empire. Fearing that the Athenian fleet would destroy his bridge of ships, he ordered his army to withdraw, leaving part of it behind with orders to conquer Greece. In the following year this army was defeated by a combined Greek army. The Persians never again attempted to invade Greece.

● *Importance of the Greek victories*

The immediate results of the Persian wars do not seem like a very great victory. Athens and much of Greece were ruined. The Greek cities of Asia Minor were free for a short time, but soon fell under Persian rule again. The Persian Empire remained very powerful, and its rulers continued to meddle in Greek affairs. It became a fixed Persian policy to try to prevent any unity in Greece. The Greek states regarded the Persians as their traditional enemies.

From a long-run viewpoint the battles of Marathon and Salamis are considered important and decisive in world history. It was a struggle between despotic, Near-Eastern civilization headed by a king-god with absolute powers, and Greek city-state civilization with representative governments of free citizens. Persian defeat meant that the Greeks could continue to develop their free culture and pass it on to Western civilization.

Athens dominates Greece

Although badly damaged, Athens was still the leading city of Greece. The city was rebuilt, with temples and public buildings even more magnificent than before. Claiming to be the "savior of Greek civilization," Athens attempted to unite all Greece. Fear of other

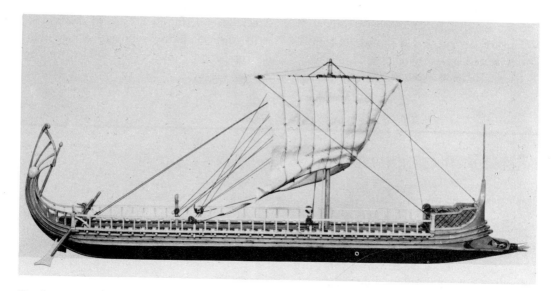

A Greek galley of the fourth century B.C. This model gives an idea of the warships used at Salamis. The large paddles at the stern were used for steering. Ports for oars can be seen along the side below the railing. The beak at the bow was presumably used to ram enemy ships.

Persian attempts at conquest made unity seem very necessary. However, Sparta wanted unity under her leadership. Too proud to use diplomacy, the Spartans tried conquest. Now the weakness of their slave system showed up. Fear of helot revolts kept them from sending expeditions far from home. Even their strong army could not extend Spartan power much beyond the Peloponnesus.

To bring about unity, the Athenians used diplomacy. In this way they were able to persuade some 200 city-states to form a system of alliances called the Delian League. The agreement gave each member one vote. Each contributed either ships or money. Funds were deposited on the Island of Delos (hence the name Delian). No state could withdraw from the league without unanimous consent. Athens was given power to decide how many ships or how much money each should contribute. In time Athens gained complete control of the Delian League. The League became an Athenian Empire, which Athens ruled as a dictator.

Now appeared the greatest of all Athenian leaders. Pericles was an aristocrat, a great-nephew of Cleisthenes who had done so much to make Athens a democracy. Pericles was a dignified, reserved person, and one of the greatest orators in a land of great orators. His ability and reputation for honesty were so great that he was chosen general for sixteen successive years. He was the real leader of Athens for thirty years, the time of its greatest power and prosperity. This period of Athenian history is called the Golden Age, or the Age of Pericles.

Pericles continued the Athenian control of the Delian League, and increased the empire. More city-states were forced to join. The League treasury was moved from Delos to Athens, and the money used openly for Athenian purposes. Revolts against these policies were crushed; land was taken from the rebels and given to Athenians who were established on it as colonists.

But Corinth (which controlled the trade with the western Mediterranean) and Sparta held out against the Athenian Empire. Athens tried to take over Corinth's trade by making alliances with Corinth's enemies. The long rivalry between Athens and Sparta increased.

You can see that Athen's policies could end in one of two ways: either she would control all of Greece, or there would be a great war. Chapter 8 will tell about this great crisis in Greek history, but first Chapter 7 will describe the wonderful culture of Athens during the period known as the Golden Age, or Age of Pericles.

Review of Chapter 6

People, places, and things

Identify: Zeus, Apollo, Cleisthenes, Solon, Delian League, Themistocles, Xerxes, helots, archons, ephors.

Locate: The routes of the barbarian tribes that invaded Greece and destroyed the Aegean civilization. Locate also Crete, Troy, Mycenae, Aegean Sea, Ionian Sea, Athens, Sparta, Marathon, Thermopylae, Salamis, Corinth, Mt. Olympus, Delphi.

Events in review

1. How did geography influence the development of Greece?
2. Why did the Greeks consider the poems of Homer important?
3. Why are the battles of Marathon and Salamis considered two of the decisive battles of the world?
4. How did the Persian Wars show both the strength and the weakness of Greece?
5. Who first had the laws of Athens written down? What other countries you have studied in this book had written codes of law?
6. What were some of the rights and powers of citizens of Athens after the time of Cleisthenes? Did all residents of Athens have these rights?
7. Why was the life of Athenians and Spartans so different? Give three examples of the contrast between the two city states.
8. In what ways were the governments of the Greek city-states similar? Were they all democratic governments?

Problems and projects

1. The greatest contribution of Greece to our civilization is said to be the development of democracy. Give examples to prove that Greece made contributions to modern democracy.
2. For how many years of military service was a Spartan "drafted"? What do you think would happen if American men had to spend this much time in the armed forces?
3. Draw a map of Greece and on it locate the city states. Show how the location of mountains and rivers affected the history of Greece.
4. Imagine yourself a Spartan youth. Write an account of your daily life.
5. As an Athenian nobleman you are interested in the development of your city state. Why?
6. Write a description of the advanced civilization that existed on the island of Crete in very early times.
7. Describe the religion of the early Greeks. Include in your description: (a) the Greek belief in oracles, (b) their idea of a future life. How did the Greek religion differ from that of the Egyptians? the Hebrews?
8. Look up information on the Olympic Games of ancient Greece. Compare the Greek games with the modern Olympic Games. Which of the modern events are carried over from ancient times? Which are new?
9. Write an essay on the battle of Thermopylae. Compare it with some famous battle of modern times (for example, the defense of Wake Island or Bastogne, or the resistance of London to German bombing, in World War II).

Chapter 7

The Golden Age: Athenian Culture in the Age of Pericles

DURING the period from about 500 to 338 B.C., Greek culture reached high levels. The highest point of all came in Athens during the Age of Pericles, the Golden Age. Reading in this chapter about the city, the people, the schools, the artists, the writers, and the great thinkers, you can see why this age came to be called Golden. You may want to ask yourself if life was always "Golden," or "Golden" for all of the people.

The city and the people

● Public buildings

The rebuilding of Athens after its destruction by the Persians was begun under Themistocles and completed during the thirty years of Pericles' leadership. Athenians showed their love of and pride in Athens by erecting beautiful public buildings: temples, gymnasiums, and theaters. They decorated buildings and all public places with their finest works of art, especially sculpture. The Greeks liked to make beautiful art part of their daily life.

The Acropolis, upper city of the ancient polis, was the scene of special beautification. At the entrance to the path up the hill was a magnificent gate. Inside the gate stood a huge bronze statue of Athena, seventy feet high. As the special protectress of Athens, she was armed with shield and spear.

On top of the Acropolis stood the Parthenon, a temple in honor of Athena. It is considered the finest example of Greek architecture. The Greek motto was: "Nothing in excess, and everything in proportion." The beauty of the Parthenon was not in its great size, but rather in its proportions. The relation of length to width, and of both to height, was perfect. At each end was a pediment, or gable, supported by columns. Along either side a row of columns supported the roof. Many works of sculpture stood outside the columns. The wall inside and above the colonnade, called the frieze, was decorated with sculpture in relief around the entire building. The relief showed an annual procession in honor of Athena. The temple itself had doors but no windows. Greek temples were shrines rather than meeting places for worshipers. The inside was seldom decorated as much as the outside. Within the Parthenon, though, stood another large statue of Athena, carved of ivory with draperies of gold decorated with jewels. (See the drawing above.)

● Homes and streets

There was a remarkable contrast between the beauty of Athenian temples and public buildings and the lack of beauty of the homes, even of the wealthy. The Athenian ideal was to spend money on buildings to beautify and benefit the whole community, not on private homes. Then, too, life in Athens was a man's life, and men spent little time in their homes. Houses were simple and plain, very close to the street, and usually of one story. They were built of sun-dried brick. The street wall was solid except for a door which led into an open court. From the court, doors opened into the living room, dining room, bedrooms, storerooms, and kitchen.

Greek homes were masterpieces of inconvenience. The only heat came from braziers

of the city. There was no sewage system, no garbage collection, no street cleaning, no paving, no sidewalks, no public lighting. Slops, rubbish, and garbage were thrown into the streets.

●Social classes

As mentioned before, there were three main classes: citizens, metics (free noncitizens), and slaves. Among the citizens there were considerable differences of wealth and social position. Some were aristocrats. They could live on the income from their lands, worked

or pans for burning charcoal. The only lighting was from dim lamps that burned olive oil. There was no plumbing and no running water. Water was carried by slaves from a well or spring in jars. There was not much furniture; but, in the Greek way; what they had was beautiful.

The streets showed another contrast in Athenian life. Great care was taken in laying out the Acropolis and public buildings, but there was no planning of streets. They were narrow, crooked, and filthy in every section

One of the buildings on the Acropolis at Athens: the Erectheum, named for the legendary founder of Athens, Erectheus. Note the Porch of the Maidens, each column being a statue of a girl.

by slaves, and give all their time to public business and social affairs. Other citizens were merchants, small shopowners, skilled workmen, and small farmers.

Citizenship in Athens was exclusive; that is, no one could be a citizen unless both his mother and father were citizens. If one parent had been a citizen, a person could become one by a decree of the Assembly, a rare and great honor.

Pericles increased the already great amount of democracy for citizens. He began the practice of paying public officials, including juries, so that every citizen could afford to take part in government. All citizens served in the Assembly, which met on the slopes of a hill about forty times a year. It decided all questions of public policy and elected the generals. They were the only elected officials. All others, including members of juries, were drawn by lot. Thus every citizen had the right to help determine policies, and an equal chance to be chosen to help administer the government.

The word *metic* meant foreigner or alien. Metics were considered foreigners no matter how long they or their ancestors had lived in Athens. Laws prohibited them from owning land or from marrying women of the citizen class. They could, of course, take no part in the government, but there were no other discriminations against them. They could move about freely, go into any occupation (except farming), and have their own religion. Most of them engaged in commerce or manufacturing, either as owners or artisans.

● Slavery in Athens

The slaves were the lowest social class and were considered to be property, dependent on their master's will. However, a slave had some legal protections. The master could not treat his slaves with constant cruelty, nor did he have the right of life and death. If the master permitted, the slave might acquire property, and even become wealthy. A slave who was freed, as many were, became a metic.

The treatment and life of slaves varied greatly according to master and occupation. Slaves in industry worked side by side with masters and free workers and were not treated differently. Much of the work in Greek in-dustry was done by manpower. The slave took the place of a machine. Household slaves were seldom badly abused. Some of them were men of education and culture, and were treated as members of the family. But there were also slaves who worked in the mines. They lived short and miserable lives—branded, beaten, and chained together in work gangs.

To the Greeks, slavery was part of the natural order of things, a necessary institution. The philosopher Aristotle reasoned that there were some people so poor in natural ability that they could be nothing else but slaves. Not all Greeks agreed. The philosopher Plato thought that all slaves should be freed. As time went on, more Greeks came to doubt the rightness of slavery.

The Greeks who spoke out against slavery were comparatively few in number. They gave early expression to an idea that was to have a long development in history. It was many centuries before the legal equality of all people became accepted over very much of the world.

● Home life

Athenian home life was almost as unattractive as the homes themselves. Athenians considered marriage a necessary institution, but there was little sentiment or romance connected with it. Its main purpose was the bearing and rearing of children. Marriages were always arranged by the parents. Often the bride and groom did not see each other until the day of the wedding. Girls married early, at fourteen or fifteen. Usually the husband was twice that age.

Women were considered definitely inferior to men. Their duty was to manage the household and the slaves and see to the upbringing of the children. They rarely appeared in public, and only by permission of the husband. They had few legal rights. If they were mistreated, they had difficulty in getting a divorce. It was easier for a man to divorce his wife. Women took no part in the social lives of their husbands. If there was a banquet or entertainment in the home, the wife withdrew to another part of the house.

The Athenian mother, aided by a woman slave, took care of both boys and girls until they were eight. At eight the boy was placed in the care of a male slave called a pedagogue, who taught him manners and went everywhere with him. Girls stayed in the home, going outside rarely, and then only when accompanied by their parents. They were trained at home in household management, but received no other schooling. They were educated to give their services to the home, just as men were trained to give their services to the state. It may be that Greek women were not particularly unhappy, for they expected life to be as it was.

● *Social life and recreation*

The Greek man had a great variety of recreation to fill his leisure time. In the open-air theaters he could watch frequent performances. There was the public business of government to be attended to. At the many athletic fields the man could watch the boys at their training or playing games. In gymnasiums he could exercise or meet and talk with friends. There were public baths. Many religious festivals were observed.

The wealthy led the most interesting lives, but others also lived well. The Athenian skilled worker did not have too hard a time. He saw to it that he had plenty of leisure time to enjoy life. Even in normal times artisans were scarce. When the great public buildings were being built, skilled craftsmen had to be imported. Therefore, there was little unemployment. The skilled worker could be quite independent. He took time off for public business or athletic events.

Unskilled workers toiled long hours at monotonous work, with little time off. Free peasants and farm workers also led dull, monotonous lives, and barely made a living.

Farming, manufacturing, trade

Farming was the most honored calling of all. More than half of all Athenians were farmers. Farming methods were very crude, and the financial rewards were not very great. Fields had to lie fallow (unplanted) every second year to regain fertility. Level land for raising grain was very scarce. Athens had to import two thirds of all the grain it used. The slopes of the hills were terraced to raise olives, grapes, and figs. The principal domestic animals were goats and sheep. Goats furnished most of the meat eaten; sheep were valued mostly for their wool. Not much meat was

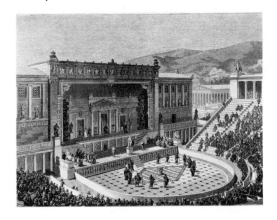

Above: The Theater of Dionysus in Athens. This is an artist's drawing of the theater as it looked when the Athenians gathered to watch the comedies of Aristophanes or the tragedies of Aeschylus. Below: A photograph showing the ruins of the theater in modern times.

eaten; fish, and cheese made of goat or sheep milk, took its place.

Athenian manufacturing was done in small shops. A shop with twenty workers was considered large. Many craftsmen worked in their own homes. Members of the family worked side by side with slaves and free employees. Work was done only to fill actual orders, and usually the customer supplied the raw materials.

Foreign trade was the most important part of the Athenian economy. The need to increase the food supply influenced all government policy and politics. It led to the building of the Athenian Empire, and made foreign trade a life or death matter. Athenian ships went everywhere in the Mediterranean, from the Black Sea to Spain. They took Athenian manufactured goods, and brought back the all-important foods and raw materials that could not be provided at home.

Cultural life in the Golden Age

●Education

The Athenians realized that if their democracy was to be successful every citizen must be educated. There were no public, tax-supported schools, but there were many private schools with very low fees. Almost all boys between the ages of six and fourteen attended elementary schools. Girls did not go to school. The schools gave what we would now call a liberal education—one that fits a person to live well.

Three main subjects were taught in these elementary schools: grammar, music, and gymnastics. Each of these included things that we consider separate subjects today. Grammar, for example, included reading, writing, and literature. The boys learned to write on a wax tablet with a stylus. Much of their reading was in such works of Greek literature as Homer's *Iliad* and *Odyssey*. Boys were taught to sing and to play musical instruments in the schools.

The Greek ideal was a healthy mind in a healthy body. Grammar and music developed the mind and the emotions; gymnastics developed the body. The boys practiced running, jumping, boxing, wrestling, and throwing the discus and javelin in open fields at the edge of the city. They usually exercised wearing only a loin-cloth.

At fourteen, when they had finished elementary education, boys of poor families were apprenticed to learn a trade. Those who could afford it went to higher schools, which were more expensive. These upper schools were conducted by men who called themselves Sophists, or wise men. Here the boys studied poetry, government, ethics (right conduct), geometry, astronomy, and rhetoric. Rhetoric was the study of oratory and debating, so important in Greek life.

Many of the Sophists were excellent teachers and truly wise men. Others, however, were pretenders. In teaching the boys to debate they were more concerned with winning by tricky methods than with sound reasoning. So today we have the word *sophistry,* from the practice of tricky argumentation in ancient Greece by the Sophists. It means reasoning which sounds good, but will not stand up when you analyze it.

When the boy was eighteen, he served a year of military training. At nineteen, in a very impressive public ceremony, he became a full citizen. The highest public officials of the city presented him with his shield and sword, the symbols of citizenship. He took a very solemn oath, swearing, among other things, to obey the laws and magistrates and defend them from attack, not to disgrace his arms or to forsake his comrades, and to leave his country in a better state than he found it. The boy then served another year in the army or the navy.

●Architecture

You have already read a little about Greek architecture. It is worth repeating that the

Left to right: Doric, Ionic, and Corinthian capitals of columns. Note the change from simple Doric to elaborate Corinthian.

beauty of a building like the Parthenon was not in its size and grandeur, but in its perfect proportions and decorations. The Greeks did not use the arch to support ceilings and roofs, but rested them on columns. A building surrounded by one or two rows of columns is considered typical of Greek architecture. There were three different types of columns. The capitals (tops) of these three types are pictured above.

Sculpture

The greatest Greek art was sculpture. Not many of the original works of Greek sculpture are still in existence. What we know about Greek sculpture has come to us chiefly through copies made during Roman times. An early artist was Myron, whose figure of the Discus Thrower is very familiar. Two of the greatest sculptors of all times lived during the Golden Age of Pericles. Phidias was artistic adviser to Pericles during the rebuilding and beautification of Athens. He was the creator of the two wonderful statues of Athena at the Parthenon, and of some of the carvings on the frieze. His greatest work was the statue of Zeus at the Temple of Olympia. Greeks who attended the Olympic Games looked at it with awe. A man who had not seen it considered himself unfortunate.

Praxiteles lived about a hundred years after Phidias, and made quite different sculpture. Phidias' works were large, formal, and dignified, as was fitting for the gods. Praxiteles made his figures more human and lifelike. Often they were life-sized. They were more graceful than those of Phidias, but lacked the feeling of awe and reverence that the work of the earlier master inspired. Above all, Praxiteles' statues gave expression to the Greek love for the beauty of the human body.

Greek philosophy: Socrates

One of the greatest thinkers and teachers of all time was a short, bald, snub-nosed little man named Socrates. Trained as a stonecutter, or sculptor, he gave up the work to be a philosopher and teacher. He would not take pay for teaching, and lived in poverty. Homely as he was, he was greatly loved because he was wise, honest, simple, and kindly.

Socrates was a critic of Athenian education, especially of the Sophists. He said they boasted too much of their wisdom, and made their pupils conceited. He would not allow himself to be called a Sophist—"wise man." He called himself a philosopher, which means a lover of wisdom and a humble seeker for knowledge and truth.

Socrates criticized the Sophists for teaching the boys to live by memorizing proverbs and imitating their elders instead of learning to think for themselves. By learning to think for himself, he said, man could learn wisdom, which would lead him to right living. Only evil could result from ignorance. Man must depend on his reason to guide his life, to show him what was truly important and what was not. Young men must be trained to reason, he said, if they were later to govern so that every citizen could lead the best possible life.

Socrates did not teach in the way that the Sophists did. They were lecturers; they told their pupils what they should think. Socrates asked questions of anyone he met anywhere. The purpose of his questions was not to get information, but to make men think in order to answer them. He especially wanted each man to understand himself. "Know thyself" was his great motto. He wanted men to understand what such ideas as love, friendship, duty, patriotism, honor, and justice really meant to them. Each man must find his own answers to these problems. This way of teaching is known as the "Socratic method."

Socrates inspired great love among his followers, but he also gained many enemies among the Sophists and the conservative people. Many people dislike having their accepted beliefs questioned. It makes them think, and this makes them uncomfortable and resentful, for thinking is hard work.

Socrates and many of his followers had come to believe that there was only one God, and that the soul was immortal. His enemies brought him to trial as a "subversive," as a man who denied the existence of the gods, and who corrupted youth. At the trial he said that his conscience, which he considered to be the voice of God, made him teach. If he were allowed to live, he would continue to teach, because his conscience would compel him to. He was condemned to die by drinking poisonous liquid made from the hemlock plant.

● *Plato*

Socrates had always been too busy teaching to write down his ideas. Later generations learned about his ideas from the writings of Plato, the greatest of his disciples. Plato was a wealthy young aristocrat. After Socrates' death, he began to teach in the grounds of the Academy, a public park and athletic field. Plato's writings are called Dialogues. Each Dialogue is in the form of an imagined conversation among several people; Socrates is usually the chief speaker. There are dialogues on government, education, justice, virtue, and religion.

To answer the question "What is justice?" Plato wrote a Dialogue called *The Republic*. This Dialogue described Plato's idea of the ideal form of government. Everyone, he said, should do the work for which he is best fitted. Men noted for bravery should be in the army. People interested in material things like food, clothing, and luxuries should conduct the business and do the labor. Slavery should be abolished. All workers should be free, though not all should be citizens, for Plato's ideal government was to be operated and controlled by a few men only. They were the

One of the most famous Greek statues, the Winged Victory of Samothrace. This sculpture was made to honor Nike, the goddess of victory. It is named for the island of Samothrace, on which it was discovered.

philosophers, to be chosen for their wisdom, ability, and correct ideas of justice. They were to own everything in common.

● Aristotle and Greek science

Plato's students in the Academy included a young Macedonian named Aristotle, whom Plato called "the mind of the school." Later, Aristotle founded a school in the gardens and gymnasium of the Lyceum.

Aristotle was probably greater as a scientist than as a philosopher. He set himself the task of investigating every kind of knowledge. He would collect as many facts as possible. Then he would arrange and organize them into a system, comparing one thing with another to find out what they meant or showed. He was especially skillful at definitions and at putting facts together in groups that are alike. This is a great part of what is called today the "scientific method."

Aristotle almost accomplished his purpose of searching every field of knowledge. He collected, described, and classified plants and animals. In order to establish principles of government, Aristotle studied the constitutions of 150 city-states. Then he wrote his book, *Politics.* For his book *Ethics,* he studied the acts and beliefs of men to learn what brought the greatest virtue and happiness. In his *Poetics* he made a study of Greek dramas to show the differences between a good and a bad play. His *Logic* is an attempt to show the principles of correct reasoning and "straight" thinking.

Aristotle was considered *the* great authority on almost everything for a thousand years after his death. If Aristotle said it, it was true.

Greek science did not reach its greatest development during the Golden Age, but the foundations of the scientific method were laid then. The thinkers of Athens were trying to find the reasons, the natural explanations, for all things. Plato and others developed ideas in mathematics and astronomy. Aristotle laid the foundations of anatomy (how the bodies of living things are made), botany, and zoology. The Greek philosopher Democritus believed that all matter is composed of moving atoms—particles so small that they cannot be divided. Modern science has proved that the atom can be divided, but still holds the theory that all matter is made of atoms.

One of the greatest scientists of the Golden Age was Hippocrates, known as the Father of Medicine. He taught that all disease comes from natural causes, not as punishment from the gods. The best healers, he said, were rest, fresh air, and proper diet. Hippocrates had very high ideals for men who entered medical practice. He wrote a pledge for them to take before they began to practice medicine. This pledge is still used. In a physician's office you may see a copy of the Hippocratic Oath.

● Literature

A surprising number of the world's greatest books were written by Greeks who lived in Athens during the Golden Age. That period of about half a century saw a great flood of creative writing. Greek writing was great because of its simple expression, its realism or truthful picture of the way people live and act even today, its beauty and grace both of style and ideas.

Greek plays were almost always written in poetic form. They were spoken or sung by two or three actors and a chorus. Plays were performed outdoors, in amphitheaters on the slopes of hills. The actors performed on a high stage which filled the end of the amphitheater. The chorus of singers or dancers were in the flat circle below the stage. There was almost no scenery. The chorus told about the scene and explained something about the action. The audience supplied the rest with their imaginations.

The actors were always men, each with a voice trained to play several parts, including women's parts. They wore elaborate costumes, with much padding and thick-soled boots to make them look larger than human beings. They used masks to show what part they were speaking.

The plays often had a religious theme, and were sometimes given in connection with a religious festival. For three successive days at the Festival of Dionysus nine short plays were given each day. Each day the audience selected the best play, judging it by the beauty of the writing and the wisdom of the ideas. The audience sat in the seats around the hillside. Pericles considered these plays so important in the education of citizens that he provided for free admission to the great festivals for all male citizens who could not afford them.

Greek tragedies

The Greeks enjoyed both tragedies and comedies. A tragedy showed the protagonist (central character) struggling against and being overcome by fate. Sometimes the protagonist was overcome by outside forces that were too strong for him, sometimes because of some weakness of his own character. The end was always inevitable; it could not be escaped. A "happy ending" was never "tacked on."

Three great writers of tragedy lived during the Golden Age. Aeschylus was called the Father of Greek Tragedy. Thirteen times he won the ivy crown as writer of the best play. He wrote of the old religious beliefs about the relationship between gods and men. Most famous of his plays to survive today are three which tell the story of Agamemnon, the king who led the Greeks against Troy, a city in Asia Minor. The second great tragedian was Sophocles. Sophocles also wrote about the old ideas.

Euripides, the third tragedian, was a realist who wrote of things as they are. Like Socrates he questioned many old beliefs and ideas. Earlier writers often glorified war for its deeds of courage and heroism. In the *Trojan Women* Euripides showed war as it really is, with all the miseries it brings.

Greek comedies

Greek comedies were what we would call *satires;* they made fun of ideas and people. The Athenians were accustomed to criticism of government leaders. Their satires often ridiculed politicians who tried to fool the people. Sometimes they praised leaders or their ideas by making fun of people who opposed them.

Aristophanes was the greatest writer of comedies. His play *Lysistrata* is sometimes performed today. It tells how the Athenian women, tired of having so few privileges and rights and of losing their husbands and sons in war, went on strike and took over the government. This idea was especially funny to the Athenians because of their low opinion of women.

Greek historians

The Greeks were the first people to take seriously the writing of history. Herodotus, whose name you have read several times, was

The famous Greek dramas are still drawing audiences. Nearly 2,400 years after the death of Sophocles, his Oedipus the King *was produced as a color movie. Notice the larger-than-life-size masks. Oedipus can be identified by his crown and scepter.*

the first great historian of the Golden Age. A great traveler, he visited Mesopotamia, Egypt, and Italy, and wrote his impressions. He also wrote the history of the Persian Wars. Herodotus was a charming writer and a wonderful storyteller. As noted on page 73, he sometimes exaggerated. He did not guarantee that his stories were true. In fact, he did not seem to care, provided they were interesting or amusing. And they are both interesting and amusing even to us today. He is called the Father of History, but since his time historians have tried to be more accurate in what they write.

The first really scientific historian was Thucydides, who wrote the sad story of the Peloponnesian War. (This was a civil war in Greece, as Chapter 8 will tell.) He wanted his history to be a guide to future statesmen, so he took care to make it accurate. If he could not check the truth of an interesting story, he did not write it.

Review of Chapter 7

People, places, and things

Identify: Pericles, Athena, Phidias, Praxiteles, Democritus, Aristophanes, Aeschylus, Sophocles, Euripides, Herodotus, Thucydides, Socrates, Plato, Aristotle, Hippocrates, the Parthenon, the Acropolis, Sophists.

Events in review

1. Name the three social classes of Athens. Describe the differences.
2. How did Pericles make Athens even more democratic than it was at the time of Cleisthenes?
3. What was the usual attitude of Greeks toward slavery? Did any Greeks disagree with the majority?
4. Why is the Periclean period of Athenian history known as "the Golden Age of Athens"?
5. Why did Socrates criticize the Sophists? What method of teaching did Socrates use?
6. "Athens was a city of contrasts." Show this statement correct by contrasting (a) homes with public buildings, (b) the position of a wealthy Athenian citizen with that of his slave, (c) the life of a nobleman with that of his wife.
7. Why was Thucydides a more scientific historian than Herodotus?
8. What subjects did Athenian boys study?
9. Did Athens have a form of universal military training?
10. Was trade important to Athens? Why?

Problems and projects

1. Did Athenians living in Athens in the Periclean Age have a greater cultural development than we have in America today? Give reasons for your answer.
2. Do you believe that the greatest Greek art was sculpture? Give reasons.
3. Which of the following made the greatest contributions to the life of *our* times: Socrates, Plato, Aristotle? Why did you select the one you did?
4. At what age did Athenian youths become citizens? Do you think this was too early an age for full citizenship? Have you heard or read any discussion about lowering the voting age in the United States?
5. Draw a plan of an Athenian house. Locate the various rooms.
6. Make a model of the Parthenon or another Greek building to scale.
7. Imagine yourself an Athenian woman. Describe your daily life. Compare the life of an Athenian woman with that of an Egyptian woman.
8. Imagine yourself an Athenian boy. Describe a typical school day. Contrast this with a day in your actual life in America.
9. If you have seen a modern production of a Greek play, write a brief description of it. Do you know of any plays written in modern times that use masks for the actors and a chorus like the Greek chorus?
10. To debate: The sentence imposed on Socrates was unjust.

Chapter 8   The Greek City-States Decline, but Greek Civilization Spreads

AS YOU HAVE LEARNED, Athens turned the Delian League into an Athenian Empire; then it came into conflict with Corinth and Sparta. In 431 B.C. a war broke out which, with brief intervals of peace, lasted twenty-seven years. It involved the whole Greek world and Persia as well; it left Greece in ruins. This war is called the Peloponnesian War because most of the fighting took place on that peninsula.

The Peloponnesian War

Athens tried to fight the war entirely on the sea where she was strongest. The Spartans invaded Attica, destroying fields and villages. The Athenian army and the entire population withdrew behind the Long Walls which protected the city and ran down to the seaport five miles away. The Spartans and their allies could not starve them out because Athens controlled the sea. However, a great plague broke out among the crowded Athenian population. Many people died, including the brilliant leader Pericles.

After that nothing went well for the Athe-

nians. Their leaders tried plans that looked clever, but nothing worked. The Spartans got help from Persia. Several Athenian fleets were lost and several armies defeated. Finally Athens surrendered. All Greece came under Spartan rule.

The Spartans proved even more harsh and selfish than the Athenians. Furthermore, Sparta lacked the men, money, and sea power to be a real ruler. Conditions were ripe for another civil war. Thebes, another Greek city-state, formed a league against Sparta. Aided by Persia, Athens, and other states, Thebes defeated Sparta and took the lead in Greece. But Theban rule was not successful, and the ruinous wars continued.

All the city-states realized that unity was necessary, but each of the leaders wanted to dominate any union that was formed. Each promised liberal, democratic rule, but gave tyranny. Many Greeks believed that union could come only under a foreign power. There seemed to be no possible outsider except Persia. However, the Persians had interfered to prevent unity, and most Greeks still distrusted them.

Macedonia conquers Greece
and spreads Greek civilization

From an unexpected direction Greek unity did finally come. Look at the maps on page 63 and on page 89. North of Greece and Thessaly is a mountainous land called Macedonia. It was then inhabited by a hardy, warlike people, closely related to the Greeks but much less civilized. They lived in small villages, each under a powerful noble. Macedonia had a king, but his power depended on his own ability and the help of the nobles. Most of the people were free peasant shepherds. They lived a herdsman's life, tending their flocks of sheep and goats. Fighting and hunting were really their main occupations.

●Philip of Macedon

In 359 B.C. a very remarkable young man came to the Macedonian throne. He is known as Philip of Macedon. In his youth he had been taken as a captive hostage to Thebes, where he spent three years. Philip learned and admired Greek ways, and learned the art of warfare from the greatest Theban general. He always kept his love and admiration for Greek culture.

Philip was determined to be a real king and to control the unruly Macedonian nobles and people. Instead of depending on the nobles to supply men for an army, he built up the first regular army in Macedonian history. It was the finest fighting unit between the time of the Assyrians and the development of the Roman legions.

After unifying his own kingdom, Philip extended his power by conquering the surrounding tribes. He increased his control of the Aegean coast by taking some Greek towns which Athens claimed as colonies. Then he turned south and began the task of unifying the Greek city-states under his rule.

Opinion about Philip was divided in Greece. In every city some men looked upon him as a savior who could assure Greece the

unity they could not get for themselves. Others opposed him as a menace to liberty. In Athens this opposition was led by Demosthenes, one of the greatest orators of all Athenian history.

Demosthenes used all his great powers of oratory to arouse the Athenians to the danger from Philip of Macedon. He attacked Philip bitterly in a series of speeches to the Assembly, and tried to get Athens to lead the Greeks once more in a fight for liberty. Today a speech which is a bitter attack on a person is called a *philippic,* from these speeches of Demosthenes. But times had changed in Athens since the Golden Age. Citizens had become more interested in money-making and pleasure than in serving the city. In spite of his great oratory, Demosthenes failed to arouse the Athenians. There was no united opposition to Macedonia.

Philip marched south with his army, conquering the Greek cities one by one. Some resisted and were defeated. Others were turned over to him by traitors. As he said: "No fortress is inaccessible if one can only introduce within it a mule laden with gold." When the Athenians did decide to fight, it was too late. Philip defeated them in a great battle and became master of all Greece.

But Greek unity was still not accomplished. Philip planned to make himself king of Greece, allowing some local self-government. He wanted Greek soldiers to join Macedonian troops in an invasion of Persia. Before these ideas could be put into effect, Philip died. His son and successor, Alexander, was only twenty.

●Alexander the Great

It did not seem likely the young Alexander would be able to carry out Philip's plans. But those who thought so were wrong. The son proved to be even more remarkable than the father. History knows him as Alexander the Great. It is said that he was so like his father that the two could never agree, and quarreled bitterly. However that may be, Philip did everything to give Alexander the best training and education possible. His military education was in the Macedonian army. Like Greek boys he was trained in gymnastics until he was a splendid athlete, with a vigorous body. And to train Alexander's mind Philip sent for the great Aristotle himself to be his tutor. Alexander's fine education made him a lifelong admirer of Greek culture.

When the time came for Alexander to command the army, he proved to be an even greater general than his father. His campaigns are considered among the greatest in history. Some of his battles were such masterpieces of tactics that they are still studied as models by army officers. He was strong and brave to the point of rashness. His dramatic acts in battle so captured the imagination of his troops that they were willing to die for him. Alexander began his military career by easily putting down rebellions in the Greek city-states and making himself master of Greece. Then he marched into Asia Minor and defeated a Persian army, conquering all Asia Minor and Syria. Next he invaded Egypt, meeting almost no resistance. From Egypt he moved into Mesopotamia, defeated another Persian army, and took control of the entire Fertile Crescent.

He was now ruler of a huge empire, but Alexander was still not satisfied. Beyond Persia lay India, the end of the world as it was then known. For four years he led his army to invade India. He met little resistance in going as far as the Indus River. He himself wanted to march on to the Ganges River, but his long-suffering army had had enough fighting. He was forced to turn and go back to Babylon. There, in the midst of a great victory celebration in 323 B.C., he became ill. In a few days he was dead of a fever. In thirteen years he had conquered all of the then-known world.

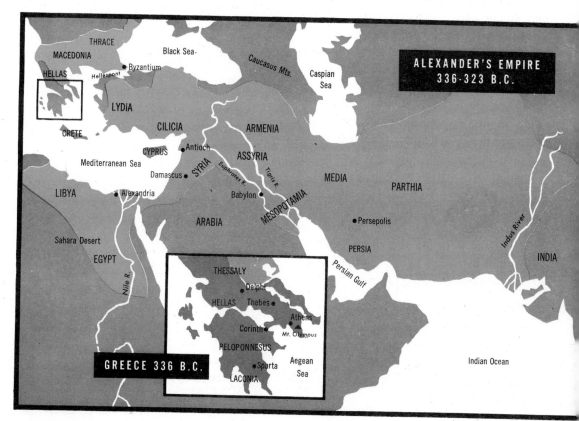

ALEXANDER'S EMPIRE
336-323 B.C.

GREECE 336 B.C.

Alexander's plan for his empire

Alexander the Great is famous as a general and conqueror, but he was even greater as a statesman. His plan was nothing less than a world empire, with himself at the head. He wanted to unite all peoples into one, combining the best of the cultures of Greece, Egypt, the Fertile Crescent, and India. Even in his short lifetime he was able to change the world. It is difficult to imagine what he might have done had he lived a normal time.

Alexander planned to accomplish his united world in two ways. The first was by founding new cities and rebuilding old cities to be the cultural centers of his empire. More than seventy new cities were built. Colonies of Greeks and Macedonians were established in each city. Alexandria, in Egypt, is one of the cities that Alexander founded over 2,000 years ago.

The second method aimed to create a united people. He did everything he could to encourage intermarriages between Macedonians, Greeks, Egyptians, and the peoples of the Near East. He himself married the daughter of the Persian king, and at times wore the robes of a Persian ruler. He took men of all religions into his army, or used them as officials in his government. He established a uniform money system for the whole empire to promote prosperity and expand trade, thus bringing the parts closer together economically.

When Alexander died, his plans for a world empire had not been completed. He left no successor, and the empire soon fell into three parts: (1) Egypt, (2) Syria, Mesopotamia, Macedonia, (3) Greece.

Leagues of city-states in Greece

Some of the Greek city-states tried a very interesting experiment after Alexander's death. They were trying to solve the problem of uniting without giving up their independence completely. Two leagues of city-states were formed. Each had a central government: a congress in which each state was represented. The congress was given power to tax and to raise an army from each state. It was limited to these powers; all other powers were kept by the individual states. Thus there was much local self-government, but there was also common government for common problems. This is called the *federal* principle of government.

The two Greek leagues did not last long. Neither Athens nor Sparta would join; so neither league accomplished its purpose. However, the principles of these two leagues were studied by the men who wrote the Constitution of the United States, for these men were trying to solve the same problem with the thirteen colonies. The Greek leagues provided a model for the American federal system of government.

Although Alexander's work was unfinished when he died, and his empire fell apart soon after, his influence was very great. The new cities he founded continued to spread Greek civilization and culture long after his death. The Mediterranean world had more unity of ideas, trade, and people than ever before. So great was his influence that the period for even two centuries after his death is known as the Hellenistic Age, or the Age of Alexander.

The Hellenistic Age of Alexander, 338–133 B.C.

Society and government

The Greeks called their peninsula Hellas, and themselves Hellenes. The Golden Age culture of the Greek city-states is called Hellenic. During the Age of Alexander Greek culture was mixed with all the cultures of the Near East. Greek was the basic strain. Educated people everywhere spoke a modified Greek language. But the cultures of Egypt and the Fertile Crescent added much to the culture that the Greeks themselves had developed. This mingled culture was called Hellenistic.

But in spite of the spread of Greek culture, the Greek idea of self-government did not spread through the other territories. In Egypt and the Near East the absolute governments of the king-god continued. Even in Greece itself there was less democracy and a lower ideal of citizenship. The wealthy and the aristocrats controlled the governments. Men came to value wealth and personal fame more than service to the state. They spent more money on fine homes than on public buildings. Greece was not prosperous, and many ambitious Greeks went out to the new commercial cities. There they became the ruling class. Most of the wealthy city-dwellers adopted Greek ways and spoke the Greek language. The mass of the people everywhere kept their own language and customs.

● *The economy*

Throughout the world of Greek culture, both industry and agriculture were largely owned by the ruler or the government. Privately owned land was usually held in large estates by wealthy aristocrats. The work was done by slaves or by poorly paid free labor. There was a small class of very wealthy people and a very large class of miserably poor people. They worked hard for long hours just to be able to live.

Commerce was the most profitable activity. The main centers were Alexandria, in Egypt; Rhodes, on the island of Rhodes off the coast of Turkey; and Antioch, in Syria. Trade routes now connected the whole Mediterranean world, and India as well. Ships were bigger and better.

The new cities were the wonders of the Hellenistic world. They were carefully planned and laid out, with straight streets. They had market squares, indoor theaters, gymnasiums, and public baths. Public buildings were larger than those in the Greek cities. Homes, especially of the wealthy, were im-

A famous example of sculpture from the Hellenistic period. This statue, produced about 100 B.C., depicts an event in the story of the Trojan War. According to the legend, a Trojan priest named Laocoön warned his countrymen not to trust the wooden horse the Greeks left outside the city. Laocoön and his sons were killed by serpents. The Trojans interpreted this as a punishment sent by the gods for refusing to trust the wooden horse. They took the horse into Troy. The Greek soldiers hidden inside the horse climbed out and opened the city gates. The Greek army rushed in and captured Troy.

proved. They had elaborate furniture, carpets, hangings, and even a private water supply and drain pipes.

Alexandria, in Egypt, was the greatest city, with a population of from 600,000 to 1,000,-000. It was a center of art, science, literature, and philosophy as well as commerce. Its library contained 750,000 volumes on papyrus rolls. Until the 1800's no modern city could equal it in size, wealth, or planning.

Education

Children of free parents, even some girls, received free elementary education in reading, writing, music, and literature. Higher education was still private, for fees. The principal higher school was called the gymnasium, a school for children of purely Greek descent. There they studied reading, writing, literature, music, rhetoric, philosophy, and physical training. University education as we know it today was given mostly in museums and libraries.

The Pharos (lighthouse) at Alexandria was built around 300 B.C. as a beacon for the harbor entrance. This structure was 370 feet high (nearly one third the height of the Empire State Building in New York City). The Pharos was one of the seven wonders of the ancient world (see page 43 for one of the others).

Philosophy

The philosophers of the Hellenistic Age are not considered as great as the thinkers of the Golden Age. There were three kinds, or schools, of philosophy.

The Cynics. These philosophers taught that men should seek virtue only. They scorned pleasure, wealth, or social position. The most famous Cynic was Diogenes, about whom there are many stories. One is that he was lying in the sunshine when Alexander the Great came by. The conqueror stood looking down at the philosopher and asked him if there was anything he could do for him. "Yes," replied the Cynic, "stand out of my sunshine."

The Stoics. Zeno, the leading Stoic philosopher, believed that the world was full of divine spirit, and that there was some of it in the soul of every man. At death the soul rejoined this universal spirit. All men were therefore brothers. The best life was one spent in working for the welfare of others. Reason, not emotions, should be the guide to conduct. Man must learn to accept whatever the laws of nature bring, and to be indifferent to grief, fear, pain, and pleasure. The Stoic philosophy had great influence later on the thinking of Romans and Christians.

The Epicureans. Epicurus taught that the aim of life was to seek pleasure and avoid pain. Pleasure, to him, was intellectual, not the physical pleasure of the senses. After his death, however, his followers came to seek the pleasures of the senses and appetites. Their motto was "Eat, drink, and be merry, for tomorrow we die." Today the word *epicurean* means a person who indulges his senses and appetites.

Mathematics and physics

The Greeks developed geometry and trigonometry far beyond the place to which Egyptians and Sumerians had carried them. Archimedes found ways to measure spheres,

A model of a compound pulley, one of the many inventions credited to Archimedes. As students of physics know, a block and tackle arrangement enables a man (or an engine) to lift heavy weights. Modern blocks have sheaves (wheels) instead of simple holes, but the principle is the same as that discovered by Archimedes.

lever, and built many machines in which levers were used. The compound pulley (the block and tackle) and cogged wheels to be used as gears were other inventions. He developed the law of floating bodies, or what is called today specific gravity.

● *Medicine*

Hellenistic scientists added greatly to the medical work of Hippocrates. The best study of medicine and surgery was done in Alexandria. The knowledge of anatomy, the structure of the body, was greatly advanced by dissection of the bodies of executed criminals. Alexandrian scientists discovered the nervous system. They learned that the brain is the center of the nervous system. Delicate surgery was performed, and anesthetics were used to deaden pain. Much was learned about the circulation of the blood and about the heart as the center of the circulatory system. Galen wrote many volumes summing up all medical knowledge. For over a thousand years Galen was the great authority on medicine, as Aristotle and Euclid were in science and mathematics.

● *Astronomy and geography*

In astronomy the Hellenistic scientists combined all the knowledge of Egyptians, Sumerians, Babylonians, and Chaldeans, and added to it. They used mathematics to calculate the position of stars and planets from day to day. One astronomer tried to prove that the earth and other planets revolve around the sun, but his theory was not accepted. Another man measured the solar year and the lunar month almost exactly, and also developed a way of measuring latitude and longitude. Ptolemy of Alexandria wrote a book on astronomy that was still used in Columbus' time.

Hellenistic geographers knew that the earth was round. A scientist at Alexandria calculated the diameter of the earth with an error of less than one per cent. He also claimed that

cones, and cylinders. The greatest work was done by Euclid. He developed geometry into a system by showing how the theorems develop logically from one another. He wrote a textbook which was used for over a thousand years, and is the basis for today's geometry books.

Archimedes was the greatest all-around scientist of Hellenistic times, and was especially important in developing physics. He used mathematics to explain the principle of the men could reach India by sailing westward around the world. It was this idea that influenced Columbus sixteen centuries later. Ptolemy made a map of the world showing latitude and longitude—a map Columbus used.

● Characteristics of Greek science

There are two amazing things about Greek progress in science. The first is that they learned so much without instruments for observing and measuring. They had not found the principle of the lens; so they had no microscopes or telescopes. They did not know of the compass, nor had they any mechanical means of measuring time accurately. They lacked delicate balances for measurement of weight. It seems fair to say that modern scientists are not better thinkers than the Greeks. They just have better instruments.

The second striking thing is that the Greeks made no effort to apply their scientific knowledge in practical ways, except perhaps in medicine and geography. They valued knowledge for its own sake, and were not interested in inventions or mechanical progress. Archimedes' clever inventions were only models. He considered them unworthy of the noble profession of philosophy and therefore regarded his inventions as interesting toys and nothing else. It was, you remember, a civilization based on slavery. Labor-saving inventions and machines would be of greatest benefit to the slaves. Scholars did not think it necessary or fitting to try to improve the lot of slaves or to make slavery unnecessary.

The Grecian heritage

Heritage means "that which we inherit," or that which is passed on from preceding generations. Greece has been called the foundation of western civilization. Let us try to sum up the heritage passed on to us from the civilization of the Greeks. The first thing to be said is that our debt is intellectual and not material. The Greeks gave us ideas rather than things such as tools or machines. The summary that follows does not try to arrange the Greek contributions in the order of their importance. Each person must do that for himself.

● Language

The importance of the Greek language cannot be overestimated. You know that the Greeks perfected the Phoenician alphabet by adding letters for vowel sounds. It is this alphabet, as adapted by the Romans, that we now use. The Greek language was used throughout the Hellenistic world. All the books of the New Testament, with the possible exception of one, were originally written in Greek. It was the language of the early Christians. In Rome it was fashionable to write in Greek. It was the language of the Eastern Roman Empire with its capital at Constantinople. Today, you can hardly write or talk about government without using Greek terms: politics, political, democracy, aristocracy, monarchy. Almost every term used in medicine comes from the Greek. For example, the Greek ending *itis* meant "an inflammation." How many diseases can you think of whose names end in *-itis?*

● Philosophy

To the Greeks, philosophy meant "love of wisdom." They tried to find the meaning of a good life—to learn how to gain the greatest happiness here and now. They believed that true happiness was something more than just having food, worldly goods, and security. Sheep could have those things. To the Greek thinkers, true happiness was in the mind, in mental activities, and such activities are possible only by reasoning human beings. The great idea was moderation: "all things in proportion"; "a sound mind in a sound body."

The ideas of Socrates, Plato, Aristotle, the Stoics, and the Epicureans are not dead things, to be found only in books. They live today in the minds of men. We all give much thought to the question of what makes a good life. Whether we know it or not, our thinking is influenced by Greek ideas.

Art and architecture

In architecture and sculpture the Greeks have never been surpassed. They excelled in the use of color and form. To them beauty was found in balance, proportion, moderation. And beauty was a thing to be lived with constantly.

Literature

Greek historical writings are read today. Greek dramas are read and performed. You would be surprised to know how many of the ideas, plots, and themes used in modern writing were first used by the Greeks. In almost every kind of writing except the novel the form and method of organization were developed by the Greeks.

Government

The idea of representative, democratic self-government was developed by the Greeks. In spite of some weaknesses which we recognize, the Greeks furnished the model for democracies to follow. The writers of the Constitution of the United States adopted the federal principle from the Greek leagues during the Hellenistic Age. Plato and Aristotle produced ideas about government that have influenced all later thinking. To us, the greatest idea that they contributed is that the individual, the citizen, has dignity, worth, and importance.

Science

The great gift of the Greeks in the field of science was the development of a scientific method—a way of thinking. The Greek mind had an eager curiosity. It wanted to know the reason for and the meaning of things. Aristotle led the way by showing that if enough facts were gathered, arranged, and classified in a system, the mind could then

An example of Greek art from the fifth century B.C. This relief of a girl holding pigeons was part of the decoration on a grave.

discover meanings and reasons. The writings of Aristotle, Euclid, Galen, and Ptolemy were studied in universities for over a thousand years. Some of them are studied today. The Oath of Hippocrates still gives us our ideal for medical practice. We have not surpassed the Greek scientists in thinking, but in our instruments and our ability and willingness to apply scientific knowledge to the solution of practical, everyday problems.

Review of Chapter 8

People, places, and things

Identify: Philip, Demosthenes, Diogenes, Zeno, Epicurus, Euclid, Galen, Archimedes, Alexander.

Locate: Hellas, Laconia, Peloponnesus, Thessaly, Macedonia, Cyprus, Thrace, Chios, Rhodes, Melos, Alexandria, Byzantium, Antioch, the Indus River, Babylon.

Events in review

1. Give three reasons for the decline of the Greek city-states.
2. What means did the Macedonians use to conquer Greece?
3. What famous Greek philosopher served as teacher for a future ruler of Greece?
4. Why are the Greek leagues of city-states of particular interest to us in the United States?
5. Why is the period of two centuries following Alexander's death called the Age of Alexander?

6. What was a gymnasium in the Hellenistic age? What activities went on in the gymnasium?
7. Describe briefly the beliefs of the Cynics, the Stoics, the Epicureans.
8. Name three great inventions or discoveries by Hellenistic scientists.

Problems and projects

1. Do you think the Greeks were wise in advocating, "Nothing in excess, and everything in proportion or moderation"? Explain the meaning of this advice as applied in daily life.
2. Make a map on which you show, in different colors, the boundaries of (a) the Egyptian Empire, (b) the Persian Empire, (c) the Empire of Alexander.
3. Make a list of twenty words now in everyday use that came to us from Greek civilization. Write a brief note on how each term gets its meaning.

Review of Greek Civilization

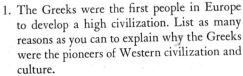

1. The Greeks were the first people in Europe to develop a high civilization. List as many reasons as you can to explain why the Greeks were the pioneers of Western civilization and culture.
2. In Egypt and the Fertile Crescent strong "king-gods" ruled over people who had no voice in their government. In what ways was government in ancient Greece different? Can you account for the differences?
3. Our political ideas are much closer to those of the ancient Greeks than to those of any other early people. In what ways are our ideas like those of the Greeks?

4. In what ways do our political ideas differ from those of the Greeks? Can you think of reasons for likenesses and differences?
5. What were the main reasons for the failure of the Greeks to unite their states? What were the results of this failure?
6. Can you think of any ways in which the condition of the modern world is like the situation of the early Greek city-states? What lessons can we learn from the Greek failure to unite? Explain carefully.
7. Are there any men in the twentieth century who might be compared with Philip of Macedon and Alexander the Great? Name

any you can think of, and explain why you think they are like Philip and Alexander.

8. Think back over all the different countries you have studied so far in this book. In which one of them would you have most liked to live? Why?

9. It has been said that one thing we learn from studying Greece is that ideas (in literature, philosophy, art, science, religion) are more important than military conquests. Do you agree? (Consider, for example, Assyria, Persia, Egypt, and the Hebrews in addition to Greece and the Empire of Alexander.)

10. Compare education in the Hellenistic Age with education in (a) Egypt, (b) the United States today.

11. Make a table or chart with the following headings: (a) architecture and art, (b) government, (c) language, (d) literature, (e) philosophy, (f) science. Under each heading, list things that are part of our heritage from the Greeks.

Books about the Greeks

Botsford, George Willis, Robinson, Charles A. Jr. *Hellenic History* (Macmillan, 1956). Greek civilization from the Bronze Age to the Roman conquest.

*Breasted, James H. *Conquest of Civilization* (Harper, 1938). A number of interesting chapters on the Greeks. Don't miss this fine book!

Coolidge, Olivia E. *Trojan War* (Houghton, 1952). A highly recommended retelling of the Trojan War.

*Davis, William S. *Day in Old Athens* (Allyn & Bacon, 1914). A readable and lively account of Athenian life in the mid-fourth century B.C. Varied and interesting information about Greek life in general.

Gardner, Helen. *Art Through the Ages* (Harcourt, Brace, 1949). A useful book, with four chapters on Greek architecture and arts. Beautifully illustrated.

Gunther, John. *Alexander the Great* (Random House, 1953). The author recounts the young Macedonian's brief and glorious years as king, giving us a sense of the interaction of Alexander's personality and the historical events of his day.

Hagedorn, Hermann. *Book of Courage* (Winston, 1942). Includes an exciting short biography of Socrates.

*Books marked with a star (*) are easy reading.

*Hall, Jennie. *Buried Cities* (Macmillan, 1922). Accounts of the excavations of Mycenae, Olympia, and other Greek sites.

Household, Geoffrey. *Exploits of Xenophon* (Random House, 1955). A Greek army's heroic and disciplined retreat after being defeated by the Persians.

Kieran, John. *Story of the Olympic Games* (Lippincott, 1952). A very readable account by a noted American sports writer.

*Lamb, Harold. *Alexander of Macedon* (Doubleday, 1946). A stirring account of a most interesting man.

Mason, Cora Catherine. *Socrates, the Man Who Dared to Ask* (Beacon Press, 1953). This book relates Socrates to his period and shows his effect on his times.

*Miller, Walter. *Greece and the Greeks* (Macmillan, 1941). A pictorial history of all phases of Greek life; a fine source for reports.

*Mills, Dorothy. *Book of the Ancient Greeks* (Putnam, 1925). A simply-written, well-illustrated, and very useful general history of Greece to the time of the Roman conquest.

*Quennell, C. H. B., and Quennell, Marjorie. *Everyday Things in Ancient Greece* (Putnam, 1954). A picture of ancient Greece, its religion, sports, houses, clothes, schools, music, travel, theatre, and warfare.

*Tappan, E. M. *Story of the Greek People* (Houghton Mifflin, 1947). Written in a fine, easy style.

SENATVS POPVLVSQVE ROMAN

Part Three ROME RULES THE WESTERN WORLD

Take a look at the time chart on pages 100–101. Note that shortly before the Age of Pericles began in Greece a new republic was established at Rome in Italy. Over the centuries Rome grew to be a great power. By the time the Empire of Alexander the Great was breaking up, the Romans were strong enough to rule the Mediterranean world. Under Augustus Caesar (pictured at the top of this page) Rome became an empire. The Romans held the Mediterranean area together under one government for nearly five centuries.

Roman civilization made many contributions to the world. One of the greatest was Roman law. The picture on the facing page shows a Roman magistrate hearing a case. From the Romans we get one of our basic ideas about justice—that a person accused of a crime is innocent unless he can be proved guilty.

The background of this picture tells more about Roman culture. The room suggests the splendor of Roman public buildings. Notice the architecture. The Romans borrowed columns from the Greek style, but they used vaulted domes and arches that the Greeks did not know how to construct.

These details, of course, suggest only a few of the things to watch for as you read the next three chapters. Chapter 9 tells of the Roman Republic, which finally became a military dictatorship and then an empire. Chapter 10 tells of strong emperors who kept their world at peace for more than two centuries. This still stands as the longest period of peace in world history. Under later rulers, men of less ability, the Roman government proved unable to preserve peace and prosperity. At last the empire decayed and fell apart.

Chapter 11 introduces a great new force in history, Christianity. Jesus was born during the reign of Augustus, in territory ruled by Rome. The Christian religion spread through many parts of the Roman Empire. In spite of persecutions, the Church grew in strength as the empire declined. When the government at Rome broke up, western Europe entered what is called the Dark Ages. The Christian Church was the one great institution to stand throughout this period.

Part Three

ROME

WESTERN EUROPE

500 B.C.	**509** Roman Republic established
400 B.C. **390** Gauls sack Rome	
300 B.C.	**270** Rome holds all Italy south of Rubicon
	264 First Punic War
	250 Roman Republic fairly democratic
	218 Second Punic War begins
	216 Hannibal: Battle of Cannae
200 B.C.	
	146 Carthage finally conquered
	Rome conquers Macedonia and Greece
	133 Rome takes Asia Minor. Beginning of civil wars
100 B.C.	
'50 Caesar conquers Gaul	**44** Julius Caesar assassinated
	29 End civil wars and Republic
	27 Augustus becomes Emperor
A.D.	
	14 Augustus dies
	50 Paul: missionary work spreads Christianity
	96-180 Good Emperors
	98-117 Trajan: Empire grows to greatest extent
100 A.D. **122-127** Hadrian's wall built in Britain	
	180-235 Commodus: the Severi
200 A.D.	**235-285** Barrack-Room Emperors
	284-305 Diocletian reigns
300 A.D.	**313** Edict of Milan
	324-337 Constantine reigns
	378 Visigoths win battle of Adrianople
	380 Christianity the official religion of Empire
	395 Final division of Empire, East and West
400 A.D.	
451 Attila and Huns defeated at Châlons	**451** Huns defeated at Châlons
476 Dark Ages begin	**476** Romulus Augustus deposed, Western Empire ends
500 A.D.	

GREECE AND NEAR EAST	INDIA	CHINA
79-404 Athenian Empire 59-404 Peloponnesian Wars	Darius annexes Indus region to Persian Empire	
38 Macedonia conquers Greece 32-331 Macedonia conquers Egypt and Persia 38-133 Hellenistic Age	326 Alexander reaches the Indus	
87? Birth of Archimedes	273-232 Asoka: the spread of Buddhism	228 Great wall begun 202 B. C.-214 A. D. Han dynasty:
		High point of ancient Chinese civilization Paper and ink invented Merit system for civil service begun
46 Rome conquers Greece 33 Rome takes Asia Minor		
1 Rome conquers Egypt ? Birth of Jesus Christ		Buddhism introduced
9? Jesus crucified		
0 Titus conquers Jerusalem and destroys the temple		
14? Trajan conquers Mesopotamia		
		214 End of Han dynasty
30 Constantinople the Eastern capital 78 Adrianople: Visigoths defeat Romans	300-535 Gupta dynasty: high civilization	
00-1100 Constantinople the greatest city of Europe 29-534 Code of Justinian		

101

Chapter 9

Rome Conquers and Rules

ITALY is the central peninsula of the three in the Mediterranean region—the Greek, the Italian, and the Iberian (Spain and Portugal). See on the map how it resembles a boot, with its top in the Alpine Mountains to the north, its toe and heel in the sea to the south. Notice that it cuts the Mediterranean almost in half. The toe is only two miles from the large island of Sicily; Sicily is only eighty miles from the African coast. Italy is the heart and center of the Mediterranean region, well located to dominate the area.

The Alpine Mountains set Italy apart from the rest of Europe. They seem good protection against land invasions, but the protection is not perfect. The mountains have a gentle slope to the north and a sharp drop to the south, and there are many passes through them. The people of Italy had to be fighters to avoid being overrun by invaders.

The Italian peninsula itself is divided by the Apennine Mountains, which run the full length of the boot. These mountains are not so rugged as those in Greece. Hence the geography of Italy was not such an obstacle to political unity as was the case in Greece.

Two-thirds of the Italian peninsula is foothill and mountain country, useful only as pasture. Except in the Po Valley and the western plain, the soil is sandy and easily washed away. Italy's temperate climate and plentiful winter rains are enough for crops of grain, vegetables, olives, grapes, and other fruits.

In the early days Italy and the nearby islands had some good natural resources, such as copper and iron. There were forests on the foothills and mountains. During Roman times the trees were cut for ships and building. The cutting of the forests allowed more rapid erosion of the sandy soil. Italy's rivers are short and shallow. Most of them are blocked at the mouth by soil washed down from the higher land, making the surrounding region swampy. Throughout history the peninsula has had epidemics of malaria and other fevers because of these marshes.

Although Italy has a long coastline, it has few good harbors. On the east the mountains rise close to the Adriatic Sea, so there are few good harbors along that coast. Along the west coast, where the land slopes more gradually, there are a number of seaports. When Rome was rising to power, the civilized part of the world was to the east of Italy, in Greece, Egypt, and the Near East. It seemed as though Italy turned her back on civilization and faced the lands of the barbarians to the north and west.

Look again at the map and find the city of Rome, in west-central Italy. It is on the Tiber, one of the short Italian rivers. The city is built on hills surrounding the river. These are the Seven Hills from which a simple farming people spread out to rule the entire Mediterranean world. The city is not at the mouth of the river, but some twenty miles inland. In early days this gave protection from pirates. There is a port, Ostia, at the mouth. For many centuries it could be used only by the smallest ships, because Tiber floods had formed a sand bar. Early Romans were not much interested in shipping.

However, the location of Rome was important for land trade. It was built where the waters of the Tiber are especially shallow and where a small island in the river makes the best crossing for many miles. Rome was the center of land trade routes which ran in all directions.

Early peoples of Italy

Even during the Old Stone Age there were people living in Italy. New Stone Age culture appeared there before 3000 B.C. After 2000 B.C. the peninsula was invaded from the north many times. Groups of people from the northern grasslands, like the invaders of Greece, moved into Italy. About 1000 B.C. the invasions increased in number. Many groups entered and settled in various parts of the peninsula. The most important in history were the Latins, who settled in the west-central plains region called Latium.

● The Etruscans

The Etruscans, a group of eastern people from the Aegean Islands or Asia Minor, entered Italy after 900 B.C. They conquered and held the coastal plains to the north of the Tiber. These Etruscans had a culture far superior to that of the natives or the Latins. They made fine clothing and jewelry, good metal work, pottery, terra cotta, and beautiful

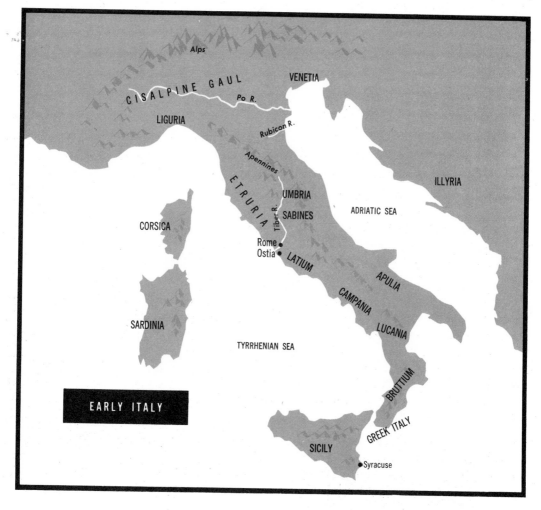

EARLY ITALY

furniture. Their written language we have not yet learned to read.

For a time it seemed that the Etruscans might conquer and rule all of Italy. They gained control of the north, ruling the Latins for more than a century. Then fortune turned against the Etruscans. They were conquered and disappeared into the mixed population of the region.

The Etruscan culture lived on, however, through its influence on the Romans. From the Etruscans the early farmers of Rome and the Latin plains learned how to pave streets, how to drain the marshes and sewers, and how to use the arch and the vaulted dome. The arch and the dome became typical of Roman building.

There were also Greeks in early Italy. Greek colonies in southern Italy and Sicily became city-states, as disunited and quarrelsome as those of the homeland. But their high culture greatly influenced the Romans, who adopted their alphabet, parts of their religion, and much of their culture.

The last of the early people to come to Italy were the Carthaginians. The Phoenicians, those great traders of early times, had established a colony at Carthage in north-central Africa. Like the mother country Carthage became a commercial power, holding territory and establishing colonies in the western Mediterranean. She had no colonies on the Italian peninsula, but had some on nearby Sicily, Sardinia, and Corsica.

The early Roman Republic

When the Latins settled in Latium, about 1000 B.C., they built villages on the Seven Hills. In time the villages were united into a city, one of many cities on the Latin plain of western Italy. For a time this city of Rome was a kingdom under Etruscan rule. In 509 B.C. the Romans drove out the Etruscans and set up a republic.

The early Romans were democratic, with little class distinction. They were farmers, and even the wealthiest men worked in the fields. No one was very rich, no one was miserably poor. They lived simply and ate simple meals, the main dish being a porridge of wheat or oats.

As time went by, Roman society became less democratic. Some families gained control of large amounts of land. A wealthy and powerful aristocratic class grew up—the *patricians*. All other citizens were called *plebeians*. They were taxed, forced to fight, sold into slavery for debt, and forbidden to marry patricians. Plebeians could not even know

A Roman soldier of the later days of the republic. This statue shows the arms and armor of the legions.

what the laws were, for they were unwritten. Laws were stated and applied by judges, who were patricians.

During the first century and a half of the republic, Rome had frequent wars with her neighbors. By making demands at strategic times, and by revolts, the plebeians found many opportunities to increase their powers. They won representation in the government. The laws were written down on wooden tablets known as the Twelve Tables. Intermarriage of patricians and plebeians was permitted. The amount of land a man could own was limited by law. By 250 B.C. the republic had become fairly democratic.

●The government

Three groups made up the government:

1. *The Assembly of Centuries.* Citizens were grouped according to military equipment, which really meant wealth. Patricians controlled it, but its importance decreased as the plebeians gained power.
2. *The Assembly of Tribes.* Citizens were grouped into thirty-five tribes according to their original residence. Plebeians controlled this assembly. It elected officials called Tribunes, and gained power to make some laws.
3. *The Senate.* Three hundred members made up the Roman Senate. They were chosen for life by the consuls from a list of qualified patricians. The Senate elected officials, passed laws, helped administer the government, and sometimes acted as a court. In the long run it was the most important and powerful governing body.

The officials who ran the government were called magistrates. Four kinds of officials had *imperium,* the power to command:

1. *Consuls.* Two patricians, elected for one-year terms by the Senate. They were chief executives and army commanders. Each could veto acts of the other.

2. *Praetors.* Patricians, elected by the Senate to be judges. They were very important because judges made much of the law.
3. *Censors.* Patricians, elected by the Senate. They registered people according to their wealth for taxes and membership in the Assembly of Centuries. They made the lists from which Senators were chosen. They let contracts and acted as moral guardians of the people.
4. *The Dictator.* A patrician, nominated by the consuls and elected by the Senate in time of need. He had absolute power for a term limited to six months.

The *Tribunes* were the most important officials *without* the power to command. There were ten Tribunes, elected annually by the Assembly of Tribes, over which they presided. They could not succeed themselves. They had to be plebeians. They could veto any act of any magistrate. (The Latin word *veto* means "I forbid.") This veto power protected the interests of the plebeians against any possible dictatorial actions by the patricians.

●The family

The family was the most important unit in Roman society. It was a larger group than our families. It included all unmarried children, married sons and their families, and all dependents. The father had absolute authority, including powers of life and death. He conducted the religious ceremonies, made all decisions, and looked after the education of the sons. In the fields he taught the boys farming and in the Forum, where the citizens met, he taught them the duties of citizenship. The mother gave instruction in reading, writing, and arithmetic. Roman women were much more honored than Greek women. The wife and mother was highly respected. She managed the household, did the buying, and shared with her husband the entertainment of guests.

The Romans were a very conservative people. They followed the customs and traditions of their ancestors. Their education aimed more at good habits than at knowledge. The children read, or were told, stories that stressed the virtues of loyalty, duty, bravery, and patriotism. They were trained to be modest, sober, silent, and, above all, obedient. They respected and obeyed authority, whether of their father or of the government.

● The army

The army was another great force in training the Roman citizen. Every man was in the militia, subject to call when needed. In the early days men fought without pay and furnished their own arms. Later, the army became much more tightly organized and highly trained. The most important unit was the legion. The strength of a legion varied from 4,500 to 6,000 men. In the days of the Republic, a usual composition was 3,000 heavy infantry, 1,200 lightly armed infantry, and 300 cavalry. A soldier of the heavy infantry is shown on page 104. Because of fine organization and training and the high morale of individual soldiers the Roman legions defeated even the great Macedonian army.

The Roman army was a citizen army. For many centuries only citizens could fight in the legions, though non-citizens could fight as auxiliaries. Discipline was strict and absolute, enforced by the soldiers themselves. If a man neglected his duty or showed that he was a coward, he was beaten and stoned by his comrades. Even if he escaped death, he could not return home. During battle a man who lost his weapons, especially his shield, was suspected of cowardice. He was punished only by public opinion, but it was a dreaded punishment. Many a man unfortunate enough to lose his weapons would throw himself into the enemy ranks, either to recover them or die, rather than face the jeers of his comrades. No man could be a candidate for high office without ten years army service.

● Religion

The early Romans believed that every force and process of nature was the expression of a spirit which had neither form nor sex. Man depended on these spirits. He must observe all the rituals and make all the sacrifices due each spirit that affected his life.

The spirits of the home were the most important. The *Lares* were guardians of the farm and fortune; the *Penates* were the guardians of the storeroom. *Janus* was guardian of the doorway and kept out evil spirits. *Vesta,* guardian of fire and hearth, was the center of family worship, most important of all. Next in importance to the spirits of the home were those that governed every part of farm life. Special festivals were held to assure the preparation of the ground, the sowing and growth of the seed, the gathering and storing of the grain. In all, there were forty-five farm and field festivals during the year.

These early religious ideas changed as the Romans came into contact with other peoples. Under Etruscan influence, Romans came to think of their spirits as having human forms and qualities. They also tried to learn the god's will by observing the entrails of animals or the flight of birds. This was called "taking the auspices." Good signs were called *auspicious,* a word with the same meaning today.

Rome's many wars brought another change in the religion. Romans had to be concerned with success in war as well as in farming. In March, month of Mars, god of war, there were great rituals to prepare for the opening of campaigns. In October, when the coming of winter ended the campaigns, there were ceremonies to purify soldiers from the taint of blood and contact with strange spirits. This was very different from the old family religion. It had become a state religion, with temples, priests, ceremonies, and processions.

Some of the old spirits remained important in the new state religion. Vesta, besides guarding hearth and fire, became guardian of the safety and prosperity of Rome itself. A great temple was built in her honor. Six maidens were chosen to be her priestesses. They promised to remain unmarried for thirty years, dedicating their lives to seeing that the sacred fire in the temple never died out. These Vestal Virgins were held in the highest honor and respect.

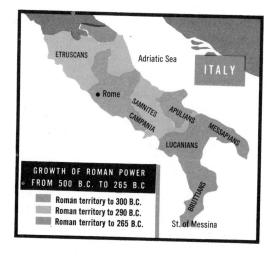

GROWTH OF ROMAN POWER
FROM 500 B.C. TO 265 B.C

Roman territory to 300 B.C.
Roman territory to 290 B.C.
Roman territory to 265 B.C.

Expansion of the Roman Republic

•Expansion in Italy, 506–270 B.C.

When the Romans formed the republic, Rome was only one among many small city-states on the Latin plain, surrounded by people who were often hostile. During the next two centuries the Romans fought many wars against their neighbors, usually to remove some nuisance or threat from their frontiers. When they conquered a threatening neighbor, they kept control of the territory so that they would not be disturbed again.

By the early part of the third century B.C. Rome held much of northern and all of central Italy. In the south the Greek states were quarreling among themselves. One side begged help from Rome, the other from a Greek city-state—so Rome conquered and then annexed the Greek colonies. By 270 B.C. Roman territory included all Italy south of the Rubicon River on the northeast coast.

The Po Valley, north of the Rubicon, was held by the Gauls, a people who were spread over most of Europe as far as the North Sea and the English Channel.

The people of some conquered towns were given Roman citizenship; others were merely made allies. Allies kept much self-government and had the protection of Roman law, but Rome controlled the allies' relations with other cities and countries. Also, they were required to furnish troops for war. However, even though the rights and privileges of Roman citizenship were given to other people, citizens could vote only in Rome. Thus great numbers of citizens were not represented in the government. Italy became a great city-state under Rome.

•Rome versus Carthage, 264–146 B.C.

With so much territory and so many new people, the Romans now faced new problems. They had to protect the entire Italian coast against invaders, and defend Italian commerce. Their commerce brought them into contact with Carthage, largest and most powerful city of the central Mediterranean. It had colonies in Sicily, Corsica, Sardinia, and Spain. With its many merchant ships and a great navy to protect them, Carthage was then the world's greatest sea power. Its people boasted that the Mediterranean was a Carthaginian lake, in which no one could wash his hands without their permission.

After Rome took southern Italy, Carthage feared that the Romans would try to take Sicily, with its Carthaginian colonies and markets. The Romans feared that the Carthaginian navy would close the Adriatic Sea and the narrow Strait of Messina between Italy and Sicily. War could probably have been avoided, but neither tried very hard—so war came. It was really a series of three wars which lasted with intervals from 264 to 146 B.C. Rome called them the Punic Wars, because the Latin word for Phoenician was *Punic.*

The "armored division" of Hannibal's army. Their war elephants helped the Carthaginians to defeat many Roman armies. However, in the Battle of Zama (shown here), the Romans under Scipio Africanus won in spite of having some of their ranks broken by the charging elephants.

The opponents were well matched. Rome had the better army, Carthage the better fleet. Carthage had more territory, but Roman lands were more compact and easily defended. Carthage had the larger population; Romans were more loyal. At first Carthaginian military commanders were more skillful, but Rome finally found generals who could win.

The first Punic War

The first war lasted twenty-five years. It went against the Romans until they built a fleet, copying a captured Carthaginian ship. The Romans used land tactics on the sea. They equipped their ships with swinging "boarding bridges." A Roman ship would ram a Carthaginian ship and let down the bridge so that heavily armed Roman soldiers could cross and take the enemy. The Carthaginian navy was defeated, after which a Roman army invaded Africa and defeated a Carthaginian army.

Carthage sued for peace, paid a large money indemnity, and gave up Sicily, Sardinia, and Corsica. Shortly afterward Rome pushed north in Italy and took the Po Valley by defeating the Gauls. To get relief from pirates she also took the eastern Adriatic coast. Thus Rome now ruled Italy, the islands, and the eastern coast of the Adriatic Sea.

The second war—Hannibal

The second Punic War was begun by the Carthaginian Hannibal, one of the great generals of all times. He planned to take Rome by surprise, invading from the north. He hoped that Rome's allies would revolt and join him.

Hannibal took his great army of infantry, cavalry, and armored elephants on the long march overland from Spain. Unfortunately he began the difficult job of crossing the Alps in the autumn. It was truly a dreadful crossing, and he lost nearly half his army there. Just as winter began he led the half-starved, half-frozen remainder of his men down into the Po Valley.

It was a strange war. The Roman armies were no match for Hannibal. He defeated several of them, after which they shut themselves up in their fortified cities. Only a few of the Roman allies revolted and joined him. Hannibal had no siege equipment, so he could not capture the fortified Roman cities. For thirteen years he ranged up and down Italy, but could not provoke the Romans to come out and fight.

Then Rome turned the tables. A Roman army invaded Africa and threatened Carthage. Hannibal's government ordered him home to defend the city. In Africa he finally met his master, the Roman Scipio. Hannibal and his army were defeated, and once more Carthage asked for peace. Again she had to pay a huge indemnity in money. She gave up her Spanish colonies and most of her African territory. The city of Carthage remained independent, but Carthaginian power was broken.

The third war—Carthage destroyed

The third war was fought to satisfy the greed of a small group of wealthy Roman landowners who wanted Rome to annex all Carthaginian territory. Their spokesman in the Senate was Cato the Elder. No matter what subject he spoke on, he always ended by saying "Carthago delenda est"—"Carthage must be destroyed." Finally, those in favor of war were successful. On a slight pretext Rome declared war, sent an army, and captured Carthage. In 146 B.C. Cato's wish was granted. The city of Carthage was entirely destroyed. It is said that the ground was plowed up and sown with salt so that nothing would grow, and a great curse was placed upon the site. North Africa became a Roman province. The Romans were now undisputed rulers of the central and western Mediterranean.

Conquest of the Hellenistic East

To the east lay the former empire of Alexander with its high Hellenistic civilization.

It was divided into several kingdoms, none strong enough to resist Roman power. Macedonia and some of the Greek city-states had joined Carthage against the Romans several times during the first two Punic Wars. Each time Rome defeated them, but did not take territory. When Macedonia broke her treaty again and attacked Rome during the third Punic War, Rome conquered both Macedonia and the Greek city-states, making them Roman provinces in 146 B.C.

Results of Roman Expansion

Between 264 and 146 B.C. the Roman state developed from a federation of Italian cities into a great Mediterranean empire. The consequences were far-reaching. The growth of the empire changed Roman culture and altered the course of European history.

Changes in government

During a period of more than 100 years, the patrician Senate regained all the powers

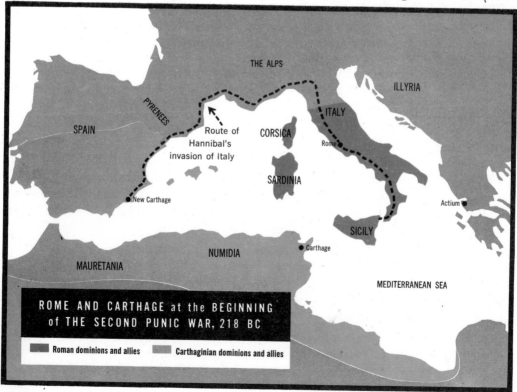

ROME AND CARTHAGE at the BEGINNING of THE SECOND PUNIC WAR, 218 BC

■ Roman dominions and allies   ■ Carthaginian dominions and allies

it had lost to the plebeians. The plebeian Assembly of Tribes could not meet on short notice, as was often necessary during the wars. The Senate could and did. Therefore, it regained control of the army, finances, and foreign affairs, and took control of the new provinces. Thus the movement toward democracy was checked. Rome was still a republic, but a patrician aristocracy ruled.

Government of the new territories was very poor. The people were not given citizenship nor were they made allies, like the Italian cities. They were treated as conquered colonies belonging to the city of Rome. Provincial cities became centers of local government under local magistrates chosen from the upper classes. New cities were built in backward regions, each controlling the surrounding country. In effect, the provinces became a collection of city-states each subject to the great city-state of Rome.

Each province had a Roman governor called a *proconsul*. He was appointed by the Senate and given absolute power, backed by a Roman army of occupation. His term was one year, and he received no salary. There-

A Roman warship in action. The Roman ship (right) has rammed an enemy vessel and dropped the boarding bridge onto its deck. The Roman soldiers are charging across the bridge. With this device, the Romans were able to use their excellent army to win naval battles.

fore, the temptation to force money from the province was very great. The system of tax collection increased the chances of corruption and bad government. It was called tax farming. In Rome the censors let contracts to men called publicans or tax farmers. They agreed to pay a fixed sum to the Roman treasury. They were allowed to keep whatever money, in excess of this fixed sum, they could collect in the provinces.

● *Agriculture*

The Roman government owned much land in the new provinces, and leased it in large estates to anyone who could pay the price. Only wealthy people could pay the leases and the cost of labor, most of which was done by slaves. The wars had brought in many prisoners, so the number of slaves increased. Since the provinces produced grain more cheaply than Italy could, they paid some of their tribute to Rome in grain. Small farmers in Italy could not compete with this cheaper grain from the provinces. Therefore, much Italian land was turned into pasture for cattle or used to grow grapes and olives. Cattle-raising and fruit-growing take more money and larger acreages than does grain-growing. Thus Italy came to depend on the provinces for most of her grain, her chief article of food.

● Trade, manufacturing, and wealth

Since Rome and most of Italy depended on imports from the provinces, the Romans encouraged commerce. Finally, Italy was importing more goods than it exported, paying its bills with wealth gained from wars. There was a steady movement of gold and silver out of Italy, to pay for importing luxuries.

Manufacturing was done in small establishments. Since most of the work was done by slaves or freedmen (slaves who had been set free), the Romans saw few reasons to invent better machines to reduce labor or increase production. The constant opening of new lands for farming shifted money and energy away from commerce and industry.

However, many businessmen became extremely wealthy. They made money from contracts for public works, tax farming, from commerce, and the loot of war. These rich businessmen were not patricians, for the senatorial class was prohibited from entering commerce. They formed a new class, the *equites* (knights), with great wealth but little political power. Landowning patricians with great estates worked by slaves or free tenants were also very wealthy. Many of them acquired a taste for luxurious living.

● Greek influence

Rome's conquest of the Greek colonies and Greece itself brought the Romans under the influence of Hellenistic culture. Educated Greeks were brought to Italy, and, although they were slaves, they became teachers, secretaries, and estate managers. The Roman who could not speak, read, and write Greek was considered uneducated. The Romans took the twenty-three letter Greek alphabet, Romanized the form, added the letters J, U, and W, and made it the alphabet that is used today. Greek literature was translated into Latin, and Latin writers imitated Greek forms. The Stoic and Epicurean philosophies had many Roman followers. As is so often the case in history, it was a question of who had conquered whom.

The Romans adopted much of the Greek religion and mythology. For example, the Greek supreme god, Zeus, became the Roman god Jupiter. His wife, Hera, was called Juno by the Romans. Aphrodite became Venus, and Hermes received the name Mercury.

The Romans copied Greek architecture to some extent, but their buildings were different. They used two features, the arch and the vaulted dome, which the Greeks had not known how to build. The Romans liked buildings to be impressive in size. The Greeks found beauty in the proportions. Characteristics of Roman buildings were large size and the use of arches and vaulted domes.

Decline of the Republic— a century of civil wars, 133–27 B.C.

By the time Rome had expanded into an empire, Roman government was completely controlled by wealthy patricians. Two other classes, equites and plebeians, lacked political power, but had aims and needs for which they wanted government action. The increasing number of slaves made life very hard for free farmers and workers. The provinces were miserably governed. There was a tendency to glorify the military hero, giving him offices for which he might not be fitted.

Solution of these problems by the government was not likely. A proper solution, in most cases, would have reduced the power or wealth of the patricians. Since the patricians controlled the government, they were not likely to permit reforms that hurt them. The failure of the ruling class to improve conditions brought attempts by other groups, and finally brought the end of the republic.

● Democratic reformers, 133–89 B.C.

Two brothers, Tiberius and Gaius Gracchus, made the first attempt to get reforms. They came from a wealthy and noble family. They had been trained by their mother to believe that service to the state was the most important thing in life. In turn, each of the brothers was elected Tribune. Tiberius gained passage of a law limiting the amount of land a man could own, and dividing up parts of large estates among those who had no land. Gaius tried to restore power to the Assembly of Tribes. He gained power for the Tribunes to use public money to buy grain and sell it to the poor below cost. He had equites replace senators on juries trying governors of provinces.

The gains brought about by the brothers Gracchus were small, and they paid for them with their lives. Tiberius was assassinated, and Gaius was forced by the patricians to commit suicide. The land reforms were not enforced. The sale of grain below cost set the example that private citizens could be supported at public expense.

The next man to appear as a leader of the democratic forces was Gaius Marius, a plebeian and a military hero. German tribes were then invading Gaul. To head the nation in this time of danger, Marius was elected consul with the backing of equites and plebeians. To defeat the Germans, Marius had himself elected consul five successive times, which broke the law prohibiting re-election.

Marius did defeat the Germans, but few of his attempted reforms succeeded. He made one change that proved dangerous. Instead of having an army of citizens serving without pay, Marius provided that the troops should be paid by their generals. Men volunteered for sixteen years. They were promised that at the end of their service they would receive a bonus of land. The armies now became loyal to their leaders instead of the government. Military leaders were able to make themselves dictators.

● The Dictators, 89–60 B.C.

Lucius Cornelius Sulla, a senator, was elected consul to repel an invasion in Asia Minor. After Sulla had gone to war, Marius seized control of Rome and executed many members of the senatorial class. After seven years of war, Sulla came home. His army marched into Rome and defeated the followers of Marius. With terrible brutality and complete disregard of the law, he executed thousands and seized their property.

Sulla ruled as a military dictator for three years. He took all powers away from the two Assemblies and gave them to the Senate. Also, he set up a new procedure for officeholding. This new procedure kept the power firmly in the hands of the patrician Senate. To be a proconsul (governor of a province) a man must first have served as consul. Before that he must have risen through the ranks of the other offices. A man could not be re-elected consul for ten years after serving. The Senate elected all officers from the patrician class. Outwardly the Senate governed, but increasingly it was in the power of army commanders who had the loyalty of their troops.

● The First Triumvirate

After three years in office Sulla retired, leaving a great struggle for power among a new group of leaders. Two generals, Gnaeus Pompey and Marcus Licinius Crassus, had become famous. When the Senate refused to elect them consuls, they threatened to use force, and the Senate gave in.

A rising politician of this time was Gaius Julius Caesar. He became a leader of the

democratic party of his uncle, Marius, although he was a member of a wealthy and noble family. In his younger days he was a playboy, but when he became interested in politics, he soon proved a master politician. Caesar was a fine orator and a liberal spender. With fine speeches and gifts of grain he built up a great following in Rome.

Caesar, Pompey, and Crassus each wanted to be sole ruler, but none of them was strong

An aqueduct in what is now Segovia, Spain, built by the Romans during the reign of the Emperor Trajan, who died in 117 A.D. Roman architects made excellent use of the arch. Roman engineers built great aqueducts like this to carry water to cities.

enough. Hence they formed an alliance. This alliance has been called a triumvirate, or rule of three men. They ruled by forcing the

Senate to do whatever they wanted. In a short time Crassus was killed in war, leaving Caesar and Pompey in control, each still ambitious to rule alone.

● Caesar's fame increases

Caesar realized that he could not win power without an army which was loyal to him, so he made himself proconsul of Gaul for two terms of five years each. Gaul included the territory which is now France, Belgium, and Holland. Rome controlled part of it, but the rest was held by tribes of Celts and Germans, who were fierce fighters. In his ten years as proconsul Caesar defeated every tribe and brought all Gaul under Roman rule. He even took an army across to England to defeat the Celts there, but stayed only a short time. He proved to be a fine military leader and organizer. Everything he did was for one purpose. He wanted to build up a strong and loyal army with which he could seize power in Rome.

Caesar carefully kept the Roman people well informed about his campaigns and victories by sending home written reports of his progress. These are known as the *Commentaries on the Gallic Wars*. They begin with the famous sentence, "All Gaul is divided into three parts." Written in clear and simple style, they are still used as textbooks by students of Latin.

Julius Caesar remains well known for what has been written about him as well as for what he himself did and wrote. His career is the basis for plays by Shakespeare and by Shaw. Below is a scene from a Broadway production of Shaw's Caesar and Cleopatra. *Caesar is about to leave Egypt and return to Rome.*

Of course Pompey became very jealous of Caesar's rising fame. To head off his rival, Pompey had himself made sole consul. Then he persuaded the Senate to order Caesar to resign as proconsul and return home without his army. Caesar refused, because to obey meant death. Instead, he led his army into Italy. When he reached the Rubicon River, he was met by a messenger from the Senate. If he crossed the river with his army, he would be declared a rebel. Caesar hesitated a short time, then made his decision: he ordered his army to march on. Since then it is said of a person who has made a decision from which he cannot turn back: "He has crossed the Rubicon."

● Caesar becomes dictator

Caesar now moved toward sole power. When Pompey and his followers fled to Greece, Caesar first made himself secure in Italy and Spain; then he defeated Pompey in Greece. He moved over into Africa, put Cleopatra on the throne of Egypt, and made Egypt an ally of Rome. In Asia Minor he drove out a dangerous tribe of barbarian invaders who had attacked Roman provinces. It was after this victory that he sent home his famous three-word message: *Veni, vidi, vici*—"I came, I saw, I conquered."

In 46 B.C. Caesar returned to Rome and took complete control of the government. He had now become so powerful that he was appointed dictator for ten years, later for life. He also had himself elected censor for life. This office allowed him to make the lists from which senators were chosen. Still not satisfied, he was made proconsul for life, with full command of the army. As a patrician he could not be elected Tribune, but the people gave him the powers of a Tribune. He was given the supreme religious office. He was called Pater Patriae—the father of his country. The form of the republic was kept, but Caesar was king in everything but name. The title was offered to him, but he refused it.

● Caesar's program of reforms

Once in power, Caesar showed himself a statesman as well as a politician and general. He made vast reforms and planned even more. His first attention went to the provinces. He granted citizenship to many provincials. As governors he chose trained men and paid them a fixed salary. Other officials were sent to check on the governors, removing those who did not rule well. Land which had been seized by wealthy men was regained and divided among landless farmers and veterans. This move established groups of Romans throughout the provinces, and thus spread Roman culture and influence. Caesar also gave membership in the Senate to many provincials.

Caesar secured laws to relieve poor farmers and men who could not pay their debts. He improved the roads so that armies as well as traders could move quickly to all parts of the empire.

To make it more nearly correct, Caesar ordered a reform of the calendar. This Julian calendar was used in Europe until the sixteenth century A.D. (in England until 1752 and in Russia even until 1917).

As you might expect, the conservative patrician families of Rome did not welcome Caesar's reforms. Trouble was bound to come. Some sixty men formed a conspiracy against him. Three of these were men Caesar considered his friends: Decius Brutus, Gaius Cassius, and Marcus Brutus. The conspirators felt that Caesar wanted to be king, and there were many things that seemed to support this idea. On the Ides of March (the fifteenth day), 44 B.C., they murdered him in the Senate building.

● The Second Triumvirate, 44–27 B.C.

A weakness of dictatorship today, as in Caesar's time, is the problem of who is to succeed to power. Caesar had named his grandnephew, Octavian, his heir. When Caesar was murdered, Octavian was only

A bedroom from the villa of a well-to-do Roman. The table is of marble. The couch and stool are of carved bone. Paintings of a town cover the walls. This room, taken from a house excavated in Italy, can be seen at the Metropolitan Museum of Art in New York City.

eighteen, had no political experience, and was studying at a school in Greece. Rome was in chaos. The conspirators tried to seize power, but Mark Antony, who was the second consul, and Caesar's general, Lepidus, drove them out and took control of Rome. Mark Antony seemed on the way to becoming dictator.

Octavian hurried home from Greece to get his inheritance. He took the name Gaius Julius Caesar Octavianus, and built up popular favor by paying the bequests of Caesar's will out of his own private fortune. But he was not sure of his power, and neither was Mark Antony. So Mark Antony, Lepidus, and Octavian came to an agreement on the rule; this was the Second Triumvirate. They defeated the forces of Brutus and Cassius, who also wanted to rule, and then divided the empire among themselves. Antony took the East, the richest part. He reconquered Syria and Asia Minor. Then he married Cleopatra, Queen of Egypt.

Lepidus took Africa, but retired from politics a few years later to take the supreme religious office, Pontifex Maximus—head priest.

Octavian got Italy, Gaul, and Spain, but he was not satisfied; so he continued to build up his popularity in every possible way. Within a few years he persuaded the Senate to declare war on Antony and Cleopatra. In a great naval battle at Actium he defeated their fleet, and both of them committed suicide. Octavian then took Egypt as his own personal province. When he returned to Rome, there was no one to dispute him. In 29 B.C. he declared that the wars were finished, which was correct. The republic was also finished, for Octavian lived long enough to establish one-man rule firmly.

Roman culture at the end of the republic

You can easily see that Rome was now very different from the Rome of early days. Nearly 500 years had passed since the Latins defeated the Etruscans and united their little villages into a city-state. It was still a city-state, but now the city controlled the whole Mediterranean area.

There was a vast difference, too, from early days when there were neither rich nor miserably poor people. Now wealthy patrician landowners had vast estates and lived in luxury both in city homes and country villas. The best men in this class had been killed in wars or in the executions during the civil wars. There were really few able patricians left. Businessmen, the equites, had also become wealthy and lived luxuriously.

The poor freedmen were in a miserable state. Competition with slaves turned them into unemployed mobs in the cities. In 50 B.C. it is estimated that 300,000 people in Rome depended on government support.

Slavery was a hard and dangerous problem. There were now 400,000 slaves in or near Rome—1,500,000 in Italy. In their treatment of slaves, Romans were more like Spartans than Athenians. The Roman attitude was that slaves were property, like cattle. They had no legal rights. Some Greek and Near-Eastern slaves, highly educated, became household servants, teachers, and secretaries. Usually they were well treated. Sometimes a master would grant freedom to a favorite. Agricultural slaves were branded like cattle, herded into the fields in the morning and home again at night to sleep chained together in dismal cellars. It is no wonder that Romans, like Spartans, lived in fear of slave rebellions.

However, in one way there was desirable progress. Roman law had developed greatly. The original Twelve Tables of the early days were laws for a small agricultural country. Their development to fit a huge empire was largely the work of the praetors (judges), usually very able men. In deciding cases they enlarged and liberalized the laws to fit changing conditions.

Review of Chapter 9

People, places, and things

Identify: Etruscans, Tribunes, Censors, Senate, Praetors, equites, Consuls, the Dictator, Gallic Wars, the Gracchi, Marius, Hannibal, Sulla, Pompey, Crassus, Caesar, Cleopatra, Antony, Marcus Brutus, Octavian, patricians, plebeians.
Locate: Rome, Tiber River, Phoenicia, Carthage, Sicily, Sardinia, Corsica, the Rubicon, the Alps, the Apennines, Actium.

Events in review

1. Were the Alps enough of a geographic barrier to protect the Romans from invasion? Explain.
2. What was important about the location of the city of Rome?
3. What did the early Romans take over from the culture of the Etruscans?
4. Name the three groups that made up the government of the Roman Republic. Which group was the most powerful? Why?
5. Why is the army of the Roman Republic called a "citizen army"? What important change in the army was made by Marius?
6. Who was Vesta? What was her importance to Rome?
7. Who said "Carthago delenda est"? What did he mean? Was his advice followed?
8. By 146 B.C. Rome had become a great empire. What changes followed in (a) Roman government, (b) Roman agriculture, (c) Roman trade and manufacturing?
9. Cite three examples of Greek influence on Roman civilization.
10. Who was the first man to become "dictator for life" in Rome? Summarize the steps by which he rose to power.
11. What men made up the Second Triumvirate? Tell what became of each man.

Problems and projects

1. Make a clay or plaster relief map of Italy. Use the map in a discussion of the influence of geography on Roman history.
2. Compare the geography of Italy with that of Greece. What significance in history is there in the fact that the harbors of Greece faced to the east and the harbors of Italy to the west?
3. Compare Greek and Roman religion. Can you account for the differences?
4. What similarities can be noted between the government of the Roman Republic and the government of the United States? What differences can be pointed out?
5. Why did Brutus oppose Caesar's one-man rule? (You can find an interesting discussion in Shakespeare's *Julius Caesar.*)
6. To debate: Hold an imaginary "United Nations" debate on the question of the Punic Wars. Should Rome be declared an aggressor against Carthage?

Chapter 10

Rome as an Empire: Greatness and Decline

ROME seemed ready for one-man rule when Octavian returned in 29 B.C., and there was no one to oppose him. Nevertheless, he proceeded cautiously. Julius Caesar had been assassinated because people thought he wanted to be king. Octavian was determined to avoid his uncle's fate. Therefore, in 27 B.C. he resigned his powers as dictator, announcing that the republic was restored. According to plan, the Senate thanked him, and then granted him a number of offices and titles. In effect, he gained complete control over the Senate, the Assemblies, and all officials. He was really the sole ruler, but the outward form of the republic was carefully preserved.

The first title granted to Octavian was *princeps*—the first man of all the citizens. From this word comes our modern word *prince*. From it also comes the name applied to the first two centuries of the Roman Empire—the *Principate*. The Senate also gave Octavian the title *Augustus,* which means exalted or sacred. He has since been known as Augustus Caesar, or just Augustus. He also became Pontifex Maximus, head priest. For all practical purposes he was emperor.

The Emperor Augustus

Augustus was made proconsul of all provinces, which he governed through lieutenants whom he appointed and removed. He com-

manded all the armies and had power to declare war and make peace. He was given the powers of a Tribune, that is, the right to propose and veto laws. The Senate kept its lawmaking powers, but the laws it passed were prepared by a committee chosen by Augustus. As princeps, he was first to vote in the Senate and the first to be consulted about the appointment of officials.

Augustus opposed taking any more territory. He thought the real problem was to rule well what Rome already had. So he began, and his successors followed, a policy of avoiding wars. Some of his successors did take more territory, and there were frontier wars against barbarian tribes. However, inside the vast region of the Roman Empire there was peace for 200 years. It was the *Pax Romana,* the Roman Peace. The world has never known another such time. Within this great empire the Pax Romana made possible the spread of both Greek civilization and the Christian religion. A great historian has said that if he had to choose a place and time other than his own in which to live, he would choose the Roman Empire during this period.

Augustus first tried to remedy the dreadful conditions left by the wars. He reorganized the provinces; he brought a large part of the empire under the direct control of the emperor instead of the control of proconsuls. As governors and other officials, he chose trained and capable men and promoted only those who showed ability. Governors served longer terms and were paid good salaries, so that there was less temptation to plunder. He continued Julius Caesar's policy of establishing colonies in the provinces and encouraged trade. Because of his great building program in Rome, he could justly boast that he found Rome a city of brick and left it a city of marble.

As always in a dictatorship, Augustus had the problem of succession. To avoid civil war, he named as his successor his son-in-law Tiberius, and allowed him to act as co-ruler during the last years of his life. In 14 A.D. Augustus died, at the age of seventy-six, after a highly successful reign.

The Julian Emperors

After Augustus' death, the empire was ruled for fifty years by men related in some way to the family of Julius Caesar. These were called the Julian Emperors. It was during this period that Britain was conquered and added to the empire. Some of the Julians were very good rulers. Two of them were insane, and ruled badly.

The Good Emperors

Five men called the Good Emperors ruled Rome for almost a hundred years during the second century A.D. Each chose an able successor. Three of them, Trajan, Hadrian, and Marcus Aurelius, are counted among the greatest Roman rulers.

Trajan was a great general and conqueror. He added Dacia, Arabia, Mesopotamia, and Armenia, bringing the empire to its greatest size.

●Hadrian

Hadrian was a follower of the Stoics, with a very high sense of duty to the state. He was a man of many talents and abilities: a patron of art, lover of Greek culture, fine conversationalist, idealist and reformer in government, able diplomat, and tolerant ruler. Born in the provinces himself (in Spain) he understood their needs and spent much time organizing and Romanizing them. To help protect the boundaries of the empire, Hadrian built fortifications along the frontiers and encouraged the natives to enter the army. He established a postal system to keep in touch with the frontiers.

The administration of the empire also needed reform. Hadrian established definite ranks in the bureaucracy. Each office had fixed requirements, duties, rank, and salary. He appointed a council of the ablest lawyers and scholars to collect the laws and organize them into a code. Hadrian was also a great builder. The most famous building put up at his order was his tomb, which still stands in Rome.

●Marcus Aurelius

Marcus Aurelius, the last of the Good Emperors, was famous as a Stoic philosopher. His book, *The Meditations of Marcus Aurelius,* is considered a fine statement of Stoic ideas of the brotherhood of man, the need to accept whatever the laws of nature bring, and the duty to work for the welfare of others. He put his ideas into practice. A wealthy man, he spent most of his private fortune in gifts to the poor. During his time the wild tribes along the frontiers caused much trouble; so Marcus Aurelius had to give much attention to the defense of the empire. German tribes invaded across the Danube and reached northeastern Italy. It took thirteen years to drive them out. In Asia Minor the Parthians invaded, and were also defeated. The troops returning from this war brought with them a great plague, which lasted many years and killed many people.

When it came to his choice of a successor, Marcus Aurelius failed to show his usual wisdom. He broke the custom of choosing able

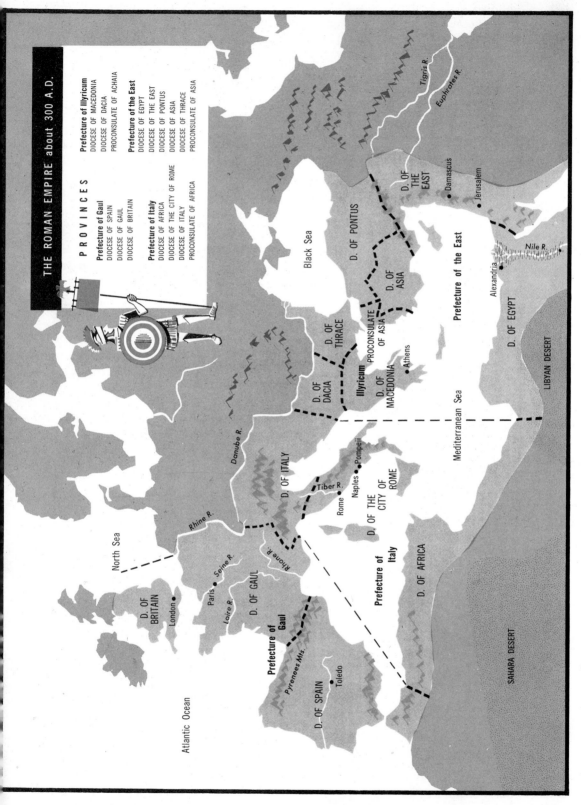

THE ROMAN EMPIRE about 300 A.D.

PROVINCES

Prefecture of Gaul
DIOCESE OF SPAIN
DIOCESE OF GAUL
DIOCESE OF BRITAIN

Prefecture of Italy
DIOCESE OF AFRICA
DIOCESE OF THE CITY OF ROME
DIOCESE OF ITALY
PROCONSULATE OF AFRICA

Prefecture of Illyricum
DIOCESE OF MACEDONIA
DIOCESE OF DACIA
PROCONSULATE OF ACHAIA

Prefecture of the East
DIOCESE OF EGYPT
DIOCESE OF THE EAST
DIOCESE OF PONTUS
DIOCESE OF ASIA
DIOCESE OF THRACE
PROCONSULATE OF ASIA

Tigris R.

Euphrates R.

D. OF THE EAST

Damascus

Jerusalem

D. OF PONTUS

Black Sea

Nile R.

D. OF ASIA

Alexandria

PROCONSULATE OF ASIA

D. OF THRACE

Prefecture of the East

D. OF EGYPT

D. OF DACIA

Illyricum

D. OF MACEDONIA

Athens

Danube R.

LIBYAN DESERT

Mediterranean Sea

D. OF ITALY

Pompeii

Tiber R.

Naples

Rome

D. OF THE CITY OF ROME

Rhine R.

North Sea

Rhone R.

Seine R.

Prefecture of Italy

Paris

D. OF BRITAIN

London

Loire R.

D. OF GAUL

D. OF AFRICA

Atlantic Ocean

Prefecture of Gaul

Pyrenees Mts.

Toledo

D. OF SPAIN

SAHARA DESERT

120

men, and appointed his son, who was weak and spoiled. This brought to an end the great days of the Pax Romana and the great period of the Roman Empire.

Culture under the early emperors

● *Agriculture*

Throughout the reigns of the early emperors agriculture remained the basic occupation of the mass of the people. In spite of the efforts of some emperors to help them, small farmers simply could not prosper. In Italy itself farming was almost entirely on large estates with vineyards or livestock. In the provinces there were more small holdings. Much grain land was worn out. Farming districts in Greece and southern Italy were abandoned, and new ones started in Gaul and North Africa. The grain supply was always uncertain. Any accident or crop failure anywhere meant a scarcity.

A new class of agricultural workers began to replace slaves on the large estates. These were the *coloni,* neither slave nor free, but bound to the land. Each colonus received a small plot of land from the owner. He had to work it, and could not leave it. He paid his rent with part of the crops he raised. The coloni worked long and hard, with little return.

● *Commerce and manufacture*

Such a vast empire, with so many different lands and peoples and so well governed, provided great opportunities for commerce. Taxes on trade were low, and the same sort of money was used everywhere, so that the exchange of goods was easy. Rome and Alexandria were great commercial centers; goods came to them from all over the known world. From the provinces Italy imported grain and raw materials such as meat, wool, and hides. From the East came silks, linens, glassware, jewelry, and furniture to satisfy the tastes of the wealthy. Italy's exports were never enough

to pay for her imports, especially from the Near East and India. During Roman times and on through later centuries, India was the source of many things that Europe had never known. Demand for her spices, cotton, and other products was so great that Europe constantly had to send out its gold and silver.

Manufacturing also increased throughout the empire. The East produced luxury goods while Italy, Gaul, and Spain made cheap goods because so much of their population was poor. Shops were small, as in Greece, and most work was done by hand.

● *Transportation*

Transportation was greatly improved during the great days of the empire. Sea trade was good and faster than land, but it was

The Romans built the finest roads ever made before modern times. This model shows the Appian Way under construction. This road was 18 feet wide, paved with blocks of lava laid on a bed of broken stone cemented with lime. Parts of this highway, begun in 312 B.C., are still in use.

risky because of pirates and lack of good charts. For land communication roads and bridges were well built, and there was a postal service from all frontiers to Rome.

But even the improved transportation and communication system was not good enough for the needs of such a large empire. It took a Roman messenger, traveling at top speed, at least ten weeks to cross the entire empire, using every known means of transportation. You can see what this meant in the problem of government. The weakness of the transportation system was one cause of the decline of the empire after the days of the Good Emperors.

● *Social classes—citizens and noncitizens*

The times of the Good Emperors were prosperous for many people, but the wealth was very unevenly distributed. There were three social classes of Roman citizens. The patrician class was composed of wealthy land-owners. They lived in fine homes, with many slaves. They wore a broad purple stripe on

The ruins of the Baths of Caracalla. These public baths had room for 16,000 persons. The Roman emperors built huge structures like this as monuments to their greatness.

their togas to show their rank. The equites were businessmen and state officials. Many of them were wealthy, but they were barred from the highest political offices. They wore a narrow purple stripe on their togas. Most of the plebeians lived in the cities. Often unemployed, they were given grain and entertainment by the government.

A Roman citizen's vote no longer had much political importance, but citizenship was still a valuable privilege in other ways. Membership in the legions was for citizens only. Roman law gave more protection to citizens than to noncitizens. Until the second century A.D. not many provincials had been granted citizenship, which made it more valuable to those who had it. However, four of the Good Emperors were born in Spain and were more liberal in granting rights in the provinces. By the time of Marcus Aurelius full Roman rights had been given to all better-class communities in the empire.

Among the noncitizens were freedmen, provincials, coloni, and slaves. During the second century of the empire large numbers of slaves were set free. These freedmen did not become citizens, but they could hold lower offices in government and enter any suitable occupation. Many became wealthy, and some were influential at court. Coloni, as you know, were neither entirely slave nor entirely free. Among the provincials there was much class distinction. Only those who could meet high requirements of wealth and land ownership could hold offices in local governments.

● Contrasts: wealthy vs. poor

Wealthy Romans not only desired comforts and luxuries. They also wanted to display their wealth. A rich patrician usually had both a city home and a country villa. Each was elaborately built and furnished, with many conveniences, such as running water and baths. Some were centrally heated.

The life of the wealthy included some time for business, both private and public, but there was much time for leisure: the siesta, exercise, the bath, and the banquet. Many wealthy Romans ate and drank enormously at banquets. Drunkenness was common.

The contrast between the lives of the wealthy and the poor was extreme. In Rome the poor lived in three or four-story wooden tenements. Danger from fire or from the collapse of these cheaply-constructed buildings was always present. Most poor people used their homes for eating and sleeping only. When they were not working, they spent their time in the streets, which were narrow and filthy. Their food was crude and monotonous. The main dish was wheat served as porridge. Sometimes they had beans and onions. Only rarely did they drink wine, and then of the poorest quality.

Men of the plebeian class found their best chance for employment in the army. Some were craftsmen or agricultural workers, but they had little security because of frequent unemployment and low wages. However, some things were in their favor. Rent was low, and the government provided grain free or below cost. Political candidates often gave gifts of grain. Both the government and the candidates furnished amusements, circuses, and public baths either free or very cheaply. Still, the life was below any standards of health and decency. Small farmers who lost their land drifted into the coloni class or outrightly into slavery.

You have already read of the miserable and hopeless lives of the slaves, especially the agricultural slaves. Rarely in history has such a large group of fairly civilized human beings lived under such bad conditions. However, the number of slaves declined greatly during the early days of the empire. The long period of peace meant fewer war prisoners; so slaves became expensive to buy. A slave was also expensive to keep. He had to be fed, clothed, and cared for. Owners of large estates found it more profitable to free their slaves and make them coloni, bound to the land. They learned that a man works better as a free individual on a small plot of land than as a member of a large slave gang. Besides, a free worker had to look out for himself.

● Government

The imperial government was the strongest tie to hold the empire together. It maintained order, established justice, defended the frontiers, and provided food and amusements. The members of the Senate still held most of the higher offices such as consul, judge, and proconsul. Equites and freedmen held the lower offices in the bureaucracy.

The position of emperor was a very demanding one. He had to make all the decisions about policies. He appointed the officials who controlled the provinces and ran the entire government. The responsibilities of the emperor's job were too much for one man, even a wise, intelligent, able man like the best of the Good Emperors. When the emperor was weak, incompetent, and selfish, good government depended entirely on the officials of the bureaucracy. From the time of Augustus on, these officials were trained men, appointed and promoted only for ability. The positions were highly prized and much sought after, not only for the salary but for the honor. The bureaucracy held the empire together when the emperors no longer could.

Taxes were much fairer and more fairly collected than under the republic. But taxes did not bring in enough money to meet all the expenses of the government. The army was, then as now, the greatest single expense. Money was also needed to buy grain, erect public buildings, and pay the expenses of the emperor's court and the bureaucracy.

Roman law was also an important tie binding the empire together. The law became uniform, just, and well suited to the needs of a complex society. It was taken into all the provinces. The praetors adapted and interpreted it to fit the laws and customs of the provincial people. Roman law was a great force for unity.

Local government in the new cities, especially in Spain and Gaul, was extremely good. Each was a small copy of Rome, with a forum, a senate building, theaters, amphitheaters, and baths. Most of the cities brought in water in aqueducts, and most had paved streets and sewer systems. Usually there were no direct taxes because the cities received income from publicly-owned land, mines, and quarries. The wealthy provincials took great pride in their cities. They gave large gifts for public buildings, streets, schools, and games.

● *The army*

The territory of the empire was held together, as it had been gained, mainly by military force. Augustus had reorganized the army into three units. The Praetorian Guard was stationed near Rome to protect the city if necessary. Its soldiers, citizens only, served sixteen years. The second unit, the Roman legions, was made up of citizens who served twenty years. The legions were stationed in great fortified camps (*castra*) along the frontiers. People often settled around the castra, so that they grew into towns and cities. In England such cities as Lancaster, Manchester, and Chester were once sites of Roman castra, and their names show it. The third army unit was the auxiliaries. These were made up of natives of the provinces or of border tribes. They enlisted for twenty-five years, with the promise of Roman citizenship when they had served their term. Soldiers of all three units were given bonuses of land along the frontiers when they had finished their enlistments. Thus there was a population of trained veterans to help guard the frontiers.

The Romans tried to establish natural frontiers wherever possible. In the west there

The remains of Hadrian's Wall. Built as a line of defense between Roman Britain and the wild northern part of the island, the wall ran from shore to shore. Compare this picture with that of the Great Wall of China (page 510) and the Maginot Line (page 628).

were the Atlantic Ocean and the North Sea; in the north, the Rhine and Danube rivers; in the east, the Black Sea and the Syrian Desert; in the south, the Sahara Desert.

In regions where neither oceans, rivers, nor deserts gave protection, the Romans built great lines of fortifications. In Britain Hadrian's Wall stretched entirely across the island in the north. There was a line of forts between the Rhine and Danube rivers. Small fortresses with permanent garrisons were placed at short intervals. The great legionary castra were further apart, with the entire distance between them protected by a ditch and wall. At first it was a wall of earth and timber, but later it was built of stone, so substantial that much of it still stands. Paved highways joined these military outposts with cities in the interior, and all provincial cities were linked to Rome by highways.

● Education

Public schools with teachers paid by city government were set up everywhere. Wealthy Romans employed private Greek tutors to teach their children to speak and write Greek as well as Latin. Every important town or city had elementary, grammar, and higher schools. In the higher schools, called rhetoric schools, children of the upper and middle classes studied the art of good writing and expressive speech in both Greek and Latin. All towns and cities had libraries; these were often teaching institutions. In many cities throughout the empire there were universities. The best were in Rome and in the Hellenistic cities of Athens, Rhodes, and Alexandria. At the Athenaeum in Rome, students from all over the empire studied law, medicine, architecture, mathematics, and engineering. The universities helped unify the peoples of the empire.

● Literature

Augustus and several of the Good Emperors encouraged art and literature, often paying for the support of good artists and writers. Roman painters and sculptors usually imitated the Greeks, and not very successfully. But Rome had a Golden Age of literature, even though its writers were not as great as the Athenians.

Virgil wrote *The Aeneid,* based on Homer's *Odyssey.* It told, in fine poetry, the story of Aeneas, supposed ancestor of the Caesars. When the Greeks captured Troy, Aeneas left, and, after many adventures, came to Italy. His descendants, Romulus and Remus, founded Rome. Horace wrote *Odes* and *Lyrics* in poetry, *Satires* and *Epistles* (letters) in prose. He had great knowledge of human emotions. Ovid wrote translations of Greek myths, the *Metamorphoses,* and love lyrics.

Tacitus was the Roman historian. His *Annals* was a history of Rome under the Julian Emperors. He was very pessimistic about the luxurious living of the wealthy and the lack of public virtue. More important still was his *Germania,* an account of the German tribes along the borders. He may have exaggerated the virtues of the Germans because he wrote the book to shame the Romans for their decay. But it is almost the only (and certainly the best) account of the early Germans.

Plutarch, a Greek who lived in Rome, wrote biographies called *Parallel Lives.* These were a series of biographical sketches, one of a famous Greek followed by one of a Roman whose life in some way resembled that of the Greek. This book is considered a classic.

● Religion

The Roman state religion grew weaker during the empire. Augustus tried to revive the old ideas of morality and virtue, to check luxury and divorce, and to encourage marriage and family life. It was a losing battle. The old Roman gods were as dead as the old Roman virtues. Augustus himself was worshipped as a god in the eastern part of the empire. By the end of the period the emperor was everywhere considered a god.

● *Amusements*

Romans enjoyed the theater, but not the Greek tragedies. Lighter comedies and satires were what they liked. Pantomimes and vaudeville acts such as jugglers, dancers, acrobats, and clowns were more popular still.

Most people liked sports more than the theater, but these sports were savage and brutal. The Romans enjoyed some Greek games like boxing, but made it more bloody by using brass knuckles. Chariot racing in the huge Circus Maximus drew large crowds. Four to seven horses drew a chariot with its driver seven times around the track. One race followed another throughout the day. At first it was a fairly civilized sport, but later foul play was permitted and almost expected. There were many accidents in which horses and drivers were injured or killed.

Animal shows and the fights of gladiators in the Colosseum were most popular of all. Wild beasts, made more savage by hunger, were let into the arena to fight one another. Men sometimes fought against animals. Often condemned criminals or slaves were thrown

A chariot race, one of the favorite Roman amusements.

into the arena to be torn by the beasts as a spectacle. Some Christian martyrs died this way.

The Latin word *gladius* meant sword. Originally, a gladiator was a man armed with a sword, although in time the gladiators used other kinds of weapons. Gladiators were trained men, sometimes free but usually slaves. They sometimes fought animals, but often fought one another, either singly or in groups. The fights usually ended in death for one or both fighters. Even Roman women screamed with delight at a death blow. When a gladiator was wounded, he appealed for mercy to the crowd. If they lifted their fists with thumbs up, his life was spared; thumbs down meant death.

Shows of this kind were given free by the government or political candidates. Chariot races or gladiatorial fights were held on all holidays. By the fourth century A.D. there were 175 holidays a year which were celebrated with public shows and games.

The decline of the empire

● *Commodus and the Severi, 180–235* A.D.

Commodus was the weak, vain, dissolute son whom Marcus Aurelius chose as his successor. Of course his thirteen-year rule was a failure, and the strength of the government declined. Finally Commodus was assassinated, and the long period of emperors chosen by those who preceded them came to an end. Three candidates, each backed by a different force in the empire, now struggled for power, and there was civil war. The winner was Septimus Severus, a general from the African provinces. He was the candidate of the legions. Severus used his power to strengthen the military dictatorship. Each of the next two rulers gained the throne as a result of an assassination. Neither man was a good ruler.

During this period all the peoples of the empire were granted Roman citizenship. At an earlier time this might have strengthened the empire. Now it was done not from a sense of justice but to get the 10 per cent inheritance tax that citizens had to pay.

● *The Barrack-Room Emperors, 235–284* A.D.

This period of fifty years was one of dreadful confusion. There were twenty-six emperors. One of them met a natural death; the rest were assassinated. The soldiers of the legions or the Praetorian Guard would murder the emperor and put their leader on the throne. These emperors have come to be called the Barrack-Room Emperors. If an emperor failed to reward the soldiers or tried to enforce discipline, they assassinated him and put in someone else. To be chosen emperor was the kiss of death. The legions did not perform their job of defending the frontiers. Every frontier of the empire was invaded by barbarian tribes.

Trade and manufacturing suffered. Travel was unsafe, and merchants hesitated to send goods by land or sea. The rural population became even poorer than before. Since the rural people had no money to buy goods, city industries suffered and unemployment increased. Population decreased throughout the empire. A great Asiatic plague spread through the provinces, causing several million deaths. Smaller families were the order of the day. The rich wanted more luxury; the poor could not afford large families.

It became very difficult to collect taxes. Money was so scarce that taxes were often paid in grain, and the army was paid in land. After 250 A.D. the government was seldom able to pay all its expenses. Some emperors tried to increase the supply of money by putting less gold and silver into the coins. This practice only made prices go higher.

The only prosperous people in the empire were the large landowners. Small farmers were forced to sell out, and estates grew in size. Many landowners left the cities and moved to their country villas. They organized and paid private armies, and defied the government officials who came to collect taxes. With the decline in population there was danger that there might not be enough labor to work the land. A new law made the position of the coloni, or serfs, hereditary. Formerly, a colonus had been forbidden to leave the land; now even his children were declared serfs.

City people were no better off. When manufacturing declined and unemployment increased, many artisans tried to leave the cities and find work in the country. To prevent this, a new law made membership in the trade college, or guild, compulsory. Furthermore, the members of the guilds were required to perform certain public services. When men tried to resign from the guilds, another law made membership not only compulsory but hereditary.

A sad fate befell the wealthy businessmen who made up the city councils of the provincial cities. They served without pay, taking great pride in the offices and often making rich gifts to their cities. When tax collection in the empire became difficult, the imperial government made these city councils responsible for taxes in their districts. If the required amount was not collected, the councils had to make up the difference. Their positions were also made compulsory and hereditary. As the amount of taxes collected grew increasingly smaller, the council members had to stay and see their personal fortunes disappear.

● Diocletian, 284–305 A.D.

The Roman Empire would undoubtedly have collapsed from inner weakness except for two able emperors who ruled during the end of the third century and the first part of the fourth century. By then it was too late to save the empire entirely. However, the reforms and reorganizations of Diocletian and Constantine postponed the collapse in the west for two hundred years, and in the east for more than a thousand years.

Diocletian was the son of a humble peasant from the eastern shore of the Adriatic Sea. He had risen through the ranks of the army to become a general. The army made him emperor, but he proved to be very different from the Barrack-Room Emperors. He was an able organizer and administrator. Diocletian's greatest work was the reorganization of the administration of the empire. It was too much for one man to manage; so he divided power with a co-emperor. Each emperor chose a man to help him rule and be his successor. Both emperors had to sign all documents to make them official.

With two emperors it was necessary to divide the territory of the empire. The most natural was division into the Latin and Greek halves. Latin was the official language of Italy, Gaul, Spain, Britain, and North Africa. This became the territory of the western emperor, whose capital, naturally, was Rome. Greek was the spoken and official language of Greece and the Near East. These became

the territory of Diocletian as eastern emperor. Each half of the empire was divided into two prefectures for the emperor and his assistant. The four prefectures were subdivided into provinces and dioceses under officials appointed by and subject to the emperors. High officials served one year; lower officials were permanent.

Diocletian ended the lawlessness within the empire, and drove out the barbarian tribes that had invaded during the time of the Barrack-Room Emperors. He tried to improve commerce and manufacturing and to increase the wealth of the empire. He needed more wealth so that taxes would produce enough money to run the government, but this problem was too much for him.

● Constantine, 312–337 A.D.

Constantine came to power in the western half of the empire seven years after Diocletian surprisingly resigned. Constantine's reign is known for two great events. The first was the legal recognition of the Christian religion. The story of his conversion is this: As Constantine led his army into battle against an early rival for the throne, he saw a blazing cross in the sky. Beneath it were the words *In Hoc Signo Vinces* "By this sign you will conquer." He is said to have pledged to become a Christian if he won the battle. He did win the battle; and he issued the Edict of Milan, in 313 A.D., by which Christianity was permitted, and protected by law. (The story of the rise of Christianity and its triumph over Roman persecution will be told in the next chapter.)

Constantine became ruler in the east as well as the west in 324. The second great event of his reign was the moving of the eastern capital to a new and stronger city which he built on the site of Byzantium, founded by the Greeks about one thousand years before. This new city was named Constantinople. The city controls the narrow passage from the Black Sea to the Aegean Sea. It is hard to attack, either from land or sea, and has been a tremendous military and commercial advantage to every government that has ever held it. Today it is the Turkish city of Istanbul.

Under Diocletian and Constantine, then, the entire empire was reorganized and in some ways strengthened. However, taxes now had to produce enough money to support two royal courts instead of one. Power had shifted away from Rome to the east where the wealth was. The fact that both Diocletian and Constantine wanted to rule the eastern empire tells its own story.

This Roman coin from the time of the Emperor Claudius is typical of Roman money.

Review of Chapter 10

People, places, and things

Identify: Pontifex Maximus, Pax Romana, Praetorian Guard, *The Meditations of Marcus Aurelius,* Tacitus, Augustus, Septimus Severus, *The Aeneid,* Ovid, Plutarch, princeps, coloni, castra.

Locate: Byzantium, Gaul, Spain, Britain, Asia Minor, the boundaries of the Roman Empire at its greatest extent.

Events in review

1. State five facts to prove that Augustus was a strong and able ruler.
2. Name two of the Good Emperors and state a contribution made by each to the Roman Empire.
3. Discuss the Roman government in terms of (a) the responsibilities of the emperor, (b) the place of the bureaucracy, (c) methods of tax collecting, (d) means of law enforcement.
4. Name the social classes that existed in the Roman Empire. Why can they be called a study in contrasts?
5. Compare Roman and Greek forms of amusements.
6. What happened to the empire during the period of the Barrack-Room Emperors?
7. What was the importance of the reigns of Diocletian and of Constantine?

8. What circumstances compelled Rome to accept a division into Western and Eastern Empires?

Problems and projects

1. Would you have enjoyed being a citizen of the Roman Empire during the period of Pax Romana? Why?
2. Was some form of one-man dictatorship necessary for Rome after she became an empire? Why?
3. Would you rather have been educated in Greece or Rome? Why? (Refer to books listed on pages 97, 144, 145.)
4. If you had lived during the latter days of the Roman Empire, what things would you have found to admire? To dislike and want to change?
5. Write an essay on the topic: The decline of the Roman Empire can serve as a warning to all great powers.
6. Write an editorial denouncing the brutality of Roman amusements.
7. In two parallel columns list the strengths and the weaknesses of the Roman Empire.
8. On a map show, in different colors, (a) the boundaries of the Roman Empire at its greatest extent, (b) the boundaries of the Empire of Alexander the Great.

Chapter 11 Christianity Rises. The Western Empire Falls

CHAPTER 10 traced the rise of the Roman Empire and the beginning of its downfall. Now we must go back to the early days of the empire and pick up the story of the rise of a great force in history, Christianity. As you have read, the Emperor Constantine made Christianity a legally recognized religion in 313 A.D. For three centuries before this date Christians struggled to spread their faith, often being treated as enemies of the Roman state. This story starts, of course, with the birth of Jesus.

The life and teachings of Jesus

Jesus was born in Bethlehem, Palestine, while Augustus was ruling in Rome. He was called Jesus of Nazareth. Later He came to be known as Christ, a Greek word which means The Anointed One, the Messiah or Savior.

Jesus lived a short and quiet life. Although Palestine was part of the Roman Empire, most Roman books on the history of the empire at that time do not refer to Him at all. Yet His teachings changed the social and economic systems of Greece and Rome, and became one of the greatest influences of the Western World.

Very little is known about the early life of Jesus. He was said to be a carpenter and a student of the writings of the Jewish prophets.

In time He became a prophet, or teacher, preaching His gospel to anyone who would listen to Him and gathering about Him a small group of disciples or followers.

The social implications of the teaching of Jesus have been tremendously important in history. He accepted the Ten Commandments as guides to right living, but He gave them a deeper meaning than they had had before. For example, he taught that the commandment "Thou shalt not kill" meant not only that one person should not murder another but also that he should not hate another. He summarized the ten rules for his followers in two great commandments: They must love God above all things, and they must love others just as much as themselves. He taught that all men were equal in the eyes of God; the soul of a poor man was just as important as that of a rich man. According to Jesus, God did not love the Jews alone, or even especially, but loved all peoples equally. Everyone should try to live a good life rather than to get wealth. His followers were told to serve their fellow men to the limit of their energy and ability. They must serve and love even enemies who treated them harshly and hatefully. The old law of Hammurabi and Moses, "An eye for an eye; a tooth for a tooth," was not for Christians. Instead, Christians must follow the Golden Rule: "Do unto others as you would have others do unto you." No man had the right to revenge, for God alone had the right to judge and punish.

Jesus taught that people must obey the government as well as God. They must be obedient to authority, pay their taxes, and learn to coöperate with one another in every kind of relationship. He disapproved of all quarreling and war, saying, "He that taketh up the sword shall perish by the sword."

The ideas and teachings of Jesus displeased the conservative, priestly class of Jews. They denied that He was the Messiah whose coming had been foretold by the prophets of old. Many Jews thought of the Messiah as a political and military leader who would defeat their enemies and set up the Jewish kingdom again. When Jesus came to Jerusalem, these people hailed him as King of the Jews. They expected Him to lead them in a war to throw off Roman rule. Instead, Jesus told them that His kingdom was the Kingdom of God. It was not political but spiritual. This was a great disappointment. The mass of the Jewish people turned against Him and supported the priestly caste. They denounced Him to the Romans, saying that He planned to make Himself King of the Jews. He was tried as a rebel by the Roman government, condemned, and executed by crucifixion.

The spread of Christianity

Jesus' disciples became missionaries and set out to convert all peoples to His teachings. At first they worked mostly in the Jewish communities of the Near East. Most of their early converts were poor people. Some years after the crucifixion of Jesus there occurred an event that was to spread the Christian religion far and wide. A Jew named Saul, a Roman citizen and a very eloquent speaker, was suddenly converted to Christianity. He had been a persecutor of Christians. Now he took the Christian name Paul and became the greatest Christian missionary.

Paul believed that Jesus' life, death, and resurrection had meaning not for the Jews alone but for all people. His inspired missionary work spread the religion rapidly. He established churches throughout Asia Minor and at Alexandria in Egypt. In Greece he founded churches at Corinth and Athens. With Peter, another disciple of Jesus, Paul did missionary work in Rome. Tradition tells that both were put to death by the emperor Nero. By 100 A.D. Rome had the largest congregation of Christians.

Conditions in the Roman Empire favored the spread of the new religion. Old religious

St. Peter, leader of the Apostles and first bishop of the Church at Rome. In this picture he is shown holding the Gospels and the keys to heaven.

beliefs were dying out. Neither emperor-worship nor Greek philosophy appealed to many people. Three Eastern religions besides Christianity had become popular in the empire. The Persian belief in Mithra promised salvation. Cybele, fertility goddess of Asia Minor, had many followers. The Egyptian worship of Isis or Osiris also promised a future life. All had some features in common. Each offered a divine being who helped mankind to find salvation. Each emphasized ideas of right conduct and right living.

Christianity had a special appeal to the poor and downtrodden. It taught that all souls were equal in the eyes of God. Mithraism excluded women; in the worship of Cybele and Isis women were more important than men. Christianity was for everyone. Unlike all others, Christianity taught respect for human labor. A man could continue his everyday life and still be a good Christian, finding that his religion helped him in his daily life. Moreover, he could look forward to salvation. Christianity promised resurrection of the body and eternal life to all who accepted God as the only God, and Jesus as His Son, the Savior.

The early Christians were very eager not only to live the good life themselves but to convert others. They were well organized, peaceful, and orderly. Their religion taught everyone to respect the government, workers to respect their employers, and even slaves to be patient in their suffering.

Persecution and triumph

You might think the Roman government would have welcomed such a group of fine, orderly, obedient, clean-living citizens. The Romans were very tolerant of religious beliefs. As long as a person observed the forms of the state religion, making his offerings of wine and incense to the statue of the emperor, he could have any other religious belief that suited him.

That was just the difficulty. Christians would worship one God only. They refused to worship the emperor as a god. To others, the offering of wine and incense to the statue was only a gesture. To Christians it was the worship of idols; no matter what the penalty, they would not do it. In addition, many of them took literally the teachings of Jesus against war. They refused to join the army.

To the Roman emperors this was a defiance of Roman law and religion. Christians were weakening the position of the emperor and therefore were a danger to the state. It became a crime to be a Christian. The property of Christians was seized, and their beliefs were punishable by death. Even the best of the Good Emperors followed this policy to some extent.

Not every emperor tried equally hard to enforce the laws. Some tried to stamp out the belief entirely and harshly persecuted the Christians. Others thought that the government should act only when Christians were denounced to it and found guilty. The terrible conditions during the civil wars of the third century turned many more people to Christianity. City people of the middle and upper classes suffered greatly, and many of them were converted to this new religion which seemed to give them hope. The government was too weak to make a consistent effort to enforce the laws, so persecution of Christians was irregular.

History seems to show that a little persecution is worse than none at all in accomplishing its purpose. Execution of Christians and seizure of their property did not stop the spread of the religion. It has been said that "the blood of the martyrs is the seed of the Church." By the end of the third century A.D., the Christian Church had become too strong for the government to try to punish all its members. So the law was changed to prohibit only the making of new converts.

The final triumph of Christianity came in the fourth century. In 313 A.D. the Emperor

Constantine issued the Edict of Milan, which ruled that Christianity would be permitted on the same basis of other religions. In 380 A.D. the Emperor Theodosius made Christianity the official religion of the empire. In 392 he forbade the worship of all heathen gods, even in private.

Organization of the Christian Church

During the first years after the crucifixion of Jesus there was little need for church organization. The few believers expected the early return of Jesus. They shared their wealth and held all property in common. Each congregation had a pastor called an *episcopus* (a Greek word meaning *overseer*; in Latin, *episcopus*). From this word came the term *bishop*. The bishop was assisted by elders called *presbyters*, from which term came the word *priest*. The bishops and priests administered the sacraments, preached, and helped the sick and needy.

The sacraments were mysteries or miracles through which men could achieve salvation. There were seven sacraments: baptism, Holy Eucharist, confirmation, penance, ordination, marriage, and extreme unction. Only a bishop could administer the sacraments of confirmation, which confirmed the recipient in the Christian faith, and ordination, which admitted members to the priesthood.

● *Bishops become important men in the organization*

In time the very simple organization of the early Church took a more definite form. Christians believed that Jesus had given the authority to continue His work to the Apostles, the first missionaries. They, in turn, commissioned others with authority to administer the sacraments and govern the Church. Bishops received power to administer all the sacraments. They gave the priests authority to administer all but confirmation and ordination. Below the priests were lesser officials. The

The Basilica of the Nativity in Bethlehem, one of the oldest Christian churches. The original church was built in the fourth century by St. Helena, mother of Constantine, to commemorate the birthplace of Jesus.

entire body of church officials was called the clergy.

The bishop was the most important church official. In time he gained other duties besides administering the sacraments. He received and managed gifts to the Church and the property of the congregation. He directed relief of the poor and needy among the congregation. He controlled the Church in all dealings with nonbelievers.

● *The territorial organization*

After Christianity became a legal religion, the Church copied the territorial organization of the Roman government. The important unit was the *diocese*, the territory of a bishop. It contained his cathedral church in the most important city. (The word *cathedra* meant the bishop's chair or throne.) The diocese was subdivided into *parishes*, each under a priest chosen and ordained by the bishop. In both church and government organization a number of dioceses were combined into a *province*, with one city as a *metropolis*. The bishop of this city was called a metropolitan, or archbishop.

● *Papal supremacy*

The Church did not follow the organization of the empire at the top, with an Emperor at Rome and another at Constantinople. The belief developed that the churches founded by the Apostles, especially at Rome, Antioch, and Alexandria, were the most important. The Church at Constantinople had not been founded by an apostle. The Church at Rome, however, had been founded by both Peter and Paul, and Peter had been its first bishop. Since Peter had been head of the Apostles, his successor, the Bishop of Rome, came to be recognized as head of all bishops, the supreme authority of the Christian Church. The Bishop of Rome came to be called the Pope, from the Latin word for father.

When the Christian Church was made the official Church of the empire, the emperors regarded it as part of the government, and its officials as subject to them. However, as the Western Empire went to pieces, the Bishops of Rome were freed from direct control of the emperors. The Church took over many governmental functions such as charity, protection of widows and orphans, control of education, marriage, and divorce. When the Western Empire broke up completely, the Church was the only organization with authority recognized throughout the West. The Bishop of Rome came to be regarded as the supreme authority.

The authority of the Bishop of Rome was never fully recognized in the East where the emperor remained powerful. Eastern emperors called Church councils to settle religious disputes. They considered Constantinople equal to Rome in the Church. The Bishop of Constantinople, called the Patriarch, claimed to be head of the Church in the East. The Churches in the East and West drifted apart. Finally, many centuries later, the East formed its own church, the Orthodox Eastern or Greek Orthodox Catholic Church.

Barbarian invasions complete the breakup of the empire

In the preceding chapter you read about the growing weakness of the Roman Empire in the third and fourth centuries. It seems likely that the Empire would have fallen apart from inner weakness without any outside pressure. However, there was much pressure from the outside to speed the decline and give the final push to the tottering government.

During the third century, while the government was weakened by the fifty years of civil wars of the Barrack-Room Emperors, there were barbarian tribes or enemy peoples on every frontier. In Africa there were the Moors and Berbers; in western Asia the Arabs and Persians; in central Asia, on the great grassland plains, numerous nomad peoples; in Europe, the Slavs, Celts, and Germans.

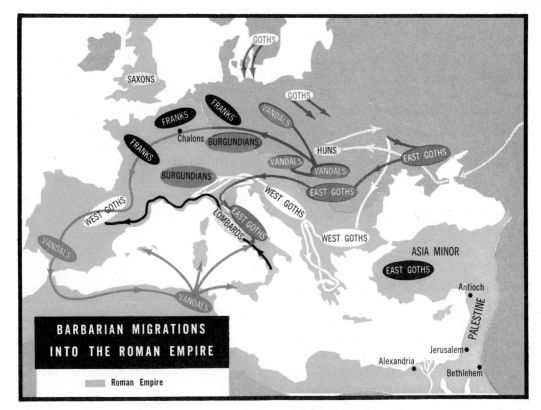

BARBARIAN MIGRATIONS
INTO THE ROMAN EMPIRE

Roman Empire

The Huns

Among the Asiatic nomads, the Huns were first to become important in the history of the Roman Empire. They were true nomads with no fixed homes, moving constantly with their flocks in search of water and pasture. Their wealth was in animals. Other belongings were limited to tents and necessary implements which could be moved easily on horseback. They were marvellous horsemen. They were organized in tribes.

The Huns made almost a profession of raiding and plundering. During the fourth century they terrorized the peoples on the Roman frontier. Historians of the empire, writing at the time, give a picture of them that shows why they were so feared. They were said to be more like beasts than men, with bowlegs, squat bodies, ugly faces with slanting eyes, prominent ears, and bristling hair. This repulsive appearance, added to their filthy habits and utter ferociousness, filled civilized people with terror.

The Germans

The Germans were far more important in history than the Huns. From their original home along the Baltic Sea they began to move south sometime after 500 B.C. They occupied western Germany, the Netherlands, and northern France, pushing the native Celts into Britain and the rest of France. Two German tribes, the Visigoths and Ostrogoths (West and East Goths), migrated across Europe to settle in the grasslands north of the Black Sea.

The Germans had no written language, so we know about them mostly through Roman writings. In his *Commentaries* Caesar told about German life and customs. Tacitus, in his *Germania,* written a century and a half later, gives a much fuller picture. His description of the Germans shows both their strong and weak points. He says they had "fierce blue eyes and reddish hair, great bodies, especially powerful for attack but not equally patient of hard work; little able to withstand heat and thirst, though by climate and soil they have been hardened to cold and hunger."

The Germans of Tacitus' time (100 A.D.) did some primitive farming, but the German was a warrior rather than a farm worker. Wars were frequent. In time of peace the men spent their time hunting, loafing, gambling, and drinking. They left the work, both at home and in the fields, to women and dependents. It was not uncommon for a man to gamble away his property and liberty, as well as the liberty of his wife and children, so that they all became slaves. Most slaves, however, were war prisoners.

Some German tribes had kings with considerable powers, but most of the important decisions were made by assemblies of all warriors. Proposals were made by king, chief, priest, or general. The warriors approved by clashing spears on shields or disapproved by shouting. When a boy reached manhood, he received his weapons. Thereafter he carried his spear and shield on all public occasions, and took part in the assemblies.

German tribesmen often formed voluntary associations for warlike adventure or plunder. A chief or great noble with a reputation for bravery usually attracted a following of young nobles who became members of his household. It was an honorable relationship on both sides. The followers received food, shelter, and equipment; the chief received a following of good fighters, hence a chance for greater deeds. They fought together, shared the profits of victory, or died together.

● *Barbarians filter into the empire*

The northern frontier of the Roman Empire along the Rhine and the Danube rivers was strongly fortified against the Germans. However, many Germans crossed the frontier peacefully. Some enlisted in the army as auxiliaries. Many veteran Roman soldiers who had received land along the frontiers married German women. Sometimes whole tribes were admitted to the empire as allies and given land in return for policing the frontier. In this way the Franks were admitted to the Netherlands, and the Visigoths were admitted to the provinces along the Danube.

In the later days of the Roman Empire, the population contained many barbarians, among them many Germans. Most of them accepted the Christian religion. They kept their own laws, but most of them spoke some form of Latin. In some ways this mingling of peoples strengthened the empire by bringing in new blood. In other ways, though, it weakened Roman culture. Most of the newcomers had little learning and cared little for Roman traditions.

● *The Germans invade in force*

The first large movement of Germans into the empire began peacefully. During the last half of the fourth century the Visigoths were living across the Danube River from the Roman line of frontier forts. The Huns were then making one of their periodic invasions of Europe. Although the Visigoths were tough fighters themselves, they, like other peoples of their time, were terrified by the Huns. When the danger neared them, they begged the eastern emperor to be allowed to cross the river for protection. They were permitted to cross and settle in return for patrolling and defending the frontier. For a time all went well. Then officials of the Eastern Empire began mistreating the new settlers, cheating them of their taxes. In 378 A.D. the Visigoths revolted. In a famous battle at Adrianople, they defeated a Roman army and killed the eastern emperor who led it. Then there was peace for a time.

Alaric, king of the Visigoths, was very ambitious. For a while it looked as though he might try to seize the throne of the Eastern Empire. However, the emperor persuaded him to march westward instead. In 395 A.D. Alaric led his Visigoths into Italy. The western emperor ordered all the troops on the northern frontier back to defend Italy, but they were not enough. The emperor shut himself up in the unconquerable city of Ravenna. Alaric captured Rome in 410 A.D., and gave his troops four days to plunder it. Then he moved his army toward Sicily, planning to take North Africa, but he died suddenly. The Visigoths later settled in southern France and northern Spain.

From 410 A.D. on the two parts of the empire grew further apart. The East revived and gained strength; the West sank to ruin. The western frontiers had been stripped of troops. Barbarians poured in everywhere, to do what they pleased in the provinces. Britain, from which the legions had been withdrawn early, was overrun by Picts and Scots from the north. Later, the German Angles and Saxons invaded Britain from the continent and established a number of small kingdoms. Northern Gaul was taken by Franks and Burgundians, southern Gaul and northern Spain by the Visigoths. The Vandals set up a kingdom in North Africa. They were a German tribe so destructive that their name has come into our modern language as a word meaning one who causes senseless destruction. Italy was overrun by the Ostrogoths, whose kingdom lasted sixty years, and later by the Lombards, who maintained a kingdom in the Po Valley for two centuries.

In the middle of the fifth century a strong leader came to power among the Huns. His name was Attila; he was so ferocious that he was called the Scourge of God. Attila led his Huns to attack Gaul. The western emperor was powerless, but one of his generals led an army against the Huns. Aided by the Visigoths, he defeated them in a great battle at Châlons, France, in 451 A.D. Attila then started to lead his army into Italy, but died suddenly two years later. His army broke up, and the Huns were no longer a threat.

● The Dark Ages follow the fall of Rome

European civilization received a terrible setback when the Western Roman Empire broke up. The German tribes that invaded and settled were not capable of setting up governments to replace the imperial government. You can imagine the conditions when there was no government to do the things which governments must do.

Roads and bridges fell into disrepair, for there was no one to see that they were kept up. Trade and manufacturing disappeared. No one had money to buy goods. It was not safe to move goods from place to place, for there was no protection against brigands. Towns and cities were regularly plundered by wandering bands of barbarians. Most people left the cities, both for greater safety and to be able to get food. Learning disappeared, for there was no government to provide schools. Libraries with their great stores of knowledge were destroyed. Crops were detroyed in the fighting, and fields were overgrown with weeds.

Savage Vandals, invading the Roman Empire, trample over a fallen Roman standard-bearer.

The Greeks have given us two fine words to describe these conditions. *Anarchy* means a complete absence of government. *Chaos* means a complete lack of order. For more than two centuries western Europe suffered the anarchy and chaos of the period that is now called the Dark Ages.

Reasons for the decline

Many reasons have been given for the decline of Roman power and glory. Among them are the great amount of slavery, the mixture of peoples, the establishment of the Christian religion, the gradual loss of fertility of the soil, the weakening of the army, and the barbarian invasions. Without doubt, each of these played some part in the story.

The bringing in of conquered people to be slaves undoubtedly weakened Roman life in many ways. It produced a class of people who were always discontented and often in revolt. Owning slaves had a bad effect on the owner. However, the number of slaves decreased greatly in the first two centuries A.D., and was lowest when the empire was weakest.

The great mixture of peoples in the later empire was both a strength and a weakness. The newcomers added physical strength, and often their customs were morally better than those of the Romans. But when they came too rapidly, they had no time to absorb Roman culture or learn loyalty to the government.

The Christian religion insisted on the worship of one God only, and taught that war was a sin. These teachings weakened the position of the emperor and lowered the morale of the army. However, the Christian teachings produced, especially in the early centuries, honest, hard-working, obedient citizens. These were not the qualities that brought the final breakup.

Loss of fertility of the soil was worst in Italy, North Africa, and the islands of Sicily and Sardinia. Cutting of timber for building

and growing grain by wasteful methods exhausted the land. These regions had to import food from other parts of the empire.

The army grew much weaker after the time of the Good Emperors. Leadership was poorer, and discipline could not be enforced. Military interference in the choice of an emperor was especially bad. It seems likely, though, that this was not the cause of the decline; it was rather the result of the weakening of the government and society.

In like manner the barbarian invasions were the result, not the cause, of weakness. They only gave the final push that toppled the tottering structure. The proof of this is that barbarian tribes were on the frontiers during the entire lifetime of both the Roman Republic and the Roman Empire. Rome was captured by German tribes in 387 B.C., and not again until about 800 years later, in 410 A.D. Not until the empire became weak were the barbarians able to break through the frontiers.

You can see that the breakup of the Roman Empire was not sudden, but gradual. It was not the result of any single cause, but of a number of very complicated causes operating during several centuries. During the third, fourth, and fifth centuries no part of Roman and imperial life was free from decay. There was political decay, economic decay, and social decay. Each influenced and acted upon the others.

●*The interacting causes: political breakdown*

Rome tried to control the entire Mediterranean world with a government meant for a small city-state. The miracle is that it worked for 600 years. The empire grew too fast and became too large for the governmental machinery the Romans could build. In an age of horseback messengers, rowing and sailing ships, and foot travel, it could not be held together. Even the fine Roman legal system could not ensure unity.

The government became more inefficient and corrupt as the territory to be governed grew. Graft and corruption became widespread in the days of the republic when the greatest expansion of territory took place. The Good Emperors were able to improve things a little, but not enough. In the later period honest administration of government was almost impossible to get. Even when the emperor was honest and able, he could not prevent his officials from stealing taxes, taking bribes, and selling justice.

The economy did not produce enough goods and wealth to support the government. The administration of Italy and the poorer provinces drained wealth from the more prosperous regions. Expenses were heavy: the erection of public buildings, the cost of giving grain to the poor, the great expense of the army, and, in the later empire, the cost of two imperial courts. Even unbearably heavy taxes could not produce enough revenue to run the government.

Attempts by the emperors to remedy these conditions only made them worse. Putting less gold and silver in the coinage brought inflation (very high prices). Gold and silver were the standards of value; less gold and silver in coins made the coins less valuable. Attempts to fix prices and regulate business activities failed. Decreased revenues meant unrepaired roads and bridges, increased piracy and brigandage, and even poorer production and trade.

The army, which had gained the territory and held the empire together, became a source of weakness in government. By the third century A.D. there were few native Romans in the army. It was recruited from the lowest classes of free noncitizens, who joined because it brought them citizenship. When enlistments fell off, men were drafted.

Lack of a fixed succession to the throne was a great weakness. After the second century A.D., the army was the strongest force in the empire. It could make and unmake emperors

A street scene in Rome. Note the patrician lady being carried on the shoulders of four slaves, with other slaves walking ahead to clear a path for her. In the later years of the empire, some Romans thought too much of wealth and luxury. Their way of life contrasted sharply with that of earlier Romans, who lived simply and held high ideals of service to their country. The breakdown of the old Roman virtues was one factor in the decline of the empire.

as it wished. The Praetorian Guard, stationed near Rome, became the greatest single force in deciding who should be emperor. Later the legions on the Rhine and Danube frontiers and in the East competed among themselves to place their generals on the throne.

It is clear, then, that for centuries the government of the empire was inefficient. It was able to last because of the rich plunder from Gaul and the East. By the time Diocletian organized an efficient government, the plunder was exhausted, and there was not enough money to run the administration.

● The interacting causes: economic decline

The economic decline of the empire, the failure to produce enough food, goods, and

wealth to allow Roman civilization to prosper, was even more important than the political weakness. It is impossible to pick a definite time and say: "Here it began." There was a gradual change from a strong empire with good trade, industry, and wealth to a time of bad distribution of wealth, depopulation of towns, decayed manufacturing and trade, and a population forced into hereditary castes of occupation.

Details of the economic decline under the Barrack-Room Emperors have already been given (pages 127–128). The bad conditions of this period were typical of a long depression that afflicted the empire. Trade and manufacturing almost disappeared. The small farmers, once the strength of Rome, gradually lost their land. Only the large landowners prospered. They evaded their taxes. Heavy taxes on the middle class in the cities could not keep up with government spending.

The empire fell apart, but Roman architects and builders left many proofs of their skill. This triumphal arch and the temple of Venus (in the background) were built by the Romans in Numidia (now Algeria).

Basically the empire produced too little wealth. What was produced went into too few hands. There was not enough wealth to support a great civilization permanently. Thus the economic decline contributed to the political weakness of the empire.

● *The interacting causes: social decay*

As time went on, there was a tremendous loss of morale in the empire's population. The early Romans were stern, virtuous, hardworking, patriotic people. They were rude and uncultured compared to the people of the East. But they had a strong sense of duty and a fine ideal of service to their government. These fine qualities were almost entirely lost in the later days of the empire. The loss showed in every class of the population. There was little patriotism, little interest in government, and a great lack of political honesty. The landowners who dodged taxes and other responsibilities were especially bad, but no single class of people was good.

The population declined as a result of foreign wars and riots, epidemics, plagues, and the lower birth rate in all classes. The gaps in the population were filled by barbarians, who were hard to unite politically and harder to absorb culturally.

Hatred and envy were everywhere: hatred of the peasant by the landlord; hatred of the army by everyone; hatred of the Christians by the pagans; hatred of the rich by the poor and the poor by the rich.

One great historian, writing about the fifth century, has pointed out that, in a world where poverty was a disgrace, poverty steadily increased, while wealth became more insolent and greedy. The poor carried brigandage to the gates of Rome itself. Parents sold their children into slavery. Public buildings fell into decay, roads into disrepair. At a time when every frontier was threatened, there was wholesale desertion in the army and frontier posts were abandoned. In a bad financial system, there was every kind of corruption. Fraud and greed flourished everywhere. The rich grew richer, the poor became poorer and more helpless. The government had lost control completely. "The most terrible chaos thus reigned throughout the Roman Empire."

The breakup of the empire at the end of the fifth century A.D. did not mean the end of Roman civilization. It lived on in Constantinople and the Eastern Empire for another thousand years. It lived on in the Christian Church, which it had greatly influenced. The barbarians whose kingdoms had once been part of the empire were influenced by its customs and civilization. Thus the heritage of the Romans, and through them the culture of the Greeks and other ancient peoples, were passed on to the modern world.

The Roman heritage

●*The preservation of other cultures*

The Roman culture was a blending of many cultures. The Romans borrowed widely from other peoples, but they borrowed wisely, taking only the best. The Greeks gave them the best of their philosophy, literature, art, and science. But the Romans often excelled the Greeks in making practical use of what they knew. As one example, the Romans did not spend as much time and thought as the Greeks did discussing what justice really is. However, the Romans developed a far better system of law, which brought practical justice to far more people than did the Greek system. The Romans destroyed the Greek city-state governments, but they created a world-state which made it possible for Greek and Hellenistic culture to live and spread.

●*Government*

The Roman Republic developed very democratic practices. All citizens could vote and be represented in the government. These good features were lost under the absolute monarchy of the empire. But even this government made possible a great civilization, the maintenance of order, the promotion of commerce, industry, science, and the arts. Even though the government of the empire was never very well organized or administered, it had many important effects. During its strong period, before the decline began, the Roman government gave all its territory the benefits of a long period of peace, the Pax Romana. The preservation and spread of Greek culture and the rise and spread of the Christian religion would have been either impossible or much less rapid without the unity and peace of the Roman Empire. Here was a step toward world peace and a world in which neighbors are not necessarily strangers or enemies.

● Law

Perhaps the greatest and most lasting Roman contribution was the system of law. During the Middle Ages it was the foundation of civil law in all countries of the former Roman Empire, and it influenced Church law greatly. It has become the basis of the legal codes of many European governments.

Roman law developed more from practical needs than from theories. The Twelve Tables were laws suited to a simple society. They were modified and expanded to fit new conditions by new laws and by the rulings and interpretations of trained judges. As Rome gained more territory, the judges often used legal practices and customs of non-Roman people if they were better suited to the cases. From this developed the idea that there were certain basic legal principles that were common to mankind. We are indebted to the Romans, for example, for the principle that an accused person is considered innocent unless and until he is proved guilty.

● Science, engineering, and architecture

The Romans were a very practical people. They were less interested in scientific research to increase knowledge than in applying knowledge to solve practical problems. Most of their knowledge of nature and natural laws came from the Greeks, but they applied it to the planning of cities, the building of water and sewer systems, the improvement of farming and livestock breeding. No Roman could match Aristotle in observing, collecting, and classifying information, nor Archimedes in working out laws of mathematics and physics. But Roman engineers applied this Greek knowledge to solve problems which the Greeks did not touch.

In engineering the Romans surpassed all ancient peoples in building roads, bridges, aqueducts, amphitheaters, and public buildings. They made wide use of the principle of the arch and vault in their bridges, aqueducts, sewers, and buildings. Roman engineers were probably the first to discover the use of cement.

Roman architecture was their greatest contribution to art. Great public buildings were erected for the emperor, the administrative departments, the Senate, and the assemblies. There were palaces, temples, amphitheaters, triumphal arches and columns. Almost every emperor did something to beautify the city of Rome, and even today people travel from all parts of the world to see what remains.

● Literature

Roman writers are not considered as great or as original as the Greeks, but there are many whose works are still read with pleasure. Among the greatest were the poets Virgil and Horace, the historians Caesar and Tacitus, the essayist and philosopher Cicero.

● Language

The Latin language continued to be used, with some changes, in most of Europe during the Middle Ages. It is the parent of all modern Romance languages (languages based on the Roman). These include Italian, French, Spanish, Portuguese, and Rumanian. For fifteen centuries Latin was the most important language of all Europe. It was the teaching language in all European universities. It became the official language of the Church (and still is used today by the Roman Catholic Church). Long after the Western Empire broke up, all government laws and decrees in western Europe were in Latin. Today scientific terms in all languages have either Latin or Greek origin. Although the English language developed mainly from the German of the Angles and Saxons, more than one-third of all English words are of Latin origin.

Review of Chapter 11

People, places, and things

Identify: Theodosius, Edict of Milan, patriarch, episcopus, presbyter, cathedra, Visigoths, Alaric, Attila, Huns, Ostrogoths, Vandals.

Locate: Palestine, Bethlehem, Jerusalem, Alexandria, Asia Minor, Antioch, Châlons.

Events in review

1. What great difference is there between the teachings of Jesus and the principle of justice taught by Hammurabi or Moses?
2. Who was the first Christian missionary? What did he accomplish for Christianity?
3. What conditions in the Roman Empire favored the spread of Christianity?
4. How long did it take Christianity to win out against persecution by Rome? What events marked the final triumph of Christianity?
5. What were the duties of a bishop? What territory did he have charge of?
6. How did the Bishop of Rome come to be regarded as the supreme authority in the Church? Did all areas accept his authority?
7. Describe the way of life of the Germans of the time of Tacitus.
8. Why are the terms "vandalism," "anarchy," and "chaos" appropriate in describing the period of the breakdown of the Roman Empire? Give examples of the conditions these words describe.
9. Were the barbarian invasions a basic cause of the decline and fall of Rome?
10. Briefly describe three interacting causes of the weakening of the Roman Empire.

Problems and projects

1. To discuss: Were the effects of the barbarian invasions entirely bad for Rome? for the rest of the world?
2. Write a biographical sketch of St. Peter, St. Paul, or another leader of the early Christian Church. (See books on pages 144–145.)
3. Prepare the script for an imaginary radio or TV newscast describing Constantine's conversion to Christianity, or announcing that Attila is approaching Rome.
4. Write an essay on the missionary zeal of the apostles, or on the decision of the Roman state to tolerate and finally to adopt the Christian faith. A class essay contest might be held.
5. Look through a magazine or newspaper. Make a list of words that have come from the Latin language. A contest or quiz program might be set up, based on identifying words of Latin origin.

Review of Roman Civilization

1. Trace the process of Roman expansion within the Italian peninsula. As the Romans came to rule over all of Italy they came into conflict with the Carthaginians. Briefly describe the nature of this long conflict. What were its results in the Mediterranean world?
2. Describe the long struggle which gradually changed Roman government from an aristocratic to a democratic republic. How was this democratic republic later changed into a

military dictatorship, and then into an empire?

3. What lessons can democratic nations learn from the experiences of Rome? Can you think of recent instances where democracy lost to military dictatorship? What circumstances seem to favor the decline of democratic government and to invite military dictatorship?

4. The period of Pax Romana—two centuries of peace—is outstanding in history. What problems and weaknesses in the empire eventually lead to the end of this unusually peaceful time?

Today, many nations are trying to preserve world peace. What lessons can be learned from the period of the Good Emperors?

5. Would you have preferred to live in Egypt during the height of Egyptian civilization, in Greece during the Golden Age, or in Rome under the Good Emperors? Give reasons.

Someone might conduct a poll of the class on this question. Note whether boys and girls give different answers.

6. Why did the Roman Empire break into two parts, each with its emperor and its capital?

What dangers did this split create for each part of the Empire?

7. A high civilization that is surrounded by barbarians is in constant danger of being undermined or destroyed. Were the Romans in any way responsible for the barbarian invasions? What might the Romans have done to save themselves from invasion?

8. Some say that our own part of the world today faces a threat of "barbarian invasion." Can you explain what is meant? Do you agree with this view? The class might hold a discussion on this question.

9. Why did the Roman government persecute Christians? Did this policy succeed? What lessons can be learned from this example of intolerance? Can you think of more recent examples of a government trying to suppress religion by force?

10. Make a table or chart with the following headings: (a) architecture and art, (b) government, (c) law, (d) language, (e) literature, (f) science and engineering. Under each heading list things that are part of our heritage from the Romans.

Compare this listing with the one made for Greece (see page 97). Which civilization made the greater contribution? Why?

Books about the Romans

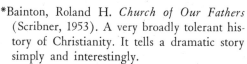

*Bainton, Roland H. *Church of Our Fathers* (Scribner, 1953). A very broadly tolerant history of Christianity. It tells a dramatic story simply and interestingly.

Bouquet, Allan Coates. *Everyday Life in New Testament Times* (Scribner, 1954). Colorful picture of all aspects of life and society in the Mediterranean world during the first century of the Christian era.

Bowie, Walter Russell. *Story of the Church* (Abingdon, 1955). This history of the Church from the time of Christ to the present day offers an understanding of the Christian heritage and its significance in the world today.

*Books marked with a star (*) are easy reading.

Burrows, Millar. *Founders of Great Religions* (Scribner, 1931). The lives of great religious leaders in easy, readable style.

Church, Alfred J. *Roman Life in the Days of Cicero* (Macmillan, 1916). See below under Treble and King.

Cowell, Frank R. *Cicero and the Roman Republic* (Penguin, 1956). More attention is paid to the economic, social, and political life of the late Roman Republic than to Cicero's life.

Cranston, Ruth. *World Faith; the Story of the Religions of the United Nations* (Harper, 1949). A recent account of world religions.

*Davis, William S. *A Day in Old Rome* (Allyn & Bacon, 1925). See below under Treble and King.

Duggan, Alfred Leo. *Julius Caesar* (Knopf, 1955). A gripping account of great events of the first century B.C. A sympathetic treatment, without hero-worship.

Forman, Henry James. *Truth Is One* (Harper, 1954). This book gives a short, clear, and pictorial story of each of the great religions.

*Foster, Genevieve. *Augustus Caesar's World* (Scribner, 1947). A very clear picture of the beginning of the empire, about the time of Jesus. Highly recommended.

Fowler, William W. *Social Life at Rome in the Age of Cicero* (Macmillan, 1909). See below under Treble and King.

*Gaer, Joseph. *How the Great Religions Began* (Dodd, 1956). Covers ten religions and their leaders.

Hagedorn, Hermann. *Book of Courage* (Winston, 1942). Contains a brief account of the great Christian missionary, St. Paul, among others.

*Johnston, Harold W. *Private Lives of the Romans* (Scott, Foresman, 1932). See under Treble and King, below.

Katz, Solomon. *The Decline of Rome and the Rise of Medieval Europe* (Cornell University Press, 1955). A simple, clear account of a very confused period.

Komroff, Manuel. *Julius Caesar* (Messner, 1955). Biography of Julius Caesar from boyhood to statesman, revealing him as a man of intelligence, courage, and vision.

*Mills, Dorothy. *Book of the Ancient Romans* (Putnam, 1927). A clear general account of Roman history.

*Quennell, C. H. B., and Quennell, Marjorie. *Everyday Life in Roman Britain* (Putnam, 1952). Excellently illustrated and very readable, with much material on early Christianity in Roman Britain.

*Tappan, Eva M. *Story of the Roman People* (Houghton Mifflin, 1910). A good general history, clearly written.

*Treble, Henry A., and King, K. M. *Everyday Life in Rome in the Time of Caesar and Cicero* (Oxford, 1930). The books by Church, Davis, Fowler, Johnston, and Treble and King give a vast amount of very interesting material on almost every phase of Roman life. Davis' book is about the period 134 A.D. during the time of the Good Emperors. The others deal with the end of the republic. The student who uses any of these books to look up material on law, religion, military organization, so-

cial customs, amusements, streets, houses, dress, food, women, slaves, children, and education, or many other subjects is in danger of not being able to put it down until he has read the entire book.

Good stories about the Romans

*Anderson, Paul L. *Pugnax the Gladiator* (Appleton-Century, 1939). Roman life in Caesar's time.

*———. *Swords in the North* (Appleton-Century, 1935). A young Roman in Caesar's army in Gaul and Britain.

Bulwer-Lytton, Edward R. *The Last Days of Pompeii* (Macmillan, 1908; also many other editions). A famous story of Roman life in the early days of Christianity. At the climax Mount Vesuvius erupts and destroys the city of Pompeii.

Coles, Manning. *Great Caesar's Ghost* (Doubleday, 1943). A mystery story which revolves around a bracelet once owned by Caesar. Much Roman history mingled with a fast-moving plot.

*Davis, William S. *Friend of Caesar* (Macmillan, 1935). This author's books always contain sound historical background, lively style, and good plot.

Powers, Alfred. *Hannibal's Elephants* (Longmans, 1944). A thirteen-year-old assistant elephant keeper tells the story of Hannibal's march. Interesting and informative.

Sienkiewicz, Henry K. *Quo Vadis; a Tale of the Time of Nero* (Little, Brown, 1943; also many other editions). A dramatic story of Christian martyrs in Nero's Rome.

*Snedeker, Caroline D. *Forgotten Daughter* (Doubleday, 1933). The story of a Greek slave girl in Rome.

———. *Luke's Quest* (Doubleday, 1947). Luke, a Greek priest and physician, spends his life collecting facts about Jesus and writing his book.

*———. *White Isle* (Doubleday, 1940). A patrician Roman family is exiled to Britain.

Wallace, Lew. *Ben Hur* (Dodd, 1953; also many other editions). A famous novel about a Hebrew boy who escaped from the galleys and won a chariot race in Rome.

Williams, Jay. *Counterfeit African* (Oxford, 1944). This mystery story gives a very good picture of Roman North Africa in the second century B.C.

Part Four

THE MIDDLE AGES

The breakup of the Western Roman Empire marks the end of ancient times. What followed was the long period known as the Middle Ages, or medieval times. "Medieval" comes from a Latin word meaning "the period in the middle." This middle era was the span between ancient times and the beginning of our modern world.

It is difficult to fix definite time limits for the great ages of history. The decline and fall of the Western Roman Empire came gradually, brought on by causes that grew up over several centuries. For convenience, though, we can say that the Middle Ages began about 500 A.D. and lasted until about 1500 A.D.

The next six chapters will describe the many sides of this important span of history. The picture on the page facing this one gives clues to several major points in the story of the Middle Ages. Here are a group of Crusaders starting from an English town on the long march to the Holy Land. Thousands of Europeans joined these expeditions in the hope of taking Palestine away from the Mohammedans. Large numbers on both sides lost their lives.

Men went on Crusades for many reasons. A very strong one was religious faith. This suggests the importance of the Christian religion in medieval times. In western Europe the institution that gave direction and meaning to the lives of the people was the great Roman Catholic Church. This mighty organization touched the lives of men at almost every point.

In the picture you can see a priest holding up a cross and blessing the warriors. The clergy were in the top rank of medieval society. Mounted on the white horse is a member of the nobility, the class that, with the clergy, dominated European civilization. Also shown are soldiers and peasants, who represent the lower orders. Thus you can see here three major groups from the world of the Middle Ages: the churchmen, the warrior nobles, the common people.

Above is sketched a castle of the kind that was needed in an age of warring lords. The feudal nobles lived in places that were fortresses first, dwelling places second.

The graciousness, the learning, and the luxury of Roman culture almost disappeared during the early Middle Ages. Throughout medieval times wars were all too frequent—though on a smaller scale than modern wars.

Take a look now at the time chart on pages 148–149. The chart lists many major events that will be covered in Chapters 12 to 17.

Part Four   THE MIDDLE AGES

ENGLAND   EUROPE AND THE CHURCH

	ENGLAND		EUROPE AND THE CHURCH
500	**410-442** Angles and Saxons to England	**496**	Clovis unites the Franks
600	**597** Augustine restores Christianity	**590**	Pope Gregory the Great
700		**732**	Charles Martel defeats Mohammedans, Battle of Tours
800	**787** Danes to England	**800**	Charlemagne crowned Emperor
		843	Treaty of Verdun: Charlemagne's Empire divided
900	**871-901** Alfred the Great		
1000		**962** Otto the Great, Holy Roman Empire **987** Hugh Capet starts Capetian dynasty	
	1066 Norman Conquest	**1054** Separation—Roman-Greek churches **1059** Cardinals elect Pope **1073-1085** Pope Gregory VII **1096** First Crusade	
1100		**1122** Concordat of Worms	
		1182 Birth of St. Francis **1198-1216** Pope Innocent III	
1200	**1215** Magna Carta **1265** Commons admitted to Parliament **1295** Model Parliament	**c. 1225** Birth of Thomas Aquinas **1273** Rudolf of Hapsburg, Emperor	
1300	**1337** Hundred Years' War begins **1387?** Chaucer writing *Canterbury Tales*	**1309-1377** Babylonian Captivity **1328** End of Capetian dynasty **1337** Hundred Years' War begins **1348** The Black Death **1378-1417** Great Schism	
1400	**1453** End of Hundred Years' War **1455-1485** Wars of the Roses	**1414-1418** Council of Constance **1431** Burning of Joan of Arc **1450** Gutenberg: printing **1469** Marriage of Ferdinand and Isabella **1492** Moors driven out of Spain Columbus	
1500	**1485** Henry VII starts Tudor dynasty		

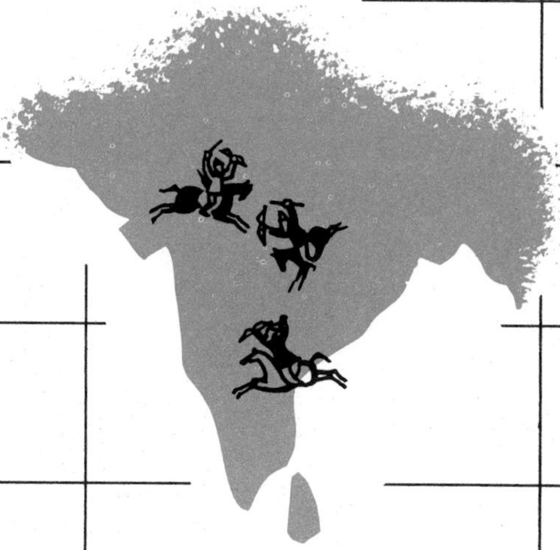

BYZANTINE EMPIRE AND NEAR EAST	INDIA	CHINA

BYZANTINE EMPIRE AND NEAR EAST

565 Reign of Justinian

Birth of Mohammed

The Hegira

Mohammedans extend conquests as far as Spain

century, Seljuk Turks to East

First Crusade
Crusaders capture Jerusalem

Saladin recaptures Jerusalem
Third Crusade

Fourth Crusade: sack of Constantinople by Crusaders

-16th centuries, Ottoman s to Near East

Turks capture Constantinople
Princes of Moscow drive out Mongols

INDIA

5th-6th century, Huns to northeast India

750-1525   Moslem invasions of India

1525   Baber-Mogul Empire

CHINA

618-907   Tang Dynasty: high culture, books printed; Li Po, Tu Fu, greatest poets

6th-8th centuries, Chinese culture spreads to Japan

960-1280   Sung Dynasty: high culture

1162-1227   Genghis Khan

1206   Genghis Khan establishes Mongol Empire
1271-1295   Marco Polo in China

1280   Kublai Khan: Mongol Dynasty

1368   Mongols overthrown
1369-1644   Ming Dynasty

Ming emperors discourage contacts with Europeans

Chapter 12

The Contrast of East and West

WHEN the Western Roman Empire broke up, about 500 A.D., western Europe entered the Middle Ages. The fall of the Western Empire left Europe in anarchy and chaos. There was no organized government, no law, no order, no industry, no commerce, no education. This Dark Age, though, did not fall over the East. There two great empires, the Byzantine and the Islamic, or Moslem, preserved the classical civilizations of the Greeks and the Romans.

The Byzantine Empire: a continuing civilization

With great difficulty, the Eastern Roman Empire managed to survive the barbarian invasions of the fifth century. Then, during the sixth century, the brilliant Emperor Justinian reorganized both the government and the army. The Eastern Empire lasted until the fifteenth century.

The Byzantine Empire survived for so long because it had strengths which the Western Roman Empire lacked. It included the lands and peoples of ancient civilizations, and it was the center of Hellenistic culture. Its economy produced enough wealth to support a great empire. Its army and navy were strong and well organized. It had Constantinople, a great and prosperous center of commerce, located where Europe and Asia come so closely together. Constantinople was built on the site of the ancient city of Byzantium. From this name we get the term Byzantine.

A great strength of the Byzantine Empire came from its highly centralized government. The emperor was all-powerful. His group of officials, the bureaucracy, were trained professionals. The government regulated trade and manufacturing very closely. Taxes raised an enormous income, so that the government could provide services to protect and encourage prosperity and maintain culture. There was no rule for succession to the throne, but the bureaucracy of officials was strong enough to carry the government through the bad times of weak emperors or civil wars. Of course, such a government preserves its strength at the expense of the rights and liberties of most of the people. To use modern terms, this was a dictatorship rather than a democracy.

Throughout its history the Byzantine Empire was surrounded by enemies. Naturally, in a period of 1,000 years it had its ups and downs, its times of strength and weakness. A list of the peoples who attacked it would be long. It survived until the Ottoman Turks captured Constantinople in 1453.

• Cultural contributions

The Byzantine Empire performed great services for civilization. Its scholars did not produce much that was original, but they preserved and passed on the learning of Greece and the Near East. The empire kept alive industry and trade with their civilizing influence. It preserved and improved Roman law. For a thousand years, while the barbarian states of western Europe were struggling to develop a new culture, Constantinople was the center of a civilization as brilliant as that of any age.

Chapter 12 continues after color supplement

ROME AND THE MIDDLE AGES

This eight-page section of pictures shows aspects of the culture of Rome and of the Middle Ages, the period that followed the fall of the Roman Empire. Compare these full-color pictures with those of Egyptian and Greek civilization in the section following page 54.

Roman civilization was influenced by that of the Etruscans (see pages 103–104). The skill of Etruscan artists is shown by these paintings. Right: A flute player (about 480 B.C.). (Photo by Braun, Paris.) Below: A scene taken from Greek mythology, showing a warrior fighting Amazons.

Above: A Roman mosaic depicting a scene in a theatrical production. Notice the masks (see page 85 for their use in the Greek theater).

Below, left: Wall decorations in the house of a wealthy resident of Pompeii.
Below, right: The courtyard of a villa at Pompeii. This great city was destroyed by an eruption of Mt. Vesuvius in 79 A.D.

emains of the Arch of Constantine and the olosseum in Rome. The great amphitheater, the olosseum, could hold 50,000 people. Note the use f the arch, a feature unknown to the Greeks and gyptians.

A present day view of the ancient Forum in Rome. This area, with its many fine buildings, was a center of Roman life.

The Temple of Vesta at Tivoli. Vesta was an important goddess in the religion of the Romans (see page 106). In many of their buildings, the Romans used columns of a style copied from the Greeks.

Above: Part of the remains of a great Roman estate, the Villa Adriana. Notice the use of both columns and archways in the colonnade at the end of the pool.

The picture at the left takes us from the Roman world into medieval Europe. The influence of the Romans was still felt. This cathedral at Worms, Germany, was built (in the twelfth and thirteenth centuries) in the style of architecture called Romanesque. Notice the rounded arches in the Roman style.

Much of the finest art of the Middle Ages was created by and for the Christian Church. *Left:* Carvings on a tomb in Canterbury Cathedral, England. *Below:* A section of a stained glass window in Canterbury.

Medieval clothing was often colorful. At left are citizens of Florence, Italy, in costumes from the Middle Ages.

Above: Equipment for a medieval soldier—a shirt of chain mail and a crossbow. The device at the right was used to draw back the cord of the crossbow. (Metropolitan Museum of Art, New York.)

Left: Medieval manuscripts were works of art. The text was painstakingly copied by hand. Then the page was decorated with elaborate capital letters and with colored illustrations.

Facing page: The elaborate armor and trappings of a knight and his charger in the late Middle Ages. (See also page 169.) This is a suit of German armor from the fifteenth century.

Masons of the Middle Ages building a tower, as shown in an illustration from a French manuscript of about 1250. Note the derrick used to hoist stones, and the man climbing the ladder with a hod of mortar on his shoulder.

A farm scene from the late Middle Ages. This picture, "April Labors on the Farm," was painted in Flanders about 1515. (Both pictures on this page courtesy of the Pierpont Morgan Library.)

The great Emperor Justinian ordered his scholars to collect and organize all kinds of Roman law. The entire collection is known as the *Corpus Juris Civilis,* the Body of Civil Law. Justinian's Code, as it is called, is in three parts. The *Code* itself was a collection, arrangement, and revision of all existing decrees of emperors. It was kept up to date by adding later decrees and laws.

The second and third parts were of even more lasting importance. The *Digest* was a summary of the writings of the great Roman experts on law. It was arranged alphabetically by ideas. It contained brief statements by the greatest writers on all legal ideas and principles, arranged so that it was easy to find them. The *Institutes* was a textbook on the basic principles of Roman law. In western Europe during the Middle Ages Roman law was studied principally from the *Digest* and *Institutes.* It greatly influenced the development of European countries, and still forms the basis of many European legal systems.

The Greek Orthodox Catholic Church was not as influential in the government of the Byzantine Empire as was the Roman Catholic Church in the West. However, it helped to bring unity in the Eastern Empire, and did very important missionary work.

During the ninth century two brothers, Cyril and Methodius, preached Christianity to the Slavs. The Slavs had no written language, and Cyril wanted them to be able to read the Bible. He made up a modified Greek alphabet for the Moravians. After further improvements, it became the Cyrillic alphabet of the Serbs, Bulgars, and Russians. These people still use Cyril's alphabet or one derived from it. The missionary work begun by Cyril and Methodius was successful. Serbs and Bulgars were converted during the ninth century, the Russians during the tenth century. Great numbers of these people still follow the Greek Orthodox faith.

Arab civilization

The second rich and highly developed civilization of the East was that of the Arabs who are called Mohammedans because of

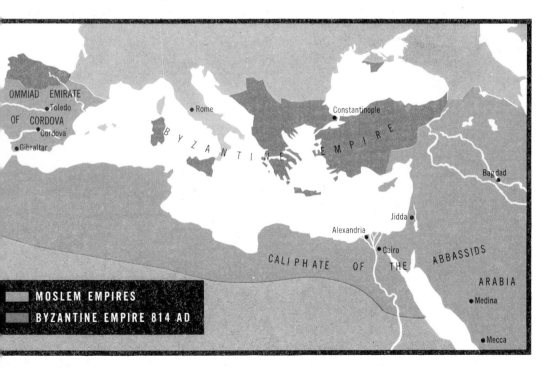

OMMIAD EMIRATE
OF CORDOVA
•Toledo
•Cordova
•Gibraltar

•Rome

Constantinople

B Y Z A N T I N E   E M P I R E

Bagdad

Jidda •

Alexandria

•Cairo

CALIPHATE   OF   THE   ABBASSIDS

ARABIA

•Medina

■ MOSLEM EMPIRES
■ BYZANTINE EMPIRE 814 AD

•Mecca

their religion. Like the Byzantine, the Arab civilization far surpassed and overshadowed that of western Europe during most of the Middle Ages.

● Arabia and the Arabs

The Arabian peninsula is a desert plateau which lies south of the Fertile Crescent. Throughout all history, even today, the scanty vegetation of the interior has supported only nomad herdsmen.

The Arabs of the interior were called Bedouins. They were organized into tribes, each under the absolute rule of a chief or sheik. The Bedouins were uneducated but very intelligent. They loved poetry and storytelling. They were dignified, courteous, and hospitable.

Some Arab tribes lived in towns along the seacoast and were traders. Goods from Asia

The Kaaba at Mecca. Now, as it has been since Mohammed's time, Mecca is the holy city for Moslems. The Kaaba is a cubical stone building which is covered with black silk hangings. This picture shows some of the millions of Moslems who have made pilgrimages to this shrine.

and Africa were brought to the port of Jidda, then taken overland to Mecca, the starting point of a caravan route running north to Syria. The town-dwelling Arabs had tribal government like that of the Bedouins, but a higher level of culture. Mecca was ruled by a rich tribe known as the Kuraish.

● Mohammed

The great religious leader of the Arabs was Mohammed. He was born in Mecca about 570 A.D. He was one of the Kuraish tribe, but his family was not wealthy. An orphan at an early age, he spent his youth in poverty, had little formal education, and probably never learned to write. He became a camel driver and caravan trader. From his contacts with other peoples he learned about religions, especially the Jewish and Christian.

While still a young man Mohammed became the commercial agent of a wealthy widow, whom he married. He then had leisure to think about a subject which interested him greatly—the problems of religion and conduct. At this time the Arabs worshipped many gods and idols. Through meditation and prayer he became convinced that the worship of many gods was wrong. There was but one Supreme Being—one God, and his name in Arabic was Allah. Thus Mohammed, like the Jews and the Christians, came to believe in one God.

When he was forty years of age, Mohammed had a great religious experience. He believed that the angel Gabriel commanded him to preach to the Arabs to bring them religious purity. Mohammed did not claim to have any supernatural powers. He considered himself to be a prophet and teacher like Moses.

Mohammed began to preach his beliefs in Mecca, but met with ridicule and bitter opposition from his tribesmen, the Kuraish. He made little progress; so he took his little band of followers to a nearby town, Medina, where he had promise of better support. This event is known as the Hegira (the Flight). Its date, 622 A.D., is important because Moslems now use it as the Year One in their calendar.

In Medina Mohammed made many converts, and became the leader of his new community. In a few years he returned to Mecca at the head of an army and captured the town. By a combination of wise policies, toleration, and force he converted the Kuraish and many of the Bedouin tribes. By 632 A.D., when Mohammed died, almost all Arabs had accepted his faith.

● The Mohammedan religion

The Koran. The Bible of the Mohammedan religion is the Koran (the Recital). It is a collection of Mohammed's teachings and accounts of his life over a period of twenty-three years, written down by scribes and collected in book form by one of his successors. It contains much that was borrowed from Jewish and Christian teachings.

The Creed of Islam. The formal name of the Mohammedan religion is Islam, which means "submission to God." One who makes this submission is called a Moslem. The creed, or central belief, is simple: "There is no God but Allah, and Mohammed is his Prophet."

The four demands of Islam. A Moslem must meet four chief obligations. He must pray at certain fixed hours of the day, facing Mecca. He must, if possible, make a pilgrimage to Mecca once in his lifetime. He must give alms to the needy. He must fast from sunrise to sunset during the month of Ramadan—the ninth month of the Mohammedan year. This is sacred because it was the month in which Mohammed had his vision.

The moral and social commands of Islam. Mohammed required and emphasized the virtues of temperance, humility, justice, generosity, tolerance, obedience to authority, and courage in moral life as well as in military conflict. A Moslem was allowed to have more than one wife. Slavery was permitted. Mos-

lems were forbidden to drink alcoholic liquors or to eat pork.

In contrast to Christian teachings, Mohammed praised what he called the Holy War. He said: "The sword is the key of heaven and hell; a drop of blood shed in the cause of God, a night spent in arms, is of more avail than two months of fasting and prayer; whosoever falls in battle, his sins are forgiven. . . ."

The heavenly rewards promised the Moslem warrior were more physical than those of the Christian heaven. The Moslem paradise had a very special appeal to desert dwellers. It was said to be a place of cool groves, green meadows, springs, and flowing streams. It promised delicacies, fruits, streams of milk and honey, perfumes, silks, and jewels. There the faithful were waited on by maidens of great beauty called Houris. Do you wonder that the good Moslems were terrible fighters, going bravely, even recklessly, into battle?

Islam has no images, no elaborate ceremonies, no priesthood. There are men learned in Islamic faith and law, but no formal priestly caste. A service in a Moslem temple, or mosque, is merely a praying together under guidance of a leader.

● The spread of Islam

When Mohammed died, an informal assembly of Moslems chose his successor. They passed over his daughter and son-in-law and picked abu-Bakr, an early convert and very able man. He was called *caliph,* successor to the prophet. When he died, an assembly chose his friend and counselor Omar as caliph. Both abu-Bakr and Omar, in order to avoid a civil war over the succession, followed a policy of holy war, that is, the conquest of neighboring territory of non-Moslems.

The Arabs had a wonderful opportunity for conquest. The governments of the Byzantine Empire and of the Persians in Mesopotamia were both weak at this period.

Everywhere the people were unhappy, with little incentive to fight. They either welcomed or did not oppose the conquerors.

Arab victories were made easier by their wise policies toward conquered peoples. They were fierce and fearless in battle but generous in victory. Non-Moslems who surrendered were allowed to keep their religion and culture. They had to accept Moslem rule and pay a special tax which the faithful did not have to pay. The caliphs opposed the slaughter or forced conversion of conquered people for a very good reason. It was only the non-Moslems who paid taxes. Every time a convert was made a taxpayer was lost. Many of the people of the conquered countries voluntarily became Moslems, and their descendants remained so.

In less than a century after the death of Mohammed his followers had overrun Arabia, Palestine, Syria, Mesopotamia, part of India, Egypt, and North Africa. Then they took to the sea, and conquered the islands of the Mediterranean. Thus the southern part of that sea was theirs for trade. They besieged Constantinople, but were turned back.

At the other end of the Mediterranean they had more success in entering Europe. The Moors of North Africa, recent converts, were eager for conquest. A general named Tarik led an expedition into Spain. In 711 A.D. Tarik led his army past the great rock that

Gibraltar. This rocky promontory has been important in world history for many centuries. Once it was part of the Moslem Empire. Then it became a Spanish fortress. The English took it from Spain in 1713 and have held it ever since as one of their naval bases. The peak of the rock rises 1,439 feet.

guards the strait between Africa and Spain. The rock was named Jebel Tarik—the Mountain of Tarik. Europeans have altered the name into Gibraltar. Spain was an easy conquest. With the defeat of the Visigoth king, the whole country collapsed. In seven years the Moors had passed beyond the Pyrenees to raid the plains of what is now central France. There, at Tours, in 732 A.D., they were defeated by the Franks under Charles Martel and driven back toward Spain. At this point the Moslems controlled the large empire shown on the map on page 151.

● The Moslem Empire

The government of the Moslem Empire left much to be desired. At the top was the caliph, supreme head of both government and religion. He was not allowed to make laws because the law of the Koran was sacred and unchanging. It was interpreted by the learned men, not by the caliph. The territory of the empire was organized into provinces, with Arabs in top government positions. Lower officials could be non-Moslems if they were loyal.

The caliph was the supreme civil, military, and religious head of the whole vast empire. In time the position became hereditary. It required a man of great ability and energy, and such men did not always appear. Later the empire was divided into three caliphates, one at Bagdad, one at Cairo, and one at Cordova in Spain.

Although the Islamic world was divided into parts, it remained united in religion, civilization, and culture. It was a very great culture. In the beginning the Arabs were a backward people, but they were intelligent and very tolerant. They were willing to adopt the best ideas, customs, and institutions they found. Language formed a common bond throughout the empire. All Moslems recognized the Koran as the sacred book. Mohammed had forbidden its transla-

tion into any other language. Therefore, Arabic became a common language among educated Moslems everywhere.

●Economic development of the Islamic world

The Arabs promoted the development of agriculture everywhere. Fruits, vegetables, and other products from any part of the empire were introduced wherever they would grow. Improved methods of fertilizing, of irrigating, and of grafting plants were discovered and spread.

Arabs had long been traders, and Mohammed in his teachings had praised and encouraged commerce. He had himself been a

A famous example of Moorish architecture in Spain: the Court of the Lions in the Alhambra, at Granada. This palace was built by the Moors while Spain was part of the Moslem Empire.

trader. Now trade could flow freely through a vast empire of great riches, with no tolls, a common language, a common money, and a common religion. Goods of India and China were brought by sea to the Persian Gulf and the Red Sea, then overland to the ports of Syria and to Cairo and Alexandria in Egypt. There was a free exchange of ideas and customs along with the exchange of goods.

Manufacturing was stimulated by the demands of trade. The empire produced textiles: silk, cotton, and linen goods, tapestries, carpets, and rugs. There were luxury products: jewelry, perfumes, and spices. Metal products included gold, silver, steel, brass, and copper. There was a great variety of pottery and glassware. Some cities specialized in making certain products. Swords of Damascus and Toledo steel became world-famous. The cotton cloth of Mosul in Mesopotamia added a word to our language—*muslin;* that of Calicut in India became known as *calico.* Morocco in Africa and Cordova in Spain made fine and famous leather goods.

● *Moslem scholarship*

The Arabs' greatest contribution to culture was their broad tolerance and willingness to accept the ideas of others. They took the science and philosophy of Greece, Rome, India, and the Orient and tried to combine them, using Arabic as a common language. Moslem scholars were interested in every field of learning.

Moslem scientists were practical men. They wrote handbooks and encyclopedias of useful knowledge on many subjects. Their geographers and navigators were the finest in their world. They introduced the compass from India and China. They themselves perfected the astrolabe, an instrument long used in navigation. From the Chinese they learned papermaking and the use of gunpowder. They added much medical knowledge to that of Hippocrates and Galen.

The Arabs were fine mathematicians. They perfected algebra (an Arabic word) as a science, and did much work in other fields. However, their greatest contribution to mathematics was the system of writing numbers, which today we call Arabic numerals. The Greeks and the Romans had represented numbers by letters, which were very awkward to work with. For problems in arithmetic they used the counting device called the abacus. Addition and subtraction were easy, multiplication not too difficult, and division difficult but possible. To write answers, though, the letters did not match the columns of the abacus.

An Arab astrolabe dating from the thirteenth century. The astrolabe was invented by the Greeks and improved by Arab scientists. This instrument was developed to measure the altitude of the stars or the sun. Explorers such as Vasco da Gama and Columbus used astrolabes for navigation.

From the Hindus the Arabs learned the use of the symbols from 1 to 9, but this did not help much. They had no zero to represent a vacant column on the abacus. A great Moslem scientist was the first to describe the use of zero to represent the vacant column. This allowed symbols to be arranged in columns, with the decimal system of forming tens, hundreds, or thousands by adding zeros. It is almost impossible to overestimate the value of this idea and method to mathematics and science. Our entire mathematical system is based on it.

● *Decline of Moslem culture*

The great days of Moslem culture were during the eighth, ninth, and early tenth centuries—that is, from about 700 A.D. to 1000 A.D. Thereafter, men who believed in "following the letter of the Koran" became powerful in the Moslem world. They opposed free thought and foreign ideas. In Spain freedom, tolerance, and progress lasted longer than elsewhere, because Spain was more independent.

An influx of new peoples also helped to lower the culture. The Arabs ruled until the mid-eleventh century. Then the Seljuk Turks, Asiatic converts to Islam, gained control. In the mid-twelfth century the Mongols, another Asiatic people, overran Syria and Mesopotamia under their great leader Genghis Khan. During the thirteenth and fourteenth centuries another Turkish tribe, the Ottomans, gained control. It was they who took Constantinople, the Balkans, and much of Central Europe.

● *Influence of Islam on western Europe*

Moslem culture made a great and lasting impression on the civilization of western Europe through two main points of contact. During the twelfth and thirteenth centuries a series of great crusades took place. Armies from Christian Europe invaded Asia in an effort to take the Holy Land away from the Moslems. These Christians from the West were amazed by and learned much from Moslem civilization. They carried back with them many ideas that helped to bring Europe out of the Dark Ages. Even closer at hand was the Moslem culture of Spain. Cordova was the Bagdad of Spain, with a university that was world-famous. Seville was a center of luxury; Toledo was famous for learning. Christian and Jewish scholars brought Moslem learning from Spain into western Europe.

The Dark Ages in western Europe

Before Christian western Europe could profit from the higher Islamic culture, it had to be ready to receive it. It had to pass through that lowest ebb of European civilization we call the Dark Ages.

Most of the Germanic tribes which invaded Italy and the Western Empire in the fourth and fifth centuries disappeared before too long. Visigoths, Vandals, Burgundians, Ostrogoths and many others helped to destroy centralized government and bring on the Dark Ages. Each tribe set up a kingdom in some part of the Western Empire. In each case the invaders were a small group ruling a much larger native population by military force. Once defeated, they vanished. They were either killed or absorbed into the population without leaving much trace.

But two groups of the Germanic tribes were destined to play a much more important role in history. They were the Angles and Saxons in Britain and the Franks in Gaul.

Britain

Pre-Roman Britain was inhabited by a people called Celts, whom the Romans called Britons. Celts lived also in Ireland and the regions of France and the Netherlands on the continent. When Caesar was conquering the Celts of Gaul, their island kinsmen came to their aid. This fact led him to invade Britain in 55 B.C. His troops defeated the natives, but stayed only a few years. About a century later most of Britain was conquered by the Romans, and it stayed a Roman province for nearly four centuries. Roman legions controlled it from their great fortified camps, or castra. The Latin language was used, and when the empire adopted Christianity, Britain became Christian.

The barbarian invasions that occurred during the fourth and fifth centuries cut Britain off from the empire. Roman legions remained until 407 A.D.; then they were called back to guard more important and valuable places. The unprotected island was raided by German tribes from the continent. Angles, Saxons, and Jutes came first as raiders, then in large numbers as settlers, especially the Saxons. The native Celts were either enslaved or driven into the highlands of Wales and Scotland. Roman culture, the Latin language,

and the Christian religion vanished. The invaders brought their Germanic tribal government, speech, and worship of the forces of nature. They were agricultural people, with little liking for town life.

● The Angles and Saxons

The Angles and the Saxons formed seven small, independent kingdoms. Later they were combined into three important ones: Wessex, Mercia, and Northumberland. Government was simple at first. The king had much power, and there was a noble class. A "council of wise men" called the Witan, made up of nobles, advised the king. Together, the king and the Witan made laws and levied taxes. The freemen were all warriors, and there were numerous slaves. In time a kingdom was divided into districts for the administration of justice and the collection of taxes. Larger districts, called shires, were under officials called shirereeves, or sheriffs.

Britain was re-converted to Christianity in the seventh century. The first missionaries came from Ireland, where the religion had not died out, but the final conversion was made by monks from Rome. Pope Gregory the Great was very eager to reclaim England for the Church. He sent a number of monks, led by Augustine, to convert the Angles and Saxons. The wife of the king of Wessex was a Christian. She persuaded her husband to allow the monks to preach, and finally Britain accepted Christianity. Canterbury, in southern England, became the religious capital. The archbishop of Canterbury was called the primate, or first officer, of the Church in Britain.

● Struggles with the Danes

By the end of the eighth century Wessex controlled almost all England. Then came new barbarian invasions by the Northmen from Scandinavia. The Saxons called them all Danes and feared them dreadfully, for they

were savage fighters. At first the Danes came as summer raiders for plunder. In time more came, and they remained through the winter, forcing the Saxons to provide for them. Finally they settled permanently. In an effort to hold the Danes in check, the kings of Wessex set aside a section of England called the Danelaw. Here the Danes could do pretty much as they pleased under a set of laws drawn up especially for them.

A great Saxon king was able not only to check the Danes but also to advance civilization greatly. Alfred of Wessex, known as Alfred the Great, became king in 871 A.D. He gave the Saxons new courage. Within a few years he led his army to the first real victory over the Danes. He was unable to drive them out of the island entirely, but he restored peace. He also began to build a navy to protect England from sea raids.

Alfred the Great is best known for his peaceful accomplishments. An educated and scholarly man, he wished his people also to be educated. He established schools and monasteries, inviting scholars from Ireland and the continent to teach. He himself translated books into the Anglo-Saxon language. At his command the monks began a history of England from the earliest times. This *Anglo-*

A model of the kind of ships the Danes used in their invasions of England. The crew did double duty as fighting men and oarsmen. While the ship was under way, the men hung their shields along the side.

Saxon Chronicle was written in the language of the people. It was continued for 250 years after his death.

The reigns of Alfred and his immediate successors make a bright spot in the gloom of the times. The work he began was continued for nearly a century. Much Danish-held land was won back. The government was strengthened and the Christian Church firmly established. One ruler, Edgar the Peaceful, was recognized as king of all England and overlord of Scotland and Wales. Then came some weak rulers, and once again the Danes.

This time the Danes conquered the whole island. Under the great Danish ruler Canute, Britain became part of a Danish empire that included most of Scandinavia and Ireland. Canute lived in England most of the time, and tried to rule wisely. Saxons were appointed to offices, and conditions throughout the empire were good. Canute's sons and successors were weak. Finally the Danish rulers were driven out, and Saxon kings again held the throne.

The Saxon kings ruled until the island was conquered by invaders from France, the Normans. This event will be described in Chapter 14. Now we will take up the history of the Franks in Gaul.

The Franks dominate Gaul

By 500 A.D. Roman Gaul had been completely overrun by barbarians. Its peoples then included native Gallo-Romans and numerous Germanic tribes: Visigoths, Burgundians, and two groups of Franks. Of all these the Franks were to have the most long-lasting importance.

● Clovis

The Franks came into the Roman Empire in the lower Rhine region. One source of their strength was that they spread slowly and permanently, without losing touch with their homeland. They established several kingdoms and began to take over the lands of the other tribes. In 481 A.D. a very able man became king of one of the Frankish tribes. He was Clovis—brutal, cruel, and conscienceless, but an excellent fighting man. Under his command his people conquered the other Frankish tribes and controlled all northern Gaul.

Not long after Clovis became king, an important event took place. Influenced by his

The victory of the Franks over the Moslems at Tours ranks as one of the decisive battles of world history. This battle prevented the Moslems from extending their empire northward from Spain into other parts of Europe. This old print shows Charles Martel leading the Franks in a charge against the Moorish forces.

Christian wife he made a vow to accept her faith if he won a battle. He did win, and not only kept his vow, but forced 3,000 of his warriors to be baptized. Clovis became a champion of Christianity, and he and his Franks came into close alliance with the popes.

At the death of Clovis his kingdom was divided among his four sons. These rulers and their descendants came to be called Merovingians because Clovis traced his family back to an ancestor named Meroveg. As time passed, the Merovingian kings became less able. They enjoyed the luxuries of court life and left the business of governing to lower officials; so they became known as "Do-Nothing" kings. One writer of the time tells that the king spent his time combing his long yellow curls with a jeweled comb. This was a far cry from Clovis, the rough-and-ready leader of barbaric tribes.

● Charles Martel

In one of the Frankish kingdoms there was an official, the chief of the royal household, whose title was Mayor of the Palace. Under the "Do-Nothing" kings the mayors of the palace became the real rulers of the kingdom. One mayor named Pepin succeeded in making the office hereditary in his family. His successors were kings in everything but name. One of them united all the Frankish kingdoms.

A very able successor of Pepin was Charles Martel (Charles the Hammer). He enforced his authority everywhere in the kingdom. When the Moslems invaded central Gaul from Spain, Charles realized that they could be defeated only by cavalry. To raise an army of cavalry he took land from the Church. He gave a part of this land to any Frankish lord who could furnish a certain number of armed horsemen.

● The Battle of Tours

With his cavalry Charles Martel met the Moslems at Tours, in central France, in 732.

He defeated them and drove them back to the region just north of the Pyrenees. Historians believe that if the Moslems had won this battle, all western Europe might have become part of Islam, with consequences that are hard to imagine.

● Pepin the Short becomes king

When he died, Charles Martel left his son, Pepin the Short, a large and strong kingdom of which he was the real ruler although he had only the title of Mayor of the Palace. Pepin wished to be king in name as well as in fact. His chance came when the pope appealed to him for help. The Lombards, a fierce German tribe, had conquered and settled in the Po valley, the Italian region still called Lombardy. They began to raid and conquer central Italy and to threaten the city of Rome. The eastern emperor could not protect Italy; so, in desperation, the pope asked Pepin the Short and the Franks to help him.

Pepin's price for his help was high. He demanded that he be declared king. The pope consented, and an assembly of Franks took the throne from the Merovingian king, sent him to a monastery, and elected Pepin king. The pope then came to Gaul and anointed Pepin. This act later became a precedent (an example to be followed) for the claims of the popes that they had the authority to install and depose kings.

King Pepin then led an army of Franks into Italy and defeated the Lombards. He took territory around Rome from the Lombard king and gave it to the pope. This was called the Donation of Pepin. It created the Papal States, of which the pope became the ruler. Pepin also waged successful wars against the Moors in southern Gaul and the Saxons in Germany. Thus Roman Gaul became the kingdom of the Franks, under a king who had real authority. The way was prepared for the greatest of all the Franks, Charlemagne, the son of Pepin.

Review of Chapter 12

People, places, and things

Identify: Justinian, the *Koran,* Islam, Mohammed, Bedouins, Caliph, Tarik, the Witan, Alfred the Great, Canute, Clovis, Charles Martel.

Locate: The Byzantine Empire, Constantinople, the Arabian Peninsula, Bagdad, Cairo, Cordova, Gibraltar, Tours, Mecca, Medina.

Events in review

1. How long did the Eastern or Byzantine Empire last? Why did it survive so much longer than the Western Empire?
2. What was Justinian's *Code?* Why was it important?
3. What was the contribution of Cyril and Methodius to the civilization of eastern Europe?
4. What was the Hegira? Why is its date important to Moslems?
5. List at least five of the teachings of the *Koran.* Point out two that conflict with Christian beliefs.
6. List facts to show that the Moslem Empire developed a great culture.
7. How much of Europe was included in the Moslem Empire? What stopped the Moslems from adding more of western Europe to their empire?
8. Why did the Christian religion vanish from Britain in the early 400's? How was Britain re-converted to Christianity?
9. What different peoples lived in Britain from the time of Caesar to the time of Canute?
10. How did Pepin the Short become king of the Franks?

Problems and projects

1. Name three men you have read about in Parts One to Three who are famous because they prepared written codes of law. Why is it so important to have laws written down? Try to imagine what life would be like if we had no written set of laws. (For example, would you like to drive a car if every local judge had his own set of traffic laws in his head?)
2. For discussion: How would the world have been different if Mohammed had never lived?
3. Draw two maps, one showing the parts of the modern world that are now predominantly Mohammedan in religion and the other showing the parts of the world that are predominantly Christian.
4. In a reference book such as the *World Almanac,* find out how many people are now members of the Christian and Moslem faiths.
5. In an encyclopedia or other source book find an account of the Battle of Tours. Imagine yourself a war correspondent covering the battle. Write a "You Are There" type of account of the battle. Stress its importance to the people of Europe.
6. Make a list of goods and products that were important in trade and manufacture in the Moslem Empire. Are any of these items still important today? Make a list of the major goods and products of the Moslem world today.

Chapter 13 A New Empire Declines into Feudalism

THE SON of Pepin the Short is claimed as a national hero by both the French and the Germans. The French call him Charlemagne; the Germans, Karl der Grosse. His Latin name was Carolus Magnus, from which comes his family name, Carolingian. All of his names translate into English as Charles the Great.

The revival of the empire: Charlemagne

Charlemagne, who ruled the Franks for forty-six years, from 768 till 814 A.D., is certainly one of the outstanding men in the political and cultural history of western Europe. He was tall, strong, handsome, and dignified. He was deeply religious. He had so little formal education that he never learned to write, but he was highly intelligent.

Charlemagne spent much of his life at war. In Italy he defeated the Lombards, who were again threatening Rome. He forced them to recognize him as their ruler. In a war that lasted off and on for thirty years, he defeated the Saxons in Germany, and forced them to accept his rule and to become Christians. In central Germany he conquered the Avars, and added that region to his kingdom. He drove the Moors back across the Pyrenees. For many years he tried to conquer Moslem Spain, but here he met his only failure. Nevertheless, by the end of his reign, Charlemagne controlled all of France, most of Germany, and some of northern Italy.

Like his father, Charlemagne helped the pope. When a revolt of Roman nobles and people endangered the pope, he called on the king of the Franks for help. Charlemagne went to Rome, restored the pope, and punished the rebels.

On Christmas Day, 800 A.D., while Charlemagne knelt at worship in the Cathedral of St. Peter, the pope placed a crown on his head and gave him the title Emperor of the Romans. Thus began the Frankish Empire, later called the Holy Roman Empire. It was not really Roman, of course. Germany was not Roman at all, and Gaul was a mixture of Roman, Celt, and German culture. Northern

North Sea · Baltic Sea · English Channel · SAXONS · BRITTANY · Paris · BOHEMIANS · FRANKISH KINGDOM · AVARS · AQUITAINE · BURGUNDY · LOMBARDS · KINGDOM OF ITALY · CORSICA · Rome

HOLY ROMAN EMPIRE of CHARLEMAGNE 814 AD

The coronation of Charlemagne. Pope Leo III placed the crown on the king's head and hailed him as "great and pacific Emperor of the Romans."

Italy had some remains of Roman culture, but much had been lost. Charlemagne himself was a warrior Frank, speaking the language, wearing the costume, and maintaining the customs of his people. However, he now had a title in keeping with his power.

● Government of the Frankish Empire

Charlemagne divided his empire into counties, each under a count, his representative. The count raised armies, administered laws, and supervised the royal estates. The emperor traveled a great deal to check on the loyalty and ability of the counts. He also sent out agents, called King's Messengers, to check up on the government and hear complaints.

Each subject in the empire contributed to the military system according to his wealth. Wealthy lords furnished cavalrymen. Freemen of the better class served as foot soldiers. Freemen of the poorer class did not serve, but had to furnish supplies. Each soldier served three months of each year, furnishing his own

weapons, armor, and upkeep. Thus the emperor had an army at no expense to himself or to his government—but it was a three-month army.

Charlemagne himself owned vast estates throughout the empire. They provided the only income for his government. There were no direct taxes on lands or people. However, since government expenses were not great, there was enough money.

● Culture in the age of Charlemagne

In spite of his own lack of education Charlemagne was greatly interested in education. Perhaps his lack of it made him realize how valuable it was. He wanted to improve the low state of learning among the clergy, both for the welfare of the Church and of the government. He also wanted to increase the knowledge and influence of his people.

To teach his own children and the young nobles, Charlemagne established at his court a school called the Palace School. The most learned men of England, Ireland, Germany, Italy, and France were invited to teach there. Bishops and abbots were also ordered to organize schools in the cathedrals and monasteries, and to collect libraries by copying the ancient books. If they showed themselves able to learn, children of the common people were admitted to the schools on an equal basis.

● Breakup of Charlemagne's empire

Charlemagne's empire was never strongly united except through the power of his own energy, ability, and personality. The local counts had to be watched constantly to see that they ruled in the interests of the emperor, not just for themselves. To keep them under control, Charlemagne had to grant *immunities* to some local rulers, especially on the far borders. This meant freedom from the visits and inspections of the King's Messengers. These local rulers became more and more independent. Charlemagne's successors granted even more immunities. The result of each grant was that the local government receiving it became more independent. The authority of the central government became that much weaker.

All but one of Charlemagne's sons died before he did. This son, Louis the Pious, inherited the whole empire. He was not a strong ruler. At his death he divided the empire among his three sons. After some quarreling among themselves, they reached a settlement. In 843, by the Treaty of Verdun (see map below), they agreed to a division that in some ways was a beginning of modern Europe. The eastern part became a kingdom; it is now Germany. The western part, roughly what is now France, was another kingdom. A strip of territory between the two became a third kingdom. It included northern Italy, and its ruler had the title of emperor.

Charlemagne's Carolingian descendants were incompetent rulers. They fought among themselves instead of uniting against invaders. Within fifty years after the Treaty of Verdun, France and Germany had become independent under elected kings. The middle kingdom broke up and disappeared. Europe suffered under invasions more terrible than those that ended the Western Roman Empire.

Invaders came from every direction. From the south the Saracens (Moslems) conquered and occupied Sicily, Sardinia, and Corsica, and terrorized the whole Mediterranean coast. From the northeast came the Slavs, moving down from the Pripet Marshes of Russia into central Europe and the Balkans. From Asia came a new group of nomads. They called themselves Magyars, but they were so much like the earlier Huns that Europeans called them Hungarians. For a century they made

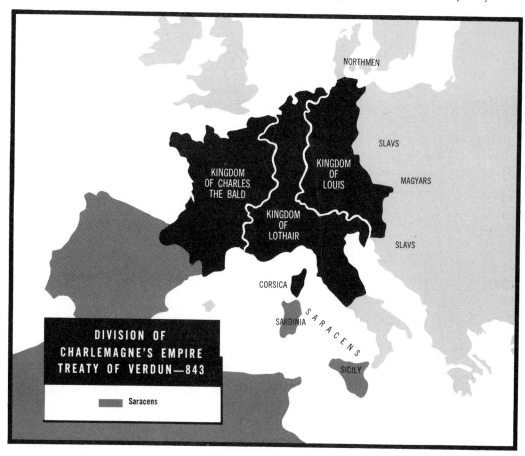

DIVISION OF CHARLEMAGNE'S EMPIRE TREATY OF VERDUN—843

Saracens

raids in every direction from central Europe, bringing terror everywhere. Then they settled down and established a kingdom on the central plains of Hungary.

• *The Northmen*

Most terrifying of all were the invaders from the north and west. The Germanic peoples of Scandinavia called themselves Vikings. The English called them Danes, and the Europeans called them Northmen. It is hard to believe that the ancestors of the modern Danes, Swedes, and Norwegians, among the most peaceful and civilized peoples of the world, could have been such brutal, bloodthirsty pirates, robbing and murdering without conscience or restraint.

The Northmen were supreme seamen. Their ships were small, but stout enough to carry the Vikings on raids to every coast of Europe, and even across the Atlantic Ocean. They could row up rivers, land, and raid the entire countryside. They were fierce and skillful fighting men. They were skilled in siege operation, and could capture even strongly fortified towns.

The Northmen settled in France just as Danes had settled in England. There was such a large settlement of Northmen in northwestern France that the region is still called for them, Normandy. A Norman chief was recognized by a French king as Duke of Normandy, in return for acknowledging the king as his overlord. The Normans eagerly adopted the civilization they found. They showed great talent for organized government; Normandy became the best organized state in France. When converted, they became ardent Christians.

In the ninth and tenth centuries, as in the fifth, organized government on a large scale disappeared in Europe. Kings were unable to hold their lands together or protect them. Local lords had to protect their own territories. They took the powers of government as well. Western Europe entered that time of small

independent local governments that is called the feudal period.

The origins of feudalism

Feudalism is a word which describes the political, economic, military, and social conditions that existed in Europe for four or five centuries after the breakup of Charlemagne's empire. Its most noticeable features were these: weak kings, strong nobles, numerous peasants, strictly local government, and much petty warfare.

A diagram illustrating the structure of feudal society.

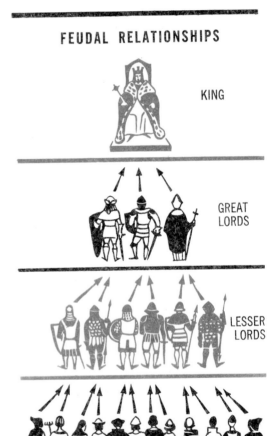

FEUDAL RELATIONSHIPS

KING

GREAT LORDS

LESSER LORDS

RETAINERS OF THE LESSER LORDS

Feudalism began when kings granted immunities to some of their lords, or became so weak that the lords simply took the power to govern their own territories. In order to get the military help of powerful lords, kings granted them the use of land from the royal lands. The strong lords, having more land than they needed, granted the use of part of it to lesser lords in return for military aid and other services. Small landholders, with no protection from the king's government, turned to their local lords. The landholder gave the ownership of his land to a powerful lord, but kept the right to occupy and use it.

All these grants were called *fiefs*. In time the fief became hereditary property. Legal *ownership* passed from the lord to his son; legal *possession and use* passed from the vassal to his son. Only the oldest son inherited, for the fief was never divided.

The Church, too, was drawn into the system. By the tenth century it owned a vast amount of land. To get the support and protection of the nobles, it gave the use of some of its land to lords, without giving up ownership. These Church grants were called *benefices*. They were supposed to last only one lifetime. A fief or benefice, then, was property legally owned by one man or by the Church but legally occupied and used by another.

By the end of the tenth century this feudal system of landholding was firmly established in France. There were about forty great feudal lords, many lesser lords, and, in all, several thousand fiefs. The king had become a feudal lord himself. He had power over, and owed protection to, the people in his own feudal lands only. Everywhere else in the kingdom, all powers of government were held by the local noble landholder.

If the organization of feudal society seems confusing, there is a logical reason: it *was* confusing. Certain basic principles about it may make it more understandable.

All society and government were based on personal relationship. Each man's loyalties and obligations were owed only to the lord immediately above him or to the vassal immediately below him. Social position and public service depended on landholding. A man who did not hold land, either as lord or vassal, simply did not count.

Every holder of land was a tenant, not an owner, until the highest rank was reached. The greater lords were vassals of the king; the lesser lords were vassals of the greater lords, and so on down. Each vassal was a tenant, not an owner, of the land he used. Private law and government replaced public law and government. Each feudal lord *was* the law and the government in his own lands.

There were distinct social classes in the feudal system. First came the clergy. The higher clergy, the bishops, and the abbots who ruled the monasteries were usually nobles. Priests and the lower clergy were usually commoners. In France the clergy were the First Estate, or first social class. The Second Estate were the nobles, a distinct and hereditary class with many special privileges. The greatest number of people were commoners, either peasants or serfs. As a social class they did not count; they could be neither lords nor vassals.

● *The feudal relationship*

In order to understand the relationship between lord and vassal, you must remember several things: It was an honorable relationship between legal equals. Only nobles could be vassals. It was a very personal relationship. Each owed certain things to the other, and to the other only. Finally, the same man might be both lord and vassal: vassal to a more powerful lord above him, lord to a less powerful vassal below him.

The granting and holding of a fief was really a contract between the lord and vassal, under which each owed certain things to the other. The lord granted the fief, the use of the land. He also guaranteed the vassal protection and justice, which was no small promise.

The obligations of the vassal were more numerous:

Military service. The vassal promised not only to fight for the lord himself but also to furnish a certain number of fully equipped horsemen and foot soldiers. He agreed to pay their expenses while at war. Military service was usually limited to forty days a year.

Feudal aids. These aids were special payment to help bear extraordinary expenses of the lord—for example, ransom if the lord was captured.

Hospitality. The vassal was expected to house and feed the lord and his companions on a certain number of days a year.

Court service. The vassal had to attend the lord's court when he was summoned. Sometimes this meant great assemblies for special ceremonies such as knighting of the lord's son or the marriage of his daughter. Usually, though, it was a court to administer justice, in which the vassal might act as a judge. Vassals, being nobles, claimed the right to be judged by their peers, or equals—that is, by other nobles.

Feudal justice was very different from Roman ideas of law and our modern laws. An accuser was not required to prove his charges against the person he accused. It was the accused who had to prove his innocence. He could do this in any one of three ways: (1) *Trial by battle.* The accused and the accuser, or champions representing each, fought a duel. The outcome determined guilt or innocence. (2) *Compurgation,* or oath-taking. The accused swore that he was innocent, and gathered a group of his nobles or neighbors, usually twelve. They took oath that they believed he was telling the truth. (3) *Ordeal.* The accused carried a piece of hot iron in his hand, or walked through fire, or plunged hand and arm into a pot of boiling water to pick up a hot stone. If his wounds healed rapidly enough, he was innocent; if not, he was guilty.

The life of the nobles

● *The castle*

The castle was of tremendous importance in medieval life. As you know, defense and protection were the responsibility of the lord. Each lord built a castle as a fortified home and a base from which to protect the surrounding country and enforce his authority.

Castles were built in places that were hard to reach, for they were places for defense rather than for pleasant living. Ideal places were the tops of hills, spurs of land almost surrounded by water, or firm ground in the middle of a marsh or a bog. If a castle had to be built in open country, a moat (a deep ditch filled with water) surrounded the high, thick outer walls. The gate to the courtyard inside the walls was reached by a drawbridge across the moat. In case of an attack the drawbridge was raised.

The principal room of the castle was the great hall. Here the lord held court, received and entertained visitors, and the family lived during the day. The lord and his family usually had a separate bedroom, but everyone else slept in the great hall. There was not much furniture. Plank tables were set up on trestles for meals. The thick stone walls with their small, usually uncovered windows made the rooms dark, damp, chilly, and drafty. Fowls, dogs, and other small animals had free run of the place. The floors were bare except for rushes in which filth and vermin gathered.

● *Food and drink*

Hospitality was a virtue among the feudal nobles. The banquet was a great part of the social life. Feudal lords and their ladies were greedy eaters and heavy drinkers. Meat was the main food; game was the favorite. Bread and cheese were important foods, with fish and eggs on fast days. Sweets were rare, for honey was the only sweetening.

When he was not fighting, the chief occupation of the noble was managing his estates. If he held several fiefs, as many did, he traveled from one to another, living on each in turn for a while.

Hunting was a favorite amusement, and was important in providing the meat which made up a large part of the diet. Deer and other large game were hunted on horseback with dogs. Birds and small game were captured by trained hawks called falcons. Indoor amusements were games: checkers, chess, and gambling with dice.

The wives of the nobles joined in the amusements and feasting. Their main duties were to superintend the household and servants, and to direct the education of the girls. There was not much romance in marriage among the nobles. It was very much a matter of business. The choice of a wife was usually made for family or financial reasons. The real obligations of a wife were, first, to bring with her the inheritance of a fief or a handsome dowry; second, to bear a son to inherit the lord's estate.

The greatest sport of the feudal lord was the mock battle or tournament. The *joust* was a fight between two knights; the *tourney* was a battle between two groups of knights. In early times these were real fights, differing from war only in being arranged in advance. As time went on, the jousts and tourneys grew to be more like pageants, with a great deal of display and a small amount of bloodshed.

During the early Middle Ages the armor of the fighting man was not very elaborate. He wore a helmet of steel and a shirt of link armor. On his left arm he carried a four-foot shield. At his belt, on the left side, he wore a cross-hilted sword. He carried an eight-foot lance in his right hand.

Armor became complicated and heavy in later medieval times. A knight in full armor

A suit of Italian armor dating from about 1400. Earlier in the Middle Ages armor was simpler. Chain mail armor and open-faced helmets can be seen in the illustration of the Battle of Hastings (page 177). The late medieval armor shown above was an ingenious and very heavy arrangement of jointed steel plates. Some chain armor was used to allow free movement.

often had to be hauled or boosted onto his horse. If he fell, he was helpless because he could not get to his feet again.

● *Feudal warfare*

War was the usual thing, not the unusual, in the feudal world. Sometimes two kingdoms fought, or a king tried to subdue a powerful, rebellious vassal. Most wars, however, were private fights between feudal lords or between lords and vassals.

By our standards they were small wars and not very bloody. Battles were small-scale, like skirmishes, and were comparatively rare.

There was not much strategy or generalship. A battle would consist of charges and counter-charges by the knights, followed by hand-to-hand fighting with sword or battle-axe. The winners gained honor, plunder, and prisoners. Indeed, it was far better to capture than to kill, for the prisoners could be held for ransom. Most of the losers escaped, however, to fight again another day.

For nobles, wars were fascinating affairs. In these little local brawls not so very many would be killed. Of course, you might be captured, but then vassals and peasants had to raise the ransom to buy your freedom. War was the business of the noble, and he loved it, but the effect on the countryside and the peasants was terrible indeed. Crops were destroyed, houses burned, cattle and animals slaughtered or driven off. War meant famine and suffering to the peasant.

The Church tried to improve conditions by limiting private wars. It tried to get all lords to accept the *Truce of God*, which forbade fighting on week ends and holy days. The prohibited time was gradually extended until there were only eighty days a year for legal fighting. By the *Peace of God*, the Church set aside certain places where fighting was not permitted. These prohibitions could not be strictly enforced even by threats of terrible religious penalties. Private wars continued until kings were strong enough to enforce peace throughout whole kingdoms.

● *Chivalry*

In one way feudalism and chivalry were like two sides of a coin: They were related to each other, but were by no means the same. Feudalism was an exchange of land or its use for protection or services. Chivalry was a code of conduct for knights. The word itself comes from the French *cheval*, horse, and *chevalier*, horseman.

In the beginning, chivalry required a knight to be brave—even foolishly brave. He must fight fairly, according to the rules. Tricks and strategy were considered cowardly. He must be loyal to his friends, keep his word, and treat conquered foes gallantly. This code was for knights only.

In the early days anyone could become a knight who had an ancestor who had performed mounted military service. He had to prove himself in battle and to receive the *accolade*. This was a stroke on the shoulder or the back with the flat of the sword, accompanied by the words "I dub [declare] thee knight." The accolade could be given by any knight.

As time went on, chivalry became much more complex, both as a code of conduct and as a course of training for fighters. In order to become a knight a boy had to pass through two preliminary stages of training. These were performed under the supervision of a knight, usually his father's lord. At the age of seven a boy became a *page*, learning manners and beginning his training in the use of weapons. In his early teens he became a *squire*, a knight's assistant, and continued his training in both manners and weapons. He took care of the lord's horses, armor, weapons, and dress. When he was considered ready, he accompanied his lord in battle to prove himself worthy to be a knight. After the squire had proved himself in battle, he was initiated into knighthood. The simple accolade of the early days developed into an elaborate, partly religious ceremony.

No one, then, was born a knight. One became a knight only after training and performance. Although all knights were nobles, not all nobles were knights unless they had been trained and had proved themselves.

Chivalry did much to soften and civilize the conduct of the feudal lords. There was a great improvement over the really rough and crude manners of the early days. However, behavior did not become perfect by any standards. You may have read stories of the brave, idealistic, moral knight in shining armor, mounted on his charging steed, going forth to rescue some beautiful, virtuous young maiden. Here again reality was often different from romance. The knight was a sworn defender of womanhood, it is true, but he married only a girl who brought a rich dowry. Wife beating was permitted by law, and was not uncommon. The courtesy of the knight was extended only to women of his own class and religion. Toward all others his attitude and actions were likely to be extremely vulgar. The feudal world was a man's world.

The manorial system

After the time of Charlemagne the center of all European rural life was the manor. Each fief was also a manor, an economic unit. Its land was divided between the lord and his tenants, the non-noble peasants and serfs. The lord kept part of the land himself, called the domain, and divided the rest. Peasants and serfs paid for the use of the land by giving the lord part of their crops and by working for him.

● The manor as an economic unit

Each manor tried to produce everything needed—that is, to be self-sufficient. In general, the manor did provide its own food, clothing, and leather goods. It might also make its own tools and implements. Some things had to be brought in. Iron, salt, tar, and millstones were usually imported. Taken as a whole, the quantity of goods exchanged was small compared to the amount produced and used locally. Trade and commerce almost died out in most of Europe during the ninth, tenth, and eleventh centuries. People tended to live in small, self-contained communities.

| *This pictorial diagram shows the parts of a typical feudal manor.*

A MEDIEVAL MANOR

FALLOW FIELDS

AUTUMN PLANTING

SPRING PLANTING

ROAD

BARNS

LORD'S CASTLE

COMMON PASTURE

MOAT

FORD

MARSH

VILLAGE

RIVER

MILL

FIELDS

BAKE HOUSE

The usual manor contained a village with houses along a single street. The manor house or castle of the lord stood a little distance away, surrounded by orchards, gardens, barns, and stables. The village was usually located on a stream which furnished water power for its mill. The land of the manor extended out from the village. These were the garden plots of the peasants, the cultivated grain fields, pasture, meadow, forest, and waste lands.

Except for the nearby garden plots, the cultivated land of the manor was divided into three large fields for growing grain. Because of poor farming methods each field had to lie fallow (unused) every third year. The weeds were plowed under and cattle allowed to graze so that it would regain its fertility. A peasant had to have land in each field, of course; otherwise he would starve in the third year. Fields were divided into strips half an acre or an acre apiece, separated by narrow, uncultivated strips. Each peasant held strips in each field. The lord's grain land was also in strips in the three fields.

By present day standards the harvests of grain were very low for the amount of seed planted. Livestock was poor, also. Cows gave little milk, which was usually made into cheese. So little hay was produced that animals almost starved in the winter. Often they were so weak that they had to be carried to the fields in the spring. Many cattle were slaughtered at the beginning of winter, and the meat was salted to preserve it.

Peasants were bound to the land. This meant that they could not leave without the lord's permission. If the land was sold, or changed lords, the peasants became tenants of the new lord. They were not slaves, for they could not be sold apart from the land. Each village had certain skilled workers: miller, blacksmith, and carpenter. There was always a priest to care for spiritual and social needs. Usually he had strips of land in the fields and did manual work himself.

The work of the peasants

All the tools and animals to work the fields were supplied by the peasants. It took eight oxen to get a field ready for planting. Since no one peasant owned that many, they worked together. All plowing, harrowing, sowing, and reaping were done by peasants working together, usually with animals and tools owned in common. Each man received only what grew on his own strips. Much of the work had to be done by hand. Medieval farming meant backbreaking work.

In addition to doing all the work on the lord's land the peasant had to perform many other kinds of service. He also paid taxes and tolls of all kinds. Thus all the lord's income came from either the work or the payments of the peasants.

Daily life of the peasants

Peasant homes were small, usually one room with an attic and cellar. Houses were built of wood with thatched roofs. The house sheltered the livestock and poultry as well as the family. Furniture was scanty. The family slept on bags of straw laid on the floor of hard-packed earth. Household equipment included only such items as a spindle for making thread, a hand loom, and a few pots and pans. There was a fireplace but no chimney, so the walls were blackened by smoke and soot.

Daily life was hard. The entire family worked in the fields to produce enough food to prevent starvation. The diet was poor. The principal foods were coarse black bread, cabbage and some other vegetables, cheese, and eggs. Home-brewed beer was plentiful in northern Europe, and ordinary wine in the grape-growing regions. Occasionally the peasant might eat a chicken, duck, or goose, but other meat was rarely seen. He was forbidden to hunt or fish. Poor diet, bad sanitation, and lack of medical care brought on diseases. The average lifetime of a peasant was about thirty years.

There were some lighter moments. Work at the manor house meant a feast and fun. Village holidays brought sport and entertainment such as archery contests, cock-fighting, bull-baiting, wrestling, and weight-throwing. But in general, surveying medieval life, you will probably agree with the verdict of history: The feudal system was a class system in which the lord of the manor was supreme. The peasants worked strenuously and lived poorly, getting almost no benefits or compensations in return for their labor.

Review of Chapter 13

People, places, and things

Identify: Carolingians, Saracens, Slavs, Magyars, Peace of God, Truce of God, chevalier, page, accolade, squire, knight, benefice.

Locate: Charlemagne's empire, the three kingdoms established by the Treaty of Verdun, the Pyrenees, Normandy.

Events in review

1. Describe the form of government established by Charlemagne.
2. Describe the relationship between Church and state in the Holy Roman Empire.
3. Who were the Northmen? Why are they important in the history of France?
4. Define feudalism. Show the connection of each of the following with feudalism: (a) fief; (b) vassal; (c) king; (d) landlord; (e) feudal aids.
5. To what extent was a manor an economic unit?
6. In administering feudal justice the following might be required: trial by battle, compurgation, or ordeal. What does each mean?
7. Name the three social classes in feudal society. Explain what place each of these held.
8. What lands, buildings, and the like, made up the usual manor in feudal times?
9. How did a man become a knight under the code of chivalry?

Problems and projects

1. Discuss the reasons for the breaking up of Charlemagne's empire. Was the major cause internal weakness or invasion by enemies?
2. Why is the Treaty of Verdun in 843 considered important?
3. Why was a system such as feudalism necessary to meet the needs of the time? Discuss as fully as you can.
4. Would you rather be tried under the feudal or the American system of justice? Why?
5. Did the manorial system offer any political or economic advantages? Carefully explain your answer.
6. Write a biography of Charlemagne, including: (a) his early life, (b) his military career, (c) his religious policy, (d) his coronation as emperor, (e) his method of controlling his empire, (f) his attitude toward education and culture.
7. Write a short essay describing life in medieval times. Include at least five of the following: indoor life, games, education, obligations of boys and girls of your age, kind of food, type of dwellings. (See pages 221–223 for source books.)
8. To debate: Under the feudal system of the Middle Ages the individual peasant enjoyed better protection than he would have under any other social system.
9. Compare life on a medieval manor with life on a modern American farm. In which would we find greater self-sufficiency? Why? What comments might a modern farmer make on the manorial system of raising crops?
10. Draw a ground plan of a medieval castle.
11. Have you read a novel, or watched a movie or TV show, dealing with "the days when knights were bold"? Did the book, or movie or TV show, give a realistic picture of chivalry and feudalism? Explain.

Chapter 14

Feudal Europe Takes the Offensive against the Moslems

THE STORY of European kingdoms under feudalism is like a tug-of-war between the kings and their powerful vassals to see who would govern the different parts of the country. During the ninth and tenth centuries kings lost almost all their power. In theory the king was the top of the feudal pyramid, vassal only to God. The reality was quite different from the theory. Kings had power and wealth only because they were feudal lords themselves. They were supreme rulers only in their own feudal lands. Each vassal in the pyramid owed allegiance and service not to the king, but only to his immediate lord. Some great lords were as strong as the king. They served him only when it was convenient.

France under the Capetian kings

By the year 1000 A.D., almost two hundred years after Charlemagne's death, the Carolingian descendants of Charlemagne had lost their kingdoms everywhere. There was no effective central government anywhere, and the feudal lords were uncontrolled. On every frontier Europe was invaded by terrible enemies. These invasions demanded some kind of strong, unified government to protect the country.

In 987 A.D. an assembly of nobles deposed the Carolingian king in the western territory that was to become France. They elected one of their number, Hugh Capet. He founded a line of French kings called Capetians. The Capetians ruled in unbroken line for over three hundred years, until 1328.

The new king ruled a territory around Paris, but even the vassals in his own lands did not recognize his authority. The rest of France was divided into powerful feudal states. In the north the greatest were Flanders, Brittany, Champagne, Burgundy, and Normandy. The powerful independent regions of Aquitaine (Guienne), Toulouse, Gascony, and Barcelona were in the south.

To become real rulers of France the Capetians had first to recover and unite all these states, either by shrewd marriages or by force. After 1066 this problem was complicated by the fact that the dukes of Normandy became kings of England while still holding vast territories in France. Regaining the territory from the feudal lords was not enough. The Capetians had also to develop a real central government capable of ruling a great territory.

The Capetians had several things in their favor. For over three centuries there was always a son to inherit the throne. They stopped the Carolingian custom of dividing the kingdom among all the sons. Only the eldest boy could inherit. Thus the Capetians were able to outlast many other noble families, taking over their lands when the family died out.

● Strong kings unite France

A number of the Capetians were extremely able kings. Some, of course, were weak, and lost power in the struggle with the lords. But the able ones came often enough and gained more than enough to make up for the losses. Thus over the long period a strong kingdom was built up.

Four Capetian kings were outstanding. Louis VI (Louis the Fat), 1108–1137, made himself supreme in his own duchy (the domain of a duke). He encouraged the growth of trade, which added to his income, and of towns, which supported him in his wars with feudal lords. He arranged the marriage of his son to the heiress of the Duke of Aquitaine, largest feudal state of France. The son, Louis VII, gave the Capetians one of their setbacks by divorcing his wife and returning her dowry. She then married Henry II, Plantagenet king of England, thereby increasing the French possessions of the English king.

Philip II (Augustus), 1180–1223, was intelligent and very crafty. He went on one of the great Crusades to the Holy Land with Richard I of England. Philip took advantage of a quarrel with Richard, came home, and took some of the English possessions in France. He also took advantage of Richard's weak successor, John, to regain still more English-held French lands. Philip strengthened

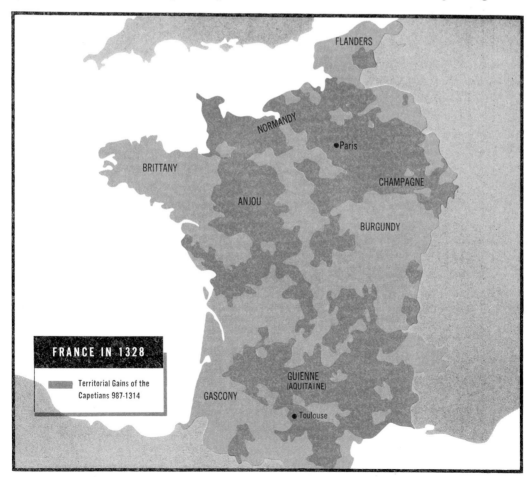

FLANDERS

NORMANDY

●Paris

BRITTANY

CHAMPAGNE

ANJOU

BURGUNDY

FRANCE IN 1328

Territorial Gains of the Capetians 987-1314

GUIENNE (AQUITAINE)

GASCONY

● Toulouse

his royal government. Instead of using feudal lords, he sent out "baillis" (inspectors) to make investigations, hear complaints, and report to the King's Council.

Louis IX, called St. Louis, 1226–1270, not only gained more territory but also reorganized and strengthened the machinery of government. The King's Council conducted general affairs of government. The Chamber of Accounts collected and looked after the revenues. The Parlement (Parliament) was the supreme court of justice, to which cases could be appealed from all parts of the kingdom. In all these bodies he used professionally trained men, not feudal lords. He continued to send out inspectors to hear complaints and make investigations. Thus a real central government capable of ruling a large kingdom was beginning to develop.

● *Philip the Fair*

Philip IV (the Fair), 1285–1314, completed the development of France into a monarchy in which the king had complete power. He inherited a strong, well-organized kingdom, and he had the ability and wealth to develop it still further. The only French territories outside his control were Flanders and Guienne, still held by the king of England.

At one time during his rule, Philip IV took an unusual step that was important in the development of the government of France. It happened because of a conflict with the pope over the taxing of the clergy. In this conflict

Scenes from the Bayeux Tapestry. This strip of embroidered cloth (231 feet long and 20 inches wide) dates from the twelfth century and shows events in the Norman conquest of England. Above: the Norman invasion forces cross the channel. Note the resemblance of these ships to Viking ships. Facing page: scenes at the Battle of Hastings.

Philip needed all the support he could get from the people. To help in the government, France had often had assemblies of the two upper classes, or Estates, the clergy and the nobles. Now, to get even wider support, Philip for the first time also called in representatives of the middle-class people—merchants and others—from the towns and cities. This assembly was called the Estates (or States) General. Philip made the beginnings of a government that represented the people more widely than ever before.

At the end of the reign of Philip the Fair, France was a strong, well-organized country. The power of the king was supreme. Philip had three sons. The sons, however, broke the long chain of the Capetian kings; each died without a male heir. In 1328 the long male line of Capetians ended.

The Normans bring feudalism to England

While a strong kingdom was being built up in France under the Capetians, another strong power was developing in England. As

Chapter 12 explained, England was invaded many times, by Angles, Saxons, and Danes (see pages 157–160). Finally, Saxon kings gained control. In the year 1066 the Saxon rule was broken by an invasion from Normandy, in northern France.

William the Conqueror

William, Duke of Normandy, claimed that the childless Edward the Confessor, Saxon king of England, had promised William the throne of England. But the Saxon nobles refused to give the throne to William. Instead, they elected Harold of Wessex as their king. The Norman duke appealed to the pope, who upheld his claim. William then gathered a fleet and an army of feudal lords from all parts of France, promising them plunder if his invasion succeeded.

At the battle of Hastings, 1066, the invading Normans defeated the Saxon forces, and Harold was killed in the battle. William and his army conquered the rest of the island with little difficulty, and he was crowned in London. Since then, he has been known as William I, or William the Conqueror.

William I (1066–1087) tried to organize his kingdom so that the king could really rule. He kept much Saxon land as his own domain, and the fiefs he gave to his followers were scattered so that the lords would be weaker. All feudal lords had to swear allegiance directly to him; thus they became his vassals. Norman government of England was more centralized (controlled by one authority) than any on the continent.

Normans and Saxons

The Saxons of England did not adopt Norman ideas, customs, and language willingly or quickly. Like any conquered people, they disliked their new masters. Anglo-Saxon, a Germanic language, remained the language of the people; Norman-French was the language only of nobles.

As time went on, the culture of England became more Norman than Saxon, and the language became an interesting mixture. The Latin language had died out almost completely after the Anglo-Saxon invasions of England. For 500 years only the Germanic Anglo-Saxon speech was used. After 1066 the Norman-French speech, based mostly on Latin, was added. The two finally blended to form the present English language. About half our words are of Anglo-Saxon, Germanic origin; 30 to 40 per cent are of Latin origin; the remainder come from Greek, Arabic, and many other sources.

Development of English government

William the Conqueror had made a strong start toward centralized government under the king. Nevertheless, the later history of England, like that of France, was a tug-of-war between kings and feudal lords.

Henry II (1154–1189) greatly increased the power of the king. To get a dependable

army he made every freeman have arms appropriate to his position and serve in the king's army. He allowed nobles to pay him money instead of military service, and used the money to hire a professional army. He required that a careful account be made of all the financial business of the government. To do this work he reorganized the court of the Exchequer (Treasury).

The greatest reforms of Henry II were made in the court system. For two reasons he wanted as many cases as possible tried in the king's courts. He wanted the king's law to replace feudal law and courts, and he wanted the fees from court trials. To do this he sent out judges to travel through the country holding court at fixed places and regular times. They were called circuit judges because they traveled in regular circuits.

> Ivanhoe, by Sir Walter Scott, tells of life in England more than a century after the Norman conquest. In this scene a Saxon peasant (Wamba) stands fearfully before a Norman lord (Front-de-Boeuf). Rivalry between Normans and Saxons persisted. Many Saxons clung to their old ways.

When the judge came into a district, he could not know what cases should be brought before him. To solve this problem, the king appointed groups of men in each district, called juries. The grand jury of twenty-five or more gave the names of suspected criminals. A petit (petty) jury of twelve decided civil cases such as disputes over land. Criminal cases were decided by the feudal procedure of ordeal or combat. In time, the petit jury came to decide criminal as well as civil cases, and the king's law replaced feudal law.

Henry II had inherited Normandy, Brittany, and Anjou in France. To these lands he added Aquitaine (Guienne) by marrying the divorced wife of Louis VII of France. English possessions in France were now larger than all of England, and these lands on the continent influenced both English and French history for centuries. English kings divided their interests instead of concentrating on building a strong kingdom in Britain. French kings schemed to regain the English-held territories.

● *The Magna Carta*

King John (1199–1216), the son of Henry II, lost much of both the land and power his father had gained. Philip Augustus defeated him in France and took some of his lands. In England John brought on a revolt among the nobles by forcing them to pay fees and taxes they considered unjust. At Runnymede in 1215 the nobles forced him to accept a document in which he promised not to do certain things. This statement is known as the Magna Carta (Great Charter). It was intended to protect the liberties of the lords. However, some parts concerned the rights of commoners as well, and these have come to be considered the most important.

The king agreed not to collect any new or special tax without the consent of his Great Council. He also promised not to take any man's property without paying for it. He promised not to sell, refuse, or delay the right of justice. Any man accused of a crime was entitled to a trial before a jury of his peers (equals). No man could be held in prison for an indefinite time without a trial. Peasants were guaranteed against unfair demands for services or seizures of property by the king. What it all meant was that the king must obey the law, the same as his subjects. The ideas in the Magna Carta have influenced many nations, including our own.

● Parliament

During this period of King John and his successors, the English Parliament began its long, gradual development. English kings had a Great Council of nobles and higher clergy to advise them. The Magna Carta provided that the king could not collect special taxes without the consent of the Council. This was an important power. In 1265, during a period of civil war, representatives of the middle class were called to meet with the higher nobles and clergy. There were two knights from each shire (county) and two burgesses (citizens) of each town. At first, lords, clergy, knights, and burgesses met together. In time Parliament, as it came to be called, divided into two houses. Higher nobles and clergy sat in an upper House of Lords. Knights and burgesses met in the lower House of Commons.

The early Parliament did not have power to pass laws. It had the important right of consenting or not consenting to new and special taxes. As the cost of the king's government increased, regular taxes became necessary, and Parliament's consent became very important. Over a long period Parliament was able to use this power to gain others.

● The Common Law

The second great English institution to begin its development during this time was the Common Law. Edward I divided the king's court into three branches: The Exchequer kept financial accounts and tried tax cases.

The Court of Common Pleas tried cases between private citizens. The Court of the King's Bench heard cases that concerned the king or the government. Below these were the circuit courts in the counties. Exceptional cases of all kinds could be taken to the king by petition. Gradually the laws of king and Parliament, with the written decisions of these courts, became the great English Common Law, the basis for the legal system of the United States as well as England.

By 1300, somewhat more than 200 years after the Norman conquest, England had developed a centralized government under the king. His power was not as complete as that of the king of France. It was checked, though only slightly, by the power of Parliament, representing nobles, higher clergy, and the increasingly important middle class of the towns.

Germany and Italy

Germany was really not a nation, but a group of German tribes. Nor was it really a kingdom, but a great number of practically independent states. There was an elected king who was only another feudal lord. Feudalism was very strongly developed; even the clergy had become entirely part of the feudal system. The last Carolingian king of Germany (the line of kings following Charlemagne) was deposed by a Saxon who was elected king of the Saxons and Franks.

Italy was in a state of feudal anarchy. Several of Charlemagne's descendants held the title of emperor without really ruling. Then no one had even the title. Some parts of Italy were held by the Byzantine Empire. The Moslems had Sicily and often invaded the mainland.

● The Holy Roman Empire

In 962 A.D. the fortunes of Germany and Italy, separate since the division of Charlemagne's empire, were joined again. A Saxon ruler, Otto I (the Great), was elected king of Germany. He was a powerful ruler, and might have started developing a strong kingdom in Germany like that of the Capetians in France—but Italy tempted him. He took territory in northern Italy, then returned to Germany. Soon he received an entreaty (petition) from the pope to come to Italy and help him. The pope was in great political trouble with the Roman nobles. Otto occupied Lombardy and was generally acknowledged as king of Italy. Then, in 962, the pope crowned him Emperor of the Holy Roman Empire of Germany and Italy.

Thus began a shadowy sort of empire that was to last, in name at least, for many centuries. It was also the beginning of a relationship between Germany and Italy that continued more than 300 years, to the great harm of both. Otto deposed the pope who had crowned him and installed his own secretary as pope. For the next forty years German kings chose the popes.

Otto the Great left his successors a fatal legacy: the lure of the title Emperor and the desire to rule Italy as well as Germany. The result was that Otto's successors ruled neither. Saxon kings tried to rule Germany but were unsuccessful, weak rulers, even in Saxony, their own homeland. They failed just as badly in their efforts to rule Italy. One writer has said that they tried to get an empire and did not even get a duchy. To gain the title of emperor, they tried to dictate who should be pope. The popes, in order to remain independent, schemed to influence the selection of German kings. At times, emperors chose and controlled popes; at other times popes controlled emperors.

● Frederick I

The greatest of the medieval German rulers was Frederick I (1152–1190), who was called Barbarossa, or Frederick of the Red Beard. Like Otto the Great he could have been a real ruler in Germany, but was lured by the Italian adventure. He forced the pope, against his will, to crown him emperor.

Frederick's attempt to rule Italy was challenged by a new power. For a long time the rich cities of Lombardy in northern Italy, prospering on trade, had become increasingly independent. There was a wealthy merchant class, and the government was partly democratic. These cities strongly opposed Frederick's rule because it threatened their independence. Frederick sent a representative to take over the government in each city. When Milan refused to receive the agent, Frederick captured the city, destroyed it, and scattered its population.

The other cities, aided by the pope, united to form the Lombard League. While a rebellion kept Frederick occupied in Germany, the League raised an army. When Frederick returned to Italy with his army, he was defeated in a battle by the League. The peace settlement was a victory for the League and the pope. Although the cities recognized Frederick as overlord, he had to agree that they could govern themselves. Frederick Barbarossa died before he could do anything .to change this result.

● Frederick II

Frederick II was in many ways the most interesting and remarkable of all the German emperors of those times. He was also the last man to try the imperial adventure. Besides being heir to the German throne, he was the grandson of the Norman king of Sicily. When he was old enough to rule, he promised the pope to go on a crusade against the Moslems if he were crowned emperor; thus he gained the title of emperor.

Frederick II was more interested in Sicily than he was in Germany. About all he did in Germany was to keep the rivalries of the great families stirred up so they would not unite against him. He granted great privileges to the German nobles in order to have his infant son accepted as king.

Frederick II tried, but failed, to unite Italy into a single kingdom. At his death his son ruled briefly as emperor. After that there was a long period of civil war in Germany. The later German rulers kept the title of Holy Roman Emperor, but they did not try to rule Italy. Thus you can see that the attempt to unite the two countries, Germany and Italy, not only failed, but also prevented either one from being united. Germany remained a jumble of independent cities and

During the Middle Ages a middle class of prosperous merchants began to gain influence. Burgesses were allowed in the English Parliament. Merchants became powerful in the Lombard League. Above: supper time in the house of a wealthy merchant.

feudal states in which the emperor had little authority. In northern Italy the Lombard cities developed into independent city-states. In central Italy the pope ruled the Papal States as a temporal ruler. The Kingdom of Sicily included southern Italy and the island of Sicily. Other parts of Europe were beginning to form strong, united kingdoms. Germany and Italy remained disunited, with bad results that lasted for hundreds of years—even up to our own times.

The Crusades

You have already read many references to the Crusades. In these great movements of the twelfth and thirteenth centuries the Christian West took the offensive against the Moslem East. The westerners attempted to regain Palestine, the Holy Land of Jesus' birth, for Christianity.

The Moslem Arabs had conquered Palestine and Syria for Islam in the seventh century A.D., while western Europe was in the depth of the Dark Ages. The Arabs were very tolerant of other religions. A Christian or Jew had to pay taxes and observe other simple regulations. Having done so, he could live in Palestine, keep his religion, and follow any business he chose. For some centuries Christian pilgrims visited the holy places unhindered. European traders from Constantinople or the Italian cities had little trouble doing business.

During the eleventh century the Seljuk Turks, new and very earnest converts to Islam, came from Asia into the Moslem Empire. They defeated a Byzantine army, broke the military power of the Byzantine Empire, took all Asia Minor, and threatened Constantinople. The eastern emperor, looking about for help, appealed to the pope at Rome. The emperor really wanted mercenary (paid) soldiers to help defend his city and regain the lost territories.

The Turks proved much less tolerant than the Arabs. Reports of persecutions of pilgrims and increasing difficulties of trade began to come back to Europe. The appeal of the eastern emperor found a welcome reception. For a variety of reasons the pope was glad to promote the idea of a great Christian

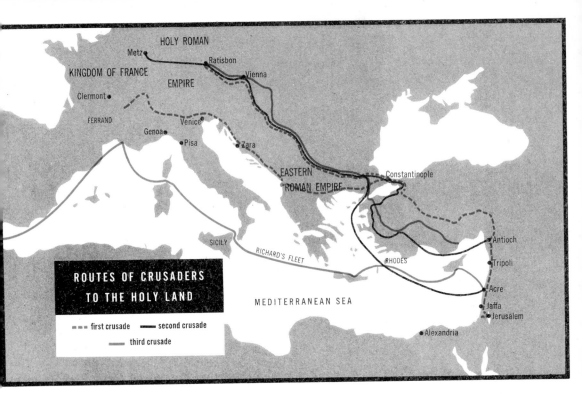

ROUTES OF CRUSADERS
TO THE HOLY LAND

--- first crusade   — second crusade
— third crusade

offensive to regain the Holy Land from the Moslems.

Pope Urban II calls for a Crusade

In 1095 Pope Urban II called a great meeting of churchmen and French nobles at Clermont, France. He urged the Franks to stop their wars among themselves and join in one great war against the unbelievers. He promised them both earthly and heavenly rewards. The great assembly joined in one mighty cry, "God wills it." From Clermont many men went all through France preaching the cause. Those who joined the expeditions sewed a cross of cloth on their garments, so they were called *crusaders*—those who bore the cross.

Men joined the Crusade for many different reasons. The pope offered great religious inducements. All the crusader's sins were forgiven. If he was killed, the crusader entered directly into heaven. His property and family were guaranteed protection by the Church. A debtor who took the cross had his debts

canceled; a criminal was relieved of punishment.

Nobles were dazzled by the lure of lands and plunder in the rich East. Merchants saw a chance for commercial gain. The Crusade was partly a religious expedition, but it also appealed to the love of adventure, the hope of gain, and the desire to escape debt, punishment for crime, or daily boredom.

The First Crusade (1096–1099)

The First Crusade was led by French nobles, or Normans from Sicily. In three organized armies they moved across Europe, reaching Constantinople by the end of the year.

It is not surprising that the crusaders were coolly received at Constantinople. The emperor had asked for some mercenary fighters, but now he saw three armies approaching the city. He feared, with some reason, that they might capture and plunder Constantinople. After much discussion the Byzantines ferried the westerners across to Asia Minor to

182

begin their long hot march toward Syria and Palestine.

With their woolen and leather garments, their heavy armor, and a shortage of pack animals, the crusaders suffered greatly. The leaders quarreled over fiefs in the lands they took. If the Turks had not also been quarreling and disunited, the expedition would have failed. The crusaders captured Antioch by means of the treachery of a Turkish officer, and after more quarrels they marched on toward Jerusalem.

Conditions improved when they reached the seacoast. Fleets of ships from the Italian cities of Genoa and Pisa brought them reinforcements, supplies, and siege machinery. Jerusalem was captured after a short siege, and the crusaders took revenge on the inhabitants for all their sufferings and hardships by a terrible massacre. One leader wrote to the pope that his horse's legs had been blood-stained to the knees from riding among the bodies of the dead.

The crusaders set up three small states: the Kingdom of Jerusalem, the Principality of Antioch, and the County of Tripoli. European feudalism was introduced; the land was subdivided into fiefs, with vassals. For almost a century the westerners held these lands. There was brisk trade with Europe, carried on mostly in Italian ships. Christians and Moslems lived in close relations and grew to respect each other. Many Christians adopted eastern customs and preferred eastern food and clothing. The governments were feudal, which is to say that they were poor; and, as usual, there was much war among the nobles. Often both sides made alliances with Moslems.

The Second Crusade (1147–1149)

The Second Crusade took place after the Turks recaptured the important city of Edessa and threatened the Kingdom of Jerusalem. In this Crusade Louis VII of France and Emperor Conrad III of Germany led armies to the Holy Land. The Second Crusade was a miserable failure.

The Third Crusade (1189–1192)

In 1187 the news reached Europe that Jerusalem had been recaptured by the famous Moslem leader Saladin. Europe's response was the famous and romantic Third Crusade, the "Crusade of the Three Kings." Richard the Lion-Hearted of England, Philip Augustus of France, and Frederick Barbarossa of Germany each started out at the head of a great army to regain the Holy Land. Again there was failure. Frederick Barbarossa was drowned while on the way, and most of his army turned back. Philip and Richard quarreled; Philip took his army home to try to take the English lands in France. Richard might have gained the whole kingdom of Jerusalem several times by diplomacy, but he preferred knightly adventure. In the end he made no gains worth mentioning.

It is estimated that 300,000 people, Christians and Moslems, lost their lives in the Third Crusade. This was the last major expedition. There were eight Crusades altogether, but none of the later ones was on a scale to compare with the third.

Results of the Crusades

Military results

From the military standpoint the Crusades were certainly failures. The First Crusade regained Jerusalem and Palestine. Christians held them for a century; then the Moslems recaptured them. When the crusading movement ended in the thirteenth century, Moslems held the entire Near East and North Africa.

However, Europeans learned many things of military importance. To mention only one, they learned the use of an explosive, gunpowder. The Moslems had probably learned of it from the Chinese. To this knowledge the Europeans added the use of the gun. At first the gun was only a crude tube of wood and metal, from which the explosion hurled stones or chunks of metal. As guns were improved, the feudal castle lost its usefulness in defense. Here was the beginning of the end of the feudal era.

● *Economic results*

The Crusades brought a great revival of trade between East and West. The Italian cities, especially Venice, Genoa, and Pisa, furnished ships to carry men and supplies to the Crusades. These ships did not return empty. They carried eastern goods, many of which had been unknown in Europe since the days of Greece and Rome.

Trade revived inside Europe, too. The new products were carried everywhere by sea, river, and overland. There was an increasingly great demand for eastern sugar, spices, perfumes, cotton and silk cloth, rice, and tropical fruits. To pay for these imports, Europeans had to produce more goods themselves: fur, hides, metals, and woolen cloth. The growth of trade and manufacturing speeded up the growth of cities. The increased demand for labor led to improvements in the conditions of peasants and serfs because they were needed to make things. Many of them became free laborers. New knowledge brought improved farming methods. New and important machines appeared: the compass for navigation, and the windmill. The barter system of the early Middle Ages began to disappear, as buying and selling with money replaced the simple exchange of goods.

● *Intellectual results*

The Crusades brought together men from every European region. Thus there was a great exchange of ideas and customs. The new things the Europeans learned from the Byzantines and Moslems were even more im-

Ships, people, and a castle of the time of the later Crusades. The ship at the right has a remarkable feature, the door that opens to allow horses to walk out onto the beach. If such a ship really was built in the thirteenth century, it anticipated by more than six hundred years the tank landing ships designed during World War II.

portant than those they learned from each other. Byzantine and Moslem science and culture brought a great intellectual revival in Europe in the twelfth and thirteenth centuries. Europeans also began to travel and to explore, with tremendous results.

● *Political results*

The Crusades hastened the growth of power of the kings and the loss of power by the feudal lords. Many nobles were killed during the Crusades. Others weakened their power by selling charters of liberties to towns they controlled in order to raise money to go on a Crusade. Towns and cities, stimulated by the increased trade and industry, grew in size, importance, and independence. The growth of cities helped to weaken feudal lords and strengthen kings. The merchants who controlled towns wanted uniform taxes and laws instead of the great variety of laws, customs, tolls, and taxes of the feudal lords. Therefore, they usually supported the king against the feudal lords. As a result, this new middle class came to be included and recognized in governments. The increasing influence of the middle class helped to weaken the power of the nobles.

Review of Chapter 14

People, places, and things

Identify: Hugh Capet, Philip II, Louis IX, Philip IV, William of Normandy, Edward the Confessor, Harold of Wessex, Henry II, Richard the Lion-Hearted, King John, Edward I, Frederick Barbarossa, Otto the Great, Urban II, Saladin, Seljuk Turks, the Parlement, Estates-General, Parliament, Lombard League.

Locate: Medieval France, Flanders, Aquitaine (Guienne), Brittany, Champagne, Burgundy, Normandy, Gascony, Anjou, Toulouse, Hastings, Barcelona, The Holy Land, Jerusalem, Constantinople, Antioch, Genoa, Pisa, Venice.

Events in review

1. What were the theoretical and real powers of the kings and of the feudal lords?
2. Name the four outstanding Capetian kings. Tell how each contributed to the unity and strength of France.
3. What steps did William I take to organize his kingdom in England?
4. What were the main provisions of the Magna Carta? What is the importance of the Magna Carta to the modern world?
5. What is English Common Law? Why is it important to us in America?
6. Who was the first European ruler to call middle-class townsmen to meet in assemblies with the nobility and clergy?
7. Why did men go on Crusades? Was religion the only motive?
8. From a military standpoint, did the Crusades succeed or fail? Why? Were military results the most important aspect of the Crusades?

Problems and projects

1. Which king did more for his country, Philip IV of France or Henry II of England? Explain your answer.
2. Compare the early English Parliament with the Congress of the United States.
3. How many provisions of the Magna Carta can be found in the Constitution of the United States?
4. How did feudalism result in unity in France and England and disunity in Germany and Italy?
5. Read an account of the Battle of Hastings. Prepare a radio or TV news broadcast in which you give the people of England an "eyewitness" description of the battle.

Chapter 15

The Roman Catholic Church in the Middle Ages

THE ROMAN EMPERORS who adopted Christianity as the official religion of the empire regarded the Church as a branch of the government. As the Western Empire of Rome grew weaker, the Church in the West freed itself from the control of the civil government. When civil government disappeared completely, the Church was strong enough to act as a substitute in many respects. In the fifth century the Bishop of Rome persuaded the eastern emperor to rule that the Church at Rome was supreme over all Christian Churches in the West.

Growth of papal power

The Bishop of Rome, or Pope, had several kinds of claims to be head of the entire Church. By the doctrine of apostolic succession, he was the successor to Peter, head of the Apostles. He could also claim that as Rome had been the center of the imperial government, so it should be head of church government.

The claims of the Bishop of Rome were not accepted everywhere. In the church organization he was a patriarch, head of several provinces of archbishops. There were other patriarchs at Jerusalem, Antioch, Alexandria, and Constantinople. Each considered himself as important in church government as the patriarch at Rome. In the West, where the empire disappeared, the Bishop of Rome was the only patriarch. His rise to be unquestioned head of the western Church was the result of the work of a number of great popes over a period of eight hundred years.

● Gregory the Great

Pope Gregory the Great was the first to hold great temporal powers in addition to his spiritual powers. Gregory was chosen pope at the end of the sixth century, when the Germanic Lombards were attacking northern and central Italy. He became the real ruler of Rome, superintending its defense. At his urging the eastern emperor recognized the Lombard conquest of northern Italy and made peace. Gregory the Great sent out the missionaries who converted Lombard Italy, Anglo-Saxon England, and Visigothic Spain to the Roman Catholic Church. He managed the vast property of the Church with great efficiency. Gregory laid the foundation for the claim of the popes to be temporal as well as spiritual rulers. At the end of his reign the papal authority was recognized throughout Italy, Spain, France, North Africa, and most of England.

From the seventh to the eleventh centuries the popes were not as powerful as Gregory the Great. Charlemagne made the Church a branch of his government. After his time the Church became feudalized. Feudal lords became bishops, abbots, and even popes. For a time the Roman nobles controlled the papacy, and it lost much of its spiritual influence.

Gregory VII

Gregory VII, another strong pope, restored the papacy to power in the mid-eleventh century. He believed that as representative of God he had supreme power not only over the Church but also over kings, emperors, and all their subjects. As pope, he controlled the most terrible punishments of the Church—excommunication and interdict. *Excommunication* was pronounced against an individual. That person was cut off completely from the Church. He could not receive any of the sacraments. He could not be buried in consecrated ground. During his life all Christians were obliged to avoid him like a leper. After his death, he was surely damned. *Interdict* was a sentence of excommunication on an entire region or country. No religious services could be held, no sacraments administered except baptism and the last rites. While interdict was in force, all souls within the region were in danger of eternal damnation. In an age of great religious faith these were terrible punishments indeed!

Gregory VII intervened in the governmental affairs of kings, emperors, and great nobles. He did not hesitate to use threats of excommunication and interdict to settle problems as he wished.

Innocent III

Pope Innocent III (1198–1216) brought the papacy to the height of its prestige and power. A very well-educated man, Innocent wrote books on law, theology, and Christian discipline. He was a skillful diplomat and one of the greatest statesmen of all European history.

Innocent III made even more sweeping claims to power than Gregory VII and was even more successful in enforcing them. He believed himself supreme over both the clergy and all worldly powers. He believed that governments of kings and emperors were only servants of the Church. He claimed the right to settle all problems, political or religious. No person or group, worldly or religious, could do more than advise him. The final decision was his.

Innocent took part in all disputes whether spiritual or political everywhere in Europe, and made free use of his powers of excommunication and interdict. When he quarreled with King John of England over the choice of an archbishop of Canterbury, he placed England under interdict. The interdict lasted until John gave England to the pope and received it back as a fief, becoming Innocent's vassal. The great pope dominated Italy as ruler of the Papal States, protector of the Lombard League, and guardian of Sicily. In Germany he deposed two kings and installed others.

Under Innocent III Europe became practically an absolute monarchy under the pope.

Mont-Saint-Michel, one of many great churches and abbeys built during the Middle Ages. On this granite rock off the Normandy coast Christians built a church and monastery in honor of the Archangel Michael. His statue stands at the tip of the spire.

It did not remain so, for a very good reason. Such a government needed a pope of almost superhuman ability and energy. Innocent III was such a man; but even so, his success came partly because conditions in Europe were favorable to his claims and activities. Later popes were less skillful, and circumstances were less favorable.

Church organization

The word *hierarchy* as used in the Church means the clergy organized in ranks according to their powers and responsibilities. The levels of the hierarchy were as follows:

The parish priest. The priest was at the

Many of the finest and most beautiful buildings of the Middle Ages were constructed by the Church. Here is the corner of a courtyard from a twelfth century French monastery. This beautiful garden has been reconstructed at the Cloisters in New York City.

bottom of the church hierarchy. In one sense he was the Church's most important officer. His was the vital duty of bringing religion to the people. He presided over the parish, conducted all church services, and administered all the sacraments except confirmation and ordination. He supervised the moral and religious instruction of his people and the moral life of the community. He also collected the tithe; this was a system by which each person had to pay to the Church one tenth of his income.

During the Middle Ages the parish priest was usually of peasant origin, with little formal education. He usually memorized the services, which were in Latin. He was the hardest working and most poorly paid member of the clergy.

The bishop. The bishop was considered the successor of Christ's Apostles. The bishop could administer the sacraments of confirmation (admission to full membership in the Church) and ordination (admission to the priesthood). He presided over a special church called a cathedral, in the most important city in his diocese. He appointed and removed parish priests, consecrated new churches, and had the very important duty of managing all church property in his diocese. Since the bishop usually controlled great wealth, the position was much sought for. In theory the clergy of the diocese elected the bishop. In practice the elections were usually controlled by kings or great nobles. Bishops were often vassals, and had vassals themselves. They were usually men of noble birth, often chosen more for their political power than for their spiritual lives and beliefs.

The archbishop. The archbishop had a diocese himself, with a cathedral church and all the powers of a bishop. In addition, he had authority over the other dioceses and bishops in his province. He could receive appeals from bishops' courts and summon provincial councils of the clergy to decide important questions of church belief and policy.

The pope and his court. At the top of the pyramid of the hierarchy was the pope, Bishop of Rome. He was the executive head of the whole organization. As already explained, the pope had great power. The pope had a court, the *curia,* to advise and assist him. He himself chose these officials. The most important were the *cardinals,* his advisers on legal and spiritual matters. After the eleventh century the cardinals had the duty of electing the new pope.

● *The position of the clergy in the Middle Ages*

The clergy made up the First Estate, the highest position in medieval society. The Church searched constantly for the best minds among all classes to enter the clergy. Churchmen were almost the only educated people. They wrote almost all the books; they conducted most of the schools. Churchmen held positions of honor and power in civil governments as advisers to kings, emperors, and great nobles.

Not all members of the clergy were priests or monks. As a class, most of them were men who had taken what were called "minor orders" so as to become students in schools, secretaries, or accountants. Such men were often employed in the households of kings and nobles. When unemployed, they lived by their wits. Taken as a group the minor clergy were not especially virtuous or pious; many of them were rascals. All of them were entitled to "benefit of clergy," the right to be tried in church courts. This right was prized because the church court could not pass a sentence of death. To prove himself a member of the clergy, a man had only to read a portion of the Bible.

Only in the clergy could the son of a commoner or peasant rise to high position. It was not a usual occurrence, for most of the higher places were filled by men of noble birth. However, a man of great ability, regardless of his birth, might rise even to be pope.

● *The Church as a state*

The medieval Church was much like a present-day government. Everyone became a member at birth, just as we become citizens. Almost everyone took the final step of admission to full membership—confirmation. Like any government the Church had its own laws and courts. It could enforce these laws even upon kings and emperors by many means, including excommunication and interdict.

The Church also resembled a modern government in having the power of taxation. It collected the tithe from all Christians. There was also "Peter's Pence," a tax of one penny per year on every household. A penny was more valuable then than now; in twelfth-century England a penny was about equal to a dollar today. The Church also received fees for the performance of ceremonies and fines from its courts. Some penances took the form of money payments. Money was obtained for *indulgences.* When a person secured an indulgence, he made a payment to the Church instead of undergoing some form of temporal punishment or penance for his sin. There was also vast income from church-owned lands. In the mid-thirteenth century, when the Church was at the peak of its power, its income was greater than that of all the kings of Europe combined.

Problems within the Church

The tremendous wealth of the Church led to abuses and corruption. When the church organization became a part of the feudal system, appointments to high church offices became the spoils of politics, involving kings and lords. Sometimes even the pope was appointed and controlled by feudal lords, kings, or emperors. Some men who became bishops or abbots were more interested in wealth and power than in spiritual and religious duties.

Feudal selection of bishops raised the problem of *lay investiture.* This term means that someone who is not a priest appoints priests. Kings or nobles chose the candidates for bishop or abbot. All the clergy did was to elect the men nominated. This caused a problem because the bishop controlled both fiefs and the symbols of his spiritual office. The symbols of the spiritual power of a bishop were his ring and crozier (cross). Kings and lords often insisted on giving both the feudal fiefs and the symbols because they saw little difference between them. However, the Church insisted that a bishop or archbishop must give the ring and crozier to the new bishop. This ceremony passed on the spiritual powers that came from the Apostles. Lay investiture led to a great conflict between popes and emperors.

The second problem in selecting church officials was *simony,* the buying and selling of positions in the church hierarchy. Under feudal control, church positions were often bought and paid for. The purchaser expected to get his money back from church income or from his subordinates. Even parish priests sometimes had to pay for appointments and recover the cost by charging high fees for church ceremonies and services.

The third great problem was the marriage of the clergy. All churchmen took vows of celibacy, that is, they pledged not to marry. Clerical marriage was condemned and forbidden by church law, but it was practiced almost everywhere. Clerical marriage threatened the Church in several ways: In church opinion, the married cleric was not able to give wholehearted devotion to his religious duties. Then, too, he might want to provide an estate for his own children from church property.

● *Reform movements in the Church*

There were many attempts to remedy the bad conditions in the Church. Pope Gregory VII was able to stop the appointment of popes by kings and nobles and secure the election of the pope by the College of Cardinals. Other problems had deeper roots.

Innocent III, in the thirteenth century, devoted himself to reform, especially the removal of control by non-clergy. As part of his efforts, he approved the formation of two new orders of monks, the Franciscans and Dominicans, both dedicated to reform.

The Franciscans were founded by St. Francis of Assisi, one of the great saints of the Church and one of the most interesting men who ever lived. Franciscans went around preaching, practicing charity, and doing nursing and social work. St. Francis believed in absolute poverty, and the Franciscans lived entirely by begging. They were called the Mendicant (Begging) Friars, or, from the color of their robes, the Gray Friars.

The Dominicans had a highly centralized organization. They were missionaries, espe-

Saint Francis of Assisi preaching to the birds. This picture from a thirteenth century manuscript shows a famous incident in the life of Saint Francis. Even the birds listened to his sermons.

cially interested in maintaining the purity of the faith. They became the greatest scholars and teachers of the later Middle Ages.

It must be said that even after three or four hundred years of effort by the Franciscans, the Dominicans, other churchmen, and many popes, the Church was still troubled by the problems of lay control, simony, clerical marriage, and the worldly lives of many clergymen.

● The Church and heresy

The Church permitted criticism of such evils as simony and clerical marriage, but it did not permit criticism of its doctrines or dogmas. A *doctrine* is a belief which is supported by great authority, usually from the Bible. In the sacrament of the Holy Eucharist, for example, the doctrine is that bread and wine, when properly blessed, actually become the body and blood of Jesus. A *dogma* is a doctrine so powerfully supported that it has to be accepted by the faithful absolutely without question.

People who questioned dogmas or became doubters because of evils in the Church, or who preached doctrines not approved by the Church, were guilty of the unpardonable sin of *heresy*. Heresy to the Church was much the same as treason to a modern government. Successful heresy meant the possibility of rebellion, secession, and the breakup of the whole church structure.

The Church developed a strong weapon to fight heresy. In the mid-thirteenth century the pope ordered the Dominican friars to seek out heretics and determine the causes of heresy. This search was known as the Inquisition. The judges sought out suspects and prosecuted them at secret trials. The defendant was not faced by his accusers, nor was he allowed to have a lawyer. Tortures were used to make him confess. If he did confess and recant (renounce his error), his penance was at most life imprisonment. If he refused to confess, or confessed and later relapsed into heresy, he was turned over to the civil government to be punished. In most countries heresy was punished by burning at the stake. These terrible penalties were thought necessary to save the soul of the heretic and to prevent heresy from spreading.

Monks and monasticism

Much of what you have read about the clergy thus far has told of only one branch of the organization. Priests, bishops, and the pope belonged to what was called the *secular* clergy. They lived, as the Latin phrase said, *in saeculo,* in the world. They had the duty of administering the sacraments and preaching the gospel to bring salvation to all the people. But you have noticed many references to monks, abbots, and monasteries. Because they lived according to strict rules (Latin—*regula*) monks were called the *regular* clergy.

Monk means "living alone." Monasticism first appeared in Egypt and the East during the third century A.D. The monks believed that the only way to live a perfect Christian life was to withdraw from the world and its temptations and gain holiness by prayer, fasting, and self-denial. The early monks were hermits who truly lived alone. Gradually, though, they came to live in communities.

● The Benedictine rule

Western monasticism lacked organization and direction until the early part of the sixth century. Benedict, a young man of a noble Roman family, became disgusted with the life of fashionable Roman society, left the city, and became a hermit. His reputation for holiness attracted so many followers that he established a monastery at Monte Cassino.

Benedict drew up a set of rules to regulate the lives of the monks. The Benedictine Rule was intended for monasteries in general, not for Monte Cassino alone. Monasteries which followed the rule were called the Benedictine

Order. Today, when you read of the Roman Catholic Church, you may notice the initials O.S.B. for Order of St. Benedict.

A monk who entered the order took three main vows. The first was *poverty*. He could own absolutely nothing. Everything he used, wore, or ate belonged to the community. All property was controlled and distributed by the abbot, the elected head of the community. The second vow was *chastity*, not to marry. The third was *obedience*. The monk gave up his own will, and swore to be subject in all ways to the abbot. He promised to remain in the monastery permanently, never going outside the walls without special permission of the abbot.

A famous Benedictine monastery, Monte Cassino in Italy. In World War II this monastery was destroyed during fighting between the Allied and German armies. It was rebuilt after the war.

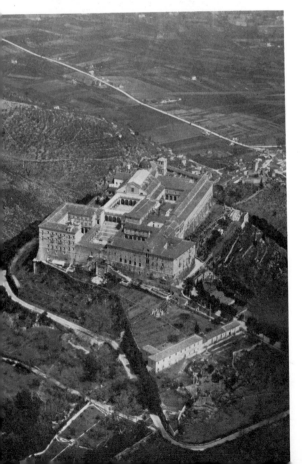

Monks spent about eight hours throughout the day in prayer. Work was a second obligation. Benedict believed that an idle monk would surely be tempted by the devil. Therefore, his rule required a fixed amount of manual labor. Gardening, repairing, cleaning, cooking, waiting on table—all the necessary tasks in and about the monastery—were assigned by the abbot to groups of monks who worked together. Scholarly work was not mentioned in the rule, but the abbot could provide for it.

●*Monks and medieval life*

Missionary work. Some monks, at the command of their superiors, left the monasteries to become missionaries. One of the famous eairly missionaries was Patrick, who converted the Irish. Two great missionaries from the Benedictine order were Augustine, who began the reconversion of England, and Boniface, who took Christianity to Germany. Monks also played an important part in the conversion of Visigothic Spain and Vandal North Africa.

Education and scholarship. Monks were among the foremost medieval scholars, and in the early period had almost a monopoly of what education there was. They had time for scholarly work, as secular priests did not, and many of them became copyists. By copying, they preserved much of the classical literature, especially that of the Romans. To relieve the tedious work of straight copying, the monks often decorated their manuscripts with enormous capital letters at the beginnings of chapters or pages, using gold and many other colors. These *illuminated manuscripts,* as they are called, were the finest art work of the early Middle Ages.

The books that were used in medieval preaching and schools were also prepared by the monks. Monastery schools were the best in Europe until universities appeared during the twelfth century. Monks did whatever scientific work there was.

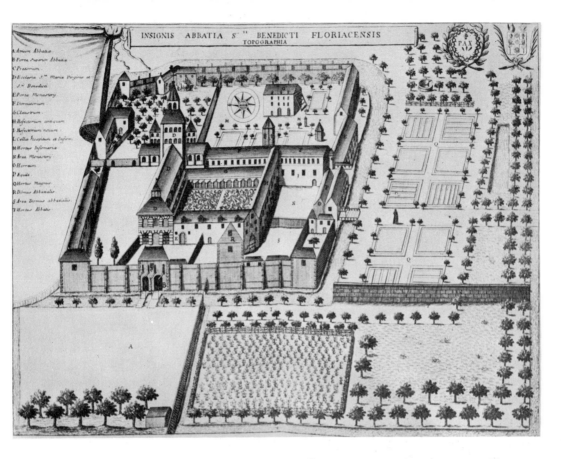

Economic life. During the early Middle Ages, monasteries were the most important centers of agriculture, commerce, manufacturing, and finance. The monks were real leaders in agriculture. They knew and continued the best Roman practices in farming. They developed better methods of raising crops, breeding cattle, and cultivating fruit, especially grapes. Their landholdings were immense. They cleared forests, drained swamps, and built dikes and roads.

During the middle and later medieval period, much manufacturing was done in monasteries. Tools, utensils, clothing, shoes, leather goods, and the best beer and wine in Europe were produced in monasteries.

Monasteries also carried on widespread trading activities. They often owned their own pack animals, ships, markets, and warehouses. Their routes were carefully mapped. Often in new regions they used roads which

A plan view of a Benedictine abbey. In the center was a courtyard with an arched cloister. To the left of the court was the church with its spire. The long building at right angles to the church was the monks' dormitory. To the right of the court was the refectory, or dining room. Around the central buildings were workshops, storage houses, gardens, and orchards.

they themselves had built. All these economic activities needed financing. The monks became the earliest bankers of the Middle Ages.

Social life. In the social life of the times monasteries were just as important as in agriculture and trade. They did much charitable work. The secular clergy were mainly responsible for charity, but the monasteries made many gifts of food and clothing to the neighboring poor. When they adopted the manorial system, monasteries were by far

193

the best landlords of the time. They also provided the best inns for travelers.

Popes versus emperors

As you have learned, popes and emperors alternated in control during the early Middle Ages. Charlemagne considered himself at least the equal of the pope. Some of his successors ruled Rome as superiors of the popes. When the Carolingian empire broke up, the popes became independent of the emperors. They also became temporal rulers of the Papal States. However, the papacy itself became a prize of local politics among the Roman nobles.

The beginning of the Holy Roman Empire in 962 brought on a great conflict between popes and emperors. The ambition of the German emperors to rule Italy brought them in conflict with the popes. Otto the Great forced the pope to recognize him as overlord. For the next forty years German rulers chose the popes.

The power of the emperors reached its peak under Henry III (1039–1056). He was stronger in Germany than most emperors. At the time, because of corrupt Roman politics, three men claimed to be pope. Henry III went to Italy, deposed all three claimants, and had a German elected. He also dictated the choice of the next three popes. Like Charlemagne, he considered the Church a branch of his royal government. He chose bishops and popes and invested them with the symbols of their offices. Henry tried to reform the Church by stopping the sale of church appointments and the marriage of the clergy.

● The great conflict

Henry III's son was only a child when his father died. Because there was civil war in Germany, the Church had a chance to increase its powers. It was then that the great Gregory VII became pope. He believed that the Church was supreme over all temporal governments and the pope supreme over the Church.

The struggle between Gregory VII and Henry IV was long and very complicated. It is enough to know that it concerned the election of church officials—whether the Church or the rulers controlled the appointment of church officials. Gregory finally excommunicated the emperor, releasing all his subjects from their oaths of allegiance, and urged them to elect another king. This was too much for Henry; so he gave in to the pope. Barefooted in the snow and dressed as a pilgrim, he came to the castle at Canossa, in Italy, where Gregory was staying. He begged forgiveness, and received it.

Thus ended the struggle over lay investiture. In 1122 at the city of Worms there was a great Diet (assembly) of churchmen, nobles, and representatives of the emperor. The emperor and the churchmen reached an agreement known as the Concordat of Worms. The emperor agreed that church officials should elect bishops and abbots and invest them with the symbols of their spiritual powers. The emperor could be present at these elections, but he promised not to try to influence them either by money or violence. He was allowed to invest the newly-elected official with the lands and secular powers by a touch of his scepter.

However, the struggle between popes and emperors was by no means ended. The attempts of the Germans to rule Italy always threatened the rule of the popes over the Papal States. It was the pope who encouraged the Lombard cities to unite and defeat the great Frederick Barbarossa. Then a new danger arose when Frederick's son married the heiress of the King of Sicily. If Germans ruled both northern and southern Italy, the papacy might be crushed between them.

This threat became an actual danger when Frederick II ruled. He made Sicily a strong, almost modern kingdom. For a time it seemed possible that he might unite all Italy into a real kingdom. Opposed to him in this ambition were several popes, successors in turn to the great Innocent III. As already noted (page 181) Italy remained disunited. In the end, the long struggle between popes and emperors ended in a complete victory for the papacy.

The influence of the Church on medieval life

The first and most important duty of the Church was to prepare people for the future life and assure them salvation in the life to come. It administered the sacraments. It regulated conduct and exacted penance for wrongdoing. It punished the unruly with threats of damnation and, in extreme cases, with excommunication. In time it gained other duties either by taking them or having them forced upon it. The Church entered widely into medieval beliefs and institutions.

● *The Church and political life*

The Church claimed to be superior to all secular governments. As God's institution for saving souls, the Church was supreme in the all-important matters of faith and morals. The Church supported monarchy, rule by a king, as the best form of secular government. It preached obedience to the laws of kings unless these laws were sinful and contrary to religious laws. The Church had its own laws, called canon laws, which it considered above civil laws. It had its own courts where clergy of any rank were tried for any offense. Many kinds of cases could be appealed to a high church court for final decision.

The Church usually supported kings against feudal lords. Through the Truce and Peace of God (page 170) it worked for peace, except, of course, in Crusades against unbelievers. The Church helped to soften the rudeness of the feudal lords and to civilize them through the institution of chivalry.

● *The Church and economic life*

The Church's moral ideas had various effects on economic practices in the Middle Ages. It taught that earthly possessions were less important than salvation. It opposed the gaining of wealth at the expense or disadvantage of others. Its insistence that labor of any kind was in keeping with the dignity of free men was very important. Many of the practices of medieval fairs and markets were influenced by the moral ideas of the Church.

● *The Church and social life*

The family. According to church doctrine the family was a sacred institution under church law. Divorce was forbidden, although under some conditions it was possible to have a marriage annulled. The Church took responsibility for all widows and orphans.

St. Patrick, one of the great missionaries of the medieval Christian Church.

Serfdom and slavery. The Church did not oppose serfdom; it had many serfs itself. The Church opposed slavery in many instances and taught that freeing a slave was a pious act of charity.

Social work. The Church took complete charge of all social work. It assumed that there would always be poor people; so it gave them relief. It did not try to remove the causes of poverty. It did teach that all men were equal in the sight of God, if not on earth. There was spiritual democracy, at least.

To relieve the sick and distressed, the Church established hospitals, orphanages, and poorhouses. Special religious orders were founded to do certain kinds of social work such as hospital care, the care of lepers, burial of the poor, and general charity. Thus that great institution, the Christian Church, was intimately connected with every side of medieval life.

Review of Chapter 15

People, places, and things

Identify: Gregory the Great, Gregory VII, Innocent III, Henry IV, St. Francis of Assisi, St. Benedict, Dominicans, Concordat of Worms, College of Cardinals, Inquisition, "Peter's Pence," tithe, "benefit of clergy," doctrine, dogma, excommunication, interdict, heresy.

Events in review

1. How did Gregory the Great and Gregory VII increase the authority of the papacy?
2. What factors helped make Innocent III such a powerful pope?
3. Briefly describe the position of the clergy in medieval society.
4. What were the problems of lay investiture and simony?
5. Explain the difference between *secular* clergy and *regular* clergy. Name one great organizer of the regular clergy.
6. Describe three great contributions the monasteries made to medieval life.
7. What major problem was involved in the struggle between Gregory VII and Henry IV? Which man won? How?
8. Did the Church preach obedience to the laws of kings? What were canon laws?

Problems and projects

1. The medieval Church had some powers and functions that now belong entirely to the civil government. List as many of these powers and functions as you can.
2. For discussion: Was the Church as much a part of feudalism as the civil government?
3. Make a chart to show the hierarchy of the medieval Church. How did this organization strengthen the Church?
4. Write a description of the daily life of a medieval monk or nun.
5. Prepare a report on the contributions of the monasteries to the development of civilization. See 221–223 for helpful reference books.
6. Prepare and present a dramatization of the meeting between Pope Gregory VII and Emperor Henry IV at Canossa.
7. Write a brief biography of a great medieval religious leader, such as St. Francis, St. Benedict, St. Ignatius Loyola, or any of the famous men or women of the Church in this era.

Chapter 16

Towns, Trade, and National States

TRADE almost died out in western Europe between the fifth and eleventh centuries. Europe became largely agricultural. Towns and cities, which lived on trade and manufacturing, decreased in population. The agricultural manors became almost, though not entirely, self-sufficient. They grew or made nearly everything they used. There was some exchange of goods, but trade was not an important economic activity.

Commerce was hindered by many obstacles. Roads were poor, bridges were few. Robbers on land and pirates at sea made travel very dangerous. Tolls charged by feudal lords were a great hindrance. In each feudal territory tolls had to be paid for the use of roads, bridges, and fords.

Church laws also made trade difficult. The Church insisted on a "just price." This price covered only the cost of labor and materials, with no profit. The Church prohibited the purchase of articles for resale at a higher price. It prohibited *usury,* the charging of interest for the loan of money.

Trade revives in the eleventh century

It was in Italy that trade began to revive in the eleventh century. Neither trade nor towns had declined there as much as elsewhere. Venice had remained under the Byzantine Empire so that its ships had some protection from the Moslems. In the first half of the eleventh century Genoa and Pisa began a Holy War against the Moslems on the sea. They gained trading privileges with Sicily, Sardinia, Corsica, and North Africa. By the end of the eleventh century and throughout the twelfth, their ships were ready to carry the crusaders and bring back rich cargoes of eastern goods.

The new trade went overland, too. New trading centers were built along roads and rivers, and many cities produced manufactured goods to supply the trade. The growing cities needed food; so more farm goods were produced. Population increased more rapidly in the eleventh century, partly because more people were needed and could be supported.

● *Markets and fairs*

The new trade needed places where goods could be exchanged. The weekly village markets did not attract enough people; so some merchants began to use religious festivals. Then some feudal lords established fairs for the sale of the imported goods. The more intelligent lords realized that they could be wealthy by charging fees on the goods sold. They guaranteed special protection to merchants for the holding of a fair. Fairs were held for several days or weeks each year.

The articles of the trade were interesting. Finer manufactured goods came almost entirely from Moslem Spain, Africa, and the

Near East. Silks, rugs, cotton and linen cloth, inlaid arms and armor, and art products in gold, silver, and ivory were on the market. There was a great demand, stimulated by the Crusades, for oriental spices, drugs, perfumes, dyes, and gems. Europe offered Venetian metal goods and glassware, fine Flemish woolen cloth, and French wine. Northern and western Europe sold food and raw materials.

The fairs helped to break down the separateness of each region and the narrow outlook of the people. A fair was very gay, and people came from great distances to attend it. A fair was more than just buying and selling. There were jugglers, clowns, and entertainers who went from fair to fair, earning money by amusing the crowds, as at our county fairs today. A person could talk to people from distant regions.

●The regions of trade

Trade flowed in many regions. Viking routes were followed to link the Baltic and North Seas with Britain, the Atlantic coast of Europe, and the Mediterranean. Flanders, now part of Belgium, grew to great commercial importance. It was the meeting point of trade routes across France, down the Rhine from Germany, across from Britain, and down from the Baltic. It became a great center of population and wealth.

Hamburg, Lübeck, and Bremen were the most important commercial cities on the coasts of the North and Baltic Seas. Because the government of the German king was so weak, the trading cities formed a league, or Hansa, for protection. The Hanseatic League was a powerful agent in the commerce of northwest Europe during the fourteenth and fifteenth centuries. It was not a political organization. It existed only to promote and protect the trade of the member cities. The Hanseatic cities had permanent trading posts, called factories, in Flanders, England, and Russia. A member who failed to keep League

The Bishop of Paris blessing a medieval fair. Around the market place are shops and stalls selling livestock and various kinds of merchandise.

agreements could be kept out of trade monopolies abroad. If a foreign country took away the privileges of Hanseatic traders, the League placed an embargo on all shipping to that country. The privileges were usually restored.

Venice became the great commercial sea power of the Mediterranean. For a while Genoa and Pisa were Venice's rivals, but in time the Venetians conquered both and became supreme. Venice monopolized the trade of the Adriatic, Aegean, and Black Seas. The Venetians also expanded on land in northern Italy and down the east coast of the Adriatic. Thus Venice became a city-state as powerful as any western European country.

When the Ottoman Turks gained control of the Near East at the end of the fourteenth century, Venice held her position for a time. However, the capture of Constantinople by the Turks in 1453 was a blow to Venetian trade, and from that time on the importance of Venice gradually declined.

Other north Italian cities, especially Florence and Milan, were important in overland trade. These independent Lombard cities also became city-states by conquering surrounding territory.

● *Portuguese navigators*

Out on the western side of the Iberian peninsula was Portugal, a small kingdom facing the Atlantic. During the fifteenth century other kingdoms of the peninsula tried to gain territory by driving out the Moslem Moors, but Portugal was more interested in land in Africa.

Prince Henry of Portugal, called Henry the Navigator, had three main interests. He hoped to gain new lands and peoples for Christianity by a crusade in Africa. He also wanted to develop Portugal's commerce, but was kept out of the profitable eastern Mediterranean trade by Venice's monopoly. Henry also wanted to get for Portugal a share of the African slave trade, which the Moors controlled. So, for the somewhat conflicting aims of more Christians, more slaves, and more trade, the Portuguese began a series of explorations along the west coast of Africa.

Henry established a school of navigation to train Portuguese sailors. His trained seamen, financed by him, worked their way slowly down the African coast and occupied the nearby islands—for example, the Azores and the Canaries. When they finally passed the end of the Sahara desert, they found a very rich commercial opportunity: trade in Negro slaves, gold, ivory, and tropical products.

Further explorations brought even greater gains. In 1487 Bartolomeo Diaz proved that Africa was not endless. He sailed around the Cape of Good Hope into the Indian Ocean. In 1498 Vasco da Gama sailed all the way to India, coming home with a rich cargo. In today's slang, Portugal had "hit the jackpot." Its ships could sail to India and the East Indies, the famous Spice Islands. Neither Arabs, Turks, nor Venetians could block them from the wealth of the Eastern trade. From that time on the importance of the eastern Mediterranean in commerce fell away, and Venice ceased to be a great power.

Revived trade stimulates the growth of towns

Towns did not disappear completely during the early Middle Ages, although they shrank greatly in population. Many Roman towns survived, especially if they were easy to defend or were important for other reasons. Some towns grew up around castles, shrines, cathedrals, or mines. However, town life was not important until the revival of trade in the eleventh century. The towns that grew rapidly were those that were important in trade. Those along the Roman roads, on the sites of the great Roman camps, around the castle of a ruling prince, at river crossings or at good harbors, developed rapidly.

● *The towns gain liberties*

Whether he was called burgess, burgher, or bourgeois, the townsman was different from other people. He was neither lord nor vassal nor serf. Manufacturing and trade, at which he made his living, played little part in the manorial system.

Since the town did not fit into the system, and since its activities were different, townsmen wanted to control their own governments. However, under the feudal system each town had its lord, with absolute powers of government. Neither nobles nor church lords were willing to give up this power; so independence and self-government for towns came only as a result of a long struggle.

Some lords, as in Flanders, gave many liberties to encourage the development of towns because they got a rich income from them. Towns sometimes bought charters of liberties from their lords. During the Crusades, when nobles needed unusual amounts of money, they were more willing to sell privileges. Often, though, it took violence and war to gain rights of self-government for the cities.

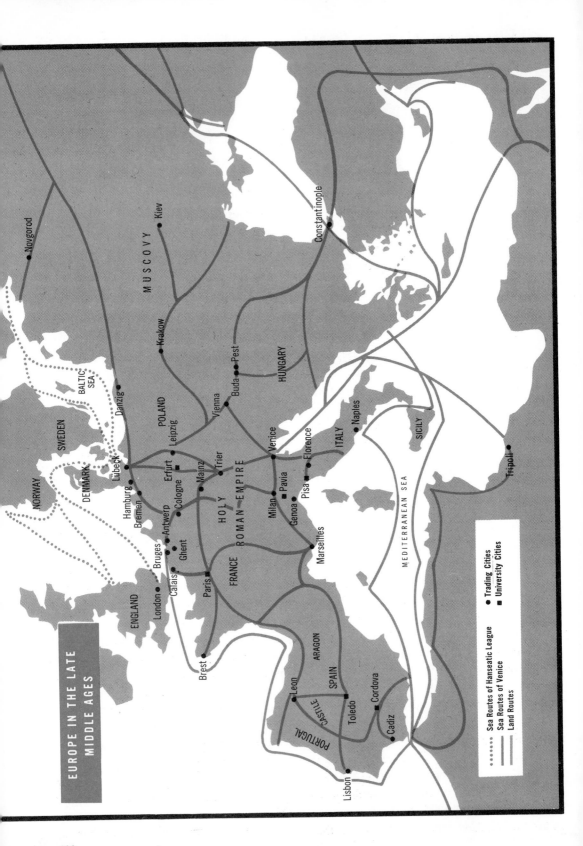

EUROPE IN THE LATE
MIDDLE AGES

Trading Cities ●
University Cities ■

Sea Routes of Hanseatic League ∙∙∙∙∙∙∙∙
Sea Routes of Venice ─────
Land Routes ─────

Novgorod

Kiev

MUSCOVY

Constantinople

Krakow

Buda
Pest

HUNGARY

Vienna

Danzig

BALTIC
SEA

SWEDEN

POLAND

Leipzig

NORWAY

DENMARK

Lübeck

Hamburg

Bremen

Antwerp

Cologne

Erfurt

Mainz

Trier

Venice

Florence

ITALY

Naples

SICILY

Tripoli

MEDITERRANEAN SEA

Milan

Pavia

Genoa

Pisa

HOLY
ROMAN EMPIRE

Marseilles

Ghent

Bruges

Calais

London

ENGLAND

Paris

FRANCE

Brest

Leon

ARAGON

SPAIN

CASTILE

Toledo

Cordova

Cadiz

PORTUGAL

Lisbon

Four liberties of townsmen

Town and city charters, in which their liberties were written, differed widely from town to town and country to country. In time, though, every bourgeois (townsman) in Europe was assured of at least four principal liberties.

The first liberty was *free status*. No matter what his birth or origin, a man who lived in a town, unchallenged, for a year and a day, was a free man. All ties to an outside lord were broken. The Germans said: *Stadtluft macht frei*—"City air makes one free." With luck, a peasant or serf who escaped to a town could become a free townsman.

The second was *free tenure*. A townsman was exempt from any duties on the manor. Services owed to the lord were owed by the entire community, not by an individual. They were always carefully written and defined.

Third came *town justice*. Towns had their own courts made up of prominent citizens familiar with local customs. Townsmen and their cases of all kinds were tried there, not in feudal courts.

Finally, townsmen had *commercial privileges*. They had the right to sell freely in the town market and to charge tolls on all outsiders trading there.

Self-governing towns

Some towns, called *communes,* gained the right of complete self-government. The officials, a mayor or burgomaster and a council, were elected by the more prominent citizens.

In Venice the doge (duke) and all other officials were elected from a closed group of certain great families which were listed in the *Golden Book*. Florence, Milan, Genoa, Pisa, and other Lombard cities were also self-governing. All of them were dominated by city-dwelling nobility or by great merchant families. Although they began as near-democracies, they all came to be ruled by dictators, called despots.

The medieval craft guilds built their own halls as meeting places. This is the Tailors' Guild Hall in Braunschweig, Germany. The building dates from the fourteenth century. The ornamental front was added in the sixteenth.

The merchant guilds

There were many reasons for merchants to unite. The dangers of travel were great; it was safer to travel in groups with armed escorts. Arranging such convoys took much planning and money. Gradually merchants founded unions called guilds or hansas.

As towns developed, the merchant guilds took the lead in getting charters of liberties from kings and feudal lords. The guilds became very powerful and exclusive. They gained a monopoly of all buying and selling in the towns. In self-governing towns it was usually the members of merchant guilds who voted to elect town officials. The guild also fixed standards of quality for manufactured goods. It made loans to and looked after members who were in trouble in any way. It provided charity for widows of members.

The guilds of skilled workers often made themselves coats of arms. Above is the coat of arms of the guild of coopers, who made barrels.

● Craft guilds

In time the artisans (skilled workers) engaged in manufacturing also formed guilds (much as the Greek and Roman craftsmen had done a thousand and more years before). Each craft guild included all men engaged in one trade, such as goldsmiths, shoemakers, or metal workers. The guild regulated wages and fixed hours and conditions of labor in the industry. It fixed the prices and conditions for selling the goods. It provided, trained, and disciplined the workers. Like the merchant guilds it looked after the welfare of unfortunate or dependent members.

Craft guilds developed the apprentice system to provide and train the skilled workers needed in industry. To become a fully accepted member of the guild (a master workman), a candidate went through two preliminary stages of training.

The *apprentice* was a boy or young man who was bound (apprenticed) by his parents to a master workman to learn the trade. He lived at the home of the master as a member of his family. The master furnished food, clothing, training in the trade, and moral guidance. The apprentice promised to obey his master, to keep his secrets of workman-

ship, and to behave himself properly. The period of apprenticeship varied from three to twelve years.

The *journeyman* was a skilled worker who, after finishing his apprenticeship, worked for a master for daily wages. The journeyman was a candidate to become a full member of the guild. After working for wages for some time, he could become a master by submitting proof of his skill—a masterpiece—and by opening a shop of his own.

Toward the end of the Middle Ages the line between masters and journeymen became much more distinct and much harder to cross. The journeyman usually remained a wage-earner all his life. Increased prosperity turned masters into a sort of industrial aristocracy. Often the master's son inherited the business and position without the required apprenticeship.

● Rise of the middle class

You can see that an important new class of people had appeared in medieval society. In early feudal times the nobles and higher clergy were at the top of the social structure, peasants were at the bottom. Now there was a class in the middle: rich merchants, bankers, master craftsmen, and artisans. They were known by various names: in England, the middle class; in France, the bourgeoisie.

The rise of the middle class was one of the most important changes in European society during the later Middle Ages. The middle class developed its own laws, especially those dealing with trade. It wanted uniform government to protect trade and property, hence it usually favored kings against nobles. To gain its support kings began to consult and use middle-class men in government positions. Wealthy merchants had high standing in the political and social life of the cities.

● Development of capitalism

Capital is money earned, saved, and invested in some business to produce profits.

The appearance of capitalism changed the economic life of Europe during the later Middle Ages. Town real estate was a fine investment. The cramped size of medieval cities meant that city land always brought a good price either by sale or from rentals. Another good investment was building a ship and financing voyages. Men with capital formed shipping companies. Each contributed part of the cost and received a share of the profit.

Banking was another capitalist activity that developed in the later Middle Ages. Merchants and manufacturers often needed to borrow money to finance business activities. During the early Middle Ages Jews had done most of the moneylending because the Christian Church forbade taking interest on loans. By the thirteenth century the great merchants had taken over the business of moneylending and other banking activities. The Lombard cities had regular agents in all important cities and at all fairs. Officially they did not charge usury (interest), but they paid themselves by rents, charges for services, or charges for damages.

● Characteristics of medieval towns

What was it like to live in one of these rapidly developing medieval towns or cities? How did they resemble, and how did they differ from, modern cities?

Medieval cities were small by modern standards. Except for Venice and several Lombard cities, no western European city had a population of 100,000. Ghent and Bruges, in Flanders, with about 50,000 each, were considered huge. London, with about 25,000, was far above average. The usual city had from 5,000 to 10,000 people.

Physically the city was very compact. It was often built on top of a hill or at the bend of a river so that it could easily be defended. It had three distinct sections. The city proper was enclosed by a wall for defense. As the population grew, sections were built just outside the wall. These were the suburbs, or, in France, the *faubourgs*. Then there was an outer strip of land of varying width that came within the law of the town.

Houses in the early towns were not much better than peasant huts. As the middle class became more prosperous, their homes were larger and better built, of stone and wood. Because land within the walls was scarce and valuable, houses were built up to five or six stories. To gain space each higher story projected out a little farther than the one below. Thus at the top the houses almost met in the middle of the street. Each city had some outstandingly fine buildings: the church, or, in an important city, the cathedral; the town hall and the guild halls.

A medieval city would have outraged both the eyes and noses of modern people. The

A famous French walled city, Carcassonne. This town was originally built by the Romans and the Visigoths. Note the towers and battlements like those of a feudal castle.

streets were dark, filthy, and full of refuse. The only way of disposing of sewage was by open gutters, which ran only when it rained. The medieval city was an excellent breeding place for disease. Plagues and epidemics (of typhoid fever, for example), were frequent and greatly dreaded.

There was no street lighting. Honest people who went out at night had to have servants to light the way with torches or lanterns and to protect them from thugs and robbers, for there was no regular police force. There was no regular fire department, though fire was a serious menace.

So far you have read only about the unattractive and disagreeable side of city life. There was also a very attractive side. The medieval city was a throbbing, lively place. By day the streets were alive with people: townsmen and visitors, merchants and strolling players, workers and jugglers. The city was a vastly different place from the manor village. The manor was a very conservative place where everything was done according to custom and tradition. The city, on the contrary, was alive, willing to accept new ideas and things, willing to grow in every way. It was much more than just a center of trade and industry. It was a political, religious, and social unit. It was the home of the cathedral and the new universities. Towns and cities helped change the civilization of Europe.

France and England become national states

By the start of the fourteenth century both France and England were well on the way to developing strong national kingdoms. In England the feudal lords could still use Parliament to check the king's power. The English Common Law, a single legal system throughout the nation, had developed. The French king had absolute power in the royal domains, about half of modern France, but he was weak outside them. French kings also used a parliament, called the Estates-General, to get the support of all classes of people. Unlike the English Parliament, the Estates-General had no real power of its own.

Feudalism was growing weaker in both countries. A feeling of nationalism, of belonging together, was growing among the people, although it was still not strong. Both countries were prosperous. The development of the woolen industry in England brought great prosperity. In France, as a result of a century of comparative peace, the population increased, trade and industry flourished, and many people prospered. However, the growing strength and prosperity of the two countries were ruined by a senseless war that lasted, with intervals of peace, for over one hundred years.

● The Hundred Years' War, 1337–1453

The basic, underlying cause of the Hundred Years' War was rivalry over Gascony and Guienne in France, which English kings still held as feudal fiefs. A second cause was the question of succession to the French throne. The male Capetian line died out in 1328 with the three sons of Philip the Fair. King Edward III of England, the son of Philip's daughter, claimed the French throne. However, the French nobles ruled that the throne of France could not go to a woman or pass on through the female line. A further problem was rivalry over the commercially rich territory of Flanders. This rivalry brought matters to a head. Edward III invaded Flanders, and the war began.

The first period of the war (1337–1380) was notable for two great battles and a dreadful plague. At both Crécy and Poitiers small English armies were attacked by much larger French armies. In each case the French feudal cavalry was completely routed, with dreadful losses, by foot soldiers armed with the new English weapon, the longbow. The days of knights on horseback as the supreme weapon in warfare were ended.

In 1348 and 1349 the terrible bubonic plague swept out of Asia to devastate Europe. (Europeans called it the Black Death.) Some towns lost from half to three-quarters of their population. Perhaps a third of all the people in England died of the plague.

During the second period of the war—about thirty-five years (1380–1415)—there was little organized fighting. Unorganized bands of brigands, robbers, and pirates ravaged France. Both countries were torn by internal troubles; in each the king lost power.

The English Parliament, by refusing to grant money until its conditions were met, forced some weak kings to recognize a number of important principles of government. Any restatement or change of a law had to be approved not merely by the king but also by the Parliament. Parliament gained the right to impose all taxes. Any tax had to be proposed first by the House of Commons. Another very important change was that the king could spend money only for the purpose for which Parliament had appropriated it. He could not take the money and do as he pleased with it. Members of Parliament were free to attend sessions, introduce bills, and engage in debate without being harmed by the king.

In France a great feud broke out between two branches of the royal family, Burgundy and Orléans, for control of the throne. This happened because the king had become insane. The French suffered a third great defeat at Agincourt in 1415. They had to agree that the English king should succeed when the insane French king died.

●*Joan of Arc inspires the French*

France's fortunes, now at their lowest ebb, were revived by one of the famous women of

> *An old print of the Battle of Poitiers, 1356. At the left are a few of the English archers whose rapid and accurate shooting slaughtered the French knights. The English used six-foot bows made of yew. Their arrows were approximately a yard long.*

Joan of Arc has inspired a number of plays and movies in recent times. Here Katherine Cornell portrays the Maid in a scene from Bernard Shaw's St. Joan. She is shown at her trial by a Church court.

history. Joan of Arc was an uneducated peasant girl of Domremy in Lorraine. During her teens she began to hear "voices" which told her what she must do. An English army was besieging the city of Orléans. Joan believed that St. Michael ordered her to help France by breaking the English siege of Orléans and seeing that the Dauphin, heir to the insane king, was crowned at Reims.

By inspiring the French to great enthusiasm and courage Joan raised the siege of Orléans and went on to other victories in the Loire valley. The French were convinced they were led by an angel; the English feared her as a devil. She escorted the Dauphin to the ancient city of Reims, the site of French coronations, and stood beside him as he was crowned Charles VII of France.

Joan had now finished the work commanded by the "voices." She wanted to go home,

but was persuaded to fight on, only to suffer a number of defeats. In a small skirmish she was captured by the Burgundians, whose ruler was an ally of the English. The Burgundians sold Joan to the English. Joan was turned over to a Church council headed by a bishop who was under the influence of the English. She was tried for witchcraft, found guilty of heresy, and turned over to the secular government to be burned at the stake. As the sentence was executed, an English leader said: "We are lost; we have burned a saint." Much later, by order of the pope, Joan's case was retried by another Church court, and she was found innocent of witchcraft and heresy. Still later she was proclaimed a saint.

Joan's death as a martyr aroused great patriotism among the people, who now thought of themselves as French instead of Burgundians, or Gascons or members of some other local group. They demanded that the English be driven out and a truly national monarchy established. By the end of the war in 1453 the English had been driven from French soil, except for the seaport of Calais.

The Hundred Years' War brought death to many men on both sides. Large areas of France were laid waste by battle, fire, and famine. Nevertheless, the war had positive results. England and France gained strong national governments. In both countries there was a revival of trade and industry. Increased national wealth meant that taxes produced enough revenue to support a strong government. The war weakened feudal lords and strengthened kings. Knights had lost military importance to commoners armed with longbows. Kings could now raise armies of common people and defeat feudal lords.

● The War of the Roses in England

The strengthening of English royal power was postponed for thirty years by a civil war in which two rival families fought for the throne. The symbol of the House of Lancaster was a red rose; that of the House of

York, a white rose. Thus the war was called the War of the Roses. It was a war of skirmishes, murders, and assassinations, fought by small bands of nobles and their retainers. Considering the small number who fought, it was a very bloody war. As a result of it, the English nobles were almost wiped out.

The war ended in 1485 when the last York king was killed in battle. Henry Tudor, who had married a York heiress, received the support of the Lancastrians. He became Henry VII, founder of the Tudor dynasty.

The story of the Tudor rulers will be told in later chapters. Here it is enough to say that the English people, tired of disorder, were willing to accept strong government. With the nobility weakened by the war, there was little effective check on the powers of the king. The Tudors ruled almost as absolute monarchs for more than a century.

● *France under Louis XI*

During the Hundred Years' War, the power of the French king had declined. For a time it looked as though the Estates-General might become a real ruling body. It gained control of finances and some power over lawmaking. However, when the war ended, King Charles VII broke the power of the Estates-General. It had not gained much popular support; so there was little complaint when it was no longer summoned to meet. Two other royal problems remained: building an effective central government administration, and breaking the power of the great vassals.

France had four great families. Each was a branch of the royal family; each ruled an entire province. The task of breaking the power of these great vassals and making the royal government supreme was done by one of the most remarkable men ever to hold the throne.

Louis XI was a powerful ruler. He avoided war except as a last resort, preferring to use diplomacy, at which he was a master. His opponents called him The Spider. He knew exactly what he wanted, and used any methods to get it. His administration was harsh and his taxes were heavy, but he did not use the money for himself; he used it to strengthen his kingdom.

Louis XI's greatest problem was Burgundy. Charles the Bold, Duke of Burgundy, was fearless and chivalrous. He was almost the opposite of the shrewd, tricky king. Charles' great ambition was to change the Duchy of Burgundy into the old Middle Kingdom of Charlemagne's successors, independent of France. To build an alliance against Charles, Louis used diplomacy. He frightened the Hapsburg Holy Roman Emperor into opposing the proposed kingdom, and he persuaded the independent Swiss that a strong Burgundy on their frontier threatened their freedom.

It was the Swiss who did Louis XI's fighting for him. They were commoners, not knights. Their army was infantry, free men who used long pikes as a defense against cavalry charges. Twice in one year the Swiss infantry defeated the knight cavalry of the Burgundians. In another battle in the following year Charles the Bold was killed.

Since Charles had no son, Louis XI seized much Burgundian territory. He wanted Flanders, but could not get it. The Flemings supported Charles' daughter, who had married Maximilian of Hapsburg. Louis had to give up Flanders, but he soon had other good fortune. The House of Anjou, another of the great French families, died out. Louis gained all of southern France for the crown. The only great fief outside royal control was Brittany, and Louis' son gained it by marriage. Thus France became a unified absolute monarchy.

Spain becomes an absolute monarchy

Down on the Iberian peninsula—now Spain and Portugal—there were three small Christian kingdoms: Portugal, Aragon, and

Castile-Leon. There was also the Moorish state of Granada. The Moorish caliphate in Spain had broken up into a number of independent feudal states, which weakened it in the fight against the Christians. However, the Christian kingdoms fought among themselves as much as against the Moors, so that progress toward building up a nation was slow.

The first real step toward the unification of Spain came in 1469. In that year Isabella, heiress of the kingdom of Castile, married Ferdinand of Aragon. This was only a personal union between the two rulers, but the two kingdoms did join in war against the Moors. In 1492 Granada, the last Moorish stronghold on the peninsula, was captured. In a short time all of Spain was conquered and united. Portugal remained independent for another century. Then Spain annexed and held it for sixty years.

Ferdinand and Isabella made Spain an absolute monarchy. They took powers away from church courts, weakened the nobles, and took away the rights of local governing bodies. They were ardent Catholics. They and their successors were the strongest royal supporters of the Inquisition. In 1492 they ruled that all Jews must either become Christians or leave Spain. Ten years later the same decree was passed against the Moors. In the long run this policy weakened Spain because Moors and Jews made up the industrial and commercial middle class. However, Spain became the greatest power in the Western World during the sixteenth century.

Developments in other countries

● *Germany and Italy fail to unite*

During the fourteenth and fifteenth centuries, England, France, and Spain developed into strong kingdoms. Germany and Italy, on the other hand, remained clusters of small local governments. As explained on page 180, Frederick II claimed to rule both Germany and Italy as Holy Roman Emperor. He failed to give either country a strong, centralized government. After his death Germany had no king for a time. Then the Hapsburg family took over the throne. The Hapsburgs did not try to rule Italy. In fact, they did not really rule Germany except in their own family lands. However, the Hapsburgs became important in the later history of Europe. By a series of well-planned marriages, they gained control of vast amounts of territory.

For centuries Germany remained a kingdom in name only, made up of more than three hundred separate and independent governments. As for Italy, there was no one country or government that fully deserved the name. It was, as a statesman said, "merely a geographic expression." Not until the nineteenth century did Germany and Italy become unified nations.

● *End of the Byzantine Empire*

After the Venetians and French knights captured Constantinople in the Fourth Crusade, it took the Byzantine emperors fifty years to regain their throne. The Byzantine Empire was fatally weakened. When a new group of invaders, the Ottoman Turks, came out of Asia at the start of the fourteenth century, the Byzantines could give little opposition. The Ottoman Turks occupied all Asia Minor and entered the Balkan peninsula, taking Bulgaria, Macedonia, Serbia, and southern Greece. In 1453 they captured Constantinople, the great bulwark of eastern Europe. The long and in many ways glorious record of the Byzantine Empire was ended.

The Turks continued their conquests. By 1529 they had conquered Egypt, North Africa, and Hungary, and were threatening Vienna in Austria when they were finally turned back.

● *The Mongols*

Another Asiatic people, the Mongols, became important in world history during the later Middle Ages. They were among the many tribes of stock-raising nomads of central Asia. In the twelfth century they were united by the great Genghis Khan, who led them on a famous career of conquests. They overran western Mongolia, Turkestan, and southern Russia. Under later rulers they conquered Persia, Mesopotamia, and moved far into central Europe.

When Mongol rulers decided to turn to the east, Europe was saved. Kublai Khan conquered China, becoming its ruler. His empire was one of the largest in world history. It was his court that Marco Polo visited. Another Mongol, the terrible Tamerlane, conquered India. At the beginning of the sixteenth century his grandson, Baber, established in India the great Mogul (Mongol) Empire that lasted 250 years.

Toward the end of the fifteenth century the princes of Moscow, in Russia, were able to throw off Mongol rule. Russia began to emerge as a European state, although it kept its oriental customs several centuries longer.

Review of Chapter 16

People, places, and things

Identify: Prince Henry the Navigator, Diaz, Vasco da Gama, Joan of Arc, Louis XI, Henry Tudor, Ferdinand, Isabella, Genghis Khan, Ottoman Turks, Mongols, Crécy, Poitiers, Agincourt, usury, bourgeois, guild, apprentice, journeyman, master.

Locate: Genoa, Sardinia, Pisa, Sicily, Corsica, Venice, Florence, Milan, Lombardy, Hamburg, Lübeck, Bremen, Flanders, Ghent, Bruges, Portugal, Aragon, Castile-Leon.

Events in review

1. Why did trade first revive in Italy during the eleventh century?
2. What was the reason for the fairs that began to be held in the eleventh century? List at least five articles traded at these fairs. Why were these fairs important in history?
3. What effect did Vasco da Gama's discoveries have on Venice?
4. What four important liberties did European townsmen acquire?
5. What were (a) the causes and (b) the important results of the Hundred Years' War between France and England?
6. What effect did the reign of Louis XI have on France?
7. Name some of the outstanding events during the period of Ferdinand and Isabella.
8. How much territory did the Ottoman Turks control by 1529?

Problems and projects

1. Discuss how the growth of towns led to the development of liberties.
2. Discuss the effect of medieval trade on (a) explorations, (b) the growth of towns.
3. How do you account for the rise of a middle class in the latter middle ages? How did this new class affect the feudal system?
4. Discuss the importance of the Hanseatic League. Is its organization similar to that of any present-day association?
5. Compare and contrast a medieval fair with a modern county fair.
6. Contrast the medieval guild system with modern trade unions. Find out some of the rules covering apprenticeship in modern trades.
7. Prepare an oral report (or write an essay) on Joan of Arc. Can you explain why many books, plays, and movies have been based on the story of Joan?
8. On a map of Europe, show the geographical reasons for the importance of Flanders as a center of trade.

Chapter *17*

The Later Middle Ages: Institutions and Culture

AFTER the twelfth century, great changes began to occur in western Europe. By the later part of the Middle Ages, changes could be seen in all the feudal institutions.

The decline of feudalism and serfdom

Many developments weakened the political power of the feudal lords. They were no longer so necessary in warfare. Infantry was replacing the feudal cavalry, and the cannon was reducing the importance of the feudal castle. Feudal lords were no longer absolute in their local governments because lords and all their people were becoming subject to the king's law and government. The new middle class was made up of free men, not subject to lords. Many of them were educated as well as wealthy. Kings often used them instead of nobles in their governments.

Commercial and industrial changes after the twelfth century led to a gradual disappearance of serfdom and the breakup of the manorial system. The growing towns and cities offered the peasant a chance to get away from his hard life. Even if he did not escape to a city and become a free man, the city changed his way of living. The city needed food; he could sell his produce for money. He could pay the lord money instead of week-work for his land. Many regions of Europe, especially those developed and settled after the twelfth century, had no serfs at all. Lords rented land for money, and hired laborers to work their domain lands. The tenants were not bound to the land; they could move away if they wanted to.

The Black Death helped to end serfdom. Rural populations were cut down. Farm labor became scarce and could command high wages. Less food was produced; so prices went up. Even though some governments passed laws to try to keep things as they were, serfdom was doomed.

The decline of both the political power of the lords and of serfdom came at different rates of speed in the different parts of Europe. Serfdom disappeared completely in England during the sixteenth century. In France most serfs had personal freedom by the fifteenth century. They still had to pay many dues and give services until the time of the French Revolution in 1789. In eastern Europe nobles remained powerful, and freedom came more slowly. Prussia had serfdom until 1807; Russia, until 1861.

Nobles as a class did not disappear with the end of feudalism. The noble class still exists in some countries. For centuries after the Middle Ages nobles had special privileges, such as exemption from taxes, and remained rich and influential.

The Church in the later Middle Ages

As Chapter 15 made clear, the Church was at times the strongest institution in the medieval world. Innocent III, most powerful of all the popes, was supreme ruler of the Church and judge of political questions throughout Europe. After his time, however, the power of the Church began to decline. Europe was changing. Kings were developing strong national governments with rich revenues from the commerce and industry of the growing cities. Their ministers were men trained for professional service, often students of Roman law. The middle class was growing in importance. It felt that its trade and industry were hampered by the restrictions of church laws. A new learning was appearing —the wisdom of the Moslems and the pagan Greeks. Much of it did not agree with the teachings of the Church, and a spirit of skepticism (questioning) began to develop.

The Church was criticized for a number of reasons. Its tremendous wealth did not seem to agree with the teaching of Jesus that worldly goods are not important. The Church's methods of raising money were criticized. Church fees and fines were high. The sale of Church offices and of indulgences was generally condemned. (An indulgence released an individual from doing penance for sin, under certain conditions.) The immoral lives of some of the clergy were a scandal everywhere. Some claims of the popes also met opposition. They claimed the exclusive right to make all appointments to Church offices. They demanded that the clergy be exempt from all national laws and all secular taxes. They also claimed the right to interfere in national political problems.

● Boniface VIII versus Philip the Fair

The first clash between popes and rulers of the new national states came over the question of the exemption of clergy and Church lands from taxation. Both Edward I of England and Philip IV (the Fair) of France demanded that the clergy pay taxes to the national treasuries. Against this practice Pope Boniface VIII issued a bull, Clericis laicos. (A bull is a formal announcement on official order of a pope. It is always in Latin, and is given a title from its first two or three words. Bull comes from the Latin bulla, a seal, which is attached to the papal order.) In Clericis laicos (1296) Boniface ordered the clergy not to pay taxes without consent of the pope. Philip the Fair struck back by forbidding the export of gold and silver from France; this cut off payments to the pope. Boniface had to modify his pronouncement slightly.

Boniface resumed his struggle with the French king later. In the bull Unam sanctam (1302) he stated that the pope was supreme on earth in both spiritual and temporal matters. He was judge of all others, but he himself was responsible to God only. To block the pope, Philip the Fair summoned the Estates-General in France. Because he needed wide support, he called representatives of the middle class for the first time. At this assembly Philip protested against Boniface's demands, accused Boniface of tyranny and heresy, and demanded that a general council of the Church bring him to trial.

Boniface replied by threatening to excommunicate Philip. The French king then had his envoy in Rome seize the pope and hold him prisoner. Although he was quickly released, Boniface died soon after. With his death the political power of the medieval papacy came to an end.

● The Babylonian Captivity, 1309–1377

Philip IV was able to have one of his French councilors elected pope to succeed Boniface's short-lived successors. The new pope left Italy and moved the seat of the papacy from Rome to Avignon, in southern France. The next six popes were also Frenchmen, and Avignon was the papal capital for seventy years.

This period of papal history is called the Babylonian Captivity, from the time in Biblical history when the Hebrews were prisoners in Babylonia. It was an unfortunate time for the papacy. For a thousand years Rome had been the center of the Church. Papal residence in France aroused suspicion among other peoples. Moreover, these popes seemed more interested in maintaining a luxurious court and raising great sums of money to support it than in the spiritual welfare of Christians. The Avignon popes lost the revenues from the Italian Papal States. To make up the deficit, church taxes became much heavier. Rome, always a hard city to govern, suffered because of the absence of the pope. It became a city of lawlessness and evil living.

● The Great Schism, 1378–1418

Now the papacy really fell on evil days. A pope was persuaded to leave Avignon and return to Rome, where he died. Eleven of the sixteen cardinals were French, but the threats of a Roman mob forced them to elect an Italian pope. The French cardinals then left Rome, declared the election void, and elected a Frenchman, who moved back to Avignon. The Italian pope excommunicated the French pope and cardinals, replacing the cardinals with Italians. The French pope excommunicated the Italian pope and cardinals.

This is the period known as the Great Schism (pronounced sĭzm, meaning a division into hostile groups). For political reasons each pope was supported by some rulers. Generally, the people and clergy of a country followed the choice of the ruler of their country.

St. Peter's in Rome. Until the Babylonian Captivity began in 1309, Rome was the "capitol city" of the Church. Rome again became the center of the Church after the Great Schism was ended in 1418.

In 1414 a church council met at Constance, where now Germany, Austria, and Switzerland come together, and remained in session for four years. It had three great tasks: to heal the schism, to deal with heresy, and to consider reforms of all the weaknesses of the Church. The schism was quickly dealt with. The council deposed the popes. It agreed that the cardinals should elect a new pope, but not until a program of reforms had been adopted.

The Council of Constance had more difficulty agreeing on a program of reforms. Everyone agreed that corruption in the Church and immorality of the clergy must be ended. But when a definite plan was proposed to deal with a problem, there was such great disagreement about the details that no conclusion could be reached.

After two years of long and bitter debate the Council compromised. It decided that a church council should be called every ten years to deal with problems, including needed reforms. The cardinals were then allowed to elect a new pope. The Council drew up a statement of eighteen matters on which reforms were to be made by the new pope with the help of councils. Then the Council of Constance wearily adjourned, and the Great Schism was ended.

●Criticism of the Church increases

You have read about religious groups who were critical of the Church. The Babylonian Captivity and the Great Schism weakened the authority and prestige of the pope and increased the criticism. Many middle-class writers ridiculed the clergy for greed, pride, laziness, and immoral living. However, criticism also came from inside the Church itself. Two members of the Franciscan order wrote a most interesting and influential book called *Defender of the Peace*. It criticized both kings and popes.

In the part of the book that dealt with temporal governments, the authors stated the democratic idea that powers of government really belong to the people, who only delegate them to the rulers. *Defender of the Peace* also expressed original ideas about the Church. The Church, it said, was made up of the entire body of believers. The only duty of the clergy was to save souls by preaching and administering the sacraments. The clergy could decide purely religious questions, but they could not fix worldly penalties for sins because God alone could punish. The clergy should not own property. According to the two Franciscan writers, the pope was only the elected head of the Church; he had no other power. All power belonged to the Christian members of the Church. They could delegate it only to a general Church council. A council had authority to make sweeping reforms in the entire Church, including the papacy.

In England these beliefs were adopted and spread by John Wycliffe, a member of the clergy and teacher at Oxford University. He attacked the wealth of the Church and the lives of the clergy. Wycliffe wrote that the pope's claim to absolute authority in the Church was unjustified. He also said that Jesus could save one's soul without the aid of a priest. The authority for salvation was in the Bible, not in the clergy. Wycliffe translated the Bible from Latin into English so that people could read it and learn what to believe and do.

Wycliffe's books were widely read both in England and on the continent. John Huss of Bohemia, a teacher at the University of Prague, was influenced by Wycliffe's writings. Huss became popular with the Czech people of Bohemia by denouncing abuses in the Church, but he angered the Czech clergy and was excommunicated. He was ordered to appear before the Council of Constance to answer charges of heresy. Huss did not have the support of his government as Wycliffe did. The emperor ordered him to appear, but guaranteed his safe return. Huss was tried by the council, condemned as a heretic, and burned at the stake in spite of the emperor's guarantee.

By the end of the fifteenth century, then, the Church was subject to widespread criticism throughout Europe. The pope elected at the Council of Constance had not tried hard to make the suggested reforms. Popes that followed him seemed interested more in Italian politics and their position as rulers of the Papal States than in the spiritual welfare of the Church. Failure to make the needed reforms helped bring on the Protestant Reformation in the next century.

Literature in the later Middle Ages

Long after it had ceased to be the vernacular (popularly spoken) language, Latin remained the written language of Europe. During the later Middle Ages, however, writing in the everyday languages began to appear. The first vernacular writings were the songs of the troubadours, lyrical poems of love and legends of romance. They were written and set to music to be sung by wandering knights and minstrels who went from court to court.

Another form of vernacular writing was the national epic, the long story in poetry of some great national hero. In England there was the story of *King Arthur and His Knights of the Round Table,* which became popular all over Europe. France had its *Song of Roland,* of the brave knight who lost his life at Roncesvalles while guarding the retreat of Charlemagne's army through the Pyrenees after a campaign against the Moslems in Spain. Germans sang the *Niebelungenlied,* the old legend of how the hero Siegfried gained the magic treasure guarded by a dragon. It forms the basis of the modern operas *Siegfried, Die Walküre,* and others by Richard Wagner.

The rise of the middle class brought a new kind of literature which the French called *fabliaux* (fables). They were stories in rhymed verse, told entirely for fun. They did not tell about beautiful maidens and brave knights; in fact, they made fun of chivalry. These stories ridiculed the foolishness of all human beings, but they were especially critical of the greediness, pride, laziness, and immoral lives of the clergy. The French series of stories about *Reynard the Fox* was especially popular.

In England John Wycliffe's translation of the Bible helped to shape the modern English language. Geoffrey Chaucer did even more to establish English in its modern form. His poem *The Canterbury Tales* pretended to be a series of stories told by a group of pilgrims on their way to Canterbury. Chaucer poked good-natured fun at the upper and middle classes, and like many other writers he satirized the clergy.

Education

The Crusades brought westerners into contact with the higher civilizations and cultures of the Byzantines and Moslems. Many translations were made of Greek and Arabic works in philosophy, mathematics, and science. Almost all the works of the outstanding Greek and Arabic writers were translated into Latin.

The study of Roman law from the Code of Justinian became very popular. Church, or canon, law was also widely studied.

By the end of the twelfth century schools in western Europe were teaching grammar as an elementary training for reading and speaking correct Latin. Higher schools taught logic (how to reason), mathematics, and science as preparations for the real professional studies: theology, law, and medicine. Learning was no longer confined to the clergy. Members of the middle class, wealthy merchants, and craftsmen were often educated. Books written in the vernacular language were beginning to appear, and laymen were beginning to write.

Establishment of universities

The universities which developed during and after the twelfth century had simple beginnings. Any man who thought he had something to teach could set himself up in a city where he might attract students. Anyone who wanted to study with him could do so by paying a fee.

As the number of both teachers (masters) and students increased, they united to form guilds to gain protection and privileges. Sometimes the guild included both masters and students; sometimes each had a separate guild. These guilds were known by the Latin word *universitas,* which meant any association of people. Gradually the word *university* came to mean an association of people for the purpose of teaching and learning.

Four great universities grew up in the twelfth century. The University of Paris specialized in teaching the liberal arts and theology. Bologna, in Italy, taught civil and canon law. Salerno, also in Italy, specialized in medicine, while Oxford, in England, resembled Paris.

Courses and degrees

The medieval university resembled a craft guild, since almost every student wanted to become a master—that is, a teacher. In time, standard courses of study were set up, with

An old picture showing Chaucer's pilgrims dining at an inn while on their way to Canterbury.

uniform requirements for the various stages of progress. These stages were shown by academic degrees. The degree of Bachelor of Arts or Science showed that the student had finished his apprenticeship and was ready to begin work to become a master, qualified to teach. The apprentice course was in the liberal arts: grammar, elementary logic, rhetoric, arithmetic, music, geometry, and astronomy.

After further study and examination the student qualified for the degree of Master of Arts; he was ready to teach the liberal arts. He was then admitted to the guild of teachers at a ceremony called commencement, which meant the beginning of his work as a teacher. In Paris the Master of Arts had to be at least twenty years of age and must have completed six years of academic work.

This was not the end. Before the Master of Arts lay the three great fields of professional study of the Middle Ages: theology, the study of religion and religious beliefs; law, either civil or canon; medicine. At Paris the degree of Master of Theology was gained only after ten more years of study. The terms master, doctor, and professor all meant the same: a man who was qualified to teach.

Theology was the greatest subject of study. The works of authority were the Bible and the writings of Aristotle, especially his work on logic. The reasonableness of the teachings of religion, as found in the Bible and the doctrines of the Church, was demonstrated by using theological methods of Aristotle.

Abelard

The first great intellect of the later Middle Ages was Peter Abelard, who taught at the University of Paris during the first half of the twelfth century. Abelard differed from other teachers of his time by encouraging his students to ask questions about church doctrine. His motto was: "For by doubting we come to inquiry, and by inquiring we perceive the truth."

A medieval scholar at work in his study. To own books and to be able to read and write were rare things in those times.

Abelard's greatest work was called *Sic et Non,* which can be translated, *Yes and No.* In it he raised a great number of questions about faith, reason, human nature, sin, and the sacraments. After each question he placed the opinions which he gathered from the Old and New Testaments, the writings of great churchmen, the decrees of church councils, and papal bulls. Many of these opinions and answers contradicted each other. Abelard allowed his students to work out the problems and conflicts for themselves. What he wanted to do was to stimulate his students to think and to inquire.

● St. Thomas Aquinas

The newly translated Greek writings, with the Arab explanations, did not always agree with the teachings of Christianity and the

dogmas of the Church. The task of reconciling, or making them agree, was performed by St. Thomas Aquinas, a Dominican, probably the greatest mind of all the medieval philosophers. His principal work was called *Summa Theologica.* In it he took up each point of church doctrine, examined it, and showed that it could be arrived at by logic. *Summa Theologica* was officially recognized by the papacy. Even today the *Summa* is the basis for all teaching of theology in Roman Catholic schools.

Science and invention

There was not much scientific progress during the later Middle Ages, but there were some men who were greatly interested. Perhaps the greatest was Roger Bacon, an English Franciscan monk. He disagreed with the method of thinking of his day. It consisted of taking an idea from an authority, such as the Bible, accepting it as a truth, and then using it as a basis for reasoning. It is called *deductive* reasoning. The way to find truth, said Roger Bacon, is to test all things by experimenting; to accept nothing as true which has not been so tested. This is the basis of our present-day scientific method. It is called *inductive* reasoning—that is, reasoning on the basis of facts.

Three great inventions helped to change life in the Middle Ages. The first was the magnetic compass, brought to western Europe by the Arabs during the twelfth century. It made the voyages of discovery and exploration possible. The second was the gun, developed by Europeans during the fourteenth century. The gun put to use in warfare the gunpowder which Europeans had learned about from the Arabs. The third invention, and possibly the most important of all, was the printing press.

The Arabs had brought from China a method of making paper and a way of printing from carved wooden blocks. The European invention was the casting of metal type, not for a whole page like the Arabs wooden blocks, but for single letters. These could be set in a frame to print a page and then used over and over again. Credit for this invention is usually given to Johann Gutenberg of Mainz, Germany. It was perfected about 1450 and spread rapidly. By 1500 there were printing presses in many places in Europe.

Art and architecture

Throughout the early Middle Ages architecture and the arts related to it were used almost entirely in the service of the Church. Since everyone belonged to one faith, the building and beautifying of the place of worship, the church, was a common interest, a community project. People could express both religious feelings and local pride.

Church builders used the round arches, domes, and low horizontal lines of Roman buildings. The style was called Romanesque. Walls had to be very thick to carry the enormous weight of the domed stone roof. Windows were small so as not to weaken the walls. The interior of a Romanesque church was always dark and gloomy. Decorations were few and simple.

● *The Gothic Style*

During the twelfth century architects in northern and western Europe developed a new style of building. They built a row of columns at the sides of the building proper. The columns were connected to the walls by arches. Thus part of the outward push of the roof was carried over to these columns. They were called *flying buttresses.* Since the walls did not need to carry so much of the outward push of a slanting roof, they could be high and thin, with very large windows. All the arches were pointed, instead of round like Roman arches. High pointed spires took the place of lower flat towers. Someone has said that everything pointed up toward heaven.

The Italians did not like this new style of architecture. They were accustomed to the low lines and rounded arches of the Romanesque style, in which they felt a local pride. Because the new style was developed in the north, they made fun of it as barbarian. They called it *Gothic,* from the barbarian Goths of the northlands. The name stuck, but since then Gothic has been considered one of the finest types of architecture ever developed.

Characteristics of the medieval world

The accepted date for the end of the Middle Ages is the end of the fifteenth century. Often the date of the discovery of America, 1492, is taken as a convenient one. All such divisions of history, however, are made by men after the events have taken place. A date

The Cathedral of Notre Dame in Paris. This view shows the flying buttresses bracing the walls.

such as 1492 or 1500 represents a useful stopping or starting point for historians. The change from medieval to early modern times took place gradually over hundreds of years.

Nevertheless, it is helpful to review Part Four by looking back over the whole medieval period. What were the main features of this civilization?

First, it seems, is what we might call "otherworldliness." The medieval era has been called an age of faith, in which the salvation of the soul was more important than any worldly affairs. Education, literature, and art all existed for the glory of God and the salvation of the soul rather than for personal satisfaction or the glory of the state. The Church was the first institution in the life of each man; the clergy were the First Estate of society.

Second, feudalism was for centuries the typical form of government. Central government disappeared, to be replaced by thousands of small, local governments in which the local lord was all-powerful. Private wars replaced public wars. Not until the late Middle Ages did strong national states begin to grow.

Third, life was rural and agricultural. Throughout most of the Middle Ages the rural manor with its serf and peasant labor, its inherited and carefully followed customs, traditions, and methods, was the prevailing pattern of life.

● Reasons for change in medieval culture

Now let us try to sum up the reasons for the decline of medieval civilization and culture. Taking them in the same order as above, we would say:

The Church was weakened by many things: the growth of national monarchies; the loss of political power of the popes; failure to reform bad conditions; the questioning attitude of the new learning. During the later Middle Ages people took at least as much

An example of medieval art, a statue of the Virgin of the Visitation in the Cathedral at Reims in France. Religious themes were outstanding in the art of the Middle Ages.

interest in the affairs of this world as in those of the next world. They were no longer willing to accept without question the authority of the Church.

In government, feudalism was replaced in some regions by national states under national monarchs. The feeling of belonging to a nation began to replace the feeling of belonging to a locality.

In economic and social life the growth of trade and manufacturing led to the development of cities. It was the revival of commerce, industry, and cities in the later Middle Ages that helped to break down the feudal and manorial systems, develop national monarchies, and create the middle class. This middle class was destined to become *the* important class of society in modern times.

The legacy of the Middle Ages

What, then, are the things which the Middle Ages have left as bequests to modern times? First, the Christian religion as organized into a great Church. In the early Middle Ages the Christian Church divided into Greek and Roman branches. At the end of the Middle Ages the Protestant groups broke away from the Roman Church. Yet the Roman Catholic Church remains the way to salvation for many millions of people in the world today. Its organization is that which developed during the Middle Ages. Its doctrines, dogmas, rituals, and ceremonies are much the same as those followed in medieval times.

In art there is the great Gothic architecture, still used in churches and public buildings throughout the western world.

In government there grew up the nation-state. The national states of the later Middle Ages were absolute monarchies which do not exist today. We also find developing, in the English Parliament, the institution that was to overthrow absolute monarchies and introduce governments in which the people govern themselves through their representatives.

In education and intellectual history there were the medieval universities, forerunners of our modern institutions. The spirit of inquiry which arose in the medieval universities helped bring the Renaissance, the Reformation, and the beginnings of modern times.

In economics we have the beginnings of capitalism, the prevailing form of business enterprise in the modern world.

Not every legacy of the Middle Ages has been admirable. Although feudalism and serfdom disappeared in most of Europe, the idea of nobles as a privileged social class and peasants as a non-privileged class continued in force for centuries. The nationalism and patriotism which developed could be harmful as well as good. It is a fine thing, you know, to love your country. But when this patriotism is carried to selfish extremes, it can cause great harm. If a citizen feels that whatever his nation does is right and whatever it wants it should have, regardless of the consequences to any other country and people, the results to the human race can be disastrous.

One part of the heritage of the Middle Ages can be seen in the many churches and cathedrals built in the Gothic style. Pointed Gothic arches are a feature of St. Patrick's Cathedral in New York City.

One bad heritage of the Middle Ages is the warfare which is such a sad feature of modern times. The strong central governments of the nation-states did stop the petty, private wars of rival feudal lords. Private war, however, was replaced by public war, on a larger scale, between nations instead of localities. War became a means by which nations could get what they wanted from other nations and peoples. Although order and law have been attained within many nations, no such law and order as yet prevail among nations. How to end this threat of chaos in the world is the greatest problem of the modern world.

Review of Chapter 17

People, places, and things

Identify: St. Thomas Aquinas, Abelard, Roger Bacon, John Huss, John Wycliffe, Geoffrey Chaucer, Avignon, Council of Constance, *Defender of the Peace.*

Events in review

1. List the factors that brought about the decline of feudalism.
2. Did serfdom disappear quickly or gradually? Explain.
3. Describe briefly the quarrel between Church and state. Include the Babylonian Captivity, the Great Schism, and the Council of Constance.
4. Name two medieval epic poems. How were the *fabliaux* different from the epics?
5. In what respects did the medieval university resemble a craft guild?
6. What Greek philosopher was relied on as an authority in medieval universities?
7. What method of teaching did Abelard favor?
8. What kind of reasoning did Roger Bacon believe in? How was this different from the medieval method of reasoning?
9. Explain the origin of the term "Gothic" as applied to architecture. How were flying buttresses used in Gothic churches?
10. List three characteristics of medieval culture.

Problems and projects

1. Discuss the rise and importance of the middle class in medieval Europe. Include the effects of the middle class on (a) literature, (b) education, (c) economic life.
2. Compare education in a medieval university with education during the Hellenistic period.
3. For discussion or debate: Which of the following inventions had the greatest share in changing medieval life—the magnetic compass, the gun, the printing press?
4. Write an editorial, "The Decline of Feudalism."
5. Write a brief explanation of the differences between Romanesque and Gothic architecture. List examples of each type that can be found in your community or your state. Bring in illustrations of each type.
6. Make sketches of (a) a Romanesque arch, (b) a Gothic arch, (c) a flying buttress.
7. On the basis of outside reading, write a description of daily life in a medieval university.
8. To debate: Medieval times were happy times.

Review of the Middle Ages

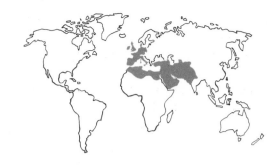

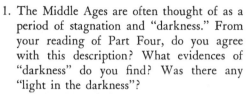

1. The Middle Ages are often thought of as a period of stagnation and "darkness." From your reading of Part Four, do you agree with this description? What evidences of "darkness" do you find? Was there any "light in the darkness"?
2. Which of the following events would you consider most far-reaching in its importance: the Battle of Tours, the founding of the Holy Roman Empire, the signing of the Magna Carta? Explain your answer.
3. What was the main purpose of the Crusades? How and why did they fail? In spite of their failure, the Crusades had great effects on world history. What were they?
4. Imagine yourself a newspaper columnist writing shortly after the battle of Poitiers (1356). Assume that you are well-informed and farseeing. What conclusions might you reach on the basis of (a) the results of the battles of Crécy and Poitiers and (b) the use of guns to attack castles? What predictions might you make for the future?
5. By the late Middle Ages, England had become an absolute monarchy under a strong Tudor king. Nevertheless, certain great steps toward democracy had been taken. Describe these steps.
6. Make a list of the contributions the Church in the Middle Ages made toward preserving and enriching civilization.
7. How did the rise of towns and the expansion of trade contribute to the decline of feudalism and the start of a new era? List as many reasons as you can.
8. As the middle class increased in power, the feudal nobles tended to lose some power. Did the kings usually approve? Explain.
9. In the later Middle Ages, what signs can you find of the beginnings of change to a new order? Consider (a) religion, (b) government, (c) economic and social life.
10. Make a table or chart with the following headings: (a) art and architecture, (b) government, (c) education, (d) language, (e) literature, (f) religion. Under each heading list items in our heritage from the Middle Ages.

Books about the Middle Ages

*Augur, Helen. *Book of Fairs* (Harcourt, Brace, 1939). A vivid description of the colorful life of medieval fairs.
*Bainton, Roland. *Church of Our Fathers* (Scribner, 1941). Simple, interesting, and dramatic—the history of Christianity.
Baldwin, Marshall W. *The Medieval Church*

*Books marked with a star (*) are easy reading.

(Cornell University Press, 1953.). A readable description of the Church in the high middle ages. Highly recommended.
*Bragdon, L. J. *Land of Joan of Arc* (Lippincott, 1952). France from earliest times.
Burrows, Millar. *Founders of Great Religions* (Scribner, 1931). A life of Mohammed, among others.
Case, Shirley J. *Makers of Christianity* (Holt,

1934). The story of the Christian religion from Jesus to Charlemagne told in the lives of important Christian leaders.

Coolidge, Olivia E. *Legends of the North* (Houghton, 1951). A spirited retelling of the myths and legends of the north countries.

Costain, Thomas Bertram. *Magnificent Century* (Doubleday, 1951). A superb narrative history of England in the turbulent days of Henry III, when England took remarkable strides in the direction of freedom and democratic principles.

*Creighton, Louise. *Heroes of French History* (Longmans, 1925). Charlemagne and Joan of Arc, among others.

Daugherty, James Henry. *Magna Charta* (Random House, 1956). The importance of the Great Charter in man's struggle for liberty and justice.

*Davis, William S. *Life on a Mediaeval Barony* (Harper, 1923). An excellent book which gives a vivid picture of almost anything you might want to know about thirteenth-century manorial life.

*————. *Short History of the Near East* (Macmillan, 1922). The Byzantine and Moslem Empire, interestingly described.

*Fitch, Florence M. *Allah, the God of Islam* (Lothrop, 1950). A beautifully illustrated objective treatment of the Moslem way of life.

*Haaren, John H., and Poland, Addison B. *Famous Men of the Middle Ages* (American Book, 1904). Brief biographies of Justinian, Attila, Clovis, Charlemagne, Gregory the Great, and many others.

Hartley, Dorothy. *Medieval Costume and Life* (Scribner, 1931). Detailed descriptions and illustrations of costumes worn by all ages and classes of society.

*Hartman, Gertrude. *Medieval Days and Ways* (Macmillan, 1937). An excellent account of the details of medieval daily life. Highly recommended.

Kelly, Regina (Zimmerman). *Young Geoffrey Chaucer* (Lothrop, 1952). An illustrated tale of Chaucer's boyhood adventures, his student days at Oxford, and his romantic training as a page at court.

*Lamb, Harold. *The Crusades: Iron Men and Saints* (Doubleday, 1946). The story of the First Crusade, excellently told.

————. *Genghis Khan and the Mongol Horde* (Random House, 1954). The story of the plundering Mongols who conquered what we now call China, Iran, Russia and Mongolia.

*Lamprey, Louise. *All the Ways of Building* (Macmillan, 1933). Romanesque and Gothic, well explained and illustrated.

*Mills, Dorothy. *Middle Ages* (Putnam, 1935). The emphasis is on the way people lived and on those things in medieval life which had the greatest effect on later periods. Highly recommended.

Power, Eileen. *Medieval People* (Methuen, 1951). Tells about the average men and women of the Middle Ages representing, among other types, a peasant, a Paris housewife, and a merchant.

————, and Power, Rhoda. *Cities and Their Stories* (Houghton Mifflin, 1927). Interesting accounts of European cities.

Previté-Orton, Charles William. *Shorter Cambridge Medieval History* (Cambridge, 1952). A history of the ten centuries between the fall of the Roman Empire and the Renaissance.

*Quennell, C. H. B. and Quennell, Marjorie. *History of Everyday Things in England* (British Bk. Centre, 1953). Deals with the period from the Norman Conquest to 1499. An excellent series, clearly written, well illustrated, with fascinating material.

Quennell, Marjorie (Courtney). *Everyday Life in Anglo-Saxon, Viking and Norman Times* (Putnam, 1955). A picture of England at the time of the great invasions.

Rayner, Edwin. *Famous Cathedrals and Their Stories* (Grossett, 1935). Short descriptions and stories, with many fine illustrations.

Sellman, Roger Raymond. *The Crusades* (Roy Publishers, 1955). A view of the Crusades, their causes, results, and effects upon Western civilization.

Strayer, Joseph Reese. *Western Europe in the Middle Ages: A Short History* (Appleton-Century-Crofts, 1955). How medieval society began, and how it finally lost its medieval character.

*Tappan, Eva M. *When Knights Were Bold* (Houghton Mifflin, 1911). This book makes the feudal age exciting. Well illustrated and well written. It can be used for reference material.

*Thorndike, Lynn. *History of Medieval Europe* (Houghton Mifflin, 1949). A valuable reference book.

West, Anthony. *The Crusades* (Random House, World Landmark Bks., 1954). An account of the amazing military expeditions which in the twelfth and thirteenth centuries tried to take the Holy Land from the Moslems and hold it in Western control.

Whitelock, Dorothy. *The Beginnings of English Society* (Penguin, 1952). English life before 1066. Interesting and easily understood. The emphasis is on social and cultural history.

Winston, Richard. *Charlemagne: From the Hammer to the Cross* (Bobbs-Merrill, 1954). Easily read and enjoyable. Western Europe in the eighth and ninth centuries.

Stories about the Middle Ages

*Andrews, Frank E. *For Charlemagne!* (Harper, 1949). The story of a boy who came to Charlemagne's palace to study at the school of the great Alcuin.

*Bolton, Ivy M. *Son of the Land* (Messner, 1946). The exciting tale of a runaway serf at the time of the Peasants' Revolt in England.

Chute, Marchette. *Innocent Wayfaring* (Scribner, 1943). A fourteenth-century English girl runs away from a convent and has many adventures on the road to London.

*Daniel, Hawthorne. *Shuttle and Sword* (Macmillan, 1932). The son of a Bruges weaver takes part in the Flemish revolt against France.

Davis, William S. *The Beauty of the Purple* (Macmillan, 1924). The defense of Constantinople against the Saracens. Historically accurate and very exciting.

——. *God Wills It!* (Macmillan, 1935). A story of the First Crusade and some of its interesting personalities.

Donauer, Friedrich. *The Long Defense* (Longmans, 1931). The last stand of the Byzantine Empire and the fall of Constantinople. A thrilling story of the siege of the city.

Doyle, Sir Arthur C. *The White Company* (Dodd, Mead, 1927. Many other editions). A company of English bowmen fight for hire in France and Spain.

Edmondston, C. M. and Hyde, M. L. F. *King's Man* (Longmans, 1948). England, France, and the Holy Land in the days of the Norman kings of England.

*Gilbert, Jane. *Imps and Angels* (Dutton, 1946). A suspense story revolving around the building of a medieval cathedral.

Gray, Elizabeth J. *Adam of the Road* (Viking, 1943). The life of a minstrel who loves the road.

*Hewes, Agnes D. *Boy of the Last Crusade* (Houghton Mifflin, 1933). A boy on the Children's Crusade finds his lost crusader father in the Holy Land.

*Hyde, Mark P. *The Singing Sword: the Story of Sir Ogier the Dane* (Little, Brown, 1930). A Danish squire in the service of Charlemagne helps free Denmark from the Saxons.

Jewett, Eleanore. *The Hidden Treasure of Glaston* (Viking, 1946). Two boys find lost pages of an ancient book about the Holy Grail. Fine, authentic background.

Lancaster, Osbert. *The Saracen's Head, or the Reluctant Crusader* (Houghton Mifflin, 1949). A hero in spite of himself. A pale, timid boy becomes a hero of the Crusades. There are many chuckles here.

Lansing, Marion F. *Magic Gold* (Little, Brown, 1928). A story of alchemy in which Roger Bacon appears as a character.

Mayer, Albert I. *Defense of the Castle* (Harper, 1937). A feudal war in tenth-century Germany.

——. *The Falconer's Son* (Ambassador, 1941). A story of the Holy Roman Empire at the time of Otto the Great.

*Pyle, Howard. *Men of Iron* (Globe Bk., 1954). A fine story of chivalry in fifteenth-century England.

Reade, Charles. *The Cloister and the Hearth* (Dodd, 1944. Many other editions). A famous historical novel of the Renaissance about the parents of Erasmus.

Reinherz, Nathan. *Trumpets at the Crossroads* (Crowell, 1948). Two young apprentice boys help in the fight to free their city from a cruel overlord.

Rosenberg, Melrich. *With Sword and Song* (Houghton Mifflin, 1937). Richard the Lion-Hearted appears in this story of a fifteen-year-old boy in twelfth-century France.

Sabatini, Rafael. *Sword of Islam* (Houghton Mifflin, 1939). The Moslem world during the sixteenth century.

Scott, Sir Walter. *Ivanhoe* (Singer, 1956). Medieval England at the end of the twelfth century. Norman and Saxon cultures were merging.

——. *The Talisman* (Dodd, Mead, 1949). Richard I, Philip Augustus, and the Third Crusade.

——. *Quentin Durward* (Dent, 1957). Louis XI of France versus Charles the Bold of Burgundy.

Part Five

THE BEGINNINGS OF
THE MODERN WORLD

The picture opposite shows Columbus going ashore at the first island he found in the new world. The date of this discovery, 1492, is (as we have said) a convenient dividing point between the Middle Ages and modern times. Of course, the world does not change overnight. Nevertheless, Columbus' voyage is a true symbol of the events that were changing the world from medieval to modern.

In the late Middle Ages men began to explore their world. Some, like Columbus, voyaged over the oceans in ships, finding new lands. Others explored the universe with telescopes. Still others explored the past through the writings of the Greeks and Romans. Many men tried to explore great problems such as religion and government by thinking and writing.

This is not to say that there was no travel or reading or thought going on in the medieval world. But in the fourteenth and fifteenth centuries, men began to show more and more curiosity about their world. They made longer voyages. They asked more questions about the nature of things. They thought more freely about the world around them. They began to make discoveries in science. They began to make changes in their religion and in forms of government. Slowly, they changed the world from old ways into the direction of our modern world.

To trace the great changes that were taking place, we will have to start in the fourteenth century. Note that some dates in the time chart on pages 226–227 overlap dates in the chart for Part Four. We will trace these changes down to the eighteenth century. Even by 1750 the world had by no means become modern in our sense. Part Five is called The Beginnings of the Modern World. In many ways the years covered in this part were a preparation for the really great changes that came later on.

Notice that one column in the time chart is headed "Renaissance and Reformation." *Renaissance* is the name given to the period of revived interest in exploration and learning and inquiry. *Reformation* refers to great changes in the field of religion.

One column is given to the new national states that increased in power.

Another column shows America playing an increasingly great role in world history. Columbus' voyage meant the start of a Spanish empire in the new world. Further down this column you will find the beginnings of English colonization in North America and the founding of our nation.

Part Five — THE BEGINNINGS OF

1300

	RENAISSANCE AND REFORMATION	THE NATIONAL STATES
1295	Polos return to Venice	
1304-1374	Petrarch	
c. 1307	Dante writing *Divine Comedy*	
1380	Wycliffe's translation of the Bible	

1400

1414-1418	Council of Constance	
1450	Gutenberg: printing	1469 Marriage of Ferdinand and Isabella, Spain
1454?	Gutenberg Bible	1480 Grand Duchy of Moscow drives out Mongols, Russia
		1485 Henry VII, starts Tudor dynasty, England
1492	Death of Lorenzo deMedici; Columbus' voyage	1492 Moors driven out of Spain

1500

1509	Erasmus, *In Praise of Folly*	1516-1556 Charles V of Spain—Holy Roman Empire
1517	Luther, the Ninety Five Theses	1529 Suleiman and Turks besiege Vienna
1534	Henry VIII, England, Act of Supremacy	1556-1598 Philip II, King of Spain
1536	Calvin, *Institutes of the Christian Religion*	1558-1603 Elizabeth I, Queen of England
1543	Copernicus publishes his theory	1571 Battle of Lepanto
1545-1563	Council of Trent	1577 Union of Utrecht: Dutch independence
1564	Death of Michelangelo; birth of Shakespeare	1580 Spain takes Portugal
		1588 Defeat of Spanish Armada
1598	Edict of Nantes issued by Henry IV of France	1589-1610 Henry IV, King of France

1600

1605	Cervantes, *Don Quixote*	1603 James I, Stuart dynasty, England
		1610-43 Louis XIII and Richelieu, France
1618-1648	Thirty Years' War	1613 Romanov dynasty, Russia
		1643-1715 Louis XIV, "the Sun King"
1648	Peace of Westphalia	
		1682-1725 Peter the Great, Czar of Russia
1685	Revocation of Edict of Nantes	1688 Death of Great Elector, Brandenburg

1700

		1713 Treaty of Utrecht: Prussia a Kingdom
		1740 Maria Theresa, Austria, and Frederick II, the Great, Prussia, begin rules
		1762-1795 Catherine the Great, Russia
		1763 End of Seven Years' War
		1772, 1793, 1795 Partitions of Poland

1800

THE MODERN WORLD

AMERICA	ASIA

	1368-1644 Ming dynasty in China Ming emperors discourage contacts with Europeans
	1405 Death of Tamerlane, Mongol Conqueror
	1460 Death of Prince Henry the Navigator, of Portugal
·2 Columbus' first voyage to America	**1486** Diaz reaches Cape of Good Hope
·3 Papal Bull of Demarcation	**1498** Vasco da Gama reaches India
·9 Vespucci visits America	
9-22 Magellan's voyage	**1510** Portuguese take Goa
1 Cortez conquers Mexico	**1516** Portuguese reach China
2 Pizarro conquers Peru	
	1590 Akbar: Mogul Empire of India at height
7-1580 Drake sails around the world, visits west coast of America	**1581** Russians reach Sibir
	1600 British East India Company founded
7 English settle Virginia	
8 French settle Quebec	
0 Pilgrims to Plymouth	
0 Puritans to Massachusetts	**1640** Russians reach the Pacific
	1644 Manchus overthrow Mings: Manchu dynasty in China
	1660 Dutch take East Indies from Portuguese
	1664 First French posts in India
2 LaSalle claims Louisiana	**1689** Russo-Chinese treaty
2 Georgia, final English colony in America	**1728** Bering sails through Bering Straits
4 Bering explores Alaskan coast for Russia	
3 End of French and Indian War, England expels France from American continent	**1763** English drive French from India
5 American Declaration of Independence	
3 End of American Revolution	

Chapter *18* # The Renaissance

SOME HISTORIANS consider the fourteenth and fifteenth centuries—the end of the Middle Ages—almost a separate and distinct period of history. Changes that had begun earlier gained so much force, became so much more rapid, produced so many new ideas and things, that it seemed that the world of the Middle Ages had been born anew. Therefore, the name given to the fourteenth and fifteenth centuries is the *Renaissance,* which means revival or rebirth.

The changes of the Renaissance took place in many fields of life. There were new ideas about government; there was a great change in the way men thought about religion. Not all these changes began or ended at exactly the same time; in fact, many of them are still going on. However, they all had great importance in this period of two or three centuries.

The new way of thinking and the search for evidence to support it began in Italy. There civilization had not sunk so low as elsewhere in the western Christian world. Rome had remained the center of this world. Neither trade nor cities had died out as completely as elsewhere. Some of the Italian cities had furnished the ships to carry the crusaders and their supplies to the Holy Land. They built up a trade with the Near East which brought them much wealth. A number of Italian cities such as Rome, Venice, Genoa, and Milan were important to the Renaissance. One, however, was outstanding. Florence, more than any other, was *the* Renaissance city.

Humanism: the Renaissance in thought

One great characteristic of the Middle Ages was the idea of "other-worldliness." Salvation of the soul in the life to come was the most important business of life on earth. Religious doctrines and dogmas and Christian virtue were the most important subjects of learning. Man was a soul to be saved; his life while on the earth was a preparation for the life to come.

Men of the Renaissance began to break away from the medieval way of thinking. They remained deeply religious, but their religion was different. They criticized the authority of the Church and protested against the abuses in its organization and administration. Above all, they were in love with life, and delighted in enjoying its pleasures.

These men were called *humanists.* They looked upon life as something more than a preparation for the life to come. To the humanists life in this world could be a thing of joy, dignity, and worth. They thought it should be made so. Man with all his faults was an intelligent individual. He could remedy his faults and solve his problems without the help of supernatural powers. We owe these humanist writers a debt of gratitude for emphasizing this idea of man as an individual of dignity and worth. This idea was not new, but during the Renaissance it gained strength and became the real revolutionary idea of modern times. Here is one of the foundations of the democratic ideal.

The humanists were greatly interested in past times, especially the civilizations of the Greeks and the Romans. They believed that the cultures of both ancient peoples held much that was attractive and valuable. Men could learn much from them, even though they contained ideas and features different from those of the Christian Church. They eagerly searched for manuscripts by Roman and Greek writers.

The Italian humanists: Dante

Dante Alighieri, the great Florentine thinker and writer, lived during the late thirteenth and early fourteenth centuries. He was the pioneer of Renaissance thought. Dante was a man of many talents: He was extraordinarily learned. He served as a diplomat, and was a very keen political observer. Above all, he was one of the world's greatest poets.

Like other scholars of his time Dante wrote much in Latin, but he preferred the dialect of his native province, Tuscany. He could express himself beautifully in the native Tuscan tongue, and he used it in his most famous works. Thus the Tuscan dialect became the written language of all Italy. Today Dante is considered the father of the Italian language.

The Divine Comedy is Dante's greatest work. It tells of a pilgrimage made by Dante accompanied by the Roman poet Virgil. Together they pass through hell, purgatory, and heaven. They meet the souls of famous people, good, bad, and indifferent. A work of this sort gave Dante a fine chance to criticize the society of his own time, and he used it fully. Thus *The Divine Comedy* is like a mirror that reflects the times of its author. The twilight of the Middle Ages and the dawn of the Renaissance both find fullest expression. It is the greatest epic of Italian literature, and among the great books of the world.

Petrarch

Another Renaissance pioneer and Italian poet was Francesco Petrarch, who lived in the fourteenth century. Petrarch studied law without much enthusiasm, and finally took holy orders and became a member of the clergy. Petrarch was a man of many interests and abilities. He approached the ideal of the Renaissance: a man of many talents all well developed. Historians consider him the founder of humanism.

Petrarch was a master of lyric poetry, which he composed in beautiful Italian and expressed with the feelings of a genuine poet-genius. He was most enthusiastic about Greek and Latin. He had a keen interest in archeology and in collecting coins and medals. He traveled widely, corresponded extensively, and severely criticized medieval educational methods. These were all earmarks of a true humanist.

The humanists of the North: Erasmus

Humanist thought could not be confined to Italy. The new ideas soon traveled across the Alps to Germany, Holland, France, and England, carried by merchants who traded with Italian cities or by students who went to Italian universities to study and then returned home.

Among the distinguished men associated with the "Renaissance of the North" was Desiderius Erasmus (1466–1536). Born in Rotterdam, Holland, Erasmus studied both in Paris and in England. He was extremely honest, both in action and in thought. He fought falsehood all his life. In Paris Erasmus encountered the Italian humanist ideas, which he accepted gladly. He devoted himself entirely to the study and publication of classical literature.

In his youth Erasmus had been compelled, somewhat against his will, to enter a monastery and take the vows. He became dissatisfied with monastic life, but found that he could not be released from his vows. It was then that he wrote his most famous book, which he called *In Praise of Folly*. It is one of the wittiest satires of any age. Erasmus ridiculed the whole system of monasticism, and went even further. He made fun of popes, archbishops, bishops, monks, and the clergy in general. He wrote against indulgences, pilgrimages, shrines, fasting on Fridays and during Lent, and even the Church's interpretation of some parts of the Bible. He believed, however, that the Church could be reformed from within.

In Praise of Folly was much more than just a criticism of the clergy and church practices. Erasmus also showed his boundless faith in man. He believed that man is basically good. His evil doings happen because of his ignorance and blundering. Erasmus offered the old Greek idea of man and salvation: that human nature is good, as are man's intentions. To find salvation man must only lead a natural life, practicing moderation.

● *Thomas More*

A great English humanist, Thomas More, wrote a book, *Utopia,* which was as popular as *In Praise of Folly.* In *Utopia* Thomas More describes his idea of a future, imaginary, ideal society. By contrast, he was criticizing the society of his own day. According to More's *Utopia,* the good society was to be made up entirely of free citizens who would elect their governing officials. Laws would be enforced not by police but by conscientious citizens themselves. Each person would work at the labor for which he was best fitted, which he himself would choose. Workdays would be only six hours long in order to enable the citizen to do other things that interested him. Each child would receive a complete education at public expense. There would be complete freedom of religion.

● *François Rabelais*

Another great man of the northern Renaissance was the Frenchman François Rabelais. He had two great loves: classical learning and the people of France. He loved the common people of his country despite all their weak-

Gargantua at dinner. This illustration from the famous book by Rabelais shows clearly the origin of our word "gargantuan."

nesses and even while he poked fun at them. He loved his native French speech and used it masterfully in his writings.

Rabelais' famous book, *The Inestimable Life of the Great Gargantua, Father of Pantagruel,* was written in the language and style of the French people he loved so well. Like *In Praise of Folly* it is a satire. Gargantua is a giant king who enjoys life on a grand scale. (The word "gargantuan" has since become a universal word, meaning huge, vast, gigantic.) With great wit and cleverness Rabelais criticized those things for which he had contempt. He ridiculed fakery and quackery, outmoded ideas, and falsehood. However, he also had things to praise. He had the highest regard for honesty and a natural way of living. He believed that man could perfect himself through reason and natural, joyous living.

The new ideas of the Renaissance were most welcome in countries where there were

230

many cities. They made slow progress where serfdom and feudal ideals still prevailed. Peasants and serfs did not even know about the new thought. Feudal lords were not interested in ideas about the dignity and worth of the individual man. Western Europe, with its greater city population, was more influenced than rural eastern Europe. Hungary was little affected, while Russia was entirely untouched.

The importance of printing

Johann Gutenberg made the modern technique of printing possible by casting movable type from metal. The new method had a revolutionary effect on European civilization. By speeding up the reproduction of books it simplified the spreading of knowledge. It helped in the setting up of libraries. It popularized the ideas and information of the Renaissance. Gutenberg's invention came at a very timely moment in history.

The craft of printing with movable type spread rapidly from Germany to other parts of the Western World. In England William Caxton began to print books in a shop near Westminster Abbey. He published the writings of Chaucer and other classics. Printing became especially popular in Italy, birthplace of the Renaissance. In less than half a century after Gutenberg's invention, there were printing establishments in many Italian cities.

The most famous Italian printer was Aldus Manutius of Venice. Aldus resolved that he would publish all the Greek and Latin classics. He wanted to be able to sell them at a price the average person could afford to pay. To do this, he printed books of convenient size on inexpensive paper. They are known as the Aldine editions.

In making the individual letters of their type, Gutenberg and his German successors copied the lettering of medieval manuscripts. Often they even reproduced the abbreviations and signs the monks had used for frequently repeated words and endings. Lettering in the manuscripts seems to run vertically, up and down. For this reason it is called "gothic." Even though it was what people were accustomed to, it was not easy to read.

Aldus wanted a type that would be clearer, more beautiful, and easier to read. The story is that he copied the handwriting of Petrarch. The Aldine type is what we call "italics." See the great differences between the two styles of type as shown below.

The Renaissance in drama

The Renaissance in England produced Elizabethan drama, so-called because Elizabeth was queen. William Shakespeare, writer and actor, took old plots and built around them masterpieces of poetic drama that have never been equalled in any language.

The Renaissance in art

Very startling changes took place in the field of painting. The most noticeable feature of Renaissance painting is an interest in natural life and forms. From this it is known as *naturalism*. Renaissance painters became increasingly interested in the world about them. In their paintings the human figures became ever more lifelike, and the landscape in the background was the countryside that the artist knew.

Renaissance painters could make both their figures and their backgrounds so lifelike because they had learned a most important trick of painting. They could show a rounded figure on a flat surface, and could show a depth

---

𝕮𝖍𝖊𝖘𝖊 𝖑𝖎𝖓𝖊𝖘 𝖘𝖍𝖔𝖜 𝖙𝖍𝖊 𝖈𝖍𝖆𝖗𝖆𝖈𝖙𝖊𝖗𝖎𝖘𝖙𝖎𝖈𝖘 𝖔𝖋 𝖙𝖍𝖊 𝖌𝖔𝖙𝖍𝖎𝖈 𝖙𝖞𝖕𝖊 𝖚𝖘𝖊𝖉 𝖇𝖞 𝕲𝖚𝖙𝖊𝖓𝖇𝖊𝖗𝖌.

These lines show the characteristics of the italic type used by Aldus.

---

and distance on canvas. This art is called *perspective*. Renaissance painters stand among the supreme artists of all times in their use of perspective, their careful attention to color, light, and shade, their portrayal of figures with rounded, human bodies, and their true-to-life landscape backgrounds.

Among all Renaissance artists the versatile genius, Leonardo da Vinci, comes first. Leonardo had so many interests and talents that he cannot be referred to only as a painter. There is hardly a field of human knowledge in which this man of many geniuses did not show his creative skill. His mural painting "The Last Supper" is universally known and recognized as a masterpiece of all time. Another of Leonardo's unforgettable paintings is the widely reproduced portrait called "The Mona Lisa."

A copper engraving by Albrecht Dürer, a German artist of the Renaissance. A knight is shown in the armor of the period. Behind him are allegorical figures representing death (with hourglass) and the devil.

Beside Leonardo da Vinci stands another master of Renaissance painting, Michelangelo Buonarroti. Millions of people have been filled with wonder as they stood in the Sistine Chapel in Rome and looked at the murals of this mighty artist. Imagine a ceiling of some 6,000 square feet on which are painted 145 huge human figures. Think of this being done by a single man within four years!

Like humanism, the Renaissance of art was not confined to Italy for very long. The new ways of painting, like the new ideas, were too forceful and their appeal too universal to remain in one country. Countries engaged in trade with the Italian cities were the first to be influenced. Merchants carried back Italian paintings just as students carried back ideas. Painters from the northern countries hurried to study with the Italian masters to learn the new techniques.

Even a summary of Renaissance art and artists would take many pages. Some famous paintings of this period are reproduced in the full-color sections of this book. The captions for these pictures give brief notes on some outstanding painters.

The age of exploration

With its eagerness for knowledge of the world, the Renaissance aroused a great interest in land and sea explorations. These explorations resulted in the discovery of new worlds and the expansion of the frontiers of human knowledge. Among the earliest explorers were the Christian missionaries, usually monks.

● *Marco Polo*

Best known among the early travelers and explorers was a Venetian, Marco Polo. Marco Polo lived before the Renaissance, but what he learned on his journeys became of great interest when the new thirst for knowledge developed. With his father and uncle, Marco Polo made the long, hard journey overland to China. There they found a friendly reception in the court of the great Kublai Khan. Marco studied the native language and became a member of the imperial council. In the service of the Khan he traveled widely, from the borders of Tibet to the borders of Burma.

The Polos spent some twenty years in the Orient, returning to Venice in 1295. Later Marco was taken prisoner in a war between Venice and Genoa. He used his time in prison to write a book describing his entire experience. It became known throughout the Western World.

In his book Marco Polo told many true stories which seemed fanciful, and some imaginary ones which sounded real. He wrote not only of China, but also of Tibet, Burma, Siam, and Japan, giving information which helped many later travelers. This information was also used by the map makers of the later Middle Ages. Their maps were of great value to the later sea explorers.

Marco Polo leaving Venice, as shown in an old woodcut.

● Atlantic explorations: Columbus

In an earlier chapter you learned that Portugal, under Henry the Navigator, took the lead in exploring the African coast and in reaching India. As a result of Portuguese exploration European ships could reach India and the East Indies and bring back their valuable goods without interference from Venice, the Turks, or the Arabs. The Portuguese established a very rich trade.

Spain soon followed Portugal's example. In 1492 Ferdinand and Isabella, the Spanish rulers, decided to finance the voyage of Christopher Columbus, an Italian navigator from Genoa. Columbus had come across the idea of Greek and Egyptian geographers that the world is round, an idea also known to scholars of his time. Columbus believed the world to be much smaller than it really is, so that a voyage westward would easily reach India.

In 1492, with three small ships, Columbus crossed the Atlantic. In the spring of 1493 he returned triumphantly to Spain to report that he had found new islands. He believed them to be off the coast of India. Therefore, he named them the West Indies and called the inhabitants Indians.

Spain and Portugal made sweeping and conflicting claims as a result of their discoveries. The dispute was referred to the pope. The Papal Bull of Demarcation, 1493, drew a line from the north to the south pole, about 400 miles west of the Azores and Cape Verde Islands. Spain was given all lands to the west of the line; Portugal, all those to the east.

The line was revised in 1494 so that Brazil became a Portuguese colony. Today the Brazilians still speak Portuguese. All the rest of Central and South America became a Spanish empire; their language is Spanish.

● Amerigo Vespucci

Columbus was soon followed by other pioneers. Amerigo Vespucci took part in a trans-Atlantic expedition. Later on he made highly

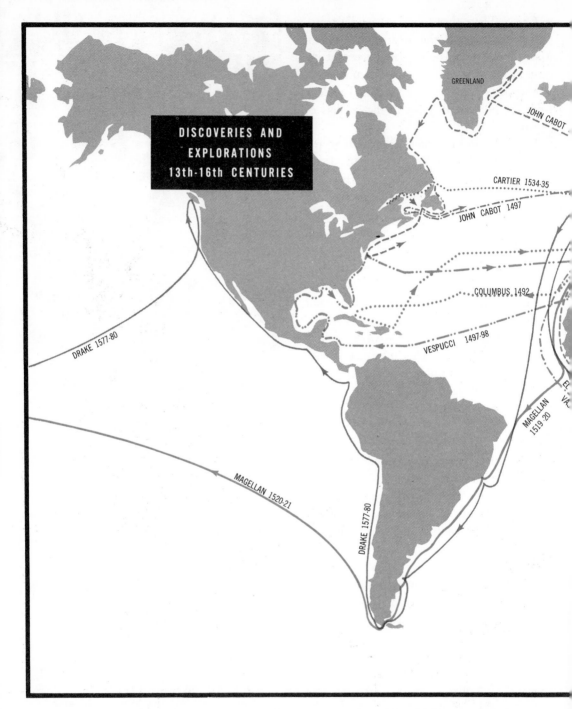

DISCOVERIES AND
EXPLORATIONS
13th-16th CENTURIES

GREENLAND

JOHN CABOT

CARTIER 1534-35

JOHN CABOT 1497

COLUMBUS 1492

DRAKE 1577-80

VESPUCCI 1497-98

EL
VA

MAGELLAN
1519-20

MAGELLAN 1520-21

DRAKE 1577-80

exaggerated claims about his discoveries. The New World was not named "Columbia," after Columbus, but "America," after Amerigo Vespucci. Vespucci became convinced that the land he saw was not India or Asia. When he returned to Europe, he wrote a

pamphlet, in Latin, about his voyage. He claimed that the land was *Novus Mundus,* a New World. His pamphlet was even more widely read than Columbus' account of his voyage. A German geographer named the new land Amerige, or America.

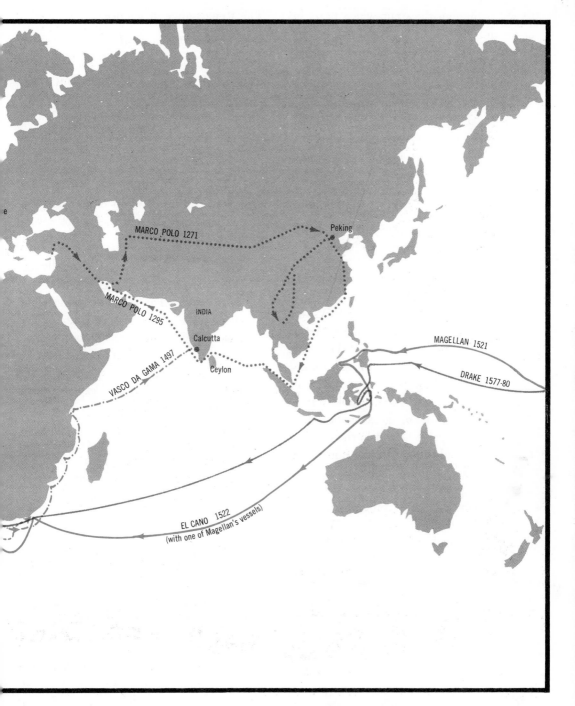

MARCO POLO 1271

MARCO POLO 1295

VASCO DA GAMA 1497

INDIA

Calcutta

Ceylon

Peking

MAGELLAN 1521

DRAKE 1577-80

EL CANO 1522
(with one of Magellan's vessels)

● *Early Pacific explorations*

Not long after the voyage of Vespucci, Vasco Nuñez de Balboa crossed the Isthmus of Panama and looked out on the Pacific Ocean. Now it seemed clear that the New World was really a continent. It was Ferdinand Magellan who really proved it so by doing what in his day seemed impossible. In 1519, with three ships, Magellan crossed the Atlantic to Brazil and sailed southward along the coast of South America. Reaching the tip, he sailed through the strait which bears his name and found a great ocean before him. He struck it at a fortunate time; the sea was so placid that he named it the Pacific (Peaceful) Ocean.

Magellan sailed westward across the Pacific and reached the Philippines. Here, in 1521, he was killed in a fight with the natives. The survivors of the crew sailed on to the west. They reached the Spice Islands and sighted Borneo. Only one ship was left, but it continued the voyage under the command of Sebastian del Cano (or El Cano) and in 1522 returned to Spain. The world had been circumnavigated for the first time in history.

Many other Spanish explorers, adventurers, and settlers sailed westward to the New World. They built a great empire for Spain. They had hoped to find spices. In Mexico and Peru they found what pleased them even more: great stores of gold and silver. Europe had always lacked the precious metals; now there seemed to be an inexhaustible supply.

The sudden flow of gold made many changes in Europe. It helped in the development of trade and manufacturing. It increased the importance of the middle class, and assisted in the growth of capitalism. It encouraged western European countries to build overseas empires. Truly, the New World of the Americas made a new world of Europe.

Magellan's voyage. Magellan and del Cano traveled about 44,000 miles in the first trip around the world. They took about 1,082 days of sailing time. A sidelight on the way these men lived at sea can be found in a list of provisions for Magellan's ships: 15 tons of ship's biscuit; 6,100 pounds of beans, lentils, and peas; 5,700 pounds of dried pork; 984 pounds of cheese; 1,512 pounds of honey; 3,200 pounds of raisins, currants, and almonds; 322 pounds of rice; 588 pounds of sugar; 100 pounds of mustard; 450 strings of garlic and onions.

The Renaissance in science

● The scientific method

We use the word *science* to mean two slightly different things. Science means a body of knowledge, facts, and truths about the universe, the world, and everything in it. Yet science also means something else, perhaps even more important: the *method* by which this knowledge and these truths are discovered and proved. The scientific method, by which men have gained all of their knowledge of the physical world, is made up of several steps:

1. *Observation:* The scientist carefully observes many facts or things.
2. *Classification:* The scientist arranges and classifies the observed facts into orderly groups which seem to belong together.
3. *Hypothesis:* The scientist tries to find some idea or theory (hypothesis) which fits all the facts in the group and explains them. It is only a *possible* solution which seems likely to be true.
4. *Experiment:* The scientist tests the hypothesis under all possible conditions and in every possible way to see whether it truly does fit all the facts and explain them.
5. *Law:* If careful and repeated experiments show that the hypothesis does prove true under all conditions, it is considered a scientific law. It can usually be stated in a language that is common to all scientists—the language of mathematics. A scientific law is often written as a mathematical formula.

You can see that the scientific method, to be truly successful, needs a number of things. The scientist needs instruments to help him observe and measure carefully. He also needs implements, instruments, and methods for conducting experiments so that they will truly test his theories. Finally, he needs different kinds of mathematics for calculating and stating his results.

During the thirteenth and fourteenth centuries much Greek and Arab scientific knowledge was brought into western Europe. Renaissance men began to test and develop the older scientific thinking. They began a steady development of modern science which has never stopped.

There is space here to tell about only a few of the leaders among Renaissance scientists. Notice that each used the true scientific method. Notice, too, how the completed work of one great man was often the starting point for the next.

● Leonardo da Vinci

Leonardo da Vinci made great contributions to science as well as to art. A man of tremendous curiosity, he experimented in many fields. He tried to discover scientific laws by using mathematics. Leonardo dissected the bodies of executed criminals in order to make his paintings of the human body more accurate. Thus he learned much about how the body is put together. He also observed the course of the blood and the relations of the bodily organs to one another. In order to draw birds more truly, he observed their flight. At the same time he tried to discover why they could fly. In his sketchbook Leonardo drew designs for a flying machine. He believed, as did Roger Bacon, that man could fly if only he could learn the natural laws that govern flight.

Da Vinci was a genuine scientist. He believed thoroughly in the value of the experimental method. In his notebook he wrote: "Those sciences are vain and full of errors which are not born of experiment, the mother of all certainty." Da Vinci kept notes and sketches to record the things he had observed and the mass of knowledge he had gathered. He did not publish his material, which was a great loss to the world. A modern scientist has said that if Leonardo da Vinci had published his work, science might have advanced in one step to a place not reached until a hundred years after his death.

● Copernicus and Kepler

The many geographical discoveries and explorations of the later Middle Ages led to a new interest in astronomy. Among the Greek writings recovered during the Renaissance

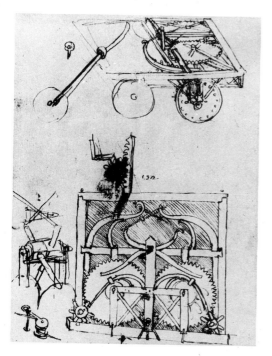

Leonardo da Vinci was an engineer and a scientist in addition to being a painter, sculptor, architect, and musician. At the top in the illustration is a sketch from his notebook, showing a design for a spring-powered car. The model was made from his drawing.

were those of a shrewd astronomer who dis-agreed with Ptolemy and other great Greek astronomers. He maintained that the center of our universe is the sun, around which the earth and other planets revolve.

In the sixteenth century a Pole named Nicolaus Copernicus came across the writings of this disagreeing Greek. The theory interested and excited Copernicus, and he began a long period of study to test it. He became convinced that all the known facts of astronomy of his time were best explained by the hypothesis of the sun-centered universe. He wrote a book telling the conclusions derived from his reasoning.

Copernicus' theory caused a great stir. Few people believed it, for it seemed to contradict the evidence of the senses. Anyone could see that the sun and planets move around the earth; anyone could feel that the earth under him was solid and stationary, not moving. Besides, the new idea was contrary to the Bible. Students and teachers of theology were violently opposed to this new idea. It is interesting that the man who published Copernicus' book felt compelled to write an introduction to it. He hinted that Copernicus was only joking, or at most stating an hypothesis.

Copernicus' idea really *was* only an hypothesis, for he could not test and prove it with either the instruments or the mathematics available to him. This proof was the work of two other men, a German and an Italian, who came later.

Johannes Kepler was able to make more careful and precise observations than Copernicus could. Since he was an excellent mathematician, he tried to test the hypothesis by mathematics. At first Kepler could not make his observed facts fit the hypothesis. It is said that he calculated the problem seventy times before he discovered the error. Copernicus had written that the earth and other planets went around the sun in orbits (paths) which are exact circles. Kepler found that the orbits are not exact circles, but ellipses (com-pressed or elongated circles). Now all the facts fell into place and fitted; the hypothesis could be proved.

● Galileo

Kepler's proof, however, could be understood only in the mind, and only by mathematicians. It could not be seen or observed. This additional kind of proof was given by an Italian professor of mathematics, Galileo Galilei, about fifty years after the publication of Copernicus' book. Galileo had read of a Dutch spectacle maker who put two glass lenses together in a tube. With this instrument he could see distant objects more clearly. Galileo made such a telescope for himself. By modern standards it was only a little one, but it allowed him to see more of the heavens than any man had ever seen before. He could see the mountains and valleys of the moon, and the rings of Saturn. When he observed that the moons of Jupiter move around the planet, the physical evidence of Copernicus' theory was revealed. The earth was a planet of the sun. Like Jupiter, it had a moon traveling around it.

Telescopes used by Galileo.

Galileo published his findings in a book which caused even more stir than Copernicus' writing. Many people wanted telescopes; many others believed them to be magic and refused to have anything to do with them. Scholars who accepted the authority of Ptolemy and Aristotle scoffed at this new theory. The Church also disapproved. Galileo was summoned to appear before the Inquisition. He was ordered to recant, or take back, his opinion. He did recant, but still the new knowledge and ideas continued to advance.

Galileo was interested in other sciences besides astronomy. He made many contributions to the science of physics. The belief of his time was that heavier bodies fall faster than lighter ones. Galileo went to the top of the famous leaning tower of Pisa and dropped a large and a small cannon ball simultaneously. When they reached the ground at the same time, the old theory was disproved.

New ideas in education

During the Renaissance and the following centuries many new ideas about education appeared. With their great enthusiasm for the classics, the humanists became promoters of the study of the Latin and Greek languages. They believed that the works of the great writers should be read in the original language. For a time it seemed that schools would be devoted entirely to the study of classic languages and classic writings.

Some of the humanist writers developed an idea that is important in modern education: the person who learns is more important than the facts he learns. The lively Rabelais believed that the student should learn manners, customs, and wisdom as well as languages. A person should be educated to meet the needs of his own time rather than to know the customs of former times. Rabelais believed that boys should learn the skills of the workshop as well as the knowledge of books.

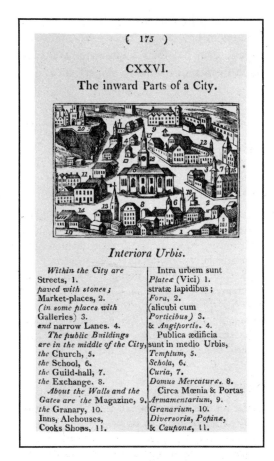

(175)

CXXVI.
The inward Parts of a City.

Interiora Urbis.

Within the City are	Intra urbem sunt
Streets, 1.	*Plateæ* (Vici) 1.
paved with stones;	stratæ lapidibus;
Market-places, 2.	*Fora,* 2.
(in some places with	(alicubi cum
Galleries) 3.	*Porticibus)* 3.
and narrow Lanes. 4.	& *Angiportis.* 4.
The public Buildings	Publica ædificia
are in the middle of the City,	sunt in medio Urbis,
the Church, 5.	*Templum,* 5.
the School, 6.	*Schola,* 6.
the Guild-hall, 7.	*Curia,* 7.
the Exchange. 8.	*Domus Mercaturæ.* 8.
About the Walls and the	Circa Mœnia & Portas
Gates are the Magazine, 9.	*Armamentarium,* 9.
the Granary, 10.	*Granarium,* 10.
Inns, Alehouses,	*Diversoria, Popinæ,*
Cooks Shops, 11.	& *Caupona,* 11.

A page from a Latin textbook prepared by Comenius in the seventeenth century. Notice how the illustration is keyed to the lesson by numbers.

Such humanist ideas of the Renaissance did not reach many people. Only the educated were affected by the new thinking, and relatively few people were educated.

During the seventeenth century a great Bohemian, John Comenius, gave a very modern turn to education. He believed and practiced the theory that a school must improve the abilities given to the pupils by nature. The student should gain full knowledge of himself and of the world about him. He should be trained in science; he should study real things and learn to meet real conditions in everyday life. The school should not be a dull place where the student was made to cram himself full of facts. He should learn many things by doing them. Knowledge and training in how to use facts were more important than the facts themselves. We may thank Comenius for many modern ideas and practices in education. He was the first man to use illustrations in a textbook. He thought they made the book more interesting. Note the illustration on page 239.

Review of Chapter 18

People, places, and things

Identify: Dante, Petrarch, Erasmus, More, Rabelais, Comenius, Gutenberg, Caxton, Aldus Manutius, Copernicus, Kepler, Galileo, Michelangelo, Leonardo da Vinci, Marco Polo, Magellan, Columbus, Vespucci, Papal Bull of Demarcation, Gargantua, *Utopia, In Praise of Folly.*

Locate: Florence, Pisa, Rome, Milan, Genoa, Rotterdam, Amsterdam, the Azores, the Cape Verde Islands, the West Indies.

Events in review

1. Define the term *Renaissance.* Why did the Renaissance begin in Italy?
2. How would you define *humanism?* To illustrate your answer cite ideas held by two famous humanists.
3. Name and briefly describe Dante's greatest work. What language did Dante use in this work? Why was his choice of a language important?
4. Did the new ideas of the humanists spread equally fast to all parts of Europe and to all classes of people? Why?
5. What were some of the outstanding qualities in the work of Renaissance artists?
6. What name did Columbus give to the new lands he discovered? Why? How did the new world receive the name "America"?
7. List the steps in the scientific method of investigation.
8. What great Renaissance man was famous as an artist and as a scientist? Name one of his paintings and one of his scientific studies.

9. What important scientific theory was stated by a Pole, who found it first in the writings of a Greek? How was the work of a German and an Italian needed to prove the theory true?
10. What modern ideas about education were expressed by (a) Rabelais, (b) Comenius?

Problems and projects

1. During the fourteenth and fifteenth centuries there were rapid changes in philosophy, science, and exploration. Some of these changes, however, can be traced back to earlier periods. How were men of the Renaissance influenced by Greek philosophers, by Greek and Egyptian geographers, by Marco Polo?
2. We are living today in what is called an age of science. How have modern scientific developments depended upon the scientific method produced by Renaissance thinkers?
3. Could the greatest Greek philosophers carry out complete scientific proof of their theories? Explain.
4. Compare the importance of (a) the invention of printing from movable type with (b) the invention of the telescope, or with (c) any modern invention such as radio.
5. To discuss: More men of genius were produced during the Renaissance than during the period from 1800 to the present.
6. On a map show the routes of the explorers discussed in this chapter. Show how the Papal Bull of Demarcation divided colonial areas between Spain and Portugal in 1493 and as revised in 1494.

Chapter 19 The Reformation

THE NEW SPIRIT of the Renaissance —the search for truth and the questioning of formerly accepted authority—was certain to affect religion and the Church. At the beginning of the sixteenth century the Church was under attack from two main sources: First, certain individuals criticized abuses in the organization and practices of the Church; others went further and criticized doctrines and dogmas of the Church. The second source of criticism was the new national governments. They opposed the Church for what they considered its outside interference in their affairs. Also, they resented having money collected in their churches and sent to Rome for use by the Church in other countries. Often they coveted the great wealth of the Church within their borders.

The Protestant Revolution in Germany

The first outright break with the Church came in Germany at the beginning of the sixteenth century. The incident which began the Protestant Revolution in Germany was a mixture of the political and the religious. Early in the sixteenth century a member of the Medici family of Florence became pope. His favorite project was the building of the great Church of St. Peter in Rome. To raise the money needed, he issued indulgences. Christians who contributed money for building St. Peter's received indulgences. These took away some of the penalties for their sins

—provided, it is important to note, they were truly penitent.

In Germany the sale of indulgences was controlled by the archbishop of Mainz, who had made a lump-sum payment to Rome for the privilege. The archbishop was very eager for the sale to go well so that he could recover his money and pay some debts which were troubling him. He employed a very enthusiastic preacher, Johann Tetzel, to travel around Germany persuading people to give generously.

Tetzel turned out to be what might be called today a "high-pressure" salesman. To build up his sales he began to claim that the purchase of an indulgence could bring pardon for sins. Then he went further, claiming that buying an indulgence could bring pardon for sins not yet committed.

●*Martin Luther*

These claims were entirely contrary to church doctrine, and they shocked and scandalized the more intelligent and truly religious Germans. One of the men who protested against Tetzel's tactics was Martin Luther, a teacher at the University of Wittenberg. Luther had been trained in law, but had given up his career to enter a monastery and become an Augustinian monk. Later he was transferred to Wittenberg to teach. He was a loyal Roman Catholic, and was shocked by Tetzel's irresponsible sales campaign. Luther protested to his church superior, but he did

A scene from a movie based on the life of Martin Luther. Here Luther (at left) is shown in his dramatic debate with Johann Eck.

not get any satisfaction. When church members came to Luther for confession, he refused to accept Tetzel's indulgences, even though ordered to do so by the archbishop.

In 1517, when Luther saw that he could not get any action from his superior, he acted on his own. On the door of the church at Wittenberg he posted a list of ninety-five statements (see the drawing at the top of page 241). They were in Latin, and were called the Ninety-five Theses. These were statements of his beliefs and position concerning indulgences. They really constituted an invitation for anyone to debate him on the question. Now the new printing press came into the picture. Luther's theses were translated into German, printed, and widely read. Even before a debate took place, the question of indulgences had stirred up a great deal of popular interest.

To meet Luther's challenge the Archbishop of Mainz brought in Johann Eck, one of the ablest church debaters. Instead of discussing the question of indulgences, Eck forced Luther to debate whether he was a rebellious clergyman. He asked whether Luther would submit to the archbishop, to the pope, or to the decision of a church council about indulgences if his own conscience taught other-

wise. In that case, said Luther, he would appeal to the teachings of the Bible itself.

● *Luther breaks with the Church*

To his shocked surprise Luther now found himself taking the very same position for which John Huss, the Bohemian priest, had been burned as a heretic. Now he could do only one of two things: recant, or break with the Church. He chose to break with the Church, and wrote an open declaration of his position to the German people. He attacked the Church both as a religious and a political institution. As a result, the pope excommunicated Luther as a heretic.

Luther continued to write pamphlets addressed to the German people and the German princes. He was an extremely able writer; he wrote in German, not Latin, so his writings had wide circulation among the ordinary people. He criticized every sort of abuse in the Church. He even attacked the papacy as a foreign power, thus appealing to German national spirit. The taxes Germans paid to Rome, he said, were an unjustified burden which helped to keep Germany poor, weak, and disunited. He appealed to the German princes to unite and destroy the power of the pope over their states.

● *Lutheran doctrine*

Luther now began to develop the doctrines of a new church, which came to be called the Lutheran Church. Its greatest difference from Roman Catholic doctrine was in the idea of how man might gain salvation. The Catholic Church taught that salvation was possible only through the sacraments administered by the clergy, and by good works done as penance. Luther taught "justification by faith"; that is, people could achieve salvation by faith alone. The clergy could help in this process, but were not absolutely necessary. A person could find in the Bible those things which he must believe, and he could be saved through his faith in them.

Many German princes accepted Luther's invitation and adopted Lutheranism. Those who did so seized all church lands and property in their states. It is a question how much their motives were purely religious and how much they were moved by hope of wealth.

It was ten years before Luther was called to answer for his rebellion. Charles V, the Hapsburg emperor, could devote little attention to German affairs for some years because he was involved in many wars. He had to fight Turkish invaders in central Europe. France was at war with the empire. There was also trouble in Spain. By the time the emperor could deal with the German problem, it was too late for peacemaking.

In 1529 Charles V summoned the Diet, a sort of parliament in the empire. The Diet declared Lutheranism a heresy. Many of the German princes who had joined the new faith protested this decision and would not accept it. From this protest the members of the new Church were called "Protestants." Luther went on to form the creed, or statement of belief, of his Church.

● War between Catholics and Protestants

Now a war broke out between the forces of the Protestant princes and those of the emperor and the Catholic nobles. It lasted twenty-five years, without a real victory for either side. In 1555 the Peace of Augsburg was signed. It had four important provisions:

1. Each German prince could decide for himself and for his subjects which religion would be followed in his state.
2. All church property taken by the Protestants prior to 1552 was considered theirs.
3. Lutheranism was the only recognized Protestant creed.
4. Lutherans living in ecclesiastical Catholic states could follow Lutheranism.

Most of the princes of northern Germany chose Lutheranism, while most of the southern German rulers remained Catholic. The wishes of the people played no part in the decisions. It was "prince's choice"; the people had to accept his decision. The church he chose became the state church in his country.

It is worth pointing out again that the Protestant Revolution in Germany was by no means strictly a religious movement. Luther succeeded in his revolt because he had the support of the political leaders, the German princes. The German princes supported the new Church for varying reasons. Some of them were probably moved more by their desire for political independence, their desire to keep all taxes collected in their lands, and their desire to take church property than by the religious differences. You must remember, though, that many who followed Martin Luther did so from purely religious motives. They wanted to set up a church that would be free from the evils and abuses they had protested against for so long. Luther's idea that man can achieve salvation by his faith alone, without the aid of any special class, had a very strong appeal. It fitted in with the new humanist thinking that man as an individual was important.

● Lutheranism spreads

Lutheran ideas spread early and rapidly to the nearby Scandinavian countries of Norway, Denmark, and Sweden. Here again the decision was as much political as religious. The principle of "prince's choice" prevailed. Within ten years after Luther nailed his Ninety-five Theses to the church door, the ruler of the united kingdom of Norway and Denmark recognized Lutheranism on an equal basis with Roman Catholicism. A few years later the Catholics rebelled, unsuccessfully, against the new order. The ruler then declared Lutheranism to be the state religion in Norway and Denmark.

A little later Sweden followed the same path. The ruler recognized Lutheranism as the state religion, and went even further. In 1604 all Catholics were removed from offices,

243

their estates were confiscated, and they were banished from the country.

Protestantism in other European nations

Lutheranism was only one form of Protestantism. The same forces and reasons that brought the break in Germany were present in many other countries. In Switzerland, the Protestant movement started under the leadership of a young humanist priest named Ulrich Zwingli. After Zwingli's death another, possibly greater, man appeared to take his place.

● John Calvin

John Calvin was a Frenchman. Like Luther he was educated for the law. He was much interested in the religious disputes of the day. Calvin saw little chance of bringing about reforms of any kind in the Church in France, so he went to Switzerland. There, in 1536, he published his book, *The Institutes of the Christian Religion*. He soon became the leader of the Protestant movement in Switzerland.

Zwingli and Calvin opposed all outward show in religion. The altars, statues, and crucifixes were removed from the churches. The wall paintings were covered with whitewash, and the stained glass windows were smashed. The greatest point of Calvin's doctrine was what he called *predestination*. Since God is able to foresee all the future, He must know that most men will be sinful, while only a few can be saved. Calvin believed that God had chosen, long in advance, those who would be saved. Calvin called these people "the elect." The only way a person could be at all sure that he was one of the elect was by living a righteous life.

Calvin became almost all-powerful in Geneva. He made the city a theocracy, that is, a government ruled by God's representatives. Because of the great importance he placed on the righteous life, he regulated the lives and

German foot soldiers of the period of the wars between the Catholics and Protestants in the sixteenth century.

conduct of the citizens down to the smallest details. There were laws prohibiting dancing, card playing, showy dress, and careless language. Violation of these laws brought extremely severe punishment. Calvinist Geneva was not a jolly place.

● Calvinist ideas spread

In France Calvinist ideas had some success among the middle class in the towns, but the great mass of the French people remained Catholic. Like Germany, France was torn by religious wars which lasted until 1598. Then a decree called the Edict of Nantes granted the Calvinists (who were called Huguenots) freedom of worship and assured them political rights.

Calvinist thinking also spread into the Netherlands and southern Germany. The southern part of the Netherlands (later Belgium) remained Catholic. The northern part, Holland, adopted Calvinism, and organized what was called the Reformed Church. Some of the people of southern Germany also adopted Calvinist ideas. However, the Peace of Augsburg had recognized Lutheranism as the only accepted Protestant creed; so Calvinism had a hard time establishing itself.

Outside of Switzerland the greatest success of Calvinism was in Scotland. John

Knox, a great admirer of Calvin, spent several years with him in Switzerland. Returning to Scotland, he succeeded in overthrowing Roman Catholic authority and setting up the Calvinist Presbyterian Church. Calvinist ideas came to England both from Scotland and the Continent, but did not meet with much success. They did influence the people called Puritans.

England and Anglicanism

The Roman Catholic Church in England had the same difficulties that it had on the Continent. Many people criticized the abuses and weaknesses. John Wycliffe, a priest and teacher, and Thomas More, famous statesman and judge, both severely criticized the clergy. When Lutheran and Calvinist ideas appeared in England, there was criticism of doctrines and of the clergy.

The greatest difficulty of the Church in England came from the growth of national government. The Tudor kings did not want interference from any outside power, and resented the influence of the Roman Church in English political affairs. They insisted on choosing the men to fill high positions in the Church in England.

● *Henry VIII*

Henry VIII, the second Tudor, became king in 1509. As a young man he showed great promise. He was handsome, well educated, pleasant, and chose able advisers. England began to enjoy great prosperity from its growing industry and trade. Henry was a devout Catholic. When the Lutheran break occurred in Germany, he wrote a pamphlet attacking Luther's ideas. Henry's pamphlet so pleased the pope that he gave him the title "Defender of the Faith." Lutherans who tried to spread their ideas in England were persecuted.

However, Henry VIII had family problems which troubled him greatly. He had married his brother's widow, Catherine of Aragon. She was the daughter of Ferdinand and Isabella of Spain. Five of the six children born to Henry and Catherine died in infancy; the other was a daughter, Mary. Henry wanted a son to carry on the Tudor line. His failure to have one convinced him that the marriage was accursed; so he asked the pope to grant him a divorce in order that he might marry Anne Boleyn.

The pope had a difficult decision to make. The laws of the Church prohibited divorce. Marriages were sometimes annulled (set aside) for technical reasons, but this one had been legalized by a special dispensation of the pope, necessary because Catherine was Henry's sister-in-law. Then, too, Catherine and her daughter Mary were close relatives of the Emperor Charles V, the most powerful Catholic ruler in Europe. The emperor wanted to protect their interests and inheritance. The pope delayed making a decision about granting the English king an annulment.

Henry VIII would not be denied. The archbishop of Canterbury, the highest church officer in England, had just died. Henry himself appointed the successor, Thomas Cranmer. The newly appointed archbishop summoned a church court which declared the king's marriage dissolved and permitted his marriage to Anne Boleyn. The pope immediately excommunicated both Henry VIII and Cranmer, but Henry refused to be frightened. In 1534 he persuaded Parliament to pass the Act of Supremacy. This act declared that the king, not the pope, was head of the Church in England. Parliament also passed a law abolishing monasteries in England, and the king seized their property.

Anne Boleyn bore Henry a daughter, Elizabeth, but no son. Henry had her tried, condemned, and beheaded for misconduct. A third wife pleased him by giving birth to a son, but she died in childbirth. In all, he was married six times; however, only his son Edward and the two daughters, Mary and

Elizabeth, survived him. In his will he provided that his son was to succeed him as Edward VI. If Edward died without an heir, Mary, the elder daughter, should succeed to the throne. If she, too, died without an heir, Elizabeth was to become queen.

Henry VIII's break with the Church was much more political than religious. Henry himself made this clear by stating that the Church in England was Catholic. No ceremony or doctrine was changed. The organization remained the same except that the king was at the head, and the authority of the pope was not recognized. Protestants were severely persecuted. The English called it "popery without the pope."

> *Henry VIII, in whose reign England broke away from the Roman Catholic Church. Henry is famous as a strong, nationalistic king. He is also remembered for his six wives: Catherine of Aragon, Anne Boleyn, Jane Seymour, Anne of Cleves, Catherine Howard, and Catherine Parr. This picture is reproduced from the famous portrait by Hans Holbein the Younger, a noted German artist.*

Religious troubles in England

After Henry VIII's death England went through troubled times. Edward VI was only ten years old, and was sickly. His advisers who ruled for him were influenced by Lutheran and Calvinist ideas; so they issued a new Book of Common Prayer and a new statement of belief. This statement was known as the Forty-Two Articles of Faith, and it contained many Protestant doctrines. Members of the clergy were allowed to marry. Priests who refused to accept these changes were removed from their offices. Catholics were persecuted. When Edward VI died after reigning only six years, England had moved far toward Protestantism.

Queen Mary, who succeeded to the throne, was a devout Catholic. She was married to Philip II, King of Spain, son of Emperor Charles V of Germany. Mary and Philip were determined that England should be restored to the Catholic Church and the authority of the pope. Under the queen's influence Parliament abolished the Act of Supremacy of Henry VIII and all the changes made during the reign of Edward VI. High church officials who had been responsible for or had accepted the Protestant reforms were removed from their positions. Archbishop Cranmer and two bishops were burned at the stake as heretics. Protestants were severely persecuted.

After reigning five years Queen Mary died childless, and her half sister Elizabeth succeeded to the throne. In a reign lasting forty-five years she proved one of the greatest of English rulers. Elizabeth I agreed with her father, Henry VIII, that the ruler should be head of the Church, with power to choose the higher clergymen. She was not as strongly Protestant as Edward VI and his advisers had been, but she wanted a strongly national church which would unite all Englishmen, end the religious troubles, and still be independent of the pope.

The Church of England

Elizabeth formed the Church of England, or Anglican Church. The ruler was head of the Church, and the Church was an "established" Church. That meant that it was supported by taxes, and the clergy were paid by the government. Not everyone was required to belong, but everyone had to pay taxes to support the Church. Nonmembers were under some handicaps, and some were harshly persecuted if they opposed the government in other ways. Persecution however, was not carried out on the same scale as in other nations.

The statement of belief of the Church of England is found in the Thirty-Nine Articles of Faith which Elizabeth caused to be written and issued. They strike a middle ground between Roman Catholic beliefs and those of the extreme Protestants. The Anglicans kept many of the ceremonies of the Roman Catholic Church, as well as the organization under bishops and archbishops.

The religious revolution in England was a conservative revolution. England did break away from the authority of the pope and set up an independent Church supported by taxes, under the ruler as head. The Church became, in a way, a branch of the government. However, its organization, ceremonies, and many of its doctrines remained closer to the Roman Catholic than any of the other Protestant churches. In America it is known as the Protestant Episcopal Church.

The Catholic Reformation

The Protestant Revolution was a terrible blow to Rome. Among other things it showed that the abuses against which men had protested for so long would have to be corrected. Reforms could not be evaded or postponed any longer or the Church would break apart entirely. The Church therefore began a program known as the Catholic Reformation or the Counter-Reformation.

Queen Elizabeth I. Daughter of Henry VIII and Anne Boleyn, she ruled England from 1558 to 1603.

Pope Paul III and the Council of Trent

Pope Paul III summoned a council of church leaders to meet in Trent, Italy, in 1545. They were to consider the Protestant criticisms of church doctrines and to make needed reforms in church customs and practices. The council remained in session for eighteen years. It re-examined all the doctrines of the Roman Catholic Church and all the customs and practices which had been criticized.

After careful consideration the Council of Trent restated all the doctrines of the Church and refused to accept any of the Protestant interpretations and doctrines. It reaffirmed its belief in all the sacraments, in salvation through the sacraments as administered by the clergy, and in the pope as the supreme head of the Church.

The Council of Trent condemned and ended some of the abuses. Simony, the sale of

247

church offices, was strictly prohibited. The sale of indulgences for money was banned. Bishops were instructed to see to it that members of the clergy were better educated and that they lived blameless lives. To guard the morals of church members the Council prepared an *Index of Prohibited Books*. The *Index* listed all books which the Church considered immoral and dangerous to the soul. All Catholics were forbidden to read them. The Council also strengthened the special courts which dealt with heresy.

● *The Jesuits*

The reformed Roman Catholic Church received strong support from a new organization led by an extraordinary man. Ignatius Loyola was a young Spanish soldier when he broke his leg during a battle. His recovery was very slow, and he devoted his time to reading and thinking about the lives of Christ and the saints. Through his reading and meditation Loyola became convinced that he should become a soldier of Christ,

spreading the teachings of Christianity among unbelievers.

Loyola spent eleven years in study and preparation for his new work. He gathered about him a group of followers. The pope gave them permission to establish a new monastic order called the Society of Jesus. Its members, known as Jesuits, take the usual monastic vows of poverty, chastity, and obedience. A fourth vow requires them to promise to obey the pope, doing any missionary work he may ask of them. A man may become a Jesuit only after a long period of education and training, which only a brilliant mind and a devoted faith can survive.

The first aim of the Jesuit order was to check the spread of Protestantism and to re-

Members of the Jesuit order in the Roman Catholic Church became famous in many fields. Some of them were missionaries, and explorers as well. Father Marquette, shown below on the Mississippi, was a pioneer of European exploration in North America.

THE RELIGIOUS SITUATION IN EUROPE ABOUT 1560

Catholic
Lutheran
Calvinist
Anglican

gain for the Church those nations that had broken away. The Jesuits were a strong force: well trained, strictly disciplined, and ardent believers in the importance of their work. Their efforts restored Poland, Bavaria, and Hungary to the Roman Catholic Church. They also checked the spread of Calvinism in France.

The Thirty Years' War

By the middle of the sixteenth century Europe had become a divided continent because of religious differences. In Germany the Peace of Augsburg, 1555, brought about an uneasy peace that lasted some sixty years and then broke down. In 1618 there began a series of wars that lasted, with intervals of peace, for thirty years and left a multitude of miseries.

Most of the causes of the Thirty Years' War can be found in the weaknesses in the Treaty of Augsburg. The principle of "prince's choice" did not allow the people of a region

any voice in choosing their religion. It limited the choice to Lutheranism or Catholicism; Calvinist and Reformed Churches were outlawed. There was no religious toleration within a state.

The problem of church property also caused trouble. According to the treaty, church property taken by Lutheran princes before a certain date was to remain theirs. No provision was made for any changes after that date. Yet there were changes, which caused great confusion and conflict over the property.

Several other conditions made peace very uncertain in Germany and other parts of Europe. There was constant rivalry among the German princes, rulers of some 300 independent states. The kings of France, surrounded by Hapsburg-held lands, took every opportunity to try to weaken the power of the Hapsburg Holy Roman Empire. Denmark and Sweden both had ambitions and looked for chances to take territory within the Holy Roman Empire.

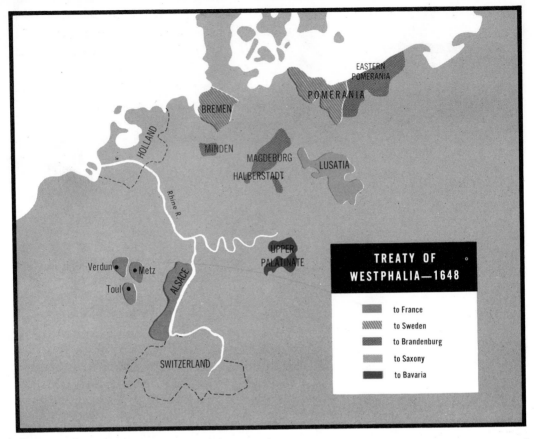

TREATY OF
WESTPHALIA—1648

to France
to Sweden
to Brandenburg
to Saxony
to Bavaria

Thus you can see that if a war broke out anywhere, for almost any reason, it was likely to spread and involve many countries. So it happened. The Thirty Years' War began as a local conflict in Bohemia, within the Holy Roman Empire. Before it ended, almost every country in Europe was involved at one time or another. Europe endured a succession of military campaigns and diplomatic deals. In 1648 the nations, nearly exhausted, sought peace, and a treaty was made.

● The Treaty of Westphalia

The Treaty of Westphalia, 1648, is a landmark in the history of western Europe. Here are some of its principal provisions (for territorial changes, see the map):

1. Each German prince was given independence in his own state. He could make war or peace without interference from the emperor.

2. Sweden received western Pomerania and the bishopric of Bremen, making it the most powerful Lutheran state in northern Europe.

3. Brandenburg, ruled by the Hohenzollern family, received eastern Pomerania and several bishoprics. This was a great step in the rise to power of the Hohenzollerns, whose reign lasted until modern times.

4. Holland and Switzerland were recognized as independent states.

5. France received Alsace, an extremely valuable territory which appears often in later European history. It also received recognition of its possession of Metz, Verdun, and Toul, three rich and strategically located bishoprics in France.

6. All former church property was to be kept by whoever held it in 1624.

7. Calvinists were granted the same privileges as Lutherans in Germany.

Results of the Protestant revolution and the wars of religion

● Religious results

The most striking result of the great convulsions of this period was that the single Christian Church of the Middle Ages was now a thing of the past. The Catholic Reformation produced a Church free of the old abuses, with a better trained and disciplined clergy. It had been able to halt the spread of Protestantism and even regain some lost territory. Southern Europe remained firmly Catholic. France and the Netherlands were divided. But Holland, Switzerland, northern Germany, Scandinavia, England, and Scotland were lost to the papacy and the Roman Catholic Church.

Religion, which had been universal in Europe, now became nationalized in the Protestant parts. Each government took responsibility for and leadership of the Church in its country. Often the state Church was supported by taxation of all the people, with the clergy paid by the government.

The wars of religion were the signs of a great intolerance. The members of each religion held stubbornly to their own views, and looked with contempt and suspicion on all others. It seemed impossible for a man to believe that anyone who disagreed with him about religion could be trusted as a friend. A man who followed a religion different from that of the majority group in his region suffered legal and social handicaps.

By the end of the Thirty Years' War Europeans had come to realize that people of different religions *could* live together peacefully in the same country. There was not yet real freedom of religion. It took long and painful education to make men realize that in order to have religious freedom themselves, they must be willing to grant it to others.

In Protestant countries there was a great increase in popular education, usually supported and controlled by the government. Protestant doctrine teaches that man can find in the Bible his own way to salvation. Men must be educated in order to be able to read and understand the Bible. Education did not mean tolerance of ideas. Luther and Calvin were as unwilling to allow free inquiry, or views differing from their own, as were their opponents.

In the Catholic countries writing and speaking were now very closely supervised. There was much less room for questioning and difference of opinion. Those who did question and differ found themselves called before the heresy courts. Their writings were placed on the *Index of Prohibited Books*.

● Political and social results

The Protestant Revolution meant a great loss of political power for the papacy. Each time a national government took control over the Church in its country, Rome lost political control.

The wars of religion brought about an era of national states—of governments each supreme in its own country. Each government claimed complete sovereignty—that is, the right to settle all its problems without any outside interference. Often this meant that wars inside the country almost disappeared. Kings who were sovereign could not permit private wars among their own people. They demanded and were able to enforce the principle that disputes must be settled peacefully according to law. However, wars between countries and nations did not cease; in fact, they seemed to come oftener.

Another political result of the wars of religion was the decline of Hapsburg power in both Germany and Spain and the rise of France as the leading European power. When each German prince was recognized as independent and sovereign, the power of the Hapsburg emperor was weakened. The possibility of Germany uniting, either under the Hapsburgs or anyone else, was made much more difficult. Spain, which had been the most powerful European country for a century or more, now began a steady decline.

Finally, what was the effect of the Protestant Revolution and the wars of religion on Germany? Politically, Germany was more divided than ever into hundreds of small, sovereign, independent states. Religiously it was split into Catholic and Protestant groups.

Economically and socially the results of the Thirty Years' War in Germany were dreadful indeed. The war was fought almost entirely on German soil. Millions of German men, women, and children lost their lives. The country was terribly devastated. It could be said of the Thirty Years' War and the peace of Westphalia: "They made a desert, and called it peace."

Review of Chapter 19

People, places, and things

Identify: Johann Tetzel, Martin Luther, Johann Eck, John Calvin, John Knox, Henry VIII, Mary, Elizabeth I, Pope Paul III, Ignatius Loyola, the Ninety-five Theses, Act of Supremacy, the *Index of Prohibited Books,* a theocracy.

Locate: Bohemia, Wittenberg, Augsburg, Westphalia, Brandenburg, Alsace.

Events in review

1. What were indulgences? How did they have an important effect on world history?
2. Give an account of the Luther-Eck debate. What position did Luther find himself in as a result of the debate?
3. List the provisions of the Peace of Augsburg. Did this treaty provide for religious toleration within the states of Europe?
4. What part did the following men take in the spread of the Protestant revolution: John Calvin, John Knox?
5. Did Henry VIII of England approve of Lutheranism? Why did he break with the Church of Rome?
6. Why can the religious revolution in England be described as a conservative revolution?
7. For what purpose was the Council of Trent summoned? What action did the Council take?
8. What country became the most powerful Lutheran state of northern Europe as a result of

the Treaty of Westphalia? What did France gain as a result of this treaty?
9. Summarize the political results of the Protestant revolution and the wars of religion.

Problems and projects

1. Could the Protestant Reformation have taken place before the Renaissance? Give reasons.
2. In what ways was the Protestant revolution a political as well as a religious movement? Give as many examples as you can.
3. Compare the development of Protestantism in Germany with the development in England. Include (a) causes of the revolution, (b) the religious settlement that resulted.
4. Compare in importance the religious, political, and social results of the Thirty Years' War.
5. To what extent were people free to worship as they chose in Europe at the end of the Thirty Years' War?
6. To discuss: The beliefs and actions of Luther had such wide effects on world history that they may be likened to dropping a pebble in a pool.
7. Write an essay on one of the following: Calvin, Luther, Henry VIII, Ignatius Loyola or one of the great Jesuit missionaries.
8. Draw a map of Europe at the end of the Thirty Years' War. Show in one color the areas that remained in the Roman Catholic Church. Show in a second color the areas that had become Protestant.

Chapter 20   The Building of the European Empires

WITH the great geographical discoveries and explorations of the Renaissance, the small world of medieval Europe suddenly expanded. New lands were waiting to be settled, new peoples had never heard of Christianity, and new possibilities of trade opened up. Any man willing to cross the sea could own land. This was like a dream come true because in medieval Europe owning land was the mark of your social position and your wealth.

Two powerful urges gave the force to European exploration and colonization: gaining wealth from trade, and spreading the Christian religion. The Spanish found rich stores of gold and silver in the Americas. The Portuguese learned that the profits of a single voyage to India could be fifty times its cost. Gradually the trade and profit motive drove the missionary purpose into the background. The desire to spread the Christian religion did not disappear but it became secondary.

The Portuguese empire

The Portuguese were the first Europeans to establish an overseas empire. Beginning with the offshore African islands and the Gold Coast of Africa, they reached the southwest coast of India, called Cochin. Portuguese ships that made the round trip successfully made enormous profits.

In about 1510 the Portuguese conquered the Cochin coast of India and used the port of Goa as a trading and administrative center. To protect the sea route they took the island of Socotra, in the Indian Ocean south of Arabia. Next they attacked and conquered Malacca on the southwest coast of Malaya. From Malacca they could easily reach the Moluccas, the fabled Spice Islands about which Europeans had dreamed. Here were found the pepper, cloves, nutmeg, camphor, sugar, tea, coffee, and indigo which were the most valuable products of the eastern trade.

Malacca gave the Portuguese a base from which to push on to China. The Portuguese

Portuguese traders in India, as shown in an old print.

PO

BUILDING OF EMPIRES
16th-17th CENTURIES

English
French
Dutch
Spanish
Portuguese

made a treaty with the Chinese which allowed them to establish a trading post at the mouth of the Canton River. Here the Portuguese built the city of Macao as a center for their trade with China.

Now the Portuguese turned backward to add another link to their chain of bases for trade and empire. This was the island of Ceylon, off the southeast coast of India. Ceylon was important as a way point between Goa and Malacca and as a source of tea and spices. With Ceylon and Malacca as bases, the Portuguese had the entire Malay group of islands as a region of trade and influence.

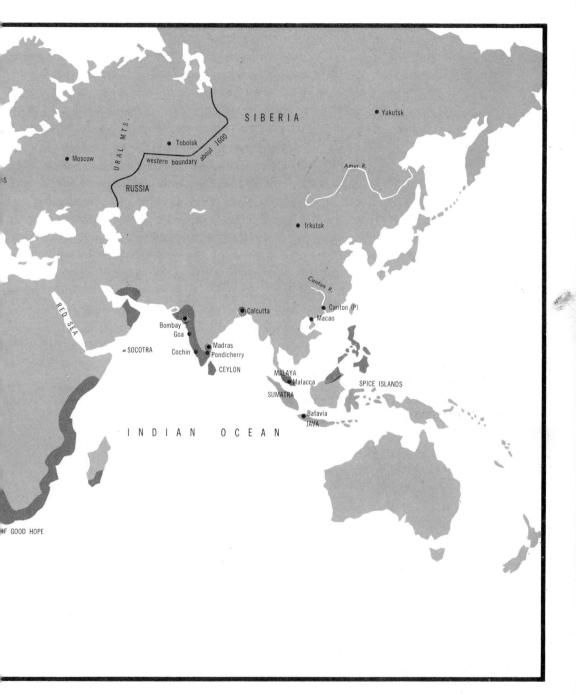

Weakness of the Portuguese empire

To set up such an empire was one thing; to hold on to it was something else. Portugal's rise to wealth and empire was rapid. The decline was almost as fast, for a number of reasons. The Portuguese government was neither strong nor well organized. The government had a hard time keeping check on and controlling its officials at home; it was impossible for it to do so in the colonies.

Both trade and settlement proved very costly in lives. Shipwrecks, battles, and diseases took a heavy toll. Each year Portugal sent out her strongest, most daring, most

255

enterprising young men. Only half, and sometimes fewer, returned. In time, the situation in little Portugal became so desperate that criminals and the lowest elements of the population were sent to the East. This had very bad effects on the colonial settlements.

Another weakness of the Portuguese as a colonizing nation was their attitude toward the native populations. Long wars against the Moslem Moors had given both the Portuguese and Spanish very narrow and intolerant religious views. The heathen, the unbeliever, was a man either to be converted or destroyed. The Portuguese set up the Inquisition in India to stamp out the Hindu religion in the land of the Hindu. Such a policy was bound to create hatred that would affect the all-important commerce.

Thus you can see that the Portuguese empire might have fallen to pieces from inner weaknesses without any attacks from the outside. In the sixteenth and seventeenth centuries, it was too much to expect that there would be no attack from the outside. The sight of such a small and comparatively weak nation controlling such a great wealth in trade was too tempting. The first threat came from Holland.

The Dutch build a colonial empire

Nature and location had turned the Dutch toward the sea; accordingly, they set up a number of companies to trade in various parts of the world. They were brave sailors, and they built very sturdy ships. When they had to fight, as they often did, Dutch ships gave a very good account of themselves against those of more powerful nations.

When Spain annexed Portugal in the mid-sixteenth century, Portuguese ships and possessions became fair game to the Dutch, who were at war with Spain. They first attacked the ships carrying goods from Portugal to northern Europe; then they preyed upon those bringing treasures from Asia to Portugal. From this it was only a step to try to take over the weak Portuguese empire itself.

At the start of the seventeenth century, the Dutch combined all their competing trading companies into one powerful organization, the United East India Company. It received the exclusive right in Holland to carry on trade between Holland, Africa, and the East Indies. This company proceeded to take over much of the Portuguese Asian empire.

Dutch colonial government was much stronger than that of Portugal. Holland appointed a governor-general of its empire. He was assisted by a council. The governor-general had great authority over local administration, but he was closely controlled by and responsible to the home government.

The Dutch tried to correct another Portuguese colonial mistake. The Portuguese had held only strategic pinpoints along coasts in order to control the sea lanes. The Dutch realized that a successful empire required much wider control over the land and the people. For example, they did not stop with establishing a trading post at Batavia on the island of Java. From there they reached out to gain control of the entire island with its large population and its valuable products: sugar, tea, coffee, and many spices. From Java the Dutch expanded westward to take the island of Sumatra, and eastward to seize the valuable Moluccas, the Spice Islands, from the Portuguese. Ceylon came next; the Portuguese were unable to hold it.

The building of the British Empire

At the end of the sixteenth century England appeared as a colonial rival of the Portuguese and Dutch. In 1600 Queen Elizabeth granted a charter to the East India Company. This charter gave the company a trade monopoly from the Cape of Good Hope in South Africa eastward to the Straits of Magellan at the tip of South America.

The English gave attention first to India because the Dutch were so firmly established in the East Indies. The East India Company set up trading posts at Madras, Bombay, and Calcutta. The company dealt mainly with local rulers, for India was divided into many little states. Where a ruler was weak and submissive, he was given aid. If bribery was a better means, a generous "gift" was extended. Where force was needed, it was used without hesitation. In the end, the English established themselves so well in India that they remained there as rulers for three and a half centuries.

The East India Company set up some trading posts in Malaya and the islands, but India was its main source of trade and wealth. Within a short time the East India Company became the largest and wealthiest company in the world. It owned a vast fleet of merchant ships and warships to protect them. The enormous profits reaped by the owners made the East India Company a universal source of envy.

The English were rather slow in establishing colonies in North America. For its woolen cloth industry England wanted the dyes and other products brought from the East by Portugal and Spain. Hence the first English ventures into North America were in search of a northwest passage to Asia. Such a seaway to the East would allow England to reach these products herself, instead of depending on foreign ships. Only after this search failed did England begin to colonize North America. Even then, the job was turned over to private companies or individuals because it was considered too expensive and risky for the English government.

During the seventeenth century English colonies were founded along the east coast of North America. They were commercial ventures; that is, they were started in the hope that they might raise the products England had to import from the East. As commercial undertakings they were disappointing. Few of the original investors got their money back, to say nothing of making profits. The English also settled in Bermuda. In the West Indies, in the Caribbean Sea, they acquired numerous islands. Here the commercial success was greater because the islands produced sugar, a very valuable and desired product.

The French in Asia and America

The end of the Thirty Years' War (1648) left France in a strong position on the continent of Europe. Under the strong King Louis XIV, France still had to give much attention to European affairs. However, Louis XIV's great minister, Jean Baptiste Colbert, was a strong believer in the value of colonies and empire. On his advice the French East India Company was established and a program of shipbuilding begun.

A reconstruction of the houses and stockade built by the English settlers at Jamestown in 1607. The reconstructed settlement was put up for the 350th anniversary of the founding of the colony.

A silver mine in Peru. This illustration from a book published in 1601 shows an artist's idea of a mine from which the Spaniards took quantities of silver ore. Day and night shifts of Indians labored in the mine.

The French East India Company set up a trading post, Pondicherry, on the southeast coast of India. The English had not reached that part of India. During the 1700's an extremely able colonial administrator, Joseph François Dupleix, set up a smoothly working administration. French trade increased rapidly, and the French expanded into new regions in India. In many places they became rivals of the British East India Company. In the eighteenth century this rivalry flared into open warfare.

Early in the seventeenth century France began to establish colonies in North America on the St. Lawrence River and in the Great Lakes region. The French developed a profitable trade in furs with the Indians. Fishing off Newfoundland and Nova Scotia became important.

The French colonies in America developed slowly until the reign of Louis XIV (1642–1715). Then a large program of exploration and settlement was begun. The entire Great Lakes region was explored. La Salle sailed down the Mississippi River to the Gulf of Mexico and claimed the entire center of North America for France. In honor of King Louis XIV, La Salle named the region Louisiana.

Now the French controlled the Great Lakes and the Mississippi River valley; so they were in a position to block the westward expansion of the English colonies. In America, as in India, the two rivals seemed bound to come into contact and conflict.

Spanish colonization

After the time of Columbus the Spanish explored the West Indies, Florida, Central America, and parts of the mainland of North and South America. They knew it was not Asia, and they knew that the islands were not the fabled Indies. They did not find the spices and dyes they wanted. However, the soil and climate were suitable for raising some of the desired products, and the natives were few enough to be controlled.

● Conquest of Mexico and Peru

The Spanish became colonizers in the true sense of the word. Unlike the Europeans in Asia, who were traders, the Spanish in the Americas were permanent settlers. They developed plantations and experimented in growing and producing various crops. Their missionaries converted the Indians, built churches, established universities, and brought European civilization to the Americas. Spanish colonization began in the West Indies, which became the center of their whole empire in the Americas. From Cuba Ponce de León went to explore Florida and Vasco Nuñez de Balboa crossed the Isthmus of Panama. Other explorers went to Yucatan and learned of the great Aztec civilization in Mexico. With his ten ships and 600 men, Hernando Cortez sailed from the islands to defeat the Aztec ruler Montezuma, capture Mexico City with its vast wealth in gold, and conquer all of Mexico.

In Mexico the Spanish heard of a great and rich civilization in South America. Francisco Pizarro, with two hundred men and fifty horses, reached the Inca empire of Peru and conquered a territory extending 2,000 miles from north to south.

Very early in their settlement of the Americas, the Spanish developed a centralized colonial administration. The colonies were ruled by viceroys and governors. These officers were responsible to a council in Spain; the council was responsible to the king. Thus the development of the Spanish colonies could be planned and directed. Mining, especially of silver, was highly developed and sent vast treasure to Spain.

The Spanish government made every effort to keep this wealth entirely for Spain. Foreigners were barred from the Spanish colonies. Silver from America could be carried only in Spanish ships and only to Spanish ports, especially Seville. It was one thing, though, to make rules, and another to enforce them. Spanish treasure ships became rich prizes. They were attacked by the many pirates who prowled the seas, and also by the ships of European nations which envied the Spanish wealth.

The English, French, and Dutch used various means to break Spain's exclusive control and to get a share of the wealth from America. They sent ships to American ports carrying manufactured goods which Spain herself was unable to supply. They made secret deals with individual Spaniards to sail the treasure ships to their ports. Instead of trying to suppress the pirates, they encouraged them to prey on Spanish ships. Nor did they do anything to keep their own sailors from making raids on Spanish ports and possessions.

● Decline of the Spanish empire

For a number of reasons, the mighty Spanish empire began to fall apart. Spain itself was not rich in either agriculture or industry.

Spanish nobles were contemptuous of both trade and industry. Their attitude prevented the development of industry which could supply the colonies with the goods they needed. France, England, and Holland did develop such industries, and they profited by selling goods to Spain. Much American gold and silver simply passed through Spain on its way to buy French, Dutch, and English goods. This gold enabled these countries to develop their industries still further, and thus strengthened them.

Although the government of Spain and the colonies was highly centralized, it was very inefficient. At home it did not allow the development of initiative by private citizens.

Acapulco, since Spanish times the most important harbor on the Pacific coast of Mexico. This old picture shows ships exchanging salutes with the fort. Ships like these carried gold and silver to Spain.

Russia once had a trading post in California. This old print shows Fort Ross as it was in 1843.

The attempt at strict colonial monopoly, shutting out all foreign trade, brought attacks by the English, Dutch, and French.

We might sum it all up by saying that Spain became great too rapidly. Her own political, social, and economic conditions did not fit her to manage such a large empire. The burdens of trying to protect and manage the empire and to carry on her many wars weakened her. At the same time her rivals became stronger, often through the wealth of Spain herself. They attacked her colonial commerce and forced her out of northern Europe. By the beginning of the seventeenth century Spain's glory had begun to decline.

Russian eastern expansion

Sixteenth century Russia was landlocked, or cut off from the sea. It was barred from overseas expansion like that of western Eu-

ropean countries. However, to the east of Russia lay a vast expanse of land, an entire continent reaching to the Pacific Ocean. This vast land was thinly settled by primitive people living at a low level of civilization. Much of it was a great plain that we call the steppes. In the north the steppes were separated from European Russia only by the low, easily crossed Ural Mountains, while in the south there was no natural obstacle at all. There were many navigable rivers to aid travel. The size of this great plain can be seen on the map on page 255.

Russia's eastward expansion was carried on mostly by people who came to be called Cossacks. Like frontiersmen everywhere, these Russians were men whom no government could hold down. They hated crowded cities and the restraints of civilization; they loved simple freedom and vast spaces. They formed their own primitive, democratic government, and won from the Moscow government many rights of self-government not granted to others.

The lure which drew the Cossacks eastward was trade, especially the fur trade. The country east of the Urals was the heaven of the trapper and fur trader. Animals were everywhere and easy to trap. Most valuable was the sable, whose fur was highly prized. In 1581 a band of Cossacks invaded and conquered a Tartar country east of the Urals, called Sibir. This opened the door to lands further east, all of which came to be known by the same name—Siberia.

Step by step the Russian pioneers forced their way eastward. The Russians faced the problem of primitive peoples—the Tungus, the Yakuts, and others. The early Russian settlers built fortified posts like the American frontier forts. As centers for trade and defense, these posts became the towns and cities of Siberia: Tobolsk, Yakutsk, Irkutsk, and others.

Russian pioneers moved eastward in two streams—one to the north and one to the south. Neither was checked by any very strong native people until the southern group reached the Amur River. Here they came in contact with the Chinese. Fifty years of skirmishes and warfare failed to overcome the resistance of the Chinese. In 1689 the two peoples signed a treaty which fixed a boundary between them north of the Amur River. The treaty allowed the Russians to trade with the Chinese. Chinese-Russian trade relations brought to China furs and raw materials. The Russians got such items as silk and the tea which became so popular in Russia.

● *The Russians reach North America*

The northern explorers finally reached the Arctic Ocean. By the mid-seventeenth century Russian frontiersmen had reached the Pacific. Hardy pioneers crossed the Bering Straits and the Aleutian Islands into Alaska, and pressed on south along the Pacific coast of North America. During the first half of the nineteenth century small bands of Russians moved into northern California and built Fort Ross, about sixty miles north of San Francisco.

Mercantilism

During the sixteenth and seventeenth centuries Europeans developed a new theory about the wealth and strength of nations. The theory is called *mercantilism*, or the mercantile theory of trade. According to this idea, the supply of money and precious metals in the hands of a government or its people was the wealth of the nation. That nation which could build up the greatest supply of gold and silver was the wealthiest, and therefore the strongest.

The most fortunate nation was the one which had deposits of gold and silver, either at home or in colonies abroad, as Spain had. A nation which lacked such a supply had to gain it by trade. This meant that it had to sell abroad (to foreign countries) more goods than it bought from foreign countries. This was called a "favorable balance of trade." It brought money into the country. This not only strengthened the country but weakened its foreign rivals by taking money away from them.

It was considered better to export manufactured goods because they brought more money. Governments encouraged the development of manufacturing and the export of manufactured goods. They discouraged the importing of foreign manufactured goods by taxes called tariffs. The tariff raised the price of the imported goods so that people bought less of them. Thus each nation tried to become self-sufficient; that is, it tried to produce all the goods its people needed and also a surplus to sell abroad to bring gold and silver into the country.

Colonies played an important part in mercantilism. Colonies which produced gold and silver were ideal. Next best were those which produced raw materials that could not be grown or produced at home. By buying these materials in its colonies, the nation could avoid buying from a foreign rival. Thus its money did not go out of the country or empire. Since the colony was also important as a market for the sale of manufactured goods, the colony should be prevented from developing manufacturing. Instead, it should be encouraged to produce the most needed raw materials. Its trade should be regulated very strictly to prevent it from buying from foreign countries or from shipping the most desired raw materials to them.

Review of Chapter 20

People, places, and things

Identify: Colbert, LaSalle, Balboa, Ponce de Léon, Cortez, Pizarro, Cossacks.

Locate: Portugal, Cape of Good Hope, India, Socotra, Madras, Bombay, Calcutta, Pondicherry, Cochin, Goa, Malay Peninsula, Malacca, Moluccas, Spice Islands, Ceylon, Java, Batavia, Sumatra, China, Canton, Macao, St. Lawrence River, Nova Scotia, Newfoundland, Louisiana (as claimed by LaSalle), Panama, Yucatan, West Indies, Siberia, Ural Mountains, Tobolsk, Yakutsk, Irkutsk.

Events in review

1. What were the original motives behind European exploration and colonization?
2. Which nation was first to establish an overseas empire? Why did this empire soon decline?
3. How did the Dutch build their colonial empire? How long did they keep control of their empire?
4. In what area did the British East India Company carry on most of its activities? Was the company successful? What French government official was responsible for setting up a rival company?
5. State briefly the reasons for the decline of the Spanish colonial empire.
6. The Russian pioneers moved eastward in two streams. How far did each one reach?
7. Define the theory called *mercantilism.* Why were colonies important in mercantilism?

Problems and projects

1. In terms of the mercantile theory, how desirable would the following colonial areas be: India, the West Indies, Alaska, Mexico, Peru? Explain.
2. Which European nations maintained their colonial empires for the longest periods? Account for their greater success in colonization.
3. How did explorations by European nations in America affect the history of the United States?
4. To debate: Mercantilism is advantageous to the country that practices it.
5. Write an editorial for a newspaper (of the sixteenth to eighteenth century) in any European colonizing country. Entitle it "A New Land Has Been Found." Tell why this news is important to your readers.
6. Prepare a dramatic sketch based on an event during one of the great voyages of discovery.
7. Has any European colony turned up in the news recently (Goa or Macao, for example)? If so, some student can report to the class on this latest event in the story of colonial empires.
8. On a world map, show the important trading posts established by Europeans during the seventeenth and eighteenth centuries. Show also the areas claimed as colonies at this time. Note distances (by land or sea) from the home country to the outposts. How did geography influence the direction and the character of colonial expansion?

EARLY MODERN TIMES

The modern world can be said to have begun with the Renaissance. Some of the accomplishments of this era are represented by pictures on this and the following pages. One of the glories of the Renaissance was its great art (see pages 231–232). Above is a section of the great painting "The Adoration of the Magi," by Sandro Botticelli, an Italian who lived from 1444 to 1510. He represents the early Renaissance, which overlaps in time the end of the Middle Ages. (National Gallery of Art, Washington, D.C.)

Facing page: At the top, "Courtyard in Delft," by Pieter de Hooch, a Dutch artist of the seventeenth century. Note the true-to-life details of people and clothing. (National Gallery of Art.) The lower picture by a great Flemish artist, Peter Breughel (1525-1569). "Winter in Flanders" is crowded with details of daily life. (Musée de Beaux Arts Bruxelles, Belgium.)

Above: "The Adoration of the Shepherds" by the great Venetian artist Giorgione (1478-1510). Note the rich detail and the masterful perspective in this and other Renaissance paintings. (National Gallery of Art, Washington, D.C.)

Right: Edward VI of England, by one of the master portrait painters of the northern Renaissance, Hans Holbein the Younger. Holbein was a German who lived from 1497 to 1543. (National Gallery of Art.)

Cities grew to new importance in the early modern world. One of the leaders in Italy and the entire Western World was Venice. Above is a modern view of the Doge's Palace, with the Grand Canal in the foreground.

From the twelfth to the fifteenth centuries the Venetians were leading merchants and fighters in the Mediterranean. Above is a Venetian galley, a long narrow ship designed for rowing and sailing. This model is of a sixteenth century galley, but it shows the appearance of ships used in earlier periods.

Right: St. Peter's Church in Rome. "The eternal city" has for many centuries played a central role in world history.

The bell tower and cathedral in Florence, a great Italian city and a center of Renaissance culture. The poet Dante and the painter and sculptor, Leonardo da Vinci, were Florentines.

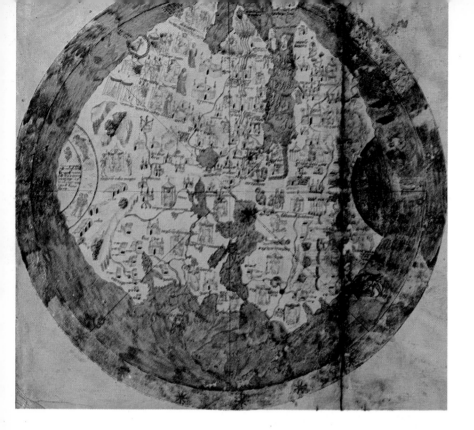

Early modern times encompassed a great age of exploration, when Europeans set out to discover the rest of the world (see pages 232–236). Above is a map of the world drawn in the late Middle Ages, showing how little some Europeans knew of geography when the Renaissance was beginning.

In the sixteenth century, Spanish explorers pushed into Central and South America. In Mexico Cortez found the great Aztec civilization (see page 258). Below are ruins of Aztec temples at Oaxaca.

From Mexico Spanish explorers moved northward into regions that are now parts of the United States, building numerous mission churches. This is San Luis Rey, near San Diego.

bove: A replica of the Mayflower, which carried English ttlers to America in 1620. (Courtesy of Plimoth antation.) By the seventeenth century, the English had tdistanced the Spaniards in empire building.

to recent times the English have kept alive some customs om earlier days. At right is a Beefeater (a guard) at the wer of London. This uniform was worn in the time of e Tudors (see page 245) and is still worn today.

The seventeenth century produced many fine artists. Sir Anthony Van Dyck (1599–1641) was born in Flanders but is best known for portraits he painted in England. At right is his "King Charles I" (see page 302). (Louvre, Paris.)

Below: "The Surrender of Breda," by the great Spanish artist Velásquez (1599–1660). This painting shows a Spanish victory in their wars with the Dutch (see page 266). The Dutch commander is offering the keys to the city of Breda to the Spanish Marquis de Spinola. (Prado Museum, Madrid.)

Chapter 21 Spain and France Dominate Europe

TOWARD THE END of the Middle Ages, Spain, Portugal, France, and England began to develop into national states. They continued to do so during the sixteenth, seventeenth, and eighteenth centuries. Each developed a strong government. In each the people came to feel that they belonged together, sharing a common history and common problems. They felt a sense of patriotism and loyalty to their country. We call such a group of people a nation.

Spain in the sixteenth century

At the beginning of the sixteenth century Spain was the most powerful nation in Europe. The reigns of two very able kings, Charles I (1516–1556) and Philip II (1556–1598), covered almost the entire century. When Charles I became King of Spain, he also became ruler of the Netherlands, the Kingdom of Naples and Sicily in Italy, the Balearic Islands and Sardinia, the province of Franche-Comté between France and Switzerland, and the vast Spanish Empire in the Americas. Three years later he was elected Emperor of the Holy Roman Empire, receiving the title Emperor Charles V. Charles V ruled Austria and had some claims to rule other German states as well.

● Problems facing Charles V

But titles and power bring with them many problems and heavy responsibilities. Charles V had certain personal problems. He was Dutch, or Flemish, by birth, and he spoke Dutch. However, as King of Spain he must be a Spaniard, and as Emperor of the Holy Roman Empire he must be a German.

The responsibilities of empire were far greater than the personal problems. As King of Spain he had to defend Spain's territories in North Africa, Italy, the islands of the Mediterranean, and the Americas. As Emperor of the Holy Roman Empire he was responsible for the defense of central Europe and the Mediterranean against the invading Turks. He was also responsible for the defense of the Christian religion in Germany. As ruler of the vast Hapsburg lands, he had to contend with fear and jealousy from other European countries, especially France.

When Charles V was elected emperor, he faced an awe-inspiring situation. The people of Spain had revolted because they did not want him as emperor, and also because he appointed men from the Netherlands to government positions in Spain. France had declared war on the Holy Roman Empire. The Turks had driven deep into central Europe; their ships were raiding the entire Mediterranean. Dutch and English ships and pirates were preying on the Spanish treasure ships from America. The Lutheran revolt had broken out in Germany, and he had to fight the Protestant princes there. All these wars had to be waged at the same time.

The wars of Charles V

Spain had some advantages in the wars. The Spanish army was then the strongest and best organized in Europe. The Spanish fleet was strong. Great amounts of gold and silver poured into Spain from America. It was possible to buy supplies and weapons, and hire soldiers to fight. However, because of the weaknesses in the empire that were noted in Chapter 20 (pages 259–260), Spain needed all her advantages. She was not able to win complete, clear-cut, victories.

Although the results of Charles V's wars may seem rather meager when measured against more than thirty years of fighting, some of them were important. The emperor was able to prevent France from taking the Duchy of Milan, but he had to give the French the important bishoprics of Metz, Verdun, and Toul. This gain strengthened France's position against the Holy Roman

Empire, as you will see on the map on this page. Charles was able to stop Turkish penetration of central Europe by driving the Turks back from Vienna. However, he had to agree to Turkish rule of the Balkans and half of Hungary. In Germany the emperor made real efforts to bring the Lutherans and the Roman Catholics into agreement. Because of the very complicated political and religious problems that existed in Germany at the time, he was unsuccessful, and the religious war broke out.

Before the German war ended with the Peace of Augsburg, 1555 (see page 243), Emperor Charles V decided to give up his throne. In 1555 he divided his vast territory. His son Philip received Spain and her possessions. His brother Ferdinand became Emperor of the Holy Roman Empire. In 1556 Charles retired to a monastery in Spain. He lived there quietly for two years; then the retired emperor died.

EUROPE AT THE TIME OF
CHARLES V   1519-1556

—— Boundaries of House of Hapsburg

Philip II of Spain (1556–1598)

Although Philip II of Spain was not Emperor of the Holy Roman Empire, he was head of a mighty state. Spain held the Netherlands, Franche-Comté in eastern France, both northern and southern Italy, North Africa, the empire of the Americas, and the Philippine Islands. Philip's close relationship to the Holy Roman Emperor often linked Spain and the Holy Roman Empire in action.

Philip II was born and educated in Spain and he proudly considered himself a Spaniard. He wanted Spain to be the leading power in Europe and the world, and he worked to make her strong at home so that she might be strong abroad. Philip had two great domestic problems: the first was the weakness of the central government, the second problem involved suspicions of heresy in religion.

Charles V had never found time to unify and centralize the Spanish government. Each of the many provinces had a separate administration; they were united only in a common allegiance to the king. Philip replaced these separate administrations with a centralized government responsible only to the king, and Spain became an absolute monarchy. The change brought opposition and even revolts in the provinces.

Philip's domestic religious problem concerned the Moors and Jews. Many people in each group had been converted to Christianity after Ferdinand and Isabella brought the Inquisition into Spain. However, Philip II suspected them of secretly practicing their former religion. He ordered the Inquisition to redouble its efforts to find and stamp out heresy. Many of those who could do so left the country, but many Moors, who considered themselves native to Spain, revolted against the savage persecution. This religious revolt, added to the political revolts in the provinces, put a heavy strain on the king's government.

With ships like this, the "Elizabethan sea dogs" of England attacked the ships of Spain. This picture shows the Golden Hind, flagship of Francis Drake. From one Spanish treasure ship that he captured in the Pacific, Drake took "thirteen chests full of royals of plate (silver coins), four score pound weight of gold, and six and twentie tunne of silver."

Spain's domestic rebellions and foreign wars were a great drain on the treasury. Even the treasure from America was not enough to pay the costs. The Spanish government levied heavy taxes, including a 10 per cent sales tax. It had a bad effect on Spanish trade and on home industries.

● Foreign problems and policies

In 1580 the throne of Portugal became vacant. Philip II of Spain claimed it, and the Portuguese were too weak to resist. The Portuguese colonies in Asia, Africa, and South America were added to the Spanish Empire, while Portugal itself became a province of the Spanish kingdom. The seizure of Portugal brought Spain more problems and expense than strength. The Portuguese people were never reconciled to the union. Spain also now had to defend the Portuguese colonies and their trade. Attacks by English, French, Dutch, and pirate ships made this a difficult task. After sixty years of Spanish rule, the Portuguese drove the invaders out of Portugal itself and again became independent.

SPAIN-NETHERLANDS-1648

Spanish Netherlands   United Netherlands

Philip II's difficulties abroad came from two main sources: the rise of national feelings and the increase of Protestantism. In two places, the Netherlands and England, he met the two things combined. In each place he suffered a crushing defeat.

Philip's position in the Netherlands was a curious reversal of that of his father. Charles V, born and raised in Flanders and speaking Dutch, was a foreigner to the Spanish. However, he received loyal support from the Netherlands throughout his reign. Philip, Spanish-born and Spanish-speaking, was a foreigner to his Netherlands subjects.

There were seventeen provinces in the Netherlands. They had no central administration, and a long tradition of local self-rule. The seven northern provinces (Holland) had accepted the Calvinist Reformed Church. This religious split of course caused trouble. Also, there was trouble over the heavy taxes which Spain levied to pay the costs of wars. The Dutch thought the taxes were aimed to kill their trade and industry.

Philip II tried to solve the problems of government and religion at the same time. In order to centralize the administration, he took away the rights of local self-government. He filled the high offices with Spaniards. These officers did not speak the language, and they neither knew nor cared for the local customs. They tried to rule the Netherlands as a Spanish colony, and the people resented them bitterly. Philip tried to stamp out Protestantism by bringing in the Inquisition from Spain. The two Spanish policies served to unite the people of Holland, almost to a man, against Spanish rule. The Spanish ruler, the Duke of Alva, used very harsh measures to try to stamp out this Dutch opposition.

● *The Dutch win freedom*

William, Prince of Orange, now became leader of the Dutch rebellion. In 1581 the seven Protestant provinces formed a league called the Union of Utrecht. They declared that they no longer owed allegiance to Spain. The Union of Utrecht is often called the Dutch Declaration of Independence. It marked the beginning of a truly national struggle, Dutch against Spanish.

The Dutch were weak on land. Several times they saved themselves from complete defeat only by cutting the dikes and letting in the sea to flood parts of their low country. On the sea the story was different. Privately owned ships, called privateers, backed by the Dutch government, went out to attack Spanish and Portuguese commerce. They raided the colonies and even the coast of Spain itself. They took over the Portuguese trading posts in the Indies.

The seemingly uneven war dragged on for many years, long after the death of Philip II. All the power of Spain was not enough to overcome the unconquerable Dutch. Holland played a part against Spain and the Hapsburg emperors during the Thirty Years' War. At last, in 1648, by the Treaty of Westphalia Spain was forced to yield. The treaty recognized the independence of the United Netherlands. The southern provinces—Catholic,

French-speaking, and industrial—remained for a time under the rule of Spain.

● *Trouble with England*

Religion and nationalism both played a part in Philip II's troubles with England. Philip was married to Mary, Queen of England (see page 246). In her reign Protestants were persecuted. The English blamed Philip and came to hate him. When Elizabeth I became queen, she set up the Church of England. This represented a swing toward Protestantism. Philip, a staunch Roman Catholic, was hostile to Elizabeth.

During Elizabeth's reign English adventurers began to try to break into the Spanish and Portuguese trade monopolies: Men like John Hawkins and Francis Drake began by seizing slaves from the Portuguese in Africa and selling them to the Spanish in America. Later they turned to attacking Spanish treasure ships. When Philip II's ambassadors protested against this piracy to Queen Elizabeth, she claimed she was helpless to control it. Secretly she supported the "sea dogs," as they were called, and shared in their profits.

Philip II decided to invade England to end this piracy and wipe out English heresy. In 1588 he sent a fleet of 130 ships, which he called the Invincible Armada. The English gathered all their ships to meet the threat, and received some help from the Dutch. The English ships were smaller but easier to handle. Their guns fired faster and had longer range. They damaged and sank a number of the great Spanish galleons. The Spanish ran low on ammunition and tried to escape. But luck was against them. A terrific storm added to the destruction the English ships had made, and only half of the Spanish ships returned to Spain. The defeat of the Armada in 1588 marked the beginning of the decline of Spanish sea power. In the later years of Philip II's life, Spain began to lose her place as a great power.

Henry IV starts France on the road to greatness

Spain dominated Europe during the sixteenth century, but the seventeenth century saw France become the most powerful state on the continent of Europe. France had some

The battle between the "Invincible Armada" of Spain and the English and Dutch fleets. The Spanish fleet is shown in a crescent-shaped formation, sailing up the English Channel.

real advantages in a struggle for European power. Facing on both the Atlantic Ocean and the Mediterranean Sea, its location was strategically strong. It had good resources for agriculture, commerce, and industry. Finally, France had a number of really great leaders. They strengthened France by dealing with two problems: (1) the religious wars between the Catholics and the Huguenots (Calvinists); (2) the power still held by the feudal nobles, which weakened the king's authority.

Henry IV came to the throne in 1589 and ruled for twenty-one years. He had been the leader of the Protestant Huguenots, but he realized that a Huguenot could not unite France. He wanted a strong, united, and peaceful kingdom. Therefore, he became a Roman Catholic, with the remark "Paris is well worth a Mass."

● The Edict of Nantes

In order to end the religious wars Henry IV issued the Edict of Nantes in 1598. It was an important edict—important both in the history of France and also in the history of religious toleration in the world. The Edict gave the Huguenots freedom of worship and equal political rights with the Catholics. It nobly asked all people to forget the past and look forward to the future. However, the Edict contained certain provisions which caused trouble in the future. Huguenots were permitted to have military fortifications and the privilege of self-government in 100 cities. All in all, however, the Edict ranks as a noble step forward toward the ideal that every man may worship as he pleases, with no legal penalties or restrictions.

Henry forced the nobles to respect his orders. He curbed their powers and reduced their privileges.

● Prosperity and peace

The great king wanted France to be prosperous. He said he wanted to "put a chicken in the pot" of every family for Sunday dinner. To do this meant that the run-down trade and industry had to be built up, the corrupt administration of the government had to be cleaned up, and the empty treasury had to be filled. Henry showed wisdom, toleration, and greatness in choosing the minister to carry out the necessary domestic reforms. The Duke of Sully was a Huguenot; therefore, he was opposed by the Catholics. However, Sully was one of the ablest men in France. The king supported him and his policies against all objections.

Sully first reformed some abuses in levying taxes and made the collection more efficient. Within a few years the treasury showed an annual surplus. He used this money to make the country more prosperous. Transportation by road, river, and canal was improved. Commerce and agriculture were helped. New industries were set up with the aid of government grants of money. Among these was the silk industry for which France was to become famous. Sully and the other ministers were strong believers in colonies. It was during Henry IV's reign that France set up the colony of Quebec in America.

The policies and works of Henry IV and his ministers brought France peace and much prosperity. The king was justly popular with most of the French people, but he still had many opponents. In 1610 a religious fanatic assassinated him.

● France declines under Marie de Medici

Louis XIII, son and successor to the great king, was only eight years old when his father was killed. His mother, Marie de Medici, became regent, that is, temporary ruler until the king became of age. She had great ambitions but lacked ability to carry them out. She did not have her husband's tolerance in religion. An ardent Catholic, she would allow no Huguenots to serve her. The able Sully lost his position. The administration of the government again became corrupt, and the nobles asserted their independence and power. The prosperity of the country declined, and the treasury again was empty.

Louis XIII and Richelieu

At the age of sixteen Louis XIII took control of the government for himself. Marie de Medici was forced into the background, and the poor councilors whose advice she had followed were banished or executed. Louis was not a strong ruler, nor did he ever develop great strength. He was interested in many things other than the art of statesmanship. He had only one quality in common with his gifted father, but this was a rare quality: he showed the ability to select good men to rule for him, and he supported them against all opposition.

Louis XIII chose as his chief minister Cardinal Richelieu, who ruled France and influenced the history of Europe from 1624 to 1642. Richelieu had started out on a military career and then had turned to the Church. His greatest interest lay in politics, diplomacy, and statesmanship. He proved to be one of the truly great statesmen of French history.

● Richelieu increases the king's power

The aims of Richelieu's policy were as simple to state as they were difficult to perform. He wanted to make the king supreme in France and France supreme in Europe. To accomplish the first aim he had to destroy the power of the nobles and to take away the political independence of the Huguenots. He also had to strengthen France economically by reviving Sully's policy of encouraging trade and industry and building a colonial empire. To make France supreme in Europe he had to reduce the power of the Hapsburgs in Spain and the Holy Roman Empire.

Richelieu's first task in France was to take away the political independence of the Huguenots. He believed that the provisions of the Edict of Nantes that allowed the Hugue-

Cardinal Richelieu, chief minister of Louis XIII of France, and one of the most powerful statesmen of Europe.

nots to govern a hundred fortified cities were politically dangerous. These cities created a state within a state, and made strongly centralized government impossible.

Fearing what might happen to them, the Huguenots sought and received a promise of help from England. Richelieu at once moved against them and besieged the strong Huguenot seaport city of La Rochelle. To prevent help from coming from England, he built a breakwater entirely across the harbor so that no ship could enter. After a stubborn resistance the Huguenots had to surrender the city. A like fate befell other fortified towns, and the Huguenots asked for peace. Richelieu took from them their independent political rights, but he left them the rights to worship freely, to hold public office, and to be admitted to schools and colleges.

The cardinal next turned to the problem of the nobles. This was even more difficult than that of the Huguenots, but Richelieu was not a man to be frightened. He moved first to crush the military power of the nobles. He ordered that all fortified castles not necessary to the defense of France be torn down.

The nobles rebelled, and he suppressed them without mercy. He set up an elaborate system of spies to watch the nobles in all their undertakings. As each plot was uncovered, he moved against the plotters. Castles were destroyed and some nobles executed as an example to others.

The next step was to reduce the nobles' political power. As governors of provinces Richelieu appointed men who favored strong monarchy, and he sent out special local administrators called *intendants*. For these jobs he chose men of the middle class. Such men of course welcomed the chance to reduce the authority of the nobles. The intendants were given strong military, political, and administrative powers. They were responsible directly to the king, who appointed and could remove them. Within a short time the intendants controlled local government completely. Thus the power of the nobles was reduced and that of the king strengthened.

● *Richelieu's foreign policy*

Richelieu's foreign policy was as determined and coldly calculated as was his policy at home. He did not allow his position as a Catholic cardinal to interfere with his main aim of strengthening France at the expense of the Hapsburgs. During the Thirty Years' War he gave France's support to Lutheran Sweden against the Catholic Hapsburgs. He did everything possible to prolong the war without involving France too deeply in it. In this way the other contestants were weak when the war ended, thus allowing France to become the strongest power in Europe.

The reign of Louis XIV

Cardinal Richelieu did not live to see the outcome of his efforts. He died six years before the end of the Thirty Years' War, and Louis XIII died a year later. Again France was left with a child as a king, for Louis XIV was a mere boy. However, France was again ruled by a great minister, once more a cardinal of the Church.

Cardinal Mazarin was an Italian by birth but French by adoption. He had been trained by Richelieu to succeed him as first minister and head of state under the new king. Mazarin proved to be an able successor. In 1648 he successfully promoted the interests of France at the Treaty of Westphalia, which ended the Thirty Years' War. He carried on the war against Spain for another eleven years and made gains for France in the Treaty of the Pyrenees (1659) that ended the war. Mazarin suppressed the last attempt of the nobles to regain their position, a rebellion in 1648. When he died in 1661, the monarchy was supreme in France, and the country was on the way to being supreme in Europe.

After the death of Mazarin, Louis XIV took the throne himself and proved to be one of the most outstanding rulers of all French history. He was determined to share his power with no one. He believed that he was God's representative on earth and therefore responsible to no one but God. We call such a ruler a king by Divine Right. Louis XIV's attitude toward government is shown by a remark sometimes credited to him, "*L'état, c'est moi*" ("I am the State").

● *Louis XIV and Colbert*

Louis XIV took himself and his work most seriously. He really worked at the job of being a king. To help him, he chose the ablest men he could find in France—men who made France great and the reign of Louis XIV glorious. Louis depended on the advice of these ministers, but the final decisions were always his alone. Two of his advisers were outstanding: Jean Baptiste Colbert was expert in the field of finance, economic development, and scientific and cultural advancement. François Louvois was expert in the field of military affairs and leadership.

Colbert, a member of the middle class, followed the ideas of Sully in promoting the economic development of France. A strong believer in mercantilism, Colbert tried to build up French industry at home and French trade abroad. Private companies were given government grants of money to build new industries or strengthen existing ones. High tariffs were placed on all foreign goods imported into France. Roads and canals were built so that goods might move easily and cheaply. Forests were preserved, and those that had been destroyed or used up were replanted. The tax system was improved so that there was enough money to finance all the improvements at home, maintain a large army, and support colonial enterprises. French companies were set up with government support to establish colonies and carry on trade in the East Indies, the West Indies, and the Near East.

It was in the field of artistic, scientific, and literary development that Louis XIV best deserved his title, "the Sun King." He was determined to make France the cultural center of Europe, so that it would be an example to be imitated by all others. He gathered about him the finest artists, writers, and musicians of France, and invited outstanding men from other countries. Any man who showed talent was given a government pension so that he could devote all his time to his art.

● Versailles

As a fitting symbol for the greatness of France and the glory of its culture, Louis XIV ordered the building of a great palace at Versailles, a few miles outside of Paris. Here were combined the finest works of French architects, painters, and sculptors. With its many fountains, its elaborate gardens, its lavish paintings, and its Hall of Mirrors, Versailles became the fitting home of the Sun King and his enormous court. It was the center of French government and the symbol to all Europe of the greatness of France.

Versailles did indeed become the ideal of European royalty. Rulers great and small tried to imitate it. A traveler in Europe will be interested and amused to see how the architecture of Versailles is copied in country after country, often with very bad results.

Versailles, the large and elaborate palace built by Louis XIV. This building has been the scene of many historic events—for example, the signing of the treaty at the end of World War I.

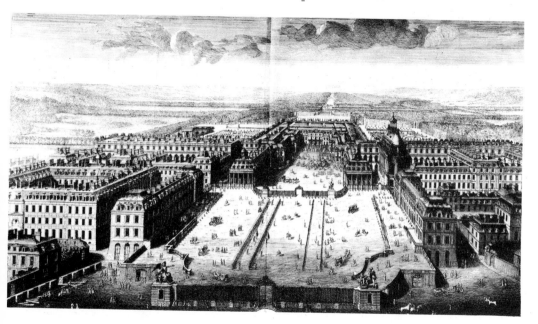

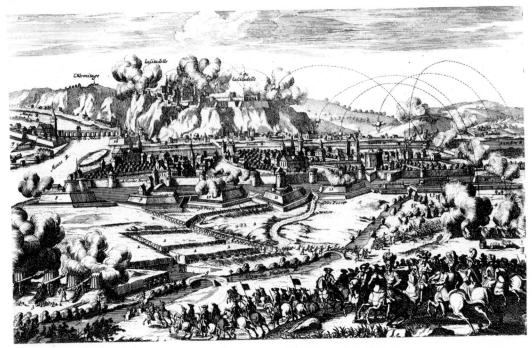

French dress, manners, style of living, and even cooking were adopted in every country by royalty and nobility. The French language became the court speech of the nobility and the language of diplomacy in all Europe.

●Louis XIV and Louvois

The darker side of the reign of Louis XIV was the work of Louvois, the military genius. Under his direction the French navy was built up and the army completely reorganized. No such army had ever been seen in Europe. Officers and men were highly trained and were equipped with standard uniforms and improved weapons. Discipline was very harsh. Today we call a person who maintains strict discipline a *martinet*. The word comes from the name of General Martinet, who was in charge of discipline. Military fortification, engineering, and siege operations were perfected by Marshal Sebastien de Vauban.

Having a large and fine army often creates a desire to use it. This was only too true of Louis XIV. It seemed almost as if his reign were a race between Colbert and Louvois.

The siege of Namur, during one of the wars fought by Louis XIV. This Dutch city was captured by the French, and the defenses were strengthened by Vauban, the French expert on fortification and siegecraft. In spite of this, the Dutch recaptured the city. The old print reproduced here shows guns (left) and mortars (right) bombarding the city. In the center, troops move up through trenches to attack the walls.

Colbert raced to build up the economy and prosperity of the country as fast as Louvois destroyed it with his war follies. During the first half of the period Colbert had more influence with the monarch, and France grew strong and prosperous. In the second half the story is sad and the picture is dark.

Louis XIV seemed to become dizzy with grandeur and power and with limitless ambitions for territorial gains. He became convinced that the security of France depended on getting what he called "natural frontiers," boundaries which nature made easy to defend. The Mediterranean Sea, the Atlantic Ocean, and the English Channel protected

272

France on the south, west, and northwest. Elsewhere Louis wanted to reach the Pyrenees, the Alps, and the Rhine River. Here his ambition came into conflict with Spain, Holland, and the Holy Roman Empire, each of which controlled some part of the desired territory.

● Military campaigns

To gain his ends Louis XIV fought four wars over a period of almost fifty years. France's power and ambitions brought into operation the diplomatic principle known as the Balance of Power. France could easily have defeated each opponent singly. Each single victory would have gained some territory France wanted and have made it that much harder for the next country to resist. The other countries of Europe, even those whose lands were not threatened, were alarmed at this prospect. To balance this great power of France, other countries united to prevent France from becoming so strong as to dominate Europe. At various times Holland, England, Sweden, Spain, Denmark, Austria, Brandenburg, and other German states were allied against the menace of France.

Between the second and third wars Louis XIV made an error which seriously weakened France. Bad advice persuaded him that the Huguenots were disloyal and a danger to France. In 1685 he revoked (canceled) the Edict of Nantes, which gave the Huguenots religious freedom. Over 100,000 French Protestants chose to leave France rather than give up their faith. Many of them were excellent craftsmen, tradesmen, and leaders of industry. They went to Holland, England, Germany, Switzerland, and even to the English colonies in America. Their skills were lost to France, and marked a gain for France's competitors abroad.

By the end of the third war many of the greatest French military leaders were dead. The large sums which Colbert's policies had brought into the treasury were gone. Taxes were heavy, and trade and industry suffered. The country was no longer prosperous.

Louis XIV's last war came about because of his attempt to unite the kingdoms of France and Spain (whose throne was vacant) under the rule of his grandson. If he had been willing to agree that the two thrones would not be joined, Louis could probably have had his grandson recognized as King of Spain. Louis insisted on trying to unite the thrones, and most of the other nations of Europe formed an alliance against him. The resulting War of the Spanish Succession was fought throughout Europe, on the seas, and in America. French armies and fleets were defeated everywhere, and Louis was forced to agree to a peace.

● The Treaty of Utrecht

The Treaty of Utrecht, 1713, ended the War of the Spanish Succession. It was important in the history of both Europe and America. Philip V, of the French Bourbon family, was recognized as King of Spain, but the treaty provided that the French and Spanish crowns were never to be united. This could have been had without a war. England, which had become France's great enemy, made large gains. From France England got Hudson Bay, Newfoundland, and Nova Scotia in America. From Spain England gained Gibraltar, a monopoly of the slave trade to America, the right to send one shipload of goods annually to the Spanish colonies, and a favorable tariff at the port of Cadiz.

The Austrian Hapsburgs also claimed their reward. They were given the Spanish Netherlands (Belgium), which then became known as the Austrian Netherlands. The Hapsburgs also received Sardinia, Naples, and Milan in Italy.

Two minor provisions of the Treaty of Utrecht had great importance for the future. The Hohenzollern Elector of Brandenburg was recognized as King of Prussia. This was the beginning of the German Hohenzollerns as a royal family. It was under Prussian, Hohenzollern leadership that all the little states of Germany were finally united into one nation. By another treaty provision the Duke of Savoy was to receive the title of King.

And what were the results of the war to the nation that started it? France gained the doubtful glory of seeing a Frenchman on the throne of Spain, which she might have had without fighting. She lost important colonial possessions in America. Economically the country was ruined. Trade and industry suffered greatly; the royal treasury was empty and heavily in debt. Taxes were crushing. The foundation had been laid for the serious economic conditions and bankruptcy which,

in about seventy-five years, were major causes of the outbreak of the French Revolution and the end of monarchy in France.

Louis XIV had lived too long and ventured too rashly. His nation's welfare and all the remarkable progress of his early years had been sacrificed to his boundless ambitions. His son, whom he had carefully trained to succeed him, had died before him. Louis had centered all powers in the king. Now these powers were to be passed on to a great-grandson who was young, weak, and incompetent.

With the powers the new king inherited a bankrupt country which had earned the fear and enmity of all Europe. It is small wonder that when Louis XIV died in 1715, the French people rejoiced.

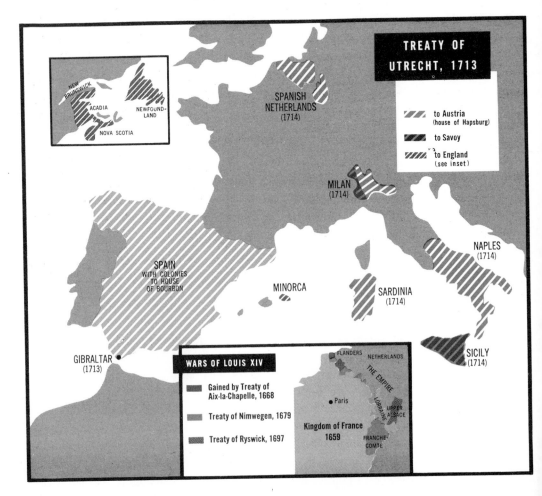

TREATY OF UTRECHT, 1713

to Austria (house of Hapsburg)
to Savoy
to England (see inset)

NEW BRUNSWICK
ACADIA
NEWFOUNDLAND
NOVA SCOTIA

SPANISH NETHERLANDS (1714)

MILAN (1714)

NAPLES (1714)

SPAIN WITH COLONIES TO HOUSE OF BOURBON

MINORCA

SARDINIA (1714)

SICILY (1714)

GIBRALTAR (1713)

WARS OF LOUIS XIV

Gained by Treaty of Aix-la-Chapelle, 1668
Treaty of Nimwegen, 1679
Treaty of Ryswick, 1697

FLANDERS NETHERLANDS
THE EMPIRE
Paris
LORRAINE UPPER ALSACE
Kingdom of France 1659
FRANCHE COMTE

Review of Chapter 21

People, places, and things

Identify: Charles V, Henry IV, Philip II, "the Sun King," William of Orange, John Hawkins, Francis Drake, Sully, Richelieu, Mazarin, Colbert, Louvois, Vauban, Huguenots, Hohenzollerns.

Locate: The Spanish Empire under Charles V, the Holy Roman Empire, the Netherlands, Metz, Verdun, Toul, Newfoundland, Nova Scotia, Gibraltar, Hungary, Vienna, Franche-Comté.

Events in review

1. Explain the term *nation*. Name four countries which, by the end of the Middle Ages, had begun to develop into modern national states.
2. What problems faced Emperor Charles V? Why did he have to fight several wars? Was he successful in his policies?
3. Philip II suffered defeats because of two great forces, nationalism and Protestantism. Show how each caused trouble for Philip in Holland.
4. Why is the defeat of the Spanish Armada (1588) an important event in world history?
5. Who said that he wanted "to put a chicken in the pot" of every family for Sunday dinner? How did he hope to make his nation prosperous?
6. What was the significance of the Edict of Nantes? Who later revoked this Edict?
7. What were the aims of Richelieu's policy? To what extent did he succeed?
8. What did Louis XIV mean when he said, "I am the state"?
9. What steps did Louis XIV take to make his court the cultural center of Europe?
10. Did France gain or lose by the War of the Spanish Succession? Explain.

Problems and projects

1. Discuss the failures of Philip II of Spain. Was he a weak ruler, or was he simply faced with forces that were too strong for Spain to overcome?
2. The success of a reign may depend upon the king's choice of advisers. Discuss, making reference to Sully, Richelieu, Mazarin, Colbert, and Louvois.
3. The Dutch are often admired for their bravery and determination. Give examples, from seventeenth and eighteenth century history, of these qualities. Can you find evidence of these qualities in the history of Holland since 1940?
4. Compare the reigns of Elizabeth I of England and Louis XIV of France. Use the following headings: (a) power of the ruler, (b) success in foreign policy, (c) cultural developments.
5. Write an essay (or prepare a dramatic sketch) on a day at Versailles during the reign of "the Sun King," Louis XIV.
6. Prepare the script for a radio or TV news broadcast announcing the approach of the Spanish Armada to England. Then narrate the battle.
7. Draw a map to show the "natural frontiers" Louis XIV wanted to secure for France.

Chapter 22

The Emergence of Russia and Prussia

FOR 250 years during the later Middle Ages Russia was a section of the great Mongol or Tartar Empire built up by Genghis Khan and Kublai Khan. The Tartars ruled the Russians, collected tribute, and influenced their culture in various ways. In 1480 the small and struggling Duchy of Moscow managed to free itself from the Tartars. Then it began a slow expansion, much like that of the Capetians in France, by conquests, marriages, and alliances.

Besides this Asiatic influence on her culture, several other factors helped to separate Russia from western Europe. Western civilization had come to her from the south—from Constantinople and the Byzantine Empire. Her religion was Greek Orthodox instead of Roman Catholic or Protestant.

Geography did much to isolate. Russia from the West. The country was almost entirely landlocked in an age when travel went mostly by sea. Russia was blocked from the Baltic Sea by Sweden and Poland, both stronger kingdoms. To the south the Ottoman Turks held the Crimean peninsula and the north shore of the Black Sea as well as Constantinople and the narrow stretches of water that separate Europe from Asia. On the north Russia had the port of Archangel on the Arctic Ocean, but it was far from Moscow and other cities, and was solidly frozen much of the year.

The wide plains of Poland and eastern Europe offered a fine chance for the invasion of Russia from the west, for they were hard to defend. But these vast expanses of land gave little opportunity for commercial contacts. Russia has many fine rivers, but they stubbornly run in the wrong directions. They flow into seas that lead nowhere, like the Caspian, or into seas that were closed to her, like the Black Sea. Others run north into the Arctic, and so are no help to overseas trade.

In 1613, after a period of social and political unrest, the Romanov dynasty gained the throne of Russia. The first three Romanovs did nothing important. Then, in 1694, there came to the throne a man who was to have great influence on Russia and Europe.

Peter the Great rules Russia

Peter I, or Peter the Great, was a remarkable man. He was crude and coarse by nature, and mercilessly cruel to opponents. But he was a born leader, a statesman, a man of great vision and imagination, and of strong convictions. He was sincere and honest, completely unselfish, and had the energy of a dynamo. Peter's intelligence told him that Russia's future lay in the west in contacts with European nations. He began a foreign policy that has continued in force in Russia ever since, even up to the present: the attempt to get warm water seaports not dominated by other nations.

At first Peter tried to get control of the Sea of Azov in the south from the Turks.

The war was only partly successful. Peter then came to realize that in order to defeat the Turks he needed two things: help from western Europe, and a strong Russia.

In 1697 a Russian mission was sent to Europe to negotiate an alliance against the Turks. In disguise, Peter the Great went along, for he wanted much more than an alliance. He was determined that Russia should be westernized, and he wanted to decide for himself which of the European arts, sciences, and institutions were best suited for his purposes. Peter and his mission visited England, Holland, Prussia, Austria, and Italy. He met scientists, artisans, craftsmen, and leaders in other fields. He lured many of them to go to Russia to work. In Holland he worked as a carpenter in a shipyard so that he could learn how ships were built. He visited schools, factories, hospitals, and arsenals to learn how things were done.

● Reforms by Peter the Great

Historians have written a great deal about some of Peter's minor reforms. He insisted that women should leave their isolated life and take part socially in the life of the community. He himself taught his courtiers to dance and to smoke tobacco. He forced the nobles to wear European style clothing; he himself cut off their long beards when they refused to do so. But these were minor things. Much more important were the changes he made in Russian industry, commerce, and government. What was even more significant, he compelled the nation to think of its future in terms of modern statesmanship—of its place in the Western World.

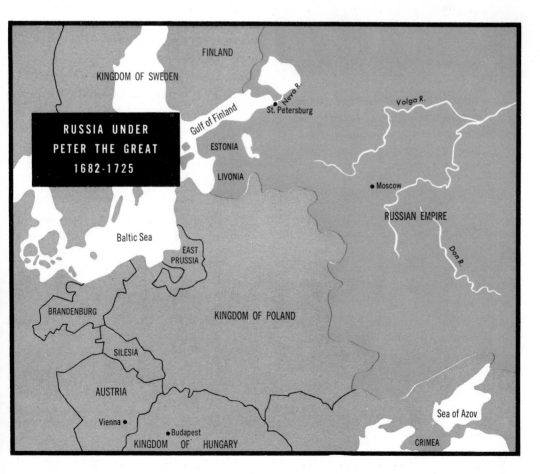

RUSSIA UNDER
PETER THE GREAT
1682-1725

These elaborate costumes were worn at the Russian court before Peter the Great introduced western European styles. This picture is from a Russian movie, Peter I.

Peter established a shipbuilding industry and began at once to build up a navy. Following French ideas he reorganized his army and equipped it with the best European weapons. He encouraged the development of trade with the West as well as with the Orient, and made great efforts to promote manufacturing.

In government Peter followed the ideas of Louis XIV of France. The Russian czar (or tsar, from *Caesar*) became an absolute monarch. He had complete control of a very highly centralized administration. The nobles were entirely subordinated to the throne. The Church became an agency and branch of the government under control of the czar.

As in France, the central government controlled local governments completely.

Peter considered the old hereditary nobility too set in their old ways to follow his reforms. By granting titles he created a new nobility of service. The title and the privileges granted depended not on birth but on the amount of service the man gave the state. To this new nobility he granted large estates, with great numbers of serfs like those of medieval Europe.

The Russian czar had failed to get European allies against the Turks, and another war started. In this second war the Turks regained their losses from the first. Peter therefore turned toward the Baltic, where Sweden blocked Russia from the sea. Here he found better fortune. In a war that lasted more than twenty years Russia gained the desired territory and ended the short span of Sweden as a great power.

Russia's new territory was at the north end of the Baltic, where the Neva River flows into the Gulf of Finland. Peter decided to build a "window to Europe," a completely new city which should be his capital. There, with terrific hardships, a city was built. It was first named St. Petersburg. (Later, after the revolution of 1917, when the Romanov rule ended, it was renamed Leningrad.) The capital was moved there from Moscow. St. Petersburg became the symbol of the new Russian policy of facing toward western Europe.

Catherine the Great

Russia still wanted to control the Black Sea and to expand westward across the Polish plains. This further expansion was carried out by a remarkable woman, Catherine II (the Great), Empress of Russia. Catherine was a princess of a petty German state who married the heir to the Russian throne. When her husband came to the throne, he died very mysteriously after ruling a short time. Catherine took over the throne of Russia and ruled for thirty-four years.

Catherine II did not earn her title "the Great" from her domestic policy. She expanded serfdom and made the lot of the peasants much worse. It is true that she patronized art, science, literature, and the theater. Court life became more Europeanized; the nobility spoke French rather than Russian. However, none of these changes reached the peasants, who lived in deep ignorance and poverty.

In foreign affairs Catherine followed the policies of Peter the Great, moving toward the sea. She fought a successful war with the Turks. Russia gained Azov, the north shore of the Black Sea, and a protectorate over the Crimean peninsula. She became protector of Greek Orthodox churches in Turkey, and gained the right to send ships through the Bosporus and Dardanelles.

● Russia and Poland

In the west Catherine II made great gains by taking advantage of the weakness of Poland. The Kingdom of Poland had much territory, but many weaknesses. The kings were elected, a process which brought both domestic and international troubles. Prussia, Austria, and Russia each plotted to put its favorite on the throne. Rival groups of Polish nobles favored Russian or French influence.

Poland contained strong minority groups of different nationalities and religions. The Polish government showed no wisdom in handling these groups. In western Poland there were large groups of German Lutherans. Ukrainians of the Greek Orthodox religion lived in the east. The Poles were Roman Catholics. They often discriminated against and oppressed the minority groups. At times there were uprisings. The minorities often appealed to Prussia, Austria, and Russia and received help from these nations. It was this foreign intervention that finally erased Poland from the map.

The First Partition of Poland came in 1772. According to a previously made agreement, Russia, Prussia, and Austria each took a slice of Polish territory. The seized land amounted to a fourth of Polish land and a third of the population.

The Polish people were shocked into trying to reform and strengthen the nation. However, before reforms could be carried out there was a Second Partition. In 1793, while Austria was busy elsewhere, Prussia and Russia took a second helping of Polish lands. Rebellions broke out among the Poles, which threatened to spread throughout eastern Europe. To prevent the spread of rebellion, the three powers got together in 1795 and performed a Third Partition. This operation was final and fatal. This time Poland was divided completely; it vanished from the map of Europe until 1919, after the First World War.

The reigns of Peter the Great and Catherine the Great established Russia as both a European and a world power. The Russian Empire now stretched from the Amur River

Peter the Great inspecting the progress of the building of his new capital city, which was named St. Petersburg.

Catherine the Great, Empress of Russia.

in eastern Asia to the shores of the Baltic and Black Seas in Europe. Russia had become a power to be reckoned with.

Austria dominates Germany

After the Thirty Years' War, Austria remained the leading state of Germany. That war was, in general, a war of the little German states and a number of other European states against the power of the Holy Roman Empire and the Hapsburg rulers whose power was centered in Austria. The Treaty of Westphalia, 1648, had weakened Austria by allowing the German states to be more independent of the Holy Roman Emperor. However, Austria maintained her position by territorial gains elsewhere, either by the Treaty of Westphalia or during the following century and a half.

Several among the many German states were important. In southern Germany, Bavaria jealously guarded its land and independence against any extension of Hapsburg power. Several times, in order to safeguard its own interests, Bavaria entered into al-

liances with France, the traditional enemy of Hapsburg Austria. Saxony also acted independently of Austrian leadership. The Prince of Saxony was one of the electors who chose the Holy Roman Emperor. Thus he had an advantage in opposing Hapsburg power.

The ruler of Hanover was also an elector. In 1715 an elector of Hanover became king of England, establishing a new dynasty there. Finally, there was the rapidly rising state of Brandenburg, whose ruler was also an elector.

● *Austria gains territory*

Austria gained considerable territory from the Turks. Emperor Charles V had relieved the Turkish siege of Vienna and had driven the Turks back a little. However, he had been compelled to recognize the Turkish conquest of Hungary and the Balkans. Charles V's successors continued to fight against the Turks. Austria, Poland, Russia, Venice, and the papacy formed a Holy League to carry on the war. The province of Bosnia, now in Yugoslavia, was freed from Turkish rule. Belgrade, capital of Serbia, and Budapest, capital of Hungary, were recovered. By 1700 Austria had gained complete control of Hungary, and the Hapsburg emperor was recognized as king of Hungary.

Austria also made gains in western Europe and in Italy. The Treaty of Utrecht, 1713, which ended the War of the Spanish Succession, favored Austria. The Hapsburgs did not get the Spanish throne, but they were given the Spanish Netherlands (Belgium) and the Duchy of Milan in northern Italy. Austria soon lost the Belgian Netherlands and Sicily, but she kept Milan for 150 years.

In the mid-eighteenth century a woman, Maria Theresa of the house of Hapsburg, became ruler of Austria. Her father, the emperor, had tried to make it safe for her to rule. At great expense he had persuaded European rulers to sign an agreement, called the Pragmatic Sanction, promising not to take her territory.

This Austria which Maria Theresa inherited was a strange state. It had great size, tremendous manpower, and strategic location down through the middle of Europe. However, it was a patchwork or crazy-quilt of territories and peoples. In addition to the ruling group of Germans there were Hungarians, Italians, Belgians, Rumanians, Poles, and various Slavic peoples such as Czechs (Bohemians), Serbs, Croatians, and Slovenes. You may be certain that this motley group of nationalities contained many conflicts of language, interests, religions, and national ambitions.

But there were strong points in the Hapsburg position. As champions of the Roman Catholic Church and defenders against the Turks, they had the strong support of the papacy. They were related by intermarriages to most of the royal families of Europe. In 1740 Maria Theresa could look to these relationships to protect her position and rights. She also had the pledges of the Pragmatic Sanction.

The Hohenzollerns of Brandenburg rise to power

The Hohenzollerns of Brandenburg had not always been rulers of a powerful state. During the Middle Ages they had only a little territory on the borders of Switzerland. This they ruled from a feudal castle on a picturesque hill called Zollern. (The name Hohenzollern means High Zollern.)

Every Hohenzollern was ambitious and eager to get more land. Often they succeeded by clever marriages, but sometimes they used other means. They were willing to use any methods as long as they increased the power, influence, and landholdings of the family. Toward the end of the Middle Ages they made a great gain. A Holy Roman Emperor named a Hohenzollern as Elector of Brandenburg. Brandenburg was then a remote frontier province in northern Germany.

During the Reformation the Hohenzollerns became Lutherans and seized all the church lands in their territories. By the end of the Thirty Years' War they had gained in various ways a number of widely scattered territories: the Duchy of Cleves, the Duchy of East Prussia, the city of Magdeburg, and the bishoprics of Halberstadt and Minden.

● *Frederick William, the Great Elector, rules Brandenburg*

In the mid-seventeenth century the fairly strong state of Brandenburg was ruled by one of the really great Hohenzollerns. Frederick

A *soldier of the Grenadier Guards, a unit of the Prussian army.*

William, called the Great Elector, ruled from 1640 until 1688. He guided Brandenburg through the difficult last years of the Thirty Years' War, and was rewarded with new territories in the Treaty of Westphalia. Then he turned to the rebuilding and further strengthening of Brandenburg.

The Great Elector first reorganized the armies of all his lands into one strong force. Then he improved the system of tax collecting, encouraged agriculture and industry, and improved transportation. By clever diplomacy he gained for Brandenburg the complete control of the duchy of East Prussia.

The Great Elector's successor, Frederick, was ambitious to have the title of king. To gain the necessary consent of the Holy Roman Emperor, Frederick supported the Hapsburgs against Louis XIV in the War of the Spanish Succession. As a reward, by the Treaty of Utrecht, 1713, he was granted the title Frederick I, King of Prussia (see page 273).

● Frederick William I, King of Prussia

Frederick I died shortly before the treaty was signed, but his successor was recognized as Frederick William I, King of Prussia. In addition to the usual Hohenzollern strengths,

GROWTH OF BRANDENBURG-PRUSSIA, 1440-1740

Brandenburg 1440-1647   acquired 1648-1740

the new king had many oddities which have endeared him to students of history. He disliked the French and French ways intensely. His father had tried to copy Louis XIV's Versailles and had furnished his palace lavishly. Frederick William I dismissed all unnecessary officials and sold much of the offending furniture.

The king was a notorious "penny-pincher" —so stingy in running the royal household and so strict in his discipline that he was called the Sergeant King. It was said that he ran all of Prussia, including the palace, like a barracks. A terrific worker himself, he had a great contempt for idleness in others. As he walked about the streets of Berlin, if he saw a man standing idle, he would chase him and beat him with his cane. His one weakness and extravagance was tall soldiers. He collected them from all over Europe. He drafted the Prussians and hired or even kidnapped foreigners to form the Potsdam Guards, a regiment of giants.

● Efficient rule by the Sergeant King

For all his quirks the Sergeant King was a true Hohenzollern in his aims and practices. He used to good advantage the money he saved. He more than doubled the standing army. It was so organized and drilled that it became the best and most efficient fighting force in Europe. The officers were drawn from the nobility, or *Junker* class, but promotion was based strictly on merit rather than birth.

In addition to strengthening the army Frederick William I improved his country in a number of ways. He reorganized the civil service, hiring and promoting efficient men regardless of birth. He promoted trade and built up industries, spending government money where necessary. The collection of taxes and the spending of money were carefully planned so that the treasury had a surplus for emergencies. The Sergeant King had no interest in philosophy or higher learning,

King Frederick William I of Prussia visiting a village school. The king liked to make unexpected visits in order to check up on teachers and students.

but he was convinced that all children should have a primary education. He issued a decree requiring all Prussian parents to send their children to school. He himself founded many village schools, and often visited them.

In spite of his great accomplishments Frederick William I had a real worry as he neared the end of his life. His only son showed little interest in either military life or government service. Instead, he spent his time writing poetry, playing the flute, and reading philosophy. The Sergeant King used the harshest methods, even including imprisonment, to force his idle and frivolous heir to be more nearly the son he desired.

Frederick II (the Great)

In 1740, the same year in which Maria Theresa became ruler of Austria, Crown Prince Frederick took the throne of Prussia as Frederick II. The Sergeant King would have been surprised to know that the Prussians would come to call his despised son "the great Fritz," while the world would know him as Frederick the Great. For, despite his flute and his love for French poetry, Frederick II turned out to be one of the greatest military leaders and statesmen of the Hohenzollerns, the true father of modern Prussia.

Prussia and Austria clash

This year 1740 was one of decision in Germany and in all of Europe. Each of the two strongest states of Germany had a new ruler. Prussia was definitely emerging as challenger to the dominance of Austria in Germany. The clash between the two states came very soon.

Austria and Prussia each had strong and weak points. Maria Theresa had the vast Hapsburg territories: Austria, Hungary, central Europe, northern Italy, and the Netherlands. As empress of the Holy Roman Empire, she had some claim on the loyalty of all German states. She had the pledges of the European rulers in the Pragmatic Sanction, the relationship of many rulers, and the support of the pope.

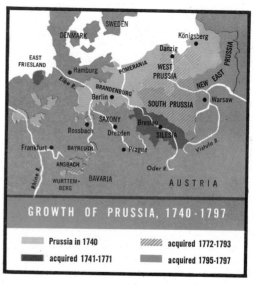

GROWTH OF PRUSSIA, 1740-1797

Prussia in 1740
acquired 1741-1771
acquired 1772-1793
acquired 1795-1797

The Holy Roman Empire had many weaknesses. Its different nationalities were almost all discontented under Hapsburg rule. Administration of the government was poor and inefficient. Maria Theresa's father had almost emptied the treasury to get signers of the Pragmatic Sanction. Despite these pledges Austria could rely for help only on Spain. There was a possibility of help from Holland and Great Britain if France opposed Austria, as it almost always did.

Prussia was smaller than Austria in population and territory. Its lands were widely scattered throughout Germany and therefore hard to defend. However, there were strengths to make up for these weaknesses. The population was solidly German. Prussia had a healthy economic system, a well organized and efficient government, and a well drilled, well equipped, and formidable army. In a conflict with Austria, Prussia could count on help or friendly neutrality from France, Bavaria, Saxony, Sardinia, and perhaps more states.

War came because of Frederick's attempt to seize Silesia from Austria. With its rich farm lands, valuable iron deposits, strategic location, and strongly German population, Silesia was so tempting that the Prussian king willingly broke his promise of the Pragmatic Sanction. After secretly making alliances with France and Bavaria he invaded Silesia without declaring war. This action started a chain of events that brought on a major war.

● The Seven Years' War

The Seven Years' War (1756–1763) finally involved almost every European country. Great Britain and France, rivals for empire, battled for colonies in America and India. At one time Frederick and Prussia were left surrounded by enemies in Europe, with only financial help from Britain. Then he showed the military genius which won him the title

"The Great." Fighting against great odds he dashed from one front to another to hold off his enemies. For all his great skill, Frederick was saved only because Russia switched sides and came to his assistance. Then his enemies were willing to agree to the Peace of Paris, 1763, which allowed Prussia to keep Silesia.

Prussia paid a high price for her gains. The seizure of Silesia started a series of wars that lasted, with some interruptions, for twenty-two years. Prussia lost almost ten per cent of her population, mostly young men. Her countryside was ravaged and devastated. The city of Berlin had been invaded three times. The royal treasury was drained, and the poverty of the population made it difficult to build it up again. Besides, the larger army that was now necessary was a heavy financial burden on the state.

In the years of peace that followed 1763, Frederick II showed that his greatness was not in military genius alone. He now showed his skill in organization and administration. The excellent civil service was maintained and expanded. Public education was continued and improved. Religious toleration was followed. Legal and court reforms were made to improve relations among the social classes. Trade and manufacturing were generously backed. By hard work and wise direction the expanded state of Prussia recovered its prosperity and forged ahead.

Prussia's territorial gains continued. Frederick the Great helped to engineer the First Partition of Poland. (His successor shared in the second and third partitions). By taking territory along the Baltic coast, Frederick was able to unite Brandenburg and East and West Prussia. Thus at his death in 1786 Frederick the Great left behind him a solidly formed, greatly enlarged, and prosperous Prussia. By the end of the eighteenth century Prussia had become a formidable rival of Austria in Germany, and a first-class power in Europe. Note the rapid growth shown on the map above.

Review of Chapter 22

People, places, and things

Identify: Peter the Great, Catherine the Great, Hapsburgs, Maria Theresa, Frederick William (the Great Elector) of Brandenburg, Frederick William I of Prussia, Frederick the Great, Junkers, the Pragmatic Sanction.

Locate: the Don, Volga, Neva, and Amur Rivers, Sea of Azov, Crimea, Black Sea, Baltic Sea, Gulf of Finland, St. Petersburg (Leningrad), Moscow, Brandenburg, Duchy of East Prussia, Duchy of Cleves, Silesia.

Events in review

1. Explain the effect of geography on Russia's relations with western Europe.
2. Why is Peter I called "the first modern czar" of Russia?
3. Did Catherine the Great improve conditions within Russia? Was her foreign policy successful?
4. What conditions in Poland made it easy for foreign powers to partition the country?
5. What different nationalities inhabited Austria at this period?
6. Why was Frederick William I of Prussia called "the Sergeant King"?
7. How was it possible for a small country, Prussia, to win a war against Austria, a larger state?

Problems and projects

1. Discuss Peter the Great's policy of westernizing Russia. Were all his changes beneficial to his country?
2. In what respects did Catherine II of Russia and Frederick II of Prussia deserve to be called "Great"? Were they "great" in the sense of being "outstanding" and "important"? Were they "great" in the sense of being "admirable"?
3. Discuss the rise of the Hohenzollerns to their position as kings of Prussia. Compare them with other rulers (Greek, Roman, French, for example). Can you explain the efficiency of the Hohenzollerns as rulers?
4. To debate: "Leaders make history." Refer to the careers of Peter I of Russia and Frederick II of Prussia.
5. Write an account of a day in the life of one of the rulers discussed in this chapter. See an encyclopedia, or books listed on pages 286–287.
6. In one column list the territorial gains made by Prussia to 1763. In a parallel column show from what country each piece of territory was taken.
7. On a map show (a) Russian expansion during the reigns of Peter I and Catherine II, (b) Prussian expansion under Frederick William I and Frederick II.

Review of the Beginnings of the Modern World

1. Can it be said that the Middle Ages ended and the modern world began at any specific date (such as 1492 or 1500)? Did any men or events of the twelfth and thirteenth centuries foreshadow the new era? Did any medieval ideas and institutions last into modern times? Cite examples to support whatever answer you give.

2. Historians have said that the basic difference between medieval and modern men is a difference in attitude of mind. Is this true in the fields of art, science, and religion? Cite examples to support your view.

3. Renaissance means "rebirth." The rebirth of what? What values or good things did mankind gain from this new spirit of the Renaissance? Were any values or good things lost because of this new spirit?

4. The Constitution of the United States includes this guarantee: "Congress shall make no law respecting an establishment of religion, or prohibiting the free exercise thereof." We have achieved religious toleration. Was the time of the Reformation an era of religious tolerance? What stand on religion was taken by the governments of Switzerland, of France, of England? by the German princes? Did the wars of religion result in freedom of worship for all groups? Explain.

5. During the sixteenth to eighteenth centuries the national state became of great importance. Point out differences between the medieval idea of a universal Christian state and the more modern national state. What gains, and what losses, resulted from the forming of national states?

6. List three countries that had become unified national states by the middle of the eighteenth century. List the countries that remained split up into small parts. Discuss why some areas were able to unite but others could not.

7. During the fifteenth to eighteenth centuries, European powers built huge colonial empires. What benefits did the European nations hope to get from their colonies? What benefits did they actually get? How did this building of empires affect the natives in the colonial areas?

8. Do any European nations still hold parts of their colonial empires? What is being said about "colonialism" today?

9. Review the famous men you have read about in Part Five: leaders in art, literature, science, philosophy, religion, exploration, government. Make a list of ten or twelve men who, in your opinion, did most to change the world from the Middle Ages to the Modern Age. Explain briefly why you selected each man on your list.

10. Suppose that you could relive one event or period from history. Which of the following would you choose: Being a citizen of Rome under the "Good Emperors," traveling to China with Marco Polo, living in Florence during the Renaissance, sailing with Columbus, joining a colonizing venture of the British East India Company? Explain your choice.

Books about the Beginnings

of the Modern World

*Antony, I. W. *Raleigh and His World* (Scribner, 1934). Raleigh the adventurer, courtier, writer, and colonizer is the focus for a study of the Renaissance world in which he lived. Highly recommended.

*Bainton, Roland. *Church of Our Fathers* (Scribner, 1941). The story of the Protestant Revolution is told impartially.

———. *Here I Stand* (Abingdon-Cokesbury, 1950). Martin Luther and his times.

*Bolton, Sarah K. *Famous Men of Science* (Crowell, 1946). Brief sketches of the lives of famous scientists, simply and clearly written.

*Carr, Albert H. *Men of Power; a Book of Dictators* (Viking, 1956). Good accounts of Richelieu, Frederick the Great, and others who helped build national states.

*Chandler, Anna C. *Story-Lives of Master Artists* (Lippincott, 1954). Short, simply written, biographical sketches of great artists. A useful reference on the great Renaissance painters mentioned in Chapter 18.

*Books marked with a star (*) are easy reading.

*Cottler, Joseph, and Jaffe, Haym. *Heroes of Civilization* (Little, Brown, 1931). Distinguished men of science, exploration, and other fields in interesting sketches: Galileo, Copernicus, Newton, Magellan, and others.

———. *Map Makers* (Little, Brown, 1936). The story of the growth of geographic knowledge. An interesting account and a valuable reference book.

*Davis, William S. *Life in Elizabethan Days* (Harper, 1930). Work, play, customs, manners, dress, food, sports, country and city life in Renaissance England.

Derleth, August William. *Father Marquette and the Great Rivers* (Farrar, Straus, 1955).

Ergang, Robert R. *Europe From the Renaissance to Waterloo* (Heath, 1954). Written in a way to interest high school students. Covers political, social, economic, and cultural developments.

*Gaer, Joseph. *How the Great Religions Began*, rev. ed., (Dodd, Mead, 1956).

Hartley, Dorothy, and Elliot, M. M. *Life and Work of the People of England: Fifteenth Century* (Putnam, 1926). An exceptionally valuable book for its fine illustrations of English life.

*Hewes, Agnes D. *Spice Ho! A Story of Discovery* (Knopf, 1941). Spices made the monotonous food of the Middle Ages more appetizing. The search for spices led both men and nations to take great risks.

*Lamb, Harold. *The March of Muscovy; Ivan the Terrible and the Growth of the Russian Empire, 1400–1768* (Doubleday, 1948). An interesting account of Russian expansion.

*Lamprey, Louise. *Building an Empire* (Stokes, 1941). The growth of the British empire told in interesting fashion.

*Lucas, Mary S. *Vast Horizons* (Viking, 1943). Exploration and discovery from the Crusades through the eighteenth century, interestingly told, with many maps and illustrations.

*Mills, Dorothy. *Renaissance and Reformation Times* (Putnam, 1939). The most readable book on the period. The illustrations are excellent. Very highly recommended.

Morison, Samuel Eliot. *Christopher Columbus, Mariner* (Little, Brown, 1955). The life and voyages of Columbus.

*Quennell, C. H. B., and Quennell, Marjorie. *History of Everyday Things in England* (British Bk. Centre, 1953). Deals with the period from 1500 to 1799.

Reinach, Solomon. *Apollo; an Illustrated Manual of the History of Art Throughout the Ages* (Scribner, 1935). The section on Renaissance art is especially good.

Syme, Ronald. *Henry Hudson* (Morrow, 1955). Story of Hudson's various explorations in search of the elusive passage to the Orient.

———. *La Salle of the Mississippi* (Morrow, 1953). An account of La Salle's first voyages, his efforts to find sites for settlement and trade, the founding of Quebec, and his experiences with the Indians.

Welch, Ronald (pseud.) *Ferdinand Magellan* (Criterion Books, 1956). In this biography we see Magellan both as a young man sailing and fighting on the first Portuguese ships seeking trade with the Far East and as a matured sea captain finding passage around South America.

Winwar, Frances. *Queen Elizabeth and the Spanish Armada* (Random House, 1954).

Good stories about the Beginnings of the Modern World

Coblentz, Catherine C. *Beggars' Penny* (Longmans, 1943). Three children, a Dutch Catholic boy, a Jewish boy, and a Dutch Protestant girl endure the siege of Leyden by the Spanish.

Dumas, Alexandre. *Black Tulip* (Temple, 1948). William of Orange fights against Louis XIV's attempt to take Holland.

———. *Three Musketeers* (Dodd, Mead. Great Illustrated Classics). An adventure classic of the days of Richelieu and Louis XIV.

*Hodges, C. Walter. *Columbus Sails* (Coward-McCann, 1939). How a monk, a sailor, and an American Indian felt toward Columbus.

Kelly, Eric P. *At the Sign of the Golden Compass* (Macmillan, 1938). Hairbreadth escapes of an English printer's apprentice who finally found refuge in a great printing house of sixteenth-century Antwerp.

Kingsley, Charles. *Westward Ho!* (Dodd, Mead, 1941, and other editions). A thrilling story of the rivalry of England and Spain in discovery and exploration. Raleigh, Hawkins, and Drake appear.

Page, Elizabeth. *Wilderness Adventure* (Farrar and Rinehart, 1946). A novel of French and English rivalry in America.

Stevenson, Robert L. *Black Arrow* (Dodd, Mead, 1949). A romantic novel about the Wars of the Roses.

Part Six THE AGE OF REVOLUTIONS

Part Six will tell about three great political revolutions. The facing page shows a high point of one of these—the American Revolution. The picture shows General Washington receiving the surrender of the British forces at Yorktown. The defeat of Cornwallis' army at Yorktown was one of the decisive victories in the struggle of the Americans to make themselves independent of Great Britain. One chapter in Part Six will describe the beginnings of our free nation.

First, Chapter 23 will describe the ideas that were behind political changes. In the seventeenth and eighteenth centuries there was a development of the critical attitude of mind that we saw in the Renaissance. A new look at government led to the concept that men have certain natural rights—among them the right to have a voice in their own government. This explosive idea contributed to revolts against autocratic government: first in England, then in the English colonies in North America, then in France. One of the men who eloquently expressed this idea is sketched above—Thomas Jefferson.

Chapter 24 tells how the English established the first representative parliamentary government. Chapter 25 describes the founding of the United States, the first federal republic. Chapters 26 and 27 describe the violent upheaval of the French Revolution and the emergence of Napoleon as an empire builder.

Later chapters tell of revolutions in Latin America, by which the colonies of Spain and Portugal won independence, and of revolutionary outbreaks in Europe in the nineteenth century.

The time chart on pages 290–291 gives a record of political changes. Notice, however, such additional items as the steam engine, the cotton gin, the McCormick reaper. Along with the political revolutions there went another kind of revolution just as far-reaching in its effects on the world. This was the Industrial Revolution. In industry and agriculture men changed from methods of work that had been followed since the Middle Ages and earlier. Power-driven machines took the place of hand work. Factories appeared and produced goods in quantities never known before. On farms, the use of machines and the application of scientific principles changed the ways of agriculture.

As a result of revolutions in government and of the Industrial Revolution, the political, economic, and social world changed rapidly and drastically. The old ways of the Middle Ages were left behind. In many important respects the world began to resemble the one we now live in.

In Part Six several of the great themes of history can be seen developing. You will read of the rapid growth of democratic government. You will learn about amazing progress in the sciences and about swift expansion in industry. On the darker side, you will find records of international rivalries and of expensive and bloody wars.

	ENGLAND	FRANCE
1600	**1603** James I begins Stuart dynasty	
	1628 Petition of Right	
	1629 Charles I dismisses Parliament	
	1642 Civil war begins	
	1649 Execution of Charles I	
	1649-1658 The Commonwealth and Protectorate—Cromwell	**1643-1715** Age of Louis XIV
1650		
	1660 Restoration of Charles II Great Navigation Act	
	1687 Newton, *Principia*	
	1688 Glorious Revolution: William and Mary	
	1689 Bill of Rights	
	1689 Locke, *Two Treatises on Civil Government*	
1700	**1701** Jethro Tull, seed drill	
	1705 Newcomen's steam engine	
	1707 Act of Union	**1713** Treaty of Utrecht
	1714 George I, of House of Hanover, King	
	1733 Kay, flying shuttle	
1750	**c. 1750** coke used for smelting iron	**1748** Montesquieu, *Spirit of the Laws*
		1752 Diderot, *The Encyclopedia*
	1765 Hargreaves spinning jenny	**1762** Rousseau, *Social Contract*
	1769 James Watt improves steam engine	**1774** Louis XVI becomes king
	1776 Adam Smith, *Wealth of Nations*	
		1789 Estates-General meets
	1785 Cartwright, power loom	**1792-1799** First French Republic
	1793 Whitney, cotton gin	**1793** Execution of King and Queen Reign of Terror
	1798 Jenner, vaccination	**1799** Napoleon becomes dictator
1800		**1804** Napoleon becomes Emperor
		1804-1815 First French Empire
		1805 Trafalgar
	1814 Stephenson, "Rocket"	**1812** Invasion of Russia
	1819 First Factory Reform Act	**1815** Waterloo
		1815 Louis XVIII restored to throne
	1832 Parliamentary Reform Bill	
	1846 Abolition of Corn Laws	
	1847 10-Hour Act	**1848** Second French Republic
1850		**1852** Napoleon III, Second Empire
	1856 Bessemer Process, iron and steel	

EVOLUTIONS

EUROPE	AMERICA	ASIA

EUROPE	AMERICA	ASIA
	1607 Virginia, first English settlement	
	1608 French in Quebec	
	1609 Henry Hudson	
	1620 Plymouth	
	1630 Massachusetts Bay Colony	**1640** Russia reaches the Pacific
	1636 Harvard College founded	**1644-1912** Manchu dynasty, China
48 Peace of Westphalia		**1644** French East India Company
		1660 Dutch take East Indies
	1663 Second Navigation Act	**1664** French to India
	1696 Enforcement Act	
3 Peace of Utrecht		
0 Maria Theresa, Austria	**1733** Molasses Act	**1736-1796** Chien Lung, Manchu Emperor Chinese territory at greatest extent
0-1786 Frederick the Great, Prussia		
2-1795 Catherine II, Russia	**1760** George III, King of England	**1763** French lose hope of Empire in India
	1763 French expelled	
	1776 Declaration of Independence	
2 First Partition of Poland	**1781** Articles of Confederation	
	1783 Peace of Paris: independence	
	1789 Constitution: Federal government	
3 Second Partition of Poland	**1793** Whitney, cotton gin	
3 First Coalition against France		
	1803 Purchase of Louisiana	
	1804 Revolution in Haiti	
Congress of Vienna	**1812-1814** U.S.-Britain, Second War	
0-1848 Age of Metternich	**1813** Bolivar in Venezuela	
-23 Revolutions	**1821** Mexico-Central America independent	
Revolutions	**1823** Monroe Doctrine	
	1826 Peru independent	
	1833 McCormick, reaper	**1839-1842** Opium War
-1849 Revolutions	**1846** Howe, sewing machine	**1842** Treaty of Nanking

291

Chapter 23   The Age of Enlightenment

THE eighteenth century is known in history as the Age of Enlightenment. Starting in the seventeenth century, but particularly in the eighteenth, men examined critically the political and social institutions under which they lived. They studied the past to learn how existing customs and institutions had developed. They analyzed the powers of kings, the special position of the churches, and the special privileges of nobles and clergy. Most of these thinkers and writers were men of the bourgeoisie, or middle class. Although they sought greater freedom, equality, and opportunity for themselves, they insisted on social justice and opportunity for everyone. They were the pioneers of many of our modern democratic ideas.

These men of the seventeenth and eighteenth centuries are often called *liberals*. They felt an urge to think and criticize. They saw the need for changes in political and social institutions to benefit all men instead of privileged groups. They proposed remedies for the bad conditions they exposed. Their ideas were opposed by many, especially by those who might lose a privileged position. People who oppose far-reaching changes in existing conditions are called *conservatives*.

In modern history the eighteenth century marks a break between the old and the new, between conservative and liberal thought. The men who influenced and brought about the change were philosophers, thinkers, and writers rather than men of action. The effect of their writing illustrates once more how powerful ideas are. Someone has said: "There is no force in history more powerful than an idea whose time has come."

Autocratic governments

By 1750 England, France, Spain, Portugal, Holland, and Sweden had become unified national states with strongly organized central governments. Russia was expanding and also developing a strong government. Germany remained divided. Prussia was emerging as a strong rival to Austria. Under the Hapsburg crown Austria united many lands and a mixed group of nationalities. These peoples were different from each other in so many ways that they lacked any natural tendency to hold together. The Holy Roman Empire was only a shadow of the past. As one wit said, it was neither Holy nor Roman nor an Empire. Italy remained a "geographic expression"—all split up in various ways. In eastern Europe the empire of the Ottoman Turks was showing signs of weakness and breakup.

Except in England, where a revolution had already taken place and the power of the king was limited by Parliament, all governments were autocratic, absolute monarchies. In this kind of government the king had all the powers. He made laws by drawing them up, signing, and proclaiming them. He appointed and removed the men who had the responsibility of enforcing and carrying out these laws. He appointed and removed judges who decided cases involving the laws and their application. In an absolute monarchy the king's will was the law. His power was based on the idea that he was God's representative on earth. He received his powers from God and was responsible only to God. This theory is known as the divine right of kings.

Social classes under the Old Régime

The people of Europe were divided into fixed and definite social classes. At the top, below the king, were the clergy, the First Estate. In most countries the clergy were paid by the government. The clergy still had much the same power and privileges they had held during the Middle Ages. They were exempted from the heaviest taxes, and stood trial only in their own special courts. On the continent of Europe the Roman Catholic Church was still a very wealthy and powerful institution with vast lands and large income. Most of this wealth was concentrated in the hands of the higher clergy: archbishops, bishops, and abbots. The lower clergy, the parish priests, were poorly paid and overworked. Often the parish priests sided with the people in favor of reforms, while the higher clergy usually joined kings and nobles in opposing changes.

The nobles, the Second Estate, enjoyed large incomes and many special privileges. These were carry-overs from feudal days. They were exempted from the heaviest royal taxes, but they still collected for themselves feudal dues of various kinds from the peasants. Nobles held the highest places in the army, church, and government. In England and France they had lost their independent political power. In parts of Germany, Italy, and eastern Europe, however, the petty princes still collected taxes, had armies, and made war on their neighbors.

Except for the king, nobles, and clergy, everyone belonged to the Third Estate. Even here there was a sharp division. At the top were the bourgeoisie—the city-dwelling middle class. They were the merchants, manufacturers, and professional people such as doctors and lawyers. Some of the most skilled workers, the artisans, were included in this class. Many of them were people of wealth and education. However, members of the middle class were always considered lower in social position than the poorest and most ignorant noble.

The manual workers—laborers, peasants, and serfs—were the lowest of all. Laborers and artisans received very low wages and lived in poor, crowded conditions. Poorest of all was the peasant. As in feudal days, he was still the bearer of all the burdens of the whole social structure. Clergy and nobles were exempt from royal taxes, which fell

A cartoon satirizing the Old Régime in Europe. The peasant (of the Third Estate) carries on his back the priest (First Estate) and noble (Second Estate).

heavily upon the peasant. He still made payments and gave service to the noble or clerical landowner. He paid the church tithe. The peasant worked long and hard, and lived in poverty, squalor, and ignorance.

This society of absolute monarchs, privileged nobles and clergy, and underprivileged workers and peasants came to be known by a general name: *The Old Régime*. Kings, nobles, and the higher clergy preferred things as they were and wanted no changes. To prevent change they tried to wipe out criticism. Speech and writings were strictly censored. Laws were vague and punishments were harsh. Death sentences were given for a great number of offenses, many of which are now considered only petty crimes.

Science influences thought

New scientific discoveries and theories had great influence on the thinking of the eighteenth century. Toward the end of the seventeenth century Isaac Newton, one of the great scientists of all times, published his book *Principia*. Newton did much to explain and expand the work of Copernicus, Galileo, and Kepler. They had shown that instead of being the center of the universe, the earth is only one of a group of planets that rotate on their axes and revolve around the sun.

● *Newton's theory of gravitation*

In *Principia* Newton stated the theory of universal gravitation. According to this theory, the force of gravity not only prevents objects from flying off the revolving earth, but also holds the whole system of sun and planets together by keeping them in their proper orbits. Newton's work had an immense influence on the thinking of his own age and on all later scientific thought. It gave, or suggested, the answers to many questions about nature that had previously gone unanswered. It also gave a great spur to scientific investigation and experimentation.

Tools for scientific investigation were developed or improved. Armed with the new tools, with better methods and improved mathematics, men made great strides in the field of astronomy, biology, zoology, botany, physics, chemistry, and medicine. For example, a Dutch scientist, Anton van Leeuwenhoek, using an improved microscope, discovered bacteria and a whole new world of microscopic life which had never been known before. An English chemist, Joseph Priestley, discovered the element oxygen. A Frenchman, Antoine Lavoisier, showed that fire, previously thought to be an element itself (a single substance), was the result of combining oxygen with fuel and heat. John Dalton, another Englishman, stated the principle that all matter is composed of basic substances

Sir Isaac Newton, the British scientist who stated the law of gravity. How important his discovery seemed to the people of his time is shown by the following lines written by the famous poet Alexander Pope: "Nature and nature's laws lay hid in night: God said, Let Newton be! and all was light."

called atoms, of a limited and definite number of types.

The scientific attitude

Even more important than any single discovery or invention was the great development of the scientific attitude of mind. The scientific mind does not accept anything as true which cannot be proved by testing and experiment. It places great importance on cause and effect. Every natural happening (phenomenon) has its cause; every cause has its effect; and this relationship can always be shown.

Influenced by the discoveries in the sciences, the eighteenth-century philosophers began to apply the scientific method to all human ideas, customs, and institutions. They believed that an idea which could not be tested by the senses or the reasoning of the mind was only a speculation, a thing to be doubted. This attitude is called rationalism—the belief that all true things can be proved by reason. Such a belief was opposed by both Church and government.

Voltaire

The outstanding rationalist writer of this period was a French philosopher, François Marie Arouet, known as Voltaire. In all his writing he insisted that reason was the only guide to human behavior. He savagely attacked all things which he considered shams and superstitions. He advocated religious toleration and freedom of speech. A great statement of the idea of free speech is attributed to Voltaire: "I do not agree with a thing that you say, but I will defend, to the death, your right to say it."

Voltaire's greatest weapon was his wit. He attacked shams and superstitions by poking fun at them, showing how ridiculous they were. This form of writing is called *satire*. Voltaire aimed his satire at autocratic government, the privileges of nobles and clergy, and the Church. He believed that the Church,

by its reliance on dogma rather than reason, and by its conservatism, was blocking the way to needed social reforms. You will not be surprised that Voltaire was forced to spend much of his life in exile from France. Eighteenth century France was not a healthy place for such a critic.

Belief in natural law arises

The philosophers of the Age of Enlightenment believed that there was a natural law which governed the universe, the world, and all its creatures. They wrote that God had created the world and given it to people to live in according to rules He had made. As it was originally created, the world was good because it was natural; it followed the rules of nature which God had made. It had ceased to be good because people had ceased to live by the rules of nature. To restore it to goodness, all that people had to do was to discover the rules by education and by using their reason. If people lived according to the laws and made their institutions and government conform to them, the world would become again the perfect place God had created.

John Locke

This belief had an enormous influence on political events at the end of the eighteenth century. It was stated by men whose writings were widely read both in Europe and America. The first statement came at the end of the seventeenth century from an English philosopher, John Locke. Locke had lived through a revolution in 1688, and he wanted to justify what had happened then. To explain his ideas he wrote a book called *Two Treatises on Government*.

Locke wrote that at some unknown time in the past men had chosen a leader or sovereign to rule them. In order to maintain a stable society they had given up some of their individual rights. However, they had kept certain rights which not even the ruler could take from them. These included the right to live, to have liberty, and to own property. If a ruler violates these rights of the people, he breaks the unwritten social contract by which the people allow him to rule them. They then have the right to overthrow the ruler and replace him with another who will pledge to observe and protect their rights.

● Montesquieu

Locke's ideas were enthusiastically adopted by a group of eighteenth-century French writers. In a book called *The Spirit of the Laws* a French baron, Charles Louis Montesquieu, tried to describe a perfect government. After a study of all existing governments, he concluded that the English form was most nearly perfect. He wrote that its greatest strength lay in the fact that power was equally divided among the executive (those who ran the government), legislative (the law-makers), and judicial (those who judged violations of the law) branches. Each was so strong that it balanced and checked the others. None could become all-powerful.

Montesquieu's praise of the English government was based on a misunderstanding of it. Even when he wrote, the legislative and executive powers were largely combined in the House of Commons. Nevertheless, his ideas were powerful. They had great influence on the formation of limited monarchies in Europe. The idea of separation of powers was adopted in the federal Constitution of the United States of 1787.

● Rousseau

Another very influential writer was Jean Jacques Rousseau. His idea was that man is born good; only his upbringing is bad. His environment (surroundings), his teaching, and his laws make him what he is. Rousseau asked how this environment, these institutions, and these laws could be changed. He gave his answer in a famous and widely read

A noble lady of the Old Régime. The wealthy nobles enjoyed many privileges, and sometimes lived in extravagant luxury. This hairdo was created for a court lady to celebrate the victory of a French warship. Such extravagance was ridiculed by writers like Voltaire.

book, *The Social Contract*. Rousseau said that the free and good state to which people are born can be preserved only if they live under a government of their own choice. Just laws and wise government must be based on *popular sovereignty,* the choice of the people themselves. Only such a government and laws can bring out man's essentially honest nature. This simple idea was simply stated, widely read, and had enormous influence on the thinking of the time.

"Benevolent despots" try to rule better

Surprisingly enough, the writings of the philosophers of the Age of Enlightenment impressed some of the absolute monarchs themselves. Some philosophers wrote that a monarch could be a perfect ruler if he had been educated to understand natural law and tried to rule in harmony with it. He would still be a despot, an absolute ruler. However, he would be "enlightened" by his education. He would be "benevolent" in his desire to rule according to the laws of nature, wisely, justly, and for the welfare of his people.

Among the more famous of the benevolent despots were Joseph II of Austria and Frederick the Great of Prussia. They worked hard and conscientiously to improve the governments of their countries. They promoted industry, agriculture, culture, and education. They tried to improve the lives and conditions of their subjects. In spite of bitter and many-sided opposition they accomplished some worthwhile reforms. For example, Joseph II freed the serfs in Austria and decreed that they could rent land. The benevolent despots, however, merely scratched the surface of what was needed, for a very good reason. Real, far-reaching reform would have required such a thorough overhauling of their governments that their own positions would have been threatened. This they were unwilling to face. They did not want to end the "good old days" of the Old Régime.

Review of Chapter 23

People, places, and things

Identify: Newton, Priestley, Leeuwenhoek, Dalton, Voltaire, Locke, Montesquieu, Rousseau, bourgeoisie.

Events in review

1. What powers were held by kings in Europe under the Old Régime? On what basis did they claim their right to rule?
2. Who made up the three estates, or social classes, of the Old Régime?
3. Did education and wealth guarantee a high position in society under the Old Régime?
4. Explain briefly what is meant by (a) the scientific attitude of mind, (b) rationalism.
5. What is meant by "natural law"? How did eighteenth-century belief in natural law differ from the medieval way of thinking?
6. Who wrote *The Spirit of the Laws?* What idea expressed in this book can be found in the Constitution of the United States?
7. What idea about government was expressed by Rousseau in *The Social Contract?*
8. Did the benevolent despots carry out thorough reforms of their governments? Why?

Problems and projects

1. Compare eighteenth-century society with feudal society. Consider (a) the powers of the king, (b) the powers and privileges of the nobles and the clergy, (c) the importance and the condition of life of various members of the Third Estate.
2. Notice where professional people stood in the eighteenth-century social order. What importance and prestige do professional men and women (doctors, lawyers, teachers, scientists, writers, and the like) have in the modern world? Can you explain why people in this group tended to gain in importance from the eighteenth century onward?
3. Write a biographical sketch of one of the following: Newton, Priestley, Voltaire, Rousseau.
4. Some of the enlightened despots tried hard to govern efficiently and to provide for the prosperity and welfare of their subjects. Are there any advantages to such a form of government? What are the disadvantages of benevolent despotism? Why do we believe that government must be "of the people, by the people, for the people"?

Chapter 24 The Revolt against Autocratic Government: England

THREE great revolutions—in England, America, and France—destroyed the Old Régime. The English completed their revolution 100 years before the uprisings broke out in America and France. This fact explains the influence of England on the eighteenth century philosophers. The government established by the English Revolution was there for Montesquieu to see and admire. John Locke had stated reasons why a nation had the right to rebel against its rulers. England stood as an example to point the way.

The Tudors rule England

In the sixteenth century England was not greatly different from the nations on the continent of Europe. The Tudor rulers of England reigned almost as absolute monarchs. Henry VIII and Elizabeth I, greatest of the Tudors, did about as they pleased. However, they were careful to get the consent of Parliament to everything they did. Parliament usually gave its consent obediently. There was not much check on the sovereign, but Parliament did not disappear completely as did the French Estates-General.

The long reign of Elizabeth, last of the Tudors, was a period of glory for England.

The Queen successfully played off her powerful enemies, Spain and France, against each other, and the defeat of the Spanish Armada in 1588 helped end the career of Spain as the dominant power of Europe. England's commerce prospered, and some industries developed. England was on the way up when Elizabeth I died, childless, in 1603. She was succeeded by her cousin, James VI of Scotland, who became King James I of England, founder of the Stuart line of English kings. Although England and Scotland had the same king, their governments were not united in any other way.

The divine-right Stuarts meet opposition

For several reasons it was safe to predict a stormy reign for the Stuart James I. He was a Scot, and many Englishmen considered him a foreigner with no real understanding of their problems. Besides, James was a firm believer in the divine right of kings. He was not willing to have his power checked or his word questioned by anyone. Furthermore, James was arrogant and tactless; he did not even wish to consult Parliament, or else he wanted Parliament to consent slavishly to his proposals.

It seemed certain that James I would meet opposition in Parliament over money. He did not have a great personal fortune, and he liked to live in lavish splendor. Unlike the Tudors, the Stuart kings were always "hard up." And they felt that bargaining with Parliament over money was beneath the dignity of their status as monarchs ruling by divine right.

Economic conditions in England were not too good at the start of the seventeenth century. The middle class was prosperous from new industries and increasing trade, but oth-ers were beginning to meet hard times. A great increase in the spinning and weaving of wool had brought a great demand for raw wool. Therefore, many landowners changed from raising grain and from general farming to raising sheep for wool. This brought unemployment among the farm population because sheep-raising needed fewer farm workers. At the same time, prices were rising. Gold and silver were coming into England from the sale of goods to Spain and her colonies and from the capture of Spanish treasure ships. The increased supply of money caused

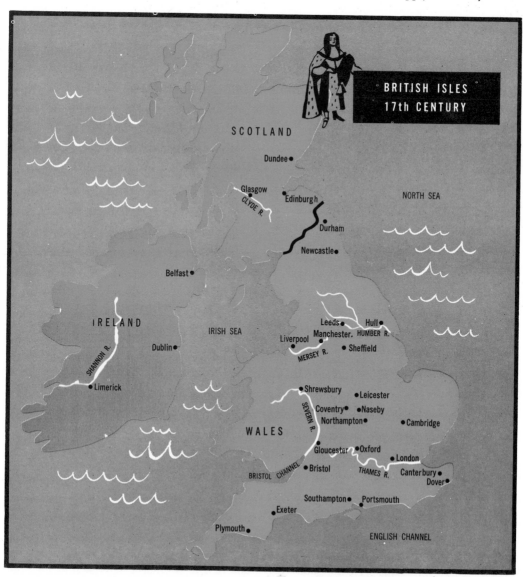

BRITISH ISLES
17th CENTURY

SCOTLAND

Dundee

Glasgow
CLYDE R.
Edinburgh

NORTH SEA

Durham

Newcastle

Belfast

IRELAND

IRISH SEA

Leeds   Hull
Manchester. HUMBER R.
Liverpool
MERSEY R.   Sheffield

Dublin

SHANNON R.

Limerick

Shrewsbury
Leicester
SEVERN R.   Coventry   Naseby
Northampton
Cambridge

WALES

Gloucester   Oxford
London
BRISTOL CHANNEL   Bristol   THAMES R.   Canterbury
Dover

Southampton   Portsmouth

Exeter

Plymouth

ENGLISH CHANNEL

a rise in prices (inflation). Distress and discontent were sure to follow when there was unemployment coupled with high prices.

● Religious problems

The religious situation in England was also unsettled. The established Church of England with its rituals, ceremonies, and beliefs midway between Roman Catholicism and extreme Protestantism seemed to satisfy most people. The "new nobility" created by Henry VIII supported the Anglican Church staunchly. Henry had given them large grants of the monastery lands he had seized. They naturally opposed any return of the Roman Catholic Church. However, there was opposition to the Church of England from two main groups. First, of course, were the Roman Catholics who remained loyal to the Church and refused to accept any of the Anglican changes. They had plotted to replace Elizabeth with a Catholic ruler; now they had hopes that the Stuarts would be favorable to their cause.

● Calvinism in England: Puritans, Presbyterians, and Separatists

The second general group of opponents of Anglicanism were followers of John Calvin. The Calvinist code of morals was very stern. Such things as games, dancing, card playing, and the theater were sinful because they were signs of idleness and pleasure. In religion the Calvinists wanted to wipe out what they considered the remnants of Catholicism in the Anglican Church. Among other things they opposed making the sign of the cross on a child's head at baptism, kneeling at communion, and the wearing of robes by the clergy. The Calvinists declared that they would "purify" both the church and the public morals; therefore, they came to be known as Puritans.

Calvinists were divided into three groups, mainly over the question of how the church should be organized. The Puritans wanted to stay in the Anglican Church, keeping its organization under bishops, but "purifying" its ceremonies and doctrines according to their ideas. The Presbyterians wanted an established (tax-supported) national church without bishops. Each congregation should elect a ruling body of elders, called presbyters. There should be district and national organizations. The smallest group was known, variously, as Separatists, Independents, or Congregationalists. They believed that each congregation should choose its own minister and make its own rules. It should be completely independent of every other congregation. The first

Mayflower II, *an almost exact reconstruction of the ship that carried the Pilgrims to America in 1620. One result of the religious problems in England under James I was that some of the Calvinists left their homeland. First to go were some of the Separatists. They emigrated to Holland, then went to the New World and founded a colony at Plymouth. Thus the history of the old world began to make history in America.*

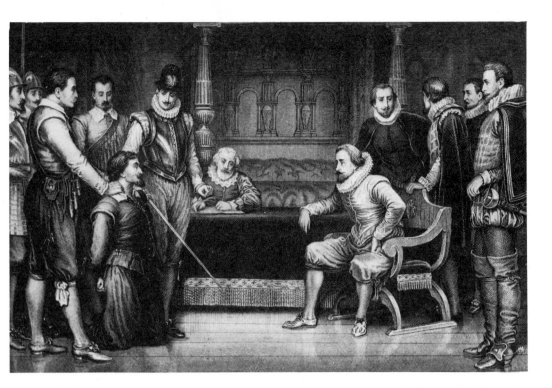

group of Separatists to come to America were called Pilgrims.

Calvinism in England was especially strong in the rising middle class—the merchants and businessmen. As city men they were strongly represented in the House of Commons. They kept a watchful eye over taxes and over anything that looked like a return to Roman Catholicism. They hoped to use their position in Parliament to accomplish their desired reforms in the Church of England.

James I has a difficult reign

During his reign of more than twenty years James I had constant difficulties with Parliament and the English people over three problems: money, religion, and foreign policy. When the House of Commons would not grant him money without question, James dismissed Parliament. He then raised money by selling titles of nobility, granting monopolies to private companies, and forcing men to make "loans" to him. When the Puritans came to him with a petition for reforms, he

A famous event in the reign of James I. A group of English Catholics plotted to blow up the Parliament buildings. The "Gunpowder Plot" was discovered before the explosion could be set off. The picture shows one of the conspirators, Guy Fawkes, kneeling while James I questions him. This plot increased anti-Catholic feeling in England, thus adding to the troubles of James I.

drove them away in a rage. There was widespread unrest in the country over a rumor that James was secretly friendly to the Catholics. His policy of friendship with Spain and his refusal to support the German Protestants in the Thirty Years' War were very unpopular. By the end of his reign James I had aroused opposition on many sides.

James' reign was marked by one great accomplishment: a new translation of the Bible. At the suggestion of the Puritans he appointed a group of outstanding scholars to do the work. The result of their labors is officially called the Authorized Version, and popularly known as the King James Version, of

301

the Bible. It is far more than a statement of religion; it is also a great work of literature. It has a simplicity, yet grandeur, of style that has influenced English speech and writing ever since it appeared.

Charles I continues divine-right rule

Charles I was as firm a believer in divine-right rule as his father, and was even more tactless. He, too, quarreled with Parliament over money and taxes. Before granting him money Parliament insisted that he sign a document called the Petition of Right (1628). By it the king promised: not to levy taxes without the consent of Parliament; not to declare martial law or to quarter soldiers in private homes in peacetime; not to imprison people without trial.

Later, when the Puritans made further demands, the furious king dismissed the Parliament and refused for eleven years to call another. To raise money during this period he adopted all the doubtful methods of his father, and found some new ones. Judges whom he appointed levied large fines, which went to the king. The Court of the Star Chamber, which held its trials in secret, without a jury, was especially hated. Charles required all towns to pay a tax to provide ships for the navy, and then used the money for his own purposes.

Charles I persecuted the Puritans so severely that many of them went to America. However, his greatest mistake was to try to establish the Anglican Church in Scotland. The Presbyterian Scots united to fight the move, and a Scottish army invaded England. In dire need of money, Charles was forced to call Parliament.

Civil War: The Puritan Revolution

The Parliament which met in 1640 lasted for twenty years and is known as the Long Parliament. Controlled by the Puritans in the House of Commons, it did many things to reduce the powers claimed by the king. Because of the need to deal with the Scottish invasion and a rebellion in Ireland Charles at first seemed to give in. Then he led troops into the House of Commons and tried to arrest the leaders of the opposition. This act led to the outbreak of a civil war between king and Parliament.

The king's supporters, called Cavaliers, were the Anglicans, the Catholics, the nobles, and all who disliked the Puritans. Supporting Parliament were the middle class and all varieties of Calvinists. Cavaliers wore their hair long and curled. Their opponents, to show their disdain, cropped their hair close and were called Roundheads. Oliver Cromwell, leader of the Puritans, drilled and welded them into an army which the Cavaliers could not match. Cromwell's "Ironsides"

King Charles I.

outfought the dashing Cavaliers. After two defeats in battle Charles I surrendered.

The Puritans end the monarchy

Now began a great jockeying among the Puritans, Presbyterians, and Independents to see who would control the government. Cromwell's army, which was strongly Independent, won the struggle. By force they kept all Anglican and Presbyterian members from entering the House of Commons. This event, called Pride's Purge because the troops were led by Colonel Pride, left only sixty Independents in the famous Rump Parliament.

The Rump Parliament abolished the monarchy and the House of Lords and proclaimed England a Commonwealth. It appointed a special court to try Charles I for treason. He was condemned and beheaded early in 1649. Oliver Cromwell became military dictator. England was without a king for eleven years.

Oliver Cromwell sets up a military dictatorship

Cromwell was a devout Calvinist of the Independent type. He was honest and upright, a powerful orator and a real statesman, but he was not democratic. He dismissed the Rump Parliament when it would not do as he wanted. He wrote two constitutions, each providing for a Parliament, and eventually dismissed both Parliaments. Finally he ruled alone for four years, with the title of Lord Protector. Cromwell suppressed all opposition, whether political or religious, with the greatest severity. His harshness in putting down rebellions in Scotland and Ireland brought him hatred in both countries.

The domestic policy of Cromwell's government was aimed to help the middle class by developing manufacturing and trade. Dutch merchants and ships had built up a profitable trade with England and her colonies during the troubled times of the civil war. Cromwell had Parliament pass two acts (the Navigation Acts of 1650 and 1651) to restore this trade to English merchants and shipowners. The acts had the effect of preventing Dutch ships from carrying goods to England or her colonies. Thus Cromwell introduced in England the policy of *mercantilism* that was to have far-reaching effects in her American colonies.

Cromwell, able but very stern, never became a popular ruler in England. As always in a dictatorship, it was difficult to provide for a successor. When Oliver Cromwell died his son Richard tried to rule, but quickly withdrew when he failed to win the support of the army. In 1660, after some hesitation, Parliament invited Charles and James, the sons of Charles I, to return to England. The elder son became King Charles II.

Charles II leads the restoration of the Stuarts

Charles II, a man of bad morals but considerable ability, had learned much from his years in exile. He believed in divine right, but, as he said, he had no desire "to go on his travels again." When his policies met determined opposition he gave in, although he often tried to gain his purposes by roundabout methods.

The policy of mercantilism begun under Cromwell was now continued and extended. It brought wars with the Dutch, during which England took the Dutch colony of New Amsterdam and renamed it New York. In foreign affairs Charles II at first supported Louis XIV of France against Holland. However, English protests forced him to switch and join the European alliance against France. This event marked the beginning of one hundred and fifty years of rivalry between England and France for mastery of the sea and for colonial empires.

Religious problems

Charles II, secretly a Catholic, hoped to relieve the English Catholics of some of their

legal restrictions. However, his attempt to do so met with such strong Parliamentary opposition that he gave up the effort. Parliament was now overwhelmingly Anglican in its make-up. It was anti-Calvinist as well as anti-Catholic. Members of the clergy were required to accept the Anglican prayer book; many Calvinist ministers were dismissed from their posts. When it seemed certain that Charles would be succeeded by his brother James, an avowed Catholic, the House of Commons passed a bill prohibiting a Roman Catholic from occupying the throne of England. The bill failed to pass the House of Lords, but it plainly showed how the people of England felt.

● *Tories and Whigs*

Parliament was divided into two groups of almost equal strength. One, called Tories, supported the Anglican Church and wanted a strong but not autocratic hereditary king. To keep the monarchy hereditary they were willing to accept a Catholic as king. Opposing the Tories were the Whigs, who favored a weak king, a strong Parliament, and greater freedom for those Protestants who did not

One major event in the reign of Charles II was the Great Fire of London, in 1666. Samuel Pepys, who kept a famous diary during this period, wrote of the fire: "September 2nd. Jane called us up about three in the morning, to tell us of a great fire they saw in the City. . . . By and by, Jane comes and tells us that she hears that above 300 houses have been burned down by the fire." Pepys described the fire that night as "one entire arch of fire above a mile long: it made me weep to see it. The churches, houses and all on fire and flaming at once, and a horrid noise the flames made and the cracking of the houses."

belong to the Anglican Church. Thus organized political parties appeared on the English scene.

● *The Habeas Corpus Act*

In 1679 the Whigs won a victory for freedom when Parliament passed the Habeas Corpus Act. This act provided that any man arrested and imprisoned must be brought before a judge within twenty days. The court would then decide whether he would be released on bail, charged and tried for a definite crime, or set free. The Habeas Corpus Act made it impossible for the king to hold his opponents in prison without a trial. It was a real step toward what we call civil liberties—rights which protect a person from unjust acts of government.

James II is dethroned in the Glorious Revolution

James II came to the throne after the death of his brother Charles in 1685. He had learned nothing from his years in exile. An avowed Catholic and an ardent believer in divine right, he antagonized both Whigs and Tories by his arrogant, headstrong speech and acts.

Again the question of the succession to the throne became very troublesome. James had two daughters, Mary and Anne. Both were Protestants, married to Protestant princes. Mary was the wife of William III of Orange, ruler of Holland and staunch opponent of Louis XIV of France. Anne had married a Danish prince. However, James' first wife had died, and he had married again, this time a Catholic princess. In 1688 she gave birth to a son, who would by law succeed his father. Since both father and mother were Catholics, it was certain that the boy would be raised in the Catholic Church. It seemed that the religious problem would continue to trouble England for many years.

● *Parliament invites William and Mary to rule (1688)*

Now all the groups in opposition to James combined. Then occurred that event in English history known as the Glorious Revolution. Both Whigs and Tories agreed that James must go. They invited William III of Holland and his wife Mary, James' daughter, to rule jointly. William III landed in England with a Dutch army, but it was hardly necessary. Unable to rally anyone to his support, James fled to France. Catholic Ireland rebelled, but William suppressed the rebellion by force. Parliament gave the crown to William and Mary as joint rulers. John Locke defended this Glorious Revolution in *Two Treatises on Government* (page 295).

William and Mary sign the Bill of Rights (1689)

The English Parliament wanted safeguards before it granted the throne to William and Mary. So, in a document famous in both English and American history, it fixed very careful conditions to which the new rulers agreed in advance. This document is known as the Bill of Rights (1689).

First and foremost, the Bill of Rights declared that the king was merely an official chosen by Parliament and subject to its laws. He could not proclaim any law, suspend any law, levy any tax, nor maintain an army

The Bill of Rights, 1689. The full name of this bill was "An Act Declaring the Rights and Liberties of the Subject, and Settling the Succession of the Crown." Of greatest interest to Americans are sections enacted by the members of Parliament to protect "their ancient rights and liberties." Compare the following with sections of the Constitution of the United States:

▶ That the raising or keeping a standing army within the kingdom in time of peace, unless it be with consent of Parliament, is against law.

▶ That the subjects which are Protestants may have arms for their defence.

▶ That elections of members of Parliament ought to be free.

▶ That the freedom of speech, and debates or proceedings in Parliament, ought not to be impeached or questioned in any court or place out of Parliament.

▶ That excessive bail ought not to be required, nor excessive fines imposed, nor cruel and unusual punishments inflicted.

without the consent of Parliament. Parliament was to meet frequently. The king promised not to interfere with the election of members, nor with their right to express themselves freely in debate and to take whatever actions they thought necessary. A standing army could be raised and kept in time of peace only with the consent of Parliament.

The Bill of Rights also gave protections to individual citizens. The rulers promised to honor the principles of free speech, the right to publish books without first submitting them to a censor, and the right of a citizen to petition the government for relief of any injustice. No man could be imprisoned without a speedy trial, nor required to give excessive bail, nor subjected to cruel and unusual punishments.

In 1689 Parliament also passed the Act of Toleration. This act granted freedom of conscience and the right of public worship to non-Anglican Protestants, whom the English called Dissenters. It was not complete religious freedom, because Catholics were still under heavy restrictions, and Dissenters could not hold public office. However, it was a step toward toleration, in the worthy tradition of the French Henry IV and the Edict of Nantes.

Shortly afterward, Parliament passed the Act of Settlement. This act provided that if William and Mary should die without heirs, Mary's sister Anne should succeed. If she died childless, the throne should go to a German princess, Sophia of Hanover, a Protestant granddaughter of James I. Thus there was great care taken to keep the Catholic Stuart descendants of James II from gaining the English throne.

Parliament as the real ruler of England

The Bill of Rights and the Act of Settlement ended the English Revolution. In summary, it was a century-long struggle between king and Parliament to see who would rule the country. Parliament was clearly the winner. In the course of the struggle it had tried and executed a king. In 1660 it restored a king to the throne. In 1688 it deposed a king and invited another to rule, having first fixed the conditions under which a king might rule. In the Act of Settlement it decided the succession to the throne. By 1700 it was clear that England was not an absolute monarchy, nor even a hereditary monarchy. Parliament emerged as the real ruler of the country.

In the Bill of Rights Parliament made sure of its supremacy over the king. It also restated the rights of individuals—to freedom of speech, press, and petition, and the rights to fair, impartial justice. The freedom of individuals in their private lives and their voice in government made great progress in seventeenth-century England.

It should be made clear that the government of England was not a democracy. Parliament did not by any means represent all the people. The House of Lords was made up

A scene in the House of Commons in the late eighteenth century.

of hereditary nobles and higher clergy. Even the House of Commons, which was becoming the more powerful of the two houses, represented only a small class: the landed gentry and the middle-class businessmen. The right to vote to elect members of Commons was very strictly limited. Workingmen and small farmers were not represented at all. It was a class government, but it did represent at least some of the people.

● Parliament continues to gain power

In the fifty years after 1689 Parliament continued to gain importance as the real government of England. The organization and institutions of English government today gradually emerged. William III knew little and cared less about the domestic problems of England. His interests lay in checking the vast ambitions of Louis XIV of France on the continent of Europe. He chose ministers to help him administer the English government. So long as he was free to handle foreign affairs, he was quite willing to allow Parliament and his ministers to deal with the domestic problems of England.

To help make the government run more smoothly, William III made a wise move. The king noticed that the government ran more smoothly when the ministers of his Cabinet belonged to the party with the most votes in the House of Commons—in those days the Whigs or the Tories. A practical man, William chose his ministers accordingly. This represented another step in Parliament's control of the executive branch of the government. The ministers who carry out the acts of Parliament must belong to the party which controls the law-making House of Commons.

Several other steps in legislative control of the government came during William III's reign. Parliament gained the right to declare war. Judges now held office "during good behavior" instead of being removable at the will of the king. It was Parliament that requested the removal of an unworthy judge. Gradually the power of the king to veto acts of Parliament was abandoned. This was not done by law but by custom. Queen Anne was the last ruler to veto an act of Parliament. Thus the ruler gave up checks on the legislative power of Parliament, while Parliament had many checks on the executive power of the sovereign.

In 1707 the Act of Union merged the separate governments of England and Scotland into the United Kingdom of Great Britain. The Scottish Parliament was abolished. Scots were given seats in the House of Lords and in the Commons, which were now called the British Parliament. There was opposition at first, but the union proved to be beneficial. It removed barriers to trade, and the resulting expanded commerce brought greater prosperity to both countries.

Parliament's complete control over the government of Great Britain developed even faster under the successors to Queen Anne. When she died childless, the throne, by the Act of Settlement, went to George I, son of Sophia of Hanover. George was Elector of Hanover, a small German state. He and his son and successor, George II, were German-born. George I spoke no English. George II spoke English but is credited with correct pronunciation of neither English nor German. Neither king was interested in British domestic affairs. They were perfectly content to leave the handling of British affairs to their ministers, who were always chosen from the majority party in Commons.

For over twenty years the Whig Party controlled the House of Commons; so its members were chosen as ministers. The recognized leader of the Whigs, Sir Robert Walpole, was always chosen as a minister. Since George I and George II showed little interest in English governmental affairs, someone had to act as head of the government. Walpole came to be recognized as the "prime," or first, minister.

307

Parliament, especially in the House of Commons. The Prime Minister presents the ruler's wishes to the Cabinet and Parliament. The ruler selects a new Prime Minister when the holder no longer controls a majority in Commons. However, the ruler chooses only the recognized leader of the party which has a majority. The Prime Minister selects the other members of his Cabinet.

The British preserve all the forms of royalty. The government operates in the name of "His (or Her) Royal Majesty." The monarch opens each session of Parliament with a speech from the throne, telling the members what laws are needed. However, the Cabinet decides what laws are needed and writes the speech which the sovereign reads. Parliament passes the laws, levies the taxes, maintains "His (or Her) Majesty's" armed forces, declares war, and approves treaties. The Cabinet, under the Prime Minister, enforces and administers the laws.

● Great Britain as a constitutional monarchy

By the middle of the eighteenth century Great Britain had become a limited, constitutional monarchy. It is somewhat confusing because the British "constitution" is not completely written in any one place. It is made up of great documents like the Magna Carta, the Petition of Right, and the Bill of Rights. But it also consists of many acts of Parliament which any succeeding Parliament may change. Many things are not written anywhere, such as the office of Prime Minister and the fact that the king does not veto laws. The British "constitution" shocks people who like things arranged and organized neatly, carefully, and definitely. But it works! It is one of the oldest constitutional governments in the world today. The limited monarchy of Great Britain furnished the model for many modern states. The British experience from 1603 to 1750 was a guide to those who wanted to abolish the Old Régime.

Traditional pomp and ceremony at the coronation of Elizabeth II. For two centuries Great Britain has been a limited monarchy, in which Parliament rather than the king or queen actually rules. Nevertheless, the British keep the forms and ceremonies of the monarchy. Note the scepter in the queen's right hand, as in the portrait of Elizabeth I (page 247). Through the time of the Stuart kings, this was a symbol of real authority.

Thus there evolved the office of Prime Minister. He became the real head of the government, because the government of Britain combines legislative and executive power in

Review of Chapter 24

People, places, and things

Identify: James I, Charles I, Charles II, James II, William and Mary, Anne, George I, George II, Oliver Cromwell, Robert Walpole, Long Parliament, Rump Parliament, Pilgrims, Cavaliers, Roundheads, Habeas Corpus Act, Act of Union.

Locate: England, Scotland, Ireland, Holland, Hanover, Plymouth Colony.

Events in review

1. What important right did the English Parliament have at the time James I became king? Why was this right certain to be a cause of trouble between king and Parliament?
2. What was the position of the Anglican Church during the reign of James I? Was there opposition to this Church?
3. Various groups of Calvinists wanted to make changes in the religious organization in England. What beliefs were held by (a) Puritans, (b) Presbyterians, (c) Separatists or Independents?
4. During the reigns of James I and Charles I, there was increasing trouble between king and country. What were the main sources of trouble?
5. Why did Charles I sign the Petition of Right?
6. Did England have a liberal or democratic government under the Commonwealth? Give details.
7. How did the Bill of Rights of 1689 (a) limit the power of the king, (b) protect individual citizens?
8. Why did the English invite a Dutch king and later a German prince to take the throne of England?
9. How did the king's ministers gain in importance during the reigns of William III and of George I and II?
10. Are the duties of the Prime Minister set down in writing in the British "constitution"? Explain.

Problems and projects

1. Contrast Charles II with the other Stuart kings as a man and as a ruler. What did he mean when he said that he had "no desire to go on his travels again"? What does the history of the Stuarts suggest about the value of tactfulness in a ruler?
2. List the powers Parliament gained at the expense of the king between the reign of James I and the reign of William and Mary. Tell briefly the steps by which Parliament acquired its powers.
3. The Petition of Right, the Habeas Corpus Act, the Bill of Rights, and the Act of Toleration covered many important rights of individual citizens. List the rights protected by these four measures. How many of the same rights are covered by the Constitution of the United States?
4. In two parallel columns make a comparison of the British Parliament after 1689 with the Congress of the United States. Consider (a) organization and membership, (b) who elected members, (c) powers held.
5. Compare Elizabeth I with Elizabeth II as to titles, privileges, duties, and powers.
6. Write a character sketch of one of the following: Charles I, Charles II, James II, Oliver Cromwell.
7. To debate: The best assurance of an individual's freedom is the preservation of the provisions of the Bill of Rights.

Chapter 25 The American Revolution

THE FOUNDING of a colony in Virginia in 1607 marked the beginning of England's colonial empire in America. By 1750 there were thirteen English colonies strung along the Atlantic seacoast of North America. These colonies were not established by the English government. Private citizens in England founded and developed all the American colonies as business ventures. In order to raise money, the Stuart kings sold monopolies for trading and colonizing to companies of stockholders. The stockholders hoped to make a profit. In other cases, kings gave large tracts of land in America to favorites. These men, called proprietors, furnished the money to start a colony. They also hoped to make a profit. To these companies and individuals the kings granted royal charters. These charters gave them the right to establish and govern colonies and to conduct business for profit.

Although the English government played little part in founding or building the American colonies, it did make certain guarantees to them. Each colonial charter promised that every colonist in America would be considered an Englishman. Colonists were promised the same legal rights and freedoms as men who were born and lived in England. This provision of the charters became very important when the colonists and the English government began to argue over who had the right to make laws for the colonies.

The American colonies were never profitable as business ventures, but they attracted many settlers from England. Some hoped to find gold or the passage to the Indies. Most of them, people of the middle and lower classes in England, came to escape the bad conditions there. The political struggles between the Stuart kings and Parliament, the religious disagreements of Anglicans, Catholics, and Calvinists, and the bad economic conditions each played a part. Englishmen came into the wilderness of America to seek a better living, peace from political strife, and freedom to worship in the way they wanted.

Men needed very strong reasons to leave England for America. Life in the New World was hard and dangerous. When the first Englishmen landed, they found an almost continuous forest that stretched from the Atlantic Coast to the Mississippi River. Land had to be cleared for farms; crops had to be raised for food. Indians resented having their hunting grounds taken away.

The English colonies develop separately

●Colonial government

Almost from the beginning, both the companies and the proprietors found it necessary to give the colonists some voice in their own government. By 1750 each colony had a government consisting of three main parts: First, a governor and, second, a council which advised him. This council also acted as the upper house of the legislature, somewhat like the English House of Lords. Third, each colony had an assembly, the lower house of the legislature, elected by the freemen or free-holders.

By 1750 many companies and proprietors had failed to make a profit; so they turned their charters back to the king. In these colonies the king appointed the governor and council, and the colonists elected the assembly. These were known as royal colonies. Three colonies, Pennsylvania, Delaware, and Maryland, were still under proprietors. The proprietor either acted as governor or appointed a governor and council. In Rhode Island and Connecticut the voters elected all officials: governor, council, and assembly.

In the royal and proprietory colonies there were many conflicts between the appointed governors and the elected assemblies. The governors had to act according to the viewpoint of the king or the proprietor. The assembly reflected the viewpoint of the voters, and these voters were usually middle-class merchants and landowners. Governors had the authority to recommend and veto laws, appoint and remove officials, and summon or dismiss the assemblies. Like the English House of Commons, the elected assemblies claimed the right to approve taxes and the spending of public money. There were many and violent disagreements over taxation, defense, the authority of royal judges, and the enforcement of laws regulating colonial trade. These conflicts helped a spirit of independence to develop in the colonies.

Conditions of soil and climate divided the colonies into three main groups. New England, where farming was less productive, developed more industries such as fishing, lumbering, shipbuilding, manufacturing, and trading. The middle colonies—New York, New Jersey, Pennsylvania, and Delaware—produced enough grain to be able to export it. They came to be called the "Bread Colonies." The southern group, from Maryland south, specialized in growing tobacco, rice, and indigo, a plant from which an important blue dye was made. From their pine forests

Governor Bradford's house in Plymouth, 1621. Note the stockade for defense against Indians. On the hillside, men are cutting trees to clear the land for farming. The colonists survived only by determination and hard work.

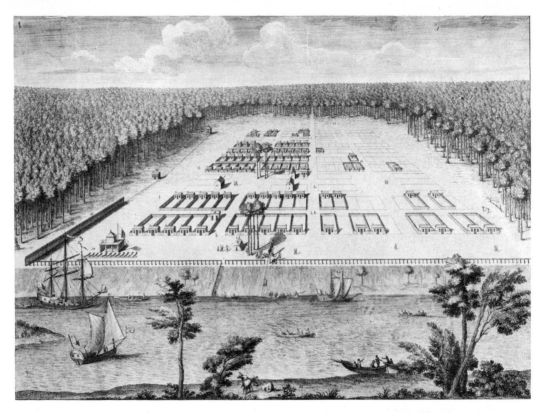

they got pitch, tar, resin, and turpentine, all important in shipbuilding and shipping. These products were called naval stores.

● Colonial trade

The colonies had to develop trade because they had to import most of the manufactured goods they needed. To get the money to pay for their imports, they had to find markets to sell their own products. The southern colonies found a good market for their tobacco, rice, indigo, and naval stores in England. In return, they bought most of their own necessities in England. England had less need for the grain, fish, and lumber of New England and the middle colonies, hence these regions sold most of their goods in Europe, Africa, and the West Indies. Much of the American commerce was carried with ships built, manned, and owned by the colonists.

Trade with the West Indies islands was especially important to the northern colonies.

A view of Savannah, Georgia, in 1734. The town is surrounded on three sides by a pine forest. From these trees the colonists got such valuable products as tar and turpentine.

Climate and soil in the islands made it possible to grow sugar cane. From sugar cane refined sugar and molasses could be made. There was a demand everywhere for these products. In time the people of the islands, using slave labor, specialized in producing sugar and molasses. They bought most of their food from outside the islands. Therefore they were good markets for the products of New England and the middle colonies.

England, Spain, France, and Holland all had colonies in the West Indies. The foreign (Dutch and French) West Indies sold their sugar and molasses a little cheaper than the British island colonies; so American shippers preferred to trade with the French and Dutch. The Americans could sell their products and buy the sugar and molasses which they needed. Because the French and the Dutch sold cheaper than the British, trade with them produced a surplus of cash. The Americans needed this badly to pay for imports from England and Europe.

Britain attempts to tighten control over the colonies

It was not long before the English government tried to set up closer ties with and controls on the colonies. The greatest attempt at imperial control was in the economic field, through the regulation of colonial commerce and industry. Oliver Cromwell had introduced mercantilism in an attempt to keep Dutch ships from trading with England or her colonies. A brief review of the mercantilist ideas about colonies might be helpful.

● Mercantilism and colonies

Mercantilism held that a colony existed for the benefit of the mother country. The colony should supply needed raw materials and buy the manufactured products of the mother country. Colonies were discouraged from producing their own manufactured products or from buying such goods from foreign countries.

English Navigation or Trade Acts required that goods shipped to or from the colonies be carried in English ships with English crews. Many American goods could be sold only in England, where they were taxed. European goods sold to America had to be landed in England, taxed, and then transported in English ships. Americans were discouraged from manufacturing. American purchases of sugar and molasses from foreign-owned West Indies islands were heavily taxed. Although some features of mercantilism brought benefits to the Americans, the over-all effects were more harmful than good.

The Navigation, or Trade, Laws were enforced by revenue agents appointed by the king or the royal governors. Cases involving the laws were tried in courts before judges appointed by the king. To make enforcement easier, cases were tried before judges alone, without juries. From a judge revenue agents could get warrants called Writs of Assistance. These warrants allowed the agents to search any place at any time to try to find smuggled goods.

● Conflicts between the colonies and England

Writs of Assistance and trials without juries led to conflicts and arguments between the colonists and the English government. The government considered them necessary to stop the smuggling of goods. The colonists, however, considered them a denial of rights guaranteed in their charters—the "rights of Englishmen." These rights included the right to a trial by jury. They also guaranteed that no man's property could be searched by government officers without a written warrant; the warrant had to name the place to be searched and the things searched for.

The purpose of the Trade Acts was to make colonial trade benefit England. For many reasons the acts failed to accomplish their purpose. Moreover, they aroused great resentment in America. Colonists found many ways to evade the restrictions. They bought and sold where they could do so most profitably. They avoided paying taxes whenever

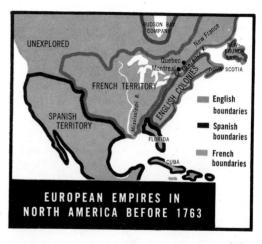

EUROPEAN EMPIRES IN
NORTH AMERICA BEFORE 1763

and however they could. Smuggling became a respectable occupation, difficult to prevent because of the long American coastline with its many harbors and inlets.

The French wars remove a danger in America

The greatest threat to the English colonies in America came from the French. Control of the St. Lawrence River and the Great Lakes allowed the French to reach the mid-continent fairly easily. The Appalachian Mountains made English expansion difficult; French control of the western waterways would have made it almost impossible.

> *A major amphibious operation in the French and Indian War—the British attack on Quebec. English troops under General Wolfe are shown landing on the shore of the St. Lawrence River and scaling the hills. The British defeated the French under General Montcalm. This battle has been called the most decisive ever fought on American soil. The British victory meant that France was no longer a power in North America. The colonies no longer faced a threat from the French.*

The discussion of the War of the Spanish Succession (page 273) and the Seven Years' War (page 284) has brought out the fact that the long series of wars between England and France were fought in America as well as in Europe. Clashes over fishing rights, the fur trade, and land claims made conflicts likely. Four British-French wars were fought in America. The most important one was an extension of the Seven Years' War in Europe. The French and Indian War (as it was named in this country) conclusively settled the British-French struggle in America. By the Treaty of Paris, 1763, France gave up Canada and the land as far west as the Mississippi River to Great Britain. The land west of the Mississippi went to Spain. Britain also gained Florida from Spain. France's American empire, and with it the French danger to the British colonies, disappeared.

England again tries to tighten control of the colonies

The French and Indian War revealed serious weaknesses in the British Empire, especially in America. Although many of the colonists fought bravely, the colonies as a whole did not make a very good record. They remained separate. Each colony preferred to have its militia (its colonial troops) used only within its own borders regardless of the common need. Colonial assemblies were very reluctant to levy taxes or grant money to carry on the war. In spite of the fact that they were at war with France, Americans continued to trade with the French both in Canada and the West Indies, and to smuggle goods as before.

The war left Great Britain with a large debt and heavy taxes. The war had been fought partly in America for protection of the colonists; therefore, the British felt that the colonists should furnish more money to pay the debt and relieve the British taxpayers of their heavy burden.

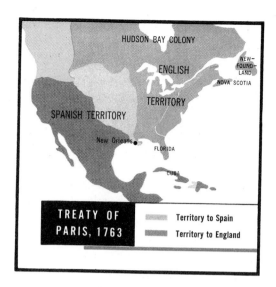

HUDSON BAY COLONY

ENGLISH

NEW-FOUND-LAND

NOVA SCOTIA

TERRITORY

SPANISH TERRITORY

New Orleans

FLORIDA

CUBA

TREATY OF PARIS, 1763

Territory to Spain
Territory to England

King George III

King George III inherited the British throne in 1760. Unlike George I and George II (his grandfather and father), he had been born, reared, and educated as an Englishman. Unlike them, he wanted to rule England in fact as well as in name. He hoped to control the government by bribing enough members to get a majority in the House of Commons, choose the Prime Minister, and have passed the laws he wanted. The men in control of the British government were determined to bring all parts of the empire under close control. They insisted that the Trade Laws be enforced; to this end writs of assistance and trials without juries were continued. To raise money to pay British officials and the army in the colonies, the colonists were required to pay special taxes such as a stamp tax.

A spirit of independence grows in the colonies

Relations between the British government and the American colonies grew steadily worse in the years from 1763 to 1776. The British were insistent that laws should be enforced, taxes should be paid, and that Americans should be obedient subjects. Americans resisted these attempts in several ways. They gave legal arguments based on

their rights as Englishmen. By refusing to buy British goods they brought pressure on British merchants and, through them, on Parliament. Some Americans resisted by acts of violence, such as tarring and feathering tax collectors or dumping tea from British ships into the harbor. Such acts made the British still more determined to have their way. British attempts to punish illegal and violent acts by the colonists made the latter even more insistent on their rights.

British pressure compelled the colonies to take some slight steps toward uniting. The Stamp Act Congress (1765), the First Continental Congress (1774), and the Second Continental Congress (1775–1781) showed an increasing degree of unity, although each was an unofficial body of representatives who could not take final action for their states.

A British tax stamp. The Stamp Act required the colonists to pay a tax for stamps that had to be placed on many kinds of documents. Here was one source of trouble between the Americans and the British government.

In the beginning almost all Americans insisted that they were loyal Englishmen trying to gain or preserve their rights. As time went on the actions and reactions of the conflict became more bitter. Many men came to feel that their rights could be assured only if the colonies became completely independent. After 1773 (the Boston Tea Party) relations went from bad to worse. In 1775 fighting broke out around Boston. On July 4, 1776, the Second Continental Congress formally adopted a Declaration of Independence written mainly by Thomas Jefferson.

The colonies declare their independence

The American Declaration of Independence became a document of world-wide importance. Its thinking was based on the writings of the Englishman John Locke, of Rousseau and other French philosophers, and even of earlier writers on the philosophy of government. Thomas Jefferson gave it a nobility of thought and a grandeur of statement that were to have far-reaching effects in the world.

The Declaration states that all men are created equal and are given by their Creator certain rights that cannot be taken from them. Among these rights are "life, liberty, and the pursuit of happiness." All powers of government belong to the people; no government can exist without the consent of its citizens. The citizens create governments to protect them in their rights. If a government fails to protect their rights, or attempts to destroy the rights, the people have a further right "to alter or abolish" that government and set up a new one that will do its duty. The Declaration then stated all the grievances of the colonists against the king. It used them as proofs that the British government was not protecting their rights, but was destroying them. It drew the conclusion that "these United Colonies are, and of Right ought to be, Free and Independent States."

In an age of autocracy and divine right of kings, these were radical ideas, indeed! They were especially bold when stated by a group of small, weak colonies against one of the most powerful kingdoms in the world. And they were bolder still when one considers that the people of the colonies were not united in wanting independence. Possibly one third of the colonists were strongly opposed to the idea. Among them were most of the wealthiest and most powerful men of the colonies: merchants, manufacturers, shippers, lawyers, clergymen, and physicians. Many of them fought for the British; the Americans called them Tories. Still more left the colonies altogether. Another third of the people were neutral; they took no active part until they saw who would win. Only about

The fight at Concord bridge, April 19, 1775. The first fighting in the Revolution took place at Lexington and Concord, in Massachusetts. The Americans turned back a British force that had marched out from Boston. In the words of Emerson, "the embattled farmers" at Concord "fired the shot heard 'round the world."

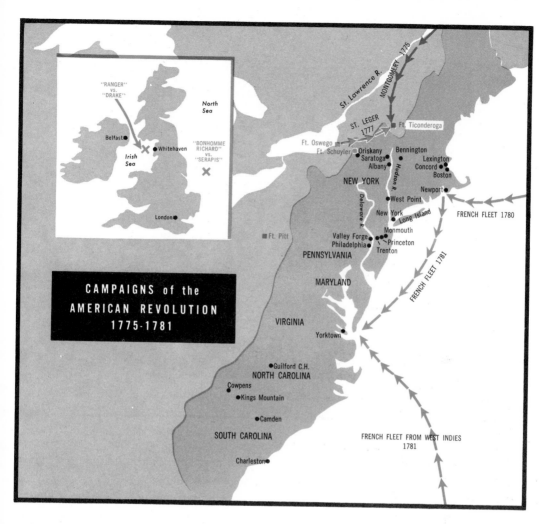

"RANGER" vs. "DRAKE"

North Sea

Belfast●

●Whitehaven

Irish Sea

"BONHOMME RICHARD" vs. "SERAPIS"

London●

St. Lawrence R.

MONTGOMERY 1775

ST. LEGER 1777

Ft. Oswego

Ft. Schuyler ● Oriskany

Ft. Ticonderoga

Bennington

Saratoga●

Lexington

Albany●

Concord●

Boston

NEW YORK

Newport●

Hudson R.

West Point●

Delaware R.

New York●

●Long Island

FRENCH FLEET 1780

Monmouth

FRENCH FLEET 1781

●Ft. Pitt

Valley Forge●

Philadelphia●

●Princeton

Trenton

PENNSYLVANIA

MARYLAND

CAMPAIGNS of the AMERICAN REVOLUTION 1775-1781

VIRGINIA

Yorktown●

●Guilford C.H.

NORTH CAROLINA

Cowpens●

●Kings Mountain

●Camden

SOUTH CAROLINA

FRENCH FLEET FROM WEST INDIES 1781

Charleston●

a third of the colonists were active independence men.

Americans fight for independence

In spite of this division in the population, the Americans had some advantages in the war. They were fighting on their own land, in defense of their own homes, in country they knew well. It was the British, not they, who had to take the offensive. The British had to fight far from home, bringing with them most of their supplies and equipment. Englishmen did not support the war very well. Many of them, opposed to King George III's attempt to rule England, felt that the Americans were fighting England's battle against the king as well as their own. Because of this lukewarm English support, the king had to hire German soldiers, Hessians, to help fight the war in America. Also, the Americans received help from England's European enemies, France, Spain, and Holland. In particular, the Americans made an alliance with France in 1778. Finally, the Americans had fine leaders. If it had not been for the inspired leadership of George Washington, the American cause would have been lost many times.

● *Problems facing the Americans*

The Americans also had weaknesses which seemed even greater than their strengths. The British fleet, strongest in the world, was

317

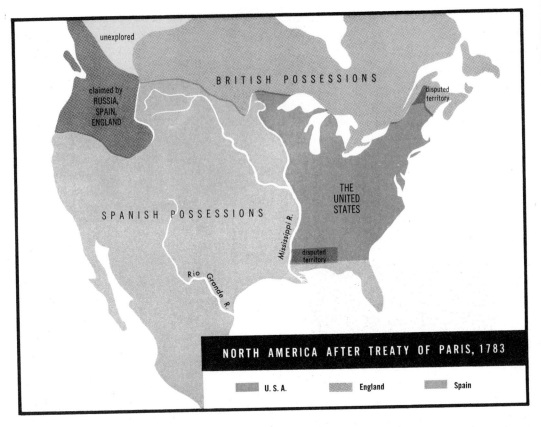

BRITISH POSSESSIONS

claimed by
RUSSIA,
SPAIN,
ENGLAND

disputed
territory

THE
UNITED
STATES

SPANISH POSSESSIONS

Mississippi R.

disputed
territory

Rio Grande R.

NORTH AMERICA AFTER TREATY OF PARIS, 1783

U. S. A.   England   Spain

a tremendous obstacle. It could land a British army anywhere on the American coast. If the army got into difficulties, the fleet could come in, take the troops aboard, and sail away again. The trained British troops were hard for the untrained, poorly organized, poorly equipped Americans to handle. Throughout the war it was almost the rule that the British could land an army and capture and hold any seacoast city they really wanted. In an open battle they could usually defeat the Americans.

The greatest American weaknesses, however, were internal. The people were divided in their opinions and feelings. Still worse, the states were disunited. The only organization to unify them was the Second Continental Congress. It was entirely a voluntary body, with no real powers. When it wanted to do anything, the proposal had to be sent to the states for approval. Few of the states gave whole-hearted support to the war unless the

fighting was within their borders. Some would not allow their militia to fight outside their own borders.

To raise money the Continental Congress had to ask the states for it or to borrow it. The Congress had no power to tax. It borrowed both by selling bonds and by printing paper money. Since it had no sure way of paying its debts, its credit was poor. Both bonds and paper money went down very much in value. At one time eighty dollars in paper money equalled only one dollar in gold.

The weaknesses of the American government made it difficult to build up a strong army. At first, the army was made up mostly of state militia, poorly trained and undisciplined. The men enlisted for only a few months at a time and then went home to carry on their ordinary duties. Congress tried to raise a Continental army of men enlisted for longer terms, who would serve anywhere.

It was hard to persuade men to enlist, especially in the early years of the war; the army was poorly paid, fed, clothed, and equipped. In the darkest days of the war it seemed that the American army might disappear altogether. In the winter of 1776–1777 Washington had only about 3,000 men fit to fight.

The American victory

In spite of all these handicaps the war was fought for seven years. The final victory came at Yorktown, Virginia, in 1781. The British General Cornwallis was forced to surrender his army to a combined force of Americans and French. The British still had more troops in America than Washington had in his army. However, Britain was tired of the American war. Also, Britain was at war with France, Holland, and Spain, and the war was going badly in other parts of the empire as well as in America. The government of the King's Friends had finally been defeated in Parliament. The Whigs, who came to power, wanted to end the American war at almost any cost. So, after almost two years of diplomatic negotiations, a peace treaty between the British and Americans was signed in Paris in 1783. The independence of the United States was recognized. Its boundaries were fixed at the Mississippi River, the Great Lakes, and Florida. Florida and the land west of the Mississippi River went to Spain.

America attempts to form a united government

The American states fought almost the whole war with only the voluntary, makeshift government of the Second Continental Congress. It was really no government at all, for it lacked all the powers which a government must have. Each state had a government with powers, but there was no central government to unite them for common action. The Continental Congress approved a constitution for a stronger government, but for various reasons it was not finally approved by all the states until 1781, six months before the victory of Yorktown.

The Articles of Confederation

The constitution was called the Articles of Confederation. It created a one-house Congress in which each state had one vote. Congress was given some powers: to declare war, make peace, conduct relations with foreign countries, raise an army, settle disputes between the states, and borrow money. It was not given power to tax. To get money Congress had to request the states to grant it. Nor was the Congress allowed to regulate trade among the states or foreign trade.

> An American victory at sea in 1779. The Americans never were able to get more than a few ships to sea in the face of the huge British fleet; however, they won some notable fights. Most famous was the capture of the British *Serapis* by the Bonhomme Richard, commanded by John Paul Jones. At one point in the battle, the British captain asked Jones if he had surrendered. Jones' reply has ever since been famous: "I have not yet begun to fight."

It was really a very strange government. There was a legislature, the Congress, with power to make certain laws. But there was no executive branch to enforce and administer these laws; that was done by the individual states. There were no United States courts. Cases involving United States laws had to be tried in the courts of the several states.

The government set up for the United States under the Articles of Confederation was too weak to do the work that a government must do. This first constitution was in effect from 1781 to 1788. In 1787 delegates from twelve states (Rhode Island not taking part) met to draft a new plan of government. The new Constitution was adopted in 1788. In the following year George Washington became the first president under the new plan of government. This Constitution is, of course, the one under which the government of the United States still operates.

● The Constitution

The writers of the new Constitution had to face certain basic problems. They had to create a central government strong enough to act for the states in those things where the states had to act together. At the same time, they had to leave the states free to act for themselves in those things which each state considered its own business. Powers had to be divided to set up a nice balance: things which only the central government could do; things which only the individual states could do; things which either or both could do; things which neither could be permitted to do. Then, too, the framers of the Constitution had to do something about the branches or departments of government. Their experience under the Articles of Confederation had convinced them that a government cannot get along without its own executive to enforce and carry out its laws, and its own courts to interpret its laws and to decide when the laws were violated.

In solving these problems, the framers of the Constitution used ideas stated earlier by Montesquieu in his *Spirit of the Laws* (page 296). They created three branches of the central government: executive, legislative, and judicial. Each one was given certain powers. Each was considered equally important. In some ways each acted as a check on each of the others, so that no one branch could become more powerful and important than the others. The central government was given power to do the things which the states acting individually could not do well. States were prohibited from doing some things which needed common action by the central government—such as declaring war, making treaties, or coining money. Both the central government and the states were forbidden to do certain things which would deny or take away the rights and liberties of the people. Then the Constitution stated that all powers not given to the central government, nor prohibited to the states, belonged to the states and the people. This is known as a *federal* form of government.

The American Revolution has world-wide effects

The effects of the American war for independence were not limited to the United States and Great Britain. The ideas of the American Revolution had a world-wide effect which is still felt today. It is worth stating these powerful ideas again.

First is the idea that all men are equal before the law, and that they have certain rights which no one can take from them—inalienable rights, as they are called. This is the very foundation of the democratic ideal. Every human being is an individual with a personality and a dignity which must be respected. No man may have a privileged position before and beyond the law; laws apply equally to all. There are no second-class people. Each human being has the right to equality of opportunity and must be treated with justice.

Another mighty idea states that all the powers of government belong to the people. It is they who create governments for the purpose of protecting their rights. The people delegate the powers to the government through their representatives. Government can exist and operate only if the people consent to it. The people can change any government which denies or fails to protect their rights. They can create whatever kind of government they think best suited for them.

These were not new ideas; John Locke and the French philosophers had written about them. However, it was the American Revolution which put them into effect for all the world to see. These ideas meant a death blow to the Old Régime: to autocracy, to divine right of kings, and the idea of a class of people specially privileged because of their birth. The ideas of the American Revolution surged through the Western world, sweeping away kings and privileged classes. Today these ideas are still at work in Asia and Africa. People who until recently have been subjects and colonists are now demanding the democratic right to govern themselves and to be treated as equal human beings.

The federal form of government created by the framers of the American Constitution has also had great influence in the world. Here is a way in which individual states or governments can be united under one central government. The central government can act for them to solve problems common to all but leave them free to act for themselves in dealing with problems that are domestic or individual. This federal form of government has been adopted in many places—in Australia, Canada, South Africa, Switzerland, Germany, and some Central and South American republics. The noble idea of democratic federalism, which was born out of the American Revolution, is a very powerful idea indeed!

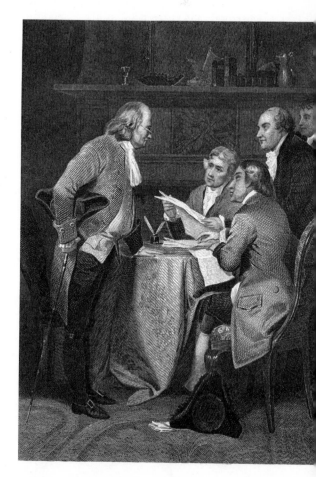

Five famous Americans who contributed to the great ideas of the Revolution and helped establish the new nation. Shown here is a committee consisting of Benjamin Franklin, Thomas Jefferson, John Adams, Robert Livingston, and Roger Sherman working on the draft of the Declaration of Independence.

Review of Chapter 25

People, places, and things

Identify: Writ of Assistance, Navigation and Trade Acts, Stamp Act, Stamp Act Congress, First and Second Continental Congresses, Declaration of Independence, Articles of Confederation, Seven Years' War.

Locate: The thirteen English colonies in America, the West Indies, Canada, Quebec, Montreal, the French Empire in America before 1763, the Spanish Empire in America after 1763, the United States after 1783.

Events in review

1. In the governments of the American colonies in 1750, which officials were elected? Who elected them?
2. What were the sources of conflict between governors and assemblies in the American colonies?
3. Why did some of the colonies have to develop trade with countries other than England?
4. Name two important "rights of Englishmen" that were guaranteed in the colonial charters. Why did the English government violate these rights?
5. Adopting the Declaration of Independence was a very bold act. Explain why this was so.
6. What advantages did the Americans have in their struggle against England?
7. Did the Continental Congress during the Revolution have any real powers? Explain.
8. The American Revolution put into effect several mighty ideas, which had world-wide influence. Briefly state these ideas.

Problems and projects

1. Why did Englishmen leave home to settle in colonies in America? Review the events that caused the Pilgrims and many Puritans to move to the new country.
2. What part did the king's government play in founding the colonies? in governing the royal colonies? Why did the English government make more and more efforts to impose controls on the colonies?
3. Sugar and molasses from the West Indies became a link in what was called the "triangular trade." Using reference books, try to find out what this term means.
4. On the basis of this and earlier chapters, evaluate the mercantile system. How much did it help and how much did it harm the British Empire?
5. Which of the ideas expressed in the Declaration of Independence had been used by Locke in justifying the Glorious Revolution in 1688?
6. Why were the Americans during and just after the Revolution reluctant to form a strong central government? What weaknesses showed up under the Articles of Confederation?
7. How did the men who wrote the new Constitution solve the problems of creating a strong central government but still protecting the rights of states? Has their plan of government influenced the rest of the world?
8. Conduct a "Who Am I" program. Use quotations from John Locke, Montesquieu, George III, Samuel Adams, Thomas Jefferson, Patrick Henry, Benjamin Franklin, and George Washington.

Chapter 26 The French Revolution

THE ENGLISH REVOLUTION of 1688–1689 established a limited monarchy. The power of the king was taken over by Parliament. The Parliament represented the nobles and the middle class. The American Revolution of 1775–1783 led to the founding of a republic—a government of elected officials without a king. The people themselves ruled through their elected representatives. The third great revolution to shake the Western World, bringing great and far-reaching changes, began in France in 1789.

The Old Régime in France

France was the outstanding example in Europe of the Old Régime. Culturally it was farther advanced than any other country on the continent. Taken as a whole its people were more prosperous than any other Europeans. But in spite of this comparatively good position, there were many very bad conditions in France.

The government of France was an absolute, divine-right monarchy. Headed by an able king who worked at his job, such a government could be fairly efficient. Under Louis XIV it was efficient. Under an indolent and wicked ruler like Louis XV the government simply drifted.

The people of France were divided into three social classes called Estates (see page 293). The First Estate (clergy) and the Sec-

ond Estate (nobles) had many privileges and few responsibilities. The Third Estate, made up of middle-class people and peasants, paid most of the taxes, did almost all of the work, and received few of the benefits.

Personal liberty did not exist in France under the Old Régime. There was no freedom of speech, press, or religion. Judges were

The Chateau of Chambord. This huge residence suggests the wealth and splendor in which members of the First and Second Estates lived under the Old Régime. These people had many privileges, few duties, and escaped most taxes.

appointed and removed by the king. Trials were secret and without jury. The king issued *lettres de cachet* (sealed letters). These ordered the imprisonment without trial of anyone who displeased the monarch. Such a person might remain in the Bastille, the famous prison of Paris, for years without trial or without even knowing why he had been imprisoned.

● Attacks on the Old Régime

The ideas and practices of the Old Régime were attacked by many French writers (pages 295–296). Influenced by the English and American Revolutions, and by Voltaire, Rousseau, Montesquieu, and many others, the French increased their critical attacks on the divine-rights monarchy, the privileges of the nobles, and the unjust taxes. They especially attacked the Church because of its vast wealth in land, its collection of tithes, and its exclusive control of education.

The success of the American Revolution had a profound effect on the thinking of the French middle class. They were delighted with the Declaration of Independence with its ideas of the equality of man and his right to control his own government. The American victory over the uncontrolled rule of a king became a guiding star. Government by the people as established in the new American republic became a great inspiration to Frenchmen.

The Old Régime in France had other troubles besides the social unrest and discontent. The long wars of Louis XIV and the wars and inefficient rule of Louis XV built up a great burden of debt. The extravagant and luxurious living of the French court used up vast sums of money. Although France was a comparatively wealthy country and the taxes were heavy, the revenue of the government seemed always too small to meet expenses.

The basic cause of France's financial problems was the failure of the wealthy people to pay taxes. Each increase of taxes made the business of the country less prosperous and the businessmen less able to pay taxes. A heavy burden fell on the peasant, least able of all to pay more. When taxes did not produce enough revenue to meet expenses, Louis XV borrowed more from the bankers with the cynical remarks, "It will last my time," and "After me, the deluge."

King Louis XVI tries reform

In 1774 a new king, Louis XVI, came to the throne in France. In ordinary times he might have been a good ruler, for he wanted to act wisely and make his country prosperous. But Louis XVI was somewhat weak and rather dull, and these were not ordinary times. The royal treasury was empty and in debt, and the people were very restless and discontented.

Marie Antoinette, wife of Louis XVI. Her frivolity and extravagance made her unpopular with many of the French people. To them, she became a symbol of many of the worst features of the Old Régime.

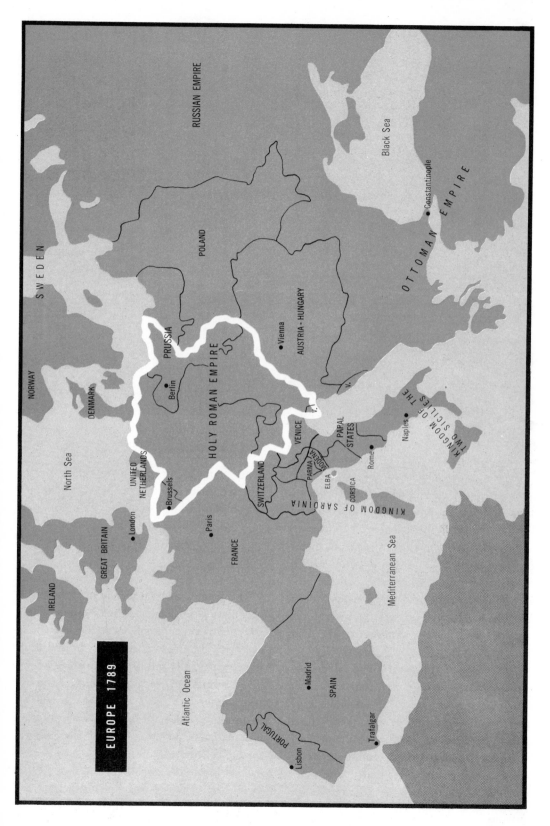

EUROPE 1789

NORWAY

SWEDEN

RUSSIAN EMPIRE

Black Sea

Constantinople

OTTOMAN EMPIRE

POLAND

PRUSSIA

Berlin

Vienna

AUSTRIA - HUNGARY

HOLY ROMAN EMPIRE

DENMARK

North Sea

UNITED NETHERLANDS

Brussels

VENICE

PAPAL STATES

Naples

KINGDOM OF THE TWO SICILIES

SWITZERLAND

MODENA

PARMA

Rome

ELBA

IRELAND

GREAT BRITAIN

London

Paris

FRANCE

KINGDOM OF SARDINIA

CORSICA

Atlantic Ocean

Mediterranean Sea

Madrid

SPAIN

PORTUGAL

Lisbon

Trafalgar

325

The attack on the Bastille

Louis XVI asked several middle-class financial experts, including Robert Jacques Turgot and Jacques Necker, to suggest ways of improving French finances. In turn each suggested real reforms: greater freedom for French industry, the payment of taxes by nobles and clergy, and less extravagant spending by the court. These proposals were resisted by the nobles who lived with the king at Versailles, and by the frivolous queen, Marie Antoinette. The reformers were dismissed; the spending continued; the debt increased.

France was heading for financial disaster and was receiving no help from those who should have given leadership—nobles, clergy, queen, and king. In 1787 the bankers refused to lend more money to the government. Paris was filled with rumors of revolution. Reluctantly the king sent out a call to the representatives of the three estates to meet at Versailles in May, 1789. Unable to solve its problems, divine-rights monarchy called on the representatives of the people. The French Revolution had begun.

The Estates-General meets and the French Revolution begins (1789)

The Estates-General met in an atmosphere of great confusion and uncertainty. There were many other problems besides the financial crisis. France was suffering from a business depression and much unemployment. The harvest of 1789 was poor, and food prices were high. All these conditions combined to produce violent protests against the government, which showed itself increasingly unable to solve the problems.

The Estates-General had not met for almost 200 years. No one knew exactly what its rules or powers were. If it were only advisory, and could not do anything, many people felt that its meeting would be useless. There was conflict and argument even over such a simple question as the method of meeting. Historically the three Estates met separately and each cast one vote. However, this allowed the conservative First and Second Estates—the clergy and nobles—to combine to outvote the Third Estate, which would probably want real reforms.

The representatives of the Third Estate were very interesting personalities. Most of them were young men; many were lawyers. A few like Honoré Gabriel de Mirabeau were men of noble birth who had consented to represent the commoners. All the representatives were greatly influenced by the eighteenth-century writers. Since they considered themselves the true representatives of the French people, they insisted on having a real voice in decisions. They were determined not to let themselves be outvoted by the other two Estates. Because the Third Estate had as many representatives as the other two combined, they wanted the Estates to meet together, with representatives voting as individuals.

The Third Estate becomes the National Assembly

The Estates-General assembled first in a combined meeting. The king greeted them and asked their help in solving France's financial problems. Then he instructed them to follow the old custom, each meeting and voting separately. The Third Estate promptly refused. They claimed that the Estates-General represented the French people, not the three classes. Therefore, they should meet together and vote as individuals.

When Louis XVI failed to take prompt action, the Third Estate proclaimed itself a National Assembly. It invited the other two Estates to join it in working for the welfare of France. When the king had the Third Estate locked out of their meeting place, they met at a nearby tennis court. They pledged (the "Oath of the Tennis Court") not to adjourn until they had written a constitution for France and seen it adopted. Finally the king gave in and ordered the three Estates to meet together.

Attack on the Bastille

Now the king tried to do secretly what he had feared to do openly. He began to bring large bodies of troops to Paris and to Versailles, where the assembly was meeting. Fearing that he planned to drive out the Estates-General by force, the people of Paris began to riot. On July 14, 1789, a Paris mob stormed and captured the fortress-prison, the Bastille, a hated symbol of the injustices of the Old Régime. In France this event is celebrated as Independence Day, or Bastille Day.

The Paris outbreak resulted in setting up a new government for the city. Under the leadership of General Lafayette, the French hero of the American Revolution, a people's army, called the National Guard, was formed. The white flag of the Bourbons with its *fleur de lis* (lily) symbols was replaced by the tricolor—red, white, and blue which has remained the flag of the French Republic.

The riots and violence in Paris soon spread out into the country. Eager to avenge old wrongs and be rid of old burdens, the peasants attacked the monasteries and the mansions of the lords. Chateaux were robbed and burned, government offices destroyed. The documents which recorded the rents, feudal dues, and obligations of the peasants to their lords were destroyed. Some nobles and their agents, and some government officials, especially tax collectors, were killed.

The National Assembly ends the Old Régime

The National Assembly meeting at Versailles now faced the problem of dealing with revolutionary violence in the country.

Many members felt that the proper way to prevent such violence was to remove the oppression and injustice that produced it. In an historic session on August 4, 1789 they abolished much of the Old Régime.

The Assembly voted to abolish serfdom and all the feudal dues and services of the peasants. It did away with all exemptions from taxes. Special feudal courts were abolished. The church tithe was repealed. All special privileges of various social groups were canceled. With one stroke this impressive law swept away all that remained of feudalism and the Middle Ages in France.

The Old Régime died hard—haughty, unyielding, and stupid to the end. Many nobles fled from France to neighboring countries. Here they plotted ceaselessly to return and undo all the revolutionary changes. These *émigrés* (emigrant nobles) were a constant source of trouble for years to come. The nobles at Versailles urged the king to use force to restore order—the old order; so Louis XVI recalled loyal troops from Flanders.

News of this event at Versailles brought new violence in Paris. A large group of women marched the few miles from Paris to Versailles. They stormed into the palace and forced the king, queen, and their children to return with them to Paris to prevent further plotting. The National Assembly soon followed. It was an important event. From that time on the entire government was increasingly at the mercy of the violent Paris mobs.

The Declaration of the Rights of Man

The National Assembly continued its momentous and revolutionary work. The abolition of feudalism was followed by another bright and shining event in man's history: the adoption of the Declaration of the Rights of Man. Strongly influenced by the English Bill of Rights, the American Declaration of Independence, and the writings of the eight-

On October 5, 1789, a mob of several thousand women, with a number of men, marched from Paris to Versailles. They demanded food, first of the National Assembly, then of the king. The next day the crowd forced the king and his family to move into Paris.

eenth-century philosophers, the Declaration of the Rights of Man stated and defined the great principles of the French Revolution.

The Declaration began by proclaiming freedom of speech, of the press, and of religious faith. It stated that men were born and remain equal before the law. They have a right to take part in their government and to resist oppression. They have a right to personal liberty, which can be taken from them only by fair trial.

Reforms in government

The abolition of feudalism and the Declaration of the Rights of Man set up the guiding principles of the new order. Now the National Assembly began to work on details.

First it reformed the national administration of France. The provinces, with their many special privileges, were abolished. France was divided into eighty-three uniform provinces called *départements*. Each in turn was divided into cantons, and the cantons were divided into communes or municipalities. Each was given power to elect its officials. This organization of the country remains basically the same today.

The Constitution of 1791

In 1791 the National Assembly finally completed the first task it had assigned itself—the writing of the constitution for France. The constitution of 1791 provided for a limited monarchy with separate executive, legislative, and judicial branches. The powers of the king were greatly reduced. He could not proclaim laws himself. He could delay laws passed by the legislative branch, but he could not veto them. The legislature was a one-house body, elected by voters who must be taxpayers. To hold office a man had to own property; thus most of the power went to the middle class.

The great events of 1789 to 1791 created a strong feeling of nationalism in France. The stirring words of the Declaration of the Rights of Man brought a feeling of loyalty and patriotism. It was loyalty and patriotism for France rather than for a small locality or region. The people began to think of themselves as Frenchmen, willing to fight to defend France and the great ideals of the revolution.

This idea of nationalism proved to be contagious. It spread first in the Western World and later throughout the entire world. Almost every group of people who felt drawn together by bonds of culture, language, or political history took as its goal the gaining of national unity. People who felt this way wanted their own government under their own control. Nationalism became one of the strong forces of the modern world.

The French constitutional monarchy falls

The new limited monarchy began its rule in most difficult circumstances. There were great problems both at home and abroad. The emigrant nobles tried to get help from foreign countries to restore the Old Régime, and they had secret dealings with the French king. Louis XVI had consented to the new constitution very reluctantly. Secretly he hoped for the success of the émigrés and the restoration of his old position.

Within a very short time the weak king was persuaded to do a very foolish thing. He and his wife and children tried to escape from France and join the émigrés. They were caught at the border and brought back. Now the French people distrusted Louis completely. They had come to hate his Austrian wife, Marie Antoinette. They considered her the chief plotter at the court, the worst influence on the king, and the real enemy of the people.

Attitudes toward the revolution

Attitudes toward the revolution divided Frenchmen into four fairly distinct groups. There were those who opposed any revolution at all and wanted a return of the old order. Led by men like Count Mirabeau, a second group thought that the revolution had gone far enough. It had achieved a limited monarchy with middle-class control. This they considered the ideal form of government. Georges Jacques Danton and Maximilian Robespierre were leaders of a slightly more radical group. They wanted to do away with the monarchy and set up a republic under middle-class control.

Most radical of all were the followers of a Parisian doctor named Jean Paul Marat. They wanted a republic representing all the people, not just the middle class. Marat wrote political pamphlets and published a paper called *Friend of the People*. By appealing to the masses for action to gain an equal share in the government, he built up a great following, especially among the people of Paris. Each of the pro-revolutionary groups formed political clubs in which they debated issues of the day. Each tried to spread its viewpoints by propaganda, either pamphlets or oratory.

The new Legislative Assembly

The new Legislative Assembly was made up of representatives of all three revolutionary groups. It faced a very considerable foreign danger. A group of European countries that feared the revolutionary spirit formed an alliance against France and gathered an army. Its commander, the Duke of Brunswick, proclaimed that the restoration of the French monarchy was a concern of all Europe. His army was prepared to invade France for this purpose.

The French Legislative Assembly compelled Louis XVI, very unwillingly, to sign a declaration of war against Austria and Prussia. Most of the republican leaders of France welcomed war. They thought it would give them a chance to overthrow the monarchy and create a republic. Only a few very farseeing men feared that war might bring military dictatorship.

War ends the monarchy

The proclamation of the Duke of Brunswick touched off a bloody uprising in Paris. A republican group led by Danton seized control of the city government. Mobs threatened the lives of the royal family. Others threatened violence to the assembly unless it abolished the monarchy. On August 10, 1792, the assembly voted to do away with the office of king. They set a date for the election of a National Convention to draw up a new constitution for France.

Thus ended the brief constitutional monarchy, amid great danger and confusion. In the midst of a foreign war, France faced a national election and a complete change of government. Louis XVI and his family were put in prison. Revolts broke out in many districts of France. Lafayette, commander of the army, was unable to accept the new situation. He gave up his command and joined the émigrés. Danton became virtually a dictator. The Austrian and Prussian armies moved into France and besieged the fortress city of Verdun.

The first French Republic is organized

When the National Convention met in Paris in 1792, it was greeted by encouraging news. The French army under its new general, Charles Francois Dumouriez, had defeated the Austrian and Prussian forces and stopped the invasion for a time. The Convention immediately proclaimed the end of the monarchy and the beginning of a republic. It had many important tasks besides its official function of drawing up a constitution. It had to suppress revolts at home and wage war against foreign invaders. By dictatorial methods the National Convention governed France for three years.

The Convention was divided into three main groups. The most moderate were middle-class republicans. They were called Girondists because many of them came from the province of Gironde. The most radical group were the Jacobins, members of a political club by that name. Between the two—both in ideas and in the assembly hall—was the largest group, with no definite views.

After declaring France a republic the National Convention tried the king for treason. By a majority vote Louis XVI was declared guilty and sentenced to death. He was publicly beheaded by the guillotine on January 21, 1793.

Foreign wars

Meantime the French armies under Dumouriez won more victories. They drove the Austrian and Prussian armies out of France. Then they invaded the Austrian Netherlands and captured the city of Brussels. Joyful over these victories, the National Convention declared that the French armies would liberate all the peoples of Europe from the Old Régime.

It was an alarming decision—to export the ideas of Liberty, Equality, and Fraternity by force of arms. The French Revolution thus became international. Great Britain, Holland, Spain, and Sardinia joined Austria and Prussia in a coalition against France. Even in France there were many who doubted the wisdom of trying to spread ideas by bayonets. The successful commander, Dumouriez, could not accept it. Following Lafayette's example, he deserted to the enemy.

For a time France's enemies were successful. French troops were driven out of Belgium, and France itself was again invaded. The National Convention met this danger by adopting conscription (the draft). The new national army was led by an able man named Lazare .Nicolas Carnot. Under Carnot, the "Organizer of Victory," the new French army was like nothing seen in Europe for many centuries. It was an army of young men, loyal and patriotic. It was willing and able to try new methods. Its officers were young men of any class who proved their ability and daring. For the first time the talents and ability of an entire nation—all classes of its people—were now used.

By 1795 the hostile coalition had begun to break up. Spain, Prussia, and Holland had withdrawn; the rest were fighting on the defensive. The French had driven the invaders out of France and had taken the country as far as the Rhine River and the Alps. The "natural boundaries" which Louis XIV had failed to gain with all his costly wars had been won by a citizen army of patriots.

But the French paid a heavy price for victory. Lives were lost and treasure was spent. In the early days of the revolution farseeing men had feared the spirit of militarism. Now their fears began to be realized. In France the army was used to crush opposition of any sort to the National Convention. Abroad, the French were so haughty in victory that the army aroused opposition among the "liberated" peoples by its conduct.

Internal troubles: the Reign of Terror

Although France was relieved of foreign dangers, there was still opposition and revolt within the country. To meet this danger the Convention set up an executive group called the Committee of Public Safety and a court called the Revolutionary Tribunal. The Committee of Public Safety directed the army in crushing rebellions. The Revolutionary Tribunal tried all who were accused of being "enemies of the revolution." Trials were swift and sentences were harsh. Many people were arrested, tried, and executed on mere suspicion. The method of execution was beheading by the guillotine, the instrument

Marie Antoinette on the way to the guillotine. The king and queen were both executed in 1793. This sketch was made from life by the famous French artist David. Contrast this view of the queen with the portrait on page 324.

The executioner waits by the guillotine, the instrument used for public executions during the revolution.

which became the symbol of the times. This Reign of Terror lasted almost ten months.

Danton and Robespierre worked together at the head of the Committee of Public Safety. Nobles and clergy suspected of disloyalty to the revolution were the first to go. Then the moderate Girondists fell under suspicion, especially after Dumouriez had deserted to the enemy. Many Girondist leaders went to the guillotine. Now the Committee turned its attention to the extreme radicals. They were demanding that France be rid of every enemy of the republic, and they considered the Church the most dangerous foe. So they demanded the execution of all higher clergy. But the radicals themselves were led to the guillotine.

Danton now felt that the Terror had accomplished its purpose and should be relaxed. But Robespierre, pitiless, fanatical republican, suspected Danton of disloyalty to the ideal. So Danton and his followers went to the guillotine. For 100 days Robespierre ruled with an iron hand, carrying out a policy of terror that aroused fear even in the Convention itself. Finally the members revolted. Robespierre himself was led to the guillotine, and the Terror was ended. The moderates, or what remained of them, were again in control.

The National Convention did much more than deal with the war abroad and the Terror at home. In spite of all the dangers and difficulties of the time, the Convention made many reforms in France. Some of them were only temporary, but many reforms were practical and permanent. The Convention began the organization and arrangement of all French laws into a code. It set up a national system of public education. It abolished slavery in French colonies. It adopted a new and superior system of weights and measures, the metric system, based on the decimal system. The metric system is now used in many parts of the world, and by scientists almost everywhere. The Convention abolished the law of primogeniture, under which only the first-born son could inherit property.

In 1795, just as the new constitution was to go into effect, there was an uprising in Paris. It was quickly suppressed by troops under the leadership of a then unknown captain of artillery named Napoleon Bonaparte. You will read a great deal more about this man as the story of the French Revolution continues.

Napoleon comes to power: 1795–1799

The National Convention drew up a constitution for a republican government. The new constitution went into effect in 1795. In the new government voting was restricted to property owners; so control was held mostly by the middle class. There was a legislature of two houses. The executive branch, which controlled the government, was a committee of five chosen by the legislature. They were called Directors; therefore, this is known as the government of the Directory.

● *The Directory and Napoleon*

The Directory governed France for only four years. Its short life was the result of a number of conditions. Most Frenchmen now longed for stable government and peaceful life. The Directory could not give them these things. France was still at war with several European powers. As a "middle of the road" government, the Directory did not satisfy either conservatives or radicals. Its problems were overwhelming and required united action. However, the Directors quarreled among themselves. Also, they were inefficient, dishonest, and corrupt. The weakness and unpopularity of the Directory paved the way for the military dictatorship which intelligent republicans had long feared.

The Directory did produce good leadership in the army. The continuing war with Great Britain, Austria, and Sardinia gave great opportunities for able military leaders. The years 1795–1799 saw the very rapid rise of that same young artillery captain whose suppression of a Paris uprising had allowed the Directory to be established.

Napoleon Bonaparte was born in 1769 of Italian parents on the island of Corsica. As a very young man he came to France to enter a military school. When he was graduated, he became a junior artillery officer. During the early days of the revolution he supported a republic. In 1793 he played a leading part in recapturing the city of Toulon from the English. In 1795 he defended the National Convention against the rioting Parisians. For reward he was given command of the French army fighting in northern Italy against the Austrians and Sardinians. Thus he became a general at the age of twenty-six.

Napoleon was a short man, vain, domineering, and overwhelmingly ambitious—but he was a superb organizer and an administrator, in both political and military affairs. Above all, he was a military genius who ranks among the great generals of all time.

Napoleon quickly showed his ability in Italy. The French army was small, weak, and poorly equipped. Within a matter of weeks he had so organized and inspired it that he forced the Sardinians to make peace. The Sardinians were followed by others: Parma, Modena, Naples, and the pope. Napoleon de-feated the Austrians twice, and in the fall of 1797 he forced them to sign a humiliating peace treaty. France gained control of all northern Italy.

Returning to France a hero, Napoleon became so popular that the Directory was greatly worried. He persuaded them to allow him to weaken the British by stopping their trade with Egypt and the Near East. Glad to free themselves of his presence in the capital, the Directory consented, and Napoleon sailed for Egypt with an army.

The Near Eastern campaign was a disaster. A French army was defeated in Syria. Worse still, a British fleet under Lord Nelson almost completely destroyed the French fleet at Aboukir Bay, near Alexandria. The French army was cut off from home. Leaving the army to its fate, Napoleon secretly returned to France. He concealed the true situation in Egypt and made exaggerated claims

The Battle of the Pyramids, one event in Napoleon's Near Eastern campaign. In this battle near Cairo, the French defeated an Arab force. In the long run, however, the whole French campaign was a failure. This fact did not stop Napoleon's rise to power in France.

of victories in the Near East. More and more Napoleon was "the man of the hour."

France was in a truly dangerous situation. The British had organized a new coalition of Great Britain, Austria, and Russia against France. French armies were driven out of Italy, and the other French-dominated states collapsed like a house of cards. It looked like total defeat, and the French people turned to Napoleon as the one man who could restore order at home and win victory abroad.

● *The Consulate*

Napoleon now organized a plot to overthrow the government and seize power. In 1799 with the aid of the army he persuaded three of the Directors to resign and placed the other two under arrest. Troops with fixed bayonets surrounded the meeting place and forced the two legislative houses to dissolve. This sort of seizure of power by force is called by the French a *coup d'état* (a stroke of state). As Napoleon himself said later: "I found the crown of France lying on the ground, and I picked it up with a sword."

Napoleon now gave France its fourth constitution in the ten years since 1789. The government was known as the Consulate because the executive branch was made up of three Consuls, appointed for ten years. Real power was placed in the hands of the First Consul; this position Napoleon took for himself. As First Consul he had command of the army and navy, the right to appoint and dismiss all officials, and the right to propose all new laws. The legislature was a farce. There were several assemblies, but none with any real authority.

Napoleon submitted the new constitution to the people for a vote, a procedure known as a *plebiscite*. They were only allowed to vote "yes" or "no"; no changes could be made. When someone asked him what was in the new constitution, he replied haughtily, "There is Bonaparte." The vote showed a vast majority in favor of the new constitution, or of "Bonaparte." Thus military dictatorship came to France, as some men had feared.

Napoleon gave a new and different meaning to the ideals of the French Revolution. Equality he accepted, but liberty meant only freedom of opportunity. He believed and practiced the idea that the leader should govern to the best of his ability. The people should obey the orders given for their own good. It was government from the top down, not from the bottom up. The French people were willing to accept this idea so long as Napoleon promised peace and security. He knew very well that he could not turn back the clock completely, and did not try to. Some of the victories of the revolution could not be erased. The ideals of the Declaration of Rights of Man remained. The abolition of serfdom and feudal privilege could not be undone. The land which the peasants now owned remained theirs.

The story of Napoleon's career will be continued in Chapter 27. The table above will help keep events in order.

Review of Chapter 26

People, places, and things

Identify: Louis XV, Louis XVI, Marie Antoinette, Turgot, Necker, Mirabeau, Danton, Robespierre, Marat, Lafayette, Oath of the Tennis Court, Directory, Consulate, Jacobins, Girondists, coup d'état.

Locate: the boundaries of France in 1789 and in 1795, Egypt, Syria, Paris, Brussels, Verdun, Toulon, Aboukir Bay.

Events in review

1. Describe briefly the French government under the Old Régime.
2. What attitude did Louis XV take toward France's financial problems? Did Louis XVI take the same view?
3. Why did the representatives of the Third Estate insist that all three groups in the Estates-General meet together?
4. List three accomplishments of the National Assembly, 1789–1791.
5. What was the purpose of the National Convention, which met in 1792? Describe the three main groups in the Convention.
6. After leading the French army to many victories, Dumouriez left his post. What was his reason?
7. Why was Danton executed during the Reign of Terror? Why was Robespierre executed?
8. Why did the government of the Directory last only four years?
9. What powers did Napoleon hold as First Consul?
10. Compare briefly the government of France under the Consulate with (a) the government of England after 1689, (b) the government of the United States after 1789.

Problems and projects

1. Draw up a balance sheet on the French Revolution, 1789–1799. Show the gains and losses of the French people.
2. In magazines and newspapers, see what you can find out about tax problems in present-day France.
3. Compare the principles of the American Declaration of Independence with those of the French Declaration of the Rights of Man.
4. Compare the Reign of Terror in France with communist tactics in Russia (or another communist-dominated country) in the twentieth century.
5. What is *nationalism?* Was the national spirit in any way a help to France? What dangers of nationalism can be shown by events in France?
6. How did Napoleon become dictator? Consider (a) the condition of France under the Directory, (b) the steps Napoleon took to increase his power. Did he simply force himself on the French people, or did he take advantage of the condition of France?
7. Draw a cartoon on the subject of the Committee of Public Safety, or the rise of Napoleon from captain to consul.
8. Prepare a "You Are There" type of broadcast covering a famous event of the revolution—for example, the attack on the Bastille, or the defense of the Convention by a young artillery officer, Napoleon Bonaparte, in 1795.
9. Note the many changes in the French government as recorded in the table on page 334. Compare developments in France with the record of the English and American revolutions. How can you account for the differences?

Chapter 27 # Napoleon and the Napoleonic Empire

THE COUP D'ETAT of November 9, 1799 made Napoleon dictator of France. The government of the Consulate kept the outward form of the republic, but as First Consul Napoleon was the real ruler. Either as First Consul or as Emperor he ruled France dictatorially from 1799 until 1814. He had such great influence on the rest of Europe that this period of fifteen years is known as the Napoleonic Era, or the Age of Napoleon. This age is noted for its almost constant warfare. Within France some of the reforms of the French Revolution were more solidly established. On the continent of Europe these reforms were spread by the victorious French armies. Old governments were overthrown; feudal ideas and institutions disappeared; the Old Régime received a fatal blow. French rule in other European countries gave the people of those countries strong feelings of patriotism, loyalty, and that desire for their own government which we call nationalism.

Napoleon rules as dictator, 1799–1804

When Napoleon seized power, France was still at war against Great Britain, Austria, and Russia. The government and the army of France had become badly disorganized under the Directory. Napoleon had deserted some of the best French troops in Egypt; the rest of the army was in a sad state. It was a situation in which Napoleon could show his

three great skills: as an organizer, as a diplomat, and as a military genius.

● War and diplomacy

He began at once to reorganize the French army. He improved military discipline and the method of selecting officers. The army was still raised by conscription (the draft), but Napoleon was an inspiring leader. He was able to create in the drafted men a great sense of patriotism and a tremendous loyalty to him.

Napoleon also engaged in some shrewd and skillful diplomacy. First he persuaded Russia to desert its allies and make peace, leaving Britain and Austria alone. He then persuaded other European countries to form a league of armed neutral states aimed at Britain. Then came the military action against the Austrians, who had been weakened by the withdrawal of Russia.

French armies struck at Austria in northern Italy and in Germany, inflicting terrible defeats. By 1801 Austria was compelled to ask for peace. As usual, the British were fighting the war on the sea rather than on the continent of Europe. The defeat of the French fleet in Egypt had reduced the chance of a French sea victory. England ruled the sea, but Napoleon controlled the continent. However, both sides were weary of war, and in 1802 peace was signed. For a short time it looked as though Napoleon would keep his promises to the French people: peace with military glory, firm and steady government, and economic prosperity.

Napoleon's ambitions, however, were overwhelming. He now moved to restore France as a great colonial power. In a secret treaty (1800) he forced Spain to give Louisiana to France. In a few years he changed his mind. There was danger of a renewal of the war with the British. Control of the sea by the British would make it very difficult for France to hold Louisiana. In 1803 Napoleon sold Louisiana to the United States. The small and young nation in the New World thus gained tremendously from the complications of Old-World wars and politics.

Reforms in France

The demands of war and diplomacy did not take all of Napoleon's time and energy, for he was a many-sided, ambitious, and tireless man. He found time to reorganize and centralize the government of France, settle

Infantry soldiers of Napoleon's Army. The motto on the flag reads "Valor and discipline."

relations between the government and the Roman Catholic Church, start a program of economic reforms to bring prosperity to the country, complete the overhauling of the laws begun by the National Convention, and make many lasting social reforms. Napoleon was not democratic. No criticism of the government was permitted. All opposition to Napoleon's authority was put down by an efficient police system.

The Code Napoléon

Under Napoleon's direction a committee of French legal scholars completed the overhauling of laws which had been started earlier. All outdated and conflicting laws were eliminated. The remaining civil laws were arranged and organized into an orderly system called the Code Napoléon. A code of criminal law and a code of commercial law were also drawn up. The civil law of the Code Napoléon was based on Roman law, but the principal ideas of the French Revolution were included. All men were declared equal before the law, with equal privileges of inheriting property and of worshiping as they chose. The Code Napoléon was such a fine piece of work that it was widely copied. It forms the foundation of the legal system of many countries in western Europe, and of the state of Louisiana in the United States.

Napoleon wanted a central, national financial institution; so he established the Bank of France. Although the bank was privately owned, it was very closely supervised by the government. It had the power to issue paper money, but was requested to keep enough gold to exchange for the paper money on demand. The Bank of France became one of the strongest financial institutions in the world.

Another lasting contribution was the French system of public education. The National Convention had drawn up a plan for such a system; Napoleon put it into effect. The school system included elementary schools, high schools, and technical schools. These were all supervised and directed by a central agency called the University of France. During Napoleon's time the schools were so conducted as to benefit him: they taught loyalty to the government and obedience to its ruler.

France becomes an empire

Although he was now the real ruler of France, Napoleon was not satisfied. He wanted his power to be permanent and hereditary, and to show before the world. He

An idealized portrait of Napoleon as emperor, showing him in his imperial robes and wearing a laurel crown like that of a Roman emperor.

quickly made two more constitutional changes to accomplish his wishes. Each change was approved by a plebiscite (popular vote). In 1802 the people approved a new constitution which made Napoleon First Consul for life, with increased powers. Two years later (1804) the French people approved a constitution which declared France an empire. Napoleon Bonaparte was accepted as Emperor Napoleon I.

The new empire was inaugurated by the coronation of Napoleon in the great Cathedral of Notre Dame in Paris, with most elaborate ceremonies. One part of the ceremony was significant. The pope had come to Paris to crown the new emperor. When the time came for the pope to put the crown on the emperor's head, Napoleon almost snatched the crown from the pope's hands and placed it on his own head. Thus he demonstrated that the power and authority were all his own, not given him by anyone.

Napoleon dominates Europe, 1804–1815

Napoleon had kept his promises to give the French people efficient government, economic prosperity, and glory. However, he did not keep the pledge to give them peace. In 1803 war broke out again, to last until the final overthrow of Napoleon in 1815.

Struggle with Britain

The English knew that Napoleon's ambition and energy threatened their commerce, their empire, and their control of the sea. French control of Belgium gave Napoleon bases from which he might be able to launch an invasion of England. Napoleon had come to realize that his domination of the continent of Europe could never be complete and safe as long as Great Britain ruled the seas and stood unfriendly and unconquered. It was a war to the death.

The emperor planned to strike at the heart of British power by defeating the British fleet and invading the island itself. He began building up the French war fleet. However, his hopes and plans received a stunning blow. In 1805 a British fleet under Admiral Horatio Nelson defeated a combined French and Spanish fleet off Cape Trafalgar on the coast of Spain. Nelson was killed at Trafalgar, but the French and Spanish fleets were almost completely destroyed.

The Continental Blockade

Now Napoleon had to change his strategy. Since he could not strike directly at England, he tried to destroy its commercial prosperity. He referred contemptuously to the British as a "nation of shopkeepers"; he believed that loss of trade would make them accept peace on his terms. Therefore, he forbade the importation of British goods into any country under French control, and put great pressure on other European countries to stop buying British products. He also declared a blockade of the British Isles.

The British answered with a blockade of France. A series of Orders in Council forbade ships of neutral countries to trade with France or her allies unless they first stopped at a British port to get a license. Napoleon's reply was a decree which stated that a neutral ship that obeyed the British order would be seized by the French.

Neutrals were thus placed in a bad position. If they disregarded the British order, they might be captured by the British navy. But if they obeyed the British order, they would be seized by the French. The United States was especially hard hit, for it depended greatly on trade with the British Isles and the continent of Europe. After a desperate effort to remain neutral, the new nation was finally drawn into the whirlpool of the Napoleonic wars. In 1812 the United States declared war on Great Britain.

The French blockade of Great Britain existed only on paper, because France lacked the ships to enforce it. The great British fleet

H.M.S. Victory, *a 100-gun ship, was Nelson's flagship when his British fleet defeated the French and Spanish at Trafalgar. The ship is now preserved at Portsmouth, England. The British fleet made it impossible for Napoleon to invade England. The fleet also imposed a blockade on France and her allies. In the words of an American historian, the British fleet stood between Napoleon and the domination of the world.*

made her blockade of Europe at least partly effective. Even though Napoleon used great pressure to prevent Europeans from buying British goods, he found enforcement very difficult. The people of Europe needed British manufactured goods; they also needed the products which British ships brought to Europe from all over the world. The French orders caused great discontent everywhere, even in France. Prices rose; smuggling and bribing custom officials became common.

Coalition against France

The blockade was not enough. Britain wanted the complete military defeat of the dangerous Napoleon. Again Britain organized a coalition against France—this time, Great Britain, Russia, Austria, Sweden, and, later, Prussia. Once more Napoleon proved himself the master general. He followed his strategy of dealing with his enemies one at a time. In turn, Austria and Prussia were defeated and forced out of the coalition. Russia withdrew next. The czar promised to observe the blockade in return for freedom to take land from Sweden and Turkey. However, the observance of the blockade hurt Russia: she needed British manufactured goods, and England was the best market for the raw materials she exported.

Napoleon now dominated Europe completely. Austria and Prussia had been forced to sign humiliating peace treaties, and Russia seemed a willing ally. Napoleon ruled Holland and forced Spain, Denmark, and the papacy into alliances. He controlled Sweden and was master of Italy. The new Duchy of Warsaw was under his protection; the states of Germany had to do as he wished. On the thrones of the conquered countries Napoleon placed his brothers, his brother-in-law, his stepson, and a marshal of his victorious armies. England was undefeated, but England could not place armies on the continent to harm him much. However, Great Britain remained always willing to support any opposition to Napoleon anywhere in Europe.

Napoleon changes the map of Europe

The victorious emperor now proceeded to make amazing changes in the map of Europe, especially in Germany and Italy. He forced the emperor of the Holy Roman Empire to give up his throne, taking, instead, the title of Emperor of Austria. He abolished the Holy Roman Empire. The 300 little German states were combined into about a third of that number. Hanover, Westphalia, Saxony, and the south German states were united

EUROPE 1812
NAPOLEON'S EMPIRE

empire of the French
states allied with Napoleon
states under Napoleonic control
boundary of Napoleonic Empire and allied states
outside Napoleon's control

into the Confederation of the Rhine, with Napoleon as Protector. All the small states of northern Italy were united into the Kingdom of Italy and made dependent on Napoleon.

These changes were not on the map alone. The Napoleonic Code was placed in effect; feudalism and serfdom were abolished. The methods of the modern French army were introduced. Without intending to, the French also instilled the spirit of nationalism. Napoleon's victories created a passion for nationalism in Europe which has lasted until today. It has not always been a blessing.

Napoleon's throne begins to totter

It was the spirit of nationalism as much as anything else that brought about the final downfall of Napoleon. At first, the French were received as liberators, but soon they became very unpopular. The French armies were often overbearing in their behavior. Taxes increased steadily to pay the costs of war and occupation. Troops were quartered in private homes, which is always a source of friction. Men were conscripted to fight in the French armies. In time, the French came to be regarded as foreign invaders. In every country people wanted to be rid of them and to govern themselves.

The continental blockade helped to stir up feelings against French rule. Everywhere it was violated, but the more it was violated, the more harshly and persistently Napoleon insisted on its enforcement. Persons who protested against it or were caught violating it, paid dearly regardless of their rank or position. Napoleon had made his brother Louis King of Holland. When Louis was negligent in stopping smuggling, Napoleon dismissed him and combined Holland directly with his Empire of France. When the pope expressed disapproval of his blockade, Napoleon placed him under arrest.

Such harshness led people in the conquered nations to try to strengthen their governments and to throw off French rule. Prussian statesmen began a far-reaching program of reforms. A brief revolt in Austria was quickly stamped out. As a penalty, Austria had to give up more land and consent to Napoleon's demand to marry the Hapsburg emperor's daughter. When she bore him a son Napoleon could rejoice at the founding of a Napoleonic dynasty.

The French emperor was now master of Europe, in a seemingly unconquerable position. However, time was working on the side of his enemies. The constant wars had sapped French manpower; the flower of the French army was gone. To get the large armies he needed, he drafted men from all the conquered countries. Often they served most unwillingly. The patriotic, revolutionary spirit of the army was gone.

●Napoleon loses Spain

In the Iberian peninsula there came trouble much worse than the brief Austrian revolt. Portugal, whose prosperity depended on trade with England, refused to observe the continental blockade. In 1808 the Spanish people revolted against Napoleon's brother Joseph, whom he had made King of Spain. England sent an army under the future Duke of Wellington to help the Spanish and Portuguese patriots. In spite of everything Napoleon could do, he could not stop the Spanish uprising or drive out the British army. The Peninsular Campaign, as it was called, lasted six years. It was a steady drain on French manpower and money at a time when they were badly needed elsewhere.

In 1812 the Spanish, with British aid, captured Madrid and drove out the French king. Then they proceeded to draw up a remarkable constitution for the country. It provided for a king with limited powers and a legislature of one house. It declared that the power of government belonged to the Spanish people. They only delegated it to the legislature

and king. The constitution abolished the Inquisition and limited the right of the Church to own land. It declared that all Spaniards were equal before the law, with certain inalienable rights. The Spanish action showed two things: the tremendous influence of the French Revolution and the rising spirit of nationalism and opposition to Napoleon.

● Napoleon invades Russia

Something even more serious than the trouble in Spain was happening. Relations between Napoleon and Czar Alexander I of Russia were growing worse. The government of Russia had several reasons for viewing with alarm and distrust Napoleon's domination of Europe. The establishment of the Duchy of Warsaw under Napoleon's protection looked like a springboard for a future attack on Russia. Napoleon's overthrow of established governments, and his annexations of territories to France, seemed to show that there was little possibility of settled conditions as long as he was in power.

Retreat from Moscow, 1812. Napoleon's invasion of Russia ended in defeat. The great distances, the hard winter, and Russian resistance were too much for the Grand Army.

The most important cause of bad relations between the two countries was the continental blockade. Alexander I had tried to keep his agreement to enforce the blockade in Russia. However, this broke up a long-established trade of Russian grain for English manufactured goods. Russian nobles suffered losses and brought pressure on the government to end the blockade. Gradually the government relaxed the enforcement. Finally Alexander I announced that trade with England would be renewed.

Napoleon could not disregard this broken agreement. He needed the blockade as his only way of striking at the hated British. Therefore he declared war on Russia and gathered an army of 600,000 men. It was a strange army, vastly different from the enthusiastic, loyal, and patriotic armies of the early French Republic. Fewer than half of the soldiers were French; the larger part of the "Grand Army" was composed of drafted Danes, Germans, Dutch, Balkan Slavs, Italians, Swiss, and Poles. In June, 1812, at the head of this international army Napoleon began his march to the east, across the vast, level plain of Russia.

To resist the enemy the Russians used a new strategy. They said that they made "distance their ally." Instead of meeting the French in open battle, the Russian army retreated slowly. Thus they drew the French deeper and deeper into Russia. As they retreated, the Russians destroyed everything that might be of value to the French. This is called the "scorched earth" policy. Behind them the Russians left bands of guerrilla troops to harass the French by hit-and-run tactics and by destroying their supply trains. The French had to leave increasing numbers of troops to garrison towns and guard their supply lines. They were unable to make the Russian army stand for a pitched battle that might be decisive.

In mid-September the French army reached and captured Moscow, but it was a hollow victory. The Russians had stripped the city; later, fires added to the destruction. Now Napoleon faced a bad choice. The terrible Russian winter was about to set in. The Russian army was still undefeated. With its burned buildings Moscow did not have enough winter quarters for the troops, and the supply line from France was long and unsafe. Napoleon could either chase the Russian army farther to the east or turn back to the west.

Retreat from Moscow, 1942. In World War II Hitler invaded Russia. His armies met many of the problems that turned back the French in 1812. The retreating Germans found the winter as bitter as the French before them.

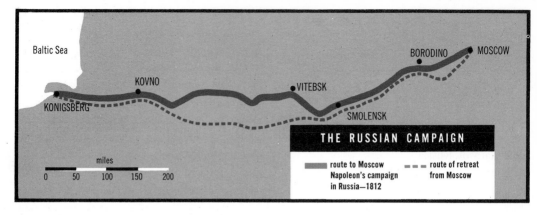

Baltic Sea

KONIGSBERG
KOVNO
VITEBSK
SMOLENSK
BORODINO
MOSCOW

THE RUSSIAN CAMPAIGN

miles
0   50   100   150   200

route to Moscow
Napoleon's campaign
in Russia—1812

route of retreat
from Moscow

He had already learned how useless it was to try to catch the Russian army. So he decided to lead his army back to western Europe.

● *Retreat from Moscow: Defeat for Napoleon*

The retreat from Moscow was one of the greatest military disasters of the century. The Grand Army had to pass again through the devastated country, this time plagued by snow and bitter cold. Now the Russians turned to pursuit. Both the Russian regulars and the guerrillas harassed the retreating French without mercy. French discipline broke down, and there were many desertions. When the retreating army reached the borders of Germany, in December, it had lost four-fifths of its numbers. The emperor himself left the army and hurried to France to raise new forces. He knew that he would now have to fight to defend his empire. Everywhere in western Europe countries were rising to throw off French rule and join the invading Russians.

Napoleon did manage to gather a new army of hastily drilled conscripts, but he faced overwhelming odds. Prussia, Austria, Great Britain, and Sweden joined Russia in a new coalition. They gathered their armies for the invasion of France. Napoleon again tried his old strategy of striking before his enemies could unite, but this time he was too late. In October, 1813, the great "Battle of Nations" was fought at Leipzig, in Germany. The new French army was decisively defeated. Napoleon retreated into France and tried to defend it, but his situation was hopeless. The allied armies captured Paris in March, 1814. Two weeks later Napoleon was compelled to give up his throne.

● *The Allies try to establish peace*

The emperor's abdication was complete. Both for himself and his family Napoleon gave up any claims to the throne of France. He was granted a pension and the small island of Elba off the western coast of Italy. Here he was allowed to rule as a sovereign. He agreed to remain there for the rest of his life.

The victorious allies now agreed that the boundaries of France should be the same as those of 1792, before the great expansion began. They restored the Bourbon monarchy to the throne. However, the king had to accept a constitution recognizing some of the gains of the French Revolution. Both of these decisions were wise. France did not lose territory which she would later want to regain. There was no attempt to restore the Old Régime completely.

This allied wisdom was due mostly to the insistence of the Russian Czar Alexander I. Behind him, though, was a remarkable man who had gained his confidence and influenced his decisions: the French minister Charles Maurice de Talleyrand. This shrewd, foxy old man was a master of diplomacy, and of always "landing on his feet" on the winning side. The record of his career shows his skill at changing sides. As a bishop, he served in the Estates-General as a representative of the privileged clergy. Then he switched to serve the revolutionary republican government. Even during the Reign of Terror he was able to save his neck. When Napoleon came to power, Talleyrand became one of his principal ministers. Now he became the foreign minister of the restored Bourbon kings.

The legitimate heir to the French throne was the Bourbon Louis XVIII, brother of the executed Louis XVI. During the Revolution he had lived in England. When Louis XVI's son died, the brother had taken the title of Louis XVIII. He skipped one number (XVII) in the pretense that the son had really been king after the execution of his father. Louis XVIII accepted a constitution which limited his powers and stated the ideas of liberty and equality. He also recognized peasant ownership of former church lands.

● Napoleon returns to France

Meanwhile, Napoleon had no intention of spending the rest of his life on the island of Elba. He plotted to return to France almost from the time he reached the island, and there were plenty of people in France who wanted him back. He did escape and landed in France on March 1, 1815. Then began the period which is called the Hundred Days. He had only a small troop of men with him; a regiment could have defeated them easily. However, the troops sent by the Bourbon king deserted to their beloved emperor, who moved on in triumph. Everywhere resistance collapsed; Louis XVIII fled the country. Three weeks after his landing Napoleon entered Paris in triumph. He declared his intention to restore constitutional government in France, and to avoid war he announced that France gave up all claims to territories formerly conquered.

France did not oppose the return of Napoleon, but the allied rulers did not intend to allow the disturber of the peace to resume his career. Napoleon hoped to benefit from the differences of opinion among the allies and disagreements over the division of territory. He soon learned, though, that on one subject they were in complete agreement: Napoleon must go. They began to move armies toward France. Once more Napoleon raised a French army and moved into Belgium to meet the combined armies of Prussia, Great Britain, and Holland. These were commanded by Napoleon's old opponent in Spain, the British Duke of Wellington.

● Waterloo

At Waterloo, Belgium, on June 18, 1815, the allied and the French armies met in a three-day battle which finally ended the career of Napoleon. From this battle we get the expression, "He has met his Waterloo." The French were badly defeated. Again Napoleon abdicated, and again the Bourbon monarchy was restored. Napoleon surrendered to the British, asking to be allowed to take refuge in England. After the experience of Elba, however, the British were unwilling to take any more chances. They sent the fallen emperor to live under constant guard on the dismal island of St. Helena in the South Atlantic. In this lonely corner of the world Napoleon lived the few remaining years of his life. He died in 1821 at the age of fifty-two.

As the years passed, there grew up a legend of Napoleon. The wars with all their miseries, the vanity of the self-crowned emperor, were all forgotten. The glories and achievements of the turbulent years of his reign were remembered. Forgotten was the military dictator, the despot, the man whose boundless ambitions brought death and misery to France and Europe. The Napoleon of the legend became the "Little Corporal," the "Corsican Eagle," the "Good Emperor," the "true patriot of the French Revolution." History proves time and again that public memory is short.

Summary: the French Revolution and the Napoleonic Era

The twenty-five years between 1789, when the French Revolution began, and 1815, when Napoleon was overthrown, are a very short time, as history goes. Yet these years brought astounding changes to the Western World. The trends and influences which began then spread throughout the whole world, and they still continue to influence the course of history.

● New ideas of government

In France the ideas of the revolution—Liberty, Equality, and Fraternity—were so well established that they could not be completely wiped out. The idea of popular sovereignty, that the real power of government rests in the people, became firmly entrenched. So also did the idea of the nation-state—a strongly centralized government responsible for the welfare of all the people. It came to be taken for granted that this new kind of government was best for the people. It would give them education and economic security, protection of their rights, equality before the law, and religious toleration.

These ideas were not confined to France. They were spread all over Europe by the French armies and conquests. In the German, Italian, and Spanish lands that Napoleon had controlled, feudalism and serfdom were abolished and the fundamental ideas of the Code Napoléon were established. The ideas of equality, of religious toleration, and the rights of the people to have a voice in their own government, were like seeds broadcast over the European continent. They continued to grow in spite of all efforts of the restored governments to suppress liberal ideas and movements.

● Nationalism

Unintentionally, Napoleon's armies also spread the spirit of nationalism. In France he worked consciously to develop loyalty and patriotism because he benefited from these sentiments. Abroad, they sprang up in spite of him. French rule over Italians, Spaniards, Dutch, Prussians, and other Germans stirred up patriotic uprisings against foreign domination. Governments in Austria, Prussia, and elsewhere tried to make reforms, to reorganize, to make their operations more efficient in order to regain control of their own national affairs. In Germany and Italy, where Napoleon combined many small states, there grew up a desire for real national unity. Poles, divided among Russia, Prussia, and Austria, wanted a Polish nation and government. The various national groups in the Austrian Empire—the Czechs, Poles, Hungarians, Slavs, and Italians—craved independence and self-government. The Slavs of the Balkan states wanted to throw off Turkish rule. The French invasion of Russia aroused a strong national patriotism there, as well as a liberal movement among the younger army officers. No efforts by the old dynastic rulers could ever "set the clock back"—restore the pattern of the Old Régime as it was before 1789.

● Modern warfare

The French Revolution and the Napoleonic Era brought another development that has profoundly affected mankind—modern militarism. Down through the centuries there had been many wars but they had been wars of a different kind, fought by comparatively small armies of professional soldiers. The revolutionary era introduced conscription, so that every able-bodied man had to serve. Later wars were to be fought not by professionals but by nations in arms. The new development was bound to have incalculable effects upon modern history.

Review of Chapter 27

People, places, and things

Identify: Czar Alexander I, Wellington, Nelson, Talleyrand, Louis XVIII, the Grand Army, Battle of the Nations, Battle of Waterloo, the Hundred Days, "scorched earth" policy.

Locate: Corsica, Elba, St. Helena, Trafalgar, Leipzig, Moscow, Waterloo.

Events in review

1. What three great skills did Napoleon possess?
2. How did the United States benefit, in 1803, as a result of wars and diplomatic deals in Europe?
3. What was the Code Napoléon? Did it have any importance outside of France?
4. How did the Battle of Trafalgar force Napoleon to change his plans?
5. How did Napoleon's continental blockade and the British Orders in Council affect neutral trade?
6. At the height of his power, Napoleon made drastic changes in Europe. List five of these changes.
7. What was the significance of the Peninsular Campaign and the Spanish constitution drawn up in 1812?
8. Why did Napoleon declare war on Russia in 1812?
9. Was the Old Régime restored in France after Napoleon's defeat? Explain.
10. The Napoleonic Era brought about a fundamental change in armies and wars. What was this new development?

Problems and projects

1. Napoleon may be said to have used the "divide and conquer" strategy to break up and defeat the European coalition. How did this method work for him? Can you give examples of the use of this policy in our time?
2. Why did Napoleon encourage a spirit of nationalism in France? How did this spirit spread to other countries? Explain the part played by nationalism in the overthrow of Napoleon.
3. Compare Napoleon's dictatorship with one of the twentieth century. Consider such items as control of the press, use of police, use of schools to teach obedience, importance of the army, importance of national feeling.
4. Compare the parts played by Great Britain, Spain, and Russia in defeating Napoleon.
5. To discuss: War is a very expensive means of solving international problems. Use the Napoleonic wars as examples (compare with other wars, if possible).
6. Review the effects of the French Revolution and the Napoleonic Era. Make a list of the permanent effects upon (a) France, (b) other nations of Europe.
7. In books on American history, look up the War of 1812. Report to the class on how the United States became involved in the Napoleonic wars.
8. Write a brief biographical sketch of Napoleon.
9. Write an editorial for an English newspaper, discussing the news that Napoleon has left Elba and returned to France.

Chapter 28

Reaction in Europe; Revolt in Latin America

THE NATIONS of Europe had been able to defeat Napoleon's France only with great difficulty. However, that had been only a military problem. In some ways it was simpler than the problems the victorious nations had to meet after Waterloo. Then the European statesmen had to decide what to do with the Europe which Napoleon left behind him.

It was a vastly different Europe from that of 1789. Ruling families had been driven from their thrones to live in exile. States had been shuffled about, boundaries moved. The Old Régime had suffered enormous blows. People had been given hope of a share in the government. National groups had been encouraged to hope for governments of their own. Above all, the Europe of 1815, exhausted by twenty-five years of bloody wars, desperately craved peace. The statesmen had to readjust boundaries and restore rulers. Most of all, they had to see that Europe did not again break down into revolution and war.

Reaction sweeps over Europe:
the Congress of Vienna

All these tasks were undertaken by the Congress of Vienna (1815). Here the leading statesmen of the European nations gathered to discuss the serious problems before them. Actually, the real decisions were made by the representatives of the four great powers which had done most to defeat Napoleon: Russia, Prussia, Austria, and Great Britain. These states were represented by their outstanding and most skillful leaders. Prince Metternich, chief minister of the Emperor of Austria, acted as chairman of the conference. Strangely enough, defeated France played an important part. This was the result of the diplomatic skill of the French minister, the sly, shrewd, and clever Charles Maurice de Talleyrand.

It was no surprise to anyone when the winning powers soon began wrangling among themselves over the division of the war spoils. The two most difficult problems concerned Poland and Saxony. From Prussia's Polish territory Napoleon had created the Grand Duchy of Warsaw, and given it to his faithful ally, the King of Saxony. Russia now demanded that all this territory be given to her. Prussia was willing to agree provided she be given all of Saxony, whose king had "backed the wrong horse." This arrangement was opposed by both Great Britain and Austria. Britain did not want to see Russia become too strong. Austria feared that the addition of Saxony might make Prussia too powerful in German affairs. For a time war seemed to threaten. Then Talleyrand was admitted to the conference, and the French diplomat suggested the compromise that settled the argument.

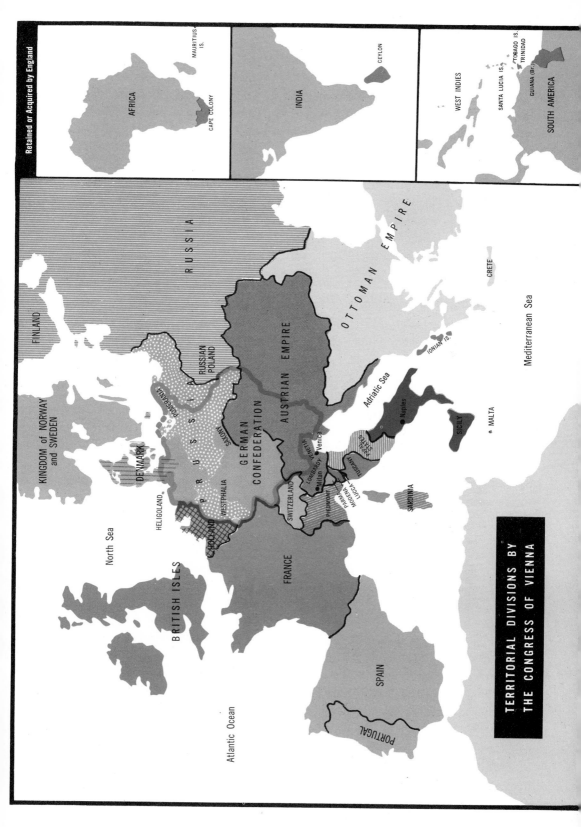

AFRICA

MAURITIUS IS.

CAPE COLONY

INDIA

CEYLON

WEST INDIES

SANTA LUCIA IS.

TOBAGO IS.

TRINIDAD

GUIANA (Br.)

SOUTH AMERICA

FINLAND

RUSSIA

KINGDOM of NORWAY and SWEDEN

RUSSIAN POLAND

OTTOMAN EMPIRE

CRETE

AUSTRIAN EMPIRE

POMERANIA

IONIAN IS.

Adriatic Sea

DENMARK

PRUSSIA

SAXONY

GERMAN CONFEDERATION

Naples

MALTA

North Sea

HELIGOLAND

WESTPHALIA

LOMBARDY

VENETIA

Venice

Milan

SICILY

BRITISH ISLES

HOLLAND

SWITZERLAND

Mediterranean Sea

PARMA

MODENA

LUCCA

TUSCANY

PIEDMONT

SARDINIA

FRANCE

Atlantic Ocean

SPAIN

PORTUGAL

TERRITORIAL DIVISIONS BY
THE CONGRESS OF VIENNA

Talleyrand urged that all settlements should be based on two principles, *legitimacy* and *compensation. Legitimacy* meant that all the former ruling families should be restored and all their former territories returned to them. Where the return of territories was impossible, they should receive *compensation:* territory taken from allies of Napoleon, like Saxony, or the weaker German and Italian states, which could not protest effectively. The strong took; the weak lost; the people were not even considered. Prussia received part of Saxony. Poland remained divided among Russia, Austria, and Prussia.

● *Kings restored to their thrones*

The rulers who had "gone on their journeys" during the revolutions now returned to their thrones in France, Spain, Holland, Sardinia, the Papal States, and elsewhere. Some of them had learned from their experiences. Others were bitter and burning to revenge their sufferings in exile. In Spain, Naples, and the states of northern Italy the restored rulers abolished the constitutions that had been set up during Napoleon's rule. They took the powers of absolute rulers, as if nothing had ever happened. Switzerland alone was allowed to regain her constitutional republican government, but had to promise that it would always remain neutral in European wars. This neutrality was guaranteed by the European powers.

● *The victors redraw the map*

The victors claimed their rewards; the map of Europe and much of the rest of the world was redrawn. Great Britain took from France most of her remaining islands in the West Indies. Elsewhere in the world Britain took Malta (in the Mediterranean), Cape Colony in South Africa, Ceylon, part of Dutch Guiana, and Heligoland (an island in the North Sea). To make up for her sufferings at the hands of Napoleon, Holland was given the Austrian Netherlands (now known as Belgium). To compensate for this loss, Austria was given the Republic of Venice and the Duchy of Milan. Hapsburgs were placed at the head of the other north Italian states of Parma, Modena, and Tuscany. In addition to the lion's share of Poland, Russia took Finland, which had been Swedish territory. Since Sweden had fought loyally against Napoleon, she was compensated by receiving Norway. Thus Denmark, which had formerly held Norway, was punished for cooperating with Napoleon. Prussia received a large share of Saxony, as well as Pomerania, Westphalia, and a share of the Rhineland.

The reason given for all this territorial reshuffling was to set up a ring of strong states around France lest she once more threaten the peace of Europe. The territories were parceled out as if they were uninhabited deserts; the desires of the people were not even considered. The nationalistic desires of many groups were disappointed. Not only was the strong desire of many Italians for a united Italy defeated, but many Italian states were placed under foreign rule. Of course the Italians hated this. The desire of the Polish people for national independence was also blocked. There was no independent self-government for the various national groups in Austria. One Austrian emperor said: "My realm is like a worm-eaten house; if a part of it is removed, one cannot tell how much will fall."

The German desire for national unity came closer to fulfillment. The number of German states was reduced to thirty-eight, and they were joined in the German Confederation. There was a Diet, or governing body, presided over by the Austrian delegate. Austria dominated the German Federation. However, her position was more than ever threatened by Prussia, for Prussia was now strong and territorially united.

The statesmen at Vienna had thwarted popular desires for independence, democratic rule, and national unity because they feared them greatly. They knew from bitter experience that these desires meant revolution, and revolution threatened everything they stood for. To prevent democratic revolutions they agreed to keep the Quadruple Alliance of Great Britain, Russia, Prussia, and Austria which had finally defeated Napoleon.

The Age of Metternich, 1815–1848

Czar Alexander I of Russia doubted that peace could be obtained and revolutions prevented simply by alliances and "sitting on the lid." Alexander was a firm believer in absolute, autocratic monarchy. However, he believed just as firmly that monarchs should be guided by Christian moral principles, with a strong sense of their charitable duties toward their subjects. He suggested that all rulers at Vienna pledge themselves to rule as Christian princes. The Holy Alliance, an agreement making such a pledge, was drawn up. It was signed by all rulers except the king of Great Britain, the sultan of Turkey, and the pope.

If the rulers of Europe had lived up to the high ideals they pledged in the Holy Alliance, the history of the next fifty years might have been different. Instead, the Holy Alliance was turned from its ideals and used for a very different purpose. This came about through the efforts of the chief minister of the emperor of Austria, Prince Metternich.

For the next thirty years Prince Metternich imposed his ideas on all of Europe so thoroughly that the time is known as the Age of Metternich. Metternich was a thorough aristocrat; as a consequence he believed that absolute monarchy under divine right was the only good government. He thought with fear and horror of democracy, constitutions, and such liberties as freedom of speech, press, and religion, and the right of people to a voice in government. To him these were truly radical and subversive ideas. They were to be suppressed without mercy because they were contrary to everything he considered good, true, and holy. Thus Metternich was what we call a *reactionary*: one who wishes to return to the conditions of former times.

● *Metternich's two aims*

During the more than thirty years of his domination, Metternich's aims were simple to state: to prevent war or revolution and to preserve the Old Régime. At home in Austria he had little difficulty in maintaining absolute monarchy. He set up an efficient system of secret police to spy on any revolutionary organizations or individuals. People who spoke out for liberty or popular rule were imprisoned, exiled, or fined. Schools were controlled in their teaching; newspapers and publishing houses were closely censored.

Austria controlled the German Confederation; so Metternich was able to have the same methods used in most German states. Hapsburg rule in northern Italy made sure that no revolutionary tendencies would succeed there. The Holy and Quadruple Alliances,

A scene in Vienna. An official is tearing down an anti-Metternich poster. Many Austrians, like other Europeans, wanted democratic constitutions, but for years the Metternich system suppressed liberal movements.

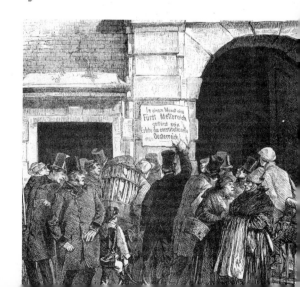

with the addition of France, were turned into instruments to carry out the same policy in the rest of Europe. Whenever there was a threat anywhere to the decisions of the Congress of Vienna, representatives of the five powers hastily gathered to discuss how to put down the disturbance. Austria, Russia, and Prussia went further: They agreed to act together to put down any attempt at revolution anywhere.

Great Britain could not agree to this last step. Under the parliamentary leadership of Prime Minister George Canning, Britain was opposed to stepping in where liberal popular movements were attempting to overthrow absolute rulers. Britain herself had a representative government, and the British people sympathized with other people in their struggles for similar governments. Then, too, Britain was a trading nation. Interfering with other countries was not good for her commerce. Therefore, Great Britain withdrew from the Quadruple Alliance. Metternich's coalition was left to act as an international, reactionary police force on the continent of Europe.

● *The Metternich system in operation*

For a time the Metternich system operated very successfully. When discontent flared up among German university students, Metternich called together the leaders of the German Confederation at Carlsbad. At his insistence they adopted measures known as the Carlsbad Decrees. Students and faculties of the universities were placed under strict watch. Newspapers were rigidly censored. An organization was formed to search for secret revolutionary activities. There were to be no political reforms that conflicted with the principle of absolute monarchy. In Italy attempts to shake off foreign rule or to set up representative governments were quickly and ruthlessly suppressed.

In France the Bourbon royal family had been restored under Louis XVIII. To his credit, Louis did not try to do away with all the reforms established between 1789 and 1815. He kept the Bank of France, Napoleon's Legion of Honor, the state-supported school system, and recognized the nobility created by Napoleon. Louis XVIII even granted a constitution to France. It recognized some individual rights and set up a legislative body to assist in governing the country. Although only very wealthy people could vote to elect the legislature, the constitution was a start in the right direction.

When Louis XVIII died, he was succeeded by his brother, Charles X. Charles was an ardent believer in absolute monarchy. As soon as he took the throne, he pledged that emigrant nobles whose estates had been seized and sold to the peasants would be paid in full by the government. This was a very unpopular policy. It meant taxing all the people for the benefit of the emigrant nobles.

● *Cracks in the Metternich system: Greek independence*

Metternich's repression led to underground movements of opposition in Germany, Italy, and Spain. In the years 1820–1823 there were revolutions in Naples, Sardinia, and Portugal, but they were quickly suppressed.

A revolt in Spain forced King Ferdinand VII to restore the constitution he had abolished. This example of successful revolution was displeasing to Metternich and the rulers of the Holy Alliance; they feared it might be contagious. Therefore, a French army crossed the Pyrenees and restored the Spanish king to full power.

In 1821 the Greeks tried to throw off the harsh, brutal rule of the Turks. Influenced by Metternich, the European rulers refused the Greeks' pleas for aid. However, many European people came to the support of the Greeks, either as volunteers or by sending arms. Finally, Russia, Britain, and France brought pressure on the sultan of Turkey. By the Treaty of Adrianople, 1829, Greece

George Gordon, Lord Byron, the British poet. He was one of many volunteers who helped the Greeks in their war for independence from Turkey. He became ill and died in Greece in 1824.

became an independent state, while the Serbs and Rumanians received some rights of self-government. These events marked the first signs of the collapse of the Turkish Empire.

Greek independence was the first cracking of the Metternich system in Europe. It showed that the sense of nationalism developed by the French Revolution could not be suppressed forever, even by strict and cruel methods. Developments at the same time in the Americas made this truth even more clear.

Latin America: the land and people

Spain had built a huge empire in Mexico, Central and South America, and the Caribbean Islands. Portugal had established a colony in the vast region of Brazil. These regions of Spanish and Portuguese colonization are known, collectively, as Latin America. They include Mexico and the six states of Central America: Guatemala, Honduras, Nicaragua, El Salvador, Costa Rica, and Panama. To the south lie ten South American states: Brazil, Ecuador, Peru, Bolivia, Chile, Venezuela, Colombia, Uruguay, Paraguay, and Argentina. Also included in Latin America are the Spanish-speaking islands of Cuba, Haiti, and Puerto Rico, as well as some smaller islands of the Caribbean Sea.

The entire area of Latin America is some eight and a half million square miles. Perhaps this figure will mean more when you realize that Brazil alone is larger than the entire United States. Venezuela is much larger than Texas, while two states the size of Texas could be tucked into Bolivia.

Latin America has many rugged and impressive mountain ranges, considerably higher than those of North America. It has a great variety of climate, ranging from the dry semi-desert areas of Central Mexico and the coast of Chile to the steaming jungles of Central America and Brazil or the open, grassy pampas (rolling plains) of Argentina. There are also vast rivers in South America. The Amazon, the Salado, the Uruguay, the Paraná, the Orinoco, with all their tributaries, make up one of the world's best river systems.

The Europeans who first came to this great region found many tribes of native people whom they called Indians. There were Indian tribes living at every stage of development from savagery to highly developed civilizations. The Aztecs of Mexico, the Mayas of Mexico and Central America, and the Incas of Peru had developed very high civilizations. They are a source of wonder to modern people who study them.

The European empires

As Chapter 20 has already noted, Spanish discoveries led to colonization, first in the islands of the West Indies, then in Mexico

and Central and South America. Many Spanish people came to the Americas hoping to make a quick fortune and return home, but there were far more Spaniards who planned to make the New World colonies their permanent home.

Spain's greatest revenue came from gold and silver, mined mainly in Mexico and Peru. Other important sources of wealth were copper and tin in Bolivia and various precious stones in Colombia. The colonists soon developed agriculture. They grew crops they had known in Europe and other crops first found in America, such as corn, potatoes, and

An Aztec calendar stone from ancient Mexico. In the center is the face of the sun god. The stone is twelve feet across. The Aztecs are believed to have had considerable knowledge of astronomy and to have known how long the earth takes to make a revolution around the sun. The Aztecs had a highly developed civilization before the first Europeans reached Mexico.

sugar cane. Portuguese Brazil contributed special products, such as coffee, cacao (the source of cocoa), tobacco, and citrus fruits. Argentina with her grassy plains became a great cattle country. In other countries the manufacture of pottery, jewelry, and textiles became important.

It was always difficult to find enough workers for mining, industry, and agriculture. Both the Spanish and the Portuguese enslaved the native Indians, but found them ill-suited for the desired work. In 1502 the first shipload of Negro slaves from Africa arrived in the West Indies. Each year thereafter great numbers of Negroes were captured in Africa and shipped to Latin America to work as slaves in mines and on plantations.

● Colonial society in Latin America

Spanish and Portuguese society in the New World was a class society, as in Europe. At the top was the governing and ruling class that came from Europe. They received many benefits and took for themselves a large share of the wealth of the countries they administered. They lived luxuriously. Their hope was always to build up a great fortune and return home to Europe to live in comfort and luxury the rest of their lives.

The governing class regarded all others with contempt. The others repaid them with hate and a strong desire to be rid of them. Next below the haughty ruling class were the white settlers and their descendants, born in the colonies and regarding them as their home. They had broken all ties with the Old World. The colonial-born whites were called *creoles*. They were often educated people and very ambitious. They resented the rigid restrictions imposed on them from abroad. Often they regarded the rulers as "foreigners," who came to America only to get rich and then return home.

Since the creoles regarded the colony as their native land, they were more friendly toward the natives than were the rulers. In general, both the Spanish and the Portuguese were more liberal in their attitude toward the Indians than were the English. Many marriages took place between creoles and Indians, which resulted in a mixed race whom the Spanish called *mestizos*. As time went by, the mestizos came to be a very numerous racial group in many parts of Latin America.

● Plantations

The economy of the Latin American colonies was one of large plantations. The ruling class were given huge grants of land, often thousands of acres in extent. The owner of the plantation lived in a luxurious home. His overseer had a less handsome house, while the workers, mostly slaves, lived in wretched hovels on the outskirts of the estate. Thus the Spanish and the Portuguese transferred the economy of the feudal manor to the New World.

Most of the colonial estates were far from towns or cities and almost self-sufficient. Often the owner spent much time in the cities of Europe, leaving his overseer to manage the estate. These absentee landlords were a haughty and idle class. The overseers who were left in charge were often inexperienced and brutal. Their cruel and harsh rule provoked much resentment.

Colonial Latin America had few towns. For the wealthy landlords these were trading centers, and a means of escape from the monotonous life of the country. Government officials, churchmen, landowners, and members of the small middle class made a social life in the towns that was much more varied than that of the countryside. Often the numerous religious festivals were times for social amusements as well. Many of the most popular amusements had been brought from Spain, such as bull fights, contests in horsemanship, dances, and singing to the accompaniment of the guitar. Almost every possible excuse for a festival was taken: weddings, births, seasonal holidays. Often a festival was held even when there was no special reason for it, just from the Spanish love for merrymaking.

The Church

Both the Spanish and the Portuguese brought with them the Roman Catholic Church. The Church and the government worked very closely together. Churchmen held high offices in the government. The government often supported the Church financially. As in Europe, there were two kinds of clergy. The secular clergy carried on the ordinary work of the Church—preaching, administering the sacraments, and ministering to the people. There were also a number of orders of the regular, or monastic, clergy—Jesuits, Benedictines, Dominicans, Augustinians, and Franciscans.

The regular clergy carried on missionary work among the Indians. They founded many missions which still exist today. The Jesuits helped to expand trade and to gain new territories. The regular clergy also taught in the schools. A number of universities were established, in which members of the clergy did most of the teaching. Education was mainly for white people, and for boys only.

A Spanish church in California. Missionaries accompanied Spanish explorers and conquerors in Mexico, South America and what is now the southwestern United States. The Mission San Diego de Alcala was built by members of the Franciscan Order.

Wealthier families sent their sons to Europe to be educated.

The independence movement

Latin America was a fertile field for the revolutionary ideas of the eighteenth century. The situation almost duplicated that of pre-revolutionary France. There were privileged classes: the governing class, the wealthy land-owners, and the clergy. There was an educated class of creoles, who resented the privileges of the rulers and the restrictions of the government. There was the great mass of peasants and slaves who might strike blows for freedom. The American and French revolutions with their stirring ideas were certain to inspire imitation in Latin America.

There were a number of reasons for the discontent of the Spanish colonies. The colonies disliked and resented the rigid restrictions of Spanish mercantilism. They protested against the transplanted feudalism with its class system. They resented the bad economic system which brought wealth to a few and poverty to the many. There was a rising feeling against the numerous heavy taxes imposed by both Church and state. When peaceful attempts to reform these conditions failed, violence was sure to follow.

Revolutionary movements in Latin America gained strength from the fact that both Spain and Portugal were very busy at home. Both had been overrun by Napoleon. After Waterloo, Spain was weakened by political troubles at home. In 1820 a revolution set up a monarchy with a constitution. It lasted only three years, but the revolution and the long years of struggle against Napoleon had left Spain weak. She was not able to offer much resistance to the independence movement in the colonies.

The first revolt—Haiti

The first successful revolt against European colonization was not against Spain or Portu-

Christophe's Citadel, in Haiti. This fortress was built between 1804, when Haiti became independent of France, and 1819. The fort could hold 10,000 men; the walls are from 80 to 130 feet high and 20 to 30 feet thick. Construction of this huge mass of masonry on a high peak was a marvelous feat of engineering and hard labor.

gal, but against the France of Napoleon. It took place on the island of Haiti, once a Spanish colony, which had been taken by France. In 1801 the Negro Toussaint L'Ouverture led a revolt against the French rulers. Napoleon sent a veteran French army to put down the uprising. However, the French suffered such heavy casualties in fights with the rebels and from malaria and yellow fever that they were forced to give up the island. The independence of the Republic of Haiti, proclaimed in January, 1804, marked the beginning of the end of colonialism in the New World.

●Independence of Mexico and Central America

The example of Toussaint in Haiti was soon followed in Mexico. Two priests, Miguel

Hidalgo and José María Morelos, led unsuccessful revolts in 1810 and 1813. The leaders paid for their failures with their lives. They had wanted more than independence from Spain. They promised reforms such as the abolition of slavery, general social improvements, and a better distribution of land. Other men took the places of Hidalgo and Morelos, and the rebellions continued until the Spanish viceroy was forced to give independence. The Spanish kings stubbornly refused to recognize the fact, but that made little difference. For all practical purposes Mexico had won national independence by 1822.

Again an example proved contagious. South of Mexico lay Central America. Here the chances of rebellion were poorer, for there were few people, and Spanish control was stronger. Nevertheless, revolts began in El Salvador, spread to Guatemala, and from there throughout the isthmus. The Spanish authorities held on grimly. By 1823, however, representatives of the five "United Provinces of Central America" joined in an assembly, drew up a federal constitution, and soon after elected the first president of the newly born national state.

The real strongholds of Spain's colonial empire were in South America—in Venezuela, Colombia, Argentina, and especially Chile and Peru on the west coast. In Venezuela and Colombia independence from Spain was won under the inspired leadership of the man known as the George Washington of South America: Simón Bolívar.

●Bolívar liberates Colombia, Venezuela, and Ecuador

Bolívar was born in Venezuela, the son of a wealthy creole family. He was educated in Europe. Here he traveled widely, seeing and studying the effects of the French Revolution. When he returned home, he was soon recognized as a leader in the independence movement.

Two leaders of the fight to make South America independent of Spain: José de San Martín and Simón Bolívar, shown meeting at Guayaquil in 1822. San Martín was a leader in the liberation of Argentina, Uruguay, Paraguay, Chile, and Peru. Bolívar is famous as the liberator of Colombia, Venezuela, and Ecuador.

Conditions in Venezuela were not too favorable; so Bolívar moved to Colombia. He raised an army, defeated the Spanish forces, and then led a march into Venezuela. In 1814, at the head of his victorious army, Bolívar triumphantly entered the city of Caracas, his birthplace. Venezuela was proclaimed a republic, with Simón Bolívar, "the Liberator," as president.

The Spanish, however, did not give up easily. The Spanish viceroy gathered an army, defeated the republicans, and forced Bolívar to flee first to Colombia and then to Haiti. In Haiti he sought help for the cause of independence, and he was able to get it. After three years he returned to Venezuela. Again there was much fighting, but after several years both Venezuela and Colombia were freed of Spanish rule and united under a federal constitution for the "United States of Colombia."

Bolívar was not satisfied. He wanted to free the entire continent of South America from Spanish rule and to unite it into one great federal republic. Ecuador came first. By 1822 the Spanish had been driven out, and Ecuador became a part of the newly formed United States of Colombia.

Argentina, Chile, and Peru

The forces of independence in Argentina had not been idle. By 1810 the creole rebels had seized control of the government, declared independence, and invited the neighboring colonies to join them. However, the Spanish were strongly entrenched in Paraguay, Uruguay, Bolivia, and especially Peru. Rivalries among the creole rebels helped the Spanish. The creoles could not agree on the kind of government they wanted. Some favored monarchy; others wanted a republic. Nevertheless, under the strong leadership of José de San Martín, Bernardo O'Higgins, and others, the states of Argentina, Uruguay, and Paraguay were able to gain independence.

San Martín was convinced that independence could not last while Spain was strongly entrenched in Peru. He also decided that the best way to get at Peru was to strike first at Chile. In Chile there was already much unrest among the people. A patriotic army was gathered, and, led by San Martín, it made the incredibly difficult crossing of the towering Andes Mountains. In spite of strong Spanish resistance, the army entered Santiago, Chile. By 1818 Chile was independent. Now it could serve as a base for the attack on Peru.

In Chile the patriots raised an army and a considerable force of ships for the final struggle. The campaign lasted more than five years. Finally, independence forces captured Lima, the capital, and proclaimed Peru an independent republic under San Martín. It took three more years of hard fighting to clear the entire country of Spanish troops. By 1825 the territory of Upper Peru had become an independent republic. It was renamed Bolivia in honor of the great Simón Bolívar. Thus by 1825 Mexico, Central America, and South America had become independent of Spain. Only in the islands of Cuba and Puerto Rico did Spanish colonialism hold on.

After French troops had put down the rebellion in Spain in 1823, there was a possibility that the Holy Alliance might try to help Spain regain her American colonies. Two things prevented this from happening. The first was objection from Great Britain, backed by the mighty British fleet. The British had built up a good trade with Latin America. If the region were restored to Spain, they feared the trade would be lost.

● The Monroe Doctrine

The United States also opposed European intervention in Latin America. The British minister George Canning offered to allow the United States to join Britain in opposing intervention. However, the United States preferred to act alone. President James Monroe made a statement which has since come to be known as the Monroe Doctrine.

Monroe said that the United States would not interfere in any European wars, nor in the affairs of any European colonies already established in the Western Hemisphere. However, no more colonies were to be established in this hemisphere. The United States would oppose any attempts to establish new colonies, add territory to existing colonies, or interfere with any Latin American governments. The combination of both British and

GAINING of INDEPENDENCE in CENTRAL and SOUTH AMERICA and CARIBBEAN to 1825

Spanish rule overthrown   Portuguese rule overthrown
under Spanish rule   French rule overthrown

United States opposition discouraged any European power from meddling in Latin American affairs. Latin America remained independent.

● Brazil wins independence

Meanwhile, in the Portuguese colony of Brazil events had taken a somewhat different course. In 1808 Napoleon's French army had invaded Portugal. The royal family fled to Brazil, settling in Rio de Janeiro. From there they ruled the colony and still claimed to rule the homeland. Even after the overthrow of Napoleon, the Portuguese king remained in Brazil. Neither the homeland nor the colony liked this. Finally, in 1821 the pressure became too great. The king returned to Portugal, leaving his son, Dom Pedro, in charge of the Brazilian government.

The people of Brazil had been influenced by the independence movement in the neighboring Spanish colonies. The departure of

This monument in São Paulo commemorates Brazil's independence.

the Portuguese king gave them their opportunity. Brazilian patriots asked Dom Pedro to become ruler of an independent Brazil, and he willingly consented. A constitutional assembly was summoned, and a constitutional empire under Dom Pedro was set up. In 1824 Brazil proclaimed its independence from Portugal, and Portugal wisely recognized the independence of its former colony.

Thus all of Latin America has followed in the footsteps of the thirteen English colonies of North America, and broken the ties of European colonialism. Only in Canada, the islands of the West Indies, and some small regions of Central and South America did imperialism remain. The greater part of the two great continents had now become independent and self-governing.

● After independence, what?

The inspired Simón Bolívar had dreamed of a great federal United States of South America, like that of the English-speaking states of North America. The patriotic San Martín had tried to bring this about by unselfishly withdrawing from his presidency in favor of Bolívar. South America had common ties that seemed to make such a union possible. Spanish was a common language in all countries except Brazil, where Portuguese was spoken. In every country the Roman Catholic Church gave a common religious faith. There was a common culture, brought from Spain and Portugal, two closely related countries.

In spite of these common ties, the dream of South American unity did not become real. Furthermore, republican independence did not bring the reforms which so many men had dreamed of and fought for. Everywhere there were rivalries and jealousies among the different parts. Within a few years after 1825, separate states began to form. Finally the region south of the United States broke up into twenty independent, sovereign republics.

Latin America was poorly prepared for self-rule. Its people had had no training in democratic government. Therefore, its republican governments failed to prove stable or beneficial to all the people. The educated creoles were less than one fifth of the population. Even they were inexperienced in government, for they had been kept out of all important positions under Spanish rule. The Spanish-Indian mestizos were less than a third of the population. The rest were Indians, except for the Negroes, who made up about one twentieth of the whole. The vast majority of these people were ignorant, and even primitive. It was not a very good basis for democratic self-government.

Independence did not bring about much change in social conditions. The Roman Catholic Church remained the official religion, and Church and government were closely tied together everywhere. Land was still owned in huge estates. The creoles simply took over from the former ruling class, or continued to hold what they already had. The landowners kept almost all their former privileges; the mass of the people were no better off than before. Slavery, poverty, illiteracy, and ignorance remained. One group of rulers had been replaced by another. The creoles were as haughty and overbearing toward the masses as the Spanish governors had been in colonial days.

Local wars were constantly breaking out. Conflicts over borders, family feuds, and the personal ambitions of dictators resulted in many small wars which brought destruction to the countryside and death to the inhabitants. Republican government was always in danger. The small ruling creole class feared that the rest of the people would seize both governmental power and land. Such conditions are an invitation to military dictatorship, not democracy. Although the South American governments have remained republican in appearance, many have actually been military dictatorships. One government

A scene in present-day Peru. This man is using a farming tool of a type that has been handed down from the Incas.

has succeeded another, not by election but by revolution or by the army seizing power—the military coup ·d'état.

The backward economic condition of the countries added to the confusion and the misery. Under Spanish rule very little industry was permitted. Most of the countries were agricultural, and the ownership of land in large estates meant that the great majority of the population continued to live in poverty and ignorance. This misery bred unrest among the people, and such unrest was exactly the condition that led to military dictatorship by the aristocratic ruling class.

It is not difficult to understand why political conditions in Central and South America have been unsettled for more than one hundred years since independence. Only within very recent years has the investment of capital from the outside begun to build up industries and to give some promise of better economic conditions. Better economic conditions might lead to more settled political conditions, more widespread education, a general raising of the standard of living, and the replacing of military dictatorships by some truly democratic form of government. But even today, in the second half of the twentieth century, these changes seem to be taking place at a disappointingly slow rate in most of South America.

Review of Chapter 28

People, places, and things

Identify: Metternich, Canning, Charles X, Toussaint L'Ouverture, Bolívar, San Martín, Dom Pedro, Monroe, German Confederation, Holy Alliance, Quadruple Alliance, Carlsbad Decrees, Incas, Aztecs, Mayas, mestizos.

Locate: West Indies, Malta, Cape Colony, Ceylon, Heligoland, Republic of Venice, Duchy of Milan, Parma, Modena, Tuscany, Finland, Poland, Saxony, Pomerania, Westphalia, Brazil, Ecuador, Peru, Bolivia, Chile, Venezuela, Colombia, the Guianas, Uruguay, Cuba, Argentina, Haiti, Puerto Rico, Guatemala, Honduras, Nicaragua, El Salvador, Costa Rica, Panama.

Events in review

1. What was Talleyrand's principle of *legitimacy?* Give an example of how this principle was put into effect.
2. What was Talleyrand's principle of *compensation?* Give an example of the application of this principle.
3. Could Czar Alexander I be called a benevolent or enlightened despot? Why? Was his advice to the rulers of Europe followed?
4. State the basic aims of "the Metternich system."
5. Why did Great Britain withdraw from Metternich's coalition?
6. Briefly describe events in Greece between 1821 and 1829. Show how these developments challenged the Metternich system.
7. Is it correct to say that a feudal society existed in the Spanish and Portuguese colonies in Latin America? Explain.
8. Where and when did the first successful revolt against European colonization take place?
9. Who were the creoles? What part did they play in winning independence for Latin America?
10. Why did the Holy Alliance in Europe not restore the "legitimate" rule of Spain's colonies in America?
11. State the main provisions of the Monroe Doctrine.
12. Did independence bring great improvement in social conditions in Latin America? Give reasons for your answer.

Problems and projects

1. List the changes in the map of Europe made by the Congress of Vienna. Note the areas where there was likelihood of trouble breaking out.
2. Discuss the problems facing the great powers at the Congress of Vienna. Try to mark out a plan for Europe that would have avoided the bad aspects of Metternich's system. Would it have been possible to preserve the peace, take care of national interests, and protect the rights and liberties of all people?
3. Debate: the Big Four at the Congress of Vienna tried to "turn the clock back" a quarter of a century.
4. Make a chart of the independence movements in Central and South America. Show leaders and dates for each country.
5. Make reports on the background, society, political life, and economy of the Latin American countries in the early nineteenth century. Discuss why these countries were not able to form a federal union, whereas in North America the colonies formed the United States.
6. After a library research period discuss the topic, "Colonies in the Western Hemisphere Today." Has the United States considered this matter? Is there any movement toward changing the status of any of the British possessions?
7. Write a biographical sketch of Simón Bolívar, comparing him with George Washington.

Chapter 29

Political Ferment in Europe, 1830-1848

THE TEN YEARS of the 1820's saw some breaks in the Metternich system in Europe and in the Americas. The American colonies of Spain and Portugal won and kept their independence. In the Balkan peninsula Greece won independence from Turkey, and the Serbs and Rumanians gained some degree of self-government. However, these gains for freedom, self-government, and nationalism were only on the fringes. In the heart of the continent of Europe Metternich was able to preserve his system through the 1820's.

France, 1830–1848

But in the 1830's Metternich's Old Régime tottered. The first real breakdown came in France. Charles X, who followed his brother Louis XVIII, tried to restore many of the privileges of the Old Régime. He did away with almost all of the weak constitution granted by his brother. In the years since 1789 France had gone too far toward self-government and learned too much about throwing off autocratic rule. In July, 1830, a revolt spread throughout the country. Charles X was forced to abdicate.

The leaders of the French rebellion of 1830 were sure that they wanted to be rid of Charles X, but they could not agree on the kind of government they desired. Those who wanted a republic were not strong enough to win. Finally all factions agreed on the choice of another king. Louis Philippe, Duke of Or-

leans, a man with a record of liberal ideas, belonged to a branch of the Bourbon family. As a compromise candidate, he was chosen king of France.

● *Louis Philippe, the "middle-class king"*

Louis Philippe was in a very delicate position. He was a king, but an elected king. From the experience of Charles X, he knew that he could be thrown out if he did not please the French people, especially the members of the middle class. Therefore, he tried hard to please everyone and be a "middle-class king." It was a difficult task in those days to be middle class and be a monarch.

Constitutional changes in 1830 favored the middle class. The right to vote and hold office in the legislative assembly was given only to a few people—to those who owned property. These people, the merchants and manufacturers, saw to it that the laws passed were beneficial to them. Louis Philippe, who called himself the "Citizen King," consented to this policy. Labor unions were outlawed, and workers were forbidden to organize themselves. The policy of high tariffs on imports was continued. It benefited the owners of industries because it kept foreign-made goods out, but it resulted in high prices to everyone. In a period of low wages and high living costs, the majority of the people are sure to be unhappy.

The French bourgeoisie also approved the new king's foreign policy. This was his attempt to build a new colonial empire, especially in North Africa. After some difficulty France established herself in Algeria and turned the country into a French possession. With Algeria as a base, France began to lay plans to extend her North African empire. She looked toward Morocco and Tunisia.

● *Opposition to Louis Philippe*

The "Citizen King" had enough opponents to be sure of rough political weather. The monarchists were divided into two groups. The outright monarchists thought that only the direct descendant of Charles X could be a legitimate, rightful king. The Bonapartists wanted to revive the empire of Napoleon, for by now the wars, miseries, and oppressions of the Napoleonic era were forgotten. Napoleon had become a hazy figure, a legend: the ruler who made France glorious.

At the other extreme from the monarchists were the republicans. They believed that France should grant political rights to all the people. France should become a republic and make social changes to benefit all the people. Most of the French workers felt this way.

Roman Catholics also were displeased with Louis Philippe. The higher clergy and many devout Catholics disliked the separation of Church and state. This policy had been started during the revolution, followed by Napoleon, and kept in force under Louis Philippe.

As the 1840's neared their end, there was widespread opposition to the régime of Louis Philippe, and great desire for change. There was no general agreement as to what kind of change should come. But it was safe to predict that the political life of the "Citizen King" would not last much longer.

Belgium versus Holland, 1830

The French rebellion of 1830 against the Metternich system spread to other parts of Europe. The Congress of Vienna had given Belgium (the Austrian Netherlands) to Holland. It was not a happy union, for the two peoples had little in common. There were differences in language, religion, and economics. The Hollanders spoke Dutch; the Belgians spoke Flemish or French. Hollanders were Calvinist Protestants; Belgians were Roman Catholics. The Dutch people were either farmers or commercial traders; the Belgians were mostly engaged in manufacturing. The Belgians wanted independence; the Dutch refused to grant it.

Inspired by news of the Paris rebellion of 1830, the Belgians in Brussels revolted and proclaimed Belgian independence. For several reasons their attempt met good fortune. Both the British and the French approved Belgian independence and refused to intervene. Austria and Russia, which might have intervened, were busy elsewhere.

The Dutch resisted Belgian independence stubbornly for some years, but in 1839 they had to give up. They signed a treaty which recognized Belgium as an independent monarchy under King Leopold. Britain, France, Austria, Prussia, and Russia also agreed to Belgian independence. Furthermore, they pledged that Belgium should be regarded as neutral in any European war. This was the pledge of neutrality which Germany violated by invading Belgium in 1914, at the beginning of World War I.

England, 1830–1848

England had been the first nation to do away with divine-right monarchy. The Glorious Revolution of 1688 made Parliament the real ruler of the country, with the House of Commons more powerful than the aristocratic House of Lords. It was representative, but not democratic, government. The right to vote for members of Commons was restricted to owners of fairly large amounts of land. Only a few places were allowed to send representatives to Commons. At the beginning of the nineteenth century, the British government was really an aristocracy controlled by the nobility and the wealthy landed gentry.

● *The need for reforms*

The following conditions in England were considered political abuses in need of reform:

1. Only property owners and a few other privileged people could vote.
2. Catholics, Jews, and Dissenters could not hold political offices.
3. Voting in elections was done by a show of hands instead of by secret ballot. This encouraged bribery and the influencing of voters.
4. The House of Commons did not fairly represent the country. The districts which elected representatives had not been changed since 1664. In some districts the population had decreased or almost disappeared, but they still sent representatives to Commons. (These were called "rotten boroughs.") In other districts choice of representatives was completely controlled by noble landowners, members of the House of Lords. (These were called "pocket boroughs" because the landowner had the representative "in his pocket.") Some of the new industrial cities, with large populations, were almost entirely unrepresented.
5. Members of the House of Commons received no pay, and had to qualify by owning large amounts of property. Thus a man

A radical paper of 1831, expressing some of the complaints of working people against the government of that time. The "William Guelph" referred to was King William IV of Great Britain.

THE

POOR MAN'S GUARDIAN,

A Weekly Paper

FOR THE PEOPLE.

PUBLISHED IN DEFIANCE OF " LAW," TO TRY THE POWER OF " RIGHT " AGAINST " MIGHT."

" IT IS THE CAUSE; IT IS THE CAUSE."

No. 25.　　Saturday, December 10, 1831.　　{ Lent to Read, without deposit, for Six Months, CHARGE ONE PENNY.

Friends, Brethren, and Fellow-Countrymen,
On Tuesday last, WILLIAM GUELPH went in state to open Parliament, and prepare for the " not less efficient" *measures* (for it is not a " measure" we perceive) of " Parliamentary Reform." We were gratified by the great moral stride which, under the short duration of our guardianship, " the mob" and "the populace," as "contradistinguished from the people", have made towards mental redemption; they have lost—thank God —lost a little of their veneration for " King" and pageantry, and!all such "royal" nonsense!　Poor WILLIAM GUELPH, notwithstanding his gilt coach and purple velvet robe, trimmed with ermine, and attended as he was, amongst even his faithful and loving subjects, by all "the pomp and circumstance of glorious war," heard, we think, very few "cheers" besides those of a few of his own trades folk, and of his own dirty troop of policemen, who formed at least three parts of the " crowd" (as tering with age, and enveloped in a large, loose-hanging wrapper of purple velvet, mounted with a small cape of " royal ermine," and tied tight round the neck, must have appeared. " Not a man present but who would have thought himself insulted by a comparison with the ' royal and illustrious person;' nor a woman who could so have far overcome her natural feelings as to wish to be the 'queen' of such ' a king!' as for myself, I inwardly exclaimed, ' and is this a king!' and felt wonderstruck that mere *accident* could have placed such a creature above so many millions of his fellow-men, so eminently his superiors!　As for his intellect, to be sure, I did not take *that* into account,—(although his family, I am told, are not very enviably celebrated for that commodity, and he himself is far, I believe, from being the Solomon even of his family)—if indeed it could be possible to associate the idea of any thing like " intellect" with such a person and expression as his own."

who was not a large landowner could not be elected, and a man without a large income could not afford to serve.

6. The House of Lords still had much power. Through their control of elections they could influence the decisions of the House of Commons.

For a number of reasons the ruling classes were able to postpone the reforms demanded by merchants, manufacturers, and workmen. Many Englishmen had become fearful of political changes because of the French Revolution, especially the Reign of Terror. The wars from 1793 till 1815 served as an excuse for putting off changes. After Waterloo, England joined the continent in fearing radical reforms. Even the long-established liberties of freedom of speech and press and the right to assemble peacefully were seriously threatened.

By 1830 the demands for reform could not be overlooked any longer. Several times the House of Commons passed a bill to give voting rights to more people and distribute election districts more fairly. Each time the House of Lords refused to pass the bill. Finally the Whig leaders of Commons forced the king to announce that he would create as many new lords as necessary to give the bill a majority in the House of Lords. To avoid this the lords grudgingly gave in and passed the bill.

A scene in London in the nineteenth century. This picture by the famous artist Gustave Doré shows how crowded and gray the slums of many great cities were. The men and women living in these tenements would not have met the qualifications for voting, even after the Reform Bill of 1832.

The Reform Bill of 1832 took representation in Commons from the "rotten boroughs" and "pocket boroughs" and gave it to the new industrial cities. Scotland was also given a larger representation in Parliament. Property qualifications for voting were lowered so that almost all members of the middle class could vote. As a result, power in Parliament was given to the owners of factories and banks, the merchants, and the shipowners. It was a step toward democracy, although not a very long step.

The Whig Party, which had forced the passage of the Reform Bill of 1832, had the support of the new voters. Since many voters favored even more liberal reforms, the party changed its name and called itself the Liberal Party. The Tory Party of the large landowners had opposed the Reform Bills, and were very reluctant to go any further. They became known as the Conservative Party. These two parties are still so called today.

The Liberal Party soon forced the adoption of other reforms. The government took a timid first step toward free public education by giving financial support to private and church schools. Parliament established the University of London so that more people could benefit by higher education. Imprisonment for debt was abolished. Penalties for criminal offenses were made less cruel. Dissenters and Catholics were allowed to hold public offices.

For more than thirty years the Reform Bill of 1832, which gave political representation to the middle class, was the only political change that could be passed. Although this act left the majority of English men and women without the right to vote, the bill was still a big step forward. It is interesting that this gain was made without revolution. The Conservatives fought the reforms of the 1830's bitterly, but when they had to yield, they accepted them without warfare. Apparently the English people had had enough of rebellion and civil war during the seventeenth century.

The English people did make one important economic gain before 1848. For many years England had had a very high protective tariff on imported grain. The country did not produce enough grain for its needs; so these Corn Laws were a great benefit to the landowners. The landowners could always sell all their grain. However, high prices were the result because everyone needed grain, and there wasn't any too much of it. This worked a hardship on everyone else except the landowners. In 1846, after a bitter fight, the Liberals forced through Parliament a bill repealing the Corn Laws. Grain could be imported into England free of tax. It was the first step in a policy of doing away with protective tariffs and making England a "free-trade" nation.

Revolutions in 1848: France

The year 1848 brought revolutions everywhere in Europe. As in 1830, trouble began in France, and events in France were the spark that touched off explosions elsewhere. Since it is not possible to write fully about all the revolts, the one in France will be discussed in some detail as an illustration of what happened in many countries.

The French trouble began over a minor matter. A meeting was to be held at which speeches critical of the government were to be made. To stop it Louis Philippe issued a decree prohibiting all meetings. The publication of the decree started riots in Paris. The disorders did not seem serious until the National Guard, summoned to restore order, joined the rioters. The disturbance grew until the king was compelled to abdicate and go to England. A temporary government was set up to restore order and draw up a constitution for France.

The temporary government was made up of various elements: ardent republicans, members of the working class, liberals, Catholic

DENMARK

NETHERLANDS

AUSTRIAN
NETHERLANDS

● Paris

FRANCE

PRUSSIA
● Berlin

RUSSIA

● Warsaw

KINGDOM OF POLAND

GERMANIC CONFEDERATION

● Frankfort

● Prague

Vienna

EMPIRE OF AUSTRIA

● Budapest

HUNGARY

PIEDMONT

LOMBARDY
● Milan

VENETIA

Venice ●

● Turin

KINGDOM OF
SARDINIA

PAPAL
STATES

CORSICA

● Rome

SARDINIA

● Naples

KINGDOM OF THE TWO SICILIES

REVOLUTIONS OF 1848

● Centers of Revolutionary Activity

groups, and intellectuals. Almost all favored a republic; therefore the Second French Republic was proclaimed. (You may remember that the first republic lasted from 1792 until the beginning of Napoleon's empire in 1804.) However, there was much disagreement over what kind of a republic the second one was to be.

The most vigorous and active group on the French political scene was the city working class. The French call them the *proletariat*. Many of their leaders believed in socialism. Among other things, this means that they wanted all industries to be owned by all the people and operated by the government for the benefit of everyone.

● Unemployment and government relief

France was then suffering from an economic depression. There was much unemployment, especially among the proletariat. The socialist members of the provisional government urged that the government do something to relieve the unemployment. Instead of trying to take over all industry, they proposed that the government set up and operate "national workshops" to give work to the unemployed. It was the first appearance in modern times of the idea that the government has a responsibility to do something about unemployment.

The "national workshops" were supposed to be regular business enterprises, where unemployed men could find useful and productive work. However, it was hard to find really useful and productive things for the workshops to do without competing with and injuring already established, privately owned businesses. So the "national workshop" scheme turned into a charitable affair instead of a sound business. Men were employed, but at work that was poorly paid, often unproductive and useless, and sometimes degrading.

Soon another difficulty appeared. To form a permanent government the temporary government called for the election of a national assembly. All men were allowed to vote; they did not have to own any property. The vote of the French nation showed that the countryside was far more conservative than the cities. The peasants had very little interest in the socialistic experiments; in fact, they were extremely hostile to many of them. The French peasants now owned their land, and they were determined to keep it. They did not intend to be taxed for the benefit of the city workingmen. They elected conservative men to the new National Assembly. When the Assembly met in June, 1848, the members voted to stop the program of national workshops.

● The Second French Republic

Again riots broke out in Paris. Fearing revolution, the Assembly gave dictatorial powers to a general. For three days Paris was a battlefield, but the army was too strong for the workers. The rebellion was crushed, and its socialist leaders were imprisoned, exiled, or executed. The socialist experiment had lasted less than six months.

The National Assembly now organized the new Second Republic of France. The Assembly tried to steer a moderate, middle course, giving each group at least some of its demands. To the workers it promised moderate social reforms. To the liberals it guaranteed freedom of the press, reforms in the courts, and abolition of slavery in the French colonies. To the Catholics it pledged greater cooperation with the Church. To the democratic elements it gave a constitution with a republican form of government.

This constitution of the Second French Republic provided for a president. He was to be elected by all the people for a four-year term and not eligible for a second term. The single legislative chamber was to consist of representatives elected by universal manhood suffrage. As constitutions go, it was liberal. It did not last long.

Street fighting in Paris in 1848. Soldiers have driven rioters back from a barricade they had made across the streets. The troops are moving onward toward a building from which civilians are firing. Many other European cities were the scenes of riots and bloodshed in 1848.

France: Louis Napoleon

At the end of 1848 there was an election of the officials of the new government. Surprisingly enough, the man who was elected president was not one of the outstanding leaders of the revolution. Instead, by an overwhelming vote, the French people chose as their leader Louis Napoleon Bonaparte, nephew of the first Napoleon.

Louis Napoleon spent most of his early years in exile because the restored Bourbons did not want any Bonapartes wandering around France. In Italy he had belonged to a revolutionary society called the Carbonari. Twice he had returned to France to take part in rebellions which failed. He was imprisoned, but managed to escape to England, where he did a little writing. Above all, he worked tirelessly to spread the legend of the glory of his uncle, Napoleon Bonaparte, Emperor from 1804 to 1815.

Louis Napoleon did not return to France until after the uprising of 1848 had taken place. No one knew just where he stood. Nevertheless, he got four times as many votes as the next highest candidate. Thus the first president of the Second French Republic was Louis Napoleon Bonaparte, whose real political opinions were unknown.

It was soon clear that Louis Napoleon wanted to be more than a president. He began to work for the support of various groups in the country. As a true Bonaparte, he did everything he could to gain the support of the army. To win over the French Catholics, he helped the pope by putting down an attempt to set up a republic in Rome. He also repealed certain laws so that the Catholic Church could have more control of French education. He favored the middle class by helping to develop manufacturing. At the same time, he tried to keep the favor of the workers by generous promises and by a program of public works that gave employment to many.

In addition to all this, Louis Napoleon was able to pose as a champion of democratic rights. In 1851 the national legislature passed a law which took from a third of the French people the right to vote. Louis Napoleon vetoed the bill, and insisted that the legislature restore universal suffrage. When the legislature refused, the president dissolved the assembly and took dictatorial powers. At the same time he issued a decree giving voting rights to all Frenchmen of legal age. Thus he could pose as a champion of the people. He stopped all criticism of his acts by strict censorship of writings and by driving his critics out of France.

Napoleon also employed the plebiscite (popular vote), a favorite trick of his famous uncle. The French people were asked to approve a plan whereby Louis Napoleon was given power to draft a new constitution for the Second French Republic. Most people thought of him as their champion; others believed that he was defending law and order. The vote was almost twelve to one in favor of his plan.

You will not be surprised to learn that the new constitution gave great power to the president, who was still Louis Napoleon. He was to serve for ten years. A Council of State appointed by the president was given law-making powers. This meant that the president really controlled the legislature through his power of appointment. The long term of ten years gave him a chance to build up his powers enormously. What looked like a republic had become a dictatorship.

Louis Napoleon was still not satisfied. He held the reality of power, but he wanted the outward show as well. He was determined to follow in the footsteps of his famous uncle, and Napoleon I had been an emperor. In 1852 there was another plebiscite on still another constitution. By cleverly handling the votes, Louis Napoleon gained the consent of the French people to allow him to drop the title of President and take the title Emperor Napoleon III. The Second French Republic was ended; the Second French Empire had begun. The emperor was really a dictator with unlimited power.

●Revolutions elsewhere in Europe, 1848

The revolt in France in 1848 sparked explosions elsewhere in Europe. In Austria there were demands for a constitution to guarantee liberties and limit the power of the emperor. The uprising was so sudden that Metternich, who for thirty years had dominated Europe, had to flee to England. Similar movements took place in Hungary and Bohemia, with the added feature that each wanted to be independent of the Austrian Empire.

People in various states in Italy tried to force their rulers to accept constitutions. Ital-ian nationalists also wanted to drive out the foreign rulers of Italian states. They were eager to unite all Italy under King Charles Albert of Sardinia-Piedmont. As a member of the House of Savoy he was the only Italian ruling an Italian state. The House of Savoy became the hope of patriotic nationalists throughout the peninsula.

The situation in Germany was like that of Italy. In Prussia, Bavaria, and other German states rulers were forced to grant constitutions. The German liberals and nationalists

Victor Hugo, a famous French writer. He was exiled from his homeland because he protested against the 1851 coup d'état by Louis Napoleon. Victor Hugo scornfully called the new ruler of France "Napoleon the Little." Today, many people the world over know Hugo as the author of Les Misérables, Notre Dame de Paris, *and other famous books. In fact, he is probably better known than Napoleon III.*

began a determined drive to unite Germany into a single national state.

The revolutionary spirit reached still other countries of Europe. The kings of Holland and Denmark accepted constitutions which established parliamentary government. In England there were demands for voting rights for more people and greater security for workingmen. Everywhere in Europe the year 1848 was marked by liberal constitutional movements, often with strong nationalistic sentiments.

Failure of the Revolutions of 1848

Revolutions seem to follow a pattern: they pass through certain stages which can almost be predicted. In the beginning, groups of people with very different ideas are able to unite and work together because they want to get rid of something they all consider bad. They do not have to agree about what they want to create, because the first task is to do away with the thing that exists.

When the existing government has been driven out, the revolutionary movement often begins to break up. The excitement and enthusiasm die down, and the task of building something new has to be faced. Differences now appear among the various groups. It is hard for them to agree about the details of the new government. Often, as the revolutionary group becomes divided, the conservative forces of the old order are able to take advantage of the splits and regain much of their former position and power.

The revolutions of 1848 were no exception to this rule. They were mostly the work of city people who wanted liberal, constitutional, parliamentary governments elected by universal manhood suffrage. When the elections

Farm scenes in the nineteenth century. These people tended to be conservative. They did not join in the revolutionary movements of 1848, which centered among city people. The farmers preferred to stick with the old order.

were held, it soon appeared that the countryside was not liberal, but conservative. Peasants joined with the clergy, the landlords, and often the well-to-do middle class to see that reforms did not go too far. As the revolutionary movement lost force and began to break up, rulers who had been forced to grant reforms were often able to do away with the changes they had agreed to.

What followed was *reaction*—a return to what had existed before. It was almost like the action of the pendulum of a clock. For a time the pendulum swung far to the left, toward liberal, democratic reforms. Then it swung back, far to the right, toward the conditions of the old order.

The failures were not complete; some gains were made. However, they seem slight in comparison to the effort and suffering needed to get them. In Sardinia King Victor Emmanuel II refused to abolish the constitution which his father Charles Albert had granted. Prussia, Holland, and Denmark adopted very conservative constitutions which did not limit the power of the kings very much. Serfdom was abolished in the Austrian Empire. Finally, the liberals who led the fight for individual rights and democratic government learned from their failures. During the second half of the nineteenth century they made great progress by putting into practice the lessons they learned in 1848.

Review of Chapter 29

People, places, and things

Identify: Charles X, Louis Philippe, Louis Napoleon, Corn Laws, national workshops, bourgeoisie, proletariat, "rotten boroughs," "pocket boroughs."

Locate: All countries in which revolutionary movements broke out in 1848.

Events in review

1. Which class of the French people benefited most from the constitution of 1830? Explain.
2. What conditions favored the Belgian revolt against Holland?
3. Why can it be said that England in 1830 had representative but not democratic government?
4. State the main provisions of the English Reform Bill of 1832.
5. List three reform measures achieved by the work of the Liberal Party between 1832 and 1846.
6. How did the French government try to relieve unemployment in 1848? Why was the plan not successful?
7. Events in 1848 can be likened to the swing of a pendulum from one extreme to another. Explain why this is so.

8. Tell briefly the steps by which Louis Napoleon transformed the Second French Republic into the Second French Empire.

Problems and projects

1. Make a list of the different governments of France from the monarchy of Louis XVI to the Second Empire of Napoleon III. Give dates and a brief description of each. What reasons can you give for the rapid turnover of French governments?
2. How much progress toward democracy did England make between 1830 and 1848? Why is this period important in English history? Were any "radical" ideas, such as allowing all men to vote, tried in England? Were they tried on the continent of Europe?
3. Make a table to summarize the 1848 revolutions. For each country, note briefly what reforms were attempted. Then note what happened when the conservative reaction took place. Note also the areas in which an effort was made to unify groups of small states.
4. Prepare a talk on the topic, "History teaches many lessons." Use the revolutions of 1848 as examples.
5. To debate: The year 1848 was a turning point in history when history refused to turn.

Chapter 30

The Industrial Revolution, 1750-1870

THE REVOLUTIONS in England, the Americas, France, and on the continent of Europe were political and social revolts. They were struggles for the rights of men to be considered as individuals, to be equal before the law, and to have a voice in their own government. Since these revolutions affected the lives of many people and were accompanied by wars and rebellions, they were widely known. During almost the same years another kind of revolution was going on. It did not attract much public notice, but it affected people's lives very powerfully and changed their ways of living almost completely. It was the Industrial Revolution.

What the Industrial Revolution was

The Industrial Revolution was a revolution in the ways of producing the goods that people use. The old way was the handicraft system of production—the making of goods by hand, usually involving skilled labor. The new way was the making of goods by machines. The new machines were driven by a new kind of power: steam power instead of animal, wind, or water power. Factories took the place of home workshops. Speedier transportation developed both on land and water. The building of the machines required great amounts of iron, and of coal to smelt it.

As a result of the Industrial Revolution, our modern world of business and industry developed. Financing the expensive new machines and building factories made opportunities to invest large sums of money (capital). Capitalists, who provided money, grew in numbers and importance. Operating the new machines required great numbers of people; hence a whole new kind of life began—that of the factory worker.

Since the new methods produced great quantities of goods more rapidly and more cheaply, it was necessary to sell them in ever-widening markets. Trade and transportation were stimulated. Since the workers had to have food and the machines needed an ever-increasing supply of raw materials, great changes also took place in agriculture.

From your reading of history you may be sure that the dates given for the Industrial Revolution, 1750–1870, are not exact. You know that the great changes in history usually occur gradually. The exact dates given are usually for the convenience of historians. Machines were used to produce goods long before 1750. However, about that time there was a rapid increase in their invention and use. Man's use of machinery did not stop in 1870, of course. Around 1870 changes became more rapid and sweeping. New sources of power, new raw materials, new methods, and new products were developed. The period after 1870 is sometimes called the Second Industrial Revolution. You will read about it later.

Why the Industrial Revolution began in England

For the Industrial Revolution to happen, there had to be certain conditions and materials: machines; sources of power; enough money for capital; enough workers for labor; iron, coal, and other raw materials; good transportation; and markets in which to sell the finished products. The Industrial Revolution began in England because England, more than the rest of the world, had these requirements.

England's island location gave protection against war. She had a good supply of coal, and some iron. Her harbors and ships gave transportation abroad. An excellent system of rivers, linked by canals, furnished inland transportation. Rivers provided water power. Men grown wealthy from trade during the sixteenth, seventeenth, and early eighteenth centuries furnished the necessary capital. Unemployment among the tenant farmers and farm laborers made available a supply of labor. The British Isles and the British Empire supplied an ample market, and there were also trade opportunities in many other parts of the world.

With all the other conditions present, machines were invented to meet the demand. It would take too long to describe all of them in detail. However, an excellent example of the Industrial Revolution was the change in the ways of making cotton cloth. This was the first manufacturing process to undergo changes. In addition, the textile industry illustrates how interrelated the process was—how one invention led to others.

● The Revolution begins in the cotton textile industry

Cotton cloth was one of the products brought into Europe from the Near East and India during the later Middle Ages. During the 1600's the traders of the English East India Company brought to England much

Regent's Canal in England. Canals were an important part of England's transportation system. Good transportation encouraged the development of industry in the British Isles.

A model of a spinning jenny, one of the machines that revolutionized the cotton textile industry.

calico (cotton cloth from Calicut, India). It became very popular in spite of its expense. Businessmen began importing the raw cotton and employing English spinners and weavers to make it into cloth. As a new industry, it was not bound by the regulations of the old trade guilds. It grew very rapidly, but not fast enough to keep up with the demand. Spinners used the spinning wheel to make the thread. Weavers used the hand weaving loom. These hand methods could not produce cloth fast enough.

The first development came in the loom for weaving. The loom is set up with a series of threads from top to bottom; this is the woof. Then a shuttle containing the thread running the other way (the warp) is pushed across the loom and back again. It is a slow process. In 1733 John Kay invented the flying shuttle; this sent the shuttle back and forth by pulling a cord. Now the weavers could weave faster than the spinners could spin, and there came a cry for more thread. Prizes were offered for a better spinning machine.

A poor English workman, James Hargreaves, won the prize in 1764 with a machine which he named the spinning "jenny"

in honor of his wife. A single wheel, turned by hand, operated eight spindles by a series of belts. It spun eight times as much thread as a single spinning wheel. Five years later Richard Arkwright improved the process by a machine called the water frame because it was driven by water power. Ten years later Samuel Crompton combined the best features of the spinning jenny and the water frame in one machine. It was called a "mule." Now there was plenty of thread of fine quality. But the weavers, even with the flying shuttle, fell far behind.

In 1785 an English clergyman, Edmund Cartwright, met the new need with a loom in which the shuttle was automatically operated by water power. Using the power loom, one man could weave as much cloth as two hundred hand-loom operators. At about the same time a cylindrical press was invented for printing colored patterns on cotton cloth. Thus cloth was cheaper to produce. As the price went down, the demand for cotton cloth increased, and so did the demand for raw cotton.

Small amounts of cotton had long been grown in the southern American colonies, which by now had become the southern United States. Cotton had never been a popular crop; it was so hard to take out the seeds in order to prepare the cotton for market. By hand, one man could prepare only one pound of cotton in a day. Even with slave labor this was too slow and costly to be profitable. Then, in 1793, the American Eli Whitney invented the cotton gin, a machine to remove the seeds. With it one man could prepare fifty pounds of cotton a day. Later, the machine was improved and driven by steam; then one operator could remove the seeds from 1,000 pounds of cotton in a day. Cotton rapidly became the leading crop in the southern United States, and the principal export crop.

The early automatic machines were all driven by water power. This was a great improvement over human, animal, or wind power, but it did have drawbacks. Factories had to be located beside a stream, preferably beside a waterfall. Water power was not constant; it was likely to vary with the seasons. Good locations on streams might not be near transportation, raw materials, labor supply, or markets.

● Steam engines

The power contained in heated water, or steam, had been observed by men since ancient times. A Hellenistic Greek had invented a steam engine in Alexandria in the third century B.C. Like so many other Greek inventions, it remained a toy in a museum. In England a steam engine, improved by Thomas Newcomen in 1705, had long been used to pump water from mines. It was a very crude machine, slow and expensive to operate. In 1769 James Watt, a Scot, patented an improved steam engine. Watt continued to improve his machine, and finally was able to make it drive other machinery. Driving the spinning and weaving machinery by steam power allowed factories to be located anywhere.

● Iron and steel

The increasing number and variety of machines brought a great demand for iron to make them. England had produced iron from early times. At first the ore was smelted with wood or charcoal as fuel. Then it was discovered that coal worked just as well, and even better. Thus appeared the twin raw materials of modern industry—iron and coal. England had these two materials in good quantity. Early in the 1700's it was discovered that a hotter fire, and better iron, could be produced by burning coke. Coke is coal from which impurities and gases have been driven off by heating it in an oven. However, coke will burn well only when it receives a blast of air, such as a blacksmith produces in his forge by a bellows. At first a leather bellows was used, but shortly after 1750 a steam blower was invented to send the air through the burning coke. This was the beginning of what came to be called a blast furnace.

Iron made in earlier days contained many impurities. Early machines were usually made by casting, that is, pouring the molten iron into a cast or mold. Many an early steam boiler blew up or a machine broke down because of the poor quality of iron. A stronger, harder material was needed. This was steel—iron from which the impurities have been removed. Often other minerals are added to form an alloy with the desired qualities.

The earliest process of steel making was called "puddling." The molten iron was stirred, or "puddled," so that the impurities could be skimmed off. This process was slow and expensive; steel remained a "luxury" product until the 1850's. During that decade an American, William Kelly, and an Englishman, Henry Bessemer, discovered a new way of making steel. A blast of cold air was blown through the molten iron; this removed the carbon and other impurities. The Bessemer process reduced the cost so much that steel became what it is today, the basic material of our industrial civilization.

Thus in the one industry of producing cotton cloth you can see how one invention called for and produced another. Improved methods of spinning brought improved methods of weaving, better sources of power, better ways of preparing raw material, and better iron and steel to build machines.

● Industrialization in other areas

The advantages of power-driven machinery in the cotton textile industry were soon copied in many other industries. The production of shoes and clothing, ammunition, furniture, iron and steel products, and many others was changed almost entirely by the use of power-driven machinery.

The three pictures on this and the facing page show steps in the history of the steam engine. Above is a model of an engine invented in the third century before Christ. Steam from the kettle passed through pipes into the sphere. Steam blowing out through the two nozzles, in opposite directions, made the sphere revolve.

Nearly two thousand years later a workable steam engine was put to use. Below is a model of a crude piston engine used to pump water. Watt's improved engine is sketched on page 374.

Some of the new inventions and processes had important by-products which developed into separate industries. Coke for smelting improved the production of iron. Then it was discovered that the gases driven off from the coal in making coke would burn to give light and heat. During the 1830's "cooking gas" was brought to London. Within a few years many homes in London and other cities used gas for lighting and for cooking.

It was during the 1830's that the modern rubber industry became possible. Rubber had been known in Europe since the days of Columbus. He had found Indians playing with balls made of the gum of a certain tree. During the 1700's Europeans learned that this substance would erase pencil marks by rubbing. Since it came from the West Indies and was used to rub, it was called "India rubber." Some Americans made shoes and coats of rubber for protection against water, but they became sticky in warm weather. In 1839, after long years of experiment, the American Charles Goodyear discovered a process for "curing" rubber to make it more elastic and usable. He mixed the raw rubber with sulfur and then heated it. He called the process "vulcanizing"; it is the basis of the modern rubber industry. For a time the industry developed slowly. It was the increased use of the automobile in the twentieth century that made the rubber industry such a necessary part of modern living.

Still another industry grew up after 1850 as a result of discovering how to use what had formerly been a nuisance. Crude oil or petroleum had been known for many years. It appeared as seepage on the ground, in streams, and into salt wells. It was regarded as a nuisance. Its only use was as a medicine, advertised as a cure for almost anything. During the 1850's men discovered that this "rock oil" could be distilled to produce paraffin, petrolatum, lubricating oil for machinery, and kerosene for lighting and heating. An important new industry grew up.

378

Thus you can see, even from the few examples you have read, that an amazing series of inventions, processes, and changes took place in industry in the century after 1750. These changes were so rapid and of such sweeping importance that they well deserve to be called a revolution. They produced more, better, and cheaper goods for man's use. They also brought with them new ways of organizing and conducting business.

● *Capitalism and the factory system*

Changes in ways of manufacturing brought changes in conditions of work. In earlier days men worked mainly in their homes. They were fairly independent: they owned their tools and produced much of their food in their own gardens. Now, because the machines were too expensive and too large to be used in homes, factories appeared. The location of the early factories was fixed by the need for water power to operate the machines. Workmen had to go to the factories instead of working at home. If the distance was great they had to find new homes near the factory.

Starting a factory took a great deal of money. Some individuals were able to raise enough money to become owners during the early period of the Industrial Revolution. However, the usual way of getting the capital was by forming a corporation. Individual men could buy shares of stock and thus become part owners of the corporation. The stockholders elected directors to decide the policies and officers to carry them out. Profits were divided among the stockholders, each receiving dividends according to the number of shares he owned.

The revolution in transportation and communication

When the Industrial Revolution began, land transportation had changed very little since the Middle Ages. Roads were little more

than deeply rutted trails, thick with dust in dry weather, deep with mud in wet. Fifty miles was a day's uncomfortable journey for a passenger in a stagecoach. Packhorses were used to carry heavy goods. Improvements in ship design had speeded up sea travel, but ships were still driven by sail, at the mercy of the winds.

The changes of the Industrial Revolution made better transportation necessary. Raw materials had to move to the factories; finished products had to move to the far-flung markets. A Scotsman, John McAdam, developed a new way of building roads. First came a roadbed of large stones; this was covered by layers of smaller and smaller stones. The surface layer was held together with mud, which was rolled with a heavy roller to make it smooth. These roads differed from modern ones only in the binding material. Today we use hot oil or asphalt instead of mud for what are called *macadam* roads.

Both England and western Europe had good networks of rivers and canals. Many

The steam engine was improved rapidly as the Industrial Revolution progressed. Besides driving machines in factories, engines were used for transportation. The locomotive below, the Stourbridge Lion, made its first trip for the Delaware and Hudson Railroad at Honesdale, Pennsylvania, in 1829.

379

A sign of the revolution in transportation
—Fulton's Clermont on the Hudson
River.

more canals were built after the discovery of the use of the lock, which regulates the level and flow of the water. The period from 1775 to 1850 was a great era of canal building. The canal furnished cheaper and a little faster transportation than the road, but it soon met with competition from a completely new form of transportation.

Locomotives and steamships

Watt's development of the steam engine was a challenge to the inventiveness of other men. If the steam engine could turn a wheel to run a machine, why could it not turn a wheel to move itself? In 1814 George Stephenson, an English engineer, perfected a steam locomotive which would run on rails and pull a load of coal. It was a crude engine, but Stephenson continued to work to perfect it. Soon a railroad was built to carry passengers as well as freight. In 1830 Stephenson's famous engine, the *Rocket,* pulled a load of cars from Liverpool to Manchester, reaching the breath-taking speed of twenty-nine miles an hour. Now began an age of railroad building throughout the world. Almost continuous

improvements—the use of steel rails, the air brake, more comfortable coaches, and special cars for different kinds of freight—made railroad transportation faster, safer, and cheaper.

Many men worked to use the steam engine successfully in ships, but credit is usually given to the American Robert Fulton, who established the first regular steamboat service. His ship, the *Clermont,* was launched on the Hudson River and at once began regular trips between New York City and Albany. Other men developed steamships which would cross the oceans. By 1838 the *Great Western,* operating by steam alone, crossed the Atlantic in fifteen days. Regular steam traffic across the Atlantic was developed by Samuel Cunard, whose "Cunard Line" still operates. The steamship, like the railroad, was improved over the years. The screw propeller replaced the paddle wheels. Ships were built of iron and steel instead of wood. Now goods could move quickly and cheaply all over the world.

● The telegraph

Communication—the transportation of ideas—also speeded up. The development of the first means of rapid communication is an interesting example both of the international character of science and of the way in which almost every invention is built upon the work of many men.

From early times many men had observed the characteristics of electricity and its connection with the power of a magnet. Magnetism had never been put to any practical use. Its working was not thoroughly understood, and no one had found a way to provide a steady flow of electric current. Around the year 1800 an Italian, Count Alessandro Volta, was able to build a battery which solved the second problem—providing a steady electric current. A Frenchman, André Ampère, worked out the laws governing the magnetic effect of an electric current. The work of both Volta and Ampère, as well as that of many other men, was put to practical use by an American, Samuel Morse. He sent electrical impulses over a wire, first in only one direction, then in either direction. These impulses could make a machine click. Morse worked out a system of dots and dashes, the "Morse code," by which these sounds could be translated into the letters of the alphabet. By 1844 Morse's telegraph had become a practical instrument, and the wires of the telegraph began to stretch out across the continents. Ideas could now travel at the speed of electricity.

Experiments were soon begun to find a way to carry the electrical impulses under the sea. Men learned that electric current could be transmitted under water if the wire was insulated with rubber. Early in the 1850's England was connected with the continent of Europe by a cable from Dover to Calais. The problem of spanning the great distance of the Atlantic Ocean presented enormous difficul-

ties. A group of enterprising Americans led by Cyrus Field refused to be stopped by the difficulties, even by several costly failures. Their first cable broke when they had almost covered the distance. A second "went dead" when the insulation failed. In 1866 they succeeded. It was not long before all the continents were joined by cables.

● Postal service

The letter postal service was probably the earliest organized method of communication. It was used by the Assyrians and the Persians to hold their empires together, and was copied by almost every later people. European governmental postal services were slow and expensive, available only to the rich. In 1840 the British government began the first modern postal service. Stamps were used for prepayment of postage. The rate was uniform regardless of distance. And it was cheap: one penny (equaling two cents in American money) sent a letter anywhere in the island. New ways of transportation made the service rapid. British methods were soon adopted by other countries. In 1879 an International Postal Union was established in Berne, Switzerland, to fix the rates for foreign postage and to promote international coöperation in handling mail.

Agriculture undergoes revolution

At the beginning of the eighteenth century, agriculture was much the same as it had been during the Middle Ages. Farmers still used hand tools much like those of ancient times. Plows were made of wood; they scratched only the surface of the soil. Seed was still sown "broadcast" by the sower scattering it far and wide with a sweep of his arm. In most countries the three-field system of strip farming was still used—only two-thirds of a farm was planted each year.

The revolution in industry made great demands on agriculture. Raw materials such as wool, flax, cotton, and leather were needed in ever-increasing quantities. The new factories and the cities which grew up around them needed both food and men from the farms. Agriculture had to change so that the farms could supply the needed raw materials, food, and labor. If agriculture had not changed, the Industrial Revolution would have died of starvation.

Improvements by English farmers

In agriculture as in industry changes began in England. The earliest improvements came from the efforts of a group of men whom we would call "gentlemen farmers." A pioneer scientific farmer was Jethro Tull. He was impressed by the wastefulness of the "broadcast" method of sowing; so he invented a seed drill which planted the seeds in regular rows. Experiments showed him that crops grew better if the weeds were removed and the soil between the rows was pulverized. To do this work he invented a cultivator which could be drawn by horses. Tull also learned that he could get larger crops by selecting the seed very carefully.

Viscount Charles Townshend, another English gentleman farmer, found a way to avoid the fallow-field practice. By repeated experiments he learned that soil fertility could be preserved by planting a field with a different crop each succeeding year. This is called crop rotation. Poor soil could be improved by using lime and various fertilizers. Turnips and other root crops, as well as hay, were valuable

A plow from the early eighteenth century, before the revolution in agriculture.

as food for cattle. Townshend was so enthusiastic in preaching the virtues of turnips that he became known as "Turnip" Townshend. His practice of crop rotation is a basic principle of modern farming.

In agriculture, as in manufacturing, machines were invented to reduce labor and increase production. Jethro Tull's pioneering seed drill and horse cultivator were followed by other improved machinery. Iron plows began to be used, in spite of the prejudice of many farmers that they "poisoned the soil." The use of the cast-iron plow was greatly increased by an American blacksmith named Wood. He produced an iron plow in three parts so that a broken part could be replaced at small cost.

American inventions

Two other revolutionary inventions of farm machinery came from America. You have already read of Eli Whitney's cotton gin (1793). It made cotton the main crop of the southern United States and met the ever-increasing demands of the cotton textile machinery. Less fortunately, it made slavery seem an absolute necessity, with tragic consequences in the United States. Another, happier invention was a machine for harvesting grain, patented by Cyrus McCormick in 1834. The McCormick reaper, drawn by horses, took the place of the old, slow, back-breaking work of cutting grain with a sickle or a scythe. The invention of the reaper was followed by other devices such as the mechanical thresher for separating wheat from its stalks and hulls. All these inventions served to lessen human labor and to increase production.

Science helps farmers

Science also helped in the improvement of agriculture. "Turnip" Townshend's early discoveries had been made largely by trial and error (keep trying until something works), not the true scientific method. About a century after Townshend's time, a professor of

The Agricultural Revolution has now progressed so far that typical farms in the United States use machinery for most operations. This is a combine in a grain field.

chemistry in a small German university, Justus von Liebig, began a really scientific study of what makes plants grow. His studies convinced him that men must not think of the soil as being only dirt. He saw that soil is a combination of chemicals that supply the food which plants need for growth. Poor soil is poor because it lacks certain chemicals. If these can be added, the soil will grow good crops. Liebig also proved that plants get their necessary carbon from the carbon dioxide in the air. By burning plants and analyzing their ashes, he learned that the three most necessary chemicals which the soil must supply are phosphorus, potash, and nitrogen. Liebig's book, published in 1840, was the real beginning of the science of agricultural chemistry. His pioneering work in chemical fertilizers led to the establishment of schools and agricultural societies, often financed by governments. These organizations carried on scientific experiments in every part of agriculture. The results in the increase in farm production and the improvement of farm products have been so great as to stagger the mind.

● *Farms become large businesses*

Two effects of the Agricultural Revolution were similar to one of the results of the Industrial Revolution. Just as the size of factories and corporations increased, so did the size of farms. The new machinery and many of the new methods could be used efficiently only on large farms. Machinery and scientific methods brought greatly increased production at lower costs. Small farmers could not use the machinery or the methods to produce at lower costs. Gradually they had to sell their farms because of the competition. They became farm laborers or moved to the cities. This development had already begun in England, and the Agricultural Revolution speeded it up. In the United States it was delayed by the great amount of cheap and free land available for settlement. However, the trend in our country has been toward fewer and larger farms with a smaller percentage of the population engaged in agriculture.

The second effect comes from the great increase in farm production. Crops must be sold in increasing quantities in wider and wider markets. The old, family-sized farm was a way of living as much as a way of making a living. The large farm, with its buildings, livestock, machinery, and scientific methods, is a business just as much as a factory is a business. It needs a great amount of capital; it needs expert management; it depends increasingly on the sale of its products in both home and foreign markets. The Agricultural Revolution has made agriculture a commercial business instead of an independent way of life.

The Industrial Revolution spreads

English industrial developments did not reach the continent of Europe for some years. There were several reasons for this slow spread. Many European countries lacked raw materials and large, easily-reached markets.

In order to keep its monopoly of the new methods the British government forbade the exportation of machines and the emigration of skilled workers. The wars of the French Revolution and the Napoleonic Era also slowed the European development.

After a late start France developed some industry. The French government helped the development in two ways. It levied high tariffs to keep out foreign manufactured goods, and it encouraged the building of a system of railroads. France did not become as completely industrialized as Britain. Her fertile farm lands, owned mostly in small holdings by peasants, kept a good balance between agriculture and manufacturing.

Belgium became highly industrialized. It was a small, very heavily populated country, rich in coal. In the later Middle Ages Flanders (Belgium) had developed a woolen industry in its thriving cities. Now this woolen industry was mechanized. A steel industry also developed, and a national system of railways spread throughout the country.

Locks on the Erie Canal at Lockport, New York. This canal, opened in 1825, was an important part of the transportation system that helped on the Industrial Revolution in the United States.

The slow growth of industry in Germany was the result of a lack, not of natural resources, but of national unity. The many small German states charged each other tariffs, making the sale of goods on a large scale difficult. In 1834 many German states, led by Prussia, formed a customs (tariff) union, so that goods could move freely. This development, and the building of railroads, caused a considerable growth of German manufacturing. However, real industrialization had to await the unification of Germany.

● *The United States*

It was in the former English colonies in North America, now the United States, that English inventions and methods were most eagerly followed. During colonial days the development of industry in America was hampered by the British system of mercantilism. After independence was won, American industrial development received a great spur during the Napoleonic Wars. American commerce was greatly hampered, and for a time we refused to import any goods from Britain. In 1812 we went to war with Britain for a second time. As a result, there was a great increase in American manufacturing, especially in New England, New York, and Pennsylvania.

The development which began then has never stopped. The United States had everything needed for a great industrial development: national unity, a vast country, a rapidly increasing population, rich natural resources, inventive genius, and a willingness to adopt, adapt, and take chances. English developments in canals and railroads were eagerly and quickly copied to solve problems of transportation. Industry moved west as transportation developed: the steel industry to Pittsburgh and the Great Lakes, the manufacture of farm machinery to Chicago. By 1869 the continent had been spanned by a railroad. By 1870 the United States was second only to Great Britain as a manufacturing nation and was beginning to rival even the mother of the Industrial Revolution.

Review of Chapter 30

People, places, and things

Identify: Edmund Cartwright, Eli Whitney, James Watt, Henry Bessemer, Charles Goodyear, Robert Fulton, John McAdam, Samuel Morse, the flying shuttle, the spinning jenny, the water frame.

Events in review

1. Briefly define *Industrial Revolution*. Why is the date 1750 used in connection with this revolution?
2. What conditions and materials were needed to produce the Industrial Revolution? Which country in the eighteenth century possessed all these advantages?
3. After the invention of Arkwright and Cartwright came into use, why were factories producing cotton usually found near streams?
4. How did the increased use of machinery lead to progress in the iron and steel industry?
5. When did "rock oil" become important? For what purposes was it used?
6. Name three important inventions in the fields of transportation and communication.
7. Which country developed the first modern postal service? What is the purpose of the International Postal Union?
8. What changes in agriculture were brought about by (a) Townshend, (b) McCormick, (c) Liebig?

Problems and projects

1. Using the textile industry as an example, demonstrate that necessity is the mother of invention. Include (a) spinning and weaving machinery, (b) sources of power, (c) iron and steel for machinery.
2. On the map locate the principal rivers and seaports in the British Isles. Note also overseas trade routes to Europe, to British colonies, and to America. Discuss the importance of geography and natural resources in the industrial growth of England. Consider the resources and the geography of England itself as well as the situation of the country on the world map.
3. Write an essay on the topic, "American contributions to the Industrial Revolution."
4. Discuss the statement that the Agricultural Revolution has made farming a business in the same sense that running a factory is a business.
5. Write a "You Are There" type of broadcast covering the first trip of the *Clermont* or the opening of the Erie Canal.

Chapter 31 The Industrial Revolution Brings Great Social Changes

FOR some centuries before 1750 the population of Europe had changed very little. There had been only a slight gain from century to century. When the Industrial Revolution began, the population of all Europe was about 140 million people. In 1914, at the beginning of World War I, Europe had a population of 463 million, more than three times as great as that of 1750. Other regions grew at different rates. The greatest population growth took place in the industrialized regions: England, western Europe, and the United States.

The changes in agriculture, industry, and transportation, with the resulting increase in trade, produced another striking result: a rapid growth of cities. The greatest spur to city growth was the coming of the factory system. Many of the early factories were located in already established cities, and these grew tremendously. Where factories were located in rural areas, cities grew up around them. Urban, or city, living became the typical way of life in the industrialized nations.

New social classes appear

The Industrial Revolution caused great changes in social classes in countries that became industrialized. In the first place, the capitalist-employer group swelled in numbers

386

and importance. The world had known employers, and even capitalist employers, before. Merchants, merchant employers, shipowners, and bankers were all early capitalists. Now they were joined by many thousands of factory owners and stockholders. Many of these people became wealthy.

● The managerial class

Two entirely new social classes were created by the revolution. One was the managerial class. Men of this group were employees, not owners. Nevertheless, they were managers who gave orders and were paid a monthly or yearly salary. This set them apart from the workers, who obeyed orders and received a daily or weekly wage. As the operation of factories became more mechanized and more complicated, the services of many expertly trained people were required. There were expert engineers, lawyers, foremen, draftsmen, scientists of all kinds doing research, superintendents, plant and office managers, and salesmen of every kind.

Almost all of the factory owners, stockholders, and the managerial class came from the bourgeois or middle class. The nobility and aristocracy gained their wealth from the ownership of land. Often, in the early days at least, they looked down on "business" as beneath them. Thus the Industrial Revolution was really the triumph of the bourgeois or middle class over the aristocracy. It put vast wealth into bourgeois hands; they gained political power as well.

● *The factory workers*

The other new social class was made up of the factory workers, city-dwelling workmen whom the French called the *proletariat*. It was a new class in society in that it owned nothing but its muscles. At first, the skilled workers refused to enter the factories, and there was difficulty in finding workers. The first factory workers were tramps, paupers, women, and poor children. Often those in charge of charity homes for orphans would "farm out" their people to the factory owner, glad to get rid of the expense of keeping them. Women and children could be used especially in the spinning mills, where much of the work consisted in watching the spindles and tying up a thread when it broke. Unbelievable as it now seems, they were also used a great deal in mines.

In time other workers entered the factories.

Small farmers, tenants, and farm workers were forced to do so because the new conditions in agriculture were taking away their jobs. Gradually, too, the artisans—the skilled spinners, weavers, and others—were forced to give in. They went into the factories, where their special skill was no longer an advantage. Some skilled hand-workers remained independent—shoemakers, tailors, and others. But factory workers greatly outnumbered the independent artisans.

Working and living conditions

In the early days of the Industrial Revolution the new class of workers had little share in the wealth or the comforts they helped produce. Working conditions were bad. Long hours were the rule. Often the factory worked

> One effect of the factory system was to crowd large numbers of people into towns and cities. This drawing by Winslow Homer shows men, women, and children going home from their work in a New England mill.

from sunrise to sunset. Sixteen- to eighteen-hour days were common; from fourteen to sixteen hours was considered a normal working day for men, women, and children alike. Factories were poorly ventilated. The air was hot and steamy in the summer, cold and damp in the winter. There were no sanitary facilities. The early machines had no safety devices. Fatal accidents were frequent, and serious or crippling injuries even more common. Accident insurance or any other form of compensation for injury was unheard of.

Wages were very low. In England as late as 1867 the average weekly wage for laborers ranged from $9.00 for the London artisan to $5.00 for a town laborer. These were men's wages; those for women and children were much lower.

Perhaps the worst feature of early industrialization was child labor. It was common for children of five to be employed in the cotton mills or the mines. Conditions in the coal mines were particularly bad. Women were hired to pull and children to push the coal carts in places where the roof was too low for a donkey to pass through. The women worked on hands and knees. The plight of the working children was most sad. They worked extremely long hours. Discipline was harsh. A child who fell asleep over his task was beaten.

If life in the mine or factory was hard and monotonous, life in the home was not much better. Poverty and long working hours meant bad living conditions and poor diet. Working people lived in shacks and tenements, cramped and crowded. Sanitary conditions were poor. Desirable kinds of recreation were hard to find. Drunkenness and immorality were common in the towns.

Workers in the factories also had to face a condition which had seldom troubled farm workers. At times there would be difficulty in selling all the production of the fast-moving machines. Goods would pile up at the factories. Employers would have to reduce wages and cut down production. This meant laying off workers. The threat of unemployment became a terrible curse for the factory worker. There was no unemployment insurance to tide him over the crisis, and no old-age pension to make up for the scanty savings that he had to spend when unemployed. Unless he could find private charity, the unemployed worker faced starvation.

Laissez faire replaces mercantilism

Perhaps you have wondered why governments did not pass laws to end these abuses and protect the workers. The answer is found

Boys dragging and pushing a cartload of coal in an English mine. Until the 1840's it was legal for women and children to labor in mines (see page 391).

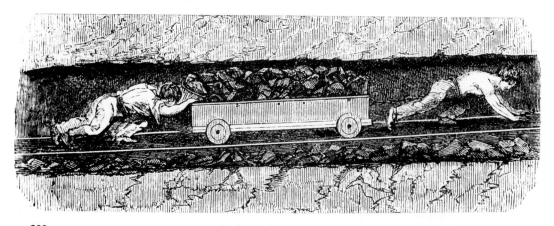

in a new economic philosophy, or way of thinking, which grew up as the Industrial Revolution developed.

During the Age of Enlightenment economic liberals attacked the ideas of mercantilism. They believed that there were certain natural laws which governed economic life. Any attempt to interfere with these natural economic laws was certain to bring disaster. The views of these economic thinkers were best stated by Adam Smith in *The Wealth of Nations,* first published in 1776.

Smith reasoned that all business and economic activity is regulated by two great natural laws—the law of supply and demand and the law of competition. In any business, prices, and therefore profits, will be fixed by the workings of supply and demand. If the supply of an article is small and there is a great demand for it, those who want it will pay more for the scarce article. Thus the price will be forced up, and the profit will go up. When this happens, men with money will invest it in factories to produce the scarce article. Soon there will be a plentiful supply of this article. Now each manufacturer will face competition in selling his goods.

In order to get people to buy his article instead of some other article, he will either have to reduce his price or improve the quality of his article, or both. If too many producers enter the same business, the price will go down so far that it may not cover some of the producers' costs of production. A producer in this case will not make any profit, and profit was the thing which tempted him to start the business. Furthermore, he may actually lose money and be forced out of business entirely. This will happen, of course, to the least efficient businesses—the ones that are so poorly organized and managed that their production costs are high. When these manufacturers have to quit, the supply of the article will decrease, and the price will go up. Then the capable, efficient, and well organized producers will make a reasonable profit.

Thus Adam Smith argued that every man should be free to do what he thinks best for himself—to go into any business he wants and to operate it for his own greatest advantage. The result would be beneficial to everyone. Investors and owners would make profits; buyers would receive better goods at lower prices. This result would come from the automatic working of the laws of supply and demand, and competition. This is the system of completely free enterprise.

The great thing about Smith's idea was that it was supposed to work automatically. In fact, he argued that if anything interfered with the absolutely free working of supply, demand, and competition, the system could not work well. Governmental laws and regulations, like those under mercantilism, were thought of as interfering with the workings of the "natural laws." The course for the government to follow was expressed in the French term *laissez faire*—let things alone. According to the theory, government should not interfere in any way with the operations of business.

The theory of laissez faire was put into practice in England during the nineteenth century. Formerly, either the government or the guilds had regulated the quantity and quality of goods produced, the hours and wages of workers, the qualifications of workers (apprenticeship), and many other business practices. Now most of these regulations were done away with. Even the tariff, which had been used to regulate trade, disappeared. By 1850 Britain had become a free-trade country. European countries and the United States adopted many of the features of laissez faire economic theory, though never as completely as Great Britain.

Laissez faire had a great appeal for employers, factory owners, and businessmen in general. They had risked their money in going into business. They felt that they should have complete charge of operating the businesses. If they bought the things they needed as cheaply as possible, they would make profits, which was the aim of business. It was easy for businessmen to think of labor as a commodity like coal, iron, or machinery. Like them, it should be bought as cheaply as possible, to keep down the costs of production.

Thus you can see that wages, hours, and all the conditions of labor for factory workers depended on the employer. The examples of two early employers will show how important the employer was to the lives of the workers.

● Richard Arkwright—organizer

Richard Arkwright was a barber, operating a shop in a basement. He was attracted by the changes in the cotton textile industry, and he invented a spinning machine. He then borrowed money to start a factory.

Arkwright was more important as a factory organizer than as an inventor. When he had difficulty in getting workers, he made arrangements to get children from orphanages and poorhouses. To manage his workers, he worked out a code of factory discipline. The code was harsh, but it was successful enough to be adopted in many places. Many of the rules and procedures of factory work throughout the nineteenth century came from this early code. Eventually Arkwright became the wealthiest of the cotton spinners. He was rewarded even beyond his wealth, being knighted by the king, thus becoming Sir Richard. Later he bought a great estate in the country and built a castle on it.

● Robert Owen—idealist

Robert Owen, a Scot, left school very young and went to work. He was extremely successful in understanding the workings of business, and in handling people. He became a mill manager. Finally, he became both owner and manager of the huge New Lanark mill, which employed 200 people.

As a factory owner, Owen felt responsible for the welfare of his workers, and devoted much time and money to making their lives happier and more secure. He built better homes for them than workers had anywhere else. He paid better wages and established a store where workers could buy food at cost. He established schools for the children—even nursery schools for the children below the school age.

However, Owen believed that workers should not be dependent on the paternal (fatherly) feelings of employers. He encouraged workers to form unions so that they could improve their working and living conditions through their own bargaining power. He also believed that workers should organize themselves into coöperative communities. The workers should own the land and factories together. Each should do the work for which he was best fitted; each should be paid according to his needs.

You can see that ways had to be found to improve the lives of workers: the low wages, the long hours, the miserable working and living conditions. During the nineteenth and twentieth centuries attempts to remedy these evils have been made in three ways: through laws; through labor unions for collective bargaining; through new ideas about the ownership of property and the distribution of the profits of business.

Living and working conditions improve

● Improvement by laws

The first attempts to improve working conditions by passing laws were made in Great Britain, where the abuses were greatest. Workers themselves played little part in this political movement; they could not vote nor could they be represented in Parliament until 1867. Indeed, members of the new middle-class factory-owning group were not represented until after the passage of the Reform Bill of 1832 (page 367).

To some extent the passage of laws to improve conditions was the work of men we call humanitarian reformers. (A humanitarian is one who loves mankind and works to promote the welfare of all humanity.) A group of writers began to tell people about the terrible conditions in mines and factories. Two powerful novels, *Martin Chuzzlewit,* by Charles Dickens, and *Sybil,* by Benjamin Disraeli, did much to arouse public sentiment. Essayists and critics like Thomas Carlyle and John Ruskin spread the word.

In Parliament factory laws gradually won the support of the Tories or Conservatives, who represented the landowning aristocracy. After 1832 these landowners were jealous of the rising political power of the middle class. They looked down on the factory owners as "newly-rich," and were willing to embarrass them with laws regulating their factories. So a series of laws slowly brought improvements during the nineteenth century. As you might expect, the earliest laws dealt with the employment of women and children.

The Factory Act of 1819 shows how far the movement had to go. It prohibited the employment of children under *nine* years of age in cotton mills. Children between nine and eighteen were limited to twelve hours of work. In 1833 this law was applied to all textile factories. No children under nine were to be employed. Children from nine to thirteen were limited to nine hours; children from thirteen to eighteen to twelve hours. Night work was forbidden to any children. About ten years later another law forbade the employment in mines of all women and girls and of boys under ten. A great advancement came in 1847 with the passage of the Ten-Hour Act. The work of all women and children in textile factories was limited to ten hours a day. Since it was not possible to run the factories without the women and children, the ten-hour day became general for all textile workers.

Other kinds of factory laws were passed before 1870. Safety devices had to be put on machines; sanitary conditions in the factories had to be improved. A real system of factory inspection was set up to enforce these laws. Better hours and more safety devices were required in mines. Gradually during the nineteenth century the doctrine of laissez faire was replaced in England by the idea that government has a responsibility for the health, safety, and welfare of its people.

● *Organized unions improve conditions*

The second way of improving living and working conditions was the organizing of

Life was hard and dirty for working people, particularly in the cities. The sketch below was drawn by George Cruikshank, who illustrated Dickens' novels. The following passage from Oliver Twist *describes a London street: "The street was very narrow and muddy, and the air was impregnated with filthy odors. There were a good many small shops; but the only stock in trade appeared to be heaps of children, who were crawling in and out at the doors, or screaming from the inside."*

A modern factory in the United States. The long hours, the child labor, and the dangerous and unhealthy conditions of early factories are not found in our twentieth-century industrial plants. Government regulations and agreements between employers and employees have revolutionized working conditions. Note that the workman shown here is protected by helmet, goggles, and gloves. In this and other ways, industry protects health and safety.

workers into unions to strengthen their ability to bargain with employers. Under the factory system the individual workman had little chance to bargain successfully with his employer. He came in contact only with foremen or plant managers, who were employees themselves with no power to fix wages or hours. If he tried to demand more pay or shorter hours, he was fired; one man was easy to replace.

The factory reform laws dealt only with the hours of work and some features of working conditions, not at all with wages. It was clear that any improvement in wages had to come through the efforts of the workers themselves. To be successful, the workers had to act together. If they formed a union, their leaders could try to meet the employer,

or the directors of the corporation, to bargain for all the workers. This is called *collective bargaining*. If the employer refused to grant better wages, they could strike: all the workers could stop work at once, and try to prevent the factory from working. When the factory was idle, the employer made no profits, while some of his expenses continued. In time he was forced to grant the increase or make some compromise agreeable to both sides. A successful negotiation usually resulted in a contract—a written agreement covering wages, hours, and working conditions for a fixed period of time.

Robert Owen had advised workers to organize unions to improve their conditions, but it was not simple or easy. Under the English common law any attempt of workmen to unite was considered illegal, as a "conspiracy in restraint of trade." When workers tried to unite anyway, employers were successful in getting Parliament to pass laws against "unlawful combinations." An Act of 1800 stated that persons who combined with others to demand higher wages, shorter hours, or better working conditions were liable to imprisonment at hard labor.

In time, efforts on behalf of the workers began to make headway. In 1824 the laws against "unlawful combinations" were repealed. In 1825 Parliament passed an act which permitted laborers to meet in order to agree on what wages they would accept and what hours they would work. Such agreements, however, could apply only to those present at the meeting. In 1871 and 1876 Parliament passed laws which said that nothing done by a group of workers was illegal unless it was also illegal when done by a single worker. If you analyze these laws, you will see that they meant that strikes were legal, as they had not been before.

● *The new doctrine of Socialism*

The third way of trying to improve the conditions of workers is more radical; that is, it requires a more basic change. It involves a change in the way in which property is owned and in which the goods produced by industry and agriculture are distributed, or divided. This third way is called *socialism*.

Many humanitarians were disturbed by the fact that the great wealth produced by the Industrial Revolution was so unevenly distributed. A few people became enormously rich, while many remained in utter poverty. A few reformers became convinced that this condition could not be changed by laws regulating working conditions or by the efforts of labor unions. They thought that a better distribution could be achieved only by changing the way in which the *means of production* were owned and operated. ("Means of production" covers everything that is used in the production and exchange of goods: land, mines, railroads, factories, stores, ships, banks, and the like.)

Under capitalism, as you know, the means of production are owned by private citizens and operated by them for their own private profit. Socialists believed that the means of production should be owned publicly, or socially, by all the people, and should be operated for the welfare of all the people. The profits of industry should go to the people in the form of better housing, better medical care, old-age and sickness care, better education, better recreation, and a host of other *social* benefits. Everyone who was able should work, receiving either wages or salary. Each person should do the kind of work for which he is best fitted. No one able to work should receive payment for idleness. Most socialists agreed that government, representing all the people, should direct and operate all production and decide on wages and salaries and on how profits should be distributed.

Socialists disagreed on many things: on how much of the means of production should be publicly owned, on how the publicly owned industries should be operated, and on what kind of government was necessary.

There were many kinds of socialists; it is possible to mention only a few.

The *Utopian socialists,* an early group, were so called because they believed that society should be made over into an ideal community like that described in More's *Utopia* (page 230). Men could be both good and happy and could live at peace with each other if they lived in small coöperative communities, owning all the means of production in common and sharing the profits. Utopian socialism was best described in the writings of a Frenchman, François Fourier, but it was the Scot, Robert Owen, who tried to put it into practice (see page 394).

● *Karl Marx and communism*

Another variety is *Marxian socialism,* which has been the most influential of all. During the Revolution of 1848 two German writers, Karl Marx and Friedrich Engels, issued a pamphlet, the *Communist Manifesto,* outlining their ideas. The failure of the revolution forced Marx to escape to England, where he wrote *Das Kapital* (Capital). This book has become a sort of "bible" of socialism.

Marx wrote that all history is the story of a struggle between classes of people. In each period of history the kind of society is determined by the economic conditions that exist. As these economic conditions change, the kind of society changes. Thus feudalism was produced by the economic conditions of the Middle Ages. When the economic conditions changed, the struggle of the middle class (bourgeoisie) against the feudal lords produced capitalism. Capitalism, he said, was like feudalism; it was a necessary stage in the development of mankind. But like feudalism, it would also change.

The Industrial Revolution brought about a struggle between the middle-class capitalists (the bourgeoisie) and the workers (the proletariat). Marx reasoned that all value (wealth) is really created by labor. But under capitalism labor receives in wages only a small

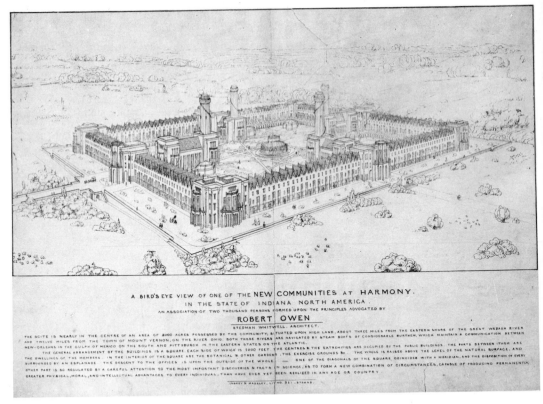

A BIRD'S EYE VIEW OF ONE OF THE NEW COMMUNITIES AT HARMONY.
IN THE STATE OF INDIANA NORTH AMERICA.
AN ASSOCIATION OF TWO THOUSAND PERSONS FORMED UPON THE PRINCIPLES ADVOCATED BY
ROBERT OWEN
STEDMAN WHITWELL, ARCHITECT.

THE SCITE IS NEARLY IN THE CENTRE OF AN AREA OF 2000 ACRES POSSESSED BY THE COMMUNITY, SITUATED UPON HIGH LAND, ABOUT THREE MILES FROM THE EASTERN SHORE OF THE GREAT WABASH RIVER AND TWELVE MILES FROM THE TOWN OF MOUNT VERNON, ON THE RIVER OHIO. BOTH THESE RIVERS ARE NAVIGATED BY STEAM BOATS OF CONSIDERABLE BURTHEN, WHICH MAINTAIN A COMMUNICATION BETWEEN NEW-ORLEANS IN THE GULPH OF MEXICO ON THE SOUTH AND PITTSBURGH IN THE EASTERN STATES ON THE ATLANTIC.
THE GENERAL ARRANGEMENT OF THE BUILDINGS IS A SQUARE, EACH SIDE OF WHICH IS 1000 FEET. THE CENTRE & THE EXTREMITIES ARE OCCUPIED BY THE PUBLIC BUILDINGS. THE PARTS BETWEEN THEM ARE THE DWELLINGS OF THE MEMBERS. IN THE INTERIOR OF THE SQUARE ARE THE BOTANICAL & OTHER GARDENS. THE EXERCISE GROUNDS &c. THE WHOLE IS RAISED ABOVE THE LEVEL OF THE NATURAL SURFACE, AND SURROUNDED BY AN ESPLANADE. THE DESCENT TO THE OFFICES IS UPON THE OUTSIDE OF THE WHOLE. ONE OF THE DIAGONALS OF THE SQUARE COINCIDES WITH A MERIDIAN, AND THE DISPOSITION OF EVERY OTHER PART IS SO REGULATED BY A CAREFUL ATTENTION TO THE MOST IMPORTANT DISCOVERIES & FACTS IN SCIENCE, AS TO FORM A NEW COMBINATION OF CIRCUMSTANCES, CAPABLE OF PRODUCING PERMANENTLY, GREATER PHYSICAL, MORAL, AND INTELLECTUAL ADVANTAGES TO EVERY INDIVIDUAL, THAN HAVE EVER YET BEEN REALIZED IN ANY AGE OR COUNTRY

INGREY & MADELEY, LITHO 31 . STRAND.

fraction of the wealth it creates. Most of the wealth goes to the capitalist owners in the form of profits. In the end, the workers would unite, overthrow the bourgeoisie, make themselves the ruling class. Then they would seize the means of production and operate them for the welfare of all. Workers in every land have interests in common. An English worker, said Marx, has much more in common with a French worker than he has with an English capitalist. The *Communist Manifesto* ended with a fiery appeal: "Workers of the world, unite! You have nothing to lose but your chains."

Marxian socialism had two main groups of followers, with many small "splinter" groups. All agreed generally on where they wanted to go: the social ownership and operation of the means of production. The principal difference was in how to get there.

To show the difference between his ideas and earlier kinds of socialism, which he sneered at, Marx called his variety *com-*

An artist's plan for a Utopian socialist community. Robert Owen spent much of his fortune trying to establish an ideal community in the United States at New Harmony, Indiana. His effort failed, as did a number of other attempts at coöperative communities.

munism. So one group of his followers call themselves *Communists.* They believe that the class struggle between capitalists and proletariat will certainly end in war. The proletariat will have to seize power by force, violence, and revolution. Since this must take place before all people are ready to accept socialism, the government will have to be a "dictatorship of the proletariat." In practice, this means a dictatorship of the communists. After a long period of education, people will become experienced in living and working together coöperatively; then the dictatorship will disappear. As you know, the Communists have been successful in seizing control of the governments of Russia and China.

There is another, more moderate group of Marxists. They call themselves *Socialists*, with a capital "S." They believe that socialism can come by gradual development, or evolution, by education and through the democratic form of government. When enough people have been educated to socialism (this theory maintains) they will elect socialist representatives to their government. When a majority of the government are socialists, the government will take over the means of production peacefully. The owners will be paid, and the government will then operate the means of production in the public welfare. Political action must come from workers organized into political parties as well as unions. In Germany the Social Democratic Party, in France and the United States the Socialist Party, and in England the Labour Party all follow socialist ideas.

The Industrial Revolution transforms man's life

In summing up the First Industrial Revolution it must be said that it had its faults and bad features. In the early days it brought dreadful conditions to the workers: long hours, the labor of women and children, bad working conditions, low wages, and poor living conditions. As time passed, though, these conditions improved. It is worth noticing that many important changes were not made by the radicals who would overthrow the capitalist system; they were made within the system of capitalism itself. The improvements came as a result of laws passed by governments, almost entirely through the democratic process. Or they came through the organization of labor into unions, and the process of collective bargaining. It was not easy. Often the passage of a law was the result of a bitter struggle. Frequently the process of collective bargaining brought long and violent strikes. But the fact remains that the improvement did take place, and without the

violent overthrow of the system of ownership. Capitalist free enterprise, rather than Socialism or Communism, still flourishes in most industrialized countries.

Neither Socialism nor Communism was destined to be tried out on any large scale for many years after the period you are studying here. In Chapter 47, you will read about the establishment of a Communist dictatorship in Russia in 1917. That dictatorship still exists today.

Looking from the vantage-point of the 1960's, we can see that few of Communism's promises of a better life have come true, and those only at a great cost. Russian workers and peasants of the 1960's were somewhat better off than their forefathers of Czarist days, although their standard of living remained below that of free Western workers. But let us see how some of the Marxist doctrines and predictions have fared in actual practice.

(1) **Marxist Theory:** *The means of production will be operated for the welfare of the people.* **Reality:** The system operates for the good of the state. The welfare of the people is not considered if it seems to conflict with the welfare of the state. If the dictators decide that the welfare of the state requires the production of heavy industrial goods and armaments rather than consumer goods, then clothing, autos, appliances, and even housing are scarce and expensive, and life is hard.

(2) **Marxist Theory:** *Economic and social classes will disappear, to be succeeded by a "classless society" of workers.* **Reality:** High party members, scientists, engineers, and other professionals enjoy larger incomes, better housing, and more privileges than other workers. The children of these privileged people have a better chance for higher education, so that class differences are likely to continue in succeeding generations.

(3) **Marxist Theory:** *Under capitalism the lot of the worker will grow constantly worse, until*

finally the workers will revolt against the system.
Reality: Even though it has taken a hard struggle, workers in capitalist nations have received an increasingly greater share of the wealth they create. Most Western workers are strongly opposed to Communism.

(4) **Marxist Theory:** *Capitalist nations will constantly wage war against each other in their struggle for control of overseas markets and colonies.* **Reality:** Communists might interpret World Wars I and II as fulfillments of this prediction. Today, however, Western nations have formed alliances to work together for peace. They have begun to draw closer together economically, as in the European Common Market (see page 731). Most of them have granted independence to their former colonies without a struggle. The reality is that almost the reverse of Marx's prediction has come about. Today the former imperialist nations free their colonies and help them to develop into strong and free nations. But the Russian and Chinese Communists have become the new imperialists. They seek to take over the new nations of Asia and Africa by subversion or conquest and to impose their dictatorship upon them.

By contrast, the achievements of capitalist free enterprise have been remarkable. It has produced more goods and services than human beings have ever before enjoyed for their health, comfort, safety, and welfare. Take a few examples: Candles and oil lamps have been replaced by electric lights. Instead of hauling water from a well, we have only to turn on a faucet. Trips that used to take days of jolting in a stagecoach or rocking on a sailing vessel can be made in a few hours by car, train, or steamer—or even faster by plane. Sanitation and medicine have made life safer and longer. Much of the toil has been taken out of factory and farm labor.

Never before in history have the average man, woman, and child enjoyed such a high standard of living as under the system of free enterprise in the industrialized countries. For the first time in human history man has solved the age-old problem of producing enough food, goods, and services for everyone. There are, of course, still problems to be solved. But there is no reason to believe that they cannot be solved by the same intelligence, ingenuity, and hard work that went into solving the problem of production.

Review of Chapter 31

People, places, and things

Identify: Adam Smith, Richard Arkwright, Robert Owen, New Harmony, collective bargaining, Karl Marx, socialism, communism.

Events in review

1. What effect did the Industrial Revolution have on cities?

2. Briefly describe the two new social classes that were brought into being by the Industrial Revolution.
3. Briefly describe working conditions, wages, and hours of work in the early factories.
4. Why did the laissez faire theory have a great appeal for factory owners and other businessmen?
5. What steps did Robert Owen take for the welfare of his employees?

6. Tell how the following contributed to the passing of laws to improve working conditions: (a) English novelists and essayists, (b) aristocratic landowners.
7. Why was the Reform Bill of 1867 important to working people?
8. What is meant by Utopian socialism?
9. Which group of Marxian socialists believe in revolution by force and violence?

Problems and projects

1. Discuss the economic views of Adam Smith about (a) the law of supply and demand, (b) competition. To what extent do his ideas apply in twentieth-century business?
2. Write a brief summary of the economic, social, and political changes brought about by the Industrial Revolution.
3. Hold a discussion, or write an essay, on the following topic: Industrial development benefits the working classes. Consider labor laws as well as industrial growth.

4. In the library, read portions of *Martin Chuzzlewit,* by Dickens, or *Sybil,* by Disraeli. Using one of these books, plus any other sources you can find, write a description of the condition of working people in the earlier days of the Industrial Revolution.
5. Individual students or committees may make reports on working conditions and labor laws in the United States today: (a) laws regulating hours of work for workers of various ages, (b) minimum wage laws, (c) Social Security and unemployment insurance, (d) safety and health regulations. (Your guidance counselor may help you find this information.) On the basis of these reports, contrast the situation today with the conditions of fifty, one hundred, or one hundred and fifty years ago.
6. Try to find figures on (a) hours worked, (b) wages, (c) value or volume of goods produced for 1800, 1850, 1900, 1950. What do these figures show about the progress made under the capitalist system?

Review of the Age of Revolutions

1. Why is the eighteenth century referred to as the Age of Enlightenment? Sometimes the same period is referred to as the Age of Reason. Why? This Age of Reason was a time of critical thinking. What institutions or ways of life were sharply attacked by eighteenth-century thinkers?
2. New political ideas appeared during this period. What was meant by "the natural rights of man"? In which countries was this idea especially important? How did this idea affect the history of these countries?

3. Explain "benevolent despotism." Can you recall rulers in other periods of history who were in some respects like these enlightened despots?
4. Review events in England from James I to the Industrial Revolution. Is it correct to say that England advanced toward democracy more by evolution than by revolution? Cite facts to support your answer.
5. Compare the American Revolution with the French Revolution. Consider (a) the situation when the revolution began, (b) the

aims of the revolutionary groups, (c) reasons for success or failure. (How much do you think the wise leadership of Washington had to do with the outcome of the American Revolution?)

6. After 1789 there were sweeping changes all over the continent of Europe. Which revolution—English, American, or French—was the most important cause of these changes? Give facts to support your answer.

7. Following the defeat of Napoleon, Europe turned to "Metternichism." What was the purpose of the Metternich system? What measures were taken to make the system work?

8. The Metternich system collapsed in 1848. Was the collapse the result of the activities of groups of rebels? Did Metternichism collapse because it was trying to suppress the spirit of the times? Explain.

9. Review the basic ideas of mercantilism. Contrast them with the laissez faire system. Why did countries like England at one time follow a mercantile policy? Why did they later shift to a laissez faire policy? Can you tell what policy they follow today?

10. The Industrial Revolution solved some problems and created others. What problems did it solve? What benefits did it bring to the world? What new problems appeared as a result of the Industrial Revolution? How many of these problems have been solved as of the present day? What is now being done about them?

Books about the Age of Revolutions

Adams, James T. *Epic of America* (Little, Brown, 1933). A fine history of the United States, useful for reference.

Baity, Elizabeth (Chesley). *Americans before Columbus.* (Viking, 1951). A study of American Indian peoples (including Aztecs, Incas, and Mayas) and cultures from the earliest Asiatic migrations to the coming of Columbus.

*Barnouw, A. J. *Land of William of Orange* (Lippincott, 1953). Highlights in the geography, history, and culture of the Netherlands. A good account of the wars against Louis XIV and the revolutionary era.

*Carr, Albert H. *Men of Power; a Book of Dictators* (Viking, 1956). Cromwell, Napoleon, Bolívar are included.

Foster, Genevieve. *Abraham Lincoln's World* (Scribner's, 1944). The events happening all over the world from 1809 to 1865 give a basis for understanding both world and United States history. Highly recommended.

*Books marked with a star (*) are easy reading.

Gershoy, Leo. *From Despotism to Revolution, 1763–1789* (Harper, 1944). An excellent study of the events leading to the French Revolution.

*Haaren, John H., and Poland, Addison B. *Famous Men of Modern Times* (American, 1906). Brief and readable biographies of many leaders of the Age of Revolutions.

Hartley, Dorothy, and Elliott, M. M. *Life and Work of the People of England: Seventeenth Century* (Putnam's, 1929). One volume of a series, well-illustrated and simply written. There is also a volume on the eighteenth century. Valuable reference works.

*Hartman, Gertrude. *Machines and the Men Who Made the World of Industry* (Macmillan, 1939). The development of industry traced from its early beginnings. Many charts and photographs.

Komroff, Manuel. *Napoleon* (Messner, 1954). The author points out how experiences in Napoleon's Corsican boyhood molded his character.

398

*Lansing, Marion F. *Liberators and Heroes of Mexico and Central America* (Page, 1941).

———. *Liberators and Heroes of South America* (Page, 1940). The men who fought for independence in Latin America in readable biographical sketches.

McGee, Dorothy Horton. *Famous Signers of the Declaration* (Dodd, 1955). Well-written reference material on the fifty-six signers.

*Mowat, Robert B., and Slosson, Preston. *History of the English-Speaking Peoples* (Oxford, 1943). The seventeenth-century English revolution is in Chapters 12–14; nineteenth-century political reform in Chapter 19.

*Osgood, Ellen L. *History of Industry* (Ginn, 1935). This readable book shows industrialism and its problems in many countries.

*Peck, Anne M. *Pageant of Middle American History* (Longmans, 1947).

*———. *Pageant of South American History* (Longmans, 1941). Rich information, told in fast-moving style.

*Quennell, C. H. B., and Quennell, Marjorie. *History of Everyday Things in England* (British Bk. Centre, 1953). Deals with the rise of industrialism. This well-illustrated book treats every phase of everyday English life. Highly recommended.

Untermeyer, Louis. *Makers of the Modern World* (Simon and Schuster, 1955). The lives of ninety-two of the great men and women of our century.

*Van Loon, Hendrik W. *Story of Inventions; Man the Miracle-Maker* (Garden City, 1934). Interesting and illuminating stories of the great inventions and their effects.

Wasserman, Louis. *Handbook of Political "Isms"* (Association Press, 1941). Brief explanations of liberalism, democracy, capitalism, socialism, communism.

Whitridge, Arnold. *Men in Crisis* (Scribner's, 1949). A good book about the revolutions of 1848. Fine character sketches of some of the leaders.

Williams-Ellis, Amabel. *Courageous Lives* (Coward-McCann, 1939). The lives and characters of "nine good citizens," including Robert Owen and Charles Dickens.

Stories about the Age of Revolutions

Boyd, James. *Drums* (Scribner's 1928). A fascinating story of the American Revolution. John Paul Jones is one of the characters.

Chambers, Robert W. *Cardigan* (Harper, 1930). A minuteman in the American Revolution, a trusted messenger to the Indians, and a very attractive character was Michael Cardigan.

*Davis, William S. *Whirlwind* (Macmillan, 1929). A young Frenchman becomes a deputy to the National Assembly and a general of the Republic.

Dickens, Charles. *Tale of Two Cities* (Dodd, Mead, 1942). A novel which stresses the Reign of Terror.

———. *Hard Times* (Houghton Mifflin, 1894). An interesting novel attacking unfair labor treatment in the First Industrial Revolution.

Forester, C. S. *Ship of the Line* (Little, Brown, 1938). Captain Horatio Hornblower commands his ship in the blockade of Napoleonic Europe.

*Hawes, Charles B. *Dark Frigate* (Little, Brown, 1934). An excellent picture of manners, customs, and language in the time of Cromwell. Very readable.

Hugo, Victor. *Les Miserables* (Collins, 1955). A novel about nineteenth-century France which has become a world classic.

*Lansing, Marion F. *Nicholas Arnold, Toolmaker* (Doubleday, 1941). The beginnings of the Industrial Revolution in New England. Eli Whitney and Samuel Slater appear as characters.

Roberts, Kenneth. *Arundel* (Doubleday, 1933). The American expedition against Quebec in 1775.

———. *Rabble in Arms* (Doubleday, 1947). The American victory at Saratoga. The book gives an interestingly different picture of Benedict Arnold.

———. *Oliver Wiswell* (Doubleday, 1940). The Tory side of the American Revolution. Roberts' books are historically accurate and very interesting.

Savery, Constance. *Emeralds for the King* (Longmans, 1945). The Puritan Revolution of 1648 in England divides a family, brother against brother.

*Trease, Geoffrey. *Trumpets in the West* (Harcourt, Brace, 1947). How Englishmen had to fight for personal and religious freedom under James II.

Updegraff, Florence M. *Blue Dowry* (Harcourt, Brace, 1948). An English girl comes to understand the meaning of American ideals and why the Americans are fighting for independence. Highly recommended.

Part Seven ADJUSTMENTS
TO THE NEW AGE

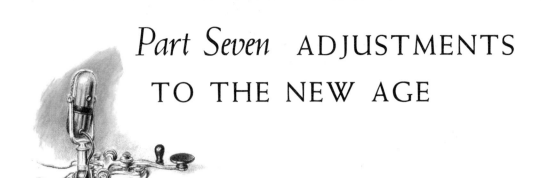

Part Six told how the tremendous forces of the Age of Revolutions made changes in the Western World from which it could never go back. The political and social ideas of the English, American, and French Revolutions proved to be irresistible forces. Reaction might suppress them for a time, but they rose again and again. Another great development—the Industrial Revolution—changed the way people lived and worked. As a result of all these changes, the world entered a new age. People had to adjust themselves to this new age. Also, they had to learn to live in a world that continued to grow and to change.

Not only did things keep happening, they also happened very swiftly. The pace of human affairs was slow in the ancient and medieval worlds. In modern times the pace has kept increasing. The illustration on the facing page shows one of the ways in which life changed suddenly. Since prehistoric times men had traveled at the pace of their own feet or of horses. Then came the Industrial Revolution and machines to speed up travel. Within a century men progressed from 20-mile-an-hour wood-burning engines to 80-mile-an-hour diesel streamliners.

It is easy to think of other ways in which life changed in a hurry—communication, for example. In the nineteenth and twentieth centuries we went from sending messages by stagecoach or Pony Express to flashing them by telegraph or radio.

Part Seven will tell how the world continued to change. Some of these changes were political. Chapter 32 describes how Great Britain, already having a representative government, achieved a democratic government as well. France turned away from democracy for a time, following the lure of nationalism and imperial glory.

The great force of nationalism played a major role in Germany and Italy. Chapter 33 tells how Germany finally became united under the leadership of Prussia. Chapter 34 relates the triumph of nationalism in Italy.

As the time chart on the next two pages shows, Part Seven is more than an account of changes in government. Chapters 35, 36, and 37 describe scientific, economic, and social adjustments to the new age. Scientific research gave the world new products, new sources of power, whole new industries. Discoveries in medical science prolonged life, causing what might be called an explosion of population.

The discoveries of science were largely responsible for the Second Industrial Revolution—a tremendous outburst of the power to produce goods and machines of all kinds. During this period such revolutionary things as the internal combustion engine (gasoline or Diesel) were invented and put into common use (as in locomotives). In this and hundreds of other ways the world became the complex, fast-moving, ever-changing, one we know in the twentieth century.

Part Seven ADJUSTMENTS

GOVERNMENT	SCIENCE AND EDUCATION

1800

1815-1848 Age of Metternich: Reaction	
	1821 First public high school, U. S.
1829 Greece independent	
1830 Revolutions: Louis Philippe, King of France	**1830-33** Lyell, *Principles of Geology*
1831 Mazzini founds Young Italy	**1831** Faraday, dynamo
1832 Parliamentary Reform Bill, Britain	**1836** First women's colleges, U. S.
1837-1901 Victoria Queen of England	**1838** Cell theory, biology
	1840 Liebig, soil chemistry
	1844 Morse, telegraph
1848 Revolutions in many countries. Second French Republic	**1846** Long, Morton, anaesthesia

1850

1852 Napoleon III, Second French Empire Cavour premier of Piedmont	**1855** Pasteur, germ theory
1853-1856 Crimean War	**1859** Darwin, *Origin of the Species*
1861 Kingdom of Italy	**1859-1952** John Dewey, educational philosopher
1862 Bismarck, chief minister of Prussia	
1864 Austro-Prussian War with Denmark	**1865** Lister, antisepsis
1866 Austro-Prussian War	
1867 Dual monarchy Second Reform Bill, Britain	
1870 Franco-Prussian War	
1871 Third French Republic	**1876** Bell, telephone
1871 German Empire	**1879** Edison, electric bulb
1871 Kingdom of Italy takes Rome	**1881-1886** Free public education, France
1878 Russo-Turkish War Congress of Berlin	
1882 Triple Alliance	
1884 Third Reform Bill, Britain	
1890 William II drops Bismarck	
	1895 Roentgen, X-ray
	1896 Marconi, wireless
	1898 Curies, radium

1900

	1903 Wright brothers' flight
1905 Revolution in Russia	**1905** Einstein, $E = mc^2$
	1907 DeForest, radio
1911 House of Lords loses power in Britain	
1914-1918 World War I	
1917 Russian Revolution	**1916** Einstein, theory of Relativity
1918 Woman suffrage, Britain	
1919 Woman suffrage, U. S.	

	1929 Fleming, penicillin
	1936 Sulfa drugs

$$E = mc^2 =$$

	1942 First sustained atomic chain reaction
	1944 Streptomycin

INDUSTRY	SOCIAL REFORM AND THE ARTS

	1770-1827 Beethoven begins break with classical music
	1775-1835 Romantic period of literature
	1810-1849 Chopin, romantic music
	1812-1870 Dickens, realism in literature
Zollverein, Germany	1813-1883 Wagner, new developments in opera
	1828-1910 Tolstoy, Russian realistic novels
Great Charter of Labor, Britain	1833 Slavery abolished, British Empire
Goodyear, vulcanization	
	1840-1926 Monet, impressionistic painting
	1841-1919 Renoir, impressionistic painting
Free trade, Britain	

Bessemer process	
First oil well, U. S.	
	1861 Emancipation of serfs, Russia
	1862-1918 Debussy, impressionist music
Atlantic cable	1863 Lincoln, Emancipation Proclamation, U. S.
First plastic; opening of Suez Canal; opening, U. S. transcontinental railroad	1869-1959 Frank Lloyd Wright, functional architecture
First commercially successful generator	
Bell, telephone	
	1881- Picasso, experimentalist painting
	1882- Stravinsky, experimental music
Gasoline engine	1883-1889 Social insurance, Germany
Diesel engine	1898-1937 Gershwin, popular and classical music
Trans-Siberian railroad completed	

Panama Canal opened	
Regular radio broadcasting	
Stock market crash U. S., followed by depression	
Invention of nylon and synthetic rubber	
	1935 U. S. Social Security Act

403

Chapter 32

Political Developments in Great Britain and France

IN CHAPTERS 32, 33, and 34 two great ideas will be shown at work in Europe—nationalism and democracy. These are such great forces in the world that they need more explanation at this point.

Nationalism

Nationalism has been defined as "devotion to or advocacy of national interests or national unity and independence." You may recall that several great movements at the end of the Middle Ages helped in the formation of national states. The Renaissance, with its development of national languages and literature, helped to bring about a national self-consciousness. The people of a country began to take pride in speaking the same language and in the works of their great writers in that language. The Protestant Revolution broke up the religious unity of Europe. Thus it ended the claims of the popes to be supreme over all kings, emperors, and other rulers, and the church no longer acted as a check on the development of strong national governments. Finally, the expansion of commerce and the development of colonial empires helped build nationalism. Trade and colonies brought in wealth; the theory and practice of mercantilism helped to build up the strong state.

But nationalism, as we understand it today, is something more than the development of strongly centralized governments. Nationalism has a mental, or psychological side, too. It means that the people, because of their common history, experiences, problems, and culture, feel that they belong together, making up a united group. This sort of feeling was not common in ancient times, and certainly not during the Middle Ages. It is a development of modern times.

A number of things work together to develop this feeling of nationality. One is the sense of shared experiences, dangers, and problems; the pride in accomplishments both political and cultural; the love of country which we call patriotism. A common race helps, but it is not necessary, as we in the United States well know. A common language also helps, but is not entirely necessary. The Swiss have a strong feeling of nationalism, although there are three official languages and several dialects in Switzerland. Nor is a common religion necessary. A common government sometimes helps develop national feeling, but is surely not necessary, nor does it always bring nationalism. When Poland was divided among Russia, Prussia, and Austria, the Polish people continued to think of themselves as a nation for a century and a quarter. Austria-Hungary had a common government, but various groups of people who lived under it thought of themselves as nations or nationalities. They never gave up the hope of breaking away and forming independent governments.

In summary, a nation is a group of people, who, whether united or divided in government, religion, race, or language, are held together mentally by the tie of nationality, the feeling of belonging together. It is also true that where a nation does not have its own independent, united, national government, it tries to get it.

Nationalism has played a great part in the modern world. In one sense it has been a good part. The sense of nationality has helped to bring about great accomplishments among the English, French, Germans, Russians, and Italians, to mention only a few. In another sense, nationalism can be dangerous. Where each people thinks only of the rights, aims, and desires of its own nation, it tends to act very selfishly, disregarding the rights, aims, and desires of other peoples. This leads to jealousy, rivalry, suspicion, and often to war. Where a sort of super-nationalism and super-patriotism exist, it is often very difficult for nations to work together to settle their differences peacefully. This sort of nationalism could be seen in the France of Napoleon Bonaparte; you will see it again in the clash between France and Prussia, described in Chapters 32 and 33. When you read the story of more modern times, particularly the period after World War I, you will note more of the dangers of nationalism. Hitler, Mussolini, and Stalin were able to establish and maintain their fascist and communist dictatorships through use of an intolerant, extreme nationalism.

Democracy

Democracy is the idea that every human being is an individual, with his own personality and with certain rights that must be respected. John Locke wrote about the right to life, liberty, and property; Jefferson wrote about "life, liberty, and the pursuit of happiness." Political democracy means that men control the government under which they live. They usually do this through representatives whom they elect to make and enforce the laws which regulate their lives. Even where the government is a monarchy under a king, as in England, his powers are limited by a constitution, and the real power of government is in the hands of the elected representatives of the people.

Democracy grows in Great Britain

Great Britain, which then included England, Wales, Scotland, and all of Ireland, was the first modern nation to develop constitutional, representative government. The English Revolution of the seventeenth century made Parliament supreme over the king. During the eighteenth century parliamentary government developed into much the form that we know now: The Cabinet (ministry) is chosen by and responsible to the elected House of Commons. Parliament is made up of two Houses: the House of Lords, composed of hereditary nobles and higher churchmen, and the elected House of Commons.

● Extending the right to vote

At the end of the eighteenth century Britain's government was constitutional and representative, but by no means democratic. Acts of Parliament prevented anyone but Anglicans (members of the Church of England) from voting or holding military or civil offices. Dissenters (Protestants who were not Anglicans), Roman Catholics, and Jews were thus barred from political life. Although Parliament ruled, Parliament itself was not democratic. The hereditary House of Lords had gradually lost power to propose laws, but it could still prevent laws from passing. The House of Commons was elected,

but not democratically elected. Property qualifications (ownership) for voting were so high that only about five per cent of the people could vote. These were the large landowners (the landed gentry). The districts represented in Commons had not been changed for over one hundred years. The rapidly growing industrial cities were often completely unrepresented, while rural villages and regions continued to send representatives to Commons.

The first steps toward more religious and political democracy came in the early nineteenth century. Political handicaps were removed from Dissenters in 1828, and from Catholics in the following year. Jews did not receive full political rights until 1858. The Parliamentary Reform Bill of 1832 improved representation in the House of Commons and gave the right to vote to more people (page 367). The property qualifications were

406

Queen Victoria with her husband Albert, Prince Consort, and five of their children. Victoria's reign, from 1837 to 1901, covered many of the events described in this chapter. This period is often called the Victorian Age.

changed so that the more prosperous farmers and middle-class city men gained voting rights. The landed gentry now found their power challenged by the rising industrial middle-class capitalists. However, even with these improvements only about one man in six could vote.

●*Social and economic reforms*

The period from 1832 to 1867 saw the adoption of social and economic reforms, but no more political changes. In 1833 Parliament passed an act which provided for the gradual abolition of slavery throughout the British colonies. All children under the age of six were declared free; all children born after 1833 were born free. Slaves over six years of age were to be freed within seven years. Their owners were to be paid from the twenty million pounds ($100,000,000) which Parliament appropriated. These same years saw the passage of acts to improve conditions of workers (pages 390–391).

The Chartists

Many people were working for further political reforms during this period. The Reform Bill of 1832 had by no means satisfied all the demands for voting rights. The industrial workers and the agricultural laborers were still voteless. In 1836 a Workingman's Association was formed. Its aim was to gain greater political and social justice. The Association drew up a petition which asked Parliament to adopt the reforms proposed in "A People's Charter." These reforms were: (1) manhood suffrage, (2) voting by secret ballot, (3) salaries for members of the House of Commons, (4) equal electoral districts, (5) abolition of property qualifications of members of the House of Commons, (6) annual election of members of the House of Commons. This "Chartist Movement" received support from many clergymen and humanitarian liberals. They saw in it a way for the workers to improve their sorrowful conditions.

Today these proposals seem so reasonable that it is hard for us to understand why the Chartists were denounced as men who threatened the very foundations of government. During the great year of revolutions, 1848, the British government took firm action against the Chartists, and the movement collapsed. The failure was due to poor leadership as well as government opposition.

Parliamentary reforms continue: 1867, 1884, 1911

Despite the failure of the Chartist movement other attempts were made to broaden the suffrage and reform Parliament still further. Workingmen continued to agitate for voting rights, and were joined by many others who favored more democratic government. Leaders of both the Conservative and the Liberal parties came to realize that reforms might gain the gratitude and the votes of the new voters. It was a Conservative cabinet, headed by Prime Minister Benjamin Disraeli, which took the initiative.

In 1867 a second Parliamentary Reform Bill was passed. Seats in the House of Commons were reapportioned again. Some thinly populated districts lost seats. These seats were given to growing cities. The right to vote was given to city industrial workers and tenant farmers. Household servants, members of the armed forces, agricultural laborers who were wage earners, and all women, were still left out. However, the addition of the new classes of voters made further reforms certain.

The tempo of political reforms now speeded up. In 1872 came the adoption of the secret ballot. Now a man could vote as he chose, without being afraid that he might suffer because someone disapproved of the way he voted. One result was to lessen the bribery which had been common in British elections. When the briber cannot be sure that he gets what he paid for, the tendency to bribe becomes less.

In 1884 another large class of men received the suffrage. This time the Liberals took the lead in giving votes to most of the agricultural workers. In the following year a Reapportionment Act divided England into electoral districts which were approximately equal in population.

Long strides had been taken to make the House of Commons a truly democratic, representative body. But there remained a great bar to the democratic process. The conservative House of Lords no longer proposed laws, but it could block a law by refusing to pass it. The ability to prevent a law from being passed was a privilege which even the king no longer had. Since the reign of Queen Anne, no monarch had vetoed an act of Parliament (see page 307). Before the government could be truly democratic, this stumbling block had to be removed.

In 1905 the Liberal Party came to power, with Herbert Asquith as prime minister and David Lloyd George as chancellor of the exchequer. The Liberals proceeded to adopt a broad program of social legislation. These changes meant that the government had to spend more money and to raise it by increasing taxes.

To meet the costs of the new program Lloyd George's budget of 1909 called for progressive income and inheritance taxes. This meant the wealthier the taxpayer, the higher the rate of taxes he paid. Lloyd George proposed to use taxes to reduce the extremes of wealth and poverty. Opposition to the bill was so strong in the conservative House of Lords that the Liberals decided to remove the Lords' power to block reforms. By the Parliamentary Reform Bill of 1911 they took away the Lords' power to veto a money bill, and to do more than delay the passage of other bills. This bill was passed over the bitter opposition of the Lords only by a threat to have the king create new Liberal peers (lords).

Now the elected representatives of the voters could really govern England. Within a month after the passage of the Parliamentary Reform Bill, liberals and workingmen gained another triumph for which they had long worked. A law was passed giving mem-

An election day scene in the United States, painted by George Caleb Bingham. By the 1830's most of our states had granted manhood suffrage. In England, the right to vote was given to an increasing number of men by reform bills passed in 1832, 1867, and 1884. Women were still left out.

bers of the House of Commons a salary of 400 pounds (at that time about two thousand dollars) a year. Now a workingman without an independent income could afford to serve in Parliament if he could be elected.

Universal suffrage in England

The reform bills of 1832, 1867, and 1884 gave the right to vote to most British men, almost without regard to their income or property ownership. A very few men, in certain occupations and services, were unable to vote. There remained, however, a very large group of people without political rights: the women. Since women paid taxes and were bound by the laws which the government passed, it seemed undemocratic to deny them a voice in choosing that government or taking part in it. All these injustices were corrected.

The Franchise Act of 1918 made all electoral districts in Great Britain completely equal in population. It gave the right to vote to every male citizen twenty-one years of age or over. It also gave the vote to women thirty years of age or over. In 1928 the qualifications for voting were made the same for women as for men: age twenty-one or over.

Thus, within less than one hundred years Great Britain made an amazing march to complete democracy. Before 1832 fewer than five per cent of British men could vote. In 1928 universal suffrage came into effect. Until 1911 an aristocratic House of Lords could block legislation. Since then the elected representatives of the people have been supreme. It is indeed remarkable that this progress was achieved peacefully, without riots or violent revolution. The whole story gives a fine demonstration of democratic triumph, and is a tribute to the good sense of the British people.

British government today

To understand the actual operations of the British government, you have to understand

From the 1880's to World War I there was much agitation in Great Britain to win for women the right to vote. The suffragettes (women who were working for the vote) used many ways to advertise their cause. This photograph shows a group of British women ready to parade with a sign and a banner. American women also demanded voting rights, as noted on page 471.

these four things: the constitution, the sovereign, the Parliament, the political parties.

The British constitution is largely unwritten, and can be amended by a simple act of Parliament (page 308). The sovereign "reigns but does not rule," having lost his power to propose and veto laws.

It would be a mistake, though, to think of the British sovereign as a meaningless figurehead. He is the symbol of national unity and sovereignty; he commands the allegiance of all his subjects. He is the principal link which holds together the independent parts of the British Commonwealth of Nations, like Canada and Australia. He has no power,

Queen Elizabeth II and her husband, the Duke of Edinburgh. Despite high-sounding titles, the queen of England does not govern the country. The prime minister, the cabinet, and Parliament run the country. The sovereign has the right to be consulted by the cabinet, the right to encourage cabinet members, and the right to warn them—but no authority over them.

but great influence. Cabinet leaders respect and consult him. He cannot command them, but his advice often influences their decisions.

● Parliament and political parties

In the Parliament the House of Commons rules supreme. Neither the king nor the Lords can veto an act of Commons. No court can declare an act of Parliament unconstitutional.

The cabinet is the executive committee of the political party which has a majority of the members of the House of Commons. All members of the cabinet must be members of Parliament and are usually members of the House of Commons. Each party chooses its own leader; the leader of the majority party becomes prime minister. The cabinet has a double job. It decides party policy, prepares the important bills to carry out the policy, and guides or steers them to passage through Parliament. The cabinet is also the executive branch of the government. Each minister acts as the head of an executive department to see that laws are properly enforced and administered. Thus the legislative and executive branches of the government are combined.

The British cabinet is said to be "responsible" to the House of Commons. This means that the prime minister and his cabinet hold their positions only so long as they command a majority in Commons. Lack of a majority is shown in two ways: (1) if an important bill proposed by the cabinet is defeated or (2) if the majority of Commons passes a vote of "no confidence" in the government. If either of these things happens, the prime minister may do one of two things: (1) He may resign and ask the king to appoint the leader of the opposition party as prime minister. The new prime minister then chooses a cabinet from his own party. Of course, the prime minister and his cabinet resign only from their positions in the ministry. They are still members of Parliament. (2) The defeated prime minister may advise the king to dissolve Parliament and call an election of a new House of Commons. This is called "going to the country." If the voters elect a majority of members of the old party, the former prime minister and his cabinet remain in office. If not, the opposition party takes over the government, with its leader as prime minister. Thus, although members of the House of Commons are elected for five years, they may serve less than that time if a new election is called before their term is up. An election must be called at the end of the five years if none has been held before.

There have been three main political parties in England. The *Conservatives* are the successors to the Tories, who represented the landowners in the eighteenth and early nineteenth centuries. The *Liberals* succeeded the Whigs, who represented the commercial and industrial middle class and the more liberal members of the aristocracy. After members of the working class received the vote in 1867 and 1884, they joined one or the other of the existing parties, or the small Socialist party. They became convinced, however, that neither party was much interested in their welfare and that they must have their own party. So, in 1901 several Socialist groups joined with representatives of the trade unions to form the *Labour Party*. In recent years it has become one of the two main parties. The Liberal Party has gradually lost strength until it now elects only a few members to the House of Commons.

France again tries empire: Napoleon III

We move now to France in the mid-nineteenth century to continue the political history of that nation. As told on pages 370–371, Louis Napoleon Bonaparte was able to rise to power in France partly because of the glorious legend of his famous uncle. Some men scornfully called the nephew "Napoleon the Little." He was elected president of the Second French Republic largely because no one knew exactly what he stood for. By clever political juggling and trickery he was able to abolish the constitution of the Second Republic and substitute another which made him emperor.

As emperor, Napoleon III had many groups against him in France. There were also other groups who would have to be satisfied or they would oppose him. The real

monarchists thought of him as only a pretender, not truly entitled to be king. Republicans were very unhappy over the death of the Second Republic. French Catholics, especially the clergy, expected him to restore the power and position of the Catholic Church. Middle-class businessmen expected favors for the growing industries. Workers wanted help in improving their very bad working and living conditions. Peasants and farmers were suspicious of any move which might reduce their control or ownership of their own land, or increase their taxes.

● *Domestic policies:*
"All things to all men"

In such a situation a ruler whose position is shaky has to make a decision. Shall he try to please everyone, even though pleasing one group may mean antagonizing another? Or shall he select those groups who will make him strong enough to hold real power, favor them, and with their support overcome all opposition?

Napoleon III chose the first way. He tried to steer a middle course: he balanced favors given to one group with favors to another. He favored the aristocracy—the aristocrats created by his uncle as well as the old Bourbon aristocracy. To win the middle class, he encouraged the building of railroads and levied high tariffs to protect the new industries. Of course this increased the cost of living, but Napoleon III was still able to pose as the champion of labor. He began a great program of public works—building roads, railroads, canals, and improving harbors. He beautified Paris with magnificent public buildings, monuments, and theaters. This program satisfied people's love of beauty and display; it also created many jobs. Napoleon III's admirers called him "the workingman's emperor." For a time, perhaps, the workers believed it. To win over the Catholics, he coöperated with the Church both at home and abroad.

France was not a republic, but on the surface the Second Empire looked like a democracy. There was a constitution, with a legislative body elected by universal manhood suffrage. What democrat could ask for more? But the reality was quite different. Members of the legislature, and other public officials, were nominated and elected under the direct supervision of the government. The legislature could not make any law unless it was proposed by the emperor. It had no power over the spending of money. It could not question the emperor's ministers and could not even publish its debates. People suspected of opposing the government could be imprisoned or exiled without trial. Newspapers were strictly censored. A paper which criticized the emperor or his government was warned twice, then suppressed. There was no freedom of speech. Liberal professors in the universities were discharged; other liberal critics of the régime were imprisoned or exiled. Organized opposition to the government was almost impossible.

● Napoleon III's foreign policies

Most dictatorships seem to follow a pattern. To quiet discontent at home, the dictator tries to win glory abroad. So it was with Napoleon III. France had two great foreign problems: with Prussia and with Russia. Nicholas I, Czar of Russia, considered the French emperor an upstart and was slow to recognize him as the real ruler of France. There was mutual suspicion and hostility between France and Russia. Napoleon III's aim in foreign affairs was to win the coöperation of Great Britain against the Russians.

Soon Napoleon had a chance to set back

> *A hospital scene during the Crimean War. At first the British and French provided almost no proper means to care for the sick and wounded, and many soldiers died for lack of treatment. The efforts of Florence Nightingale had much to do with the organizing of adequate hospitals, such as the one shown here.*

the Russians and at the same time win British friendship. This chance came in connection with the fast-weakening Turkish Empire. The Russian czar claimed the right to protect all Christians living under Turkish rule. Napoleon III had several reasons for opposing this claim. He wanted to increase French prestige abroad. He wanted to win an alliance with Britain, which feared Russian expansion toward the eastern Mediterranean. By posing as the defender of Catholic Christians against Russian control he would gain the support of French Catholics. He could claim to be supporting minority groups, thus winning the support of the Poles against Russia.

The Crimean War

The outcome of all this planning was that France and Great Britain came to the support of Turkey against Russia. In 1854 a war broke out. Since it was fought in the Black Sea peninsula of the Crimea, it is known as the Crimean War. On both sides the war was conducted with terrible inefficiency and waste. Tennyson's poem, "The Charge of the Light Brigade," describes one tragic event of this war. After two years of terrible fighting, with great losses from battle and disease, Russia was defeated.

By the treaty, signed in Paris, Russia had to give up her claims to protect the Christians in the Turkish Empire. She was forbidden to build up a navy in the Black Sea. The right to use the Danube River was given to all nations, with a special commission set up to supervise this international navigation. Turkey was to be "protected" as a member of the European family of nations.

And what did France win to repay her cost in lives and money? Well, glory, perhaps! Certainly none of the peace terms was of any benefit to France. In fact, supporting Turkey was bound to mean trouble in the future. In spite of all efforts to bolster the shaky empire, Turkey was growing hopelessly weaker, fully justifying its nickname, "The Sick Man of Europe." The government was weak, corrupt, and inefficient. The various Christian minorities under Turkish rule in the Balkans were unhappy and dissatisfied. Nationalism was strong among them. Nothing less than freedom and national independence could satisfy them. As time went on, it became clear that no force could check Turkey's weakness. Furthermore, no force could stop Russia's gain in strength and her quick recovery from the shock of the war.

Intervention in Mexico

Napoleon III now turned to the establishment of a French colonial empire. In North Africa he took advantage of a native revolt to establish French rule over Algeria. In the Far East he set up a French protectorate over Cambodia, thus beginning French control in Indo-China. His greatest colonial adventure was in the Western Hemisphere.

In Mexico, in 1861, an Indian named Benito Juárez led a revolt and overthrew the existing military dictatorship. Juárez announced that his government would not repay money which former governments had borrowed from European bankers. To force payment of the loans, Great Britain, Spain, and France sent troops to Mexico to seize the customs houses. In a short time Britain and Spain reached agreement with Juárez and withdrew their troops, but French troops did not withdraw. Napoleon III saw an opportunity to set up a French colony, and decided to try it.

In 1863 French troops overthrew the Juárez government. Napoleon III installed a ruler of his choice, Archduke Maximilian, brother of the Emperor of Austria. However, Maximilian was met with revolts, and was kept in power only by French troops.

The United States vigorously protested this violation of the Monroe Doctrine. It was prevented from taking action by the War Between the States. When the war was over,

The end of one of Napoleon III's adventures in foreign intrigue—his effort to make Maximilian Emperor of Mexico. This picture shows Maximilian, followed by an officer with a white flag, walking out to surrender to the Mexican army.

the United States sent an army to the Mexican border, and then asked the French emperor when he would withdraw his troops.

The combination of the American warning, the Mexican revolt, and a threatening situation in Europe persuaded Napoleon III to give up the Mexican adventure. Maximilian was defeated, captured, and executed by the Mexicans. The French emperor was blamed on all sides for the ruinous venture.

The diplomatic adventures of Napoleon III in Italy are part of a story to be told later. Here it is enough to say that he tried to be on every side and only succeeded in antagonizing everyone: French republicans, French Catholics, and Italians of every school of thought. It was a diplomatic disaster.

The Franco-Prussian War ends the Second French Empire

In 1869 Napoleon III faced great opposition. His disastrous foreign adventures in Italy and Mexico were displeasing to almost all parties and groups in France. Liberals and republicans could not forgive him for killing the republic, nor for his tyranny as emperor, nor for his playing politics with the Catholic Church. Catholics were discontented with his wavering policy toward the papacy in Italy and his abandonment of Maximilian. Elections held in that year showed strong opposition from both conservatives and liberals.

Napoleon III decided to regain the support of all groups in France by another bold and risky venture. By opposing the unification of Germany under Prussia he could unite behind him Frenchmen of every school of thought, because Prussia was almost universally disliked in France. This scheme was risky in that it might bring war. If war came France could not count on any outside help. The emperor's foreign policy had antagonized all European countries.

● Bismarck

To make things worse, the man who was leading the Prussian government and directing foreign policy was one of the shrewdest diplomats and outstanding statesmen in Europe. He was Otto von Bismarck. Napoleon III was surely no match for him; if Louis Napoleon did not know it, Otto von Bismarck did. He considered the French emperor "the greatest unrecognized mediocrity in Europe." Napoleon III was willing to risk war to prevent German unification. Bismarck had decided that war with France was the last step necessary to achieve German unification. It would pull the German people together. When two nations reach this point, only an excuse for war is needed. It came soon from a part of Europe where it would have been least expected.

A revolution had taken place in Spain. The queen, Isabella II, was driven out, and the Spanish began to search for a new ruler. In 1870 they offered the throne to a German, Prince Leopold, cousin of the king of Prussia.

Leopold was not impressed; he refused the offer. When Bismarck heard this news, he persuaded the Spanish to renew the offer and Leopold to accept it.

In Paris Napoleon III, urged by members of his court, took a strong stand against this development. If Leopold accepted the invitation, France would be threatened by the fact that Germany and Spain would be under the same royal family. So the French emperor dispatched strong notes to Spain and Prussia, asking that Leopold again turn down the offer.

Leopold did withdraw, and Napoleon III had won an easy diplomatic victory. But, as a gambler, he decided to "push his luck." Members of his court urged, and he agreed, that the Prussian royal family should be thoroughly discredited. To do this the reckless French emperor made further demands. He insisted that King William I of Prussia pledge publicly that no member of the Hohenzollern family should ever be a candidate for the Spanish throne.

The king of Prussia was vacationing at a place called Ems. There the French ambassador delivered Napoleon's demand. The king's reply was not positive, but noncommittal. The ambassador, not satisfied, asked for another meeting to discuss the matter. The king replied that since he was returning to Berlin, he would be unable to see the ambassador.

● The "Ems dispatch" and the war

Bismarck was following the developments carefully. When he learned of the last meeting, he performed one of his greatest diplomatic tricks. He released to the newspapers an account of the meeting between the Prussian king and the French ambassador. This "Ems dispatch," as it was called, was accurate except for one thing. By omitting a few words of what the king said, the despatch was made to sound as though the French ambassador had been dismissed offensively and contemptuously. Bismarck knew that French public opinion was already aroused over the Prussian question. So he reasoned that it would be kindled to a hot flame by this incident. Before releasing his story to the press, he made certain that the Prussian army was ready for anything.

The timing of the "Ems dispatch" was perfect. The news reached Paris on Bastille Day, July 14, a great national holiday like our Independence Day. At such a time a patriotic people is in no mood to accept national humiliation. There were public demonstrations amounting to hysteria. Crowds raged through the streets of Paris demanding war on Prussia. Napoleon III was by now hesitant to carry the adventure as far as war, but he was helpless against the public passion. When the legislature met next day, a declaration of war against Prussia was proposed and adopted by an overwhelming vote. The gamblers on both sides had produced a war; now it remained to be seen whose gamble would "pay off."

It was a short war, but a decisive one. As was expected, no outside nation made any move to help either side. The Prussian army was superbly trained and equipped, and ably led. The French army from the start showed appalling inefficiency and confusion. Within a month it suffered terrible defeats and was

FRANCO-PRUSSIAN WAR 1870-71

Direction of Prussian drive

forced back from the border, especially in Alsace. Though ill at the time, the emperor went in person to take command. The decisive battle took place at Sedan, near the Belgian border, six weeks after the outbreak of the war. Napoleon III himself, with an army of 80,000 men, fell into the hands of the enemy.

The defeat at Sedan was a political as well as a military disaster. It was the end of the empire of Napoleon III. When news of the defeat reached Paris, rebellion broke out and the republicans seized control. They declared the emperor deposed, and proclaimed France, for the third time, a republic. Thus began the Third French Republic.

Review of Chapter 32

People, places, and things

Identify: "Napoleon the Little," Juárez, Maximilian, Herbert Asquith, Bismarck, "The Sick Man of Europe," "The Charge of the Light Brigade."

Locate: France, Prussia, Austria, Turkey, Lombardy, Spain, Mexico, Crimea, the Black Sea, the Bosporus, the Dardanelles, the Danube River, Sedan.

Events in review

1. What factors usually contribute to nationalism? Are all these factors necessary? Explain.
2. Can a monarchy have democratic government? Explain.
3. What groups of Englishmen received the right to vote under the Parliamentary Reform Bill of 1867? What groups still could not vote?
4. Explain how the Reform Bill of 1911 took away the political power of the House of Lords.
5. When did women first receive the right to vote in England? When were the qualifications for voting made the same for women as for men?
6. How is the British prime minister selected? In what way are he and the rest of the cabinet "responsible to the House of Commons"?
7. Did France have democratic government under Napoleon III? Give details.
8. What did France gain as a result of the Crimean War?

9. Why was the United States concerned over Napoleon III's attempt to set up an empire in Mexico? What action did the United States take?
10. Why did Napoleon III oppose the unification of Germany under Prussia?
11. How was Spain involved in the events leading up to the Franco-Prussian War?
12. Briefly describe the "Ems dispatch" incident.

Problems and projects

1. Make a list of events in the growth of democracy in Great Britain from 1832 onward. Using this list, try to show how the English continued to advance toward democracy by evolution, not revolution.
2. The sovereign in England is head of the state, but the president of the United States is both head of the state and of the government. Explain.
3. Compare the cabinet in the United States with the British cabinet. How are members selected? What duties and powers do they have?
4. Discuss the foreign policy of Napoleon III. What were his aims? Did he succeed or fail? Give details. Can you think of recent examples of dictators engaging in foreign adventures for similar reasons?
5. Write a report on one of the leaders in the votes-for-women movement in England or the United States.
6. Write a short sketch of one of the following: (a) Maximilian, (b) Juarez, (c) Florence Nightingale (telling of her work in army hospitals during the Crimean War).

Chapter 33

The Formation of the German Empire

THE Franco-Prussian War changed French history, as Chapter 32 has just shown. This war was also a turning point in German history—the point at which the German states finally united into a powerful empire. To get the background for this story it is necessary to review events in Germany, and especially in Prussia, from the time of the French Revolution. That is, we will go back for a bit from the period of Napoleon III to the era of Napoleon Bonaparte.

Prussia during the French Revolution and the Napoleonic Era

At the time the French Revolution began (1789) Prussia was a fairly well united, strong, and prosperous state as a result of the gains made by the Sergeant King and Frederick the Great. During the next twenty-five years two weak rulers lost all these gains. They allied themselves with Austria to try to wipe out the revolutionary gains in France. Frederick William II helped to form the First Coalition of Prussia, Austria, Great Britain, Spain, and Holland against France. He was defeated by the French armies. In 1795 Prussia had to give up all claims to territories west of the Rhine River.

Ten years later a still weaker ruler, Frederick William III, allowed himself to be drawn into the Third Coalition against Napoleon Bonaparte. Prussian armies were disastrously defeated, and the peace that followed almost wiped out Prussia. Napoleon took all of Prussia's Polish lands and formed the Grand Duchy of Warsaw. This was ruled by his loyal ally the king of Saxony. Napoleon also took all Prussian territory in west Germany and formed the state of Westphalia. This state was ruled by his brother Jerome. The Prussian army was limited in size. The country had to pay a large indemnity, support an army of occupation within her territory, and contribute soldiers to the French armies.

● *Nationalism in Prussia*

Strangely enough, this almost complete disaster brought about the birth of the modern state of Prussia. There was a great patriotic outcry for national revival, for reforms to rebuild the nation in every way. The feeling of nationalism became very strong. Statesmen arose to give force and direction to these demands for reforms. Serfdom was abolished, and medieval class distinctions were removed. Local self-government was established, and municipal government was improved. Reforms were made in education, in the levying and collection of taxes, and in the relations between the peasants and the former feudal landlords.

Vital changes were made in the Prussian army. Conscription was begun. Men were called into service for short periods of intensive training and then put in the reserve army. Thus Prussia observed the limits placed on her standing army by the French, but at the same time she built up a large force of trained men. Discipline was improved. Regardless of class origin, able men were given a chance to advance.

Thus the revived Prussian state with its reborn army was in a position to be in "at the death" of Napoleon Bonaparte's power. When Napoleon Bonaparte retreated into western Europe after his disastrous Russian campaign, Prussia joined the other European powers in war against France. Prussian armies played their part in the battles of Leipzig and Waterloo. Prussia earned the right to be one of the "Big Four" powers at the Congress of Vienna.

Prussia and Austria, 1815–1860

At the end of the Napoleonic Wars, Prussia was still the main rival of Austria in Germany. The treaties of the Congress of Vienna gave her much important territory. She received territory along the east bank of the Rhine, two thirds of Saxony, and a part of Westphalia. Prussian lands now stretched continuously from the Russian border to the Rhine River. The Prussian population was overwhelmingly German. The government was well organized and efficient; the economy was strong.

Napoleon had made great changes in Germany which worked in Prussia's favor. He had abolished the Holy Roman Empire in which the Austrian Hapsburg rulers had been so powerful. The Hapsburgs now had to content themselves with the title of Emperor of Austria. Napoleon had also reorganized and consolidated many small German states into fewer larger ones. The Holy Roman Empire was replaced by a German Confederation of thirty-eight states, still under the leadership of Austria.

Napoleon Bonaparte had done more than reorganize and consolidate German states. He had let loose in Europe all the forces and ideas of the French Revolution. One such force was nationalism, the desire for a united German people under a single government. This feeling favored Prussia more than Austria. The population of Prussia was strongly German. In Austria the Germans were a minority ruling group. There were many other national groups: Hungarians; the Slavic Czechs, Slovaks, Slovenes, Serbs, Poles, Croats; the Rumanians, and the Italians. Most of them wanted independence and their own national governments. Austria therefore opposed a united Germany. She preferred to keep it as it was—a loose confederation of states under her leadership. Thus she put herself into opposition to one of the great forces or trends of the time: the idea of nationalism.

● Obstacles to German unity

Austria's opposition was not the only stumbling block to German unity. France also was opposed. The traditional French policy was to keep Germany weak and divided. Within Germany itself there was opposition to unification. Many groups of people favored the status quo (things as they are). In the various German states the royal families and nobility feared loss of social position and privileges. Government workers in the states feared loss of their jobs. The religious division of Germany was an even greater problem. Prussia and northern Germany were Protestant; Austria and the south German states were overwhelmingly Catholic.

● Forces favoring unity

However, there were also strong forces working for unity among the Germans. Many of the early German nationals were liberals. Believing in the democratic ideas of the French Revolution, they wanted Germany to be a constitutional, democratic monarchy. Some favored a German republic. The beginnings of the Industrial Revolution in Germany strengthened the desire for unity. Industrial development was hindered by the

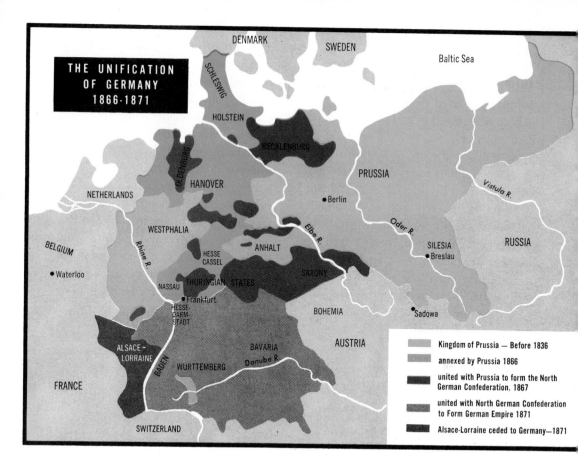

THE UNIFICATION
OF GERMANY
1866-1871

DENMARK
SWEDEN
Baltic Sea
SCHLESWIG
HOLSTEIN
MECKLENBURG
OLDENBURG
HANOVER
PRUSSIA
NETHERLANDS
Berlin
Vistula R.
WESTPHALIA
Oder R.
Elbe R.
BELGIUM
ANHALT
SILESIA
RUSSIA
HESSE CASSEL
Breslau
Waterloo
NASSAU
THURINGIAN STATES
SAXONY
Frankfurt
HESSE-DARM-STADT
BOHEMIA
Sadowa
ALSACE-LORRAINE
BAVARIA
AUSTRIA
BADEN
WURTTEMBERG
Danube R.
FRANCE
SWITZERLAND

Kingdom of Prussia — Before 1836

annexed by Prussia 1866

united with Prussia to form the North German Confederation, 1867

united with North German Confederation to Form German Empire 1871

Alsace-Lorraine ceded to Germany—1871

many German states with their different laws and their tariffs. Businessmen came to want national unity. The people felt the effects of the tariff barriers in the increased prices of the goods they bought.

Prussia took the lead in forming an economic union. In 1819 she got other German states to agree to a *Zollverein* (customs union). Tariffs were charged only when goods moved to or from the group of economically united German states; there were no tariffs within the union. By 1848 all the German states except Austria and the city of Hamburg had joined the union. Prussia gained greatly from the Zollverein. Industrial development had gone further in Prussia. The railroads radiated from Berlin. The other German states became more and more dependent economically upon Prussia.

The liberal movement for German unification received a tremendous setback during the revolution of 1848. You will remember that for a time it looked as though Germany would be united under a liberal democratic constitution. However, the forces of reaction and disunity proved to be too strong. The liberals failed, and many of them gave up the struggle and left Germany for good.

Germany becomes unified

In 1860 a new and very different kind of man took the lead in the drive for German unification. He was Otto von Bismarck, the man who had such contempt for Louis Napoleon. Bismarck was a member of that aristocratic, landowning, Prussian group whom the Germans call *Junkers*. He was no liberal; on the contrary, he had all the conservative ideas of his class. In 1848 he strongly opposed the parliamentary movement, and he remained undemocratic throughout his life. He was a devoted and devout Protestant Prussian.

● Bismarck's policies

Bismarck believed thoroughly that Prussia had been predestined to lead the German people to unity. He was willing to assist this "divine will" by the use of money, trickery, bribery, and military force. A convinced monarchist, he served his beloved king, William I of Prussia, to the very best of his abilities. And those abilities were truly great. Bismarck was highly intelligent and well educated. Unlike many of his class he was very well informed regarding what went on in other countries. He studied foreign developments carefully, and was able to put his knowledge to good use.

Bismarck had great contempt for socialists and liberals. He regarded them as talkers only, not men of action. His own ideas he stated thus: "The great questions of the hour will not be settled by votes or by the parliamentary resolutions, but by blood and iron." This statement won him the nickname of the Iron Chancellor.

Bismarck became chief minister of the king of Prussia in 1860. He had the thorough cooperation of the king and the two generals in charge of the army. Count Helmuth von Moltke and Count Albrecht Theodor von Roon were great both as organizers and as military strategists. Bismarck, the king, and the generals all agreed that it was necessary to reorganize and strengthen the Prussian army. First, however, an increase of taxes was needed.

The Prussian parliament refused to appropriate the money for the military expansion program, but Bismarck solved this problem easily. He dismissed the parliament and collected the taxes anyway, paying no attention to the protests of the liberals and the strict constitutionalists. His plan was to stop the criticism with military victories, on the theory that "Nothing succeeds like success."

Bismarck, von Moltke, and von Roon proceeded to make the Prussian army a great war machine. New weapons were provided, especially a new breech-loading rifle called the "needle gun." This gun fired faster and more accurately than the old muzzle-loaders. The great aim was efficiency. Everything was done to make the military force operate like a machine, with the precision of clockwork. An attempt was made to plan in advance for every possible development. Suppose an enemy blew up a bridge to delay the Prussians. To his amazed dismay, the enemy would find that the Prussian engineers were ready with the parts of a bridge to fit that exact spot. No such planning had ever been known.

● The Danish war, 1863

Prussia's problem was twofold: first, to drive Austria out of leadership in Germany, and, second, to overcome the unwillingness of the south German states to accept Prussian leadership. Bismarck was as careful and far-seeing in diplomacy and statesmanship as his generals were in military affairs. Instead of attacking Austria directly, he chose a roundabout way. He began his campaign for German unification with a war against Denmark.

On the border between Denmark and Germany lay two duchies, Schleswig and Holstein. The population was a mixture of Germans and Danes. The duchies were ruled by the Danish king under a constitution which provided that they were not part of Denmark, but separate. In 1863 a new king came to the Danish throne. At the insistence of many Danes, he issued a new constitution which provided that Schleswig and Holstein were part of Denmark. This act gave Bismarck his chance.

Both Prussia and Austria protested against the new Danish constitution. Acting together they demanded that it be revoked. When Denmark refused, Prussia and Austria declared war. Denmark had hoped for help from France and Great Britain, but neither acted. The little country went down to defeat before the two powerful enemies. The peace treaty gave the two duchies to Prussia and Austria jointly. Austria demanded that the two duchies form a single state within the German Confederation. Prussia refused this settlement. After some bitter wrangling, it was decided that Prussia should rule Schleswig, and Austria should rule Holstein.

● Bismarck plots his next move

The second step in the process was to drive Austria out of the German Confederation. Bismarck prepared the way by a series of masterful diplomatic actions. He persuaded Emperor Napoleon III of France to remain neutral if war came between Prussia and Austria. The French emperor stated his demands in writing: territory held by the South German States. Bismarck's promises were oral, and very hazy. Next the German Chancellor made an alliance with the Kingdom of Italy. In return for fighting against Austria, Italy was to receive Venetia. Finally, by complicated and tricky moves, he provoked Austria into declaring war on Prussia.

● The Austrian war, 1866

Austria had not counted on the superb Prussian army. In fact, the swift Prussian victory came as a surprise to the whole world. It is known as the Seven Weeks' War, for it lasted just that long. Everywhere Prussia took the initiative, and everywhere she was victorious. The Italians failed to hold up

their end, but because of Prussian victories, they gained Venetia anyway. The war ended with a great Prussian victory over the Austrian army at Sadowa, in Bohemia.

By the Treaty of Prague, which ended the war, Austria approved the dissolution of the

Three types of the "needle gun" used by the Prussian army. This weapon was a single-shot, bolt-action, breech-loading, rifle. It was called "needle gun" because of its long firing pin. This rifle gave the Prussian troops an advantage over the Austrians, armed with muzzle-loading guns, in the Seven Weeks' War, the "blitzkrieg" victory for Bismarck's forces in 1866.

German Confederation and the cession of Holstein to Prussia and of Venetia to Italy. Many Prussians wanted Bismarck to go farther—to crush Austria completely and seize the south German states which had fought with Austria. However, this did not fit in with the shrewd diplomacy of Bismarck. He wanted Austria out of the German Confederation, but not as a permanent enemy. And he wanted the southern states to join Prussia willingly, not by force. There were no seizures of territory and no indemnities. Considering the completeness of the Prussian victory, it was a very lenient peace. This, too, was part of the plan.

In north Germany it was different. Here Prussia had everything to gain and nothing to lose. The provinces of Schleswig and Holstein, the states of Hanover, Cassel, and Nassau, and the free city of Frankfurt were all added to Prussia. Now Prussia included forty per cent of German territory, with seventy-five per cent of the population. There were twenty northern states that were allowed for a time to remain independent, but they were united into a North German Confederation. Each state had self-government,

The loser in the Franco-Prussian War, Napoleon III, sits with the triumphant Bismarck the day after the great German victory at Sedan in 1870.

though the king of Prussia was hereditary president of the confederation. Since Prussia was the largest state, Prussian representatives dominated the legislature. Only the four southern states of Bavaria, Baden, Württemberg, and Hesse remained outside. If they could be persuaded to join, German unity would be complete.

Austria's defeat and her expulsion from the German Confederation brought a reorganization there also. For a time it looked as though the various national groups might take advantage of the defeat to try to gain independence. The two most numerous groups in the motley empire were the Austrian Germans and the Hungarians. They realized that unless they stood together, they would face revolts of the Slavic groups. Such revolts would cost them both dearly. So, in 1867 they reached a compromise agreement which allowed both of them some degree of self-government but kept them united against the Slavs.

The state was divided into two parts: the Empire of Austria and the Kingdom of Hungary. Each had its own constitution, its own parliament, and a considerable degree of self-government. But they had a common army, and they acted together in foreign relations. The same person ruled in both countries: in Austria as emperor, in Hungary as king. This strange creation, two bodies with one head, was called the Dual Monarchy. It worked fairly satisfactorily for the Austrians and Hungarians. However, it left all the other national minorities dominated by either Austria or Hungary; so they were discontented. The Dual Monarchy lasted from 1867 until 1918, when it collapsed as a result of defeat in World War I.

● *The Franco-Prussian War and final unification, 1870–1871*

In Germany, Bismarck had taken a long stride toward his heart's desire: a nation united under the dominance of Prussia.

Prussia dominated the North German Confederation. Now the problem was to get the four southern states to join. Catholic and Austrian influence was strong there; it would take some great outside danger to persuade them to unite willingly.

As you have read, Bismarck had persuaded Louis Napoleon not only to remain neutral between Austria and Prussia, but also to state in writing the price of his neutrality. That price, although vaguely stated, was to give France gains in southern Germany. Therefore, when France declared war on Prussia in 1870, Bismarck showed this document to the leaders of the southern German states. Thus he persuaded them that their greatest danger was France, not Prussia. He converted them from rivals into allies against France. As allies they contributed their share toward the Prussian victory.

At the end of the Franco-Prussian War the allied German states took a further step. On January 18, 1871, they met in the Hall of Mirrors of the Palace of Versailles. There they issued an official proclamation declaring the formation of the German Empire with William I of Prussia as German emperor.

Bismarck had been lenient with Austria because Austrians were Germans and he did not want them as enemies. He had no such feeling about France. He did not hope or want to make friends of the French. The terms of the treaty were harsh. France had to give to the new German empire the rich border provinces of Alsace and Lorraine. In addition, France was to pay an indemnity of five billion francs (one billion dollars) within three years. As a final humiliation a German army of occupation was to remain in France. Its costs were to be paid by the French government until the indemnity was paid. The French had to accept the terms, but they did not forget the humiliating experience. Their desire for revenge played a considerable part in the period leading up to the First World War.

The government of the German empire

The new German empire, born of the policy of blood and iron, was not all that Bismarck desired. He was forced to make many compromises in order to accomplish his purpose. Much as he disliked constitutions, it was a constitutional government. Since it was composed of twenty-five states, with the newly annexed provinces of Alsace and Lorraine in a special separate class, it had a federal form of government. Each state had its own ruler, whatever his title might be. And each state had full right to handle its own local, domestic matters: land laws, public health, public education, police, and local taxation.

The imperial government was given control of all common problems such as national defense, foreign affairs, tariffs, and commercial matters. At the head of the imperial government was the emperor, or kaiser, who was also king of Prussia. He was not, as Bismarck would have liked, an absolute monarch, but he had tremendous power. He could appoint the chief executive officer, the chancellor, who was responsible to him. The emperor commanded the army and navy and controlled foreign affairs. He could declare a defensive war on his own authority; he could wage offensive war with the consent of the upper house of legislature. He appointed twenty of the sixty-one members of the upper house. Since fourteen votes could block a change in the constitution, Prussia, or the emperor, could defeat any amendment. With the consent of the upper house, he could dissolve the lower, popularly elected, branch of the legislature.

The legislative branch of the government was composed of two houses. The *Bundesrat,* or federal council, was the upper house. It was composed of sixty-one members appointed by the hereditary rulers of the various states. The *Reichstag,* or imperial parliament, was the lower house of the legislature. Its

423

An iron works in nineteenth-century Germany. Such small plants were soon replaced by a huge iron and steel industry.

nearly 400 members were elected by universal manhood suffrage. The federal council drew up all the bills which the lower house could consider. It could also veto bills which the lower house passed. Actions of the lower house could be vetoed by the federal council. And it could be dismissed by the emperor and federal council acting together.

As you can see, the constitution "loaded the dice" in favor of Prussia in imperial affairs. Prussia had the greatest number of delegates in the appointive Bundesrat. Also, as the most populous state, it had the greatest number of delegates in the elective Reichstag. There was little chance that the Reichstag would pass any liberal, democratic laws to upset the status quo. It was too well controlled by the Bundesrat.

Prussian dominance made the chance of democratic action even less likely. Prussia was still governed by the very conservative constitution adopted in 1850. This constitution, unchanged until 1918, placed power in the hands of the king and the Junkers, the aristocratic great landowners. So, although the government of the German Empire was

federal and constitutional, it was unlike any other state in that it was aristocratic, not democratic. Nationalism and democracy had become completely divorced in the formation of the German empire. A new great power appeared on the continent of Europe.

Bismarck faces domestic problems

•Industrial development

German unification brought a tremendous spurt of industrial development. As you have learned, the Industrial Revolution started in Germany rather late. The economic union of the Zollverein in 1819 had aided industrialization. Political unification proved a real spur. The victory over France brought with it not only the rich mines of Lorraine, but also a billion dollars in gold for capital.

The railroads of Germany were government owned and were wisely managed to promote industrial development. The government also constructed a system of canals for cheaper, although slower, transportation. Even without the iron of Lorraine, there were good natural resources. When the iron of Lorraine was added to the coal of the nearby Ruhr Valley, a tremendous steel industry grew up. In one way the late industrial development was an advantage: German industries could use the most improved machinery and best methods developed elsewhere. Also, German scientists produced even greater changes and improvements. German workmen received excellent training in industrial and technical schools.

Under Bismarck's leadership the government helped in many ways. Money and banking laws became uniform throughout the empire; postal and telegraph services were centralized. A high tariff policy was adopted to protect German industries from foreign competition. The government encouraged German industrialists to form huge trusts, called cartels, to do away with competition inside the country. It worked wonderfully for the industrialists, but the lack of competition brought a rise in prices which was not so beneficial to consumers. Very rapidly Germany became an industrial nation, exporting manufactured goods, importing food and raw materials. By 1900 it was threatening the positions of Britain and the United States as leading producers of steel and machinery. It was also rivaling them for leadership in world trade.

Agriculture did not disappear in Germany; quite the contrary. By using scientific methods and the fertilizers produced by the rapidly developing chemical industry, even the poor, sandy, shallow soil of the North German Plain became very productive.

Berlin became increasingly the center of the new empire—both the industrial center and the political capital. Connected with all parts of the country by rail and canal, Berlin became a tremendous industrial city with rapidly growing population. Germany was a power to be reckoned with, economically as well as militarily.

● Political problems

In spite of the close control of the aristocratic Prussians, the new imperial government soon ran into difficult political problems. Political parties which opposed Bismarck's policies were formed. Some wanted more liberal and democratic imperial government, with social reforms. Many feared Bismarck's military policy, with its ever-growing army and navy, and his foreign policy which so often threatened war. Often the Catholic deputies from the southern states, especially Bavaria, raised issues concerning the federal principles. They resented the interference of the imperial government in what they considered local and domestic affairs. They thought their own state government should deal with such affairs. Sometimes the Catholic deputies would join with the liberals and socialists. They did not especially agree with the ideas of the socialists

and liberals but they joined with them in order to get their support for policies of their own.

Bismarck came to feel that the Catholic Church was a threat to his beloved empire. The claim of the pope to administer German church property seemed like foreign interference in German domestic affairs. In 1872 diplomatic relations between the imperial government and the papacy were broken off. Strict measures were passed to control the Catholic clergy and Catholic schools. Clergymen who opposed these measures were imprisoned or banished.

This religious policy stirred up a hornet's nest of opposition. A Catholic Party was formed to oppose the religious acts and to work for other reforms. Many non-Catholic liberals also joined the opposition. Bismarck realized that he had made a mistake and was big enough to admit it. He re-established diplomatic relations with the papacy, and repealed all the laws against Catholics.

● Bismarck vs. the socialists

The rapid rise of socialism in Germany was a result of the progress of the Industrial Revolution. The swift industrialization followed the same pattern as in England. Cities increased greatly in population. An industrial working class appeared, detached from the soil, owning nothing but their labor. They had the same problems as in England: obtaining better housing, decent wages, shorter working hours, and providing security against accidents, sickness, old age, and the fear of unemployment. Many men felt that these were problems for government action, in the form of what is called social legislation. Socialists banded together to form the Social Democratic Party and championed the cause of the workers. As a result, the party grew rapidly, with its members coming mostly from the city workers. In 1875 they elected deputies to the Reichstag; within five years they increased their representation

The railroad terminal in Berlin, photographed about 1880. Berlin was the capital of the new German nation and was growing into one of the world's great industrial centers.

greatly. They strongly opposed many of Bismarck's policies, and they demanded more democracy and many social reforms.

Of course, representation in the Reichstag did not mean much. That body was powerless to pass the laws its members demanded if the upper, federal council, the Bundesrat, was opposed. And, since the Bundesrat represented the hereditary rulers, there was little chance that it would propose any "radical" laws or allow any to pass. The most the socialists could do was (when they had enough votes) delay or prevent passage of laws Bismarck wanted. Yet the Reichstag made a good public platform for the socialist members to air their grievances and complaints, and to make their promises of what they would do if they only had the power. Every gain in socialist voting strength, every demand for reform, alarmed the old chancellor.

Bismarck decided to use all his weapons to fight the socialists. Two attempts were made to assassinate the emperor. Although Bismarck knew that neither would-be assassin had any connection with socialism, he took advantage of the public excitement. He accused the Social Democrats of plotting the attempts. The emperor and the Bundesrat dissolved the Reichstag and called for new elections. There was a great propaganda campaign against socialism and socialists.

The election greatly reduced Social Democratic representation in the Reichstag. The chancellor now had a majority there, and was able to push through laws aimed at the socialists. It was made unlawful to spread socialist propaganda through newspapers, books, or pamphlets. Socialists were forbidden to hold public meetings.

● Social reforms in Germany

But the grievances of the workers were too real and their needs were too great to be wiped out by such restrictive laws. In spite of all the handicaps the socialists continued their fight successfully. In the ten years after the laws were passed, the Social Democratic representation in the Reichstag increased threefold. Again, as in the fight against the Catholic Church, the Iron Chancellor had to take stock of his tactics, and see how to achieve what he wanted. Repression had failed; he decided to try something else. He studied what it was that attracted people to socialism. He decided that the reforms which the socialists proposed were less dangerous than a powerful socialist political party, which might later make even more radical demands. If the government granted the social reforms, people would have less reason to join the socialists and the party would lose strength.

Bismarck called his new policy "stealing the socialists' thunder," or "killing socialism with kindness." He put through a program of social reforms as wise as it was far-seeing. First came insurance against sickness, then insurance against accidents. Other laws limited working hours and provided for certain holidays from work. The final step was an act which provided insurance against old age and inability to work. It was a pioneering program of government-directed social reforms. It did not stop socialism in Germany, but it did remove many of the workers' fears and grievances. German social legislation has since been copied in many other industrial nations.

Bismarck's foreign policies

We shall have to put off discussing the foreign relations of the German empire until you come to the period leading up to the First World War. However, you must understand Bismarck's basic foreign policies. Militarism continued to be glorified. Conscription (the draft) was adopted throughout the empire. The army constantly increased in size, and the most modern weapons and equipment were provided. Professional military men were given important places in the civil service as well as in the army. Imperial Germany continued to be a strong military power during and after Bismarck's era.

United Germany now wanted something which some other European nations had achieved several centuries earlier: a colonial empire. The disunited Germans had taken no part in the imperial race for colonies during the sixteenth, seventeenth, and eighteenth centuries. Now they found most of the desirable regions already occupied. Here was a possibility of future trouble.

Bismarck analyzed the European situation thus: France was a natural and permanent enemy; every attempt must be made to keep her isolated, without allies. Germany must always keep France and Russia separated so that in case of war Germany would not have to fight on two fronts. Bismarck made every attempt to keep up a long-standing friendship between the Hohenzollerns and the Romanovs of Russia. Austria he considered a natural ally; you will recall the lenient terms he gave the defeated Austrians in 1866. He promoted friendship between Hohenzollerns and Hapsburgs. Prussia had helped the Kingdom of Italy to gain Venetia in 1866. Bismarck strengthened this friendly relationship, so that Germany and Italy became allies. In 1882 Bismarck succeeded in forming the Triple Alliance of Germany, Austria, and Italy.

Emperor William II drops Bismarck

Bismarck's beloved Emperor William I died in 1888, and was shortly succeeded by William II. The young monarch and the old chancellor soon disagreed violently. William

One of the most famous political cartoons ever drawn, this is a British comment on Bismarck's retirement. This Punch *drawing of 1890 shows the young emperor, William II, watching the veteran statesman leave the post he had held since 1860.*

DROPPING THE PILOT.

427

II felt that Bismarck was too powerful. He insisted that cabinet ministers be more responsible to himself, the emperor. Bismarck felt that the young man was taking away powers which he had exercised wisely for many years. He feared that William was too rash and undisciplined to use power discreet-

ly. When Bismarck, thinking himself indispensable, offered his resignation, William II accepted it. Bismarck retired with a great feeling of bitterness. His fears of the rashness of Kaiser William II proved justified. A later chapter tells of the Kaiser's troubles after "dropping the pilot."

Review of Chapter 33

People, places, and things

Identify: Bismarck, von Roon, von Moltke, William I, William II, Zollverein, Reichstag, German Confederation, North German Confederation, Triple Alliance, cartels.

Locate: Prussia in 1789, Austria in 1789, the Grand Duchy of Warsaw in 1807, Silesia, Saxony, Westphalia, Schleswig, Holstein, Hanover, Cassel, Nassau, Bavaria, Baden, Württemberg, Hesse, Venetia, Alsace-Lorraine, Leipzig, Frankfurt.

Events in review

1. What effect did the defeat of Prussia by Napoleon Bonaparte have upon that country?
2. List (a) the forces opposing the unification of Germany and (b) the forces working toward unification.
3. Tell briefly how Bismarck drove Austria from her position of leadership in Germany.
4. How did Bismarck persuade the four southern states in Germany to accept Prussian leadership of Germany?
5. What was the Dual Monarchy? When and why was it established?
6. Briefly describe the terms of the treaty that ended the Franco-Prussian War.
7. What powers were held by the emperor of the new German Empire? by the Bundesrat, or federal council?
8. How was Prussia able to hold a dominant position in the German Empire?
9. Why did German industry develop rapidly after the unification of Germany?

10. Explain why Bismarck decided to put through a program of social reforms. What laws did his program include?
11. What were Bismarck's basic foreign policies?

Problems and projects

1. Historians have said that leaders appear at a time of crisis to direct and stimulate national feeling. Does the story of the rise of Prussia and the unification of Germany bear out this theory?
2. Make a chart of German unification. Show what each of the following contributed: (a) the conquest of Prussia by Napoleon Bonaparte (b) the Zollverein, (c) political and military leadership (d) gain of territory through three wars.
3. On a map of Europe show Prussia in 1860. Then add the territories acquired by Bismarck. Show when and from whom each piece of territory was won.
4. Compare the government of Britain as of 1867 with the government of France under the Second Empire and the government of the German Empire. Which nation or nations had universal manhood suffrage? Which had made the greatest progress toward democracy? In which was the legislative body really strong? Give details.
5. Do some reading about Napoleon III and Bismarck. Contrast the personalities and the policies of "Napoleon the Little" and "the Iron Chancellor."

Chapter 34

The Unification of Italy; Nationalism in Central Europe

DURING the revolutionary years of 1848–49, the Italians tried hard to form a united country, but they failed. This failure did not end the hopes of the Italian patriots. Many of them worked harder than ever to gain their dearly wanted goal. There was general agreement on the principal aim: a united Italy. There was much less agreement about how they should gain unity, and how the unified nation should be governed when it was established. There were three large groups, each with a plan.

Many Italians, including the Catholic clergy, wanted a federation of Italian states headed by the pope. This plan found little support among the liberals, especially after 1849 when the papal policy completely disapproved any form of liberalism. Many of the liberals were ardent democrats; they wanted a democratic, republican government for Italy.

A third large group of Italian patriots rejected both the republic and the papal federation. They wanted Italy to be a constitutional monarchy under the House of Savoy, rulers of Piedmont-Sardinia. King Charles Albert had been forced to abdicate after the defeat by Austria in 1849, but his son, Victor Emmanuel II, was a success as a constitutional monarch. Men of the third group wanted the Kingdom of Piedmont-Sardinia

to be extended throughout the entire peninsula, thus becoming the Kingdom of Italy.

Three great leaders unify Italy

● *Mazzini*

Most Italian patriots belonged to one or another of the three groups, and many of them made great sacrifices to reach the goal. But unified Italy was really the work of three great leaders. They agreed about the main aim, but they were unlike in almost every way. Possibly you would not think of a poet as a great revolutionary leader. Yet Giuseppe Mazzini was both. He devoted his entire life toward an ideal: a united Italy freed from all foreign rule and from kings. He wanted a republic, a nation in which rich and poor would have equal rights. Mazzini was slender, charming, and intense. His faith in his ideal was so great, and his eloquence so persuasive, that he made the idea of nationalism become almost a religion in Italy. Even Germany, Hungary, Bohemia, and South America were deeply influenced by him.

Mazzini spent much of his life from 1820 to 1860 either in prison or in exile. The Italy of that day was no place for such a firebrand. In Switzerland he organized exiled Italian patriots into a secret society called Young Italy. Patriots of other countries copied this

429

idea of a nationalistic secret society. It is no wonder that rulers in Austria and Germany, as well as Italy, considered Mazzini a dangerous enemy. When revolutions broke out in Europe in 1848, it was he who gave the signal for an uprising in Italy. His followers seized the cities of Rome and Venice and set up republics. But at that time they were not strong enough. Austrian troops reconquered Venice; French troops destroyed the republic of Rome. Mazzini fled to exile in London. In greatest poverty he continued to spread the twin faiths of nationalism and democratic republicanism.

● *Garibaldi*

The second leader was also a republican, but a very different kind of man. Giuseppe Garibaldi was born in Nice, and early became a sailor. He joined Mazzini's Young

> *Giuseppe Garibaldi, one of the three great patriot leaders in the unification of Italy.*

Italy, and at the age of twenty-five he was condemned to death for his work in the secret society. He escaped and went to South America, where he fought in the revolutionary struggles for independence. In 1848 he returned to Italy and played a great part in the establishment and defense of Mazzini's Roman republic. He and his followers adopted the red shirt as their symbol. With his red shirt and shaggy beard, Garibaldi looked like a desperate bandit, but he was really a very simple and kindly man. He told his followers that he could offer them "not pay, nor quarters, nor provisions; but hunger, thirst, forced marches, battle, and death." He himself refused to take anything more than the poorest private soldier had. The failure of the revolution of 1848 made him a fugitive again. After a time in exile he settled down quietly as a farmer on a small Italian island.

● *Cavour*

The third man was different still. Count Camillo di Cavour was an aristocrat, well educated and widely traveled. But he was a different kind of aristocrat. Cavour had learned to dislike the idea of absolute monarchy and to admire the English system of parliamentary government. He also admired the English ideas of business. Cavour's ambition was not only a united but also an industrialized Italy. At home in Piedmont he managed his family estates so well that they were among the most profitable in Italy. But Cavour wanted more than wealth; he was also a patriot. He entered politics and became a minister in Piedmont-Sardinia, serving both King Charles Albert and his son, Victor Emmanuel II.

Cavour's plan for Italy was different from that of Mazzini and Garibaldi. Both of them wanted a united, independent Italian republic. Cavour wanted to work through the Kingdom of Piedmont. If he could make it strong and liberal, nationalists in the other

Italian states could seize control by revolutions and then annex them to Piedmont. This was the plan that was tried during the revolutions of 1848–49. It failed then because Piedmont was not strong enough to defeat the Austrians. However, the kings of Piedmont had granted a constitution with a parliament whose elected representatives had a considerable voice in the government.

● Piedmont takes the lead

In 1852 Cavour became prime minister of Piedmont and began to put his ideas into practice. At home he reorganized and strengthened the army and started a program of economic development. He helped to establish factories and banks and to build railroads. He encouraged shipbuilding, and negotiated treaties with other countries to increase trade. He disliked the very strong influence of the Roman Catholic Church on the politi-

A modern view of the city of Naples, with Mt. Vesuvius in the background. Before the unification of Italy, Naples was in the Kingdom of the Two Sicilies. In 1860, Garibaldi drove out the king of the Two Sicilies. Garibaldi then met Victor Emmanuel II in Naples and handed over the conquered territory to him. Mt. Vesuvius has been a famous volcano since Roman times. The first eruption, in 79 A.D., buried the Roman city of Pompeii.

cal life of his country. Under the neat slogan, "a free church in a free state" he tried to reduce this influence. He did so by dissolving the Jesuit order, which was very powerful politically, and some of the monastic orders as well.

Some of Mazzini's followers had been convinced by the failure of 1848–49 that Cavour's plan offered the best chance to unite Italy; so they began to work with him. If he could make Piedmont strong enough to defeat Austria, they could plot the revolutions in the other Italian states. Of course, as an official of a government at peace with its neighbors, Cavour could not join openly in these plots. He did meet the conspirators secretly and took part in the planning.

The greatest obstacle to Italian unity was Austria's control of part of northern Italy. In order to increase Piedmont's prestige in Europe, and perhaps to gain help against Austria, Cavour joined Great Britain and France in the Crimean War. A small Piedmontese army was sent to fight there. At the peace conference he hoped to be able to raise the question of Austria's withdrawal from northern Italy. It did not turn out that way; therefore, he tried something else.

Louis Napoleon, Emperor of France, was still on his search for glory abroad. To him Cavour proposed an alliance of France and Piedmont against Austria. Napoleon was at first reluctant to take this step, fearing it would antagonize the pope and the French Catholics. However, with Austria driven out, there was a chance that France could dominate a weak confederation of Italian states. Cavour believed that, with Austria out, the other Italian states would join Piedmont and make it strong enough to take care of itself.

● Cavour's deal with Napoleon III

The gaudy emperor and the patriotic prime minister met secretly at Plombières in 1858, and a deal was made. In return for French help against Austria, Cavour promised to give France the duchies of Nice and Savoy. They lie between the two countries—Nice, along the Mediterranean coast: Savoy, to the north, controlling some of the approaches to the Alpine passes. He also agreed that he would not declare war on Austria. However, he would maneuver things so that Austria would declare war on Piedmont. Napoleon III agreed that if Austria did declare war,

France would send troops to help drive the Austrians out of Lombardy and Venetia. These could then join "a large Italian state."

Everything went according to plan. Cavour began a great program of military preparation in Piedmont. Convinced that such preparations could be directed only at Austria, the emperor of Austria became frantic and played directly into Cavour's hands. He sent a note to the government of Piedmont, flatly demanding that the military preparations be stopped. Cavour was delighted. He firmly rejected Austria's attempt to interfere in the affairs of Piedmont. Austria chose to enforce her demand: she declared war.

The war also went according to plan, at least to Cavour's plans. The combined Italian-French forces quickly drove the Austrians out of Lombardy and marched on into Venetia. Now the plotted revolts began to take place. Other north Italian states rebelled, overthrew their governments, and asked to be annexed to Piedmont. Throughout the entire peninsula there came a cry for a unified Italy.

This was more than the rash Napoleon III had planned for. He did not want a strong, united Italy, just as he did not want a united Germany. A unified Italy would include the Papal States. To take these from the pope would further antagonize the French Catholics, who had already warned him against helping Piedmont. If there were a long war with Austria, Napoleon feared that Prussia might help Austria for her own selfish ends.

● Napoleon III changes his mind

Without warning, Napoleon III broke his agreement. He met the Austrian emperor and signed an armistice without consulting his ally, Piedmont. According to its terms, Piedmont received Lombardy, but Austria kept Venetia. The other Italian states were to have their Hapsburg rulers restored, but they were to be allowed to form a federation under the pope.

It was a bitter pill for Cavour and the Italian nationalists. Napoleon III insisted on receiving his full price of Nice and Savoy, but would deliver only half of his side of the bargain. Cavour was so indignant that he resigned as prime minister and retired to his country estate. Victor Emmanuel II feared that he would lose his half victory if he continued the war; so he agreed to the terms.

● Nationalism gains strength in Italy

But a movement had been started which no armistice or peace treaty could stop. The Italian people refused to give up their aims. Popular feeling ran far ahead of governmental caution. Cavour returned to office to try to quiet the clamor. But other rebellions took place throughout northern and central Italy. The restored rulers were again driven out; popular temporary governments were set up. When elections were held, the votes were overwhelmingly in favor of joining Piedmont and of Italian unity.

Napoleon III was completely opposed to any such arrangement. For a time there was a chance of war between France and Piedmont; then Cavour arranged another deal. France was to keep Nice and Savoy. In return, Piedmont was to be allowed to annex the duchies of Parma, Modena, and Tuscany, and the papal province of Romagna. At the treaty signed at Turin in 1860, both sides agreed.

It was a harsh blow to Italians. Nice and Savoy had long been Italian provinces. They had been held by the French for only a short time under Napoleon Bonaparte. The king of Piedmont was from Savoy; his family was called the House of Savoy. Garibaldi, born in Nice, cried out against the deal, saying it made him a foreigner in his own country. But Victor Emmanuel II made the decision. By giving up Nice and Savoy, Piedmont took a long step toward Italian unity.

Now the aroused force of Italian nationalism moved from the north to the south. Here

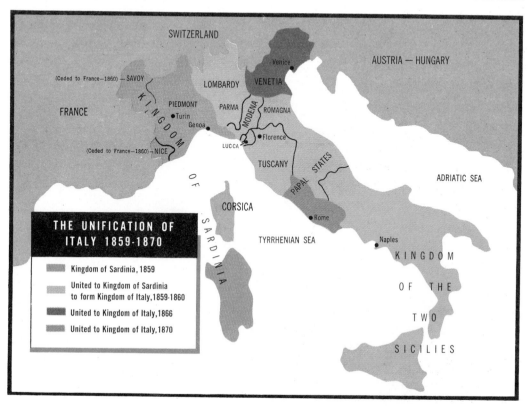

THE UNIFICATION OF
ITALY 1859-1870

Kingdom of Sardinia, 1859

United to Kingdom of Sardinia
to form Kingdom of Italy, 1859-1860

United to Kingdom of Italy, 1866

United to Kingdom of Italy, 1870

lay the Kingdom of the Two Sicilies, under a government which was probably the most harsh and oppressive in the entire peninsula. Garibaldi now came out of his retirement. With Cavour's approval he began to gather his legion of redshirts at Genoa. When his force numbered a thousand men, he sailed for the island of Sicily. A host of enthusiastic people welcomed his arrival and joined his army. Within a short time he held the entire island. Crossing to the mainland, he seized Naples and drove the king of the Two Sicilies north to the border of the Papal States. From there Garibaldi planned to march to Rome. It was his intention to make the city of Rome and the Papal States part of Italy.

Fearful that Garibaldi might set up a republic instead of turning the territories over to Victor Emmanuel II, Cavour decided to send an army south. To reach Garibaldi the Piedmontese army crossed the Papal States.

Cavour acted with mixed boldness and caution. He annexed most of the Papal States to the rapidly growing Kingdom of Piedmont. However, he left the city of Rome, with a small territory around it, under the control of the pope.

The half-feared trouble between the king and Garibaldi did not arise. They met in Naples. Without hesitation Garibaldi turned over his conquered lands and his army to the king. Refusing all offers of honors and titles, taking only a little money and a bag of seed, Garibaldi returned to his farm.

● The new Kingdom of Italy

Elections were held everywhere in Italy except in Venetia and Rome. The people voted overwhelmingly for national unity under the House of Savoy. Representatives met in Turin in 1860 and elected Victor Emmanuel II king of Italy. The new kingdom included every part of Italy except Venetia,

NATIONALITIES—
AUSTRO-HUNGARIAN
EMPIRE—1866

RUSSIAN EMPIRE

GALICIA

GERMAN

MORAVIA

BOHEMIA

Vienna ●

● Budapest

HUNGARY

TRANSYLVANIA

RUMANIA

EMPIRE

AUSTRIA

CROATIA-SLAVONIA

SERBIA

TYROL

BOSNIA

DALMATIA

ITALY

Adriatic Sea

Germans
Slavs
Magyars
Rumanians
Italians

still under Austria, and Rome, still ruled by the pope.

European governments were now faced with what the French call a *fait accompli*—an accomplished deed. They had only two choices: to recognize the new state or to fight it. Most embarrassed of all was Napoleon III. Unwittingly he had helped to bring about a development which he did not want at all. As he had done so often in the past, he wavered. He decided against helping Austria; however, he did send French army units to Rome to prevent the Italians from taking over that city.

The unification of Italy was not complete in 1860, but the end was in sight. Cavour, the great architect of unity, died, but there were other leaders to finish the task. By allying herself with Prussia against Austria in 1866, Italy was able to take Venetia. French troops in Rome still prevented the seizure of the city. However, when the Franco-Prussian War broke out in 1870, Napoleon III had to recall his troops. The Italians entered the city, and in 1871 Rome was proclaimed the capital of the Kingdom of Italy.

The pope protested bitterly. He excommunicated the king and forbade Catholics to have anything to do with the Italian government. He shut himself up in his Vatican palace, saying that he would remain "the prisoner of the Vatican" until the Papal States were restored to him. For many years the problem of the relations between the Church and the government in Italy was a very difficult one.

After nearly 1500 years of division and struggle, Italian unity had been accomplished. Perhaps the strangest thing in the whole story is the part played by Napoleon III, Emperor of France. Misjudging completely the driving force of Italian nationalism, he helped to start the movement toward victory. Then he turned against it and made futile efforts to prevent it. You can understand why his wavering and fitful policy gained him the enmity of so many groups in both France and Italy.

Nationalism in central Europe— the Austro-Hungarian Empire

In 1848–1849 the twin forces of nationalism and democracy forced Prince Metternich to flee for his life from the Austrian Empire. However, the revolutions of 1848–49 failed. Little gain was made for either democracy or the nationalistic hopes of Hungarians, Slavs, and Italians. After her defeat by Prussia in 1866, Austria tried to prevent other nationalistic outbreaks by forming the Dual Monarchy, under which the Hungarians had some self-government.

The Dual Monarchy had plenty of problems. The other national minorities—the Czechs of Bohemia, the Serbs, Croats, Rumanians, Poles, and Italians—received no such favors as Hungary received. They remained discontented, hoping and working for independence and self-rule. Economic differences between Austria and Hungary created troubles, too. Austria was beginning to develop manufacturing industries, but Hungary remained almost entirely agricultural. Hungary was therefore in favor of low tariffs and freer trade, while the industrialists of Austria wanted high protective tariffs. There were also problems in the common army over command and language. The Austrians spoke German; the Hungarians spoke their native Magyar language.

The Dual Monarchy had elements of strength, too. It lasted over fifty years and presented to the outside world an impressive imperial sight. The most powerful force to hold it together was economic. The various parts of the empire fitted together. Some were agricultural, furnishing raw materials and food; others were industrial, producing manufactured products. Each furnished a good home market for the other. With all its political problems of clashing nationalities, the Dual Monarchy made sense from an economic viewpoint. It knitted all central Europe into one economic unit. Someone has said that if the Dual Monarchy had not existed, someone would have had to invent it.

The Ottoman Empire and the Balkans

Further south, in the Balkans, nationalist and political feelings were also strong. This region was known as the "powder keg" of Europe. Much of the Balkan peninsula was still ruled by the empire of the Ottoman Turks. "Misruled" might be a better term. The government of the Ottoman Empire was harsh, tyrannical, inefficient, and unbelievably corrupt. There were religious differences. The Turks were Moslems, while most of the native population in the European part of the empire were Christians, either Roman or Greek Orthodox Catholics. Political misrule and religious oppression

A church of the Greek Orthodox faith, in the Balkans. Many people in the Balkans and Russia belong to this branch of the Christian faith.

caused resentment that often led to outbreaks of rebellion.

● *Russia vs. Turkey*

The Ottoman Empire often seemed near collapse, but outside forces held it together. Turkey had become a football of international power politics. For several reasons Russia supported the national groups in the empire that were trying to gain freedom. The Russians were Slavs; so were the Bulgarians, Serbians, and Bosnians, who wanted independence from Turkey. The Russians worshipped in the Greek Orthodox faith; so did many of the discontented Balkan groups. Finally, and most important, if Turkey collapsed, Russia could gain control of the water route from the Black Sea to the Mediterranean. (The Bosporus strait leads from the Black Sea to the Sea of Marmora. The Dardanelles strait leads to the Aegean.) Control of this route had been a goal of Russian foreign policy since medieval times. Russia, with free access to the Mediterranean, would no longer be landlocked.

This Russian drive toward the Mediterranean brought in other European powers to try to hold the crumbling Turkish Empire together. Great Britain did not want the Russians in the Mediterranean where they might challenge her sea power. The British did not want to fight a war to take and hold Constantinople; so they tried to prop up the feeble Turks. It made a strange picture: the autocratic Russian government championed the cause of freedom and independence of the Balkan peoples. Britain, the most democratic government in western Europe, supported the oppressive Turks in preventing that freedom. Truly, "politics makes strange bedfellows."

All these international political maneuvers and nationalist desires finally caused war between Russia and Turkey in 1877–78. The Turks were defeated and forced to sign a treaty giving independence to several of the

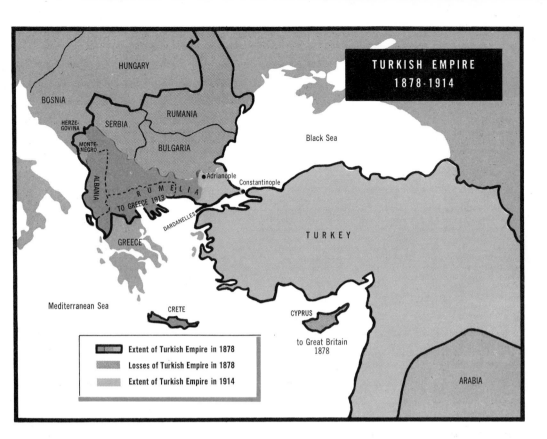

TURKISH EMPIRE
1878-1914

HUNGARY

BOSNIA

HERZE-
GOVINA   SERBIA

RUMANIA

MONTE-
NEGRO

BULGARIA

Black Sea

ALBANIA

R U M E L I A

TO GREECE 1913

• Adrianople
Constantinople

DARDANELLES

T U R K E Y

GREECE

Mediterranean Sea   CRETE

CYPRUS

to Great Britain
1878

ARABIA

Extent of Turkish Empire in 1878

Losses of Turkish Empire in 1878

Extent of Turkish Empire in 1914

Balkan groups. Before the treaty could go into effect, the European powers, led by Austria and Great Britain, forced the Russians to consent to an international conference to rewrite the treaty. The congress met in Berlin in 1878, with Bismarck acting as "honest broker." It approved the following terms: Serbia, Montenegro, and Rumania became completely independent. Bulgaria was given self-government, but it was still a part of the Turkish Empire. She received much less territory than the Russo-Turkish treaty had given her. Great Britain was given the right to occupy and administer the island of Cyprus, long held by Turkey. Though the Turkish sultan still officially ruled the island, Britain actually took it over. Having this island as a naval base increased Britain's power in the eastern Mediterranean. Austria was given the right to govern two former Turkish provinces in the Balkans, Bosnia and Herzegovina, but she was not allowed to

annex them. Newly independent Serbia did not like to have Austria ruling Bosnia, for Bosnia lay between her and the sea. There was some chance of Serbia's gaining the territory from the failing Turks, but much less chance of her getting it from Austria.

No amount of "propping up" could save the failing Ottoman Empire. In 1882 the British occupied Egypt, formerly a Turkish dependency. Several years later the Bulgarians who had been left under Turkish rule rebelled and joined the self-governing part of Bulgaria. After a long and bitter rebellion in Crete, the European powers forced Turkey to grant that island self-government. In 1908 Bulgaria became completely independent. In that same year Austria broke the agreement of the Congress of Berlin by annexing Bosnia and Herzegovina outright.

By 1914, when World War I broke out, Turkish territories in Europe had shrunk to a very small but very important holding. It still included two things of immense strategic value: Constantinople and the straits.

Revolution stirs in Russia

Russia was one great European power where the democratic movement had made very little progress. The czar ruled the sprawling Russian empire with unlimited power, but political developments in western Europe were bound to have some effect on Russia. Western influence had been strong in Russia since the time of Peter the Great. Improved transportation and communication made it stronger still.

Russia was by no means a nation like England or France. The huge empire took in a great variety of peoples and national groups. Some were akin to each other racially and religiously. A majority of the whole population belonged to three interrelated groups: the Great Russians, living in the central and northern parts; the Ukrainians (sometimes called the Little Russians), living in the southern part; and the White Russians, living in the western part. They all belonged to the Greek Orthodox Church. Scattered throughout the empire there were smaller racial, national, and religious groups speaking many languages.

So the Romanovs, czars of Russia, were faced with problems of restless nationalities and of democratic tendencies from the West. They met these problems with very harsh measures. There was a very strict censorship of speech and press, enforced by secret police, the army, and by officials with unlimited powers. The domestic program of the czars aimed to keep their autocratic powers. They did this by suppressing all demands for a constitution and a lawmaking body. They made the Greek Orthodox Church an official state religion, with the czar as head. They also began a program of "Russification." This meant that the non-Russian subject peoples —Poles, Jews, even the Finns, who enjoyed a special position, and the Asian peoples— were compelled to use the Russian language, accept the Greek Orthodox religion, and follow Russian customs and culture.

The foreign policy of the Romanovs was twofold. The program of expansion eastward into Asia and southward into the Turkish Empire was pushed steadily. In the Balkans, they backed what was called Pan-Slavism— the union of all Slavic peoples under Russian leadership. Probably the greatest single aim of their foreign program was to gain control of Constantinople and the straits leading out of the Black Sea and giving access to the Mediterranean.

● Emancipation of the serfs, 1861

Serfdom had come late to Russia. It had begun to disappear in western Europe before it became firmly established in Russia. By the mid-nineteenth century it was very firmly fixed. Millions of peasants were "bound to the land." They could not leave unless ordered by government officials or permitted by their landlords. The land they worked belonged to the landlord. To pay for the use of part of his lands, the serfs worked for the landlord about three days a week. Sometimes they paid a rent "in kind," that is, in grain, flour, or other produce. The lord enjoyed every privilege at the cost of the masses.

For several hundred years these conditions had led to scattered rebellions and uprisings among the peasants. They wanted the right to move about freely, to seek employment wherever they could find it, and even to own the land on which they worked. The government was usually able to suppress these revolts without difficulty, and it acted with great cruelty.

Toward the middle of the nineteenth century the peasants began to receive some support from a new class of people in Russia: the middle-class industrialists. As industries came to be established, the capitalist factory owners began to urge that the serfs be freed. They were not liberals nor humanitarians; they needed workers in their factories. So long as the serfs were bound to the land, they could not move into the cities to be factory workers.

The defeat in the Crimean War in 1856 was a blow to the Russian government. Furthermore, discontent among the peasants was increasing. Finally, the old order had to give way to the ideas of the new age. Czar Alexander II decided to end the centuries-old bondage by freeing the serfs. First he freed those on the vast estates of the royal family. Then, in 1861, he issued his famous Emancipation Proclamation. By its terms the government bought sections of the lands owned by the nobles and then sold small tracts of farmland to the peasants.

Emancipation of the serfs did not really improve their conditions very much. Indeed, the situation of the peasants seemed to prove the arguments of the moderate liberals that reforms must go much further. The government bought land from the nobles at high prices. This land was sold to the peasants in small strips at high prices. The peasant did not receive enough land to allow him to earn the payments on the land, pay the taxes, and still live. Therefore, he had to rent additional land from the noble landlord. Rents were very high. In some ways the peasants were worse off after emancipation than before.

● *Other reforms*

The czar carried out a number of liberal reforms. The courts were reformed, new courts were set up, and trials were held in

> *Tolstoy, a famous Russian author and liberal thinker. He freed the serfs on his own lands before the emancipation act of 1861. Though he was a member of the nobility, he spent years working in the fields. Note the crude plow and harrow he is using. He is widely known for two great novels,* War and Peace *and* Anna Karenina.

public, with juries. The army, the schools, and many other institutions and agencies were also changed. Probably the most far-reaching reforms were made in local government in thirty-four provinces. Local governing bodies were elected directly by the nobility and indirectly by the peasants. They were given control over public health, education, social welfare, and some public works in the communities. These local governments were given the right to tax.

● *Assassination and reaction, 1881–1905*

Alexander II now had a considerable reputation as a liberal reformer. However, his policies were criticized from both directions.

Defeat for Russia in the war with Japan. This photograph shows Japanese troops taking over from Russian troops as the Russians surrendered their fortress at Port Arthur.

Liberals considered them as only modest first steps, and pointed out further needed reforms. Reactionaries bemoaned them, and tried to convince the czar that they endangered the position and privileges of the ruler and the nobles.

In 1863 the Poles revolted against Russian rule in an attempt to regain their independence. The revolt was crushed, but Alexander II was frightened. The liberal reforms were taken away or whittled down. Now a radical group of reformers appeared. They were called *Nihilists*, from the Latin word *nihil*, meaning nothing. They wanted nothing kept of the Old Régime unless it was analyzed and accepted. The czar's government took strong measures against nihilism, and the Nihilists turned to terrorism. In 1881 Alexander II was assassinated.

The assassination marked the end of liberal reforms and the beginning of an intensive campaign of reaction. Censorship, control of church and education, spies and informers, imprisonment and exile were used to stamp out radical nihilism and even moderate liberalism. Finns, Jews, Poles, and other national minorities were distrusted and oppressed under the slogan "One Czar, One Church, One Language."

The attempt to preserve the old order of things met with much opposition, open or underground. The development of industry produced a class of city workers who wanted the right to form unions and to strike. Middle-class industrialists wanted a voice in the government. Liberals and radicals were more than ever determined to gain reforms. The government's attempt to "sit on the lid" produced an explosive revolutionary situation.

● *The Revolution of 1905*

In 1904–1905 Russia fought a war with Japan in the Far East. To the surprise of the world, the Russians were badly defeated by the small, recently westernized Japanese nation. One thing was clear: The Russian defeat was the result of incredibly poor and inefficient government. This fact furnished a spark to all the discontented groups in the country. The result was an explosion—the Revolution of 1905. The Old Régime was forced to yield in order to survive.

In a special edict (The October Manifesto), Czar Nicholas II announced that he was granting a constitutional charter. It would set up a parliament (Duma) with limited powers. There was also a Bill of Rights, with limited guarantees of personal liberties. These grants calmed the turmoil. However, after the peace treaty with Japan, the czar's government was in better position to deal with its critics at home. Two Dumas were dismissed because they insisted on a written constitution which would make the czar's ministers responsible to the Duma. Then the qualifications for voting were changed so that only large landowners could vote. The result was a conservative Duma.

Under Nicholas II, Czar of all the Russias, the government remained just about what it had been—an absolute, autocratic monarchy. The reactionaries learned nothing from the revolution of 1905. The revolutionary leaders were hunted out, imprisoned, exiled, or executed. All the measures to keep down or wipe out the reform movement were used as before. The Old Régime held power until World War I.

Review of Chapter 34

People, places, and things

Identify: Mazzini, Garibaldi, Cavour, Charles Albert, Victor Emmanuel II, Alexander II, Nicholas II, Nihilists, the Duma.

Locate: Austria, Piedmont, Nice, Savoy, Lombardy, Venetia, Turin, Sicily, Kingdom of the Two Sicilies, the Papal States, Genoa, Naples, Serbia, Montenegro, Rumania, Bulgaria, Bosnia, Herzegovina, the Dardanelles, Constantinople, Cyprus, Crete.

Events in review

1. Italian patriots agreed on the aim of a unified Italy; they disagreed on methods of gaining unity. State the different plans held by three large groups of Italians.
2. Why did Cavour make a deal with Napoleon III? What did the French emperor hope to gain?
3. By 1860 unification of Italy was not complete but the end was in sight. Explain this statement.
4. What events in 1866 and 1871 completed the unification of Italy?
5. List the elements of strength and of weakness in the Dual Monarchy.

6. What was taken away from Turkey at the Congress of Berlin in 1878? What was left of the Turkish Empire in Europe by 1914?
7. What was the importance of Constantinople and the straits to Russia?
8. What reasons led Alexander II to emancipate the serfs? Did freedom improve their condition?
9. Which way did the liberal—reactionary pendulum swing in Russia after 1881? Why?

Problems and projects

1. What is meant by the saying that Mazzini was "the soul of Italian unification," Garibaldi "the sword," and Cavour "the brains"?
2. In what respect was Piedmont especially fitted to be the leading state in Italy? Compare the role of Piedmont in Italy with the role of Prussia in Germany.
3. Compare the diplomacy of Cavour with that of Bismarck in dealing with Austria and France.
4. Make a report on places discussed in this chapter that are still "of strategic importance" and turn up in the news (Cyprus and Turkey, for example).

Chapter **35** # Developments in the Fields of Science, Population, and Education

THE PERIOD of the Middle Ages is sometimes called the Age of Religion. The nineteenth and twentieth centuries are often referred to as the Age of Science. This new age did not spring to life suddenly, all at once. Human knowledge, like human history, changes slowly and gradually. Discoveries, inventions, and ideas which seem new and startling in themselves are usually built upon the painstaking work of men who went before. This is especially true of science.

The word science is used in two ways: science, meaning a body of knowledge; and science, meaning a method of gaining that knowledge. You have already read how Greek and Arab thinkers of ancient times contributed to scientific knowledge. The scientific method developed during the Renaissance. (You may want to review page 236.)

Scientists speak of two kinds of science: There is *pure science,* which attempts to gain knowledge for the sake of knowing. Pure science tries to learn the laws which govern the operations of man and the universe— the laws which regulate all natural things. The pure scientist is not interested in whether the laws he learns have any practical use; he just wants to know "what makes things tick." *Applied science,* on the other hand, is

interested in using knowledge to solve practical problems—to make life easier and better, to help man control nature and his environment.

Science makes great advances

The advances in both pure and applied science within the last 100 years make a startling story. Almost every field of human life or activity has been changed by science. The food we eat, the clothes we wear, the new things we buy to make life easier or pleasanter, the methods of travel, transportation, and communication we use, the schools we attend to fit us for the changing world in which we live—all these carry a deep imprint of scientific developments. Our religious faith, our ways of thinking about government, social groups, the family, or the place of the individual in the world, have all been affected. Science and scientific research have invaded not only schools, from high school to university, but also business, industry, and government itself. Our story here can tell only the highlights.

● *New views of the universe*

You have already read how the work of Copernicus, Galileo, Kepler, and Newton led

442

to a new conception of the universe (pages 237–239 and 294). Later astronomers, chemists, and physicists have worked out ways of discovering what sort of matter makes up the universe and of measuring the speed at which it travels.

Within our own century Albert Einstein, the great German-Jewish physicist who came to the United States to escape persecution in Germany, developed still another theory concerning the universe: the theory of relativity. Formerly, men had thought of all matter as having only three dimensions: *length, breadth,* and *thickness.* Not so of the universe, said Einstein; there is a fourth dimension, *time.* According to Einstein's theory, time, space, and motion are not absolute things. They are relative. They depend on one another, so that a change in one brings changes in the others. Einstein worked out complicated mathematical formulas to explain his idea of relativity and how it governs the operations of the universe.

Biology and the "life sciences"

Astronomers, physicists, mathematicians, and geologists built a wider knowledge of the earth and its place in the universe. Biologists undertook the study of life itself. They studied both plants and animals to try to understand how living things live—the process of life itself. Their study convinced them that all living organisms, both plant and animal, have certain common needs and certain body processes.

Here again, the seventeenth and eighteenth centuries prepared the way for progress in the nineteenth century. A seventeenth-century scientist had built a better microscope. While he was observing a drop of water through it, he was amazed to see a host of tiny creatures whose existence had never been suspected. Since they moved, ate food, and reproduced themselves, he concluded that they were living. An eighteenth-century Swede had carefully classified plants to make botany an orderly study. A Frenchman had founded zoology by doing the same thing for animals. The working out of the *cell theory*—that all living things are made up of cells, which contain protoplasm, the basis of life itself—made the modern science of biology possible. The discovery of the useful and harmful properties of bacteria was important in several fields of science.

● *Darwin's theory of evolution*

The nineteenth century brought forth a new theory of how life developed—how the various plants and animals had come to be

> Albert Einstein. His theory of relativity is considered one of the greatest intellectual achievements in the history of scientific thought. The announcement of his famous equation $E = mc^2$ might be called the starting point of our atomic age (see page 446 and the illustration on 445).

as they now are. Since Greek times men had been observing the likenesses and differences between living plants and animals and the fossils found in rocks. Many men came to believe that every species—every kind of living thing—had developed gradually from earlier forms. Since this was a belief in evolving, or growing out of, it was called the *theory of evolution.*

The man who gave the idea of evolution a new force was Charles Darwin. From his early youth Darwin was interested in collecting and studying birds, flowers, insects, and rocks. When he had finished his university work, he went on a trip around the world on a government surveying ship, collecting specimens of living things on sea and land and gathering fossils everywhere.

Darwin's study of fossils and living organisms convinced him that the theory of evolution was true. Also, it gave him an idea of how the changes had taken place—how the present species had evolved or developed from the different forms found in the fossils. He published his conclusions in 1859 in a book that had a long, impressive title: *On the Origin of Species by Means of Natural Selection, or the Preservation of Favored Races in the Struggle for Life.*

● *Natural selection*

All species—all kinds of living things—both plants and animals, wrote Darwin, have to struggle to gain the food and other things necessary to maintain life. Some individuals in each species are born slightly different from the rest. For example, some horses can run faster, some giraffes have longer necks, some plants are more resistant to disease. These favored individuals have a better chance to survive than the others. Therefore they are the ones that live and pass on their favorable characteristics to their descendants. Those who are best fitted to adjust themselves to their environment (their surroundings) will survive; the weaker will perish.

Thus in nature there is a kind of natural selection going on all the time. This is the process of "natural selection," or the "survival of the fittest."

Darwin later applied the theory of natural selection to man himself. Many parts of the human body are enough like those of lower animals to suggest that evolution has taken place in man, too. Studying the many likenesses between the ape and man, Darwin came to the conclusion that both had developed, or evolved, from some common ancestor. Since the common ancestor was undiscovered, it came to be called, popularly, "the missing link."

You can easily imagine what a tremendous stir the publication of Darwin's book created. To religious people, evolution by natural selection seemed a complete denial of the story of creation in the Bible. Darwin was attacked as an atheist and an advocate of the Devil himself. Not even all the scientists agreed with Darwin. Almost all agreed with the theory of evolution itself. But many doubted that natural selection was the only way, or even the most important way, by which new species evolved.

The physical sciences

The physical sciences of chemistry and physics had their foundations in the eighteenth century. For example, an Englishman, Joseph Priestley, discovered oxygen. Another Englishman, Henry Cavendish, proved that water is a compound of two gases, hydrogen and oxygen.

Modern ideas of the nature of matter and the true foundation of both chemistry and physics stem from the work of an early nineteenth century Englishman, John Dalton. He stated that all kinds of matter are made of atoms. These atoms, he said, are themselves unchangeable and indivisible. Dalton said that there are different kinds of atoms. Each kind is a chemical element. Each atom

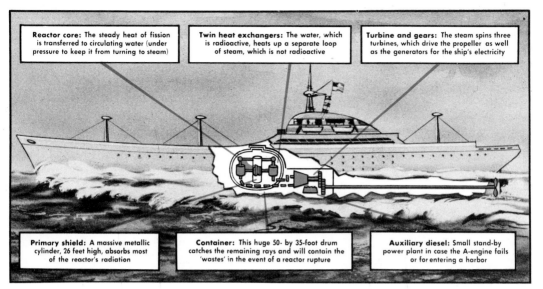

Reactor core: The steady heat of fission is transferred to circulating water (under pressure to keep it from turning to steam)

Twin heat exchangers: The water, which is radioactive, heats up a separate loop of steam, which is not radioactive

Turbine and gears: The steam spins three turbines, which drive the propeller as well as the generators for the ship's electricity

Primary shield: A massive metallic cylinder, 26 feet high, absorbs most of the reactor's radiation

Container: This huge 50- by 35-foot drum catches the remaining rays and will contain the 'wastes' in the event of a reactor rupture

Auxiliary diesel: Small stand-by power plant in case the A-engine fails or for entering a harbor

has its own weight; thus the different atoms can be distinguished one from another. Atoms unite one with another in fixed, measurable proportions to make compounds. Two atoms of hydrogen united to one atom of oxygen form a molecule of water.

● *The study of electricity*

The widespread use of electric power was made possible by a discovery of the Englishman Michael Faraday during the 1830's. He did experiments with a horseshoe magnet and a copper disk. When the disk was placed between the arms of the magnet and rotated, it built up an electric current. Faraday had discovered the principle of the electric generator, or dynamo. (The word dynamo comes from the Greek word for power.) Other scientists built large and usable dynamos. These dynamos could be run by steam power or the power of falling water. Thus the energy of heat and the energy of falling water could be changed into electrical energy. This new kind of energy played a great role in the Second Industrial Revolution (see Chapter 36).

Men could now generate electricity, but they still did not know what it was or where it came from. Many tried to answer the questions, without full success. Finally, in

An application of scientific discoveries to practical problems. This drawing shows how atomic energy could be used to generate steam to drive the turbines of a passenger liner.

1895, a German scientist, Wilhelm Konrad Roentgen, started a completely new path of investigation. Roentgen discovered that when he sent an electric current through certain gases, he produced radiations which would penetrate solid matter. He did not know what the radiations were, so he called them X rays, since X in algebra represents an unknown quantity. Soon afterwards the Frenchman Pierre Curie and his Polish wife, Marie, isolated the element radium. They found that this element produced exactly the same sort of radiations.

Other scientists excitedly took up the search. They proved that both Roentgen's X rays and the radiations from radium were made up of particles of electricity. These particles, or electrons, are part of every atom. Atoms are not indivisible, as Dalton thought; atoms are made up of at least three particles; protons, electrons, neutrons. Protons and neutrons form a nucleus, or heart; electrons whirl around the nucleus at tremendous speed. Some atoms, like radium, are in a constant process of breaking up. As they

445

break up, the atoms throw off particles of electricity.

● *Einstein—$E = mc^2$*

Albert Einstein first stated that this breaking-up process meant that the mass (the substance) of the atom was being changed into energy. He also stated that the process could be reversed: Energy could be converted into mass. All matter, he said, is composed of atoms; the nucleus of an atom is a tremendous amount of energy. To determine the amount of energy, Einstein developed a formula, or equation. The equation looks simple, but is probably the most revolutionary statement a man has ever made: $E = mc^2$. Energy (E) equals the mass (m) multiplied by the speed of light squared. When you know that the speed of light is 186,000 miles a second, you will begin to realize how vast an amount of energy is stored in such a small particle. When even a small mass is multiplied by 186,000 squared (34½ billions), the result is going to be huge.

The whole story of the development of atomic energy illustrates two things which have already been mentioned. The first is this: The discovery of one man is built on the work of those who went before him, and becomes, in turn, the basis of the work of those who come after. The second is that science is truly international in character. Here are the names and countries of only a few of the many scientists who have contributed to the knowledge of the energy locked in the atom and how to release it: Dalton, England; Mendeleev, Russia; Roentgen, Germany; Pierre Curie, France; Marie Curie, Poland; Thompson, Mosely, and Rutherford, England; Bohr, Denmark; Einstein, Germany; Lawrence and Oppenheimer, United States of America; Hahn, Strassman, Meitner, Germany; Fermi, Italy.

Edward Jenner, discoverer of vaccination. He is shown here vaccinating a baby from the arm of a girl who had cowpox.

From their combined research came the first "practical" use of atomic energy—the dreadful atomic bomb.

Medical science preserves and lengthens life

It is difficult to say what field of science benefited mankind most. But surely the tremendous advance in medical science has most closely touched the life of each of us. It has saved life itself and has made better health and longer life possible. Again you will be interested in noticing how science is interrelated—how almost every field of science has contributed to the development of one field.

● *Jenner—vaccination*

Using the scientific method, Edward Jenner brought great good to humanity. In his day smallpox was one of the most feared diseases in the world. Dreadfully contagious, it swept through cities in terrible plagues; it respected neither rich nor poor, noble nor commoner. It was most common among children. In fact, it was so fatal that it was said that mothers did not count children until their children had smallpox and lived through it.

Jenner made a thorough investigation of smallpox in the hope of finding a way to prevent it. There seemed no sure cure once the disease started. He learned that milkmaids who had once had cowpox, a disease of cows similar to smallpox, did not get the dreaded killer even when there was an epidemic. Jenner experimented for almost fifteen years before he was ready to try his theory on human beings. Then he took pus from a cowpox sore, scratched the skin of a boy's arm, and put the pus on the scratch. The boy had a mild case of cowpox, but quickly recovered. Jenner then took the boy with him when he treated patients with smallpox; the boy did not contract the disease. Then he made his critical test: he scratched the boy's arm again and put pus from a smallpox sore on it. The boy remained healthy. So Jenner could announce to the world in 1796 that he had discovered a way to prevent the dreaded smallpox by inoculation, or vaccination.

● *Pasteur—germs as the cause of disease*

Jenner had discovered a method, but he did not know the scientific principle that made it work. That principle lay undiscovered until the day of Louis Pasteur. Pasteur was not a physician. He was a chemist who, with a microscope, made studies of bacteria. Scientists had believed that these bacteria, and even some other kinds of living things, came to life out of nothing. They called the process "spontaneous generation." Pasteur's experiments convinced him that bacteria and other microscopic living things were not "spontaneously created." They reproduced themselves like other living things. After a long campaign, Pasteur and other scientists convinced the scientific world that bacteria were carried from place to place in the air, on the hands or clothes, and in other ways.

Working on the theory that bacteria cause human illnesses, Pasteur discovered the bacteria that cause rabies, the disease carried by the bite of a "mad" dog. Pasteur now applied his knowledge of a principle to the method developed by Jenner. Jenner's vaccination had worked because cowpox is a mild form of smallpox. When the milder germ enters the body, the system builds up "antibodies" to fight and kill the disease germ. These "antibodies" remain, able to fight and kill the more deadly germs of smallpox.

Pasteur found a way of weakening the germs of rabies without killing them entirely. His theory was proved when he injected this vaccine into a boy who had been bitten by a rabid dog; the boy did not get rabies.

Thus the chemist, Pasteur, had made several great contributions to medical science: He showed that germs are not spontaneously created out of nothing. They reproduce themselves, as all living things do. They can be killed by heat and by other means. He developed the theory that germs can cause disease. He revealed the principle by which germs may be made to fight germs.

● Progress in medicine and surgery

Pasteur's work was the starting point of a great international fight against disease. The cause of and treatments for cholera, tuberculosis, yellow fever, and diphtheria were found. The use of anesthetics and properly sterile methods, as well as the discovery and use of the X ray, made surgery safe. The development of new medicines like the *sulfas* and the *antibiotics* helped in the fight against germs and viruses.

The great killers of a century ago: cholera, bubonic plague, yellow fever, diphtheria, scarlet fever, typhoid fever, and tuberculosis have been controlled. In some cases they have been almost wiped out. Today the most frequent causes of death are the diseases of middle and old age: heart disease and cancer.

● Life expectancy increases

The lengthening of the life span during the past 350 years has been astounding. In 1600 the average English boy at birth could expect to live only twenty years. By 1850 this *life expectancy* had increased to about thirty-five years in the United States and western Europe. Today in the United States a boy at birth can be expected to live sixty-six years; a girl, seventy-two years.

Population increases and cities grow

Since 1750 the population of the entire world has tripled. This great world-wide growth has taken place most rapidly in Europe and the United States. There seems to be a relation between industrialization and the increase of population. Just as the Industrial Revolution speeded up after 1870, so did the increase in population. From 1870 to 1900 England gained 10,000,000 people, Italy 6,000,000, Russia 30,000,000, and the United States nearly 38,000,000. These rapid increases did not come from an increasing birth rate; they came from the great improvements in medical science about which you have read.

● The shift to the cities

Along with the increase in population came a shift to the cities. This happened for several reasons. The growing industries were located in or near cities. There was the chance for employment, which was declining on the farms. Machinery and scientific methods made it possible for a smaller farm population to produce more food. Thus large cities could be fed. Furthermore, new methods of preserving and transporting food made it available where needed.

City life became typical of the age of industrialization. Where once a vast majority of people lived in rural areas and in very small villages, now more people lived in the cities than in the country. The United States offers striking figures in this respect. In 1790 there were only six cities of 8,000 or more population. They contained only a little over three per cent of the population. Today more than half of our population lives in towns and cities of 8,000 or more population. New York City, which had a population of 60,000 in 1800, has grown to around 8,000,000.

Graph showing how world population has grown in three centuries. The small inset graph shows the world total. The large colored bars in the main graph show the population by areas in 1956. The lines running across from the dates show the numbers in each area at each date.

GROWTH OF WORLD POPULATION

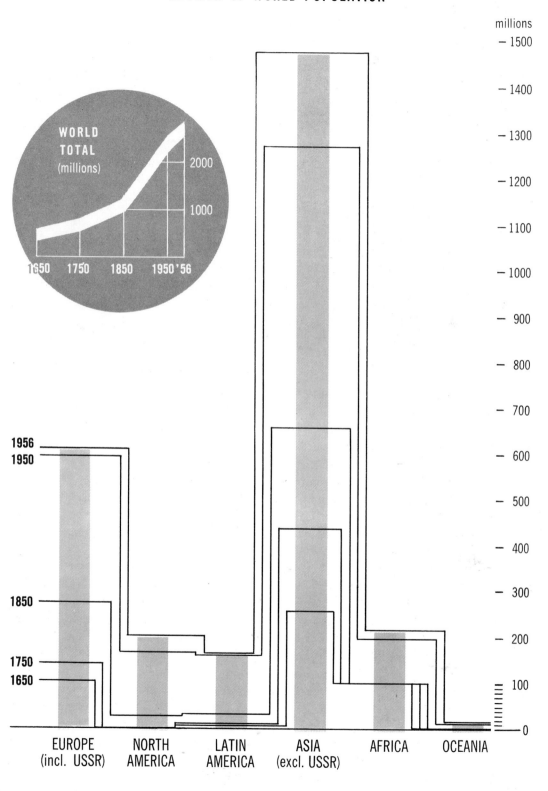

millions
- 1500
- 1400
- 1300
- 1200
- 1100
- 1000
- 900
- 800
- 700
- 600
- 500
- 400
- 300
- 200
- 100
- 0

WORLD
TOTAL
(millions)

2000

1000

1650 1750 1850 1950 '56

1956
1950

1850

1750

1650

EUROPE
(incl. USSR)   NORTH
AMERICA   LATIN
AMERICA   ASIA
(excl. USSR)   AFRICA   OCEANIA

City life created many problems, not only of food supply but of housing, health, sanitation, and recreation. The spaciousness, the fresh air, the beauty of the countryside, and its simpler life and environment were gone. The cities were places of congestion, cramped quarters, slums, less friendly neighborhoods. People "minded their own business"; one might live in an apartment house for a long time without knowing his neighbor. But there were some compensations: libraries, schools, many kinds of entertainment, playgrounds, and parks. City governments, forced by necessity and public opinion, began to improve living conditions: require better housing, pave streets, improve sanitation and water supply, provide utilities such as street lighting, gas, water, electricity, and garbage disposal.

● Emigration

Another feature of population growth was impressive. That was the movement of pop-

European immigrants arriving in the United States toward the end of the nineteenth century. The population of this country was swelled by people coming here from abroad.

ulations across national boundaries to foreign lands. Like so many other things, this movement also speeded up after 1870. The great movement was away from Europe to North and South America, Africa, and Australia. Europe was literally invading the other continents, peacefully. Between 1870 and 1900 more than 25,000,000 people left Europe for the United States; others went to South America, South Africa, and Australia. Such a mass migration (movement) of people has no equal in the history of the human race. Much of the emigration (movement away) came from countries where economic conditions were poor, like Ireland and Italy, or where there were minority groups who were oppressed, such as the Jews, Armenians, and Slavs.

Developments in education

Three great forces—nationalism, democracy, and industrialization—have influenced the history of the world since the eighteenth century. Each has played a part in the development of mass education—popular education supported by government and available to everyone.

The philosophers of the American and French Revolutions realized that democratic government requires that all citizens be educated. However, the growth of free public education was slow both in the United States and in Europe. Many people opposed the idea for several reasons: they feared that education would encourage revolutionary ideas; that it would make men less willing to do manual work; that it would be costly, and increase their taxes. In 1850 illiteracy—the inability to read and write—was widespread even in the industrialized nations. In Asia and Africa it was almost complete.

● *Public education increases*

After 1850 new forces produced more public education in the industrialized nations. Larger towns and cities made the establishment of schools easier and cheaper. As more people gained the right to vote, they voted for more education. Liberals, who had always favored better education for everyone, were now joined by other groups. Industrialists wanted literate workers as well as more engineers and skilled technicians. Military leaders wanted educated soldiers for mechanized armies. Nationalists wanted schools to develop patriotic citizens. After seizing control of Russia, the Communists made free education available to everyone.

Whatever the reasons, after 1870 governments in western Europe and the United States began to adopt laws making some form of education universal and compulsory. In some countries it was only elementary education; in others, public education

Schoolrooms of the early nineteenth century and of the middle of the twentieth century. Above: a New England classroom, restored to show how it looked about 1820. Free public elementary schools were established early in the history of New England. In many parts of the world, however, children received no schooling. In the present century, many nations give tax-supported education. The United States offers public education to all. Below is a model schoolroom constructed at the University of Michigan. Note the television set and the other features of this "classroom of tomorrow."

extended through the secondary, or high schools. In the United States the idea has been extended even further. Public, tax-supported education is now available to everyone from the kindergarten through the university. At the same time, better training has been provided for teachers.

In general, the amount and effectiveness of public education have followed, very closely, the degree of industrialization. Economic backwardness has seemed to hold back educational progress. But whatever the speed, the general picture is much more encouraging. Illiteracy has gradually been reduced, and, in some countries, almost eliminated. It has been a magnificent undertaking, carried out by a legion of teachers. These men and women, though often underpaid and working under conditions far from ideal, have faithfully rendered valuable service to their communities, their nations, and the world.

The spread of literacy has had many results. It promises to produce a more informed citizenry, and a higher level of moral and political behavior. A larger reading public has made possible the modern newspaper, the modern magazine, and the greatly increased publication of books. The quality of newspapers, magazines, and books has not always remained high. Perhaps, though, more and better education will result in higher standards among the reading public, and this, in turn, will raise the quality of reading matter.

Review of Chapter 35

People, places, and things

Identify: Charles Darwin, John Dalton, Michael Faraday, Wilhelm Roentgen, Pierre and Marie Curie, Albert Einstein, Edward Jenner, Louis Pasteur.

Events in review

1. What is the difference between *pure* science and *applied* science?
2. Was the Age of Science a sudden, new development in the nineteenth century? Explain.
3. Was the theory of evolution a new one in Darwin's time? What was Darwin's theory of natural selection?
4. Name contributions to our knowledge about electricity and radiation made by an Englishman, a Frenchman, and a German.
5. Name discoveries in medical science made by men from the following countries: France, England, Germany, the United States.
6. What has happened to life expectancy since 1600? What accounts for the change?
7. Briefly describe the increase in and shifts of population in the later part of the nineteenth century.

Problems and projects

1. The medieval period has been called the Age of Religion. The nineteenth and twentieth centuries have been called the Age of Science. Go back to the Renaissance and review the development of the scientific method. Try to show how scientific ideas were built up by many men in many countries.
2. Were the Greek philosophers primarily concerned with pure science or applied science? What about the scientist of the seventeenth to twentieth centuries? Give examples.
3. To discuss: In how many ways does science affect daily life in the twentieth century? How important is it that we have an understanding of scientific methods and laws? Can "average people" understand science?
4. Make a graph of population growth for one of the cities in your state. Can you show that the population grew more rapidly as industries became more important?
5. Make a report on the history of the public school in your town. Try to find out how many people lived in your town fifty or one hundred years ago, how many went to school, what they studied, and so on. Note changes from then until now.

Chapter *36*

The Second Industrial Revolution

THE FIRST Industrial Revolution brought a great increase in the production of goods and much more rapid methods of transportation and communication (see Chapters 30 and 31). The Industrial Revolution did not stop in 1870. In fact, after 1870 its progress became so rapid that the period from 1870 to the present is sometimes called the Second Industrial Revolution.

Transportation becomes more rapid and comfortable

During the First Industrial Revolution steam power for transportation produced both the railway locomotive and the steamship. Since then, sea travel has been speeded by the building of two great canals, the Suez and the Panama. In 1869 the Suez Canal made it possible (for the first time since early Egyptian days) for a ship to go from the Mediterranean to the Red Sea and thence to India and the Orient. Around South Africa the distance from Liverpool, England to Bombay, India, is 12,470 miles. By Suez it is 7,156 miles. In 1914 the narrow Isthmus of Panama joining North and South America was cut by the opening of the Panama Canal.

On land, also, new routes appeared. The first transcontinental railroad across the United States was completed in 1869. In 1905 Russia completed the Trans-Siberian Railroad. This spanned the entire Eurasian Continent from St. Petersburg (Leningrad) on the Gulf of Finland to Vladivostok on the Pacific. The completion of the Cape-to-Cairo Railroad, crossing Africa from south to north, had to wait until after the First World War. Britain's plan for such a road, running completely through British colonial territory, was blocked by Germany's possession of a colony in East Africa.

Almost continuous improvements have been made in the speed, comfort, and safety of both rail and sea transportation. Improvements in the steam engine made it possible to carry heavier loads even more speedily. Other means of transportation appeared. The bicycle came during the nineteenth century, as did the streetcar in the cities. After the electrical industry developed, the early horse-drawn cars were replaced by electrically driven trolley cars.

Perhaps the greatest development in transportation resulted from the invention of the internal-combustion engine in the 'nineties. An internal-combustion engine produces its power by an explosion of fuel—gasoline or Diesel oil—inside a cylinder. This explosion drives the piston. The internal-combustion engine has been truly revolutionary in what it has done for road, rail, air, and water travel.

Communication is improved

During the first seventy years of the nineteenth century came improvements in postal

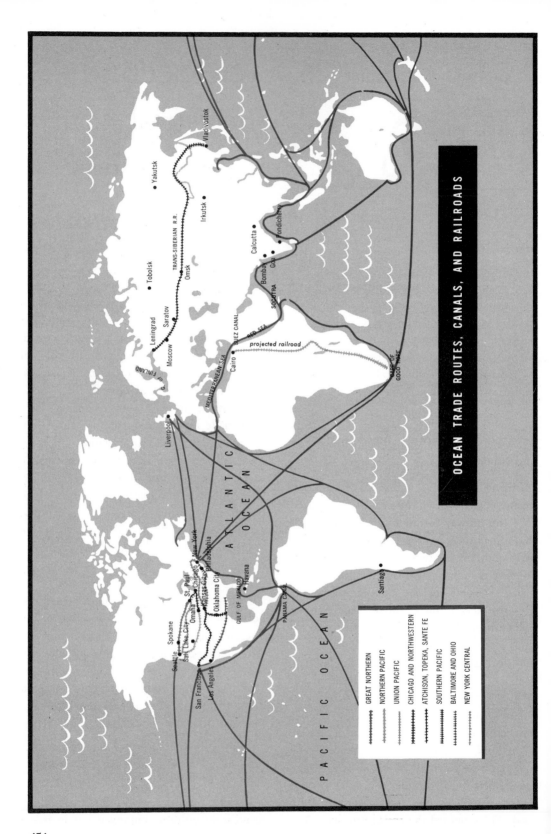

OCEAN TRADE ROUTES, CANALS, AND RAILROADS

GREAT NORTHERN
NORTHERN PACIFIC
UNION PACIFIC
CHICAGO AND NORTHWESTERN
ATCHISON, TOPEKA, SANTE FE
SOUTHERN PACIFIC
BALTIMORE AND OHIO
NEW YORK CENTRAL

Vladivostok
Yakutsk
Irkutsk
Tobolsk
Omsk
TRANS-SIBERIAN R.R.
Saratov
Leningrad
Moscow
G. OF FINLAND
Calcutta
Pondicherry
Bombay
Goa
SOCOTRA
SUEZ CANAL
RED SEA
Cairo
MEDITERRANEAN SEA
projected railroad
CAPE OF GOOD HOPE
Liverpool
ATLANTIC OCEAN
New York
St. Paul
Chicago
Philadelphia
Kansas City
Oklahoma City
Omaha
Havana
GULF OF MEXICO
Salt Lake City
Spokane
Seattle
San Francisco
Los Angeles
PANAMA CANAL
Santiago
PACIFIC OCEAN

454

service, the International Postal Union, and the invention of the telegraph and cable. Morse's electric telegraph provided rapid communication, but its use, either for sending or receiving the code messages, was only for specialists. Alexander Graham Bell, a Scotch emigrant to the United States, invented a form of electrical communication, the telephone, which anyone can use. Bell was a teacher, interested particularly in helping the deaf. While studying speech and hearing, he found that by using electrical magnetism he could vibrate a thin diaphragm of iron so that it sent out sound waves exactly like those of the human voice. Bell's telephone was first publicly displayed at the Philadelphia Centennial Exposition of 1876. Emperor Pedro II of Brazil, a visitor to the exposition, picked up the instrument and held it to his ear. Then he started back in amazement, crying: "It talks!"

● Radio

The telephone and telegraph both depend on the endless wires which span continents and sometimes lend ugliness to cities. Communication without wires was a discovery of the Italian Guglielmo Marconi. Marconi's wireless enabled ships at sea to communicate with stations on land and with other ships. However, the communication was by a series of dots and dashes—the Morse code. With further developments by Marconi, Lee De Forest, and others, it became possible to transmit the human voice and other sounds through the air. The radio industry was born. Commercial radio broadcasting began at station KDKA in Pittsburgh, Pennsylvania, in 1920.

● Other means of communication

Printing was another communications industry that developed spectacularly during the Second Industrial Revolution. The linotype, the rotary press, and cheap paper made faster and cheaper printing possible. With the addition of rapid communication by wire and radio, it became possible to produce great newspapers for the large city populations. The printing of books and magazines of all kinds also increased greatly.

The motion picture, a development chiefly of the twentieth century, also became a powerful force of communication. The successful addition of sound and color to the original black and white silent film made even more effective this means of communicating ideas.

Press, radio, television, and other means of communication have caused a shrinking of our world. We are in close contact with peoples we hardly knew of before. The world has become so much smaller because of more rapid transportation and communication that in a sense all peoples have become neighbors. Knowing these neighbors has become a necessity rather than a mere curiosity.

Science speeds the Second Industrial Revolution

Even more than the First, the Second Industrial Revolution is the product of applied science. In industry after industry—electrical, electronics, steel, chemical, agricultural, and all the industries that sprang up from the internal-combustion engine—you will see that the great outburst of productive energy after 1870 depended on the application of scientific knowledge and methods to the problems of production and transportation.

● Steel and other metals

The first Industrial Revolution made steel *the* basic industry—the one on which all others depend. Bessemer's process of steelmaking, first used in 1856, depended on the use of iron ore containing very little phosphorus. Where such deposits were available, as in the United States, great steel-making industries sprang up. Other countries were handicapped until scientists worked out processes to use lower-grade iron ores. Chemists

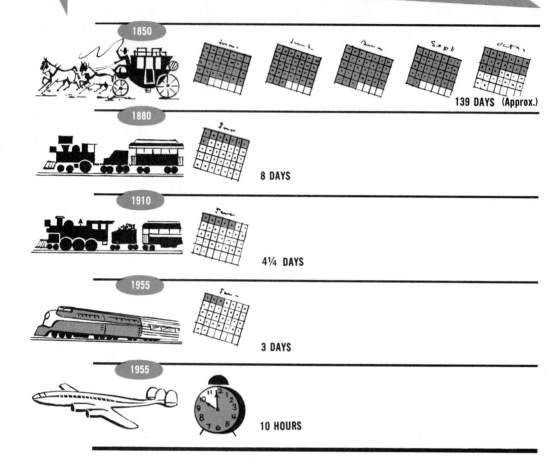

THE SPEED-UP IN TRANSPORTATION

SAN FRANCISCO   TIME NEEDED FOR A TRIP FROM NEW YORK TO SAN FRANCISCO   NEW YORK
(Regular travel, not record-making trips)

1850   139 DAYS (Approx.)

1880   8 DAYS

1910   4¼ DAYS

1955   3 DAYS

1955   10 HOURS

who specialized in metals—metallurgists—learned new ways to remove impurities from iron. They also learned how to add new metals to steel to give it added hardness, strength, or other desirable qualities. A similar development took place in the production of light metals such as aluminum, magnesium, and beryllium.

● *Modern uses of electricity*

The modern electrical industry is based on Faraday's invention of the dynamo in 1831. Faraday did not make his discovery practical, because he was more interested in basic re-

This chart demonstrates improvements in transportation by showing how travel time across the United States has been shortened since 1850.

search into the nature of electricity. The dynamo was only an interesting scientific toy for forty years; then a Belgian engineer produced a commercially successful generator.

Perhaps no man did more to make the use of electricity practical than an American, Thomas A. Edison. Edison was not a trained scientist. In fact, he had very little formal education, for he went to work at the age of twelve. But he did not stop his real education. He read everything he could, and was especially interested in scientific books, particularly on electricity. By chance he got hold of Faraday's book explaining the principle of the dynamo; he sat reading it all night. Faraday mentioned the possibility of producing light by electricity, and Edison took this as his particular problem. The difficulty was to find a material cheap enough to use, which would glow continuously when an electric current was passed through it and not burn out too soon. After experimenting with many materials, not discouraged by many failures, Edison got the desired result from carbonized cotton thread, or filament. It glowed continuously for more than forty hours. Better filaments have since been developed, of course.

To make electricity practical for city use there had to be a central power house where the energy of the steam engine could be changed by the dynamo into electricity. The electricity then had to be carried on wires to the place of use. Edison worked long and hard on the many problems connected with the central powerhouse and the transmission of electricity. In 1882 he achieved success. The streets of New York City were lighted with his lamps, with electricity provided from his powerhouse. The same year saw Edison plants completed in London, England, and Milan, Italy.

The first big generators were driven by steam engines, and a great deal of our electricity is still produced this way. But there is a less costly kind of energy for producing electricity—the energy of "white coal," that is, the energy of falling water. Much of our electric power is now produced at great dams such as those in the Tennessee valley, Bonneville and Grand Coulee on the Columbia River, and Hoover (Boulder) Dam on the Colorado River. Hydroelectric power—electricity produced by water power—has been a blessing to countries like Italy, Switzerland,

The picture above shows a model of the device which Michael Faraday, an English scientist, built to produce an electric current. The disk was rotated, by the hand crank, between the arms of the magnet. Faraday's discovery in 1831 prepared the way for the large-scale use of electricity. Until the principle of the dynamo was discovered, electric current was produced by batteries (page 381). Faraday was more interested in pure science (basic research) than in applied science. Later scientists and engineers, following his lead, developed generators capable of producing electric current in large quantities.

Below: generators in a modern hydro-electric plant in the United States. This powerhouse in a dam in Tennessee contains six generators with a capacity of 216,000 kilowatts.

the Scandinavian countries, and many others which have good rivers but little coal. In such countries, "white coal" makes large-scale industry possible.

You do not have to be told how important electrical energy has become in our modern life. All you have to do is think what happens in millions of homes when the power fails: no light, no heat, no refrigeration, no cooking, no washing of clothes, or mixing of foods by machine, no vacuum cleaning, no radio, no television; almost, one might say, "no anything."

● The chemical industry

Chemistry, too, has come out of the research scientist's laboratory to become a vast, many-sided, far-reaching industry which touches our daily lives at many points. The modern chemical industry, or chemistry in some form, helps to produce the food we eat, the clothes we wear, many of the articles we use, and even the homes we live in. As with electricity, the list of uses and products of chemistry would fill a book in itself. Let us look at only a few of the branches of the chemical industry, and see from them how important it is.

Before the invention of the internal-combustion engine, oil was refined chiefly to produce kerosene for lamps. However, the numerous uses of the internal-combustion engine have made the products of the oil industry—gasoline, Diesel fuel, and lubricating oil—necessities of modern life. There are, of course, many other products of oil and the oil industry.

The rubber industry also depends on chemistry, and also had to wait for the invention of the automobile to reach its present development. The large demands of the automobile industry for rubber made the supply of natural, or crude rubber very important. Chemists in the rubber manufacturing nations searched for a replacement of the crude rubber, which came from distant sources in Malaya and the East Indies. During World War II the Japanese conquered these regions. Inability to get natural rubber speeded the search for a substitute, and American chemists produced a synthetic (artificial) rubber made mostly from oil.

● Synthetics and by-products

No side of the chemical industry is more fascinating and exciting than the use of by-products, and the development of synthetics. A by-product is something produced in the process of making something else. The amazing story of coal tar is an example. As you know, the coke used in making steel was produced by heating coal to drive off the gases and certain impurities. The gases, of course, were a by-product. Eventually they came to be used for lighting and heating. Another by-product was a black, sticky substance called coal tar. It was a nuisance until the chemists began to experiment on it. What a treasure-chest they unlocked! They found so many derivatives—things derived from coal tar—that it would be hard to name them all. The dyestuff that gives your clothing its color is a coal-tar derivative. The perfume that makes you smell the way you want to is a coal-tar derivative. The naphthalene flakes that keep away the moths; the saccharin that sweetens your food, if you are reducing; the extracts that flavor your food; the aspirin that deadens your headache; the sulfa drugs that heal; the carbolic acid that will kill you if you drink it; and the TNT that will blow you up—all these are coal-tar derivatives. A similar development in chemistry has produced plastics, so extensively used in the modern world.

● Chemistry and farming

Agricultural chemistry has had an amazing development, too. The soil can be analyzed, the proper fertilizers produced and added, entirely by chemical processes. It is even possible to grow plants without soil at all; they can be grown in water to which the proper chemicals have been added. Great increases in food production have resulted from the use of farm machinery and the better methods of planting and harvesting crops and the care of animals learned by chemists, biologists, and other scientists. One example is enough to prove the case. In the United States from 1900 to 1950 total farm production increased by one third. Yet there was actually less land under cultivation in 1950 than in 1900. The increase came almost entirely from the application of the results of scientific research by the federal and state governments and in the many colleges and universities in the land.

● *The automobile industry and related industries*

A few moments of thought will show you that many industries sprang up around the internal-combustion engine. There are not only automobiles, trucks, buses, and air-planes. Farm and road machinery, construction equipment, locomotives, and ships are some of the other uses to which gasoline and Diesel engines are put. Probably the industries which produce the internal-combustion engine in all of its forms and uses have a greater amount of money invested, and employ more workmen, than any other industries in the industrialized nations. Add to these the subsidiary, or related, industries (such as garages, battery makers, tire makers) which depend for their existence on the first group, and you can see what a vast change has taken place in the economic life of nations in the comparatively short time since the 1880's, when the first one-cylinder putt-putting gasoline engine was developed.

The early days of mass production as applied to the automobile industry— the assembly line at the Ford Motor Company plant.

Businesses grow big

● *Mass production*

A workman operates most efficiently when he performs one rather simple operation over and over. Knowledge of this fact led Henry Ford to improve the technique of *mass production*. Mass production depends on three things: (1) division of labor, (2) interchangeable parts, and (3) assembly-line production. Through the use of mass production methods Ford was able to produce an automobile at a very low cost. Thus he transformed the automobile from a luxury to what it is today: a necessary means of transportation, owned and used by vast numbers of people.

> *Oil is one of the world's most important raw materials, and huge tankers are used to transport it. This ship, one of the Cities Service fleet, is 707 feet long and can carry 14,112,000 gallons of oil.*

Such production methods did not suit small companies. The small company could not afford to buy the machinery necessary nor hire the industrial engineers and other trained managers to plan its production. Nor could it employ scientists for research to improve the quality and cut the costs of its products. These things required great amounts of capital; only very large firms had the money. Large companies have other advantages in using mass production. They can make savings by buying raw materials in large quantities at lower prices. Sometimes they can own their own sources of raw materials—mines and forests, for example. And they can use the mass-production method: dividing up the operations of their labor to make it more efficient. All of these things are costly, but they produce the desired result. Each article of the finished product is produced at a lower cost than is possible for a smaller company.

● *Large corporations*

As the Second Industrial Revolution progressed, the size of corporations, in both capital invested and size of factory or factories, increased greatly. For example, in 1901 J. P. Morgan and his associates formed the United States Steel Company to buy out Andrew Carnegie. The new company had a capital of a billion dollars. (A billion, you should remember, is a thousand million.)

Increasing size did not solve all the problems of corporations. The large corporation could produce goods at a lower cost than a small one. However, to get lower costs it had to operate at full capacity, turning out as much goods as it was able to produce. There was then the problem of selling the goods. If a number of corporations were producing the same products, competition became very keen. If they tried to sell the products by cutting prices, the smaller and less efficient businesses suffered. Often they were forced to sell out to one of the larger firms.

As a result, although the size of individual corporations increased steadily, the number of individual corporations decreased just as steadily. The world had entered an era of "Big Business." For instance, in 1950 five per cent of all the manufacturing companies in the United States employed seventy per cent of all manufacturing workers and produced ninety per cent of all the manufactured goods. Even the giants found that competition was not the blessing which Adam Smith had proproclaimed—at least, not to the owners. Competition which reduced the selling price also reduced profits to the stockholders; so corporations tried to find ways to do away with competition. They found ways of getting together to form monopolies. (A monopoly has complete control of the production of an article or a service.) The advantage of a monopoly, to the owner, is that it can control production and fix the price. If the consumer does not want to pay that price, he must do without.

Monopoly, both on a national and international scale, has created a problem of control. People who favor the control of monopolies reason this way: the monopoly keeps the price of goods high by eliminating competition. But when the price is kept high, not as many goods can be sold. When goods cannot be sold, fewer goods are produced; this means that fewer people are employed. When there is unemployment in one industry, still fewer people have money to buy goods; so other industries suffer as well. When unemployment increases, it leads to a depression. In a depression all the people of a nation suffer.

● Depressions

Our industrialized system of business does not always run smoothly. "Good times" and "bad times" alternate. Prosperity changes to depression, and back again. This is a process that we call the "business cycle." Industrialization seems to have made depression both more frequent and more severe. More peo-

ple suffer because of unemployment. Bad conditions in one industry have a tendency to spread to other industries, and also to spread rapidly from nation to nation.

There are many theories as to what causes the ups and downs of the business cycle, and just as many about how to prevent them. One thing seems clear, however. Man, through the use of intelligence, has solved the problem of how to produce enough goods. The same intelligence should enable him to solve the problem of how to distribute and use the goods he produces.

Trade faces new problems

Mass production needs mass consumption in widespread markets. This problem has been made international by the great increases of production resulting from the Second Industrial Revolution. The industrial nations produce more goods than they themselves can consume. Even the tremendous market of the United States, the largest single market in the world, is not large enough to use all the goods we produce. If our farms and factories are to continue to operate at a high level of activity and prosperity, we must export from ten to twenty per cent of our total production of both manufactured and farm products. We are more fortunate than many nations because we produce so much of our food and raw material at home. Even so, we are far from being self-sufficient.

● The need for raw materials

The enormous use of raw materials in the industries of the industrialized nations has become a major international problem. No nation is self-sufficient; every nation needs to import raw materials, some nations more than others. Each wants to be sure that it will always be able to get the materials it needs. The result has been a scramble to get control of a sure supply of raw materials wherever they may be found.

Oil is an example. Without it, all the internal-combustion engines would stop for lack of fuel, all the machinery would grind to a halt for lack of lubrication. There are a number of regions where fields, or deposits, of crude oil are found: the United States, Canada, Venezuela, the Soviet Union, the Near East, and the East Indies. In 1945 three nations controlled over ninety per cent of the world's oil reserves. The United States controlled fifty-eight per cent, Great Britain (which has no oil within its own borders) twenty-two per cent, and Soviet Russia eleven per cent. Except for Russia, this does not mean that the governments controlled the oil reserves; they were owned and controlled by the private oil companies. Governments are concerned, however, both in the owning and the non-owning countries. The non-owning countries especially must be certain that they receive their necessary supply of oil. Some of the international diplomatic crises in the Near East result from the concern of the great powers over the oil fields in that area.

The importance of oil supplies was demonstrated when the Suez Canal was closed for a time in 1956–57. The tankers that carry oil from the Near Eastern oil fields to Europe were unable to follow their usual route through the canal. France and Britain feared that their transportation services and their industries might be crippled by lack of oil. Emergency plans for shipping oil to these nations were prepared.

Problems of international trade

The whole problem of trade among nations is of great importance. Nations that have to buy goods abroad must sell goods abroad to pay for their purchases. There is a reverse side to this picture, too. Nations that sell goods abroad must buy from abroad. Let us try to simplify a very complicated process this way:

When an American corporation sells products in England, it wants to be paid either in gold or in American money. Gold is accepted as payment everywhere, but the world supply is limited. Therefore, buying nations usually do not have enough gold to pay for their purchases. The American firm wants payment in American money because British paper money does not "spend" in the United States; the corporation cannot pay its workers' wages or its taxes or buy its raw materials with British pounds.

Now there are only two ways in which the British can get American money to pay for the goods they buy from us. We can, of course, lend it to them. As you can see, this does not make much sense. How can they then get the money to repay the loan? We would want that to be American money, too. The only sensible way for them to get our money is to sell us goods or services. Thus you can see that if the United States (meaning all our business firms) wants to sell goods abroad, it must also buy goods abroad. In this way the foreign countries can get our money to pay us for the goods they buy. Possibly this sounds complicated. If you analyze it, you will see that in the long run international trade is an exchange of goods for goods. One who wants to continue to sell must also continue to buy.

The problem is even more complicated. The businessmen of a nation do not like to see goods brought in from abroad, if those goods are already being produced at home. They do not object to the importation of goods that they cannot produce. No one in the United States objects to the importation of coffee. But producers of goods want to keep the home market for themselves. If goods are bought from abroad, there is the danger that they will not be able to sell their products so profitably in the home market.

Tariffs

Businessmen in the industrialized countries, therefore, have persuaded their governments to "protect" them from foreign competition by charging high taxes, or tariffs, on imported goods. The tariff, of course, is paid by the person who brings in the goods from abroad. If he brings them in to sell, he adds the amount of the tariff to the price at which he sells. Thus imported goods become more expensive. Since they are higher priced, less of them can be sold and therefore less will be imported.

See how this affects the problem of international trade. If the United States, for example, passes high tariff laws to keep out foreign goods, it makes it more difficult to sell American goods abroad. For if people in foreign countries cannot sell us their goods, they cannot get the money with which to pay for our goods.

Tariffs and other restrictions on international trade have made it much more difficult for nations to sell their surplus production. This, in turn, has made it difficult to keep industries running in full production and to prevent depressions. It is probably one more problem which will have to be solved by international coöperation.

Review of Chapter 36

People, places, and things

Identify: Alexander Graham Bell, Guglielmo Marconi, Thomas Edison.

Locate: Sea routes from England and Europe through the Mediterranean and the Suez Canal to the Far East; sea routes from Europe and from New York through the Panama Canal to San Francisco and the Far East; the Trans-Siberian Railway.

Events in review

1. Name five changes in means and routes of transportation during the Second Industrial Revolution.
2. Name five developments in communication during the Second Industrial Revolution.
3. What contributions did Faraday and Edison make to the Industrial Revolutions?
4. What are *by-products*? What are *synthetics*? Give examples.
5. What is the purpose of a protective tariff?
6. What three factors are involved in mass production? Who applied the technique to automobile-making?

7. Why is oil of great importance in international trade and in international diplomatic relations?

Problems and projects

1. Compare the First Industrial Revolution with the Second. What are the major differences? To what extent is the second simply a continuation of the first?
2. Explain how the Second Industrial Revolution can be called the product of applied science.
3. Discuss the effects of the internal combustion engine upon transportation. In what sense can these effects be called revolutionary?
4. Remember that the history of the Second Industrial Revolution is still going on. Watch the newspapers and magazines for reports of current advances in pure and applied science —in medicine, electronics, and design of aircraft and rockets, for example. What revolutionary developments seem to be on the way?
5. Write an essay on the development of radio, or talking movies, or radar.
6. Prepare a report on (1) the use of atomic energy in power plants, to drive ships, etc., or (2) earth satellites.

Chapter 37

The Arts, Religion, and the New Social Teachings

EVERY age expresses itself in the art and literature it creates. Art and literature seem to form a mirror in which the life and thought of the time are reflected. Thus, during the Middle Ages the arts reflected the profoundly religious character of the period. The art and writing of the modern period are far less devoted to religious idealism. They place much more emphasis on economic, scientific, and political themes, on the immediate world around us.

Literature—the art of words

In the period after 1750 many more people became readers. Literacy greatly increased as the period progressed. City people, denied the pleasures of nature, may have turned more to books in order to live in their imaginations. The literature of the period from 1750 to the present can be discussed under several headings.

● *Romantic writers*

At the beginning of the period, the *romantics* held full sway in both poetry and the novel. A romantic writer is one who presents life-as-it-should-be. He appeals to sentiment, fancy, and the imagination. Often he departs from the present to tell wonderful tales of the past. Novelists such as the British Sir

Walter Scott and the French Alexandre Dumas told fine, brave, adventurous tales of bygone days. The German poets Heinrich Heine and Johann Friedrich Schiller and the English John Keats and Percy Bysshe Shelley wrote of love, beauty, and freedom.

Goethe, a very great German poet and philosopher, and one of the truly great writers of mankind, was concerned with ideas of order, freedom, and liberty. His best known work is *Faust,* the story of an aging scholar who sells his soul to the devil (Mephistopheles) so that he may again have the joys of youth and love. Faust undergoes many sorrowful experiences, but Goethe points his moral thus: in the end Faust finds peace in the joy of useful work. The writings of the romantics helped their readers to escape, in their minds, from their own lives and surroundings, which were all too often ugly, grim, and boring.

● *Realistic writers*

As the nineteenth century progressed, a new school of writers appeared: the *realists.* They pictured life as it really is. Instead of love, beauty, and adventure, the realists made social and economic conditions their theme. War, slavery, and serfdom became subjects of novels, as did the idea of democracy, the inequalities of social and economic life, the miseries of the city workers and the landless peasants. Honoré de Balzac pictured nineteenth-century French society in a tremendous series of novels called *The Human Comedy*. In his monumental novel *War and Peace,* the Russian Count Leo Tolstoy showed war not as a romantic adventure but as a vast confusion of mistakes, misery, and death. In picturing the grim ugliness of much of real life the realists often pointed the way to needed reforms.

Other modern writers

Of course, not all modern writing is realistic. There were many people who felt that it was bad enough to have to live with the harshness, grimness, and problems of life without having to read about them. They wanted to get away from reality, and they found a way in the "literature of escape." The "great detective" appeared on the literary scene, and the mystery story became increasingly popular. The "literature of escape" has been very popular. The detective novels of Conan Doyle with their hero, Sherlock Holmes, have been followed by a host of rivals and imitators. The "western," the tale of cowboys, Indians, and badmen, found a great following among both readers and moviegoers.

The realities of nineteenth- and twentieth-century life had critics, but they also had defenders. The novels and poems of England's Rudyard Kipling praised the expansion of the British Empire. They showed the white man, especially the British white man, taking the responsibility of ruling the other races in all parts of the world. According to Kipling, the white man has superior qualities, and it is proper that he should govern the other races in their own interest; this is "the White Man's Burden." The scene of many of Kipling's poems and stories is India, then part of the mighty British Empire and described as the "greatest jewel in the British crown."

Music—the art of sound

Music has been called an "international language." Although each nation's music is a part of its own culture, it also enriches the culture of the whole world. The great composer can speak to all people, and all will understand his message and enjoy the beauty he has created.

Until the beginning of the seventeenth century, music was written almost entirely for religious use. Composers wrote for the voice alone, or for voices accompanied by instruments which were kept very much in the background. Secular, or nonreligious, music developed greatly during the seventeenth century and has continued to develop ever since. Composers began to give instruments equal importance with voice; then they began to compose for solo instruments and for orchestras. During the eighteenth and nineteenth centuries music reached great heights, especially in Germany and Italy, with musicians of other nations also contributing. There were two great schools of composition, the *classical* and the *romantic*.

Grand opera—Giuseppe Verdi's famous Rigoletto.

Classical and romantic music

Musically speaking, the word *classical* has two meanings. A loose meaning is used to distinguish any serious music from *popular* music. By the stricter, second meaning, the classical school of composers wrote according to fixed and established rules of form. The Germans Bach, Haydn, and Mozart were among the world's greatest classical composers.

Beethoven began the change to *romantic* music. This kind of music pays more attention to the passionate expression of feelings and emotions than to the strict rules of form. Other great romantic composers were the Germans Schubert, Mendelssohn, Wagner, and Brahms, the Polish Chopin, the Russian Tchaikovsky, the Finn Sibelius, and the Italians led by Rossini and Verdi. Some of these men contributed greatly to the combination of drama, vocal, and instrumental music which is called grand opera.

Modern schools of music

During the late nineteenth and early twentieth centuries a new kind of music appeared —first in France with the works of Claude Debussy and Maurice Ravel. The style is called *impressionism*. It had no program, or story, as some of the romantic music had. It tried to create impressions in its listeners— moods which were developed through very rich harmonies. Like impressionist writing and painting, it paid little attention to details or to the rules.

During our century, the twentieth, composers have done a great amount of experimenting in music. Earlier music had been written on the octave, or eight-toned, scale. It followed certain rules of harmony, in certain keys. Experimental music was written on different scales, the six-, ten-, and twelve-tone scale. Instead of harmony it often used dissonance, or discord. Some music was written without key. The Russians Sergei Prokofiev, Igor Stravinsky, and Dimitri Shosta-kovich, the Americans Arnold Schoenberg and Aaron Copland, and the Hungarian Béla Bartók have all composed experimental music which critics believe has lasting value.

Just as there has always been a wide audience for the popular "literature of escape," so there has always been a wider audience for "popular" music than for classical. The ballad of love and sentiment has many admirers. The harmonies and rhythms of the American Negro produced "jazz," which has gone through many variations since the early days of the twentieth century. There has been interplay between the classical and the popular. The American George Gershwin tried to combine both fields. An amazingly successful composer of popular music, he also tried his hand at serious composition. His *Rhapsody in Blue, An American in Paris,* and *Porgy and Bess* have won a wide acceptance from both kinds of listeners here and in Europe. Another development of the mid-twentieth century is the vastly greater audience for serious music. The phonograph, the radio, and even school bands and orchestras have made millions of people understand and love good music.

Painting—the art of line, form, and color

Through their discovery of the rules of perspective the great artists of the Renaissance were able to give depth to their paintings. Thus both landscapes and the human figure were shown much more realistically. This trend toward *realism,* or *naturalism,* continued through the seventeenth and eighteenth centuries. The artist, whether portraitist or landscapist, tried to make his work "true to nature" in every detail. More and more, art became "photographic."

The seventeenth and eighteenth centuries produced great painters. The seventeenth century Spanish painters El Greco and Velásquez and the Dutch Rembrandt rank among the world's greatest painters of portraits. The eighteenth century English Gainsborough and Reynolds and the Spanish Goya are not considered as great as the earlier men, but they were very able. In the early nineteenth century landscape painting became very popular. The French Corot and the English Constable and Turner painted landscapes of great beauty and careful detail.

After the middle of the nineteenth century a new style of painting called *impressionism* appeared. Like impressionism in music, impressionism in painting tried to capture quick impressions, or moods, without paying great attention to details. The French Monet and Renoir were the founders of the impressionist school. Most of their great disciples have been French also: Cézanne, Matisse, Degas, and Gauguin. There was also the Dutch Van Gogh. Picasso, a Spaniard living and painting in France, is well known in our times.

Examples of the work of several of the painters named here are reproduced in full color in this book.

Religion in the modern world

Religious toleration—the right of a man to worship as he chooses—has been a development of modern times in the Christian world. Slow at first, it increased rapidly as the centuries passed. During the Middle Ages, heresy was a crime punishable by death. Even after the Reformation most countries had an established church with which it was a crime to disagree.

There are many milestones in the slow progress toward religious toleration. The French Edict of Nantes of 1598 (page 268) preceded by almost 100 years the English Act of Toleration. In the late 1700's Frederick the Great granted religious toleration in Prussia, the United States adopted the First Amendment to the Constitution, and the French, in the Declaration of the Rights of Man, proclaimed that no one should be disturbed in his religious beliefs.

The nineteenth century saw religious toleration spread to most countries in Europe. Partly this was the result of liberal ideas; partly it was the result of the indifference to religion. In any case, there are now few places in the world where a man may not follow whatever religious beliefs he chooses, even if that means no religious beliefs at all.

The spread of religious toleration brought a movement against the established church; that is, the church that is practically a branch of the government and is supported by taxation. Men rebelled against paying taxes to support a church they did not accept. Gradually church and state became separate in most countries. There are still established churches in a few countries: the Lutheran Church in Scandinavia, the Roman Catholic Church in Spain and Italy, the Anglican Church in England.

The twentieth century has brought startling developments in the arts of music and painting. Other striking changes are everywhere seen in the art of architectural design. One example of modern design is this industrial building in Racine, Wisconsin.

Another feature of modern religious life has been the great increase in sects, or organized churches. This has taken place mainly in the Protestant churches. It is a basic belief of Protestantism that every man can find his own way to salvation through the Bible. There is no official authority to interpret the Bible, as the pope does for Roman Catholics. Different men interpret various parts of the Bible differently. Men who agree among themselves break away from an existing church and form a new one. For example,

The places of worship shown on these two pages suggest two facts about religion in the modern world: First, there are many different religions, and numerous sects within these religions. Second, in most countries all these groups are allowed to worship freely. All over the world men have built churches. Above is a Roman Catholic church in the mountain town of Pescadore, Colombia. Below is a place of worship of the Jewish faith, Beth El Synagogue, in New London, Connecticut.

there are Unitarians, Baptists, Methodists, Friends (Quakers), Adventists, Mormons, and Christian Scientists. You may know of numerous others.

Modern times bring new ideas about the functions of government

You have already read (page 389) about Adam Smith's view of the proper purpose of government. The state, said Smith, should limit itself to three duties: (1) to protect the people from violence and invasion from outside; (2) to protect each individual from the injustice or oppression of other individuals, by establishing courts of justice; (3) to set up and maintain certain public works and institutions which individuals or groups cannot profitably set up and maintain. Beyond this, Smith reasoned that the government should allow every individual the freedom "to pursue his own interest in his own way"—the doctrine of laissez faire.

Abraham Lincoln took a different viewpoint. He said it should be the purpose of government to do for its people whatever they need to have done, but cannot do at all or cannot do as well for themselves as individuals.

The past 200 years have seen a steady movement away from Adam Smith's idea of limited government toward the broader view of Lincoln. As more people gained the right to vote and the right and privilege of education, they came more and more to look upon government as "their government." They came to regard government as an instrument which should solve problems too big or too complicated to be solved by individuals or groups. This changed viewpoint of the functions of government has resulted in a great increase in the activities of government.

● *Governments and economic activity*

Governments in the modern world have engaged in many economic activities. They

Above: a church of the Eastern Orthodox faith, on one of the Greek islands in the Aegean. This branch of the Christian religion includes almost 129,000,000 people. The Roman Catholic Church has more than 484,000,000. The Protestant churches include a total of almost 208,000,000. Below is a Protestant church building at Longmeadow, Massachusetts.

This cartoon from Punch *makes fun of the British Labour Party's policy of taking over industries. The coal, steel, and other industries were run by national boards. The caption for the cartoon reads: "The Round Table was abolished last month—we're the National Distressed Female Protection Board now."*

have regulated working conditions in industry and tried to prevent monopolies. They have owned and operated businesses themselves. Governments on the continent of Europe have owned and operated railroads, telephone, telegraph, and radio systems, and water, gas, and electric utilities. In England, under the socialist Labour Party, the government bought and operated the coal, electric, transportation, and steel industries. Federal and state governments in the United States have built dams to improve navigation, furnish water for irrigation, and produce electric power for sale to farms, cities, and private industries. Many governments have passed laws to regulate relations between labor and employers and to try to prevent strikes. Some governments have tried to help favored industries or groups of people by giving subsidies—special payments of money

for special purposes. Finally, governments have tried to improve the social welfare of their people by such programs as public education, free medical care, and low cost housing.

● *Rising government cost brings higher taxes*

All of this increased activity of governments has caused a great increase in the number of people employed by government and in the cost of government. The money to pay the increased costs can come only from taxation. The result has been that many people formerly not taxed at all now have to pay taxes. Those formerly taxed are now more heavily taxed, and the list of taxable commodities has steadily lengthened.

New kinds of taxes are used, too. Some of them have great social importance. The income and inheritance taxes produce great amounts of revenue for governments. They also spread the wealth of a country, and, to some extent, prevent the formation or growth of large fortunes.

You can see that the whole problem of the activity of government has become increasingly complicated and difficult in the modern world. How much should government control and regulate the economic activities of industry, labor, and farmers? How much should governments engage in business activities themselves? How much, and what, services should a government provide for its people? What sort of taxes should a government use to pay for the services it does provide? These are complicated, difficult problems to solve. Every question has arguments of merit on both sides. Yet they are questions which the citizen must be prepared to answer.

The change in the position of women

One of the most interesting developments of the past century has been the improvement in the social and political condition of women. In the Western World of 1800, women had few rights and privileges, and many handicaps. Before marriage a woman was subject to her father; after, to her husband. Legally, she could not own property. A married woman's children belonged legally to her husband. The law barred a woman from voting or holding office; custom barred her from education or from entering business or the professions.

When the Industrial Revolution got under way, women entered the factories to work. From this start better positions opened in industry, nursing, teaching, social service, and other professions. The growth of public schools made education available to more girls; colleges and universities gradually opened to them.

Today in Great Britain and the United States women enter all the professions and every sort of occupation and business. Most of their legal handicaps have disappeared. In other countries conditions vary but there is a trend toward equality of rights.

The drive to win equal rights for women caused many amused comments—by men. This cartoon—entitled "Woman's Kingdom Is At Home"—was drawn by the famous American cartoonist Thomas Nast.

Women voting in Cheyenne, Wyoming. The Wyoming Territory granted women the right to vote 51 years before the Nineteenth Amendment made their right nationwide.

Women get the right to vote

As they gained better educational and economic opportunities, women also demanded political equality: the right to vote and hold office. The campaign for woman suffrage received the support of some men, but most of the leaders were women: in England, Mary Wollstonecraft and Emmeline Pankhurst; in the United States, Lucretia Mott, Elizabeth Cady Stanton, and Susan B. Anthony.

It was an uphill fight against scorn, ridicule, and abuse. Gains came slowly: Wyoming in 1869, Australia and New Zealand in the 1890's, the Scandinavian countries in the early 1900's, Great Britain in 1918 and 1928, and the United States in 1920. Today women may vote in the above-mentioned countries, in most European countries, some Central and South American countries, and some Asian countries. Other countries will surely follow, because political equality for women has come to be regarded as another step on the way to social justice.

Review of Chapter 37

People, places, and things

Identify: Goethe, Ludwig von Beethoven, George Gershwin, Monet, Renoir, Emmeline Pankhurst, Susan B. Anthony.

Events in review

1. What view of the world was taken by the following writers: (a) Alexandre Dumas, (b) Leo Tolstoy, (c) Rudyard Kipling?
2. What is meant by an established church?
3. Name the three duties of the state as set forth by Adam Smith. How is the view of Abraham Lincoln different from that of Smith?
4. List three of the ways in which governments now engage in economic activities.

5. How does the increased activity by government affect taxes?
6. When did women win the right to vote in (a) Australia, (b) Great Britain, (c) France, (d) the United States?

Problems and projects

1. From your reading, find representative passages from romantic and realistic novels. Read these to the class and discuss why they are typical of two kinds of writing.
2. Find reproductions of art works that represent different schools or styles of painting. Present these for class discussion.
3. Obtain records that will give samples of classical music, impressionism, and jazz.

Review of Adjustments to the New Age

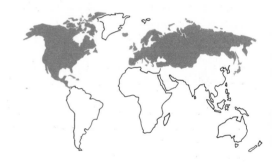

1. Review the rise of nationalism in Europe from the wars of Napoleon Bonaparte through the unification of Italy and Germany. Show how nationalism influenced history.
2. Which countries made the greatest progress toward democratic government during the nineteenth century? In which countries was there little or no progress? Can you explain why some countries progressed more rapidly?
3. Make a summary of the career of Louis Napoleon. What was the effect of his reign on France? What part did he play in the unification of Germany? of Italy?
4. Compare the unification of Germany with the unification of Italy. To what extent did unification depend on one leader? Compare Bismarck and Cavour. Which man do you consider greater? Why?
5. Make a list of ten outstanding events in the political history of the nineteenth century.

Tell in one or two sentences why you think each event was noteworthy.
6. Make a list of ten men and women who made outstanding contributions to the world during the nineteenth century. The list can include people who were important in political affairs, in science and invention, or in the arts.
7. Compare the First and Second Industrial Revolutions. Were they separate historical developments, or was the second revolution really a continuation and speeding-up of the first?
8. Try to picture for yourself daily life in the later years of the nineteenth century. If you could be transported to 1880 or 1890, how "modern" would the world seem? What familiar things would you miss?

   Suppose you went back to 1820 or 1830. What would life be like? If you could choose, would you prefer to live in the 1820's or the 1880's? Explain your choice.

Books about the New Age

*Bakeless, Katherine, *Story-Lives of Great Composers* (Lippincott, 1953). Clearly written biographical sketches.

*Bolton, Sarah K. *Famous Men of Science.* (Crowell, 1946). Brief biographies written interestingly.

*Cottler, Joseph, and Jaffe, Haym. *Heroes of Civilization* (Little, Brown, 1931). Brief biographies of Lavoisier, Pasteur, Lister, Metchnikoff, Einstein, and others.

Darrow, Floyd L. *Masters of Science and Invention* (Harcourt, Brace, 1938). Galileo, Jenner, Darwin, Pasteur, and others.

De Kruif, Paul. *Microbe Hunters* (Harcourt, Brace, 1939). This book has long been popular for its lively accounts of the personalities and work of Pasteur, Koch, and other bacteriologists.

Foster, Genevieve. *Abraham Lincoln's World* (Scribner's, 1944). Highly recommended for a fine discussion of the events that were happening simultaneously all over the world.

*Fox, Ruth. *Great Men of Medicine* (Random House, 1947). Readable accounts of Harvey, Lister, and other medical pioneers.

Garland, Joseph. *Story of Medicine* (Houghton Mifflin, 1949). Richly filled with information and human interest. Highly recommended.

*Hagedorn, Hermann. *Americans: a Book of Lives* (John Day, 1946). Ford, Burbank, Edison, and Carver, among others. Very interestingly written.

Hogben, Lancelot. *From Cave Painting to Comic Strip* (Chanticleer Press, 1949). Full of chuckles, facts, and beautiful illustrations. A historical study of man's communication by means of pictorial symbols.

Meyer, Jerome Sydney. *World Book of Great Inventions* (World Publishing Company, 1956). The story of man's great inventions from prehistoric times to the present.

*Books marked with a star (*) are easy reading.

*Nazaroff, Alexander I. *Land of the Russian People* (Lippincott, 1953). A simply written history of Russia.

*Osgood, Ellen L. *History of Industry* (Ginn, 1935). A clearly written story of the Second Industrial Revolution.

*Quennell, C. H. B., and Quennell, Marjorie. *History of Everyday Things in England* (British Bk. Centre, 1953). Includes much on the Second Industrial Revolution and its effects. Food, clothing, amusements, and architecture as well as agriculture, industry, and transportation. Excellent illustrations.

*Seeger, Elizabeth. *Pageant of Russian History* (Longmans, 1950). A well written, simple account of Russian history.

Victor Book of Opera (R.C.A. Manufacturing Co., 1936). The stories of the operas.

Good stories about the New Age

Dickens, Charles. *Life and Adventures of Nicholas Nickleby* (Dodd, Mead, 1949. Great Illustrated Classics). Dickens points the finger of scorn and indignation at England's neglect of education.

Harper, Theodore A. *Red Sky* (Viking, 1935). Life in Russia before the revolution.

Kyle, Anne D. *Red Sky over Rome* (Houghton Mifflin, 1938). Garibaldi and Mazzini appear in this story of an American girl living in Rome at the time of the unification of Italy.

Laguna, Frederica de. *Thousand March* (Little, Brown, 1930). The adventures of a young American volunteer with Garibaldi's Red Shirts.

Meigs, Cornelia L. *Railroad West* (Little, Brown, 1937). The many difficulties in building the Northern Pacific Railway in the United States.

Orczy, Baroness Emmuska. *Spy of Napoleon* (Putnam's, 1934). Plots and counterplots in the empire of Napoleon III.

473

Part Eight GREAT POWER RIVALRIES

Earlier parts of this book concentrated on certain areas on the globe. Even the great empire of Rome covered only a section of the earth. In modern times, history is in the fullest sense *world* history, and Part Eight covers events that affected all lands and peoples. Notice that the time chart on pages 476–477 takes in Europe, Africa, Asia, and America.

Part Eight tells how world problems built up to a dreadful climax in World War I (1914–1918). This was the first of two wars that we describe as world conflicts. As an example of how international a war this was, the British Empire brought men from as far away as India, Australia, and New Zealand to fight Germans and Austrians in France. The picture on the opposite page shows Australian troops, from "down under" on the other side of the world, marching through a French village. Englishmen, Canadians, Frenchmen, Belgians, Germans, Turks, Austrians, Russians, Serbians, and others were in the war from the start. A new power in the Far East —Japan—took a hand. Later the United States became involved.

The causes of war were many and complicated. One of the causes was introduced in Part Seven. Nationalistic feeling was strong in many of the great powers of Europe. After the Franco-Prussian War, France was left with a grievance against Germany. The new and strongly nationalistic German Empire

was led by an ambitious and rash man, William II. The chances for rivalry and friction were clear.

The earlier chapters in Part Eight tell how rivalries developed among the great powers. One source of trouble was a race for colonies and trading privileges in Africa and Asia. Chapters 38, 39, and 40 tell of this new wave of imperialism. In addition, you will find accounts of the lands and people of three highly important areas: India, Africa, and China.

Chapter 41 describes the amazing transformation of Japan from an isolated feudal country into an industrialized nation and a military power. Japan quickly followed the Western powers into the race for empire.

Chapter 42 tells how the United States took her place among the great powers in the world.

Chapter 43 describes how the rivalries among nations in Europe and the rest of the world ended in the outbreak of war, and how the war was won. Chapter 44 shows the victors struggling with the problems of making peace. Chapter 45 sums up the damage the war caused to peoples and places. World War I was a lesson on a huge scale in the fact that modern war creates more problems than it settles. In Part Eight you will find much stress on two of the great themes of world history: the causes and effects of war, the problems of making peace.

EUROPE   AFRICA

1800

1806   British take Cape Colony from Dutc

1815-1848   Age of Metternich

1830   Revolutions   **1830**   French in Algeria

1836   Boer republics recognized

1847   Liberia founded

1848   Revolutions
Second period of imperialism begins

1850

1852   Second French Empire
1853-1856   Crimean War

1867   Dual monarchy, Austria-Hungary
1870   Imperialism speeds up. Franco-Prussian War
1871   German Empire   **1871**   Cecil Rhodes to Africa

1881   French take Tunisia
1882   British take Egypt
1878   Austria, protectorate over Bosnia, Herzegovina   **1884**   German Southwest Africa
1882   Triple Alliance   **1885**   Belgian Congo, German E.
Africa, British East Africa

1886   British Nigeria, French Guinea
1890's   Italy takes Eritrea, Somaliland
1894   Russo-French   **1896**   Italy defeated by Ethiopia
Alliance   **1898**   Anglo-Egyptian Sudan
1899-1902   Boer War

1900

1907   Triple Entente
1908   Austria annexes Bosnia, Herzegovina   **1910**   Union of South Africa
1912-1913   Balkan Wars   **1912**   French Morocco-Italian Libya
1914-1918   World War I   **1914-1918**   World War I
January 1919   Versailles conference
February 1919   Weimar Republic
June 1919   Versailles Treaty
1923   Second Treaty with Turkey. Kemal, dictator

1931   British Commonwealth of Nations
1933   Hitler in Germany. Failure of military
disarmament
1936   Failure of naval disarmament

1950

IVALRIES

ASIA		AMERICA	
00-1858	Rule in India by British East India Company	1789	Federal government under the constitution

		1814	End of second U. S. War with Great Britain
		1815-1915	U. S. isolation
		1823	Monroe Doctrine

39-1842	Opium Wars in China	1839	Durham Report: self-government in Canada
		1846-1848	War between U. S. and Mexico

52	Taiping Rebellion, China.		
54	U. S.-Japanese Treaty		
57	Sepoy Rebellion, India		
58	India ruled by British government	1860	Election of Lincoln
		1861-1865	Secession and War
		1863-1864	Slavery abolished
67	Japanese revolution, Shogun overthrown	1867	Purchase of Alaska
		1867	French troops withdrawn from Mexico. Juarez, president
77	Victoria becomes Empress of India		
89	Japanese constitution	1890	Pan-American Union formed
94-95	Chinese-Japanese war		
99	Open Door Policy		
00	Boxer Uprising	1898	Spanish-American War. U.S. adopts imperialism
02	Anglo-Japanese Alliance	1904	U. S. gains Panama Canal Zone
04-1905	Russo-Japanese War. Treaty of Portsmouth		
11	Chinese rebellion	1914	Panama Canal opened
12	End of Manchu rule. Chinese Republic	1914-1917	U. S. neutrality, World War I
14-1918	World War I Twenty-one Demands	1917-1918	U. S. in World War
		1919	Senate rejects Versailles Treaty
		1922	Washington Disarmament Conference
27	Chiang breaks with Communists, Civil War		
31	Japanese invade Manchuria		
37	British grant constitution to India Japanese invade China		

Chapter 38 The New Imperialism: India

IMPERIALISM is the policy of building up an empire by getting colonies—the lands of other peoples. The first great period of European imperialism came during the sixteenth, seventeenth, and eighteenth centuries. Europeans established colonial empires in the Americas, in India, and in the East Indies. Their imperial ventures were stimulated by the theory of mercantilism. This theory taught that colonies added greatly to a nation's wealth.

After 1800, however, European statesmen came to be a little doubtful of the value of empires. England and Spain lost great colonial empires in the Americas. Perhaps colonies were not good permanent investments of either money or men. The Industrial Revolution in Europe created great needs for capital and labor. Europeans were giving most of their time and attention to political movements—the struggle for more democratic government, labor and land reforms, and the attempts at unification in Germany and Italy. Liberals in Europe were pointing out that the position of a colonist did not fit well with the ideas of the French and American Revolutions about the dignity and equality of man.

The new attitude showed in several ways. Trade with colonies became free and open to all nations instead of just the mother country. For the most part, governments did not make much attempt to add to their empires. The British tried to avoid repeating their mistake in America by granting a great degree of self-government to Canada.

Reasons for a new interest in empires

In spite of the doubts of some people about the value of colonies, certain forces of the early nineteenth century helped to produce a new interest in empires.

1. *Nationalism.* Taking colonies (nationalists argued) added to the strength and prestige of their country. In addition to providing wealth and glory, overseas outposts were important as naval bases in time of war.
2. *The hope of self-sufficiency.* The Industrial Revolution created a demand for huge supplies of raw materials. Nations sought colonies in the hope of controlling the sources of important raw materials, such as rubber.
3. *New markets.* Colonies could serve as markets for the mother country's manufactured goods. Here was another effect of industrialization.

4. *Places for investment.* Some men in the industrialized nations had gained wealth from their businesses. The so-called backward nations were attractive places to invest surplus capital.
5. *Outlets for surplus population.* A frequent excuse for taking colonies was to have a place where surplus population could go and still be under the national flag.
6. *Missionary motives.* Religious people urged that it was their duty to carry the Christian religion to the heathen.
7. *"The White Man's Burden."* It was argued that the white European peoples had an obligation to civilize backward peoples.

As you read Part Eight you will be able to see how much value there was in these various arguments for taking colonies. One fact must be remembered: whether or not the reasons listed proved to be sound, many men believed in them. They acted on their motives by trying to build empires. This new imperialism was the result of a complex mixture of political, economic, and social forces. These forces stirred up public opinion and drove governments to try to expand overseas.

Characteristics of the new imperialism

The result of all these forces was a second great wave of imperialist expansion. It began about 1850 and speeded up tremendously after 1870. France began a drive for overseas colonies in Africa and Asia. England followed the same course. Russia drove in two directions: toward the Near East, and into Central and Eastern Asia. Smaller nations like Holland and Portugal, which already had possessions in the East Indies and Africa, stepped up their colonial activities. Belgium moved into Africa. The United States joined the imperial adventure, taking colonies in the Caribbean and the Pacific.

Two nations deserve special mention. Neither Germany nor Italy had taken any part in the first wave of imperialism during the earlier centuries. Neither country gained national unity until the early 1870's. For ten years thereafter each was busy with affairs at home. Even in the second wave of imperialism, they "came late to the party." When they did begin, they searched furiously for colonies. But by that time most of the desirable places had been taken by others. Much of the course of modern history is explained by this fact.

There were many motives for taking colonies—some selfish, some unselfish. Religious people believed in trying to teach their beliefs to other peoples. Many missionaries worked to improve the health and welfare of those they were trying to convert. Shown here are Christian missionaries in India about 1900.

How the European powers divided the "Dark Continent"—Africa—will be told in Chapter 39. Imperialism in China will be described in Chapter 40. The present chapter gives general details of the new colonialism and then tells of the great British imperial venture in India.

Colonies, protectorates, concessions, and spheres of influence

There are some terms used in connection with imperialism that need explanation. A *colony* gives the imperial nation total control over the land and the native population. It is gained by discovery, settlement, or conquest, and is *annexed,* becoming a part of the empire. In a *protectorate* the native ruler keeps his title, but officials of the foreign power "pull the strings." The "protecting" power keeps out other foreign nations. A *concession* is the grant of economic rights and privileges in the "backward" country. The grant is given to foreign merchants or capitalists who want to trade, build railroads, or develop mines or natural resources. A *sphere of influence* is a region where other nations recognize that one nation has special, sometimes exclusive, economic and political privileges.

Steps in the new imperialism

The new colonialism was very different from the old. In the beginning it was not actively planned by governments. Often it was the work of individuals: merchants who set up small trading posts or explorers and scientists in search of adventure and scientific data. Missionaries went out to convert native populations to the Christian religion. Sometimes the missionary, the merchant, or the scientist was abused by the natives. When word of the incidents reached their governments, soldiers were sometimes sent to protect them. Often the soldiers established themselves permanently. Soon government officers appeared, and a new "protectorate" came into being.

Cynical people made up a formula: "First the missionary and the trader, then the soldier, then the governor with the flag."

Loans to native rulers were often the entering wedges of colonialism. When the chieftains spent the money recklessly, as they often did, they found themselves heavily in debt, and they were forced to grant economic concessions. Economic penetration often led to political control, as Egypt, Tunisia, Indo-China, and many other places were to learn.

There was another difference in the new colonialism. In the Americas and Australia white Europeans had occupied and settled the colonies, pushing aside the sparse native population. India, China, and Africa, the new imperial regions, were in many areas already crowded by their own populations. In many regions the climate was ill-suited to European settlement. It was typical of the new imperialism to find small groups of whites dominating vast native populations because their governments were weak. Sometimes, as in much of Africa, the natives were extremely backward. However, some of the new colonials were people with a long history of civilization and a profound culture.

The new colonialism stirred up bitter jealousies and rivalries among the imperial nations. Nations came to the verge of war, and actual wars did occur. One reason for the bitterness was a revival of the old idea of mercantilism—of exclusive monopoly control of the new colonies. The vital and valuable raw materials were for the benefit of the mother country. Others might buy them in peacetime, but at a price. It was the goods of the mother country that were sold to the people of the colony. This exclusive attitude made the struggle for possession very bitter.

The story of India

The colonization of India dates from the first imperialist period. Chapter 20 told how the Europeans came to India and how, after

a struggle, the British were able to drive out the French and dominate the peninsula. The present discussion will tell something of the ancient and honorable civilization of India. A small force of Europeans was able to conquer and rule a huge, densely populated, highly civilized region. Many developments took place in India during the second period of imperialism.

● *The land and the people of India*

If you look at the map of Asia, you will see why India is often called a sub-continent. It is a triangular peninsula on the southern Asiatic coast line, more than half the size of the United States. Its western shores are washed by the Arabian Sea. The southern tip projects into the Indian Ocean. To the east lies the Bay of Bengal. On the north, where it joins the mainland of Asia, lies the great chain of the Himalaya Mountains, the highest in the world. Like the peninsulas of the Mediterranean, India is set apart from the mainland by towering mountains. As in Eu-

The early days of imperialism in India. A ship of the British East India Company off Bombay in 1780.

rope, the mountains did not provide complete protection. In the long course of history numerous passes have allowed hordes of peoples to invade the peninsula from the north.

These snow-clad mountains and the seasonal rains feed the great rivers of northern India: the Indus, the Ganges, and the Brahmaputra. The southern half of the peninsula is a rough, rocky plateau. The rainy season, brought by the southwest winds, called *monsoons,* lasts from June through September. The monsoon rains are the heaviest in the world. In some places rainfall of 800 inches in a season has been recorded. Excessive rainfall sometimes means floods which do indescribable damage, destroying property and washing away the valuable topsoil. There are also years when the prayers for rain are not answered. Drought also means disaster. The land is parched, the irrigation system fails, springs, wells, and streams dry up, and misery results. Famine is a problem as old as India.

The present population of the entire peninsula is about 465 million. Only China has more people. People of every race, color, and creed have invaded India in the course of her long history. All of them have left their imprint on the language, customs, and religious beliefs. The people of India are divided in race, language, and religion. The three main races of mankind—white, yellow, and black —have mingled freely, so that traces of all three are found in many people. There are fifteen major languages, and no less than 720 dialects. In religion, two thirds of the population follow Hinduism. About one fourth is Mohammedan.

● Early civilization in India

In the Indian valley of the Indus River, there are remains of a civilization which probably goes back to 3000 B.C. There were towns and cities with houses made of brick. Many of the houses contained baths. The people of that day used copper and bronze tools. They wore clothing of woven cotton and produced beautifully decorated pottery of great artistic value. That ancient people invented a system of writing which unfortunately we are not yet able to read. Some scientists think that this high civilization of the Indus was in some way connected with the culture of the Sumerians in Mesopotamia.

Between the fifteenth and thirteenth centuries B.C., India was invaded from the northwest by waves of Caucasian people like those who invaded Persia, Greece, and Italy. These invasions probably destroyed the high culture of the Indus Valley. Like any invading group, the Caucasians in India had their problems. They were less numerous than the natives whom they dominated. These natives were a dark-skinned people called Dravidians. There were differences in language and religion, too. To preserve their rule and their racial difference, the invaders used military force and two other methods: a caste system and a religion which included the caste system.

● The caste system

There is nothing anywhere else in the world like the caste system of India. In the true sense of the word it is unique. People are divided into very fixed and rigid social classes. These are hereditary; a man is born into a caste and dies in that caste. The people of each caste are similar in occupation, social position, religion, and, for the most part, color. Originally there were four castes in descending order of importance: (1) Brahmans —the priests, scholars, and wise men; (2) the rulers and warriors; (3) the merchants and landowners; (4) the servants, peasants, and humble workers.

Each caste has its own rules about eating, marriage, labor, and worship. A person must not eat or drink with a person of a lower caste, nor can he render any service to any

A bronze statue of Siva dating from the twelfth century A.D.

person of a lower caste. He can work only at the occupations recognized for his caste. He may not marry outside his caste. He eats only food which the rules of his caste recognize as pure. A person who violates any of the rules of his caste may become an outcast (a person of no caste at all). Such a person is considered an "untouchable." No member of any caste may associate with him in any way. He may not enter the temples, attend the schools, or use the wells or bathing places of people of the castes. He can do only degrading work, which no one else will do.

As time passed, the original four castes were multiplied. Subdivisions were made and completely new castes appeared with the coming of new occupations. Today there are between 2,000 and 4,000 hereditary castes, each with its own position and fixed rules.

You can see how useful the caste system would be to a ruling group that wanted to maintain its rule. Membership in the three upper castes went to the invaders; the Dravidians formed the fourth caste. Since caste rules made it impossible for a person to leave his caste, and since caste was hereditary, it made a very fixed, unchangeable society. There was always the penalty of being made an outcast for anyone who rebelled against the system.

The Caucasians who came into India brought their own religion, and they found many different religious beliefs among the Dravidians. Both groups worshipped many gods, especially those representing forces of nature: fire, earth, storm, lightning, and so forth. In time, the religions of the two groups combined into *Hinduism*. It is not really a religion as much as it is a group of related religions. Because Brahma is a principal god, and the caste of Brahmans are the priests, it is sometimes called *Brahmanism*.

● *Hinduism*

There are three supreme gods in Hinduism: *Brahma* the Creator, *Vishnu* the Pre-server, and *Siva* the Destroyer. Below these come a host of other gods: the spirits of trees, animals, and persons. Various groups of Hindus pay special reverence to certain animals: monkeys, snakes, and dogs. Cows are especially sacred. No Hindu will eat the flesh of a cow, although milk, cheese, and butter are eaten.

A principal doctrine of Hinduism is *reincarnation,* or the *transmigration of souls.* According to this belief, the soul does not die with the body. At death the soul enters the body of another being, either human or animal. *Karma,* the Hindu law of life, teaches that the progress of the soul depends on the life one lives. The good are rewarded; the evil are punished. Reward means that the soul enters the body of someone of a higher caste. A person of evil life is punished by having his soul reborn as a person of a lower life, or an animal. Some Hindus take this belief so seriously that they will not kill any animal, even a poisonous snake, a tiger, or even an insect, because it may be the bearer of a human soul. You can see how caste is woven into the religion. The belief is that men were divided into castes at creation; the soul moves upward or downward through the castes according to the sort of life its bearer leads. The good life, of course, means acceptance of caste and observance of all caste rules. The goal of the progress of the soul is *nirvana,* where the soul is united with that of Brahma and personal existence ceases altogether.

Civilization in India reached a great peak in the 800 years from about 300 B.C. to 500 A.D. During that time the greatest literature of India was created. Its poetic, religious, and philosophic writings have influenced Western as well as Oriental thinkers and writers. Art was at a high level. Architecture, painting, music, and sculpture flourished. In the handicrafts there was beautiful work in weaving, pottery, and metal work. The textile industry was outstanding. As you know, Indian cotton textiles

An example of Indian architecture, the "Tower of Victory," built centuries ago in Rajputana.

were highly desired in the Mediterranean world; such names as calico, cashmere, cotton, chintz, all originated in India.

● Buddhism

During this great period of civilization a new religion appeared in India. Buddhism was an offshoot of Hinduism. It started as a movement to reform Hinduism, just as Christianity began as a movement to reform the Jewish religion. Buddha is not a name, but a title, just as Christ is a title. Christ means "The Anointed One"; Buddha means "The Enlightened One."

Buddha's name was really Gautama. He lived during the fifth century B.C., and was the son of a wealthy Indian prince. Gautama lived the life and enjoyed all the pleasures of a man in his position, until, at the age of twenty-nine, he became deeply troubled by an age-old problem. Why, he asked himself, should life bring joy to a few and poverty and suffering to so many? Why must there be misery and death? The problem troubled him so that he resolved to spend the rest of his life searching for answers to his questions. He put aside all his possessions, left his wife and infant son, and traveled as a beggar in search of the truth.

Gautama followed all the paths which were recommended as leading to wisdom. He lived as a hermit and a scholar. He tried fasting and self-torture. None brought him the answers he sought. Then one day, as he sat meditating under a banyan tree, light came to him, and he found the truth, the Way of Life. In that moment, according to his followers, he ceased to be Gautama, and became Buddha, the Enlightened One.

Buddha accepted the Hindu doctrine of karma, that Good comes from Good, and Evil from Evil. Men must seek the good, and avoid the evil. Since only deeds, good or bad, are important, salvation cannot come through self-torture or from animal sacrifice, as some Hindus thought. Salvation comes from knowing and following the Four Truths. They are as follows: (1) All human life is full of suffering and sorrow. (2) Sufferings and sorrow are the result of sins. Evil and sins come from man's cravings and desires. (3) Nirvana is the perfect peace, in which the soul is released from having to be born again. (4) Nirvana can be reached by moderation in conduct in eight ways: (*a*) right views, (*b*) right intention, (*c*) right speech, (*d*) right action, (*e*) right livelihood, (*f*) right effort, (*g*) right mindfulness, (*h*) right concentration.

Buddha made unselfishness the key to his religion, and he gave very definite rules for unselfish behavior: "Not to kill, to steal, or to commit adultery; not to lie, to gossip, to indulge in faultfinding, or to use profanity; to abstain from covetousness (greed) or hatred; and to avoid ignorance."

As you see, Buddhism is closely related to Hinduism, but there are differences. For example, Buddha accepted the Hindu ideas of karma and nirvana, but he did not accept the Hindu gods as sacred. According to Buddha, man alone could do the supreme thing—change good to evil and evil to good. He could do it by following the Way of Life on the path of the Four Truths. He did not need the help of gods or priests or temples or idols. Buddha taught that there are only two kinds of people, the good and the bad. Thus, although he did not attack the caste system openly, he did not accept it. Buddha did not claim to be a divine being. He claimed to be only a philosopher and teacher who pointed out to men the way they should follow for right conduct and salvation.

Buddhism gained some followers, but did not make much headway for several centuries. The Brahmans naturally opposed it. The Brahmans were the priests; they ruled the temples and performed the religious ceremonies. Buddhism made these things unnecessary. Brahmans were the highest caste. Their position depended on people's accepting the idea of reincarnation—rebirth into a

higher or lower caste according to the life they lived. Buddhism taught that everyone could reach nirvana, regardless of caste, if he were good.

● *The reign of Asoka—Buddhism spreads*

In the third century B.C., the empire of Alexander the Great in India was taken over by a native king. This man had learned from the Macedonians both the science of government and their methods of war. He and his son were able to extend their rule greatly, so that Asoka, the third ruler in the family, ruled over almost all of India. Asoka became a devout Buddhist. He did not force people to accept the religion, but many did. During the time of his reign India had many contacts with other countries of the Orient. Asoka himself sent out missionaries to teach Buddhism, and the religion spread to Tibet, China, Burma, Java, Ceylon, and Indo-China.

Although Buddhism spread widely in India during the reign of Asoka and for some time afterward, it did not replace Hinduism. The caste system remained. Gradually the Brahmans were able to absorb and take over the new ideas into the old. A thousand years after Buddha's death, there were fewer Buddhists in India than in China and Burma.

The later history of Buddhism in other countries is very interesting. Gautama himself did not claim to be divine, but he was turned into a deity. He taught only a Way of Life, in which temples, priests, and shrines were unnecessary. But Buddhism became an organized religion with temples, monasteries, priests, monks, elaborate ceremonies, and holy shrines and sacred places which attracted hosts of pilgrims. Buddha had condemned idol worship, but his own image was worshipped by his followers.

At the end of the fifth century A.D., the great period of civilization ended. India entered a period of decline, much like the Middle Ages of Europe. The land was invaded by many peoples, among them the Huns, the Moslem Arabs and Turks, and the Mongols. The country broke up into small states. Learning and the arts declined.

In those dark days religion became the great consoler, for Hinduism teaches, above all, *resignation*—the acceptance of what is, in the hope of better things in the next incarnation. Centuries of poverty made men regard poverty as virtue and wealth as sin. Thus the people came to have enormous endurance, but little will to change or improve things. Hinduism was almost always able to absorb its conquerors. Each invading group was absorbed into the population. Each man became a member of a caste. Religious beliefs were taken over, adapted, and fitted in, just as

This seventeenth century painting shows a Moslem emperor of India seated on a throne. Before him are three of his subjects and a European explorer or trader.

Buddhism had been. This was true of everyone but the Moslems.

India became a nation of small isolated village communities. It was a rural society, engaged in the most primitive kind of agriculture. Transportation was very poor; there was little exchange of goods or ideas. Villages were almost self-sufficient. Each maintained its caste system. The family was the strongest unit; the elders administered the community. Life became stagnant; things were done according to tradition and custom.

The Moslem invasion of India

The one religion that Hinduism could not absorb was *Islam,* the faith of the Moslems. The followers of Mohammed, who taught that all men are equal, detested Hinduism with its caste system and its worship of idols. From the beginning of the eighth century onward, the Moslems came in successive waves. As raiding invaders they tried either to convert the Hindus or to slaughter them. Eventually the Moslems settled down in the northeast and the northwest and became part of the population. However, they clung fiercely to their religion.

During the sixteenth century A.D. the Moslem Mongols, or Moguls, as the Indians called them, invaded India. They took over an existing Moslem kingdom and ruled most of northern India. In many ways the Mogul Empire was a great improvement over previous conditions. Government was stable, with able administrators. For several centuries Hindus and Moslems lived side by side in peace. The Moguls built cities, promoted education, and erected many fine buildings.

How fine their architecture was may be seen in the Taj Mahal. This is not only the finest example of Islamic art in India, but also one of the world's great examples of architecture. The Taj Mahal is a tomb. It was built for his wife by a seventeenth-century Mogul ruler. It is a marble building, placed

| The Taj Mahal, at Agra.

in a colorful garden and enclosed by a stone wall. To see the Taj Mahal is one of the great experiences the world offers to the lover of beauty.

During the second half of the seventeenth century, Mogul sultans tried to unite the entire peninsula. There was a renewed effort to convert the Hindus; resistance brought slaughter, with widespread revolts and uprisings. The Mogul Empire began to break up into small independent states. In the northeast and northwest they were Moslem; in the rest of the peninsula they were Hindu. Neither people was able to convert the other, and neither was able to conquer the other. Between them they produced a weak, divided India just at the time that the Europeans began to appear on the scene.

India becomes a British colony

In 1498 the Portuguese Vasco da Gama reached the coast of India after sailing around Africa, and established contact between India and Europe. The Portuguese set up small trading posts at various places on the coast of India, and enjoyed a near-monopoly of Indian trade for 100 years. In 1600, Queen Elizabeth I of England gave a charter to the London East India Company; soon thereafter a French East India Company was chartered. Both established "factories," or trading posts, in India.

The Europeans were able to take advantage of the feudal conditions that followed the breakup of the Mogul Empire. The British and the French companies formed alliances with native princes and slowly increased their territorial control. There was probably trade, wealth, and glory enough for both, but in the world of the eighteenth century things were not done that way. The two companies clashed, and in 1763 the British expelled the French from India.

India ruled by the East India Company

It was the British government that fought the war and signed the treaty, but it was not the British government that took over affairs in India. For nearly 200 years the world saw the strange spectacle of a huge land with an ancient civilization controlled by a private corporation, the British East India Company. By one means or another, the Company gradually extended its control. It administered and collected the taxes in one native state; it controlled the diplomatic relations of another; it ruled other territories directly. The religious hatreds of Hindus and Moslems as well as the caste system made it difficult for Indians to unite against the foreigners. There were never more than a handful of British in the country. When fighting was necessary, they used native troops to do their fighting.

India in the period of the new imperialism

There was plenty of resentment in India against the autocratic rule of the British officials. In 1857 the native troops, or *sepoys,* mutinied. The Sepoy Rebellion almost drove the British out of India altogether. Troops

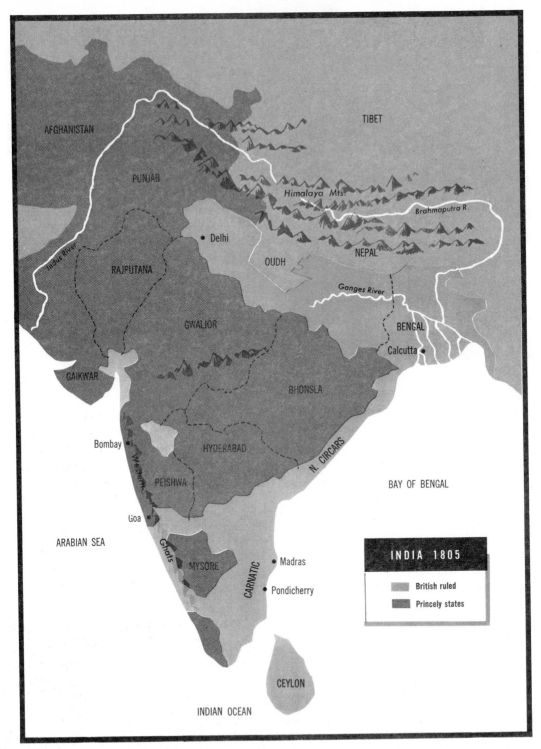

INDIA 1805

British ruled

Princely states

were sent out from Britain, and the rebellion was finally put down. In the following year Parliament passed an act which dissolved the British East India Company and transferred rule of India to the British crown. About twenty years later, Queen Victoria was proclaimed Empress of India. British India made up about five-eighths of the peninsula. The rest consisted of many states, headed by native princes, with varying degrees of self-government. Usually the British controlled the foreign policy of the native princes.

To control India, both British and native, the British used the old Roman device of "divide and rule." They played off one prince against another, granting favors to those who coöperated with the colonial rule and dealing harshly with those who did not. They did not need to do anything to keep the religious feelings stirred up. They treated Hindu and Moslem equally, but they did little to try to appease the hatreds. They did give unity, and put an end to the many local wars and massacres.

British rule brought India into closer contact with the Western World. The British were chiefly interested in profitable trade. To get it, they maintained public order, good administration, and guarded India against foreign invasions. They built roads, bridges, railroads, hospitals, and schools. They tried to improve agricultural methods and to introduce better health and sanitation.

Much of this benefited the Indians, of course, but other effects of British rule were harmful. The Indian handicraft industry almost disappeared. British cotton mills could make cloth so cheaply that it could be carried to India, the home of cotton cloth, and undersell the product of the Indian hand weavers. Local artisans had to go to the city in search of work, or depend on a miserable livelihood from farming.

British land policy also proved bad for India. Much of the land of the Indian villages had been owned in common; it was supervised by a village official whom the villagers chose. The British, probably mistakenly, thought that these officials were owners of the land and that the villagers were tenants. They gave the officials title to the land, and often appointed them tax collectors as well. Thus they created a class of little economic dictators. These men often became money-lenders, too. They loaned money to the villagers to pay their rent and their taxes. The interest rates were exorbitant. The land did not produce enough wealth to pay the debt; so the peasant sank deeper into a debt that often passed on from generation to generation.

● The rise of Indian nationalism

Nineteenth-century British civilization had a terrific impact on India. It was a land of primitive agriculture and handicrafts in isolated villages. It was a land of the Hindu religion, with its rigid caste system and its stubborn holding to tradition. Western industrial culture and Western political ideas clashed with native pride in an ancient civilization and its culture. To the Indian, especially the educated Indian, the Westerner was a materialist, a money-grabber. The Westerner seemed interested only in things; he cared nothing for what were to the Indian the higher values: of mind, soul, and spirit.

When the movement for Indian nationalism arose, it had two distinct wings. Some Indians, especially those who had been educated in British schools and universities, preferred independence gained by Western methods. India would have to advance toward

In 1857 the native troops in India rose against the British. This painting shows Maharini Lakshmi Bai of Jhansi leading her troops in a battle with British cavalry.

independence gradually, by democratic methods. Others wanted not only to break all ties with Britain, but to drive out all Western influence. They wished to revolt not only against the alien British philosophy, but also against the alien religious ideas of Islam in India.

The views of this second group alarmed the Indian Moslems. They were a minority in the land. British rule protected them against discrimination and violence. If British rule were removed, Hindu patriotism might produce an ugly situation. The Moslem was therefore much less enthusiastic about driving out the British than was the Hindu. The independence movement gathered strength very slowly. Down to the time of World War I, the British kept India under a very tight rein.

Review of Chapter 38

People, places, and things

Identify: Buddha, Brahmans, karma, nirvana, Dravidians, Moguls, Asoka, Taj Mahal, sepoys.

Locate: India, Himalaya Mountains, Arabian Sea, Indian Ocean, Tibet, Burma, Java, Ceylon, Indo-China, China, Indus River, Ganges River, Brahmaputra River.

Events in review

1. Name the forces that caused a new wave of imperialism in the nineteenth century.
2. Why did Germany and Italy get a late start in the race for colonies?
3. Define: (a) colony, (b) protectorate, (c) concession, (d) sphere of influence.
4. What was the original purpose of the caste system in India? How was the system kept rigid?
5. Why did the Brahmans oppose Buddhism?
6. What people conquered India during the sixteenth century? What happened to their empire during the seventeenth century, just at the time the Europeans came on the scene?
7. Who dominated India after the French were driven out in 1763? When did the British government take over the rule of India?
8. List beneficial and harmful effects of British rule in India.

Problems and projects

1. Compare the new imperialism of the nineteenth century with imperialism of the sixteenth to eighteenth centuries. Why was India important during the old and the new periods of imperialism?
2. Discuss the differences between Hinduism and Buddhism. How does the Moslem faith differ from Hinduism and Buddhism? (Review Chapter 12 for details on the Moslems.)
3. How did the division between Hindus and Moslems make it easier for the British to control India? Why were the Moslems less eager than the Hindus to drive out the British? What is the situation today? Is there still trouble between Moslems and Hindus? Report on the present situation.
4. Set up a debate on imperialism. One speaker will take the role of a nineteenth-century British statesman defending the duty of his country to carry "the White Man's Burden." Another speaker, in the role of a patriotic Indian, will challenge him.
5. Write a war correspondent's account of one of the events during the Sepoy Mutiny—the relief of Lucknow or the Siege of Delhi, for example.
6. Read one of Kipling's stories about India, or several of his poems. Discuss what his writing shows about the relations between the British and the Indians.

Chapter 39 — The Partition of Africa

IN THE FIRST PERIOD of imperialism Europeans had made little entry into Africa except along the Mediterranean coast and a few scattered coastal trading posts elsewhere. The vast, unexplored interior of the continent was marked on maps as Terra Incognita (unknown land). But during the second half of the nineteenth century the huge land of Africa, the Dark Continent, became the white man's domain.

The white man looks to Africa

Geographically, Africa is divided into three main regions. The northern strip along the Mediterranean Sea can almost be considered a part of Europe. One of the oldest civilizations in the ancient world had existed in the valley of the Nile River, in Egypt. In Roman days North Africa had been a valued part of the empire. Thereafter it had become part of the vast empire of Islam, held by the Arabs and then by the Turks.

South of the Atlas Mountains and the cataracts of the Nile lies tropical Africa: first a vast desert, then dense tropical jungles. Besides the Nile, the tropical region is drained by three great rivers: the Niger and Congo on the west and the Zambezi on the east. Much of Africa is a high plateau, whose edges come very close to the seacoast; therefore, these rivers do not give an easy way into the interior. At the edge of the plateau there are rapids and waterfalls, usually hemmed in on both sides by dense jungles.

Below the tropical region lies South Africa, a region of grasslands and temperate climate. The southern tip, the Cape of Good Hope, was settled by Europeans during the first search for an all-water route to India and the Orient. Ships going to India and the East Indies stopped there for food and water.

The European colonies on the east and west coasts of Africa were trading posts only, with very vague boundaries. The British, French, Portuguese, and Spanish all had claims along the coast. The slave trade was the most valuable. When it was prohibited early in the 1800's, interest in Africa died down.

●The new imperialism in Africa

The division of Africa into colonies is a good example of the new kind of imperialism. Usually the first to come were explorers, scientists, traders, or missionaries. Often they brought back reports of the wealth of the regions. These reports influenced others to follow them. Sometimes they met with resistance and violence from the natives. Then the

soldiers appeared, followed by the consul, "to protect the interests of his nationals." The military were usually followed by builders, engineers, technicians, to open mines, build roads, railroads, bridges, and dams. Then the region would be exploited and developed for the benefit of the developers.

The early explorers discovered that there were regions where white men could live, and that they were rich in business opportunities. There was rich trade with the natives for desirable products, such as ivory. There were minerals to be mined and natural resources to be developed by very cheap native labor. Control could be taken at very little cost.

Africa illustrated the new imperialism in another way: not many Europeans settled in the new regions. Usually a few Europeans controlled great native populations, often through the use of native troops whom they trained and equipped. Even in South Africa, where European settlement was heaviest, the proportion of white to native was very small. In 1950, only one out of every five in South

Two great African explorers meet, Henry M. Stanley and David Livingstone. Livingstone, a missionary as well as explorer, pioneered in probing into "the Dark Continent," starting in 1840. Many years later he disappeared, and Stanley, a reporter for the New York Herald, *went to look for him. In 1871 the two men met in Tanganyika. Stanley's first words—"Dr. Livingstone, I presume"—are famous.*

Africa was white. Elsewhere the proportion was much less.

The partition of Africa will be easier for you to follow on the map if it is arranged geographically, coast by coast. (You will realize that it did not actually happen that way.) We shall begin with the west coast—the side of Africa that faces South America.

West Africa is colonized

● Belgium: the Congo

In the late nineteenth century, Leopold II, King of the Belgians, became interested in the Congo River region of Africa. After much national and international jockeying, he established his authority there, declaring it was his duty "to open to civilization the only part of our globe where it has not yet penetrated, to pierce the darkness which envelops whole populations."

The vast territory of some 900,000 square miles became Leopold's personal property, not a colony of Belgium. It had rubber and ivory to be exploited, but much capital was needed. Leopold formed a corporation and sold stock. The development of the Congo was very profitable, but very hard on the natives. Whole regions were set aside as absolute monopolies of the corporation. Natives were forced to work and were treated with great brutality. The exploitation of the Belgian Congo became an international scandal. There were so many protests that King Leopold finally transferred his colony to the Belgian government.

In their haste for quick profits, the Belgians carelessly destroyed the rubber trees without replanting for the future. However, there was other wealth in gold, diamonds, copper, palm oil, cocoa, rice, cotton, and timber. Today the Belgian Congo is important because it has the largest known deposit of uranium.

The Belgian government improved the treatment of the natives and trained them to do skilled mechanical work. However, the Belgians opposed any degree of self-government, and when the Congo became independent in 1960 it was totally unprepared for it. The Congolese army mutinied, Belgians fled in panic, hunger and disease spread widely, and United Nations troops were sent in to quell violence between battling Congo leaders.

Great Britain: Nigeria

The Niger, second great river of the tropical west, flows into the ocean at the base of the "hump" of western Africa. Control of the river meant control of a vast region with rich resources. A British company set up a trading post at the mouth of the river and pushed steadily inland. For a time there was sharp rivalry with a French company, but the British were able to buy out the French. After a few years the British government bought out the Niger Company and declared Nigeria a protectorate of Great Britain.

France: Senegal, the Ivory Coast, the Gold Coast, French West Africa

France had long held the port of Dakar at the very tip of the "bulge" of West Africa. Using this as a base, they worked inland along the Senegal River and took complete control of the region called Dahomey. In the process they deposed and exiled a protesting native chieftain. A French military force pushed aside the Portuguese, who also claimed the region. The French have since made much use of native troops from this region in their armies. When trained and well equipped, Senegalese have proved themselves fierce fighters.

In the first imperialist period the French had established the colony of French Guinea on the southwest shore of the "bulge." Now they became interested in the nearby Ivory Coast, so called from the abundance of elephants. They seized control of the region and began to expand northward toward Guinea.

The French seaports in Senegal, Guinea, the Ivory Coast, and Dahomey were separated by the possessions of other nations. Therefore, the French worked tirelessly and dangerously to join them in the interior. From the commercial outposts they pushed inland with small military forces, disregarding native opposition and the claims of other countries. They clashed with the British, Portuguese, and Germans. In the explosive European situation of the late 1800's, it seems amazing that they did not touch off a major war. By 1900 the French had rounded up an enormous inland empire called French West Africa. Since it included the Sahara Desert, the size did not necessarily mean wealth. However, there were products of great value in some parts of the region, and the numerous French seaports gave them outlets.

● Germany, Togoland, the Cameroons, German Southwest Africa

For some years after the unification of Germany in the 1870's, Bismarck was not interested in colonies because he doubted their value. Industrial Germans wanted to raise the German flag in Africa and elsewhere, but Bismarck was cool to the suggestions. About 1884 he yielded. Once in the scramble, Germany went the whole way. After Emperor William II dropped Bismarck in 1890, Germany drove even harder for her "place in the sun," for colonies and empire.

A German explorer raised the flag in Togoland, on the south shore of the African bulge. A little farther south a German merchant gained entrance to the Cameroons from a native chieftain and began to push inland. Still farther south, near Britain's Cape Colony, Germans began to establish themselves in Southwest Africa. By cleverly playing Great Britain and France against each other, Bismarck was able to overcome British opposition and gain recognition of German Southwest Africa.

Although Germany's African empire was twice as large as the homeland, the Germans really got only what was "left over." Togoland and the Cameroons were tropical jungles with small populations which could provide few workers. Both water and labor were scarce in Southwest Africa, but the climate made white settlement possible. However, the natives clung to their land, and it was both painful and costly to dislodge them. Throughout Germany's occupation there was much violence and occasional uprisings which had to be put down by force. The Germans begrudged the more valuable possessions of the British and French. They coveted the Belgian Congo and Portuguese Angola, which

they thought they could exploit more efficiently than the Belgians and Portuguese. However, German attempts to buy the Portuguese or Belgian colonies were unsuccessful.

● Spain and Portugal in West Africa

To complete the roundup of the west coast of Africa, it should be mentioned that Spain acquired two colonies: the narrow strip along the northwest coast called Rio de Oro, and Spanish Guinea, just north of the Cameroons. Spain also held the Canary Islands in the Atlantic, and the island of Fernando Po off the coast of the Cameroons. Portugal held two territories: Portuguese Guinea, south of Senegal, and Angola, north of German Southwest Africa.

● Liberia

With only one exception the entire west coast line and vast regions of the interior of Africa had been divided up in the scramble for empire. Look at the southwest shore of the bulge and see the small section marked "Liberia."

The Republic of Liberia had been established in 1847 by freed Negroes from the United States, under the protection of our government. It was a rare political experiment: a Negro republic of former slaves. The republic had many economic difficulties, which at times made its continued independence doubtful. There is little question that it would have ended as the "protectorate" of some ambitious European colonial power if the United States had not intervened and helped Liberia maintain independence.

South Africa becomes colonized

The story of European settlement in South Africa began in 1652, when Capetown was settled as a Dutch naval station. Gradually more Dutch came, mostly farmers, or *Boers,* as the Dutch call them. They were hardy, thrifty pioneers. With Negro labor they built

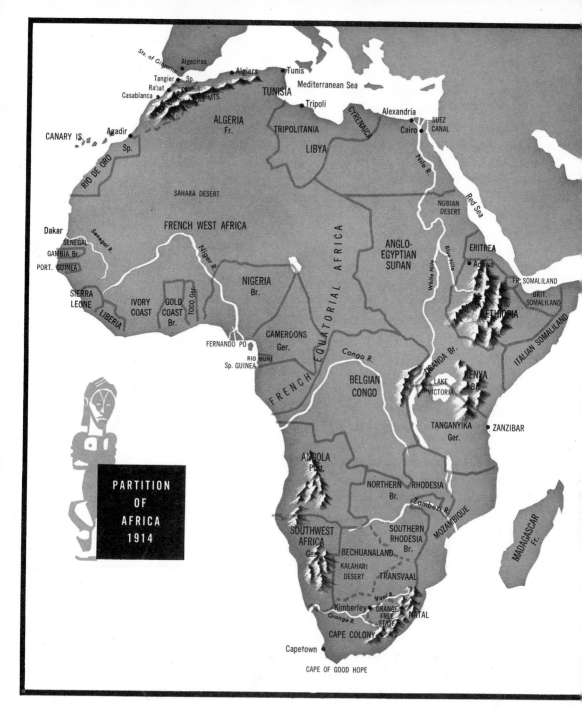

Sts. of Gibraltar
Algeciras
Sp.
Tangier
Rabat
Casablanca
ATLAS MTS.
CANARY IS.
Sp.
Agadir
Sp.
RIO DE ORO
Sp.

Algiers
Tunis
TUNISIA
Tripoli
ALGERIA
Fr.
TRIPOLITANIA
LIBYA
Mediterranean Sea

CYRENAICA
Alexandria
Cairo
SUEZ CANAL

Nile R.
Red Sea
NUBIAN DESERT

SAHARA DESERT

FRENCH WEST AFRICA

Dakar
SENEGAL
GAMBIA Br.
PORT. GUINEA
SIERRA LEONE
LIBERIA
IVORY COAST
GOLD COAST Br.
TOGO Ger.

Senegal R.
Niger R.

NIGERIA
Br.

FERNANDO PO
RIO MUNI
Sp. GUINEA

CAMEROONS
Ger.

FRENCH EQUATORIAL AFRICA

Congo R.

BELGIAN CONGO

ANGLO-EGYPTIAN SUDAN

White Nile
Blue Nile

ERITREA
Adowa
FR. SOMALILAND
BRIT. SOMALILAND
ETHIOPIA
ITALIAN SOMALILAND

UGANDA Br.
LAKE VICTORIA
KENYA
Br.

TANGANYIKA
Ger.
ZANZIBAR

ANGOLA
Port.

NORTHERN RHODESIA
Br.
Zambezi R.

MOZAMBIQUE

MADAGASCAR
Fr.

SOUTHWEST AFRICA
Ger.

BECHUANALAND

SOUTHERN RHODESIA
Br.

KALAHARI DESERT

TRANSVAAL

Vaal R.
Kimberley
Orange R.
ORANGE FREE STATE
NATAL

CAPE COLONY

Capetown
CAPE OF GOOD HOPE

PARTITION
OF
AFRICA
1914

up a colony that was profitable as well as strategically located. They were settlers, planning to found homes, rather than wandering hunters or explorers.

In 1806, during the Napoleonic Wars, Great Britain seized Cape Colony and established British authority. Disliking foreign rule many of the Boers left and trekked to the north. There they carved out settlements for themselves across the Orange and Vaal rivers: the Orange Free State and the Boer Republic of Transvaal (across the Vaal). By 1850 both these states had won recognition of their independence.

Cecil Rhodes

The way in which British Cape Colony expanded to take the Orange Free State, Transvaal, and much more of South Africa is largely the story of one man. In 1870 Cecil Rhodes arrived in Cape Colony from England. He was a clerk, with little money or education and in poor health. The discovery of diamonds in Kimberley, on the north border of Cape Colony, gave Rhodes his chance. He showed a great talent for business and a genius for organization. Within ten years a corporation formed by Rhodes gained a complete monopoly of South African diamond production. The discovery of gold in Transvaal in 1886 was another opportunity for Rhodes' organizing talents. By the mid 1890's Cecil Rhodes, the sickly son of an Anglican minister, had become fabulously wealthy.

Rhodes was a firm believer in the glories of British civilization and culture. He thought that in time it would prevail throughout the world. In his will Rhodes provided a fund for scholarships to Oxford University for students from the British Empire, the United States, and Germany. The purpose was to prepare the way for the peaceful union of all Anglo-Saxon peoples under British leadership. These are the famous Rhodes Scholarships.

Rhodes' dream for Africa was a chain of British colonies from the Cape of Good Hope north to the Mediterranean. He wanted to build a railroad running from Capetown to Cairo through British territory all the way. He began to push the northward expansion of Cape Colony. The first step was the establishment of a protectorate over Bechuanaland, an unclaimed region between Cape Colony, Southwest Africa, the Orange Free State, and Transvaal. Next he organized the British South Africa Company, which gained the huge territory of Rhodesia, north of Bechuanaland and Transvaal.

The Boer republic remained a roadblock in the path of "progress." Transvaal was especially so. After the discovery of gold, the Boers regarded the rush that followed as an invasion of their territory and property rights. They were very religious people, and they regarded the miners as godless, lawless, and destructive, even though they found the miners a profitable source of revenue. Rhodes began to plot the overthrow of the Transvaal government, and organized a raid for this purpose. The raid failed.

The Boer War

Relations between the British and the Boers now became openly hostile. Transvaal allied itself with the Orange Free State, and sought protective alliances with Holland and Germany. The Boers passed high tariffs and other laws discriminating against the British. Grievances were allowed to pile up, until they resulted in a war that began late in 1899 and lasted almost three years.

Twenty-five pounds reward for Churchill, dead or alive. This poster was issued by the Boers during the Boer War. Winston Churchill, later to become famous as prime minister of England, was then a war correspondent. He was captured but escaped from a Boer prisoner-of-war camp.

The Boers fought bravely. As underdogs they had the sympathy of much of the world. In the end, British might prevailed. Transvaal and Orange Free State were annexed to South Africa. The British allowed the Dutch language to be used in schools and courts. Within five years they kept a promise made at the time of the peace and granted self-government to the two Boer states.

In 1910 Cape Colony, Natal, Transvaal, and Orange Free State drew up a federal constitution. In 1920, after the British Parliament had approved the constitution, they united in the federal Union of South Africa. Relations between British and Boers have improved, but they are not too friendly. This problem is small beside the racial problem which has developed within South Africa. This situation is part of a later story.

The east coast of Africa becomes colonized

● German East Africa

While the British were occupied in Bechuanaland, Rhodesia, and with the Boer War, the Germans appeared on the east coast of Africa. Using bribery with cheap trinkets and some threats of force, a German adventurer persuaded some east-coast chieftains to sign agreements placing themselves under his protection. Returning to Germany he persuaded the German government to recognize the documents and declare the regions protectorates of Germany.

Both the British and French had plans for eastern Africa. However, the three nations were able to reach an agreement. France received the large island of Madagascar. A strip of coastland 1,000 miles long and ten miles deep was placed under the rule of the Sultan of Zanzibar, a tiny island off the east coast. The northern half of the strip was recognized as a British "sphere of influence." The southern part became a German "sphere of influence."

A German officer and a tribal chieftain in German East Africa.

East Africa proved to be the most attractive of Germany's African possessions. Germans settled there in some numbers, and the colony produced cotton, hemp, rubber, and other crops. There was a "native problem." As in Southwest Africa there were serious labor problems and unrest. The white settlers took land freely from the natives, which did not make for friendly relations. A rebellion by the native Hottentots required a German army of almost 20,000 to subdue. Some 100,000 natives lost their lives in the rebellion. Despite its promise, the colony never paid its way as a business venture. However, it did block the British dream of a Capetown-to-Cairo railroad through British territory.

● The struggle for Uganda

North of German East Africa lay the attractive territories of Uganda and Kenya. These were objects of the ambition of both Britain and Germany. Christian missionaries had begun to enter the country, but they were badly received by the natives, who were Moslems. In protest against the activities of the Christian missionaries, the natives rebelled

497

and overthrew their ruler. He appealed to the British for help. The British were willing, but they arrived too late. Ambitious Germans from East Africa had hurried to Uganda and occupied the capital. They signed an agreement with the deposed ruler, placing him and his country under the "protection" of Imperial Germany.

This on-the-spot action by Germans was reversed in Berlin. At that time the German government was negotiating with the British to get the small island of Heligoland in the North Sea. In return for Heligoland the British received Uganda, the island of Zanzibar, and favorable border adjustments elsewhere in Africa. The Germans made Heligoland a strong fortress and naval base.

● Italy in East Africa: Somaliland, Eritrea, Abyssinia (Ethiopia)

Like Germany, Italy entered the colonial race late. Her need for colonies as suppliers of needed raw materials and places for surplus population was greater than that of other imperial nations. However, by the time she had become united and could give attention to imperialism, the desirable regions were taken.

After some adventures on the Mediterranean coast, Italy turned her attention to the east coast. Sad to say, there was little of any value on which the "claim-stakes" had not already been put up. All that remained was the uninviting 1,200-mile-long coast of Somaliland facing the Indian Ocean, and an equally unattractive desert region called Eritrea, along the Red Sea. Still, they were better than nothing. An Italian company asked for a lease from the sultan of Zanzibar. After the company had established itself, the Italian government took over the company. Thus Italy satisfied her imperialistic urges with two strips of desert coast line which proved an annual expense to the Italian treasury.

However, there was a chance to expand into the interior. Touching each of the new coast colonies was an interior region, Abyssinia (better known as Ethiopia), ruled by a native emperor. The French were trying to get a concession for a railroad in Ethiopia. When the Italians began to make moves in that direction, the French persuaded the emperor of Abyssinia to cancel a treaty he had made with Italy. Seizing this as a pretext, the Italians invaded Ethiopia from Somaliland. However, the Ethiopian army had been trained and equipped by the French. To the amazement of the world, and especially of the Italians, the invading army was decisively defeated at the battle of Adowa. The Italians withdrew from Ethiopia.

Thus Ethiopia joined Liberia as one of the two sovereign, independent states in Africa. The Western powers, including the United States, sent diplomatic representatives to the Ethiopian capital. Such recognition was a rare experience for a "backward" country in the world of the late nineteenth and early twentieth centuries.

● The Sudan

Below Egypt, and toward the interior from Abyssinia, lies a wide region called the Sudan. It was inhabited by Ethiopians and backward Arab tribes, mountaineers and excellent fighters. Since Great Britain had taken over Egypt, the Sudan became important to her for two reasons: The Nile River rises in the Sudan. Control of the region gave a chance to build dams to control the flow of the vital river. Then, too, control of the Sudan was a step toward the British dream of a Capetown-to-Cairo railroad.

Britain was not alone in wanting the Sudan; the French had ambitions there. Views and threats were exchanged, and war seemed a possibility. Conquering the Sudan did not look like an easy project. Both the British and the Egyptians had already tried to enter the country. They promised better administration and abolition of the slave trade, the curse of the country. However, the warlike

tribes had resisted these attempted intrusions successfully. Nevertheless, both Britain and France regarded the Sudan as a prize worth the risk of war, and both took steps to gain it.

Britain ordered a force in Egypt to push southward along the Nile and establish its authority in the Sudan. The French sent an expedition from their west coast colony, French Congo, and another from Abyssinia. The two-year journey of the western force was a daring one, through some 3,200 miles of tropical jungle. It reached its destination first. A French officer with a small force of Senegalese troops raised the French flag at Fashoda, on the upper Nile.

The British force had fought its way slowly through stiff native resistance. When it reached Fashoda, the British commander insisted that the French flag be lowered and the British and Egyptian flags raised. The tension was relieved when both officers decided to ask their governments for instructions.

Neither government really wanted war; so they negotiated. The French were willing to recognize the British as masters of the Sudan. In return, the French received a vast terri-

The Battle of Omdurman, a British victory during the conquest of the Sudan in 1898. Shown here is the charge of the 21st Lancers. One of the officers of this regiment was Winston Churchill.

tory west of the Sudan adjoining French Congo. The entire area was called French Equatorial Africa. The British also recognized French possession of the Sahara Desert, which united all French possessions in Africa into one contiguous (touching or adjoining) region.

The British then proceeded to suppress all native resistance in the Sudan. Britain pretended that it was a joint occupation by the British and Egyptians, but there was little doubt which held the upper hand. Under British management the region made considerable progress. Public order was maintained; the slave trade was suppressed; the constant local wars which had torn the country were stopped. An irrigation system brought much agricultural improvement. The Sudan produced the world's finest cotton. In contrast to some of the other African colonies, the Sudanese people received considerable benefit from the economic improvements introduced by the British. But it was still colonial rule, and the people seemed to prefer freedom.

North Africa: the Mediterranean Coast

● The French in Algeria

The Mediterranean coast of Africa was long a part of the Arab and Turkish empires. In the nineteenth century most of its people were Moslems—either Egyptians, Arabs, Berbers, or Moors. They had successfully resisted European force for centuries. For a long time the famous Barbary pirates, who operated off the coast of Algeria, had taken a toll of Mediterranean shipping, including ships of the United States.

It was partly the operations of the pirates that gave the French the excuse for their first conquest. In 1830 a French force occupied the country, put the king (dey) under arrest, and settled down to stay. For more than forty years the French fought fairly constant rebellions and widespread violence. Economically, it was worth the price. It was rich land, especially along the coast. The Moslem population was small compared to the size of the country. Many French people moved in, taking over the best land and running the businesses. Algeria became an exporter of farm products, wine, and meat, playing an important part in French economic life.

● The struggle for Tunisia

East of Algeria lies Tunisia, a country of ancient glory. Its capital, Tunis, had once been the formidable Carthage which dominated the central Mediterranean until the Romans, after a century of warfare, captured and destroyed it. In the later 1800's Tunisia was a poor and backward country under Turkish rule. Its ruler, the bey of Tunis, was a lavish spender on his own pleasures. Because the revenues of Tunisia did not support his style of living, he borrowed widely from European bankers. When the loans came due, he was unable to pay. Sensing a chance, the French government gave him financial aid. Thus he was able to meet the financial crisis.

The bey continued his carefree life. When loans fell due, he levied higher taxes. This policy finally brought rebellion in Tunisia. The bey was unable to restore and maintain order. The French government demanded that the bey's creditors set up a commission to keep order and reorganize Tunisia's finances. Reorganization was really needed. The yearly charges to pay the interest and principal of the debt were larger than the entire country's revenue from taxes. After very complicated negotiations a commission was set up with French, British, and Italian members.

All three of the commission nations wanted Tunisia, and the diplomatic maneuvering became quite complicated. In the end, the British and French were able to arrange a trade. The French were given a free hand in Tunisia; in return, they consented to the British occupation of the island of Cyprus. The Germans were consulted. They consented, thinking French success in Tunisia might soften their bitterness over the defeat by Germany in 1870. Only Italy had nothing to trade.

A disturbance by Tunisians along the Algerian border gave the French an excuse. A French army marched in to "restore and maintain order." They forced the bey to sign a treaty which permitted the French to maintain public order, protect the country against foreign influences, and settle the debts to foreign creditors. A few years later another treaty declared Tunisia a French protectorate. The bey still remained ruler in name. However, the French resident-general took charge of foreign affairs, had some voice in local government, and could veto all orders of the bey.

The French made many improvements in Tunisia. They restored order, built roads and schools, set up industries, and put the public finances on a sound basis. Land that had formerly been unused was now made productive, and Tunisia became a healthy place, economically. This was done by Frenchmen, who received the greatest benefits. But some of the improvements benefited the natives as well. However, Tunisians did not completely accept French rule. Religious differences, local pride, and a rising spirit of nationalism made them resent foreign government and aim for either home rule or complete independence.

Italy was bitterly disappointed with the outcome in Tunisia. She was an inexperienced newcomer in the game of imperialism. She had tried to play with the veterans, and she had met the usual fate of the beginner. For years there was ill feeling between Italy and France. When the European powers began to line up and take sides, Italy chose to ally herself with Germany and Austria rather than with Britain, Russia, and France.

The struggle for Morocco

Colonial imperialism was a sort of chain reaction. A gain in one place created a demand for a move somewhere else. Getting Tunisia seemed necessary to protect and extend to the east the French influence in Algeria; so now France thought it needed Morocco for protection to the west.

Look at the map to see the immensely valuable strategic location of Morocco. It forms the south side of the narrow Straits of Gibraltar, the entrance to the Mediterranean. It borders on both the Mediterranean and the Atlantic. The oceans give cooling breezes; the Atlas Mountains cut off the hot winds from the Sahara Desert. The climate is pleasant; the soil is rich.

The Arabs and Moors of Morocco were a warlike people. They had ruled Spain for many centuries, and had successfully defended their own country against invasion. The riches of the country and its strategic location made it a valuable prize for imperialism,

A warship of the early twentieth century. The race for colonies made strong navies important to the great powers. France, Germany, and Great Britain all added to their fleets. Shown here is a British cruiser.

but this in itself was a sort of protection. So many European countries wanted Morocco that each feared to try to take it. Doing so might touch off diplomatic and military dynamite. It finally fell to France.

Because of the very complicated and dangerous situation in Morocco, France proceeded with great caution. The French government first made Italy some promises. If Italy would remain neutral in any struggle over Morocco, the Italian government would have a free hand in Tripoli and Cyrenaica, east of Tunisia. Then came a deal with Britain. France agreed that the British were to have a free hand in Egypt. It also promised that Tangier, the south shore of the Straits of Gibraltar, would go to Spain, which would not fortify it. In return, Britain promised to remain neutral in case of French aggression in Morocco.

For all their diplomatic caution the French had overlooked Germany. Emperor William II was a fiercer imperialist and a much less cautious diplomat than Bismarck. When he learned of the French deals about Morocco, William made a public declaration that Germany considered Morocco a sovereign state, not to be attacked. Because of the great international tension, it was decided to call a

A view in the harbor of Tripoli, largest city in Libya. The minaret of a Mohammedan mosque can be seen in the background. Tripoli was part of the Turkish Empire from 1551 until Italy took it in 1912.

conference of all Western powers to try to settle the Moroccan question without war.

The Algeciras Conference was attended by representatives of thirteen nations, including the United States and Morocco. It was a diplomatic triumph for France. All the participants agreed to a compromise. Morocco was to be "independent," but under international control. Its nearly bankrupt finances were to be controlled by an international bank in Tangier. This bank was to be operated by representatives of the national banks of Britain, France, Spain, and Holland. There was also international control of the Moroccan tariff collection. A Moroccan army was to be under French and Spanish officers and commanded by a Swiss inspector-general. Germany was blocked from any effective claim in Morocco. If France moved carefully, the diplomatic and financial provisions of the agreement gave her a great advantage.

France makes Morocco a protectorate

Morocco continued to be a trouble spot. Natives rose in rebellion against the sultan for accepting European control. There were numerous attacks upon Frenchmen and other Europeans and their property. In 1907, after one such attack, a French warship bombarded Casablanca. French troops then occupied the town and surrounding region. France exacted a heavy indemnity from the sultan.

In 1911 the sultan of Morocco was besieged in his capital city of Fez by rebel forces. He asked the French for help; the French sent an army and occupied the city. Germany protested this move as a violation of the Algeciras agreement. She sent a warship to the port of Agadir "to protect German lives and property." It soon became evident that Germany was willing to allow France to have Morocco if she were given something elsewhere. A bargain was made: France gave Germany part of French Equatorial Africa, and promised again that all nations would have equal rights in Moroccan trade and economic development. Germany withdrew her opposition, and Morocco became a French protectorate like Tunisia.

Italy in North Africa

In the French-Italian deal over Morocco, Italy agreed to be neutral in Morocco, and France was to be neutral in Tripolitania and Cyrenaica. These two desert provinces belonged to the Turkish Empire. They had almost no economic value, but they would be easy to take because Turkish rule was weak and poor. As one diplomat put it, when Italy came to the table, only the crumbs were left. So Italy decided to feast on the crumbs. First she secured guarantees of neutrality from the European powers. Then, on a very flimsy pretext, she declared war on Turkey.

Again, as in Ethiopia, Italy received an unpleasant surprise. The "Sick Man of Europe" made a surprisingly strong resistance. The war, which had been planned as a short one, dragged on for over a year. Trouble in other parts of the empire and pressure from European powers finally made the Turks yield.

Italy took the two provinces and united them into Italian Libya. It was a profitless victory. Except for a narrow strip along the coast, the land is barren. The population was small, but the people violently opposed Italian rule. As a result, the Italian government had the military expense of keeping the country "pacified" for many years.

● Egypt and the Suez Canal

Like most of the rest of North Africa, the ancient land of Egypt was part of the Ottoman Turkish Empire. When the Ottoman Empire was crumbling during the nineteenth century the Turkish khedives (viceroys) in Egypt became almost entirely independent. They still paid tribute to the sultan, but they were absolute, hereditary rulers in Egypt.

Egypt's first great contact with the Europeans during the 1800's came when a French company gained a concession to build a canal through the Isthmus of Suez. Almost half of the stock of the company was bought by the governments of the Ottoman Empire and Egypt. French purchasers bought most of the rest. The canal was completed in 1869.

During the second half of the century the Egyptian government fell into great financial difficulties. The cause was much like that in Tunisia. Egypt's ruler, Ismail Pasha, was a great admirer of Western ways. He began a program of very extensive improvements in the country, far greater than its revenues would pay for. Ismail had very expensive habits himself, and very little concern with financial management. When money was scarce, he had two solutions: raise the taxes and borrow. In the ten years of his rule, he increased the foreign debt of his government by more than twenty times. In time foreign banks refused to lend him more money, even at the highest rates of interest.

Ismail's solution was to sell the Egyptian stock in the Suez Canal. This was an opportunity for the British. On the advice of the

The opening of the Suez Canal, November 17, 1869.

503

great Conservative prime minister, Benjamin Disraeli, the British government bought the Egyptian stock and thus became the largest single stockowner in the canal. The British holding was so large and the rest of the stock so widely scattered, that the British gained virtual control of the canal.

Ismail soon spent the British money, and his government was bankrupt. The next event was both familiar and threatening. The creditors set up an international commission, with representatives from Britain, France, Austria, and Italy, to take over the financial problem. The commission controlled Egyptian borrowing abroad and carefully audited revenues and spending. When a serious crop failure in Egypt reduced the tax revenue, the British and French decided to take drastic steps.

The two governments appealed to the sultan, demanding that Ismail be replaced. It was done. Finances were placed entirely in the hands of the British and French; no other power was permitted to interfere. These arrangements met with considerable resistance among the aristocratic Egyptian upper classes. The resistance was the result of religious differences and national pride. Also, the taxes were not only heavier, but were efficiently collected, even from the aristocrats themselves. When a revolt threatened, the British and French took further action.

● The British take over Egypt

In 1882, as a warning that they were prepared to back their administration with force, the two powers sent a combined naval force. The Egyptians met the threat with rebellion. The British fleet bombarded Alexandria. British troops occupied the city, and soon held the entire country. Because of a crisis at home, the French withdrew. On the other hand, in spite of considerable criticism and opposition at home, the British government refused to withdraw. They said that they had to maintain order and safeguard the canal.

By now the canal was the main highway to India; it was Britain's lifeline of empire. Besides, retreat might mean that British purchasers of Egyptian bonds, to the amount of 150 million dollars, might lose their money. Thus ancient Egypt became a British protectorate. The khedive and his officers were restored to their places. There was a cabinet and an assembly. Behind each, though, was the poorly concealed power of Great Britain.

Many constructive things were accomplished under British rule. Finances were put on a sound basis. The building of the Assuan Dam and an extensive irrigation system placed much more land under cultivation. Courts became less corrupt and more efficient. Forced labor and the more degrading forms of corporal punishment were abolished. There were better roads and harbors. Public education was begun. Even though the improvements reached only a few, it was a beginning. Probably the worst feature of British occupation was that it bolstered up the already wealthy aristocratic class. The Egyptian peasants, the *fellahin,* continued to live in poverty, misery, and ignorance.

The Egyptian aristocrats disliked British rule even though they benefited by it. Here was a vicious circle: The longer the British remained, the stronger became the nationalist feeling against them, and the more the British feared to pull out. The aristocrats used the British as a scapegoat. When there was unrest among the lower classes because of bad conditions, they could always blame it on the hated foreigner. Every concession the British made toward more home rule and self-government was used as the stepping stone to the next demand—that the British withdraw and leave Egypt to the Egyptians. This was the situation on the eve of World War I.

Thus, in the short space of half a century the Dark Continent of Africa was carved and sliced and divided up among the European powers. It was a dangerous process; many times the imperialist rivalries brought the nations to the verge of war. It was done with a complete disregard for any geographic and tribal differences or rights of the natives. During this period the same process was going on in China.

Review of Chapter 39

People, places, and things

Identify: Cecil Rhodes, Boers, Ismail Pasha, Benjamin Disraeli, Hottentots, Berbers.

Locate: Atlas Mountains, Nile, Niger, Congo, Zambezi, Cape of Good Hope, Belgian Congo, Nigeria, Dakar, Senegal River, Dahomey, French Guinea, the Ivory Coast, Togoland, the Cameroons, German Southwest Africa, Canary Islands, Rio de Oro, the Island of Fernando Po, Spanish Guinea, Portuguese Guinea, Angola, the Orange and Vaal Rivers, Transvaal, Orange Free State, Cape Colony, Kimberley, Capetown, Cairo, Bechuanaland, Rhodesia, Zanzibar, Madagascar, Uganda, Kenya, Heligoland, Somaliland, Eritrea, Abyssinia (Ethiopia), Egypt, the Suez, Sudan, Algeria, Tunisia, Morocco, Tripoli, Cyrenaica, Tangier, Libya, Cyprus.

Events in review

1. Geographically, Africa can be divided into three regions. Briefly describe these three.
2. In what ways did the partition of Africa illustrate the "standard operating procedure" of the new imperialism?
3. How and by whom was the Congo exploited?
4. How valuable was Germany's "place in the sun" in Africa?
5. How was Liberia founded? How was it able to remain independent?
6. What powers fought the Boer War? What was the outcome of the war?
7. Explain how the island of Heligoland became a factor in the partition of Africa.
8. What was "the Fashoda incident"? Describe the settlement that followed the affair.
9. Tell briefly how France acquired control of Tunisia.
10. How did the Germans enter into the dealings over Morocco?
11. How did the British become virtual owners of the Suez Canal?

Problems and projects

1. Compare the degree of success of the European powers that partitioned Africa. Which nation got the greatest area of land? Which got the most valuable colonies? Which nations got the "crumbs from the table"? Can you explain why some nations got so much more than others?
2. In Tunisia and Egypt inefficiency in handling taxes and paying debts gave European powers a chance to "get a foot in the door." Describe the pattern of events by which financial problems led to intervention, and intervention turned into domination. Give specific details for two countries.
3. Make a summary of the steps by which France acquired control of Morocco. Include French maneuvers and international bargains.
4. History is being made at a rapid pace at present. Watch the newspapers and magazines for the day-to-day history of Africa. Report to the class any significant developments in such areas as Algeria. What is happening to "the White Man's Burden" in Africa?
5. Discuss the British policy that resulted in the establishment of Ghana as a new nation in 1957. What benefits have the people of Ghana received from the British? Could the case of Ghana serve as a model for ending colonialism in the rest of the world?
6. The history of Africa in the nineteenth century contains more famous events than can be covered in one book. Look up one of the following and write a report on it: Stanley's explorations and his meeting with Dr. Livingstone, the Jameson Raid, the death of General Gordon at Khartoum, Winston Churchill's adventures as a soldier in the Sudan or as a correspondent during the Boer War.
7. Make a map of Africa in 1914. Show by different colors, shading, crosshatching, etc.: (a) the colonial possessions of Great Britain, France, Germany, Portugal, Spain, Italy, Belgium, (b) the remaining independent states.

Chapter 40

The New Imperialism: China

THE ANCIENT LAND of China was a fertile field for the new imperialism. The methods of imperialism were not the same as in Africa. The Europeans found in China a great civilization and a government that had at times been powerful. Instead of dividing the country into colonies, the outside powers staked out claims for special interests and spheres of influence. To understand what went on, you need to know something of China's geography, history, and civilization.

The land and the people of China

Look at the map on page 507. The Chinese Empire, which lasted until 1912, took in the area bounded by the heavy colored line—a region larger than the United States. Within the empire there were subdivisions. The major ones have their boundaries marked by lighter colored lines. The heart of China, with its eastern edge the seacoast, is called China Proper. Surrounding this in a semicircle are regions called the vassal states: Tibet to the west, Sinkiang to the northwest, Mongolia and Manchuria to the north. Though not included within the empire, Korea was dominated by the rulers of China.

Nature has set China Proper off from surrounding regions by high mountain ranges, desolate deserts, and the sea. This isolation is found everywhere except to the north. Here, in the third century B.C., the Chinese tried to protect themselves from invasion by a man-made barrier, the Great Wall of China. This amazing structure runs across plains and mountains for more than 1,500 miles. (See the map on page 523.)

Chinese isolation did not protect it from foreign invasion and conquest, even before the Europeans came in the nineteenth century. Many times during the long centuries of its history it was conquered and ruled by foreigners: Tartars, Mongols, and Manchus. Sometimes foreign rule lasted for several centuries, but invariably it broke down. Then the invaders were absorbed into the Chinese population.

In the western regions of China there are some of the highest mountains in the world. From there the elevation of the land descends gradually until it reaches the Great Plains in the north and the Pacific Ocean in the south. A very important mountain range runs through the center of the area from west to east. It separates the valleys of the two greatest rivers, and divides China Proper into two regions which are rather different from each other. North China is a wheat-growing region; South China a rice-growing region. There are differences in language and culture, too.

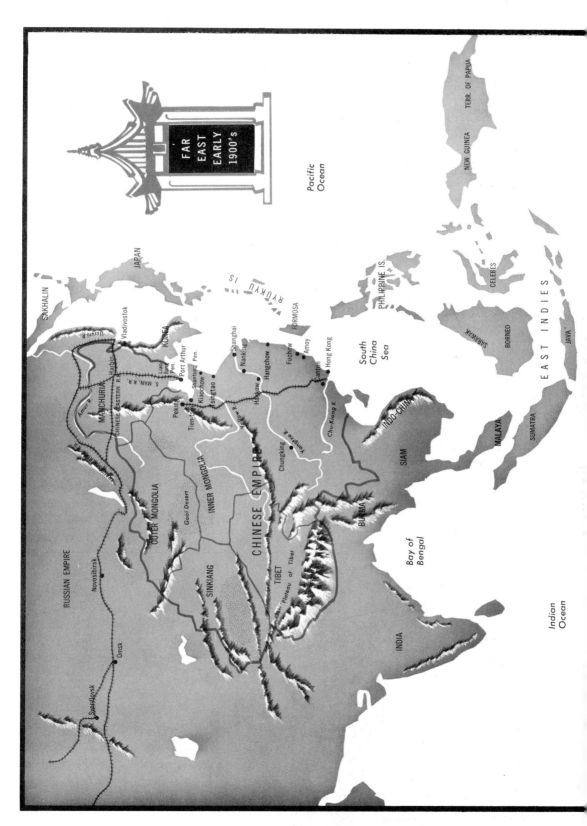

FAR
EAST
EARLY
1900's

Pacific Ocean

SAKHALIN

JAPAN

RYUKYU IS.

SAKHALIN

Vladivostok

KOREA

Harbin

Amur R.

MANCHURIA

CHINESE EASTERN R.R.

S. MAN. R.R.

Port Arthur

Liao Tung Pen.

Shantung Pen.

Peking

Tientsin

Kiaochow

Tsingtao

FORMOSA

Shanghai

Nanking

Hankow

Hangchow

Fuchow

Amoy

Hong Kong

Canton

PHILIPPINE IS.

South
China
Sea

Yellow R.

Yangtze R.

Chungking

Chu-Kiang R.

OUTER MONGOLIA

Gobi Desert

INNER MONGOLIA

CHINESE EMPIRE

TIBET

Plateau of Tibet

SINKIANG

RUSSIAN EMPIRE

Novosibirsk

Omsk

Sverdlovsk

BURMA

SIAM

INDO-CHINA

MALAYA

SUMATRA

NEW GUINEA

TERR. OF PAPUA

CELEBES

SARAWAK

BORNEO

JAVA

EAST INDIES

INDIA

Bay of
Bengal

Indian
Ocean

● Rivers and seaports

China has many rivers, but two of them have played the most important parts in its civilization and culture. In the north is the Yellow River, with a total length of 2,700 miles. Because of its shallowness it is almost useless for navigation. It carries a great burden of silt, which settles rapidly to the bottom. This river is very hard to keep within its banks. The Chinese build dikes, but when the dikes break, as they sometimes do during the summer floods, the river runs wild. Because of the destruction it causes, the Yellow River is called "China's Sorrow." Sometimes it cuts a completely new channel to the sea.

The Yangtze River in central China is 3,200 miles long, and very deep through most of its course. Large ocean-going ships can go up the river 600 miles to the great city of Hankow. Ships of shallower draft can go to Chungking, more than 1,300 miles from the sea.

China has excellent seaports: Hong Kong; Shanghai, near the mouth of the Yangtze; Canton, near the mouth of the Chu-Kiang River; Tientsin, Hangchow, Swatow, Amoy, Fuchow, and Dairen. These seaports and the broad highway of the Yangtze River offered a chance for invasion from the sea. The imperialist powers used these openings when they began to exploit China.

River steamers in the gorges of the Yangtze River, more than one thousand miles from the sea.

● Population and resources

China has a population of at least 450,000,-000 people in its vast area. It has some resources which are valuable in modern industry, such as coal and tungsten. The great resource is the land itself. At least three fourths of the people are farmers. They live in villages rather than scattered farmhouses. You can understand how dense the population is, if you can imagine that every isolated farm in the United States were a village of some 200 families.

The population of China is not spread evenly throughout the area. About two-thirds of China's area is mountainous or barren; it can support only a small percentage of its population. As a result, *six-sevenths (about 85 per cent) of the people live on one-third of the land*. In the valleys of the Yangtze and Yellow rivers, on the North China Plain, and along the southeastern coast, the population varies from 400 to almost 900 persons to the square mile.

Of the provinces surrounding China Proper, Manchuria is the most valuable. It has good mineral resources, and the soil of its plains is fertile. It produces enough of its staple crop, the soybean, to feed a growing population, and more for export. Millions of Chinese have moved into Manchuria.

Chinese civilizations rise and fall

China today is dominated by a Communist government. It is hard to say what course the history of this new China will take. The present chapter goes back to China as it was in the old days of the empire. Old China was a land of twenty-four dynasties (successions of emperors of the same family). China could claim the oldest continuing civilization in the world, with records going back some 2,000 years before the time of Christ. (The records of ancient Egypt go back even further; but this culture did not endure until modern

times, as China's did.) Chinese civilization began in the great bend of the Yellow River. Its economic life, based on agriculture, and its well organized form of government allowed it to spread gradually. Thus the original Chinese people were able to take in the whole of China Proper, and at times, some of the surrounding regions.

A mighty civilization it was! A written language was developed. Chinese works of poetry and philosophy rank among the world's greatest. Chinese painting was exquisite. Chinese handicrafts in metal, stone, embroidered silk, pottery, and porcelain show that her craftsmen were patient, skillful, and had a deep sense of grace and beauty. Chinese scientists discovered the art of paper-making, and invented block printing—printing from carved wooden blocks. They discovered gunpowder and used it for fireworks to drive away evil spirits. The Chinese developed a

Chinese architecture—a temple originally built during the Ming Dynasty (1368–1643 A.D.).

style of architecture which is not only practical but beautiful, and which fits lovingly into the landscape. They delved deep into mathematics and astronomy, and were among the first to develop a solar (sun) calendar.

The daily lives of the people were regulated according to the teachings of the greatest philosophers. It was, for the most part, a peaceful and orderly civilization. The highest social position went to scholars, the lowest to soldiers. For many centuries its system of agriculture supported a much larger population than the agriculture of Europe could support. It gave us, among so many other things, the blessing of tea.

Chinese civilization needed little from the outside, either materially or spiritually. Countries that wanted to trade with China were

509

allowed to do so only if they recognized the emperor as "the Son of Heaven, ruler of the world." Foreign ambassadors had to kneel before him and touch their foreheads to the floor nine times. As late as the eighteenth century, when King George III of England sent an ambassador to ask for trade privileges, a Chinese emperor could reply that China had no use for English products. However, the emperor said that he had heard that the English could not live without China's tea and silk; so he would allow a few ships to come and trade.

● Cycles in Chinese history

China's history is not one of an even, gradual rise of civilization over 4,000 years. It is a story of cycles. A gradual rise of civilization would take place during a period of orderly government, reach a peak, and then decline as government became weaker. The decline would reach a low point of confusion, disorder, and rebellion. Then usually the dynasty would be overthrown and a new one established.

It was usually during these low ebbs that outside invaders were able to conquer the country and set up their dynasties as rulers. Between the mid-thirteenth and the mid-fourteenth century, A.D., the Mongols conquered China. It became part of the vast empire of Kublai Khan and his successors. More recently, the Manchus from Manchuria were

The Great Wall, built to protect China against invaders from the north. Running more than 1,500 miles, the wall is the longest fortified defense line ever constructed. Compare Hadrian's wall (page 124) and the Maginot Line (page 628).

able to cross the Great Wall and set up a dynasty which ruled China from 1644 until 1912.

To understand why the imperialistic powers were able to exploit China so easily, you have to understand the law of the cycle more fully. During the period of chaos that marked the end of one dynasty and the beginning of another, there were floods, famines, wars, and rebellion. Farms were destroyed, and land went out of cultivation. It was usually a period of complete disorder, and it sometimes lasted several hundred years. During this period millions of people died of starvation or were killed in war; the population was greatly reduced. This had one good effect: there was enough good land to go around, and this land was redistributed. When the new dynasty gained control, most people had enough land to support themselves. Thus they could pay enough taxes to support the new government.

● *Taxes and landholdings*

Local government in China was in the hands of an official class, the landlord-gentry. They owned rather large amounts of land, which they usually rented to tenants. The rental was high. Fifty to sixty per cent of the harvest was fairly common rent. These officials had charge of tax collection. Usually they used tax collectors who did the job personally; sometimes this position was hereditary. The collectors naturally paid themselves well by squeezing the peasants for everything they could get.

The large landlords were usually too powerful to be forced to pay much in taxes. At the most, they paid only small amounts. Therefore, the great burden of taxation fell on the poorer peasants. Often the landlords and officials were also moneylenders, making loans to tide the peasants over from seedtime till harvest. Rates of interest were high.

The Chinese family also played a part in the cycle. The father had complete control.

The family included his wife, his unmarried daughters, and his sons with their wives and children. The father owned the land; the family worked for him. When he died, the land was equally divided among the sons. Each son then became the head of his own family unit. In an agricultural country, this equal division of land among the sons was necessary; there was no other way for them to live.

As time passed, the individual landholdings became smaller and smaller. Taxes remained high, and had to be paid. Sometimes when the government was having financial troubles, taxes were collected years in advance, by force. Eventually, the landholding of the family became too small to support it and pay the taxes. Money had to be borrowed. When the debt could not be paid, the owner lost his land and became a tenant. Sometimes he was forced to leave the land altogether.

● *Bandits and war lords*

In a farming region there were few places for a landless man to go. He might go to a city and try to find work as a laborer, but jobs of this sort were scarce. He might become a beggar. But many proud men took another course. They took to the hills and became bandits. Increasingly, the division of land, the high taxes which fell most heavily on the peasants, the loans at high interest rates, the high rentals, forced more and more men into banditry. Groups of them banded together under leaders. Sometimes a bandit leader would become powerful enough to try to get control of a region, or a whole province. He was called a war lord.

This meant, of course, that the imperial government was faced with rebellions. As time went on, rebellions became more numerous, and the emperor's government had to give more of its attention and spend more of its revenue to put them down. Dikes and irrigation systems were neglected; floods and famines followed to make the whole situation worse. Eventually, the dynasty was overthrown, and a period of anarchy, confusion, and civil war followed. War lords struggled among themselves for power. Eventually some one of them was able to extend his control over several provinces and make his position hereditary. In time, his sons and grandsons extended the family rule. After a long period a new dynasty emerged, and the cycle began again.

At the time the Europeans came in the mid-1800's, the Manchu dynasty was reaching the lowest ebb of its cycle. It had ruled China since about 1644. The Europeans took advantage of the Manchu weakness, but they probably kept the Manchus in power longer than they would have stayed otherwise. European influence probably kept the fall of the Manchus from being as violent and sweeping as it might have been. The fall of the Manchus in 1912 was the beginning of modern China. Modern China began without the redistribution of land that usually accompanied the overthrow of a dynasty. Perhaps that is one reason why lately the slogan "Land for the peasants" had such a great appeal in China.

Chinese civilization is influenced by three philosophers

The Chinese people's ideas about life and living were based on the teachings of their greatest philosophers. This was also true of their attitude toward government. Therefore, in order to understand Chinese life and government, you must know something of the lives and teachings of three great philosophers.

● Lao-tze

Lao-tze, who was born sometime around 500 B.C., was the founder of a way of thinking called *Taoism*. It got its name because its central idea is *Tao,* which means the Way of Nature. Lao-tze said that Tao is an indescribable something which governs the universe and all nature. Man may bring himself into harmony with Tao by practicing three great virtues: humility, frugality, and contentment. Men should not strive for learning, riches, or power. Such efforts, he said, do not bring the Tao into harmony with man. People should try, rather, to bring themselves into harmony with the Tao by being quiet, thoughtful, and humble. As Lao-tze said, "He who overcomes others is strong; he who overcomes himself is mighty."

Lao-tze himself did not believe in temples or a formal religion. However, after his death his teachings were organized into a religion. He had laughed at the idea of gods; yet he came to be worshipped as a god. He had taught that life is a sorry sort of vanity at best; yet Taoist priests sold charms which would give life everlasting! Taoism had a great appeal for the masses of peasants. It declared that wealth and power were meaningless, and peasants were surely poor and weak. They could not, of course, follow the main idea, and remain inactive; they could not leave everything to nature, for that meant starvation. But Taoism's veneration for one's ancestors, and the belief that the ancestors are closely associated with every act of the descendants, were powerful influences in Chinese life.

● Confucius

Even more powerful were the teachings of Kung-fu-tze, which means Kung the Philosopher, or Reverend Master. Westerners translate this name as Confucius. He lived, perhaps fifty years after Lao-tze, in a time of great disorder and confusion. The central government had broken down, and there were war lords everywhere. Confucius had little to say about the idea of god, the meaning of death, or the idea of life after death. He was not a religious prophet, nor especially a religious man, as we use the term. But he did have ideas about life, and the good life. Because of the times in which he lived, he believed that the good life depended on order, and that order depended on good government.

Confucius was the son of an aristocrat. His father died when the boy was only three years old, and the family was left in poverty. In spite of this, Confucius managed to get a good education. At the age of twenty-two he set himself up as a teacher, and soon gained a great following. He gathered and edited much of the wisdom and writings of earlier men, which were published in nine books now called the Confucian Classics.

Confucius taught that government depends on good example. If the prince lives and rules virtuously, he will be obeyed by a virtuous people. Virtue, in the Confucian teaching, consists of correct behavior toward others. Its greatest statement resembles the Christian Golden Rule, although stated negatively: "What you do not like when done unto yourself, do not do unto others." There are five important relationships in virtuous behavior: the relation between husband and wife, between younger brother and older brother, between father and son, between prince and minister, and between friend and friend. These relationships form a code of behavior which stresses loyalty, charity, propriety, justice, wisdom, and, above all, obedience.

Confucius hoped to put his ideas into practice by becoming minister to a war lord. The story is that he was given a high post, minister of crime, in his native province of Shantung. Within a year, according to the story, he had supplied the people with an elaborate system of rules to regulate their daily behavior, and crime had almost disappeared. But, again according to the story, neighboring war lords became jealous of the progress of the province. To upset things, they sent a troupe of beautiful "singsong" girls and handsome horses to Confucius' master, who promptly began to neglect the business of government. Things gradually grew worse; the people ceased to obey the code. Finding his advice unheeded, Confucius retired and lived the rest of his life in disappointment.

But the teachings of Confucius lived on. They taught right living. They were not based on some divine idea, but on the deep Chinese family feeling of reverence for ancestors and ancient wisdom. They have had a powerful influence on Chinese life and thought in the 2,500 years since Confucius' time.

● Buddhism in China

The third great influence on Chinese thought and religious belief was Buddha. By the third century B.C., Buddhism had been carried out of India by missionaries. A strong dynasty ruled China from 200 B.C. to 200 A.D. During this time China had many contacts with other countries. It was then that missionaries from India brought in Buddhism. When this dynasty was breaking up and Tartar nomads from the north were raiding China, the Buddhist teachings found many

A Buddhist shrine in China. This copper statue, weighing more than fifty-five tons, was made during the Sung Dynasty (960–1278 A.D.).

converts, especially among the peasants. Neither Taoism nor Confucianism offered them much consolation in this time of crisis. Buddhism, with its idea of nirvana, which the Chinese interpreted as immortal happiness after death, offered an escape from the miseries of the present. By then temples, ceremonies, rituals, priests, music, and incense had been added to Gautama's ideas, and they had a strong appeal.

All of these ideas influenced the attitude of the Chinese people toward life itself, and toward government. In time, the three philosophies all became religions of a sort. They were so much alike that people could accept more than one at a time. Many considered themselves followers of all three. Confucianism, with its reverence for the past and emphasis on the family, was probably the most widespread. The Chinese had always revered their ancestors, and worshiped the emperor as almost a divine being. These things continued. The other ideas—humility, contentment, loyalty, justice, wisdom, and obedience—made the Chinese of all classes a patient, enduring person. He was resigned to his lot. He resorted to violence and rebellion only when that lot became unendurable.

In Chinese society it was the family, not the government, that was the center of national life. There were relationships between family and family. The government was a sort of overseer of these relationships. Within the family the father was the head, the guardian of the welfare of all the members. As head of the family, the father was greatly concerned that all of the individuals under his control lived up to their obligations, the standards of conduct as prescribed by Confucius. If the family units were properly administered, general affairs were bound to be healthy.

● Local government

This meant that local governments had a great deal of freedom and responsibility. As

Sun	Moon	High	Elephant

Chinese writing, showing steps in the development of characters from the fourteenth century B.C. to modern times. The four columns show how the symbols for Sun, Moon, High, and Elephant evolved from simple pictures to complicated characters.

long as local authorities met their tax collecting responsibilities and did not question any vital principle, they could carry on their administrative duties in any way that they saw fit.

The system of appointing local officials was very interesting. Confucius considered politics and government a very honorable profession. A person entered it only after rigid training. Officials shared with scholars the highest social rank in the system; scholars and officials were really the same. No man could receive a government position unless he took an extremely difficult examination based on the classics.

Education was not a responsibility of government, either national or local. Children were educated by tutors. In those families which could not afford to hire a tutor, the children went uneducated. It is estimated that down to the year 1900 not more than five per cent of the Chinese people were literate. The reason for this was partly financial: the expense of paying a tutor. In part, though, it came from the difficulties of the Chinese writing. Although the Chinese developed a written language very early in their history, they never did reduce it to an alphabet. The written symbols stood for entire words; a person had to memorize thousands of symbols to be able to read the classics.

● *The civil service*

In earlier times the small percentage of educated people meant that the officials of the civil service were, in practice, members of the wealthy, landlord-gentry class. They were scholars, for they had to be highly educated in the classics to pass the examinations. In making appointments of successful candidates, two rules were followed: no official could serve in the locality in which he was born. No official could serve more than three years in any one locality.

At first glance, this system seems admirable. Only highly educated, intelligent scholars could serve as government officials. Further examination shows that it had several possible weaknesses. The knowledge needed to pass the examinations was not practical knowledge of the day-to-day problems of government, especially the kinds of problems which the Chinese came to face in their contacts with the West during the nineteenth century. Also, in actual practice positions in the government were open to a very small minority. This minority was already a wealthy class, and they often used their official positions to increase their wealth.

● *The emperor*

At the head of the entire government was the emperor, the Son of Heaven, whom the Chinese believed to be divinely inspired. He was not a divine-right ruler in the Western sense. Confucius taught that the ruler has duties and responsibilities to his people; he also must act and rule virtuously. As long as he ruled in accordance with the interests of the people, he could be either Chinese or foreign. If he failed to rule properly, he lost his divinity and his position as well. His subjects had the right to depose him and replace him with someone else more fitting.

The Chinese developed a written language early in their history. This inscription comes from a bronze vessel made as early as 1000 B.C. Translation: "Po Che-fu made this precious vessel to be used for offerings when royalty is formally received."

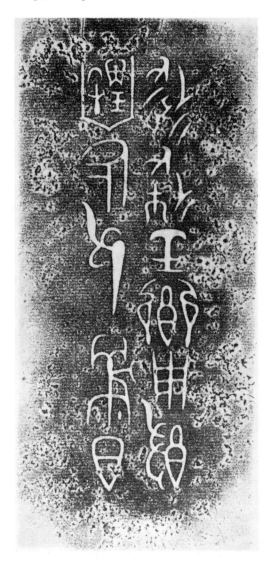

● *Attitudes toward war*

One other feature of Confucian and Chinese thinking had great influence on their struggle with the West. Confucius and later Chinese thinkers taught that no one could gain virtue and righteousness by military force. If an idea or a practice was right, it was bound to win out. Chinese people of all classes followed this practice in their lives. A Chinese peasant would argue endlessly with a neighbor. They might stand in the middle of the village street and argue forcefully, paying no heed to the crowd that gathered. But neither would strike the other. If one did, he "lost face" because by using force he admitted that his cause was not just or right. Thus the old philosophy denied the policy of war except as a last resort of defense. The wars which China at times waged against her neighbors were conducted by rulers who were not followers of Confucius.

The Chinese remain an isolated people

When the European powers began their drive for colonies, protectorates, and spheres of influence in the mid-nineteenth century, China was isolated both externally and internally. There were a few European merchants in some of the port cities, but they had little influence on the life and thought of the country. There was almost no knowledge of the world beyond the borders. Within the country, poor transportation made each village an isolated community, with little contact beyond its neighbors.

The entire philosophy which governed the life of the country was different from that of the West. The Western ideas of nationalism, government, and sovereignty were beyond the comprehension of the Chinese. They simply did not fit the system of thought. Then, too, China was an agricultural country. There had been no Industrial Revolution to produce the goods, weapons, and means of transportation on which the West now depended.

The national government of China was then very feeble. The Manchu dynasty was rapidly declining; its cycle had about run out. Land ownership had become concentrated in too few hands; the tax system was failing; and banditry was increasing. When the Manchus failed to stop the intrusions of the West, there was only one solution according to the Confucian thinking: the rulers had failed in their duty, and so ought to be replaced. Thus, after the 1850's the dynasty was under attack by the Europeans from without and also by groups from within. In 1852, the Taiping Rebellion began in the south and spread rapidly to the north. It lasted twelve years. Although it was finally put down, the position of the Manchus was hopelessly weakened.

The Europeans end Chinese isolation

Chinese isolation really ended in 1839–1842 through a war with England which is often called the Opium War. British merchants at Canton had built up a profitable trade bringing in opium from India and selling it throughout South China. It was profitable to the British, but it did much physical and moral damage to the Chinese. So the Chinese authorities ordered the sale of opium stopped and all opium turned over to them. When the British merchants refused, they were put under arrest by the Chinese officials. There was a bitter exchange of demands and counterdemands between the two governments. At the end of a three-year war, the British occupied Canton and the nearby coastal region.

Then came the first of the treaties which China was forced to sign, which the Chinese therefore call "the unequal treaties." China was compelled to open the ports of Canton, Shanghai, Fuchow, Amoy, and Ningpo to British trade; these were then known as "treaty ports." No tariff of more than five per cent could be charged on British goods. A further provision stated that British subjects in these ports were under British, and not Chinese, law. The implication was that Chinese laws were too primitive to be applied to foreigners. The foreigner came under his own laws, and was tried in his own courts. This sort of provision came to be known as *extraterritoriality*.

In the world of the 1850's Britain could not hold her privileged, monopolistic position in China very long. France and other Western powers, including the United States, demanded and received similar treaties with similar privileges. Western influence, both of merchants and missionaries, penetrated the country still farther. The Taiping Rebellion was a revolt against both this increasing foreign influence and the Manchus who failed to prevent it. The Western governments insisted on "protecting their nationals." When the Manchus failed to do so, there was another short war with Britain and France. Again the Chinese were thoroughly defeated. Again, in 1858, an "unequal treaty" had to be signed.

The treaty of 1858 opened additional "treaty ports" on the coast and also along the Yangtze River. A British embassy was opened in the capital at Peking, soon to be followed by embassies of all the other powers. The Chinese government pledged proper protection to Christian missionaries and their converts. Britain took the rocky island of Hong Kong at the mouth of the Pearl River, and a small section of the mainland. Russia, in separate treaties, received even more than trade privileges and extraterritoriality. It got all territory north of the Amur and east of the Ussuri rivers. Thus Russia gained eastern Siberia, and with it the Pacific port of Vladivostok.

Japan and China quarrel over Korea

Now a new country appeared in the picture. In the mid-1800's Japan had been opened up to the Western nations. Soon it had

A pavilion in the Summer Palace of the Chinese emperors, at Peking.

learned so much from the Europeans that it outdid the West. The territory that interested Japan was the nearby peninsula of Korea. During the second half of the nineteenth century Korea was isolated from foreign penetration. It was still a dependency of China. Korean authorities had to refer all questions of foreign relations to the Chinese emperors. It was clear that this Korean isolation could not last long. Russia, France, and the United States were all interested in gaining trade privileges there. Japan feared that if Korea fell under control of some Western power, this nearby foreign base would be a threat to her safety. Therefore, Japan also began to press for privileges in Korea.

The Koreans feared and hated Japanese influence and interference. They referred Japanese demands to China; the Chinese authorities referred them back to Korea. When the Japanese did get a treaty which opened some Korean ports to Japanese trade, they maintained that Korea was entirely independent. China still maintained that Korea was a dependency. To counteract Japanese gains, the Chinese allowed Korea to make trade treaties with six European nations.

The Sino-Japanese War

There followed a long story of moves and countermoves in which Japan tried to increase her influence in the peninsula. In 1894 a rebellion broke out in Korea. Both Japan and China sent armed forces to put it down. It was an explosive situation, and it exploded. There was a short war. In a few weeks the seeming giant, China, was defeated by the seeming pygmy, Japan.

Japan now imitated the West still further with an "unequal treaty." The Chinese were compelled to recognize the complete independence of Korea. They had to cede to Japan the long chain of islands which extends to the south: the Ryukyus, the Pescadores, and the great island of Taiwan, or Formosa. There was another provision of great importance. Look on the map at the southern coast of Manchuria. See how the Liaotung Peninsula extends southward into the ocean (the Yellow Sea). It has great strategic value to Japan, and China had to cede it to Japan. In addition, China agreed to pay Japan an indemnity of 150 million dollars.

The Western powers were not especially pleased to find that Japan had learned her lessons so well. Russia, especially, had plans of her own for Manchuria and the Liaotung Peninsula. She wanted no strong power in

Korea or Liaotung, close to her new naval base at Vladivostok. Also, she hoped to link her Trans-Siberian Railroad to Liaotung by a line from Harbin, in Manchuria, to Port Arthur, at the tip of the peninsula. France backed Russia because of an alliance. Germany, strangely enough, did so in the hope of weakening the French-Russian alliance, which she felt was aimed at her. For different and conflicting motives, the three powers came to the "aid" of China.

When the terms of the Japanese treaty were announced, Russia, Germany, and France united to bring pressure to keep Japan off the Asiatic mainland. In a joint note they "advised" the Japanese government to withdraw. The Japanese were furious, but they were not ready to face such an array of force. They gave Liaotung back to China in return for an increased indemnity. The Japanese had won the war, but not the peace.

China goes to pieces

More than any previous event, the victory of Japan showed the world the complete weakness of China. Now she became more than ever the helpless battleground of conflicting imperial ambitions. France and Russia gave her further "aid"—a loan to help her pay the indemnity to Japan. Of course, there was a catch to it. China had to pledge that no foreign power would be given any rights in Chinese financial matters unless the same rights were given to France and Russia. Britain and Germany hastened to make similar loans with the same provisions.

China had still more bills to pay for her foreign "aid." France demanded and received special rights to develop mineral resources of south China, trading privileges, and the right to link China with the French protectorate in Indo-China. Germany was given a 99-year lease of Tsingtao on the wonderful Bay of Kiaochow, on the south shore of the Shantung Peninsula. She also received min-

The Trans-Siberian Railway under construction.

ing rights and the right to build a railway in Shantung. Great Britain would not be left out. She took more trading privileges in the Yangtze Valley and the right to build a naval base at Wei-hai-wei, in Shantung. This was to balance the German base on the Shantung Peninsula. The price the Russians exacted for their "aid" calls for a longer explanation.

● *Russian interests in Manchuria*

Look once more at the map of the northern part of China and the province of Manchuria. See how the northern border of Manchuria follows the long, curving line of the Amur River. See that Manchuria's eastern border is the Ussuri River. All territory north of the Amur and east of the Ussuri rivers had been given by China to Russia. At the southern tip of the eastern Russian territory was the seaport, Vladivostok, where the Russians had built a naval base. Manchuria extends up, in a great hump, into Russian Eastern Siberia.

In 1891 the Russians had begun a gigantic project, the building of a railroad from western Russia all the way to Vladivostok. If this Trans-Siberian Railroad had to follow the long curving line of the Amur, it would be 350 miles longer than if it could cut straight across Manchuria to Vladivostok. The Manchurian route also offered fewer difficulties in the form of rivers and mountains.

Therefore, Russia's bill for "aid" was a leased right of way, tax free, across Manchuria. She was to have the right to "maintain order" along the entire route, and certain other extraterritorial privileges. Thus northern Manchuria would be under Russian economic and military domination. The result of that sort of thing was an old story. In a further and secret treaty, Russia and China formed an alliance for mutual aid in case either should become involved in war with Japan.

When the Germans and British seized their bases in Shantung, Russia wanted entry to the Yellow Sea, too. She forced China to lease her the southern part of the Liaotung Peninsula and built a naval base at Port Arthur. She also built the South Manchurian Railway, the branch of the Chinese Eastern Railway, from Harbin to Port Arthur.

The fury of the Japanese can be easily imagined. They had been forced to give up the spoils of their victory by the Western powers, and now they had to watch those same spoils and more, too, being divided up among those same powers. Japan's time had not yet come.

The Western powers now turned to further division of China. Thus far they had operated only along the coast and up the Yangtze River. Now they began to carve up the interior into "spheres of influence."

● *The Open Door Policy*

The United States watched this new development with some concern. The United States did not herself want leases, naval bases, or spheres of influence in China. But she did not want to be shut out from Chinese trade by the seizure of exclusive rights by the European powers. In 1899 the American Secretary of State appealed to the powers interested in China to recognize what he called the *Open Door Policy*. This meant that all would agree that no nation would claim exclusive rights, but that all would have equal rights to trade anywhere in China. The powers agreed. No one wanted to stand out before the world as the only one to refuse, but no power really intended to observe the Open Door. By 1900 the fate of China seemed to be sealed.

The Boxer Rebellion breaks out

The Chinese had been unable to prevent the numerous grants of special privileges to the foreign powers, but they bitterly resented what had happened. For all their patience and resignation, they were proud people. They resented the indignities heaped upon their common interests and teach China to respect Western power. By an unheard-of joint action, Britain, Germany, Russia, Japan, and the United States sent a combined army to China. They relieved the besieged embassies, put down the rebellion, and imposed heavy penalties, including the payment of a large indemnity. By its treatment of the indemnity, the United States won much Chinese friendship for many years to come. Our share of the indemnity was much larger than was needed to pay all the damages. We returned about half of it to the Chinese government, with an understanding that it was to be set aside as a Boxer Indemnity Fund to pay the expenses of Chinese students to study in America.

Russia and Japan go to war

The Boxer Rebellion had an indirect effect. It sharpened the rivalry between Japan and Russia and brought on a war between them. When the foreign troops were withdrawn from China after the rebellion, the Russians lingered on in Manchuria. Japan regarded this with displeasure. She looked on Manchuria as a future Japanese sphere of influence. Despite several protests by the Japanese government, the Russians were in no hurry to keep their promise to withdraw. The Japanese prepared to force them out.

In 1902 Great Britain signed an alliance with Japan. Each agreed to the right of the other to defend its special interests in China, Manchuria, and Korea against the aggression of any third power (Russia). In the event one became involved in war with a third power, the other agreed to remain neutral unless some fourth power entered the war against its ally. In that case it was pledged to give aid.

The alliance meant great prestige for Japan. She no longer stood alone, but now had the support of a first-class European power. Japan now stepped up her demands on Russia. Not only did she demand the withdrawal of troops; she proposed that she would leave

American troops in Peking during the Boxer Rebellion. In the background is part of the Temple of Agriculture.

them, and the foreigners' contempt for their ancient race and culture. Antiforeign sentiment ran very high. In 1899 the old Manchu Dowager Empress (mother of the emperor) forced her son to leave the throne, and took it herself. Partly to stop Chinese attacks on the Manchus, she did everything she could to stir up hatred for foreigners, especially the missionaries. Within a year there were widespread attacks on foreigners in every part of China. They were led by a patriotic society which called itself the "Righteous Fists," translated as the Boxers. Foreigners who could do so fled to the protection of their embassies at Peking (now Peiping) and were besieged there by an army of angry Chinese.

Despite their jealousies and rivalries the Western nations were determined to protect

Manchuria to Russia if Russia left Korea to Japan. The Russians reluctantly agreed to negotiate, but they were slow. Early in 1904, without any declaration of war, Japan attacked the Russian naval force at Port Arthur and sank a number of ships. The Russians later sent a force from their Baltic Fleet all the way around to Asia, but it, too, was defeated.

The Japanese army marched up through Korea and reached Manchuria. Another force landed on the Liaotung Peninsula and forced its way inland. The Russians were fighting at a disadvantage, 5,000 miles from their supplies. Russian public opinion was divided; probably a majority of the people opposed the war. The czar's imperial government mismanaged the war badly, both in the training and leadership of troops and the provision of supplies.

The Japanese had the advantage of nearness, better preparation, and the united support of the war by the population. However, her victories were costly, especially as the Russians fell back farther inland. Her economy was seriously drained, and there was danger that it would collapse entirely. Therefore, the Japanese government requested Theodore Roosevelt, President of the United States, to act as mediator in bringing about peace negotiations. In 1905 the treaty was signed at Portsmouth, New Hampshire.

Russia gave Japan her lease on the Liaotung Peninsula, the lease on Port Arthur, and the southern part of the Chinese Eastern Railway. She recognized Japan's special position in Korea. She agreed to withdraw her troops from Manchuria, except the railway guards. Instead of paying an indemnity, Russia turned over to Japan the southern half of the island of Sakhalin, and gave the Japanese special fishing rights on the Siberian coast.

● *China loses to both sides*

Two years later, in a secret treaty, Japan and Russia divided Manchuria into two

The Russo-Japanese War. Above: an 11-inch howitzer used by the Japanese to bombard the Russian fortress and ships at Port Arthur. Below: a Russian warship in the harbor, just after being struck by an 11-inch shell.

spheres of influence—the northern half to Russia, the southern to Japan. Japan promised not to interfere with Russia's ambitions in Outer Mongolia; Russia, in return, promised not to interfere with Japan's control of Korea. Three years later Japan proclaimed the annexation of Korea; there were no protests.

China had to watch the Russo-Japanese War, a helpless but not disinterested spectator. Whichever side won, China lost; for it was Chinese territory they were fighting for. It was only one more step in the long humiliation.

There was a difference between the Western imperialism in China and in India or even Africa. In India and Africa Western powers took control of governments and exercised authority. They exploited the regions they controlled. However, along with authority they also took certain responsibilities. They protected the regions from outside attack and stopped internal wars. And they did take some responsibility for the people within the regions they controlled. In China this was not so. The imperial powers took authority, but no responsibilities. They did not protect the country from war. They assumed no responsibility for the people. They exploited, but did not protect.

The Chinese overthrow the Manchus

Among the Chinese people there grew up increasing demands for a change. In many cases the leaders of the movement were Chinese who had been educated in western Europe or the United States. They wanted not only the overthrow of the Manchus but also a complete break with "Old China." Influenced by Western ideas, they wanted constitutional, democratic government, with freedoms guaranteed by a bill of rights. They also wanted an Industrial Revolution—better transportation and communication, expanded industry, and improved agriculture.

These demands meant trouble. Industrialization was not possible without both foreign capital and foreign skills, but these meant outside influence. The political changes would meet opposition, not only from the Manchus and the ruling class, but from the deeply imbedded conservatism of the Chinese people themselves.

The Manchus themselves saw the need for change. They tried to make some reforms, but they were too little and too late. In 1910 and 1911 there were crop failures, the result of a very dry year followed by disastrous spring floods. Misery brought violence and the overthrow of the dynasty.

●Sun Yat-sen and the Republic

During 1911 rebellion spread through south China. As a last desperate gesture, the Manchu ruler decreed the establishment of a constitutional monarchy, but it was too late. The revolutionaries would accept nothing but a republic. At the head of the republicans was Dr. Sun Yat-sen, who had lived in the United States, attended school in Hawaii, and graduated in medicine at Hong Kong. He was a republican from deep conviction. He believed that much of Old China would have to go in order that a New China could face the world on equal terms. Sun Yat-sen founded the Chinese People's Party, which is called the Kuomintang.

In February, 1912, the Manchus were forced to abdicate. The Kuomintang proclaimed the Chinese Republic. In his book, *The Three Principles of the People,* Sun Yat-sen stated these principles as, "The People's Government, The People's Rights, The People's Livelihood." Briefly expanded, they meant (1) political unification and the ending of foreign influence; (2) a gradual change to democratic government with full personal liberties and rights for all; and (3) economic improvements, including land reforms and industrialization. This opened a new and turbulent era in China, about which

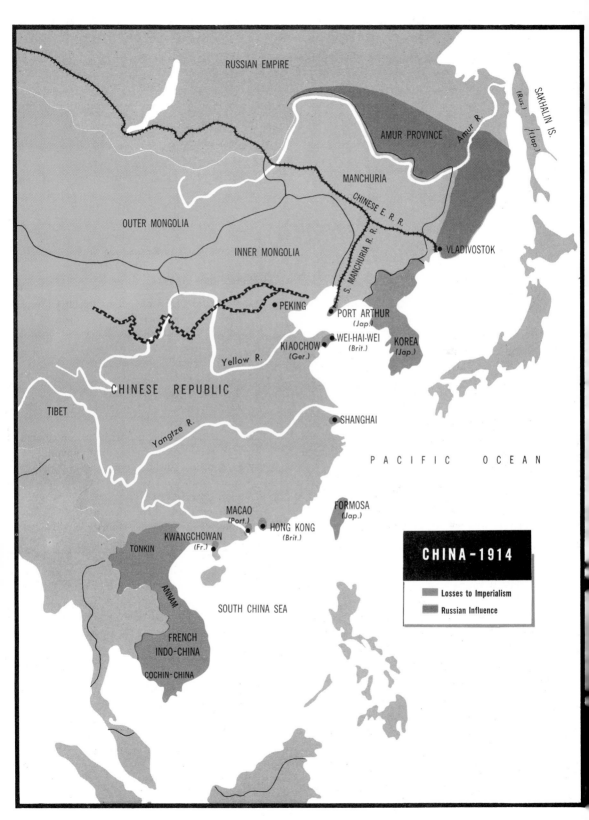

RUSSIAN EMPIRE

SAKHALIN IS.
(Rus.)
(Jap.)

AMUR PROVINCE

Amur R.

MANCHURIA

CHINESE E. R. R.

OUTER MONGOLIA

INNER MONGOLIA

S. MANCHURIA R. R.

VLADIVOSTOK

PEKING

PORT ARTHUR
(Jap.)

WEI-HAI-WEI
(Brit.)

KOREA
(Jap.)

KIAOCHOW
(Ger.)

Yellow R.

CHINESE REPUBLIC

TIBET

Yangtze R.

SHANGHAI

PACIFIC   OCEAN

MACAO
(Port.)

FORMOSA
(Jap.)

KWANGCHOWAN
(Fr.)

HONG KONG
(Brit.)

TONKIN

CHINA—1914

ANNAM

SOUTH CHINA SEA

Losses to Imperialism

Russian Influence

FRENCH
INDO-CHINA

COCHIN-CHINA

you will learn in a later chapter. Before we go on with China, we shall learn more about Japan, which had come late but powerfully onto the stage of international power politics. Chapter 41 tells how this small feudal country became a great power.

Review of Chapter 40

People, places, and things

Identify: Lao-tze, Taoism, Confucius, Nirvana, Buddha, Manchus, Taiping Rebellion, Sun Yat-sen, Kuomintang, "treaty ports," "unequal treaties."

Locate: China Proper, Tibet, Manchuria, Yellow and Yangtze Rivers, Hankow, Chungking, Peking, Hangchow, Tientsin, Hong Kong, Shanghai, Canton, Swatow, Amoy, Fuchow, Dairen, Indo-China, Korea, Japan, Amur and Ussuri Rivers, Vladivostok, Liaotung Peninsula, Harbin, Trans-Siberian Railway, Manchuria, Port Arthur, Formosa, Shantung, Sakhalin, Outer Mongolia, Inner Mongolia, Ryukyus, Pescadores.

Events in review

1. What foreigners invaded China before the Europeans?
2. Name the two main regions of China Proper. Name the two most important rivers of China.
3. Why was the organization of the Chinese family important in Chinese farming and Chinese history?
4. Which of the religions that became important in China was brought in by missionaries from India? Why did this belief appeal to the Chinese?
5. What title did the Chinese give their emperor? Was he considered to rule by divine right?
6. What is meant by *extraterritoriality?* Give examples.
7. How did China lose Formosa?
8. Why did Russia "come to the aid" of China after the Japanese won their war with China?
9. Who proposed the Open Door Policy? What was its purpose?

10. Tell briefly what caused the Boxer Rebellion. What was the outcome?
11. What did Japan gain from the Russo-Japanese War?
12. List the "Three Principles of the People" in Sun Yat-sen's program for China.

Problems and projects

1. Discuss the effects of geography on Chinese history. Include: (a) the routes open to invaders, (b) the division of China into regions, (c) the importance of rivers, (d) China's natural resources.
2. Make a list of Chinese contributions to world civilization. Discuss their importance.
3. Chinese history is said to fall into cycles. Explain and discuss.
4. Make a list of the factors that contributed to the weakness and the final downfall of the Manchus. Include both the weaknesses within China and the pressures exerted by foreign powers.
5. Which of these three great powers—Great Britain, Russia, Japan—contributed most to the weakening and cutting-up of China? Give facts to support your answer.
6. Imagine yourself a Chinese scholar, and a follower of Confucius, living in the 1840's. Describe your reactions to the Opium War and the treaty that followed it.
7. Make a report to the class on the life and teachings of Lao-tze or Confucius.
8. Try to find out which of the long-standing problems of China (floods, famine, land reform, for example) are still problems under the present regime.
9. On a map of China show what China lost through (a) concessions to foreign powers (extraterritorial rights and spheres of influence), (b) the Sino-Japanese War, (c) the Russo-Japanese War.

Chapter *41*

The Rise of Modern Japan

THE COUNTRY of Japan consists of four principal islands. Honshu is called the main island; the six largest cities are located there. The others are Shikoku, Kyushu, and Hokkaido. Altogether these four islands have an area slightly less than that of the American state of California. There are no rivers of any size, but there are plenty of good seaports. The climate is good and there is ample rainfall for the principal agricultural crop, rice. The three southern islands have a temperate climate, but Hokkaido, the northern one, is colder. Japanese people prefer a warm climate; so they have not settled Hokkaido as thickly as the other three. The attractiveness of the climate is offset to some extent by two natural forces which have caused great destruction and loss of life throughout Japanese history: earthquakes and typhoons.

The islands of Japan are very mountainous, which makes them places of great natural beauty. This beauty has its penalty, though. Only about one-seventh of the land can be cultivated. The *total* land area of Japan is less than that of the state of California. When ninety million people try to support themselves on the food produced by such a limited farming area, problems obviously arise. There are few natural resources aside from the land. As an industrial nation, Japan has

to import almost all of its raw materials, which makes another difficult problem.

The people and the civilization of Japan

The Japanese are a comparatively young people, historically speaking. Little is known of the origin of the race. Scientists believe that they have developed from three main

> Ainus, a primitive group living on the island of Hokkaido.

525

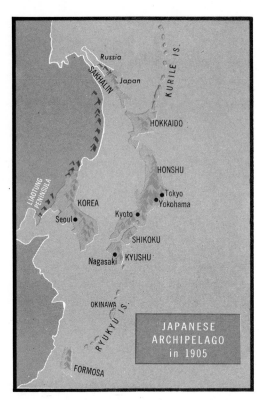

groups. The original inhabitants of the islands are thought to have been people of the white race, the Ainus. Primitive groups of Ainus are still found on the northern island, Hokkaido. Through the centuries they have mixed with two other groups: Mongols who came from the mainland of Asia and Malays who moved north from the islands of the South Seas.

Even in Japanese legends the records go back only to the seventh century B.C. The empire was founded then (according to the legends) by Jimmu Tenno, a descendant of the sun goddess, who became the first emperor. As a descendant of the goddess, he was himself a god. He was so sacred, in fact, that the Japanese did not look directly at him or even at his picture. They did not call him by name, but used the title *Mikado,* which means "Exalted Gate." You may recall the Egyptian title *Pharaoh*—"Great House."

The worship of the emperor was a part of the religion called *Shinto,* or *Shintoism.* Believers in this religion worshipped beauty,

and saw a divine spirit in every beautiful object—tree, rock, or mountain. Cleanliness was so much a part of the religion that Japanese are noted for it today. The worship of ancestors also became part of the religion; the ancestors became divine spirits. In the religion there also developed a deep patriotism and love of the homeland. It was Nippon, the place where the sun rises, or the Land of the Rising Sun. The national flag, a red ball on a white field, stands for the rising sun. To the Japanese man, nothing could be more honorable than to die on the battlefield in the service of the emperor, the homeland, and the ancestors.

● *Chinese influence on Japanese civilization*

Until the middle of the sixth century A.D. the Japanese had no written language. Our knowledge of the history of the islands before that time comes from the stories and legends handed down from generation to generation. About 550 A.D., Buddhist missionaries began to enter Japanese islands from Korea, bringing with them not only the religion but the civilization and culture of China and India.

The Japanese welcomed both the religion and the culture. Many people became Buddhists. The Japanese borrowed the Chinese written language, changing it for their purposes. Like the Chinese, Japanese writing is not alphabetical; the characters stand for complete words. A person who can read Chinese writing has great difficulty with Japanese because of the changes or adaptations. The same character may mean different things in each language.

The Japanese adopted many other features of Chinese civilization, but they seemed to be much more interested in the practical, applied things than in the philosophical teachings. During the seventh century A.D. a Japanese emperor created a centralized government. He was influenced by the structure of the Chinese Empire. He tried to establish an official class and to make very detailed rules for the living habits of the people. Japan has developed no great philosopher nor religious leader, nor any great literature.

Japanese art has been greatly influenced by China. Anyone who studies the artistic development of the two countries sees many similarities. Like the Chinese, the Japanese introduce their art into every part of living. Even the pottery of the peasant is decorated with simple but graceful designs. It has been said that the Japanese do not touch anything without beautifying it. Japanese prints and other art works are exquisite; their lacquer work is very fine; they have developed gardening into a magnificent art. The Japanese inject an idea into everything they create: their poetry, their decorations, and even their flower arrangements, which they have developed into a serious, formal study.

As in China, the father is head of the family. The system is based on the submission of woman to man, and of the young to the old. The older and more successful male members have authority over the younger and poorer, but they also take responsibility for helping and protecting needy relatives. Few decisions are made by individuals. Usually any important decision concerning an individual is made by a family council. This custom of group rather than individual decisions runs through all Japanese life, whether it be economic, political, or military.

Japan develops feudal government

After a brief period of dictatorship, Japan developed a feudal form of government. There was still an emperor, the Mikado, Son of Heaven. In theory he was still divine, and the supreme ruler. In practice he remained shut up in his palace at Kyoto. Often he was neglected, ignored, and lived in poverty.

The country was divided into feudal districts, ruled by lords called *daimyos*. They were served by a special military class, like knights, called *samurai*. The profession of both daimyo and samurai was military. Like European nobles, they did no other work. They developed their own special code of conduct, called *Bushido*—the code of the warrior. Bushido called for a strict life of exercise and training to make the samurai an effective fighter. There was not much chivalry in the European sense. The samurai were merciless fighters. It was not uncommon for a samurai to kill a defenseless peasant because he thought the peasant had not shown him proper respect. Beneath the samurai, in the social scale, came the commoners, with merchants well down toward the bottom. At the bottom, of course, came the peasants.

Japanese feudalism developed another difference from the European. In time, one feudal lord was able to enforce his power over the others and make himself a military dictator. Strangely enough, he did not make

An ancient figure of a Japanese warrior in armor. From the feudal era to World War II the Japanese military caste had a reputation for being fierce warriors.

himself emperor. Instead, he took the title *Shogun,* which meant something like "Barbarian-Subduing Great General." The position of shogun became hereditary, like that of emperor. The shogun was the real ruler of the country, but the emperor was kept as a convenient figurehead. His supposed divinity was useful.

The Europeans come to Japan

Europeans first came to Japan by accident. In the middle of the sixteenth century a Portuguese ship was forced to seek refuge in a storm. Other vessels followed, and trade sprang up between the Portuguese and Japanese merchants. Catholic missionaries, Portuguese Jesuits, soon followed. At first they were welcomed by the Japanese, who thought they were European Buddhists. However, since the custom of ancestor worship had never been part of the Christian religion, the Portuguese Jesuits did not make very many converts in Japan.

The Portuguese were soon followed by Spanish and Dutch merchants, and by Spanish Franciscan missionaries. Friction developed among the Christians over the right to carry on missionary work. This aroused Japanese suspicions of political as well as religious interference. Early in the seventeenth century the Japanese authorities ordered the missionaries to go home and urged the Japanese converts to return to their original faith. Restrictions were placed upon trade. When the foreign traders protested, the Japanese government expelled them and closed its ports entirely to foreigners. From 1638 until 1854 Japan was completely isolated, refusing any contacts with the outside world.

Japanese isolation ends

As you know, the Western World did not stand still during those two centuries. European nations and the United States became increasingly industrialized and began to search for new markets and new sources of raw materials. The isolation of China was broken down in the 1840's.

Even within isolated Japan changes took place. The strict class pattern of feudalism began to break down. Economic life, based on agriculture, began to change to trade and commerce. Just as in Europe, a middle class of merchants, traders, and bankers appeared. It did not fit into Japanese feudal society any better than it had in Europe. The middle class began to play an increasing part in economic life. The daimyos and samurai, unable to stop this development, turned to a policy of oppression of the helpless peasants. Side by side with the growing wealth of the middle class, there was increasing poverty among the peasants. It was a time of great social unrest.

By the 1850's it was impossible for Japan to remain isolated any longer. The world of the nineteenth century would not permit it. During the first half of the century there had been a few hesitant, individual efforts to open trade with Japan, but the Japanese government was able to resist them successfully. American whaling and merchant ships, seeking shelter in Japanese harbors from storms or trying to get provisions there, were refused entry and harbor facilities. Sailors who were shipwrecked and cast ashore were treated harshly.

● *The United States sends an expedition to Japan*

In these circumstances the government of the United States took action. In 1853 President Pierce sent a naval force under Commodore Perry to negotiate a treaty. Perry took a personal letter from the president to the shogun. He told the shogun's representative that he would return for an answer. In Japan there was much argument. A treaty with the United States meant the end of the policy of isolation. Opinion was divided. Some wanted military resistance; others realized that Ja-

pan could not hold out long. When Perry returned next year with a larger naval force, the shogun reluctantly agreed to negotiate.

The treaty signed by representatives of the two nations in 1854 was a turning point in Japanese history. Two Japanese ports were to be opened to foreigners, not only for shelter but also for trade. Japanese isolation was broken down. As you would expect, the United States could not keep a monopoly. Within two years similar treaties with Japan were signed by Great Britain, Russia, and Holland. In general, the representatives of foreign nations were given rights to live, trade, purchase naval supplies, and send consuls to several Japanese seaports.

For a time the conservative isolationists of Japan took a position of "thus far and no farther." Foreign consuls were isolated; contacts with foreign traders were kept to a minimum. It took patience and tact to win greater favors, trust, and understanding. The first consul general of the United States, Townsend Harris, was equal to the task. With patience, understanding, honesty, and sincerity,

Commodore Matthew Calbraith Perry lands to negotiate with the Japanese. Perry's honor guard of seamen and marines is forming ranks in the center. Two steam warships of the American squadron can be seen at the left.

he gradually gained the confidence of the Japanese officials. In 1858 his success was shown in another treaty. The Japanese government consented to exchange diplomatic representatives with the United States. More foreign consuls were admitted; more treaty ports opened. Tariff regulations were set up. Foreigners living in Japan were given the right to observe their own religious ceremonies. Similar treaties followed with other nations, and Japanese isolationism began to collapse.

Japan goes Western

These changes in foreign relations were bound to produce domestic changes in Japan. Japan, like China, was at a crossroad; the great question was, Which way should Japan take? If she tried to resist Western influence by force, she would probably suffer the fate of China and be carved into colonies and spheres of influence by the imperial powers. To prevent this, she would have to change, and become strong in the only way the imperial powers would respect. Japan would have to become industrialized and copy Western methods and equipment in business, industry, and the armed forces.

The decision was not made without a struggle. The more conservative feudal lords rebelled against the shogun and also attacked the foreigners. They were soon taught a lesson. A combined naval force from the fleets of Great Britain, France, and Holland entered southern Japanese ports. They put down the rebellion and forced the rebels to pay an indemnity.

A group of younger and more progressive nobles now took matters into their own hands. In 1867 they staged a successful revolution. They overthrew the shogun. With him the feudal order collapsed. They restored complete authority to the emperor, the mi-

A Japanese junk. In the 1860's the Industrial Revolution had not begun in Japan. Steamships were a strange foreign marvel. The Japanese were still in the age of sails and oars. Yet within two generations the Japanese made themselves over into a powerful, modern nation. Contrast the wooden sailing craft below with the steel warship on the facing page.

kado. Japan became an absolute monarchy, in fact as well as in theory.

● *Westernizing industry and education*

This younger group believed that Japan must take the second road—toward Westernization and industrialization—if their country were to avoid the fate of China. Once the decision was made, it was carried through in the most thorough fashion. Foreign experts were invited to come to Japan to help modernize transportation and communication, set up modern industries, and reorganize the legal and political systems. Commissions of Japanese scholars were sent abroad to study American and European governments, military and naval organizations, and systems of education. They wanted to learn the best that the West had to offer. Young Japanese were sent abroad to study and to observe Western ways of life.

A great industrial development took place. A steel industry was built up, as well as various kinds of manufacturing establishments. The cotton and silk textile industries were especially important. Shipbuilding and foreign trade were expanded. It was not long before Japanese cotton goods began to compete with British cottons throughout the Far East. The railroad, the telegraph, the telephone, and the radio appeared in Japan. Banking also developed rapidly. It is an amazing story. Within a third of a century the Japanese had almost duplicated the development which in the West had taken 150 years.

A complete system of compulsory education was set up for girls as well as boys. Girls were educated in ways of making home life happy, boys in vocations. Technical and industrial education was especially stressed for boys. Both boys and girls were strongly indoctrinated as loyal subjects of the mikado. The educational system wiped out illiteracy almost completely, thus placing Japan far ahead of other Asian countries in the number of its people who could read and write.

The new government

It is interesting and revealing to notice what the Japanese copied from the West. They wanted to be strong militarily; so they copied the organization and methods of the Prussian or German army and the British navy. They wanted to be strong industrially; they copied methods, machines, and techniques in England, Germany, and the United States, taking the best they could find. Their greatest dilemma was in government. They wanted to keep the supreme, divine position of the emperor. At the same time they wanted to give the appearance, at least, of following the democratic, constitutional forms so widespread in the West. Therefore they copied the constitution of the German empire.

The Japanese constitution was drafted by an appointed commission. They first made an extensive study of the reports of Japanese groups which had studied Western political philosophies and governments. Their draft of a constitution was accepted by the emperor and proclaimed in 1889. The people were not given a chance to vote on it.

First came an Imperial Law, which provided the method of succession to the throne. Then came Imperial Ordinances, which defined the powers of the emperor. Briefly stated, they were complete. The emperor remained the sacred descendant of the gods. His will and his orders were superior to any acts of the legislature. There was also a Cabinet of Ministers, appointed by and responsible only to the emperor.

There was a two-house legislature: the House of Peers, or lords, whose positions were mostly hereditary, and an elected House of Representatives. The two houses were of equal rank, except that the lower house approved the annual budget which was presented to it by the cabinet. However, if the House of Representatives refused to approve the budget, the cabinet, with the emperor's permission, could enforce the budget of the

A Japanese battleship of the time of the Russo-Japanese War. A people who were used to small sailing boats learned in a remarkably short time to be skilled handlers of steam warships. Many of Japan's ships of this period were bought from foreign shipyards; however, Japan was creating her own steel and shipbuilding industries.

preceding year without approval by the house.

Neither house could consider anything except legislation presented by the cabinet, which was, of course, responsible only to the emperor. As a further safeguard against any "excess of democracy," the emperor had an absolute veto over all laws passed by the legislature. He could also negotiate all treaties, and these did not have to be approved by either house. He could summon the legislature at his pleasure and dissolve the lower house when he pleased. He commanded the armed forces and could declare war and make peace. He was supposed to act only on the advice of his cabinet, but he appointed and could remove these advisers.

The influence of the military

A strange feature of the new constitution concerned the position of the military. The emperor was supreme commander. He was advised in military and naval matters by the Supreme War Council and Supreme Navy Council of top-ranking officers. They recommended the men who served as Minister of

War and Minister of the Navy in the emperor's cabinet. They were always army and navy officers. Thus the military was in no way controlled by the civil government. No cabinet could be formed unless the candidates approved by the Chiefs of Staff were given the War and Navy posts. They had more influence than any other cabinet ministers. Their resignation, if their advice or policy was not followed, might force the resignation of all other ministers. This lack of responsibility of the army and navy to the civil government, and the great influence of the military over the emperor, was to be very important in the years leading to World War II.

This was the government that controlled the destiny of Imperial Japan in the years between 1889 and 1945. This was an absolute monarchy with a constitution—a constitutional democracy which was not democratic, with a parliament which could not make laws except on subjects given to it. The parliament could not make any laws on the supremely

Rice fields. Raising enough food became a problem when Japan's population began to increase. Japanese farmers learned to use all the available land for rice or other crops.

important matters of war, peace, and foreign relations. In practice Japan was a dictatorship without a dictator, with a cabinet at the mercy of military men.

● Problems resulting from Westernization

The Westernization of Japan was successful in preventing the country from falling victim to Western imperialism. In fact, Japan herself soon joined the imperial race. The Westernization caused many internal problems, for Western ideas came into conflict with long-held Japanese customs and traditions. This created psychological problems among the people themselves. There were other problems, too.

As in Europe, industrialization and scientific development produced a sudden increase in population. Cities grew very rapidly. Every inch of land capable of being farmed was put to use. As in China, individual landholdings became very small and were farmed by intensive methods. This means that the work was done by hand, as we might cultivate a small garden. Food supply did not increase as rapidly as population.

There was, in fact, a surplus of population —more than the land would support, more than could possibly find jobs to allow them to live. Therefore, Japanese people began to emigrate (to leave the country). After Japan gained Formosa and Korea, many went there. Many went to islands of the Pacific. Many came to the United States. In time, countries began to pass laws against Japanese immigration. Such laws were passed by the United States, Australia, and Canada. Many of these laws were racial in nature. The United States, for example, prohibited the immigration of Japanese and Chinese entirely, while still permitting the immigration of Europeans. As proud people, both Japanese and Chinese resented this discrimination.

Japanese industrial development created another problem. The islands lack almost all of the raw materials necessary to modern industry; these must be imported from abroad. The only way for a nation to pay for its imports is by selling its own goods abroad. Since a good percentage of food must also be imported, Japan had to export or die. Few nations die willingly, or quietly.

In exporting goods Japan met with restrictions, just as in its export of people. Many countries passed tariff laws, to protect their own home markets against Japanese competition. They could plead the excuse that Japanese labor was cheap, and it was true. Such a poor nation cannot pay high wages or maintain high standards of living. Industrialization in Japan followed much the same pattern as industrialization in Europe and the United States. Great monopolies developed. In the period after World War I steel, railroads, banks, textiles, electric power, shipbuilding, and merchant shipping were all controlled by five great family-owned corporations. Collectively, they were called the zaibatsu.

Japan feels forced to imperialism

Monopoly control did not solve the problems of surplus population and the necessity to export. These two problems help to explain Japanese imperialism in Korea, Manchuria, and the islands to the south. Japan found herself in much the same position as Germany and Italy: the Japanese had "come late to the party." There were few rich lands with sparse population left. Japan's successes in the war with China and the later war with Russia gave her some gains, but these did not completely solve her problems. Japan's attempts to solve these problems caused two more explosions of Japanese imperialism in two World Wars.

In 1914 Japan could look at her record of less than fifty years with some pride. She had industrialized and Westernized, and had saved herself from the fate of China. She had defeated China, her great tutor in civilization. The Anglo-Japanese Treaty of 1902 recognized her as a power worthy of equal standing with great European powers. In the Russo-Japanese War she had defeated one of the great powers, even though it was a narrow scrape. She had gained imperial holdings: the peninsula of Korea, the island of Formosa, the southern part of the Liaotung Peninsula with its naval base of Port Arthur, and a "sphere of influence" in southern Manchuria. There was more rich plunder to be had in China if only the European powers and the United States could, in some way, be driven out or diverted. This Japan tried, too. Here is where in the end she came to invite disaster, as you will learn in the later part of the story of Japan.

Review of Chapter 41

People, places, and things

Identify: Mikado, Nippon, Ainus, daimyos, samurai, shogun, *zaibatsu*, Commodore Matthew Calbraith Perry, Townsend Harris, Anglo-Japanese Treaty of 1902.
Locate: Honshu, Kyushu, Shikoku, Hokkaido, Korea, Kurile Islands, Sakhalin, Formosa, Manchuria, Port Arthur.

Events in review

1. What is the importance of geography to Japan in terms of (a) climate, (b) land area, (c) natural resources?
2. List the main characteristics of Shintoism.
3. How much did Chinese culture influence Japan? Give examples.
4. What was accomplished by the 1854 treaty between the United States and Japan? by the 1858 treaty?
5. After their isolation ended, the Japanese copied from Western nations. What did they copy from (a) Germany, (b) Great Britain, (c) the United States?
6. Describe briefly the powers held by the emperor under the constitution proclaimed in 1889.
7. Explain why military men had such great influence in the Japanese government after 1889.
8. What two problems help to explain Japan's imperialism in Asia?

Problems and projects

1. Compare feudalism in Japan with feudalism in medieval Europe. Did any European country ever have an official with powers like those of the shogun? How was the mikado finally restored to a position of real power?
2. Make a summary of the changes that took place in Japan after the nation started on the road to Westernization and industrialization. Can you explain how the Japanese were able to make such thorough changes so rapidly?
3. Describe the Japanese government as set up by the Constitution of 1889. How was the constitution prepared? What were the functions and powers of the emperor? the cabinet? the legislature? Did the legislature have any of the powers held by the British Parliament or the Congress of the United States?

   Compare the Japanese government with the government of the German Empire.
4. Discuss the end of Japan's isolation. Why did Japan preserve her isolation from 1638 until 1854? For what reasons did the United States want to make a treaty with Japan? How did the United States go about "opening" Japan?
5. Bring to class reproductions of Chinese and Japanese art. How much does the Japanese work resemble the Chinese? Contrast Oriental art with European and American art.

   If recordings of Japanese music are available, make a comparison of Japanese and Western music.

Chapter *42*

The United States Becomes a World Power

AFTER the United States gained its independence from Great Britain, it expanded very rapidly. Within seventy years its original boundaries had been pushed west to the Pacific Ocean, south to the Gulf of Mexico and the Rio Grande, and north along the Canadian border all the way to the Pacific. The new territory was gained in different ways: by purchase, by the threat of war, by annexation of the independent Republic of Texas, by actual war, and by recognition of the right of settlement.

The greatest contributions of the American Revolution were the democratic ideas of the equality of man before the law, his right to a voice in his own government, and the federal form of government. The federal form is an attempt to unite a group of independent governments under a national, or federal, government. It means that powers have to be divided up. The federal government receives power to deal with common problems which the individual states cannot handle as well for themselves. But the states keep the powers to deal with individual, domestic problems.

Problems of the federal form of government

In practice, the federal form of government was not easy to operate. Sometimes it was hard to decide which problems were national

and which were local, to be dealt with by the states. The powers of the federal government were stated in the Constitution in simple words, but the words could be interpreted in different ways. If they were interpreted strictly, the government was denied a power unless it was definitely stated in exact words. Strict interpretation limited the number of things the federal government could do. However, the Constitution could be interpreted liberally by "reading between the lines." Liberal interpretation allowed the federal government to do anything the words implied, or hinted at. Thus it became more powerful in relation to the states.

During its first seventy years under the Constitution, the United States went through several bitter arguments over the power of the federal government to pass certain laws. Once, during the Napoleonic Wars, the federal government tried to prevent the United States from being drawn into the war between the French and British by stopping our trade with foreign nations altogether. These laws brought many protests; a group of New England states threatened to secede. Another time, the argument was over the protective tariff. Agricultural states in the west and especially the south, believed that the protective tariff increased the price of the manufactured goods they had to buy from the industrial and commercial northeastern

535

The United States expands westward. This scene shows pioneers climbing the corduroy road to the mining town of Leadville (now in Colorado). The discovery of minerals was one motive for the settling of the West.

states. The protective tariff also brought threats that the southern states would secede (withdraw) from the Union. Both questions, however, were settled without actual secession or fighting.

● The issue of slavery

The most serious argument over the division of powers between states and the federal government came over the question of slavery: should slavery be permitted in the territories? Territories were lands which had not yet become states; they were owned and controlled by the federal government. Slavery had existed in the American colonies almost

from the beginning. The Constitution recognized it as legal, but it was a state problem, not a federal problem. In states where it existed it could be abolished only by action of the state itself. Some states had done this, and Congress had prohibited slavery in the first territory to belong to the United States.

The problem of slavery had been dealt with more from the economic than the moral standpoint. Slavery had been abolished in states where it was not profitable or where it was not thought necessary. It remained and increased in states where it was thought necessary, especially after Eli Whitney's cotton gin made cotton a profitable crop. In the southern states the principal crops, cotton and tobacco, were thought to require slave labor.

The problem of slavery in the territories became so important and so difficult to settle because both cotton and tobacco were crops that wore out the soil. Southerners wanted to have new lands to which they could move when their soil was exhausted. They did not want to have to change their economy, or way of living. Therefore, they opposed any attempt in Congress to prohibit slavery in the territories. In time they came to believe that Congress did not have the power to do so.

During the period before 1860, this dispute over the power of the federal government flared up twice with great bitterness. Each time it concerned the right of individuals to take slaves into territories. Each time it brought threats of secession. Each time it was settled by compromise, so that secession, and perhaps war, were avoided. Then in 1860 the United States elected a president, Abraham Lincoln, of a new party. The Republicans had pledged to prevent the spread of slavery into the territories. They were also pledged to pass a high protective tariff. These were both matters that had brought threats of secession before. The Republicans elected Lincoln, but they did not win a majority in either house of Congress. So they would have had great difficulty in putting their ideas into effect. However, secession took place even before the newly elected officials had taken their offices.

Internal war tests the democratic and federal ideas

A group of states, eventually eleven, seceded from the United States, and set up a new government called the Confederate States of America. President Lincoln and Congress maintained that the Constitution did not give a state the right to secede. They declared the act of the southerners a rebellion, which it was the duty of the government of the United States to suppress. Efforts to compromise proved useless. War came in 1861.

The war lasted for four years, the most bloody and costly war that had ever been fought up to that time. In the end the superior manpower and industrial resources of the North prevailed. The Confederacy was defeated; the Federal Union was preserved. During the course of the war the Constitution was amended to prohibit slavery anywhere in the United States or its territories. Later amendments gave the freed slaves citizenship, and granted them the right to vote. Thus the doctrine of the equality of all men before the law was maintained and strengthened, and the union, with its federal form of government was preserved.

These things were done, but at a tragic cost. The southern states were devastated. Their property in slaves was gone, with no compensation. The northern and southern forces together lost nearly 500,000 men (killed, died of wounds, or died of disease). Families had been torn apart; brother had fought against brother. The war, and the sad

Destruction in the South as a result of the War Between the States. This photograph by Mathew Brady shows a blown-up railroad trestle at Fredericksburg, Virginia.

period that followed it in the South, left deep scars on the national life that were to remain for a long time.

Industrial development after 1865

The economy of the United States developed tremendously in the period after the War Between the States. Industry and manufacturing, transportation and communication, mining, agriculture, and the production of new materials all increased at a rapid rate. Industry had begun to develop in the United States before the war, but the country had remained mainly agricultural. By 1890 manufacturing had equaled agriculture in value, and was to become increasingly important in our national economic life.

A number of conditions made this great industrial development possible. There were rich natural resources: land, coal, iron ore and other minerals, especially oil. There was enough labor, either from immigration or from farm workers who left the soil. There was enough capital, either from the savings of Americans or surplus capital from Europe.

Many new machines were invented to produce more goods while using less labor. The rapidly increasing population furnished a market for the sale of the goods. Railroads were built rapidly to furnish transportation. There were no tariff walls within the United States; the entire country was one enormous market.

The governments, both federal and state, were especially friendly toward business. They granted subsidies, and the federal government levied high protective tariffs. Although there were some laws passed to regulate industries, they were not very effective. In general, both the federal and state governments maintained a laissez-faire policy. As a result of all these favorable factors American agriculture and industry not only kept pace with the rapidly growing population but even produced large surpluses for export.

After the War Between the States, this nation rapidly built up its industry and its transportation system. Railroads crossed the continent from sea to sea. Below is a Santa Fe Railroad scene in the 1880's.

We adopt a policy of isolation

The end of the Napoleonic Wars, in 1815, was the beginning of a long period during which the people of the United States did not need to pay much attention to the rest of the world. Americans wanted only to be left alone, to live their lives and develop their country as they saw fit. Any desire for territory was satisfied by expansion on the thinly settled and weakly held continent of North America. We had neither need, nor much desire, for possessions elsewhere.

● *The Monroe Doctrine*

Early in our history this policy of isolation was expressed in the Monroe Doctrine. You may recall that at one time the Holy Alliance schemed to overthrow the newly independent Latin American republics and restore them as colonies of Spain. President Monroe's statement declared that the Western Hemisphere was closed to further European colonization (page 359). Any attempt to establish new colonies or expand existing ones would be considered "dangerous to the peace and safety" of the United States.

The Monroe Doctrine became the basis of our foreign policy for a century. We avoided becoming involved in any European affairs. We showed little interest in any world affairs unless they touched us directly, or threatened to do so. But we considered ourselves guardians of the Western Hemisphere. Any move to increase European power and influence in North or South America or the nearby islands brought an immediate reaction from the government of the United States. You will recall that our government forced the French Emperor Napoleon III to give up his attempt to set up a French dominated colony in Mexico.

Our policy of isolation continued almost till 1900. However, the Second Industrial Revolution brought about some conflicting ideas. Some people in the United States urged that we join the new imperialism by taking island possessions in the Caribbean and the Pacific. It was argued that such possessions were necessary to our commerce, industry, and defense. They would provide markets for our products, sources of raw materials, and, above all, coaling stations and naval bases for our merchant ships and fleet. In 1867 the United States purchased Alaska from Russia, but we did not make any serious attempt to expand outside the continent until the end of the nineteenth century.

The Spanish-American War ends our isolation

In 1898 the United States became involved in a war with Spain. The main cause of the war was the condition of Cuba, a Spanish colony in the West Indies. For many years the Cubans had been discontented with Spanish rule. There were several rebellions, which the Spanish government suppressed only with great difficulty. Many United States citizens and corporations had invested money in Cuba, in sugar plantations, refineries, and railroads.

When a new rebellion broke out in the middle 1890's, some American property was destroyed, and our government protested. This alone would not have been a cause for war, but public feeling had been aroused in the United States. Cubans who had settled here spread much propaganda against the Spanish. Two American newspapers, which were competing with each other for circulation, printed sensational stories about Spanish misrule and the cruelty with which the revolt was being put down. Many of these stories later proved to be false, although the truth was bad enough. People in the United States were very sympathetic toward the Cubans. There was a strong feeling that Cuba must gain her independence.

Two incidents brought American public opinion to a fever pitch. A private letter of the Spanish ambassador to the United States was stolen and printed in one of the newspapers. In the letter the ambassador had expressed a very poor opinion of President McKinley. Spain sent an apology and replaced the ambassador. American indignation had not yet died down when the second incident happened.

The United States had sent the battleship *Maine* to Havana to "protect American citizens" and their property. The *Maine* was blown up by an underwater explosion and sank with much loss of life. An investigation was made, but it could not be determined who or what had caused the explosion. However, people in the United States took it for granted that the Spanish were to blame, and demanded a declaration of war.

● *The war—April to August, 1898*

President McKinley and his cabinet did not want war. Yet they felt unable to resist the popular demand, even though Spain showed some willingness to meet American terms about Cuba. The President asked Congress to declare war, and it was done. In the resolution declaring war we said that we were

> *The wreck of a Spanish warship in the Philippines. On May 1 1898, Commodore George Dewey's force destroyed the Spanish squadron in Manila Bay, including the small cruiser* Isla de Cuba, *shown here.*

fighting to gain independence for Cuba, and denied any intention of taking the island for ourselves. The last provision was adopted at the demand of members of Congress who opposed American imperialism.

The war itself did not last long, and the result was never much in doubt. It was fought not only in Cuba and Puerto Rico, Spain's West Indian colonies, but also in Spain's possessions in the Pacific, the Philippine Islands. There a Spanish squadron was destroyed, and the city of Manila besieged. A Spanish squadron which came to Cuba was destroyed by the American navy off Santiago in July. Units of our army had already landed in Cuba and engaged the Spanish forces around Santiago. Our troops in Cuba suffered seriously from disease—far more than from enemy action. An army-navy expedition took the island of Puerto Rico. Spain was unable to continue the war and asked for peace, fighting stopped in August, and a treaty was signed in December.

● *Cuba becomes a protectorate*

In the peace the United States observed the promise not to take Cuba as a colony. We recognized the independence of Cuba, and helped to restore order, rebuild the country, and set up a republican government. However, we kept a naval base there. Also, we made the Cubans state in their constitution that the United States had the right to intervene in Cuba to protect the independence of the island and to maintain an orderly government. The Cubans promised not to make any treaty which might weaken the independence of the island, and not to borrow any money from any foreign power unless they could pay the money back out of the ordinary revenues of their own government. This was done to keep any foreign country from using the debt as an excuse to move in on Cuba. Thus Cuba did not become an American colony, but it did become a protectorate of the United States.

The United States acquires overseas possessions

Our pledge concerning Cuba did not apply to the rest of the Spanish colonies. We insisted on keeping Puerto Rico in the Caribbean and Guam and the Philippines in the Pacific; Spain reluctantly consented. When the treaty came before the American Senate for ratification, there was a long debate, and much opposition to the taking of colonies and protectorates. Finally, however, the treaty won the necessary two-thirds vote. Apparently the American people approved the policy of imperialism. In an election in 1900 President McKinley and his supporters in Congress were re-elected by a large vote.

Thus the United States had given up half of its policy of isolation. The war showed the new position of the United States as a world power. Even though Spain was, by then, one of the weaker European powers, our easy victory made other nations recog-

The end of the war with Spain did not bring peace in the Philippines. The United States had to put down a rebellion by Filipinos who demanded independence at once. Shown here is the Utah Light Artillery in action with insurgent Filipinos in 1899.

nize our growing strength. A few years later our navy had grown enough to be ranked third or fourth among the world's navies.

The United States builds the Panama Canal

The United States faced many new problems as a result of the Spanish War. We were now responsible for the welfare of peoples of different races, languages, religions, civilizations, and cultures, in places far from our shores. We had to find a way of governing these colonies. (We called them territories, possessions, or dependencies.)

There was also the problem of defense. During the war we had annexed the Hawaiian Islands, until then an independent state. So in the Pacific we had Hawaii, Guam, and the Philippines. In the Caribbean lay the protectorate of Cuba and the colony of Puerto Rico. Obviously, defense of the empire was a naval problem.

● The need for a canal

Before the war the American battleship *Oregon* had been stationed on the Pacific Coast. When war became likely, this ship was needed to strengthen the American force in the Caribbean. The *Oregon* had to go at high speed all the way around South America, a distance of 12,000 miles. It was clear that we would have to build two complete navies to protect our empire, or find some easier and quicker way to move warships between the Atlantic and Pacific oceans.

A canal across the Isthmus of Panama had long been talked about. After a French company had built the Suez Canal, it tried also

> The Panama Canal under construction, June, 1913. The Culebra Cut (now called Gaillard Cut) is the deepest excavated portion of the canal. At the right is Gold Hill. For a view of the same stretch of the canal after completion, see page 543.

to build one across Panama, but failed. The United States government now began negotiating for permission and a right of way to build a canal.

● Diplomatic negotiations

First, we arranged with the British to be released from a treaty which pledged that any canal should be built jointly by Great Britain and the United States. We bought the rights of the French company. Then we began to negotiate with the Republic of Colombia for the lease of a strip of land across the isthmus. At that time, Panama was a province within Colombia.

Here, however, we struck a snag. After a treaty had been negotiated, the Colombian Senate adjourned without ratifying it. There was great indignation in the United States. People felt Colombia was trying to "hold us up" for more money. The United States government began to investigate another possible route, through Nicaragua.

There was also indignation in Panama. The people of the region were eager to have the canal built because it promised them great benefits. When the negotiations between the United States and Colombia seemed to break down, the people of Panama began a revolution to gain independence. They wanted the canal. American warships stationed there kept Colombian troops from crossing the isthmus. Thus the revolution succeeded. The United States very quickly recognized the independence of Panama. A treaty between the two governments was drawn up and speedily ratified. We now had all the rights to build a canal.

● The canal is completed

The building of the Panama Canal was one of the world's greatest engineering projects of the time. It would probably have been impossible without the new machines which had been invented. Medical science, too, played a great part. Cuban and American scientists had discovered that mosquitoes carry the yellow fever which had done so much to cause the French failure. By wiping out the mosquitoes, they controlled the disease and thereby enabled the men to work in Panama. The canal was opened in 1914. It shortened the distance from New York to San Francisco by 7,900 miles, and the distance from New York to the new Territory of Hawaii by 6,700 miles. Fleets in the Atlantic and Pacific could be combined into one unit when necessary. Commercially the canal was also very useful. The shorter distances lowered the operating costs of a ship many times the amount of toll it paid to use the canal.

The policy and tactics of the United States in gaining the right to build the canal were widely criticized, especially in the countries of Central and South America. There is no evidence that Americans actually stirred up the revolution in Panama, but it is clear that our navy did prevent the Colombian government from moving its troops to suppress the revolt. We also showed much greater speed than usual in recognizing a new government which came into power by revolution.

The Latin American countries felt that the United States had become completely imperialistic, and a threat to their independence any time they stood in the way of what we wanted. They called us the "Colossus of the North." They resented our calling ourselves Americans, as if we were the only Americans. They lived in America, too, and felt that they were Americans. They resented the Monroe Doctrine, by which we claimed the right to interfere in their affairs, to "protect" them from other nations.

United States foreign policy in the Caribbean

The building of the canal had a great effect on the attitude of the United States toward the countries in Central and South America bordering on the Caribbean Sea.

A tanker in the Panama Canal passing Gold Hill in the Gaillard Cut. The trip of 44 nautical miles through the canal cuts nearly 8,000 miles from the sea distance between the Atlantic and Pacific coasts of the United States.

Formerly this region had been a sleepy backwater of the world, a dead end of commerce. Now the canal made it a highway of trade.

The canal also became the most vital link in our naval defense. It was just as though we had moved our southern border 2,000 miles to the south. Indeed, the defense of the canal became far more vital to our welfare and our safety than the Gulf of Mexico or the Rio Grande had ever been. Thus, everything about the countries that bordered on the Caribbean Sea, and the islands of the Caribbean, became of great importance in American foreign policy.

The governments of the countries in this region were very unstable, and this was a matter of great concern to the United States. They were republics only in name. The man in power was usually a military dictator. He was removed from power only by a revolution which brought in another military dictator. These revolutions were very frequent.

Another cause for concern was the fact that the Caribbean governments often borrowed money from European banks and private lenders. A government which gained power by revolution sometimes refused to pay the debts of the former government. They gave a reason which was often true enough: the money had not really gone to the country, but into the pockets of the president and his supporters. Finances of the countries were often in a bad state. Revenues from taxes often went into private pockets, too.

European lenders were often able to get their governments to bring pressure to get payments. Sometimes warships were sent and troops were landed to compel payment. A typical method was to take over the collection of the customs, the principal tax, and hold out enough money to pay the debts. You will recognize that these were common situations in the new imperialism. Loans that were not repaid often led to intervention by the imperial powers. All too often intervention ended with the taking of a colony or the establishment of a protectorate or sphere of influence.

The United States would have objected to such happenings in the Western Hemisphere at any time after the Monroe Doctrine. Now, however, there was the added fear that a strong European power with a foothold in the Caribbean region could threaten the canal or the sea lanes to it. President Theodore Roosevelt made a new statement concerning the Monroe Doctrine.

Roosevelt said that if any situation threatened the independence of any country in Central or South America, the United States would intervene to stop a foreign country from stepping in. In practice, this is what it meant: If a Caribbean country were threatened by revolution, or if nonpayment of debts brought threats from abroad, the United States would establish a protectorate over the Caribbean country. In several cases we landed marines and took over and operated the government of the country, at least the treasury. We collected the taxes and supervised the spending of money. Then we saw to it that the country's foreign debts, including those owed to American banks and corporations, were paid.

Often the protectorates established by the United States brought benefits to the Caribbean countries. Roads and schools were built, medical and sanitary facilities were improved from the tax money, which was honestly administered. Probably the countries were never better governed or enjoyed greater freedom from wars, revolutions, financial crises, and national bankruptcies. Yet these benefits were not always welcomed by the Latin Americans. They resented the fact that the Caribbean had become practically an American lake, in which our influence was supreme. No Caribbean government could come to power or stay in power without our approval. The Latin-American countries tended to be suspicious of the great power in the north.

The United States as a world power

By the first decade of the twentieth century the United States had taken its place as one of the great powers of the world. It had established an empire of colonies and protectorates in the Caribbean and the Pacific. It had begun to drop its isolation to play a part in world affairs. It had forced the Japanese to end their isolation. With its Open Door Policy, it had tried to prevent the complete division of China into colonies and spheres of influence. President Theodore Roosevelt had taken part in the Algeciras Conference, which tried to solve the explosive problem of Morocco without war. He had acted as mediator to end the Russo-Japanese War. Our fleet was one of the strongest; our agriculture and industry made us one of the wealthiest and most productive of nations.

However, power brings responsibilities as well as benefits. How well was the United States prepared to take the responsibilities of

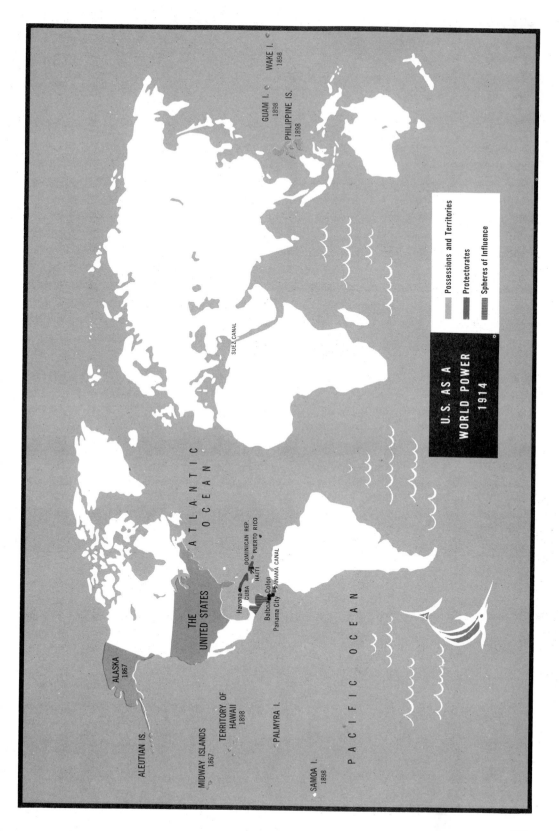

ALEUTIAN IS.

ALASKA
1867

MIDWAY ISLANDS
1867

TERRITORY OF
HAWAII
1898

PALMYRA I.

SAMOA I.
1898

PACIFIC OCEAN

THE
UNITED STATES

ATLANTIC
OCEAN

Havana
CUBA
HAITI
DOMINICAN REP.
PUERTO RICO
Colon
Balboa
Panama City
PANAMA CANAL

SUEZ CANAL

GUAM I.
1898
WAKE I.
1898

PHILIPPINE IS.
1898

PACIFIC OCEAN

U.S. AS A
WORLD POWER
1914

Possessions and Territories

Protectorates

Spheres of Influence

545

a great power? And how willing was it to do so? Those questions were to be answered in the second decade of the 1900's, when the whole world was torn by a great war.

Review of Chapter 42

People, places, and things

Identify: James Monroe, Abraham Lincoln, William McKinley, Theodore Roosevelt, Open Door Policy, Algeciras Conference, U.S.S. *Maine.*

Locate: Colombia, Panama Canal Zone, Colón, Balboa, Panama City, Cuba, Havana, Santiago, Puerto Rico, the Philippines, Guam, Hawaii.

Events in review

1. What group of states threatened to secede from the Union during the time of the Napoleonic Wars? What issue were these states protesting about?
2. What invention increased the importance of slavery in the southern states?
3. There were many underlying causes for the War Between the States. What action by a group of states was the immediate cause— that is, the event that led to the start of fighting?
4. List the conditions that made possible the rapid industrial development of the United States after the War Between the States.
5. What statement became the basis of United States foreign policy during most of the nineteenth century?
6. Briefly describe two incidents that aroused American indignation against Spain and led to the Spanish-American War.
7. List the territories acquired by the United States as a result of the war with Spain.
8. To what extent was Cuba a protectorate of the United States after the island became independent from Spain?
9. Briefly describe (a) the commercial and (b) the military importance of the Panama Canal.
10. How did a great medical discovery contribute to the building of the Panama Canal?

Problems and projects

1. The Industrial Revolution proceeded rapidly in the United States after 1865. Compare developments in the United States with developments in Europe. Did any European countries have natural resources and other advantages equal to those of the United States?
2. Review (in Chapter 32) the attempt of Napoleon III to interfere in Mexican affairs. What did Napoleon III try to do? What attitude did the Mexicans hold? What action did the United States take?
3. Why did the United States take a strong interest in the financial troubles of Central and South American governments? Can you describe instances in Africa of European nations using debts as an occasion for moving into a country?
4. Write a report on George W. Goethals or Walter Reed, telling the part he played in the construction of the Panama Canal.
5. Write a biographical sketch of one of the great leaders during the War Between the States, or of one of the leading figures in American industry in the nineteenth century.
6. On the map, locate the United States and all its possessions as of 1914. Include the Panama Canal Zone and show some of the important trade routes passing through the canal.
7. In an American history textbook, look up the Clayton-Bulwer Treaty, the Hay-Pauncefote Treaty, and the Hay-Bunau-Varilla Treaty. Report to the class on what these treaties provided.
8. Prepare a report on the Panama Canal. Cover such topics as the locks, Gatun Lake, the height of the canal above sea level at various points, problems in constructing the canal. (Incidentally, note on the map that the western end of the canal is the Atlantic terminus.) Can you explain why there has been discussion in recent years of a plan to build a sea-level canal?

Chapter 43   The First World War

TENSIONS among the great powers built up during the late nineteenth century and the early twentieth century. Finally these tensions burst out in World War I. The causes of this war were numerous, complicated, and interrelated, and whole volumes have been written about them. Here we will sort out and discuss certain basic factors: nationalism, imperialism, militarism, and a system of alliances. These conditions acted together to produce in 1914 a situation in which war seemed the only way out.

Nationalism as a cause of war

Nationalism is the feeling among a group of people that they belong together, bound by the ties of a common culture, a common history, and common problems. You may recall that at first national groups tried to unite under governments controlled by the people themselves. Nationalism and democracy went together. During the late nineteenth century the movement became more nationalistic and less democratic. For instance, the German people were united under a government which was far from democratic.

The desire to unite all the people of a nation within its boundaries had very explosive possibilities in a Europe where nationalities were so mingled. Two examples will serve.

In the Balkans the new Slavic kingdom of Serbia was eager to bring the Slavs of neighboring regions under its rule. However, Austria, which had reason to fear independent Slavic states, was much opposed. In France after 1871 there was a strong desire to regain the "lost provinces" of Alsace and Lorraine. Any attempt to do so was bound to produce fear and opposition in Germany.

Nationalism, carried to extremes, produced a sort of supernationalism and a very exaggerated idea of "national honor." These ideas caused tension and made it difficult to settle international disputes peacefully.

Imperialism as a cause of war

The rapid industrialization of the late 1800's and early 1900's brought the return of an old idea: the desire for national self-sufficiency. This led to high protective tariffs at home and a wild rush for colonies abroad. The partition of Africa led nations to the brink of war several times. In the Orient the rival ambitions of Russia and Japan did produce war, but it was limited to the two nations. Imperialistic rivalries in Africa and China were very dangerous to peace. Both nationalism and imperialism appeared in conflicts over the division of the weakening Ottoman Empire. National groups—Greeks, Slavs,

Arabs—wanted independence and self-government. Imperial nations—Great Britain, Russia, Austria-Hungary, Germany, and Italy —were each eager for a share of the spoils.

Militarism as a cause of war

Both nationalism and imperialism depended on a strong army and navy. The nation strong militarily got what it wanted, as the Prussians showed in their wars with Denmark, Austria, and France. The nation that was weak lost out, as Italy found to her sorrow.

Prussia had led the way with two military ideas. The first was conscription and a military reserve force. The drafted man, after a period of military training and service, was placed in a military reserve. He was subject to call at any time and to "refresher" training from time to time. Arms and equipment for the reserve army were kept at convenient places throughout the country. It was a very important and serious step, internationally, for a nation to call its reserves into active service. It was known as *mobilization,* and was the last step before actual fighting. Once mobilization had begun, it was difficult to prevent the outbreak of war.

The second Prussian change in established military methods was the General Staff. This was a super-military organization, made up of the best trained and most brilliant officers. Their duty was to perfect the organization, equipment, and training of the army and to prepare plans for any war which might possibly come. Every nation in Europe except Great Britain copied the Prussian ideas of conscription and the General Staff.

As the international situation became increasingly tense, a great armament race developed. Standing armies were increased in size and equipped with new and more destructive weapons. Great sums were spent for the fortification of national boundaries. There was also a naval race. Germany began very rapidly to build up a large and modern navy. Her example was followed by France, the United States, and especially Great Britain. The British depended on their navy rather than upon their army. For many years they had followed a policy of maintaining a navy equal in size to the combined navies of France and Russia, the two European powers with the largest navies. Germany's attempt to rival Great Britain on the sea was certain to affect British policy.

The armaments race was very expensive; so it meant great increases in taxation. The heavier taxes were justified to the people of the nations in two ways: pride in the nations' strength, and the desire for security and protection. Increases in military and naval strength were always "for defense." If it made itself strong enough, a nation could remain peaceful and secure because other nations would be afraid to attack it. That was the reasoning. However, you can see that an increase in army or navy by one nation would surely produce a round of increases by all others. Each wanted to equal or surpass the others, always "for defense," of course. It was a race that seemed to have no end. In a very tense world, it was terribly dangerous.

The system of alliances as a cause of war

During the late 1800's the balance of power in Europe was upset by the unification of Germany and of Italy. Germany, especially, created an entirely new situation. Instead of a group of relatively weak states divided into rival groups by Prussia and Austria, there now appeared a unified German Empire. It was militarily strong, with rapidly developing industries, and it was led by a diplomat, Bismarck, who was both ruthless and skillful.

● *The Triple Alliance*

In order to secure peace so that unified Germany could grow strong, Bismarck tried to do two things in his foreign policy. The first was to keep France isolated and without allies so that she could not seek revenge and the recovery of Alsace and Lorraine. To accomplish this, Bismarck first formed the Dual Alliance with Austria-Hungary and later the Triple Alliance to include Italy (page 427). Both were "defensive" alliances. Each country promised to come to the assistance of the others if they were attacked.

Italy's joining the Triple Alliance was a strange move. For many years Austria had been the great Italian enemy. Austria held the Dalmatian coast, across the Adriatic from Italy. Here lay the province of Istria and the city of Trieste, which Italy had long desired. Austria held the province of Tyrol, which contained the famous Brenner Pass, the chief invasion route from the north into Italy. It was Italy's disappointment over the French seizure of Tunisia (pages 500–501) which led her to join the Triple Alliance. Bismarck counted Italy a weak link, but the forging of the Triple Alliance in 1882 did isolate France in Europe.

Bismarck's second aim, closely related to the first, was to keep Germany's relations friendly with both Great Britain and Russia. Britain was much more interested in overseas expansion than in events on the continent of Europe. Bismarck was perfectly willing that Britain should control the seas and have a free hand in gaining new colonies, but he wanted Britain to stay out of continental European affairs. He doubted the need for or the value of colonies, and was pushed into the colonial struggle with great reluctance. As for Russia, Bismarck had a horror of an alliance between France and Russia, for this might force Germany to fight on two fronts at the same time. He was willing to make many sacrifices of German policy to prevent such an alliance.

The formation of the Triple Alliance completely upset the balance of power in Europe. France became very uneasy and began to seek allies. For some time Bismarck's skill-

H.M.S. Invincible, *launched in 1907 when the great powers were racing to build up their navies and armies. This ship cost the British about 1,740,000 pounds (about 8,700,000 dollars). In World War I the* Invincible *was sunk during the Battle of Jutland.*

ful diplomacy prevented any French gains. Russia also was displeased, but Bismarck was able to keep her from trying to do anything. Then, in 1888, Kaiser William II came to the throne of Germany. He was a vain, conceited, arrogant, and domineering young man. A firm believer in divine right, he insisted on ruling personally. It was certain that two such proud and dominating personalities as William II and Bismarck would clash, and they did. In 1890 the Iron Chancellor resigned. From then until his abdication in 1918 William II ruled Germany through chancellors of his own choice.

Kaiser William II reversed Bismarck's polices toward Britain and Russia. He entered the race for colonies with full force, demanding that Germany be given her "place in the sun." He began a great naval building program. Germany, said the Kaiser, should have a navy "second to none."

● *The Triple Entente*

France's opportunity came soon. Russia needed foreign capital, and she sought a loan from Germany. For reasons that would not have satisfied Bismarck, the German government refused the loan. The French hurried to lend the money, and to take other steps to win Russian friendship. In 1894 France and

MAJOR ALLIANCES IN 1914

Triple Alliance ▓ Triple Entente

Russia formed an alliance. French isolation was ended, and Bismarck's great fear of facing enemies on two sides became a reality.

The rapidly increasing German navy upset Britain's established balance of naval power. She tried to reach agreement with Germany to stop the naval race, but could get no agreement. Germany also began to interfere with some of Britain's imperial schemes. The goods of the rapidly expanding German industries gave stiff competition to British goods in world markets. Britain, too, began to look for friends. The British and French were able to reach an agreement over Morocco and Egypt (page 501). It was an entente, or agreement, rather than an alliance. To close the circle and balance the Triple Alliance there had to be agreement between Britain and Russia. Because of their rivalry in the Near East, it was difficult for these nations to get together. However, with French help an agreement was made.

In 1907 the powers of Europe faced each other in two great systems of alliances: the Triple Alliance of Germany, Austria, and Italy; the Triple Entente of Great Britain, France, and Russia. Each side had its strengths and weaknesses. The Entente looked more powerful, although it was less firmly joined than its rival. It controlled the seas. However, the still unsettled rivalry over the control of Constantinople and the Bosporus might easily develop into a source of Entente weakness. The Alliance of Germany, Austria, and Italy had the advantage of a central position on the continent. Furthermore, the lands of the three allies bordered on each other. But the Alliance had its weak link. Italy could not be depended on; the hostility between Italy and Austria-Hungary continued despite the alliance. Also, the Triple Alliance had strong powers on both its eastern and western fronts.

Rivalry in the Balkans touches off war

● German policy in the Balkans

Germany now began to look for added strength to make up for the weakness of Italy as an ally. She did not find the new strength, but in trying to do so she made one of Bismarck's fears come true. She strengthened the relation between Britain, Russia, and France. This is what happened. Germany began negotiations with Turkey; thus she entered the troubled scene of the Balkans and the Near East.

To extend her influence into the region, Germany planned a railroad from Berlin through the Balkans to Constantinople and on to Bagdad on the Tigris River. The railroad was finally to reach the head of the Persian Gulf. To the British this meant a threat to her Mediterranean "lifeline" to India. It also meant a strong competition for the trade of the Near East. To the Russians it meant that Turkey would now have a strong protector, and that Russian hopes of gaining Constantinople and the Bosporus would be dim.

The Balkans had long been a region of many conflicts and ambitions, both of nationalism and imperialism. These nations were well named "the powder keg of Europe."

After centuries of Turkish rule the Balkan peoples longed for independence and self-government. During the nineteenth century Greece, Rumania, Bulgaria, and Serbia did become independent. The Slavic independence movements had the support of Russia. The Russians were Slavs of the same Greek Orthodox religion as many of the Balkan Slavs. Russia promoted a Pan-Slavic movement—an attempt to unite all Slavic peoples under Russian leadership. Pan-Slavism was bitterly opposed by Austria-Hungary because it would strengthen the discontent and independence movements among the Slavs of the Austro-Hungarian Empire. Therefore Austria usually supported Turkey in opposing the independence movements. However, when opportunity offered, she took Turkish territory that was occupied by Balkan Slavs.

In 1878 Austria was authorized to administer two provinces, Bosnia and Herzegovina, that were right next to her own lands. In 1908, in violation of an earlier promise, she annexed the two provinces outright.

Britain opposed Russia's Pan-Slavism and her moves toward Constantinople. Britain's fears became greater after she secured a controlling interest in the Suez Canal. The Suez became the main highway, the lifeline, to India, and India was the most valuable possession in the empire. Neither the British nor the Russian government was willing to see Germany penetrate the area. Neither wanted the other to have Constantinople, but neither wanted Germany to have it. When, therefore, Germany commenced her drive to the east, Britain and Russia found themselves in agreement to resist German expansion.

Perhaps the greatest rivalry in the Balkans was between Austria and Serbia. With aid

EUROPE IN 1914

from Russia the Slavic Serbs had gained complete independence from Turkey in 1878. But Serbia was landlocked. She hoped to gain Bosnia and Herzegovina as a step toward the unification of the southern Slavs. The establishment of the Austrian protectorate disappointed the Serbs; the Austrian annexation in 1908 infuriated them.

In 1912 and 1913 two wars were fought in the Balkans which almost but not quite touched off the world explosion. Their causes and events are far too complicated to go into here. It is enough to know that, as a result of the first war, Serbia gained her port on the Adriatic. As a result of the second war, Austria forced Serbia to give up the seaport she had gained to the newly formed kingdom of Albania. The hatred of the Serbs for the Austrians was so great that patriotic secret societies were formed to spread anti-Austrian propaganda and to plot against Austria.

●*Effects of Germany's Balkan policy*

The new ambitions of Germany in the Balkans and the Near East added to all of these long-established rivalries and ambitions. Austria found a strong supporter in Germany. Russia and Britain found a strong opponent. When Austria annexed Bosnia and Herzegovina in 1908, the Russians at first moved to stop any further moves by Austria. But Kaiser William II sprang to the side of Austria, as he put it, "like a knight in shining armor," and the Russians had to give in.

The events that took place from 1870 to 1914 seem to have the same terrible logic as the plot of a Greek tragedy. In the Greek plays the tragic ending is inevitable. All the events march with terrible force toward a conclusion that could be foreseen but could not be avoided. So it was in the period you have been studying.

The rapid development of the Industrial Revolution created beliefs in the possibility of national self-sufficiency, the desirability of colonies, "national honor," and "peace

through strength." These ideas and forces produced a Europe divided into two rival alliances. Furthermore, it was staggering under the burden of armaments. Reasonable, peaceful solutions to problems became increasingly difficult to achieve. Compromise was scorned; it was called a policy of weakness.

Europe was like an immense room filled with open barrels of powder in which fools and madmen were allowed to play with matches. The slightest spark in the right place meant the explosion, and there were so many "right places." It is not surprising that the spark touched powder in the Balkans. The result was a tragedy for Western man.

●*Assassination at Sarajevo*

The spark that touched off the explosion of World War I came on June 28, 1914, at Sarajevo in the disputed Austrian province of Bosnia. The Austrian Archduke Francis Ferdinand, heir to the throne, and his wife were assassinated. The assassin was a member of one of the secret societies called the Black Hand. Its members included many Serbians, among them high government officials.

The assassination brought to a head the long struggle between Serbia and Austria. The Austrian government was determined that the unruly Serbs should be punished and finally put in their places. However, before Austria acted, she made sure of German support in case the Russians should try to protect their fellow Slavs. Germany gave Austria assurance of German backing in anything she did. The Austrian government now made sure of the backing of all parts within the empire. Then it presented the Serbian government with an ultimatum (the "last word"—either do this or face war).

●*Austria and Serbia go to war*

In the ultimatum Austria demanded that the Serbian government officially condemn all anti-Austrian propaganda, suppress all

"All the News That's Fit to Print."

The New York Times.

THE WEATHER
Fair to-day and Tuesday; diminishing northwest winds.

VOL. LXIII...NO. 20,647. .... NEW YORK, WEDNESDAY, AUGUST 5, 1914.—TWENTY PAGES. ONE CENT In Greater New York, Jersey City and Newark. | ...

ENGLAND DECLARES WAR ON GERMANY; BRITISH SHIP SUNK; FRENCH SHIPS DEFEAT GERMAN, BELGIUM ATTACKED; 17,000,000 MEN ENGAGED IN GREAT WAR OF EIGHT NATIONS; GREAT ENGLISH AND GERMAN NAVIES ABOUT TO GRAPPLE; RIVAL WARSHIPS OFF THIS PORT AS LUSITANIA SAILS

Kaiser Hurls Two Armies Into Belgium After Declaring War.

LIEGE ATTACK REPULSED

German Guns Are Reported to be Bombarding Both That City and Namur.

BELGIANS RUSH TO ARMS

Parliament Acclaims King's Appeal and Votes $40,000,000 for National Defense.

FRENCH BORDER CLASHES

Stronger German Forces Crossing the Border Near Mars-la-Tour and Moineville.

RUSSIANS ATTACK MEMEL

Seaport Town of Germany Objective of Attempt of Enemy to Capture It.

Over 17,000,000 Fighting Men of Eight Nations Now Engaged in the Colossal European War

DUAL ALLIANCE

	Regular Army.	Reserves.	War Strength. Total.
Germany	870,000	4,430,000	5,300,000
Austria-Hungary	390,000	1,610,000	2,000,000
Total	1,260,000	6,040,000	7,300,000

TRIPLE ENTENTE AND ITS ALLIES.

	Regular Army.	Reserves.	War Strength. Total.
Russia	1,290,000	3,300,000	4,590,000
France	720,000	3,280,000	4,000,000
England	254,500	476,500	731,000
Belgium	42,000	180,000	222,000
Servia	32,000	208,000	240,000
Montenegro			50,000
Total	2,388,500	7,444,500	9,833,000
Grand Total			17,133,000

The above figures do not include the naval forces of the allies.

Cunarder Slips Out; Will Pick Up British Cruisers as Escorts.

GERMAN WARSHIPS NEAR

Liner to Head for Newfoundland, Where Other English Ships Will Meet Her.

FRENCH CRUISERS OUTSIDE

Wireless Code Messages from Telefunken Station at Sayville Aid German Cruisers.

TO BE SENT TO WASHINGTON

Another German Detachment also outflanking the village of Molsonville, in the Department of Moerthe-et Moselle. A parish priest was killed.

Other detachments visited outlying farms at Lepuix, near Belfort, and requisitioned cattle. Several Germans were taken prisoners and brought into Belfort.

German troops today cut the telephone and telegraph wire on French territory along the border.

No engagement in force was reported, but the French outposts have been hurried since last night by repeated attacks on their outposts on the...

GERMAN FLEET SINKS A BRITISH MINE LAYER

Scout ship Pathfinder Is Chased By the Kaiser's Warships But Makes Its Escape.

LONDON, Aug. 4.—A British mine-laying ship has been sunk by a German fleet.

The Pathfinder scout ship was pursued by the fleet, but managed to make her escape.

There are some mine-layers in the German Navy. On being bombarded at Helgoland, all of them were lost.

BATTLE IN THE NORTH SEA

London Paper Reports One Going On, Says Wounded Are Landed.

LONDON, Aug. 4.—A special of the London Daily at 11 P. M. asserts that a naval battle has been going on some hours off the north of Scotland and that several wounded marines and seamen have been landed at Cromarty.

TWO GERMAN WARSHIPS TAKEN, ANOTHER SUNK

French Fleet in the Mediterranean Reported to Have Won a Victory.

PARIS, Aug. 4.—An unofficial report from Algiers says that a French...

State of War Exists, Says Britain, as Kaiser Rejects Ultimatum.

MUST DEFEND BELGIUM

King George Issues Call to Arms and Thanks the Colonies for Their Support.

ENVOY LEAVES BERLIN

British Foreign Office Makes Final Announcement One Hour Before Time Limit.

VOTE $525,000,000 FUND

JAPAN TO AID ENGLAND

To Smash the Kiel Canal Probably English Fleet's First Attempt Against Germany Would Smash Kiel Canal.

British Declaration of War With Germany, Following Rejection of Her Demand

LONDON, Aug. 4.—Great Britain declared war on Germany at 7 o'clock tonight.

An earlier announcement that Germany had declared war on Great Britain was due to an error in the Admiralty's statement.

The Foreign Office's Statement.

The British Foreign Office has issued the following statement:

"Owing to the summary rejection by the German Government of the request made by his Britannic Majesty's Government that the neutrality of Belgium should be respected, his Majesty's Ambassador at Berlin has received his passports and his Majesty's Government has declared to the German Government that a state of war exists between Great Britain and Germany from 11 o'clock P.M., Aug. 4."

Declaration Announced to Germany.

BERLIN, Aug. 4.—Shortly after 9 o'clock this evening William Edward Goschen, the British Ambassador, went to the Foreign Office and announced that Great Britain had declared war with Germany. He then demanded his passports.

England Calls All Unmarried Men From 18 to 30 To Serve King and Country in This Hour of Need

LONDON, Wednesday, Aug. 5.—A War Office advertisement appears in the morning papers headed: "Your King and Country Need You."

The advertisement says that the empire is on the brink of the greatest war in the history of the world, and appeals to all unmarried men between the ages of 18 and 30 years to join the army immediately.

---

anti-Austrian publications and societies, eliminate all anti-Austrian books and teachers from her public schools, and dismiss the officials involved in the propaganda Also, it was to arrest at once two Serbian officers, who were named. The most excessive demands were these: Austrian officials must be allowed to help in suppressing the propaganda; Austrian judges must be allowed to sit in trial of those accused of the crime at Sarajevo. These terms had to be accepted within forty-eight hours, or Austria would declare war.

The reply of the Serbian government was mild and conciliating. Serbia accepted all the terms except the last two. She pointed out that to allow Austrian officials to operate in Serbia and Austrian judges to sit in Serbian courts would be a denial of her rights as a sovereign nation. However, Serbia expressed willingness to submit the entire dispute to the recently created international court at the Hague, in Holland.

Taking no chances on reasonableness, the Serbian government ordered mobilization of all troops. It was a wise step. In spite of the mildness of the Serbian reply, Austria announced that her terms had not been met. She declared war on Serbia when the time limit of the ultimatum was reached.

The chain reaction spreads the war

The system of alliances sent nations down into war like a row of dominoes when the first one topples. All attempts to get Austria to continue negotiations were in vain. Germany showed some hesitation, but continued to support Austria. When it was sure that the Austrians would attack, Russia ordered partial mobilization in order to be in a position to help the Serbs. Immediately Germany sent an ultimatum to Russia. She demanded that Russia cancel mobilization within twelve hours or face war. Although the Russian czar tried to explain his peaceful intention, Germany declared war at the end of the twelve hours.

On the same day as the ultimatum to Russia, Germany also sent one to France. She demanded that France at once declare herself neutral. When the French ignored the ultimatum, Germany declared war on France.

Now the position of Great Britain became all-important. Some believe that if the British government had taken a firm stand with her allies when the Austrian ultimatum was first made public, the war might have been avoided, because the Germans might have been more cautious. Others doubt it. They argue that the Germans expected to win before the British could do anything effective. Understandably, the British did not want a European war; and if one came, they wanted to stay out if possible. The British did not act even when Germany declared war on Russia and France. Then the Germans took a step that brought Britain into the war.

The neutrality of Belgium had been guaranteed by all the European powers (page 364). Belgium agreed to stay out of any European war and not to help either side. The other powers agreed not to attack Belgium. However, a glance at the map will show you the strategic importance of Belgium. It is on the flat European coastal plain, with borders on both France and Germany.

A German "secret weapon" of 1914. When the Germans drove through Belgium toward France they used these heavy howitzers to smash the Belgian fortifications. Guns of this size had never before been moved with an army on the offensive. They fired a projectile 42 centimeters (nearly 17 inches) in diameter.

Germany's diplomacy since the end of the nineteenth century made it necessary for the German General Staff to plan for Bismarck's nightmare—a two-front war against France and Russia. The General Staff counted on German efficiency to allow them to mobilize, strike, and knock France out of the war before the Russians could attack from the east. However, the Franco-German border was mostly hilly, wooded country, very heavily fortified on both sides. It was not favorable terrain for a swift blow. The German master plan called for only a feint there, to draw the French army out of position. The main German drive was to be made across the flat, open plain of Belgium. If the Germans could smash into France at the lightly fortified Franco-Belgian frontier, they could swing around and capture Paris before French mobilization could be completed. Such an attack would violate the guaranteed neutrality of Belgium, but that did not disturb the German planners. It was their job to win wars, not to worry about treaties.

As soon as the German government had declared war on France, it sent an ultimatum to Belgium. The Germans demanded that German troops be permitted to cross Belgian territory. The British protested this demand and insisted that the guarantee of neutrality be observed. The German foreign minister replied that surely Britain would not fight a war over "a scrap of paper." The Germans marched into Belgium; Great Britain declared war on Germany and Austria.

● The contest for allies

All the nations of the two sets of alliances were at war except Italy. The Italian government took the position that the Austrians and Germans were the attackers; therefore her defensive alliance did not require Italy to help them. Italy declared herself neutral. Whatever Italy could expect to gain from the war had to come at the expense of Austria: the Tyrol, the ports of Trieste and Fiume,

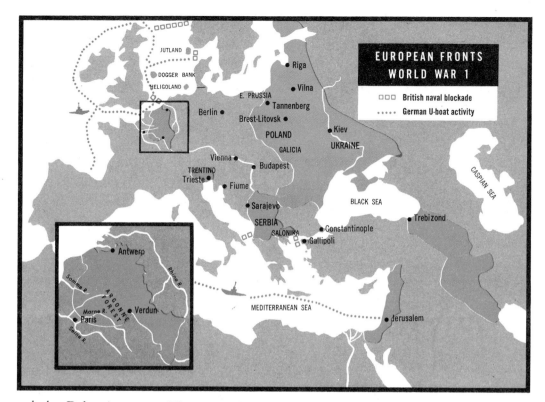

EUROPEAN FRONTS WORLD WAR 1

□□□ British naval blockade
····· German U-boat activity

and the Dalmatian coast. There was little chance that Austria would give them up, but her opponents might offer them as spoils of victory. The nine months of Italy's neutrality saw some desperate bargaining by each side: the Allies (Britain, France, Russia) and the Central Powers (Germany and Austria-Hungary). Finally, secret treaties were drawn up among Britain, France, Russia, and Italy, dividing the spoils of war in case they defeated the Central Powers. Italy then entered the war against her former allies, Germany and Austria.

Japan declared war in 1914, siding with Great Britain in accordance with the terms of the Anglo-Japanese alliance of 1902 (page 520). This help Britain was reluctant to accept, but she had no choice. Japan hoped to destroy the German Pacific Fleet which was stationed at the leased base of Kiaochow on the Shantung Peninsula. This would be of aid to Britain, to be sure, but there was another side to the coin.

An ally often has a disturbing way of serv-ing his own interests rather than yours. Japan had her own plans for the Far East; she was only waiting until the European powers were busy elsewhere. The war was a golden opportunity which the Japanese were quick to seize. They captured the German base of Kiaochow, and then moved on to occupy the entire Shantung Peninsula.

To balance the loss of Italy Germany redoubled her efforts to win Turkey over. In the middle of October, 1914, Turkey plunged into the war on the side of the Central Powers. It was a serious blow to the Allies. Turkey was not a strong military power, but she had a strategic position. Control of Constantinople and the straits bottled up Russia's Black Sea fleet, just as German control of the entrance to the North Sea bottled up the Russian Baltic fleet. Furthermore, Russia lacked the industry to allow her to fight a modern war very long without help from her allies. Turkey's entrance made it impossible for such help to reach Russia through the Mediterranean and the Black seas.

There were other diplomatic maneuvers. The belligerents bid desperately with offers to the neutrals. The neutrals tried just as hard to get the best offer. Even more important, they tried to pick the winner. Germany won Bulgaria, which gave the Central Powers an immensely strong strategic front. With Bulgaria in the line-up, the front stretched from the North Sea through Central Europe, the Balkans, Constantinople, and on through the Turkish Empire to the Persian Gulf. However, the Allies were able to persuade Greece and Rumania to join them.

By 1917, the war involved almost the entire continent of Europe. Spain, Portugal, Holland, Switzerland, and the Scandinavian countries managed to maintain the difficult position of neutrality. The war had also reached out into the Far East to involve Japan and helpless China as well as the British possessions: Australia, New Zealand, and India. It reached across the Atlantic to draw in Canada, the United States, and many of the Latin American countries. It was, in every sense of the words, a world war—the first of its kind.

"The war behind the front"—German women working in a munitions factory.

How World War I was fought

It was very different from any war in the past. Weapons were more destructive than ever before. It was industrialized warfare. All the industries of the warring powers had to be mobilized and organized to the one end: production to win the war. More men than ever before fought in actual combat. Never had so many people, both men and women, taken' part in the "war behind the front"—the industrial and agricultural production needed to supply the armed forces.

● *War as an endurance contest*

Former wars had been wars of movement, with columns of troops marching and countermarching to outmaneuver and outflank the enemy. Sometimes they met in pitched battles. Occasionally they settled down into siege operations before some fortress city. World War I began as a war of movement; then it settled down into a gigantic siege operation of trench warfare. The two armies faced each other in lines of trenches behind barbed wire extending all the way from the Swiss border to the English Channel. It became what is called a war of attrition; victory goes to the side that lasts longer and wears the other out.

The Central Powers had many advantages in such a war. Germany was superbly prepared. Her army was excellently organized and trained, and equipped with superior weapons, and fought in enemy territory and not on her own soil. German industry and transportation were geared to war. Her lines of communication with her allies were far better than those of her enemies. The solid front from the Baltic Sea to the Persian Gulf was a tremendous advantage. However, for a long war the real advantage lay with the Allies. They had more manpower and greater industrial resources. Above all, they controlled the seas; therefore, they could bring in food and raw materials they needed and could blockade and eventually starve the Central Powers.

● *The war drags on—1914-1916*

The German attack on France through Belgium came very close to success, but it did fail. German troops reached the Marne River, almost within sight of Paris. Here the French stood fast. Reserves were moved out from Paris in taxicabs. The French army counterattacked. The Germans were forced to withdraw for some distance, and Paris was saved.

The Russians mobilized much more quickly than the Germans had expected. One Russian army moved westward toward Budapest; another moved through East Prussia, threatening Danzig. Although the Russians had plenty of manpower, they were no match for the Germans in equipment or training. The armies met in a terrific battle at Tannenberg in East Prussia. The Russians were defeated and driven back with terrible losses. Soon after, the Germans were able to launch an offensive in the east and drive the Russians out of Germany into Russian Poland.

It was clear that Russia's greatest weakness was lack of equipment. To meet this problem the Allies decided on a daring venture: an attempt to force their way through the Dardanelles and capture Constantinople. The Turks resisted stubbornly, and the attack failed with great losses. The originator of the plan was Winston Churchill, First Lord of the Admiralty (Secretary of the Navy) in the British cabinet. Churchill had to take the responsibility for the failure and resign his cabinet post.

The greatest naval battle of the war was fought off Danish Jutland in the North Sea, in May, 1916. Neither side could claim a complete victory, but the German navy retired into the Baltic and there were no fleet battles during the rest of the war. The British and French fleets were able to keep control of the Atlantic and the Mediterranean. Thus they could throw a blockade across the North Sea

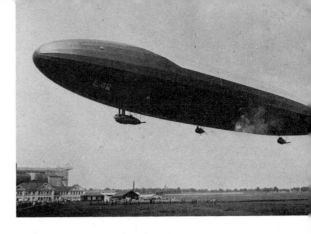

War in the air. Germany used zeppelins like the one shown here to bomb England. German naval dirigibles made 40 raids on England, dropped 220 tons of bombs, killed 557 people and wounded 1,358. The damage done was too small to have any effect on the course of the war.

to prevent supplies from reaching Germany. The Germans struck back with their best available weapon, the submarine, trying to sink all ships going to Britain and France.

By 1916 the war had reached a deadlock. The British naval blockade was more effective than the German submarine blockade. On the land there was the gigantic stalemate of trench warfare. There was little chance that either side could break through, start a war of movement, and force a decision. The machine gun dominated the war. Neither side dared to risk an offensive all along the line. At a ghastly cost both sides had learned that an offensive could drive the enemy back a certain distance in a given sector, if the offensive side were willing to spend the men and munitions. However, it could not break through; it succeeded only in establishing a wedge-shaped salient.

At the end of 1916 a balance sheet of the war seemed to favor the Central Powers. Under the heavy weight of the war, Russia was rapidly reaching the point of total collapse. If this happened, the Central Powers could move all their troops from the eastern front and concentrate on the west. There was terrible war weariness in Austria, but the same was true in Italy and even in France. Germany stood firmly, suffering less damage since she was fighting on enemy territory. Britain was beginning to feel fear and despair, because German submarines were sinking ships faster than they could be built. There was a danger that Britain might be starved for raw materials and food. The start of 1917 was a dark period for the Allies. Then the entry of the United States proved to be a turning point in the war.

The United States enters the war

When the European War began in 1914, the government of the United States immediately declared neutrality. Many of our people sympathetically followed the course of the war, favoring one or the other side, but the sentiment in the country was almost unanimous that the war was "none of our business." Overwhelmingly the American people favored staying out of the war.

●*Economic involvement in the war*

However, the war soon affected the United States considerably. As the only industrialized neutral nation we became a supplier of food, raw materials, and munitions. The United States government insisted on the right of our citizens and business firms to sell non-war supplies to either side without interference. But we agreed that if an American ship carrying contraband (war munitions) to one side was captured by the other side, the captors had the right to seize both ship and cargo without interference. However, we insisted on the right of American citizens to travel in safety on ships of any nation, neutral or belligerent (warring). As a neutral, the government could lend money to either side, and it made no effort to stop banks, corporations, or private citizens from doing so by buying the bonds of foreign gov-

ernments. Of course, buying a bond is simply lending money to the government that issues the bond.

The United States soon had a tremendous economic stake in the war. American industry entered a "war boom," working overtime to fill the orders of warring countries. American farmers had never been so prosperous. There was a demand for everything they could raise, and more, because the warring nations could not produce enough at home. Prices and wages both went up far and rapidly.

As the British blockade tightened, American trade became more and more one-sided. Soon we were trading with the Allies only. Payment for these supplies became a problem. At first the British and French paid in gold, but this could not continue long, for they did not have enough gold. Then they called in all the stocks and bonds in American corporations which their citizens owned, and sold them in the United States to pay for the needed goods. When this money ran out, they sold their government bonds to American investment bankers. The bankers, in turn, sold them to their customers. This meant that the British and French governments were borrowing from American citizens the money to pay for the American goods.

●*Wilson tries to arrange peace*

President Woodrow Wilson made many attempts to get the warring powers to agree to stop the war. He offered his services as a mediator, or go-between, to try to arrange peace terms. He appealed to both sides to state their war aims—what they wanted from the war. In this way he hoped to find some basis for negotiation. Neither side would accept him as mediator. The Allies demonstrated at times their willingness to state their war aims. The Germans refused to show their hand. One reason for this was the fact that the Allies had their postwar plans

This famous recruiting poster was the work of James Montgomery Flagg.

fairly well laid out; it is doubtful if Germany had any specific postwar plans.

● Trouble with the blockades—particularly German submarine warfare

The United States soon ran into difficulties with the two blockades. The British stopped our merchant ships and took them into port to be searched for contraband. They added greatly to the list of articles that could be seized as contraband. American protests were met with the reply that in such a war almost anything was useful as a war supply. When our trade with neutral Holland and Scandinavia increased, the British stopped it on the grounds that the goods must be going on into Germany.

Our troubles with the British over war trade were nothing compared to those with Germany over the submarine blockade. British seizures of American ships and cargoes meant loss of property. If circumstances com-

pelled a British warship to sink a merchant ship, it could (in theory at least) carry the passengers and crew to safety. The submarine could neither take a ship into port nor carry the passengers and crew to safety. At first the Germans stopped and searched ships. If they found contraband, they allowed passengers and crew to escape in lifeboats; then they sank the ship. When British anti-submarine warfare became more effective, this procedure proved too dangerous for the German submarines. Then the submarines sank ships without warning, which meant loss of life of passengers and crew.

British merchant ships carrying American passengers were sunk, the most famous being the *Lusitania*, on which 124 Americans were lost in 1915. The United States protested against this and other incidents. In 1916 Germany promised to stop sinking ships without warning, provided the United States would use its influence to persuade the British to end their blockade. President Wilson would not accept this condition.

Sentiments in the United States changed considerably as the war progressed. The sinking of ships, with the loss of American lives, influenced the thinking of many people. British and French propaganda was much more convincing than that of the Germans. The great prosperity of the industrial and agricultural booms depended increasingly on the Allies, and the British and French bonds which people had bought had an effect on their sympathies. Many Americans came to think of Allied victory as a triumph of democracy over tyranny and militarism. Wilson's saying, "The world must be made safe for democracy," became a deep conviction with many people. They felt that only American entry could prevent a German victory.

● The declaration of war—April, 1917

In January, 1917, the German government announced that it would sink without warning any ship of any nation found in a large

The home front: Alma Gluck, a well-known opera singer, selling bonds for the Third Liberty Loan. This photograph was taken on Broad Street, in Philadelphia. Note the German helmet on the post.

zone around the British Isles. President Wilson then broke diplomatic relations by recalling the American ambassador from Germany and sending home the German ambassador. He appealed to the Germans to repeal their order, but they refused. Therefore he summoned a special session of the Congress. On April 6, 1917, by an overwhelming vote, the Congress declared war on Germany.

As a warring power, the United States faced many problems. Its navy was well prepared, and could go into the war at once. But its army was very small. Conscription was adopted almost immediately, but it was a question whether a large enough army could be raised, trained, equipped, and transported to Europe in time to prevent an Allied collapse. For the first time in our history, our industry, agriculture, and transportation were organized for a single purpose: the winning of a war. They performed miracles indeed.

When the Germans declared unrestricted submarine warfare in January, 1917, they reasoned that the United States would not declare war. Even if we did, they believed that their submarines could starve Britain and force her to surrender before an American army could be raised, trained, and landed in Europe. If Britain surrendered, none of the other Allies would continue the war. The German reasoning came dangerously close to being right. It was not until the spring and summer of 1918 that troops of the newly drafted and trained American army arrived in Europe in any numbers. Meanwhile, the hard-pressed Allies had to hold on.

The Central Powers collapse

The boost to Allied morale given by the American entry was badly needed. Already—in March, 1917—the long-feared Russian collapse had begun. The czar's government was overthrown. Eight months later the Communists seized control and made a separate peace with Germany. Even worse, they published, for all the world to see, the terms of the secret treaties in which the Allied Powers agreed to divide up the loot of victory. Now men in the Allied countries could see what they were really fighting for, and they did not like it.

● War aims—the Fourteen Points

In a speech to Parliament Prime Minister David Lloyd George tried to undo the bad impression by stating somewhat more idealistic aims. But it was President Woodrow Wilson who gave the noble statement of what he thought the Allied aims should be.

This he did in the Fourteen Points, which he stated in a speech to the Congress. There were six points of a general nature, and eight which dealt with definite countries and regions, such as Russia, Belgium, Alsace-Lorraine, Italy, the Balkans, Turkey, and Poland.

Wilson's general proposals were as follows:

1. No secret treaties; all treaties should be not only public, but negotiated in public.
2. Freedom of the seas for all nations, in peace and war.
3. The removal of all economic barriers (tariffs); equal opportunity for trade among all nations. All nations to have an equal chance to buy raw materials.
4. Reduction of national armaments "to the lowest points consistent with domestic safety."
5. Fair adjustment of all colonial claims. The interests of the people of the region were to be considered equally with those of the nation claiming the title.
6. A League of Nations, which would give mutual guarantees of political independence and protection of territories to large and small states alike.

The Fourteen Points caught the imagination of people everywhere as a statement of aims worth fighting for. They raised the morale of Allied fighting men. Copies were dropped behind the German lines; they made the German people more willing to surrender. Historians have felt, though, that President Wilson made a serious mistake. He did not use his influence during the war, when it was greatest, to get the Allies to agree definitely to the Fourteen Points and to renounce publicly the terms of the secret treaties.

● German attacks fail in 1918

The collapse of the Russians allowed the Germans to stage a huge offensive on the western front during the spring and summer of 1918. It was their last desperate gamble to break through and end the war before the Americans could turn the tide. It was a gamble the Germans had to take, because their submarine blockade was failing. American troops and supplies were reaching Britain and France in increasing numbers and quantities. The German offensives of 1918 lasted until mid-July. They failed by a very narrow margin. Then, strengthened by increasing numbers of American troops, the Allies counterattacked and drove on to victory.

Things were going badly for the Central Powers in the Near East and the Balkans. Bulgaria, seeing little hope for victory or for aid from her allies, caved in first. Turkey soon followed, suing for peace. In Austria-Hungary a revolution brought the old empire to an end. Austria and Hungary formed separate governments.

The battle front: men of the United States Army advance through the French village of Montfaucon, near Verdun. The wrecked house shown here was at one time used as a German observation post. A periscope can be seen sticking up close to the two weather vanes on the peak of the roof.

"All the News That's Fit to Print."

The New York Times.

THE WEATHER
Fair today and Tuesday; diminishing northwest winds.

VOL. LXVIII...NO. 22,206. .... NEW YORK, MONDAY, NOVEMBER 11, 1918. TWENTY-FOUR PAGES. TWO CENTS ...... THREE CENTS ...... FOUR CENTS

ARMISTICE SIGNED, END OF THE WAR!
BERLIN SEIZED BY REVOLUTIONISTS;
NEW CHANCELLOR BEGS FOR ORDER;
OUSTED KAISER FLEES TO HOLLAND

SON FLEES WITH EX-KAISER

Hindenburg Also Believed to be Among Those in His Party.

ALL ARE HEAVILY ARMED

Automobiles Bristle with Rifles as Fugitives Arrive at Dutch Frontier.

ON THEIR WAY TO DE STEEG

Belgians Yell to Them, "Are You On Your Way to Paris?"

Kaiser Fought Hindenburg's Call for Abdication; Failed to Get Army's Support in Keeping Throne

By GEORGE RENWICK

GERMAN DYNASTIES MORE WARSHIPS BEING WIPED OUT | JOIN THE REDS

King of Wuerttemberg Abdicates — Sovereign of Saxony to Follow Suit.

PRINCES MAY BE EXILED

Socialists Are Demanding That Every Sovereign in the Empire Shall be Dethroned.

Four Dreadnoughts in Kiel Harbor Espouse the Revolutionary Cause.

GUARDSHIPS ALSO GO OVER

Those Protecting Mines in the Great Belt and the Baltic Abandon Their Posts.

BERLIN TROOPS JOIN REVOLT

Reds Shell Building in Which Officers Vainly Resist.

THRONGS DEMAND REPUBLIC

Revolutionary Flag on Royal Palace—Crown Prince's Palace Also Seized.

GENERAL STRIKE IS BEGUN

Burgomaster and Police Submit—War Office Now Under Socialist Control.

Socialist Chancellor Appeals to All Germans To Help Him Save Fatherland from Anarchy

---

WAR ENDS AT 6 O'CLOCK THIS MORNING

The State Department in Washington Made the Announcement at 2:45 o'Clock.

ARMISTICE WAS SIGNED IN FRANCE AT MIDNIGHT

Terms Include Withdrawal from Alsace-Lorraine, Disarming and Demobilization of Army and Navy, and Occupation of Strategic Naval and Military Points.

By The Associated Press

WASHINGTON, Monday, Nov. 11, 2:48 A.M.—The armistice between Germany, on the one hand, and the allied Governments and the United States, on the other, has been signed.

Things were going badly with Germany, too. The German army fought fiercely, took a heavy toll of life, and made its withdrawals in orderly fashion. Although German forces were still within the borders of France, a point was being rapidly reached where these forces would have to retreat into their own country and allow Germany to be invaded.

Weary from the long war, and beginning to taste defeat, the German people rebelled. Kaiser William II was forced to abdicate, and a republic was proclaimed. On November 11, 1918, the new Socialist chancellor of the German Republic signed an armistice. For years after the war, the victorious powers remembered this date as Armistice Day.

An armistice is not a peace treaty; it is an agreement to stop fighting until a treaty can be drawn up. However, the terms of the armistice which Germany had to sign left no doubt about her defeat, and no chance that she could renew the war. She had to cancel the severe and humiliating peace treaties which she had forced the Russians and Ru-

manians to sign. She had to surrender all her submarines and a large part of her surface fleet. She had to give up all war prisoners, and hand over certain munitions which might make it possible for her to fight again.

Thus the Central Powers were defeated, and the bloodiest war, until then, in human history ended. It left Europe and the whole Western World poorer, weaker, and suffering from bad effects that are still felt.

Review of Chapter 43

People, places, and things

Identify: William II, David Lloyd George, Winston Churchill, Woodrow Wilson, ultimatum, contraband, secret treaties.

Locate: The Central Powers, the Allies, Serbia, Bosnia, Herzegovina, Sarajevo, the Dardanelles, the Bosporus, Paris, the Marne, Jutland, Berlin, Bagdad.

Events in review

1. Give an example of the nationalist feeling that was one of the causes of the First World War.
2. Give an example of the growth of militarism before World War I.
3. What nations made up the Triple Alliance? What was the purpose of this alliance?
4. Name the nations that joined the Triple Entente. For what reasons did they join this alliance?
5. What region came to be called "the powder keg of Europe"? Give an example of the conflicts in this area.
6. What event can be said to have "lit the fuse" in 1914, setting off the war?
7. Did all members of the two big alliances enter the war at once? Explain.
8. What advantages did the Central Powers have in the war? What advantages did the Allies have?
9. Describe briefly the situation in the war at the end of 1916.
10. In what ways was the United States affected by the war even while remaining neutral?

11. What development in 1917 contributed directly to the declaration of war by the United States?
12. List the six general proposals included in Wilson's Fourteen Points.

Problems and projects

1. Review Bismarck's ideas about German foreign policy. Why did he form the Triple Alliance? Why was he opposed to the policies of Emperor William II? Could it be said that unwise moves by William II led to the forming of the Triple Entente?
2. Explain as fully as you can the chain reaction that followed the assassination of the Austrian archduke in June, 1914.
3. On a map of Europe show the route of the German attack through Belgium in 1914. In a second color show the route of the German offensive against France in 1940.
4. Draw a map to show (a) the main fighting fronts, 1914–1918, (b) the supply routes from the United States to Great Britain and France.
5. Discuss the general proposals in Wilson's Fourteen Points. Which of these six points do you think most deserved to be put into effect? Why?
6. On a world map show (a) the nations that fought in World War I (at any time during the war), (b) the neutral nations. Try to find the population of the warring and neutral nations at that period. Use the map and the population figures in a discussion of the statement that this was truly a *world* war.

Chapter 44 The Shaping of the Peace

AFTER the armistice in November, 1918, the Allies faced the task of arranging peace terms. For us it is difficult to realize how much the hopes and longings of the peoples of the world centered around the writing of the peace treaty. There was hardly a person who had not been affected in some way by the tragedy of the four years of war. The announced ideals of the Allies, democracy in a peaceful world, caught the imagination and stirred the hopes of men and women everywhere. The great slogans of Woodrow Wilson—"a war to end wars," or "a world safe for democracy"—had expressed an almost universal longing. The terms of the Fourteen Points seemed to chart the way to such a world. They were accepted by people in the defeated countries as well as among the victors.

The treaty makers face difficult problems

There were serious and difficult problems to be settled in a treaty. Some of them were so complex that they would have been almost impossible to settle to everyone's satisfaction, even if all those who had a share in writing the treaties had agreed that they had to ensure that the peace was "a peace of justice to all."

Three great empires, the German, Austro-Hungarian, and Russian, had crashed. In Germany and Russia, hereditary emperors had been replaced by socialist republics. The Dual Monarchy was now split into the two republics of Austria and Hungary. A fourth empire, that of the Ottoman Turks, was tottering. Everywhere there were problems of territories and boundaries, and the conflicting claims of the nations were difficult to reconcile justly. Nationalist groups everywhere in Europe—in Poland, the Baltic Coast, the old Austro-Hungarian Empire, the Balkans, and the Near East of the Ottoman Empire—were pressing their claims for independence, self-government, and the union of all their national groups inside the boundaries of one state. Nationalism was strong in the colonial empires, too. The Arabs of North Africa, the Egyptians, the Indians, and the Chinese all had strong desires for independence.

The destruction caused by the war also brought up the problem of reparations (payments for damage). In the west the war had been fought principally in French and Belgian territory. Four years of trench warfare had created havoc over a wide strip of land. Who was responsible, and who should pay for restoring the land?

Finally, there was the problem of a world organization to keep the peace. This was the last of Wilson's Fourteen Points, and it probably had more widespread appeal than any other. Everywhere people agreed upon the need for such an organization. Would they agree as easily upon the details of its formation? How should such a body be organized? What power should it have? Would nations that had always been sovereign (having complete right to settle all problems as they saw fit) be willing to give up any of their sovereignty to a world organization? Would they be willing to give it the power to deal with problems which concerned them, and to accept its decisions?

● *A peace of justice or a peace of vengeance?*

It would have been difficult to write a "peace of justice," even though everyone wanted such a peace. Woodrow Wilson believed it was possible, and he reasoned that only a peace of justice could be a lasting peace. Unless all peoples, including the defeated powers, were treated justly, the treaty would only create new problems and stir up new hatreds and desires for revenge. In time, these would surely lead to another war.

There were many people, however, who disagreed. The war had left much bitterness, hatred, and longing for revenge. Among the victors there was a strong feeling that the defeated must be taught a lesson. Only by harsh treatment, they reasoned, could Germans and Austrians be taught the penalty for starting a war. Some went further and argued that Germany should be divided up and disarmed completely. This sort of feeling was strong in France. Twice within fifty years Frenchmen had seen their country overrun, occupied, and devastated by the Germans. Belgians also had good reason to hate the Germans. Had they not invaded and devastated Belgium in violation of a treaty promise? Should not the treaty make it impossible for Germany ever to do these things again?

Thus there were two viewpoints about what sort of treaty should be written. On one side were those who favored a peace of justice based on the Fourteen Points—a peace which would be lasting because everyone accepted it. On the other side were those who wanted a peace of vengeance and punishment, which would be lasting because it would make it impossible for the defeated to fight again. So important was the decision that President Wilson decided to go in person to the peace conference. He wanted to use all his influence to bring about a peace of justice, especially one which would include a League of Nations to keep such a peace, and end the threat of war.

● *The peace conference at Paris*

The conference met in Paris, in January 1919. It was a large gathering. The Allied

This scene in a French town suggests the extent of the destruction caused by the war.

President Woodrow Wilson and General John J. Pershing reviewing troops in France after the Allied victory.

and associated powers which had won the war had eventually included thirty-one countries in Europe, Asia, Africa, and the Americas. They were almost all represented. Russia was in the midst of a civil war and was the only ally that did not take part in the conference. The Soviet government had signed a separate, harsh, and humiliating peace treaty with Germany. In spite of Russia's valiant fight against heavy odds in the war and her heavy losses, the country was barred from participation in the Paris Conference.

The defeated powers were not represented either. The victors decided to work out and agree upon the terms among themselves. Then they would call in representatives of the defeated powers to accept the terms. It was also decided that each defeated power

should have a separate treaty. The Central Powers had included Germany, Austria-Hungary, Bulgaria, and Turkey. Since Austria and Hungary now had separate governments, this would mean five different treaties.

Outwardly, the work of writing the treaties was done by the representatives of all the thirty-one nations. Actually, the real work was done in advance and behind the scenes by the representatives of the five great powers: Great Britain, France, Italy, the United States, and Japan. It was really the first four who shaped the treaty. The Big Four leaders, as they were called, were: Britain, Prime Min-

THE EIGHTEENTH TO
TWENTIETH CENTURIES

Above: The colonial
Governor's palace,
Williamsburg, Virginia.
The architecture and
costumes are authentic
reproductions of the
styles of the early
eighteenth century.

Right: The kitchen of
"Kenmore," built near
Fredericksburg,
Virginia, in 1752.
George Washington's
sister lived here.

Facing page, top: A clipper ship, typical of American merchant ships in the middle portion of the nineteenth century. American merchants established a busy trade with foreign lands, and Americans became interested in Eastern lands. (Museum of the City of New York.)

Facing page, bottom: A sample of Eastern art, "Prince Riding an Elephant." (Metropolitan Museum of Art.)

The eighteenth and nineteenth centuries produced many styles of painting. Above: A portrait of a boy by Francisco José de Goya (1746–1828), a Spanish artist. (Metropolitan Museum of Art.)

Right: Lafayette in the uniform of the American army during the Revolution, painted by F. G. Casanova. (New York Historical Society.)

As trade with the Orient developed, Chinese textiles became famous for color, design, and workmanship. Above is a Mandarin Square, a piece of embroidered silk representing a mythological beast. (Metropolitan Museum of Art.)

Right: Japanese armor of the kind worn by the samurai warriors of feudal Japan in the era described on page 527. The face of the helmet suggests the fierceness that often marked these Japanese fighting men. (Metropolitan Museum of Art.)

Left: "The Kinryungan Temple," a print by Hiroshige (1797–1858). This delicate, peaceful work of art shows an aspect of Japanese culture that contrasts sharply with the militarism of the samurai. (Metropolitan Museum of Art.)

Rapid change has characterized the world in the last few centuries. Above: Costumes of New Yorkers in 1780. (Museum of the City of New York.)

Below: A Saratoga, New York, parlor in the nineteenth century. (The Brooklyn Museum.)

Facing page: A Ford of the early twentieth century, and a General Motors "car of the future," built in the second half of the century.

New styles of painting have developed in the modern world (see page 467).

Above: "The Bridge at Arles," by Vincent Van Gogh (1853–1890), a Dutch artist. (Rijksmuseum, Horskamp, Holland.)

Below: "Tahitian Mountains," by Paul Gauguin. This French artist (1848–1903) did some of his greatest work in the South Pacific islands. (The Minneapolis Institute of Arts.) Compare the paintings on this page with those on pages 262A, 262B, and 262C.

ister David Lloyd George; France, Premier Georges Clemenceau; United States, President Woodrow Wilson; Italy, Premier Vittorio Orlando.

Very early in the work of the conference the two conflicting viewpoints came out. The British, French, and Italian governments had given lip service to the Fourteen Points, but they had never given up the aims stated in the secret treaties. The idea of a peace of justice came to be represented by the Fourteen Points; the idea of a peace of vengeance by the terms of the secret treaties.

Wilson wins a League of Nations

In order to make his viewpoint prevail, Wilson insisted that the first work of the conference should be the writing of a covenant, or constitution, of a League of Nations. This covenant should be included as part of the German treaty, the first treaty to be drafted. Wilson and his chief adviser, Colonel Edward House, were appointed as the American representatives on a commission to draft the covenant. The work was done in a month, and the result was promptly and unanimously adopted by the entire conference in mid-February, 1919.

According to the covenant, the League of Nations had two main aims: to promote international coöperation, and to maintain peace by settling disputes peacefully and by reducing armaments. It was to include all independent, sovereign powers. It was to function through three main agencies: an Assembly, a Council, and a Secretariat, and to work closely with a separate and independent body, the Permanent Court of International Justice, or World Court.

The Assembly was a sort of lower house. It was to be made up of representatives of all member nations. Regardless of size, each had one vote. The Council served as an upper house of the League. It was composed of nine nations (later increased to fifteen). Of these Council members, five nations were to be permanent members—the representatives of the Big Five powers: Great Britain, France, Italy, Japan, and the United States. The settlement of almost all important matters was to require a unanimous vote of the Council, and usually of the Assembly.

The Secretariat, or secretarial staff, was to be made up of the permanent employees of the League. They were to do the clerical work, act as expert advisers, keep the records, and guard the file of pacts, treaties, agreements, and conventions drawn up by the League and its members. A Permanent Court of International Justice, or World Court, was also set up. The judges were to be elected by the Assembly and Council.

The League provided an interesting way for trying to deal with the problem of imperialism and the so-called "backward" peoples. Where a people were considered not yet ready for independence and self-government, they were made trustees of the League. The League gave the area as a mandate to the government of an advanced nation to administer. The administering nation was pledged to prepare the people for independent self-government, not to fortify the territory, and to make annual reports to the League concerning progress. The administering nation was also pledged to treat the area not as a colony but as a trust.

The members of the League of Nations accepted an obligation not to resort to war; they were to submit any disputes to arbitration. Arbitration could be carried on by the World Court, or by special boards or commissions set up for each particular case. The covenant also provided that, if a member broke his promise to submit to arbitration, and went to war, the League could impose penalties on him. These could include breaking diplomatic relations, economic sanctions (refusal to buy anything from or sell anything to the offending member), blockade, or, as a last resort, military force.

ARCTIC OCEAN

GREENLAND
(Danish)

ALASKA
(U.S.)

CANADA (Br.)

NEWFOUNDLAND
(Br.)

UNITED STATES

NORTH
ATLANTIC
OCEAN

PACIFIC OCEAN

HAWAII (U.S.)

WEST INDIES

MEXICO

CUBA
DOMINICAN
REP.
Br.HONDURAS   HAITI   PUERTO RICO
(U.S.)
GUATEMALA
HONDURAS
EL SALVADOR   NICARAGUA
COSTA RICA
PANAMA

VENEZUELA
(Br.)
(Du.)   (Fr.)
GUIANA COLONIES
COLOMBIA
ECUADOR

PERU

BRAZIL

BOLIVIA

PARAGUAY

CHILE

URUGUAY

ARGENTINA

North Sea

Baltic Sea

ESTONIA

LATVIA

LITH.
MEMELAND (Ger.)
E. PRUSSIA

DENMARK

NETHERLANDS

BELGIUM

EUPEN
MALMEDY
LUX.
SAAR
LORRAINE   ALSACE

GERMANY

POLAND

U.S.S.R.

CZECHOSLOVAKIA

FRANCE

SWITZ.

TYROL

AUSTRIA

HUNGARY

RUMANIA

Trieste   Fiume

ITALY

YUGOSLAVIA

BULGARIA

NEW ZEALAND
(Br.)

ALBANIA

GREECE

SICILY

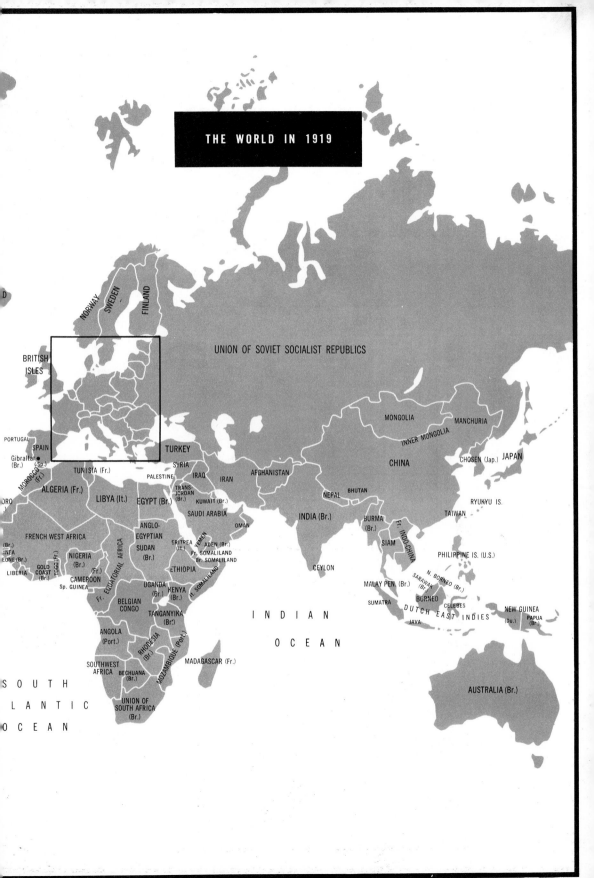

THE WORLD IN 1919

NORWAY
SWEDEN
FINLAND

BRITISH
ISLES

UNION OF SOVIET SOCIALIST REPUBLICS

PORTUGAL
SPAIN
Gibraltar (Br.) (Sp.)
TURKEY
SYRIA
PALESTINE
IRAQ
IRAN
AFGHANISTAN
MONGOLIA
MANCHURIA
INNER MONGOLIA
CHOSEN (Jap.) JAPAN
CHINA

MOROCCO (Fr.)
ORO
TUNISIA (Fr.)
ALGERIA (Fr.)
LIBYA (It.)
EGYPT (Br.)
TRANS-JORDAN (Br.)
KUWAIT (Br.)
SAUDI ARABIA
NEPAL
BHUTAN
RYUKYU IS.
TAIWAN
INDIA (Br.)
BURMA (Br.)
Fr. INDO-CHINA

FRENCH WEST AFRICA
(Br.)
INEA
EONE (Br.)
LIBERIA
NIGERIA (Br.)
GOLD COAST (Br.)
TOGO (Fr.)
CAMEROON (Fr.)
Sp. GUINEA
Fr. EQUATORIAL AFRICA
ANGLO-EGYPTIAN SUDAN (Br.)
ERITREA (It.)
YEMEN
ADEN (Br.)
Fr. SOMALILAND
Br. SOMALILAND
OMAN
ETHIOPIA
It. SOMALILAND
CEYLON
SIAM
PHILIPPINE IS. (U.S.)
N. BORNEO (Br.)
SARAWAK (Br.)
MALAY PEN. (Br.)
SUMATRA
BORNEO
CELEBES
DUTCH EAST INDIES
NEW GUINEA (Du.)
PAPUA (Br.)
JAVA

BELGIAN CONGO
UGANDA (Br.)
KENYA (Br.)
TANGANYIKA (Br.)

ANGOLA (Port.)
RHODESIA (Br.)
MOZAMBIQUE (Port.)
MADAGASCAR (Fr.)

I N D I A N

O C E A N

SOUTHWEST AFRICA
BECHUANA (Br.)
UNION OF SOUTH AFRICA (Br.)

S O U T H

A T L A N T I C

O C E A N

AUSTRALIA (Br.)

The Allies quarrel over peace terms

President Wilson, after a journey to the United States, returned to Paris to resume work on the territorial revisions of the treaty. He found the advocates of a harsh peace much stronger. The opposition to his leadership in the United States weakened his position. In contrast, both Lloyd George of Britain and Clemenceau of France had the strong support of their parliaments. Lloyd George had been overwhelmingly re-elected in 1918 on a platform that included a promise to hang the kaiser. Both he and Clemenceau had promised to make Germany pay the costs of the war. In this atmosphere the difficult problem of territorial adjustments had to be taken up.

● *French territorial demands*

France demanded, above all, security from German attack in the future. She insisted on the return of Alsace and Lorraine, which had been guaranteed in the Fourteen Points. France also demanded that the French boundary should be the Rhine River, and that the Saar Valley with its valuable deposits of coal be occupied by the French. Great Britain and the United States opposed these claims on the ground that they would create more problems than they would solve. Both the Saar Valley and the Rhineland, the German territory on the west bank of the Rhine, were solidly German in population.

● *Italian demands*

Italy demanded the Tyrol region, between Italy and Austria, and the Dalmatian coast, including the ports of Trieste and Fiume. These had been promised her in the secret treaties. She insisted on having them. Here again there were problems of population and nationality. There were Italians in the Tyrol, but there were also some 250,000 German-speaking Austrians. Along the Dalmatian coast the cities had heavy Italian populations but in the surrounding countryside the people were almost all Slavs. Most of the Slavs wanted to join the newly formed Kingdom of Yugoslavia. Fiume, especially, would make a convenient seaport and railroad terminal for Yugoslavia, which had none. Italy had many ports.

Lloyd George and Wilson were willing to give in on the Tyrol, but Wilson steadfastly opposed giving Fiume to Italy. The controversy over this point became so bitter that Orlando left the conference and went home in disgust. The Big Four became the Big Three.

● *Demands by other nations*

Britain demanded that all Germany's African colonies be turned over to her, that the German navy be surrendered and Germany prohibited from building warships.

Belgium demanded two small bits of German territory, Eupen and Malmédy, along her borders, and reparations for damages to her land and cities.

Poland, according to the Fourteen Points, had been promised her own government and access to the sea. This would mean taking former Polish territories from Germany, Russia, and Austria. Access to the sea, however, was difficult. The Baltic seacoast cities were solidly German, and Poland was shut off from them by German-inhabited East Prussia.

Japan had occupied the German-held port of Kiaochow, and most of the rest of the Shantung Peninsula. She had also seized the German island colonies in the Pacific—the Marshall, Caroline, and Marianas archipelagoes. She now demanded that all of these be turned over to her permanently. She also demanded that the powers recognize Japan's "special position" in respect to China. This meant, in very polite words, that in any further seizure of Chinese territory, Japan was to have the first choice and largest share.

President Wilson fought valiantly against this return to imperialism. So bitter was the

fight that Japan threatened to follow Italy's example: she would withdraw from the conference and take the territories anyway. In order to keep Japan at the conference and in the League, Wilson gave in on Shantung. He also agreed that Japan should have the islands, but only as mandates of the League of Nations.

●*Reparations*

The problem of reparations concerned payment for war damages. The great question was what to include as war damages. Did it mean damage to property only? Did it mean also the payment of pensions to wounded war veterans, widows, and orphans? If all of these were included, how could the total amount be estimated? It was finally decided that all the things mentioned above must be included. However, at the time the rest of the German treaty was ready, there was still complete disagreement about the total amount of reparations.

Allied occupation troops in the Rhineland. One intention of the peacemakers after the war was to make France safe from future threats by Germany. The Rhineland was patrolled by Allied troops until 1926.

Germany signs the Treaty of Versailles

The chances for a "peace of justice" with Germany, as Wilson saw it, were not very great. Many times President Wilson had to give way. For a good part of the time he was ill with a very bad case of influenza. Where he did give way, he consoled himself with the thought that the League of Nations would be able to remedy the injustices after the hatred and bitterness had died down. With that in mind he was willing to sign the completed treaty, even though it differed in many places from the letter and spirit of the Fourteen Points.

At the end of May, 1919, the German representatives were called in, presented with the

571

completed treaty, and told to sign it. The Germans bitterly complained that the treaty did not follow the Fourteen Points, which they regarded as promises to them. Especially they complained about the clause concerning war guilt, and the "blank check" they had to sign as reparations. But protests were in vain. The representatives of the new German republic had no choice but to sign. On June 28, 1919, at the famous palace at Versailles, in the outskirts of Paris, Germany signed the treaty of peace.

● *The terms of the treaty*

By the terms of the Treaty of Versailles, Germany acknowledged that she was solely guilty of beginning the war, and therefore was liable to pay reparations. She would pay five billion dollars in two years, and an unnamed sum later. In 1921 the Reparations Commission set the total bill at thirty-three billion dollars.

Germany gave Alsace and Lorraine to France. She agreed not to fortify the Rhineland, or to have troops there. The territory was to be occupied by Allied troops for an unstated time. The Saar Valley was to be administered by the League of Nations for fifteen years. During this time its coal was to go to France in part payment of reparations. At the end of fifteen years the people of the district could vote as to whether they wished to continue under the League of Nations, rejoin Germany, or join France. Germany gave Eupen and Malmédy to Belgium, northern Schleswig to Denmark, and German Poland to Poland. She also agreed that the German seaport of Danzig should become a Free City, administered by the League of Nations, available to Polish use. Poland could reach Danzig by means of a "corridor" cut through West Prussia. The corridor was to be a part of Poland.

Germany's colonies were made mandates of the League of Nations and divided up among the victor nations. Britain received German East Africa and part of the Cameroons. German Southwest Africa went to the Union of South Africa. Togoland and part of the Cameroons went to France. In the Pacific the German-held islands north of the equator went to Japan. Those south of the equator went to Australia and New Zealand. Japan took Kiaochow and Germany's rights in Shantung.

Germany had to abolish conscription. The German army was limited to 100,000 men, of whom 4,000 could be officers. Privates had to enlist for twelve years, officers for twenty-five. No reserve army could be built up. The famous General Staff was abolished. The manufacture of big guns, tanks, military airplanes, and poison gas was forbidden. The navy was similarly restricted; there were to be no battleships bigger than 10,000 tons, and only a limited number of surface ships. No submarines at all were allowed.

Thus you can see that the treaty writers tried to make sure that Germany would be, if not a peace-loving, then certainly a peace-keeping nation. Germany was stripped of colonies and strategic territories, some of which contained the coal and iron so necessary for industry. She was strictly limited in armaments, she was forced to pay a huge sum in reparations, and parts of her territory were occupied by foreign military forces.

The United States rejects the treaty

When President Wilson returned to the United States with the German treaty, he found a hornet's nest of opposition. Some of the American people were beginning to wonder whether the war had been worth the effort, and whether their venture into internationalism had not been a mistake.

Many Americans of foreign birth and ancestry opposed the treaty. Irish-Americans feared that the League of Nations might prevent Ireland from winning her independence from Great Britain. German-Americans were dismayed at the treatment of Germany. Italian-Americans felt that Wilson had insulted Italy. Liberals looked with concern at how far the treaty was from the Fourteen Points, which they had supported. Conservatives were very dubious about the League of Nations because it was such a great departure from traditional American isolation.

● Opposition in the senate

When the treaty was submitted to the Senate, three main attitudes quickly appeared. A fairly large group, mostly Democrats, were willing to vote for it as it stood, though few of them approved of it entirely. A fairly small group, called "irreconcilables," were completely opposed to the treaty in any form. They either thought it fundamentally bad and beyond repair, or, they were convinced isolationists. Between these two, a fairly large group of senators was willing to accept the treaty if certain reservations, or qualifications, were added to it. Most of these reservations were completely unacceptable to President Wilson. All of them, of course, would have had to be accepted by all the nations which had signed the treaty.

● Wilson's appeal to the nation fails

It was soon clear that there were not enough senatorial votes to ratify the treaty as it stood; so President Wilson went on a speaking tour through the country. He chose a route which would take him through the states of the strongest senatorial opponents of the treaty. For three weeks, in the heat of September, he spoke to large audiences, arguing strongly for the ratification of the treaty as it stood.

It is impossible to say whether the speeches did what he wanted them to do, but it seems certain that they were the end of President Wilson. He was never a strong man physically, and he was weakened by an illness in Paris and the strain of the long treaty negotiations. The speaking tour in the hot summer proved to be the last straw. When he returned to Washington, he suffered a paralytic stroke. For three months he was unable to carry on any of his presidential duties.

In the interval, however, his enemies in the Senate had their way. They drew up a list of fourteen reservations to the treaty. First, the treaty with the strong reservations was voted down. Next, the treaty without any reservations was voted down. Then a final vote was taken on the treaty with mild reservations acceptable to the president. It received a majority of the votes, but not the necessary two thirds. Technically, the United States remained at war with Germany until 1921.

No one can say how much the Senate opposition to the treaty was purely political, or how much represented a real fear that the United States would become hopelessly entangled in the affairs of foreign countries. We cannot say why the senators voted as they did, or why the people apparently felt as they did, but there seems little doubt of the meaning and the effect of the act. The world was about to make its first attempt at peace through coöperation, and the United States refused to coöperate. During the fight over ratification President Wilson said that if the United States did not join the League, the war would have to be fought again. In this he was a prophet.

Austria, Hungary, and Bulgaria sign treaties

Separate treaties were made with each of the Central Powers. Since Austria and Hungary had formed independent republics, they had to sign separate treaties. To see what happened to the old Dual Monarchy, you must compare the maps of Central Europe of 1914 and of 1920. The independent republic of Austria was recognized. The treaty provided that it should never be united with Germany. It became, as the saying went, a capital without a country. There were six million people

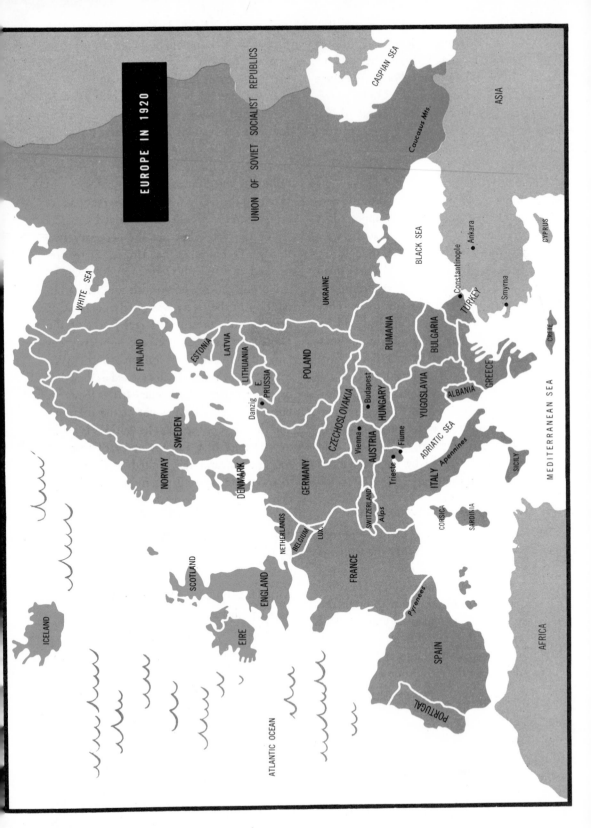

EUROPE IN 1920

UNION OF SOVIET SOCIALIST REPUBLICS

CASPIAN SEA

ASIA

Caucasus Mts.

BLACK SEA

• Ankara

CYPRUS

WHITE SEA

UKRAINE

Constantinople

• Smyrna

TURKEY

FINLAND

ESTONIA

LATVIA

LITHUANIA

POLAND

RUMANIA

BULGARIA

CRETE

E. PRUSSIA

Danzig

CZECHOSLOVAKIA

Budapest

GREECE

SWEDEN

Vienna

HUNGARY

YUGOSLAVIA

ALBANIA

NORWAY

AUSTRIA

Fiume

ADRIATIC SEA

DENMARK

GERMANY

Trieste

Apennines

ITALY

MEDITERRANEAN SEA

SWITZERLAND

Alps

SICILY

NETHERLANDS

BELGIUM

LUX.

CORSICA

SARDINIA

SCOTLAND

FRANCE

ICELAND

ENGLAND

Pyrennes

EIRE

SPAIN

AFRICA

ATLANTIC OCEAN

PORTUGAL

574

in all of Austria; one third of them lived in Vienna. The nation could produce neither the food nor the raw materials to feed its people or its industries. Austria rapidly sank into a state of financial crisis and poverty.

Hungary also lost much territory—those parts with populations of other nationalities. It became a landlocked country. It remained agricultural, able to produce enough food for itself, but little more. Beautiful Budapest, like Vienna, became a painful reminder of past glories.

● New nations: Czechoslovakia and Yugoslavia

Two new states were created: the republic of Czechoslovakia, in central Europe, and Yugoslavia, in the western Balkans. These were created for the Slavs of the old empire. Czechoslovakia included Czechs, Slovaks, and Ruthenians. Yugoslavia united the old kingdoms of Serbia and Montenegro, the former provinces of Bosnia and Herzegovina, and some of the Dalmatian coast.

In the Fourteen Points the Slavic people of central Europe had been promised that they would be given independence and self-government in states created along the lines of nationality. This promise was kept. Politically, the treaties recognized the centuries-long nationalist ambitions of the Slavic peoples. In that way, this new deal was admirable. In another sense, it was tragic.

Whatever its political weakness and injustices, the old Austro-Hungarian Empire did make sense economically. It had areas that produced agricultural and raw materials; it had industrial areas. They fitted together well. Each was a market for the products of the other. The old empire was a prosperous region. There was an outlet to the sea, the port of Trieste on the Adriatic. All this was now gone. Austria and Hungary were landlocked. If they could coöperate and exchange goods freely, they might still enjoy their former prosperity. But each was now a sovereign state, and there were many old enmities. The prosperity of the whole was succeeded by the misery of the parts.

Bulgaria, too, paid the penalty for picking the loser, as you will see if you compare the two maps (1914 and 1920) again. Her most severe loss was her outlet to the Aegean Sea, which went to Greece.

A new Turkey rises after the war

In some ways, the treaty with Turkey was the most difficult of all to write. Negotiations took more than a year. It was not that the Turkish government offered resistance. Like its allies, it did not sit in on the negotiations. But here was a region where the religious, nationalistic, and imperialistic problems and rivalries were centuries old.

Almost all the European powers wanted influence and domination in the Near East. Russia, of course, was temporarily out of the picture; so there was no chance that she would get her long-sought control of the Dardanelles. Britain wanted control of regions that had rich oil resources. France wanted similar control, especially in Syria. Italy wanted islands which belonged to the Turkish Empire. Greece, with British backing, hoped to gain control over the west coast of Asia Minor; some even dreamed of Constantinople. Within the Turkish Empire, the long-oppressed Christian Armenians wanted independence, and so did the Arabs.

● The first treaty with Turkey

Because Turkey had "backed the wrong horse" in the war, it was now possible to take her territory and move her out of Europe completely. That is, it could be done if the victorious powers could decide who should take over Turkey's European territory. For a time there was talk of giving the United States the authority to administer Constantinople and the Straits for the benefit of all nations. When the United States withdrew completely from European affairs, the powers had to fall back on their old solution: leave Constantinople, at least, in Turkish hands.

The rest of the terms of the treaty were severe. The Dodecanese islands went to Italy. The island of Cyprus, in British possession since June, 1878, and annexed in November, 1914, was to be formally recognized as a British colony. In 1925 Cyprus was declared a crown colony of Great Britain. On the European mainland, Thrace went to Greece. It extended all the way along the Aegean coast to within a few miles of Constantinople. On the coast of Asia Minor, Greece took the city of Smyrna, and the territory around it. Constantinople and the Straits remained in Turkish hands, but the Straits were to be unfortified, and to be administered by an international commission.

In Asia Minor Turkey kept only the northern province of Anatolia along the Black Sea. The sultan had to give up all claims to land in North Africa, including Egypt and the Sudan. The Arab states of Palestine, Transjordan, and Iraq went to Great Britain; Syria and Lebanon went to France. But Britain and France were to hold them as mandates of the League of Nations.

Like the leaders of his allies, the sultan of the Ottoman Empire had no choice but to sign the treaty. However, when the terms were known in Turkey, there was a violent protest, especially against the transfer of Thrace and Smyrna to Greece. For some years a group of nationalists who called themselves the Young Turks had been trying to bring reforms in the weak, inefficient, and corrupt government of Turkey. Discontent over the terms of the treaty brought all problems to a head.

The new treaty, 1923

Led by a very able man named Mustafa Kemal, the nationalists now rose to power. After a brief war, they drove the Greek army out of Smyrna. Then they demanded that the treaty of 1920 be cancelled and a new one written. By now the European powers had no taste for another war; so they agreed. In 1923 the new treaty returned eastern Thrace and Smyrna to Turkey. She also regained full control of Constantinople. The Straits were still to be unfortified and administered by a commission of the League of Nations. They were to be open to the vessels of neutral nations in war as in peace.

The nationalists overthrow the sultan

Kemal and the nationalists now went on to overthrow the government of the sultan, and set up a republic with Kemal as dictator-president. He was convinced that Turkey must become a progressive Westernized nation. Therefore he began a program of very broad, sweeping reforms to accomplish this purpose. The capital was moved from Constantinople to Ankara, in Asia Minor. The church and the government were separated. The Moslem caliphate, which united both church and state under the religious leader, was abolished. Religious orders were also abolished. Polygamy (more than one wife) was prohibited. Women were set free from the harem, and given the right to vote. Western dress was adopted; the fez, traditional hat of Turkey, was prohibited. More important still, the Western calendar, the metric system of weights and measures, and the Latin alphabet were adopted. This last, which was far easier to use than the difficult Arabic script, made literacy much more possible to many people. Kemal also began a program of economic development. The government paid subsidies to farmers to improve agriculture, and to "infant industries" to help industrialization.

The treaties leave problems unsolved

If you compare, once more, the two maps (1914 and 1920), you will see four new states along the Baltic, in what was formerly Russian territory. They were Finland, Estonia, Latvia, and Lithuania. In 1918 they had declared their independence of Russia, and were recognized by the victorious powers at the end of the war. You will notice that the new state of Poland included what was formerly Russian Poland, and that Rumania gained the large, formerly Russian province of Bessarabia. Thus Russia, the former ally, actually lost more territory than Germany, the defeated enemy. There were two reasons for this: Russia had withdrawn from the war and signed a separate peace with Germany. And the government of Russia was now controlled by the Communist Party, which was bitterly opposed to the Western powers.

There were many problems still to be solved; in fact, World War I was a classic example of the fact that modern war creates far more problems than it solves. There were boundary problems and places where the principle of nationality was sacrificed to national ambitions. You may remember the 250,000 German-speaking Austrians in the Tyrol, which Italy demanded and got from Austria. There were also the Germans in Danzig and in the Polish Corridor.

● *National minorities*

No matter how hard the statesmen tried to draw boundaries to meet the promise of "national self-determination" which the Fourteen Points had made, many people found themselves living under governments controlled by other nationalities. They became "national minorities." How could they be assured of equality, freedom, and justice? After the war between Greece and Turkey, the two governments agreed upon an exchange: Turks living in Greece for Greeks living in Turkey. But such an exchange was not always possible.

At the suggestion of President Wilson, an attempt was made to meet the problem in the treaties. Each treaty contained a clause in which governments pledged to treat national

minorities fairly. The minority people were guaranteed political rights, such as the right to vote, special representation in lawmaking

A view from Constantinople (now Istanbul) across the Bosporus strait. For centuries Turkey was a major concern of European statesmen because of her location commanding the Bosporus and the Dardanelles. As the map shows, Turkey controls the water route from the Black Sea to the Mediterranean. The tower in the foreground of the picture is the minaret of a Mohammedan mosque.

bodies, the use of their language in their own schools, and the right to practice their own religion. These privileges were to be guarded by the League of Nations. In case of violation, the League was bound to take appropriate action. To a great extent, then, the protection of national minorities had to depend on how well the League of Nations worked.

The mandate system of the League of Nations was an attempt to protect the rights of people in Germany's former colonies and the Arabs in the former Turkish Empire. Here again, everything depended on the League. If the League became a really effective body, then the people of these regions would move toward independence and self-government at a rate depending on their level of civilization. If the League did not work well, then the lands would become colonies, thinly disguised under the name of mandate.

Review of Chapter 44

People, places, and things

Identify: David Lloyd George, Georges Clemenceau, Vittorio Orlando, Woodrow Wilson, Colonel Edward House, Mustafa Kemal.

Locate: Alsace-Lorraine, Saar Valley, Tyrol, Trieste, Fiume, Coast of Dalmatia, Yugoslavia, Schleswig-Holstein, Eupen, Malmédy, Danzig, Togoland, German East Africa, Cameroons, German Southwest Africa, Union of South Africa, Kiaochow, Shantung, Anatolia, Palestine, Transjordan, Iraq, Syria, Lebanon, Ankara, Cyprus, Dodecanese Islands, Iran, Marshall Islands, Caroline, and Marianas.

Events in review

1. What were the major problems that needed to be settled by the peace treaty at the end of World War I?
2. Which of the nations that had fought in the war were *not* represented at the Versailles Conference?
3. List the three main agencies that made up the League of Nations. State the functions of each.
4. What demands did Japan make at the peace conference? What action did President Wilson take? Why?
5. What did France ask for at the peace conference? Were all her demands granted?
6. Why was Danzig made a free city? Why was a corridor cut through Germany?
7. How did the Allies try to make sure that Germany would be a peace-keeping nation?

8. Give three reasons for objections in the United States to the Treaty of Versailles.
9. Name the four empires that vanished as a result of the war. Name two new states that were created by the treaty-makers.
10. Who were the Young Turks? What changes did they bring about in Turkey?
11. What was the problem of "national self-determination"? Was this problem solved?

Problems and projects

1. Discuss President Wilson's aims and his accomplishments at the peace conference. What sort of peace did he hope for? On what points was he compelled to compromise? On what points did he win? Can you explain his difficulties in trying to achieve his goals?
2. Suppose that the Treaty of Versailles could have been rewritten in the light of later events. What changes should have been made to improve the treaty?
3. Make a report on any localities mentioned in this chapter that have been in the news recently as "trouble spots" (Cyprus, or Transjordan, possibly).
4. Study the maps of Europe, before and after World War I. To what extent did the peace treaties "remake the map of Europe"? Explain the reasons for the major changes.
5. Interview a veteran of World War I. Write for the class a report of his experiences. Note whether he met any of the famous leaders or took part in any of the major battles or other events.

Chapter 45

The Aftermath of World War I

WHEN we think about war, it is natural to think first of the cost in lives. In World War I the cost was shocking and staggering. The estimates show that between eleven and twelve million men lost their lives in the fighting. That many more were wounded. Thousands were crippled for life. These were mostly young men, of course.

The cost in lives and property

But for the first time in history, the loss of lives among the civilian population was at least as great as in the armed forces. The blockade, artillery and aerial bombardment, the disruption of economic life with resulting famine and starvation, political violence, and social unrest all took their toll. An exact count is impossible. Germany, France, and Russia suffered most severely. A large part of a generation was lost. Among them were certainly many future leaders of government, science, industry, and the arts. This is the sort of cost which cannot be estimated. There is no yardstick with which to measure such losses.

The destruction of property was just as terrible. In areas of actual combat entire cities and the surrounding countryside were wiped out. Homes were left in ruins, fertile fields

and orchards laid waste, cattle and livestock killed or driven off. Factories, mines, and railroads were wrecked. Ships, with their cargoes, lay at the bottom of the sea. There is

War widows in Belgium. This drawing by a Dutch artist, Louis Raemaekers, suggests some of the effects of the war. The death of husbands and fathers left broken homes. Widows had to face both grief and the problem of making a living.

only one yardstick to measure these losses: money. An exact figure is impossible. Certainly it would run to many billions of dollars.

Political and economic problems

The period immediately after the war was one of political, economic, and social confusion. The nations of the world faced overpowering problems. They had to take care of the sick, wounded, and crippled. Armies had to be demobilized and their men given peaceful employment. Refugee people scattered by the war had to be resettled. Farmers had to begin again to cultivate their devastated lands.

Hunger, unemployment, and disease encouraged much unrest. Angry and despairing, many people tried to find a way out by rebelling, to set up what they hoped would be a better form of government. Very often their troubles were not the result of any particular form of government. They were the result of a set of general conditions which any kind of government would find it hard to meet. Nevertheless, the last year of the war and the period after the war saw political revolutions in many parts of Europe. Especially among the defeated nations, governments were overthrown and new forms set up.

● *Unstable governments*

By mid-November, 1918, the Germans had declared their country a republic and formed a temporary government, which signed the armistice. The leaders were mainly moderate men, including the Social Democrats, the German socialist party.

In February, 1919, an assembly met in the city of Weimar and drafted what came to be known as the Weimar Constitution. Germany became a federal republic. Democracy in Germany had a hard row to hoe. Almost at once the republic had to fight off the radicals of the left, the communists. During 1920

severe communist riots broke out in Berlin and in southern Germany. The government had to put down uprisings by force. The republican government also faced rising opposition from the radical right; these were the monarchists and the group later known as Nazis.

Austria also became a republic before the end of the war. You already know something of the position of postwar Austria. The prospects for any economic prosperity were dim, and that seems always to mean little chance for stable government. The early government was under strong socialist influence. However, socialists were soon suppressed by Catholic, monarchist, and conservative nationalist groups. The government kept its republican form, but it really became a fascist dictatorship of the extreme conservatives. Some Austrians wanted union (*Anschluss*) with Germany as a solution to their economic problem, but this was forbidden by the peace treaties.

In Hungary, a liberal republic was overthrown by a communist dictatorship. The communists, in turn, were overthrown by conservatives. Hungary was declared a monarchy with the throne "temporarily vacant." Actually, it was a dictatorship supported by the great landowners and the army officers.

A period of poverty follows the war

One damaging effect of World War I was the general spread of poverty. This was felt not only in the defeated nations, but also among the victors. The only exception was the United States. Here the economic system seemed to have become stronger during the war. The world situation illustrated a great truth of our times: in a modern war, no one wins; some just lose less than others.

Economic recovery was slow and difficult. Much productive power had been destroyed. What was left was in worn-out condition. World trade was disrupted. Demobilization and unemployment caused serious problems. It was natural, perhaps, that every nation tried to solve its own problems in a way that seemed best for it. However, the result was a form of economic nationalism that made the recovery of the whole much slower and more difficult.

●High tariffs

To protect its home market, every country passed high tariffs. Some adopted quotas on imports. These limited the amount of goods that could be brought in. The United States, whose productive power had actually increased during the war, took the lead. Every nation followed. Even Great Britain gave up the free-trade policy which she had followed since the middle 1800's. First Britain adopted mildly protective tariffs, and then a system of "imperial preferences." This meant that products of the British Empire and Commonwealth were given special preference within the empire and commonwealth countries.

In a world where international trade was so vitally important, economic nationalism was bound to bring bad results. One example should be enough. Between 1926, when recovery began, and 1939, when World War II came, world production of manufactured goods increased thirty-four per cent. World trade in manufactured goods declined thirteen per cent.

●Financial troubles: inflation

As a result of the general poverty, the revenues of governments declined in spite of heavier taxes. The need for revenue was just as great, and even greater. Governments had to pay the continued heavy expenses for armies and navies. There were also the costs of the new social programs: old age pensions, unemployment insurance, and the like. To fill the gap, many governments adopted two disastrous financial policies: They borrowed heavily by selling bonds. They printed vast quantities of paper money, which could not

This German bank note for one billion marks (1,000 million) was very small change during the period of inflation.

be exchanged for gold or silver. As you know, when the supply of money in circulation is increased without an increase of the amount of goods to be bought, the result is certain. With lots of money and few goods, up go the prices of the goods. Therefore, although taxes produced more money, the money bought less. The gap between income and expenses continued; so more money was borrowed and printed.

This condition is known as inflation. In many countries, such as Russia and the states of central Europe, it reached fantastic limits. Let us take Germany as an example. In 1913, before the war, one German mark was worth twenty-five cents, American money. In 1923,

A scene in a German bank in the early 1920's. Instead of wallets, Germans needed large hampers and sacks to carry their paper money. At this point, twenty-five cents in United States money was worth one trillion marks.

an American quarter was worth one trillion marks. (This means 1 followed by 12 zeros: 1,000,000,000,000.) In the following years the German government issued a new kind of money. The old marks could no longer be used; they must be exchanged for the new at the rate of one trillion for one.

These figures may make you gasp, or even laugh. But they were no laughing matter to the people who "went through the wringer" of inflation. Imagine your condition if you had had, in 1913, the tidy sum of 500,000 marks in savings. You had left it untouched

Newspaper headlines on "black Friday," a disastrous day for the New York stock market. The optimism mentioned in the newspaper stories did not last long. Years of depression followed the crash.

for ten years. When you went to the bank to draw it out, you would have received it in one 5,000,000-mark bill because nothing of a lower denomination was printed. Instead of buying $125,000 worth of goods, it would have been worth less than a penny. You can see what happened to savings, whether in money, bonds, or insurance policies.

● *War debts and reparations*

Another very troublesome problem hindered economic recovery and helped spread poverty. It was the puzzling question of war debts and reparations. During and immediately after the war, the United States government had loaned its allies some ten billion dollars. (This was different from the loans the American citizens made by buying foreign government bonds.) In the postwar period the United States insisted that these government loans be repaid. It did not, of course, want payment in any of the cheap paper money. It demanded either gold or American money. However, European governments did not have enough gold. If they paid what they had, their paper money, already greatly depreciated in value, would have become worthless. There were only two ways to get American dollars: either sell goods in the United States or borrow money there. Selling goods was made very difficult by the high American tariff. During the 1920's, Europeans, both governments and private corporations, borrowed American money by selling bonds to American banks, corporations, and private citizens.

There was also the problem of reparations. Germany had been ordered to pay thirty-three billion dollars in war damages. Most of this was to go to Belgium, France, and Britain. The Belgians, French, and British maintained that they could pay their war debts to the United States if Germany paid its reparations and war debts. The United States argued that there was no connection between reparations and war debts. The Allies had borrowed

rk **Times.**

	THE WEATHER
₪ Times Company.	Cloudy and continued cold today; tomorrow fair and warmer.

OBER 25, 1929. TWO CENTS

ORST STOCK CRASH STEMMED BY BANKS; 2,894,650-SHARE DAY SWAMPS MARKET; EADERS CONFER, FIND CONDITIONS SOUND

CIERS EASE TENSION

Wall Street Bankers d Two Meetings at Morgan Office.

BREAK 'TECHNICAL'

t Lays It to 'Air Holes' ws Low Prices Do Not ict Situation Fairly.

MARGINS BEING MET

Market 'Susceptible to ment'—Mitchell, Potter, in, Prosser at Talks.

Wall Street Optimistic After Stormy Day; Clerical Work May Force Holiday Tomorrow

LOSSES RECOVERED IN PART

Upward Trend Starts With 200,000-Share Order for Steel.

TICKERS LAG FOUR HOURS

Thousands of Accounts Wiped Out, With Traders in Dark as to Events on Exchange.

SALES ON CURB 6,337,415

Prices on Markets in Other Cities Also Slump and Rally —Wheat Values Hard Hit.

BIG DROP IN WHEAT; PIT IN A TURMOIL

TREASURY OFFICIALS BLAME SPECULATION

Break of 12 Cents a Bushel to New Season Low and 8-Cent Rally Mark Wild Trading.

Drastic Market Decline Found Not Due to Any Basic Business Weakness.

STOCKS TUMBLE IN CHICAGO

Selling Swamps Exchange in 1,200,000-Share Day—Part

STILL PLAN TAX REDUCTION

Reserve Board Meets Twice in Day and Keeps in Constant

the money, and should repay it regardless of whether Germany paid reparations. Germany asserted that the total of reparations was entirely beyond her ability to pay.

Historians disagree as to whether Germany actually intended or tried to pay. She did make some reparations payments. The coal of the Saar Valley, which France took, counted as a reparations payment. Germany, too, borrowed money in the United States by selling bonds to American citizens. She used some of this money to pay reparations. The Allies then used the reparations money to make payments on their American war debts. However, if you will take a close look at this interesting game of musical chairs, you will see that there was not much future in it.

● *The depression starts: 1929*

In the fall of 1929 an event occurred that was destined to stop all payments of reparations and war debts, and spread poverty world-wide. The New York stock market crashed. Many American banks, factories, mining companies, and business firms went bankrupt. The stock market collapse was the sign of the beginning of a world-wide depression. Some 25,000,000 workers throughout the world were unemployed and hungry. The United States, both the government and the people, refused to lend any more money to Europe. Germany stopped paying reparations. The Allied nations stopped debt payments.

The unbelievable thing about the poverty of the depression was this: it was poverty in the midst of plenty. Even though the prices of goods fell very low, the goods could not be sold, and people went hungry. Manufactured goods piled up in warehouses, farm crops were ploughed under because existing crops could not be sold. Canada burned part of her wheat crop. Brazil dumped coffee into the sea. People simply did not have the money to buy. Economic nationalism, in the form of high tariffs and quotas, now reaped a bitter harvest. European exports and imports declined over sixty per cent in three years. The imports and exports of the United States went down as much as sixty-eight per cent.

The causes of the world-wide depression are many and complicated. The main ones can be summarized as follows:

1. Increased use of laborsaving machinery produced more goods, but it caused less employment. Fewer people had the money to buy goods.
2. Monopoly in industries increased production, but also prices and unemployment. Even in the depression the prices of manufactured goods, where there were monopolies, fell less than those of agricultural products, where there was no monopoly. The higher prices meant that, although the monopoly might be able to produce more goods, less could be sold.
3. The war debts decreased the ability of European nations to buy goods.
4. Tariff walls and quotas cut down international trade.
5. Most of the world's gold was in the treasuries of the United States and France.
6. Economic nationalism made every nation try to be self-sufficient.
7. A great share of the world's wealth came to be concentrated in the hands of relatively few people. They could not possibly buy and use all the goods produced. Poorer people lacked the money to buy the goods needed.

There were other causes, but you have read enough to realize that they might be summed up briefly in a statement which is not new to you. The world, at least in the industrial nations, had learned how to produce enough goods for all. It had not yet learned how to distribute, or divide up, these goods among the people who needed and wanted them.

The depression seemed only to intensify and make worse many of the sad and ugly postwar developments. Unemployment and poverty brought unrest and violence. Democratic governments were undermined as people sought for new solutions to their desperate problems.

The feeling of nationalism increases

The war brought a great upsurge of nationalism, often of the narrowest, most superpatriotic sort. This result must surely be counted as one of the immeasurable costs. It was a strange development, for in many ways nationalism seemed an outmoded fashion.

> *Lawrence of Arabia, an Englishman who was important in Arab affairs. During World War I he took a leading part in the Arab revolt against Turkish rule. At the Versailles conference T. E. Lawrence urged that Arab nationalist desires get attention. However, the great powers failed to grant what the Arabs wanted.*

The League of Nations was a world organization. Economically the world had become a great interrelated únit. Every part depended on every other part. New methods of transportation and communication brought all parts of the world close together. It was in this world, united in so many ways, that nationalism divided nations and peoples into little hating, fearing, suspicious splinters. National policies and propaganda of the war period have to bear a heavy responsibility for this development.

Each national group began to live its own life within its borders, with its own government, army, frontiers, tariffs, and foreign policy. It was good to see each nation, small as well as large, free to enjoy its rights to self-government. But many almost unsolvable problems arose. Trade and travel became difficult. As frontiers multiplied, clashes and disputes also increased; as a result, so did armed forces, with their heavy burden of expense.

Stronger nationalism was not at all confined to Europe. It was world-wide. In the imperial and colonial regions the desire for independence and national self-government became ever stronger. The Arab regions of the old Turkish Empire, in North Africa and Asia Minor, seethed with revolt. The natives of Morocco and Tunisia rebelled against the French, and were put down by force. In Lebanon and Syria, Arab revolts forced the French to give up their mandates there. Britain was forced to give independence to Egypt, although she kept a force in the Suez region to defend the canal.

Nationalism in India

Strong nationalist movements appeared in Asia, too. A nationalist movement for independence from Great Britain had already risen in India. Britain had taken India into the war, receiving great support both in men and money. In return, she had promised India a greater degree of self-government. However, a constitution for India had to satisfy many conflicting groups. Indian nationalists demanded complete self-government (dominion status). British conservatives opposed giving up the empire. Many religious and social groups in India—Hindus and Moslems, Brahmans and untouchables—were hostile to each other. There were the native princes, who were absolute rulers in their domains, and liberal Indian political groups.

● Mahatma Gandhi

A great leader appeared among the Indian nationalists. Mohandas Gandhi, called by the Indians *Mahatma,* or "The Saintly One," wanted complete self-government for India. He also wanted Indians to give up Western ways and ideas and return to their ancient culture and religion. Gandhi was opposed to all use of force or violence. He believed that India could gain her ends by passive resistance, or, as he called it, "non-violent noncoöperation."

It may seem strange to think of offering no resistance, no matter how much force is used against you. But when you realize what it meant, you will see that it could be very effective. It meant refusal to buy any British goods. It meant refusal to pay taxes. If you were taken to jail, you went peacefully. But the jails could hold only so many. There were many other features to "civil disobedience." The British, who are not a brutal people, found this form of resistance hard to deal with.

After much trouble and many conferences and investigations, Britain did grant a federal constitution with provincial self-government, in 1937. However, the British viceroy still controlled national defense and foreign affairs. The nationalists were not satisfied; they now insisted on complete independence. But the Moslems, fearing Hindu rule, demanded a division of India so that there could be an independent Moslem state.

Mahatma Gandhi picked this picture as the most characteristic photograph of himself.

Nationalism in China

In China also a nationalist movement was well under way. Various groups of nationalist Chinese had united into the National People's Party, or Kuomintang. In 1912, led by Dr. Sun Yat-sen, they had overthrown the Manchu dynasty and set up a republic. Sun Yat-sen planned to make China a democratic country. He wanted to liberate the Chinese people from the injustices they suffered under their own rulers and from foreign domination under the "unequal treaties."

The Republic of China, however, existed mainly on paper. It controlled the southern region around Canton. The rest of the country was divided up among various war lords. The Nationalists asked help from foreign powers to overthrow the war lords and give China a strong central government. The United States, Great Britain, Japan, and other powers remained indifferent to the plea.

585

Communist intervention in China

The only country that offered help was the new communist government of Russia, or the Soviet Union. The Communists had voluntarily given up their special rights and privileges under the unequal treaties, an act which had won them much good will in China. Now they sent technical and political advisers to help reorganize the Kuomintang (the party of Sun Yat-sen) and build up an army. The young Communist Party of China was admitted to the Kuomintang. The communists began to organize the workers of the new factories in Canton and Shanghai and the peasants of the provinces to help in the revolution.

Under the leadership of a young general, Chiang Kai-shek, a nationalist army grew until, in 1926, it was strong enough to move against the war lords of the north. The first

Chiang Kai-shek, leader of the Nationalist Chinese forces, in 1927.

move was to Hankow, the great "interior seaport" on the Yangtze River. It was a very successful campaign. Using the communist techniques, the regular army was preceded by many propagandists. They urged the peasants to rise against their landlords and against the war lords who ruined the country and forced Chinese to fight against Chinese. The Nationalist government was moved north to Hankow. The Russian advisers became very influential.

The Nationalist Party

The Nationalist Party was made up of many different groups with different aims. All agreed that it was good to be rid of the Manchus and that China must be united and independent. Here the agreement ended. There was a "right wing" of conservatives: landowners, merchants, bankers, and owners of the new industries that had grown up in the seacoast cities. They wanted a strong China, but they did not want to change the system of land ownership. Nor did they welcome strong labor unions. The "left wing" was made up of the Communists and of students and intellectuals who accepted the viewpoint of the Communists. They wanted to base the power of the new China on the peasants and workers. The army, or at least its officers, generally favored the conservatives. Many of them came from the landlord-gentry class. Naturally they opposed any division of land among the peasants.

While Dr. Sun Yat-sen lived, he was able to keep these different groups united under his leadership. He died in 1925, just before the march to the north. General Chiang Kai-shek, after a struggle, made himself leader of the right wing of the party. The conservatives had been greatly alarmed during the "march to the north." Peasants had been stirred up to violence against the landlords, and workers to go on strike. Foreign governments, especially Britain and the United States, helped the split to develop because they did not want a Chinese government under Russian communist influence.

● The Nationalists break with the Communists

In 1927 the break came. The right wing of the Nationalist Party drove out the Communists and sent the Russian advisers home. They set up a Nationalist government in Nanking, with no representatives from the left wing. It was not done peacefully. It was the beginning of a civil war that was to last for many years. The Communists and some parts of the army moved first to a southeastern interior province. Here they set up a Chinese Soviet Republic. They were under repeated attack by the Nationalist army. Finally they were driven out altogether. After a famous "Long March," which took them 6,000 miles on a roundabout route, they established themselves in a poor province west of the great bend of the Yellow River.

● Chiang Kai-shek

The Nationalist Nanking government was a one-party government, and really a one-man government of Chiang Kai-shek. Through his control of the army he was able to control the Kuomintang, the Nationalist Party. In general, he shared the views of his officers. They wanted a strong China, with reform of the abuses that had sapped the country's strength. They were not much interested in democracy, and they hated communism. In general, they wanted to keep the old ways in the countryside and the villages, for they came from the class which had benefited most by them.

Chiang needed the support of the bankers, merchants, and industrialists too. They felt that China could be strong only if it were Westernized, and industrialized, with a greatly improved transportation system. You can see that Chiang had to be somewhat of a juggler to keep the groups in his party balanced. For the most part he did this ably.

By 1937, in spite of continued civil war with the Communists, opposition from Japan, and very lukewarm support from the Western powers, Nationalist China had made progress. The Nationalists were able to make a small beginning at a system of roads and railroads. They improved the financial system, and also reformed and improved the educational system. Some slight beginnings were made in industrialization. Progress was slow because of lack of capital. Also, many of China's natural resources were controlled by foreign powers. Japan, for example, controlled Manchuria with its rich minerals. Some of the foreign powers were willing to give up a few of the special privileges they held. The Nationalists were allowed to collect China's tariff, and two or three of the smaller foreign-held concessions were given back.

Because of differences of opinion within their own ranks, the Nationalists did not deal with two very ancient problems. No changes were made in the very unequal land ownership, nor in the system of collecting taxes in the provinces. You may recall that these were two of the greatest problems of Old China. Through the centuries they had produced the situation that led to the overthrow of dynasties.

China lived in fear of aggression by Japan. Chiang considered that he was running a race, trying to answer a great question: Could China be organized and strengthened before Japan struck? Much of the revenue which might have been used for other improvements was spent on organizing, equipping, and strengthening the Chinese Nationalist army.

You can see, then, that the war brought about a great increase of nationalism in a world whose problems—economic, social, and political—could only be solved internationally. In Europe a narrow kind of nationalism grew stronger—an attempt by each nation to settle all problems strictly in its own national interest, without regard for the consequences to anyone else. In Africa, the Near East, and

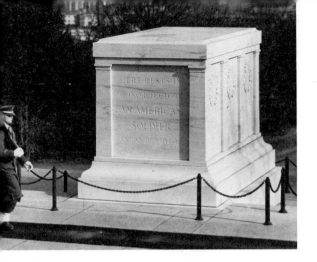

One reminder of the cost of World War I is the Tomb of the Unknown Soldier in Arlington, Virginia. Of the United States forces, 126,000 men died. France counted 1,357,800 dead; Great Britain, 908,371; Germany, 1,773,700; Russia, 1,700,000.

Asia, there was a great upsurge against colonial imperialism.

Summary: the costs of World War I

How can the results of this first world-wide war be summed up? It must be admitted that it is a very uneven balance sheet. The loss figures, in red, far outnumber the gain figures, in black.

On the gain side may be mentioned those national groups which realized long-sought aims for independence and self-government. Democratic republicans would count it a gain that hereditary monarchies tottered and collapsed. Among the unemployed, in the postwar period, were a number of unemployed royal families. For a time it looked as though the democratic idea had actually gained in the world, for many of the new governments started out as liberal, democratic forms. Greatest gain of all, it seemed, was the formation of an organization for world coöperation. There was a chance, at least, that conflicts which had in the past led to wars might now be settled in peace, with justice. If this were

to prove true, then possibly all the sacrifices might not have been in vain.

The loss side of the balance sheet is so long that it can hardly be set down, even in brief summary. The appalling death roll was not only a loss to the present, but a loss which the future could never make up. The destruction of property was a similar loss. Destroyed land may be reclaimed; destroyed buildings rebuilt. But the raw materials which go into the weapons of war—the sunken ships, the exploded shells—are gone. Mankind has used up these resources for no gain. Assigning a money value to these losses, and saying that the future can repay them, is very deceptive. The real wealth, the thing itself, is gone. It can never be repaid. The postwar world was a poorer place. It had spent, not just its income, but its capital.

Although it is impossible to arrive at an exact figure for the cost of the war in dollars, estimates have been made. One scholar estimates that the total cost to all the warring powers was 400 billion dollars. In a day when dollars were worth more than in recent years, 400 billion of them could have done the following things:

1. It could have built a $2,500 home, with $1,000 worth of furniture, on five acres of land worth $100 an acre, for every family in the United States, Canada, Australia, England, Wales, Scotland, Ireland, France, Belgium, Germany, Italy, and Russia.
2. It could have furnished each of these countries with a $5,000,000 library, a $10,000,000 university, endowed salaries for 125,000 teachers and 125,000 nurses.
3. It could have bought all the land in France and Belgium at $100 an acre.

Another estimate which can be grasped is this: one half of the expenditure of the United States in the war could have bought an automobile and a tractor for each of the 6,500,000 farmers then in the country, and have left over $600,000,000 to spend for roads.

There is another loss which is intangible (impossible to touch or grasp). What of the loss to culture and civilization itself? As students of history, who know something of the decline of the Roman Empire, you will be interested in the following words of a careful and scholarly observer, written in 1938:

"Spiritually and morally, civilization collapsed on August 1, 1914—the civilization in which people now middle-aged grew up, a culture which with all its shortcomings did give more satisfaction to more people than any other yet evolved. Young people cannot realize how the world has been coarsened and barbarized since 1914; they may feel the loss of security into which their parents were born, but they cannot appreciate how much else has been lost; even we who once had it cannot recall it now without an effort. But the collapse of a great culture is a long process; it took the Roman world four or five centuries to hit bottom. Since 1914 we have slipped back as far perhaps as the Romans slipped between the Antonine age [the time of the Good Emperors] and the days of Alexander Severus [the beginning of the period of the Barrack-Room Emperors]." *

Review of Chapter 45

People, places, and things

Identify: Mohandas Gandhi, Sun Yat-sen, Chiang Kai-shek, Kuomintang.
Locate: Germany, Austria, Hungary, India, China, Manchuria, Hankow, Nanking.

Events in review

1. What problems did the new German and Austrian governments face after World War I?
2. What is meant by inflation? What causes inflation?
3. Why did problems develop over a) war debts, b) reparations?
4. Name three of the major causes of the worldwide depression that started in 1929.
5. Who advocated the policy of "non-violent non-coöperation"? What does this term mean?
6. Why was there civil war in China in the 1920's and 1930's?
7. What were the major problems facing Chiang Kai-shek's government?
8. Give one estimate of the cost of World War I measured in dollars.

Problems and projects

1. Discuss the losses the world suffered as a result of World War I, including the cost in lives, the cost of the war itself measured in terms of money, and the economic and social problems that followed the war. Which losses do you consider the most serious? Explain.
2. Summarize the policy of the United States toward China up through the time of the Nine-Power Treaty. (Review Chapter 40.) What was the basic idea of American policy? How did this compare with the policies of other nations?
3. Write a brief biography of Sun Yat-sen, emphasizing his influence on Chinese history.
4. Write a brief report on Chiang Kai-shek.
5. Write a brief biography of Gandhi.
6. Read descriptions of the depression that began in 1929. Ask friends and relatives to tell you what they can remember of it. Write for the class a "You Were There" account of the stock market crash in 1929, or of the effects of the depression on daily living in the early 1930's.

* Davis, Elmer. "We Lose the Next War." *Harper's Magazine*, March, 1938, p. 342. Quoted by permission of Mrs. Elmer Davis.

Review of Great Power Rivalries and World War 1

1. Compare the pattern of imperialism in India, Africa, and China. In which regions did the imperialist nations establish colonies? In which regions did they establish spheres of influence? Did the European nations do anything to benefit the native population? In which area did they exploit the native peoples most and give least?

2. The new imperialism brought on sharper international rivalry. In what parts of the world was the rivalry most serious? What issues were involved?

3. In 1854 Japan was an isolated feudal country. By 1921 Japan was able to claim second rank among the great naval powers. How did Japan make this rapid change? What did she gain from three wars during this period? What effect did the rise of Japan have on China?

4. To what extent did the United States join in the imperialist race? Did the United States oppose and restrain the imperialistic policies of other nations? Consider events in Central America and the Caribbean, South America, and the Far East.

5. To what extent was militarism and the building up of large armed forces a cause of World War I? What efforts were made in the Versailles treaty to limit the armed forces of Germany?

6. Compare the First World War with the Napoleonic Wars. How much did nationalism have to do with these wars? Compare the plus and minus sides of the balance sheets on these wars. Compare the problems faced by the treaty makers in 1815 and at the close of World War I.

7. Discuss the statement that World War I created more problems than it settled. Give as many specific details as you can to show what problems were created by the war or left unsettled by the peace.

Books about Imperialism and World War 1

Benns, F. Lee. *Europe Since 1914: in Its World Setting* (Appleton-Century-Crofts, 1954). A valuable reference book.

*Browne, Lewis. *This Believing World* (Macmillan, 1944). Readable accounts of the Oriental religions.

Burrows, Millar. *Founders of the Great Religions* (Scribner's, 1931). Lao-tze, Buddha, and Confucius.

Clark, Grover. *Place in the Sun* (Macmillan,

*Books marked with a star (*) are easy reading.

1936). The expansion of Europe; the two eras of imperialism. An excellent reference.

Crow, Carl. *China Takes Her Place* (Harper, 1944). Sun Yat-sen, the revolution of 1911, and much later history.

*Davis, William S. *Roots of the War* (Century, 1918). The background and underlying causes of World War I in very readable form.

*Dilts, Marion M. *Pageant of Japanese History* (Longmans, 1947). Almost every phase of Japanese life in every age is described in this well-written, well-illustrated book.

*Ekrem, Selma. *Turkey, Old and New* (Scribner's, 1947). Most of the book deals with the changes begun by Mustafa Kemal.

Fish, Carl R. *Path of Empire; a Chronicle of the United States as a World Power* (Yale University Press, 1919). An excellent book for reference on American imperialism.

Fitch, Florence M. *Their Search for God; Ways of Worship in the Orient* (Lothrop, 1947). The essentials of Hinduism, Buddhism, Confucianism, Taoism, and other religions, well and simply described.

*Gaer, Joseph. *How the Great Religions Began* (Dodd, rev. ed., 1956).

*Gatti, Ellen, and Gatti, Attilio. *Here Is Africa* (Scribner's, 1943). Well and simply written, beautifully illustrated. There are chapters on the partition of Africa.

*Kuo, Helena. *Giants of China* (Dutton, 1944). Biographies of Confucius, Sun Yat-sen, Chiang Kai-shek, and other Chinese leaders. Here are truly fascinating stories.

*Lamprey, Louise. *Building an Empire* (Stokes, 1941). How the British Empire grew.

Liddell Hart, Basil. *War in Outline* (Modern Library, 1939). World War I briefly told.

Lin Yu-t'ang. *Wisdom of China and India* (Random House, 1942). Selections from the writings of the great sages and philosophers of the Orient.

*Modak, Manorama. *Land and People of India* (Lippincott, 1952). Much valuable information about India in clear and simple writing.

Moon, Parker T. *Imperialism and World Politics* (Macmillan, 1947). A very useful reference book.

Nicolay, Helen. *Bridge of Water; the Story of Panama and the Canal* (Appleton-Century, 1940).

*Quinn, Vernon. *Picture-Map Geography of Asia* (Lippincott, 1955). A valuable geographical aid.

*Seeger, Elizabeth. *Pageant of Chinese History* (Longmans, 1947). How the Chinese reacted to the Western powers. An entertaining and informative book.

*Yaukey, Grace (Cornelia Spencer, pseud.). *Land of the Chinese People* (Lippincott, 1951).

*———. *Made in India* (Knopf, 1946).

*———. *Understanding the Japanese* (Aladdin Books, 1949). Three interesting and informative books, simply and clearly written.

Stories about Imperialism and World War I

Buchan, John. *Thirty-Nine Steps* (Longmans, 1947).

———. *Greenmantle* (Nelson, 1957).

Buck, Pearl. *Good Earth* (World Publishing, 1947). The story of a Chinese family's love for the soil and their struggle to cultivate it.

———. *Young Revolutionist* (John Day, 1932). A young Chinese boy fights in the Revolution of 1911.

*Carpenter, Frances. *Tales of a Chinese Grandmother* (Doubleday, 1937). Much lore concerning Chinese ways, manners, and morals.

*Chandler, Anna C. *Dragons on Guard* (Lippincott, 1944). Stories of art and history during three dynasties, which give a good interpretation of China.

Forester, C. S. *Sky and the Forest* (Little, Brown, 1948). The central character, an African chieftain, allows the reader to see imperialism from the native's side.

Hobart, Alice T. *Oil for the Lamps of China* (Grosset, 1933). A touching novel dealing with Chinese life and American "big business" abroad.

Jagendorf, Moritz A. *In the Days of the Han* (Messner, 1945). China in the second century B.C. The adventures of two fearless young Chinese make good reading.

Kipling, Rudyard. *Something of Myself; for My Friends, Known and Unknown* (Doubleday, 1937). Kipling's own story of his life in India.

*Nordhoff, Charles B. and Hall, James N. *Falcons of France* (Little, Brown, 1945). Flying during World War I.

Remarque, Erich M. *All Quiet on the Western Front* (Putnam, 1948). A famous novel about a young German soldier in World War I.

*Sugimoto, Etsu I. *Daughter of the Samurai* (Doubleday, 1947). This book gives a picture of Japanese feudal customs.

Part Nine

THE WORLD BETWEEN
TWO WARS

After the end of World War I, the people of the earth hoped to settle down to a time of peace. What they got was twenty-one years of uneasy truce. By the 1930's, violence was breaking out in many parts of the world. Mankind was living again under the threat of war. The nature of the threat might be symbolized by a weapon of growing importance, the aerial bomb. In 1939 the bombs began to fall and World War II was on.

The causes of this war were many and complicated. To a considerable extent, World War II was a struggle between democratically governed nations and dictatorships. After the first war, Great Britain, France, and the United States preserved their democratic forms of government. Other nations, however, tried to solve their problems by letting dictators take over their governments. A dictatorship of the left—communism—established itself in Russia. Italy and Germany fell to the dictatorship of the right—fascism. Japan, already an autocratic state, became increasingly militaristic.

The fascist, militaristic states wanted to expand by seizing new territory. They were willing to risk war to gain their ends. The democratic nations, on the other hand, longed to keep the peace at almost any price.

The picture on the facing page dramatizes one of the reasons why the peace was not kept. The upper sketch shows the signing of a pact by which the great powers agreed to outlaw war. Men of good will tried to solve international problems by talking, making promises, and signing papers. Unfortunately, treaties proved useless because they were not enforced. While the statesmen talked, the dictators were on the march, taking what they wanted by force of arms. The lower sketch shows Hitler, dictator of Germany, reviewing some of the troops he used in his effort to dominate Europe.

The League of Nations, mankind's first attempt to maintain peace through coöperation, proved too weak to stop Italy, Germany, and Japan. The democracies failed to join together to work for peace. Eventually they were forced to go to war. In Chapters 46–50 you will be able to trace the interplay of three great themes of history: concepts of government, the problems of peace, the sources of war. For a quick preview of Part Nine, look at the time chart on pages 594–595.

THE RISE OF TOTALITARIAN STATES IN EUROPE

OTHER EUROPEAN NATIONS AND THE LEAGUE OF NATIONS

1915

1917	March, Nicholas II of Russia abdicates November Bolshevik revolution
1918	Armistice, World War I
1919	Bolsheviks consolidating power in Russia Weimar Constitution, Germany

1918	Armistice, World War I
1919	Peace conference at Paris

1920

1921	End of civil war in Russia. New Economic Policy begins
1922	Fascists march on Rome, Mussolini seizes power in Italy
1923	Rivera dictatorship in Spain Inflation in Germany Hitler's *Mein Kampf*
1924	Lenin dies, Russia

1920	League of Nations holds first session
1921	Irish Free State established
	European nations at Washington Conference on Naval Disarmament (1921-1922)

1925

1925	Financial crises in France Locarno Treaties
1926	General strike in Great Britain Germany admitted to League of Nations
1928	Stalin established as dictator in Russia First Five-Year Plan
1929	World-wide depression

1928	Pact of Paris (Kellogg-Briand Pact)
1929	World-wide depression

1930

1931	Spanish Republic established
1933	Hitler becomes Chancellor of Germany Nazis dominate country Second Five-Year Plan in Russia

1930	Naval disarmament conference meets at London
1931	British Commonwealth established Great Britain abandons free trade
1932	League of Nations investigates Japan's aggression in Manchuria General Disarmament Conference at Geneva (ends in failure 1934)
1933	Germany withdraws from League of Nations and from Geneva Disarmament Conference Japan withdraws from League

1935

1935	Hitler announces rearmament Saar rejoins Germany Italy invades Ethiopia
1936	German troops occupy Rhineland Spanish Civil War begins; Italy and Germany help fascist side Rome-Berlin Axis announced Russia puts emphasis on military production
1937	"Non-intervention" policy toward civil war in Spain; Germany and Italy continue to aid Franco Rome-Berlin-Tokyo Axis formed
1938	Germany annexes Austria Munich meeting: Czechoslovakia loses Sudetenland
1939	March—Germany and Hungary occupy remainder of Czechoslovakia April—Italy seizes Albania August—Hitler-Stalin pact September—Germany invades Poland, World War II begins December—Russia invades Finland

1935-1936	League declares Italy an aggressor in Ethiopia; economic sanctions fail
1937	Great Britain and France agree to "non-intervention" in Spain Italy withdraws from League
1938	Great Britain and France accept Munich accord
1939	Great Britain and France declare war against Germany after invasion of Poland

1940

ASIA AND AFRICA	UNITED STATES

1917 Balfour declaration: Palestine a homeland for Jews

1918 Armistice, World War I

1917-1918 United States in World War I

1920 Woman suffrage (19th Amendment)

1921-1931 Period of moderate civilian government in Japan

1921-1922 Washington Conference on Naval Disarmament

1922 Fordney-McCumber tariff (high protective)

1923 Kemal comes to power in Turkey, westernization program begins

1924 Quotas limit immigration; Japanese excluded

1926 Kuomintang party moves to take control in China

1927 Chiang Kai-shek breaks with communists Establishes National government at Nanking

1927 President Coolidge suggests disarmament conference at Geneva Conference fails

1928 Kellogg-Briand Pact

1929 World-wide depression

1929 Stock market crash Depression begins

1930 Ghandi leads "civil disobedience" movement in India

1931 Militarist government in Japan Japan invades Manchuria

1932 Japan attacks Chinese forces at Shanghai Manchuria becomes Manchukuo, a Japanese puppet state Iraq granted independence

1933 Japan defies League of Nations and withdraws

1930 Hawley-Smoot tariff (high protective) United States accepts London Naval Treaty

1932 F. D. Roosevelt elected for first term

1933 United States refuses to recognize Japanese seizure of Manchuria Reciprocal Trade Agreement Act Good Neighbor Policy, United States and Latin America

1935-1939 Neutrality laws passed

1939 President proclaims state of limited national emergency because of war in Europe

1936 Egypt becomes independent

1937 Government of India Act gives India partial self-government Japan attacks China, begins an eight-year war

Chapter 46

The Search for New Solutions: Dictatorships

TO UNDERSTAND what happened in various nations in this "world between two wars," you must see clearly the basic differences between democracy and dictatorship. They are much more than just differences in forms of government. They are completely different philosophies—two completely different ways of thinking about life and the meaning of the individual citizen.

Democracy depends on the individual, free citizen

The democratic ideal is really a way of thinking about the meaning and importance of a person, an individual, in relation to society as a whole. It teaches that every individual is a person of inborn dignity and worth. His rights cannot be taken from him, and they must be observed and protected by his fellow citizens. He is entitled to fair and just treatment under the law. He has the opportunity to develop his abilities, and to share in the rewards of life according to his abilities and what he does with them.

To be sure that his rights and liberties are protected by his government, each individual in a democracy has an equal voice in that government; in fact, he *is* the government. Government is his creation and his servant.

Its very existence depends on his "consent to be governed." Government exists only to serve the individual citizen. It regulates, controls, and judges the actions of people only to make sure that they do not violate the rights of others. Each citizen gives up some of his rights to complete freedom of action so that all citizens may have both freedom and security. Government is the judge of this ideal as well as the means of accomplishing it.

Democracy does not achieve its ideal in every respect. But this is a noble ideal. No other kind of government comes as close to realizing the basic teachings of all the great religions. People in a democracy should always strive to remedy imperfections in their countries. They should always try to make the actual practice come closer to the great religious and philosophical idea that "All men are brothers." Citizens in a democratic society also have obligations to be informed and objective; they must be unemotional in exercising their rights. There are two possible approaches for each citizen: "What will be good for me?" and "What will be good for the whole community?"

Political democracy allows men to unite in political parties to elect their representatives in the government. These government officers will put the ideas of the people into effect in the form of laws. You have already read a description of how parliamentary democracy operates in Great Britain (see pages 405–411).

This kind of parliamentary democracy works best when there are only two major political parties. Then one party is almost always sure to elect a majority of the members of the lower house. Thus they can "form a government." "The government" will be able to govern, for it will always have a majority of votes to put its policies into effect. At the next regularly scheduled general election the voters will be able to show whether they approve of the policies and action. When national unity is very important, such as in a war or a depression, it is necessary to have a coalition government. This is a cabinet made up of members of different parties.

This kind of majority government requires a great deal of fair play from both the major- ity and the minority party. It demands much self-discipline and coöperation among opponents. The minority must be willing to accept the decision of the majority. They may work to win the next election so as to put the party out of power. In Britain the minority party is called "His [or Her] Majesty's Loyal Opposition." That word "loyal" is perhaps the very heart of democratic government. The party out of power must be loyal to the nation. When the opposition refuses to accept the decisions of the legally elected majority, and uses forceful and violent means to compel adoption of its ways of thinking, democratic government ends. A nation in which such events occur is headed for dictatorship, of one kind or another.

Parliamentary democracy in action: the Canadian House of Commons in session.

Dictatorship makes the citizen a servant of the state

In the nations where the economic, social, and political situations were worst, dictatorships replaced democracy. It can almost be stated as a law that people will accept a dictatorship, or allow one to establish itself, only when their problems seem unsolvable by any other method. Dictatorship takes root and thrives in countries where people can see no other way out—where life is filled with poverty, hunger, disease, bitterness, frustration, and hopelessness. Poverty and hunger may make a people willing to give up deep spiritual and philosophical ideas in return for food.

Dictatorship, of whatever kind, is a complete denial of the democratic ideal. In a dictatorship it is the state, the government, which must be served and must succeed. The rights and dignities of the citizen must be sacrificed to the welfare of the state. You can see the absolute and fundamental oppositeness: In a democracy the government is the servant of the people; it exists for their welfare. In a dictatorship the people exist for the welfare of the state. To be sure, the state promises the citizen material things: food, clothing, a job, a better standard of living. But to get them he must be willing to give up his fundamental rights and liberties, and many of his spiritual beliefs.

●Characteristics of dictatorship

1. Dictatorship is always totalitarianism. A totalitarian government allows only one political party to function openly. The government goes through the motions of holding elections, but all candidates are picked by the dictator. Those who are elected have only one job—to approve decisions the dictator has made.

2. The dictatorship is always a police state. The dictator controls the armed forces and the police and uses them to stamp out opposition. People can be arrested without a warrant and punished without a trial. Secret police spy on all citizens.

3. The government controls newspapers, magazines, books, and radio and television stations. The people are not told the news as it happens; they are told what the dictator wants them to think happened.

4. The people are trained to conform to the will of the dictator. Expressing contrary opinions is made dangerous. Children are educated to believe and obey, not to think.

5. Dictatorship appeals strongly to nationalism and superpatriotism. The glories of the nation are played up. The ambitions of the nation are pictured as right and just. Other nations are often presented as menacing villains.

6. War is presented as honorable and glorious. All wars, of course, are fought to defend the fatherland or to gain what the

Modern dictators, like the Spartans in ancient Greece, believe in training children at an early age to be obedient followers. Shown here are junior Fascists—"The Roman Wolf's Sons"—parading past Mussolini in the days when he was dictator of Italy.

nation deserves. The dictator expects men to be willing to die to gain what he wants.

Dictatorships are alike in the methods they use to gain or keep power. But they differ in their aims, both in theory and to some extent in practice. There can be dictatorships of the "left" (socialist and communist dictatorships) and of the "right" (capitalist and fascist dictatorships).

Communism

The dictatorship of the left is communism. Under communism all the means of production—the farms, mines, factories, railroads, business enterprises—are owned in common by all the people. They are operated by the government, for the welfare of everyone. So the communists say. Under communism everyone who is able must work. In theory, at least, he works at the thing he is best fitted to do. The communist does not believe that the proceeds of production should be divided up equally. Instead, each person should receive only as much as he needs. The communist slogan is "From each according to his ability; to each according to his needs."

If you examine this doctrine a little, you will see that it goes against certain human instincts. A person likes to be paid somewhat according to the value of the work he does. He would not be happy to see a man who does less useful, less skillful, or less efficient work receive more pay just because he needs more.

Much of communist theory developed from the ideas of Karl Marx (page 393). "Pure communism" cannot be put into practice until people have been trained to accept it. Thus the communists argue that they must overthrow the capitalist system by revolution. A dictatorship of the communist party will run things until everyone is ready to accept communist philosophy. Chapter 47 will tell of the communist dictatorship that has been dominating Russia since World War I.

Life in a dictatorship: women soldiers marching in a Communist demonstration in Moscow. Dictatorships stress military organization and obedience to the state. Having large numbers of people wear uniforms stresses the idea of conforming to the will of the dictator.

Fascism

The dictatorship of the right is fascism or Nazism—except for minor differences, the same thing. Fascism does not involve any change in the system of ownership. The means of production are owned by private individuals. They still receive profits in the form of dividends, interest, or rent. But the means of production are managed and regulated by the state, the dictatorship. Thus fascism is a sort of capitalist dictatorship.

The fascist dictators have almost all come to power in the same way: They make promises to two very different groups of people. To the capitalists, the big industrialists, they promise prosperity, high profits, the prohibition of strikes and labor troubles, the control or abolition of labor unions. A successful revolution needs a popular, mass support, too. So the would-be dictator tries to appeal to a great mass of people. He promises them jobs, better wages, a higher standard of living. He is usually not very successful with the workers who are organized into unions. They distrust his speeches against strikes and "labor troubles." But such promises have great appeal to one particular class: the lower middle class of small businessmen, merchants, shop owners, and "white-collar" workers. They suffer terribly as a result of war and postwar inflation. They are ripe for promises.

The would-be fascist dictator makes other promises, too. He promises a return to ancient glories and former prosperity. He promises to regain lost territories or remedy old international injustices. To desperate and hopeless people these promises are very alluring.

Thus communist and fascist dictatorships have both likenesses and differences. Each kind is totalitarian, with all the trappings and methods of the police state. But there is a fundamental difference in their aim, in where they say they are going. The next two chapters will give you a chance to compare and contrast the communist dictatorship in Russia with fascist dictatorships in Germany and Italy.

Review of Chapter 46

People, places, and things

Identify: communism, fascism, totalitarianism, police state.

Events in review

1. What is the relation of the individual citizen to the government in a democracy?
2. What is the relation of the individual citizen to the government in a dictatorship?
3. What conditions tend to make it possible for a dictator to take over a country?
4. List five characteristics of dictatorship.
5. According to communist theory, who owns the means of production?
6. According to fascist theory, who owns the means of production?

Problems and projects

1. Review earlier parts of this book. What governments of the past had some or all of the characteristics of dictatorships? For example, was Sparta a dictatorship? Was France a dictatorship under Napoleon I and Napoleon III? Explain.
2. Compare the dictatorship of the left with the dictatorship of the right. Consider (a) what the aims of the state are said to be, (b) the methods used by the government.
3. In two columns, draw up a contrast of dictatorship with democracy. Use the following headings: (a) elections, (b) powers of elected lawmaking bodies, (c) arrests, trials, and sentences, (d) freedom of the press, radio, etc., (e) education, (f) in summary, the importance of the individual vs. the importance of the state.
4. Read reports of the experiences of men and women who escaped from Hungary in 1956 and 1957. How do their stories illustrate the methods of a police state?
5. Write an essay on this topic: Under a democratic form of government, the citizen has the greatest opportunity to live a happy, successful, useful life.

Chapter 47 # The Russian Revolution

THE RUSSIAN REVOLUTION of 1905 brought some changes in the czar's government. There was a legislative body, the Duma. It was of little value; the czar remained an absolute ruler with almost full powers. The early 1900's also saw a respectable beginning of industrialization, but it was only a beginning. Russia was far behind the western European countries in industrial power. Of her 170,000,000 people in Russia, only about 2,500,000 were industrial workers. Like the rest of the population they had much to complain about, and were denied all the usual liberties of citizens elsewhere.

Russia's participation in World War I was a sad story. The Russo-Japanese War of 1905 had shown the country's economic weakness. The war which began in 1914 exposed it still further. There were not enough railroads or good roads. Russian industry could not equip and supply the army. Turkey's entrance on the side of Germany had cut Russia off from outside supplies. The Russian "steam-roller" (the mass of armed men) on which the Allies had counted so heavily, proved to be poorly equipped and badly used. There was no doubt about Russian courage, but in a modern mechanized war courage is not enough. Behind the army was a government that was inefficient and corrupt, completely unfit to deal with the problems of modern warfare.

"Old Russia" collapses

Considering all these handicaps it is not surprising that Russia collapsed. The amazing thing is that she held out as long as she did. For more than three years Russian troops on the eastern front held down more than half of the armies of the Central Powers.

> Russian troops marching to do battle with the Germans in 1914. By 1917 more than three quarters of the men in the Russian armed forces were on the casualty lists—killed, wounded, or prisoners. See the figures given at the top of page 602.

During this time Russia's battle losses were 1,700,000 killed, 5,000,000 wounded and crippled, and more than 2,000,000 taken prisoner by the enemy. It seems probable that if Russia had not fought so well during these three years, the Central Powers would have won the war.

By the spring of 1917 the Russians were weary of hardships and disheartened by the terrible losses of the war. They had lost all faith in their government. A factory strike broke out in Petrograd (St. Petersburg). The stubborn Czar Nicholas II ordered it put down by force. The weak Duma demanded reforms in the government; Nicholas II dissolved the Duma. If he had been more willing to compromise when demands for reform were comparatively moderate, he might have saved his throne and spared Russia the horrors that were to follow. But Nicholas II lacked foresight and skill of statesmanship. All he could think of was to preserve autocracy.

● The Provisional Government

By March 15, 1917, the uprising in Petrograd forced Nicholas II to give up his throne. The Romanov monarchy was ended. A Pro-

Street fighting in Petrograd during the revolution.

visional Government was set up to carry on until a constitutional assembly could form a permanent government.

There was another group working for change in Russia. It was the Soviet (council) of Workers, Peasants, and Soldiers. It was made up of moderate socialists, with a small group of the extreme, or radical, socialists: the Communists. They were called Bolsheviks. The first Soviet was formed in Petrograd, but soon there were similar councils of workers, soldiers, and peasants throughout Russia. By June, 1917, they had held an All-Russian Congress of Soviets and set up a Central Executive Committee to act as a parliament. The radical Bolsheviks were a small minority at first. As time went on, they were able to gain leadership and control.

The Provisional Government and the Soviet soon clashed over policy. It was the old disagreement between the liberal and radical. The Provisional Government was made up of moderate liberals, with a strong sprinkling of conservatives. They wanted a democratic constitution with all the guarantees of individual liberties. However, they opposed any basic changes in the ownership of property. The radicals, on the other hand, wanted complete nationalization—government ownership—of all industry. They demanded that the government of Russia be made up of Soviets (councils) of workers, peasants, and soldiers.

The two principal disagreements between the Provisional Government and the Soviet were over the continuation of the war and the distribution of land among the needy peasants. The Provisional Government held that the war must be continued until the Central Powers were defeated. They also argued that they had no power to take and distribute land because they were only a temporary government. That decision must wait until the constitutional assembly had formed a permanent government.

The Soviet took exactly the opposite stand on both questions. There must be an immediate peace. It could be a negotiated peace among all the warring powers. If that were not possible, then Russia must make a separate peace with Germany. On the land question, the Soviet demanded that the huge estates of the czar and the nobles be taken by the government and distributed immediately among the peasants. These disagreements played into the hands of the Bolsheviks, the Communists. At first they did not control either the All-Russian Congress or the Central Executive Committee. They did have a program that appealed to great numbers of the Russian people. Furthermore, the Bolsheviks had very able leaders, such as Lenin.

Lenin and the Bolsheviks

Nikolai Lenin was an extremely intelligent and forceful man. He came from the ranks of the lower nobility, and had been educated in law at a university. Yet he was a fanatically devoted Communist. He was also a very shrewd politician. His slogan, "Land, Peace, and Bread," had an enormous appeal to the Russian masses. He promised, also, immediate and favorable laws for the industrial city workers. In the months after March, 1917, when the Provisional Government was set up, the war had continued, still unsuccessfully for the Russians. Gradually the army became completely demoralized and unwilling to fight on. The Bolsheviks were able to gain control of the Central Executive Committee. Their slogan was "All Power to the Soviet." They claimed that only the Soviets, the true representatives of the Russian people, were entitled to govern Russia. On November 7, 1917, they overthrew the Provisional Government by force and seized control of the government of Russia.

The Communists at once tried to silence all opposition and carry out their program. They signed separate and very harsh peace treaties with Germany, Austria-Hungary, Bulgaria, and Turkey. In the treaties they gave up much Russian territory. The Communists

United States troops near Vladivostok. In 1918–1919, British, Japanese, and United States forces were sent into Siberia to support the White Russian armies.

called on the workers of all countries to revolt, seize control of their governments, and take over the means of production. One of the main doctrines of communism is that the revolution must be world-wide; otherwise communism cannot succeed anywhere. It is the doctrine of world revolution.

However, the Communists faced many problems within Russia. Many groups of Russians opposed the Communist policies and actions, and considered the Soviet government illegal. In scattered groups, under various leaders, they attempted to overthrow the Communists. Because of their opposition to the Red Russians (the Communists), they were called White Russians.

Civil war

The civil war lasted three years and completed the devastation begun by the world war. The Red (Communist) and White (opposition) armies fought many battles and left an appalling trail of destruction. Angered by both the separate peace and the Communist appeal for world revolution, the Allies aided the White forces. They gave them arms and money, and even sent small forces of troops to help them. Allied troops were sent to Russian seaports and into Siberia to aid the White forces. But the Allied effort was a half-hearted one; their troops were too few in number and too poorly equipped to effectively support the White forces. As a result, Allied help only prolonged the civil war, but could not change the result: The Communists defeated the White Russians.

● *The Communists win complete control*

In 1921 the civil war ended, and the Communists took complete control of the devastated country of Russia. The royal Romanov family had been executed. Many nobles and middle-class people were also executed in a "Red Terror" closely resembling the Reign of Terror of the French Revolution. Many other lives had been lost in battle, in raging epidemics of typhus, or through starvation. Agriculture had declined until it was no more than a struggle to raise enough to keep alive. City population was brought down to the starvation level. The transportation system was ruined. Of the comparatively small number of prewar industrial factories, only thirteen per cent remained. Russia in 1921 resembled Germany at the end of the Thirty Years' War, when "They made a desert, and called it peace."

The hoped-for revolution in other countries had not taken place. By 1921 Europe was beginning to recover from the damages of war without the results which Communist leaders had expected. In Russia the Soviet regime had survived, but at a frightful cost. During the civil war the leaders had put communism into practice. Whatever food could be seized from the peasants, whatever industrial commodities could be produced, had been distributed on a basis of need. The first need

was that of the Red Army. Civilians were left to do without, to starve if need be, because the army had to fight to "save the revolution." Now, with a sort of "peace" at hand, the Communist leaders had to develop a program to "build a new society" in Russia. The rest of the world would have to wait.

Russia tries to build a Communist society

In 1921 the problems of trying to build communism in Russia, or any other governmental and economic system, were many and complex. Russia is a huge country of tremendous distances. A traveler from Petrograd on the banks of the Neva River to Vladivostok on the Pacific shore covers almost twice the distance from New York to San Francisco.

Even the terrific losses of the world war followed by the civil war left a large population. It was not a unified, or homogeneous, population. By one count there were people of two races and 182 national groups. The "Old Russian" policy of "one language, one church, one czar" had been a failure. In spite of that policy, 149 different languages were spoken, and all the great religions had their followers. There were vast differences in civilization and culture, too. In European Russia there were people thoroughly in tune with twentieth-century, industrialized society. On the far peninsula of Kamchatka, in the Pacific, there were tribes just emerging from Stone-Age culture. Almost every level of development in between could be found somewhere.

● *Communist theory vs. the facts*

The Communists faced a tremendous contradiction between economic theory and economic reality. Communism preached of a society in which there would be no social classes. Every person would work and contribute according to his ability. He would receive according to his needs. It is doubtful

This Russian poster was made during a famine caused by failure of grain crops. The Russian word on the poster means "Help!"

whether people will ever accept such a way of dividing up the results of labor and production. The Communist leader, Joseph Stalin, had a favorite saying, "Facts are stubborn things." The Communist theory of wages bumped up against an economic reality, a stubborn fact of human nature.

There was another, even greater, contradiction. The Communists talked of nationalizing industries and then sharing the wealth produced. But the stubborn fact, the economic reality, was that there were almost no industries to nationalize and no wealth to share. Arguments over how to divide the results of production were meaningless when there was no production.

Lenin, the dictator, was a devoted Communist, but he was also a very practical man. He realized that to build a better society Russia needed fewer theories and more cultivated farms, more factories and mines in actual operation, more schools and higher literacy, better machinery in both agriculture and industry, more workers trained to operate this machinery, more houses, and modern cities. These things could not be produced by fine speeches about Communist theory, but only by money and work.

Capital, you recall, is wealth which has been saved out of present production to be invested in further production. It is invested in the hope of making a profit, of receiving more income. There was not much capital in the Russia of 1921. The owners of what savings there were would not be attracted by the promise of no private profits, no return on their investment. Even if all Russian savings could be seized and put to use, they would not be enough. The needed capital must come from abroad. However, foreigners would not be willing to invest their savings in a country whose government promised to confiscate all capital and abolish all private profits. Nor would Russian workers and peasants be willing to work hard if they knew that what they produced would be taken from them and divided according to a theory they did not believe in.

In a conflict between theory and facts, something has to give; this time it was Communist theory. If Russia were to attract the capital and get the work she needed, the Communists would have to return, at least to some extent, to capitalist ideas. They would have to permit private ownership of property, personal profit, and wages based on the value of the worker's efforts. Therefore, in 1921 Lenin announced the adoption of the New Economic Policy (N.E.P., for short).

● *The New Economic Policy*

The N.E.P. called in all the old, inflated currency, and issued a new, more stable money. Individuals were permitted to buy, sell,

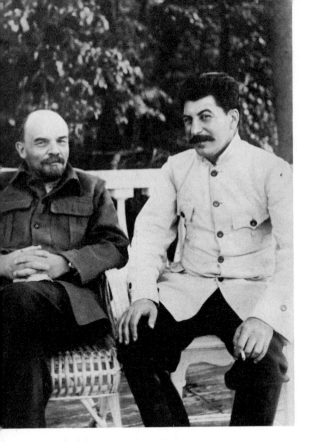

Present and future dictators of Russia: Lenin and Stalin in 1922.

and trade farm products. "Big industries" remained under government ownership and management. These included the production of oil, coal, iron, and other minerals, steel, and the railroads. Smaller business shops and home industries were declared free. Individual private enterprise for private profit became lawful. Foreign capital was invited and welcomed for the development of the state industries, and promised a high rate of dividends. Foreign technicians were invited to come to help, with the promise of high salaries.

Agriculture, the industry of the great majority of the people, was a problem. Most Russian peasants still farmed much as their ancestors had done. Now the land seized from the landlords was divided among the peasants. The promise of the revolution—land to the peasants—was carried out. How-

ever, agricultural production had to increase to feed the growing population of the cities. Under N.E.P. the government tried to persuade the peasants to pool their land into large collective farms. Large farms could be equipped with modern farm machinery. Those who did so were promised a share of the harvest based on the amount of land they contributed and the amount of work they did.

But the stubborn Russian peasant stuck to the old ways of farming. A few joined the collective farms, but not nearly enough to satisfy the government planners. The great majority held on to their small strips of land. They were free to produce and sell as they saw fit as long as they paid their taxes. For the time being, the government did not force them to join the collective farms. Compulsory measures were to be adopted about a decade later.

The N.E.P. was the third stage, or phase, of the Russian Revolution. First came the Provisional Government, with its moderate, liberal attempt to set up a democratic republic. Second came the Communists and the civil war, with its "war communism." Then came the N.E.P., from 1921 till 1928.

Stalin succeeds Lenin

Lenin died in 1924. One of the problems of dictatorship is that there is no fixed law of succession to power. Lenin's death, therefore, brought a struggle for power among the high officials of the Communist Party. It was bitter, savage, and merciless even though it was concealed. As a result of a series of betrayals, double crosses, and assassinations, Joseph Stalin made himself dictator.

By 1928 Stalin felt that he was securely in power. He was not as broadly intelligent and educated as Lenin nor nearly as flexible in his thinking. But he was shrewd, crafty, calculating, and merciless. He was convinced that the N.E.P. was no longer useful. Stalin broke with the accepted communist doctrine.

He believed that communism did not have to become world-wide in order to succeed. Of course, he considered world-wide communism still desirable and even sure to come. But for the time being, it could be made to succeed in one nation alone, and that nation was Russia. What was needed was a return to state ownership and state planning.

In 1928, therefore, Stalin announced the return to a planned economy; he issued the First Five-Year Plan. All the concessions of the N.E.P. to private industry were cancelled. Henceforth everything was to be owned, controlled, and managed by the state. The Russian Revolution entered its fourth stage.

Russia sets up the Five-Year Plans

In a planned economy everything, down to the smallest detail of the whole economic system and society, is planned in advance. The master plan of the First Five-Year Plan was a large volume in itself. In addition, there were specific, detailed plans for each industry. Nor did the plan apply to industry alone. There was a plan for agriculture, a plan for a vastly increased education system, a plan for housing, a plan for the development of recreational facilities, a plan for medical care and hospitals.

It was a gigantic plan; there had been nothing like it in history. The backward, agricultural Russian people had to raise themselves by their own bootstraps to the level of modern industrialized and mechanized society. Because of the threatening international situation, they had to do it fast. With the usual dictator's appeal to outside danger, Stalin said, "We are in a race. We are from fifty to one hundred years behind the advanced countries. We must run through the distance in ten years. Either we do this, or they will crush us."

According to the plan, manufacturing was to be increased about 130 per cent and agriculture 50 per cent within the five years. Be-

cause of the danger of war the great increase in industrial production was to be in the so-called heavy industries: roads and railroads, steel plants, tractor factories, oil wells, dams and power plants to electrify the country. These are "producers' goods"—goods to be used in further production—rather than "consumers' goods"—things used by people in their daily living. The vast amount of money to finance the program was to be raised by taxes, by the sale of bonds, and by profits from the state trusts. Every government official and every citizen was called upon to give his utmost effort to reach the goals. The Russian people were called upon to sacrifice in two ways: They would have to work very hard. They would have to "do without." Production of the kind of goods that make life easier and pleasanter would have to wait.

The program for agriculture was a harsh one. There was to be no more individual farming; all farms were to be merged into collectives. With modern machinery and methods enough food would be produced to feed the entire population, with a surplus for export. The money from these exports was to be used to pay for the machinery and equipment that had to be bought abroad to build up industries. It would also pay the salaries of the foreign experts and technicians who were brought in to help. This time the peasant had to join the collectives. Those who refused or who did not coöperate were liable to be imprisoned, exiled, or executed.

● Results of the First Five-Year Plan

The First Five-Year Plan was carried out successfully in most industries. Many exceeded their quotas; a few reached their goals in four years. Seventy per cent of all the good farm land was collectivized. However, many defects appeared. They had to be remedied if the program of planned economy were to continue and succeed. Rates of increase varied. Sometimes slow progress in one kept back several others. Quality of goods was poor because of the lack of skilled labor, lack of labor discipline, poorly constructed machines, and hasty work. In spite of the building program, there were not enough railroads. Poor transportation held back all industries.

There were heavy costs, too. The grain, oil, and timber sold to pay for foreign goods were often vitally needed at home. Hunger, even starvation, at home was considered of no importance beside the success of the plan. Often, too, these exports were "dumped" abroad (sold at a price below the market). Foreign producers of the same goods were more unfriendly than ever toward Russia. At home the Russians suffered almost indescribable hardships. Shoes, clothing, housing, fuel, and food were very scarce. The people were asked to endure these hard times for the sake of a better future. But, as a good, earthy, Russian proverb says: "Fine promises fill no bellies."

The Second and Third Five-Year Plans

The Second Five-Year Plan was begun in 1933. It was even larger than the first, for it counted on the skill and experience gained by labor during the first. The program again called for a great increase in transportation and the heavy industries. However, it also recognized the need for more consumer goods as a reward to the people, who had worked so hard, suffered so much, and contributed so greatly to the first success. For a time it looked as though the worst hurdles had been passed. There was even some relaxation of the heavy hand of dictatorship. Things once forbidden, such as attractive clothes, cosmetics, and jazz music, were now permitted. Food and merchandise rationing was repealed. Greater freedom was allowed in education, newspapers, motion pictures, and plays.

Once more the international situation caused a change in Communist plans. This time Stalin did not have to invent a foreign danger. A very real one existed. Adolf Hitler

A shepherd in Turkmen Soviet Socialist Republic tending sheep belonging to a collective farm. Contrast this scene with the one on page 609.

came to power in Germany in 1933. His greatest threats were against communism and Russia. At first he did not look dangerous, but when he had had several years to establish himself, he no longer looked like a shouting, ranting lunatic. Mad, perhaps, but dangerous.

By 1936 the danger seemed so great that much of the consumer program of the Second Five-Year Plan was given up. Far greater attention was paid to the production of military goods. Need for clothing, refrigerators, and the like had to take second place to the production of guns, tanks, planes, and ammunition. The Third Five-Year Plan, begun in 1938, was almost entirely devoted to military needs. It was necessary, because in the summer of 1941, without a declaration of war and in violation of a nonaggression treaty, German armies poured into Russia.

From 1928 until 1941 the Russian people received very little in better living for all the sacrifices they had made for the Five-Year Plans. Life continued to be hard and grim. City populations lived under very crowded conditions. Peasants were forced into the collective farms. Many of those who resisted were exiled or executed. These included many of the most prosperous and successful farmers. Almost eighty per cent of all peasants were included in the collectives, but they were bitter, resentful, and uncoöperative.

There was no doubt that farming in large collectives did increase production. Machinery and scientific methods could be used in a way that was impossible in small strips individually owned and operated. But peasant opposition was so great that in 1936 the government had to ease up on its policy. It allowed peasants to own their houses, garden plots, and a few animals, and to sell the produce.

The Russian police state

Hard material conditions were not the only costs of the communist program. There were other costs, difficult to measure in any of the usual terms. How could we measure the cost to the individual of the "police state," with all that it means? It involves a life of constant fear and suspicion, a distrust of friends, neighbors, fellow workers, and even members of one's own family. A person never knew who might be an informer, or a member of the secret police. People had to conform, to agree, to express no opinion at all, or express only the opinion of the dictators. It was not always safe to accept and advocate the opinion of the moment. The "party line," the policy of the Communist Party, which controlled the government, did change from time to time, often rapidly and very greatly. A person who did not change with the "party line," who continued to express yesterday's or last week's accepted opinion, became, therefore, a critic of the government. He was an "enemy of the state."

The actual membership of the Communist Party was always small—possibly 2,500,000 out of the more than 200,000,000 people of the Soviet Union. Admission to the party was difficult. Expulsion was easy for any slightest violation of the very strict party regulations. At intervals there were "purges" during which party members, including high leaders, were tried and executed for suspected "deviations," or disloyalties. Of course, the Communist Party remained *the* party; no opposition party was tolerated. There were elections, but there was only one list of candidates. They were always men or women approved in advance by the party.

The official name of the government is the Union of Soviet Socialist Republics (U.S.S.R.). The Union is made up of fifteen republics, of which the Russian Socialist

A trolleybus stop in Revolution Square, Moscow.

Federated Soviet Republic is the largest. The constitution has a Bill of Rights which states sweeping protection to the rights of individuals. Outwardly it looks like a representative, democratic, parliamentary government. In practice, this "parliament" exists only to give rubber-stamp approval to the decisions of top Communist Party leaders. The guarantees of individual liberties mean little.

The dictatorship became harsher as time passed. At the beginning of the second Five-Year Plan there were signs that it was relaxing. But the increasing foreign danger brought a stiffening dictatorial control. Historians and students of Russian communism disagree as to whether the relaxations of 1933 and 1934 were really meant to be the beginning of free living. Communists promised a "classless society," but the communist leaders had made themselves a ruling class. They had great power, authority, and prestige. It seems natural that they should try to hold on to it, and make themselves ever more secure. An English historian once stated what seems to be a universal truth: "All power corrupts, and absolute power tends to corrupt absolutely." The Soviet leaders wield absolute power.

● *Opposition to the dictatorship*

The fact that there was no permitted opposition did not mean that no opposition existed. In such cases opposition "goes underground." The factory worker works slowly and is absent regularly because of "illness." He may damage machinery "by accident," or spoil the articles he works on. This is called sabotage. Soviet law regards sabotage as a grave offense, but it is hard to detect and combat such deliberate abuse. On the farm, sabotage may take the form of planting less, slaughtering cattle, underfeeding cattle and poultry to cut down production of milk, other dairy products, and eggs. The Russian peasant has shown a genius for this sort of resistance and for evading government orders.

Foreign relations

● *The Comintern*

The Communist government of Russia could find no allies in Europe. The capitalist nations in western Europe, and the United States, feared Russian communism. They feared that the communists would take advantage of the disturbed conditions of a post-war world to stir up widespread communist revolutions. The communists gave them enough reason to fear. There were communist parties in many lands. In Moscow there was a world organization known as the Communist International, or Comintern. Working through the local communists in other lands, it tried to arouse workers, and especially colonial peoples. The Comintern urged them to overthrow their governments and set up societies with no privileged classes. Peasants were promised the estates of large landowners. Industrial workers were promised a fairer share of the things they produced. Such an open call to violence and revolution was bound to create fear, suspicion, and hostility in the outside world.

● *Buffer states isolate Russia*

The reaction was to isolate Russia in Europe—to try to make it impossible for Russian influence to spread. There was established what the French call a *cordon sanitaire,* or quarantine. A line of hostile states was set up all around European Russia to act as buffers, or shock absorbers, in case the Russians attempted to march westward. Look at them on the map. Beginning with Finland on the north, running down through Estonia, Latvia, and Lithuania along the Baltic, then swinging overland through Poland and Rumania, the buffer states isolated Russia completely from western Europe by land.

The rulers of the buffer states had to make some reforms so that communist propaganda would have less appeal. Some of the large estates were divided among the peasants. Of

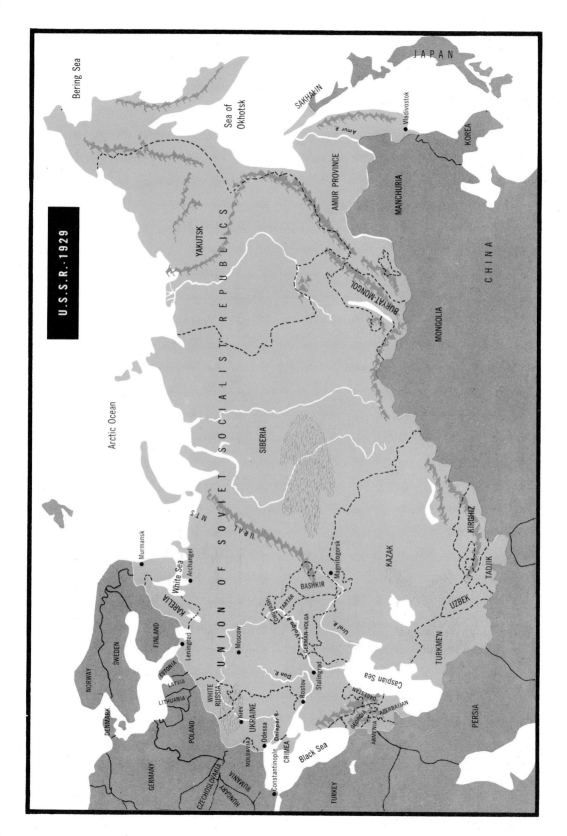

U.S.S.R. · 1929

Bering Sea

Sea of Okhotsk

JAPAN

SAKHALIN

Vladivostok

KOREA

Amur R.

AMUR PROVINCE

MANCHURIA

YAKUTSK

BURYAT-MONGOL

CHINA

MONGOLIA

Arctic Ocean

SIBERIA

REPUBLICS

SOCIALIST

SOVIET

OF

UNION

UR·A·L MTS

KIRGHIZ

TADJIK

KAZAK

Magnitogorsk

BASHKIR

UZBEK

CHUVASH

TARTAR

GERMAN-VOLGA

Volga R.

Ural R.

TURKMEN

Murmansk

White Sea

Archangel

KARELIA

FINLAND

SWEDEN

NORWAY

ESTONIA

LATVIA

LITHUANIA

DENMARK

POLAND

GERMANY

CZECHOSLOVAKIA

HUNGARY

RUMANIA

Leningrad

Moscow

WHITE RUSSIA

Kiev

UKRAINE

Odessa

Dnieper R.

MOLDAVIA

CRIMEA

Constantinople

Black Sea

Don R.

Rostov

Stalingrad

Caspian Sea

DAGESTAN

GEORGIA

AZERBAIJAN

ARMENIA

TURKEY

PERSIA

611

course, the former owners were well paid. An attempt was made to raise standards of living for workers. It was not easy. Much of the territory of the buffer states had belonged to prewar Russia, and had natural economic ties with Russia in transportation, marketing, and the exchange of products. These ties had to be broken for fear economic relations might lead to political control. But economic relations are stubborn things. They do not change easily. The new states had to spend much money for armies and defense preparations against a possible Soviet military move to regain the lost territory. All in all, the economic condition of the buffer states was not very healthy. It is doubtful that they could have stayed free through the 1920's and 1930's without financial help which they constantly received from the Western nations.

To the south, also, Russia found no allies. Turkey, greatly reduced in territory, had become a republican dictatorship under Mustafa Kemal. His program of reforms and industrialization aimed to Westernize Turkey. The old Turkish fear and suspicion of Russia did not change. Czarist or communist, the Russians still cast longing eyes at Constantinople and the straits leading out of the Black Sea. These were stubborn facts of economics and geography, not of political government. Fear of Russian interference and influence was found in Turkey, too.

Much the same things happened in Persia, or Iran as it was now called. A limited constitutional government had been set up. Power was carefully held in the hands of the large landowners, who kept almost feudal conditions on their great estates. They offered a good chance for communist propaganda, but the official government remained strongly anti-communist.

Thus from the tip of land in the Arctic Ocean all the way around beyond the Black Sea the Soviet Union found itself ringed with a solid barrier of hostile buffer states. Behind them were the openly hostile and aggressive Germany and Italy. France, Britain, and the United States were strongly anti-communist, and gave needed financial and military support to the buffer states.

● Communist propaganda in Asia

In Asia, however, the situation was entirely different. Japan, to be sure, was strongly anti-communist and threatened to be aggressive. In other Asiatic countries there were all the materials for a two-way revolution. People in the colonial empires—in India, Indo-China, and the East Indies—were in revolt against colonial imperialism. They wanted national independence from the West. Within these countries another movement was taking shape. The poor people, especially the peasants, were ripe for revolution against the wealthy landowners, on whom they blamed so much of their poverty and misery. Asia seethed, not only with nationalism but also with a demand for economic improvements, for a better way of life.

This was a situation that looked good for Soviet propaganda. Communism, they could say, opposed imperialism and favored economic improvement of the masses. The Soviet government could point to the fact that under communism land had been given to the peasants and that great strides were made toward industrialization. They did not, of course, speak of the lack of freedom under dictatorship, nor of the price the Russian people paid for whatever achievement had been attained. And even if this had been known, it might not have carried much weight with the people of Asia. They had never known much freedom of the sort that was lacking in Russia. Then, too, many of them were at the point where rice—the next meal—might be far more important than abstract ideas like freedom, justice, and the rights of the individual. Asia presented a great opportunity for the Russian communists in this struggle for the minds of men. It still offers an opportunity for communism.

Review of Chapter 47

People, places, and things

Identify: Nikolai Lenin, Joseph Stalin, Soviet, U.S.S.R., Comintern, Duma, Bolsheviks, "party line," collective farms, Five-Year Plan.

Locate: Estonia, Latvia, Lithuania, Finland, Turkey, the principal states of Russia. The boundaries of Russia in 1914 and in 1921. Note where Russia lost territory and to what nations.

Events in review

1. What weaknesses in the Russian Empire showed up during World War I?
2. After the fall of the Romanov monarchy, what two groups began to struggle for power in Russia? Which group won?
3. What is meant by the doctrine of world revolution?
4. When the Communists became masters of Russia, they faced two great contradictions between their theories and the actual facts. What were these contradictions?
5. Briefly describe Lenin's New Economic Policy.
6. What is meant by a planned economy? When did Russia change from the N.E.P. to a planned economy?
7. Briefly describe the effects of the Five-Year Plans on Russian farmers.

8. What sort of elections are held in Russia? What is the function of the "parliament"?
9. Approximately what proportion of the population of Russia belonged to the Communist Party?
10. What was meant by the *cordon sanitaire*?

Problems and projects

1. The Russians claim that economic freedom (the right to work) is far more important than political freedom (the right to vote, hold free discussion of issues, and the like). How would you reply to this claim?
2. What were the aims of the First and Second Five-Year Plans? What factors contributed to the failure of these plans? Why was so little attention given to producing such consumer goods as cosmetics and attractive clothes. Do you think that a less harsh policy might have led to greater production of all kinds of goods?
3. Discuss the ways in which the communist regime is typical of the "police state" described in Chapter 46.
4. Discuss the claim of Soviet Russia that a "classless society" was created.
5. Review the section on Karl Marx in Chapter 29. How much do you think the communist state in Russia resembles the sort of state Marx proposed?

Chapter 48

The Fascist Dictatorships

THE SEARCH for new solutions to the old problems of peace, security, and a better way of life may lead peoples in many directions, under many ideas. The Russians took the direction of dictatorship of the left: that is, communism. The Italians followed another guidepost to the dictatorship of the right: fascism.

Problems of postwar democracy in Italy

Parliamentary government runs into trouble in countries where there are more than two major political parties. In order to get a majority in parliament, two or more parties have to combine into a coalition. A coalition is very hard to hold together long enough to carry out any sort of long-range program. Often a coalition government can remain in power only by doing nothing. It avoids problems because the parties to the coalition cannot agree on a solution. Such was the case in Italy.

Italy's problems were tremendous, complicated, and almost insolvable. They would have been hard to solve even if some one party had controlled the government with a large majority. There was, first, the basic problem of a poor land with a large population. There

was not enough food to supply the needs of the people, and the country lacked the raw materials to support industries. The soil of Italy had begun to wear out and run down even in the days of the Roman Empire. The long centuries following had done little to improve it.

Italy entered World War I with the expectation of imperial gains in the Tyrol, the Dalmatian coast, Albania, Africa, and the Near East. The Versailles treaties did give her some of the Austrian Tyrol, Istria, and a few islands near the coast of Turkey. Still the Italians felt that these were not enough and thought that they had been deceived. These lost lands became "Italia Irredenta"—Italy Unredeemed.

World War I and the postwar period took their toll in Italy, as elsewhere. There was heavy loss of life, a crushing burden of debt, unemployment, and inflation. There were labor troubles, including many violent strikes. All sorts of groups promised solutions of all kinds, from the most reactionary people on the right to the most radical communists on the left. The democratic Italian government (a constitutional monarchy) seemed paralyzed and helpless to meet the pressing needs of the situation.

The rise of Fascism

The man who came out from obscurity with promises to solve all problems, to save Italy from confusion, division, civil war, and communism, was Benito Mussolini. He came from a humble family; his father was a blacksmith. He was self-taught, and his education was scanty. In his younger days he had belonged to the extreme left wing of the Socialist Party, and had published a newspaper. He had served a term in jail, and had had to flee into exile because of his views. During the war his views changed. He was expelled from the Socialist Party and became an extreme nationalist. During Italy's neutrality he had strongly advocated entrance on the Allied side. When this happened, he joined the army, fought, and was wounded.

● *Mussolini's program*

When Mussolini returned from the war, his political views had shifted still further. He did not rejoin the socialists, but began to organize his own party. He called it *Fascisti,* or *Fascist.* The words *fascist* and *fascism* come from the Latin word *fasces.* The fasces was a bundle of rods and an axe, the symbol of governmental authority in Roman days. Mussolini found his first followers among the veterans and discontented nationalists. His first program advocated many liberal, and even socialist, ideas, but it expressed complete opposition to socialism and communism.

Gradually, however, the Fascists attracted another following. Businessmen, especially the large manufacturers, were attracted by the anti-communist program. They gave the Fascists much financial support. Professional men also joined. There was great support among the lower middle classes, grievously hurt by the inflation, and also among the unemployed.

Now there came a change in the program. Mussolini announced the protection of private property and of the middle class. He came out firmly against the proletariat, the industrial working class. The anti-communist and anti-socialist pledges were stronger than ever. Of course, there were promises for everyone: full employment, public order, social security, and national glory. Italy would gain all her war aims, and there would be a return to all the glories of the Roman Empire.

The Fascist Party began a violent campaign against its opponents, especially the socialists and communists. Fascists broke up strikes, assaulted individual opponents, attacked opposition political meetings and beat up the speakers and anyone who attempted to defend them. This violence was carried on, they said, because the government could not defend the state from these enemies within. Fascists adopted a black shirt as their uniform. The more confusion and discontent there was in Italy, the stronger became the black-shirted ranks.

● *Mussolini becomes dictator*

By 1922 the party had become so strong that the king was persuaded to choose Mussolini as prime minister, and ask him to form a government. By the end of the following year Mussolini had changed the government of Italy to a fascist dictatorship. Fascists were appointed to all official positions, both in the central government and in the provinces. A new election law was passed. The party that received the most votes got two thirds of the seats in the Chamber of Deputies, the lower house of parliament. Winning the election was a matter of controlling the voting places by Fascists. Once the Fascists had their majority, they voted "decree powers" to Mussolini. He could pass a law just by signing a decree. He became *Il Duce*—The Leader.

Now all the trappings of dictatorship appeared. The opposition parties were wiped out by intimidation, kidnapping, assault, and actual murder. Local democratic governments in towns and cities were abolished, to

Mussolini and a group of his Fascist followers in 1922. The civilian suit he wore when this picture was taken was soon replaced by a military uniform. From 1923 until World War II Mussolini ruled Italy as dictator.

be replaced by officials appointed from Rome. Freedom of speech, press, assembly, and trial by jury were suspended. Free labor unions were abolished and strikes were prohibited. Labor unions were reorganized under the control of the government. The police, both regular and secret, were everywhere. Mussolini became commander in chief of the army, navy, air force, and police. The powers of both Senate and Chamber of Deputies were reduced. They could consider only laws which Il Duce introduced. The real power was concentrated in the hands of the Grand Council of the Fascist Party. This Council was made up of some twenty of the leaders. At the head, of course, was Mussolini. The government, controlled by the Fascist Party, regulated every phase of the life of the people. The individual was ordered to serve the welfare of the state. The slogan "Believe! Obey! Work!" appeared everywhere.

● *The corporate state*

The Fascists did have a philosophy of government and a plan for reconstruction. When they had established themselves firmly in power, they put their idea into practice. In most governments men are chosen to represent the people of a geographic area. In the Congress of the United States there are two senators from each state and a representative from each congressional district in a state. In the Italian Fascist state, men did not represent geographic regions; they represented occupations. The principal economic activities such as agriculture, manufacturing, commerce, and transportation were formed into thirteen syndicates, or corporations. In each field there was a syndicate for employers and another for employees. These syndicates were united and controlled by a Ministry of Corporations. The first Minister was, naturally, Benito Mussolini. All strikes or lockouts were forbidden; all labor disputes were arbitrated by the government. Workers now had to belong to the syndicate of their trade, and this syndicate was controlled by the government.

In 1927, to improve the sorrowful condition of Italian workers, Il Duce had his parliament enact a Charter of Labor. It had many fine provisions. Night workers were to be paid more than day workers. All workers were to have annual paid vacations. Sunday was a day of no work. The government provided social security and insurance. The workers were still waiting for the complete enforcement of the Charter twelve years later, when World War II broke out. But employers found little to complain of.

The Fascist government did solve some problems. It restored public order, eliminated strikes, and suppressed violence of all kinds. It did reduce unemployment. Industry and agriculture were both increased and made more prosperous. A great program of public works was begun: buildings, schools, roads, the draining of marshes. The famous Pontine

Marshes at the mouth of the Tiber River had been a source of malarial mosquitoes since Roman days. They were drained and turned into farm land. Education was greatly increased. School attendance was made compulsory to the age of fourteen. Illiteracy, which had been 40 per cent in 1913, was reduced to 25 per cent by 1939. The education, of course, was Fascist. Children studied lessons specially prepared to teach the doctrines of fascism, the virtue of Il Duce, the glories of Italy, and the evils of those who denied Italy her "rightful claims." The army and navy were greatly increased. This program of building up armaments achieved a double purpose. It added to the military strength of Italy and helped reduce unemployment. War was advertised as being a glorious, patriotic adventure.

The picture had its other side, too. Such a program is costly, and the treasury of the Italian government was never well filled. The standard of living of the people, already low, went down even more. The old basic problem remained: too many people, too little food, too few natural resources. The expanded armed forces placed a heavy financial burden on the people. When the depression hit Italy at the end of the 1920's, the new government faced a severe test.

● Foreign policy: the colonial solution

The only solution the Fascist government could find for this basic problem was colonies. The Italian colony of Libya, in North Africa, was developed to some extent. It was a poor place, mostly desert. In the 1930's, colonial expansion seemed a little out-of-date except to the "have-not" nations. There was not much colonial territory left to take in the crowded world. To try to take some that was already occupied was risky business. But there was one African territory not held by any great power. Furthermore, it adjoined two existing Italian colonies. It was Ethiopia, about which you will learn more later.

Mussolini decreed that fascist leaders must be rugged, and he made them prove their toughness by diving through flaming hoops. This photo was taken in 1938.

Difficulties of the Weimar Republic in Germany

Germany's defeat in 1918 brought the end of the German Empire. The kaiser abdicated and sought safety in neutral Holland. The temporary government called a constitutional assembly at Weimar. Under the constitution adopted there, Germany became a federal democratic republic. It had an elected president and an elected two-house legislature.

In the lower house, the Reichstag, political parties were represented directly according to the number of votes they received. In the upper house, the Bundesrat, the seventeen states were represented. No state, not even Prussia, was now allowed to have more than two-fifths of the total number of members. There was a cabinet, or ministry, made up of members of the majority party in the Reichstag. The prime minister was called the chancellor. There was universal suffrage for both men and women.

In the first election there were seven political parties, ranging from the Spartacists (Communists) on the extreme left to the Nationalists, who wanted a return of monarchy, on the extreme right. There were two socialist parties, which differed concerning the speed with which industry and property were to be nationalized. In 1919 and 1920, the moderate socialists controlled the government. Thereafter there was a swing to the right. The parties representing big business, the middle class, and the Nationalists gained power.

The Weimar Republic had a hard time from the very beginning. There was much opposition in Germany to the idea of republican government. At first the communists tried to seize the government, and were put down only by force and bloodshed. A year later, in 1920, the monarchists attempted to overthrow the republic. An armed force marched on Berlin and forced the republican government to flee to safety. This movement was crushed by a general strike of the people. Thereafter the socialists were kept out of the cabinet. Two prominent liberal leaders were assassinated.

The difficulties of the republic did not spring from political opinions only. They were really reflections of the great economic, social, and political problems that came from the war. Germany, like other nations, went through all the troubles of the postwar period. Unemployment was very great; inflation reached dreadful proportions. In the Versailles treaty the country lost much in territory and resources. There was also the difficult problem of reparations. People had a natural tendency to blame everything on the loss of the war, especially on the harshness and injustice (from the German point of view) of the treaty. The Weimar Republic had the added burden of having signed the treaty for Germany; so it had to take part of the blame. (See pages 571–572 for the terms of the treaty.)

In spite of these handicaps, the republic did survive. From 1924, when the inflation was ended, until 1929, when the depression began, conditions actually improved. But they were still bad enough. There was still much unemployment, and the lower middle class was in a wretched condition. The depression, of course, made things very much worse.

Economic conditions always affect politics. Conditions in Germany are shown by the fact that in the election of 1930 twenty-seven parties presented candidates. The moderate socialists received the most votes, but two opposite extreme parties made great gains. Out of some 500 members of the Reichstag, the extreme leftist communists held seventy-six seats. A new party of the extreme right, the National Socialists, gained ninety-five seats.

The rise of Nazism

The new party was the personal creation of a most extraordinary man, Adolf Hitler. He was born in Austria in 1889, the son of a minor customs official. Little is known of his early career. He tried to be an artist, but failed and became a house painter. He served as a volunteer in the German army during World War I. Although he received an Iron Cross for bravery, he did not rise above the rank of corporal.

●Hitler's program

When the war ended, Hitler was an unhappy, bitter, and frustrated man. He publicly criticized the republican government for accepting the humiliating peace terms. In 1923 he joined the German General von Ludendorff in an attempt to overthrow the government. The revolt was quickly put down, and Hitler served almost a year in prison. While there, he wrote a very curious book called *Mein Kampf* (My Battle). In it he set down his idea of how he would make Germany once more a great power in Europe and the world.

Mein Kampf is a very poor book, judged either by its style or what it has to say. It is full of bad writing and pompous preaching. In places it resembles the ravings of a madman. But it was to become almost a Bible in Germany. That a highly cultured people like the Germans should accept such drivel, and raise its writer almost to the level of a divine being is a dangerous and a troubling thing.

Hitler was a gifted orator. Wherever he found an opportunity and an audience, he harangued. His National Socialist Party promised all things to all people. This is shown even in its full name: The German National Socialist Workers' Party—something there for everyone. It came to be known as the Nazi Party, for short. The Nazis wore brown shirts as a uniform.

In *Mein Kampf* and in his speeches Hitler justified the "socialist" part of the party name by such promises as land reforms, better working conditions, social legislation, nationalization of big business, and the abolition of unearned profits. But there was much heavier emphasis on the "National" part. He promised to repeal the Versailles Treaty, especially the "war-guilt" clause. He would restore Germany to equality in armaments, regain all the lost territory and colonies, and

Hitler and von Hindenburg in 1933, when Hitler became chancellor of Germany. Hitler (a corporal in World War I) wears formal civilian clothes. Von Hindenburg, one of the great generals of the war, wears his uniform. The spiked helmet recalls the Prussian uniforms of Bismarck's day.

even build a "Greater Germany." This would come at the expense of Poland and the rich wheat fields and natural resources of the Soviet Union. Although he made some "socialist" promises and favored dictatorship, he was completely opposed to communism.

To these promises Hitler added another, and uglier, side to his policies—his garbled philosophy of the "master race." According to this philosophy, the Germans were the Aryans, the master race. All other peoples were inferior. The Slavic Poles and Russians were fit only to serve the Aryan masters. The Negro race he considered hardly human, while the Jews were to be totally exterminated.

● *Hitler becomes dictator*

Until 1929, when the depression came, the Nazis made little impression on the German people. The depression changed the picture

A rally of Nazi Storm Troopers in Hitler's Germany. The mass of steel-helmeted men lined up facing the swastikas shows several of the characteristics of dictatorship: emphasis on military might, and stress on extreme nationalism.

entirely. The hardships, unemployment, and miseries of the depression brought a great increase in Nazi strength. People saw no solution to their problems. In despair they turned to Der Fuehrer, "The Leader," the man who promised prosperity, security, and glory if they would trust everything to him. In elections in 1932 the Nazis became the second largest party in the Reichstag. In a crucial election in March, 1933, they gained the largest number of seats, although not a majority. In these elections both the communist and socialist vote declined greatly.

The president of Germany, General Paul von Hindenburg, offered Hitler a cabinet position in a coalition government under a Nationalist chancellor, but the Nazi leader arrogantly declined it. So the aged president reluctantly appointed Hitler chancellor and allowed him to form a cabinet. Once in command as chancellor, Hitler was able to seize power in much the same way Mussolini had in Italy. He also was given "decree power." Thus Germany followed Italy to dictatorship of the right.

The Nazi system

The Nazi regime had all the usual accompaniments of dictatorship. Opposition political parties were immediately dissolved, as were all labor unions. All government—national, state, and local—was centralized under the Nazi Party and Der Fuehrer. Labor organizations were "coördinated" under the government. Even the churches, both Catholic and Protestant, were placed under state control. Opposition newspapers were suppressed; those allowed to publish were heavily censored. The government took control of all radio stations. There was a death penalty for broadcasting without a license. The schools were also taken under control so that children would be brought up as believers in Nazi doctrine and the wonders of Der Fuehrer.

Members of opposition groups—liberals, socialists, communists—were thrown into concentration camps. A goodly number managed to escape abroad. The worst punishment went to the Jews. A series of laws, the Nuremberg Decrees, took away all their civil and political rights, and they were subjected to hideous persecution.

The Nazis managed to reduce unemployment, thanks to a great program of public works, buildings, roads, and canals. Industry expanded, especially war industry. Hitler declared that Germany would rearm, and his promise did not take long to be put into effect. The Allies did nothing to enforce the disarmament provision of the Versailles Treaty. The slogan throughout Germany was, "What Germany needs is not butter, but guns." Only thus, Hitler argued, could Germany win the respect of the world. Although more people were actually at work, the standard of living in Germany slowly went down.

Nazi foreign policy

Hitler's nationalist program stated several main goals. The Versailles Treaty was to be canceled and all German territory regained. Even this would not be enough. Germany, said Hitler, needed *lebensraum*—living space. According to the Nazis, it was not right that the great German "master race" should have to live in such cramped quarters when the "inferior" Slavs in eastern Europe had so much precious land. After this Greater Germany had been attained, leadership in Europe would be snatched from France. Great Britain would be forced out from any influence on the Continent. Once Europe was mastered, the world of Africa and Asia lay beyond. There were no limits to the expansion of the "master race." The first step toward fulfillment of such an ambitious program was rearmament.

Germany marches into the Rhineland

In 1936, after three years of rearmament, Hitler was ready to try out both his own strength and British and French willingness to resist it. According to the Versailles Treaty the Rhineland, German territory on the west bank, the French side, of the Rhine, was to be demilitarized. There were to be no fortifications or German troops there. In the spring of 1936 the new German army marched into the Rhineland and occupied it. The other powers watched the act and did nothing. Only France sent a diplomatic note of protest. The first step proved successful. It was only natural that the next step was to follow. For a while, however, Hitler stopped, getting himself ready for further moves. You will soon learn what these further moves were. For the present, we shall take a look at happenings in Spain.

Fascist dictatorship in Spain

On a small scale, developments in Spain during the 1930's really represented the rest of Europe. A young democracy grew up, struggling hard with grave political, social, and economic problems. It was killed by a fascist movement from within, aided by the fascist dictators in Italy and Germany. It received some aid from the Russian communist dictatorship, but the democracies followed the course of appeasement and allowed the fascist cause to win.

● Spain in the nineteenth and twentieth centuries

Spain had lagged far behind the rest of Western Europe in the developments of the nineteenth and early twentieth centuries. It was a poor country. Much of the land was barren, and it did not have many mineral resources. There was some industrial development, but the country was mainly agricultural. Much of the land was owned in large estates by the nobility. The Catholic Church was very powerful. It was an established Church, supported by taxation, with the clergy paid by the government. The Church controlled the educational system; it also controlled much wealth.

The government of Spain was a constitutional monarchy. The power of the king was limited by an elected parliament, the Cortes. The history of Spain up to the beginning of World War I was a troubled story. There were strikes, violence, political assassination, suspension of constitutional guarantees and declaration of martial law, military plots, separatist movements in the provinces, and much radicalism of every variety.

Many radical movements were directed against the Church. Opponents felt that the Church was too conservative, using its great power and influence to prevent needed political, social, and economic reforms. However, they found it very difficult to criticize the Church on these grounds without being accused of heresy and attacks on the faith.

In the period after World War I the disordered conditions in Spain grew worse. From 1923 to 1931, with the unspoken approval of the king, a military dictatorship tried to stamp out all liberal and democratic movements. Opposition pressures built up, and in 1931 the dictator resigned. A local election showed a republican landslide, and the king left the country. Political leaders declared Spain a republic and set up a provisional government.

● The Spanish republic

A general election chose a constitutional assembly dominated by liberal republicans, who wrote a very democratic constitution. Spain was to be ruled by a one-house Cortes (legislature), with a president, premier, and cabinet responsible to it. Elections were to be by universal suffrage. There was to be freedom of religion. Church and state were to be separated, and education was to be secular (non-Church). The government was given much control over industry and property, and public utilities were to be government-owned and operated.

The elected republican government put these reforms into effect very rapidly. Land taken from the Church and the nobles was given to landless peasants. Clergymen were barred from teaching in schools, and were no longer paid by the government. Workers were given shorter hours, better wages, the right to organize, and a voice in the management of business.

These sweeping reforms brought conservative opposition both in Spain and abroad. The religious changes were bitterly opposed,

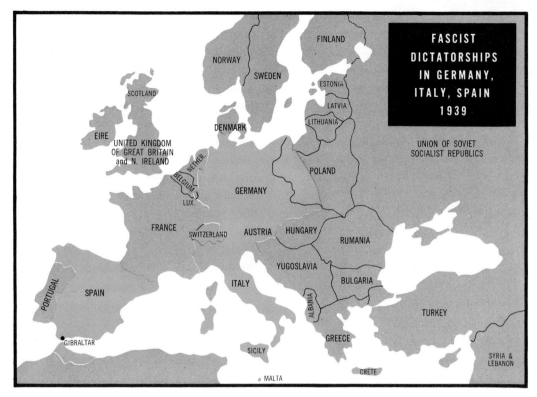

as were the seizures of land and the new rights of labor. Many people, including most of the officers of the army, wanted to return to a monarchy.

The most extreme radicals—communists and anarchists—wanted even more drastic changes. To achieve them, and to prevent a feared seizure of the government by the conservatives, the radicals stirred up strikes and riots, which the government suppressed by force. Successive elections produced more conservative governments and slowed down changes and reforms.

● Rebellion and civil war in Spain

In 1936 a general election was won by a Popular Front (coalition) of liberals and radical groups. A coalition government of liberal republicans, distrusting the loyalty of many army officers, discharged some with pensions and transferred others to the colonies. This move touched off a revolt of army groups in Morocco, the Canary Islands, and

Spain itself. The rebel army was led by General Francisco Franco. The rebels received help from the German and Italian dictatorships, in the form of fully organized and equipped "volunteer" units.

The Loyalists—the supporters of the elected republican government—had few loyal troops and fewer military leaders. To get the support of radical groups in Spain they admitted socialists and communists to their government. This added to their problems, for the communists then worked from within to gain control, so that the republicans had to fight a double war. After admitting communists to the government the Loyalists received some help from Soviet Russia, although it was difficult for Soviet aid to reach Spain. It was a war of unequal forces, for the Loyalists were more poorly organized, equipped, and disciplined than their Spanish, Italian, and German enemies.

The Spanish civil war became a small scale European war. Germany and Italy saw a

The Spanish civil war: Republican fighters with shotguns and automobiles in the street of Valencia.

fascist Spain as a link in their chain around France. Soviet Russia saw Spain as a possible ally, perhaps even a communist state, in Western Europe. Both sides used the Spanish war as a sort of testing ground for new weapons and tactics.

"Nonintervention"

The British and French did not want to see Spain go to either side. More than anything else, they feared that the Spanish war might spread to the rest of Europe and involve them. In 1937, Great Britain and France called a conference of European nations, including Germany and Italy, but not the Soviet Union. All agreed to a policy of nonintervention in Spain, with a blockade to stop the flow of "volunteers" and supplies. The agreement proved to be a diplomatic fraud. The blockade stopped most of the aid to the Loyalists, but not German and Italian aid to Franco. To Hitler and Mussolini this was one more proof that Britain and France would do nothing to stop aggression unless it directly involved their own territory.

Victory for Franco's forces

The Spanish civil war ended in March, 1939, with a Franco victory. It was during his campaign to capture Madrid that one of Franco's generals used an expression which has since come into every language. He an-

nounced that he had four columns marching on Madrid, and a "fifth column" of people within the city who would rise against the defenders when the right time came. Since then the expression "fifth column" is universally used to mean traitors within a country who give aid to its enemies.

The three-year war nearly bled Spain white. The country was devastated, and more than a million people had lost their lives. The sufferings of the Spanish people during the war, and long after, can hardly be imagined. Many years would have to pass before the country could recover from the economic destruction and from the bitterness and hatred caused by the war.

Spanish fascism

The Spanish government of General Franco closely resembled the fascist dictatorships in Italy and Germany. Like Mussolini and Hitler, Franco became head of the state, with unlimited power. He was responsible, as one decree said, "only to God and history." Like his teachers, he assumed a title: El Caudillo—the Chieftain. His party, the *Falange,* was the only one permitted. Its National Council, chosen by Franco, "advised" him on legislation. The economic organization of the country resembled that of Fascist Italy, with syndicates, or corporations, organized by occupations and economic activities. There were all the police activities and suppressions customarily found under an autocratic form of government.

The changes made by the republicans were all done away with. All property was restored to those who had held it before the republican reforms were put into effect (see page 622).

Needless to say, the army occupied a privileged position under the new government and gave loyal support to the dictatorship of General Franco. Thus, on the eve of World War II one more democracy went down the road to dictatorship.

The Spanish civil war: Italian infantry with rifles and tanks advancing through olive groves near Toledo. Franco's forces were strengthened by numbers of Italian and German technicians, by combat troops, and by supplies of modern artillery, aircraft, tanks, and other weapons and materials of war. In the picture at the right, note the tracks in the foreground, made by tank treads.

Review of Chapter 48

People, places, and things

Identify: Benito Mussolini (Il Duce), Italia Irredenta, Black Shirts, Adolph Hitler (Der Fuehrer), Brown Shirts, Reichstag, Nuremberg Decrees, *Mein Kampf,* Lebensraum, the Falange, Francisco Franco, the Popular Front.

Locate: Libya, Ethiopia, the Rhineland, Spain, Morocco, Canary Islands, Madrid.

Events in review

1. What did Italy hope to gain from World War I? What did she actually receive?
2. What powers did Mussolini hold after he became dictator in Italy.
3. What happened to labor unions after the Fascists came into power?
4. List the problems that faced the Weimar Republic in Germany.
5. What was the connection between the depression (beginning in 1929) and the rise to power of the Nazis?
6. Why did the Fascist and Nazi parties start large programs of public works?
7. Briefly describe the goals of Hitler's foreign policy.
8. What important step did Hitler take in 1936?
9. What groups in Spain opposed the reforms put into effect by the republic after 1931?
10. Explain why the Spanish civil war became a European war on a small scale.

Problems and projects

1. What problems did both Mussolini and Hitler promise to solve? To what extent did they solve certain problems after coming to power? What was the cost to the people of Italy and Germany of these "solutions"?
2. Why did Mussolini's program appeal to many groups in Italy? What conditions in Italy made the people ready to accept a dictator?
3. Compare the Communist, Nazi, and Fascist dictatorships in terms of their effects on individual rights and liberties (freedom of speech, freedom of worship, the right to vote, and the like).
4. What was the Fascist and Nazi policy concerning education? Can you give examples of similar policies used by dictatorial governments in ancient Greece and in nineteenth-century Europe?
5. Write a brief biographical sketch of Mussolini, covering the period from his youth to the time when he became dictator.
6. Write a similar biographical sketch of Hitler. Compare and contrast his career with that of Mussolini.
7. Draw a cartoon to satirize the Fascist or Nazi systems.
8. Make a large chart (poster size) covering the Fascist and Nazi dictatorships. Show effects on labor unions, industry, elections, schools, churches, the press and radio, and minority groups.

Chapter 49   The Postwar Democracies Fail to Support Peace

BY THE TIME the postwar period ended in 1939, only three of the world's great powers were still democracies. Some of the smaller states, such as Holland, Belgium, the Scandinavian countries, Switzerland, and Czechoslovakia, still followed the democratic form of government and way of life. But among the "majors" there were only France, Great Britain, and the United States. The postwar world had not proved "safe for democracy." The difficult and complex problems of the war and postwar period led nation after nation to accept the totalitarian solution of dictatorship. It is interesting to see how the three democratic countries weathered the storm.

France faces problems

The Third French Republic was a typical European parliamentary democracy. There was an elected president, with little power. In the two-house legislature real power was found in the lower house, the Chamber of Deputies. Its members were elected by universal male suffrage for four years. It selected the premier and cabinet to act as the executive. They remained in power only as long as they had a majority of votes in the Chamber. Any time one of their major proposals was defeated, or the Chamber passed a vote of "no confidence," they had to resign their cabinet positions. Then the leaders of another party or parties tried to "form a government" by setting up a cabinet which could command a majority in the Chamber.

●Instability in the government

There were from ten to fifteen important political parties. They ranged from fascists and monarchists on the extreme right to communists on the extreme left. There were also a number of smaller "splinter groups." As a result, coalition governments were always necessary and usually lasted only a short time. In the seventy years between 1870 and 1940, there were 106 different ministries. Thus the average life of a government was less than a year.

French government was a little less shaky and unstable than it looked. The overthrow of a ministry seldom resulted in a general election of a new Chamber of Deputies. It simply meant a reshuffle of cabinet positions among the leaders of the political parties. Often the same coalition of parties would be able to form a new cabinet with a new man as premier and the other positions reshuffled.

626

It was like a game of musical chairs. A large bureaucracy of civil servants kept their jobs regardless of the party in power. However, the short average life of French governments made it hard for any political group to put into effect and carry out a long-range, planned political program.

Gains and losses from the war

France seemed to come out of World War I with great gains. She regained Alsace and Lorraine and took a share of Germany's colonies. She could claim the coal of the Saar Valley for fifteen years, with a chance of getting the territory permanently if the Saarlanders should vote that way after fifteen years. Her former enemy, Germany, was limited in military strength by the treaty. Germany had to pay reparations for war damages and war costs. Two of the newly created states, Poland and Czechoslovakia, were free partly because France had demanded that they be independent; they became her allies. They enabled France to encircle Germany in order to keep the Germans weak and in bounds.

But there was a dark side to the picture, too. Nearly a million and a half French people had died during the war. Much of this loss was from the youngest and strongest men of France. The remaining population was less than thirty-nine millions. The German population was almost twice as great. This gap between the French and German populations troubled France greatly, especially because the French population remained about the same or actually declined during the postwar years. The German population steadily increased.

Northern France had to be rebuilt. Even if Germany had paid reparations, they would have stretched out over a long period of years. Rebuilding of the devastated areas—farms, factories, roads, homes, villages, towns—had to be done quickly and at the expense of the French government.

Financial troubles

Though France managed to lessen her debt, still the country had to face a serious financial problem. It had borrowed from its citizens and from the United States. Inflation took its toll, too. In 1913 the French franc was worth about twenty cents. By 1926 it had fallen to two cents, and it was finally "stabilized" at four cents. This meant that anyone who had bought government bonds in 1913 had lost eighty per cent of the money invested.

The finances of the Third Republic had always been bad. The landowners and the industrialists were able to avoid paying their fair share of taxes. The taxes fell mostly on the industrial workers and the lower middle class. The French tax rate was the highest in western Europe, but taxes did not fall where the wealth really was. Therefore, they did not produce enough money to pay the heavy expenses of the postwar years. The government did not dare to try to make the taxes fairer, for this seemed politically impossible. No party or coalition which proposed such a measure could have stayed in power. Instead, France borrowed more money by selling bonds or printing more paper money. These actions made the value of the franc go down and prices go up.

The expenses of the French government continued to be heavy for several reasons. The number of civil servants—that is, government employees—increased during and after the war. There was also the cost of repairing the damaged areas and the heavy debt payments. Most important, perhaps, was security. Twice in less than fifty years France had been invaded by Germans. Frenchmen seemed willing to make many sacrifices to prevent this from happening again.

Defense: the Maginot Line

The French army was kept large, and the navy was built up. A line of steel and concrete

A section of the Maginot Line: barbed wire, to stop infantry, and steel rails, to stop tanks. Behind these rows of obstacles was a complicated system of underground forts. Turrets for guns projected from the surface of the ground. Under them were living quarters, magazines, power plants, storerooms, hospitals, and communications centers, all buried in concrete and earth.

fortifications about 360 miles long was built solidly along the German and Luxembourg frontiers. This fortification was named, for the engineer who planned it, the Maginot Line. It had a great and disastrous influence on French thinking, both military and civilian. The French were prepared to fight the last war over again. Since defense—trench warfare—had been its greatest feature, they planned to make French defenses impregnable so that the country could never again be invaded by land from the east. They built a huge trench system between France and Germany.

● International affairs

The weakness of French governments in the thirties—the shifts in political leadership and the failure to solve economic problems—

took its toll, especially in international affairs. For all the size of her army France seemed an unreliable ally because she was weak financially and lacked a firm policy. She had an alliance with Belgium, but by the mid-1930's the Belgians canceled this alliance. Also, they declared themselves neutral in any future war. France's prewar ally, Russia, was now under communist rule. Although France and the U.S.S.R. formed an alliance, it was a very shaky one because the economic beliefs of the two nations were so different. France's wartime ally, Italy, was now under fascist rule, and Italy's old-time opposition to France reappeared. By 1938 Hitler and Mussolini had formed an open alliance; so France could not count on help there. France's postwar alliances with Poland, Czechoslovakia, Yugoslavia, and Rumania were less dependable. Their strength certainly did not replace that of Russia and Italy.

Only Great Britain was left for France to depend on. But British foreign policy during the 1920's and 1930's was not entirely consistent, either. Postwar France seemed to lose all sense of direction and to drift wherever British policy carried her. During the 1930's the drift was slowly and surely toward war.

What happened especially during the 1930's was a complete shift in the old "balance of power." Prewar France had been backed by strong alliances with Great Britain and imperialist Russia. So she was at least as strong as, and probably stronger than, her rivals. By the mid-1930's the old balance of power was gone, and France had lost leadership. The leadership had been seized by two fascist dictators, Mussolini and, especially, Hitler. Each of them was willing to risk war to gain his aims. France and Britain wanted peace at almost any price.

France lacked the power to resist Germany by force, or she feared that she lacked it. So she chose to bargain for peace. She gave in to each demand of Hitler in the hope he would be satisfied and not ask for more. This policy is known as appeasement. It has never worked in dealing with a strong, ambitious, and unprincipled man like Hitler. Each gain became the stepping stone for the next demand. Each appeasement strengthened the receiver and weakened the giver. This had already been shown by the way Germany was allowed to rearm and to reoccupy the Rhineland.

Problems of the British Empire

Like France, Great Britain seemed to have won a great victory. But as with France, the cost had been great. British colonial possessions were greatly extended. She took the former German colonies as mandates, and she gained in the Near East at the expense of Turkey. She no longer feared Germany as a naval rival. The German fleet had been seized, and the treaty had limited the size of the German navy. Germany had also been removed as an industrial competitor and rival for the world markets, at least for the time being.

The cost was indeed great. First, of course, was that incalculable cost, the loss of lives. Britain, alone among the warring powers, did not have conscription at the beginning of the war. Conscription was not adopted until 1916. Under conscription there is a selection. Men are taken or not, partly according to some estimate of their value to society, or at least to the war effort. In a volunteer war it is often the most patriotic, the "bravest and the best," who go first. The war wiped out the very flower of a generation in Britain. How much poorer the British nation has been since as a result, no one can say.

Britain was not invaded; therefore it did not suffer the destruction of land, farms, towns, and cities that other countries did. But there were heavy losses among the merchant ships on which so much of British prosperity depends.

● *Demands for self-government*

Although the British Empire was larger as a result of the war, it began to show many weaknesses. From all over the world came demands from colonial peoples for more freedom, self-government, or complete independence. In the face of these demands the cost of maintaining the empire became a serious problem. The first really serious trouble came close to home.

Ireland had never been happy under British rule. Centuries of misrule and oppression had given the Irish much reason to hate the English. During the late nineteenth century Britain had given southern Ireland a degree of home rule, but not enough to satisfy the Irish. They wanted complete independence. During the war, with Britain in trouble, the Irish seized the chance to rebel, and a bloody and bitter struggle took place. In 1921 the British gave in. Southern Ireland became the Irish Free State, a self-governing dominion within the British Commonwealth. In 1937 the Irish declared themselves a completely independent republic, taking the name Eire, and Britain made no move to stop them. The six northern counties of Ulster chose to remain in the United Kingdom, with representation in the British Parliament. This division of the island is religious as well as political, and it still troubles the relations between Britain and Eire.

There were similar developments elsewhere. In 1922 Britain was forced to give Egypt, her protectorate, complete independence. The British kept a base to defend the Suez Canal. Then unrest in India forced Britain to give India some self-government, although the British kept control of finance, military affairs, and foreign relations. Iraq, which had been a British mandate in the Near East, was recognized as an independent nation in 1932. Elsewhere in the Near East, mainly in Palestine and Transjordan, people clamored for greater freedom.

The British Commonwealth of Nations

Even in those parts of the empire which already had almost complete self-government, there were demands for more. After the American Revolution the British had followed a wise policy. They had granted much self-government to those parts of the empire which had large English-speaking populations, such as Canada, Australia, New Zealand, and South Africa. For each country Britain still appointed a governor general. He had a veto power over laws, although he did not use it much. Britain also kept control of foreign policy—the making of treaties and the declaration of war. Now these dominions demanded complete self-government. The British showed a genius for accommodation, adjustment, and acceptance of the necessities of life. They gave in without a struggle.

In 1931 an act of the British Parliament, called the Statute of Westminster, recognized the Dominions of Canada, Australia, New Zealand, and South Africa as completely self-governing. The British Parliament has no power to make laws for them in any way. They are still linked with the United Kingdom in a very loose organization called the British Commonwealth of Nations. All recognize the British monarch as their sovereign. Of course the sovereign has no more power in the dominions than at home in Britain. It is the sort of unwritten arrangement which only the British seem able to manage. It works, and it has held together through the strains of World War II and the postwar difficulties.

Economic problems

Britain's economic problems were even more difficult to solve than the political troubles. There was a heavy war debt, both at home and to the United States. The extremely heavy taxes were based mostly on ability to pay. British income and inheritance taxes achieved what it took revolutions to do else-

The governor general of Canada leaving Canada's Parliament buildings. The governor general acts as the representative, in Canada, of the reigning monarch of Great Britain. Just as the monarch has no real power in Britain, the governor general has no major role in Canada. The real head of the government is the prime minister. The governor general serves as a connecting link between Canada and England.

where: the reduction of great fortunes and the breaking up of great estates.

The coal mines on which so much of Britain's industry depended were beginning to be worked out. The remaining seams of coal were narrow and of poor quality. British factories were badly run down. Machinery was worn out or inefficient compared to newer American or Japanese machines. During the war American and Japanese industries had taken over many of the British world markets. Under the handicap of a run-down and less efficient industry, these markets were hard to regain. Yet Britain had to sell abroad to pay for needed imports of food and raw materials. Like Japan, she had to export or die.

In the prewar period British people received a very considerable income from money they had invested abroad. For example, a great many of the stocks and bonds of American corporations were owned in Britain. The dividends and interest on these investments helped Britain to pay for her vital imports. However, during the war the British government had to call in these foreign stocks and bonds and sell them to get money to pay for war supplies from the United States. She could no longer count on this income to help her solve her difficult problem of foreign trade.

● Politics and foreign policy

The war had its effects on British politics and foreign policy. In the period before the war the Liberal Party had carried out a program of reform in political, social, and economic affairs. The war ended this progressive movement. The postwar period was one of Conservative control. The Liberal Party almost disappeared. Most of its members either joined the new Labour Party, representing the socialists and the trade unions, or became Conservatives. The Labour Party grew greatly in strength, but was not yet large enough to win a majority and form a government.

With difficult political and economic problems both at home and in the empire, the British Conservatives had a hard time maintaining any strong and consistent foreign policy. At almost any cost they wished to avoid being drawn into another European or world war. So, with the rise of the dictators, Britain usually followed the policy of appeasement.

Yet the amazing thing is this: Despite all its problems and hardships, Britain did not drift into dictatorship, either of the left or the right. On the contrary, democracy increased in Great Britain. Women were given the right to vote. The socialist Labour Party grew in strength without any official handicaps, and without revolution. The formation of the British Commonwealth was a triumph for democracy and for common sense. Britain gave way slowly to the demands for colonial independence. She held on as long as she could, but she did give way, without trying to use force.

The United States after World War I

The end of World War I found the United States in a much stronger economic position than it had held in 1914. There had been no devastation. Both industry and agriculture had expanded tremendously. The war boom had brought a great deal of prosperity to the country, although the wealth seemed more unevenly divided than ever. Wages had increased greatly; but, generally speaking, prices had gone up even more. People living on wages and salaries were not much better off. Profits, of course, had been enormous.

But our country had its problems to solve. Many parts of the economic system were out of gear. Taxes had increased greatly, though they were mild in comparison to those in European countries. The government had borrowed a great deal of money by selling bonds during the war. The national debt (the money owed by the government to the holders of its bonds) had increased from a little over one billion dollars in 1915 to twenty-five and one-half billions in 1920. There were problems of demobilizing the army and navy and changing industry from wartime to peacetime production. There was considerable inflation; prices had more than doubled between 1913 and 1920. Again, this was mild compared to Europe.

● Foreign policy: isolation

After the war the United States had chosen isolation rather than world coöperation. In addition to its policy of political isolation— "no entangling alliances"—the United States also chose economic isolation. During the 1920's and early 1930's it raised its tariffs to the highest level in history. It was a strange policy, in a way. The United States had a surplus of farm and manufactured goods which it had to sell abroad. It had also loaned money to foreign nations, and it wanted the debts paid. It wanted the payment for the debts and the goods in American money. The best way for foreign people to get American money is to sell goods in the United States. However, American manufacturers were so insistent on high tariffs to keep foreign-made goods from competing in the American market that foreigners could not sell goods to get the money to buy our goods or pay the debts. So we—individual Americans—loaned them more money by buying bonds of foreign governments or foreign corporations. It didn't make much sense, economically, and the depression stopped it. The depression also stopped our sales of goods abroad almost completely.

During the administration of President Franklin D. Roosevelt an effort was made to revive world trade. In 1933 the Reciprocal Trade Agreements Act was passed. It allowed the president to make special agreements with foreign countries. If a foreign nation would lower its tariff rates on some American products, the American government would lower its tariff rates on some of that country's products. United States foreign trade began to recover.

● *Attempts to preserve peace*

Although the United States, in refusing to join the League of Nations, had chosen isolation, it sincerely wanted peace. Its early policy of completely ignoring the League was later modified; American "observers" took part in many League activities concerning labor problems and the drug traffic. In its search for a way to peace the United States, in 1928, joined with France in promoting the Kellogg-Briand Treaty, or Paris Peace Pact.

The signing nations agreed not to go to war with each other, to fight only in self-defense, and to settle all disputes by arbitration. Within five years some sixty-three nations had signed the pact. It was a fine gesture toward peace, but it soon proved meaningless. Treaties and agreements which can be enforced only by public opinion were not worth much in the world of the 1930's.

● *A move for disarmament: the Washington Conference*

The experience of the period before World War I seemed to prove that an armaments race did not necessarily bring peace. Both the Fourteen Points and the covenant of the League of Nations called for a reduction of armaments.

For a time after the war it seemed that Great Britain, Japan, and the United States would engage in a naval building race. This possibility was prevented by a bold diplomatic move by the United States. The secretary of state invited all naval powers interested in the Far East (except the Soviet Union) to send representatives to a conference at Washington. There the nine powers present agreed to a ten-year "holiday" in the building of capital ships (large warships). Total tonnage in capital ships was to be limited to a ratio of $5 : 5 : 3 : 1.67 : 1.67$—that is, the United States and Britain should have the same number, Japan three-fifths as many, France and Italy less, but equal to each other. Aircraft carriers were similarly limited, but smaller surface warships and submarines were not.

Several other treaties dealt with Far Eastern possessions and policies. In a Four-Power Treaty, the United States, Great Britain, France, and Japan agreed to recognize each other's rights in the lands around the Pacific. They also agreed that if any of the four violated these rights, the others should meet to discuss methods of punishing the violator. The Nine-Power Treaty was signed by all nations present. It guaranteed the independence and territorial integrity (territory and boundaries) of China. Existing spheres of influence and leases were left untouched. All signers reaccepted the principles of the Open Door Policy, that China should not grant special privileges to any nation.

● *Failure of attempts at disarmament*

The brave example of naval arms limitation at the Washington Conference was not followed. Later attempts to extend limitations to cruisers, destroyers, and submarines failed. When the ten-year holiday ended it was extended with so many escape clauses as to be almost useless. In 1936, when Britain and the United States refused her equality, Japan withdrew. By then Germany was rebuilding her navy, and the attempt to limit naval armaments was given up.

The League of Nations took the lead in trying to bring about a reduction of land armaments. After five years of preparatory work, a conference met at Geneva in 1932, attended by the representatives of sixty nations. Conflicting viewpoints soon produced a deadlock. France would not reduce her armies unless Britain and the United States would guarantee her security. Neither nation would give the guarantee. Germany announced that if other nations did not reduce armaments, as they had agreed to do in the Versailles Treaty, Germany would consider rearming.

The conference met again in 1933. By then Hitler had come to power in Germany, and the German delegation defied the convention. If the nations did not agree to a program of total disarmament, Germany would disregard the Versailles Treaty and rearm. When no action came, Germany left the conference. Secretly for two years, then openly, she began to build up her army and navy. The world of the 1930's was not a good climate for disarmament. A new arms race began and continued until World War II.

MAYBE IT'S A CASE OF TOO MANY COOKS.

Making foreign policy for the United States was a complex task in the 1930's. This cartoon shows President Franklin D. Roosevelt being bombarded with advice—to make reciprocal trade agreements, to keep isolated from foreign troubles, to keep neutral.

● *Attempts to ensure American neutrality*

During the middle 1930's Congress passed a whole series of acts aimed to prevent the United States from repeating the mistakes of the 1914–1917 period. By 1937 the following acts had been passed: The government was prohibited from making loans to any nation which had not paid its war debts. If war broke out, neither our government nor our citizens could lend money to a warring power. The United States would not sell munitions of war to either side. Raw materials might be sold, but the country that bought them had to carry them in its own ships and pay cash for them. American merchant ships were not permitted to be armed nor to enter war zones. American citizens were forbidden to travel on the ships of a warring power.

This legislation meant that the United States had given up its long-held claim to "freedom of the seas"—the right of a neutral to trade with either side. The American people and their representatives in Congress were determined to stay out of war even though some principles had to be sacrificed. But it didn't work. World War II was swiftly building up.

The League of Nations tries but fails

The League of Nations was a noble idea, but it failed. It failed, but it did accomplish many things. What did it accomplish and why did it fail?

You already know that the League failed in its main purpose: It could not prevent a second world war. In the minds of many people this failure has overshadowed many fine and constructive things the League did, and caused them to be forgotten.

● *Achievements of the League: financial aid*

The League gave help which prevented complete financial collapse in Austria and Hungary. Twice, in 1922 and 1932, Austria had to appeal for help to prevent complete bankruptcy. After making Austria reduce some of its governmental expenses, the League arranged for a loan to Austria by several League members. Austria was thereby saved from financial bankruptcy, although its important economic problems were not solved. In Hungary much the same thing happened in 1923, also with encouraging results. Similar financial aid had been given to Greece, Bulgaria, Estonia, and Danzig.

● *Settling boundary disputes*

Several times the League was able to bring about the settlement of international disputes which might otherwise have become serious. There was a boundary agreement between Turkey and Iraq (formerly Mesopotamia), which had become a British mandate. Brit-

ain and Turkey could not agree, and the problem was turned over to the League. After an investigation, the League made a recommendation which both countries accepted. A somewhat similar question arose between Germany and Poland over Upper Silesia. After careful study a League commission recommended division according to the wishes of the local population. Again both countries agreed, and the League conducted the necessary voting.

● *Labor laws and humanitarian work*

Under the League constructive work was done to provide labor legislation. The International Labor Organization (I.L.O.) made recommendations to governments concerning labor laws. Its governing board consisted of sixteen men; eight represented employers and eight represented employees. From its central office in Geneva, Switzerland, it dealt with problems of unemployment, working hours, child labor, employment of women, protection in dangerous work, sanitary conditions, and similar problems of the welfare of workers. Its recommendations were especially helpful in eastern Europe, the Near East, and Asia, where bad labor conditions prevailed. These recommendations led to the adoption of progressive labor legislation by many governments.

The League accomplished much in humanitarian activities. The enormous task of returning both war prisoners and refugees was carried out. Fine relief work was done in areas where there was famine. Much was done to prevent the smuggling of drugs and to combat diseases by health and sanitary measures. This sort of work receives few headlines in newspapers, and people know little about it. But it represented a fine accomplishment, just the same.

● *Mandates*

As you know, parts of the Turkish Empire and the German colonies became mandates of the League. They were turned over to trustee nations. These nations were League members who accepted the obligation to care for the inhabitants, rule them justly, and prepare them for self-government.

Mandates were classified A, B, or C according to the level of civilization and the degree of readiness of the people for self-government. The Arab states of the Turkish empire were classified A. Their people were considered almost ready. The League member was to assist them in organizing governments. In most African states the people were less advanced and a longer preparation was necessary; they were classified B. Islands of the Pacific, where conditions were very primitive, were class C. The trustee nation pledged to report progress to the League each year. The way of assigning mandates was criticized and the system did not work perfectly, but it was much better than the former colonial rivalry and scrambling.

● *Failures of the League*

To understand the failure of the League of Nations, you must understand its basic weaknesses. The first weakness was that it was made up of "sovereign, independent states." It was not a federal union like the United States, where the federal government is granted the power to make and enforce laws on certain matters. The League was not a government at all, in that sense. It could not make laws; it could only recommend certain actions. Whether these recommendations were carried out depended on whether the member nations wanted to carry them out. Also, the vote on important matters had to be unanimous in the Council, and usually in the Assembly; so the vote of one member could prevent even a recommendation from being made. Thus the League might condemn the conduct of a member, but it could do little to enforce or carry out its decision.

The League could usually persuade or compel the smaller, less powerful nations to accept its decisions. But when it was faced with the national ambitions of a major power, it was seldom successful.

Even if the League had been much different—if it had had far greater powers—it would still have worked under a tremendous handicap. The United States never joined the League; Germany joined the League in 1925; Soviet Russia came in belatedly in 1934; Japan, Italy, and Germany, because of disagreement, withdrew from the League in the early 1930's. In 1939, as a result of the Soviet-Finnish war, Soviet Russia was expelled from the League. The Soviet leaders departed without much protest or sorrow. The absence of five major powers weakened the organization most seriously.

Hitler's coming to power in 1933 undermined the League further. As soon as he

> The weakness of the League of Nations is emphasized by this cartoon comment on Japan's aggression against China. (See page 636.) The title of the cartoon is, "The unarmed cop."

came to power, Hitler began to insist on the right of Germany to rearm and to fortify the Rhineland. He demanded the return of the Saar to Germany. He started a policy that led to the annexation of Austria by Germany. This act led to other territorial gains. All this Hitler accomplished despite the League's disapproval of his rash actions. The League was helpless to block Germany's policy, mainly for two reasons: It could not get all the powers to join. It could not get willing coöperation of the members it did have.

Japan attacks Manchuria and defies the League

Japan's conduct in Asia was a further illustration of the fatal weakness of the League. From about 1930, when the military party in Japan came into power, the League tried to check Japanese aggression on the mainland of Asia. Japan's greatest aim was toward Manchuria, the province that adjoined Korea. It was here that a blow was struck, and it soon showed the grave weakness of the League. It was here, according to some historians, that World War II really began.

In September, 1931, there was a mysterious explosion near Mukden, Manchuria, which damaged the Japanese-controlled railroad. Without warning and without the consent of the Manchurian or Chinese government, Japanese troops occupied Mukden. The Republic of China appealed to the League for help. The Japanese delegate stated that it was purely a local, domestic matter, and warned the League not to interfere. Japan maintained that she was not violating any treaties, nor was the Japanese government declaring war on China, or conquering her territory. Japan was only "suppressing banditry." The conflict which began in 1931 and which became a regular war in 1937 was to last, with intervals, until 1945. However, in Japan it was never referred to as a war. It was always "The China Incident".

● *Other nations fail to stop Japan's aggression*

Japan's action was in clear violation of the Nine-Power Treaty and of the Kellogg-Briand Pact. It was a test of what happened to treaties when there was no means of enforcing them. In this case, the United States, although not a member of the League, proved willing to play its part. Through its Secretary of State, Henry L. Stimson, the United States declared that the Japanese action was a violation of existing international agreements, and that it would not recognize any change in the status of Manchuria. It is possible that the United States would have coöperated in stronger measures against Japan if the League had taken such action.

But the members of the League, especially Britain and France, were timid and cautious. They advised Japan and China to avoid war and settle their differences peacefully. Japan ignored the advice; the Japanese army began to occupy all of Manchuria. The League sent an investigating commission, headed by the English Lord Lytton, to study and report on the controversy. The Japanese at the same time continued their conquest. They declared Manchuria an independent state, under the name of Manchukuo. The ruler was the deposed Manchu emperor of China. As you might guess, he was a puppet; he danced when the Japanese pulled the strings.

After a nine-month investigation the Lytton Commission report was submitted to the League. The report condemned Japan's action and recommended that Manchuria be restored to China. Only Japan voted against the report and the recommendation not to recognize Japan's puppet state of Manchukuo. As a result of their defeat the Japanese withdrew from the League entirely. The League was helpless to do anything else but to sign a paper protest.

The "Manchuria Incident" can be summarized thus far as follows: The League was too weak to check a definite act of aggression by a big power. The major powers, especially Britain and France, acted timidly, and so encouraged Japan to press further. The lesson of Manchuria was that the League would take no strong action against aggressor nations, and that they could withdraw from the League and follow any policy they wanted. The League's inability to check aggression resulted in great loss of prestige. Japanese aggression, unchecked, started a chain reaction of other aggression that brought the collapse of peace in the East as well as in the West.

Italy attacks Ethiopia

The lesson of Manchuria was put into practice first by Mussolini. His solution for the basic problems of Italy lay in colonial expansion. The object of his ambition was Ethiopia (Abyssinia), the independent African state that had been admitted to League membership. Ethiopia bordered on the Italian colonies of Eritrea and Italian Somaliland. In 1896 it had defeated one Italian attempt to seize it. Ethiopia's League membership was not enough to discourage Mussolini, and the defeat of 1896 was only something to be wiped out for the "glory of Italy."

As in Manchuria, a "border incident" provided the pretext. In December, 1934, an Italian border patrol in Somaliland clashed with an Ethiopian border patrol. There was every indication that the Italians had provoked the incident. Mussolini at once ordered the Italian army in Eritrea and Somaliland to invade Ethiopia to "restore order."

Ethiopia had little ability to resist such an invasion; so she appealed to the League of Nations for protection. Emperor Haile Selassie appeared in person before the League Assembly. He was a dignified but pathetic figure as he appealed to the members to live up to their obligations and stop the aggression. Here was an even clearer test case than Manchuria, for Ethiopia was an independent gov-

ernment and a League member. If the League failed here, it was clearly futile as a peace-keeping organization.

As in Manchuria, selfish national interests weakened League action. Neither Britain nor France wanted to increase Italian unfriendliness toward them. They had little enthusiasm for strong League action. The League made a mild effort to bring the dispute to arbitration. Mussolini replied with an all-out campaign to conquer and colonize Ethiopia.

Haile Selassie, Emperor of Ethiopia, appeals to the League of Nations for help against Mussolini's attack.

The League had no choice but to declare Italy an aggressor and to apply economic sanctions against Italy. This meant that the League members would refuse to sell Italy any materials useful for war. They would also refuse to buy anything from Italy. These were only halfhearted sanctions, however. Oil, coal, and other minerals continued to be sold to Italy by League members. Certain non-League members—Germany, Austria, Hungary, Switzerland, and the United States—traded freely with Italy. The United States, following its neutrality laws (see pages 633–634) would not sell munitions of war to either

637

warring power, but private corporations continued to sell basic raw materials, especially oil, to Italy.

In a long war Italy might have been weakened by even these halfway sanctions, and have been forced to give in to the demands of the League. But the Ethiopian army was not equipped to make it a long war. The Italians entered the Ethiopian capital, Addis Ababa, in the spring of 1936. Mussolini then declared Ethiopia a part of the Italian Empire and proclaimed King Victor Emmanuel III Emperor of Ethiopia.

● Another defeat for the League

The League of Nations could see nothing to do but admit a second defeat. During the summer of 1936 it called off the boycott on Italy. Again it had failed to check aggression. Mussolini, of course, could not forgive even the halfhearted action. Hitler's Germany recognized the Italian conquest at once. In the fall of 1936 the two fascist dictators entered an open alliance. This alliance came to be referred to as the Rome-Berlin Axis. An axis is a line, real or imaginary, which passes through an object, about which the object

turns or revolves. It meant that the world revolved about the "axis" between Rome and Berlin. Thus the old system of alliances began to reappear. The plan for collective security, or peace through coöperative action, had broken down. By the end of 1937 Mussolini's Italy also withdrew from the League of Nations.

In spite of its very considerable accomplishments, the League of Nations failed in its main purpose: keeping peace through international agreement and coöperation. In part, the failure resulted from the facts that the League was made up of completely sovereign nations and that a unanimous vote was required for action. This was only the surface reason. The League of Nations was weak because the great powers were fearful of a strong international organization which might interfere with their own private aims and ambitions.

This map shows Ethiopia, which Mussolini conquered in defiance of the League of Nations. More details of aggression by the Rome-Berlin-Tokyo Axis will be found in Chapter 50.

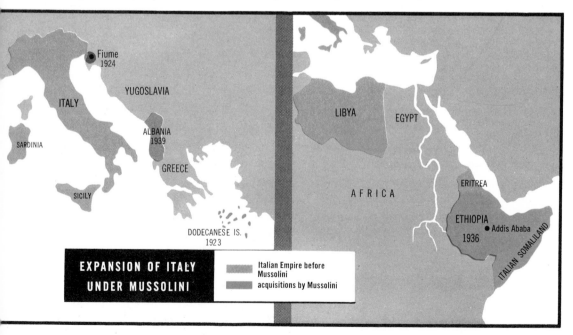

EXPANSION OF ITALY UNDER MUSSOLINI

Italian Empire before Mussolini

acquisitions by Mussolini

The members of the League had not created an organization which could keep the peace by making laws and enforcing them. It is doubtful if any of the major powers would have been willing to join such an organization. Not all were willing to join even the much weaker organization that was set up. Nor were all the nations who joined it willing to support the organization and coöperate to any full extent with it. The price for this unwillingness to stand solidly behind collective security was a second world war, longer, bloodier, and in all ways more terrible than the first one.

Review of Chapter 49

People, places, and things

Identify: Henry L. Stimson, Kellogg-Briand Treaty, Haile Selassie, Lytton Commission, Rome-Berlin Axis, sanctions.

Locate: Manchuria, Mukden, Ethiopia, Addis Ababa, Eritrea, Italian Somaliland.

Events in review

1. Name three major powers, and four smaller ones, that preserved democratic government during the period between world wars.
2. What gains did France make as a result of World War I?
3. What were the economic and political weaknesses of France in the period after World War I?
4. What was the Maginot Line?
5. What is meant by a policy of appeasement?
6. Describe briefly the effects of World War I on the British Empire.
7. In what ways did democracy increase in Great Britain during the period between world wars?
8. What was the Statute of Westminster?
9. What laws passed in the 1930's were intended to keep the United States neutral in wartime?
10. What agreements did Japan violate when she invaded Manchuria?
11. What did the "Manchuria Incident" suggest about the powers of the League of Nations?
12. Briefly describe how the League of Nations suffered a second serious defeat in the case of Ethiopia.

Problems and projects

1. Did the United States remain wholly isolated from world affairs during the 1920's and 30's? Did this country take any steps toward international coöperation and keeping the peace? Explain and discuss.
2. Name three points at which the aggressive, dictator nations might have been stopped during the 1930's. Can you explain why other nations followed a policy of appeasement? Were the risks involved in a firm policy any greater than the long-range risks of an appeasement policy?
3. Discuss the statement that the League of Nations was only as strong as its members wanted it to be.
4. Prepare a "You Are There" type of news broadcast covering the start of the "Manchuria Incident" or the Italian attack on Ethiopia.

NOTE: A map of the world in 1939 will be found on pages 640–641. This map will be a useful reference while you read Chapter 50.

ARCTIC OCEAN

GREENLAND
(Danish)

ALASKA
(U.S.)

CANADA (Br.)

NEWFOUNDLAND
(Br.)

UNITED STATES

NORTH

ATLANTIC

OCEAN

PACIFIC OCEAN

HAWAII (U.S.)

MEXICO

WEST INDIES

CUBA
DOMINICAN
REP.
(Br.)HONDURAS HAITI
PUERTO RICO
(U.S.)
GUATEMALA HONDURAS
EL SALVADOR NICARAGUA
COSTA RICA
PANAMA
VENEZUELA
(Du.)
(Br.) (Fr.)
COLOMBIA GUIANA COLONIES
ECUADOR

PERU
BRAZIL
BOLIVIA
PARAGUAY

URUGUAY
CHILE ARGENTINA

NEW ZEALAND
(Br.)

ESTONIA
LATVIA
DENMARK
LITH.
MEMELAND (Ger.)
E. PRUSSIA
NETHERLANDS
GERMANY (POLAND) U.S.S.R.
BELGIUM
LUX.
CZECHOSLOVAKIA
(AUSTRIA)
FRANCE TYROL HUNGARY
SWITZ.
Trieste Fiume RUMANIA
YUGOSLAVIA
ITALY BULGARIA
ALBANIA
GREECE

SICILY

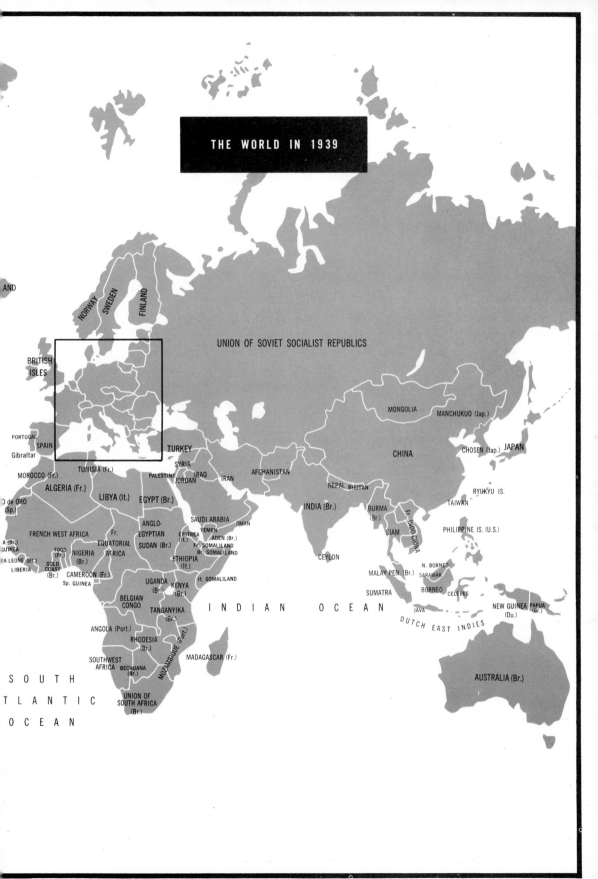

THE WORLD IN 1939

UNION OF SOVIET SOCIALIST REPUBLICS

AND

NORWAY
SWEDEN
FINLAND

BRITISH
ISLES

PORTUGAL
SPAIN
Gibraltar

MOROCCO (Fr.)
TUNISIA (Fr.)
ALGERIA (Fr.)
LIBYA (It.)
EGYPT (Br.)

TURKEY
SYRIA
PALESTINE
JORDAN
IRAQ
IRAN

AFGHANISTAN

MONGOLIA
MANCHUKUO (Jap.)

CHINA

CHOSEN (Jap.) JAPAN

RYUKYU IS.

NEPAL BHUTAN

INDIA (Br.)

BURMA
(Br.)

TAIWAN

PHILIPPINE IS. (U.S.)

O de ORO
(Sp.)

FRENCH WEST AFRICA

Fr.
EQUATORIAL
AFRICA

ANGLO-
EGYPTIAN
SUDAN (Br.)

SAUDI ARABIA

YEMEN
ERITREA
(It.)

OMAN
ADEN (Br.)
Fr. SOMALILAND
Br. SOMALILAND

ETHIOPIA
(It.)

SIAM

Fr. INDO-CHINA

CEYLON

MALAY PEN. (Br.)

N. BORNEO
SARAWAK
BORNEO
CELEBES

NEW GUINEA PAPUA
(Du.)   (Br.)

A (Br.)
GUINEA
RA LEONE (Br.)
LIBERIA

TOGO
(Fr.)
NIGERIA
(Br.)
GOLD
COAST
(Br.)
CAMEROON (Fr.)
Sp. GUINEA

UGANDA
(Br.)
KENYA
(Br.)

It. SOMALILAND

BELGIAN
CONGO

TANGANYIKA
(Br.)

SUMATRA

JAVA

DUTCH EAST INDIES

INDIAN   OCEAN

ANGOLA (Port.)
RHODESIA
(Br.)

MOZAMBIQUE (Port.)

MADAGASCAR (Fr.)

AUSTRALIA (Br.)

SOUTHWEST
AFRICA BECHUANA
(Br.)

UNION OF
SOUTH AFRICA
(Br.)

S O U T H
A T L A N T I C
O C E A N

Chapter 50 Japan and Germany Bring the War

CHAPTER 49 has told how, in Europe and in the Far East, world tensions were building up. In the 1930's the fascist states began a series of acts of aggression. Japan's attack on China has been discussed as an example of the failure of the League of Nations to preserve peace. Now it is time to take a closer look at Japan's development into a militaristic, aggressive world power that had much to do with bringing on World War II.

Japanese policies

You may remember what has been said about the Japanese government. At the head was the emperor, the mikado, sacred and divine. Outwardly he had full power. He chose his own cabinet of advisers; he could propose and veto acts of the legislature; he could declare war and make peace; he had some power to rule by decree. In practice, however, the emperor did only what his cabinet decided. So the struggle for control of government policy was a struggle to control the cabinet.

This was difficult, for until 1918 the cabinet was not responsible to the legislature. Thus the elected civil government was weak. It did not have very much voice in controlling the policies of the country. For the most part, the

elected government was dominated by the Japanese industrialists and large landowners.

The special position of the military was a thing of great importance in Japan. The secretaries of the army and navy, in the cabinet, were always selected by the high-ranking officers of the two services. The two positions were always filled by a general and an admiral. Even when the rest of the cabinet became responsible to the parliament, the military leaders did not. Therefore, the civil government had no actual control over the military leaders. The army and navy could make their own policy. The higher officers of both army and navy were filled with representatives of the old samurai class. They were fanatically loyal to the emperor, superpatriots, and great believers in war as the solution of all problems.

●*The gains of World War I*

World War I gave Japan the chance she had been waiting for. The powers of Europe and the United States were fighting among themselves; therefore they could not pay much attention to Asia. Japan took over the German rights in Shantung and the German islands in the Pacific. She presented a list, the Twenty-one Demands, to China. If accepted, the demands meant that China would be subjected to Japan. When the United States and European countries protested, Japan softened her demands slightly. She forced the president of the Chinese Republic to sign two treaties which were national suicide to China. The assembly of the Chinese Republic refused to ratify either treaty.

The Treaty of Versailles recognized Japan's control of the German leases in Shantung. The Allies also recognized her "special position in China." She received the German islands north of the equator (the Marshalls, Carolines, and Marianas) as mandates of the League of Nations.

● *The era of civil control in Japan,*
1921–1931: moderate policies

From the end of World War I until 1931 the moderate elements seemed to control the Japanese government. During the war the Allies had great need for Japanese manufactured goods. The Japanese industries had developed very rapidly. After the war, therefore, Japan had even greater need than before for raw materials, markets, and space for her rapidly growing population. Giving government subsidies, using much laborsaving machinery, and paying very low wages, Japan was able to increase exports greatly to pay for her needed imports. But this government support and the heavy costs of the army and navy meant very heavy taxes.

During this period the Japanese government showed great moderation in international affairs. Japan returned Shantung to China in 1922. She signed the Washington treaties which provided for limitation of navies, the guarantees of China's territory, and the Open Door Policy. She also signed the Kellogg-Briand Treaty which outlawed war.

Historians disagree about the meaning of these Japanese actions. Perhaps Japan really did want international peace. Again, they may have been only paper pledges, to be observed until the "right time" came. There is no doubt that the Japanese military leaders disapproved of and resented them, especially the naval limitation.

Japan turns toward militarism

The difficulties of Japanese trade during the 1920's increased because of high tariffs. The difficulties were made worse by the immigration policies of other nations. The world-wide depression which began in 1929 brought additional burdens. All told, it added strength to the military leaders who urged action and the use of force. They demanded a larger army and a navy second to none. They insisted on taking the mandated islands as outright Japanese possessions. They also cast longing eyes at the Chinese province of Manchuria. For this reason the Japanese prevented the armies of the Chinese Republic from taking over Manchuria; it was still controlled by a war lord. The militarists also advocated a Japanese "Monroe Doctrine for Asia." This would allow Japan to control the destinies of the Far East. For the same reason the Japanese created "incidents" in Manchuria in order to justify their outright invasion of Chinese territory.

When Japan invaded Manchuria, China could make little military resistance. She was torn by many factions. Manchuria itself was ruled by a war lord who gave only a surface allegiance to the Nationalist government at Nanking. China's only real weapon was a boycott of Japanese goods. China was Japan's second best customer; only the United States bought more Japanese goods. It was not long before China's refusal to buy Japanese goods began to hurt. Some of the Japanese merchants in Shanghai asked the home government for help. In 1932 a Japanese army occupied the city, after considerable fighting with the Chinese, and gave it up only when the Chinese agreed to end the boycott.

After Japan left the League of Nations, she soon showed that she intended to dominate the Far East. She refused to return the island mandates, and, against the agreement, fortified them. She started an extensive program of development in Manchukuo. British and American oil companies were excluded from the territory in spite of their protests that the action violated the Open Door pledge. Even before the naval limitations of the Washington Treaty ended, Japan began a great naval building program. She had already enlarged her army considerably. A spokesman for the Japanese Foreign Office unofficially announced a sort of Monroe Doctrine for Asia. He said that Japan took exclusive responsibility for Eastern Asia, although she might allow China to share the burden of her responsibility.

Japan had insisted that China withdraw all troops from the region south of the Great Wall, which was the southern boundary of Manchuria. At the same time Japan announced her intention of extending her influence over the vassal states of Inner Mongolia, Sinkiang, and two Chinese border provinces. One of these includes the great cities of Peiping (the former imperial capital) and Tientsin.

● Japan invades China

Early in 1937 Chiang Kai-shek and the Chinese communists agreed to stop their civil war and form a common front against the Japanese in north China. It was probably this event that influenced the Japanese war leaders to strike. It was not hard to find an excuse. On July 7, 1937, a clash between Japanese and Chinese troops took place near Peiping. It was one of those murky incidents in which it is almost impossible to fix responsibility. The Japanese armies at once began to move southward.

The conquest of the great Chinese cities did not take too long, although the Chinese made a brave and stubborn resistance. By 1939 the Japanese occupied about one-fourth

Dictatorship on the offensive in Asia: Japanese troops march into Harbin in northern Manchuria.

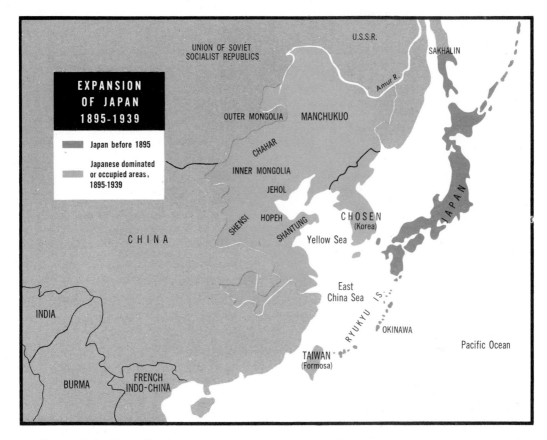

EXPANSION OF JAPAN 1895-1939

- Japan before 1895
- Japanese dominated or occupied areas, 1895-1939

U.S.S.R.

UNION OF SOVIET SOCIALIST REPUBLICS

SAKHALIN

Amur R.

OUTER MONGOLIA MANCHUKUO

CHAHAR

INNER MONGOLIA

JEHOL

SHENSI HOPEH SHANTUNG

CHOSEN (Korea)

CHINA

Yellow Sea

JAPAN

East China Sea

RYUKYU IS.

INDIA

OKINAWA

Pacific Ocean

TAIWAN (Formosa)

BURMA FRENCH INDO-CHINA

---

of China, including all the seaports, the Yangtze Valley as far as Hankow, and many interior cities. Still the Chinese refused to give up. Wherever they had to fall back, they followed the "scorched earth" policy which the Russians had used against Napoleon. They moved their capital far up the Yangtze River to Chungking. Everywhere they fought a guerrilla war, cutting off Japanese supplies, making lightning raids in the supposedly occupied regions behind the Japanese lines. The war proved a great drain on Japan. Even before World War II began in Europe, Japan had lost a million troops in China and spent ten billion dollars. Chinese losses were uncountable. But Japan could find no way to end "The China Incident."

The United States and the European powers continued to play it safe. The United States government followed its neutrality laws, and prohibited the sale of munitions to either side. But private companies in the United States and Britain continued to sell vital scrap iron and gasoline to the Japanese. They sold to China, too. A trickle went overland into China, across the famous Burma Road which had been built. Another trickle came overland from Russia. But the Chinese fought on.

Now let us leave Asia and go back to Europe, where the dark clouds of war were swiftly gathering.

Germany rocks Europe

World War II came principally as a result of Germany's conduct under the leadership of Adolf Hitler. The boundless ambition of Hitler—his determination to build the Greater Germany, the "Thousand-Year Reich," his utter disregard of promises, treaties, and the rights of others—made either

645

complete submission to Hitler's wishes or world conflict inevitable.

You already know the first steps. In 1933 Hitler took Germany out of the League of Nations and announced his intention to rearm. In 1935, after a strong campaign of Nazi propaganda, the people of the Saar voted to return to German rule. In 1936 the Rhineland was reoccupied and its fortification begun. The failure of Britain and France to take any determined action against either rearmament or the Rhineland move convinced Hitler that he could do almost as he pleased. He did not really want war, provided he could get what he wanted without it. But he was willing to risk war in order to gain what he wanted. It was what military men call a "calculated risk." He counted on the fact that if he stood firm and seemed prepared to go to war, his opponents would always back down at the last moment.

● *Hitler's technique of aggression*

Hitler had a regular, planned technique for conquest without actual war; it has been well named a "war of nerves." It was accomplished step by step. We shall trace it a bit so that you can see how it worked and why it succeeded so well for a time. After the victim had been selected, these steps followed:

1. In the nation to be attacked a Nazi party was formed. This was accomplished either among the German minority, if there was such in that country, or it was formed among some discontented people led by native traitors and supported in every way by Germany.
2. "Atrocity" stories of the mistreatment of Germans were sent out in a stream to Germany and the world.
3. The antiwar and appeasement sentiments in Britain and France were nourished by German propaganda. Those who favored a strong stand against Hitler were branded as warmongers.

4. A "crisis" of some kind would be cleverly built up by Hitler, and he would demand a "German solution to the question." He would also promise that it would be the "last demand" for any readjustment of territory.
5. Warlike demonstrations would begin in Germany: the mobilization of reserves, shifting of troops to the frontier, mass flights of airplanes.
6. Any yielding by the victim became the first step toward complete control by a Nazi dictatorship. All pledges and promises were violated; the entire country was taken over.
7. The conquered country became the base for the next conquest.

Danzig was almost a laboratory example of the method in practice. In addition, here the campaign was against the League of Nations, which Hitler detested. The Treaty of Versailles had made the German city of Danzig a Free City, protected by the League. It was to be a port for both Germany and Poland. The Free City had its own elected government, and the League appointed a commissioner to settle disputes between Danzig and Poland. It was a "setup" for the Nazi technique. There was a heavy German population. The city had been torn from the "fatherland." The commissioner was a foreigner. The despised Poles were given rights.

A strong Nazi party sprang up in Danzig, encouraged by propaganda and financial help from Berlin. By 1937 it had won control of the city government, using the usual Nazi tactics where they seemed necessary. The city government then demanded things that made relations with Poland increasingly difficult. The position of the League commissioner became almost impossible. Danzig was "ripe for the plucking" any time Hitler demanded that it be returned to Germany. But Danzig was not the first step in the program which Hitler stated so frankly in *Mein Kampf* and in his speeches. Several other gains had to be made first.

Hitler's move into Austria

The peace treaties had left Austria in an impossible condition economically. About the only hope for the future lay in some sort of union with Germany. Some among the heavily German population of Austria favored such unification (*Anschluss*). However, such a step was definitely prohibited in the treaty. Here again was an ideal chance for the Nazi technique. A Nazi party was formed in Austria. The Austrian government, by then extremely conservative and a near-dictatorship, could do little to resist the Nazi inroads. In fact, it did not seem to want to do much.

By 1938 threats by both Hitler and Mussolini forced the Austrian government to include Nazi members in the cabinet. Once there, they began to "bore from within,"

while Nazi Germany stepped up the pressure from the outside. The Austrian chancellor offered to take a vote of the Austrian people on the question of unification. Hitler feared to take this chance, and refused to permit it. The chancellor resigned, and the German army marched in unopposed. In March, 1938, Hitler proclaimed Austria a state of the German Reich. The League of Nations took no action; another member had lost its independence. Britain and France sent protests to Hitler; he disregarded them. No other action was taken; the technique had worked perfectly.

The addition of Austria enlarged Germany's population, territory, and resources. It also raised Hitler's influence in Europe. Strategically, Germany had now penetrated

Dictatorship on the offensive in Europe: Joyful Nazis celebrate Hitler's coup in Austria.

the heart of central Europe and reached a common border with her ally Italy. A single glance at the map will show what it did to Czechoslovakia, which Hitler had announced as the next step in the program. The annexation of Austria meant that Germany almost completely encircled the Czech republic. Of course it was not so in Nazi propaganda. To Hitler, Czechoslovakia became "a dagger aimed at the heart of Germany."

Hitler moves against Czechoslovakia

Around the western rim of Czechoslovakia, in a region known as the Sudetenland, there lived more than three million Germans. This territory had been included in Czechoslovakia by the peace treaty because it is separated from Germany and Austria by a rim of mountains. These mountains would give the new state a natural and defensible frontier. It was one of the many instances in the treaty where nationalism and the self-determination of peoples gave way to the claims of defense. The Czech government made a fairly honest effort to protect the rights of this German minority. They were allowed to use their own language in the schools, and given proportionate representation in the Parliament, the civil service, and the army. Still, it is not surprising that many of the Sudeten Germans wanted to be united with Germany.

With the victory of Nazism in Germany, a strong Nazi party grew up among the Sudeten Germans. By the usual tactics they increased their membership in the Czech Parliament. After 1935 they actually had more votes than any other party, although not a majority. After the annexation of Austria the troubles in Czechoslovakia steadily mounted toward a climax. Stories of discrimination and atrocities against the "poor Sudetens" were innumerable. In September, 1938, the situation became so critical that the Czech government placed the country under military law.

• Hitler demands the Sudetenland

This was Hitler's signal. Immediately he announced that the German army would invade Czechoslovakia to protect the "Sudeten brothers" and return them to the loving care of the fatherland. Of course their territory would have to come with them. The Sudeten territory included the protective rim of mountains, which the Czechs had fortified heavily. Without it, the country was defenseless against encircling Germany. The usual mobilization and troop movements took place; the stage was set.

Now it was a question what action Europe would take. Czechoslovakia was a League member, but this had proved no protection to Ethiopia and Austria. However, the Czechs had other resources. They had defensive alliances with both France and Russia. The Russian alliance provided that Russia would aid the Czechs only on condition that France did. So what would France do?

France turned to Great Britain to see if she could find support there. If so, the Czechs would have help from France, Britain, and Russia. This combination would be strong enough, perhaps, to make Hitler back down. However, Britain and France were so fearful of war that they would not take the chance. Neville Chamberlain, prime minister of Great Britain, sent a personal representative to investigate and "advise" the Czech government. He advised the Czechs to make every possible concession to avoid war.

PARTITION OF CZECHOSLOVAKIA 1938-1939

to Germany, Oct. 1938
to Hungary, Nov. 1938
to Hungary, Mar. 1939
to Poland, Oct. 1938

Concessions, however, were useless with Hitler. To him every concession was a sign of weakness and a signal to increase his demands. He also increased Germany's military preparations. War seemed almost inevitable. Chamberlain asked Hitler for a face-to-face talk, and he flew to meet the German Fuehrer. Thus began the three meetings—Berchtesgaden, Godesberg, Munich—each more humiliating than the preceding one. Each time Chamberlain learned only that Hitler was determined that the Sudetenland should be returned to Germany. If it were not, he would invade it and take it.

With the approval of France, Chamberlain warned the Czech government that all territories more than half-German in population would have to be handed over. If they were not, he warned, Czechoslovakia would have to face Germany alone. France agreed, and Czechoslovakia had no choice but to yield.

● *Appeasement at Munich*

Now, of course, Hitler stepped up his demands. The Czechs would have to withdraw faster than they wanted to. No new line of defense must be built. To settle these differences, the heads of the governments of Great Britain, France, Germany, and Italy met at Munich at the end of September, 1938. The Czech government was not represented. Nor were the Russians invited. They had steadfastly stated that they would live up to their agreement. They would come to the defense of the Czechs if France did. To the communist leaders, the Munich conference was another sign that the Western powers, Britain and France, were trying to buy Hitler off with appeasement in the hope that he would attack Russia.

Since 1938 the word "Munich" has become a byword and a symbol for appeasement and surrender. You will undoubtedly hear it used often, and now you will understand its meaning. The Czechs were given ten days to give up the Sudeten territory. For what it was

Prime Minister Neville Chamberlain of Great Britain smiles and waves on his return from the Munich meeting. For a time it was believed that he had succeeded in appeasing Hitler.

worth, Britain and France guaranteed the borders of what was left of Czechoslovakia. Mr. Chamberlain returned to England to tell the British people: "I have brought you peace in our time." How far, far wrong he was!

● *The end of Czechoslovakia*

When the lion had feasted, the jackals came to take their share. Poland and Hungary took parts of the dismembered country, claiming that those parts were occupied by their people. What remained of Czechoslovakia became a defenseless nation in the heart of Europe, at the mercy of Hitler any time he chose to move. And he chose, very soon. By supporting disagreements within Czechoslovakia, he divided the country into three parts.

Then, accusing them of plotting to overthrow the Munich agreement, he sent the German army in. The western part was annexed outright to Germany; the central part became a German "protectorate"; the eastern part was given to Hungary.

Thus within a period of six months an independent republic, probably the most prosperous and democratic of the postwar states formed after World War I, had been wiped completely from the map of Europe. The League of Nations was compelled to cross another name from its list of members. Still another was to come soon. Mussolini, once a model for other dictators, had by now become the imitator of Hitler, the tail of the kite. In April, 1939, he invaded Albania on the east coast of the Adriatic. In a few days the country was taken. The King of Italy and Emperor of Ethiopia gained an additional title: King of Albania.

The fall of Czechoslovakia marked the high point of Hitler's diplomatic victories and bloodless conquests. It had the most serious effects on European and world affairs. Germany became the strongest power, the most

The cartoonist David Low comments on the propaganda techniques used by the dictators. One side of their policy was to tell the people what they wanted them to believe (under communism, there is the "party line"). The other side of their scheme was to prevent people from hearing the truth about world affairs. President Roosevelt and other leaders in the democratic nations denounced cases of aggression by the fascist states such as Hitler's grabs at Austria and Czechoslovakia. The fascist leaders did their best to keep these comments from reaching their people.

strategically located, in Europe. The Axis powers, Germany and Italy, completely upset the balance of power and the hope for peace through collective security. The prestige of the League of Nations had received still another blow. Those people who had been unwilling to see it before, now knew that Hitler's promises were absolutely worthless. Reliance on Great Britain and France was seriously weakened. Suspicions were aroused among the Russians.

Germany threatens Poland; France and Britain prepare to resist

By now it was clear that Hitler would never be satisfied and that his promises were worthless. Appeasement and concessions only increased his appetite. No sooner had Czechoslovakia been swallowed than he began making moves toward Poland. The strength of the Nazi party in Danzig now began to pay off. The Polish Corridor, that strip of territory cut through Prussia to allow Poland to reach the seaport of Danzig, was Hitler's pretext. There were "mistreated" Germans to be "protected" both in the Polish Corridor and in Danzig.

In France the premier was given dictatorial power to prepare the country for war. In England, the father of the policy of appeasement, Neville Chamberlain, at last became doubtful of the "peace in our time." He rushed through Parliament a huge armaments program and a conscription law. France already had a defensive alliance with Poland. Britain now announced that she would help Poland if Germany attacked. Britain and France soon made similar announcements concerning Greece, Rumania, and Turkey.

Britain and France also began negotiations for an alliance with Soviet Russia. Until then Russia had been excluded from all major decisions in Europe and the rest of the world. The British and French found that the communists were suspicious and hard bargainers. The Soviet leaders knew that they had a place on Hitler's timetable. But they had little reason to trust, and much reason to suspect, the British and French. Alliance or no alliance, they feared that the Western powers

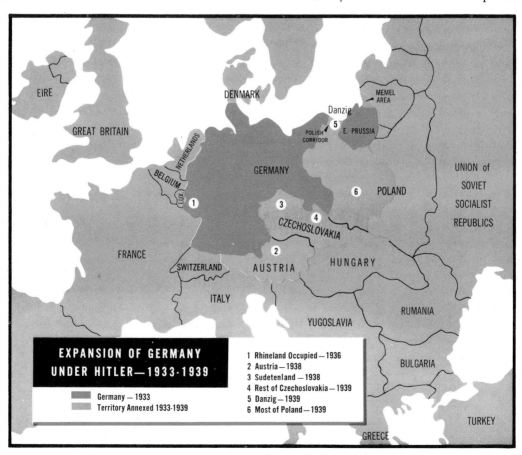

EXPANSION OF GERMANY UNDER HITLER—1933-1939

Germany — 1933
Territory Annexed 1933-1939

1 Rhineland Occupied — 1936
2 Austria — 1938
3 Sudetenland — 1938
4 Rest of Czechoslovakia — 1939
5 Danzig — 1939
6 Most of Poland — 1939

would welcome a chance to turn Hitler loose on them.

The Soviet leaders therefore insisted that the independence of the Baltic states of Finland, Estonia, Latvia, and Lithuania be guaranteed, as well as the independence of Poland. They also wanted a military alliance among all these states to work out a strategy so that they could act instantly in case Germany attacked any of them.

This arrangement sounded reasonable enough, but it brought instant protests from the Baltic states, and especially Poland. All of them had common borders with the Soviet Union, but not with Britain or France. A common military agreement would mean that in case of a German attack Russian armies would move into their countries to meet the Germans. All of them, and especially Poland, feared such protection. They were afraid that they might never be able to get rid of the protectors. For this reason the negotiations dragged on till they reached an apparent stalemate.

Meantime the German war of nerves on Poland was increasing in volume and intensity. The Nazis of Danzig were demanding unification with the fatherland. There were cries from the Germans of the Corridor about mistreatment by the Poles. Hitler was screaming his demands that these atrocities must be stopped by a "German solution of the question."

The Hitler-Stalin Pact

In August of 1939 the tense and nervous world received a great blow. Hitler proudly announced that Germany and the Soviet Union had signed a nonaggression treaty; Moscow confirmed the news. It was a tremendous shock. It was about the most unlikely treaty, between two of the most openly declared bitter enemies, that could have been imagined.

However, a little thought shows that it was not so unlikely. In any case, it had happened.

When negotiations with the British and French seemed completely stalled, the Soviet government had hinted that it was ready to sign a nonaggression treaty with any nation, including Germany. Hitler was hesitant at first, even though treaties meant little to him. Finally he sent his foreign minister to Moscow to complete the arrangement.

Publicly, the Hitler-Stalin Pact pledged each of the two never to attack one another, and to remain neutral if the other were involved in war. Secretly, they agreed to divide eastern Europe into spheres of influence. Germany was to take western Poland. Russia was given a free hand in the Baltic states, eastern Poland, and the province of Bessarabia which she had lost to Rumania in 1918. There was little doubt of the meaning of the pact. The Western nations had lost a possible ally in the east. Germany was sure of Russia's neutrality. It was a tremendous military advantage, which Hitler was not slow to use.

Many theories have been advanced to explain this agreement between two deadly foes. It is certain that neither of them trusted the other; they knew each other too well. So each must have counted on something which did not depend on the other's keeping his word.

The most believable explanation goes something like this: Hitler counted on a quick victory in the west. Even if Britain and France declared war, they could not help Poland. He counted on an easy victory there. With that in hand, he counted on his submarines and air force to keep Britain off the Continent so that he could knock France out of the war. He believed that Britain would then bargain for peace. All this time he could count on being free from danger from the east, from Russia—provided events moved as fast as he thought they would. When he had mastered the West completely, he could use all his forces to conquer Russia.

Crafty Stalin, master of Russia, believed that Hitler would get bogged down in the west; so that war would take longer than Hitler expected. The longer Hitler was pinned down in the west, the longer Russia would have time to prepare. Stalin did not care much which side won so long as both were weakened and drained. If both sides were bled white, Russia would be proportionately stronger when the end did come.

Crisis over Poland; World War II begins

These are speculations, guesses. If this is what Hitler and Stalin thought, time proved that neither was right. Whatever were their reasons, the fact is that the Hitler-Stalin pact marked the beginning of events that led directly to the most frightful war mankind has ever experienced. Within a week after the signing of the pact, the Polish situation reached a crisis. Hitler demanded that the problem of Poland must receive the "Ger-

man solution": Danzig must be returned to Germany, and the problem of the Corridor must be settled by a vote of the inhabitants. Messages flew back and forth between Germany and Poland, but neither side would give in.

On the morning of September 1, 1939, Hitler declared that Danzig was annexed to the Reich. At the same time his air force made a massive attack on Poland, and Nazi troops, led by tank columns, struck across the border. Two days later Great Britain and France kept their promises to Poland. They declared war on Germany. Within forty-eight hours the "local" war in Poland became the beginning of World War II.

Thus ended the uneasy truce of the 1920's and 1930's. Thus began the most destructive war men had known. How the war spread from Europe to take in the world will be explained in Chapters 51 and 52 of Part Ten.

Review of Chapter 50

People, places, and things

Identify: Neville Chamberlain, the Anschluss, Twenty-one Demands.
Locate: Manchuria, Outer Mongolia, Inner Mongolia, Shantung, Sinkiang, Peiping, Shanghai, Yangtze Valley, Austria, Czechoslovakia, Sudetenland, Danzig, Polish Corridor, Albania, Munich.

Events in review

1. What did Japan gain from the Treaty of Versailles?
2. Why was the period from 1921 to 1931 known as the era of civil control in Japan?
3. The start of World War II is usually set in 1939. How long had China and Japan been involved in war by that date? Was the war a drain on Japan?
4. Briefly describe how Hitler took over Austria.
5. How did the term "Munich" become a symbol for appeasement?

6. What changes in British and French policy followed the final destruction of Czechoslovakia?
7. What were the public and the secret provisions of the Hitler-Stalin Pact?

Problems and projects

1. Discuss: How much did events in the 1930's represent the power and success of Hitler, Mussolini, and Japan? How much did they, instead, represent failure on the part of other countries to stop aggression at the first sign of trouble?
2. List the techniques Hitler used in his "war of nerves." Compare them with Russian techniques in the "cold war" in the 1950's.
3. Bring to class newspaper articles, editorials, cartoons, and magazine articles from the years 1938–39. Discuss what they show of reactions to Hitler's moves, opinions on what the United States and Britain should do, and so on.

Review of the Period between Two World Wars

1. During World War I it was often said and believed that the war was being fought "to make the world safe for democracy." How safe was democracy in the period between 1918 and World War II? Give details of what happened in democratically governed countries.

2. Another hope during World War I was that that conflict would be "the war to end all wars." Twenty-five years after the outbreak of the First World War a second world conflict began. Compare the causes of the two wars. Can it be said that one nation, or group of nations, deserves to be held guilty of starting the first war? the second?

3. The League of Nations was an experiment in world coöperation. Did the League function successfully in any ways? Describe three times when the League failed to face and solve a problem that threatened world peace. How can you explain the weakness and failure of the League of Nations?

4. Compare the dictatorships that appeared in Russia, Italy, and Germany. What circumstances favored the growth of police states in these countries? Name the men who became dictators. What powers did they hold? What was their view of the rights of the individual versus the powers of the state? Why did they stress nationalism and preparation for war?

5. When Germany, Italy, and Japan made aggressive moves during the 1930's, the democracies followed a policy of appeasement. Give examples of appeasement. Can you explain why this policy was followed? What were its results? What lessons can be learned from it?

6. The immediate cause of World War II seems a minor problem in comparison to the six-year global struggle that developed. What factors other than the immediate issue of Poland caused nations to enter the war? List as many fundamental reasons as you can to explain why the major Axis powers and the major Allied powers engaged in war.

Books about the period between the wars

Allen, Frederick L. *Only Yesterday* (Harper, 1931). The United States in the 1920's. Revealing and entertaining.

———. *Since Yesterday* (Harper, 1940). Many details on life in the United States in the troubled 1930's.

*Books marked with a star (*) are easy reading.

Benns, F. Lee. *Europe Since 1914: in Its World Setting* (Appleton-Century-Crofts, 1954).

*Carr, Albert H. *Men of Power; a Book of Dictators* (Viking, 1956). Mussolini, Hitler, and Stalin, among others.

Crain, Maurice. *Rulers of the World* (Crowell, 1942). Chapters on Mussolini, Hitler, Stalin, Franco, and the "Men Who Rule Japan."

Fry, Varian. *Peace That Failed* (Headline Book No. 21. Foreign Policy Association, 1939). Why the Treaty of Versailles broke down.

———. *Bricks Without Mortar; the Story of International Coöperation* (Foreign Policy Association, 1938). The failure of the League of Nations.

Gould, Kenneth M. *Windows on the World* (Stackpole, 1940). Chapters on democracy, communism, and fascism.

Gunther, John. *Inside Africa* (Harper, 1955). An examination into the future of Africa in the light of current social, economic, and political conditions.

Harcave, Sidney Samuel. *Russia, a History* (Lippincott, 1956). Coverage of the period before 1682 is brief; of that after 1917, full.

*Ives, Vernon. *Russia* (Holiday House, 1943). A clear and simply written history.

Kalp, Earl S., and Morgan, R. M. *Democracy and Its Competitors* (Ginn, 1940). The contrast between democracy and dictatorships is clearly shown.

Lauterbach, Richard. *These Are the Russians* (Harper, 1945). Chapters on the leaders and much material on Russian life under communism.

Library of Congress. *Communism in Action* (U. S. Government Printing Office, 1946). A government document describing the actual operation of communism in Russia.

*Living Democracy Series. *Isms and You* (Civic Education Service, Inc., Washington, D.C.).

*———. *Capitalism—Way of Freedom*. A very readable series of pamphlets explaining the different political and economic philosophies.

Loder, Dorothy. *Land and People of Spain* (Lippincott, 1955). A history of Spain with a guidebook view of cities, culture, and customs.

Mowrer, Lilian. *Rip Tide of Aggression* (Morrow, 1942). How the world conflict was brought on by the dictatorships.

Pratt, Helen G., and Moore, Harriet L. *Russia: a Short History* (John Day, 1947).

Price, Willard. *Japan Rides the Tiger* (John Day, 1942). An especially good account of the training of young Japanese.

*Seeger, Elizabeth. *Pageant of Russian History* (Longmans, 1950). Clearly written and excellently illustrated.

Untermeyer, Louis. *Makers of the Modern World* (Simon and Schuster, 1955). Biographies of ninety-two men and women who formed the pattern of our century.

*Vaughan, Josephine B. *Land and People of Japan* (Lippincott, 1952).

White, William C. *Made in U.S.S.R.* (Knopf, 1944). A general picture of the geography, history, and social conditions as well as handicrafts.

———. *Report on the Germans* (Harcourt, Brace, 1947). Conditions in postwar Germany.

Wohlrabe, Raymond A. and Werner Krusch. *Land and People of Austria* (Lippincott, 1956). Fine background material for understanding the Anschluss.

Stories about the world between the wars

Albrand, Martha. *Endure No Longer* (Little, Brown, 1944). This novel shows how the desperate conditions in postwar Germany led people to accept a Fuehrer.

Almedingen, Martha E. *Frossia* (Harcourt, Brace, 1944). The conflicts and adjustments of the early years of the Russian Revolution.

Crew, H. C. *Under Two Eagles* (Little, Brown, 1929). Life in Poland during the 1920's.

Daugherty, Sonia. *All Things New* (Nelson, 1936). The experiences of Russian refugees in America during the 1920's tell much about both countries.

Hess, Fjeril. *Mounted Falcon* (Macmillan, 1933).

———. *House of Many Tongues* (Macmillan, 1935).

Two novels which tell much about Czechoslovakia between the two wars.

*Kuo, Helena. *Westward to Chungking* (Appleton-Century-Crofts, 1944). The Chinese-Japanese war. "Scorched Earth" on the retreat to Chungking.

*Lewis, Elizabeth F. *China Quest* (Winston, 1937).

*———. *Ho Ming, Girl of New China* (Winston, 1934).

*———. *When the Typhoon Blows* (Winston, 1942).

*———. *Young Fu of the Upper Yangtze* (Winston, 1932).

These novels for younger readers give a good picture of life in twentieth-century China and tell much about the Chinese philosophy of life.

*Savery, Constance. *Enemy Brothers* (Longmans, 1943). An English boy educated by the Nazis has a hard time getting used to English ways.

Part Ten THE GLOBAL WAR AND AFTER

Part Nine told how the stupidity, fears, deceit, and greed of certain nations built up into forces that plunged mankind into war. Part Nine ended with the outbreak of fighting in Poland. Now, in Part Ten, Chapter 51 tells how the Germans conquered almost all of western Europe and besieged the British in their fortress island. Chapter 52 tells of the Japanese attack that brought the United States into the war and of Hitler's invasion of Russia. After the dark years from 1939 to 1942, the tide began to turn. Chapter 53 describes how the allied nations moved slowly but surely to defeat Italy, Germany, and Japan.

The picture on the facing page shows three of the leaders of the free world. In 1944 the Allies landed in Normandy and began a drive that eventually crushed the German armies in western Europe. Shortly before D-Day, Winston Churchill, Prime Minister of Great Britain, General Dwight D. Eisenhower, Supreme Commander of the Allied Expeditionary Forces, and General Charles de Gaulle, leader of Free France, met at General Eisenhower's headquarters. The artist has re-created the conference with General Eisenhower pointing out the objective of the enormous land, sea, and air forces he commanded.

Even before the war ended in victory, the nations began work on a plan to prevent future wars. The allies opposed to Germany and Japan formed an organization, the United Nations, to try to maintain peace through coöperation. Chapter 54 tells of the formation, organization, and the successes and failures, of the United Nations.

The final chapters bring the record of history on from the end of World War II into the second half of the twentieth century. Wartime coöperation among the United Nations disappeared. It was replaced by the fears and suspicions of the cold war. The world tended to divide into communist and anticommunist blocs, with uneasy neutrals between. The war of ideas between democratic and communist nations became world-wide. In Korea and Indo-China the cold war became a shooting war, though a limited war. Mankind lived with the risk of more "small wars"—or of a total war, fought with hydrogen bombs and guided missiles.

In Asia and Africa old-style imperialism faced its end. A possibility developed that it might be replaced by a new imperialism of communist domination. Rising forces of nationalism among African, Near-Eastern, and Asian peoples, plus the stresses of the cold war, kept the world in ferment.

Meanwhile, science and technology made wonderful advances, taking man into the age of nuclear power and to the frontiers of space. A great question remained: would man's discoveries and skills be used for war or for peace?

EUROPE

AFRICA AND THE NEAR EAST

EUROPE		AFRICA AND THE NEAR EAST	
1939	World War II begins with German invasion of Poland Russia moves into Poland and Finland		
1940	German blitzkrieg overwhelms Denmark, Norway, Holland, Belgium, and France Italy enters war Air Battle of Britain Battle of the Atlantic vs German submarines	1940	Italy invades Egypt; British drive Italians back into Libya
1941	Germany invades Balkans, takes Greece and Crete Germany invades Russia	1941	British defeat Italians in Ethiopia British take Iraq. British and Free French take over Syria Hard fighting in North Africa
1942	Air and sea war continue Russians stop German advance at Stalingrad	1942	Germans drive deep into Egypt Stopped at El Alamein United States and British forces land in Morocco and Algeria
1943	Russians begin to drive back German armies Conferences of Allied leaders at Casablanca Quebec, Cairo, and Teheran Allies invade Sicily and Italy; Mussolini ousted; Italian government surrenders	1943	Allies defeat Axis forces in North Africa
1944	Heavy air raids on Germany D-Day, Allies land in Normandy Russians drive Germans out of Russia and push into Czechoslovakia and Hungary Battle of the Bulge (ends January 1945)		
1945	Allies drive back Germans, cross the Rhine Yalta Conference V-E Day, Germany surrenders Potsdam Conference		
1946	United Nations holds first meeting (London) Italian Republic established Nuremberg war crime trials Fourth French Republic established	1948	Great Britain withdraws from Palestine Arab-Israeli war begins
1947	Russians control satellites in Eastern Europe Cominform organized Truman Doctrine announced Aid to Greece and Turkey The "Cold War" develops	1949	United Nations arranges cease-fire in Palestine
1948	Marshall Plan—aid for sixteen European nations Berlin blockade Communists take over Czechoslovakia Yugoslavia breaks with Cominform	1952	Libya becomes independent Revolts in Tunis and Morocco King Farouk of Egypt abdicates
1949	Council of Europe formed NATO set up West Germany becomes a republic	1954	Great Britain agrees to withdraw from Suez Canal Zone France faces unrest and violence in Algeria
1951	Schuman Plan adopted		
1953	Stalin dies Malenkov, Molotov, Khrushchev at top of Soviet state Russians announce they have tested H-bombs	1956	Morocco and Tunisia gain independence Egypt seizes Suez Canal Great Britain, France, and Israel invade Egypt, defeat Nasser's troops. United Nations orders cease-fire and withdrawal, sends United Nations force to Egypt
1954	West Germany joins NATO Trieste question settled		
1955	Bulganin takes the place of Malenkov as premier of Russia "Conference at the Summit" held by Big Four leaders at Geneva	1957	Eisenhower Doctrine announced for Mid-East
1956	Revolt in Hungary crushed by Soviet troops. United Nations General Assembly denounces Russian actions	1958	Egypt and Syria merge as United Arab Republic (UAR) American troops sent to Lebanon
1957	Khrushchev becomes top man in Russia Russians launch sputniks I and II	1960	Cypress and fourteen African nations gain independence Congo becomes independent, civil war begins among tribes, United Nations forces sent to Congo
1958	DeGaulle becomes first President of new Fifth Republic in France		
1961	First Russian space flight		
1961	Berlin Crisis—Russians wall off East Berlin	1961	Syria withdraws from UAR

AND AFTER

ASIA AND THE PACIFIC	THE UNITED STATES
1939 Japan takes Hainan	**1939** Arms embargo section of Neutrality Act repealed Declaration of Panama forbids hostile acts within 300 miles of the shores of any of the American nations
1940 Japan occupies Indo-China Japan joins German-Italian Axis	**1940** Large increases in national defense spending: two-ocean navy planned Congress passes first peacetime draft law Destroyers-for-bases deal with Great Britain
1941 Japanese-Soviet non-aggression treaty Japanese attack Pearl Harbor, the Philippines, Singapore, other bases	**1941** Lend-Lease Act, aid to Britain Roosevelt and Churchill draw up Atlantic Charter Pearl Harbor Attack. United States declares war
1942 Japan's advances checked at Coral Sea, stopped at Midway United States forces land on Guadalcanal	**1942** Allied nations meet in Washington and sign pledge to fight for victory
1943 United States forces start pushing back Japanese: retake Attu, Kiska, take Tarawa; heavy fighting in Southwest Pacific	
1944 United States forces take Marshalls, Saipan, Guam, land in Philippines B-29's bomb Japan	**1944** Dumbarton Oaks Conference
1945 Landings on Iwo Jima, Okinawa Atomic bombs dropped on Hiroshima and Nagasaki V-J Day, unconditional surrender of Japan	**1945** San Francisco Conference draws up Charter for United Nations Roosevelt dies, Truman becomes President
1946 Philippines become an independent Republic Civil war starts again in China	**1946** United Nations General Assembly meets in New York
1947 India granted independence from Great Britain United Nations arranges cease-fire in Kashmir	**1947** Truman Doctrine announced
1948 Burma granted independence United Nations recognizes Republic of Korea	**1948** Extensive aid to Europe under ERP President Truman re-elected
1949 Chinese Communists win civil war. Chiang Kai-shek withdraws to Formosa	**1950** United States supplies bulk of armed forces for Korean War
1950 Republic of Indonesia formed North Koreans invade South Korea. United Nations orders withdrawal. United States sends forces into Korea. Chinese Communists aid North Koreans	**1952** Eisenhower elected President First H-bomb test
1951 Peace treaty with Japan signed Negotiations for truce in Korea begin	**1953** Armistice ends active fighting in Korea
1953 Korean armistice signed	**1954** First atomic-powered submarine (U.S.S. Nautilus) launched
1954 French losing war in Indo-China, agree to settlement SEATO formed	**1955** Deadlock on United Nations membership broken
1955 Bandung Conference of Asian and African nations	**1956** President Eisenhower re-elected
1957 Malaya independent, joins United Nations	**1957** Eisenhower Doctrine announced International Geophysical Year begins July 1
1958 Chinese Communists shell off-shore islands of Quemoy and Matsu	**1958** Earth satellites launched Disarmament talks in United Nations Alaska becomes 49th state
1959 Chinese Communists conquer Tibet	**1959** Hawaii becomes 50th state
1961 Communists start civil wars in Laos and Viet Nam	**1960** John F. Kennedy elected President
	1961 First American space flight

659

Chapter 51

The War in the West

WORLD WAR II was fought on so many fronts and involved so many nations that the narrative of events has to seem complicated. In following the course of this global war, make full use of the headings in the text, the maps that accompany the text, and the time chart on pages 658–659.

The German blitzkrieg in Poland

In Poland the Germans showed that they had studied, and learned from, the experience of World War I. They had no intention of "fighting the last war over again." The campaign in Poland revealed new tactics which came to be called blitzkrieg—lightning war. The airplane dive bomber had been developed into a form of artillery. It worked closely with advancing ground troops by knocking out machine-gun and artillery emplacements. Other planes bombed cities to spread panic, and hit at railroads and bridges to disorganize communications. The ground troops were led by columns of tanks. These, plus specially trained engineer troops, cleared the way through trenches and light fortifications. Trench warfare was as out-of-date as the medieval castle.

It was a return to the war of movement, with new and terribly effective weapons. The classic military movement of encirclement

was much used. While one column attacked from the front, others swept around to attack from the sides or broke through to the rear to destroy communications and supply routes. The aim was to cut the enemy force into small groups which could be destroyed singly or forced to surrender.

In less than two weeks western Poland was under German control. Warsaw, the capital, was surrounded and besieged. Fighting bravely but outmaneuvered and bewildered, the Polish army was cut up and pressed back. Then came a fatal blow. The Soviet army, which had gathered at the eastern border, marched across to occupy eastern Poland. The resistance of the Polish army collapsed. On September 27, 1939, there was an armistice. The fighting had lasted less than a month, and a stunned world saw Hitler triumphant in the east. Now the secret parts of the Hitler-Stalin Pact were revealed. Once again Poland disappeared completely. Germany took the larger, western part. A smaller, eastern section, inhabited largely by Ukrainians, was added to the Soviet Union.

Russia, the Baltic states, and Finland

Russia went on to take the Baltic states. By diplomatic pressure and threats, Estonia, Latvia, and Lithuania were compelled to grant land, sea, and air bases. This was only the first step to a complete loss of independence. By mid-1940 all three were added to Soviet territory.

The Soviet communist leaders tried the same tactics in Finland, but here the story was different. The Finns proved stubborn. They refused the Soviet demand for a naval base at Hangö, on the peninsula that juts out into the Baltic Sea at the mouth of the Gulf of Finland. Negotiations and diplomatic blackmail proved fruitless. On November 30, 1939, the Russian army attacked Finland. The Finns appealed to the League of Nations, which condemned Soviet aggression and expelled the Soviet Union from membership. It was a belated and futile gesture.

The Russians received a surprise, though. They had expected an easy victory and had used a fairly small army, poorly equipped. The Finns put up a magnificent fight. The war proved to be a bloody and costly struggle lasting more than three months. Finally the Soviet leaders realized that they would have to use the "first team," and Finnish resistance was crushed. Finland was forced to give in to the Soviet demands on March 12, 1940.

The Soviet Union took Hangö and with it control over the entrance to the Gulf of Finland. The Finnish-Soviet border was demilitarized and pushed farther north, thus strengthening the Soviet in that region.

The "phony war"—France and Britain

The Germans had not been disturbed in their campaign in Poland by any need to fight on two fronts. France and Great Britain had tried no offensives. The British landed an expeditionary force which took up a position behind the French-Belgian border. The French moved into the Maginot Line of fortifications. They seemed to be following the strategy of World War I—the strategy of wearing the enemy out. There was so little action on the western front that the newspapers began to call it a "phony war." It seemed that it might end in a deadlock or some uncertain peace.

On the seas things were much the same as in World War I. The British navy commanded the sea as far as surface warfare was concerned. Yet they faced a serious challenge from German submarines, which were sinking enemy and neutral merchant ships on sight. The strategy seemed to be the same as in the earlier war—a British blockade to starve out the Germans, and a submarine blockade of England.

However, the British and French underestimated their opponents. In World War I the kaiser's Germany had seemed savage and ruthless in its attack on neutral Belgium, but the Germany of 1914 had respected the neutrality of Holland and the Scandinavian countries. In World War II Hitler saw that the long North Sea and Atlantic coastlines of Norway and Denmark would make blockade very difficult if the Germans controlled them. They would also furnish fine offensive bases for submarines. Hitler was not the man to let a thing like a declaration of neutrality stand in his way of gaining such prizes.

Germany attacks—the blitzkrieg again

Early in April, 1940, the "phony war" ended with a sudden German invasion of Denmark and Norway. Again it was blitzkrieg, aided by another strategy, the "fifth column." (See page 624 for the statement made by one of Franco's generals when he was attacking Madrid during the Spanish civil war.) Hitler had prepared his way in Scandinavia by a fifth column of native traitors. In addition, Germans had entered the country as workmen and lived there for some years innocently. When the time came, these fifth columnists seized power plants and radio stations, doing everything they could to disrupt transportation and communication.

Denmark and Norway fall

In a few weeks German troops controlled both Denmark and Norway. The German navy had numerous ships sunk or damaged in battles with the Norwegians and the British. Germany, however, made enormous gains. The long Norwegian coastline with its narrow, deep fiords gave good bases for submarines. There were many sites for airfields. Blockade became much more difficult; in fact, the tables began to turn. Shipping to France and Britain was in grave danger.

It was a rude awakening for the Allies. The British now realized that the war was a life and death struggle. In Parliament, Prime Minister Chamberlain, of Munich fame, was forced to resign. Winston Churchill became the leader. During the 1930's he had made many speeches in the House of Commons, calling upon the government to increase armaments and making gloomy predictions of the folly of appeasement. Now, when his predictions seemed to be coming true, the British turned to him for leadership.

The beaches at Dunkirk. In the period from May 29 to June 4, 1940, 336,000 men were evacuated to England. Men waited for days on the beaches. To take them off, 801 ships ranging from destroyers to fishing boats ran a shuttle service across the Channel.

Holland, Belgium, Luxembourg

The stunned Allies were not given a chance to regain their balance. The conquest of Norway and Denmark had hardly been completed when the Germans invaded Holland, Belgium, and Luxembourg. Again it was blitzkrieg. The German columns moved with such speed and power that local defense was caught unawares and completely paralyzed. The combination of tank battalions and dive bombers seemed irresistible. Tiny Luxembourg fell in one day to panzer (armored) columns, Holland in less than five days, and Belgium in a week.

The British army on the Continent had moved into Belgium to meet the Nazi attack, but the speed and power of the Germans was too great. The British force was rolled back against the sea at Dunkirk. Only the fact that the British Royal Air Force was able to hold temporary control of the air over the small region kept the army from being wiped out completely. It was in an impossible position. There was nothing to do but surrender or get out.

The retreat from Dunkirk was a stirring story of great courage. All available ships and boats were used to carry troops to England. The courage of the English was unsurpassed. A surprisingly large proportion of the British Expeditionary Force and some French troops were transported to England. It was a military disaster, though. All the military equipment was left at Dunkirk. The army which was saved could not fight again until it was completely re-equipped.

The situation of the Allies was now desperate indeed. The British had been driven from the Continent. The French were left to fight alone. What was worse, the costly Maginot Line, on which they had counted so heavily, was now useless. The Germans were making an end run around it. They could now attack through the flat, lightly fortified plain from Belgium.

The fall of France

The blow came soon. Early in June, 1940, Germany began the offensive against France. It was a desperate battle. The French fought against so many odds that it seemed hopeless from the start. They fought with bravery, but they were not trained or equipped for the kind of war they had to meet. The German panzer columns cut the French forces into ever smaller groups. Northern France was a scene of utmost confusion. Everywhere the civilian population tried to flee before the advancing Germans, carrying whatever goods they could save, in every sort of vehicle. They blocked roads, thus adding to the difficulties of the French army. The German air force

added to the confusion by bombing and machine-gunning the roads to make the blocks worse.

● *Italy enters the war*

Until this time Mussolini had kept Italy neutral. Now, with French resistance weakening, he declared war on France and Britain. President Roosevelt called it "the stab in the back." Four days later the Germans entered Paris. From there on, it was a triumphant march. The French government now had only two choices: either to surrender or flee to North Africa and try to carry on the war from there. Rather than surrender, the French ministers resigned.

● *Pétain's government surrenders*

There were Frenchmen who were willing to surrender, though. A new government was formed under the aged Marshal Henri Philippe Pétain. He was given dictatorial powers. His vice premier, Pierre Laval, had a long

As the German Army drove into France, civilians tried to escape from the battle zone. These men, women, and children of a French village crowded the street, carrying clothing and bedding.

record of urging collaboration, or coöperation, with Hitler. On June 22, the Pétain government signed an armistice with Germany. Two days later they signed one with Italy.

The German armistice terms were as severe as those the Allies had imposed on Germany in 1918. Under the terms the northern half of France was to be occupied by Germany. The French people paid the costs of the occupation. The French navy was to be handed over to the Germans. There were other humiliating terms; France was left completely at the mercy of Germany. The Pétain government moved to the city of Vichy; the "Vichy Government" became associated with appeasement and surrender.

Even in those tragic days there were many Frenchmen who wanted to fight on, to keep the alliance with Britain and continue the war. Some escaped to North Africa, some to England. The man who rose as the leader of this resistance movement was General Charles de Gaulle. From London he urged the French people to stand firm. When the Vichy government surrendered, those who wanted to continue the fight formed a government of their own. It was called the Provisional French National Committee, or, popularly, the Free French Government. Its main support came from France's African colonies.

Thus there were three Frances: occupied France, fascist Vichy France, and Free France. The last did not have much of a force, but it had the will and determination to fight on until France was freed and Germany defeated. Within France was formed an underground force called the maquis. In the dark days of 1940 joining the ranks of the Free French forces required great faith and courage.

● *Dark days for the democracies*

The days of the summer of 1940 were dark indeed. They illustrated the truth of the expression much heard in those days: "Eng-

land prepared for no war; France prepared for the old World War; Germany prepared for the new World War." In less than three months the Germans had conquered Norway, Denmark, Holland, Belgium, Luxembourg, and France. They now controlled the long Atlantic coastline of Europe from the tip of Norway to Spain. They also controlled the northern Mediterranean coast from Spain through Italy. In Spain dictator Franco made no attempt to conceal his contempt for the democracies and his sympathy for the fascist dictators. German submarines were allowed to use Spanish ports. Spain, Franco said, was a "nonneutral nonbelligerent"—not actually fighting but not neutral.

Britain's former hold over the Mediterranean was now reduced to her possession of certain key bases: Gibraltar, the islands of Malta and Cyprus, and Alexandria in Egypt. The Axis powers now controlled the coasts and extended their power deep into the heart of Europe, for the dictatorship in Hungary was coöperating fully with Hitler and Mussolini.

In September, 1940, came another blow. The Japanese government announced an alliance with Hitler and Mussolini; it now became the Rome-Berlin-Tokyo Axis. It did not fit in very well with Hitler's "master-race" propaganda, with its contempt for Orientals. However, he was equal to the situation. The Japanese, he announced, were "yellow Aryans."

Britain faces Hitler

Britain was left alone, fighting for her life. She was now in danger of being blockaded. Submarines and bombing planes from bases along the coastline of western Europe ranged far out into the Atlantic to attack any ship heading toward the British Isles. German planes, in greater number than British, could strike at British industrial centers from nearby bases, whereas German industry was much farther away from Britain. Germany had 3,500,000 seasoned troops, England's 1,500,000 soldiers were poorly equipped. If the French navy should happen to fall into the hands of Germany, Britain's mastery of the seas might indeed be in imminent danger. Thus the invasion of Britain across the narrow English Channel seemed a possibility. Hitler planned such an attack, to be called "Operation Sealion."

The "master plan" of *Mein Kampf* now seemed a reality. Germany dominated the continent of Europe. Now it remained to be seen whether Britain would follow the plan. According to *Mein Kampf,* Britain was to make peace. In return for being allowed to keep the British Empire intact, she was to recognize German dominance of the continent of Europe. All former German colonies were to be returned, and Germany was to be given the Belgian Congo. Italy was to have the entire Adriatic Coast, and was to dominate Spain and Greece. Hitler confidently expected the British to yield to such a plan.

Hitler began his air attacks on Great Britain even before the French-German armistice was signed. Industrial centers, ports, and cities were bombed. After about a month of this, he made a peace offer to Britain, stating his terms.

● *Britain refuses to surrender*

Hitler had underestimated his opponents, as he so often did. The British people refused to surrender; they showed dogged courage in fighting against odds. They were now led not by Chamberlain the Appeaser but by Winston Churchill, a magnificent and inspiring war leader. In a noble speech to the British people Churchill replied to the Nazi offer: "We shall defend our island, whatever the cost may be. We shall fight on the beaches, we shall fight on the landing grounds, we shall fight in the fields and in the streets, we shall fight in the hills; we shall never surrender. . . ." To the United States he addressed

an appeal for supplies, arms, and ammunition. As he put it, "Give us the tools, and we will finish the job."

The first British move was to make sure that the Germans did not get the French fleet. A number of French warships were in two groups, one at Alexandria, in Egypt, the other at Oran, the port of Algeria. The squadron at Alexandria refused to return to France and remained in port. These ships took no further part in the war. At Oran the French admiral, Jean François Darlan, favored collaboration with the Germans and refused to join the British. Having no choice, a British squadron sank or damaged most of the French ships. Only a few managed to get away. British naval superiority was preserved, and the cross-channel invasion became less of a threat.

● *The Air Battle of Britain*

When his peace offer was rejected, Hitler determined to knock Britain out of the war without invasion. British troops were still fighting in the Near East, Egypt, and North Africa, but they would be useless if the homeland had to surrender. So the bombing raids on the vulnerable British industrial cities were stepped up. The aim was to destroy

A German fighter of World War II, the Me (Messerschmitt) 109. The Germans easily smashed the Polish and French air arms. The Royal Air Force of Great Britain proved tougher.

and fire bombs, but other British cities received their full share. Coventry was almost leveled, and the port of Liverpool was dreadfully damaged.

The British fought back. Although few in number, their fighter planes were better in quality, and they were piloted by daring and skillful flyers. As the dreadful months of the summer and fall of 1940 passed, they took an increasingly heavy toll of the German bombers. Of these fighter pilots of the Royal Air Force, Churchill said, so aptly, "Never in the field of human conflict was so much owed by so many to so few." The loss of bombers forced the Germans to shift from day to night attacks. For two years Britain was attacked from the air almost every night. Docks, airfields, factories, and residential areas were bombed constantly. But the British doggedly dug out of their ruins and continued the fight.

● The Battle of the Atlantic

Although the air attack was the most spectacular, it was not the greatest danger to Britain. There was also the "Battle of the Atlantic." German planes, new-type mines, and long-range submarines took a dreadful toll of British, Allied, and neutral merchant ships. By early 1941 more than 7,000,000 tons of ships had been sunk. Sinkings were averaging more than 500,000 tons a month, much faster than new ships could be built. Germany was building more submarines at a very rapid rate. Although Britain might not be bombed into submission, there was every possibility that she might be starved out. It is likely that this would have happened if the United States Navy had not given help. Let us see how this happened.

United States' policy toward the war

Chapter 49 described the determination of the United States to stay neutral in another war. This was a very strong sentiment;

A radar-controlled searchlight in England. In a few respects, the British were prepared for war. They had an advantage in the fact that their scientists had developed effective radar sets by the outbreak of war. This radar-searchlight combination helped locate night bombers. Radar helped the outnumbered Royal Air Force defeat the Germans in the Air Battle of Britain. Far more than any earlier conflict, World War II was a contest between scientists. Churchill calls this phase "the wizard war."

Britain's ability to fight and to lower British morale—their will to fight. Each day the German planes came over to drop their deadly loads—tons of explosives. British planes fought back with bombing raids on German industrial cities. The nightmare of air warfare began in full force. London was most intensively bombed, with both explosive

666

it was best expressed in the Neutrality Act of 1937, passed by large majorities in both houses of Congress. In the event of war anywhere, industrial corporations in the United States were forbidden to sell munitions to either side. They could sell raw materials, but the warring nation had to pay cash and take the cargoes away in its own ships. American merchant ships were forbidden to arm or to go into war zones. American citizens were prohibited from traveling on the ships of a warring country without special governmental permission. No loans could be made to warring nations, either by the United States government or by private banks, corporations, or citizens.

Intervention or isolation?

The steps in Hitler's rise to power had troubled many people in the United States. Many Nazi acts and policies influenced American thinking: the "master-race" policy, the persecution of Jews and other religious groups, the persecution of labor, the aggressive imperialism, the violation of promises and treaties. Even before he began to extend his power, many people felt that the Hitler ideas were a menace to civilization. Each step in German aggression increased their concern for the future of Europe and possibly of the free world. Many Americans felt that the United States should intervene in some way to stop this menacing philosophy.

There were others, of course, who disagreed. A Nazi party, the German-American Bund, made some headway among Americans of German descent. Some people were in concealed or open sympathy with the Nazi policy towards Jews and toward labor. Others believed that it was folly for the United States to concern itself in European quarrels. No matter how much they disagreed with his philosophy and actions, they felt that Hitler was "Europe's business." Many of these groups were represented in a very loose organization which grew up under the name of

Radar helped the British to locate German raiders. To attack them the British had some excellent fighters, such as this Spitfire.

America First. It had some respectable, patriotic leaders. It represented, as you can see, the isolationist point of view.

The differences between the interventionists and the isolationists came to a head with the outbreak of World War II. Interventionists maintained that the Neutrality Act of 1937 was not neutral. It prevented the British and French, who could come and get them, from buying munitions and war supplies here. This helped the Germans, who could not come and get them anyway. Isolationists reasoned that to change the act after the war had begun would favor the Allies, and so be un-neutral.

The Neutrality Act of 1939

After several months of debate in the country and in Congress, the interventionists won a limited victory. By good majorities in both houses, the Neutrality Act of 1939 was passed. It repealed the embargo, or prohibition, on the sale of munitions and war supplies. Warring nations could buy them if they came and got them and paid cash. It was "cash-and-carry." None of the other provisions was changed, but once more the United States became a supplier of munitions to belligerents.

The disaster at Dunkirk and the fall of France aroused great concern in the United States. There was increased feeling that a Nazi victory would be a blow to all democratic ideals everywhere. Aid to besieged Britain seemed more than ever a necessity. Many people felt that Britain was really fighting our battle. It was not a unanimous sentiment, by any means. The isolationists still opposed any move that might bring the United States any closer to active fighting.

More aid to Britain, 1940–1941

Steps were taken, nevertheless. In September, 1940, by an executive agreement, President Roosevelt transferred fifty over-aged American destroyers to Great Britain. The Congress did not have to approve the "destroyer deal." In return for the destroyers the United States got ninety-nine-year leases on air and naval bases in Newfoundland, the British West Indies, and British Guiana in South America. Thus the British anti-submarine campaign was strengthened, and the United States was able to strengthen the defenses of the Western Hemisphere.

●Defense preparations

The Congress showed its concern for the world situation by passing huge appropriations for building up the American armed forces.

In the same month of September, 1940, the United States took a step never before known in our peacetime history. Congress passed a peacetime Selective Service Act. Every man between 21 and 36 became liable to one year of military training and service. The National Guard was called for active service at once. Shortly afterward, the task of organizing the industrial resources of the country for defense was given to the newly created Office of Production Management for Defense, jointly headed by an industrialist and a labor leader.

●"The arsenal of democracy"

As the terrible Battle of Britain continued, and as the Germans stepped up their Battle of the Atlantic, sentiment in the United States shifted still further, to a point of "all aid to Britain short of war." President Roosevelt stated that the United States must become "the arsenal of democracy." There was a great deal of self-interest in this anti-German sentiment. Many Americans keenly felt that if Britain fell, and especially if the British fleet fell into German hands, the Axis powers would gain mastery of the seas. The United States would then be in danger of attack from two directions—from Europe and from the new Axis partner, Japan, in the Pacific. Many people had now come to feel that the Axis aimed at nothing less than world domination. Unless one understands this feeling, he cannot possibly understand the United States' action in 1941.

The problems of American foreign policy are suggested by this cartoon. The artist parodied a famous Greek sculpture (page 91). Uncle Sam struggles with isolation. One man urges aid to Britain and France. Another wants strict neutrality.

The Lend-Lease Act, 1941

The Neutrality Act of 1939 had permitted the British to buy, for cash, war supplies in the United States. Just as in World War I, cash was hard to come by. As in World War I, the British called in all the stocks and bonds of American corporations owned by British citizens, and sold them in the United States. This time there were not so many, and the dollars did not last long. In March, 1941, President Roosevelt proposed, and the Congress passed, the Lend-Lease Act. It authorized the president to sell, lease, lend, *or otherwise dispose of* war supplies to any government he thought essential to the safety of the United States, on any terms he considered satisfactory. An appropriation of eight billion dollars was made available at once, mostly for aid to Britain.

There was, of course, the problem of getting supplies across the submarine-infested Atlantic Ocean. The United States Navy began making an anti-submarine patrol far out into the Atlantic, "to protect neutral merchant ships." During the spring of 1941 the value of this patrol increased when Denmark's government-in-exile granted us the right to establish air and naval bases in Greenland and Iceland. In May, 1941, a German submarine sank an American merchant ship. President Roosevelt immediately froze all German and Italian assets in the United States, making it impossible for them to get at and use such things as bank deposits. He also ordered all German and Italian consulates in the United States closed.

The Atlantic Charter

President Roosevelt and Prime Minister Churchill were in very close touch with each other. They wanted to avoid any repetition of the "secret treaties" incidents of World War I. In August, 1941, they met on a British battleship at Argentia, Newfoundland, and drew up the *Atlantic Charter*. This was a pronouncement of democracy's aim in time of war.

The Atlantic Charter began with a statement that neither nation sought any gains, territorial or otherwise. They wanted no territorial changes made that were not approved by the people of the territory concerned. They respected the rights of all people to choose the form of government they wanted, and pledged themselves to restore self-government to peoples who had been deprived of it. They promised to do everything they could to see that all nations, great and small, victor or conquered, should have equal rights to trade and to get raw materials. They promised to try to promote economic coöperation in the world, so that all peoples could have security and good living standards. They promised to work for a peace that would bring all peoples security, and freedom from fear and want, a peace that would give all men freedom of the seas. They stated their belief that all nations, for realistic as well as spiritual reasons, must give up the use of force.

It was a noble statement of aims. It held out hope to those nations which had been conquered by Germany and Italy, and even hope to the people of Germany and Italy themselves, once the dictatorships had been overthrown.

The United States an ally of Britain

The United States had moved a long way from its position of neutrality as stated in the Act of 1937. After the passage of the Lend-Lease Act the only remaining restriction on American action was the part of the 1937 act which prohibited American merchant vessels from being armed or from entering war zones. In November, 1941, the Congress passed an act which removed both of these limitations. Thus the relationship of the United States to Great Britain became that of a nonbelligerent ally. The United States was giving the British "all aid short of war."

The sentiment of the American people was still by no means unanimous. Each step toward closer participation in the war brought strong criticism from influential people and newspapers. In the summer of 1941, when the first Selective Service Act was about to expire, a bill to extend it for another year passed the Congress by the narrowest possible margin: one vote in the House of Representatives. Other acts relating to the war caused long and bitter debates when they were proposed to the Congress. Most of them were passed by substantial majorities; nevertheless, it was clear that a proposal of an actual declaration of war on Germany and Italy would find the nation bitterly divided.

Review of Chapter 51

People, places, and things

Identify: Marshal Pétain, Pierre Laval, Admiral Darlan, General Charles de Gaulle, Neville Chamberlain, Winston Churchill, Franklin D. Roosevelt, the maquis, isolationists, Rome-Berlin-Tokyo Axis.

Locate: Estonia, Latvia, Lithuania, Finland, Hangö, Poland, Warsaw, Norway, Denmark, Holland, Belgium, Luxembourg, France, Dunkirk, Vichy, Sicily, Malta, Gibraltar, Egypt, Alexandria, Oran.

Events in review

1. Why did Poland's resistance collapse so quickly?
2. What was the "phony war"? When did it end?
3. What outstanding event took place at Dunkirk?
4. When did Italy enter the war?
5. Which French government surrendered to Germany? Which French government continued fighting?
6. "Give us the tools, and we will finish the job." (a) By whom was this said? (b) To whom was it said? (c) Were the tools delivered?
7. What was the "Battle of the Atlantic"? Why was it of critical importance in the war?
8. What was the purpose of the Neutrality Act, passed by the Congress of the United States in 1939?
9. What was the Lend-Lease Act, passed in 1941?
10. When and by whom was the Atlantic Charter drawn up?

Problems and projects

1. Discuss the blitzkrieg tactics used by the Germans in 1939–1940. How did the fighting in this war differ from the fighting in 1914–1918? Can you explain how Germany won these "lightning victories"?
2. It has been said that "England prepared for no war; France prepared for the old World War; Germany prepared for the new World War." Is this true, in whole or in part? Give evidence for your view.
3. How was Poland partitioned in 1939? What earlier partitions of Poland have you read about in this book? What is the situation of Poland today?
4. According to *Mein Kampf*, what did Hitler expect England to do after he became master of the continent of Europe? In what ways did he underestimate the British? How was England able to stand up to the German attack?
5. Write an essay on the provisions of the Atlantic Charter. Why could this be called a document of world-wide significance?
6. On a map of Europe show the advance of Hitler's armies in 1939 and 1940. Show the names of countries conquered and the dates of conquest. Compare the area controlled by Italy and Germany in July, 1940, with the area controlled by Great Britain.

Chapter 52

The War Spreads Eastward

FOLLOWING the course of World War II is like watching a three-ring circus. You have to try to keep track of many events going on in different places. Chapter 51 covered the start of the war in Europe and the American reaction to that conflict. Now it is necessary to take a look at the Far East and see how tensions were building up toward war in that part of the world arena. Then we will take another look at Europe.

Japan moves to the south

Japan was involved in her war against China. However, she was still able to make grabs at other territory. During the early months of 1939, she took Hainan Island. This island cuts the sea route between the British-held ports of Hong Kong and Singapore. Japan also took some islands off the coast of Indo-China. It seemed clear that Japan was moving steadily toward the rubber, tin, oil, and other riches of the Netherlands East Indies and the adjoining countries.

France and Britain were greatly concerned, but by then the situation in Europe was so tense that they could do nothing but protest. The United States was also concerned. We needed these raw materials ourselves, and did not want to see them in Japanese hands. Ja-

pan had announced the New World Order in Asia, or the Greater East Asia Co-Prosperity Sphere. We feared that such an organization might endanger our possessions in the Philippines. In an effort to threaten the Japanese, the United States moved part of its Pacific fleet to Hawaii. In July, 1939, we gave Japan the required six-months' notice that we were canceling our commercial treaty with her. Private American corporations, however, still continued to sell oil, gasoline, and scrap iron to the Japanese.

The outbreak of the European war gave the Japanese militarists and imperialists the chance they had been waiting for. Now they could clear the British and French out of China, and go on to take the lands to the south. To prevent Russia from interfering with these plans, the Japanese made a treaty with the Soviet government. They settled a dispute over the boundary between Siberia and Manchukuo. On the other hand, to stop the supplies that came to Nationalist China over the Burma Road and from Indo-China, Japan put pressure on the British and French.

When France and the Netherlands both fell, Japan seized her golden opportunity. She declared that the Netherlands Indies were under her "protective custody." Japanese pressure forced Marshal Pétain of Vichy to consent to Japanese supervision of all traffic to China through Indo-China, which France owned. Within a few months Indo-China had become an economic and military protectorate of Japan. Britain was forced to close Hong Kong and the Burma Road to all shipments of war materials to Nationalist China. In September, 1940, Japan formed the Rome-Berlin-Tokyo Axis by an alliance with Hitler and Mussolini.

● United States-Japanese relations

The United States made a steady stream of protests against the Japanese territorial moves, as violations of the Four-Power and Nine-Power Treaties. The United States also bought tungsten from and made loans to Chiang Kai-shek's government. In September, 1940, in a move obviously aimed at Japan, President Roosevelt placed an embargo on the shipment of oil and scrap iron from the United States to any region but Britain or the Western Hemisphere nations.

The relations between Japan and the United States grew steadily worse during 1941. In April the Soviet Union and Japan made another nonaggression treaty, this time for five years. In the summer, a strong pro-Axis, militarist government came to power in Japan under Premier Tojo. Attempts to reconcile differences between Japan and our country met increasing difficulties.

The demands of the two countries were opposite. The United States insisted that Japan stop the war in China, and observe her promises of the Nine-Power Treaty not to take Chinese territory and to keep the Open Door Policy. We also insisted that she observe her promise of the Four-Power Treaty, in which Britain, France, Japan, and the United States pledged to respect each other's rights and possessions in the Pacific and Far East.

Japan, on the other hand, demanded that the United States stop trying to "encircle" Japan, stop giving help to Nationalist China, and lift all embargoes on the sale of goods.

She insisted that we recognize Japan's dominant rights in the Far East: the Japanese Monroe Doctrine. Late in 1941 the Japanese government sent a special representative, Saburo Kurusu, to Washington for the announced purpose of trying to settle all differences peacefully. Chances for such a settlement did not seem very good.

Now, with Japan and the United States on the brink of war, we shall switch back to the other side of the world for new developments in Europe and Africa.

The struggle for the Balkans and the Near East

The Nazi blitzkrieg victories in western Europe were an unpleasant surprise to the Russian communist leaders. If Stalin had counted on a long, costly war to entangle Hitler in the west, he had guessed badly. Stalin had moved in quickly to seize his agreed share in eastern Poland and the Baltic states. Even Finland's unexpected resistance did not delay him too long. Now he turned to the south to claim his spoils there. By pressure on Rumania he forced that nation to give up the two provinces of Bessarabia which Rumania had taken from Russia in 1918, and northern Bukovina (which had never belonged to Russia).

● German penetration of the Balkans

This move had been agreed to in the Nazi-Soviet Pact, but it did not please Hitler. His gains in Austria and Czechoslovakia had put him firmly in central Europe. Hungary had become a satellite state, which allowed him to begin a penetration of the Balkans. He wanted the entire region for himself. It had valuable food supplies and raw materials to feed the German industrial machine. Rumania, especially, had the only extensive oil fields on the continent of Europe outside Russia, and oil is the very lifeblood of the modern, mechanized army.

When the British disabled the French fleet, Hitler's best chance to invade the British Isles passed. Britain would have to be knocked out from the air and by blockade. This meant that a large part of the German army was free for other uses. As soon as the French surrender had been obtained, the German army moved into Rumania and took over the remainder of the country.

● Italy attacks in Africa and Greece

Now Mussolini decided to get into the act. He had been forced to stand by and see his boasted position as a world-shaking dictator shrink. Hitler had grown greater and greater, and had pushed the Italian hero ever further into the background. Mussolini wanted Greece, the entire eastern shore of the Adriatic, and vast territories in Africa: Suez, Egypt, the Sudan, Kenya, and Tunisia. In the fall of 1940, with France safely out of the war and Britain fighting for her life, Italian troops in East Africa moved into neighboring British Somaliland; others from Libya invaded Egypt. At the same time, using conquered Albania as a base, an Italian army invaded Greece.

For Italian armies life seems to be filled with unpleasant surprises. The Greeks put up a stout resistance, routed the invading Italian army, and threw the entire timetable out of gear. The British army in Egypt met the invading Italians and drove them back. Then a British counterattack pushed on to capture the principal seaport of Italian Libya. Finally, the British sent troops to help Greece against the Italians. In East Africa the British also counterattacked. They regained British Somaliland, and went on to drive the Italians out of their short-lived "empire" in Ethiopia. Emperor Haile Selassie was restored to his throne. By June, 1941, the Italians had surrendered all their East African territories to Britain. Mussolini could "talk a good war," but apparently he lacked the touch when it came to the real thing.

War in the Libyan desert: British infantry advancing. A shell has just burst in front of them.

● Hitler takes Bulgaria

With Hitler, however, it was different. Once started in the penetration of the Balkans, he went the limit, as always. Bulgaria followed Rumania. Pressure on the Bulgarian government resulted in another bloodless conquest, another satellite state for the Nazis. It also brought the Germans within striking distance of Istanbul (formerly Constantinople) and the Straits. Italy was in trouble in Greece. Hitler was willing to help, because Greece, in his hands, was a jumping-off place for the Suez Canal and the Near East with its rich oil resources.

● Yugoslavia and Greece

Between Greece and the German-held territories in central Europe and the northern Balkans lay the state of Yugoslavia. It was an uncomfortable position. No one could feel secure with Hitler as a near neighbor. The Yugoslav Regent, Prince Paul, was willing to

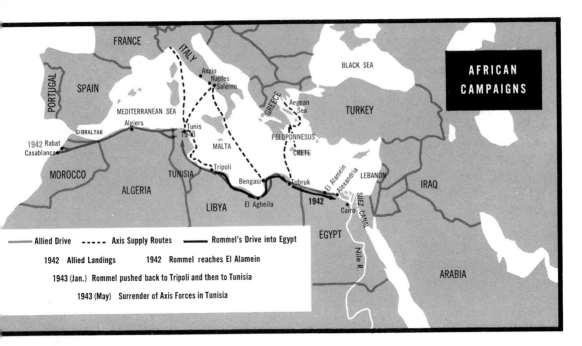

AFRICAN CAMPAIGNS

——— Allied Drive   - - - - - Axis Supply Routes   ━━━ Rommel's Drive into Egypt

1942   Allied Landings   1942   Rommel reaches El Alamein

1943 (Jan.)   Rommel pushed back to Tripoli and then to Tunisia

1943 (May)   Surrender of Axis Forces in Tunisia

make a deal with Hitler in return for a promise of political and territorial preservation. The Yugoslav people had little faith in Hitler's pledges; there was an uprising. The young King Peter II was placed on the throne, and a new ministry given power. Such an "insult" was, of course, more than Hitler could stand. Yugoslavia was invaded by German troops from the north and Italians from Albania. In less than two weeks a typical German blitz had crushed Yugoslavian resistance with tremendous bloodshed and destruction.

Greece came next. Despite the help of British troops from Australia and New Zealand, and stubborn fighting by the Greeks, the air power and mechanized strength of the Nazis were too great. Greece was conquered. The British withdrew to the island of Crete, where British sea power seemed to make them safe.

Now one of the new military techniques of the war was used. German parachute troops and air-borne troops in transport planes and gliders swarmed into Crete. After heavy fighting, remnants of the Greek and British forces had to abandon the island and move to Egypt. Thus Germany controlled the entire Balkan Peninsula except the narrow tip, Istanbul and the Straits, where Turkey remained determinedly neutral.

● The campaign in North Africa and the Near East

The British success in North Africa proved to be brief. Once Greece had been conquered, the Germans were able to move powerful forces across the Mediterranean by air and in ships that ran the British blockade. Led by General Erwin Rommel, the "Desert Fox," the Axis forces drove the weakened British out of Libya and back into Egypt. Here the British were able to make a stand at a place called El Alamein, only seventy miles from the great port and naval base of Alexandria.

The German plan was clear: a gigantic "pincers movement" against the Suez Canal. One jaw of the nutcracker came through North Africa; the other was to come through the Near East: Lebanon, Syria, Iraq, and Palestine. In this region they would have the added advantage of vast oil fields. The Nazis had made the usual preparations in the Near East, with Nazi parties and fifth columnists in readiness. Lebanon and Syria could be taken from Vichy France.

This time, however, the plan broke down. The British and Free French were able to hold fast in Iraq, and to drive out the Vichy French from Lebanon and Syria. In spite of great German pressure, Turkey remained neutral. The German North African force was stalled at El Alamein. Vigorous efforts by the British navy in the Mediterranean made it difficult for Axis supply ships to reach Africa.

● The end of German-Russian coöperation

The German triumph in Rumania and Bulgaria had come without fighting, but Yugoslavia and Greece had been much more costly. German victories were costly in another sense, too. The seizure of Bulgaria and Rumania alarmed the Soviet Union. There was now a long, common German-Russian frontier from East Prussia to the Black Sea. The Russians regarded the Balkans, especially Rumania and Bulgaria, as their own sphere of influence.

In November, 1940, after the Germans had taken Rumania, but before the Bulgarian victory, there was a Soviet-Nazi conference in Berlin. The Russians demanded that Bulgaria, Istanbul, and the Straits be an exclusively Soviet sphere of influence. Hitler suggested a vast division of Europe and Asia: Germany was to have all of Europe; Russia was to have Asia, including India. Neither would yield, and there was a deadlock. After the German conquest of Bulgaria, relations between the two signers of the nonaggression pact became steadily worse.

Germany attacks Soviet Russia

On June 22, 1941, the great war entered a second stage. Without a declaration of war German armies invaded Soviet Russia along the entire western border. They received help from Finnish, Hungarian, Italian, and Rumanian armies. The Spanish dictator Franco, although he did not openly enter the war against Britain, sent a division of troops to fight against Soviet Russia. Thus in eastern Europe a new 1,800-mile front was opened. Britain, fighting alone from her island, now had help in the east, possibly an ally with enormous manpower and resources. On the day of the invasion Prime Minister Churchill declared that although he did not admire communism, any nation that fought the Nazis was an ally. Such a nation should receive all possible aid from Britain and the freedom-loving nations. The United States also declared its willingness to extend Lend-Lease aid to the Russians.

Willingness to give aid was one thing; getting actual help to the Russians was another.

War comes again to the Pyramids (pages 31, 333). The British set up a radar station on the Great Pyramid. The Khepren Pyramid is in the background.

Convoy to Russia. Seamen on a British ship watch smoke pour up from a merchantman hit by a German bomber. In spite of four days of attack, this convoy kept on to Murmansk to carry supplies to the Russians.

As in World War I, Russia was blockaded against Allied aid. Although Turkey remained neutral, help by way of the Straits and the Black Sea would have to run the gauntlet of German air and submarine power in Greece, Rumania, and Bulgaria. There were two Russian ports in the Arctic, at Murmansk and Archangel. Convoys to them had to pass the long, Nazi-held coast of Norway. From this coast both planes and submarines took a terrific toll. But another route was developed. From the head of the Persian Gulf supplies crossed Iran by train and truck to southern Russia in the Caspian and Caucasus region. This Persian route was developed into a lifeline over which trucks, guns, planes, munitions, food, and lubricants from Britain and the United States poured into Russia to keep the Russians fighting.

● *The Russian defense scheme*

The Russians needed all the help they could get. The initial force of the Nazi panzer columns was terrific. Everywhere the Russian armies were rolled back. For a time it seemed

as though Hitler would have another swift victory. Within a very short time the great cities of Moscow and Leningrad (formerly Petrograd and St. Petersburg) were under siege. Here, however, the attack bogged down. For the first time in the war the German armies found themselves in a real fight to the finish, instead of a quick, easy victory. There were several reasons for the stronger Russian resistance.

The first reason, undoubtedly, is the vast size of Russia. Countries like Rumania, Yugoslavia, Poland, and even France are comparatively small. A defending army has little chance to "roll with the punch," as the boxers say. A powerful attack can overrun the entire country in a short time. Not so in Russia, which is almost two and a half times the size of the United States. A defending army can retreat long distances, and still have behind it vast areas of its own land. Here it can recover, regain momentum, and launch a counterattack. The attacker, on the other hand, has an ever longer line of transportation, communication, and supplies. Napoleon learned this to his sorrow.

The Russians used the same scorched-earth tactics against Hitler that their forefathers had used against Napoleon. The retreating armies and the civil population destroyed everything of value as they went. Homes were burned, factories carried away or demolished, railroad, telegraph and telephone lines destroyed, cattle driven away or slaughtered, grain and other foodstuffs burned. Thus the land which the enemy gained was more of a hindrance than a help. Many of the civilians fled before the invaders, but many men remained behind. They hid out in the swamps and forests, and made guerrilla attacks on railroads, bridges, trains, supply lines, and water lines. These were lightning attacks; the guerrillas struck, destroyed, then scattered. They terrorized individuals who collaborated with the conquerors, forced the Nazis to use many troops to guard their supply and communication lines, and made administration of the occupied areas most difficult.

Hitler's famous "intuition" and his previous easy successes led him to expect a Russian surrender after a short campaign. The Russian stand at Leningrad, and especially at Moscow, wrecked his timetable. As the struggle lasted through the summer and short Russian fall, Hitler was faced with the decision Napoleon had to make: He could either retreat, leaving the Russian army weakened but still organized, or he could stand. Unlike Napoleon, Hitler chose to stand.

Now the Germans had to face a new enemy—what the Russians call Generals January and February. Inadequately supplied for a winter campaign, the Nazi troops were numbed by the bitterly cold winter of 1941–1942. The cold also played havoc with their equipment. The Russians, accustomed to such hardships and better equipped for them, chose this time for a counterattack, especially to relieve pressure on Moscow. For the first time the Germans had to retreat. All along the line they were forced back, with great losses of men and material. (See the picture on page 343.)

Nevertheless, the year 1941 ended with the Germans deep in Russian territory. They had plenty of force left for another great campaign when spring and summer again made their kind of fighting possible. Meantime, the Russians and British had gained a great and powerful ally in the west: the United States had entered the war.

Japan attacks the United States

By the end of November, 1941, the United States had become, for all practical purposes, a nonfighting ally of both the British and the Russians (see pages 666–669). The United States had given most of its attention to the war in Europe. In 1941, however, relations with Japan reached the critical state described on page 672.

Part of the United States naval base at Cavite, in the Philippines, after Japanese air bombing. Manila was hit the same day as Pearl Harbor.

The people of the United States were still greatly divided in their attitude toward the war. It may seem that a declaration of war was only a short step beyond what we were actually doing, but it would have been a difficult step to take, politically. Isolationism was still strong, and an unprovoked declaration of war would have found the country divided.

● The attack on Pearl Harbor

On December 7, 1941, Japan did the one thing that would unite American public opinion completely. Without warning, without any declaration of war, and while "peace conferences" were still going on in Washington, planes from a fleet of Japanese carriers attacked the United States navy base of Pearl Harbor, Hawaii. The attack came as a complete surprise. Some of the American ships were sunk or so badly damaged as to be put out of commission. The American dead totaled 2,403.

677

Arctic Ocean

ALASKA

UNION OF SOVIET SOCIALIST REPUBLICS

KAMCHATKA

ATTU   ALEUTIAN IS.   Dutch Harbor

SAKHALIN

KISKA

MONGOLIA   MANCHURIA

Vladivostok

Mukden •

KOREA

MIDWAY

• Hiroshima

CHINA

Nagasaki •

RYUKYU IS.

OKINAWA

BONIN IS.

IWO JIMA

HAWAIIAN
ISLANDS

Pearl Harbor •

BURMA

WAKE IS.

THAI-
LAND

INDO-CHINA

PHILIPPINE

ISLANDS

LEYTE

MARIANAS

SAIPAN

GUAM   TINIAN

CAROLINE IS.

TRUK

MALAYA

• Singapore

KWAJALEIN

MARSHALL IS.

EAST INDIES

NEW GUINEA

SOLOMON IS.

TARAWA

GILBERT IS.

GUADALCANAL

Coral Sea

SAMOA IS.

AUSTRALIA

**FAR EAST and
PACIFIC 1941-45**

Furthest extent
of Japan's conquests

NEW

ZEALAND

Now there was no question as to whether the United States would declare war. The problem was out of American hands. On December 8, 1941, the Congress declared war on Japan, as did the British Parliament. Four days later Germany and Italy declared war on the United States, and the Congress re-

plied in kind. Thus the United States became a full-fledged belligerent in the second world war.

It was a question, though, what kind of a war the United States could fight, and how it could be fought. The Pacific war against Japan would have to be primarily a naval war, but the United States navy had been seriously damaged at Pearl Harbor. To get men and supplies to the war in Europe was a naval problem, too. Although American industry had some start in providing Lend-Lease to Britain and Russia, it was still largely on a peacetime basis. Now we had to supply the British and Russians, and also provide for an enormous American war effort on two fronts.

Japanese victories in the Far East and the Pacific

The Japanese were quick to take advantage of American inability to defend the seas. On the same day as the attack on Hawaii Japan began aerial attacks on the Philippines; on the third day the first landings on Luzon started. The American defenders had known for some hours of the attack on Pearl Harbor. For some reason that has never been explained the planes of the American air force, on which much of the defense against invasion depended, were carefully drawn up in formations on the air fields. They were "sitting ducks" to the attacking Japanese.

Within a month the American island outposts of Guam and Wake had been captured. In less than three months the mainland areas of Burma, Thailand, and Malaya, with its mighty British fortress of Singapore, had been added to already-conquered Indo-China. The Japanese went on to conquer a vast island empire: the East Indies, the Philippines, and the Gilbert Islands. Australia stood out as the last stronghold of resistance in the southwest Pacific, but it could be supplied only over a long line from Hawaii. Japanese landings on New Guinea and the Solomon Islands threatened even this supply line.

Thus, in an amazingly short time Japan had taken over a million square miles of land with more than one hundred million inhabitants. The region was rich in resources: copper, manganese, tin, rubber, iron, hemp, quinine, and oil. The area was the world supplier of some of these commodities, especially tin, rubber, and quinine. Their loss was a serious handicap to the war effort of the United States and its allies.

The Japanese had shown themselves to be skillful, determined, and resourceful fighters. It was certain that they would fortify their new positions and defend them fiercely. Regaining all this territory and striking at the Japanese homeland would be a tremendous task, as you can see by looking at the map of the Pacific region.

The Allies' darkest hour

Thus you can understand why the first half of 1942 was a period of darkest gloom for the Allies. Japan had overrun much of the South Pacific and was at the doorstep of India. The Germans were still deep in Soviet territory, preparing for another great drive. They were also in Egypt. The great pincers movement was still a possibility, if the Germans drove into the Caucasus region to cut the Iranian supply line, and then down through the Near East. An even greater pincers movement could take place if the Japanese drove overland through India to meet a German drive into Asia. Britain was still besieged on her island; the Battle of the Atlantic was a terrible one indeed. During the first six months of 1942 Axis submarines sank 506 merchant ships, totaling 2,783,316 tons, in the Atlantic and Arctic areas. Only 28 German and Italian submarines were destroyed.

Review of Chapter 52

People, places, and things

Identify: Premier Tojo, Saburo Kurusu, Prince Paul of Yugoslavia, General Erwin Rommel.

Locate: Egypt, Suez Canal, Alexandria, El Alamein, the Sudan, Kenya, Tunisia, British Somaliland, Ethiopia, Libya, Hungary, Rumania, Yugoslavia, Greece, Albania, Crete, Lebanon, Syria, Iraq, Palestine, the Persian Gulf, Murmansk, Moscow, Leningrad, Pearl Harbor, the Philippines, Manila, Wake, Guam, Indo-China, Dutch East Indies, Australia, New Guinea

Events in review

1. What action did Japan take after France and the Netherlands were defeated by Germany?
2. Tell briefly the attitude taken by the United States toward the Japanese war with China.
3. In the fall of 1940, Italy started three offensives. Tell where these attacks were made and whether or not they succeeded.
4. Why did the Germans invade Greece? Did the German attack succeed?
5. Briefly describe the German plan for a "pincers movement" in North Africa and the Near East.
6. Why can it be said that the war entered a second stage in June 1941?
7. Explain the importance of Murmansk and the Persian Gulf in the war.
8. How did "Generals January and February" play a part in the war?
9. How much territory did the Japanese conquer in the early months of their participation in World War II?
10. Why was the early part of 1942 a dark period for the Allies?

Problems and projects

1. Discuss relations between Germany and Russia from the signing of the Hitler-Stalin Pact to the invasion of Russia. How did the German invasion of the Balkans influence German-Russian relations? Why did Hitler attack Russia?
2. Why did the Nazi blitzkrieg strategy, which had been so successful in the west, fail in Russia? Compare the problems of Hitler's armies in Russia with those faced by Napoleon's forces in 1812. What was the effect (in both cases) of the Russian scorched earth policy, of guerrilla warfare, and of severe weather?
3. Discuss the increasing tension between the United States and Japan from 1939 to 1941. What was Japan trying to do? Why did the United States object? What moves did the two nations make?
4. What did the Japanese expect to accomplish by their strike on Pearl Harbor? What was the major effect of their attack? Why could this date be called a turning point in the course of the war?
5. On a map of North Africa and the Near East, show the route of the pincer movement planned by the Germans. Show how far General Rommel's armies drove into Egypt before they were defeated.
6. On the basis of research in books and atlases, draw a large war map of the European theatre in 1940–1941. Show key bases such as Malta and Alexandria. Show supply routes from England to Egypt, from Germany to North Africa, from England and the United States to Russia. Show the lines taken by German offensives, and the scenes of battles. Show, for the Battle of the Atlantic, the areas where German submarines were most active.

Chapter 53 The Coming of Victory

THE SECOND HALF of 1942 saw the tide of war begin to turn. The Allies had tremendous forces, both of manpower and production. The job was to organize for war and unite in a common purpose. The first step came at Washington on January 2, 1942, when twenty-six nations, at war with the Axis, pledged themselves to a common victory, subscribed to the principles of the Atlantic Charter, and signed a declaration to that effect.

Objectives of the Allies

In the years that followed, there were numerous other conferences at which either the leaders of the Allied nations—Roosevelt, Churchill, Stalin, Chiang Kai-shek, or their foreign ministers—met to discuss the conduct of the war and the peace to follow. Such conferences were held in Washington in 1942; and in Casablanca (Morocco), Quebec (Canada), Moscow, Cairo (Egypt), and Teheran (Iran), during 1943. In 1945 came two of the most important ones, at Yalta, in the Crimea, and Potsdam, in Germany. All of these meetings made important contributions to the war effort in achieving a common purpose and healing disagreements among the Allies. A coalition war is hard to fight successfully.

The Allied nations were able to agree both on immediate plans and on a statement of ultimate objectives. These were issued as the Seven Points. You will notice that while they resemble the statements of the Atlantic Charter, there are differences. The points were:

1. The organization and maintenance of world security.
2. The joint enforcement of the terms of peace.
3. Joint action in the surrender and disarmament of the enemy.
4. The establishment of a world order based on the principle of equal sovereignty of all nations, great and small.
5. Joint action to maintain peace and order until an international organization could be established.
6. No military occupation of foreign countries except with the consent of the other Allied nations.
7. Reduction of world armaments.

Much suffering had to be endured, many lives lost, before any of these objectives could be attained.

NOTE: The world map on pages 682–683 shows the areas in which the major campaigns of 1942–1945 were fought.

ARCTIC OCEAN

KAMCHATKA

ALASKA

ATTU
KISKA I.
ALEUTIAN IS.

PACIFIC OCEAN

UNITED STATES

NORTH
ATLANTI
OCEAN

MIDWAY

WAKE I.
Pearl Harbor
HAWAII

MARSHALL IS.

GILBERT IS.
MAKIN
TARAWA

SOLOMON IS.
ELLICE IS.
GUADALCANAL

NEW ZEALAND

NORWAY
SWEDEN
Hango
G. of FINLAND

ESTONIA

DENMARK
LATVIA

GREAT BRITAIN
Memel
Danzig
LITH.

Liverpool
Coventry
NETHERLANDS
Berlin
E.
PRUSSIA

London
GERMANY
Potsdam
Warsaw
POLAND

Dunkirk
Aachen
Torgau
Vistula R.

BELGIUM
LUX.
Prague
CZECHOSLOVAKIA

Paris
Moselle R.
Vienna

FRANCE
Loire R.
SWITZ.
AUSTRIA
HUNGARY
RUMANIA

Vichy
Po R.
Belgrade

YUGOSLAVIA

Toulon
ITALY
BULGARIA

ALBANIA
Istanbul

GREECE
Athens

SICILY
MALTA

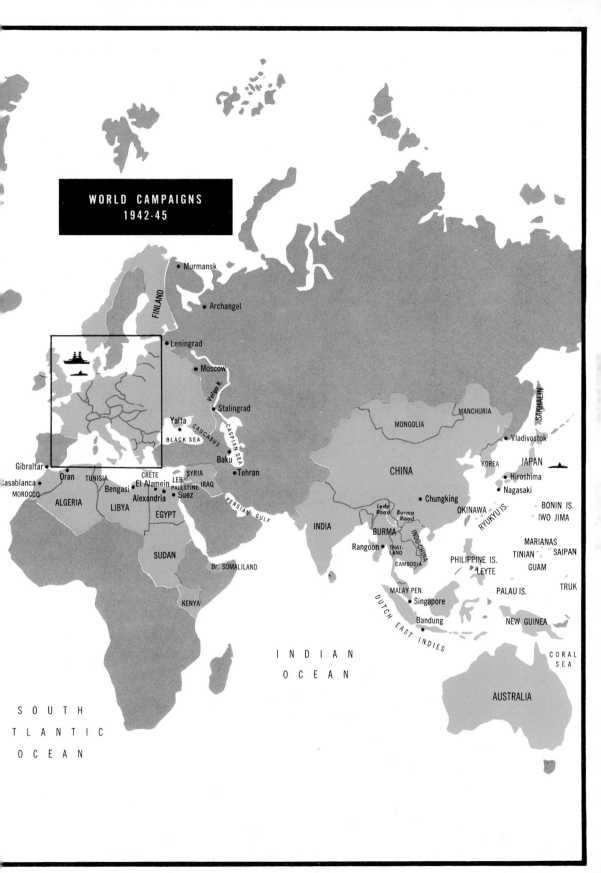

WORLD CAMPAIGNS
1942-45

Murmansk

Archangel

FINLAND

Leningrad

Moscow

Volga R.

Stalingrad

Yalta

CAUCASUS

BLACK SEA

CASPIAN SEA

Baku

Tehran

Gibraltar

Oran

TUNISIA

CRETE

SYRIA

LEB.

PALESTINE

IRAQ

Casablanca

El Alamein

Bengasi

MOROCCO

Alexandria

Suez

ALGERIA

LIBYA

EGYPT

PERSIAN GULF

SUDAN

Br. SOMALILAND

KENYA

MONGOLIA

MANCHURIA

SAKHALIN

Vladivostok

KOREA

JAPAN

CHINA

Hiroshima

Nagasaki

Chungking

OKINAWA

BONIN IS.

IWO JIMA

RYUKYU IS.

Ledo
Road

Burma
Road

INDIA

BURMA

INDO-CHINA

Rangoon

THAI-
LAND

CAMBODIA

MARIANAS

TINIAN

SAIPAN

PHILIPPINE IS.

GUAM

LEYTE

TRUK

MALAY PEN.

Singapore

PALAU IS.

Bandung

NEW GUINEA

DUTCH EAST INDIES

INDIAN

OCEAN

CORAL
SEA

AUSTRALIA

SOUTH

ATLANTIC

OCEAN

Generalissimo Chiang Kai-shek, President Franklin D. Roosevelt, and Prime Minister Winston Churchill at their Cairo conference, November, 1943. This was one of the meetings (see page 681) that helped guide the Allies to victory.

The turn of the tide: North Africa, 1942–1943

The Nazis had been checked first before Moscow in the fall of 1941. The next sign that they were not invincible came in North Africa. Rommel's desert fighters had pushed deep into Egypt before they were stopped at El Alamein. If they could push on to Alexandria, all the control of the eastern Mediterranean would be lost, and the Suez Canal threatened. Allied reinforcements, equipped with quantities of American tanks, were rushed to Egypt. In a decisive battle that lasted more than a week at the end of October, 1942, the Allied troops under the British General Bernard Montgomery almost destroyed Rommel's force. Montgomery followed his advantage and pushed the weakened Germans across Italian Libya toward Tunisia. This victory in the desert was the first encouraging sign of Allied superiority in military equipment. It was an equally good proof of superior strategy, morale, and will to win.

● *Landings in Morocco*

At about the same time a huge American force gathered in the Atlantic off the shores of Morocco. It was commanded by the American General Dwight D. Eisenhower. Early in November British and American forces landed in French North Africa and began to drive east. Both forces joined in Tunisia in a common effort to drive the enemy out of Africa. President Roosevelt appealed to Admiral Darlan, commander of the Vichy French in North Africa, not to resist. Some of the French fought hard against the first landings, but a truce was soon arranged. For this the Vichy government paid dearly. Hitler ordered that all of France be occupied by the Germans. Supreme authority in France was given to the German Marshal von Rundstedt. Pétain and Laval became more than ever puppets of the Nazis.

The Allied forces then began to push eastward toward Tunisia to apply the pincers on Rommel's forces. The Germans rushed reinforcements by air and made the campaign a hard one, but by mid-May, 1943, the German forces surrendered. North Africa was cleared of enemy troops. The Italian empire in Africa disappeared, and the French colonies were now held by the Free French. The Mediterranean route to the Middle and Far East was now secure.

The turn of the tide: Russia, 1942–1943

The Germans had suffered losses of men, materials, and territory in Russia in the bitter winter of 1941–1942, but they were still strong enough for another great offensive. This time they struck toward the south with two main aims. One spearhead drove toward the Caucasus, the oil region of Russia. Another drove toward Stalingrad on the Volga River to cut the all-important supply line north from Iran.

As always, the initial German drive had tremendous force. The southern group pushed deep into the Caucasus toward the Caspian Sea. Fighting fiercely, the Russians stopped it before it reached its goal, the city of Baku. North of the Caucasus the Russians were forced back until they reached Stalingrad.

Here a life and death battle was fought for about six months. The city had been under siege for almost a month when the Germans began what was to be almost their last offensive. Suffering terrible losses, they penetrated the city, but the Russians did not retreat. Fighting went on from street to street and house to house. Again the Germans spent their strength without conquering Russia. Even worse, the Allied landings in North Africa had forced them to shift part of their air force and ground troops from Russia to the Mediterranean. Again Hitler had his choice: He could withdraw from his long and exposed position in Russia before the oncoming winter, or he could stand. Once more he chose to stand.

● Russian victory at Stalingrad

The Russians almost stripped Siberia of reserves. In November, 1942, they began a counterattack with an encircling movement. The battle raged for two months. On February 3, 1943, the entire German army before Stalingrad was forced to surrender. The heroic defense of Stalingrad was certainly one of the turning points of the war. The victory was most significant, not only for the Russians but for the entire Allied cause.

Russian infantry in the rubble of Stalingrad.

The German losses in men and material were stunning. The Nazis never completely recovered from the blow of this decisive defeat.

After the victory at Stalingrad, the Russian army never again lost the initiative. However, the Germans were able to meet almost the supreme test of an army: They were as able and skillful in defense and retreat as in attack. But they were forced to retreat, steadily and continuously. The relentless Russian advance continued throughout 1943. By the beginning of 1944 the Germans had been forced back into Poland. From here on it was a slow but sure agony for an army which, two years before, had marched triumphantly across the continent of Europe.

This victory, clearing Russian soil of the invaders, came at a cost that can hardly be estimated. It was paid, in Churchill's words, in the "blood, sweat, toil, and tears" of millions of men, women, and children. Every member of society paid in some way for every victory on every front, either in lives or in the untold quantities of lend-lease supplies that helped to make the victory possible. All the sacrifices were pooled for a common cause: victory over Nazism and Fascism.

● *Russia demands a second front*

From the beginning of the German campaign in South Russia in 1942, Stalin had made constant and ever-stronger demands that the British and Americans open a second front in western Europe. He wanted to relieve the German pressure on Russia. This problem was one of the greatest points of disagreement among the Allied nations. The British and Americans believed that they were not ready, and that an attack when they were not fully prepared might set them back a long time. The Russians, ever suspicious, thought that the Western powers were allowing the Germans and Russians to kill each other off, while the others sat back to claim the spoils of victory.

The landing in North Africa had relieved the German pressure at Stalingrad a little, but not enough to satisfy Stalin. Once North Africa was cleared, he renewed his demands for a landing on the coast of western Europe. Churchill, on the other hand, insisted on an attack on what he called the "soft underbelly of the Axis": Italy and the Balkans. Churchill won out.

The turn of the tide: Sicily and Italy

In July, 1943, after much preparation by air bombing, the Allied armies from North Africa landed on the strategic island of Sicily. The natives welcomed the invaders. In spite of strong German resistance the island was cleared in a little over a month. From here the bombing of the Italian mainland was stepped up in preparation for a landing there.

In Italy the political results of the conquest of Sicily were swift. Mussolini was forced to resign. The king appointed a new premier, General Pietro Badoglio. His first act was to dissolve the Fascist Party which had ruled for more than twenty years. When the Allied army landed on the toe of the Italian boot, the Italians surrendered unconditionally. The Italian forces under Premier Badoglio now turned on their former ally and declared war on Germany. The Italian government was recognized as a "cobelligerent" (one who fights the same enemy, but is not an ally). There were signs of discontent with Nazi rule elsewhere: in Finland, Hungary, and Bulgaria.

The "underbelly" of Italy did not prove to be very soft. Despite Italian surrender, the Germans resisted the Allied advance with skill and determination. For a time it seemed likely that the Allied forces would be pushed off their second beachhead, at Anzio, on the central coast of the Italian mainland. They held on grimly until reinforcements could come. Then came a slow advance up the peninsula, every gain paid for in the lives

of American, British, and Canadian soldiers. Mussolini retreated with the Germans. Il Duce, the "strong man" of Italy, now proved to be a "Sawdust Caesar."

The turn of the tide: the Pacific

The Japanese were threatening Australia and pushing southward to menace the supply line to Australia. In May, 1942, they got their first check. A Japanese fleet thrusting at the supply line, between New Guinea and the Solomon Islands, was met by American and Australian air and naval forces. In the five-day battle of the Coral Sea, the invaders were turned back. Soon thereafter a larger Japanese fleet pushed eastward to try to capture Midway Island, the major outpost for the great American base in the Hawaiian Islands. The Japanese fleet was met near Midway by an American fleet. In a crucial battle (June 3–June 6) fought chiefly by carrier-based planes, the Japanese were defeated. In these two battles the American fleet began to "cut the Japanese down to size."

The joy of these victories was somewhat dampened by the news that Japanese troops had landed at Kiska and Attu, on the long chain of the Aleutian Islands in the North

U.S.S. Enterprise, *photographed shortly before the United States entered World War II. This carrier and two others, the* Yorktown *and the* Hornet, *were the main strength of the fleet that won the decisive Battle of Midway in June, 1942. Their planes sank four Japanese carriers. The* Enterprise *fought on through the whole Pacific war, taking part in other crucial battles such as those around Guadalcanal.*

Pacific. Their planes had bombed the naval base at Dutch Harbor, the nearest American base to the main islands of Japan. This represented the high point of Japanese advance.

To realize how immense this operation was, look once more at the map on page 678. See how the Japanese line encloses the "fortress of Japan." It runs from Russian Vladivostok at the south tip of Siberia, across Sakhalin, to Paramushiro, off the base of Kamchatka, east to Kiska in the Aleutians. Then it makes a great sweep southward through the Marshall Islands and Gilberts to the Ellice Islands. Thence it turns westward through the Solomons and eastern New Guinea and curves around the East Indies to reach the India-Burma border. On the mainland of Asia it includes Burma, Thailand,

Malaya, Indo-China, the whole coast of China, most of northern China, Manchuria, and Korea. As striking points against the Japanese heart-land, Midway was 2,600 miles from Japan, and Dutch Harbor almost as far. The northern tip of Australia was nearly 1,000 miles farther from Japan. These are "air miles." All the intervening seas were held by the Japanese fleet and submarines, with many islands strongly held by Japanese troops and planes.

The naval victories of Coral Sea and Midway had been defensive. The next move was defensive also. In early August, 1942, American marines landed on the Solomon Islands, seizing Tulagi and the airfield at Guadalcanal. Holding Guadalcanal meant safety for the life line to Australia from Hawaii and the United States. This hitherto unknown jungle island was so important that four times in the next four months the Japanese launched savage attacks on the United States forces. All were repulsed, with terrible losses on both sides.

● The United States on the offensive

The year 1943 saw the Allied nations take the offensive in the Pacific. Sea, air, and land forces of the United States (helped by Australian and New Zealand forces) turned to the attack. In the South Pacific, a long series of battles drove the Japanese entirely out of the Solomon Islands. In the Central Pacific, Tarawa, in the Gilbert Islands, was captured after a savage fight. In the Aleutians, American forces regained Attu and Kiska.

For the continued offensive against Japan, the Allies adopted a strategy called "island-hopping." The plan was to advance across the Pacific by capturing certain Japanese-held islands. Other Japanese positions were to be bypassed. Once these islands were cut off from Japan they could be left to sit out the rest of the war. One of the greatest Japanese bases, Truk, was left to wither on the vine.

By 1944 the American navy had been greatly enlarged; it now outnumbered the Japanese. From the start of the war, the aircraft carrier had replaced the battleship as the "backbone of the fleet." In 1944, many new carriers joined the fleet. The army and marine corps were now large enough to supply men not only for the Italian fronts and the proposed landing in Normandy, but also for new offensives in the Pacific. The Marshall Islands in the Central Pacific and New Guinea in the South Pacific were cleared of Japanese. The Marianas, in the west-central Pacific, were taken to provide, in northernmost Saipan and Tinian, bases for the long-range bombing of Japan. In October, 1944, an American army commanded by General

United States Marines on the beach at Kwajalein, during the conquest of the Marshall Islands in 1944. The Americans had 1,954 killed and wounded out of 41,446 troops used. Of the Japanese garrison of 8,675, only 265 survived the battle.

Douglas MacArthur landed at Leyte in the central Philippines. Shortly after the landing the Japanese fleet suffered a crushing defeat in a great air and sea fight—the Battle of Leyte Gulf. The Japanese ground forces fought on, but after six months of hard and bitter fighting the entire Philippine archipelago was recovered.

● *China and the Burma Road*

In China, the war from 1940 to 1943 had been a deadlock. During 1944 the truce between Chiang Kai-shek and the Chinese Communists broke down. Each side accused the other of fighting it rather than the Japanese. Undoubtedly there was fault on both sides. Chiang was still receiving a trickle of supplies flown "over the hump" from India. General Joseph Stilwell, his American military adviser, urged Chiang to take the offensive against the Japanese, but Chiang seemed more interested in storing up supplies for a fight with the Communists. At Chiang's insistence Stilwell was removed. It seemed clear that China would not be able or willing to make much of an offensive as long as the China coast and the Burma Road, her principal supply routes, were still in Japanese hands.

The Burma Road might have been reopened if Britain had been able to get assistance from India. Here, however, she ran into difficulties with both the independence movement and the Hindu-Moslem hostility. In return for military help, Britain offered India dominion status after the war. But Gandhi and the India Congress Party demanded immediate self-government. The Moslems demanded a separate, independent state if India were granted self-government. When Britain refused immediate self-government, Gandhi and his followers turned to "civil disobedience" and urged nonresistance to Japan. American engineers began building a new road, the Ledo Road, to China, west of the Burma Road.

After the assault forces came the Seabees to build air and naval bases. Each island captured was rapidly turned into a base for pushing the attack closer to Japan. The United States forces did a remarkable job of building and supplying bases thousands of miles from home.

Steps to victory

● *Increased production*

In 1942 American industry made a slow start at changing over to the production of war supplies. During 1943 industrial and farm production increased at a rapid rate. By 1944 the "miracle of American production" was again taking place. Statistics are cold, often meaningless things, and for this reason may be omitted. It is enough to think of the wide-flung fronts that had to be supplied: the Russian, the North African, the Italian, the Pacific, and the Chinese. Of course, every commander felt that he did not receive enough; that is the way it is in war. But every front was supplied, and a reserve built up for the last push.

American lend-lease supplies did not travel entirely on a one-way street after the United States entered the war. There was also a "reverse lend-lease." The British, especially, furnished many supplies and much equipment to American troops in Europe. They provided bases for ships and planes and quarters for troops. It was real pooling of supplies for a common cause.

● Defeat of the submarines

More important still, the supplies were reaching their destination in increasing quantities. The Battle of the Atlantic was being won. The convoys of troop and supply ships were protected both by destroyers and other escort ships and by land-based and carrier-based planes. New scientific devices were perfected to locate submarines. The "wolf-packs" of Nazi submarines were turned from hunters into hunted.

● Air attacks on Germany

The Allied air attack against Germany and the occupied countries rose steadily in

The home front. World War II was a contest between the factories of the warring nations as well as between planes, ships, and men. Industry in this country and in Great Britain turned out enormous quantities of weapons, supplies, and equipment. Shown here is a Ford Motor Company assembly line manufacturing "Liberator" bombers (B24's) for the United States Army Air Force. At its peak strength, in 1945, the air arm had more than 80,000 planes in service.

fury and intensity. German cities were bombed more ferociously than the Germans had bombed England. At first the Allies tried "pinpoint" bombing, aimed at industrial targets only. Later they switched to "area-bombing" to weaken both the ability and the will of the Axis to fight. Some cities, like Hamburg, were almost wiped out. There was scarcely a single German city that did not feel the terror from the air. Industries in the occupied countries were also bombed. It was sad to have to destroy the productive power of peoples who had been on the side of the free nations. In fact, the inhabitants may have wondered which was worse: being conquered or being "liberated." Most of them, though, were not bitter about the costs of regaining freedom.

Victory in Europe

● D–Day: the second front

On June 6, 1944, came the long-awaited event: the Allied landing in western Europe. The Germans had called their defense line along the coast the Atlantic Wall of Fortress Europe, and had boasted that it could not be taken. The landing was preceded by months of careful planning of every detail by the Allied military staff, commanded by General Eisenhower. The engineering ingenuity behind the transfer of more than a million men and their equipment across the English Channel reads like a story from science fiction. Carried and guarded by the greatest gathering of ships in history, screened in the air above, almost a quarter of a million men landed on the first day to breach the Atlantic Wall and carry the battle into Fortress Europe.

The landings were made on the beaches of the French peninsula of Normandy. Within a month the Allies had poured into Europe more than 1,000,000 men, 150,000 vehicles, and 650,000 tons of supplies. The Germans fought stubbornly, trying to bottle up the Allied army on the narrow, heavily wooded peninsula. At the same time they tried again to destroy British morale, this time by an attack with two new weapons. The V-1 was a pilotless, jet-propelled, flying bomb. The V-2 was a rocket-propelled missile.

Both German attempts failed. After several weeks of hard fighting, Allied troops broke out of the peninsula and began a blitzkrieg of their own to free northern France. The French underground resistance forces, the maquis, harassed the Germans with guerrilla warfare. The Allied forces in Italy had fought their way up the peninsula to the German line protecting the Po River Valley. Now they also made a landing on the Mediterranean coast of France and fought their way up the Loire River valley. On August 25, 1944, Allied troops entered Paris. The Allies now blasted their way across northern France into Belgium. By the beginning of September they faced the dreaded German West Wall and Siegfried Line that ran through Belgium, Luxembourg, and along the west bank of the Moselle River.

● The Russians drive from the east

In June, 1944, the Russians made a gigantic attack on the Germans. They struck along the eastern battle front which stretched for 2,000 miles. Attacks came all along the line. By mid-September Finland surrendered. In the next three months the Baltic states of Estonia, Lithuania, and Latvia were recaptured. A southern Russian spearhead struck through the Balkans. By the end of August Rumania was out of the war. Bulgaria followed at the end of October. The exposed position in Greece now caused the Germans to withdraw from the Aegean Islands. A British force landed in Greece and drove the Germans out. Yugoslavia was freed by Russian and Yugoslav guerrilla troops under Marshal Joseph Tito. Albania was also conquered. In Hungary, the dictator, Admiral Miklos Horthy recommended surrender, but he was overthrown by Hungarian and German fascists.

The heaviest Russian fighting and the strongest German defense were on the central front, in Poland. The German Fatherland Line was very strong. It took heroic attacks by the Russians to break through. By July they had reached the Vistula River, not far from Warsaw.

Despite the loss of their allies, the Nazi leaders of Germany would not give up. Both the military leaders and the people realized that further fighting meant only disaster. In

Three of the leaders of the drive across France: Lieutenant General George S. Patton, Lieutenant General Omar Bradley, and Field Marshal Sir Bernard Montgomery.

July, 1944, there was an unsuccessful attempt to assassinate Hitler. Still Hitler insisted on continuing the war. To the very last he talked of working his way out of Germany's plight and going on to victory. There was no choice for the Allies but to finish the job of subduing Germany by force.

● The Americans and British drive from the west

In the west the "unconquerable" West Wall was pierced by an American army at Aachen (Charlemagne's old capital) after five weeks of fighting. In Belgium the British were able to take the port city of Antwerp. Now supplies could be brought directly for the attack. The Allies cleared Alsace and Lorraine of Germans and prepared for an attack all along the line.

The Germans were not through, however. They made a terrific counterattack in Belgium and drove a fifty-mile bulge into the Allied lines. The fighting of this Battle of the Bulge, which lasted two weeks, was some of the hardest in the war. The Allies rallied and held the German drive. They were

helped by the fact that the Russians, in the east, launched the greatest winter attack in all history. In three weeks they advanced 265 miles into German territory.

When the Bulge was eliminated, the Allies encircled the West Wall at either end and moved on to the Rhine. By sheer good luck the American army found a bridge undestroyed at Remagen. They pushed across the river quickly and established a bridgehead on the other side. Simultaneously the British army made an important crossing farther north.

Now Germany felt the blitz on the ground as well as from the air. American and British columns from the west and Russian columns from the east sliced and slashed the crumbling German army into smaller and smaller bits. In early spring of 1945 the whole front simply caved in.

On April 25, 1945, a momentous event took place at the city of Torgau. The Russian and American armies made their first contact. It was agreed that the Russians, who had suffered most from German occupation and had made the greatest sacrifices in the fighting, would be given the honor of entering Berlin first. Still the German command refused to surrender. It still tried to save something by separating the Allies. The Nazi generals were especially reluctant to surrender to the Russians. Toward the end of April the German command offered to surrender to the British and Americans. Allied unity prevailed; the offer was refused.

● V–E Day

Now the German commanders in the field began to give up. At the end of April the German army in northern Italy surrendered unconditionally. Italian guerrillas at once pursued and captured Mussolini. The fallen idol was shot and his body hung in public. On May 1 came the news that Hitler had either committed suicide or been killed in the struggle for Berlin. The following day the Russians captured the battered and devastated city. Within a week the German high command surrendered unconditionally. May 8, 1945, was V–E Day: the day of victory in Europe.

Victory in the Pacific

There was still a war to be won in the Pacific. Allied island-hopping had brought the main islands of Japan within the range of long-range bombers (the B29 superfortresses) from Saipan. By early 1945 these raids became systematic. The Japanese industrial cities were being devastated. Effective bombing needed closer islands, though, both for medium-range bombers and as a landing-place for superfortresses crippled in the long-range attacks.

The first move was into the Bonin Islands, directly south of Tokyo and not far away as a bomber flies. The one picked for assault was the small, volcanic island of Iwo Jima. Here the American marines landed, and some of the bitterest fighting of the war took place. It was a long, bloody month before the small island was cleared of Japanese defenders. From here the attack shifted to the nearby Ryukyu Islands. The largest island, Okinawa, was taken, again after bitter fighting. Japanese resistance became more desperate the more closely the home islands were approached. Thousands of fanatical Japanese pilots volunteered to crash their planes into Allied ships. Off Okinawa, nearly 250 vessels were damaged by air attacks, most of them suicide crashes.

Japanese cities, factories, and bases were now subjected to destructive raids by army long-range bombers and by navy carrier planes. Japan could hardly move a ship out of port in the face of the Allied fleets. (United States submarines, for example, sank 524 Japanese merchantmen in 1944–1945). Nevertheless, the government refused all urging to surrender.

The Battle of the Bulge. Infantrymen of the United States 2nd Division take shelter from a German artillery barrage.

● Problems of defeating Japan

You have to understand the military situation of the entire Far East in the spring of 1945, *as it looked at the time,* to understand two important decisions that were made then. Although Japanese cities and industries were under constant and heavy bombing, there was no sign of Japanese surrender. Germany had shown that an industrial nation can endure several years of heavy air attacks, and still have to be conquered on the ground, making conquest bloody and costly. There was every indication that this would have to be done in Japan. The main islands would have to be invaded and conquered. The experience in the Marshalls, the Gilberts, Iwo Jima, and Okinawa showed that this would be a dreadfully costly business. The Japanese had proved themselves desperate fighters. They did not surrender, even when their situation was absolutely hopeless. They fought to the death.

Military experts at the time had another problem. The Japanese army was firmly entrenched on the mainland of Asia, especially in Korea and Manchuria. The Manchurian army was reported to be the pick of all the

Japanese military forces. It might continue to fight even though the homeland was conquered. This would require a landing on the mainland of Asia and possibly a long campaign there.

● Yalta: the decision to get Russia to enter the war against Japan

The best solution of the Manchurian problem seemed to be to persuade the Soviet Union to enter the war against Japan. They could attack Manchuria from Siberia while the other Allied nations attacked the main islands. Russia was not at war with Japan. She had a nonaggression treaty with Japan which did not expire until April, 1946. She had given warning that she might enter the Japanese war sooner. While the Russians were fighting for their lives against the German invasion, they had no desire for an additional war in Asia. They had resisted all urging to declare war on Japan.

In February, 1945, before the conquest of Iwo Jima and Okinawa, President Roosevelt and Prime Minister Winston Churchill met Marshal Stalin at Yalta in southern Russia. They agreed that after surrender Germany should be temporarily divided and occupied by Allied forces. They also planned democratic governments for the liberated areas of Europe. Most important, they promised Stalin that if he would declare war on Japan within

Amphibious landing in the Pacific war. Men of the 124th Infantry wade ashore from U.S. Navy landing craft. In 1945 it seemed probable that the greatest amphibious operation of the Pacific campaign would have to be carried out against the home islands of Japan.

two or three months after the German surrender, Russia would receive compensation: (1) Russia would get the southern part of the Island of Sakhalin and (2) the Kurile Islands; (3) Port Arthur would be leased to Russia as a naval base; (4) the port of Dairen would be internationalized; and (5) the Chinese-Eastern railroad would be operated jointly by Russia and China. Chiang Kai-shek did not attend the Yalta conference, but he did accept the terms later. This was the first decision: to make concessions to Russia in the Far East in return for a declaration of war on Japan and an invasion of Manchuria.

● Potsdam: the decision to use the atomic bomb

The second decision concerned an equally serious problem: the use of the atomic bomb. You may recall that nineteenth-century scientists had discovered that all matter is composed of atoms. Later research had convinced men that the atom itself was composed of energy, and that it could be split to release this energy. In the 1920's Albert Einstein had stated the possibilities of the production of energy from atomic fission, or splitting, in the terrifyingly simple equation $E = mc^2$: the energy in the atom is equal to its mass multiplied by the square of the speed of light. During the 1920's and 1930's scientists everywhere were working on the problem of splitting the atom. Just before the beginning of World War II, German scientists had succeeded in splitting an atom of uranium, although they did not release energy in any usable form.

In 1941 Einstein persuaded President Roosevelt that the free nations should make a great effort to produce an atomic weapon. German scientists were known to be working on the problem and must not succeed first. Prime Minister Churchill agreed. Scientists from all over the free world, many of them refugees from Germany, Italy, or the conquered countries, gathered in the United States to work with American scientists on the supersecret "Manhattan Project." Four years of work and billions of dollars went into the project. By the early summer of 1945 a usable atomic bomb had been produced.

The question immediately arose in Washington: should the bomb be used? The scientists predicted that it would be the most terribly destructive weapon ever known in warfare.

After the German surrender, the Allied leaders met at Potsdam, in July, 1945. President Roosevelt had died; President Harry S. Truman represented the United States. Winston Churchill's party had been defeated in an election. Prime Minister Clement Attlee of the Labour Party represented Great Britain. Premier Joseph Stalin still represented Russia.

The decision was to issue an ultimatum to Japan. Unless she surrendered, new and more terrible blows would be struck at the main islands. Japan must agree to give up all territory taken since 1894. She must return Manchuria, Formosa, and the Pescadores Islands to China, and allow Korea to become independent. The Japanese government refused to surrender.

●Hiroshima, Nagasaki, and surrender

On August 6, 1945, the world entered a new age. A single American bomber dropped an atomic bomb on Hiroshima, Japan. It exploded with the force of 20,000 tons of TNT. More than 60 per cent of Hiroshima was smashed into scorched ruins. On August 8 Russia declared war on Japan, and Russian armies swept down into Manchuria. Contrary to expectations, they met little resistance. On August 9 a second and even more powerful atomic bomb was dropped on the city of Nagasaki. Next day the Japanese sued for peace, asking only that the emperor could keep his throne. The Allies agreed, provided that the emperor would accept the orders of the Supreme Allied Commander. On September 2, 1945, the unconditional surrender was signed on board the American battleship *Missouri* in Tokyo Bay. The most terrible war in history came to an end.

The decisions of the Yalta and Potsdam Conferences have been bitterly criticized since the end of the war. It has been said that the Russian entry into the war with Japan was not necessary. Therefore, the concessions to Russia were simply "gifts to communism." It has been said that the use of the atomic bomb was not necessary. Japan could not resist much longer and would have surrendered without the devastation of two cities by the appalling new weapon.

You will have to make up your mind for yourself concerning these problems. It is possible that both criticisms are correct. All an individual can do today is to remember that decisions must be made in the light of *what is known at the time,* and not what becomes clear later. It is not possible for the man who makes the decision to be a "Monday-morning quarterback." He does not have the advantage of knowing what will happen later.

World War II: A summary

What can be said of the costs of World War II? There is almost no way to estimate them. The cost of destroyed property alone would run into billions and billions of dollars. This would, of course, overlook that dreadful and incalculable cost of lives, the toil and the suffering, not only during the war itself but for many years afterward. Placing a dollar value on this sacrifice is a poor sort of honor to pay to those who gave their lives, either in battle or behind the lines.

In the discussion of the price humanity paid for World War I you read of another intangible cost: the decline of civilization and culture. The quotation used there (page

A view of Hiroshima, showing some of the effects of the atomic bomb. A few buildings (those of reinforced concrete construction) still stand; others have been swept away. Of the Japanese men, women, and children in the city, 78,150 were killed; 37,425 were injured; 13,983 are listed "missing."

589) called attention to the relapse toward savagery and barbarism, and compared it with the decline of the Roman Empire. It also pointed out the fact that the people who live during such a period are seldom conscious of what is happening. This trend during World War II could be illustrated by one example.

At the beginning of the war the German

bombing of the Dutch city of Rotterdam and of the British cities caused a wave of horrified, shocked protest to run through the free world. An attack on helpless civilians was considered the height of savage brutality. By 1943, however, Allied air attacks on German cities were welcomed. "Area bombing" to destroy civilian morale found many defenders. The use of the atomic bomb on Hiroshima and Nagasaki did not bring any great public protest.

This is not to say these acts should be condemned as wrong. That is a decision which every individual must make for himself.

What it shows is only this: A practice, the attack on civilians—men, women, and children—was considered at the beginning of the war to be unspeakably brutal and barbarous. By 1945 it had come to be accepted as the normal practice of war.

No, the fixing of a money price is a poor way to honor those who died. A better way is to accept the words of Abraham Lincoln: "That we here highly resolve that these dead shall not have died in vain." Unless a better world can be created in which wars are impossible, then all the sacrifices were, indeed, in vain.

Review of Chapter 53

People, places, and things

Identify: Field Marshal Bernard Montgomery, General Dwight D. Eisenhower, Pietro Badoglio, "Sawdust Caesar," Marshal Joseph Tito, General Douglas MacArthur, Clement Attlee, Harry S. Truman, the Burma Road, the "soft underbelly" of Europe, the second front, Albert Einstein, Manhattan Project, Yalta conference, D-Day, V-E Day.

Locate: Egypt, El Alamein, Libya, Tunisia, Algeria, Morocco, Casablanca, the Caucasus, Baku, The Volga river, Stalingrad, Sicily, Anzio, New Guinea, the Coral Sea, Australia, New Zealand, the Solomon Islands, Guadalcanal, Tulagi, the Aleutian Islands, Kiska, Attu, Dutch Harbor, Vladivostok, Sakhalin, Marshall Islands, Gilbert Islands, Ellice Islands, Burma, the East Indies, Hawaii, Midway, the Marianas, Saipan, Tinian, Leyte, Normandy, the D-Day beaches, Paris, the Moselle River, the Rhine, Antwerp, Aachen, Torgau, Iwo Jima, Okinawa, Hiroshima, Nagasaki, Formosa, Korea

Events in review

1. What was the United Nations Pact of 1942?
2. What was the significance of the Battle of El Alamein?

3. What happened in France as a consequence of the Allied landings in North Africa?
4. Tell briefly why the Battle of Stalingrad was a crucial point in the war.
5. What changes in the government of Italy took place after the Allied landings in Sicily and Italy?
6. Name two defensive victories won by the United States forces in the Pacific in 1942.
7. Why did the Allied commanders, in 1945, expect to have to invade the home islands of Japan? Why did they expect the invasion to be bloody and costly?
8. What major decision was reached at the Potsdam Conference?

Problems and projects

1. Do you note any similarities and any important differences between the Atlantic Charter and Seven Points, of World War II, and Wilson's Fourteen Points in World War I?
2. Winston Churchill wrote of events in 1942 as "The Hinge of Fate" of the war. Explain what he meant. Events in 1943 have been called "the turn of the tide." How and where did the tide turn in the war?
3. Report on the importance of "the miracle of American production" in winning the war.

Chapter 54   The United Nations: a New Hope

THE POSTWAR WORLD revolves entirely around two great, all-encompassing facts. One is this: For the second time the nations of the world tried to build an organization to establish and maintain peace and security for the entire world by the process of international coöperation. The second is this: The nations of the world, with a few exceptions, have divided themselves into two bitterly hostile camps, mutually distrustful and suspicious, given to making increasingly strong accusations against each other.

The split has not come between the victorious Allies and their defeated enemies. It has come among the victors themselves. The division is mainly along the lines of ideologies, or systems of belief. On one side stand the democratic, capitalist countries, led by the United States, Great Britain, and France. On the other side are the communist dictatorships and their captive satellites led by Soviet Russia and Communist China.

The Allies were able to hold together until the wars in Europe and the Pacific had been won. Even before the Pacific war ended, they had succeeded in writing a charter for a world organization called the United Nations. Their common experiences in the period between the two wars and during World War

II made them willing to try international coöperation again. At various conferences and in numerous declarations they pledged themselves to form an international organization for collective security and peace.

During the summer and fall of 1944 a preliminary conference was held at Dumbarton Oaks, in Washington, D.C. Representatives of Great Britain, Russia, China, and the United States drew up a provisional charter to be submitted to the governments of all the United Nations. At Yalta, Roosevelt, Stalin, and Churchill discussed this proposed charter and agreed on the time and place for the first General Assembly of the United Nations. At this general assembly the final charter was to be drawn up.

The San Francisco Conference draws up the United Nations Charter

In April, 1945, representatives of fifty nations met in San Francisco. After two months work they agreed to and signed the final charter. It was then submitted to the governments of the nations for their acceptance. Within four months fifty-one nations had ratified the charter. It became effective on October 24, 1945.

President Roosevelt did not live to take part in the San Francisco Conference. However, he had made careful plans to avoid the misfortunes that befell President Wilson's League of Nations covenant in the United States. The charter of the United Nations was kept entirely separate from the peace treaties. The task of drawing up the treaties was not given to the United Nations, but to the Council of Foreign Ministers of the five leading Allied Powers: the United States, Great Britain, Soviet Russia, France, and Nationalist China. In the United States delegation to the San Francisco Conference, President Roosevelt, a member of the Democratic Party, included three leading Republican members of the Senate Committee on Foreign Relations.

Their experiences in the period between the wars and in the second war had apparently convinced the American people that isolation is impossible in the modern world. When the United Nations Charter was presented for ratification, the Senate debated for only six days. The time was spent mostly with speeches in favor of the organization. Then, by the overwhelming vote of 89 to 2 the Senate ratified the charter.

In ratifying the charter, the nations agreed to the purposes and accepted the obligations of membership. The purposes were: the maintenance of peace and security, the promotion of equal rights and the self-determination of peoples, the development of international coöperation, and the encouragement of respect for human rights and fundamental freedoms. These were to be achieved without distinction as to race, sex, language, or religion.

The obligations which member nations undertook were: to respect each other's sovereignty; to settle disputes peacefully; not to use force or the threat of force for purposes contrary to the charter; to back up the United Nations when it called upon them; not to help any country against which the United Nations was taking action. Unless the United Nations was acting to prevent aggression or a threat to the peace, it should not interfere in the internal affairs of any nation.

The charter permits the member nations to form agreements among themselves for mutual coöperation, both economic and military. These agreements are usually among nations within a region. One such regional pact is the OAS (Organization of American States) among the United States and the Latin American countries. It is for mutual economic help and common defense of the Western Hemisphere.

How the United Nations is organized

● *The General Assembly*

The charter created a fairly simple structure for the organization. The General Assembly is made up of representatives of all the member nations. It meets once a year unless a special session is called. Each member nation is entitled to five delegates, five alternates, and as many advisers as it wishes. The large representation allows the nations to be represented on the various committees, where much of the work of the Assembly is done. When the Assembly votes as a body, each nation has one vote. On comparatively unimportant matters a simple majority vote is needed. On *substantive* matters (decisions of importance) a two-thirds vote is required. For example, with the total membership at ninety-nine, if all members voted, it would take only fifty votes to pass an unimportant matter but sixty-six votes to adopt a substantive resolution, such as the recommendation of collective action or the admission of a new member. Nations may *abstain* (not vote either way) if they want to.

The Assembly is given the duty of fixing the budget of the organization and each nation's share of the cost. It elects the members of the Security Council, the International Court of Justice, and the Secretary-General.

It receives and considers the reports of the various agencies of the United Nations. It promotes the development of international law. The Assembly may consider and discuss any problem that relates to world peace unless that problem is already being considered by the Security Council.

The General Assembly was planned as a deliberative body. Here any problem could be discussed, and every member could speak his mind. It was thought of as a great forum, where the public opinion of the whole world could be expressed. But it was not planned as an organ for action; it can only discuss and recommend.

● The Security Council

The Security Council is the action organ; its chief responsibility is the maintenance of peace. It is made up of eleven members. Five of them (usually called the Big Five) are permanent members: the United States, Great

The General Assembly of the United Nations in session. This view shows President Eisenhower making a speech to an emergency meeting of the Assembly held in August, 1958. When a critical situation developed in the Near East (in Lebanon and Jordan) the Assembly was called into session (see Chapter 56, page 762).

Britain, Soviet Russia, France, and Nationalist China. The six temporary members are elected for two-year terms by the General Assembly, and cannot be immediately re-elected. Each member nation on the Council has one representative and one vote. The Council must be ready to meet at any time.

The Council may take any action necessary to maintain peace, settle disputes, or prevent or meet aggression anywhere. It was given a power which no other body received. It can order members to take action to maintain peace; they are pledged in advance to carry out such orders. When once a dispute is before the Council, it may get more information by asking questions of the parties involved or by sending representatives to investigate. However, the nations concerned must agree to having such representatives sent. Often, after the dispute has been discussed, the Council urges the disputing nations to get together and work out their own solution. Sometimes it appoints mediators, or go-betweens, to help in the process of getting together. The Council itself may suggest some kind of a compromise, or it may send the case to the International Court of Justice for decision. Only when these measures have been tried, and when the Council finds that a nation has broken the peace, or is threatening to do so, does it use more forceful measures.

The Council can order the United Nations members to break diplomatic relations with an offending nation. It can also call for economic sanctions: an embargo on the sale of any or all goods, a boycott on buying goods. As a final step, the very last resort, it can ask the members to provide the armed forces and facilities that may be necessary to stop armed aggression.

It is very important to understand the voting in the Security Council. It takes seven of the eleven votes to adopt any measure. On procedural, or unimportant matters, the votes of any seven will pass a resolution. But on substantive, or important matters, *the seven must include the unanimous votes of the five permanent members.* Thus you can see that any one of the Big Five may prevent the Council from taking an important action by voting against it. This is the much discussed veto power.

The veto power was included in the charter at the insistence of both the United States and Russia. It was confidently predicted that the United States Senate would refuse to ratify the charter if the veto were not included. However, the Soviet Union has used the veto very often. People in the United States feel that the power has been abused.

● *The Secretariat*

The third agency of the United Nations is the Secretariat. This body is made up of clerical and administrative workers, advisers and technical experts, who are permanent employees of the United Nations itself. The Secretariat is divided into several departments, each under an assistant secretary-general. The members of the Secretariat come from various parts of the world and are carefully selected. A member of the Secretariat pledges to serve the interests of the United Nations and to take no orders from the government of his own nation. The nations, in turn, have agreed in the charter not to try to influence members of the Secretariat in the performance of their duties.

The head of the Secretariat is the Secretary-General. He is nominated by the Security Council and elected by the General Assembly for a term of five years. He has many responsibilities: He attends all meetings of

The Security Council of the United Nations in session. Representatives of the member nations are seated around the horseshoe table. This photograph was taken in October, 1956. The topic being discussed was a proposal to arrange a truce between Egypt and Israel (see Chapter 56, pages 758–759, for details of this crisis).

A village in British Togoland, one of the United Nations trust territories in Africa. A United Nations observer is talking with two women who are working in front of their houses.

the Council, Assembly, and the other organs; he carries out all tasks given him by any of these groups, and reports annually to the General Assembly on the work of the United Nations organization. The Secretary-General may bring to the attention of the Security Council any matter which he thinks may threaten international peace and security. This gives him certain powers and obligations more than those of an administrative officer only.

● The International Court of Justice

The International Court of Justice replaces the old World Court. The Court is made up of fifteen judges elected by the Security Council and General Assembly for terms of nine years; they may be re-elected. Like the members of the Secretariat, the judges are elected as individuals, distinguished jurists, not as representatives of government.

The Court may decide any dispute brought before it by national governments. It cannot deal with cases of individuals or groups of people. The Court does not have compulsory jurisdiction. It can decide only those cases which national governments bring to it voluntarily. Governments which do submit disputes are pledged to accept the decision. However, if either or both refuse to do so, the Court has no way to compel them. The Court may also give advisory opinions—advice on international legal problems—to any of the organs of the United Nations which ask for such aid.

● The Trusteeship Council

The Trusteeship Council is a body set up to deal with colonies and dependent areas. Trust territories are the former mandates of the League of Nations which have not yet become independent. The mandate powers have voluntarily placed them under the United Nations trusteeship system. For each trust territory, the trustee nation signs an agreement with the United Nations. It promises to carry out the purposes of the United Nations: to maintain order, to develop free political institutions, to develop education, to protect native rights, and to guarantee free speech and worship.

The trustee nations send in yearly reports on their trusteeships. These reports are received by the Trusteeship Council. It has a varying number of members. The Big Five are represented. Each trustee nation has a place on it. Then, to insure fair consideration and action, there is an equal number of members from non-trustee nations. Each member has one vote, and there is no veto.

The Trusteeship Council has some actual powers to do its job. It receives and debates the annual reports. The membership of non-trustee nations makes certain that the reports will be studied critically. The Council can send out questionnaires to the trustee nations. It can receive petitions, both written and oral, from people in the trust territories. And it can send visiting missions to make on-the-spot investigations and report back.

The Economic and Social Council

The Economic and Social Council was created to carry out the promise that the United Nations will work to improve the economic and social conditions of all peoples everywhere. In accepting the charter, the members agreed to work together to promote higher standards of living, employment for everyone, and social and economic progress everywhere. The Economic and Social Council has eighteen members elected by the General Assembly for three-year terms. Each member has one vote; there is no veto. The Council may recommend action, but it has no power of enforcement except the good will and self-interest of nations, and the force of public opinion.

The Council has approached its work in three different ways. It has set up a number of commissions to consider and recommend on definite subjects: on population, on transportation and communication, on human rights, on the status of women, on narcotics, and so forth. It has set up a technical assistance program to help underdeveloped countries. And it has created, or allowed to associate with it, a number of specialized agencies, each dealing with a single problem or a related set of problems.

In the next section of this chapter you will learn a little about the work of several of these special agencies. It is regrettable that this work is little known to people in general. It is one of the most interesting parts of the work of the United Nations. You can get an idea of the purposes of the specialized agencies from a reading of their names: Food and Agriculture Organization (FAO); United Nations Educational, Scientific, and Cultural Organization (UNESCO); World Health Organization (WHO); International Labor Organization (ILO; taken over from the League of Nations); International Civil Aviation Organization (ICAO); International Bank for Reconstruction and Develop-

ment (BANK); International Monetary Fund (FUND); Universal Postal Union (UPU); International Telecommunication Union (ITU); World Meteorological Organization (WMO); United Nations International Children's Emergency Fund (UNICEF).

An interesting thing about the specialized agencies is that a nation does not have to be a member of the United Nations to belong to a specialized agency. In fact, United Nations members do not have to belong to any of them. Membership in the agencies varies from fifty-four members of BANK and FUND to ninety-three members of UPU.

Political problems facing the UN

Unlike most newborn infants, the United Nations was not given a chance to grow up and gain strength and wisdom before it had to handle serious problems. Almost from the moment of its formation it was faced with political problems which no "infant" should ever have had to handle. This is the reason for the spotty record. However, there have been some real successes. In its first eight years of life, the United Nations helped to stop four regional wars: in the Balkans, Palestine, Kashmir, and Indonesia. The solutions were not as swift and as clear-cut as everyone would have liked, but the fighting did stop before it spread. The United Nations has also officially fought a war itself in Korea. But there have been failures, too. In the following account are a few instances of both the successes and the failures.

Soviet troops in Iran, 1946

The United Nations had hardly been organized in 1946 before Iran complained that Soviet Russia was keeping in Iran the troops she had moved there during the war. Iran considered these Russian troops a threat to her independence, and asked United Nations help in having them withdrawn. The United

Street scene in Indonesia—a busy inter-section in Batavia, Java.

States and Great Britain supported Iran. The Security Council accepted the case. There was a public debate in which Iran, Britain, the United States, and the Soviet Union presented their cases. The Soviet Union decided to withdraw the troops. Probably the world-wide publicity played a part in the decision.

Even more interesting than this dispute are the cases where the United Nations has been able to stop wars that were actually in progress.

●Indonesia

During World War II Japan drove the Dutch out of their empire in the East Indies. When the Dutch returned at the end of the war, they found that the native feeling of nationalism and desire for independence had reached a fever pitch. The Dutch investments in the islands were very large. Almost the whole economy of the Netherlands was built around the East Indian empire. Therefore the Dutch used force to try to regain and hold their colonies. The result was an outright war between the Dutch and the Indonesians.

Public opinion in the world, especially in the United States, was strongly against the Dutch. The United Nations provided a place for this opinion to be expressed—and felt. The Security Council appointed a commission to deal with the problem on the scene. It was able to get a cease-fire agreement which called for the setting up of an independent Indonesia. During the negotiation of terms of the independence, the agreement broke down. The Dutch resumed the war. Once again the fighting was stopped through the efforts of the Security Council commission.

The agreement concerning Indonesian independence was successfully drawn up at The Hague. Indonesia became independent and was admitted to membership in the United Nations in 1950. Indonesia would undoubtedly have won its independence without the aid of the United Nations. Colonialism is on the retreat everywhere, and seems to be vanishing in today's world. However, without United Nations help the process would have been much longer, far bloodier, and in all ways costlier.

●Palestine

For many years there has been a movement among the Jews throughout the world, known as Zionism. It favors a return of the Jews to Palestine, their homeland in Biblical days, and the establishment of a Jewish national state. Zionism grew stronger in the period between the two wars. Many Jews did return to Palestine. They bought land from the Arabs and established businesses in the cities. They met some opposition from the

Arabs of Palestine, although they had little difficulty buying land from them.

It was really a conflict of vastly different civilizations and cultures. The Jews brought with them the civilization of the twentieth century. The Palestinian Arabs were living in a feudal culture much like that of the Middle Ages. A few wealthy landlords owned most of the land. Most of the peasants lived in poverty and ignorance. Therefore the opposition was not only religious, Moslem against Jew, but also economic. Jewish knowledge of modern techniques of agriculture, industry, commerce, and science gave them a higher standard of living. This caused discontent among the Arab peasants. The feudal landlords were faced with demands for a better way of life.

Great Britain held the mandate over Palestine from the League of Nations. Now she found herself in an embarrassing position. To get help during World War I she had made conflicting promises to both groups. Jews had been promised a homeland in Palestine. Arabs had been promised that they would have an independent state if they would help defeat the Turks.

The Zionist movement gained more strength because of the Nazi persecution of Jews in Germany before and during World War II and in the conquered countries during the war. A host of Jews from all over Europe and the rest of the world began to pour into Palestine. They claimed it as their homeland, both from Biblical times and because of the British promise. The Arabs, however, pointed out that they had held the country for thirteen centuries and had more right there than the Jews. They demanded that the influx of Jews be stopped, or they would stop it by force. Both sides bitterly criticized the British.

In 1947, the British turned the whole problem over to the United Nations General Assembly. Britain announced that no matter what decision the Assembly reached, she would withdraw from Palestine in the following year. The Assembly recommended that Palestine be divided into an Arab and a Jewish state. The Jews proclaimed their part as the state of Israel. This was opposed by both the Palestinian Arabs and also by the neighboring Arab and Moslem states of Syria, Jordan, and Egypt.

In 1948 the British withdrew their troops from Palestine. War broke out between Israel and the Arab states. The Security Council ordered the fighting stopped, and appointed a mediator to try to bring the two groups into agreement. The first United Nations mediator, the Swedish Count Folke Bernadotte, was assassinated; however, his

United Nations observers keep watch in the Gaza strip, an area where there has been much trouble between Egypt and Israel. This photograph shows Indian troops of the United Nations Emergency Force stationed in this area in 1957 (see Chapter 56).

successor, Dr. Ralph Bunche, an American, was able to bring the two sides together and get an armistice agreement. The problems were not settled, but the war was stopped for a time.

● *The Balkans*

The Balkan Peninsula has long been the "powder keg" of Europe. Tensions, "border incidents," and wars there have always the dangerous possibility of spreading, like the incident at Sarajevo in 1914. In the years after World War II the Balkans became one scene of the conflict between the communist East and the democratic West.

In 1946 there was a rebellion in Greece. The Greek government complained to the Security Council that the neighboring communist countries of Albania, Bulgaria, and Yugoslavia were helping the communist rebels in Greece. The Security Council sent a commission to investigate. It reported that the Greek charges were true. However, the Security Council was prevented from taking any further action by a veto by Soviet Russia. The case was transferred to the General Assembly.

The General Assembly sent "watchdog" teams to the Balkans to study developments and make reports. These reports placed the responsibility for the trouble on Greece's neighbors. They gave moral support to the action of the United States in giving financial support and sending military advisers to Greece. Through a combination of United Nations moral force and United States material aid the so-called civil war in Greece was ended. Greece and her former enemy, Yugoslavia, have since entered into a defensive military alliance and closer economic relations.

● *Kashmir*

After World War II India gained independence from Great Britain, and the separate Moslem state of Pakistan was set up.

From your knowledge of Indian history you could have predicted that relations between the two states would be troubled.

When the partition between Moslem and Hindu states was made, it was provided that the rulers of the "princely states" could decide for themselves whether to join India or Pakistan. Trouble came in Kashmir, in the high mountainous border region of north-central India. The Maharaja of Kashmir was a Hindu; he chose to join India. But the vast majority of the Kashmiri people are Moslems; they wanted to join Pakistan. A civil war broke out. Troops came in from neighboring Pakistan to help the rebels, and India sent troops also. It was a dark and threatening picture.

Through United Nations efforts a cease-fire line was established. Both sides agreed that the future of Kashmir should be determined by a vote of the people. However, the United Nations representatives were never able to get India and Pakistan to agree to conditions for this plebiscite. In January, 1957, India announced in the Security Council that it considered Kashmir already part of India, and that a plebiscite was impossible. The Security Council passed a resolution renewing the call for a plebiscite. However, India refused to heed the call, and formally declared the accession of Kashmir to India. Thus the United Nations was successful in preventing what might have been a very bloody religious war, but unsuccessful in having its recommendation for a solution carried out.

● *War in Korea*

In 1950 the North Koreans were under the dominance of a communist regime. They invaded South Korea. This was declared an act of aggression by the Security Council. The Council called upon the members of the United Nations for military help in stopping the aggression. The various member nations gave help in varying degrees. The North Koreans were driven back beyond the established border. When Communist China entered the war to help the North Koreans, the United Nations declared China, also, an aggressor.

The war reached an armistice, with the two armies on their respective sides of the established border. The armistice has not yet resulted in a peace treaty, and may not for many years. It is not a clear-cut, well-defined solution. But an act of aggression was declared, met and stopped, and driven back, through the action of some, at least, of the members of an international organization.

The League of Nations was very weak in dealing with Japanese aggression in Manchuria and Italian aggression in Ethiopia during the 1930's. This weakness was probably its death blow. The United Nations was not weak in dealing with aggression in Korea. As a result, its chances for survival are better.

The problem of UN membership

The United Nations has had its definite failures and deadlocks on political problems. It is a question whether they can properly be blamed on the organization. Like the League of Nations, the United Nations can be no stronger than its members are willing to make it. And the great fact of the postwar world has been the bitter and growing split between the two most powerful members of the United Nations: the United States and the Soviet Union.

This split is mainly ideological: a split between democratic capitalism and dictatorial communism. It has affected conditions throughout the world. Very naturally it has affected the actions and capabilities of the United Nations. Many deadlocks have resulted, of which two were most noteworthy: membership and disarmament.

The United Nations began with fifty-one members. These were the nations which had allied themselves during World War II to fight against the Axis powers. The charter provided that the other nations would be admitted later. A prospective new member must show that it is "peace-loving," able and willing to carry out the obligations of members. The recommendation of a new member is made by the Security Council, where it is subject to the veto. Admission of recommended nations comes by a two-thirds vote of the General Assembly. The aim is for universal membership. A world organization can operate successfully only if all nations belong to the group.

Nine nations were admitted during the first four years, ending with the new state of Indonesia in 1950. After that there was a complete deadlock on membership. Nations favored by the Western powers were vetoed by the Soviet Union in the Security Council. Therefore they could not be recommended. Nations favored by Russia were unable to get the required seven votes of the Security Council for recommendation. Twenty-one nations applied for membership and failed to be admitted.

After some five years of wrangling that deadlocked the United Nations a compromise was finally reached in mid-December of 1955.

War in Korea. United States infantry in the front line, firing at communists on the next hill.

Originally eighteen candidate nations were recommended by the General Assembly for membership in the United Nations. Two applicants, Japan and Outer Mongolia, were blocked by the vetoes of the Soviet Union and Nationalist China (Formosa). Sixteen others were finally admitted. The new members are as follows: Albania, Austria, Bulgaria, Cambodia, Ceylon, Finland, Hungary, Ireland, Italy, Jordan, Laos, Libya, Nepal, Portugal, Rumania, and Spain. During 1956 the log jam was broken still further by the addition of four more members: Morocco, Sudan, Tunisia, and Japan. In 1957 the new states of Ghana and Malaya joined. 1958 brought membership to Guinea, while Egypt and Syria merged to form one state, the United Arab Republic. In 1960 seventeen new members including several new African states brought the total membership to ninety-nine.

The admission of Red China was a subject of sharp political controversy, especially in the United States. It became much more difficult to deal with after Communist China entered the Korean War and was declared an aggressor. Naturally, the communist countries favored having Red China in the United Nations. They thought the communist government should have the permanent seat on the Security Council which the charter gives the Republic of China. A number of other countries, including some of the new Asian nations, also favored having the Chinese Communists in the organization. However, the United States was firmly opposed to their membership.

The problem of disarmament

The Charter of the United Nations expressed the eagerness of the nations to relieve the world's people of the crushing burden of armaments. The charter directed the Security Council to make plans for the regulation and reduction of armaments. The solution of the problem was made more urgent by the knowledge of the vast destructive power of atomic and hydrogen bombs.

Early discussions of the disarmament problem were divided into two sections: conventional armaments and atomic weapons. Later, however, the two were combined under a Disarmament Commission made up of the members of the Security Council and Canada. The success of the disarmament talks depended on reaching agreement on a method of preventing nuclear warfare. No such agreement could be reached in the years of meetings after 1946.

The negotiations stalled on the problem of how to make sure that an agreement to give up the production and use of atomic weapons would be kept. The United States insisted that there must be a complete system of inspection to see that the weapons were not secretly produced and hidden for a surprise attack. This inspection could be either on the ground or by means of aerial photographs. The Soviet Union wanted first an agreement to outlaw the production and use of atomic weapons, followed by the destruction of all existing weapons. Then, they said, there could be discussion of methods of inspection. In spite of many proposals and counterproposals there was no agreement.

While the disarmament negotiations went around like a squirrel in a cage, the armaments race continued. Both sides developed atomic and then hydrogen weapons. Both worked as fast as possible to develop long-range guided missles which could carry nuclear warheads from continent to continent at tremendous speeds. It was said that, so long as they remained about equal in strength and kinds of weapons, neither side would dare attack the other. No matter how successful the surprise attack, the attacker would also be destroyed by the retaliation (striking back) that was certain to follow. Winston Churchill said that the world had reached a "balance of terror." People who remembered their history were uneasy over the idea that

The problem of disarmament has been particularly urgent since the appearance in the world of long-range missiles that can carry nuclear warheads. Shown here is the United States Army's Redstone missile. The Soviet Union is believed to have made rapid progress in developing missiles with intercontinental range.

an arms race could be depended on to keep the peace.

The deadlock over inspection led to disagreement even over the membership of the Disarmament Commission. After some years of fruitless efforts, the Commission turned over the negotiations to a subcommittee of five: the Soviet Union, the United States, Great Britain, France, and Canada. Later the Russians announced that they would no longer meet with the subcommittee. They proposed a commission consisting of all members of the United Nations. The Western nations refused this plan, fearing that the Soviet Union would use the larger committee only as a platform for propaganda.

Faced with this new deadlock, the General Assembly, after considering numerous compromise suggestions, approved a Western proposal to add fourteen nations, thereby increasing the Commission to a total of twenty-five. Still not satisfied, the Soviet representative announced that his government would not take part unless seven more nations of its choosing were added.

● *Tests of weapons and radioactive fall-out*

Another stalemate occurred over the testing of atomic and hydrogen weapons. The United States and the Soviet Union both conducted extensive tests; Great Britain made some. Testing brought up the problem of the fall-out of radioactive materials. The explosion of a nuclear device carried such material high into the stratosphere. It was then carried around the earth, falling in widely scattered places. A heavy exposure to such radiation brings death to human beings, animals, and vegetation. A lesser exposure may injure the genes involved in heredity, so that more abnormal children may be born in later generations. Even among scientific experts there was no general agreement on how much radiation a human being could take without ill effects. People all around the world demanded that the testing be stopped. Others replied that the testing was necessary to keep up in the arms race, and that the danger from fall-out was a risk that had to be taken.

Proposals to stop testing bogged down over the same problem of inspection: could there be certainty that the agreements would be kept. Early in 1958, after completing an extensive series of tests, the Soviet Union announced that it would make no more. However, the Russians said they reserved the right to resume their testing if the Americans and British failed to stop their tests. The United States made its own offer to stop testing. During the summer of 1958 it conducted tests to determine the success of its attempt to produce a "clean" bomb—that is, a bomb that produces a limited amount of radioactive fall-out.

During the summer of 1958 atomic scientists from both Eastern and Western countries held meetings. Their purpose was to investigate whether there were reasonably sure methods of detecting nuclear explosions at great distances. If they agreed that atomic explosions could be detected, it might be possible for the opposing sides to agree to end testing.

In the late 1950's a ray of hope came from the establishment of the International Atomic Energy Agency of the United Nations. In December, 1953, in an address to the General Assembly, President Eisenhower urged the major powers to coöperate in developing peacetime uses of atomic energy. He proposed that all nations able to produce atomic energy give part of their atomic stockpile to an international pool. These materials could then be used for peacetime research and production, even by nonproducing nations.

An atomic energy agency, supervised by the United Nations, should be set up to accept contributions of nuclear material.

For several years action on this proposal was bogged down in cold war wrangling. Then, early in 1956, representatives of twelve nations, including both the United States and the Soviet Union, drew up a charter for an International Atomic Energy Agency. Later in 1956 representatives of all member nations of the United Nations approved the charter unanimously. It was to go into effect as soon as it was ratified by the governments of eighteen nations, including at least three of the five atomic powers. These conditions were fulfilled in July, 1957, and the new Agency began operations in October, 1957. Vienna, Austria, was chosen as permanent headquarters.

This cartoon by David Low suggests the problems involved in making use of atomic power.

The function of the Agency was to receive nuclear fuel from producing nations and allocate the material to nations wanting to use it for peaceful purposes. It could also distribute needed equipment and technical knowledge. It had the power to set up inspection and safeguards to protect public health and prevent use of the material for military purposes. The United States, the Soviet Union, Great Britain, and several other nations gave nuclear materials and scientific equipment to the Agency.

The joint conference of scientists and the formation of the International Atomic Energy Agency were both hopeful signs, but they really had only slight connection to the problem of disarmament. As in so many other matters, it must be said that the United Nations has failed to bring about disarmament because of the inability of its two most powerful members to agree. The United Nations has been valuable as a place where there could be discussions in which all nations could express opinions. It is to be hoped that world opinion and the efforts of men of many nations will solve this problem.

The work at the specialized UN agencies

You have read that the economic work of the United Nations is carried on through the Technical Assistance Program and the work of the specialized agencies. The Technical Assistance Program has one main aim: to help nations to help themselves. It gives assistance only when asked to do so by a government. It works mainly in the underdeveloped countries. The technical assistance experts try to teach people new, easier, and more productive ways of doing things. In 1957 there were more than 2,500 of these experts. They came from seventy-seven different countries, and gave assistance in one hundred and thirty-two countries.

The money for the program comes from voluntary contributions from governments. These contributions usually amount to about $20,000,000 a year.

India, as you know, has a tremendous problem of food supply, yet for various reasons less than half of the land of this subcontinent is cultivated. One area at the base of the Himalaya Mountains has rich soil, but it was covered with jungle and filled with malarial mosquitoes. At the request of the Indian government, the Technical Assistance Program officials agreed to a combined project there. The World Health Organization supplied a Greek expert on malaria and an English public health nurse. The supplies and equipment were provided by the United Nations International Children's Emergency Fund. Working in an area of 2,000 square miles, the World Health Organization team reduced the malaria rate considerably. The United Nations International Children's Emergency Fund carried on a mother-and-child health program. The Indian government sent in tractors and bulldozers to clear the jungle. The Food and Agriculture Organization sent in experts to work with Indian agricultural specialists. As soon as part of the land was cleared, people began moving in from other parts of India. A whole new region had been rendered productive, and so a step has been taken to lower the starvation rate of India.

The work of the specialized agencies is just as exciting when they work alone as when they combine under the Technical Assistance Program. The World Health Organization has been one of the most successful. Staffed by physicians, nurses, sanitation experts, and public health workers from many nations, it has fought cholera in Egypt and malaria all over the world. It has fought other diseases and improved health conditions in many parts of the globe. The World Health Organization also conducts research and coordinates health information. Thus a new treatment for disease can soon be put into operation everywhere.

The World Health Organization fighting malaria. A priest watches a worker for this United Nations agency spray DDT on the walls of a temple in Thailand.

The Food and Agriculture Organization tries to increase the production of farms, fisheries, and forests, to improve the distribution of food and to raise the levels of nutrition among the world's peoples. It sponsors seed-improvement programs, helps to reclaim land, as in India, helps to fight insect plagues, and helps develop better ways of producing food.

The purpose of the United Nations Educational, Scientific, and Cultural Organization (UNESCO) is to encourage education and increase the international exchange of knowledge, thus bringing better international understanding. In its early years it undertook a great variety of projects. More recently it has concentrated mostly on trying to reduce illiteracy. The method is to set up fundamental education centers in many countries. There people are trained to teach reading, writing, and the basic knowledge of health, sanitation, and the management of a home. The first such center was set up at Patzcuato, Mexico, to train people from many Latin American countries.

Even these few examples show you how important and stirring the economic and social work of the United Nations is. Compared to a national government, the organization works on a very small budget. The American contribution to the entire organization averages out to about seventy-five cents per person in our country. Most people consider the money well spent. However, it is not the question of finances that troubles people about the United Nations. The great question is whether it can really do its main job. Thus far in history many methods of preventing war have been tried. None have succeeded. If international cooperation through the United Nations can do it, people will care little about the cost.

What about the future of the United Nations?

Most of the doubts concerning the United Nations center around one main point: It is not really a government; it is only an organization of sovereign nations. In accepting the charter, each nation has agreed to do certain things and behave in certain ways. However, each nation decides for itself whether it will live up to these obligations. If it decides not to live up to them, the United Nations has little power to compel it.

Many people are critical of the veto power of the Big Five in the Security Council, especially of the way it has been used by Soviet Russia. However, the veto power and its use or misuse are outward signs of a deep problem. Of greater importance, though more difficult to see, is the fact that the United Nations has to rely mainly on world opinion to get its proposals accepted and carried out.

The United Nations cannot pass laws, as the government of a nation or a state can. It can draw up conventions or covenants. These are proposals for international treaties. Each must be ratified or accepted by the member nations in the same way that a treaty is ratified. No member is compelled to ratify.

Even those treaties or proposals that are ratified to become international laws must be enforced by the individual, sovereign nations. Each decides for itself whether to obey the law. If a nation decides not to obey, discussions in the General Assembly or Security Council may bring the force of public opinion to bear. The United Nations has certain weapons to compel the observance of law and prevent aggression. They are diplomatic boycott, economic boycott, and military force. However, their use may be prevented by a veto. Thus the United Nations can only be as strong and as effective as its members, the individual, sovereign nations, will permit it to be.

Review of Chapter 54

People, places, and things

Identify: Dumbarton Oaks Conference, San Francisco Conference, Secretariat, Secretary-General, Ralph Bunche, Zionism, plebiscite.
Locate: Iran, Palestine, Greece, Yugoslavia, Pakistan, India, Kashmir, Indonesia, Korea.

Events in review

1. What events led to the writing of the United Nations Charter?
2. Was the drawing up of the United Nations Charter combined with the writing of peace treaties?
3. How many nations had ratified the charter by October, 1945? What purposes of membership did they agree to?
4. What obligations did the member nations accept?
5. Describe briefly (a) the membership and (b) the duties of the General Assembly.
6. Describe briefly (a) the membership and (b) the duties of the Security Council.
7. What is the veto power in the Security Council?
8. What are the functions of the International Court of Justice?
9. What territories, formerly in the charge of the League of Nations, came under the care of the UN? What group in the UN is responsible for these territories?
10. Cite two instances in which the United Nations was able to prevent a local crisis from spreading into a major crisis or a war.
11. What happened to the early efforts of the UN to control armaments, particularly atomic weapons?
12. What is the purpose of the World Health Organization, (b) the Food and Agriculture Organization?

Problems and projects

1. Trace the steps taken by the Allies of World War II to form the United Nations, from the Declaration of London through the ratification of the UN charter.
2. The history of the United Nations is still being made while you read this book. You will want to watch for and report on important developments. Has there been any recent change in the membership of the UN? If so, what is the total number of members? What nations now make up the Security Council?
3. In the library, go through newspaper or magazine files for the past two or four weeks. How many stories about the UN do you find? What problems for the UN are mentioned?
4. Compare the record of the United Nations from 1945 to the present with the record of the League of Nations between World Wars I and II.

Chapter 55 Allied Unity Vanishes

THE WORLD that emerged from World War II in 1945 was not exactly the kind that human beings had hoped for, and had suffered all the bloodshed and destruction to gain. Some gains had been made. Fascism, with its tyranny over the minds and bodies of men, its hateful doctrines of race and religion, and its threat to all man's best ideas about the dignity and worth of the individual, had been defeated. The Allied nations had made a brave second start toward world coöperation. This time they had the strong support of two of the great dissenters of 1919: Russia and the United States.

Problems left by the war

● Economic dislocations

Like all wars, World War II created terrible problems. The loss of life and destruction of property amounted to many times that of World War I. Fighting had ranged over a wider area, and the bomber plane had spread death and devastation far beyond the battle lines. Cities were ravaged, rural areas laid waste, industries destroyed, transportation and communication systems wrecked. Millions of war prisoners, refugees, and other displaced persons had to be given homes and helped to earn a living.

The most immediate need was to prevent famine and epidemic diseases. Late in 1943 the Allied nations had wisely formed a temporary body, the United Nations Relief and Rehabilitation Agency (UNRRA). As soon as countries were freed of Axis control it went into action, and it was still working nobly when the war ended.

The problem of restoring the economic systems, rebuilding the destroyed homes and public buildings, draining the flooded lands, and repairing the devastated areas was certain to take time. There was every reason to suppose that it would require all of Europe's energies and resources for many years. While it was being done, life for most Europeans would be drab and grim, with few comforts and no luxuries.

● Political dislocations

There was a vast political job to be done, too. The solidly established governments of Great Britain and the United States had survived the test of war. In Russia the Communist dictatorship was firmly in power. Almost everywhere else political reconstruction or political change took place. The Nazi government was not restored to power in Germany. The Italians had overthrown Mussolini and Fascism as well as the king and the monarchy. The Vichy fascist regime had abolished the Third French Republic, but the French people proceeded to write a constitution for the Fourth French Republic. Many other changes took place. Politically, the world was in a state of flux.

Many political problems of boundaries and territories had to be settled. The government of Poland had to be reorganized, and the Polish boundaries fixed. Yugoslavia claimed the city of Trieste and other areas formerly held by Italy. The future of Germany was uncertain. Monarchies in Greece, Rumania, and Yugoslavia were tottering.

During the war communist Russia and capitalist, democratic Britain and the United States had coöperated very well—as well as any allies in a coalition could be expected to work together. There had been differences, of course, but in general the alliance had worked well. At the end of the war there were bright hopes that this coöperation could and would continue. Many people believed and said that it was possible for democracy and communism to exist together peacefully in the same world.

There were others who were not so hopeful. They believed that two such different ideologies or philosophies or ways of life were bound to clash at some time. They were, however, in the minority. The entire United Nations Charter was written with the idea that coöperation was possible. The Big Five powers were required to be unanimously in agreement on all important decisions. It was expected that they would be unanimous on those questions that concerned peace.

● The rise of nationalism

Throughout all of Asia and Africa nationalism was on the rise. In their conquest of Asia the Japanese had used a slogan that appealed to the people of that area: Asia for the Asians. Asian people soon learned, to their sorrow, that Japanese imperialism was no better than European imperialism. In many

ways it was much worse. The European rulers had been driven out of many of their colonial territories by the Japanese. When Japan was defeated and driven out, the native people had no desire to see the Europeans return. They wanted no imperialism at all; they wanted independence and self-government.

In many of the former colonies there was another movement as well. Millions of people were existing just a little above the starvation level. They began to demand more food, more goods, a better way of life—things that most of us in this country take for granted. This movement was not directed primarily against the Europeans, although they had to bear the force of it when they stood in its way. It was aimed largely at the wealthy natives: the owners of large estates who charged enormous rentals, the moneylenders who charged such high interest rates that they kept peasant families in debt to them from one generation to another. To understand the postwar world, you must know

Relations with Russia have long been a problem for the Western World. Since World War II particularly, the free world has faced the puzzle of guessing what the leaders of Russia propose to do.

'A RIDDLE WRAPPED IN A MYSTERY INSIDE AN ENIGMA'—Churchill

about this double movement in the former colonial areas: the demands for independence and for a better way of life.

The problem of the peace treaties

• *The Potsdam Conference*

After the surrender of Germany and before the Japanese war had ended, the heads of the three leading powers met at Potsdam, near Berlin, Germany. Premier Stalin represented Russia. Clement Attlee, leader of the Labour Party, was prime minister representing Britain. President Truman represented the United States.

These heads of state made a number of important decisions about postwar policy and the writing of the peace treaties. Peace treaties were to be written by a Council of Foreign Ministers representing the major powers. At first there were only three; later, France and China were admitted, and other nations among the Allies were given representation.

The Potsdam Conference continued arrangements agreed to at Yalta in 1945. Germany and Austria were each divided into four zones. Each zone was occupied by one of the four major allied powers. In each country unified administration was to be given by an Allied Control Council. This was made up of the military leaders of the occupying armies. The decisions of the Council had to be unanimous.

The Potsdam Conference also reached certain preliminary agreements over postwar German boundaries. East Prussia was to be given to Russia. The Russians were also to keep certain parts of eastern Poland into which their armies moved in 1939. To pay Poland for this loss of territory, she was given the right to administer prewar German territory up to the Oder and Neisse rivers. This territory comes close to the city of Berlin. Germany was also to lose the territory in the west which she had seized from France, Belgium, and Denmark.

At Potsdam it was decided that Germany should pay reparations for war damages. However, payments should be in the form of industrial plants and equipment rather than cash. During the war the Germans had looted the occupied countries of wealth in the form of art treasures, plants and machinery, and almost everything else that was movable. This wealth was to be returned, as far as it could be. Also, Germany was to give up plants and machinery that could be used for war production. Postwar Germany was expected to concentrate on agriculture and peacetime industries—"light" industries to produce consumer goods. The Nazi leaders were to be tried as war criminals.

• *Treaties with Germany's allies*

Early in 1947, after months of debate, the Council of Foreign Ministers reached agreement on treaties for Italy, Rumania, Hungary, Bulgaria, and Finland. The terms of all these treaties were much alike. The defeated countries had to return territory they had taken, and their prewar boundaries were reduced. They had to pay reparations to nations their armies had invaded. Their armed forces were reduced and limited. Italy was stripped of her African colonies and of islands in the Adriatic and Aegean seas. All except Italy (which had already abolished its monarchy and set up a republic) were to choose their forms of government at free, democratic elections.

The Italian city of Trieste, on the Adriatic coast, was an especially difficult problem. Supported by the Soviet Union, Yugoslavia demanded Trieste. Great Britain, the United States, and Italy opposed the transfer. The solution in the Italian treaty was a compromise. Trieste was made a Free City under United Nations administration. However, Tito, the Communist dictator of Yugoslavia, continued to make threatening demands about Trieste. Until his break with Moscow in 1948 he had Russian support. Trieste remained a danger spot of Europe until 1954, when an agreement was reached. Trieste and its surrounding territory were given to Italy. A small adjoining territory inhabited by Slavs was given to Yugoslavia. Each side promised to respect the rights of national minorities in its territory.

The ideological split between East and West made the negotiation of these minor treaties very difficult. Agreements about Germany and Austria proved to be almost impossible. The four-way occupation of these two countries continued as months and years passed without agreements on peace treaties having been reached.

● *The problem of Germany*

On the map you can see the division of Germany into four zones of occupation. Notice that Berlin lies entirely inside the eastern, Russian zone. The city itself was divided into four occupation zones. Supplies for the city and its Western occupation forces had to pass through Russian-held territory.

The end of the war found Germany a devastated country, greatly reduced from its prewar size. Its population was constantly increased by Germans who had formerly lived outside the boundaries of prewar Germany. They were now forced to return to their homeland. Czechoslovakia, for example, insisted that the Sudeten Germans, the cause of Czech downfall, must get out of Czechoslovakia. The Russians adopted the same policy toward Germans in the Baltic states (Estonia, Latvia, and Lithuania) which they had taken back, and in East Prussia, which they had gained in the war. Poland followed suit, forcing out Germans from prewar Poland and her new administrative territories east of the Oder and Neisse rivers. She replaced them with Poles transferred from that part of eastern Poland which Russia took.

Although these moves were not surprising, in the light of prewar troubles with German minorities, the dumping of these refugees into shrunken postwar Germany created a terrible problem. These people had to be kept alive, and jobs had to be found for them.

● *Trial of Nazi war criminals*

The military occupation of Germany revealed to a shocked world the horrible picture of the German concentration camps. The Nazis had followed a systematic policy of mass murder and extermination. More than 6,000,000 of the estimated 10,000,000 Jews living in Europe were murdered by the Nazis. They died of disease and starvation in concentration camps, were suffocated in gas chambers, and were burned in crematoriums. Others were subjected to horrible tortures, serving as "guinea pigs" for scientific experimentation on the human body. Their bodies were frozen, their bones broken, their blood injected with poisons. At the end of the war, only a few thousand Jews were left in Germany and the conquered countries.

A special international court was set up at Nuremberg to try those Nazi leaders who had survived and been captured. Hitler was not alive, and some of his lieutenants had escaped, to find refuge in fascist Spain and Argentina. But many of the top leaders had

NETHERLANDS

BRITISH ZONE

BELGIUM

Berlin ●

LUX.

RUSSIAN ZONE

POLAND

ZONE

FRANCE

FRENCH ZONE

U.S. ZONE

CZECHOSLOVAKIA

SWITZERLAND

AUSTRIA

ITALY

OCCUPIED GERMANY AFTER WORLD WAR II

been captured. Late in 1946 the court sentenced twelve of the principal leaders to death and seven others to life imprisonment. It also declared the Nazi Party a criminal organization. In each occupation zone special courts were set up to try lesser people responsible for atrocities committed during the war. The trial and punishment of war criminals was a warning to future leaders not to start wars, or at least not to lose them.

"DeNazification"

There was a much more difficult problem to solve: How could the German people themselves be "deNazified"—rid of the "master-race" ideas—and re-educated in democratic ways? Children who had grown up during the Nazi period had had these ideas constantly hammered into them. Education is a powerful force in shaping character and ideas. Many Allied observers found that most adult Germans refused to admit that they were in any way responsible for the Nazi crimes. They criticized Hitler mainly for having lost the war. Changing such a people, whose modern history has been so militant and warlike, into a peaceful nation was not a simple problem.

German industrial plants

The immediate problem of keeping Germany peaceful was easily solved. The Allied

Street scene in postwar Germany. Citizens of Worms, standing between rows of shattered houses, look at the gap left when a bridge was destroyed during a battle. The war left much of Germany devastated. The Allies still intended that Germany pay for the damage she had caused in other nations during World War II. It became evident, however, that the Allies would have to let the Germans rebuild their own country.

Control Council moved swiftly to disband all German land, air, and sea forces. The General Staff, with all its military schools and institutions, was abolished. German industry was forbidden to manufacture big guns, tanks, or airplanes, even private or commercial planes. The plan was to make sure that Germany could not rearm. All plants and industrial equipment which could be used for war production were to be dismantled and taken away.

In the decisions about German industry, the Allies soon ran up against the truth of one of Stalin's favorite sayings: "Facts are stubborn things." They soon found themselves in complete disagreement. There was, first of all, the very difficult question of what a war industry is in these days of industrialized warfare. A factory which manufactures tractors may easily be converted to the production of tanks. A steel plant may turn out armor plate as well as steel beams.

There was also an even more basic problem. In their zone the Russians began by dismantling industrial plants and shipping them east to replace those destroyed during the war. Soon, however, they changed. They allowed the factories to remain, and took their reparations out of the goods produced. In the western zones the British and Americans faced a very stubborn fact: An agricultural Germany, with light industries only, simply would not support the German population. There seemed to be only two choices: Either allow Germany to industrialize fully, or face the prospects of having to feed and support the German population indefinitely.

The British and Americans constantly moved toward an easier treatment of Germany and her industries. This policy was violently opposed by the French, who had good reason to fear the industrial power of Germany.

The Allied Control Council, therefore, found it increasingly hard to reach unanimous decisions on German industry, or, for that matter, anything else about the combined administration. In Austria the story was much the same, although on a smaller scale. The Council of Foreign Ministers could reach no agreement on peace treaties. Their meetings became a series of violent accusations and counter-accusations. Early in 1948 the Council of Ministers adjourned indefinitely. In 1950 a meeting to consider an Austrian treaty alone made no progress and was abandoned.

● *The Austrian treaty*

After long delays the four occupying powers finally signed an Austrian treaty in May, 1955. After seventeen years of occupation, first by Germany, then by the Allies, Austria once more became a "sovereign, independent, and democratic state." The treaty forbids any political or economic union between Austria and Germany in "any form whatsoever." The boundaries of Austria were defined as those that existed on January 1, 1938.

Austria pledged to respect the rights of the Slavic minorities, to maintain a democratic government, and to enact laws to prevent the revival of the Nazi Party. The Austrian government also promised to coöperate with the Allied powers to ensure that Germany would not be able to get arms in Austria. The treaty provided that Austria would not have to pay any reparations.

The cold war develops

● *The satellite states*

When the Russians fought their way up through central Europe and through Poland, they set up communist-controlled temporary governments in Rumania, Bulgaria, Hungary, Albania, Yugoslavia, and Poland. All of these territories except Yugoslavia were occupied by the Red Army after the end of the war. The peace treaties promised that there would be free elections in which the peoples could

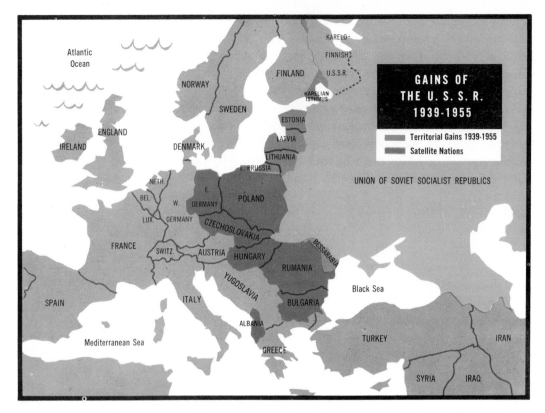

Atlantic Ocean

NORWAY

SWEDEN

FINLAND

KARELO-FINNISH U.S.S.R.

KARELIAN ISTHMUS

ESTONIA

LATVIA

LITHUANIA

E. PRUSSIA

ENGLAND

IRELAND

DENMARK

NETH.

BEL.

LUX.

W. GERMANY

E. GERMANY

POLAND

CZECHOSLOVAKIA

FRANCE

SWITZ.

AUSTRIA

HUNGARY

BESSARABIA

RUMANIA

YUGOSLAVIA

ITALY

BULGARIA

SPAIN

ALBANIA

GREECE

Mediterranean Sea

Black Sea

TURKEY

IRAN

SYRIA

IRAQ

UNION OF SOVIET SOCIALIST REPUBLICS

GAINS OF THE U.S.S.R. 1939-1955

■ Territorial Gains 1939-1955
■ Satellite Nations

choose their governments, but these promises were not truly observed. Every country had at least a coalition government which included communist representatives. Working from within by their usual tactics, the communists got rid of all opposition. By 1947 each of these states had been declared a "People's Democratic Republic." Translated, this means a communist dictatorship.

They were called the "satellite states." In astronomy a satellite is a small planet which revolves around a larger planet; the moon is a satellite of the earth. In political language a satellite does exactly what some powerful state tells it to do. In all matters of both domestic and foreign policy the satellite states are completely subordinated to Soviet Russia.

During 1947, also, the old communist international organization was revived once more. It had been dissolved in 1943. Now it took a new name: the Communist Information Bureau (Cominform). Outwardly its purpose was the exchange of information. Ac-

tually it was a way of maintaining links between Russia, her satellites, and the communist groups in other countries.

Thus it became clear that Russia was following a double policy. In countries where the Red Army was in occupation, communist dictatorships were set up with all the features of the police state. For all practical purposes Russia had now extended her boundaries far into western Europe, for the communists in the satellite states ran their governments only to serve Russian ends. The other edge of the sword was the Cominform. Its aim was to stir up dissension and revolution in countries which the Russian army did not control, using the local communist parties as willing tools.

● *The division of Germany*

By 1948 the situation in Germany had reached a point where joint government had become impossible. The economic situation in the country was in a sad state. In the Western zones the problem was complicated by the fact that German refugees made their way west from the Russian zone in a constant stream.

The three Western occupying powers decided to unite their zones economically in the hope of solving this difficult problem. They announced that if Germany was not united by a peace treaty they would allow the Germans in their zones to write a constitution and set up a democratic government. The western Germans held a constitutional assembly at Bonn and set up the German Federal Republic. It was still under the control of the Western occupation authorities. The Western powers also unified their zones in Berlin and permitted the election of a democratic city government.

The Russians now took three steps which showed their purposes and methods more clearly than anything they had done so far. First they set up a Communist government in Eastern Germany, including Eastern Berlin. Then, in June of 1948 they stopped all land and water traffic into Berlin from the west. It was the "Berlin Blockade." There was no doubt that its purpose was to force the Western powers to abandon Berlin.

● Czechoslovakia falls to communism

In the same months the communists in Czechoslovakia seized power. Prewar Czechoslovakia had been the most democratic of all the central European states. The postwar government was democratic, too, although the communists were strongly represented. Czechoslovakia was in a difficult position. It was not occupied by the Russian army, but it had common borders with occupied Poland, east Germany, and Hungary, and even with the Soviet Union itself. The government therefore tried to do a very difficult thing: to act as a "bridge between east and west." They tried to keep friendly relations with both the Western democracies and the communist bloc. Elections had shown that communist

strength in Czechoslovakia was declining, and new elections were coming soon. The Czech communist leaders manufactured a "crisis" and seized control of the government. When the elections were held, the voters were offered a single list of candidates, all selected by the communists. The foreign minister of the country, Jan Masaryk, son of its founder, Thomas Masaryk, was reported to have committed suicide. President Eduard Beneš resigned and was replaced by a communist dictator. Thus, unwillingly, Czechoslovakia became a satellite state.

There was nothing the Western powers could do about Czechoslovakia without going to war, and they were not ready to do that. When the Japanese war ended, the United States had demobilized its army very rapidly. Britain's forces were widely spread and very busy in many parts of the world. The Russians still had many divisions under arms and ready to strike. They could have overrun all of western Europe easily. War would have been suicidal.

The Western powers could not help Czechoslovakia, but they could and did refuse either to be starved out or bluffed out of Berlin. Instead, Britain and the United States organized an airlift to supply western Berlin by plane. It was a costly but brilliant success. The two million inhabitants of the western part of the city were supplied with food and coal. After the lift really began to operate well, they also got raw materials for their industries. In ten months the Russians gave up. Without formal announcement, the blockade was gradually lifted.

● The iron curtain divides the world

There was no doubt that, as Winston Churchill said, an "iron curtain" had fallen between East and West. The world was engaged in a cold war, a war of nerves, a war fought by means that stopped short of all-out, shooting war. By every kind of force, threat, intimidation, and subversion the communists

had taken over a great bloc of nations. They were trying to stir up communist-led revolutions in the countries they could not reach by more direct means.

Only one break appeared in the iron curtain. During the spring of 1948 there was a disagreement between Marshal Tito, dictator of Yugoslavia, and Stalin. Communist Tito objected to having the policies of his country directed by Russia, as was the practice in the satellite states. By June, 1948, the split became definite; Yugoslavia was expelled from the Cominform.

Here was another of the many fuzzy situations of the postwar world. Tito still maintained, stoutly, that he was a communist. He even tightened his dictatorship in Yugoslavia. But he had broken with Stalin's Russia. What policy should the West follow toward Yugoslavia? The decision was that we would "play along with Tito." We would give him aid, cautiously, as long as he continued to oppose Russia, even though we disliked his communism.

The Berlin airlift. German children wave and cheer as an American plane brings in supplies over the Russian blockade. Note that they are standing on the beams and rubble of a building bombed during the war.

As the cold war of nerves developed, one thing became increasingly clear: If the communist sweep were to be stopped, the United States would have to play the main part in doing it. America had come out of World War II as the only undevastated major power. Our productive machine had greatly increased, even though the supply of raw materials had been used up at a terrifying rate. In 1945, even more than in 1939, the United States could supply her own needs for food and manufactured products, and still have vast amounts to export to a needy world.

The rest of the Western powers were exhausted. In addition to all other postwar problems France and Italy had to reorganize their governments. Furthermore, among their people there were serious differences in political and economic opinion. In both countries there were large communist parties with many supporters. Great Britain had spent almost all her strength in fighting the war. In the post-war period she had many problems to deal with throughout the world, as well as the most serious domestic problems.

It all came to this: The world had become a two-power world. No matter how much the fact might be covered up by alliances and satellites, there were only two major powers: the United States and the Soviet Union. The Soviet Union seemed determined to spread her power and influence as widely as possible. In fact, she wanted to dominate the world. If she were to be prevented from doing this by picking off one country at a time, as Hitler had done, the United States must take the lead in opposing her. Americans suddenly found themselves thrust into the new role of world leadership.

The Western counterattack

One of the many difficulties of writing about a very complicated period is that so many things happen at the same time. It is easier for you to understand if they are arranged in logical groups, one after another. But that is not the way things happened. For example, you must not think that the Western powers waited until the fall of Czechoslovakia and the Berlin blockade to defend democratic countries against the spread of communism. Nearly a year before those events the United States took two very important steps to strengthen the West.

● The Truman Doctrine: aid to Greece and Turkey

The first shock which stirred the United States into action came early in 1947. Great Britain had been giving large-scale military and financial support to the Greek govern-

ment against the rebels there. Britain was unable to carry on. In spite of a large United States loan, she was almost bankrupt. Therefore she announced that she could no longer defend the eastern Mediterranean region against the spread of communism. In addition to Greece, this might mean the fall of Turkey and of the whole Near East with its rich oil supplies.

In March, 1947, in a message to Congress, President Truman announced what came to be known as the Truman Doctrine. The United States, he said, considered the further spread of communism a menace to American democracy. The United States would not try to stamp out communism in Soviet Russia or the nearby states, or in any country which freely chose communism. It would, however, use its money, materials, technical assistance, and influence to help countries threatened by communism if they wanted to oppose it. He asked Congress for an appropriation of 400 million dollars to help defend Greece and Turkey from communist domination. The Congress was more willing to approve the grant of money when it was reported by the United Nations investigating committee that communist countries were helping the Greek communist rebels.

With American financial and technical aid, the Greek government slowly put down the rebellion. The process was hastened by Yugoslavia's break with the Cominform. Yugoslavia then closed her borders to all traffic with Greece. Later, Greece, Yugoslavia, and Turkey signed a military and economic alliance. Thus the policy of "containment"— of stopping the spread of communism— scored its first important victory.

● The Marshall Plan: the European Recovery Plan

Experience in Greece, in postwar loans to Britain and France, and with UNRRA, seemed to show that the great need was for economic aid, not political aid. Also, such aid had to be on a continent-wide scale. There must be a general European recovery. It had to be brought about by a coördinated plan, not country by country. And the nations of Europe would have to help in the process.

Several months after the announcement of the Truman Doctrine, Secretary of State George C. Marshall made a new statement of policy: The United States was prepared to give aid to Europe on certain terms. The European countries must get together and determine their needs on a continental basis. They must show what resources they could put into a common pool for economic rebuilding. They must end inflation and put their money on a sound basis. And they must make all efforts to remove the barriers to trade—tariffs or other means—and allow trade to flow freely throughout the continent.

President Harry S. Truman confers with Secretary of State George C. Marshall. General Marshall was Chief of Staff of the United States Army during World War II. Retiring from service after the war, he served in President Truman's Cabinet as Secretary of State (1947–1949) and Secretary of Defense (1950–1951).

Britain and France took the lead in lining up the European countries to meet their part of the agreement. The offer was officially made to all countries on the continent of Europe, which would include the Soviet bloc. Britain and France tried hard to persuade the Russians to join. Speaking for Soviet Russia, Foreign Minister Vyacheslav Molotov refused. The need for economic aid was just as great in eastern Europe, but the satellite nations were compelled to refuse, also. The communist newspapers and radio attacked the Marshall Plan as "dollar imperialism," an attempt of the United States to bind Europe to "Wall Street capitalism."

There were probably two reasons for the Soviet refusal. The Marshall statement did not directly say that there would be some form of inspection of its working, but it hinted at it. This the suspicious Russians would never permit. The other reason probably went deeper. A continent which was economically united and strong offered a much smaller chance for communist expansion than one that was divided and poverty-stricken. The Russians did not want to see Western Europe recover.

Sixteen European nations took part in what came to be called the European Recovery Plan. The communist bloc stayed out; Spain was not invited. The three western zones of Germany were added later. By September, 1947, the European nations had worked out their program. Three months later President Truman asked the Congress to appropriate 17 billion dollars to carry out the plan for four years. In April, 1948, the Economic Cooperation Act was passed and went into effect.

The Truman Doctrine and the Marshall Plan now seem to have been wise, statesmanlike moves. The United States accepted the challenge of leadership in the free world. It even offered economic assistance to the communist states in return for peaceful coöperation. As the only nation in the world able to do so, it offered its wealth in goods and supplies to help others become once more prosperous. Americans knew that economic prosperity is a much better basis for stable, peaceful governments than poverty and misery.

Reasons for aid to Europe

The humanitarian instinct played a part in influencing Americans to support the Marshall Plan, but there was also another motive. It was "enlightened self-interest," which means looking out for oneself in an intelligent way. It worked in two ways. First, American aid allowed American industries, paid by their government, to send their surplus goods to Europe, thus avoiding a depression on the United States. In so doing the United States helped European countries, always the best foreign customers of American industry, to build up more rapidly so that they could once again be self-supporting and good customers.

The second point of self-interest has to do with safeguarding the American way of life. If the continent of Europe had been allowed to remain in poverty and misery, with great numbers of people jobless, homeless, and hungry, it is doubtful that democracy and free institutions could have survived. Communism grows best in poverty-stricken lands. When the Marshall Plan went into operation, the communist parties in France and Italy were the largest in the two countries. By the time the plan had operated for several years, their strength was reduced, although they still remain large and dangerous. The United States was certainly helping the free world by preventing the rest of Europe from going communist.

Steps to increase Western unity

By the end of 1947 the cold war had reached a point of unofficial, undeclared political and economic warfare between East and West. The two sides were lining up in blocs, groups of states united in some ways for closer ac-

International coöperation: the United States ships sugar from the Caribbean to help Europe recover from the effects of the war.

tion. The Eastern (communist) bloc had the advantage of being more strongly united. They had a common political, economic, and social doctrine. They were able to act quickly and together. As the saying went, when Moscow had a cold, all the satellite states sneezed.

Such speedy action is seldom possible in the democratic nations of the West. Congresses and parliaments must first act to grant authority to the leaders. Such proposals require lengthy debates and, usually, compromises. Nor could any nation dictate the policy for the whole group, as Soviet Russia did for the Communist bloc. Although the United States furnished most of the money and materials, it could not, and did not want to, whistle the tune and make the others dance. It wanted allies—partners—not satellites. Each nation had to decide for itself whether to accept proposals of policy.

In spite of these handicaps to speedy and united action, alarm over the aggressive Soviet policy made Western Europe show a degree of economic and political unity surprising in view of its long history of nationalistic separation. Many steps were taken, voluntarily, toward creating a federal union of Europe.

Benelux and the Council of Europe

Early in 1947 Britain and France signed a fifty-year treaty of military alliance. Late in the same year Belgium, Holland, and Luxembourg entered into an economic customs union, aimed at doing away with all tariffs on each other's goods. This group became known as the Benelux nations.

The shock of the communist seizure of Czechoslovakia brought further Western unity. Early in 1948 Britain, France, and the Benelux countries signed a fifty-year treaty pledging economic coöperation and military assistance to each other in case any one was attacked. By this treaty a Council of Europe was set up. There was a definite statement that it would be the nucleus of a federal parliament for Europe. In mid-1949 the original five states were joined by Sweden, Norway, Denmark, Eire, and Italy.

NATO is formed

In April, 1949, the unity of the free West was carried one step further. Twelve nations signed a twenty-five-year treaty, creating a North Atlantic Treaty Organization (NATO). The signers were the United States, Great Britain, France, the Benelux states, Italy, Portugal, Norway, Denmark, Iceland, and Canada. In 1953 Turkey and Greece joined NATO. It was a mutual defense pact. The signers agreed that an attack on one should be considered an attack on all. If such a thing happened, they agreed to consult together immediately on what steps to take.

Some idea of the comparative strength of the two blocs, NATO and Soviet, can be gained by these figures on world economic strength. As is well known, the three basic industrial materials are coal, oil, and steel. Electric power and shipping facilities are of

RESOURCES: NATO VS. SOVIET

per cent of world total

OIL

MERCHANT SHIPPING

COAL

ELECTRICITY

STEEL

POPULATION

*(INCLUDES COMMUNIST ASIA)

726

equal importance. The figures shown in the chart on page 726 are percentages of the total world resources.

In some other ways the figures are not so encouraging. The Soviet bloc has 32 per cent of the world's population, compared to NATO's 16 per cent. The Soviet bloc produces 39 per cent of the world's grains, compared to NATO's 38 per cent.

● *The Coal and Steel Community*

During the early 1950's an amazing step was taken toward the economic unity of Europe. The French Foreign Minister, Robert Schuman, proposed that the six nations which produce almost all of western Europe's steel and coal unite all their facilities and production. The Schuman Plan proposed the formation of a European Coal and Steel Community among France, Germany, Italy, and the Benelux nations. A central authority would regulate production and prices. The members would not charge each other tariffs on coal or steel. None of them would charge more for coal and steel sold outside the country than for that sold inside. This pact was ratified by all six countries; it went into operation early in 1953.

The West needs greater military strength

None of these moves reduced the cold war. On the contrary, the fury and bitterness of the attacks, accusations, and charges on both sides increased with the passage of time. It was a dangerous and explosive situation, resembling that of 1914. Thoughtful people feared that some incident, somewhere, might prove to be the spark that would light the powder train to a world explosion.

Although the Western bloc had greater economic strength, the communist bloc was far superior in military power, especially in ground troops. The West's great fear was that the Communists would overrun Western Germany, possibly all Western Europe. Rus-

EUROPEAN COAL-STEEL COMMUNITY

■ COAL   ▲ STEEL CENTERS   □ IRON-ORE DEPOSITS

sian possession of the industrial regions of the German Ruhr and of northern and eastern France would make their economic strength equal to that of the West.

The United States had clearly indicated that a Russian drive to the west would bring atomic bombing of Russia's cities and industries. After the Russians developed their own atomic bombs, any conflict between the two powers was likely to be a two-way nuclear war.

From the West's standpoint the only solution seemed to be to build up military strength so that it could stop a Communist drive. The European Recovery Program was switched increasingly from economic to military aid. Even so, the United States came to believe that German troops would be needed to help stop a Russian attack. Remembering the history of 1870, 1914, and 1940, you will not be surprised that France objected strongly to German rearmament. Yet the French could see the need of strengthening Western defenses.

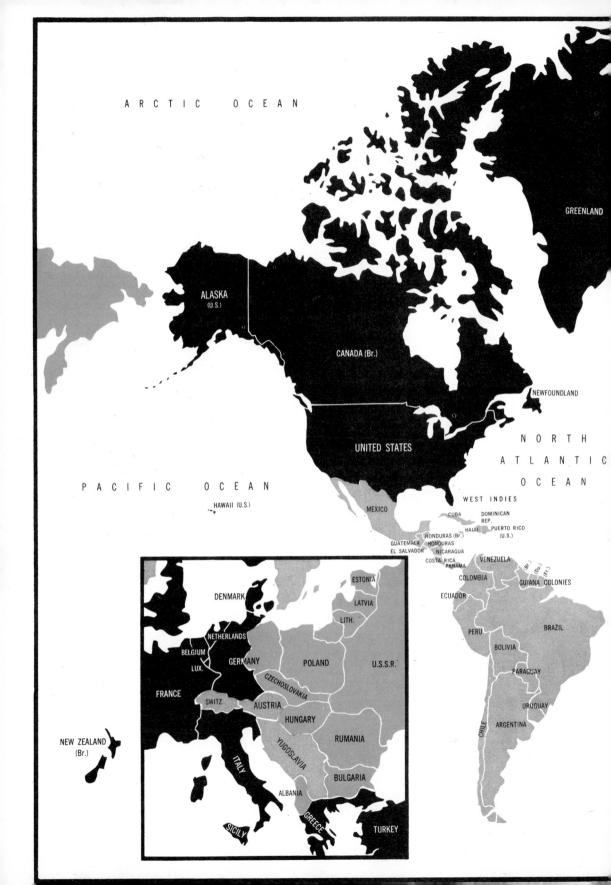

COMMUNISM,
ANTI-COMMUNISM
and the NEUTRALS,
1957

NORWAY
SWEDEN
FINLAND

BRITISH
ISLES

PORTUGAL
SPAIN
Gibraltar
MOROCCO (Fr.)
TUNISIA (Fr.)
ALGERIA (Fr.)
LIBYA
EGYPT

O de ORO
(Sp.)

FRENCH WEST AFRICA
A (Br.)
GUINEA
RA LEONE (Br.)
LIBERIA   GHANA
TOGO
(Fr.)
NIGERIA
(Br.)
Sp. GUINEA
Fr.
EQUATORIAL
AFRICA
CAMEROON (Fr.)

BELGIAN
CONGO

ANGLO-
EGYPTIAN
SUDAN

ERITREA
Fr. SOMALILAND
Br. SOMALILAND
It. SOMALILAND
ETHIOPIA

UGANDA   KENYA
(Br.)   (Br.)
TANGANYIKA
(Br.)
ANGOLA
(Port.)
RHODESIA
(Br.)
SOUTHWEST
AFRICA   BECHUANA
(Br.)
UNION OF
SOUTH AFRICA
(Br.)
MOZAMBIQUE (Port.)
MADAGASCAR (Fr.)

UNION OF SOVIET SOCIALIST REPUBLICS

TURKEY
SYRIA
LEB.
PALESTINE
JORDAN
IRAQ   IRAN
AFGHANISTAN
PAKISTAN
SAUDI ARABIA
OMAN
YEMEN
ADEN (Br.)

NEPAL
BHUTAN
INDIA (Br.)
PAKISTAN
BURMA
CEYLON

MONGOLIA

CHINA

KOREA
JAPAN
RYUKYU IS.
TAIWAN

N. VIETNAM
LAOS
THAI-
LAND
S. VIETNAM
CAMBODIA
PHILIPPINE IS.
N. BORNEO
MALAYA   SARAWAK
SUMATRA (Du.)   BORNEO
CELEBES
Bandung
JAVA (Du.)

INDIAN OCEAN

INDONESIA

NEW GUINEA
(Du.)
PAPUA

AUSTRALIA (Br.)

SOUTH
ATLANTIC
OCEAN

Neutral
Communist Bloc
Anti-Communist Bloc

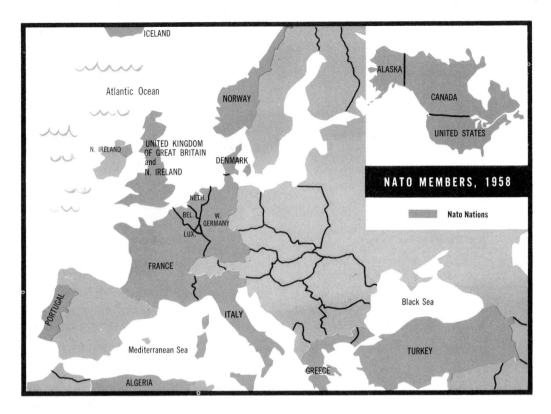

ICELAND

Atlantic Ocean

NORWAY

N. IRELAND

UNITED KINGDOM
OF GREAT BRITAIN
and
N. IRELAND

DENMARK

NETH.

BEL.

LUX.

W.
GERMANY

FRANCE

PORTUGAL

ITALY

Mediterranean Sea

ALGERIA

GREECE

TURKEY

Black Sea

ALASKA

CANADA

UNITED STATES

NATO MEMBERS, 1958

Nato Nations

● EDC fails and NATO is strengthened

The French idea was that Western Europe should form a European Defense Community (EDC). It should be modeled on the Coal and Steel Community, but should apply to armies and defense instead of steel production. There should be a supreme military authority to control a combined European army. The nations should provide troops to this army according to an agreed schedule. However, the troops should have a common uniform and a combined command under the military authority. German troops could be recruited, armed, and included in the army, but they would not come under German command.

This plan proved to be too bold for Britain, and even for France herself. The British refused to commit troops to a combined European army. Nevertheless, early in 1952 France, Italy, West Germany and the Benelux nations signed an EDC treaty. In 1954, how-

ever, the French national assembly refused to ratify the treaty, and the EDC plan collapsed.

The other Western powers were greatly disappointed over this development, but they continued to work for increased military unity and strength. In October, 1954, the Western nations agreed to integrate West Germany and Italy politically and militarily into a European plan of defense. This plan provided for (1) a settlement of the Saar question involving France and Germany; (2) restoration of full sovereignty to Germany and permission to establish a 500,000-man army in Germany; (3) a new Western Union in which the armies of Germany and Italy would be combined with the armed forces of Great Britain, France, Belgium, the Netherlands, and Luxembourg; (4) guarantee of British troops and air force for defense of Western Europe; (5) granting Germany full membership in the North Atlantic Treaty Organization.

The Saar joins West Germany

During the same month of October, 1954, France and Germany signed an agreement concerning the Saar region. It was agreed that politically the Saar would remain a "European territory." The administration of the Saar would be headed by a European commissioner. He would be responsible to a Committee of Ministers of the Council of Europe. Economically, however, the rich Saar Basin would be allied with France by tariff and financial ties. The Saar agreement helped make France willing to accept the rearmament of West Germany.

In 1955 the Saarlanders were again allowed to vote to choose their country. As in 1935, they voted to rejoin Germany. A French-German agreement covered the change-over period. It provided that Saarlanders were citizens of the German Federal (West German) Republic, subject to all of its laws. The rail and postal systems operated under German laws. Until the end of 1959 the coal-mining industry was to be under joint French-German regulation. Until that time Saarlanders paid tariff duty on goods imported from Germany, while trade with France was duty free. On January 1, 1957, the Saar became the tenth state of the German Federal Republic.

Euratom and the Common Market: more steps toward unity

The formation of the International Atomic Energy Agency (page 710) was accompanied by another step toward European economic unity. France, Italy, West Germany, and the Benelux nations joined to form another agency similar to the Coal and Steel Community (page 727). It was called the European Atomic Energy Community, commonly known as Euratom. It was given power to do all the trading within the group in nuclear ores and fuels for peaceful uses. The Community set up among the six nations a common market in atomic equipment and materials, and took over their foreign relations in atomic energy matters. Euratom was given power to conduct atomic research and development. One of the first projects considered by the Community was a ten-year program to run from 1957 to 1967, for the production of electrical power by means of nuclear energy.

In March, 1957, the same six nations took another momentous step. They concluded a treaty establishing the European Economic Community, usually called the Common Market. The treaty provided that, over a fifteen-year period, tariffs and import quotas among the six nations would gradually be abolished. A common tariff was to be placed on goods coming from outside. An investment bank, with capital contributed by the member governments, was created. Its purposes were to finance projects beyond the means of a single nation, to finance any changes in industries made necessary by the formation of the common market, and to help develop industries in the less developed areas of the community. The treaty created a fairly elaborate federal system to govern the European Economic Community.

Now we shall switch back to Asia. How was communism getting along in the Orient?

Communism triumphs in China

The truce between Chiang Kai-shek and the Chinese Communists broke down even before the end of the war with Japan. Each side accused the other of bad faith. The Communists claimed that Chiang was using lend-lease supplies and placing his troops in position to attack them rather than the Japanese. Chiang replied that the Communists were spreading their propaganda and undermining the Nationalist Government.

The end of the Japanese war gave the Chinese Communists a sudden advantage. They were established in northern China, near

Manchuria. When the Russians invaded Manchuria and took the surrender of the Japanese armies there, the Chinese Communists were nearer than the Nationalists. The Russians turned over to the Communists the great store of arms and ammunition taken from the Japanese. The Communists were soon complete masters of northern China, under their leader, Mao Tse-tung.

When open war broke out between the two Chinese groups, the Allies tried to prevent China from falling into chaos. The United States sent General Marshall as a special envoy. He was able to arrange a truce, but it was a brief one. Each side accused the other of truce violations and the war broke out again.

The Communists rapidly gained the upper hand. Their propaganda slogan, "Land for the Peasants," had a great appeal. The Nationalists seemed to have lost control. Large groups of Nationalist troops deserted to the Communist side, taking with them their supplies and equipment. In battle, too, the Communists were victorious. City after city, province after province, fell into their hands. Each victory brought them more strength.

Life on Formosa: farmers hoe their field while soldiers of Chiang Kai-shek's army man an antiaircraft gun, watching for a possible Communist attack. The gun was supplied by the United States.

The United States was alarmed at the prospect of a Communist China in the Far East, allied with Soviet Russia; so the American government made many attempts to bolster up the fading Nationalist strength. Over 400 million dollars was appropriated for aid to Nationalist China. But the Nationalist government seemed to have lost the loyalty of the Chinese people. It had become very corrupt. American observers reported that much of the aid was taken for private use by high officials of the Nationalists. Some war material was even sold to the Communists. When the position of Chiang Kai-shek seemed hopeless, American aid was discontinued altogether. It seemed that nothing could be done to change the outcome except to send a large force of American troops to fight against the Chinese Communists.

By 1950 Chiang Kai-shek and the Nationalist government had been driven completely off the mainland of China to the island of Formosa. The Communists held the entire mainland. They proclaimed the Central People's Government of the People's Republic of China, with Mao Tse-tung as president-dictator. Britain, India, the Soviet bloc, and other nations have recognized the Communist government. The United States and many others have refused to do so.

There is much disagreement in the United States over the reason for the Communist victory in China. One thing is certain. The Communist victory was a serious defeat for the United States and the free world.

A question of major concern to the world is the extent to which Russia and Communist China will continue to coöperate. Will China move toward more independent policies, as Yugoslavia has done under Tito? The free world watches Sino-Soviet relations closely, for upon them may depend its fate.

The United States continued to regard Chiang Kai-shek's regime as the lawful government of China. Supplies and military equipment were sent to Formosa. The Nationalists fortified their positions on Formosa and on Quemoy and Matsu, islands close to the mainland. Chiang announced his intention to return to the mainland.

The Chinese Communists threatened to "liberate" the Nationalist-held islands. In 1957 and again in 1958 it seemed likely that Red China might attack. President Eisenhower and his Secretary of State, John Foster Dulles, announced that United States forces might be used to defend the islands. Sea, air, and land forces were moved into the area. United States ships helped move supplies to Quemoy while the island was being bombarded. Thus the Formosa Strait became one of the world's areas of tension.

Review of Chapter 55

People, places, and things

Identify: George C. Marshall, V. M. Molotov, Jan Masaryk, Eduard Beneš, Mao Tse-tung, Cominform, iron curtain, Berlin airlift, Benelux countries, Schuman Plan, ERP.

Locate: Russia and the satellite states, the NATO nations, the People's Republic of China, Formosa, Hong Kong.

Events in review

1. When and for what purpose was UNRRA formed?
2. Name three countries that faced the problem of setting up new governments to replace fascist regimes after the war.
3. Name one important effect of the war and Japanese imperialism on the people of Asia.
4. Which two nations were divided into four occupation zones? Name the four occupying powers.
5. Why did Trieste cause a problem in writing the peace treaty for Italy? What arrangement was made in 1947? What agreement was reached about Trieste in 1954?
6. Name five central European nations in which the Russians set up communist-controlled temporary governments during World War II.
7. What was the purpose of the Nuremberg trials?
8. What did the victorious powers first propose to do with German industrial plants? What problems developed?
9. How long did it take the Council of Foreign Ministers to agree on a treaty for Austria? What were the terms of the treaty?
10. How did Russia extend her power through (a) satellite states, (b) the Cominform?
11. Tell briefly what happened in Czechoslovakia in 1948. Why were the Western powers unable to take action?
12. Where did a break in the iron curtain appear in 1948?
13. What was the purpose of the Truman Doctrine? Where was this doctrine first put into effect?
14. Briefly state the purpose of the Marshall Plan. How many European nations took part in it? To what extent were they asked to help themselves?
15. What policy was agreed on by the signers of the NATO pact?
16. What event at the end of World War II gave the Chinese Communists an advantage in their rivalry with the Nationalist government?

Problems and projects

1. Self-interest is one of the main guides for a nation's foreign policy. To what extent was the Marshall Plan based on the self-interest of this nation?
2. Compare the Truman Doctrine with the 1957 plan often referred to as "the Eisenhower Doctrine." How similar are the purposes and methods of the two plans?
3. On the basis of newspaper and magazine articles, make a report to the class on current events in the Far East. What is the current situation regarding Formosa? Communist China? Has the United States taken any recent action? Has the United Nations acted?

Chapter *56* # The World in Ferment

YOU HAVE READ of the two-way revolutionary movement in the colonial world. Colonial people demanded national independence—self-government—and a better way of life. These two aims played a large part in the Communist victory in China. The Communists did not create the revolutionary situation in China. They took advantage of conditions that already existed.

After World War II imperialism was in retreat throughout the colonial world, at different rates of speed in different places. It was to be expected that such a revolutionary situation would affect the course of the cold war. This involvement led to two minor wars, each of which threatened to develop into a world war.

The "little wars": Korea

When the war with Japan ended in 1945, it was arranged that the Russians would take the surrender of the Japanese in northern Korea, the Americans in southern Korea. For convenience, a dividing point was fixed at the thirty-eighth parallel of latitude. Thus postwar Korea had two occupation armies.

At the Moscow Conference, 1945, the Allies agreed that Korea should be independent.

The United States, the Soviet Union, Great Britain, and China were to act as trustees in Korea for five years while a constitution was being written and the country prepared for independence.

Forming a government for Korea proved difficult. The Russians and Americans were unable to agree about a temporary government, or about anything else. In 1947, the United States requested the General Assembly of the United Nations to supervise elections in Korea. Russia boycotted the United Nations commission, refusing to allow elections in her zone.

North and South Korea

The Russian-American disagreements led to the formation of two governments. In 1948, in the American zone, Koreans elected an assembly which wrote a republican constitution and chose Dr. Syngman Rhee as president. Some seats in the legislature were left open for representatives from northern Korea if elections were held there. The United Nations General Assembly recognized the Republic of Korea (South) as a legal government. A proposal to admit it to the United Nations was blocked by a Russian veto. Meantime, a People's Republic of

North Korea had been formed in the Soviet zone. It was, of course, a communist government. Its proposed admission to the United Nations was blocked by the Western powers.

American and Russian occupation forces were now withdrawn, but each continued to have much influence in its former zone. In North Korea the Russians had two advantages. They had a government and an army led by disciplined communists. They had an economic advantage, too: North Korea had almost all the industries of the country.

● Invasion and war

The following years brought many clashes and border incidents along the thirty-eighth parallel. On June 25, 1950, the North Korean army crossed the border and moved southward in a well-organized invasion in force. The plan was obviously to seize the south quickly and present the world with an accomplished fact. On the invasion day, at the request of the United States, the Security Council of the United Nations met. The Soviet Union was then boycotting the meetings to try to enforce its demand for the admission of Communist China. With the Rus-

sians absent the Council was able to issue a demand that the North Koreans withdraw. Two days later, when they had not done so, the Security Council declared North Korea an aggressor, and called upon United Nations members to furnish troops to stop the aggression.

The conflict was a United Nations war as well as a small-scale world war. General Douglas MacArthur was placed in command of a United Nations army. Sixteen nations sent men and materials in varying amounts. The United States furnished most of the supplies and equipment, and more troops than any nation except South Korea. The United States Navy supported the ground forces. The Russians sent supplies and equipment to the North Koreans.

The actual war was a seesaw affair. At first the North Koreans drove the United Nations forces into a small area around the southern port of Pusan. Then, in a brilliant counterattack, the United Nations drove all the way to the Yalu River, the border between Korea and Manchuria. At this point several hundred thousand "volunteer" Chinese Communist troops entered the war. The United Nations troops were again driven south of the thirty-eighth parallel.

In a move that caused great controversy in the United States, President Truman removed General MacArthur from the United Nations command. Under his successor the army regrouped and counterattacked, driving slowly north across the parallel. Progress was slow and costly because of the mountainous terrain and also because the enemy was supplied with Russian equipment, especially planes. These planes operated from bases across the Yalu River in Chinese Manchuria. There were strong demands in the United States that these bases be attacked and destroyed. The United Nations Allies, strongly supported by President Truman, took the position that this could not be done for fear of spreading the war.

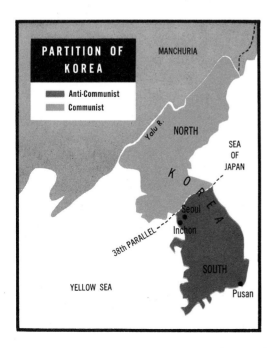

PARTITION OF KOREA

■ Anti-Communist
■ Communist

MANCHURIA

Yalu R.

NORTH

SEA
OF
JAPAN

K
O
R
E
A

Seoul
Inchon

38th PARALLEL

SOUTH

YELLOW SEA

Pusan

War in Korea. A minesweeper of the Republic of Korea forces blows up as she strikes a mine in Wonsan harbor. Several minesweepers of the United States Navy were also destroyed or damaged. Mines swept up in Korean waters were found to be of Russian types.

● *Truce negotiations and the armistice*

The United Nations army was making slow progress north of the thirty-eighth parallel when the enemy called for negotiations for peace. Although it meant giving up the advantage of a successful offensive, the Allies agreed to negotiate. Attempts to agree on the terms of an armistice dragged out for more than two years. Finally, on July 27, 1953, an armistice was signed.

Among other things, the armistice provided for a peace conference to be held within three months. Five years later the conference had not been held. There had not been agreement on what nations should attend, or on the subjects of negotiation. Thus the Korean War came to an inconclusive end.

The war was costly to everyone, most of all to Korea, which was left badly devastated. It taught one great lesson: local wars and aggressions can be stopped, and aggressors made to pay dearly, if nations stand united against lawless conduct. If it is known in advance that they will stand united, the aggressions are less likely to occur.

The "little wars": Indo-China

Indo-China was made up of three states: Laos, Cambodia, and Viet Nam. The French had held Indo-China as a colony for over a century before they were driven out by the Japanese during World War II. After the war, when the French tried to return, they found that a strong independence movement had developed in Viet Nam. This drive for independence was led by a man named Ho Chi Minh.

In order to return without a fight, the French promised Viet Nam a large degree of self-government, with mixed French and native representation. In practice this combined government did not work well. Eventually the Indo-Chinese withdrew and declared Viet Nam an independent republic under Ho Chi Minh. The French landed troops; the republican forces withdrew to the north. France set up a federation of the three states under a weak native emperor, really controlled by the French high commissioner.

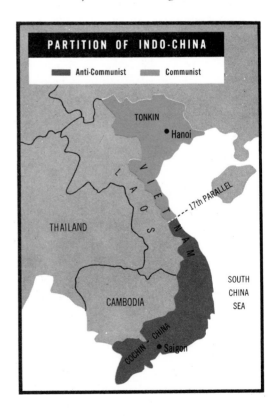

PARTITION OF INDO-CHINA

■ Anti-Communist   ■ Communist

TONKIN
● Hanoi

LAOS

17th PARALLEL

THAILAND

VIETNAM

SOUTH CHINA SEA

CAMBODIA

COCHIN-CHINA
● Saigon

After a series of offers and counterdemands, fighting broke out.

It was jungle guerrilla war, a very difficult kind to fight. The French could hold the cities, but only "strong points" in the country. They used the famous French Foreign Legion, and Senegalese troops from Africa. Some Indo-Chinese fought with the French, but without much enthusiasm. The war was a terrible drain on the none-too-healthy treasury and economy of France.

● Intervention by the Chinese Communists

After their victory in China the Chinese Communists helped the Indo-Chinese rebels with equipment and training. The armistice in Korea made more Chinese help possible. The Indo-China War became less a guerrilla fight and more a conflict between regularly trained and equipped divisions. Early in 1954 the rebels began an offensive which the French could not stop.

Until then France had insisted that the war was entirely a domestic affair. She had refused to allow any United Nations action, or any interference from outside nations. The successful rebel drive forced her to change her tune. France now declared the Indo-China War an attack on her by international communism, and appealed for aid to the Western powers.

Few of the countries which had fought with the United Nations in Korea were willing to help the French. France had proclaimed the war a domestic uprising, not a United Nations problem. The United States wavered in its position, but finally decided not to do more than furnish supplies and equipment unless the others would join in. The others would not. The rebel drive continued, and France had to make peace.

● The Geneva Conference of 1954

Pierre Mendes-France, who became premier of France in 1954, was determined to

Indo-China. A French soldier crouches in a muddy ditch, watching for snipers.

end the Indo-China War. He called for a conference of France, Great Britain, the United States, Soviet Russia, and Communist China to meet at Geneva to settle both the Indo-China and the Korean problems. The Communists were in a strong bargaining position at Geneva. They were willing to continue the war; the French were not willing to keep on fighting.

In mid-1954 the Geneva Conference reached an agreement. Laos and Cambodia became independent states within the French Union. Viet Nam was divided in the middle. The Communists took the northern half, Viet Minh, which contains rich resources and the second-largest seaport. People who wished to leave this region were allowed to do so before the communists took over. The southern half, Viet Nam, became an independent republic. It was agreed that elections should be held within two years to create a unified government for the two parts. Years went by, but the proposed elections to unite Viet Minh and Viet Nam were not held.

The Korean problem was also discussed at the Geneva Conference. Differences of opinion over how to conduct an election throughout Korea were so conflicting that the subject was dropped altogether. Korea remained divided, with no formal peace treaty.

The Indo-China War and the Geneva Conference represented communist victories in terms of gaining territory and in terms of impressing the world with communist strength. Both the Indo-China affair and the refusal to form the European Defense Community (page 730), which happened at about the same time, showed a weakening of the unity of the Western powers. Such a weakening had been a principal aim of Soviet foreign policy since the end of World War II.

Japan after World War II

The situation in postwar Japan was quite different from that in Germany and Austria (pages 717-719). Because the United States had carried the major burden of the Japanese war, its troops occupied the defeated country. There was no conflict of authority.

●*The American occupation*

The real ruler of occupied Japan was General MacArthur. Although the Japanese government operated throughout the occupation, all its actions had to have his approval. As in Germany, the aim of the occupation forces was to demilitarize Japan. Control of industry was to be taken away from the zaibatsu, a group of five families that had dominated Japanese industry before the war. Only industries suited to peacetime pursuits were to be allowed to function.

The occupation of Japan went very smoothly. In spite of atomic bombing, industry had not been as badly damaged as in Germany. The Japanese people proved amazingly cooperative. They accepted their defeat, and the political reforms forced on them, without apparent resentment.

●*Writing the peace treaty*

Writing a Japanese peace treaty proved much more difficult than the occupation. The Russians insisted that the treaty be written by the four powers most concerned with the war—the United States, China, Great Britain, and the Soviet Union. Agreements would have to be unanimous. The American government maintained that the treaty should be written by the eleven nations which had fought the Pacific war, with equal votes and majority decisions.

After six years of deadlock, the United States summoned a peace conference to meet in San Francisco in 1951. The Western powers consented to this move; the Russians did not. Forty-eight nations signed the treaty with Japan, but it was a strange ceremony. The Soviet Union, Poland, and Czechoslovakia attended the conference but refused to sign the treaty. China, the nation which had suffered most from Japanese aggression, was not present. The Western powers could not agree which Chinese government to invite, and decided not to invite either.

By the treaty Japan gave up all rights and titles to Formosa and the Pescadores, and all claims to special rights in China. She also gave up her rights to the mandated Pacific Islands, to the southern half of Sakhalin, and to the Kurile Islands. She renounced all claims to Korea and acknowledged the independence of that country. The Japanese government accepted obligations to settle international disputes peacefully, to give aid to the United Nations, and to pay reparations for the war damages Japan had caused.

The treaty provided for the end of American control and the withdrawal of occupation troops. An additional treaty between Japan and the United States allowed American troops to remain in the islands until Japan was ready to take over her own defense.

War between Japan and the Soviet Union did not officially end until 1956. The two nations then agreed to restore diplomatic relations. The Soviet government promised not to oppose Japan's application for membership in the United Nations. Many problems of territories and trade relations were left to be settled by further diplomatic negotiations.

● Problems of postwar Japan

To Japan, peace brought the end of bloodshed, destruction, and occupation, but not the end of her problems, which were even worse than before the war. She had lost all territory gained since 1875. Her growing population, now nearly ninety million, had little more than the four main islands for living space. Even the most intensive farming of the small amount of arable land did not produce enough food. Most of the raw materials for Japanese industry had to be imported and paid for by exports. It has been said before that Japan had to export or die (page 533). This statement was even more true after World War II.

China had been Japan's best customer before the war. When China fell to the Communists, the Western powers, especially the United States, insisted that Japan not sell to China any supplies that might be useful in war. This made it difficult for Japan to buy Chinese raw materials. She could buy American raw materials, but at a much higher cost. The purchases were financed mainly by American loans.

The problem of Japanese reparations was simple for the Russians but difficult for everyone else. The Russians had suffered no war damage from Japan, but they paid themselves well by taking and carrying off Japanese-built factories from Manchuria. For the other countries it was not so simple.

At first the Allies seized Japanese shipyards, munitions plants, and many large factories. The plan was to distribute them as reparations, at the same time reducing Japan's ability to make war. When division of these plants proved difficult, some repara-

General Douglas MacArthur and Emperor Hirohito of Japan in the United States Embassy, Tokyo.

tions payments were taken in Japanese-produced goods. In 1949, the United States announced its opposition to any further reparations payments. The Americans claimed that such payments prevented Japan from recovering and becoming self-sufficient.

To understand this American policy you must comprehend one of the great dilemmas of modern war. Japan's conquerors had three choices: to allow a great part of the Japanese population to die; to support them; or to help them to support themselves. The first was unthinkable; the second unacceptable as a long-range solution. Thus the United States

DROPPING THE PILOTS

Change of command in Russia. After Khrushchev became top man, he demoted four of the high-ranking men in the Soviet state. The British magazine Punch *ran this cartoon. Kaganovitch, Shepilov, Malenkov, and Molotov are being dropped. Compare the cartoon on Bismarck's retirement (page 427).*

faced the strange solution of paying to help rebuild the destruction it caused during the war.

The cold war complicated the problem of Japanese trade, as you have seen. It also produced a strange military situation. The United States had insisted that Japan adopt a constitution pledging them never to go to war, and to have only a few troops for domestic police purposes. After the communist victory in China and the war in Korea, American statesmen came to believe that Japan must be rearmed. She must be able to defend herself and to help against the communists if war came.

The Japanese were not eager to build up military forces again. They had found it more profitable to spend their money to build up industries and export their goods. They knew that the United States would not see them fall to the communists. Therefore, they went very slowly in rearming, and allowed the United States to bear most of the burden of defending them. Truly, war produces ironic situations.

The cold war continues

●*The change in Soviet leadership*

The death of Joseph Stalin early in 1953 raised once again the great problem of dictatorship: who succeeds when the dictator is gone? During the next five years a series of triumvirates (groups of three men) headed the Soviet government. The personnel changed fairly rapidly, but during 1957 and 1958 Nikita Khrushchev emerged as top man in the Communist Party and the Russian state.

Soviet foreign policy shifted many times during this period. At times the Soviet leaders blustered, called names, and threatened dire things if the Western powers attacked Russia. Then they would speak sweet words about the possibility of "peaceful coexistence" —living together peacefully in the same world. Soviet policy in these five years seemed to be aimed at convincing the neutral nations that the communists were peace-loving, whereas the West, led by the United States, were "capitalist-imperialist warmongers."

●*The Warsaw Pact: the communist NATO*

In May, 1955, in Warsaw, Poland, the Soviet government held a meeting of representatives of the communist bloc: the Soviet Union, Poland, East Germany, Czechoslovakia, Hungary, Rumania, Bulgaria, and Albania. The purpose was to form a military organization like the West's NATO. The nations adopted the Warsaw Pact, by which each nation pledged to furnish troops in proportion to its population in the event of war. The satellites pledged almost one hundred divisions, a large army when added to the vast manpower of the Soviet Union.

The Geneva "Summit" Conference of 1955

After Stalin's death many people urged that the way to prevent the ever-threatening war was to hold a meeting of the heads of the four main powers. Winston Churchill urged "a conference on the highest level"; the expression "a summit conference" was widely used. The theory was that, meeting face to face around a table, the heads of state could reach general agreements, leaving the details to be worked out later by the foreign ministers.

In July, 1955, the heads of government of the United States, Great Britain, the Soviet Union, and France met at Geneva, Switzerland. For six days they discussed four great problems, the underlying causes of the cold war: (1) Unification of Germany, (2) European security, (3) Disarmament, (4) How to improve relations between East and West by such means as greater freedom of travel and exchange of cultural and scientific ideas. There was no doubt that, if the first three of these problems could be solved, the world could heave a sigh of relief. Unfortunately, although a little progress was made on the fourth point, almost nothing was accomplished about the other three.

Ferment among the communist satellites

It is easy to think of the communist bloc as a solid, firmly knit group of states, strongly united by a common purpose. This viewpoint overlooks the fact that the satellites were national states, some with long histories of independent rule, national heroes, and cultural glories. Poland and Hungary had long-

standing antagonisms toward Russia. Communist policies of forcing peasants onto collective farms, speeding the development of industry, and taking the products for Soviet advantage, were certain to produce hostile feelings. Now and then an event occurred to remind the world that communist bloc unity was a forced thing, and that the satellites longed to be free.

The first such event came in 1948 when Yugoslavia's Tito, although himself a communist, broke with Moscow. After that Yugoslavia followed its own course, a fact that apparently aroused envy among the satellites and rage in Moscow. "Titoism" became a great fear to Soviet leaders. In 1953 the East German workers revolted against their communist leaders. Russian troops suppressed the revolt. Under their protection the East German Communist government survived.

Trouble came next in Poland, where the Poles demanded the right to follow a nationalist policy as Yugoslavia had done. Defying Moscow, they chose as their leader Wladislaw Gomulka, a communist out of favor with

Uncle Sam showing doubt about the Russian leaders: Did they want friendship or trouble?

"We Play Hot And Sweet"

741

the Russians. Gomulka warned Moscow to give in to Polish demands in order to stop the rising discontent. The Soviet leaders consented, and order was restored. After that relations between Poland and the Soviet government were on an uneasy tightrope. Gomulka knew that if he went too far in his independent policy, the Russians would destroy Poland either by force or by cutting off Russian raw materials and markets from Polish industries. Moscow knew that if it went too far, the Poles would rise in frantic revolt.

Escape from Hungary after the uprising against Russian domination of that country. A woman refugee makes her way across a river to enter Austria. More than 120,000 people left their homes rather than live under communism.

Revolt in Hungary

The next uprising took place in Hungary. Students and workers expressed their sympathies with the Poles by street demonstrations. In October, 1956, the police fired on one such demonstration. A protest demonstration took place. Hungarian troops, sent to suppress the protest, joined the demonstrators. Before long the rebels controlled all of western Hungary.

As in Poland, the revolt brought a new premier, Imre Nagy, to power. Nagy was forced to make many anti-Soviet moves. He promised a free election, with opposition parties permitted. He announced Hungary's withdrawal from the Warsaw Pact. He appealed to the United Nations for help. The rebels tried to wipe out completely the much-hated secret police. They demanded the complete withdrawal of Russian troops from Hungary. Soviet troops did withdraw from Budapest. After receiving reinforcements, they re-entered the city, seized Nagy and most of his cabinet, and installed a new government under a man they could trust.

The Hungarians opposed these moves, first by passive resistance and general strikes, then by violence. They appealed for help to the Western powers and to the United Nations. No help came. The Hungarians paid dearly for their spirit of independence. Soviet troops with tanks, guns, and planes crushed the revolt with great slaughter.

During the revolt and after its defeat, more than 120,000 Hungarians fled across the borders into Austria and Yugoslavia. Nearly half of these refugees were resettled throughout Europe, South America, and the United States. However, many could not find new homes. In despair, some returned to Hungary. Two years after the revolt there were still 50,000 Hungarians living in crowded refugee camps in Austria, Germany, France, Yugoslavia, and Switzerland. They were left with little hope for the future.

The Russians had seized Imre Nagy and General Pal Maleter, leader of the rebel army, in violation of promises of safekeeping. In mid-1958 Khrushchev announced that both men had been tried, condemned, and executed.

The unrest among the satellite states seems to prove several things. First, the satellite peoples accepted their communist governments and their domination by the Russians very unwillingly. However, it was doubtful that they could gain independence without outside help. Second, it was likely that the satellite divisions promised by the Warsaw Pact would be more of a hindrance than a help to the Soviet Union in case of war. Third, the brutal suppression of the revolts in East Germany and Hungary showed the world the merciless determination of the Soviet government to hold on to its empire at all costs. Neutral states became more doubtful that the Russians were peace-loving and opposed to imperialism.

● Sputnik, Explorer, and Pioneer

On October 4, 1957, the world entered a new era—The Space Age. The Soviet government announced that it had successfully launched an earth satellite—an artificial moon which would revolve around the earth on a fixed orbit. The Russian word for satellite is *sputnik*. Within a few hours the word came into international use.

A month later came another announcement: a second satellite, weighing half a ton, was circling the earth on an orbit reaching 1,000 miles out in space and at a speed of nearly 18,000 miles an hour. In the second satellite was a small dog, Laika. Later in August, 1960, there was sent into space the 10,143 lb. "flying zoo," with two dogs, several rats, mice, and insects. The latest sputnik returned safely to earth.

The launching of the satellites had real scientific importance. To scientists they promised help in the study of cosmic rays,

A satellite and final stage rocket being assembled at the United States Army's Ballistic Missile Agency in Huntsville, Alabama. The satellite shown here is of the same type as Explorer I, successfully launched January 31, 1958.

the distribution of chemical elements, and the actions of heart, lungs, digestive functions and blood circulation under conditions of low gravitation.

Politically the satellites had immense psychological and propaganda value to the Russians. Neutrals were impressed by this proof of the advanced state of Soviet science. In the West, especially in the United States, it came as a rude awakening that the Russians should be first in a scientific achievement. There were many demands for a reform of the American educational system in order to train more engineers and scientists to equal the Russian progress.

From a military standpoint Sputnik was interpreted to mean that the Russians had perfected a very powerful rocket fuel and an accurate guiding system. It was freely stated

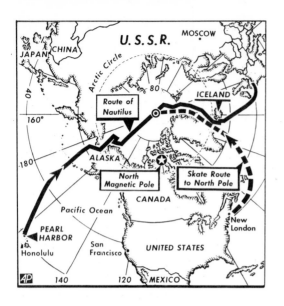

U. S. S. R.

MOSCOW

JAPAN CHINA

Arctic Circle

80

ICELAND

Route of
Nautilus

160°

180

ALASKA

North
Magnetic Pole

Skate Route
to North Pole

CANADA

Pacific Ocean

New
London

PEARL
HARBOR

Honolulu

San
Francisco

UNITED STATES

140

120

MEXICO

Confidence in American scientific ability and technical skill was boosted by the history-making voyages of two atomic-powered submarines of the United States Navy. In August, 1958, U.S.S. Nautilus and U.S.S. Skate made passages under the polar icecap.

that they would be able to send intercontinental ballistic missiles, carrying nuclear warheads, anywhere in the world. The military importance of this development need hardly be pointed out.

After several disheartening failures the United States succeeded in launching its first satellite, called Explorer, on January 31, 1958. Within the next six months three more American satellites were put in orbit.

The competition for the conquest of space was sure to continue. In mid-1958 the Russians sent up a third satellite, weighing more than a ton. In October the United States Air Force attempted to fire a rocket around the moon. Pioneer failed to reach the moon but attained a record distance, more than 71,000 miles from the earth. More "moon shots" were predicted. Scientists discussed manned rockets and manned satellites, and trips to other planets. Many people urged "crash programs"

—all-out efforts without regard to cost—to be the first to accomplish these things. Others, however, warned that men should not neglect the problems of this world, such as poverty and hunger, in their eagerness to conquer new worlds.

On November 3, 1960, Explorer VIII soared into orbit and began beeping back signals that may lead to important discoveries concerning the ionosphere, the "roof" of ions that controls long-range radio.

American science and technology scored a notable first in another field with the exploits of atomic-powered submarines (see the map on this page).

● *The contest for the neutral nations*

In the war of ideas between East and West, each aimed its propaganda mainly at those nations which had not lined up on either side. Each tried to convince these neutrals that it had the better kind of government, that its economic system was more productive, and that it was truly working for peace.

Most of the neutrals were located in Africa and Asia. India, Pakistan, Burma, Indonesia, Ceylon, Egypt, and the Arab states were all newly independent nations. Almost all of them hesitated to take a definite stand for either bloc. They felt that both were too warlike; they preferred not to be drawn into the struggle.

The new nations did not fully trust the West. Most of them had been colonies of Western powers, and they feared a return of the old colonialism. Such incidents as France's fight to keep Indo-China and her North African colonies, and American aid to France, made the neutrals doubt that the West was really as favorable to freedom and self-government as it said. Many of their peoples were of colored races; they were quick to resent any signs of racial discrimination among the Western powers. They seemed to fear a return of colonialism more than the spread of communism. Still, they were shocked by incidents such as the Russian suppression of the German and Hungarian revolts.

Most of the new nations were underdeveloped industrially. For some years after World War II the United States spent a great deal of money to help them improve their economic systems. Some of this money went as gifts, some as loans. Some was granted on a nation-to-nation basis, some through the United Nations Technical Assistance Program.

After 1955 the Soviet Union gave increasing amounts of economic aid to the underdeveloped countries. Most of it was in the form of long-term, low-interest loans, for projects such as roads, factories, dams, and power plants. Thus the propaganda war developed an economic side. Whichever made the grant or loan to build a project sent engineers and other experts to help. These men surely influenced the thinking of people they met and worked with.

●SEATO

The communist victory in Indo-China led the West to try to prevent further communist expansion in southeast Asia. Shortly after the Geneva Conference on Indo-China, representatives of a number of nations met at Manila, Philippine Islands. On September 8, 1954, the Southeast Asia Defense Treaty was signed, setting up an organization (SEATO) similar to NATO, but not so closely knit. Signers of the document included the United States, Great Britain, France, Australia, New Zealand, Pakistan, the Philippines, and Thailand. They joined to resist the spread of communism, especially in Cambodia, Laos, and Viet Nam. The signers agreed to meet and consult when action seemed needed. It was a disappointment to the West that India, Burma, Ceylon and Indonesia would not join the organization.

The map on this page shows the SEATO members. Several of these nations also signed

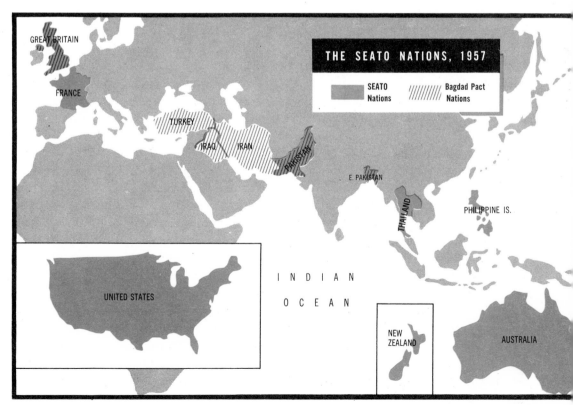

THE SEATO NATIONS, 1957

SEATO Nations

Bagdad Pact Nations

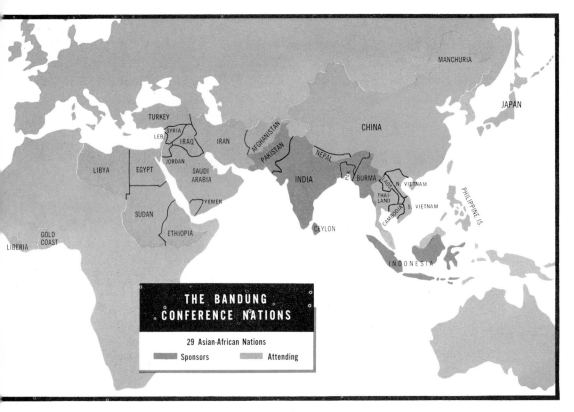

THE BANDUNG
CONFERENCE NATIONS

29 Asian-African Nations

Sponsors   Attending

the Bagdad Pact, another phase of the effort to block communist aggression (see page 760).

● The Bandung Conference

In April, 1955, representatives of almost all independent Asian and African nations met at Bandung, Java (Indonesia). The delegates discussed such matters of common interest as colonialism, segregation, racial discrimination, and cultural coöperation. They agreed unanimously to support the principle of national independence.

The conference adopted a number of resolutions. Among other things, the delegates urged the formation of a United Nations fund for economic development, and the provision of more funds for the development of Asian-African countries. They condemned such practices of racial discrimination as the current policy in South Africa. With great emphasis they condemned colonialism in every form.

The Bandung Conference served notice to the world that the people of Africa and Asia were no longer to be considered "second class nations." These nations were prepared to play their part in the world on a basis of equality with all others. With a loud voice they said "colonialism is dead."

IGY: coöperation in science

From the political and military standpoints the nations of the world were divided into three groups: East, West, and neutrals. The cold war made any kind of political or military coöperation almost impossible. However, it was still possible to get world-wide coöperation in science.

The International Geophysical Year (IGY) was an example of such coöperation. For eighteen months, from mid-1957 until the end of 1958, 8,000 scientists from sixty-four nations joined to make observations and exchange information about the earth. Men and women from almost every branch of physical science took part. The projects were financed by half a billion dollars pledged by the various nations, principally by the Soviet Union and the United States.

The vast range of IGY was shown by a few of the projects undertaken. Rockets and artificial satellites gathered information about the ionosphere and measured the radiation of the sun in the stratosphere. There were observations of the sediment at the bottom of oceans, of tides and currents and their effects on climate. Observations in the polar regions aimed to learn the effect of the Antarctic on the world's weather, and the melting rate of glaciers. Scientists tried to learn whether islands and continents were stationary or drifting.

Each participating nation had its own committee of scientists. There was also a combined committee to coördinate the work,

receive data, and report progress. All facts from the observation stations went to the coördinating committee, were assembled, and were given out to scientists throughout the world.

The International Geophysical Year was a fine example of world-wide coöperation. It was a sad thing that there was so little of this spirit in other fields of human life.

Preparations for scientific research during the International Geophysical Year, 1957–1958. Fifty-five nations coöperated in the most extensive study ever made of our world. As part of its share in the study, the United States made extensive explorations and observations in Antarctica. The photograph reproduced below shows United States Navy personnel setting up a ground control approach radar unit at a landing strip for aircraft.

The twilight of imperialism

The two-way revolution by which colonial people worked for a better way of life and self-government began long before World War II. The enormous dislocations caused by that global conflict speeded the process. In the postwar period colonies and empires disappeared rapidly. Imperialism seemed to be on the way out.

● *The Philippines*

The United States made an early and graceful retirement from one of its colonial ventures. In 1934 the United States Congress passed an act granting independence to the Philippines after ten years. When the independence date came World War II was being fought and the Japanese still held the islands. President Roosevelt announced that independence would be granted as soon as possible after the war.

The independent Philippine Republic was born July 4, 1946, with a constitution like that of the United States. The United States received 99-year leases on certain military bases, which it placed under the supervision of the Security Council of the United Nations. The United States appropriated large sums of money to help repair the war devastation in the islands and gave the Philippines favored tariff treatment for twenty years.

After granting independence to the Philippines the United States still kept a number of possessions. She still held Puerto Rico and the Virgin Islands in the Caribbean and the Canal Zone in Panama. Guam and Samoa in the Pacific remained in American hands. The Marshall and Caroline archipelagoes were granted to the United States by the United Nations as exclusive trusteeships. The Americans still held the island of Okinawa which they had taken from Japan.

The Territory of Alaska was admitted to the Union as a state in 1958. A year later Hawaii added the fiftieth star to the flag.

● *Burma and Ceylon*

Burma had been overrun by the Japanese during World War II. After the war Burma opposed the return of British rule. The British made no effort to regain their former colony, granting independence without a struggle. In 1946 Ceylon, which had always been separate from India, was granted a constitution as a self-governing dominion of the British Commonwealth of Nations.

The end of imperialism in India

The British refused to free India during the Second World War. In 1947 they kept a wartime promise and granted independence. The British tried to provide for a unified, federal India, but the Moslems insisted on a separate state. Therefore, the British granted independence to two states: the large, mostly Hindu, Dominion of India, and the five Moslem states of *P*unjab, *A*fghanistan, *K*ashmir, *S*ind, and Baluchi*stan*. These were united into the Republic of Pakistan. It takes its name from the first letter of the names of first four states (with an *i* added) and the final syllable of the last.

India and Pakistan were made dominions of the British Commonwealth, with the privilege of withdrawing if they desired. India later gave up dominion standing, and kept only economic ties with Great Britain. Both India and Pakistan were quickly admitted to the United Nations.

The independence and partition of India were accompanied by dreadful violence and bloodshed. Moslems fled from India to Pakistan; Hindus in Pakistan tried to escape to India. It was a vast, sad migration of terrified people. Religious riots and massacres took place in both countries. During this turmoil the great Hindu leader Gandhi was assassinated while trying to persuade the two groups to live together in peace. His assassin was not, as you might expect, a Moslem, but a member of a fanatic Hindu sect who thought Gandhi was being false to his religion in calling for peace with the Moslems. Eventually a truce was arranged, and the religious fighting stopped. Fighting later broke out in Kashmir over the question of whether this state should be part of Pakistan or of India. The United Nations stopped this civil war (see page 706).

● The Republic of Pakistan

Of the two states, Pakistan seemed to face the more difficult future. It was divided into two separate parts: the Indus River valley in the northwest, and the region at the mouth of the Ganges River, 1,000 miles to the northeast. East Pakistan had a population of 42 million, 54 per cent of the total, but the capital was located in West Pakistan, which largely controlled the government.

There were great cultural and economic differences between the two regions of Pakistan. They had different languages, and could not agree which should become the national tongue. English was still the official language. Both sections were almost entirely agricultural; they lacked the raw materials for many industries. The population was not too large for the area. By improving its agriculture the country might feed itself and produce a surplus for export. Both the United States and the United Nations helped with loans and technical assistance.

The Pakistani disagreed sharply over the kind of government they wanted. Some ardent Moslems wanted to be governed by the laws of the Koran. Others wanted a Western type of non-religious, democratic government. After two years of debate, an assembly wrote a constitution for the Islamic Republic of Pakistan. It decided to remain in the British Commonwealth. Pakistan does not pay allegiance to the British Crown, but accepts the British sovereign as a symbol of its "free association" with the other commonwealth nations.

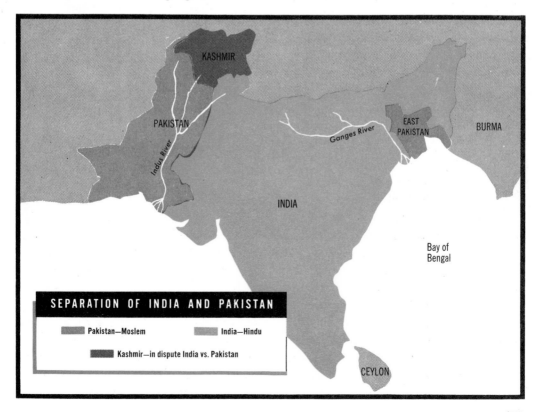

SEPARATION OF INDIA AND PAKISTAN

Pakistan—Moslem　　　India—Hindu

Kashmir—in dispute India vs. Pakistan

● *The new government of India*

India decided to become a parliamentary democracy. Jawaharlal Nehru was chosen as the first Prime Minister. The problem of languages made parliamentary government difficult. India had four major languages and many minor ones. It was necessary to conduct sessions of the parliament in English,

This dense crowd in modern India suggests one of the problems of that country: overpopulation.

the only language common to all representatives.

India had grave social problems. It was estimated that 85 per cent of the people were illiterate. A program of compulsory education was started, but it faced many difficulties. In elections, the parties used pictures of animals as symbols so that the illiterate voters could make their choice. The Hindu caste system was legally abolished, but it was thought that it would remain in practice for a long time.

The economic problems of India were even more serious. The population was much too large for the food supply. More than three hundred million people occupied an area about half the size of the United States. Agriculture was handicapped by primitive methods and tools and an uncertain water supply. Millions of people lived daily on the verge of starvation; many died of diseases caused by poor nutrition. The infant death rate was shockingly high. Average life expectancy was about thirty years, less than half that in the United States. It was estimated that at least one hundred million people had no regular jobs, because their labor was not needed. Miserable conditions like these made fertile soil for communist propaganda.

India had started a program of technical and industrial development in five-year plans. Some industries were owned and operated by the government. The great need was for capital. The United States made some loans; the Technical Assistance Program of the United Nations also helped.

Many people in the West believed that it was very important that India succeed in building up its industries and raising its standard of living. Two great nations, India and China, were competing for leadership in Asia. China was a communist dictatorship; India was democratic, and a mixture of capitalism and mild socialism. If India's efforts failed, it would probably not remain either democratic or mildly socialistic.

● *Foreign policy*

The two new nations differed in foreign policy as in so many other ways. Pakistan chose the Western side, becoming a member of SEATO and the Bagdad Pact. Nehru insisted that India remain neutral. He said the world must choose between peaceful coexistence or no existence at all. Eventually, he thought, the world must be governed by enforceable law. Until then, Nehru tried to act as a mediator between the opponents.

Thus two new nations, India and Pakistan, were born in violence and bloodshed. Each faced many difficult problems. Relations between them would probably be strained for a long time. Nevertheless, they represented the voice of a new Asia, a voice already listened to in the United Nations.

The changing order in the Far East

● *Malaya*

The movement away from empire and toward independence was world-wide. In southeast Asia the British had ruled the Malay states for over a century. It was an extremely important part of the British Empire for several reasons: its great wealth in tin, rubber, and iron, and its strategic location.

After the end of World War II the British met with many difficulties in Malaya. The population was made up of about three million Malays and two million Chinese. Most positions in government were held by Malays, but the more enterprising Chinese had most of the capital and controlled most of the business. There was considerable friction between the two groups. Among the Malays there was a strong movement for independence. Among the Chinese there were many communists and sympathizers. For more than ten years the British fought a jungle war against communist guerrillas.

Early in 1956 the British signed an agreement with the Malayans, promising full independence within the British Commonwealth. In mid-1957 the promised event took place. Another former colony became an independent nation, and was admitted to the United Nations.

Mao Tse-tung, head of the government of Communist China and a powerful figure in Far Eastern affairs.

• The rise of Communist China

In a relatively few years, the situation in the Far East went through radical changes. Through the period of World War I the Western powers, particularly Great Britain, dominated the Orient. In the 1930's Japan made a bid to become master of eastern Asia. This effort was one cause of World War II, in which the United States and her allies stopped Japan's imperialist moves. After this war, the Western powers could not restore the old order in the Far East. As just noted, the trend was toward independence for former colonial areas.

A threatening new power arose in the Orient—Communist China. The old spheres of influence, once held by Western powers in China, were obviously gone forever. Red China showed signs of planning to extend her influence in the Far East, as by helping the North Koreans and the Indo-Chinese Com-

munists. The Communist régime also threatened to attack Formosa (or Taiwan) and other islands held by the Nationalist Chinese government of Chiang Kai-shek (see pages 732–733). In the Formosa area, Communist China faced a United States policy of supporting Chiang's government. Whatever course events might take, the ruler of Red China—Mao Tse-tung—had emerged as a powerful figure in the world.

The twilight of imperialism in Africa and the Near East

• The Sudan

In Africa, too, empires were vanishing. Until early 1953, the Sudan was under the joint rule of Britain and Egypt. Each of these powers wanted to keep the territory for itself, but the Sudanese wanted to be independent. In 1953 the two countries agreed that a plebiscite should decide whether the Sudan would be independent, join Egypt, or have self-government within the British Commonwealth. In 1955 the Sudanese Parliament disregarded the plan for a plebiscite and unanimously adopted a resolution declaring the Sudan an independent republic. Neither Britain nor Egypt opposed the move; both recognized Sudanese independence.

• Libya

The Italian colony of Libya was taken by the Allies during World War II. When the Italian peace treaty was written, the Big Four were unable to agree what should be done with the territory. They turned the problem over to the United Nations General Assembly. The Assembly voted that Libya should become independent in 1952, and sent a commissioner with an advisory council to prepare the way. In 1952 the independent kingdom was established with an Arab king and a federal constitution.

Libya was a very poor country. Without the economic help given by Great Britain, the United States, and the United Nations its future would have been dim. It stood, though, as an example of independence gained under the auspices of the United Nations.

Kenya, Central Africa, and Ghana

In the East African colony of Kenya a native antiwhite society had terrorized the country since 1952. After many months of fighting the British finally managed to restore order, but the problem of independence remains unanswered.

Elsewhere Britain was more successful. In 1953 the Federation of Rhodesia and Nyasaland was formed. The newly created state was given a large degree of self-government. In March, 1957, the former colonies of the Gold Coast and British Togoland were merged as the independent state of Ghana. The new state became a member of the British Commonwealth of Nations and of the United Nations.

Congo

When, in 1960, Congo was granted independence by Belgium, and the Belgian authorities withdrew, chaos rapidly developed. Belgium had not trained leaders among the native people of the Congo. Rival political leaders could not control the country, and terror and destruction were widespread. The country lacked technicians of all types, including doctors. United Nations troops were finally sent into the Congo to attempt to restore law and order.

The new nations of Africa face numerous problems. Among these may be mentioned the serious conflict between the old tribal and the new nationalistic loyalties. Another, as in Congo, is the absence of trained leaders in government and in technical fields. A third is the deep-seated antagonism between native and the former colonial population. The presence in these countries of resources vital to the world creates other problems.

In Africa, the conflict between the free and the communist worlds is keenly felt, as the Soviets bid for the attention and eventual control of new nations and the free world tries to cope with the continent's tragic problems.

Cyprus

An exception to the British policy of graceful withdrawal was the island of Cyprus in the eastern Mediterranean. Great Britain had held Cyprus since 1878. Four-fifths of the inhabitants were Greek Christians; the rest, Turkish Moslems.

The people of Cyprus (Cypriots) had opposed British rule for a long time. After World War II, the Greek inhabitants, led by Archbishop Makarios, demanded enosis—union of Cyprus with Greece. Turkish inhabitants opposed this idea, fearing domination by the Greeks. The Turkish government also opposed the union, pointing out the nearness of Cyprus to Turkey and the fact that the island had been part of the Turkish Empire for three centuries before the British gained it.

The British also opposed the enosis movement. After they were forced out of their Suez base by Egypt, Cyprus became very important as a base of British operations in the eastern Mediterranean. For this reason Britain could offer Cyprus only home rule. After a long and often violent struggle, Cyprus won its independence, though the British retained their right to the maintenance of naval bases. Archbishop Makarios was named president of Cyprus, which became the fifteenth state in 1960 to win its independence; the other fourteen were in Africa.

The Union of South Africa

An extremely grim and dangerous situation existed in the Union of South Africa. Here the white population was divided between British settlers and Dutch Boers, many of whose ancestors had lived in the country

more than three hundred years. Negroes out-numbered the whites by five to one, and con-siderable numbers of Indians lived in South Africa. There was also a group of people of mixed white and Negro, mixed white and Indian, or mixed Indian and Negro ancestry. These people were called the Coloreds.

Fearing domination by the Negroes, the whites refused to grant them political or so-cial equality. The Boers, who controlled the government, enforced a policy called *apart-heid* (segregation). Natives were forced to live in separate communities—agricultural reservations in the country, or native slums near the cities. Their labor was needed on the land or in the mines, but they were allowed to do only the most menial kinds of work. They were not allowed to be educated, nor to have any political rights. At one time the Coloreds had limited political rights, but the Boer Nationalist Party abolished them.

The strength of nationalism in the Arab world is suggested by this mob of Egyptians parading in Cairo. They carried banners and shouted slogans denouncing the Western powers.

The Arab world

The Arab world extends from the Atlantic coast of Morocco all the way across North Africa through Egypt and the Middle East. It is a huge territory with some seventy mil-lion inhabitants. It has always been important in world history because of its strategic loca-tion. The middle eastern portion has become even more important in recent years because of the discovery of oil there. Nearly two-thirds of the world's known oil reserves are located in the Arabian Peninsula, around the Persian Gulf, and in the ancient land of Mesopotamia (now Iraq).

As you see on the map (page 758), the

Arab world is divided into a number of national states. Most of the people of the region are united by a number of strong ties. They are Moslems, following the religion of Islam. They speak the Arabic language. They have been increasingly in revolt against the old colonialism of the British and the French, and feel strongly that all Arab peoples should be united. This Arab nationalism, a drive for uniting or federating the Arab states, is a mighty force within the region. Another force that has united the people, especially in Egypt and the Near East, is their bitter hostility to the Jewish state of Israel.

There are also forces of division and disunity among the Arab states. Disputes over borders go back into history. Even more divisive are family feuds and dynastic rivalries. The Hashemite rulers of Jordan and Iraq claim descent from Mohammed. The Saud family, which rules Saudi Arabia, is a rival of the Hashemites. In recent years there has appeared a new claimant to the leadership of all the Arabs: Gamal Abdel Nasser, President of Egypt and the United Arab Republic (page 761). Because of its strategic location, its wealth of oil, its strong nationalistic drives, and its many tensions, the Arab world is a most important part of the modern world.

French North Africa

A strong independence movement has stirred the Moslems in the three French colonies of Morocco, Tunisia, and Algeria. After World War II French governments made gradual and grudging concessions in Morocco and in Tunisia, the most recently acquired of the three. In 1956 both Morocco and Tunisia became almost independent. They gained complete control of their domestic affairs, but France kept some powers over their foreign affairs and defense. Tunisia voted to become a republic; Morocco remained under the rule of a sultan.

In Algeria a solution was more difficult to find. The territory had been a French possession since 1830. It is four times as large as France, although only the land along the coast is good for farming. Some of the rest of the country contains important minerals. During the 1950's valuable oil deposits were found in the Sahara Desert, which makes up about four-fifths of the area of Algeria. The population of the country was about ten million. Four-fifths of them were Moslems—Arabs and Berbers. The Europeans, besides the French, included Spanish, Italians, and some Jews. Many of the French colonists (called *colons*) were descendants of French people who had settled in Algeria as early as the 1830's.

The French made many improvements in Algeria: roads and railroads built; land reclaimed; education, sanitation, and health improved; agriculture modernized. Most of the benefits of these measures went to the French colons. They owned the best one-third of the land under cultivation. The native population, which had increased rapidly

Trouble in Algeria. French police round up men suspected of belonging to the nationalist revolutionary movement. The sign on the garage advertises "Washing . . . Greasing."

because of advances in medicine and sanitation, could not support itself on its poorer land. There was a mass migration to the cities or to France. Less than half of these new city dwellers found employment, and then only at very low wages. There were few schools for Moslems; not more than one Arab child in five attended primary schools.

After 1871, Algeria was considered a department, or state, of France, with the right to send representatives to the National Assembly. Natives had no political rights till 1919, when suffrage was given to a few carefully selected Moslems.

●Revolt in Algeria

The nationalist revolutionary movement found many supporters in Algeria. Moderates demanded home rule; radicals wanted complete independence from France. Late in 1954 the radicals formed a National Army of Liberation and began fighting for independence. It was a guerrilla war, which the French seemed unable to stop, and which caused much destruction in the country. Fighting this elusive sort of war cost the French many lives and a staggering sum of money.

After two years of war the French were willing to yield a little. The French National Assembly passed the Algerian Statute of 1957. It allowed Algerians to elect an Algerian Assembly as well as representatives to the French parliament. However, the system of voting was such that one million Frenchmen elected more representatives than nine million Moslems. This was not good enough for the National Army leaders, and the war continued.

A peaceful settlement of the Algerian problem was very difficult to reach. The rebels demanded complete independence. The French colons would accept no plan which would give Moslems equal voting rights. They had the support of conservative parties in France, who were unwilling to see any

more of the French empire vanish. The problem was made more complicated by the nature of the French government.

The Fourth French Republic, like the Third, was a parliamentary democracy. It had one of the same weaknesses: the large number of political parties represented in the National Assembly made it difficult for a government to keep a majority and stay in power. The Fourth French Republic had twenty premiers in twelve years. A premier who tried to settle the Algerian war by a proposal which the rebels might accept was overthrown by the votes of the Algerian representatives and the French conservatives, usually supported by the communists, the largest single party in the assembly. Thus France was burdened with a costly war, which the army could not win, but which no government could settle by compromise.

●De Gaulle becomes premier

In May, 1958, General Charles de Gaulle accepted the assignment of forming a government, on condition that he be given the power to reform the constitution. The new constitution, giving greater executive power, was approved on September 28, 1958, and in December de Gaulle became the first president of the fifth republic of France.

As de Gaulle faced national problems, he requested more power. In February, 1960, the Assembly and Senate gave him additional power to handle the seemingly insoluble Algerian problem, where fighting between the French and the Algerians, who wanted independence, had been going on for several years. For the coming year de Gaulle was entrusted with the power to issue decrees with the force of law for the following purposes: 1) maintain law and order; 2) provide national security; 3) seek peace in and administer Algeria. When this power expires in February, 1961, Parliament will be able either to reject or to give approval to the decrees which de Gaulle issued.

Egypt and the Suez crisis

The modern history of Egypt has been stormy. Discontent with British rule became effective in 1922, when the British ended their protectorate and recognized Egypt as a sovereign state with some reservations about defense. In 1936 the two countries signed a treaty of alliance which allowed the British to keep troops in the Suez Canal zone for twenty years.

Egypt's royal government left much to be desired. There was unrest in the country over royal extravagance, corruption in government, and delays in promised reforms. The younger officers of the army were dissatisfied over the very poor Egyptian showing in the war with Israel (page 705). In 1952 a group of officers led an uprising which forced King Farouk to abdicate. A constitution declared Egypt an Islamic republic with a democratic form of government. In 1954, Colonel Gamal Abdel Nasser came to power as premier, and in 1956 he was overwhelmingly elected Egypt's first president. Although the forms of democratic government were observed, Egypt was really a military dictatorship under Nasser.

The new ruler took strong stands in foreign policy. After much agitation by Egypt, Great Britain agreed in 1954 to withdraw all troops from Suez within twenty months. On June 13, 1956, the last of the British troops left the canal zone. Thus ended seventy-four years of military occupation to defend this section of the British sea route to the Persian Gulf and the Far East.

President Nasser negotiated with the United States for arms, and with the United States, Great Britain, and the World Bank for loans to build the Aswan dam on the upper Nile. In mid-1956, finding the United States slow to furnish him arms, he announced an agreement with Czechoslovakia to buy Czech arms with Egyptian cotton. The Western powers were shocked at this evidence

President Nasser of Egypt announcing that he was taking over the Suez Canal.

of communist penetration into the Middle East. This alarm was increased a few months later by the announcement that the Soviet Union was furnishing arms to Syria.

● Nasser takes over the Suez Canal

In July, 1956, possibly in reproof to Nasser for the arms deal, the United States and Great Britain announced that they were withdrawing their offers of loans to build the Aswan dam. The World Bank then withdrew its offer. Nasser's reaction was immediate. On July 26, 1956, he announced that Egypt was taking over the Suez Canal Company. He said that the stockholders would be paid. The canal would be run by Egyptians, and the profits used to build the dam.

Egyptian nationalization of the Suez Canal raised many problems. The stockholders lost a very profitable venture for an indefinite promise of later payment. Half the total oil supply of Europe goes from the Middle Eastern fields through the canal. With Suez in possibly unfriendly hands, this vital supply was threatened. Some oil could be shipped in tankers around the Cape of Good Hope, but this added greatly to the distance and the expense. Equally serious, from the viewpoint of the West, was the prospect of increased Soviet influence in the sensitive Middle East. Each of these points was a cause of alarm and concern to the governments and people of Great Britain and France.

The Egyptian move was especially alarming to Israel. Her relations with the neighboring Arab states had been bad since the truce ending the Palestine war. There were constant border incidents—raids and reprisals—across all the Israeli borders. In violation of the Convention of 1888 regulating the Suez Canal, Egypt refused to allow Israeli ships or ships of other countries with cargoes bound for Israel to pass through. Egypt's shore batteries controlled the entrance to the Gulf of Aqaba, where Israel tried to set up a port on the Red Sea. From the Sinai Peninsula and the narrow Gaza Strip along the Mediterranean, guerrilla attacks were made across the border into Israel; the Israeli often replied in kind. Israel was especially alarmed over the Soviet-Egyptian arms deal. She feared that the arms would be used against her.

ARAB COUNTRIES

1. Suez Canal
2. Lebanon
3. Israel
4. Gaza Strip
5. Sinai Peninsula
6. Aqaba Gulf

● Israel, Britain, and France invade Egypt

When negotiations through the United Nations failed to improve the situation, Israel acted. On October 29, 1956, the Israeli army struck across the border. In a lightning campaign they seized the Gaza Strip, cleared the approaches to the Gulf of Aqaba, defeated the Egyptian army in the Sinai Peninsula, and reached a point only twenty-five miles from the canal. Britain and France then made demands on both belligerents: a cease-fire; withdrawal of troops ten miles from the canal; Egypt's consent to the temporary occupation of key points along the canal. Israel consented; Egypt refused. The British and French then began an air attack on Egypt and seized the Mediterranean end of the canal. The Egyptian army seemed powerless to resist either the British-French or the Israeli invasion. The Suez Canal was blocked by ship sinkings by both the British and the Egyptians.

● The UN orders a cease-fire

Another force now came into action. On the day after the Israeli invasion the Security Council of the United Nations met. Several resolutions calling for a cease-fire were supported by the United States and the Soviet Union, but were vetoed by Britain and France. An emergency session of the General Assembly then met. Here the United States again voted in support of a cease-fire, which the General Assembly adopted over British, French, and Israeli opposition. The General Assembly also adopted a resolution setting up a United Nations Emergency Force to patrol the cease-fire line.

In addition to the pressure of world opinion, as shown in the United Nations, the British faced much opposition at home. There were also threats of intervention by the Soviet Union and of boycotts by Arab and Moslem nations. All these pressures proved too great. In spite of their military successes, the British and French agreed to a cease-fire after only three days of fighting.

With amazing speed the Secretary-General of the United Nations, Dag Hammarskjöld, formed an international police force, made up largely of Norwegian, Danish, and Yugoslav troops. They were flown to the war area. Britain and France withdrew their troops fairly quickly, but Israel was more reluctant to give up Aqaba and the Gaza strip.

● Results of the Suez crisis

The results of the Egyptian war were many and varied. The canal was closed for three months while United Nations-directed salvage crews cleared the wreckage. In spite of his poor military showing, President Nasser kept power in Egypt and control over the canal. He became a hero to many of the Arab people, and more than ever the leader of Arab nationalism. Britain, France, and Israel suffered a major moral defeat. Western unity suffered a great blow when the United States opposed the actions of her British and French allies. The Soviet Union gained, both from the weakening of Western unity and in prestige as a supporter of Arab independence. The Suez crisis helped to divert attention from the Hungarian revolt which was going on at the same time.

One bright spot about the Suez affair was the formation of the United Nations Emergency Force. By its use the world organization succeeded in stopping a "little war" that might have grown into a major disaster. Many people felt that the U.N.E.F. should be made permanent and expanded into a truly international peace force.

Continuing cold war tensions in the Middle East

The Middle East, site of the ancient Fertile Crescent, is one of the important and sensitive regions of the modern world. The meeting place of three continents, the loca-

Soldiers of the Israeli army, which quickly defeated the Egyptians in the Sinai desert.

tion of two-thirds of the world's oil reserves, the center and focus of Arab nationalism, the region has become the scene of many conflicts, tensions, and stresses.

Many of the countries of the Middle East were formerly parts of the Turkish Empire. The treaties ending World War I broke up the empire and created from it the states of Syria, Lebanon, Palestine, Jordan, and Iraq, mandates of Britain and France. It was not long before they left their mandate status and became wholly independent.

The oil of Iran, Iraq, Saudi Arabia, and the small Persian Gulf States was taken from the ground and refined by British, Dutch, and American companies. The royalties which they paid were the main source of revenue of the governments of these Middle Eastern countries. Much of the oil was carried to the Mediterranean in pipelines which crossed Syria, Jordan, Israel, and Lebanon. If for no other reasons, these facts made the Middle East vitally important to Europe and the United States. Geographically, it is at the doorstep of the Soviet Union. Small wonder that it became involved in cold war conflicts.

The Bagdad Pact

The Western powers built up a chain of alliances to block further Soviet expansion. NATO included Greece and Turkey in the eastern Mediterranean. SEATO began with Pakistan in northern India. Between them lay a gap—the Middle East.

This gap was filled by the Middle East Treaty Organization (METO). In November, 1955, at Bagdad (in Iraq), Britain, Turkey, Iran, Iraq, and Pakistan signed the Bagdad Pact. They agreed to coördinate their defense policies, act together to prevent the overthrow of governments by subversion, and coöperate in economic activities. The United States approved of the organization, helped to form it, sent observers to all but the economic meetings, but did not join. Jordan was invited but did not join. You can see

Clearing the Suez Canal, January 1957. After the fighting stopped, a major salvage job began in order to reopen the canal. Here United Nations salvage craft are removing sections of a wrecked bridge.

how the Bagdad Pact linked the two existing systems of alliances.

The Soviet Union's reply to the Bagdad Pact was the arms agreements with Egypt and Syria. Soviet influence seemed to grow in the two countries. The Soviet government encouraged Nasser's efforts to extend his influence at the expense of leaders of pro-Western Arab states, especially King Faisal of Iraq and King Hussein of Jordan. The Russians strongly supported Nasser in the Suez crisis, and helped make possible his survival. From Cairo his radio made attacks on the "Western imperialists," and on his rival Arab leaders. Radio Cairo stirred up unrest against the Iraq and Jordan governments, and called for the Arab states to unite under Nasser's leadership and destroy Israel. Egypt and Syria coöperated closely in foreign affairs.

● The Eisenhower Doctrine

Alarmed by the spread of communist influence, and fearing the overthrow of friendly states, the United States tried to save the situation. At the request of President Eisenhower, Congress adopted a resolution which stated that the United States was prepared to use its armed forces to assist any Middle East nation which asked for such assistance against communist aggression. The president was authorized to give economic and military financial aid to Middle Eastern nations. President Eisenhower signed the document on March 9, 1957.

There was some doubt whether the Eisenhower Doctrine could lessen the dangers of the Middle East. The hazards seemed to come, not from outright communist aggression, but from revolts stirred up inside countries. Much of the stirring up was done by Nasser of Egypt, but there was a question whether this could be called communist aggression.

● The United Arab Republic

In February, 1958, came two steps toward the union which so many Arabs wanted. On February 1, President Nasser announced that Egypt and Syria were merging to form the United Arab Republic. Nasser became the president, and there was a combined legislative body which he appointed. The combined armies were put under the command of Egyptian officers. To all appearances Egypt had swallowed Syria.

The new state immediately appealed for all the forces of Arab nationalism to join it. The small state of Yemen, at the lower end of the Arabian peninsula, was the first taker. Yemen joined with reservations: it did not become a republic, but remained an absolute monarchy.

President Nasser announced that the foreign policy of the new state would be one of "positive neutrality" between East and West. He continued his strong attacks on "Western imperialism," and on the pro-Western Arab states. Outwardly he was friendly toward the communist bloc, but it was considered unlikely that he was under communist domination.

● The Arab Union

Two weeks after the formation of the United Arab Republic, Kings Hussein of Jordan and Faisal of Iraq announced the joining of their two countries into the Arab Union. Each country kept its own government, but the armies were put under a combined command. Faisal was to be head of the Arab Union, but if anything happened

The presidents of Syria and Egypt celebrate the merger of these nations as the United Arab Republic.

to him, Hussein of Jordan was authorized to speak for the two governments. In spite of the single military command, it was agreed that Iraq should remain as a member of the Bagdad Pact, but that Jordan need not join. The Arab Union remained generally pro-Western in foreign policy. It opposed communist influence and the attempts of Nasser to stir up revolt in its region.

Arab nationalism and the movement for Arab unity had produced two conflicting unions. Each claimed to be the true ruler. They differed in foreign policy and in government. Each had elements of strength and weakness. Two other Arab states, Lebanon and Saudi Arabia, remained apart from either union.

● Lebanon, Iraq, and Western intervention

In mid-1958 a series of events threw the Middle East and the whole world into a turmoil. Trouble began in the small republic of Lebanon. This state, on the site of the ancient land of Phoenicia, was also a trading nation. It was among the most prosperous of all the Arab states; its prosperity did not depend on oil alone. Its population was about evenly divided between Moslems and various sects of Christians. Its politics were very involved and complicated; its foreign policy was pro-Western.

In May, 1958, President Chamoun of Lebanon announced that he was proposing to the legislature, which he controlled, a revision in the constitution. The change would permit him to serve a second six-year term in the presidency. A revolt broke out in Lebanon, directed in part against the proposed second term, in part against the pro-Western policies of Chamoun. Radio Cairo broadcast encouragement to the rebels, who made statements praising Nasser. Chamoun complained to the United Nations Security Council that his government was in danger of being overthrown by "massive interference from out-

side." He said the rebels were receiving both arms and men across the Syrian border.

The Security Council instructed Secretary-General Hammarskjöld to take a group of observers to investigate the Lebanese complaint. In due time the Secretary-General reported that the revolt was an internal affair, with little aid coming from outside. The observers remained in Lebanon. The rebellion dragged on, with neither side apparently fighting very hard.

A new crisis came in mid-July, 1958. In an apparently well-planned army coup d'état in Iraq, King Faisal, his uncle, and the pro-Western premier were killed. The army took control of the government. There were official announcements that the new régime had withdrawn from the Arab Union with Jordan, and had signed a pact with the United Arab Republic to act together for defense and to coöperate in economic and cultural matters. It seemed highly doubtful that Iraq would remain in the Bagdad Pact organization.

On July 15, 1958, the United States announced that, at the request of the government of Lebanon, it had landed marines to protect American lives and property, and to prevent the overthrow of the Lebanese government by outside agents. The marines took control of the airport and the seaport of Beirut. Other groups of American troops landed in Turkey to be ready as reinforcements. Soon after the American landing the British sent troops to Jordan at the request of King Hussein.

The United Nations General Assembly was called into emergency session to consider the crisis in the Near East. In a speech to the Assembly, President Eisenhower outlined United States policy for the area. He stated that the United States would not oppose Arab nationalism and moves for unity unless such moves endangered world peace. He proposed a UN-sponsored agency to raise the standard of living in the Arab world. He asked that a United Nations "peace force" be created for the Middle East. The organizing of such a force would allow the United States and Great Britain to withdraw their troops. United States forces started to leave Lebanon during October.

Opinions on the American and British intervention and the Eisenhower proposal were numerous and varied. The situation was so troubled and complex that it was hard for anyone to be sure of the right path to peace and order. One prediction seemed easy: the Middle East would continue to be the scene of tensions and conflicts which might embroil all nations.

● Plans for peace continue

A proposed East-West summit conference to be held in Paris in May failed to materialize.

On May 1, 1960, a United States U-2 high-altitude jet reconnaissance plane was shot down while on a photographic reconnaissance mission across Soviet Russia. The pilot was captured.

The U-2 case had an immediate effect upon the planned East-West summit conference. Soviet Premier Khrushchev barred talks without prior United States apology for the U-2 incident. This President Eisenhower refused

to do. Neither Prime Minister Macmillan nor President de Gaulle was able to persuade Khrushchev to resume negotiations. Thus the planned conference was bound to fail.

● Trouble in Cuba

In Cuba the government of the dictator Batista was overthrown in 1959 by a popular young revolutionary, Fidel Castro, who promised the Cuban people many reforms. Castro, however, proved to be incompetent and dictatorial. Free elections were denied the people and Communists held positions of influence. Thus another trouble spot confronted the Free World, as communism sought a foothold only a few miles off the coast of the United States.

● The Act of Bogotá

In 1960, representatives of twenty Latin American states met at Bogotá, Colombia, where they made bold plans for raising the standard of living and bringing social justice to all the people of Latin America. The plan called for outside help, and for labor and sacrifice on the part of the Latin American people themselves, to bring about reforms through democratic processes.

The Prospect Before Us

And so you have reached the end of the book, but not the end of the story. History is a tale that never ends. Each day's headlines bring reports of new developments. If they were really new—with no connection to anything that existed before—the world would be impossible to understand. But the new grows out of and is built upon the old. Knowing what has gone before, you are better able to understand what happens next.

Ours is a dangerous world, but endlessly

interesting, and a great challenge. If the world seems full of signs of danger, it is also full of signs of progress. If there is fear of possible war, there is also hope of victory over disease, ignorance, and hunger.

Will peace come through larger military forces, more deadly weapons, and stronger alliances? Or will it come through international coöperation? For the present, both methods are necessary. For which course will you choose to work for the long future?

Review of Chapter 56

People, places, and things

Identify: Jawaharlal Nehru, Gamal Abdel Nasser, Ho Chi Minh, Pierre Mendes-France, Imre Nagy, Nikita Khrushchev, Charles de Gaulle, Dag Hammarskjöld, Sputnik, Explorer, Pioneer, U.S.S. *Nautilus.*

Locate: the Philippine Republic, India, Pakistan, Kashmir, Burma, Ceylon, the Sudan, Libya, Tunis, Morocco, Algeria, Suez, Israel, the Gaza Strip, Union of South Africa, Southwest Africa, Ghana, North Korea, South Korea, Seoul, Yalu River, Indo-China, Laos, Cambodia, Viet Nam, Thailand, Formosa, Lebanon, the members of the United Arab Republic.

Events in review

1. When the North Korean army attacked South Korea, what action did the United States take? the United Nations? On what terms was an armistice arranged?

2. What part did the Communist Chinese take in the war in Indo-China? What effect did the armistice in Korea have on this war?

3. Was the Geneva Conference on Indo-China a victory for communism or the Free World? Did the Geneva "Summit" Conference accomplish any of its four aims?

4. Why was China not represented at the conference that signed the peace treaty with Japan?

5. Did the Russians collect reparations from Japan? Did the United States?

6. Name one communist satellite which revolted successfully against the communist leaders in Moscow and one which revolted unsuccessfully. What three things does this unrest indicate about the communist bloc?

7. What event on October 4, 1957 blasted the world into the Space Age? Tell one fact about the political meaning of this event and one fact about its meaning to science.

8. What was the purpose of SEATO? of the Bagdad Pact?

9. What was the world significance of the Bandung Conference? Which nations were represented at this gathering?

10. What was the IGY? Mention three of its projects. How many scientists from how many nations participated?

11. When did the United States promise independence to the Philippines? When was the Philippine Republic established?

12. How did India gain her independence? Why was India divided into two states?

13. What problems did Pakistan face after becoming independent?

14. How did events in Algeria contribute to the end of the Fourth French Republic?

15. What changes took place in the control of the Suez Canal between 1954 and 1957?

16. What part did the United Nations take in the dispute over the Suez Canal?

17. Briefly describe the events that led to Western intervention in Lebanon and Jordan.

Problems and projects

1. Compare the policies of the United States, Great Britain, and France about granting independence to former colonies. What have been the results of these policies?

2. Compare the NATO and SEATO pacts. What were the aims of the two agreements? How does the strength of the nations in NATO and SEATO compare with the strength of possible opponents?

3. To what extent can the Geneva Conference on the war in Indo-China be compared with the Munich "deal" of 1938?

4. Make a report on "the New World" of twentieth-century science. Your topic might be the results of the International Geophysical Year, discoveries in medicine, peaceful uses of atomic power, or plans for space travel.

5. On the basis of outside reading, make a report to the class on the Philippine Republic. Compare this nation with its neighbors. Can you explain why it has been said that "the Philippines represent a window for democracy in the Far East"?

6. Make a report on what you consider the most dangerous situation in Africa, the Near East, or the Far East today—that is, the one most likely to lead to international trouble and possibly to war.

Review of
the Global War and After

1. There is an old saying, "to the victor belong the spoils." In ancient times (the wars of the Assyrians, of Alexander the Great, or of the Romans, for example) did the victors gain enough loot to make a profit? What was the situation with the Napoleonic Wars? World War I? In World War II, did the Germans and Japanese collect spoils when they were winning? What about the Russians? the United States and her allies? What does the case of Japan show about the "spoils for the victor" in a modern war?

2. The United Nations was created in an effort to make the world more peaceful and orderly. Compare this organization with its predecessor—the League of Nations. To what extent was the plan for the UN an improvement on the plan of the League? What serious problems still hamper the UN? What might be done to make the UN more effective?

3. How many new, independent nations have been added to our maps since 1945? How many of these new states are in Africa? How many in Asia? What does the rise of these young countries show about the force of nationalism in the world?

4. In 1945 the world was divided into two groups: The Allies versus the fascist Axis powers. After the war a different division of the world developed: the free nations versus the communist bloc. Which of the wartime totalitarian powers have now joined the "free world"?

   Name some of the main events that increased the gulf between the free world and the communist world. When and where did the cold war have its hot periods?

5. Discuss the problem of the coexistence of the free and communist worlds. Have any steps been taken toward disarmament, or toward increasing trade between the worlds? Can such steps be taken in spite of the fundamental differences between the two worlds in beliefs about individual rights and about the nature of government?

6. The Introduction to this book is called "History and You." Explain why "You" (the individual citizen) are more involved in the making of history now than was ever the case in the past. What can the citizen of a democratic nation do to help solve the problems facing the world of man?

7. Re-read the introductions to and reviews of Parts One to Ten of this book. As you think back over the story of men and nations, what lessons do you find from history to guide us today? How many times in the past has the world faced—*and survived*—such menaces as intolerance toward religious and personal freedom or "total war"?

8. Make charts or lists in which you compare the world of today with the world of one or more past eras (the height of the Roman Empire, the Renaissance, the mid-eighteenth century, the mid-nineteenth century, for example). In making the chart or list, you might use as topic headings the great themes of history listed in the Introduction to this book. In what ways has the world made progress under each heading?

9. It has been said that our world continually grows smaller and that the parts grow more and more interdependent. Events in any country are likely to concern all countries. Discuss these statements. As background for the discussion, review World War II and the years since that war. Do any nations now keep isolated from world affairs?

10. The launchings of the Sputniks, the Explorers, and the Pioneer have been compared in importance with the great voyages of discovery of earlier days. Review such feats of exploration as Magellan's voyage and Columbus' discovery of America. Do these seem more or less important to you than man's first explorations of space?

Books about
the Global War and After

Allen, Frederick L. *Big Change* (Harper, 1952). The changes in American life and institutions in the first half of the twentieth century.

*Arne, Sigrid. *United Nations Primer* (Rinehart, 1948). Wartime conferences at Yalta, Teheran, and Potsdam. The peace aim of the Atlantic Charter. A fine foundation for the study of the United Nations organization.

Beckel, Graham. *Workshops for the World* (Abelard-Schuman, 1954). Describes clearly the work of the eleven specialized agencies of the United Nations.

Benns, F. Lee. *Europe Since 1914: in Its World Setting* (Appleton-Century-Crofts, 1954).

Bowles, Chester. *Ambassador's Report* (Harper, 1954). Experiences of the Bowles family in India. Interesting reading.

Bowles, Cynthia. *At Home in India* (Harcourt, 1956). Excellent report on the young people of India written by the daughter of Ambassador Bowles.

Castro, Josue de. *Geography of Hunger* (Little, Brown, 1952). The story of hunger in the underdeveloped areas of Asia, Africa, and Europe, and the need for a world food program.

Commager, Henry S. *Pocket History of the Second World War* (Pocket Books). A brief but adequate account of the war.

Crain, Maurice. *Rulers of the World* (Crowell, 1942). Short biographical sketches of the leaders of democratic and dictatorial nations.

De Jong, Dola. *Return to the Level Land* (Scribner's, 1947). How a Dutch family struggled to overcome the destruction of World War II.

Dewey, Thomas E. *Journey to the Far Pacific* (Doubleday, 1952). A report on conditions in Asia after World War II.

Eisenhower, Dwight D. *Crusade in Europe* (Doubleday, 1952). General Eisenhower's own account of World War II in Europe.

Epstein, Beryl (Williams). *Rocket Pioneers, on the Road to Space* (Messner, 1955). Survey of the development of rocketry during the last 150 years.

Espy, Willard R. *Bold New Program* (Harper, 1950). A discussion of the part to be played by the United States in helping to build up the underdeveloped areas.

Fenichell, Stephen Sydney and Phillip Andrews. *United Nations, Blueprint for Peace* (Winston, 1954). The whole story of the United Nations since its founding in 1945.

Fischer, John. *Why They Behave Like Russians* (Harper, 1947). How economic, social, and historical conditions have influenced Russian national characteristics.

Foreign Policy Association, Headline Books. *Africa; New Crises in the Making; Changing Far East; East and West of Suez; European Jigsaw: Atlas of Boundary Problems; Look At Africa; Look At Latin America; Restless India; Shadow Over Asia.* Each pamphlet is scholarly and is clearly and simply written, presenting an account of the problem with which it deals. They are inexpensive. The Foreign Policy Association will send a complete list of its Headline Books.

*Gatti, Ellen, and Attilio. *Here Is Africa* (Scribner's, 1943). A fine history of Africa in its many aspects, illustrated with excellent photographs.

Gunther, John. *Behind the Curtain* (Harper, 1949). Personalities and problems on both sides of the "curtain."

Hailey, Foster B. *Half of One World* (Macmillan, 1950). Mao Tse-tung, Ho Chi Minh, and Soekarno are among the Asian leaders discussed.

Hersey, John. *Hiroshima* (Knopf, 1946). How the atomic blast affected six survivors.

———. *Into the Valley: a Skirmish of the Marines* (Knopf, 1943). Fighting on Guadalcanal, reported sensitively.

Higgins, Marguerite. *War in Korea* (Doubleday, 1951). The Korean War as reported by a woman reporter on the scene.

*Books marked with a star (*) are easy reading.

*Hoffman, Gail. *Land and People of Israel* (Lippincott, 1955). Palestine from Old Testament days to the present.

Hoffman, Paul G. *Peace Can Be Won* (Doubleday, 1951). The operation of the Marshall Plan in Europe, by one of its directors.

Johnsen, Julia E. (Comp.) *Dilemma of Postwar Germany* (Wilson, 1948).

——. *Federal World Government* (Wilson, 1948).

——. *Palestine: Jewish Homeland?* (Wilson, 1946).

Kirk, Lydia. *Postmarked Moscow.* (Scribner's, 1952). The wife of an American ambassador to the U.S.S.R. (1949–1952) tells of conditions in letters to her children.

Kugelmass, Joseph Alvin. *Ralph J. Bunche, Fighter for Peace* (Messner, 1952). Readable biography of the distinguished United Nations figure.

Lauterbach, Richard E. *Danger from the East* (Harper, 1947). The problems of Asia threaten the peace of the world.

Lie, Trygve, and others. *Peace on Earth* (Hermitage House, 1949). The first Secretary-General of the United Nations writes on the problem of preserving peace through international coöperation.

The editors of *Life, Life's Picture History of Western Man*. An excellent summary of the history of the Western World, with splendid illustrations.

McClellan, Grant Samuel. (ed.) *The Middle East in the Cold War* (H. W. Wilson, 1956). The story of the Middle East up to 1956.

Michener, James A. *Voice of Asia* (Random House, 1951). Interviews with Asians of all classes. The author feels that all Westerners must know and understand Asia's problems.

*Modak, Manorama. *Land and the People of India*, rev. ed. (Lippincott, 1952). A good chapter on Gandhi and Nehru.

Moraes, F. R. *Jawaharlal Nehru* (Macmillan, 1956). A political biography of India's nationalist leader.

*Roosevelt, Eleanor, and Ferris, Helen. *Partners —the United Nations and Youth* (Doubleday, 1950). How the specialized agencies of the United Nations help the young people in many lands.

*Rosenthal, A. M. *United Nations; Its Record and Prospects* (Manhattan, 1953). A pamphlet which gives a very good account of the success and difficulties of the organization.

Shirer, William L. *Midcentury Journey* (Farrar and Rinehart, 1951). Conditions in Europe in 1950 as seen by an experienced foreign correspondent.

Streit, Clarence. *Union Now* (Harper, 1949). A proposal for a federal union of the democracies to bring peace through strength.

Todd, Lewis P. *Marshall Plan* (Economic Coöperation Administration, Washington, D.C.). A free pamphlet telling about the working of the program.

United Nations. *Handbook of the United Nations* (Columbia University Press, 1949). Information of all sorts about the UN.

White, Theodore H. *Fire in the Ashes: Europe in Mid-Century* (Sloane, 1953). Europe from the end of World War II to 1953. An excellent presentation of events, people, and basic problems. For better readers.

Stories about World War II and after

Bates, H. E. *Fair Stood the Wind for France* (Little, Brown, 1944). A study of the French underground and English spies.

Bottome, Phyllis. *London Pride* (Little, Brown, 1941). A novel of courage during the London blitz, 1939–1941.

*Forester, C. S. *The Ship* (Little, Brown, 1943). What happens on a warship during a naval engagement. Highly recommended.

Hersey, John. *A Bell for Adano* (Knopf, 1944). A famous short novel of how an American officer helped an Italian village.

*Huggins, Alice M. *Red Chair Waits* (Westminster Press, 1958). The conflict of old and new ways in modern China.

Levin, Meyer. *My Father's House* (Viking, 1947). A young Jewish boy escapes the Nazis in Poland and tries to find his father in Palestine.

Michener, James. *Tales of the South Pacific* (Macmillan, 1947). Both the darker and the lighter sides of the war in the Pacific.

Orwell, George. *Animal Farm* (Harcourt, Brace, 1954). The animals stage a communist revolution. A bitter satire for better readers.

*Rankin, L. S. *Daughter of the Mountains* (Viking, 1948). An exciting story of a Tibetan girl who made her way to the coast of India in search of her stolen dog.

Shute, Nevil. *Most Secret* (Morrow, 1945). The British Intelligence Service during the war.

Index

Key to Pronunciation of Vowels				
china,	fāte,	băd,	cärd,	fair
fern	mĕt	thēse		
if	nīce			
more	hŏt	nō	mōōn	cŏŏk	out
cut	tūne			

Haydn [hī'd'n], Franz Joseph, 466
Hebrews, 42, 43, 45, 49–54. *See also* Jews
Heidelberg man, 13
Heine [hī'nĕ], Heinrich, 464
Hejira [hē·jī'ra], 153
Hellenistic Age and culture, 90–95, 111, 125, 150
Helots [hĕl'ŏtz], 69, 75
Henry II, king of England, 175, 177–178
Henry VII, king of England, 207
Henry VIII, king of England, 245–246, 247, 298
Henry IV, king of France, 268, 306
Henry III, emperor of Germany, 194
Henry IV, emperor of Germany, 194
Henry the Navigator, 199, 233
Hera [hē'ra], 66, 111
Heresy, 191, 206, 213–214, 242–243, 265, 467, 622
Hermes [her'mēz], 66, 111
Herodotus [hē·rŏd'ō·tus], 85–86; quoted, 20, 44, 73
Herzegovina [her'tsĕ·gō·vē'na], 437, 551, 552, 575
Hieroglyphics [hī'ĕr·ō·glif'iks], 23–24, 25, 32, 50, 64
Himalaya [hi·mä'la·ya] Mountains, 481, 711
Hinduism, 157, 256, 482, 483, 486, 489, 490, 585, 689, 748–749
Hippocrates [hi·pŏk'ra·tēz], 84, 93, 95, 156
Hirohito [hē'rō·hē'tō], 739
Hiroshima [hē'rō·shē'ma], 695–696
History: themes in, 3–5; importance of, 3–6; how to study, 4–6
Hitler, Adolf, 405, 592–593, 608, 618–622, 628–629, 635–636, 638, 645–653, 664, 665, 672–674, 692
Hittites, 18, 41, 44
Ho Chi Minh [hō chē' mēn], 736
Hohenzollern [hō'ĕn·tsŏl'ern] family, 250, 273–274, 281–284, 415, 427
Holland, 244, 250, 251, 256–257, 266, 273, 292, 303, 312, 317, 319, 331, 340–341, 345, 364, 479, 529, 556, 559, 617, 626, 661, 662. *See also* Netherlands
Holy Alliance, 351–352, 359, 539
Holy Land, in Crusades, 147, 157, 175, 181–185
Holy Roman Empire, 163–165 (map), 179–181, 194, 207, 208, 249, 250, 263–265, 269, 280, 282, 292, 340, 418
Homer, 65, 81, 125
Hong Kong, 508, 517, 522, 671–672
Horace, 125, 142

House of Commons, 179, 205, 296, 301–306, 307–308, 311, 315, 364–367, 405–407, 409–411, 662
House of Lords, 179, 303, 304, 306–307, 310, 364–366, 405, 407, 408, 409
Huguenots [hū'ge·nŏts], 244, 268–269, 273
Humanists, 228–231
Humanitarians, 390–391, 393
"Hundred Days," 334, 345
Hundred Years' War, 204–206
Hungarians, 165–166, 346, 418, 435
Hungary, 166, 208, 231, 249, 264, 280, 283, 371, 422, 429, 564, 566, 573, 575, 580, 634, 637, 649, 650, 664, 672, 675, 686, 691, 708, 716, 719, 740–743, 759
Huns, 135–137, 486
Huss, John, 213–214, 243
Hussein [hoŏ·sān'], king of Jordan, 760–762
Hyksos [hik'sŏs], 28

Iberian [i·bēr'i·ăn] Peninsula, 62, 102, 199, 207–208, 341–342
Ikhnaton [ik·nä't'n], 29, 41, 51
Il Duce [ēl doō'chä], 615, 687
Illiteracy, 451–452, 514, 530, 576, 617, 712, 750
Immortality, belief in, 13, 34–35, 40–41, 45, 66, 83, 132, 195, 228, 514
Immunities, granting of, 164–165, 167
Imperialism, 253–284; as cause of World War I, 475, 547–548; in India, 478–480, 487–490, 748–751; in Africa, 491–505, 752–756; in China, 516–524; difference between that in China and in other regions, 522; Japanese, 533–534, 752; return to, after World War I, 570; revolts against, 612; old style replaced by communism, 657, 743. *See also* Colonies and colonization, Empires
Incas, 259, 353, 361
Independents, 300, 303
India, 91, 375, 475, 478–490, 675, 679, 752; Alexander's invasion, 89; trade with, 121, 199, 253–258; Moslem conquest, 154; Mongol conquest, 209; search for route to, 233, 491; British colony, 465, 480–481, 487–490, 551, 556; missionaries in, 479; caste system, 482–483, 751; religious division, 483–487, 490; French expelled, 487; map in 1805, 488; in World War I,

556, 584; striving for self-government, 564, 585, 612, 629, 689; in World War II, 687, 689; independence, 706, 748–751; trouble over Kashmir, 706; technical assistance program, 711, 751; as neutral in cold war, 744–745, 751; separation from Pakistan, 748–749 (map), 750; social problems, 750–751
Indians, American, 233, 310, 311, 378; in Central and South America, 258–259, 353–355, 361
Indo-China, 413, 480, 485, 612, 671–672, 679, 688, 744, 745; war in, 736 (map)–737, 738, 744
Indonesia, 745, 746; UN action in, 703–704
Indulgences, 189, 211, 230, 241–242, 248
Indus [in'dus] River and Valley, 16–17 (map), 44, 89, 481, 482, 749
Industrial Revolution, 289, 374–396, 453–463, 538–539
Industry: in France, 268, 271; shipbuilding 278, 380, 530; in Latin America, 361; textile, 375–376, 387, 390–391, 483–484, 530; government and, 389, 469–470; gas and oil, 378, 458, 460, 462; rubber, 378, 458; woolen, 384; plastics, 396, 458; in Germany, 424–425, 621, 719; in Russia, 438–439, 440, 601, 605–608; electric, 445, 456–458; chemical, 458; auto, 458–459; in Japan, 530, 643; in U.S., 538; in Great Britain, 630; in World War II, 689–690
Inflation: in 17th century England, 299–300; after World War I, 581–582, 614, 618, 627, 631
Innocent III, 187–188, 190, 194, 211
Inquisition [in'kwi·zish'un], 191, 208, 239, 256, 265, 266, 342
Intendants, 270
Interdict, 187
International Atomic Energy Agency, 710–711, 731
International Court of Justice, 699, 702
International geophysical year (IGY), 746–747
International Postal Union, 381, 455
Inventions, 13, 15, 16, 18, 32, 39, 41, 92–93, 142, 156, 183–184, 216–217, 231, 238–239, 289, 294, 374, 376, 377, 378–379, 382, 443, 445, 453, 455, 456–457, 556, 666–667
Investiture [in·ves'ti·tūr], conflict over, 189–190, 194
Iran [ē·rän'], 44, 612, 676, 681, 685,

Voting rights: in England, 365–367, 372, 390, 405–409, 631; in France, 370; in United States, 408; for women, 409, 471; in Germany, 617: in Algeria, 756

Wagner [văg′ner], Richard, 214, 466
Wales, 158, 159, 405
War, problem of, 4, 118, 131, 138, 220, 579–583, 589, 696–697, 714–723
War of 1812, 339, 385
War Between the States (Civil War), 413, 536–538
War of the Roses, 206–207
War of the Spanish Succession, 273–274, 280, 282, 314
War lords, Chinese, 511–512, 585–586, 643
Warsaw, 660, 691; Pact, 740–742, 743
Warsaw, Grand Duchy of, 340, 342, 348, 417
Warships: ancient, 75; 18th century, 501, 521, 529, 540; 20th century, 531; Germany prohibited from building, 570, 572
Washington, George, 288, 289, 317, 319, 357
Washington Disarmament Conference, 632
Waterloo, battle of, 345, 366, 418
Watt, James, 377; steam engine, 374
Weaving, 375–376
Weimar [vī′mär] Republic, 580, 617–618
Wellington, Duke of, 341, 345
West Germany (Federal Republic), 721–722, 724, 727, 730–731
West Indies, 233, 257, 258, 312, 314, 350, 354, 378, 539–541, 668
Westphalia, 341, 350, 417, 418
Westphalia, Treaty of, 250 (map), 252, 266, 270, 280, 282
Whigs, 304–305, 307, 319, 366–367, 411

"White Man's Burden," 479
White Russians, 603–604
Whitney, Eli, 376, 382, 536
William I, king of England (William the Conqueror), 177
William III of Orange, king of England, 305–307
William IV, king of England, 365
William II, emperor of Germany, 427–428, 494, 501, 549, 552, 562, 617
William I of Prussia, emperor of Germany, 415, 420, 423, 427
William, prince of Orange, 266
Wilson, Woodrow, 558, 560–561, 564, 565, 566, 567, 570–571, 573, 577
Women: in ancient Egypt, 28, 30; in Sumeria and Babylonia, 39, 40; in Sparta, 70; in Athens, 79–80; in Rome, 105; in feudal times, 169, 171; Peter the Great's reforms, 277; employment in factories, 388, 391; suffrage, 407, 409, 471, 617, 631; improved status, 470–471; in China, 511; in Japan, 526; in Turkey, 576; in Russia, 599; employment of, and I.L.O., 634
World Court, 553, 567, 702
World War I, 271, 279, 364, 405, 422, 423, 437, 453, 475, 547–563, 584; causes, 547–553; on the sea, 549, 557, 559; fronts, 555 (map); secret treaties, 555, 560, 561, 567; blockades, 556–559; purchase of bonds, 558–559, 560; destruction, 561, 565, 579, 588; peace treaties, 565–567, 570–573, 575–578, 759; map of world after, 568–569; Treaty of Versailles, 571–573, 575–576; reparations, 572, 582–583; aftermath, 579–583; costs, 579–580, 584, 588–589; international debts, 582–583, 669; promises to Jews and Arabs, 705
World War II, 192, 342, 458, 527, 532, 593, 636, 639, 752; events leading up to, 642–653; campaigns in Europe, 660–666, 672–674, 675–677, 685–686, 690–693; United

States as a neutral, 667–670; campaigns in Pacific, 671–672, 677–678 (map), 679, 687–689, 693–696; campaign in North Africa and Near East, 674 (map)–675, 684–685; entry of United States, 677–679; Allies' objectives, 681; map of 1942–1945 campaigns, 682–683; industrial production for, 689–690; costs, 696–697; peace treaties, 699, 716–721; problems left, 714–723
Writing, 19, 23–25, 49–50, 64, 514–515, 526
Württemberg [vür′těm·berg], 422
Wycliffe [wī′klif], John, 213, 214, 245

Xerxes [zerk′sēs], King, 44, 46, 74
X rays, discovery of, 445

Yalta Conference, 681, 694, 695, 698, 716
Yalu [yä′loo′] River, 735
Yangtze [yăng′tzē′] River and Valley, 508, 517, 519, 586, 645
Yellow River and Valley, 16–17 (map), 508, 509, 587
Yemen [yěm′ěn], 761
Yucatan [yoo′ka·tăn′], 258
Yugoslavia, 280, 570, 575, 628, 673–674, 676, 691, 706, 723, 715–717, 719, 722, 741

Zaibatsu [zi·bät′soo], 533, 738
Zambesi [zăm·bē′zi] River, 491
Zanzibar [zăn′zi·bär], 497–498
Zeus [zoos], 66, 71, 83, 111
Zionist [zi′un·ist] movement, 704–705
Zollverein [tsŏl′fěr·īn′], 419
Zoroaster [zō′rō·ăs′ter], 45
Zwingli [tsving′lē], Ulrich, 244

Acknowledgments

The publisher is indebted to the following for illustrations reproduced in the text:

Alinari, page: 91
Aluminum Company of America, page: 392
American Museum of Natural History, pages: 15, 16, 24, 238, 354
Arabian American Oil Company, page: 152
Art Institute of Chicago, page: 527
Austrian Information Service, New York, page: 421

Bettmann Archive, pages: 137, 195, 230, 248, 294, 311, 351, 358, 446, 471, 518
Black Star (Kreider from Black Star), page: 577
British Information Services, pages: 124, 246, 247, 300, 301, 302, 306, 308, 339, 372, 375, 388, 406, 410, 492, 662, 666, 667, 673, 675
Brown Brothers, pages: 43, 139, 205, 409, 598, 616, 619

Caisse Nationale des Monuments Historiques, page: 83
California Historical Society, page: 260
Capital Press Service, Ottawa, Canada, page: 630
Cities Service Company, page: 460

Eastfoto, pages: 508, 509, 513, 517
European, pages: 620, 625, 649

Fine Arts Department, International Business Machines, Inc., page: 237 (both)
FLO (Frances L. Orkin), page: 321
Ford Motor Company, pages: 459, 690

Foto-Enit-Roma, pages: 122, 192
Fotokhronika Tass, page: 279
Freer Gallery of Art, pages: 486, 514, 515
French Cultural Services, pages: 324, 331
French Embassy, Press and Information Division, pages: 176, 177, 269
French Government Tourist Office, pages: 203, 217, 218, 296, 337

Ewing Galloway, pages: 154, 219, 431, 585
Philip Gendreau, pages: 360, 510
Giraudon, page: 293
Government of India Information Services (Washington, D.C.), pages: 482, 484
Greek Government Tourist Bureau, page: 469 (top)

Photo-Hachette, pages: 198, 370
Haiti Government Tourist Bureau, page: 357
Herblock and The Washington Post (copyright by The Washington Post Co.), page: 741
Historischer Bilderdienst Berlin-Wilmersdorf, page: 281
Historisches Bildarchiv Handke, Berneck, Germany, pages: 49, 69, 80 (both), 92, 108, 126, 129, 201, 244, 283, 422, 424, 426, 497, 503, 554, 581 (both)
Hudson and Delaware Railroad Corporation, page: 379
Hulton Picture Library, page: 233

International Coöperation Administration, page: 725
International News Photos, pages: 687, 722
Israeli Armed Forces, page: 759
Italian State Tourist Office, New York, pages: 104, 212, 430

Japan Tourist Association, pages: 525, 532
S. C. Johnson & Son, Inc., page: 467

Reproduced from the Collections of the Library of Congress, pages: 304, 314, 315, 316, 326, 338, 394, 412, 471 (top), 536, 559, 633, 635, 668
Lutheran Church Productions, Inc., page: 242

The Manchester Guardian and The Register and Tribune Syndicate, Des Moines, Iowa (Low, world copyright), pages: 650, 710
Methodist Missions, page: 479
Metropolitan Museum of Art, pages: 18 (top), 42, 68, 72, 95, 156, 169
Ministry of Information (India), Publications Division, page: 750
Museum of Fine Arts, Boston, page: 131

National Archives, pages: 520, 537, 540, 541, 556, 560, 561, 565, 602, 603
National Film Board of Canada, page: 597
National Gallery of Art, Washington, D.C., page: 408
National Maritime Museum (Greenwich, England), pages: 184, 265, 481, 501, 549
National Park Service (Abbie Rowe), page: 588
New York Historical Society, pages: 380, 384
New York Public Library, pages: 85, 110, 160, 215, 239, 253, 258, 259, 267, 271, 272, 280, 312, 333, 342, 353, 365, 371, 387, 391, 414, 741
New York Public Library Prints Division, pages: 328, 366
The New York Times, pages: 553, 562, 582, 715. Copyright by The New York Times and reproduced with permission
Newsweek—Van Dyke, page: 445

Oriental Institute of The University of Chicago, pages: 38, 40

Panama Canal Official Photo, page: 542
Paul Thompson Photo, page: 531
Percival Goodman, page: 468 (bottom)
Pierpont Morgan Library, pages: 181, 216
Polychemicals Sales Service Laboratory, page: 396
Press Association, Inc., page: 718
Press Information Bureau, New Delhi, India, page: 489
Punch, pages: 427, 470, 740. Reproduced by permission of *Punch*.

Quick, Mrs. Elsie A., from *Raemaeker's Cartoons*, Doubleday, Page and Co., page: 579

Rapho Guillumette Pictures (Copyright by A. L. Goldman), pages: 53, 133

Santa Fe Railway, page: 538
The Science Museum, London, pages: 75; 378 (top) British Crown Copyright.
Sedge Le Blang Photo, page: 465
SIB Photo Service, Moscow, page: 343
Smithsonian Institution, Freer Gallery of Art, pages: 93, 121, 159, 376, 378 (bottom), 382, 451 (top), 457, 530
Sovfoto, pages: 278, 439, 606, 608, 609, 685
Standard Oil Company, New Jersey, pages: 383, 468 (top), 469 (bottom), 543

Tennessee Valley Authority, page: 457 (bottom)
Trans World Airlines, Inc., pages: 18 (bottom), 31, 32, 78, 113, 140, 155, 323, 487
Triangle Photo Service, pages: 361, 502, 584, 601, 605, 624

Underwood and Underwood, pages: 440, 521 (both), 566, 599
Union of South Africa Government Information Office, page: 496

Union Pacific Railroad, page: 356
United Nations, pages: 701, 702, 704, 705, 712, 760
United States Air Force, pages: 665, 667
United States Army, pages: 684, 692, 693, 696, 707, 709, 724, 739
U.S. Naval Institute, Annapolis, Md. page: 557
United States Navy, pages: 319, 529, 677, 688, 689, 694, 736, 747
University of Michigan, Research Laboratory, page: 451 (bottom)

Vandamm, pages: 114, 206
Virginia Department of Conservation and Development, page: 257

Walker Art Gallery, Liverpool, England, page: 499
Wide World Photos, Inc., pages: 14, 66, 67, 443, 571, 586, 617, 628, 637, 644, 647, 663, 676, 700, 732, 737, 742, 743, 744, 752, 753, 754, 755, 757, 761

Yugoslav State Tourist Office, New York City, page: 436

The publisher is indebted to the following for the reproductions in the color supplements:

Jacques Braun, Paris, pages: 54A, 150A
The Brooklyn Museum, Brooklyn, New York, page: 534F

Colonial Williamsburg, Williamsburg, Virginia, page: 534A

Otto Done, page: 262F

Col. Louis H. Frohman, pages: 54G, 150F, 534A, 534B, 534C, 534F

Marcello G. Garavaglia, Milan, Italy, pages: 54D, 54E, 54F, 150A, 150B,

150C, 150D, 150E, 150F, 150G, 262D, 262E, 262F, 262G
General Motors, page: 534G

Kenmore, Fredericksburg, Virginia, page: 534A

Long Island Automotive Museum, Southampton, New York, page: 534G

The Metropolitan Museum of Art, New York, New York, pages: 54G, 54H, 150F, 534C, 534D, 534E
The Minneapolis Institute of Arts, Paul Gauguin. *Tahitian Landscape*, 1891, oil on canvas, $36\frac{3}{8} \times 26\frac{3}{4}$ inches (Julius C. Eliel Memorial Purchase Fund), page: 534H
The Jules S. Bache Collection, 1949, page: 534B
Musée Beaux Arts Bruxelles, Brussels, Belgium, page: 262C
Museum of the City of New York, New York, page: 534C, 534F
Museum of Fine Arts, Boston, Massachusetts, page: 54G

National Gallery of Art, Washington, D.C., Samuel H. Kress Collection, page: 262B; Mellon Collection, pages: 262A, 262B, 262C
New York Graphic Society, pages: 262A, 262B, 262C, 262H, 534B
New York Historical Society, New York, New York, page: 534B

The Pierpont Morgan Library, New York, page: 150H
Plimoth Plantation, Plymouth, Massachusetts and Dickson Studios, page: 262G

Rijksmuseum, Horskamp, Holland, page: 534H

Union Pacific Railroad, page: 262G
United Nations Educational, Scientific, and Cultural Organizations, *Unesco World Art Series II, Egypt*, pages: 54B, 54C

Map Supplement

The following sixteen pages contain twelve full-color maps prepared by C. S. Hammond & Co. These maps are intended to supplement the text maps by presenting a large number of historical and geographical facts—for example, routes of exploration, place names, and physical features. The twelve maps relate to the text as suggested in the following list:

MAP 1. Upper left section: Part One, Chapters 1 to 4. Upper right section: Part Two, Chapters 6 to 8. Lower left section: Part Three, Chapters 10 to 11. Lower right: Part Five, Chapters 20 to 22.

MAP 2. This map ranges over Asian and Near Eastern history from the Sumerians (Chapter 2) to Hiroshima (Chapter 53) and Formosa (Chapters 55 and 56). Map 2 is particularly useful in relation to Chapters 12 (Part Four), 18, 20 (Part Five), 38, 40, 41 (Part Eight), 53 to 56 (Part Ten).

MAP 3. Chapters 18, 20, 21 of Part Five.

MAP 4. Chapters 18, 20 (Part Five), Chapters 25, 28 (Part Six).

MAP 5. Chapter 20 (Part Five), Chapter 25 (Part Six), Chapter 42 (Part Eight). Also, general reference for United States geography and place names.

MAP 6. Chapter 39 (Part Eight). Also general reference for the geography of Africa.

MAP 7. Chapters 38, 40, 41 (Part Eight). Also general reference for the geography of Asia.

MAP 8. Chapters 44 and 45 (Part Eight), Chapters 46 to 50 (Part Nine). Also general reference for world geography.

MAP 9. Chapters 51 to 56 (Part Ten). Also general reference for European geography.

MAPS 10 and 11. For general reference, showing the two hemispheres and their physical characteristics. Note the key. The colors show the height of land above sea level.

MAP 12. Chapters 54 to 56 (Part Ten).